THE STARMAN OMNIBUS

VOLUME FOUR

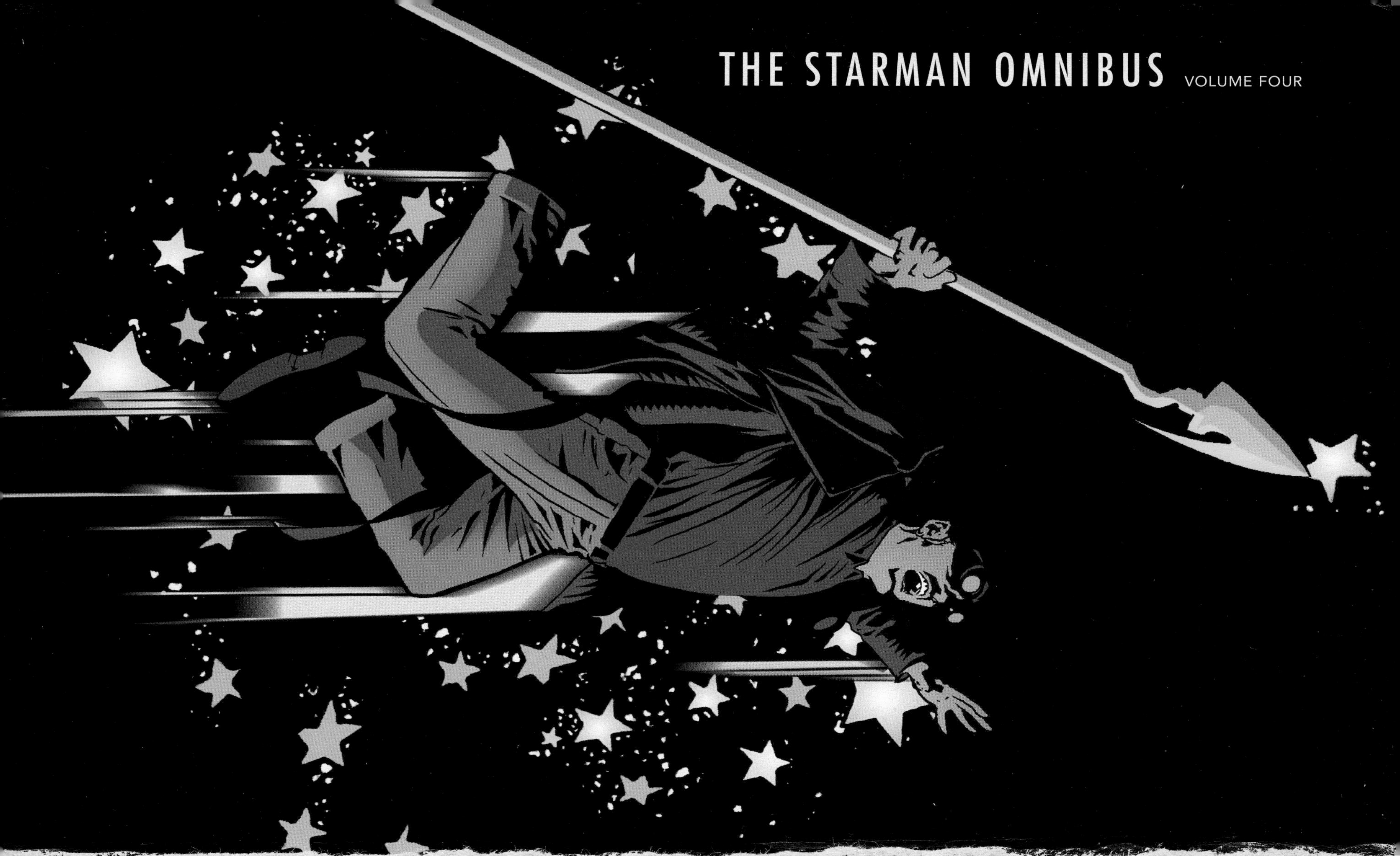

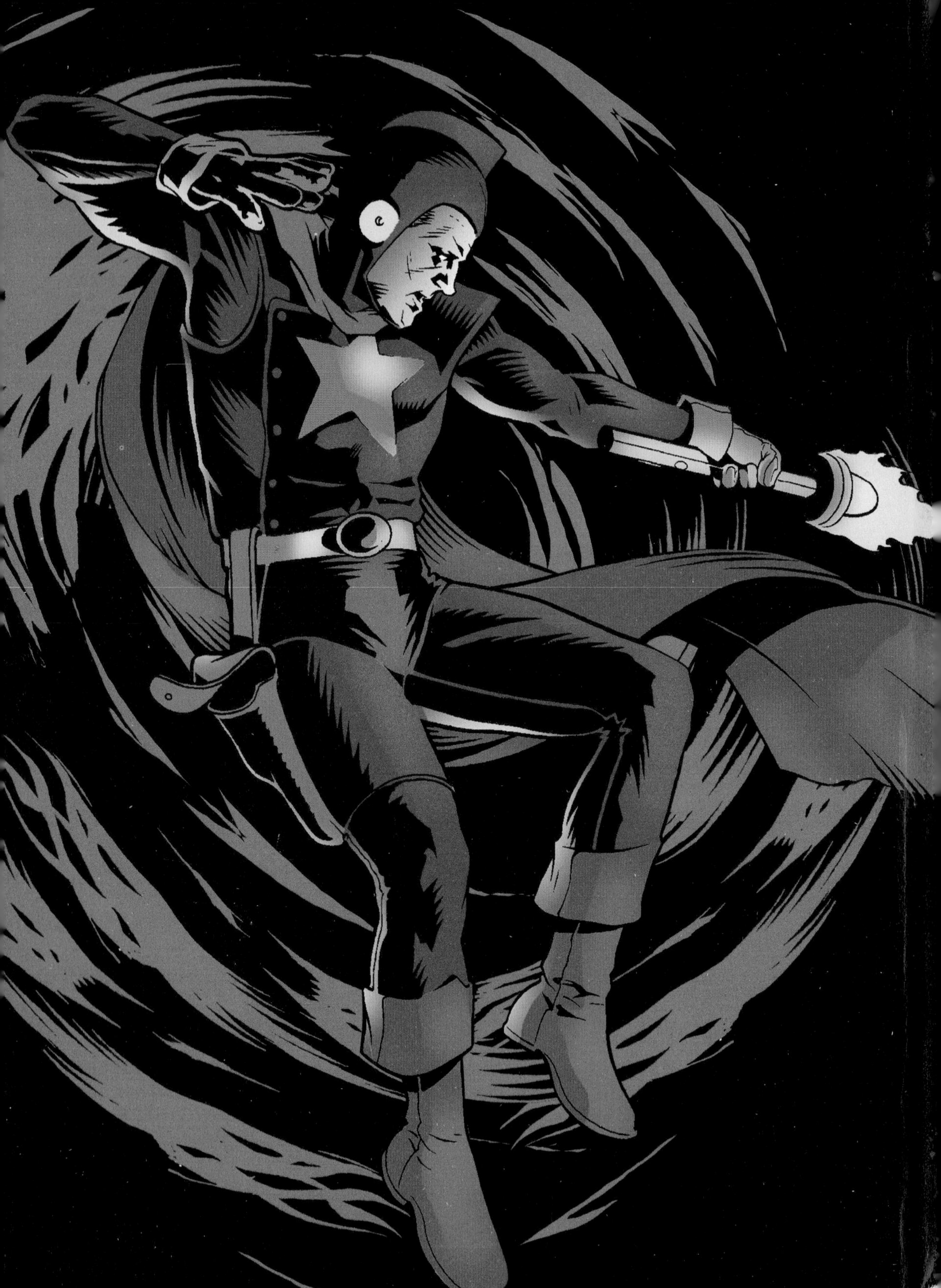

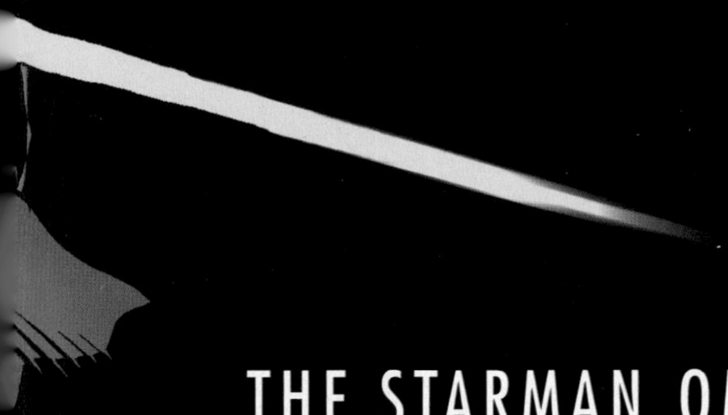

THE STARMAN OMNIBUS VOLUME FOUR

James Robinson Jerry Ordway Writers

Tony Harris Mike Mignola Pete Krause John Lucas Mike Mayhew Gary Erskine Matt Smith Gene Ha Steve Sadowski Wade von Grawbadger Dusty Abell Tim Burgand Pencillers

Wade von Grawbadger Mike Mignola Dick Giordano Gary Erskine Richard Case Gene Ha John Lucas Mike Mayhew Tom Nguyen Drew Geraci Tim Burgand Ray Snyder Inkers

Gregory Wright Carla Feeny Matt Hollingsworth Glenn Whitmore Pat Garrahy Gene Ha Colorists

Bill Oakley Kurt Hathaway Willie Schubert John Costanza Letterers

Jack Knight created by James Robinson and Tony Harris
Batman created by Bob Kane Hellboy created by Mike Mignola

Dan DiDio
SVP-Executive Editor

Archie Goodwin
Peter J. Tomasi
Mike Carlin
Editors-original series

Chuck Kim
Frank Berrios
Assistant Editors-original series

Georg Brewer
VP-Design & DC Direct Creative

Bob Harras
Group Editor-Collected Editions

Anton Kawasaki
Editor

Robbin Brosterman
Design Director-Books

DC COMICS

Paul Levitz
President & Publisher

Richard Bruning
SVP-Creative Director

Patrick Caldon
EVP-Finance & Operations

Amy Genkins
SVP-Business & Legal Affairs

Jim Lee
Editorial Director-WildStorm

Gregory Noveck
SVP-Creative Affairs

Steve Rotterdam
SVP-Sales & Marketing

Cheryl Rubin
SVP-Brand Management

Cover by Tony Harris

Select interior color separations by
GCW and Digital Chameleon

THE STARMAN OMNIBUS
Volume Four

DC Comics, 1700 Broadway
New York, NY 10019
A Warner Bros. Entertainment Company
Printed by RR Donnelley, Salem, VA, USA
1/20/10. First Printing.

HC ISBN: 978-1-4012-2596-4
SC ISBN: 978-1-4012-2597-1

JAMES ROBINSON SET OUT TO WRITE HIS ULTIMATE COMICS SAGA BY STAYING TRUE TO THE REAL WORLD —

DON MURPHY

Of course, his "real" world is different from others that have gone before him. His involves collectibles and tattoo ink as opposed to, say, biker rings and snake gods. Oh, and Jack Knight is a lot like James was, at least when these stories were coming out, whereas I doubt certain people were ever much like Rorschach.

I first met James not long after the new Starman emerged in ZERO HOUR #1. He was doing a signing at LA's premiere comics book shop, Meltdown Comics on Sunset Boulevard, and I just went up and introduced myself. A friendship slowly emerged from that, and literally for years James, myself and Gaston the shop's owner trekked one hour south every Saturday to buy comics we didn't need down in a town called Walnut. By the time the comics collected herein were published we had been friends for years, looking to work together on something.

I can't believe that over a decade has gone by since I first read these books. Upon re-reading, I was struck by how easy James makes it look. He manages to shift tone almost imperceptibly, going from serious to cartoonish when dealing with the Big Red Cheese, to dark and brooding with the Hellboy books and then to everything and the kitchen sink with the 80-Page Giant. In a world in which most writers excel at one thing only, this is no easy feat. James can write funny scenes, romantic interludes and action before most people finish their outlines.

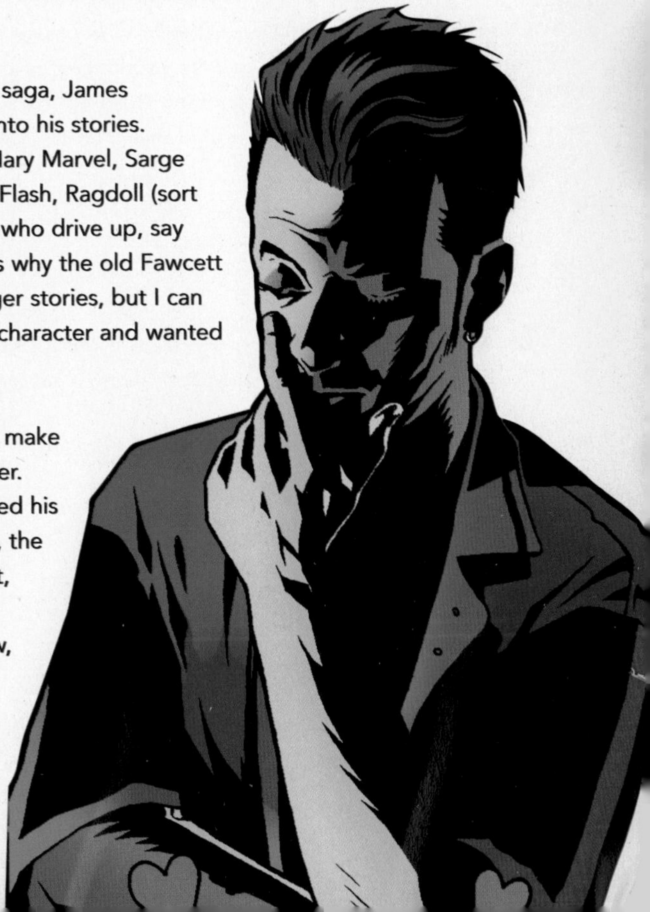

I was struck too by how, at this point in the saga, James is damn good at working other characters into his stories. There's Batman, Hellboy, Captain Marvel, Mary Marvel, Sarge Steel (who the hell was that?), Golden Age Flash, Ragdoll (sort of) and dozens more from the DC Universe who drive up, say hello, and then move on. I could ask James why the old Fawcett hero Bulletman shows up in one of the longer stories, but I can already guess the answer. James liked the character and wanted to use him. Simple as that.

It's not the use of incidental characters that make this volume of STARMAN stand out, however. You can tell in this volume James has reached his stride. He has sorted out, for the first time, the mishigas of the Starman legacy. Ted Knight, son Jack, the Kirby Starman, the blue guy, Mikaal, etc. Maybe you didn't care to know, but thanks to James it all makes sense for the very first time. If, like me, you read comics because of the continuity of the characters which link to your memories growing up, then this Herculean task is one to tip your hat to. You see, like Swamp Thing and Daredevil and Sandman before him, no one cared too much about Starman before James came along. This left a history that was convoluted, to say the least.

This volume, thanks to the vagaries of fate, is episodic. A lot of self-contained short stories. James is having the most fun with the 80-Page Giant. While tracking the history of an idol/weapon he manages to do short tales of all the major characters in the new Starman mythos. Gangsters, druggies and the like populate the adventures, as James flexes his muscles and writes many stories about one story. But my personal fave is the "Times Past" story with Phantom Lady. Not just because she's a cool character. James manages to take this almost ancient super-heroine and effortlessly tie her into the present Starman world. You'll like it.

Though episodic, the stories all build toward James' masterwork, "Stars My Destination," which will really get going in the next volume. This saga, I feel, is still underrated and more than holds its own against WATCHMEN, A GAME OF YOU or *That Yellow Bastard*, similar comics high points. But you have to work to get your saga. You can't have *Empire* without *New Hope*. You can feel the cornerstones of the upcoming saga being laid all about you in this book.

James and I eventually did work together on a film that I produced and he scripted called *The League of Extraordinary Gentlemen*. The Sean Connery starrer grossed $200 million worldwide and tons more on DVD. I'm proud of it. If you liked it, credit James' smart screenplay with making it work. If you are a hater, then blame someone other than the hard-working screenwriter. Either way, if you are reading this volume I think you should check out the film.

If you read the amazingly introspective final essays in these volumes, you can learn what happened to Jack Knight's real life counterpart in the ensuing decade. He's now happily engaged and living in San Francisco. Kismet. He's also writing some of the best comics out there every month. And I am glad that after all these years we remain friends.

Don Murphy
Los Angeles, California
October, 2009

Don Murphy is a movie producer whose credits include the films Natural Born Killers, Apt Pupil, From Hell, The League of Extraordinary Gentlemen, Transformers, Shoot 'Em Up, *and* Transformers: Revenge of the Fallen, *among others.*

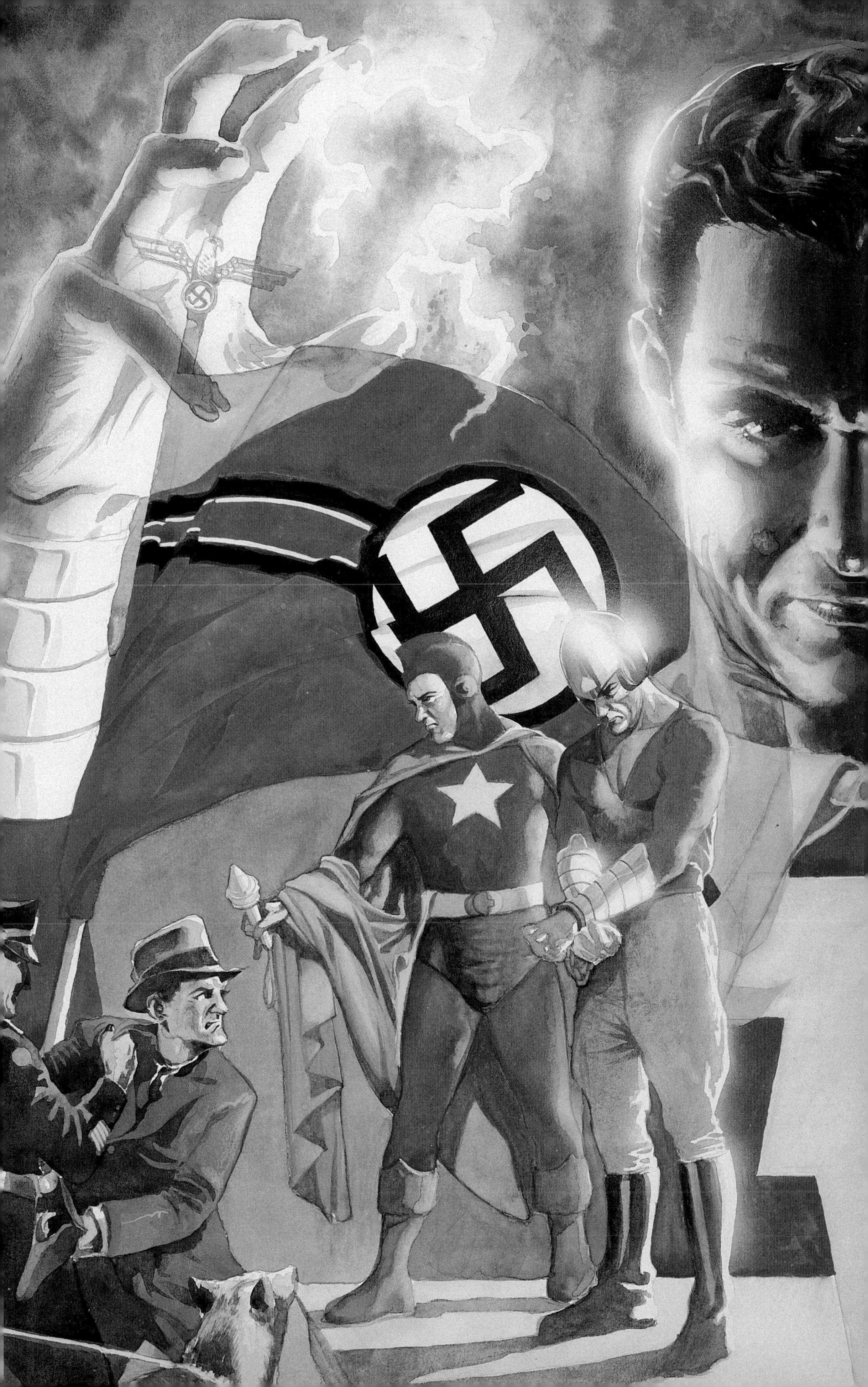

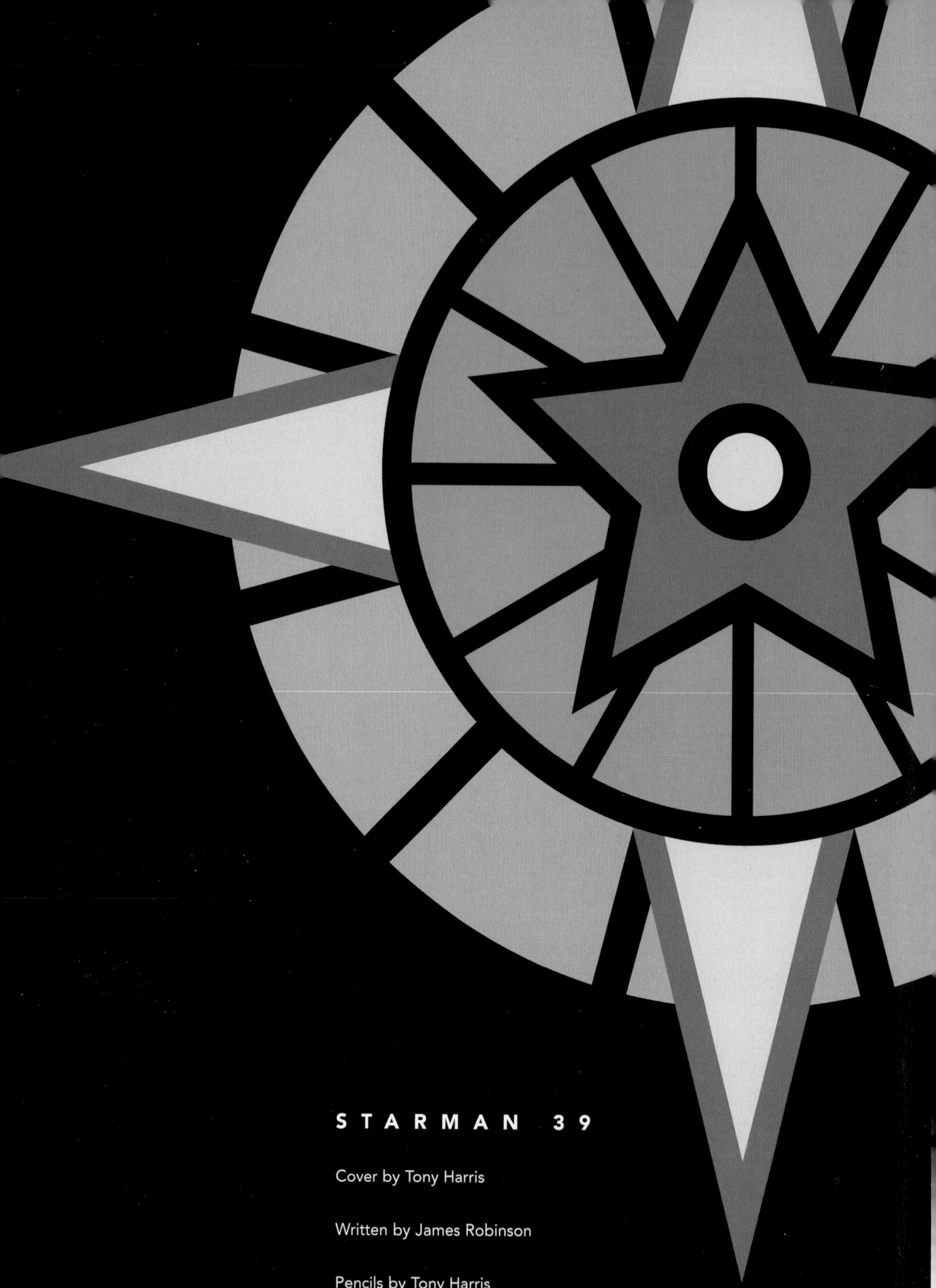

S T A R M A N   3 9

Cover by Tony Harris

Written by James Robinson

Pencils by Tony Harris

with inks by Wade von Grawbadger

and colors by Gregory Wright

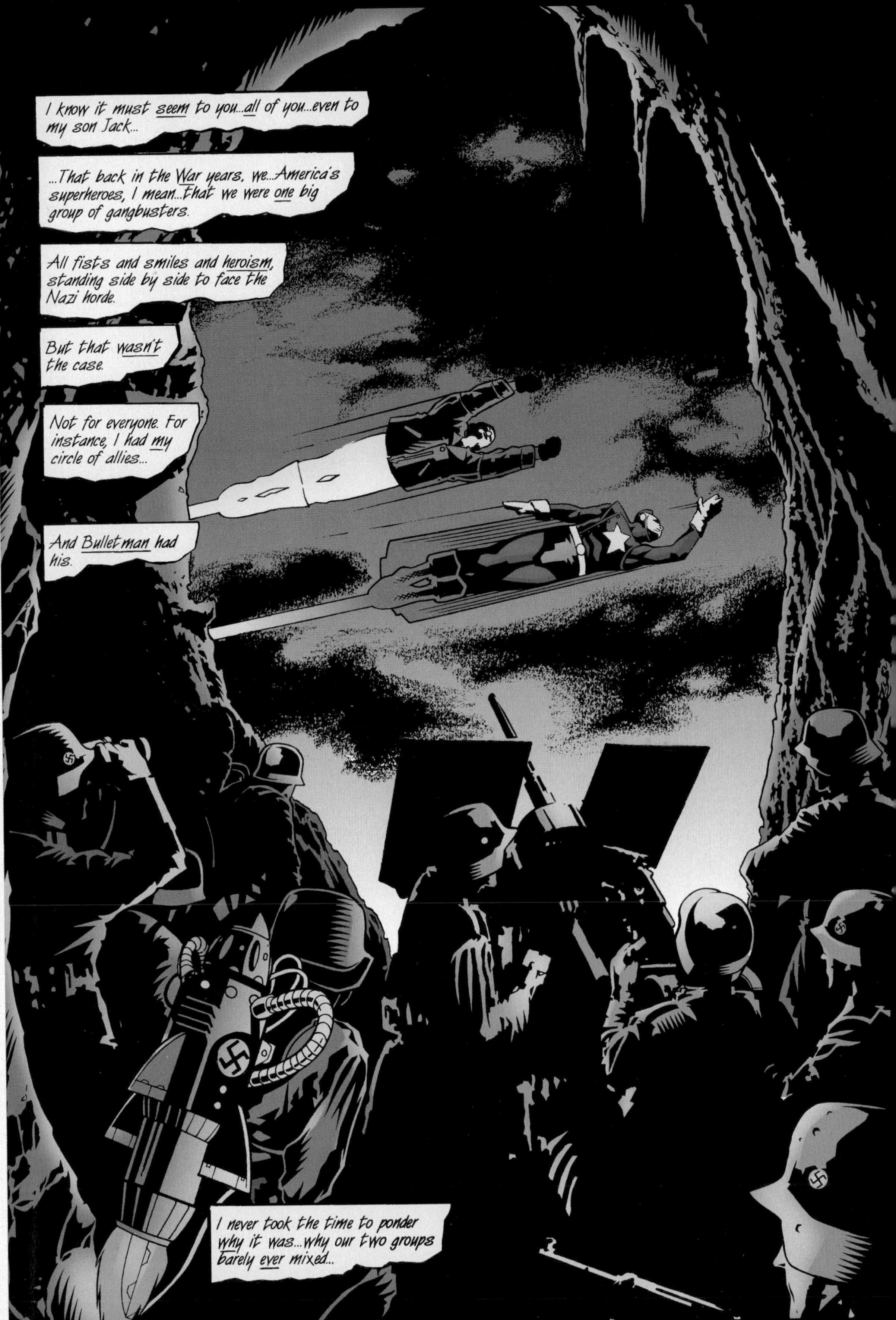
I know it must seem to you...all of you...even to my son Jack...
...That back in the War years, we...America's superheroes, I mean...that we were one big group of gangbusters.
All fists and smiles and heroism, standing side by side to face the Nazi horde.
But that wasn't the case.
Not for everyone. For instance, I had my circle of allies...
And Bulletman had his.
I never took the time to ponder why it was...why our two groups barely ever mixed...

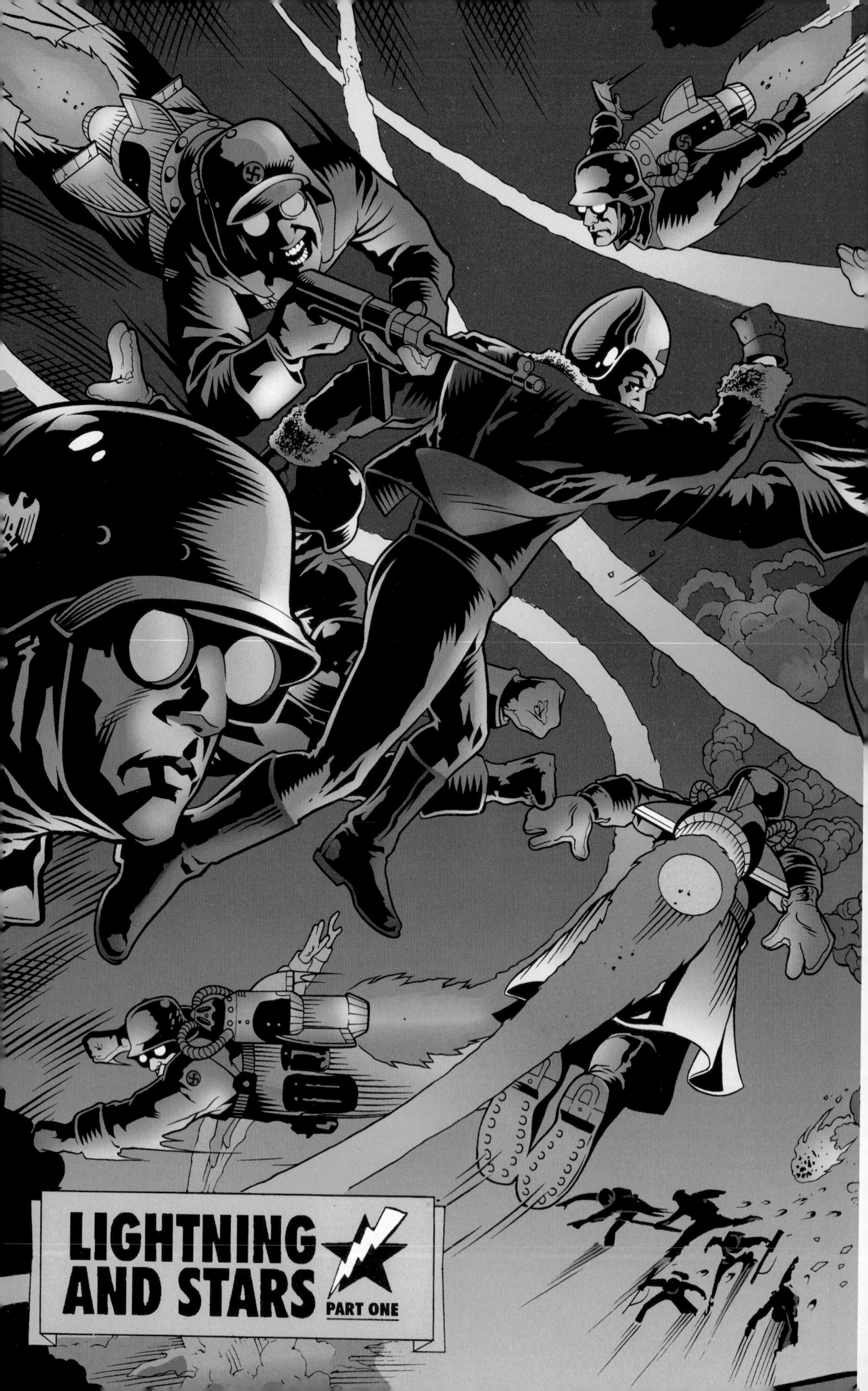
LIGHTNING AND STARS
PART ONE

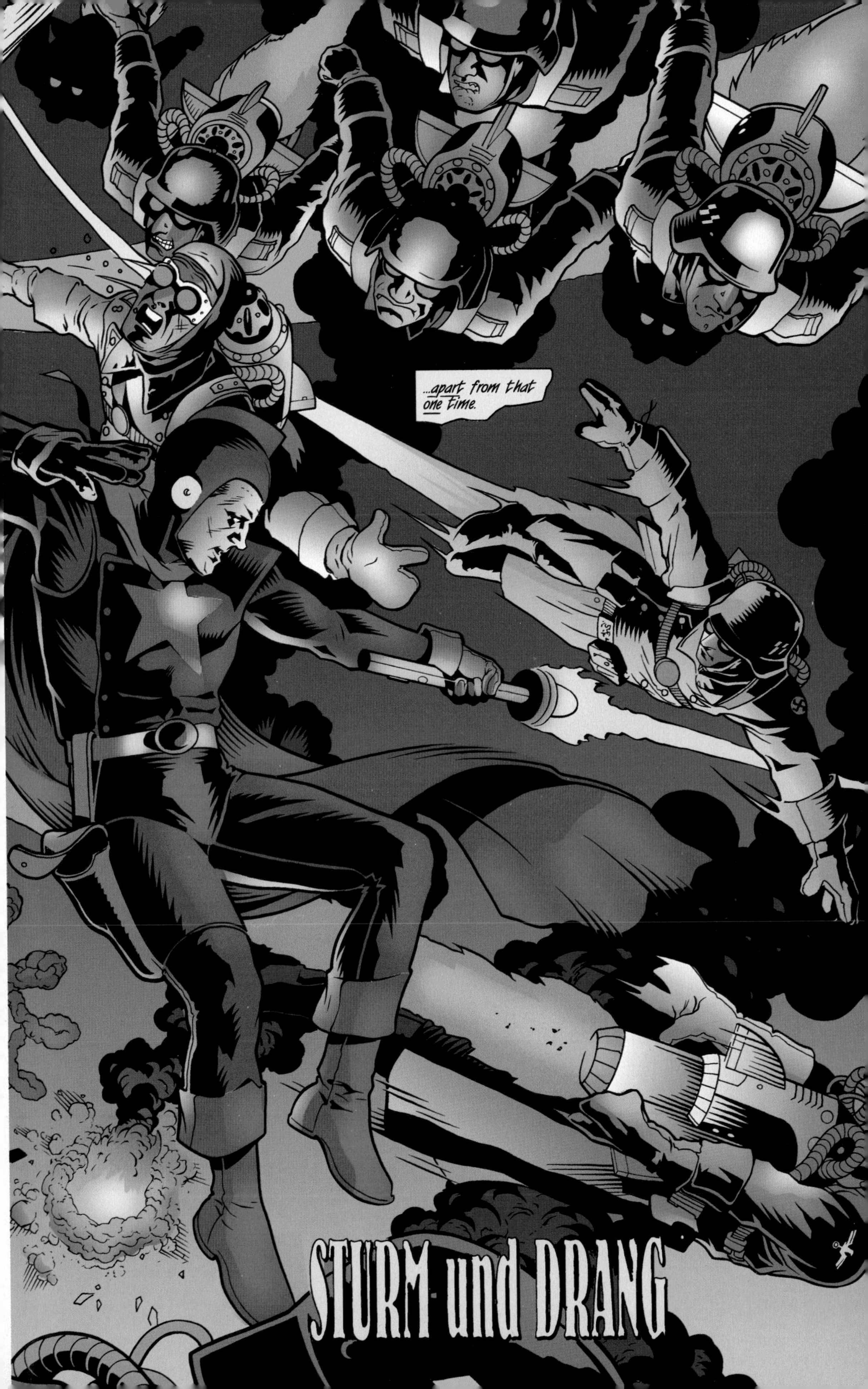
...apart from that one time.
STURM und DRANG

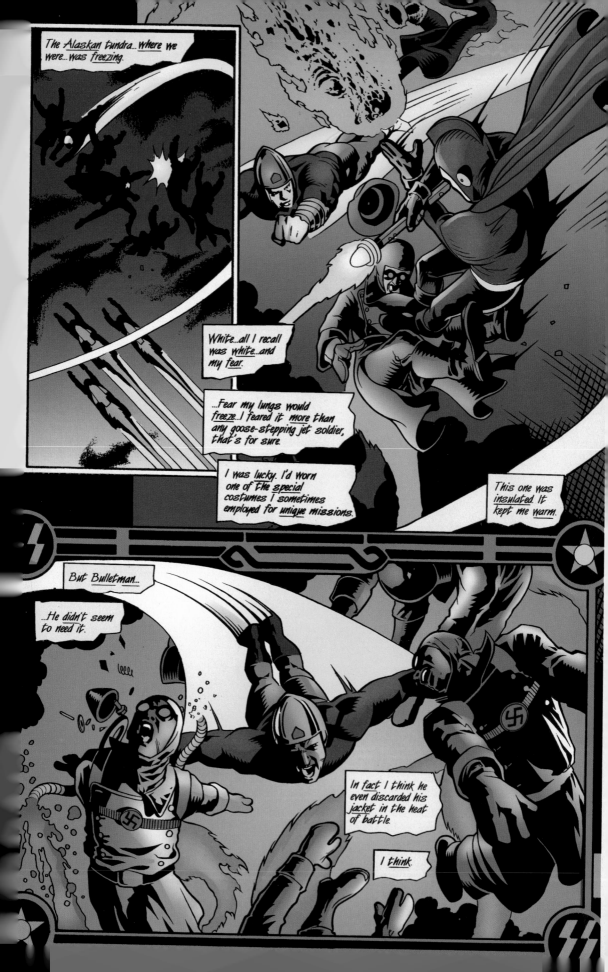

The Alaskan tundra...where we were...was freezing.

White...all I recall was white...and my fear.

...Fear my lungs would freeze...I feared it more than any goose-stepping jet soldier, that's for sure.

I was lucky. I'd worn one of the special costumes I sometimes employed for unique missions.

This one was insulated. It kept me warm.

But Bulletman...

...He didn't seem to need it.

In fact I think he even discarded his jacket in the heat of battle.

I think.

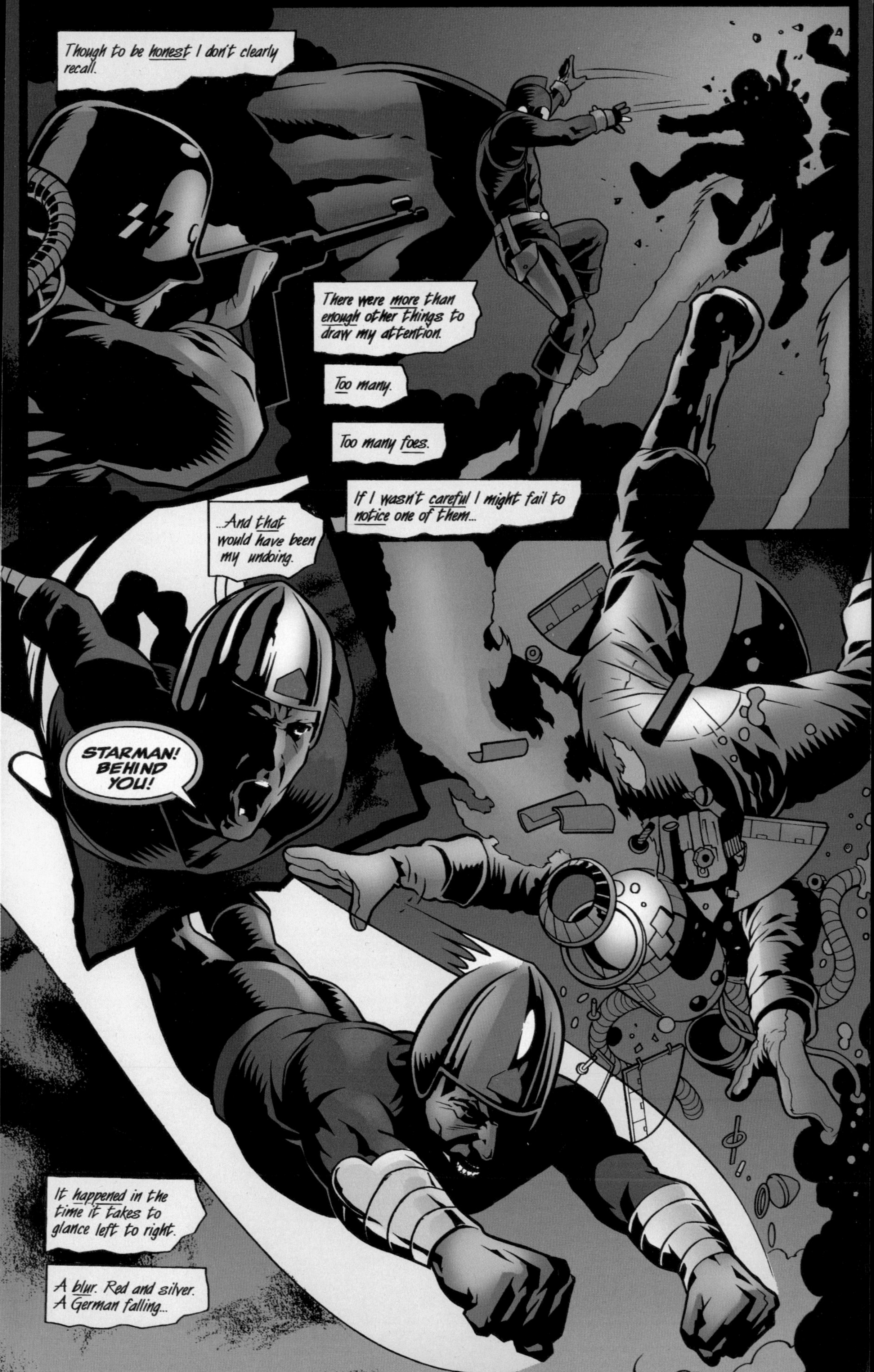
Though to be honest I don't clearly recall.
There were more than enough other things to draw my attention.
Too many.
Too many foes.
If I wasn't careful I might fail to notice one of them...
...And that would have been my undoing.
STARMAN! BEHIND YOU!
It happened in the time it takes to glance left to right.
A blur. Red and silver. A German falling...

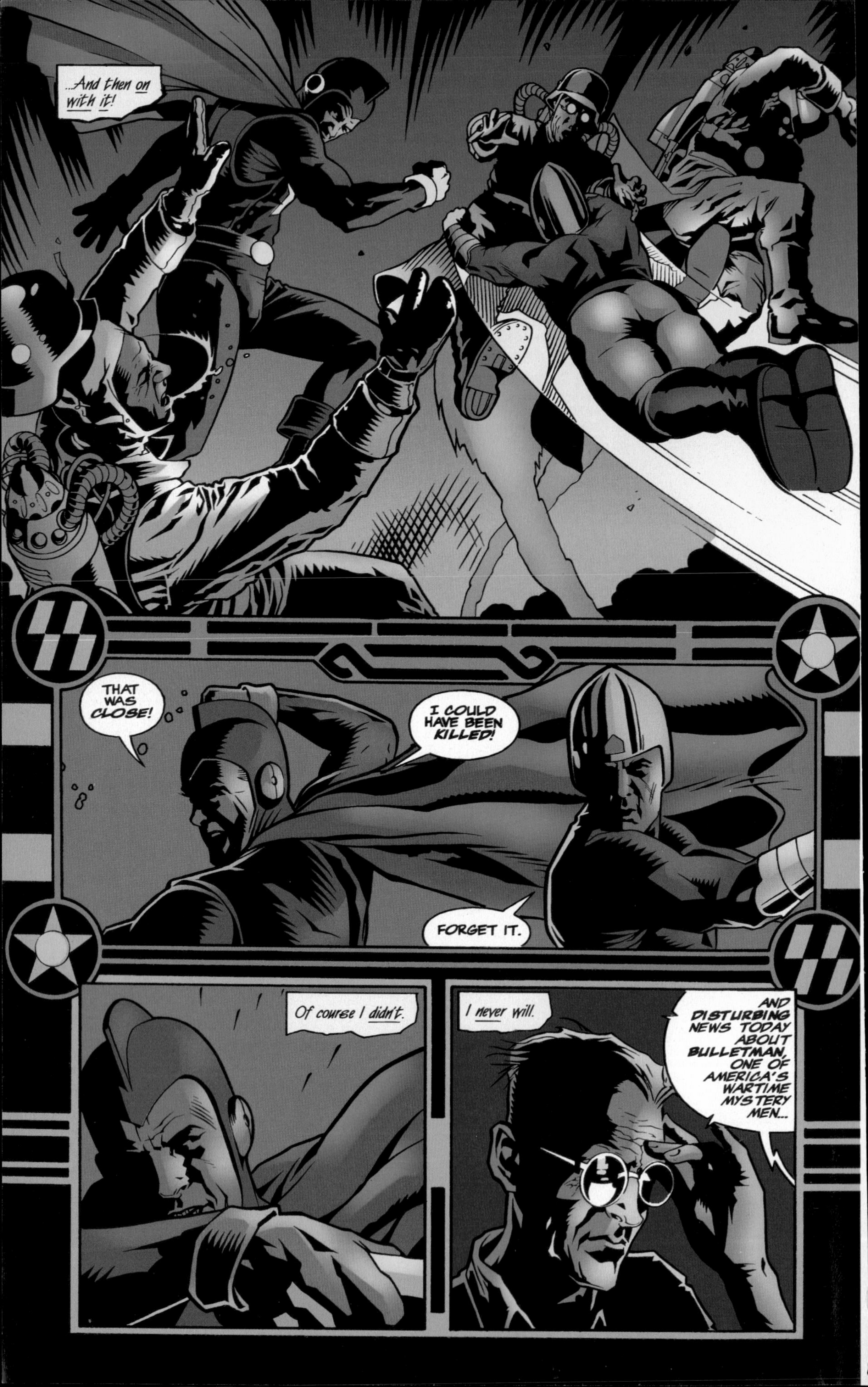
...And then on with it!
THAT WAS CLOSE!
I COULD HAVE BEEN KILLED!
FORGET IT.
Of course I didn't.
I never will.
AND DISTURBING NEWS TODAY ABOUT BULLETMAN, ONE OF AMERICA'S WARTIME MYSTERY MEN...

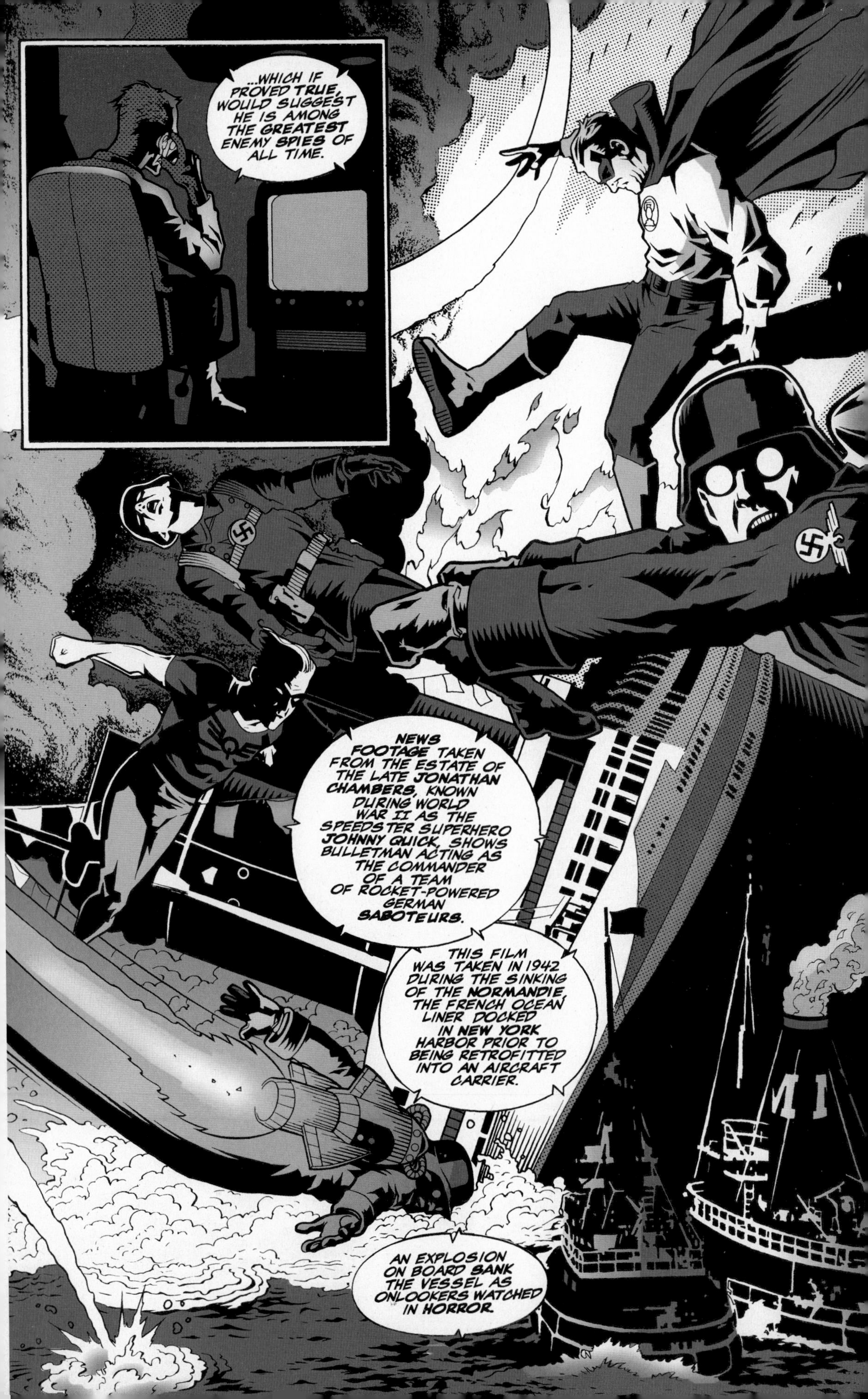
...WHICH IF PROVED TRUE, WOULD SUGGEST HE IS AMONG THE GREATEST ENEMY SPIES OF ALL TIME.
NEWS FOOTAGE TAKEN FROM THE ESTATE OF THE LATE JONATHAN CHAMBERS, KNOWN DURING WORLD WAR II AS THE SPEEDSTER SUPERHERO JOHNNY QUICK, SHOWS BULLETMAN ACTING AS THE COMMANDER OF A TEAM OF ROCKET-POWERED GERMAN SABOTEURS.
THIS FILM WAS TAKEN IN 1942 DURING THE SINKING OF THE NORMANDIE, THE FRENCH OCEAN LINER DOCKED IN NEW YORK HARBOR PRIOR TO BEING RETROFITTED INTO AN AIRCRAFT CARRIER.
AN EXPLOSION ON BOARD SANK THE VESSEL AS ONLOOKERS WATCHED IN HORROR.

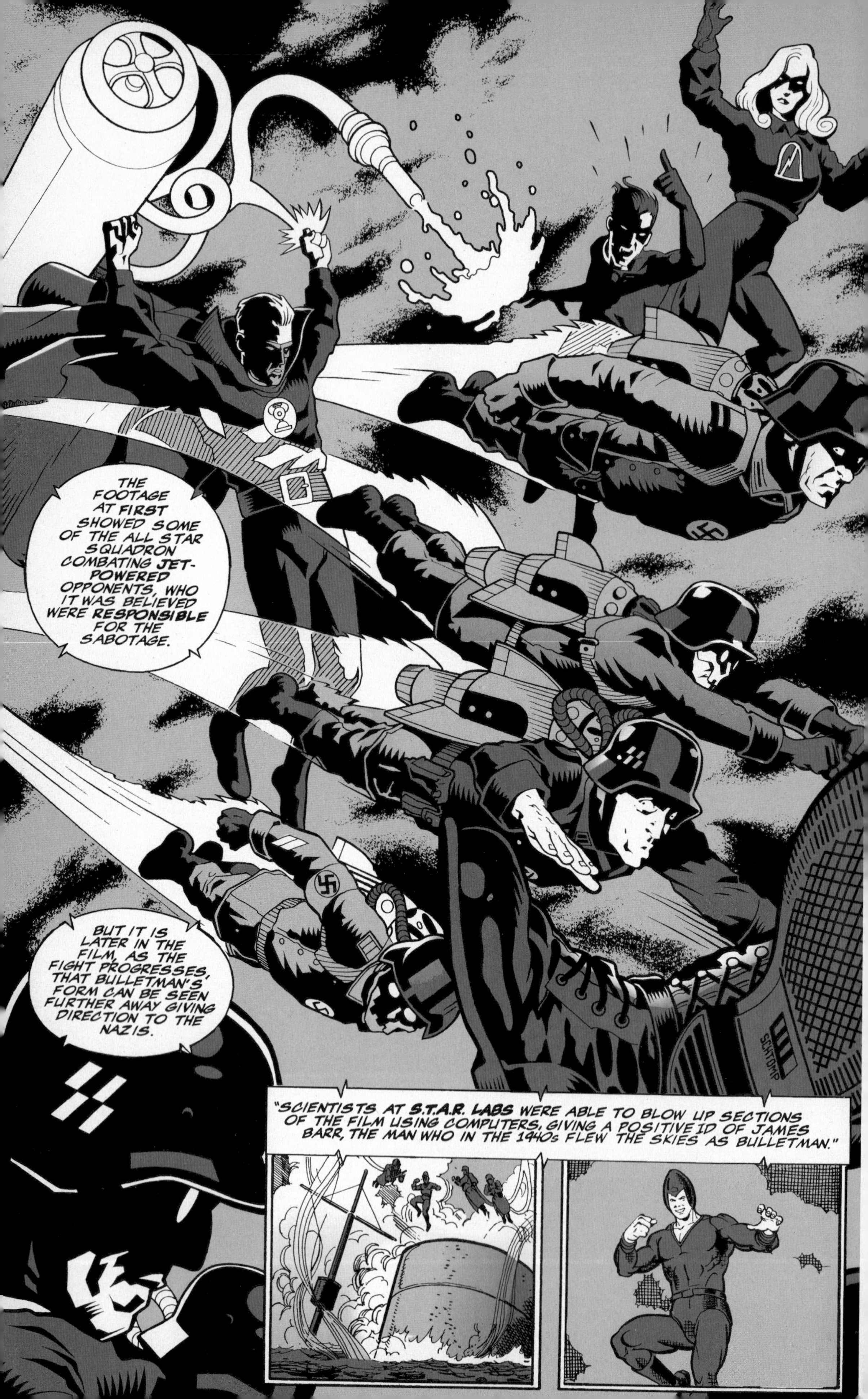
THE FOOTAGE AT FIRST SHOWED SOME OF THE ALL STAR SQUADRON COMBATING JET-POWERED OPPONENTS, WHO IT WAS BELIEVED WERE RESPONSIBLE FOR THE SABOTAGE.
BUT IT IS LATER IN THE FILM, AS THE FIGHT PROGRESSES, THAT BULLETMAN'S FORM CAN BE SEEN FURTHER AWAY GIVING DIRECTION TO THE NAZIS.
"SCIENTISTS AT S.T.A.R. LABS WERE ABLE TO BLOW UP SECTIONS OF THE FILM USING COMPUTERS, GIVING A POSITIVE ID OF JAMES BARR, THE MAN WHO IN THE 1940s FLEW THE SKIES AS BULLETMAN."

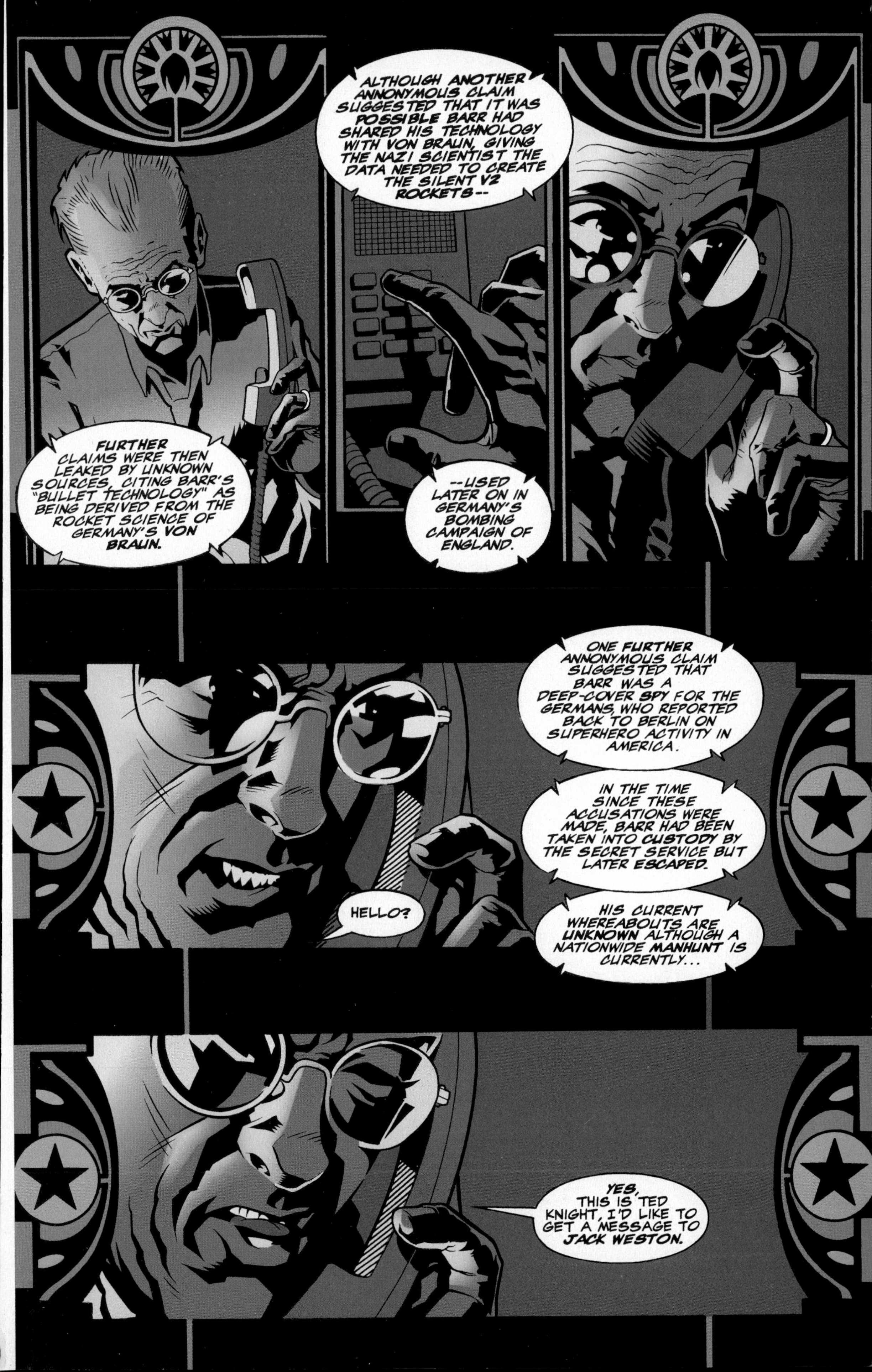

ALTHOUGH ANOTHER ANNONYMOUS CLAIM SUGGESTED THAT IT WAS POSSIBLE BARR HAD SHARED HIS TECHNOLOGY WITH VON BRAUN, GIVING THE NAZI SCIENTIST THE DATA NEEDED TO CREATE THE SILENT V2 ROCKETS--
FURTHER CLAIMS WERE THEN LEAKED BY UNKNOWN SOURCES, CITING BARR'S "BULLET TECHNOLOGY" AS BEING DERIVED FROM THE ROCKET SCIENCE OF GERMANY'S VON BRAUN.
--USED LATER ON IN GERMANY'S BOMBING CAMPAIGN OF ENGLAND.
ONE FURTHER ANNONYMOUS CLAIM SUGGESTED THAT BARR WAS A DEEP-COVER SPY FOR THE GERMANS, WHO REPORTED BACK TO BERLIN ON SUPERHERO ACTIVITY IN AMERICA.
IN THE TIME SINCE THESE ACCUSATIONS WERE MADE, BARR HAD BEEN TAKEN INTO CUSTODY BY THE SECRET SERVICE BUT LATER ESCAPED.
HELLO?
HIS CURRENT WHEREABOUTS ARE UNKNOWN ALTHOUGH A NATIONWIDE MANHUNT IS CURRENTLY...
YES, THIS IS TED KNIGHT, I'D LIKE TO GET A MESSAGE TO JACK WESTON.

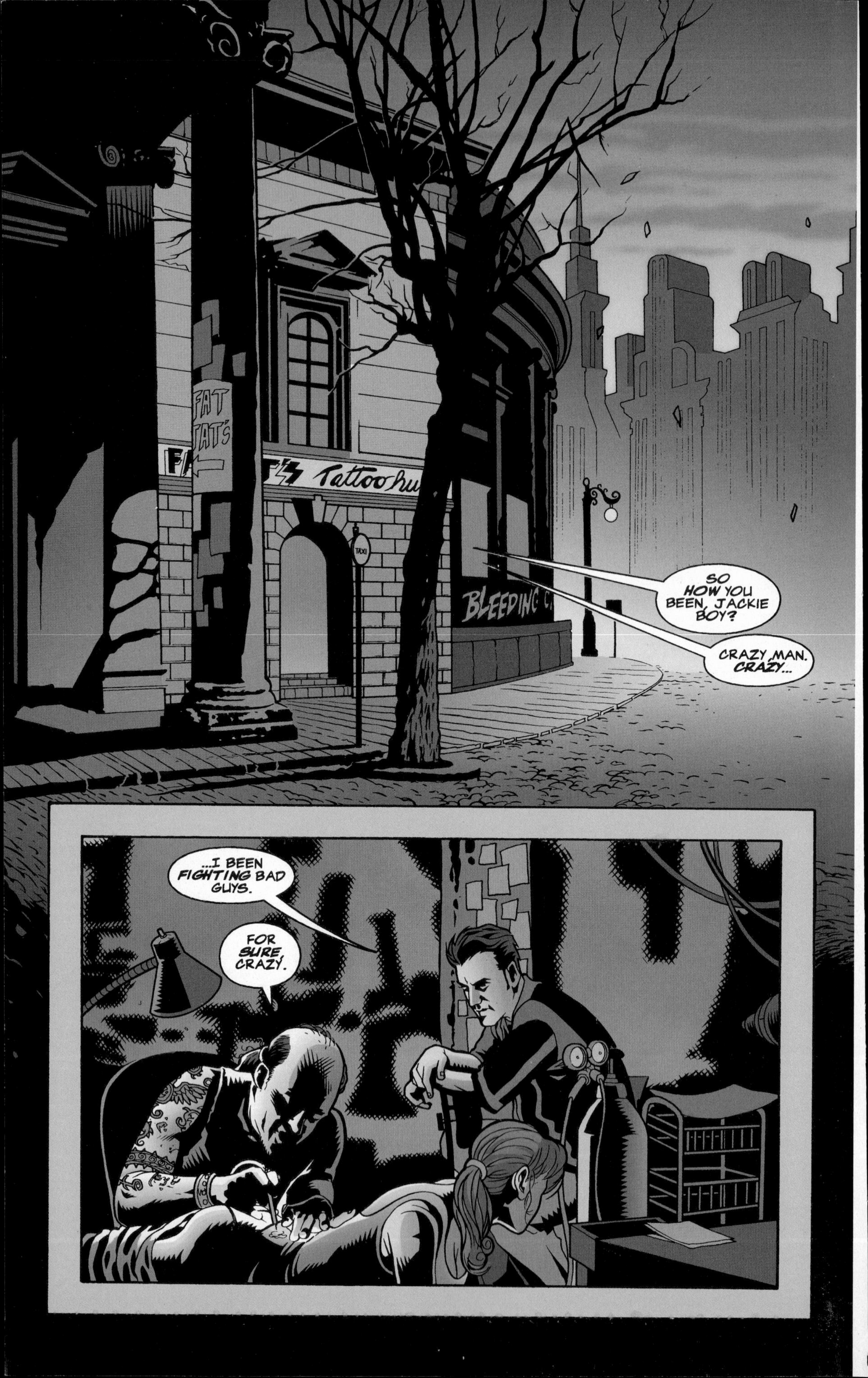
FAT TAT'S
FAT TAT'S Tattoo Hut
TAXI
BLEEDING
SO HOW YOU BEEN, JACKIE BOY?
CRAZY, MAN. CRAZY...
...I BEEN FIGHTING BAD GUYS.
FOR SURE, CRAZY.

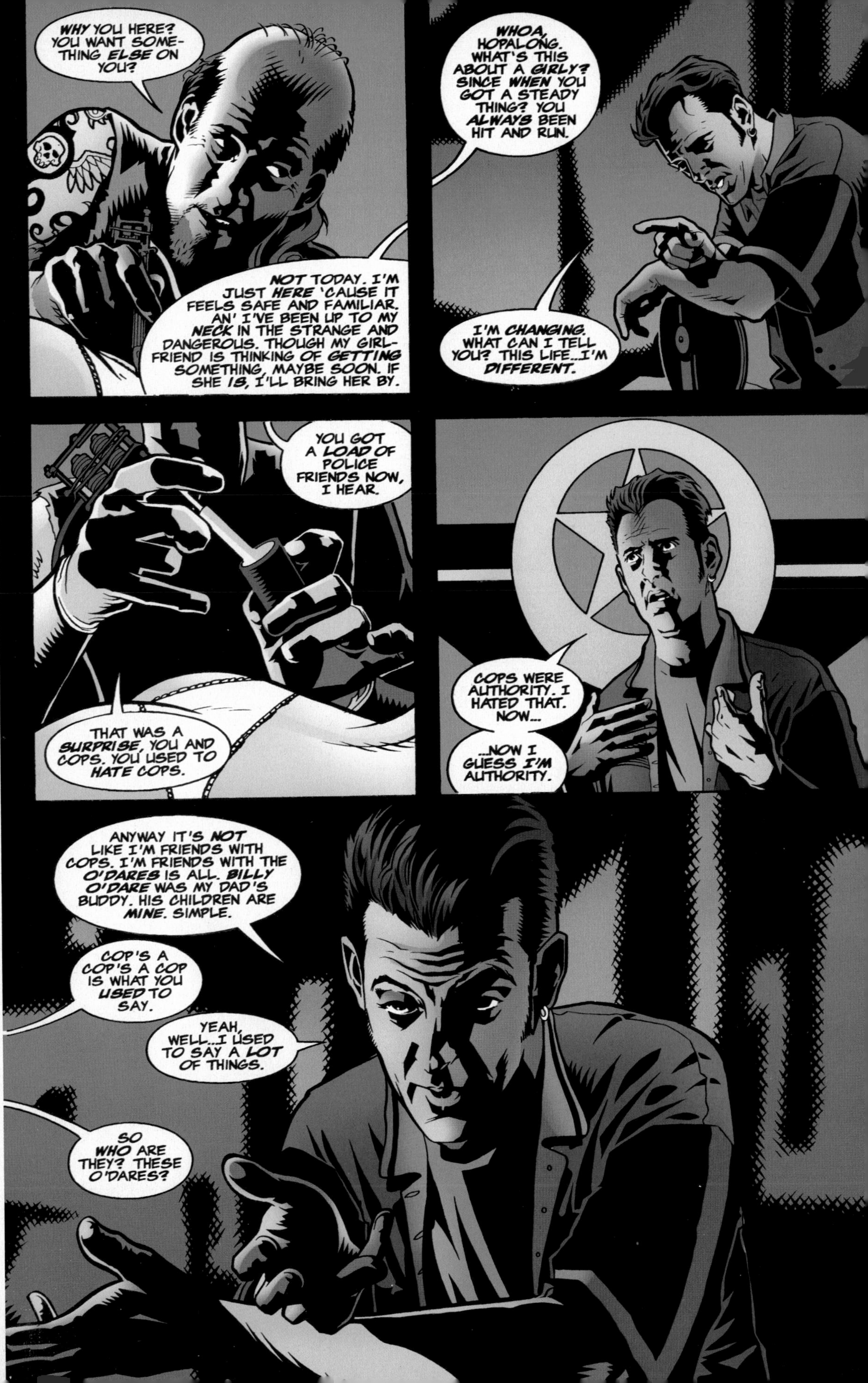
WHY YOU HERE? YOU WANT SOMETHING ELSE ON YOU?
NOT TODAY. I'M JUST HERE 'CAUSE IT FEELS SAFE AND FAMILIAR. AN' I'VE BEEN UP TO MY NECK IN THE STRANGE AND DANGEROUS. THOUGH MY GIRLFRIEND IS THINKING OF GETTING SOMETHING, MAYBE SOON. IF SHE IS, I'LL BRING HER BY.
WHOA, HOPALONG. WHAT'S THIS ABOUT A GIRLY? SINCE WHEN YOU GOT A STEADY THING? YOU ALWAYS BEEN HIT AND RUN.
I'M CHANGING. WHAT CAN I TELL YOU? THIS LIFE...I'M DIFFERENT.
YOU GOT A LOAD OF POLICE FRIENDS NOW, I HEAR.
THAT WAS A SURPRISE, YOU AND COPS. YOU USED TO HATE COPS.
COPS WERE AUTHORITY. I HATED THAT. NOW...
...NOW I GUESS I'M AUTHORITY.
ANYWAY IT'S NOT LIKE I'M FRIENDS WITH COPS. I'M FRIENDS WITH THE O'DARES IS ALL. BILLY O'DARE WAS MY DAD'S BUDDY. HIS CHILDREN ARE MINE. SIMPLE.
COP'S A COP'S A COP IS WHAT YOU USED TO SAY.
YEAH, WELL...I USED TO SAY A LOT OF THINGS.
SO WHO ARE THEY? THESE O'DARES?

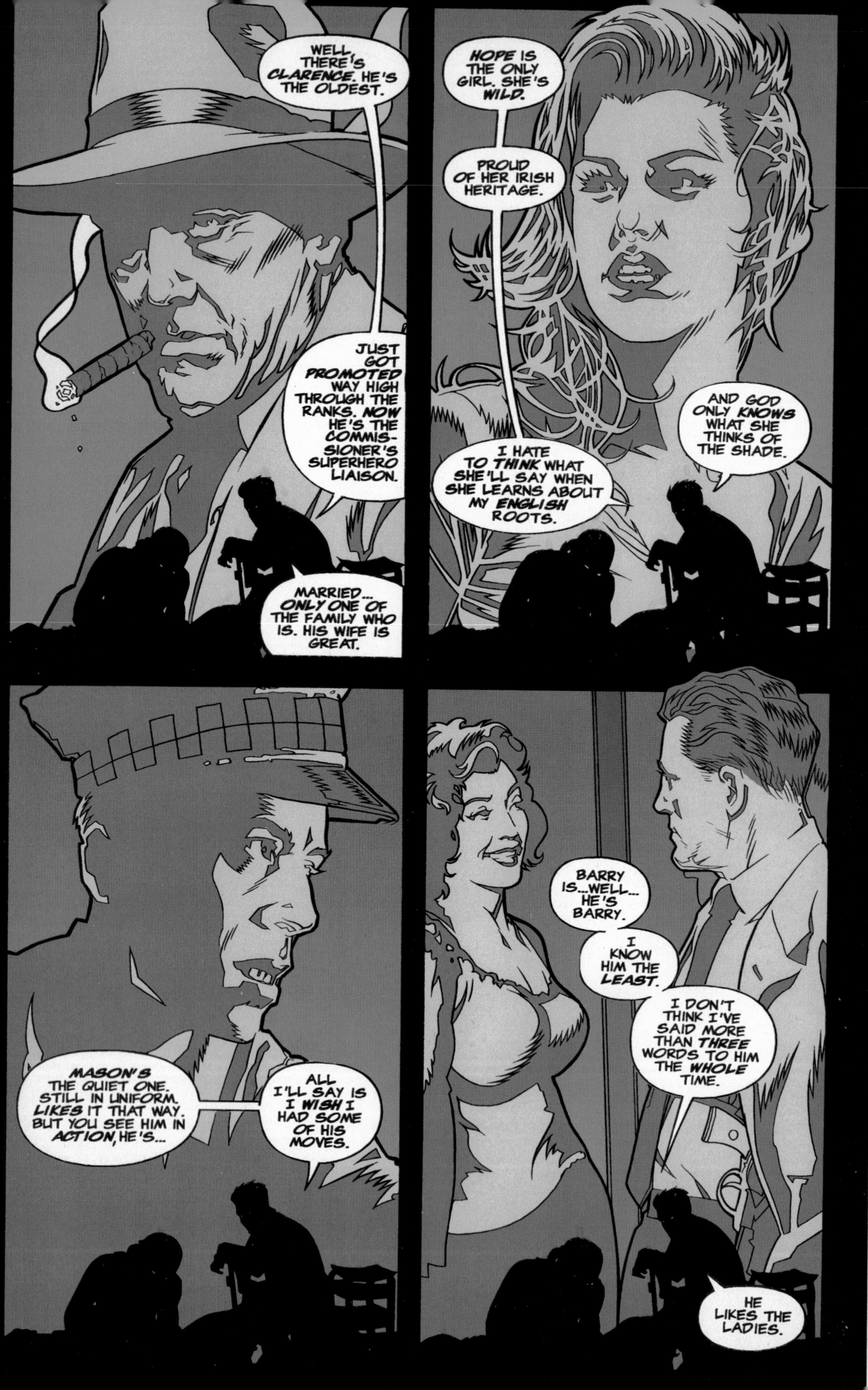
WELL, THERE'S CLARENCE. HE'S THE OLDEST.
JUST GOT PROMOTED WAY HIGH THROUGH THE RANKS. NOW HE'S THE COMMISSIONER'S SUPERHERO LIAISON.
MARRIED... ONLY ONE OF THE FAMILY WHO IS. HIS WIFE IS GREAT.
HOPE IS THE ONLY GIRL. SHE'S WILD.
PROUD OF HER IRISH HERITAGE.
I HATE TO THINK WHAT SHE'LL SAY WHEN SHE LEARNS ABOUT MY ENGLISH ROOTS.
AND GOD ONLY KNOWS WHAT SHE THINKS OF THE SHADE.
MASON'S THE QUIET ONE. STILL IN UNIFORM. LIKES IT THAT WAY. BUT YOU SEE HIM IN ACTION, HE'S...
ALL I'LL SAY IS I WISH I HAD SOME OF HIS MOVES.
BARRY IS...WELL... HE'S BARRY.
I KNOW HIM THE LEAST.
I DON'T THINK I'VE SAID MORE THAN THREE WORDS TO HIM THE WHOLE TIME.
HE LIKES THE LADIES.

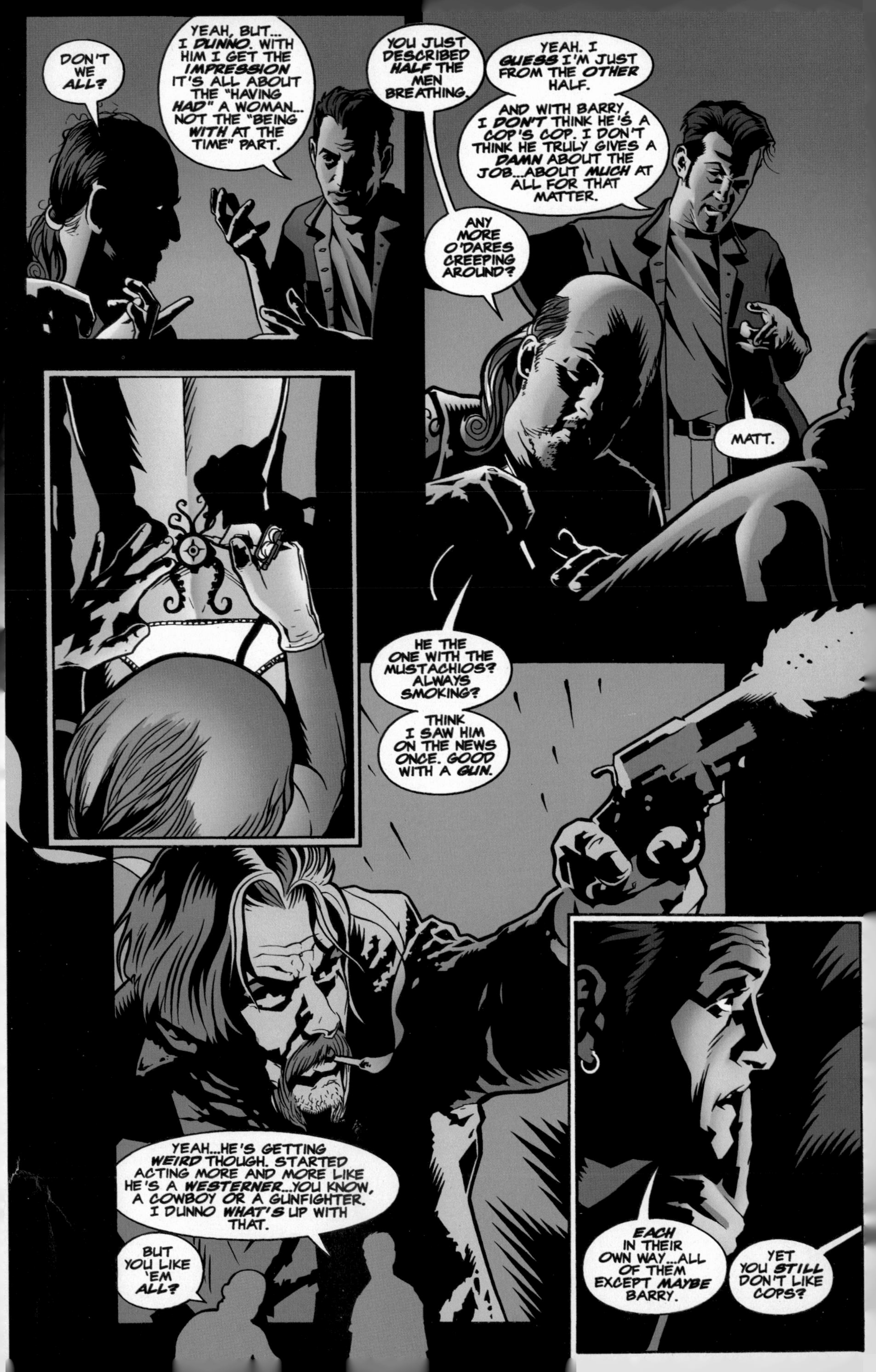
DON'T WE ALL?
YEAH, BUT... I DUNNO. WITH HIM I GET THE IMPRESSION IT'S ALL ABOUT THE "HAVING HAD" A WOMAN... NOT THE "BEING WITH AT THE TIME" PART.
YOU JUST DESCRIBED HALF THE MEN BREATHING.
YEAH. I GUESS I'M JUST FROM THE OTHER HALF.
AND WITH BARRY, I DON'T THINK HE'S A COP'S COP. I DON'T THINK HE TRULY GIVES A DAMN ABOUT THE JOB...ABOUT MUCH AT ALL FOR THAT MATTER.
ANY MORE O'DARES CREEPING AROUND?
MATT.
HE THE ONE WITH THE MUSTACHIOS? ALWAYS SMOKING?
THINK I SAW HIM ON THE NEWS ONCE. GOOD WITH A GUN.
YEAH...HE'S GETTING WEIRD THOUGH. STARTED ACTING MORE AND MORE LIKE HE'S A WESTERNER...YOU KNOW, A COWBOY OR A GUNFIGHTER. I DUNNO WHAT'S UP WITH THAT.
BUT YOU LIKE 'EM ALL?
EACH IN THEIR OWN WAY...ALL OF THEM EXCEPT MAYBE BARRY.
YET YOU STILL DON'T LIKE COPS?

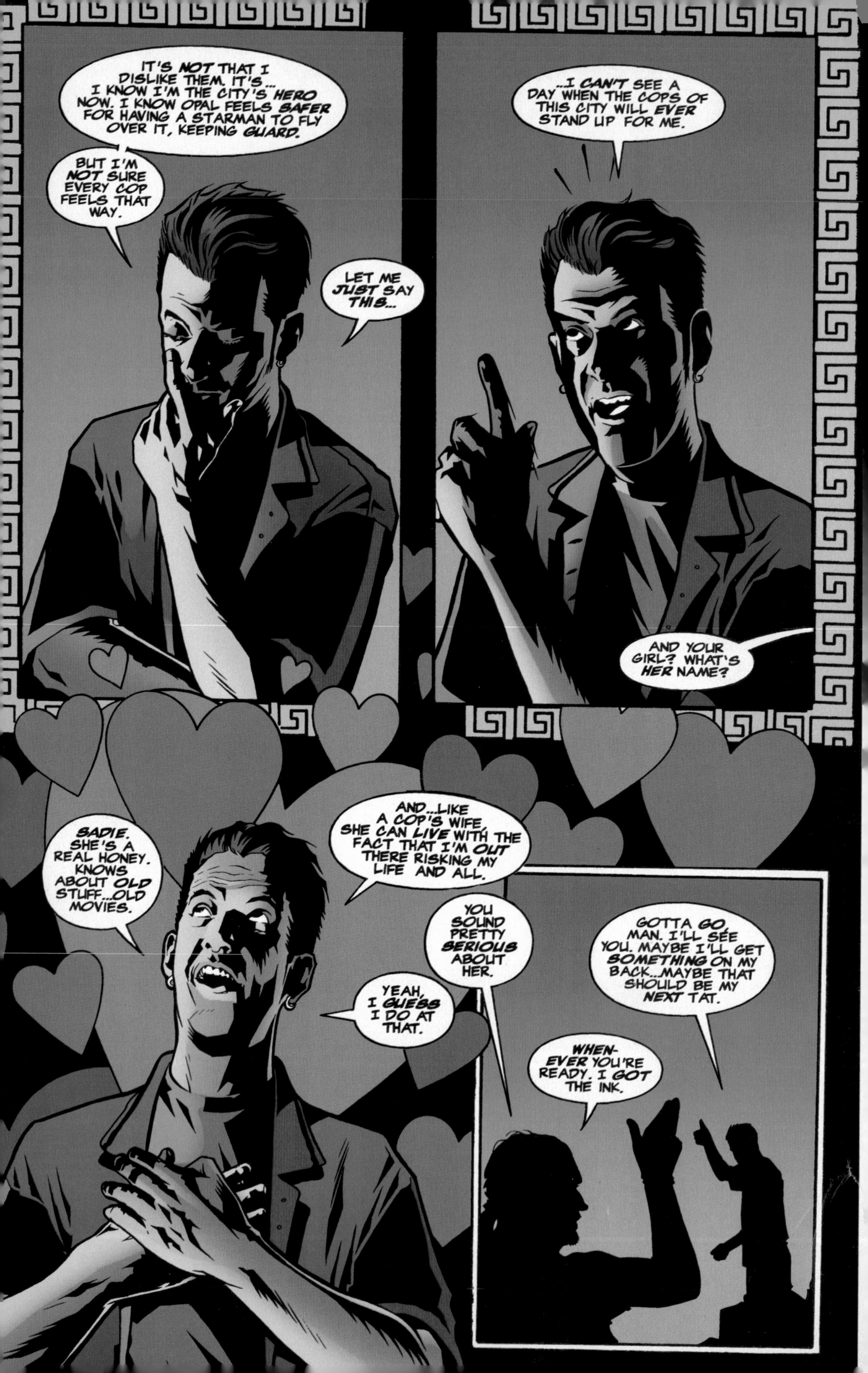
IT'S NOT THAT I DISLIKE THEM. IT'S... I KNOW I'M THE CITY'S HERO NOW. I KNOW OPAL FEELS SAFER FOR HAVING A STARMAN TO FLY OVER IT, KEEPING GUARD.
BUT I'M NOT SURE EVERY COP FEELS THAT WAY.
LET ME JUST SAY THIS...
...I CAN'T SEE A DAY WHEN THE COPS OF THIS CITY WILL EVER STAND UP FOR ME.
AND YOUR GIRL? WHAT'S HER NAME?
SADIE. SHE'S A REAL HONEY. KNOWS ABOUT OLD STUFF...OLD MOVIES.
AND...LIKE A COP'S WIFE, SHE CAN LIVE WITH THE FACT THAT I'M OUT THERE RISKING MY LIFE AND ALL.
YOU SOUND PRETTY SERIOUS ABOUT HER.
YEAH, I GUESS I DO AT THAT.
GOTTA GO, MAN. I'LL SEE YOU. MAYBE I'LL GET SOMETHING ON MY BACK...MAYBE THAT SHOULD BE MY NEXT TAT.
WHEN-EVER YOU'RE READY. I GOT THE INK.

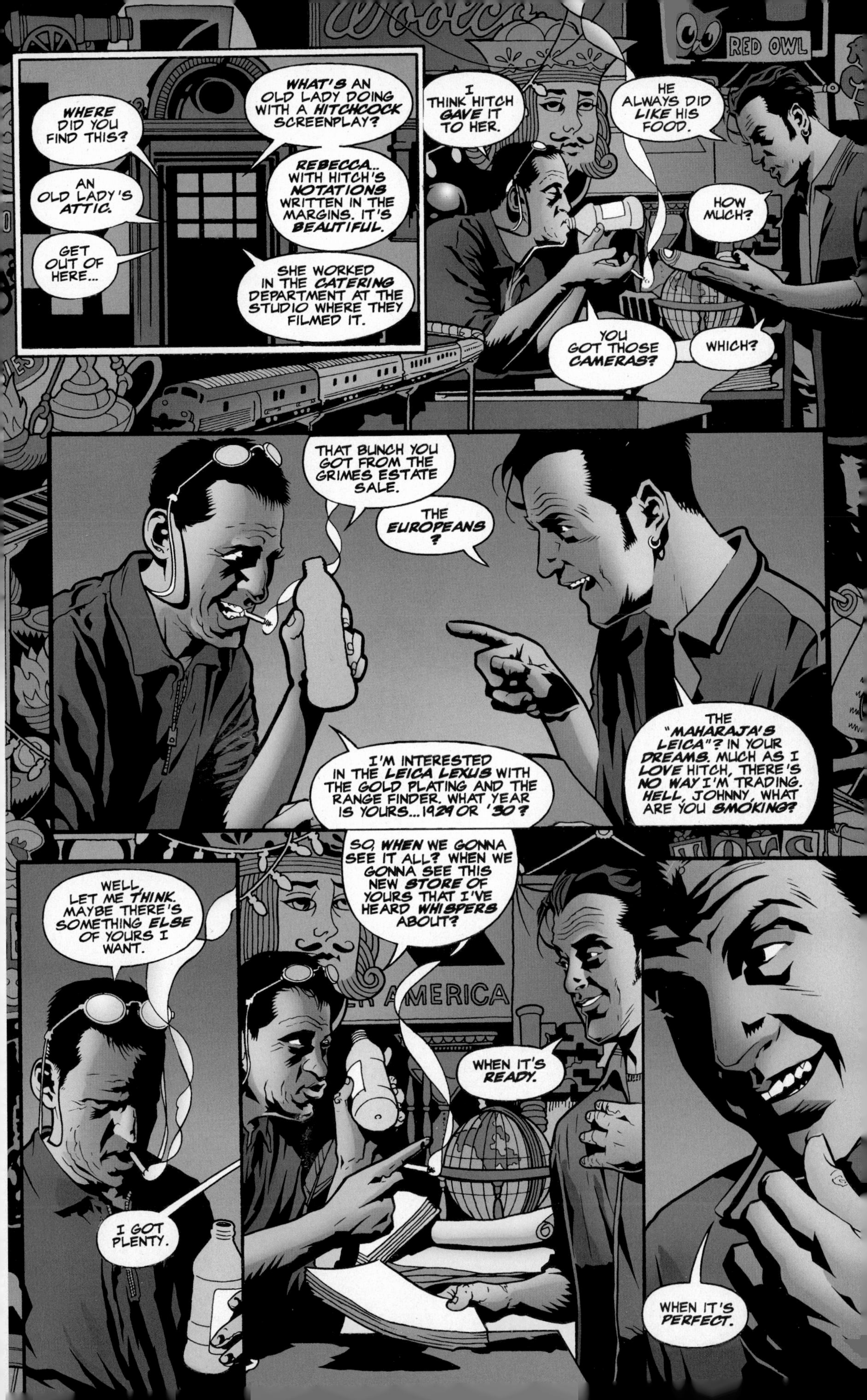

WHERE DID YOU FIND THIS?
AN OLD LADY'S ATTIC.
GET OUT OF HERE...
WHAT'S AN OLD LADY DOING WITH A HITCHCOCK SCREENPLAY?
REBECCA... WITH HITCH'S NOTATIONS WRITTEN IN THE MARGINS. IT'S BEAUTIFUL.
SHE WORKED IN THE CATERING DEPARTMENT AT THE STUDIO WHERE THEY FILMED IT.
I THINK HITCH GAVE IT TO HER.
HE ALWAYS DID LIKE HIS FOOD.
HOW MUCH?
YOU GOT THOSE CAMERAS?
WHICH?
RED OWL
THAT BUNCH YOU GOT FROM THE GRIMES ESTATE SALE.
THE EUROPEANS?
I'M INTERESTED IN THE LEICA LEXUS WITH THE GOLD PLATING AND THE RANGE FINDER. WHAT YEAR IS YOURS... 1929 OR '30?
THE "MAHARAJA'S LEICA"? IN YOUR DREAMS. MUCH AS I LOVE HITCH, THERE'S NO WAY I'M TRADING. HELL, JOHNNY, WHAT ARE YOU SMOKING?
WELL, LET ME THINK. MAYBE THERE'S SOMETHING ELSE OF YOURS I WANT.
I GOT PLENTY.
SO, WHEN WE GONNA SEE IT ALL? WHEN WE GONNA SEE THIS NEW STORE OF YOURS THAT I'VE HEARD WHISPERS ABOUT?
WHEN IT'S READY.
WHEN IT'S PERFECT.

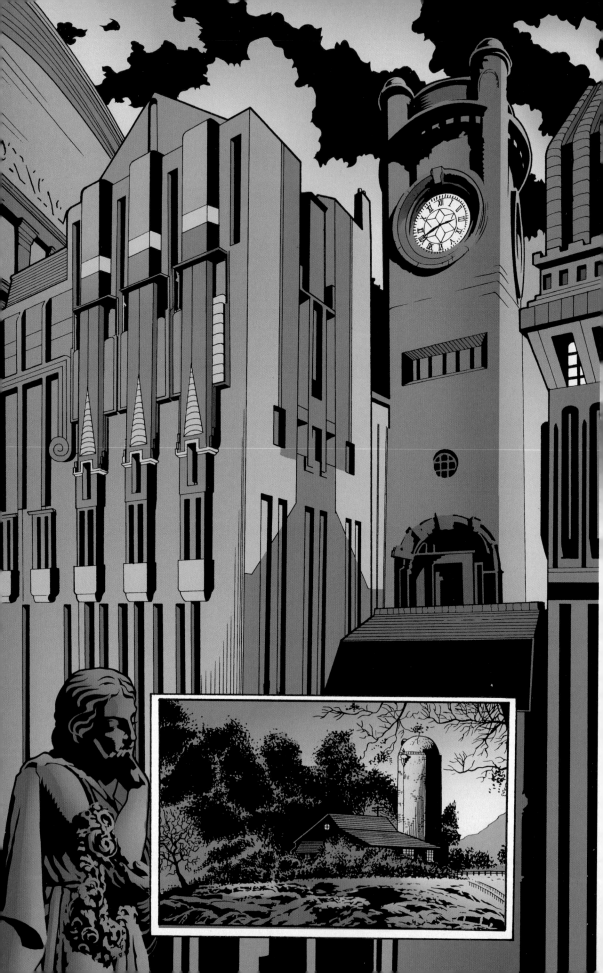

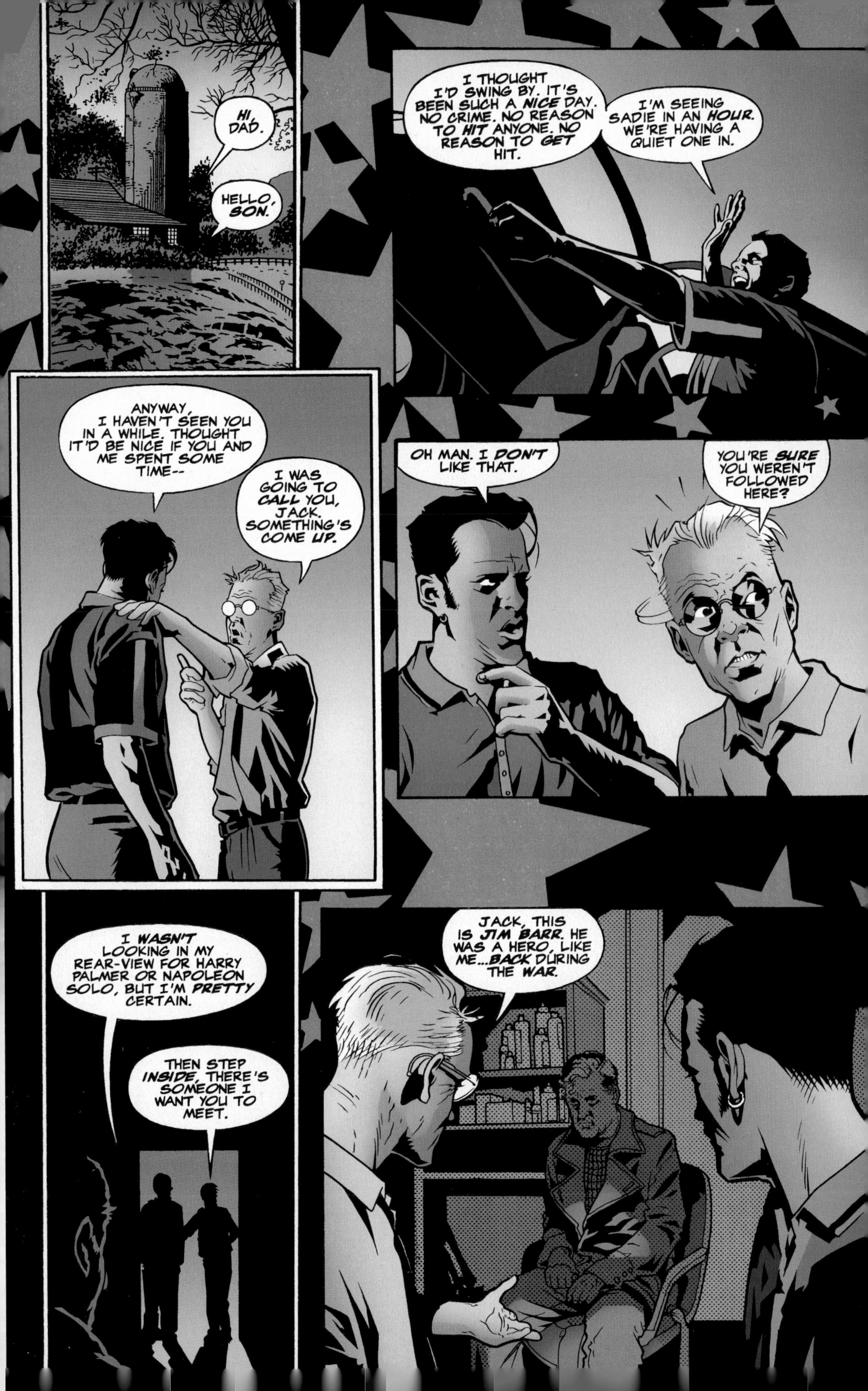
HI, DAD.
HELLO, SON.
I THOUGHT I'D SWING BY. IT'S BEEN SUCH A NICE DAY. NO CRIME. NO REASON TO HIT ANYONE. NO REASON TO GET HIT.
I'M SEEING SADIE IN AN HOUR. WE'RE HAVING A QUIET ONE IN.
ANYWAY, I HAVEN'T SEEN YOU IN A WHILE. THOUGHT IT'D BE NICE IF YOU AND ME SPENT SOME TIME--
I WAS GOING TO CALL YOU, JACK. SOMETHING'S COME UP.
OH MAN. I DON'T LIKE THAT.
YOU'RE SURE YOU WEREN'T FOLLOWED HERE?
I WASN'T LOOKING IN MY REAR-VIEW FOR HARRY PALMER OR NAPOLEON SOLO, BUT I'M PRETTY CERTAIN.
THEN STEP INSIDE, THERE'S SOMEONE I WANT YOU TO MEET.
JACK, THIS IS JIM BARR. HE WAS A HERO, LIKE ME...BACK DURING THE WAR.

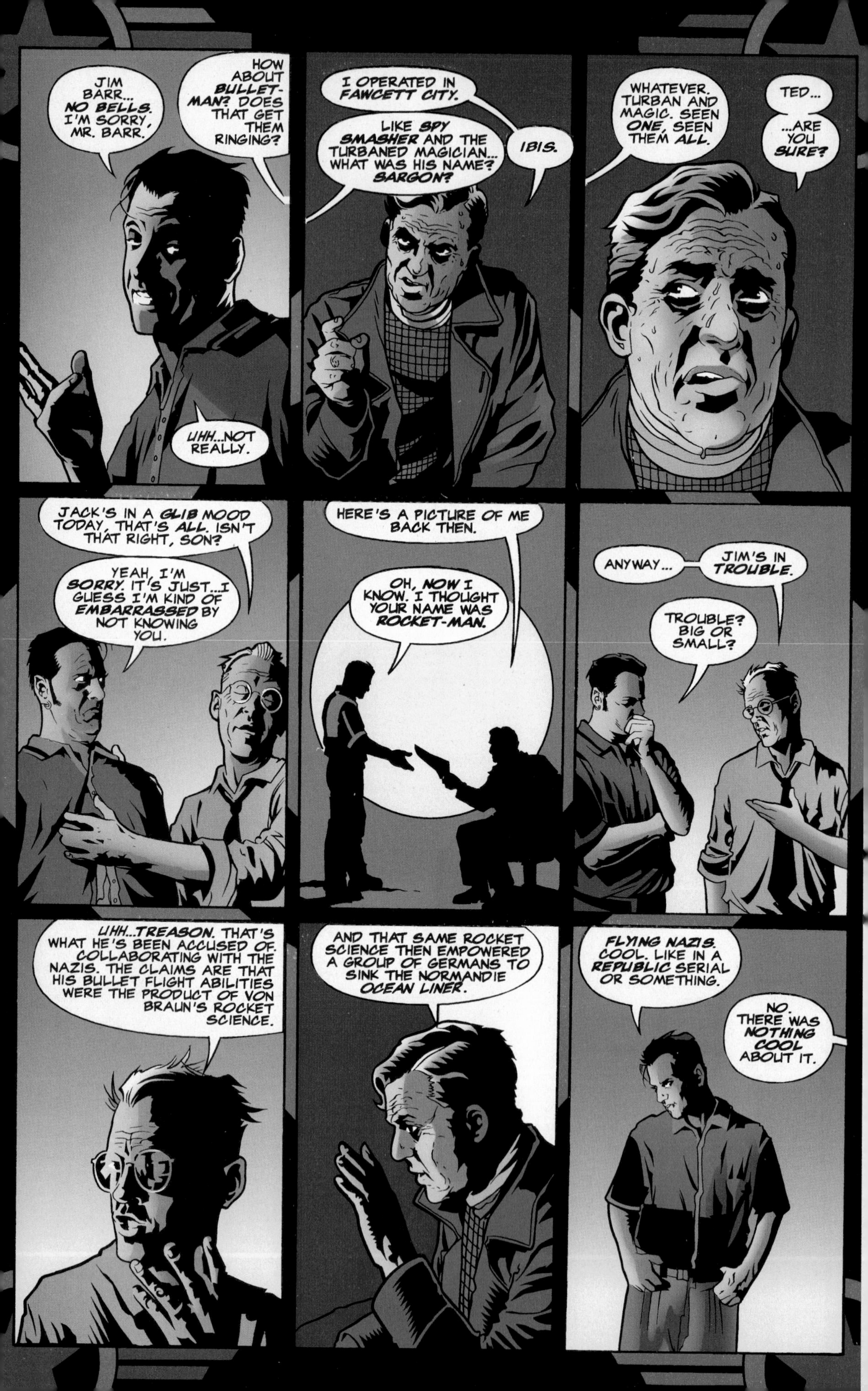

JIM BARR... NO BELLS. I'M SORRY, MR. BARR.
HOW ABOUT BULLET-MAN? DOES THAT GET THEM RINGING?
UHH...NOT REALLY.
I OPERATED IN FAWCETT CITY.
LIKE SPY SMASHER AND THE TURBANED MAGICIAN... WHAT WAS HIS NAME? SARGON?
IBIS.
WHATEVER. TURBAN AND MAGIC. SEEN ONE, SEEN THEM ALL.
TED...
...ARE YOU SURE?
JACK'S IN A GLIB MOOD TODAY, THAT'S ALL. ISN'T THAT RIGHT, SON?
YEAH, I'M SORRY. IT'S JUST...I GUESS I'M KIND OF EMBARRASSED BY NOT KNOWING YOU.
HERE'S A PICTURE OF ME BACK THEN.
OH, NOW I KNOW. I THOUGHT YOUR NAME WAS ROCKET-MAN.
ANYWAY...
JIM'S IN TROUBLE.
TROUBLE? BIG OR SMALL?
UHH...TREASON. THAT'S WHAT HE'S BEEN ACCUSED OF. COLLABORATING WITH THE NAZIS. THE CLAIMS ARE THAT HIS BULLET FLIGHT ABILITIES WERE THE PRODUCT OF VON BRAUN'S ROCKET SCIENCE.
AND THAT SAME ROCKET SCIENCE THEN EMPOWERED A GROUP OF GERMANS TO SINK THE NORMANDIE OCEAN LINER.
FLYING NAZIS. COOL. LIKE IN A REPUBLIC SERIAL OR SOMETHING.
NO. THERE WAS NOTHING COOL ABOUT IT.

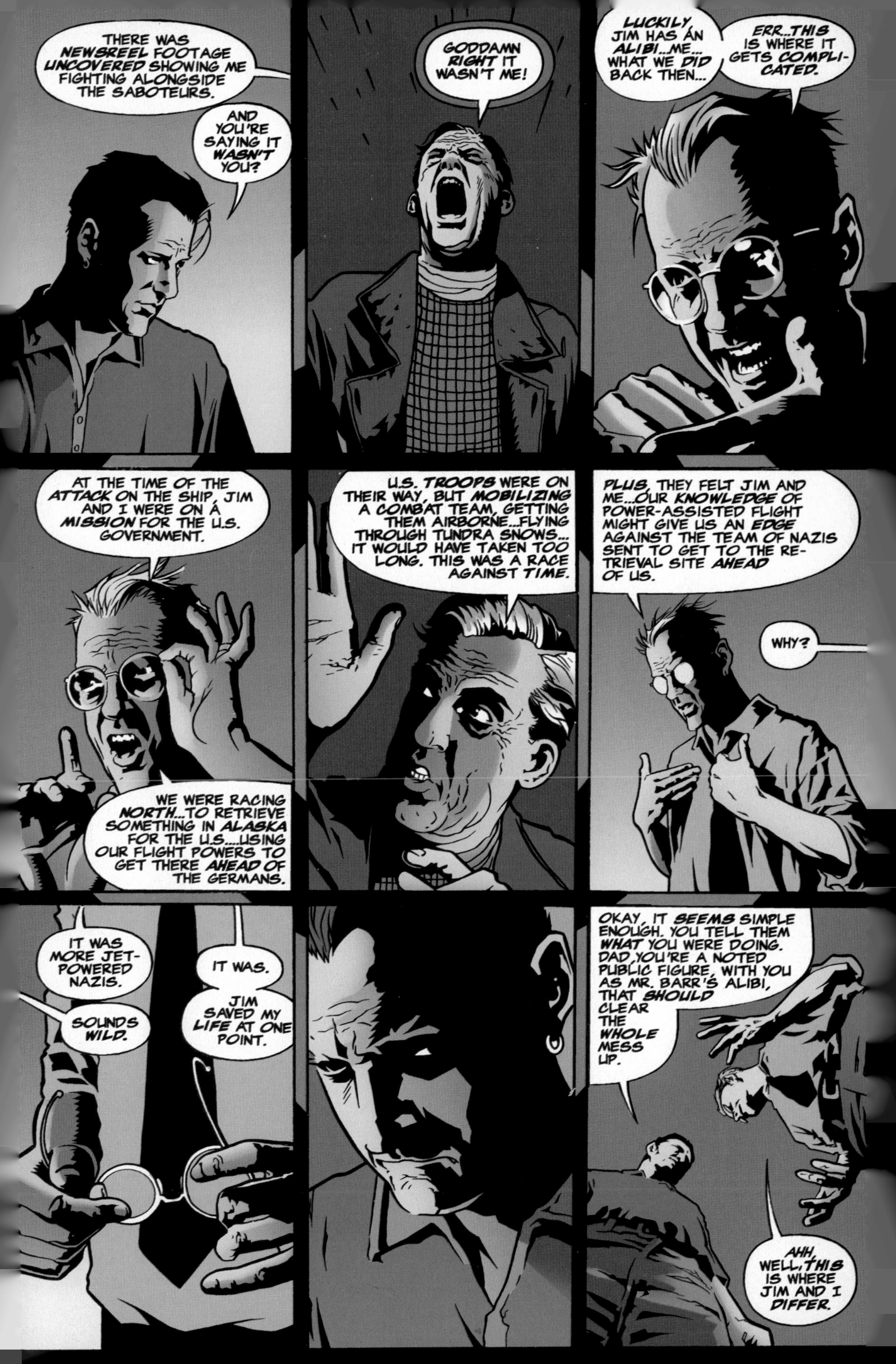
THERE WAS NEWSREEL FOOTAGE UNCOVERED SHOWING ME FIGHTING ALONGSIDE THE SABOTEURS.
AND YOU'RE SAYING IT WASN'T YOU?
GODDAMN RIGHT IT WASN'T ME!
LUCKILY, JIM HAS AN ALIBI...ME... WHAT WE DID BACK THEN...
ERR...THIS IS WHERE IT GETS COMPLI-CATED.
AT THE TIME OF THE ATTACK ON THE SHIP, JIM AND I WERE ON A MISSION FOR THE U.S. GOVERNMENT.
WE WERE RACING NORTH...TO RETRIEVE SOMETHING IN ALASKA FOR THE U.S....USING OUR FLIGHT POWERS TO GET THERE AHEAD OF THE GERMANS.
U.S. TROOPS WERE ON THEIR WAY, BUT MOBILIZING A COMBAT TEAM, GETTING THEM AIRBORNE...FLYING THROUGH TUNDRA SNOWS... IT WOULD HAVE TAKEN TOO LONG. THIS WAS A RACE AGAINST TIME.
PLUS, THEY FELT JIM AND ME...OUR KNOWLEDGE OF POWER-ASSISTED FLIGHT MIGHT GIVE US AN EDGE AGAINST THE TEAM OF NAZIS SENT TO GET TO THE RE-TRIEVAL SITE AHEAD OF US.
WHY?
IT WAS MORE JET-POWERED NAZIS.
SOUNDS WILD.
IT WAS.
JIM SAVED MY LIFE AT ONE POINT.
OKAY, IT SEEMS SIMPLE ENOUGH. YOU TELL THEM WHAT YOU WERE DOING. DAD, YOU'RE A NOTED PUBLIC FIGURE, WITH YOU AS MR. BARR'S ALIBI, THAT SHOULD CLEAR THE WHOLE MESS UP.
AHH, WELL, THIS IS WHERE JIM AND I DIFFER.

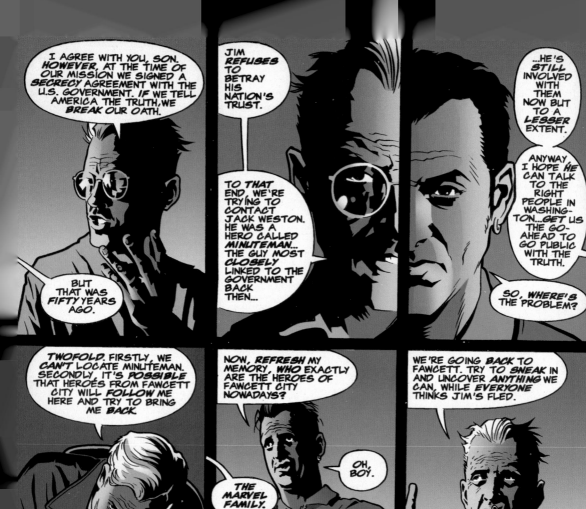

I AGREE WITH YOU, SON. *HOWEVER,* AT THE TIME OF OUR MISSION WE SIGNED A *SECRECY* AGREEMENT WITH THE U.S. GOVERNMENT. *IF* WE TELL AMERICA THE TRUTH, WE *BREAK* OUR OATH.

BUT THAT WAS *FIFTY* YEARS AGO.

JIM *REFUSES* TO BETRAY HIS NATION'S TRUST.

TO THAT END, WE'RE TRYING TO *CONTACT* JACK WESTON. HE WAS A HERO CALLED *MINUTEMAN...* THE GUY MOST *CLOSELY* LINKED TO THE GOVERNMENT BACK THEN...

...HE'S *STILL* INVOLVED WITH THEM NOW BUT TO A *LESSER* EXTENT.

ANYWAY I HOPE *HE* CAN TALK TO THE RIGHT PEOPLE IN WASHING-TON...*GET* US THE GO-AHEAD TO GO PUBLIC WITH THE TRUTH.

SO, *WHERE'S* THE PROBLEM?

TWOFOLD. FIRSTLY, WE *CAN'T* LOCATE MINUTEMAN. SECONDLY, IT'S *POSSIBLE* THAT HEROES FROM FAWCETT CITY WILL *FOLLOW* ME HERE AND TRY TO BRING ME *BACK.*

NOW, *REFRESH* MY MEMORY, *WHO* EXACTLY ARE THE HEROES OF FAWCETT CITY NOWADAYS?

THE *MARVEL* FAMILY.

OH, BOY.

WE'RE GOING *BACK* TO FAWCETT. TRY TO *SNEAK* IN AND UNCOVER *ANYTHING* WE CAN, WHILE *EVERYONE* THINKS JIM'S FLED.

SO IF CAPTAIN MARVEL AND HIS CREW TURN UP HERE, YOU WANT ME TO *RUN* INTERFERENCE?

NOTHING TOO EXTREME, SON. JUST *DELAY* THEM.

I HEAR THEY HAVE *POWER* TO RIVAL SUPERMAN'S, SO *NOTHING* I CAN DO IS GONNA BE *TOO* EXTREME.

DO YOUR BEST.

NICE MEETING YOU, MR. BARR.

YOU HAVE MY *GRATITUDE,* JACK.

IF YOU *SAVED* MY DAD'S LIFE, MR. BARR, THEN IT'S *YOU* WHO HAVE MINE.

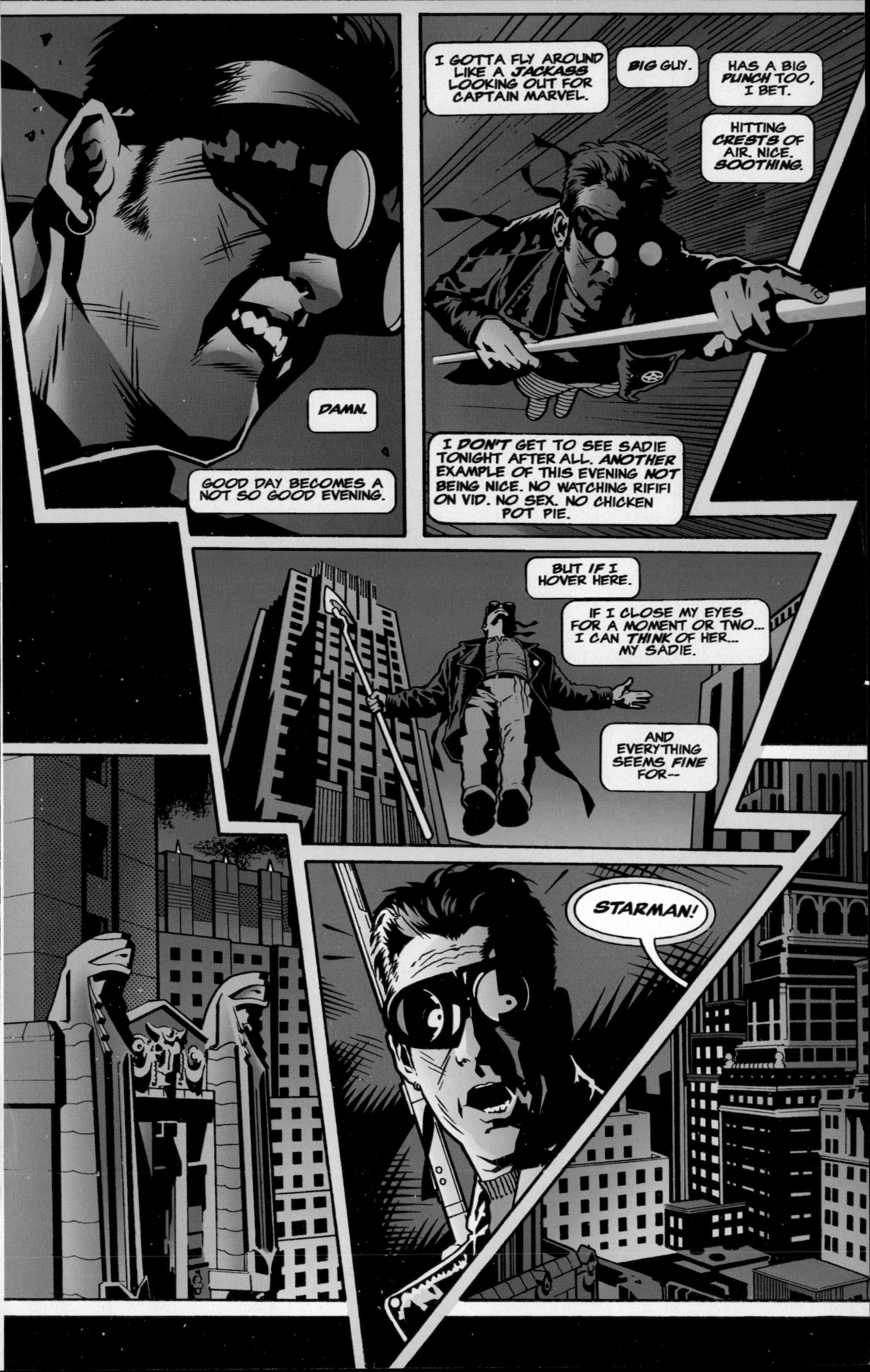

DAMN.
GOOD DAY BECOMES A NOT SO GOOD EVENING.
I GOTTA FLY AROUND LIKE A JACKASS LOOKING OUT FOR CAPTAIN MARVEL.
BIG GUY.
HAS A BIG PUNCH TOO, I BET.
HITTING CRESTS OF AIR. NICE. SOOTHING.
I DON'T GET TO SEE SADIE TONIGHT AFTER ALL. ANOTHER EXAMPLE OF THIS EVENING NOT BEING NICE. NO WATCHING RIFIFI ON VID. NO SEX. NO CHICKEN POT PIE.
BUT IF I HOVER HERE.
IF I CLOSE MY EYES FOR A MOMENT OR TWO... I CAN THINK OF HER... MY SADIE.
AND EVERYTHING SEEMS FINE FOR--
STARMAN!

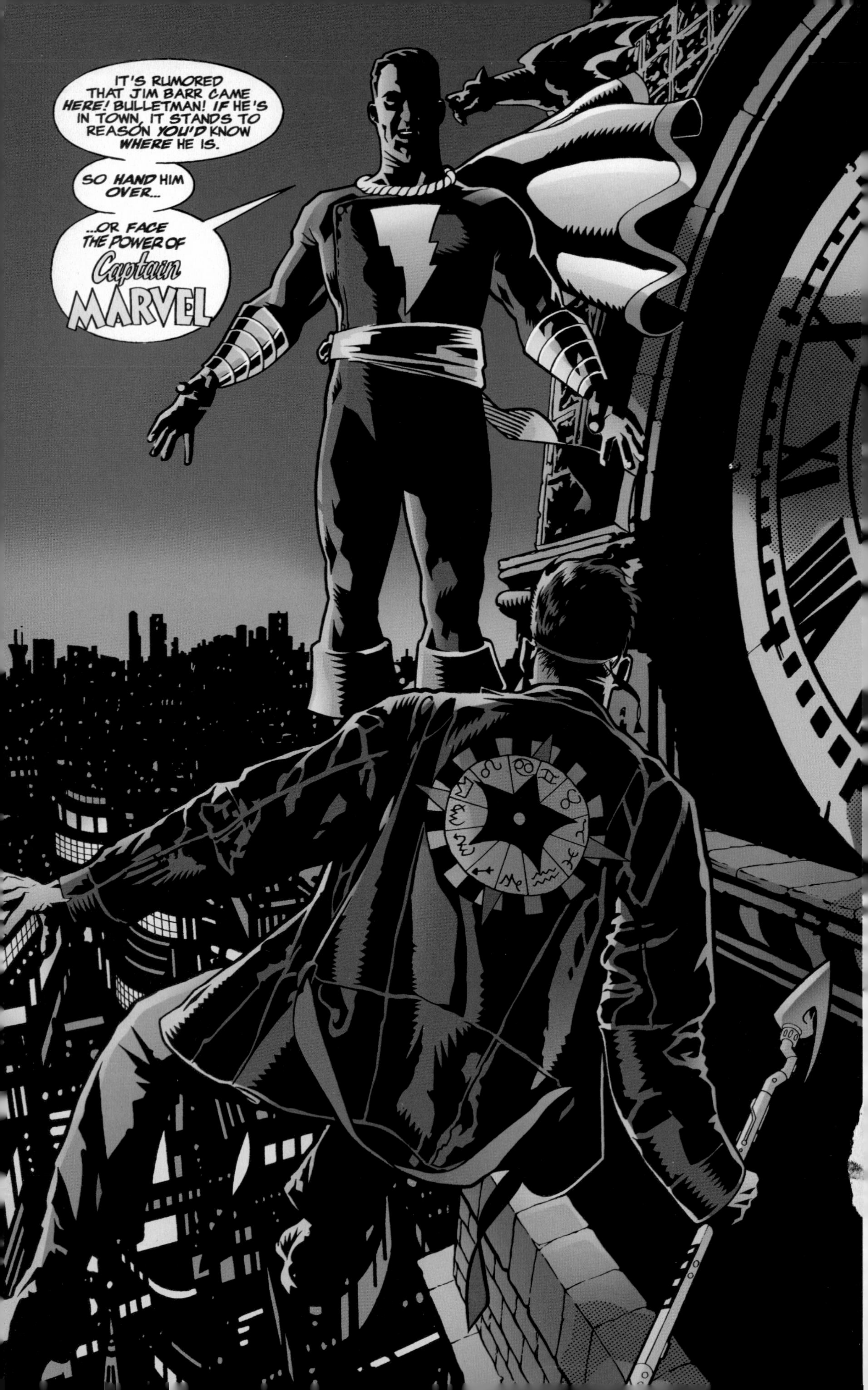
IT'S RUMORED THAT JIM BARR CAME HERE! BULLETMAN! IF HE'S IN TOWN, IT STANDS TO REASON YOU'D KNOW WHERE HE IS.
SO HAND HIM OVER...
...OR FACE THE POWER OF Captain MARVEL

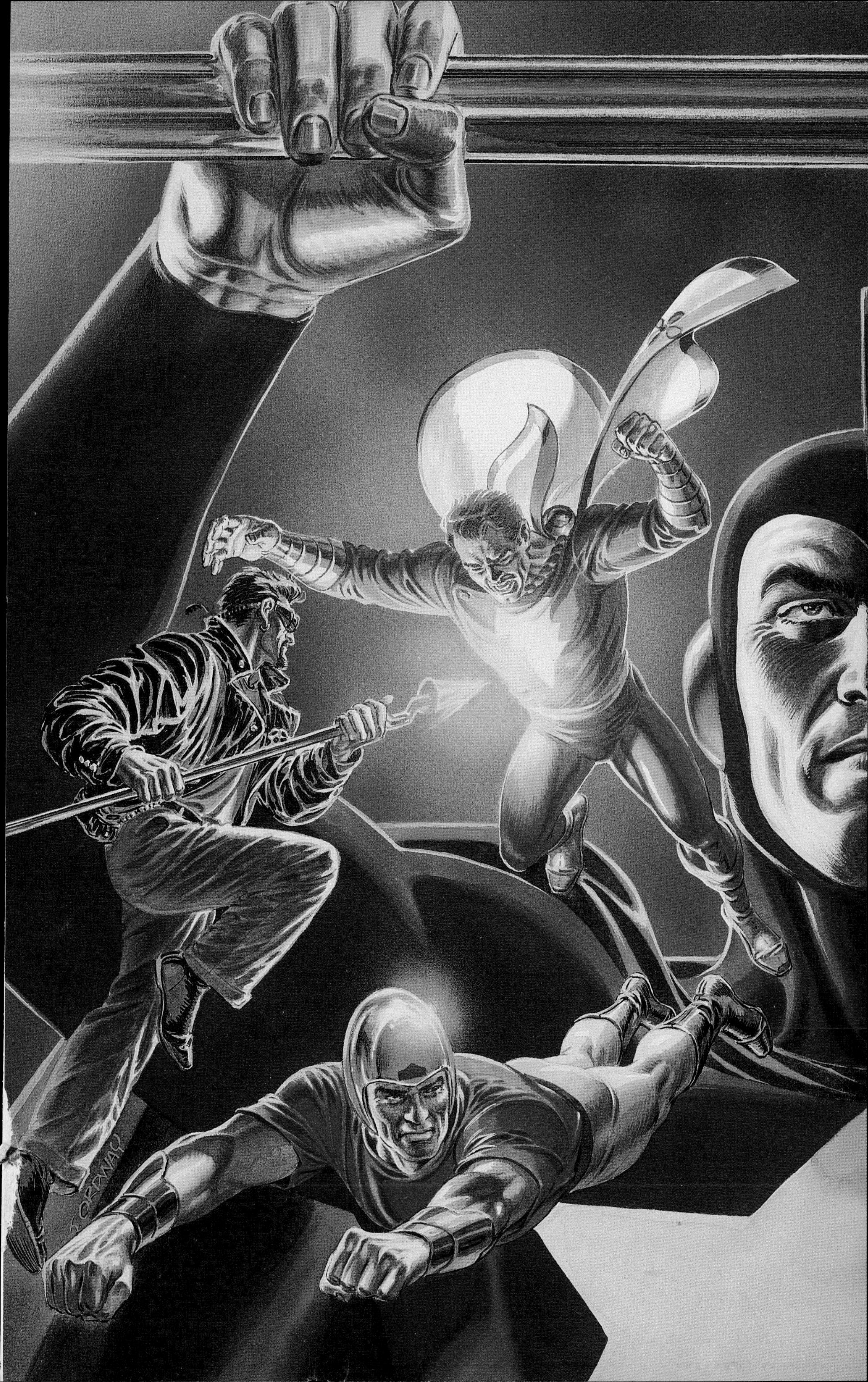

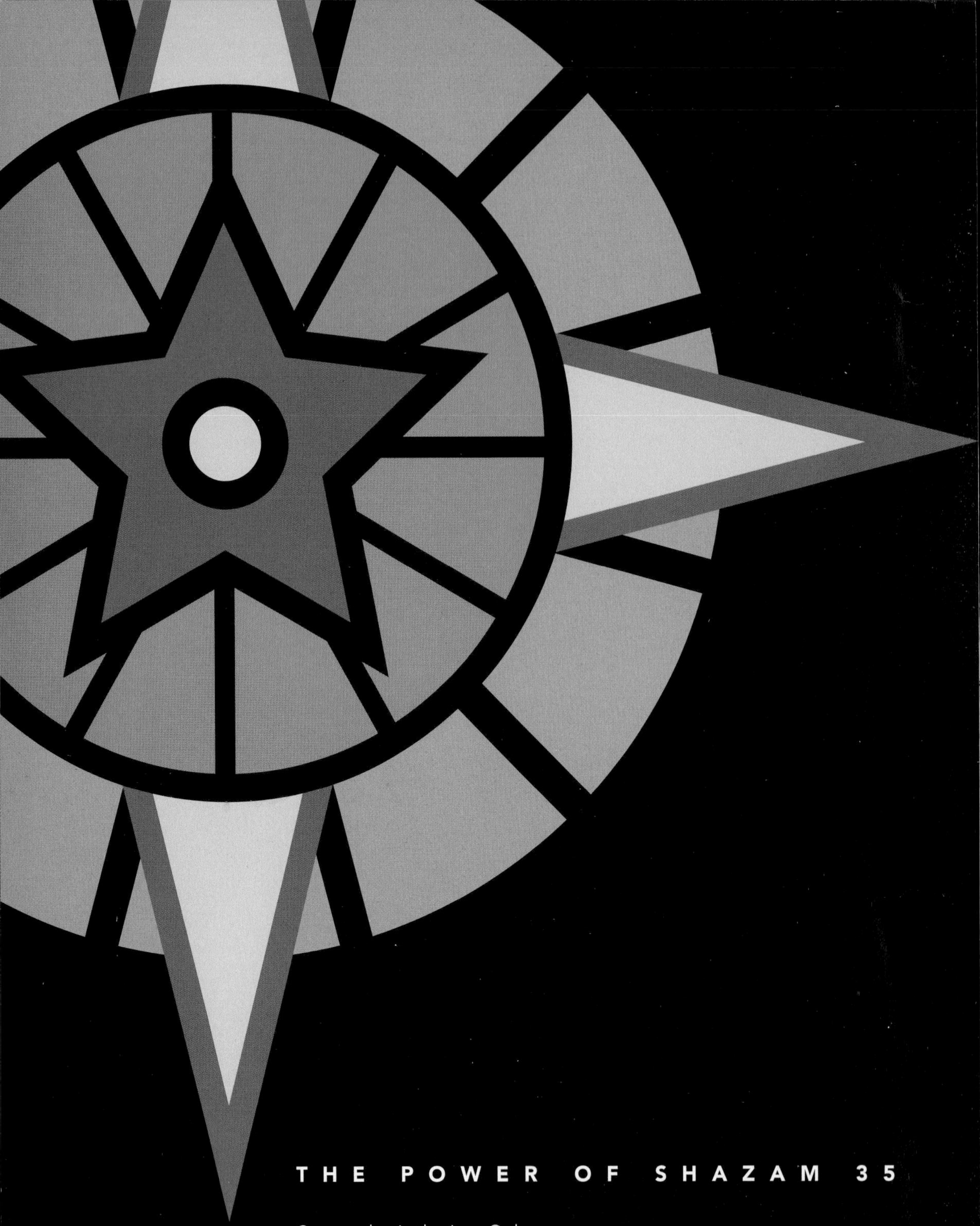

THE POWER OF SHAZAM 35

Cover and script by Jerry Ordway

Pencils by Pete Krause

with inks by Dick Giordano

and colors by Glenn Whitmore

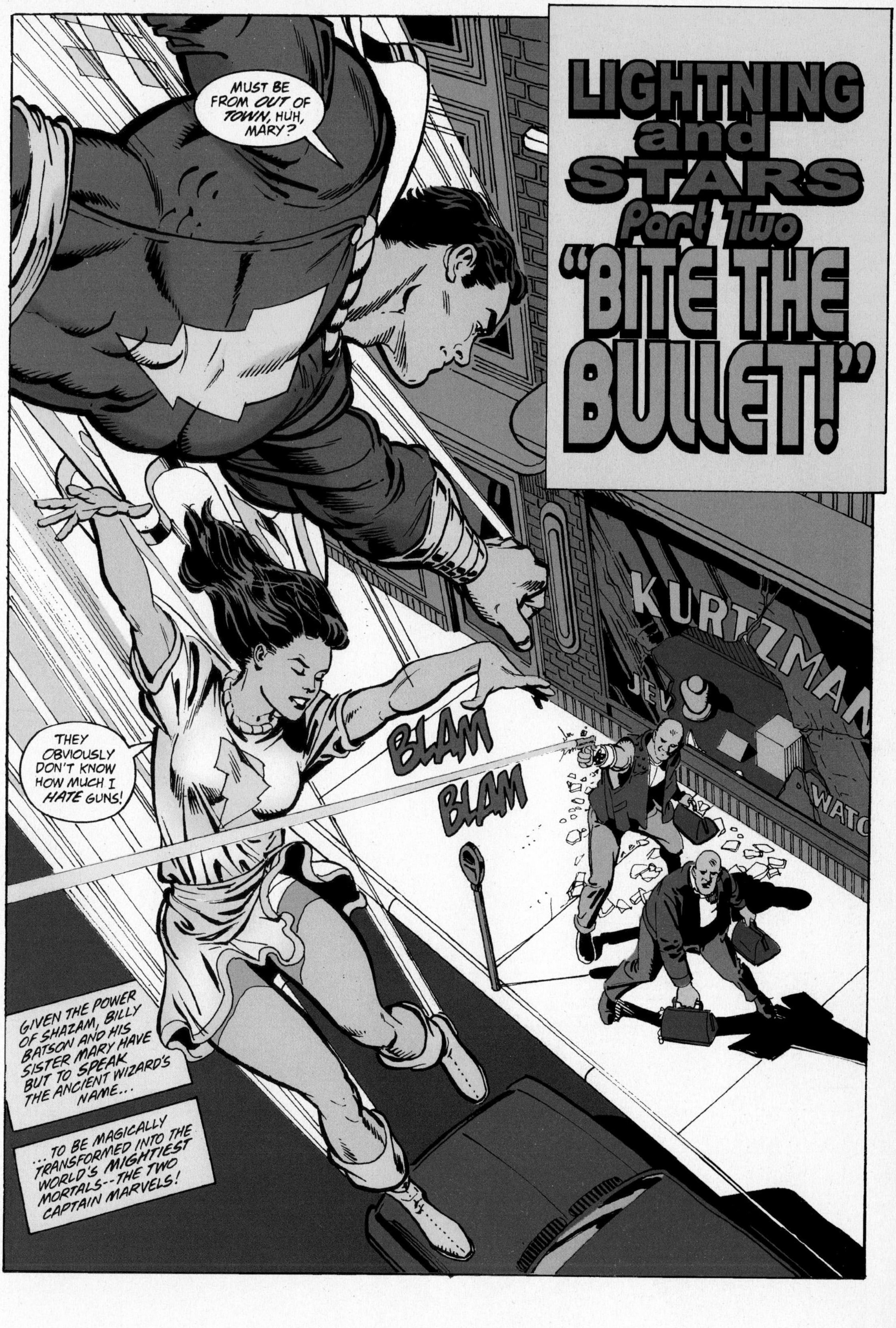
LIGHTNING and STARS
Part Two
"BITE THE BULLET!"
MUST BE FROM OUT OF TOWN, HUH, MARY?
THEY OBVIOUSLY DON'T KNOW HOW MUCH I HATE GUNS!
BLAM
BLAM
KURTZMAN
GIVEN THE POWER OF SHAZAM, BILLY BATSON AND HIS SISTER MARY HAVE BUT TO SPEAK THE ANCIENT WIZARD'S NAME...
...TO BE MAGICALLY TRANSFORMED INTO THE WORLD'S MIGHTIEST MORTALS--THE TWO CAPTAIN MARVELS!

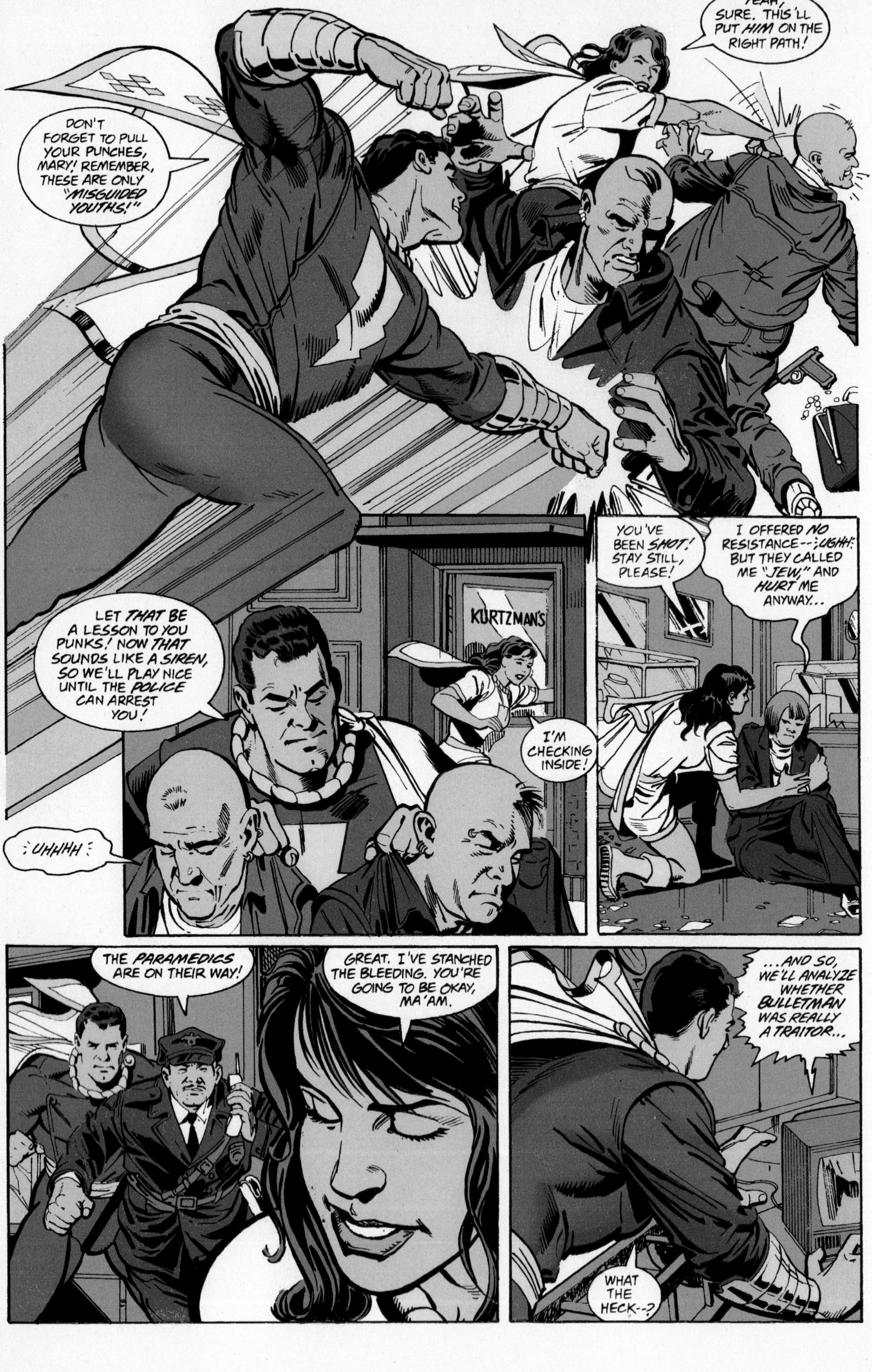
DON'T FORGET TO PULL YOUR PUNCHES, MARY! REMEMBER, THESE ARE ONLY "MISGUIDED YOUTHS!"
YEAH, SURE. THIS'LL PUT HIM ON THE RIGHT PATH!
LET THAT BE A LESSON TO YOU PUNKS! NOW THAT SOUNDS LIKE A SIREN, SO WE'LL PLAY NICE UNTIL THE POLICE CAN ARREST YOU!
KURTZMAN'S
I'M CHECKING INSIDE!
UHHHH
YOU'VE BEEN SHOT! STAY STILL, PLEASE!
I OFFERED NO RESISTANCE-- UGHH! BUT THEY CALLED ME "JEW," AND HURT ME ANYWAY...
THE PARAMEDICS ARE ON THEIR WAY!
GREAT. I'VE STANCHED THE BLEEDING. YOU'RE GOING TO BE OKAY, MA'AM.
...AND SO, WE'LL ANALYZE WHETHER BULLETMAN WAS REALLY A TRAITOR...
WHAT THE HECK--?

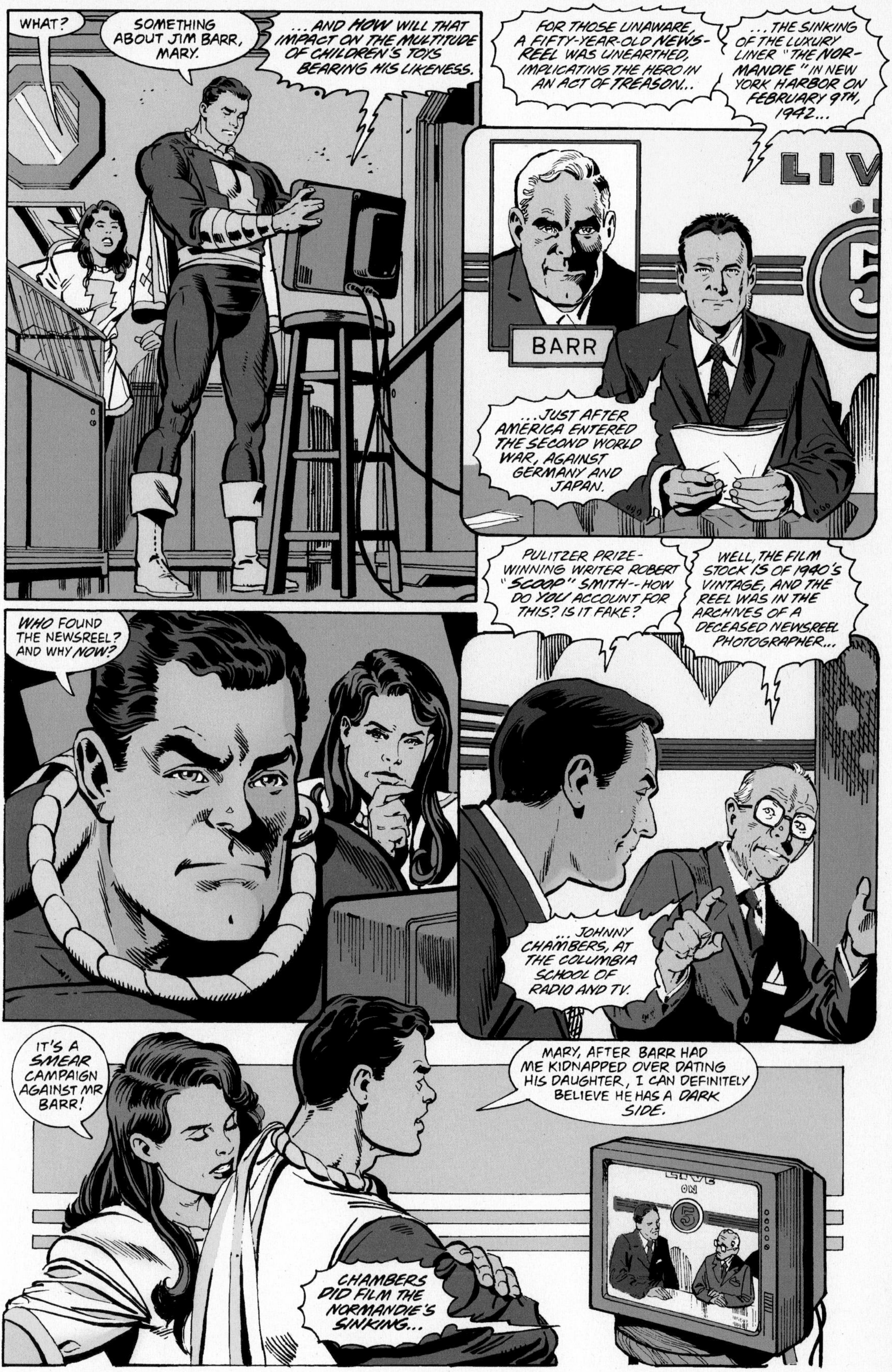
WHAT?
SOMETHING ABOUT JIM BARR, MARY.
...AND HOW WILL THAT IMPACT ON THE MULTITUDE OF CHILDREN'S TOYS BEARING HIS LIKENESS.
FOR THOSE UNAWARE, A FIFTY-YEAR-OLD NEWS-REEL WAS UNEARTHED, IMPLICATING THE HERO IN AN ACT OF TREASON...
...THE SINKING OF THE LUXURY LINER "THE NORMANDIE" IN NEW YORK HARBOR ON FEBRUARY 9TH, 1942...
LIV
BARR
5
...JUST AFTER AMERICA ENTERED THE SECOND WORLD WAR, AGAINST GERMANY AND JAPAN.
PULITZER PRIZE-WINNING WRITER ROBERT "SCOOP" SMITH--HOW DO YOU ACCOUNT FOR THIS? IS IT FAKE?
WELL, THE FILM STOCK IS OF 1940'S VINTAGE, AND THE REEL WAS IN THE ARCHIVES OF A DECEASED NEWSREEL PHOTOGRAPHER...
WHO FOUND THE NEWSREEL? AND WHY NOW?
...JOHNNY CHAMBERS, AT THE COLUMBIA SCHOOL OF RADIO AND TV.
IT'S A SMEAR CAMPAIGN AGAINST MR BARR!
MARY, AFTER BARR HAD ME KIDNAPPED OVER DATING HIS DAUGHTER, I CAN DEFINITELY BELIEVE HE HAS A DARK SIDE.
LIVE ON 5
CHAMBERS DID FILM THE NORMANDIE'S SINKING...

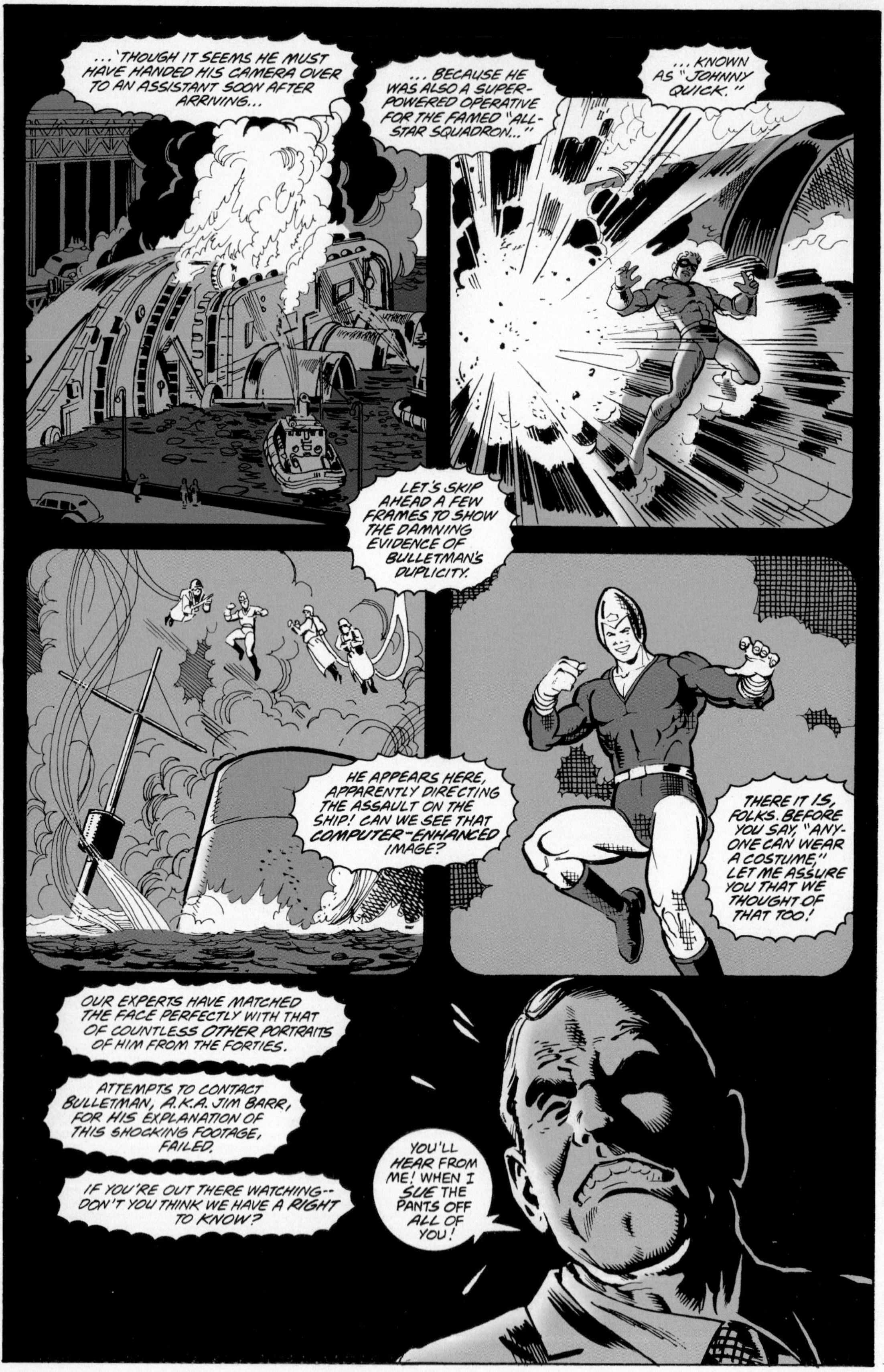
...'THOUGH IT SEEMS HE MUST HAVE HANDED HIS CAMERA OVER TO AN ASSISTANT SOON AFTER ARRIVING...
...BECAUSE HE WAS ALSO A SUPER-POWERED OPERATIVE FOR THE FAMED "ALL-STAR SQUADRON..."
...KNOWN AS "JOHNNY QUICK."
LET'S SKIP AHEAD A FEW FRAMES TO SHOW THE DAMNING EVIDENCE OF BULLETMAN'S DUPLICITY.
HE APPEARS HERE, APPARENTLY DIRECTING THE ASSAULT ON THE SHIP! CAN WE SEE THAT COMPUTER-ENHANCED IMAGE?
THERE IT IS, FOLKS. BEFORE YOU SAY, "ANY-ONE CAN WEAR A COSTUME," LET ME ASSURE YOU THAT WE THOUGHT OF THAT TOO!
OUR EXPERTS HAVE MATCHED THE FACE PERFECTLY WITH THAT OF COUNTLESS OTHER PORTRAITS OF HIM FROM THE FORTIES.
ATTEMPTS TO CONTACT BULLETMAN, A.K.A. JIM BARR, FOR HIS EXPLANATION OF THIS SHOCKING FOOTAGE, FAILED.
IF YOU'RE OUT THERE WATCHING-- DON'T YOU THINK WE HAVE A RIGHT TO KNOW?
YOU'LL HEAR FROM ME! WHEN I SUE THE PANTS OFF ALL OF YOU!

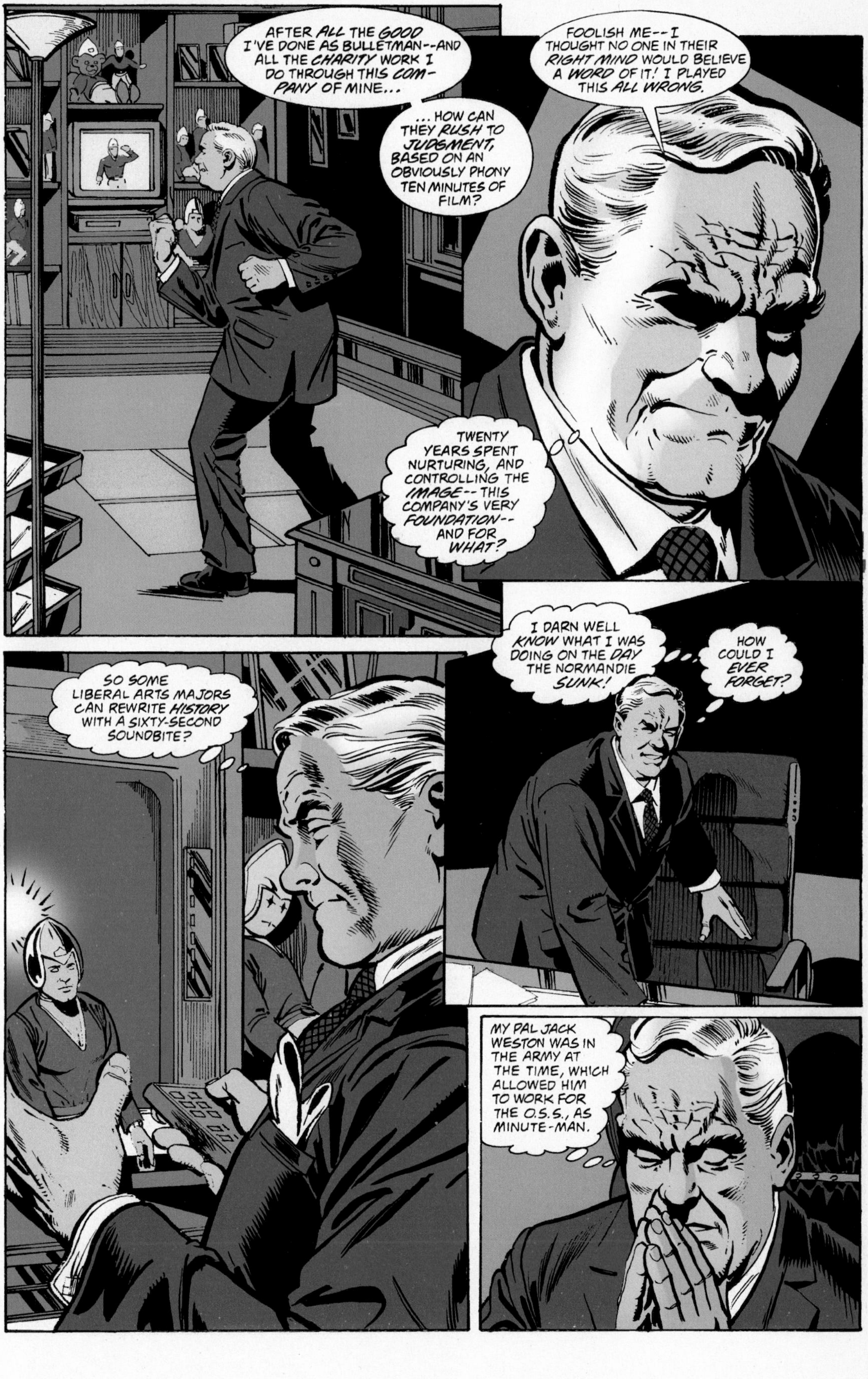
AFTER ALL THE GOOD I'VE DONE AS BULLETMAN--AND ALL THE CHARITY WORK I DO THROUGH THIS COMPANY OF MINE...
...HOW CAN THEY RUSH TO JUDGMENT, BASED ON AN OBVIOUSLY PHONY TEN MINUTES OF FILM?
FOOLISH ME--I THOUGHT NO ONE IN THEIR RIGHT MIND WOULD BELIEVE A WORD OF IT! I PLAYED THIS ALL WRONG.
TWENTY YEARS SPENT NURTURING, AND CONTROLLING THE IMAGE--THIS COMPANY'S VERY FOUNDATION--AND FOR WHAT?
SO SOME LIBERAL ARTS MAJORS CAN REWRITE HISTORY WITH A SIXTY-SECOND SOUNDBITE?
I DARN WELL KNOW WHAT I WAS DOING ON THE DAY THE NORMANDIE SUNK!
HOW COULD I EVER FORGET?
MY PAL JACK WESTON WAS IN THE ARMY AT THE TIME, WHICH ALLOWED HIM TO WORK FOR THE O.S.S., AS MINUTE-MAN.

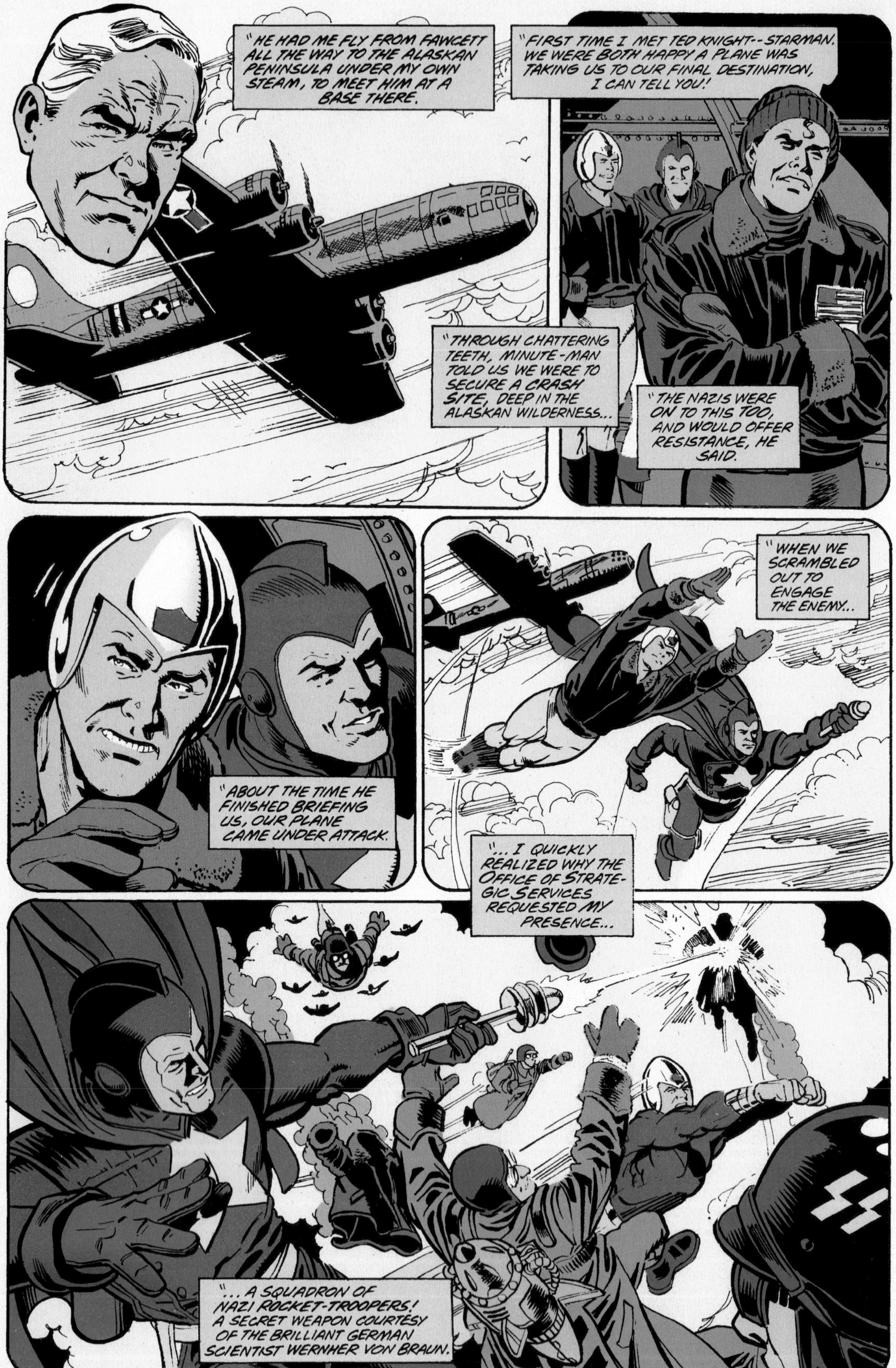
"HE HAD ME FLY FROM FAWCETT ALL THE WAY TO THE ALASKAN PENINSULA UNDER MY OWN STEAM, TO MEET HIM AT A BASE THERE.
"THROUGH CHATTERING TEETH, MINUTE-MAN TOLD US WE WERE TO SECURE A CRASH SITE, DEEP IN THE ALASKAN WILDERNESS...
"FIRST TIME I MET TED KNIGHT--STARMAN. WE WERE BOTH HAPPY A PLANE WAS TAKING US TO OUR FINAL DESTINATION, I CAN TELL YOU!
"THE NAZIS WERE ON TO THIS TOO, AND WOULD OFFER RESISTANCE, HE SAID.
"ABOUT THE TIME HE FINISHED BRIEFING US, OUR PLANE CAME UNDER ATTACK.
"WHEN WE SCRAMBLED OUT TO ENGAGE THE ENEMY...
"...I QUICKLY REALIZED WHY THE OFFICE OF STRATE-GIC SERVICES REQUESTED MY PRESENCE...
"...A SQUADRON OF NAZI ROCKET-TROOPERS! A SECRET WEAPON COURTESY OF THE BRILLIANT GERMAN SCIENTIST WERNHER VON BRAUN.

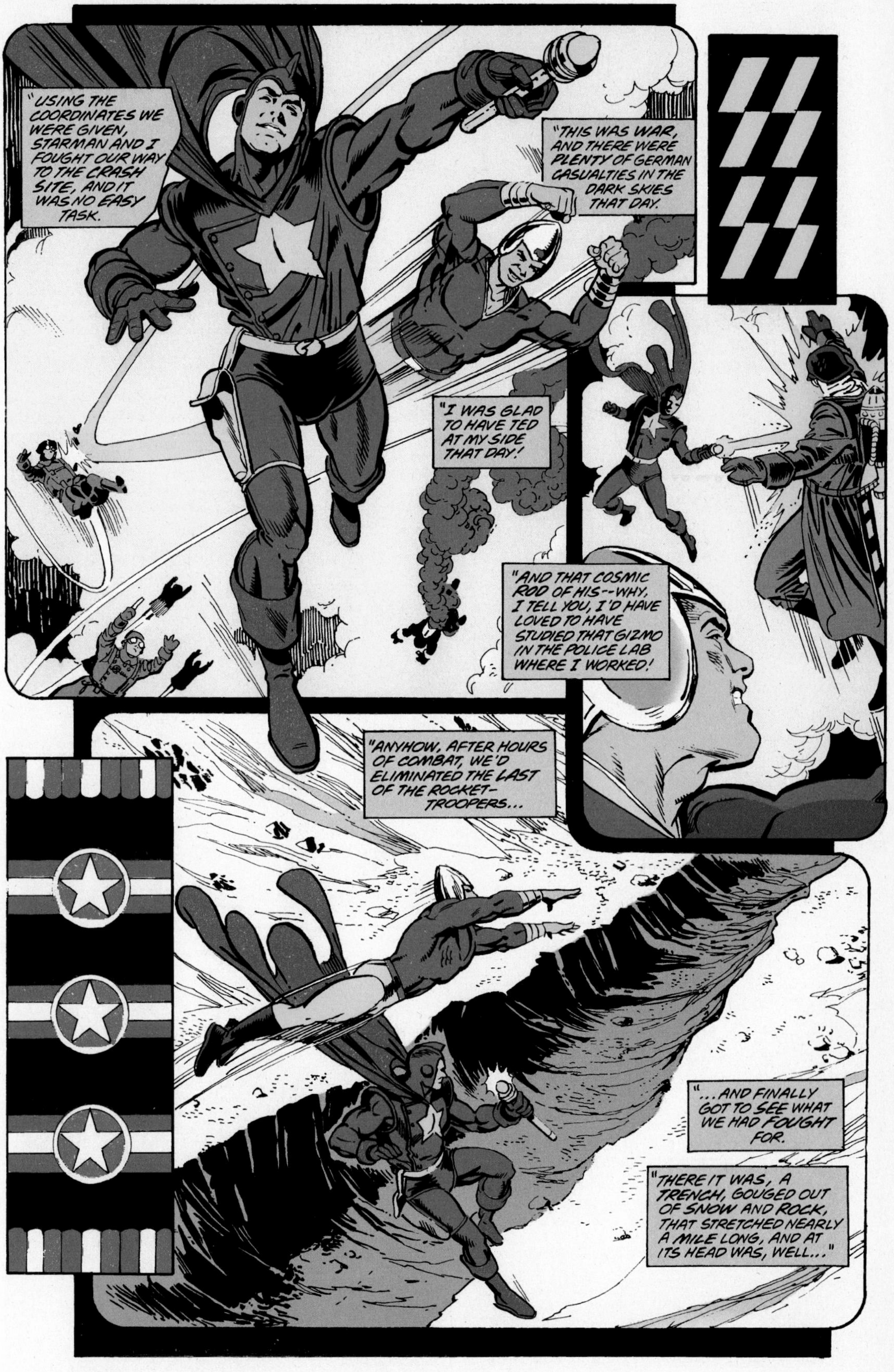
"USING THE COORDINATES WE WERE GIVEN, STARMAN AND I FOUGHT OUR WAY TO THE CRASH SITE, AND IT WAS NO EASY TASK.
"THIS WAS WAR, AND THERE WERE PLENTY OF GERMAN CASUALTIES IN THE DARK SKIES THAT DAY.
"I WAS GLAD TO HAVE TED AT MY SIDE THAT DAY!
"AND THAT COSMIC ROD OF HIS--WHY, I TELL YOU, I'D HAVE LOVED TO HAVE STUDIED THAT GIZMO IN THE POLICE LAB WHERE I WORKED!
"ANYHOW, AFTER HOURS OF COMBAT, WE'D ELIMINATED THE LAST OF THE ROCKET-TROOPERS...
"...AND FINALLY GOT TO SEE WHAT WE HAD FOUGHT FOR.
"THERE IT WAS, A TRENCH, GOUGED OUT OF SNOW AND ROCK, THAT STRETCHED NEARLY A MILE LONG, AND AT ITS HEAD WAS, WELL..."

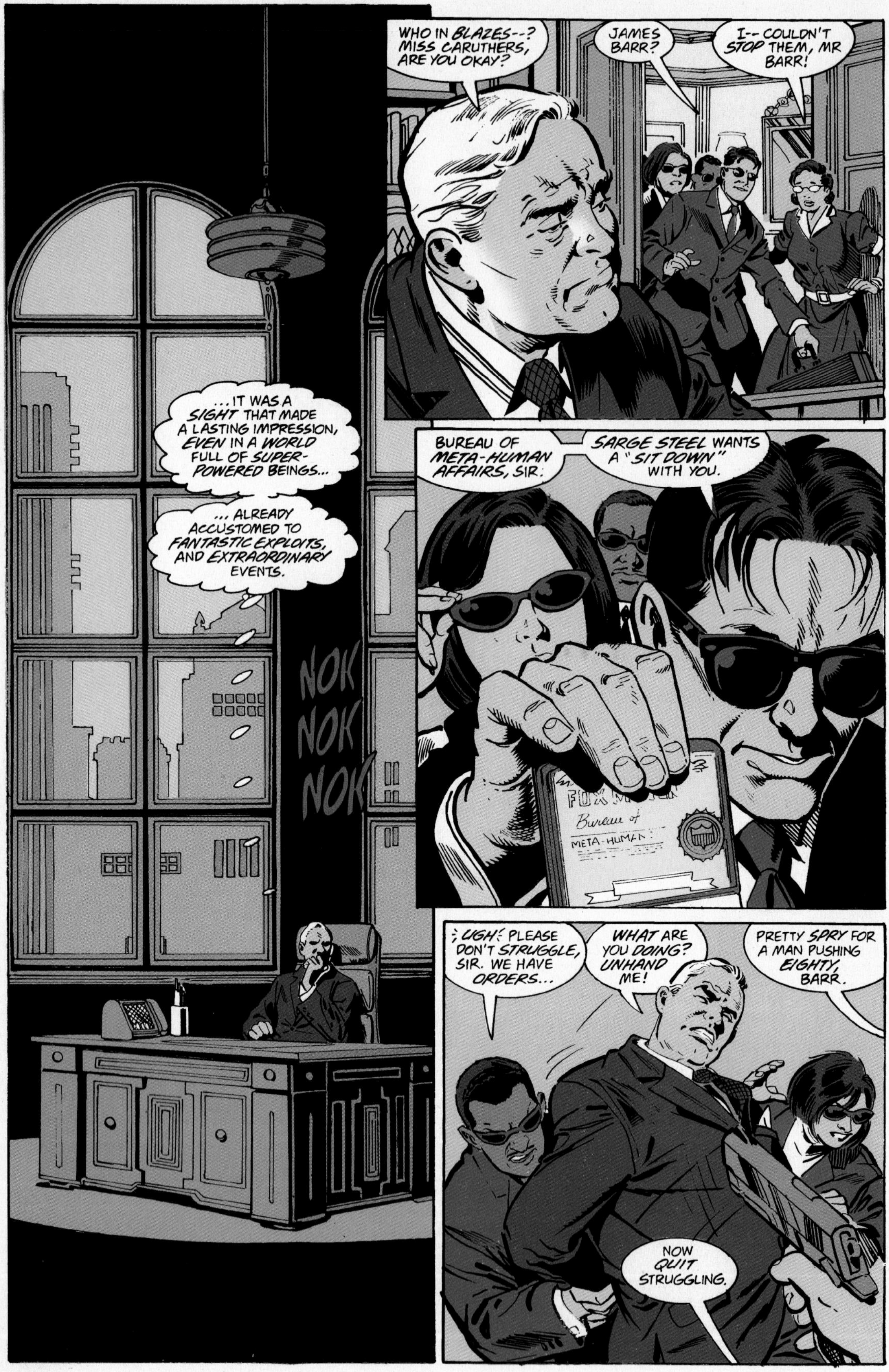
...IT WAS A SIGHT THAT MADE A LASTING IMPRESSION, EVEN IN A WORLD FULL OF SUPER-POWERED BEINGS...
...ALREADY ACCUSTOMED TO FANTASTIC EXPLOITS, AND EXTRAORDINARY EVENTS.
NOK NOK NOK
WHO IN BLAZES--? MISS CARUTHERS, ARE YOU OKAY?
JAMES BARR?
I-- COULDN'T STOP THEM, MR BARR!
BUREAU OF META-HUMAN AFFAIRS, SIR.
SARGE STEEL WANTS A "SIT DOWN" WITH YOU.
Bureau of
META-HUMAN
UGH! PLEASE DON'T STRUGGLE, SIR. WE HAVE ORDERS...
WHAT ARE YOU DOING? UNHAND ME!
PRETTY SPRY FOR A MAN PUSHING EIGHTY, BARR.
NOW QUIT STRUGGLING.

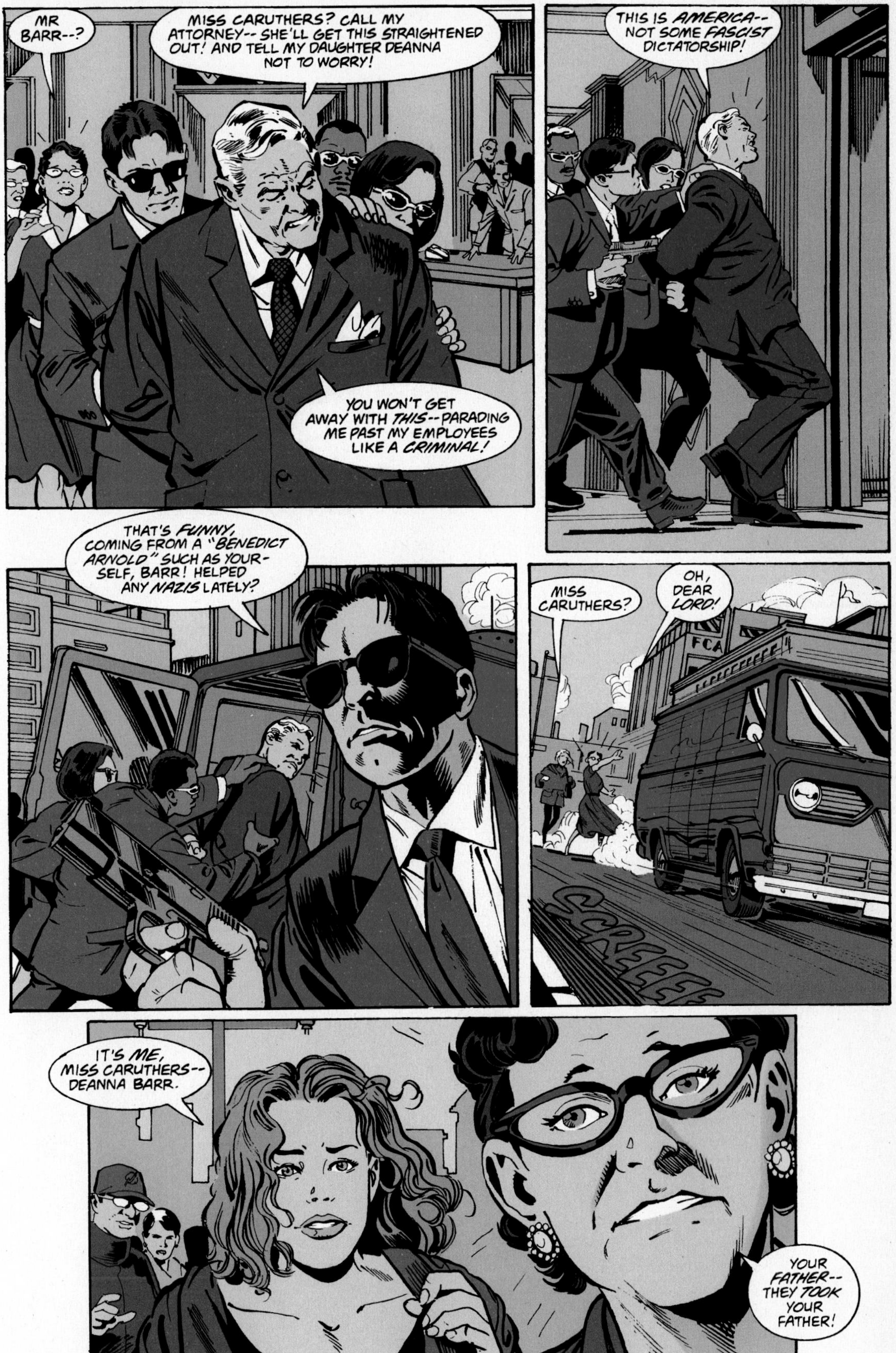
MR BARR--?
MISS CARUTHERS? CALL MY ATTORNEY-- SHE'LL GET THIS STRAIGHTENED OUT! AND TELL MY DAUGHTER DEANNA NOT TO WORRY!
YOU WON'T GET AWAY WITH THIS--PARADING ME PAST MY EMPLOYEES LIKE A CRIMINAL!
THIS IS AMERICA-- NOT SOME FASCIST DICTATORSHIP!
THAT'S FUNNY, COMING FROM A "BENEDICT ARNOLD" SUCH AS YOURSELF, BARR! HELPED ANY NAZIS LATELY?
MISS CARUTHERS?
OH, DEAR LORD!
FCA
SCREEEE
IT'S ME, MISS CARUTHERS-- DEANNA BARR.
YOUR FATHER-- THEY TOOK YOUR FATHER!

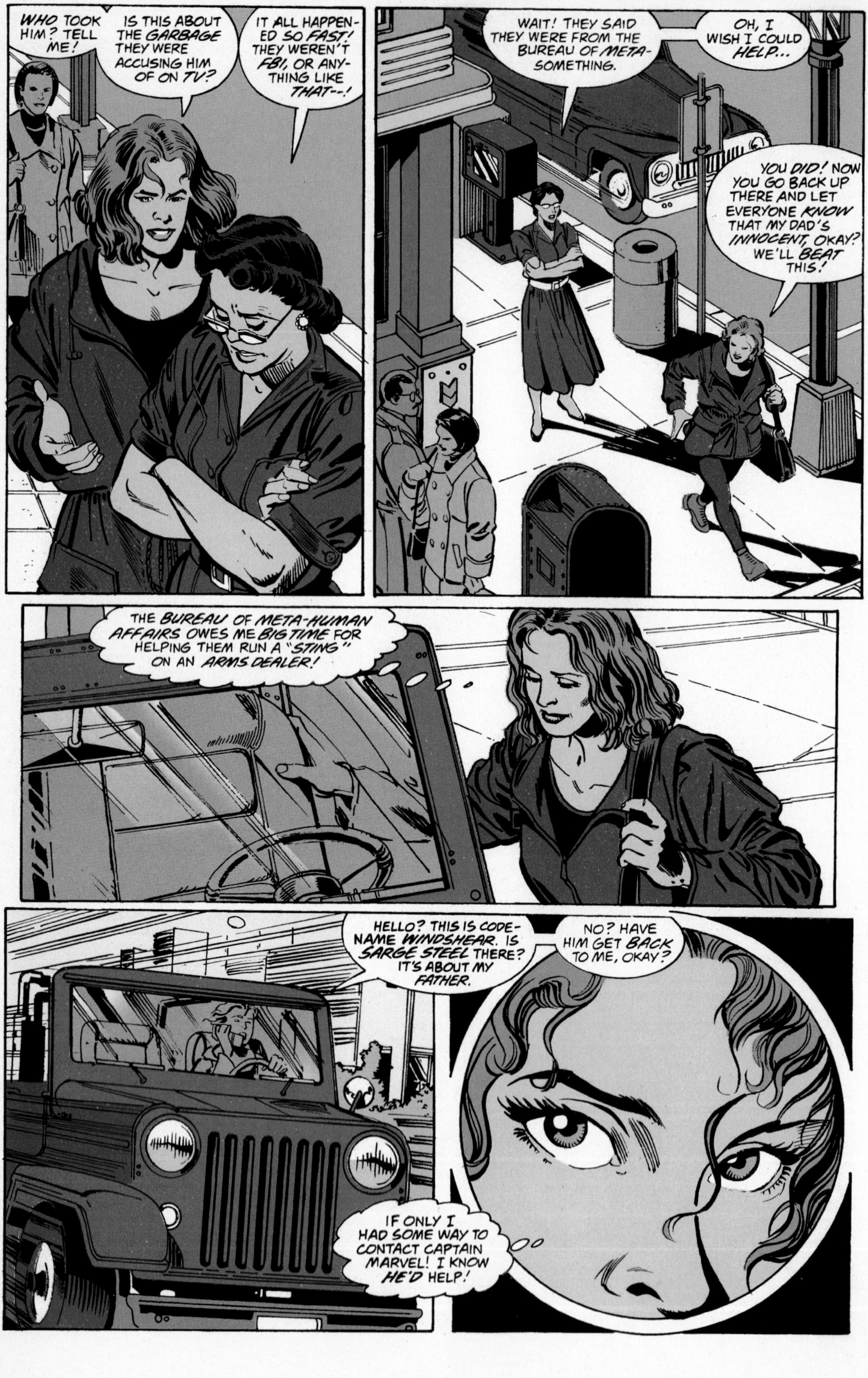
WHO TOOK HIM? TELL ME!
IS THIS ABOUT THE GARBAGE THEY WERE ACCUSING HIM OF ON TV?
IT ALL HAPPENED SO FAST! THEY WEREN'T FBI, OR ANYTHING LIKE THAT--!
WAIT! THEY SAID THEY WERE FROM THE BUREAU OF META-SOMETHING.
OH, I WISH I COULD HELP...
YOU DID! NOW YOU GO BACK UP THERE AND LET EVERYONE KNOW THAT MY DAD'S INNOCENT, OKAY? WE'LL BEAT THIS!
THE BUREAU OF META-HUMAN AFFAIRS OWES ME BIG TIME FOR HELPING THEM RUN A "STING" ON AN ARMS DEALER!
HELLO? THIS IS CODE-NAME WINDSHEAR. IS SARGE STEEL THERE? IT'S ABOUT MY FATHER.
NO? HAVE HIM GET BACK TO ME, OKAY?
IF ONLY I HAD SOME WAY TO CONTACT CAPTAIN MARVEL! I KNOW HE'D HELP!

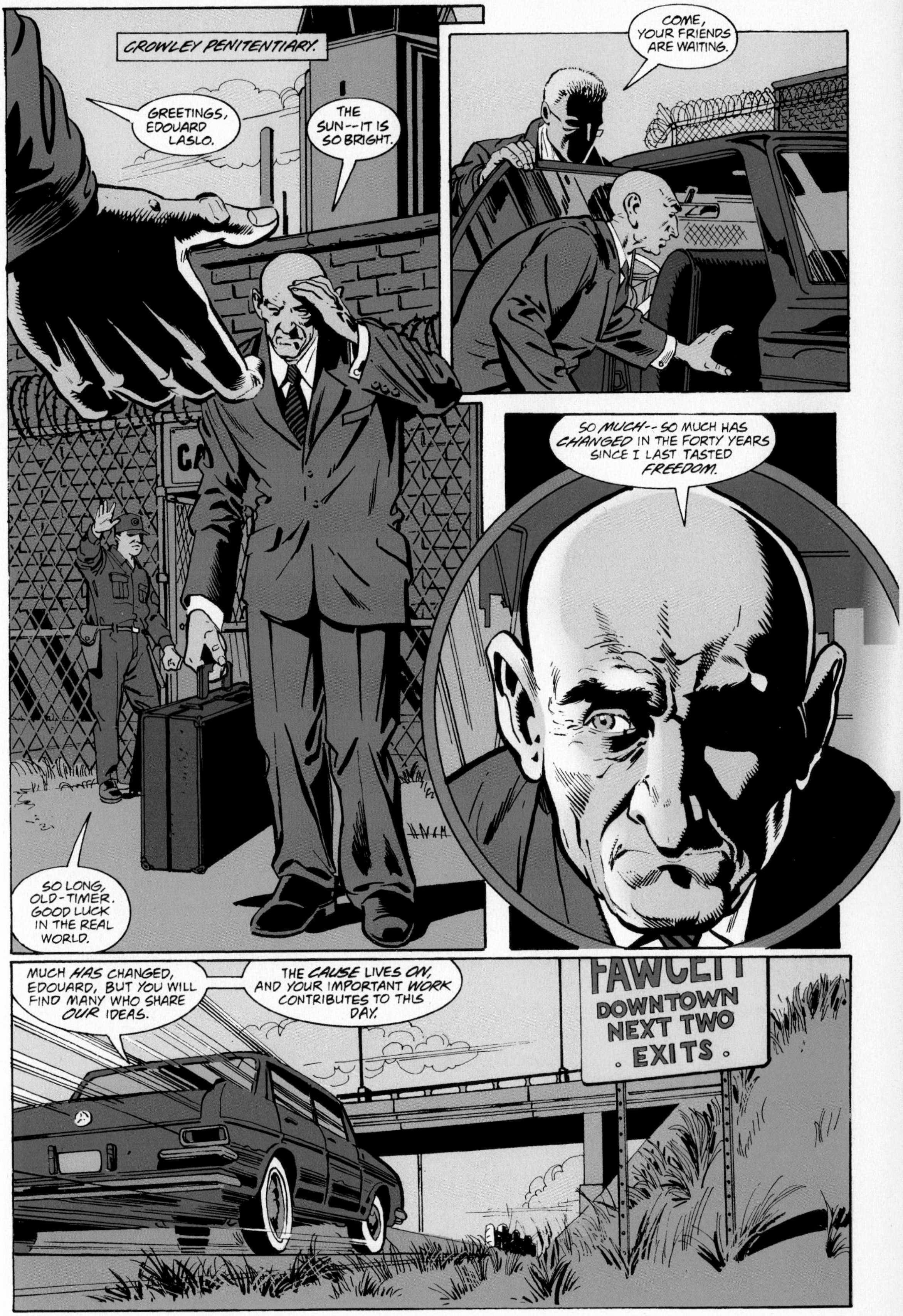
CROWLEY PENITENTIARY.
GREETINGS, EDOUARD LASLO.
THE SUN--IT IS SO BRIGHT.
COME, YOUR FRIENDS ARE WAITING.
SO LONG, OLD-TIMER. GOOD LUCK IN THE REAL WORLD.
SO MUCH--SO MUCH HAS CHANGED IN THE FORTY YEARS SINCE I LAST TASTED FREEDOM.
MUCH HAS CHANGED, EDOUARD, BUT YOU WILL FIND MANY WHO SHARE OUR IDEAS.
THE CAUSE LIVES ON, AND YOUR IMPORTANT WORK CONTRIBUTES TO THIS DAY.
FAWCETT
DOWNTOWN NEXT TWO EXITS

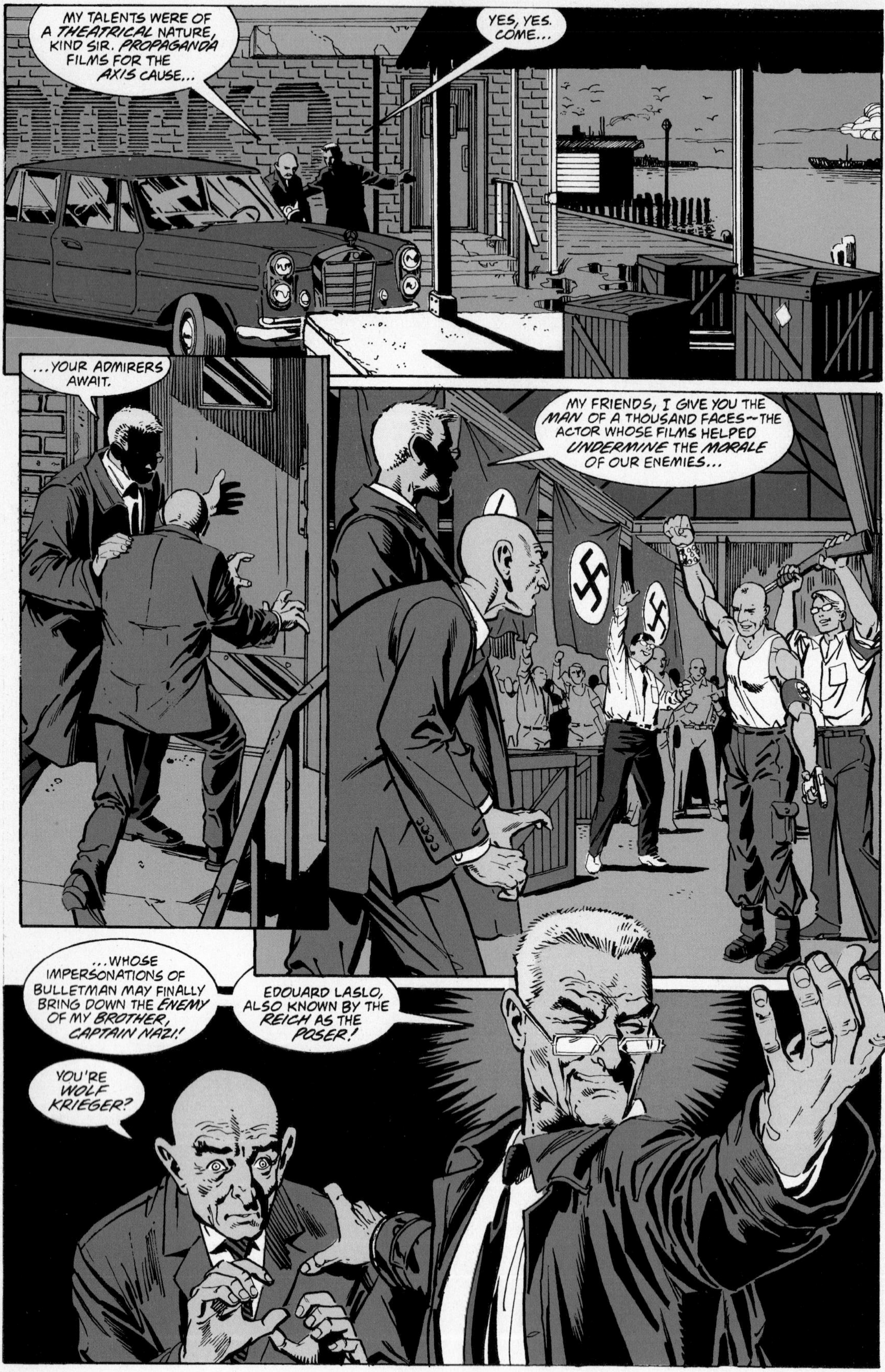
MY TALENTS WERE OF A THEATRICAL NATURE, KIND SIR. PROPAGANDA FILMS FOR THE AXIS CAUSE...
YES, YES. COME...
...YOUR ADMIRERS AWAIT.
MY FRIENDS, I GIVE YOU THE MAN OF A THOUSAND FACES--THE ACTOR WHOSE FILMS HELPED UNDERMINE THE MORALE OF OUR ENEMIES...
...WHOSE IMPERSONATIONS OF BULLETMAN MAY FINALLY BRING DOWN THE ENEMY OF MY BROTHER, CAPTAIN NAZI!
EDOUARD LASLO, ALSO KNOWN BY THE REICH AS THE POSER!
YOU'RE WOLF KRIEGER?

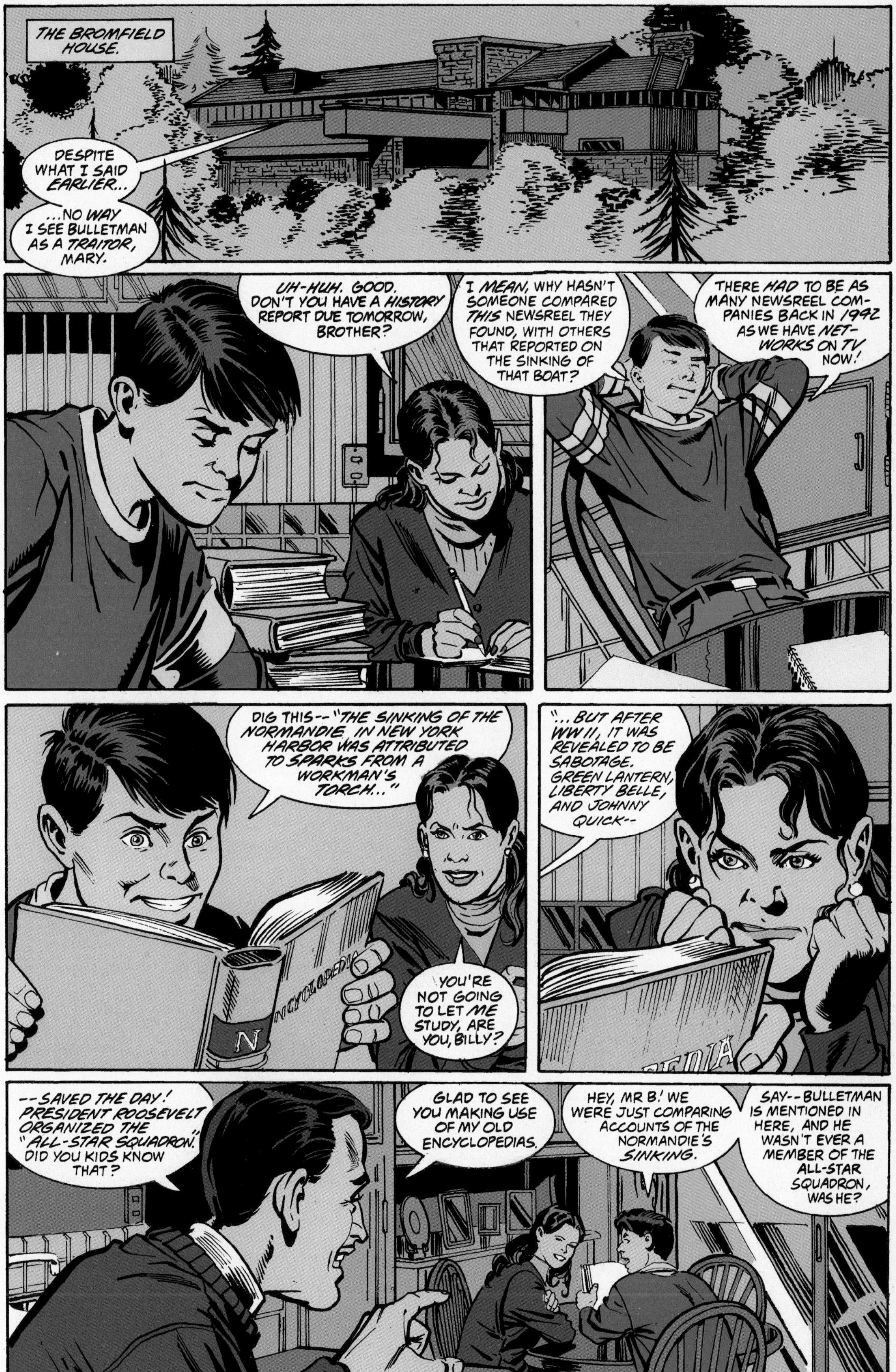
THE BROMFIELD HOUSE.
DESPITE WHAT I SAID EARLIER...
...NO WAY I SEE BULLETMAN AS A TRAITOR, MARY.
UH-HUH. GOOD. DON'T YOU HAVE A HISTORY REPORT DUE TOMORROW, BROTHER?
I MEAN, WHY HASN'T SOMEONE COMPARED THIS NEWSREEL THEY FOUND, WITH OTHERS THAT REPORTED ON THE SINKING OF THAT BOAT?
THERE HAD TO BE AS MANY NEWSREEL COMPANIES BACK IN 1942 AS WE HAVE NETWORKS ON TV NOW!
DIG THIS-- "THE SINKING OF THE NORMANDIE IN NEW YORK HARBOR WAS ATTRIBUTED TO SPARKS FROM A WORKMAN'S TORCH..."
YOU'RE NOT GOING TO LET ME STUDY, ARE YOU, BILLY?
"...BUT AFTER WW II, IT WAS REVEALED TO BE SABOTAGE. GREEN LANTERN, LIBERTY BELLE, AND JOHNNY QUICK--
--SAVED THE DAY! PRESIDENT ROOSEVELT ORGANIZED THE "ALL-STAR SQUADRON." DID YOU KIDS KNOW THAT?
GLAD TO SEE YOU MAKING USE OF MY OLD ENCYCLOPEDIAS.
HEY, MR B.! WE WERE JUST COMPARING ACCOUNTS OF THE NORMANDIE'S SINKING.
SAY--BULLETMAN IS MENTIONED IN HERE, AND HE WASN'T EVER A MEMBER OF THE ALL-STAR SQUADRON, WAS HE?

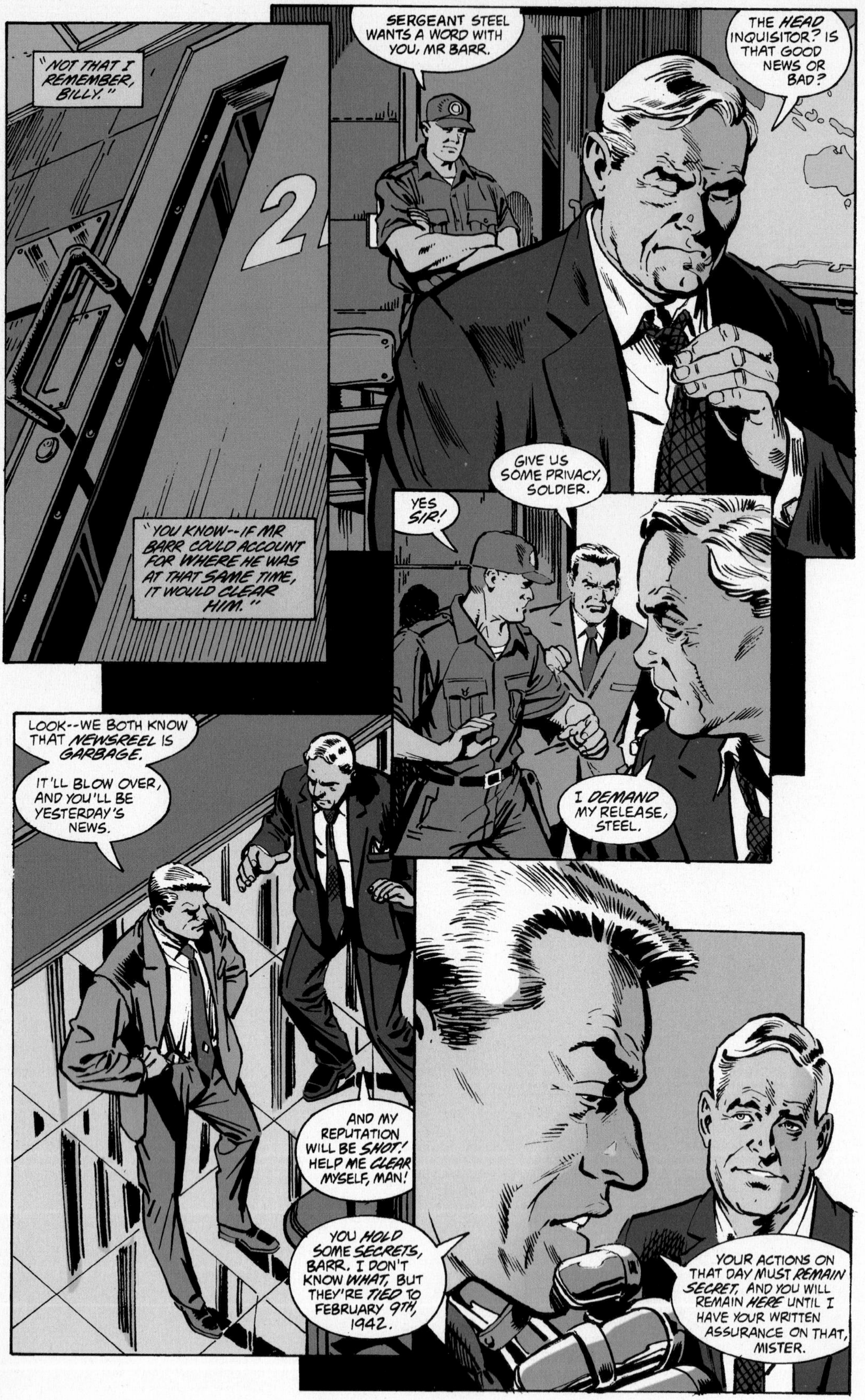
"NOT THAT I REMEMBER, BILLY."
"YOU KNOW--IF MR BARR COULD ACCOUNT FOR WHERE HE WAS AT THAT SAME TIME, IT WOULD CLEAR HIM."
SERGEANT STEEL WANTS A WORD WITH YOU, MR BARR.
THE HEAD INQUISITOR? IS THAT GOOD NEWS OR BAD?
GIVE US SOME PRIVACY, SOLDIER.
YES SIR!
I DEMAND MY RELEASE, STEEL.
LOOK--WE BOTH KNOW THAT NEWSREEL IS GARBAGE.
IT'LL BLOW OVER, AND YOU'LL BE YESTERDAY'S NEWS.
AND MY REPUTATION WILL BE SHOT! HELP ME CLEAR MYSELF, MAN!
YOU HOLD SOME SECRETS, BARR. I DON'T KNOW WHAT, BUT THEY'RE TIED TO FEBRUARY 9TH, 1942.
YOUR ACTIONS ON THAT DAY MUST REMAIN SECRET, AND YOU WILL REMAIN HERE UNTIL I HAVE YOUR WRITTEN ASSURANCE ON THAT, MISTER.

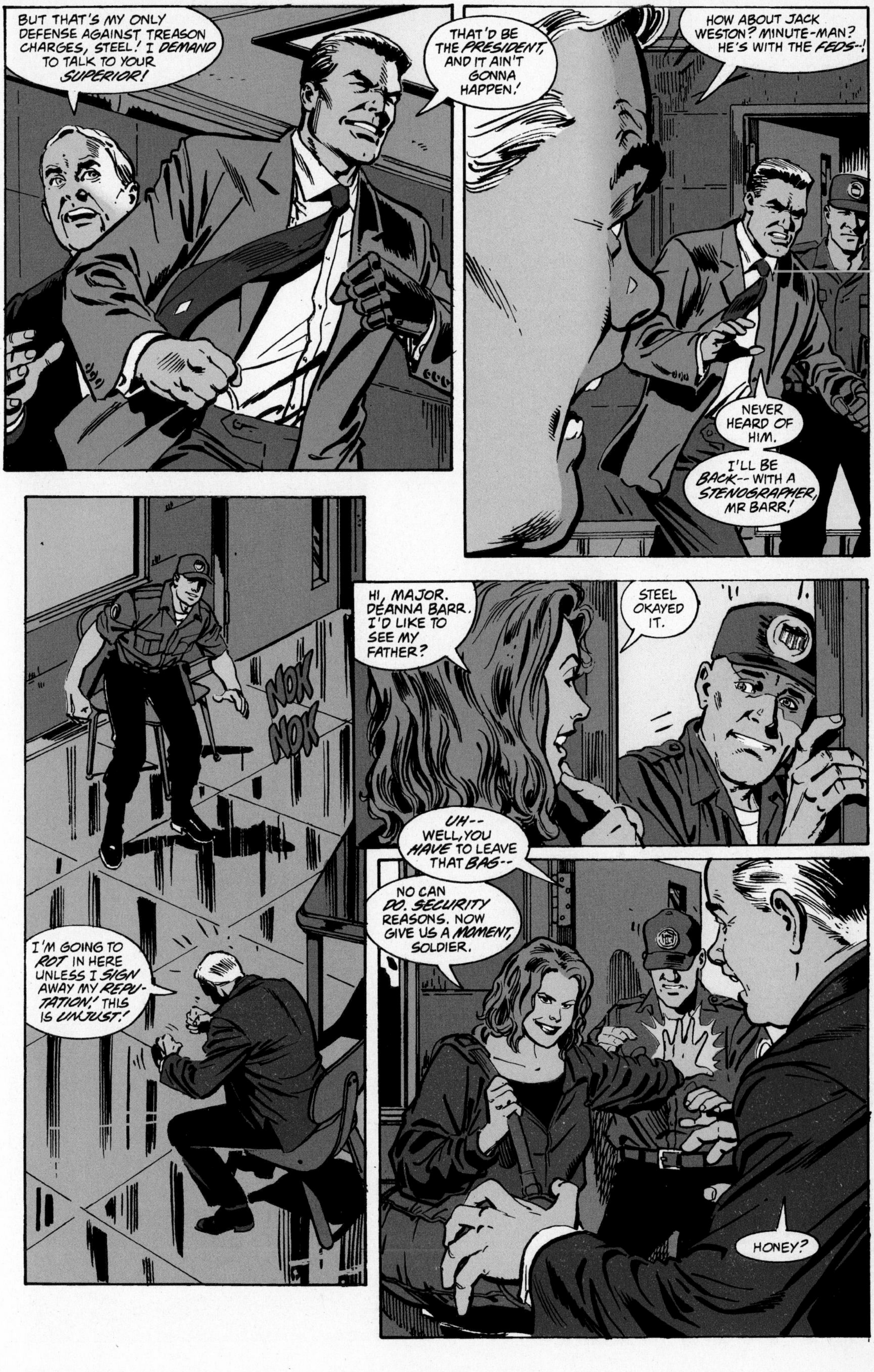
BUT THAT'S MY ONLY DEFENSE AGAINST TREASON CHARGES, STEEL! I DEMAND TO TALK TO YOUR SUPERIOR!
THAT'D BE THE PRESIDENT, AND IT AIN'T GONNA HAPPEN.'
HOW ABOUT JACK WESTON? MINUTE-MAN? HE'S WITH THE FEDS--!
NEVER HEARD OF HIM.
I'LL BE BACK-- WITH A STENOGRAPHER, MR BARR!
NOK NOK
I'M GOING TO ROT IN HERE UNLESS I SIGN AWAY MY REPUTATION! THIS IS UNJUST!
HI, MAJOR. DEANNA BARR. I'D LIKE TO SEE MY FATHER?
STEEL OKAYED IT.
UH-- WELL, YOU HAVE TO LEAVE THAT BAG--
NO CAN DO. SECURITY REASONS. NOW GIVE US A MOMENT, SOLDIER.
HONEY?

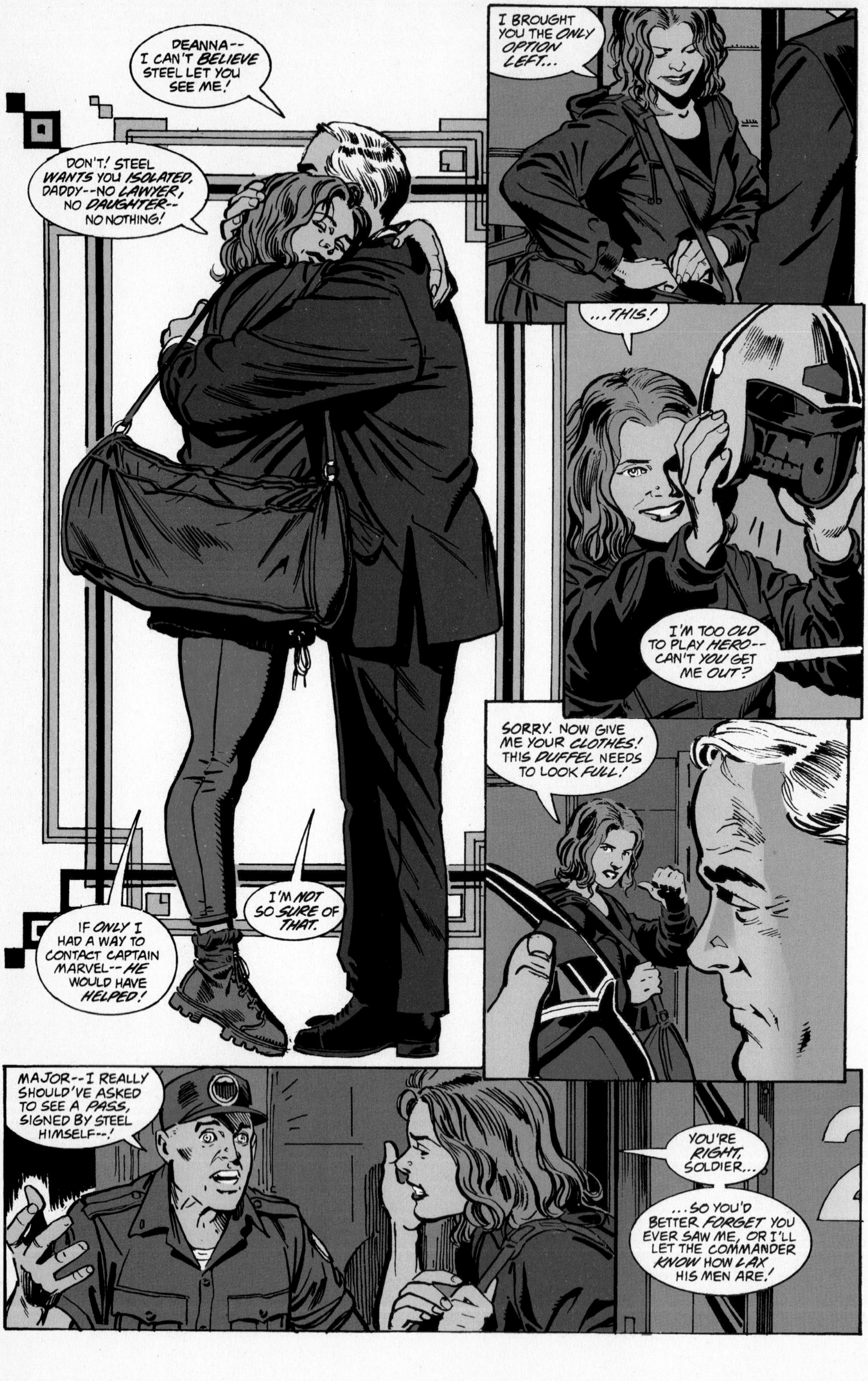
DEANNA-- I CAN'T BELIEVE STEEL LET YOU SEE ME!
DON'T! STEEL WANTS YOU ISOLATED, DADDY--NO LAWYER, NO DAUGHTER-- NO NOTHING!
IF ONLY I HAD A WAY TO CONTACT CAPTAIN MARVEL--HE WOULD HAVE HELPED!
I'M NOT SO SURE OF THAT.
I BROUGHT YOU THE ONLY OPTION LEFT...
...THIS!
I'M TOO OLD TO PLAY HERO-- CAN'T YOU GET ME OUT?
SORRY. NOW GIVE ME YOUR CLOTHES! THIS DUFFEL NEEDS TO LOOK FULL!
MAJOR--I REALLY SHOULD'VE ASKED TO SEE A PASS, SIGNED BY STEEL HIMSELF--!
YOU'RE RIGHT, SOLDIER...
...SO YOU'D BETTER FORGET YOU EVER SAW ME, OR I'LL LET THE COMMANDER KNOW HOW LAX HIS MEN ARE!

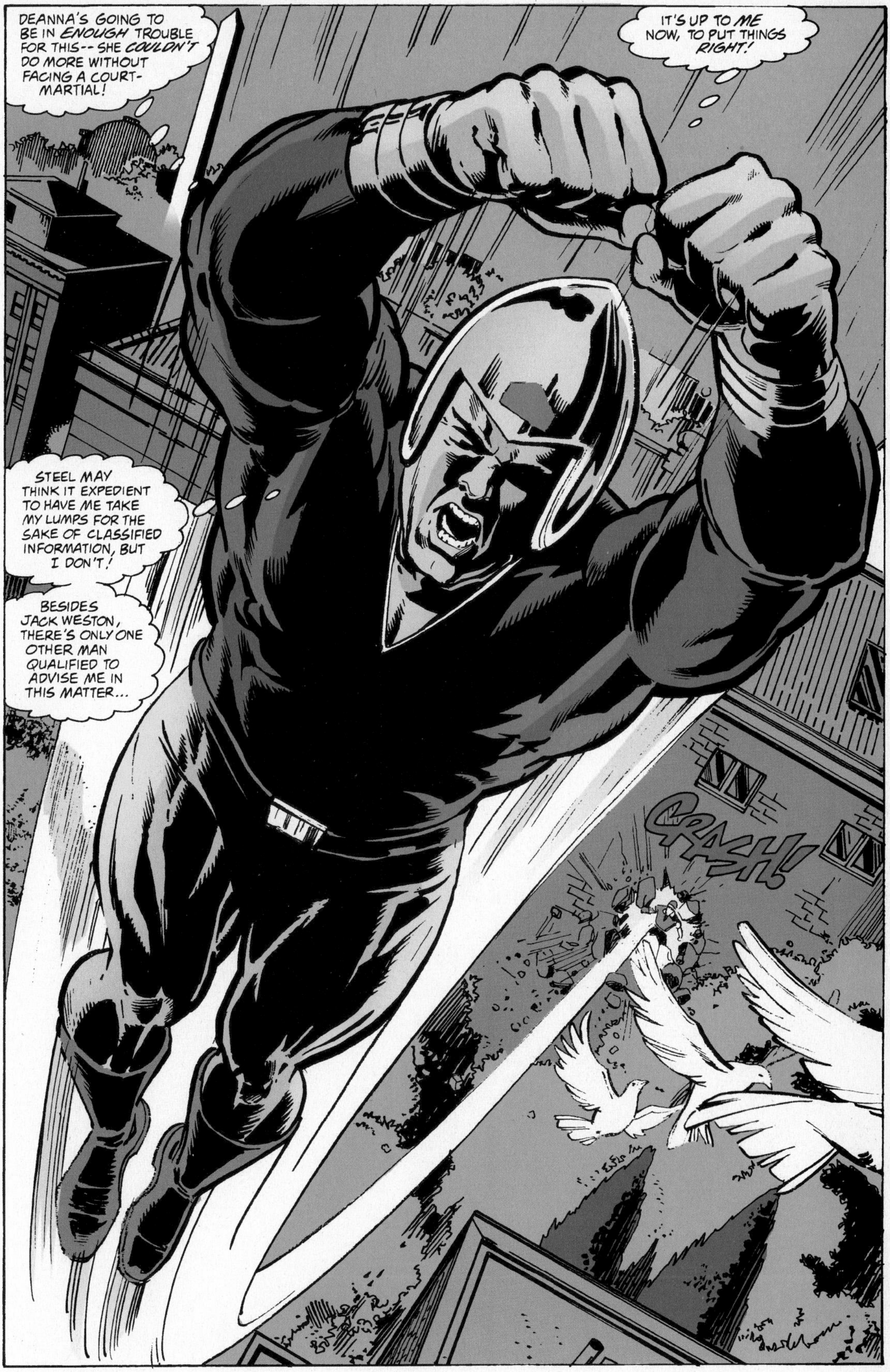
DEANNA'S GOING TO BE IN ENOUGH TROUBLE FOR THIS-- SHE COULDN'T DO MORE WITHOUT FACING A COURT-MARTIAL!
IT'S UP TO ME NOW, TO PUT THINGS RIGHT!
STEEL MAY THINK IT EXPEDIENT TO HAVE ME TAKE MY LUMPS FOR THE SAKE OF CLASSIFIED INFORMATION, BUT I DON'T!
BESIDES JACK WESTON, THERE'S ONLY ONE OTHER MAN QUALIFIED TO ADVISE ME IN THIS MATTER...
CRASH!

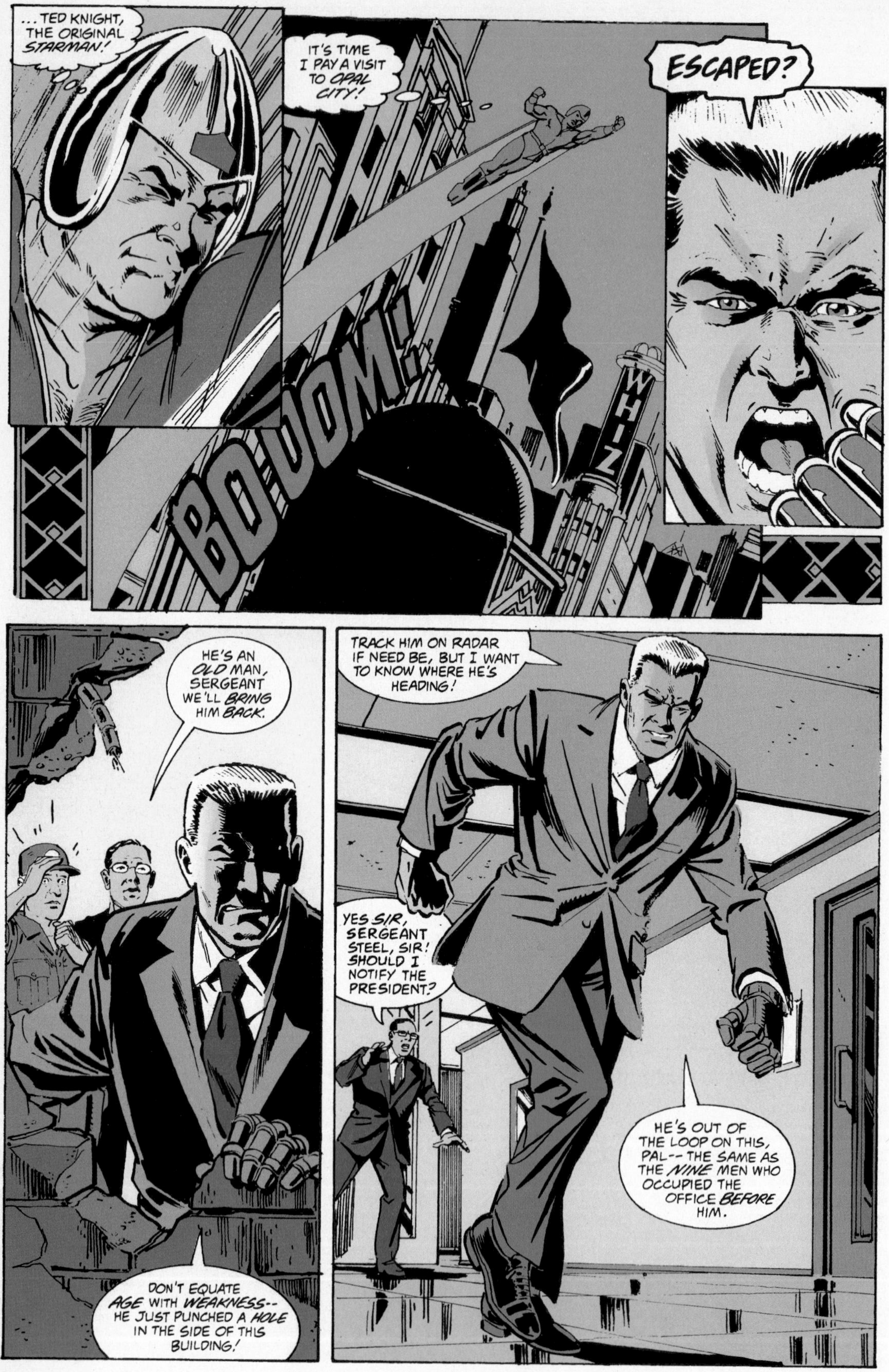
...TED KNIGHT, THE ORIGINAL STARMAN!
IT'S TIME I PAY A VISIT TO OPAL CITY!
BOOOM!
WHIZ
ESCAPED?
HE'S AN OLD MAN, SERGEANT WE'LL BRING HIM BACK.
DON'T EQUATE AGE WITH WEAKNESS-- HE JUST PUNCHED A HOLE IN THE SIDE OF THIS BUILDING!
TRACK HIM ON RADAR IF NEED BE, BUT I WANT TO KNOW WHERE HE'S HEADING!
YES SIR, SERGEANT STEEL, SIR! SHOULD I NOTIFY THE PRESIDENT?
HE'S OUT OF THE LOOP ON THIS, PAL-- THE SAME AS THE NINE MEN WHO OCCUPIED THE OFFICE BEFORE HIM.

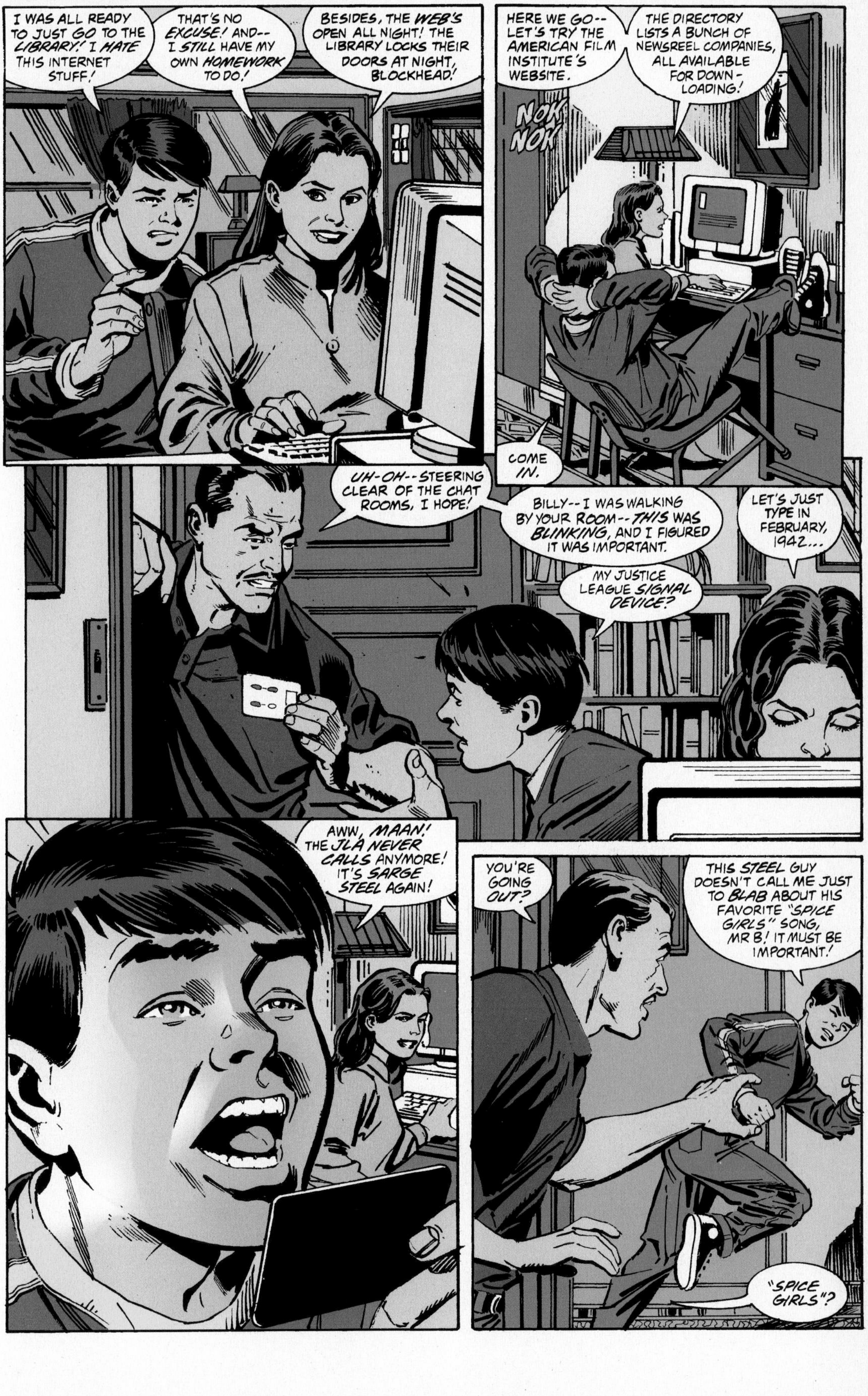
I WAS ALL READY TO JUST GO TO THE LIBRARY! I HATE THIS INTERNET STUFF!
THAT'S NO EXCUSE! AND-- I STILL HAVE MY OWN HOMEWORK TO DO!
BESIDES, THE WEB'S OPEN ALL NIGHT! THE LIBRARY LOCKS THEIR DOORS AT NIGHT, BLOCKHEAD!
HERE WE GO-- LET'S TRY THE AMERICAN FILM INSTITUTE'S WEBSITE.
THE DIRECTORY LISTS A BUNCH OF NEWSREEL COMPANIES, ALL AVAILABLE FOR DOWN-LOADING!
NOK NOK
COME IN.
UH-OH--STEERING CLEAR OF THE CHAT ROOMS, I HOPE!
BILLY--I WAS WALKING BY YOUR ROOM--THIS WAS BLINKING, AND I FIGURED IT WAS IMPORTANT.
LET'S JUST TYPE IN FEBRUARY, 1942...
MY JUSTICE LEAGUE SIGNAL DEVICE?
AWW, MAAN! THE JLA NEVER CALLS ANYMORE! IT'S SARGE STEEL AGAIN!
YOU'RE GOING OUT?
THIS STEEL GUY DOESN'T CALL ME JUST TO BLAB ABOUT HIS FAVORITE "SPICE GIRLS" SONG, MR B! IT MUST BE IMPORTANT!
"SPICE GIRLS"?

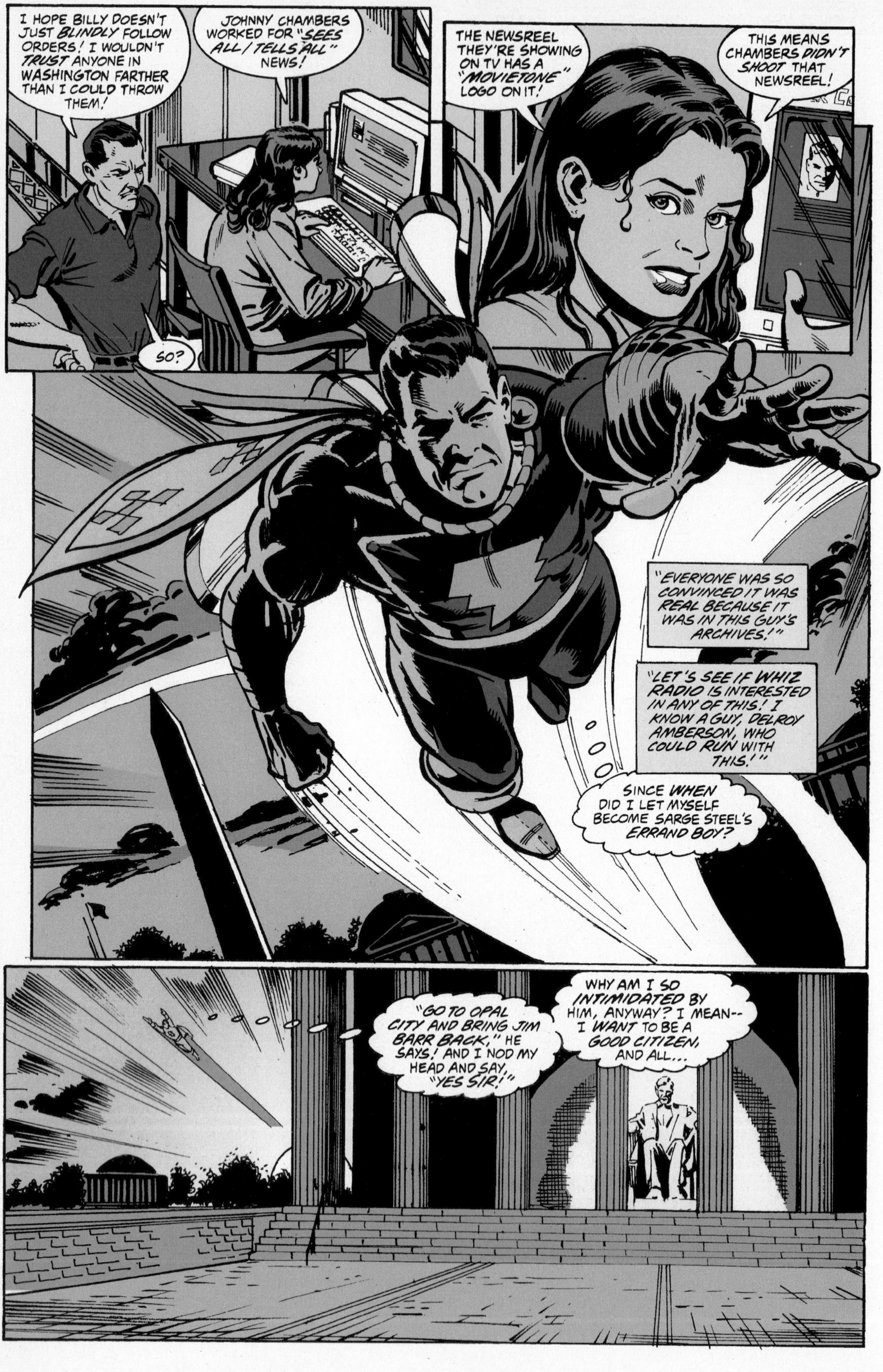
I HOPE BILLY DOESN'T JUST BLINDLY FOLLOW ORDERS! I WOULDN'T TRUST ANYONE IN WASHINGTON FARTHER THAN I COULD THROW THEM!
JOHNNY CHAMBERS WORKED FOR "SEES ALL/TELLS ALL" NEWS!
SO?
THE NEWSREEL THEY'RE SHOWING ON TV HAS A "MOVIETONE" LOGO ON IT!
THIS MEANS CHAMBERS DIDN'T SHOOT THAT NEWSREEL!
"EVERYONE WAS SO CONVINCED IT WAS REAL BECAUSE IT WAS IN THIS GUY'S ARCHIVES!"
"LET'S SEE IF WHIZ RADIO IS INTERESTED IN ANY OF THIS! I KNOW A GUY, DELROY AMBERSON, WHO COULD RUN WITH THIS!"
SINCE WHEN DID I LET MYSELF BECOME SARGE STEEL'S ERRAND BOY?
"GO TO OPAL CITY AND BRING JIM BARR BACK," HE SAYS! AND I NOD MY HEAD AND SAY, "YES SIR!"
WHY AM I SO INTIMIDATED BY HIM, ANYWAY? I MEAN-- I WANT TO BE A GOOD CITIZEN, AND ALL...

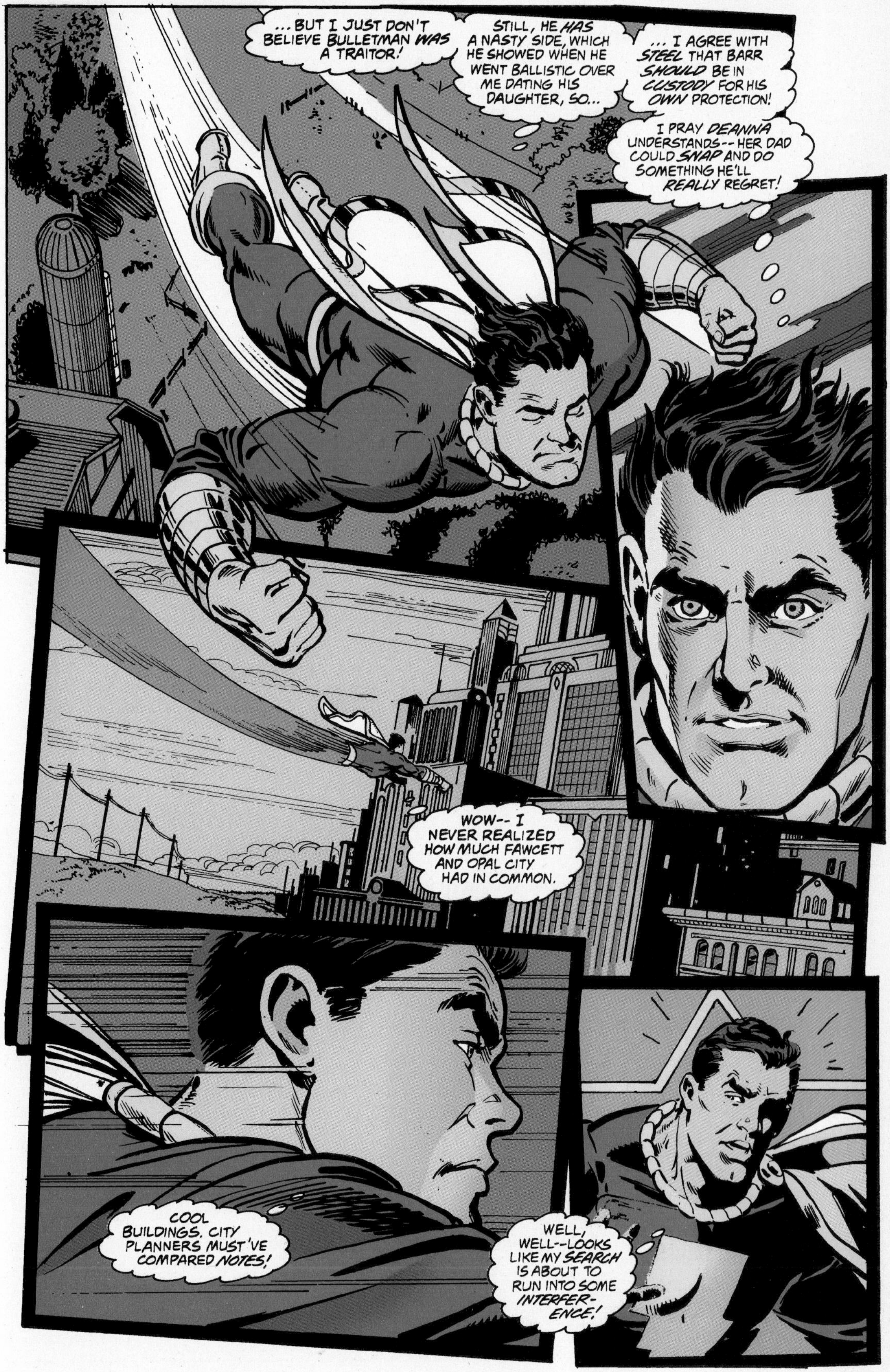
...BUT I JUST DON'T BELIEVE BULLETMAN WAS A TRAITOR!
STILL, HE HAS A NASTY SIDE, WHICH HE SHOWED WHEN HE WENT BALLISTIC OVER ME DATING HIS DAUGHTER, SO...
...I AGREE WITH STEEL THAT BARR SHOULD BE IN CUSTODY FOR HIS OWN PROTECTION!
I PRAY DEANNA UNDERSTANDS--HER DAD COULD SNAP AND DO SOMETHING HE'LL REALLY REGRET!
WOW--I NEVER REALIZED HOW MUCH FAWCETT AND OPAL CITY HAD IN COMMON.
COOL BUILDINGS. CITY PLANNERS MUST'VE COMPARED NOTES!
WELL, WELL--LOOKS LIKE MY SEARCH IS ABOUT TO RUN INTO SOME INTERFER-ENCE!

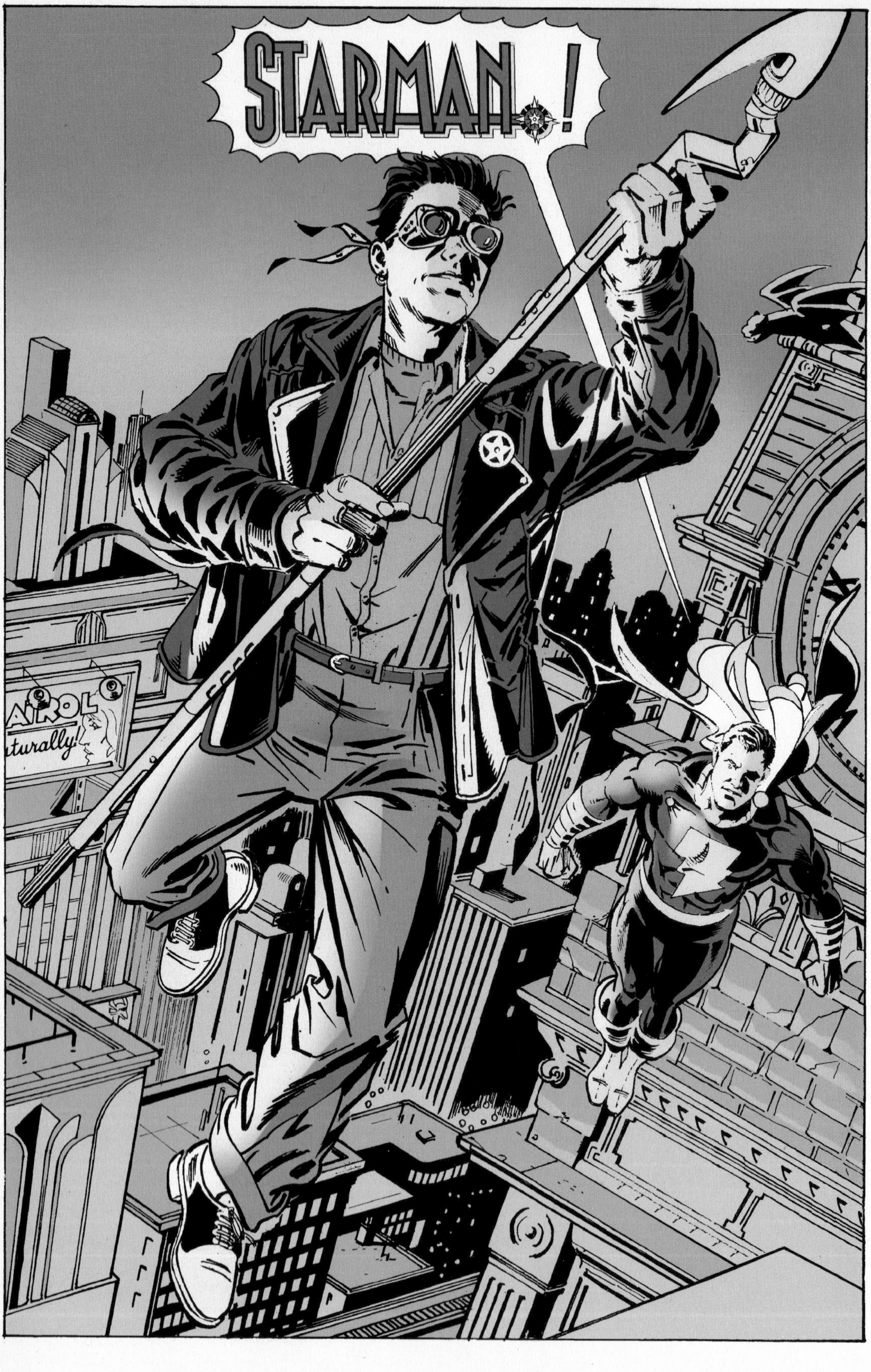
STARMAN!

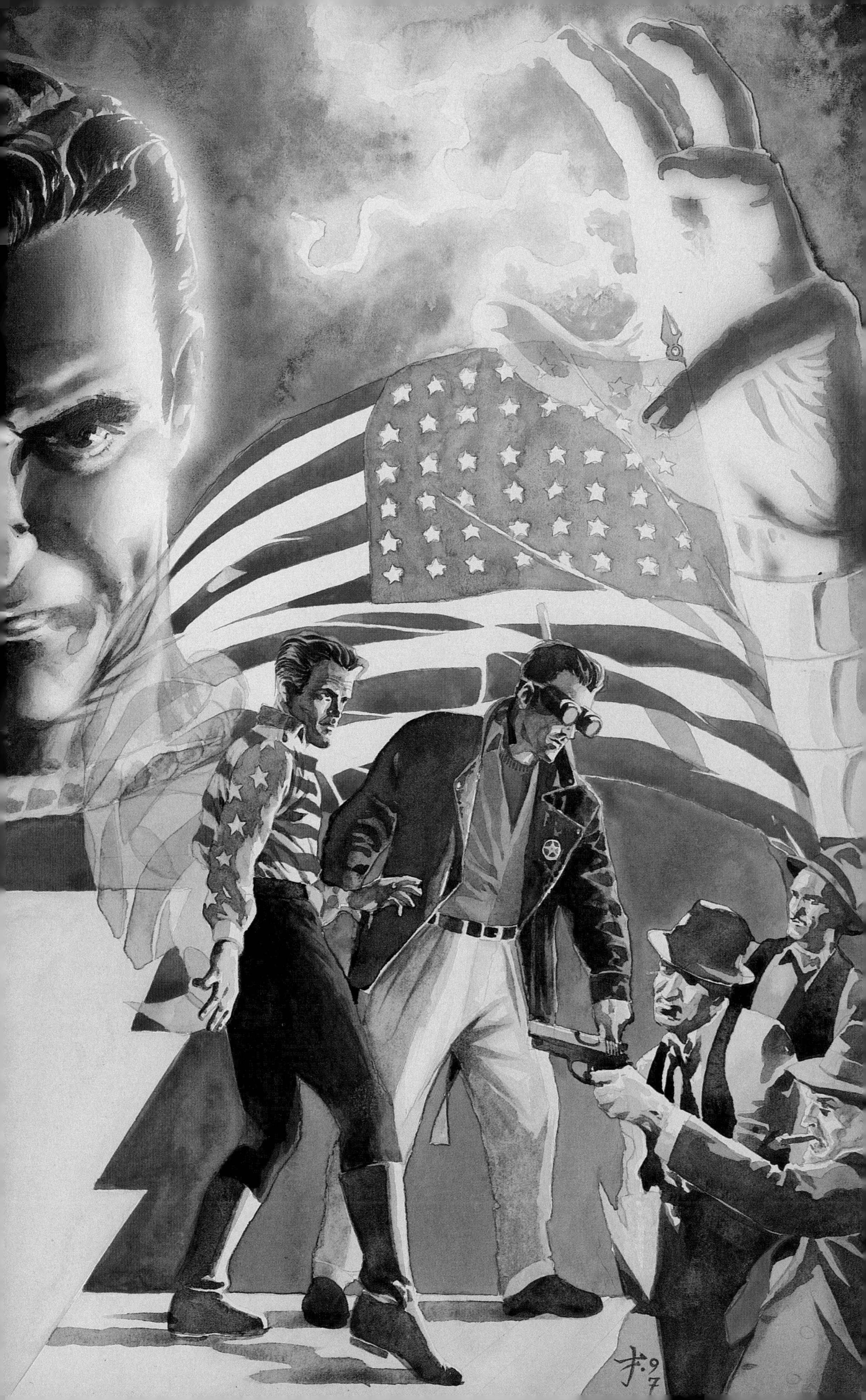

S T A R M A N   4 0

Cover by Tony Harris

Written by James Robinson

Pencils by Tony Harris

with inks by Wade von Grawbadger & Ray Snyder

and colors by Gregory Wright

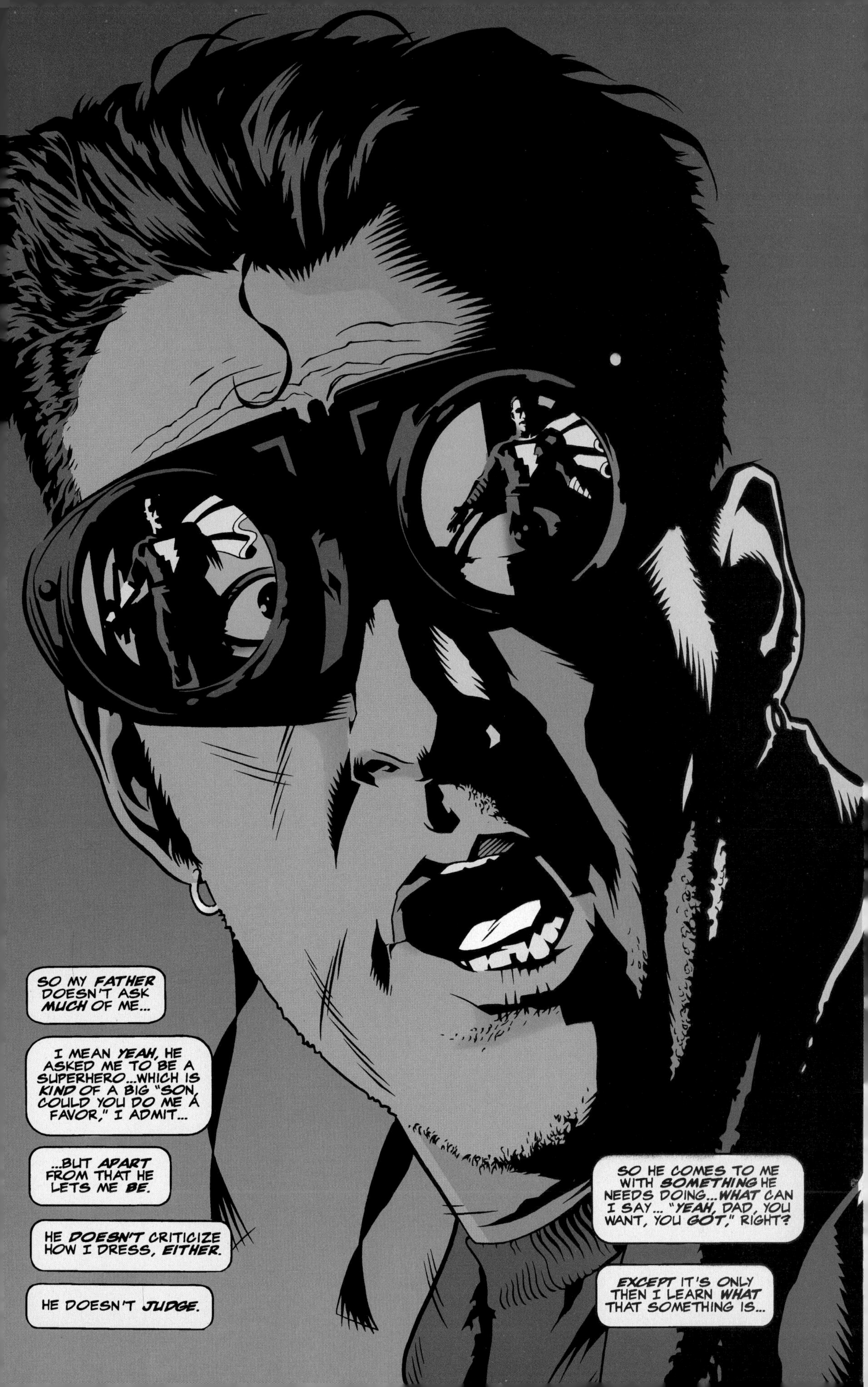

SO MY FATHER DOESN'T ASK MUCH OF ME...
I MEAN YEAH, HE ASKED ME TO BE A SUPERHERO...WHICH IS KIND OF A BIG "SON, COULD YOU DO ME A FAVOR," I ADMIT...
...BUT APART FROM THAT HE LETS ME BE.
HE DOESN'T CRITICIZE HOW I DRESS, EITHER.
HE DOESN'T JUDGE.
SO HE COMES TO ME WITH SOMETHING HE NEEDS DOING...WHAT CAN I SAY... "YEAH, DAD, YOU WANT, YOU GOT," RIGHT?
EXCEPT IT'S ONLY THEN I LEARN WHAT THAT SOMETHING IS...

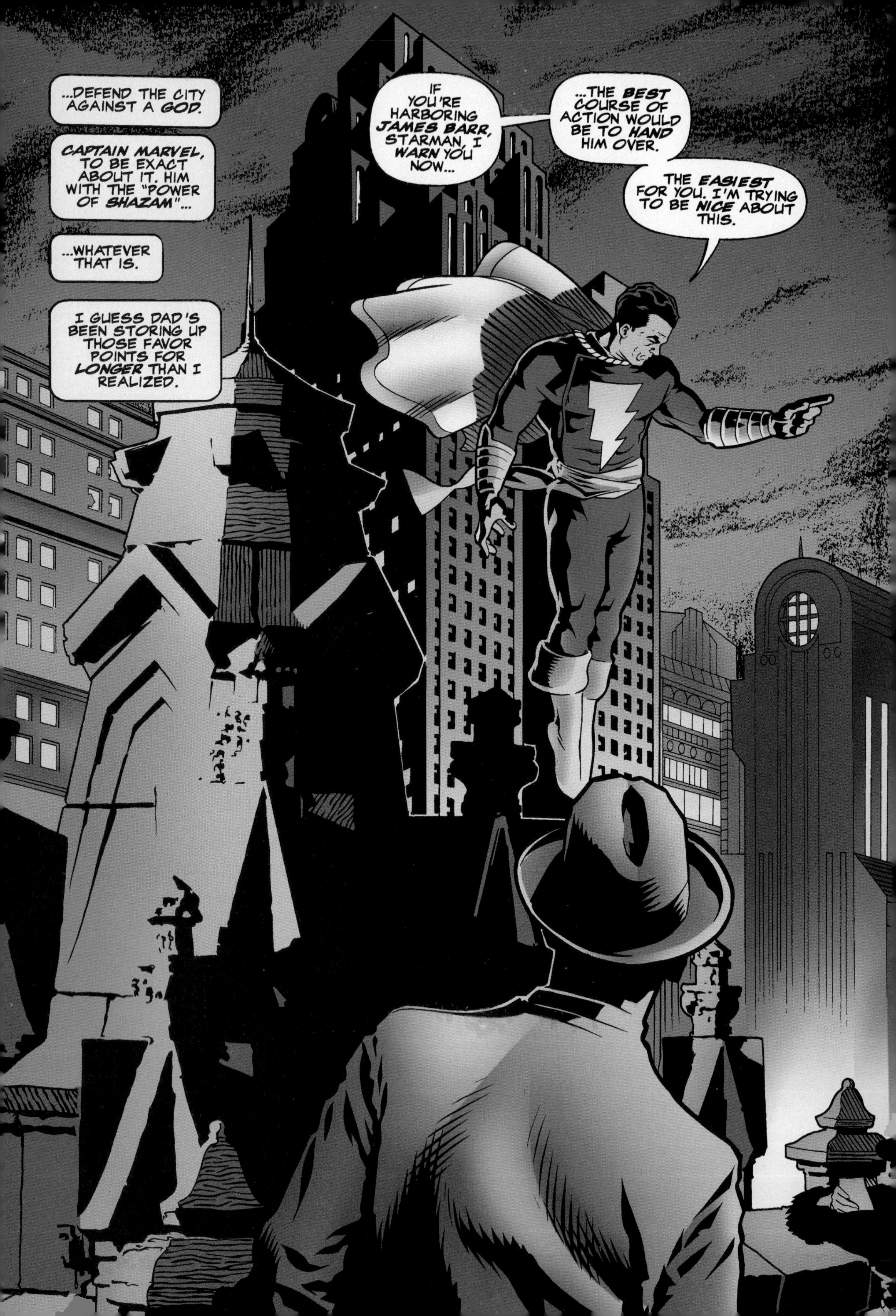
...DEFEND THE CITY AGAINST A GOD.
CAPTAIN MARVEL, TO BE EXACT ABOUT IT. HIM WITH THE "POWER OF SHAZAM"...
...WHATEVER THAT IS.
I GUESS DAD'S BEEN STORING UP THOSE FAVOR POINTS FOR LONGER THAN I REALIZED.
IF YOU'RE HARBORING JAMES BARR, STARMAN, I WARN YOU NOW...
...THE BEST COURSE OF ACTION WOULD BE TO HAND HIM OVER.
THE EASIEST FOR YOU. I'M TRYING TO BE NICE ABOUT THIS.

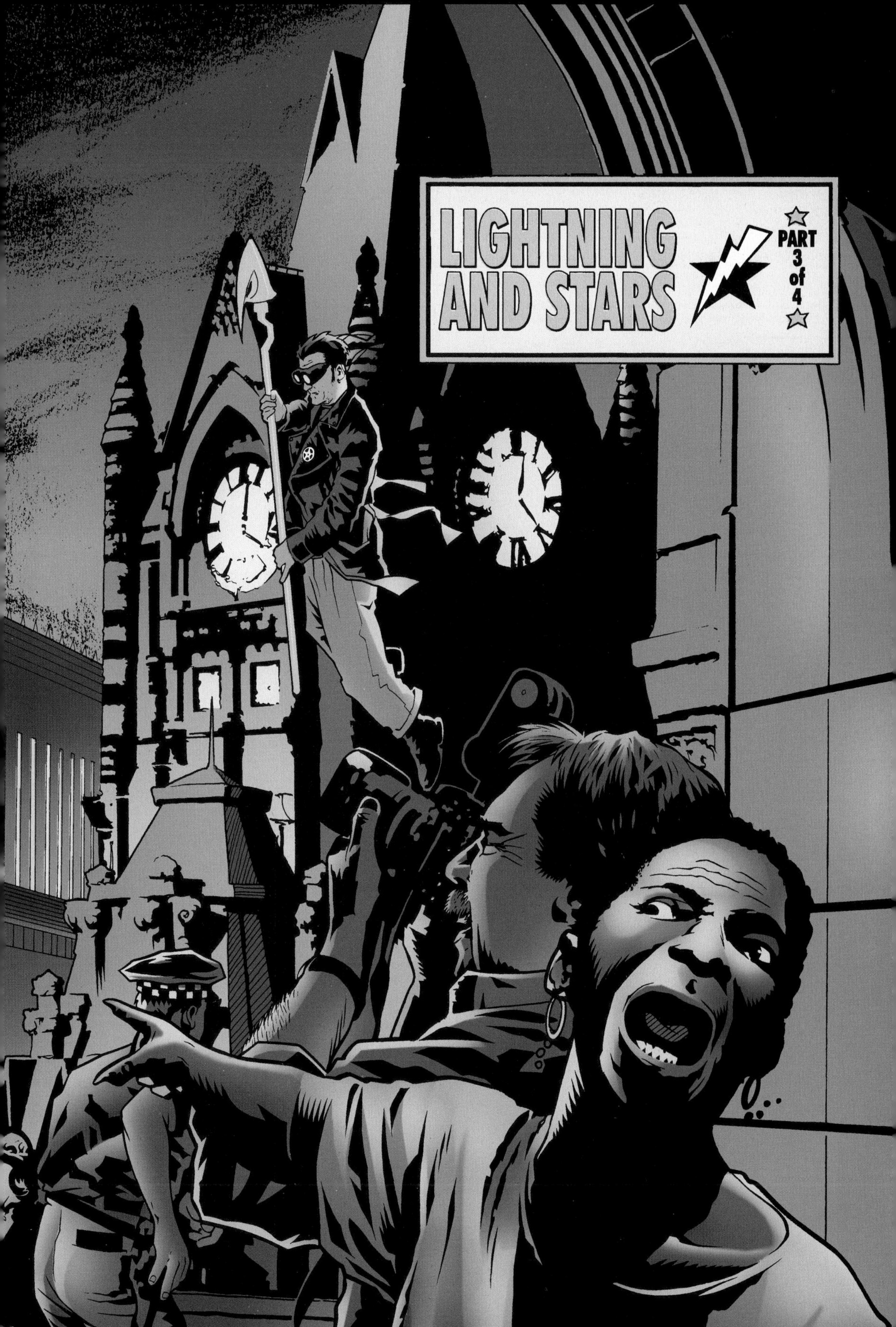
LIGHTNING AND STARS
PART 3 of 4

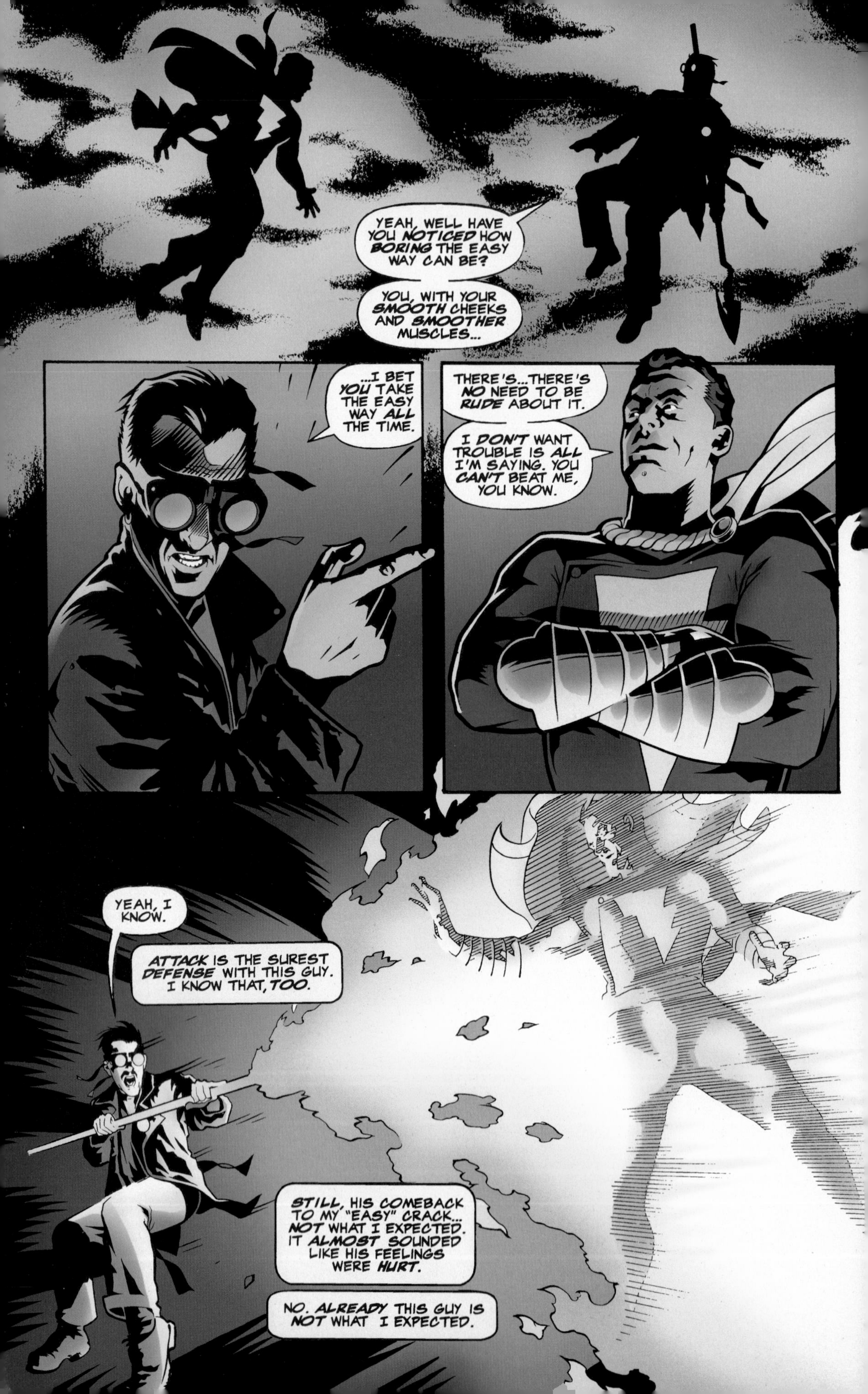
YEAH, WELL HAVE YOU NOTICED HOW BORING THE EASY WAY CAN BE?
YOU, WITH YOUR SMOOTH CHEEKS AND SMOOTHER MUSCLES...
...I BET YOU TAKE THE EASY WAY ALL THE TIME.
THERE'S...THERE'S NO NEED TO BE RUDE ABOUT IT.
I DON'T WANT TROUBLE IS ALL I'M SAYING. YOU CAN'T BEAT ME, YOU KNOW.
YEAH, I KNOW.
ATTACK IS THE SUREST DEFENSE WITH THIS GUY. I KNOW THAT, TOO.
STILL, HIS COMEBACK TO MY "EASY" CRACK... NOT WHAT I EXPECTED. IT ALMOST SOUNDED LIKE HIS FEELINGS WERE HURT.
NO. ALREADY THIS GUY IS NOT WHAT I EXPECTED.

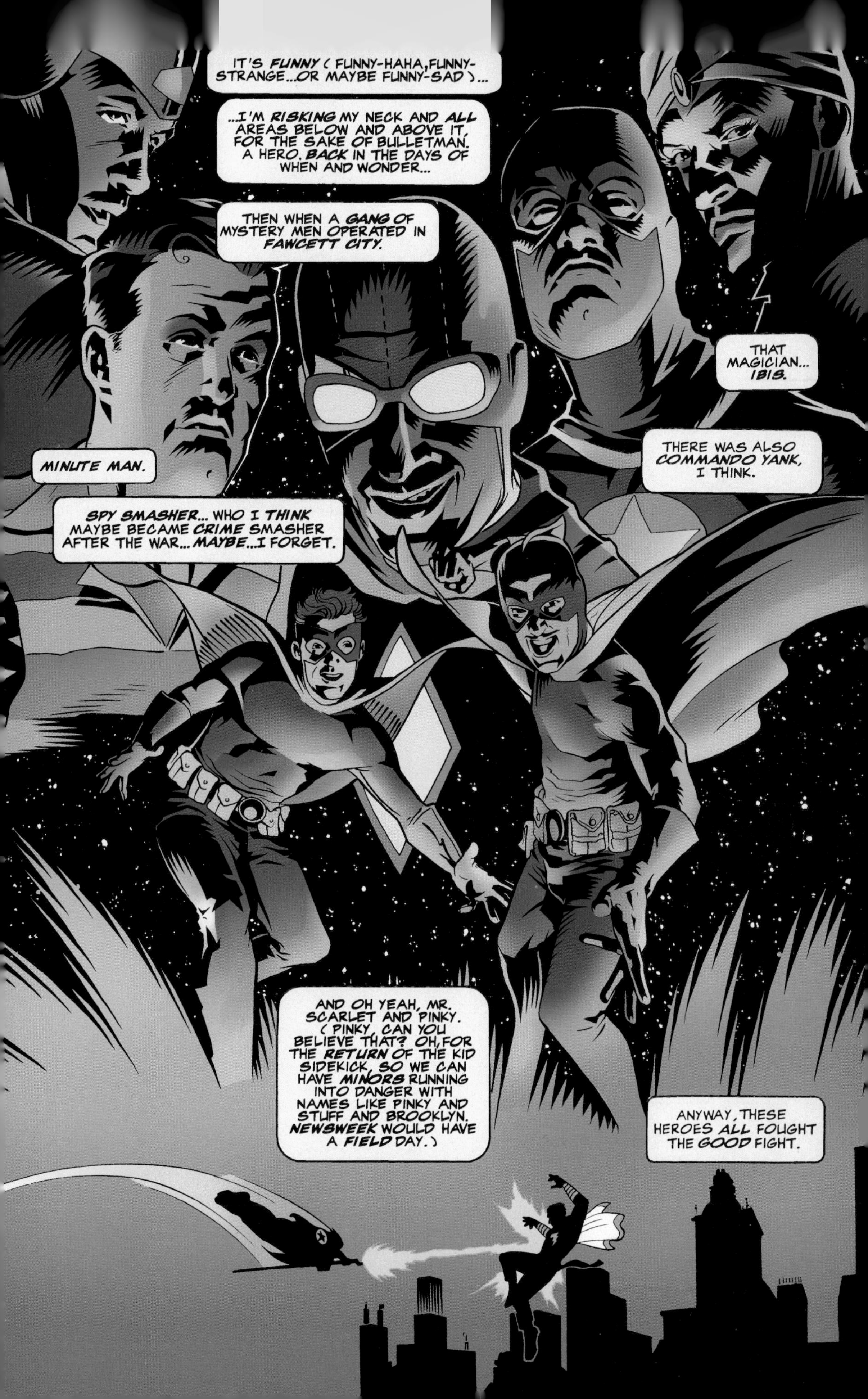

IT'S FUNNY (FUNNY-HAHA, FUNNY-STRANGE...OR MAYBE FUNNY-SAD)...
...I'M RISKING MY NECK AND ALL AREAS BELOW AND ABOVE IT, FOR THE SAKE OF BULLETMAN. A HERO. BACK IN THE DAYS OF WHEN AND WONDER...
THEN WHEN A GANG OF MYSTERY MEN OPERATED IN FAWCETT CITY.
THAT MAGICIAN... IBIS.
THERE WAS ALSO COMMANDO YANK, I THINK.
MINUTE MAN.
SPY SMASHER... WHO I THINK MAYBE BECAME CRIME SMASHER AFTER THE WAR... MAYBE...I FORGET.
AND OH YEAH, MR. SCARLET AND PINKY. (PINKY, CAN YOU BELIEVE THAT? OH, FOR THE RETURN OF THE KID SIDEKICK, SO WE CAN HAVE MINORS RUNNING INTO DANGER WITH NAMES LIKE PINKY AND STUFF AND BROOKLYN. NEWSWEEK WOULD HAVE A FIELD DAY.)
ANYWAY, THESE HEROES ALL FOUGHT THE GOOD FIGHT.

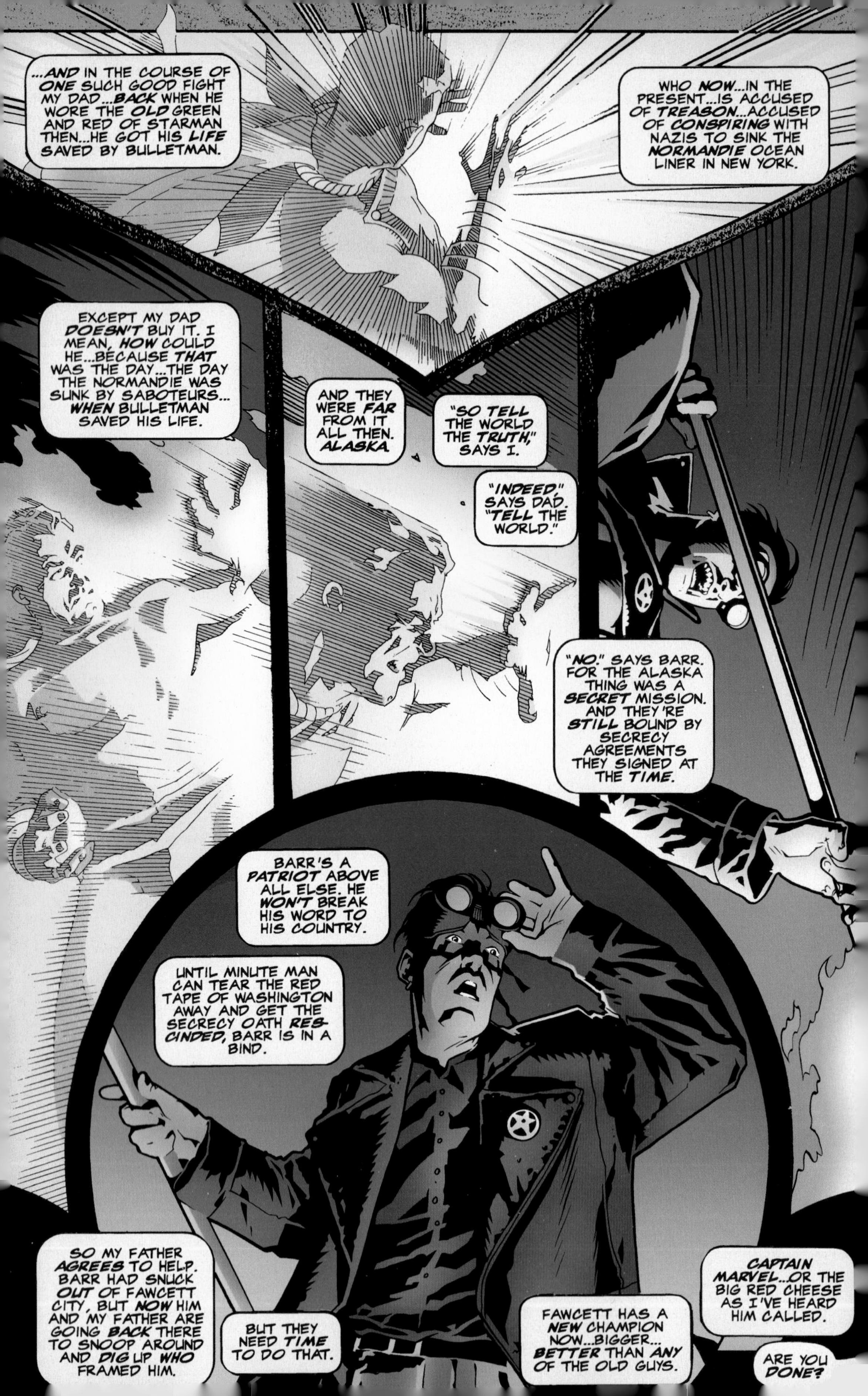
...AND IN THE COURSE OF ONE SUCH GOOD FIGHT MY DAD...BACK WHEN HE WORE THE OLD GREEN AND RED OF STARMAN THEN...HE GOT HIS LIFE SAVED BY BULLETMAN.
WHO NOW...IN THE PRESENT...IS ACCUSED OF TREASON...ACCUSED OF CONSPIRING WITH NAZIS TO SINK THE NORMANDIE OCEAN LINER IN NEW YORK.
EXCEPT MY DAD DOESN'T BUY IT. I MEAN, HOW COULD HE...BECAUSE THAT WAS THE DAY...THE DAY THE NORMANDIE WAS SUNK BY SABOTEURS... WHEN BULLETMAN SAVED HIS LIFE.
AND THEY WERE FAR FROM IT ALL THEN. ALASKA.
"SO TELL THE WORLD THE TRUTH," SAYS I.
"INDEED," SAYS DAD. "TELL THE WORLD."
"NO." SAYS BARR. FOR THE ALASKA THING WAS A SECRET MISSION. AND THEY'RE STILL BOUND BY SECRECY AGREEMENTS THEY SIGNED AT THE TIME.
BARR'S A PATRIOT ABOVE ALL ELSE. HE WON'T BREAK HIS WORD TO HIS COUNTRY.
UNTIL MINUTE MAN CAN TEAR THE RED TAPE OF WASHINGTON AWAY AND GET THE SECRECY OATH RESCINDED, BARR IS IN A BIND.
SO MY FATHER AGREES TO HELP. BARR HAD SNUCK OUT OF FAWCETT CITY, BUT NOW HIM AND MY FATHER ARE GOING BACK THERE TO SNOOP AROUND AND DIG UP WHO FRAMED HIM.
BUT THEY NEED TIME TO DO THAT.
FAWCETT HAS A NEW CHAMPION NOW...BIGGER... BETTER THAN ANY OF THE OLD GUYS.
CAPTAIN MARVEL...OR THE BIG RED CHEESE AS I'VE HEARD HIM CALLED.
ARE YOU DONE?

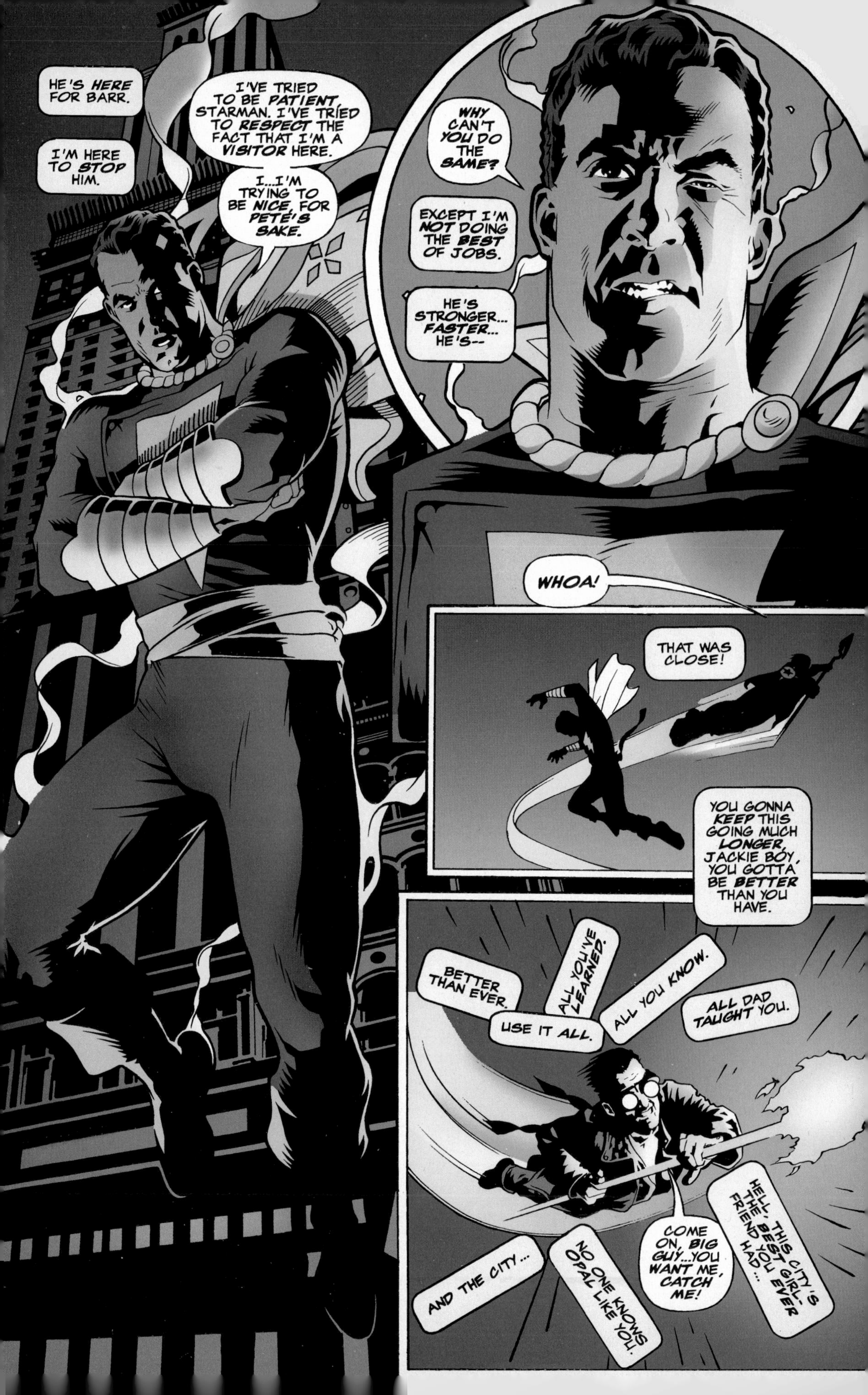
HE'S HERE FOR BARR.
I'M HERE TO STOP HIM.
I'VE TRIED TO BE PATIENT, STARMAN. I'VE TRIED TO RESPECT THE FACT THAT I'M A VISITOR HERE.
I...I'M TRYING TO BE NICE, FOR PETE'S SAKE.
WHY CAN'T YOU DO THE SAME?
EXCEPT I'M NOT DOING THE BEST OF JOBS.
HE'S STRONGER... FASTER... HE'S--
WHOA!
THAT WAS CLOSE!
YOU GONNA KEEP THIS GOING MUCH LONGER, JACKIE BOY, YOU GOTTA BE BETTER THAN YOU HAVE.
BETTER THAN EVER.
USE IT ALL.
ALL YOU'VE LEARNED.
ALL YOU KNOW.
ALL DAD TAUGHT YOU.
HELL, THIS CITY'S THE BEST GIRL-FRIEND YOU EVER HAD...
COME ON, BIG GUY...YOU WANT ME, CATCH ME!
NO ONE KNOWS OPAL LIKE YOU.
AND THE CITY...

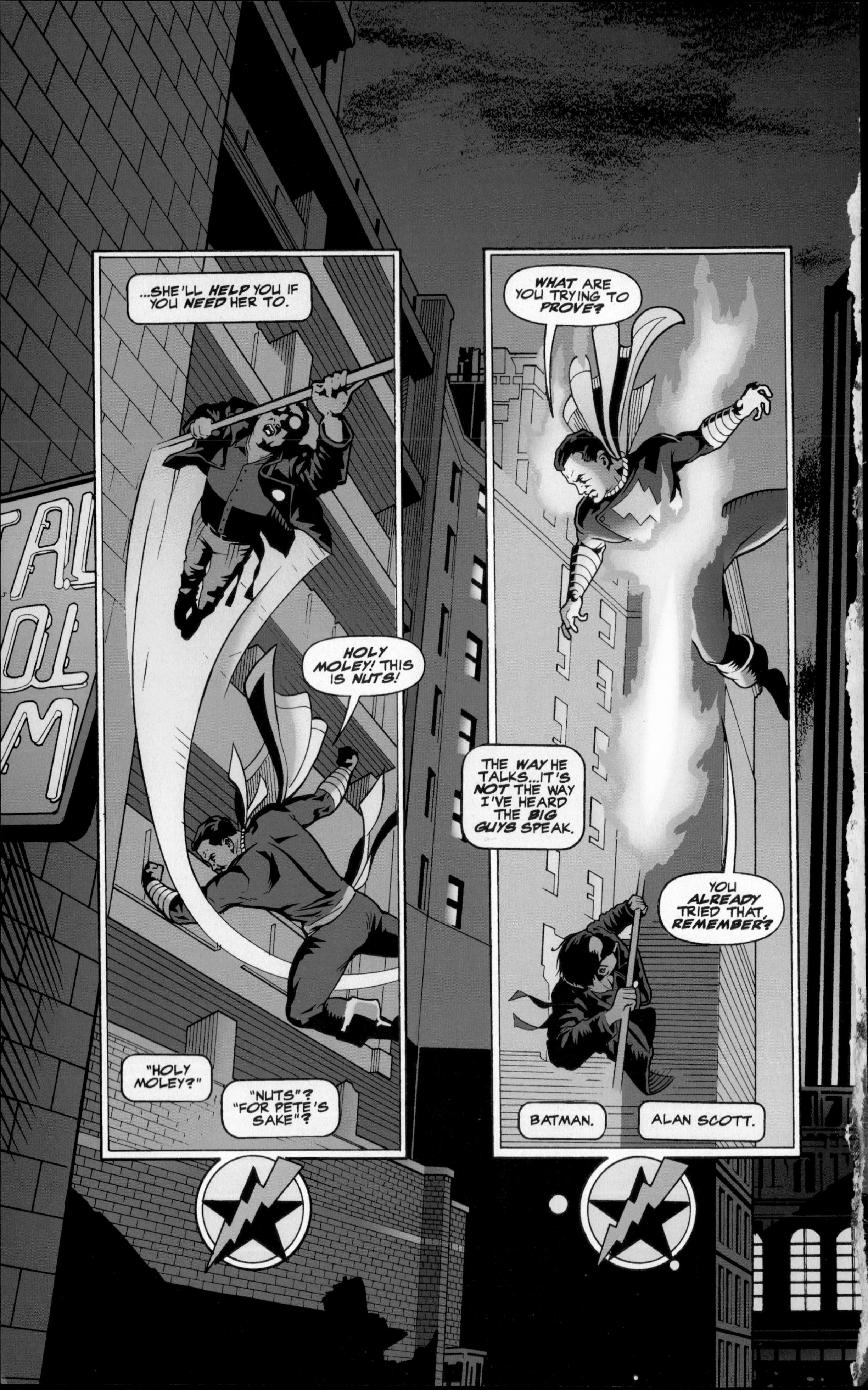
...SHE'LL HELP YOU IF YOU NEED HER TO.
HOLY MOLEY! THIS IS NUTS!
"HOLY MOLEY?"
"NUTS"? "FOR PETE'S SAKE"?
WHAT ARE YOU TRYING TO PROVE?
THE WAY HE TALKS...IT'S NOT THE WAY I'VE HEARD THE BIG GUYS SPEAK.
YOU ALREADY TRIED THAT, REMEMBER?
BATMAN.
ALAN SCOTT.

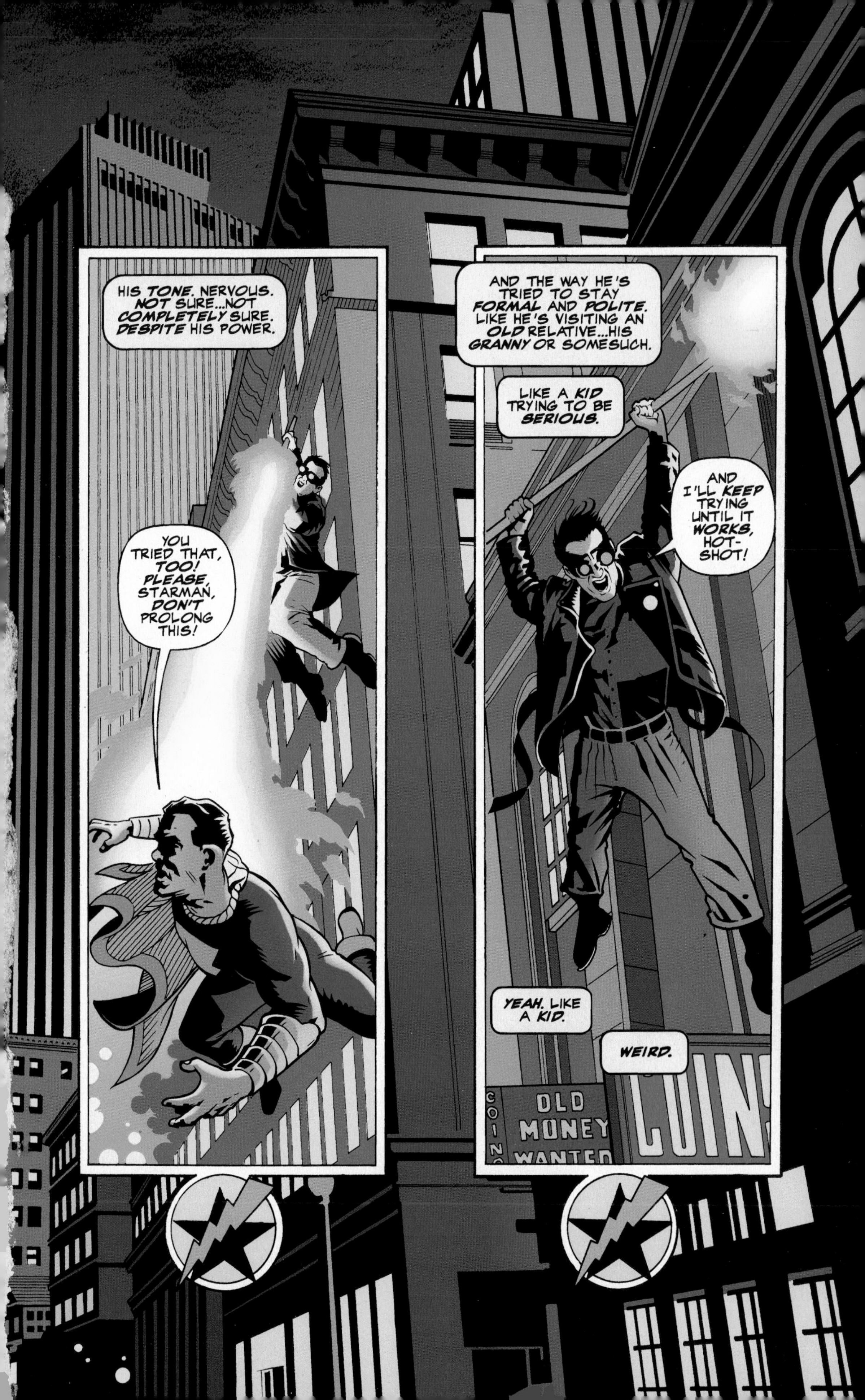
HIS TONE. NERVOUS. NOT SURE...NOT COMPLETELY SURE. DESPITE HIS POWER.
YOU TRIED THAT, TOO! PLEASE, STARMAN, DON'T PROLONG THIS!
AND THE WAY HE'S TRIED TO STAY FORMAL AND POLITE. LIKE HE'S VISITING AN OLD RELATIVE...HIS GRANNY OR SOMESUCH.
LIKE A KID TRYING TO BE SERIOUS.
AND I'LL KEEP TRYING UNTIL IT WORKS, HOT-SHOT!
YEAH. LIKE A KID.
WEIRD.
OLD MONEY WANTED
COINS

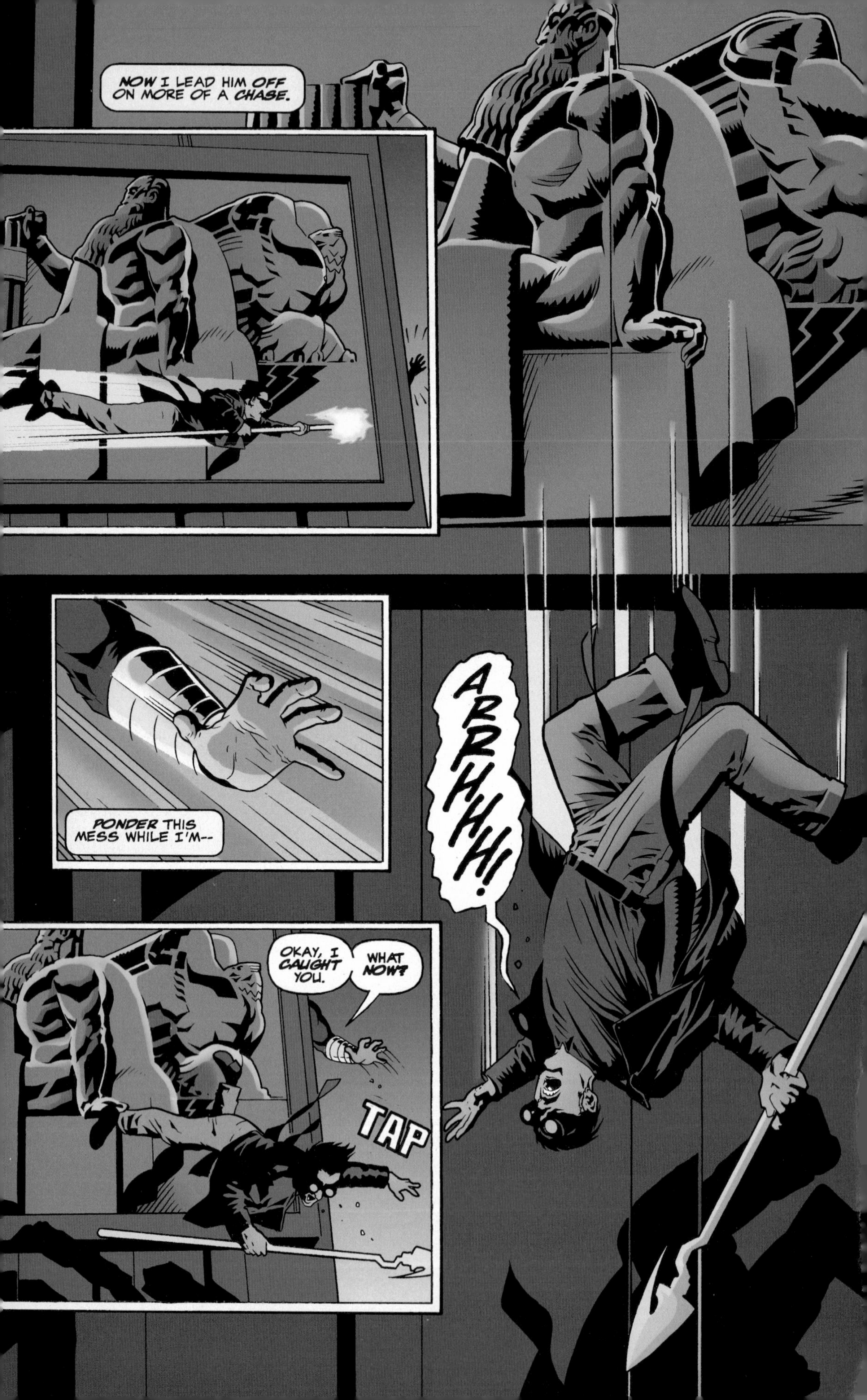
NOW I LEAD HIM OFF ON MORE OF A CHASE.
PONDER THIS MESS WHILE I'M--
ARRHHHH!
OKAY, I CAUGHT YOU.
WHAT NOW?
TAP

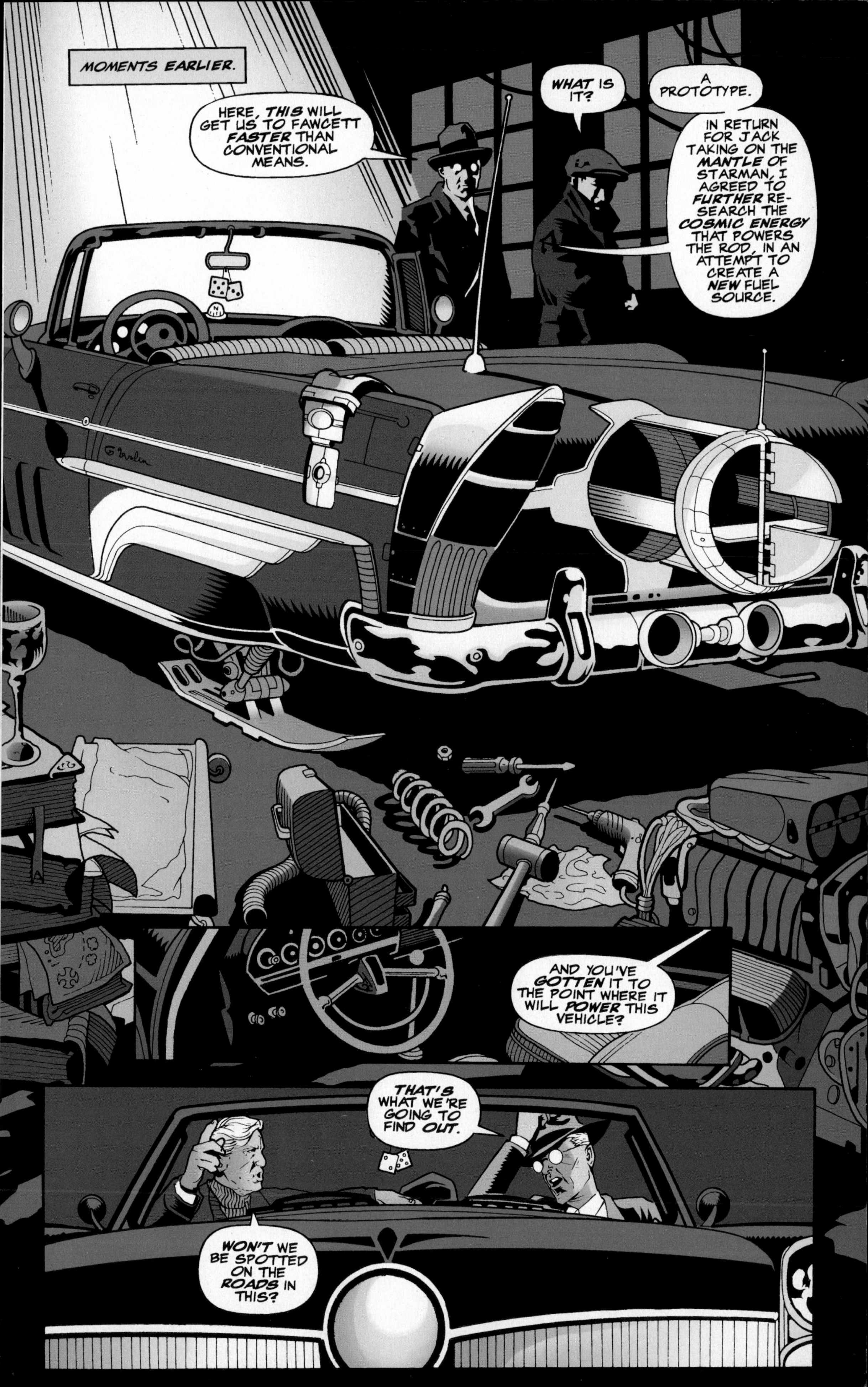
MOMENTS EARLIER.
HERE, THIS WILL GET US TO FAWCETT FASTER THAN CONVENTIONAL MEANS.
WHAT IS IT?
A PROTOTYPE.
IN RETURN FOR JACK TAKING ON THE MANTLE OF STARMAN, I AGREED TO FURTHER RESEARCH THE COSMIC ENERGY THAT POWERS THE ROD, IN AN ATTEMPT TO CREATE A NEW FUEL SOURCE.
AND YOU'VE GOTTEN IT TO THE POINT WHERE IT WILL POWER THIS VEHICLE?
THAT'S WHAT WE'RE GOING TO FIND OUT.
WON'T WE BE SPOTTED ON THE ROADS IN THIS?

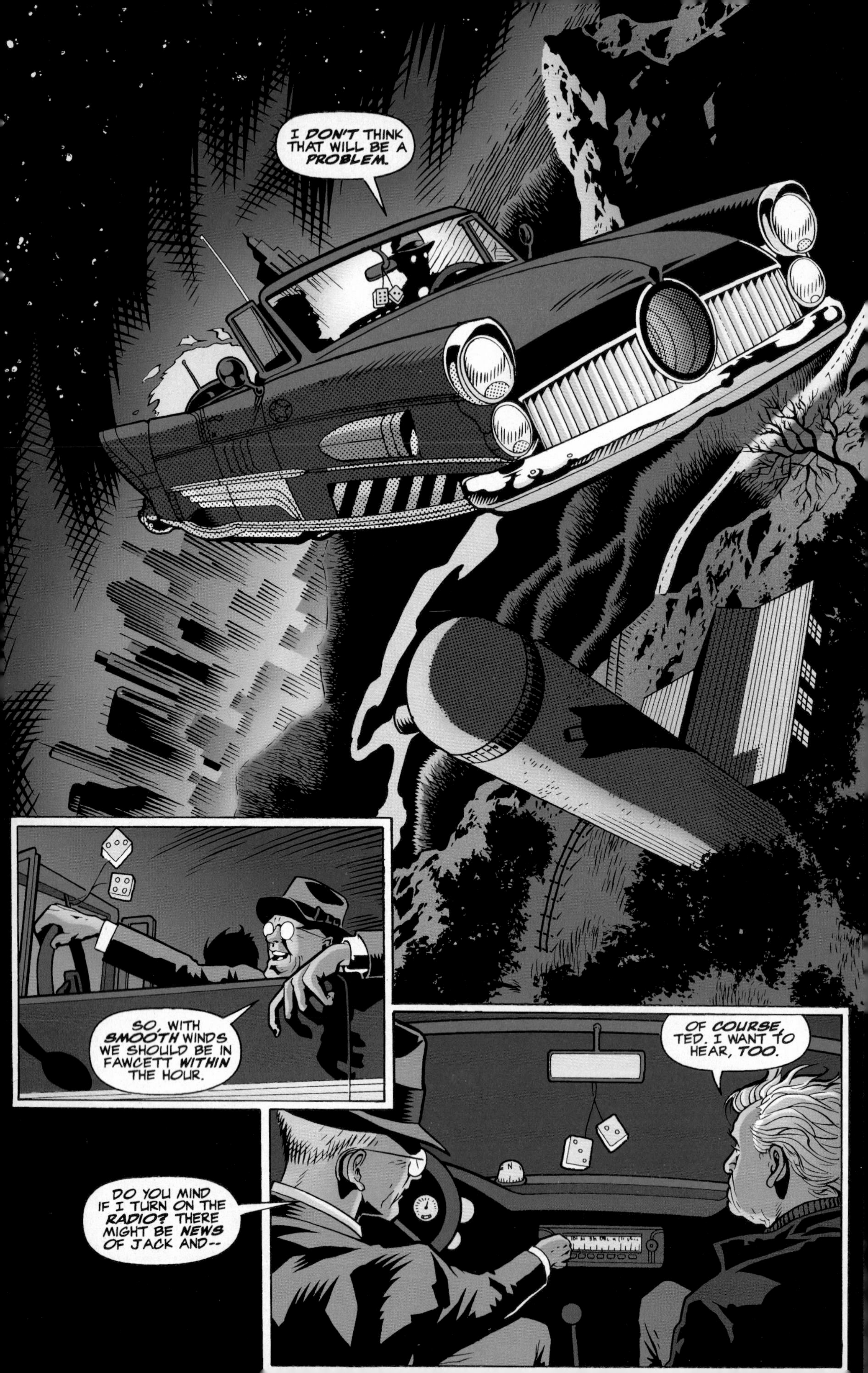
I DON'T THINK THAT WILL BE A PROBLEM.
SO, WITH SMOOTH WINDS WE SHOULD BE IN FAWCETT WITHIN THE HOUR.
DO YOU MIND IF I TURN ON THE RADIO? THERE MIGHT BE NEWS OF JACK AND--
OF COURSE, TED. I WANT TO HEAR, TOO.

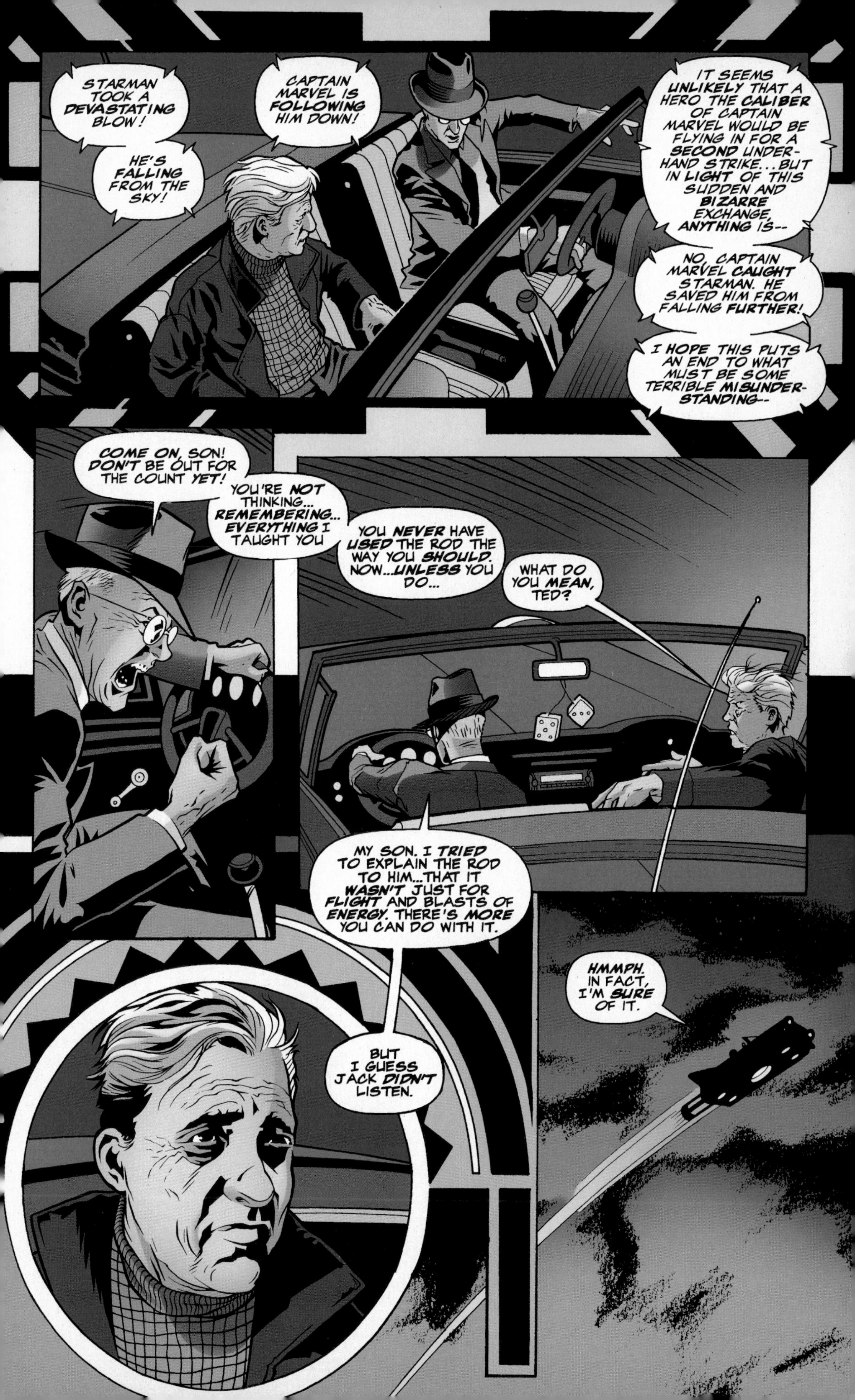
STARMAN TOOK A DEVASTATING BLOW!
HE'S FALLING FROM THE SKY!
CAPTAIN MARVEL IS FOLLOWING HIM DOWN!
IT SEEMS UNLIKELY THAT A HERO THE CALIBER OF CAPTAIN MARVEL WOULD BE FLYING IN FOR A SECOND UNDER-HAND STRIKE...BUT IN LIGHT OF THIS SUDDEN AND BIZARRE EXCHANGE, ANYTHING IS--
NO, CAPTAIN MARVEL CAUGHT STARMAN. HE SAVED HIM FROM FALLING FURTHER!
I HOPE THIS PUTS AN END TO WHAT MUST BE SOME TERRIBLE MISUNDER-STANDING--
COME ON, SON! DON'T BE OUT FOR THE COUNT YET!
YOU'RE NOT THINKING... REMEMBERING... EVERYTHING I TAUGHT YOU
YOU NEVER HAVE USED THE ROD THE WAY YOU SHOULD. NOW...UNLESS YOU DO...
WHAT DO YOU MEAN, TED?
MY SON. I TRIED TO EXPLAIN THE ROD TO HIM...THAT IT WASN'T JUST FOR FLIGHT AND BLASTS OF ENERGY. THERE'S MORE YOU CAN DO WITH IT.
BUT I GUESS JACK DIDN'T LISTEN.
HMMPH. IN FACT, I'M SURE OF IT.

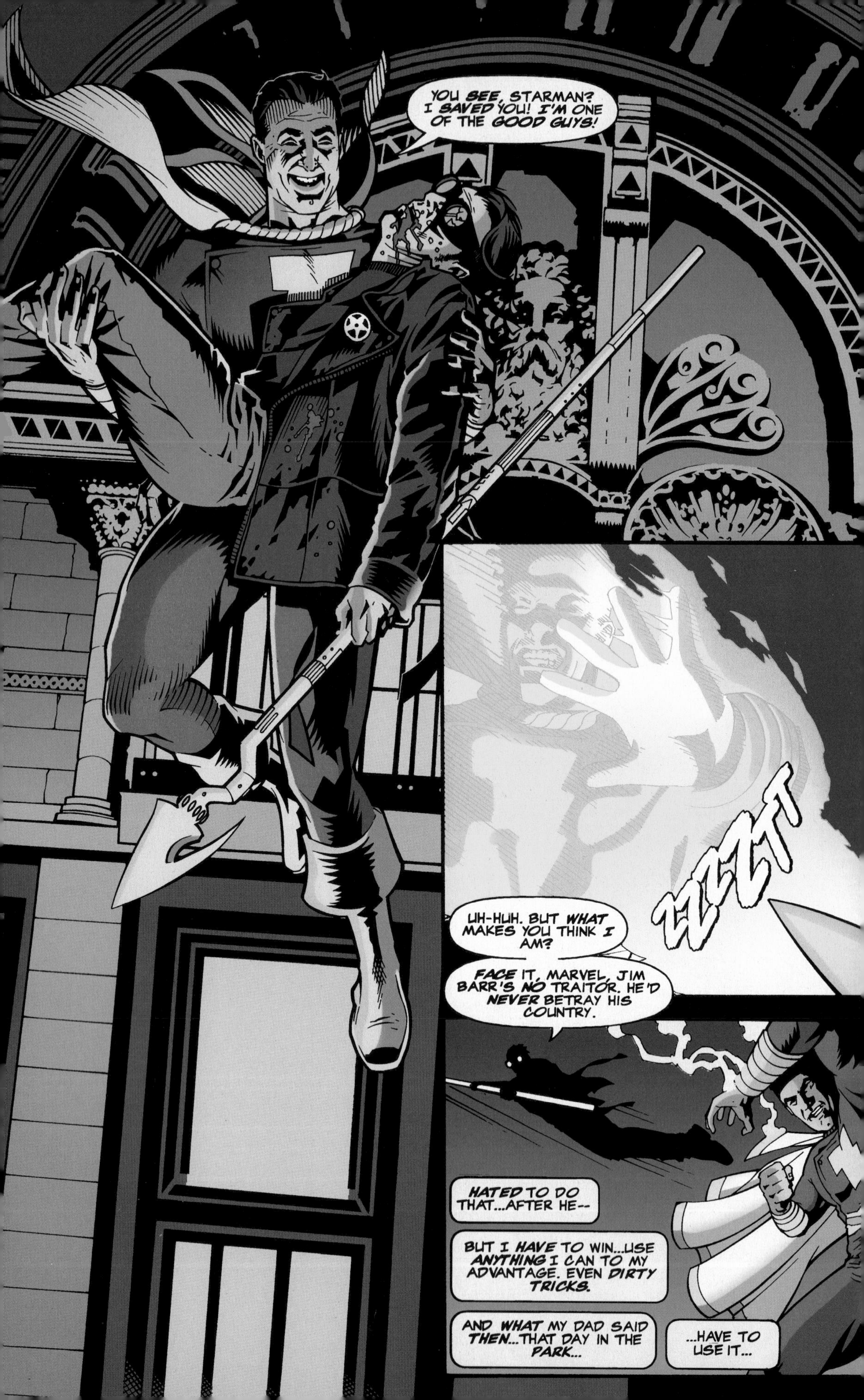
YOU SEE, STARMAN? I SAVED YOU! I'M ONE OF THE GOOD GUYS!
ZZZZT
UH-HUH. BUT WHAT MAKES YOU THINK I AM?
FACE IT, MARVEL, JIM BARR'S NO TRAITOR. HE'D NEVER BETRAY HIS COUNTRY.
HATED TO DO THAT...AFTER HE--
BUT I HAVE TO WIN...USE ANYTHING I CAN TO MY ADVANTAGE. EVEN DIRTY TRICKS.
AND WHAT MY DAD SAID THEN...THAT DAY IN THE PARK...
...HAVE TO USE IT...

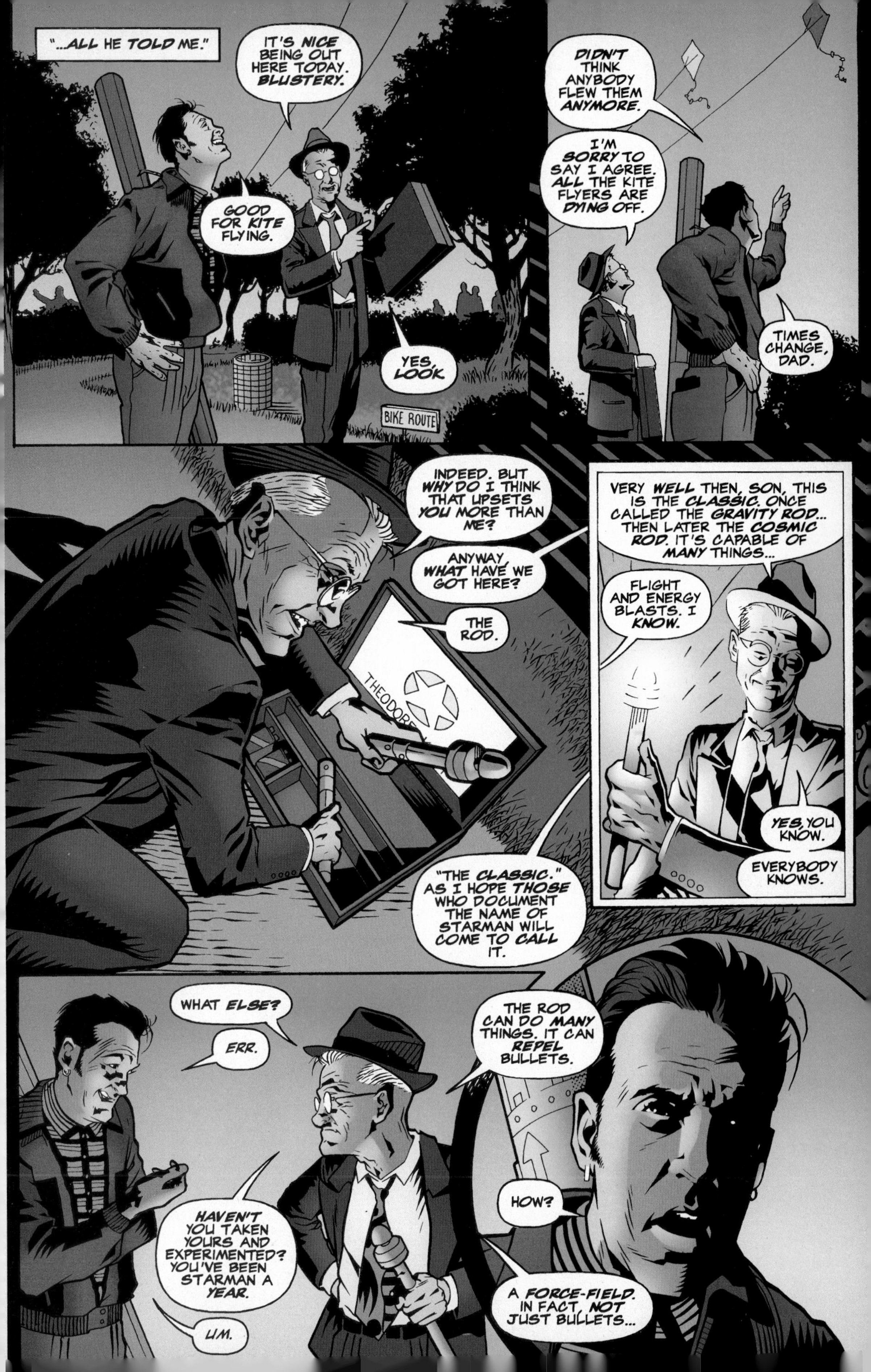
"...ALL HE TOLD ME."
IT'S NICE BEING OUT HERE TODAY. BLUSTERY.
GOOD FOR KITE FLYING.
YES, LOOK
BIKE ROUTE
DIDN'T THINK ANYBODY FLEW THEM ANYMORE.
I'M SORRY TO SAY I AGREE. ALL THE KITE FLYERS ARE DYING OFF.
TIMES CHANGE, DAD.
INDEED. BUT WHY DO I THINK THAT UPSETS YOU MORE THAN ME?
ANYWAY, WHAT HAVE WE GOT HERE?
THE ROD.
THEODORE
VERY WELL THEN, SON, THIS IS THE CLASSIC. ONCE CALLED THE GRAVITY ROD... THEN LATER THE COSMIC ROD. IT'S CAPABLE OF MANY THINGS...
FLIGHT AND ENERGY BLASTS. I KNOW.
YES, YOU KNOW.
EVERYBODY KNOWS.
"THE CLASSIC." AS I HOPE THOSE WHO DOCUMENT THE NAME OF STARMAN WILL COME TO CALL IT.
WHAT ELSE?
ERR.
HAVEN'T YOU TAKEN YOURS AND EXPERIMENTED? YOU'VE BEEN STARMAN A YEAR.
UM.
THE ROD CAN DO MANY THINGS. IT CAN REPEL BULLETS.
HOW?
A FORCE-FIELD. IN FACT, NOT JUST BULLETS...

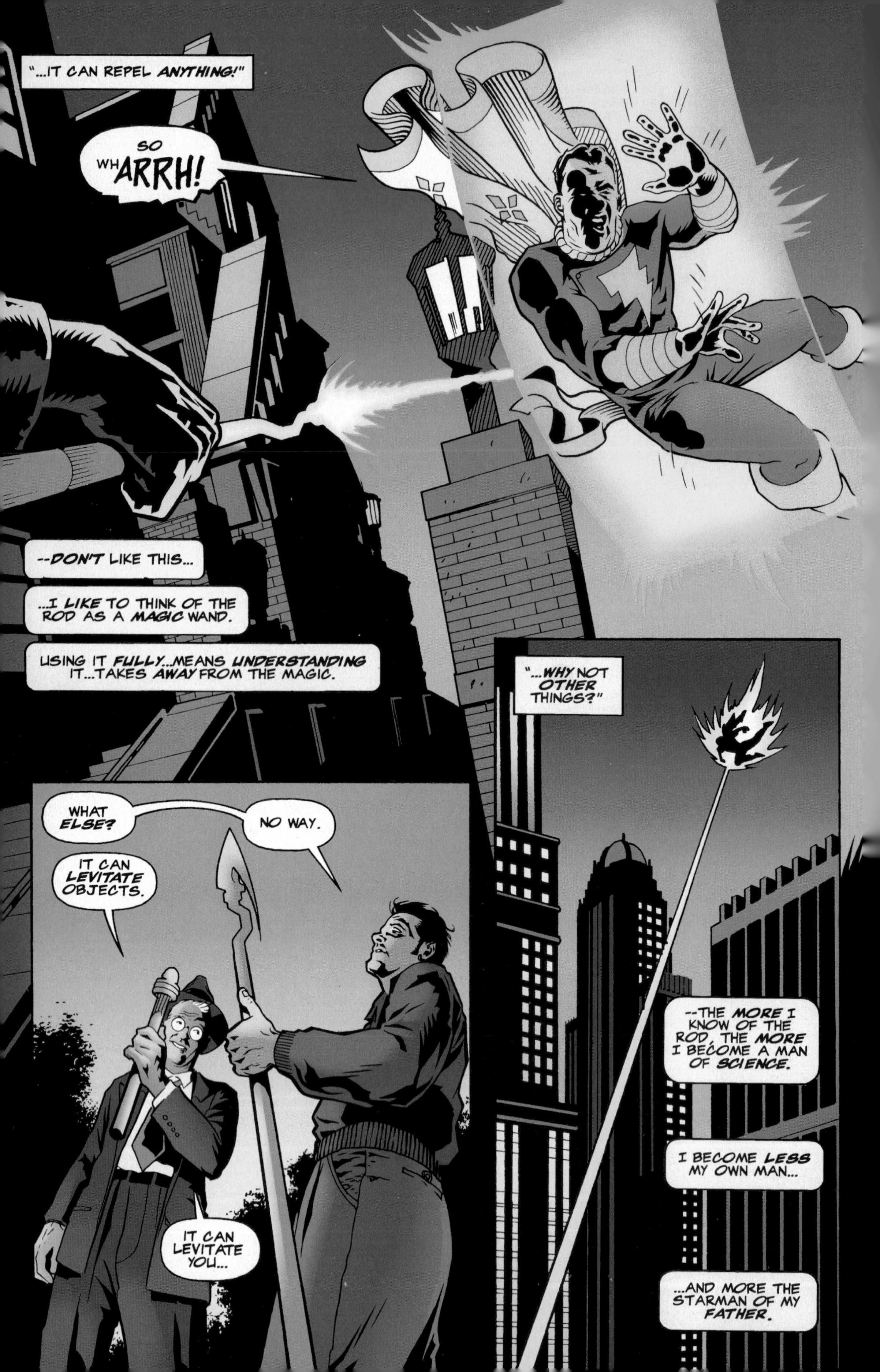
"...IT CAN REPEL ANYTHING!"
SO WHARRH!
--DON'T LIKE THIS...
...I LIKE TO THINK OF THE ROD AS A MAGIC WAND.
USING IT FULLY...MEANS UNDERSTANDING IT...TAKES AWAY FROM THE MAGIC.
WHAT ELSE?
NO WAY.
IT CAN LEVITATE OBJECTS.
IT CAN LEVITATE YOU...
"...WHY NOT OTHER THINGS?"
--THE MORE I KNOW OF THE ROD, THE MORE I BECOME A MAN OF SCIENCE.
I BECOME LESS MY OWN MAN...
...AND MORE THE STARMAN OF MY FATHER.

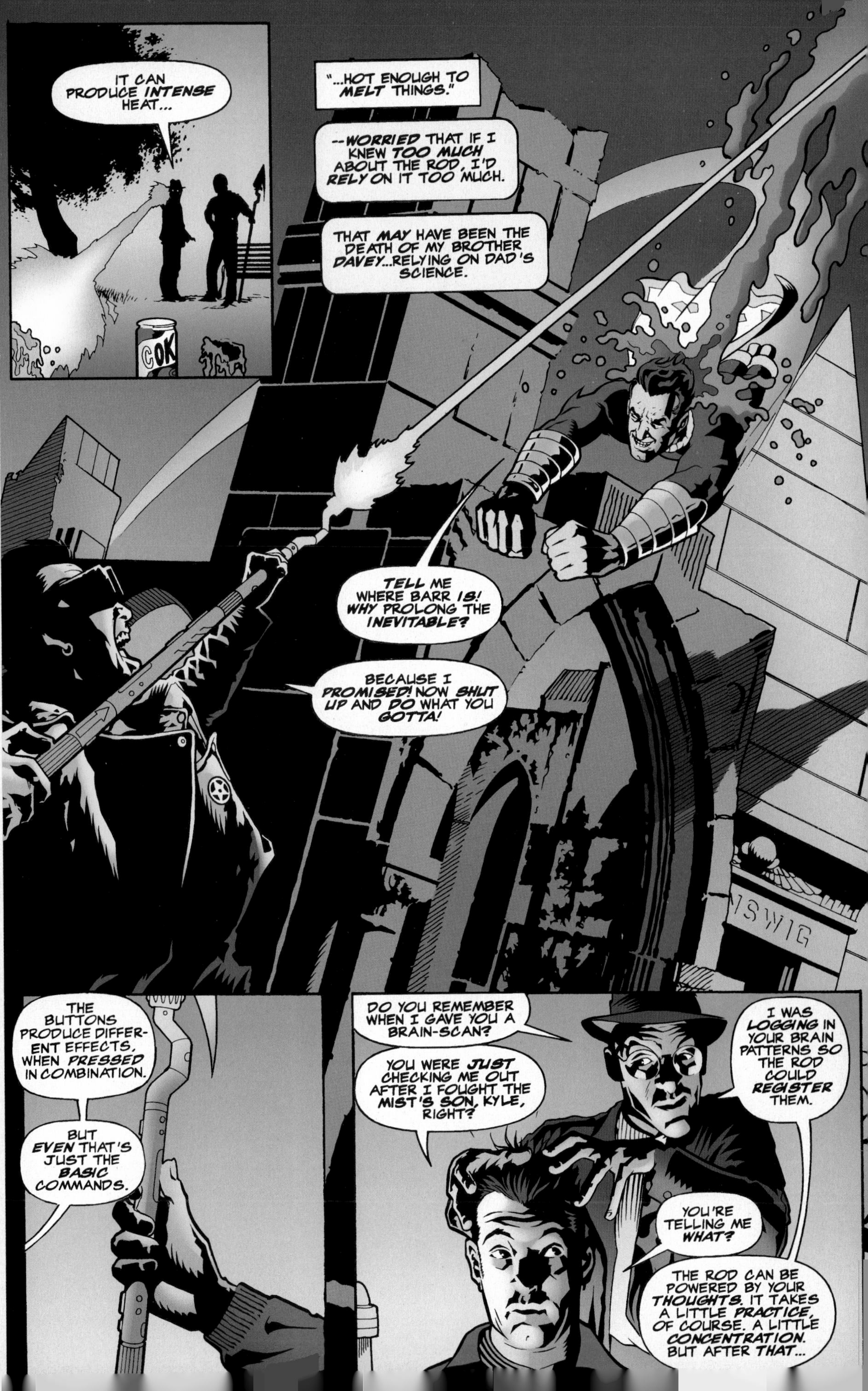
IT CAN PRODUCE INTENSE HEAT...
COK
"...HOT ENOUGH TO MELT THINGS."
--WORRIED THAT IF I KNEW TOO MUCH ABOUT THE ROD, I'D RELY ON IT TOO MUCH.
THAT MAY HAVE BEEN THE DEATH OF MY BROTHER DAVEY...RELYING ON DAD'S SCIENCE.
TELL ME WHERE BARR IS! WHY PROLONG THE INEVITABLE?
BECAUSE I PROMISED! NOW SHUT UP AND DO WHAT YOU GOTTA!
SWIG
THE BUTTONS PRODUCE DIFFERENT EFFECTS, WHEN PRESSED IN COMBINATION.
BUT EVEN THAT'S JUST THE BASIC COMMANDS.
DO YOU REMEMBER WHEN I GAVE YOU A BRAIN-SCAN?
YOU WERE JUST CHECKING ME OUT AFTER I FOUGHT THE MIST'S SON, KYLE, RIGHT?
I WAS LOGGING IN YOUR BRAIN PATTERNS SO THE ROD COULD REGISTER THEM.
YOU'RE TELLING ME WHAT?
THE ROD CAN BE POWERED BY YOUR THOUGHTS. IT TAKES A LITTLE PRACTICE, OF COURSE. A LITTLE CONCENTRATION. BUT AFTER THAT...

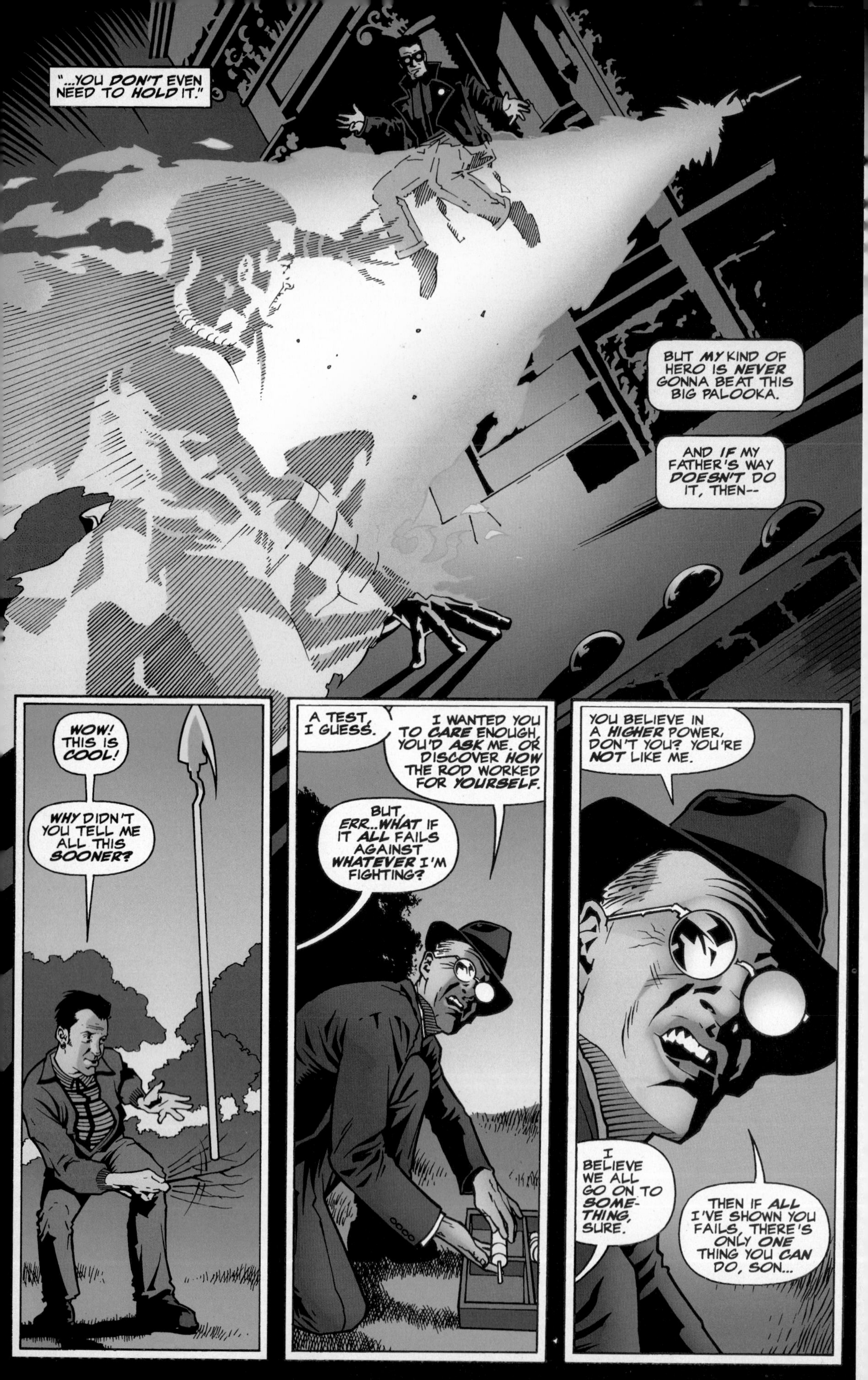
"...YOU DON'T EVEN NEED TO HOLD IT."
BUT MY KIND OF HERO IS NEVER GONNA BEAT THIS BIG PALOOKA.
AND IF MY FATHER'S WAY DOESN'T DO IT, THEN--
WOW! THIS IS COOL!
WHY DIDN'T YOU TELL ME ALL THIS SOONER?
A TEST, I GUESS.
I WANTED YOU TO CARE ENOUGH, YOU'D ASK ME. OR DISCOVER HOW THE ROD WORKED FOR YOURSELF.
BUT ERR...WHAT IF IT ALL FAILS AGAINST WHATEVER I'M FIGHTING?
YOU BELIEVE IN A HIGHER POWER, DON'T YOU? YOU'RE NOT LIKE ME.
I BELIEVE WE ALL GO ON TO SOME-THING, SURE.
THEN IF ALL I'VE SHOWN YOU FAILS, THERE'S ONLY ONE THING YOU CAN DO, SON...

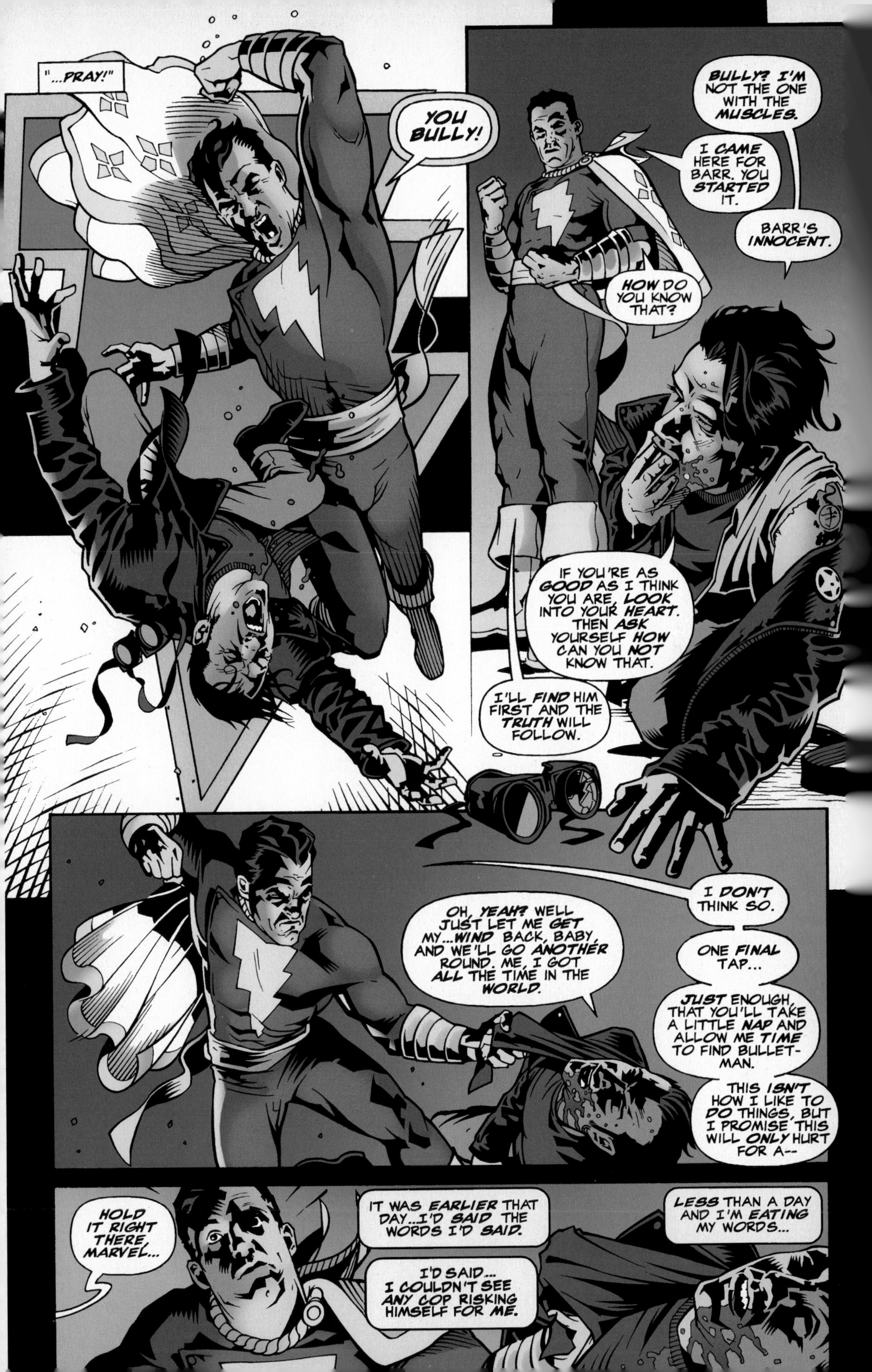
"...PRAY!"
YOU BULLY!
BULLY? I'M NOT THE ONE WITH THE MUSCLES.
I CAME HERE FOR BARR. YOU STARTED IT.
BARR'S INNOCENT.
HOW DO YOU KNOW THAT?
IF YOU'RE AS GOOD AS I THINK YOU ARE, LOOK INTO YOUR HEART. THEN ASK YOURSELF HOW CAN YOU NOT KNOW THAT.
I'LL FIND HIM FIRST AND THE TRUTH WILL FOLLOW.
OH, YEAH? WELL JUST LET ME GET MY...WIND BACK, BABY, AND WE'LL GO ANOTHER ROUND. ME, I GOT ALL THE TIME IN THE WORLD.
I DON'T THINK SO.
ONE FINAL TAP...
JUST ENOUGH, THAT YOU'LL TAKE A LITTLE NAP AND ALLOW ME TIME TO FIND BULLET-MAN.
THIS ISN'T HOW I LIKE TO DO THINGS, BUT I PROMISE THIS WILL ONLY HURT FOR A--
HOLD IT RIGHT THERE, MARVEL...
IT WAS EARLIER THAT DAY...I'D SAID THE WORDS I'D SAID.
I'D SAID... I COULDN'T SEE ANY COP RISKING HIMSELF FOR ME.
LESS THAN A DAY AND I'M EATING MY WORDS...

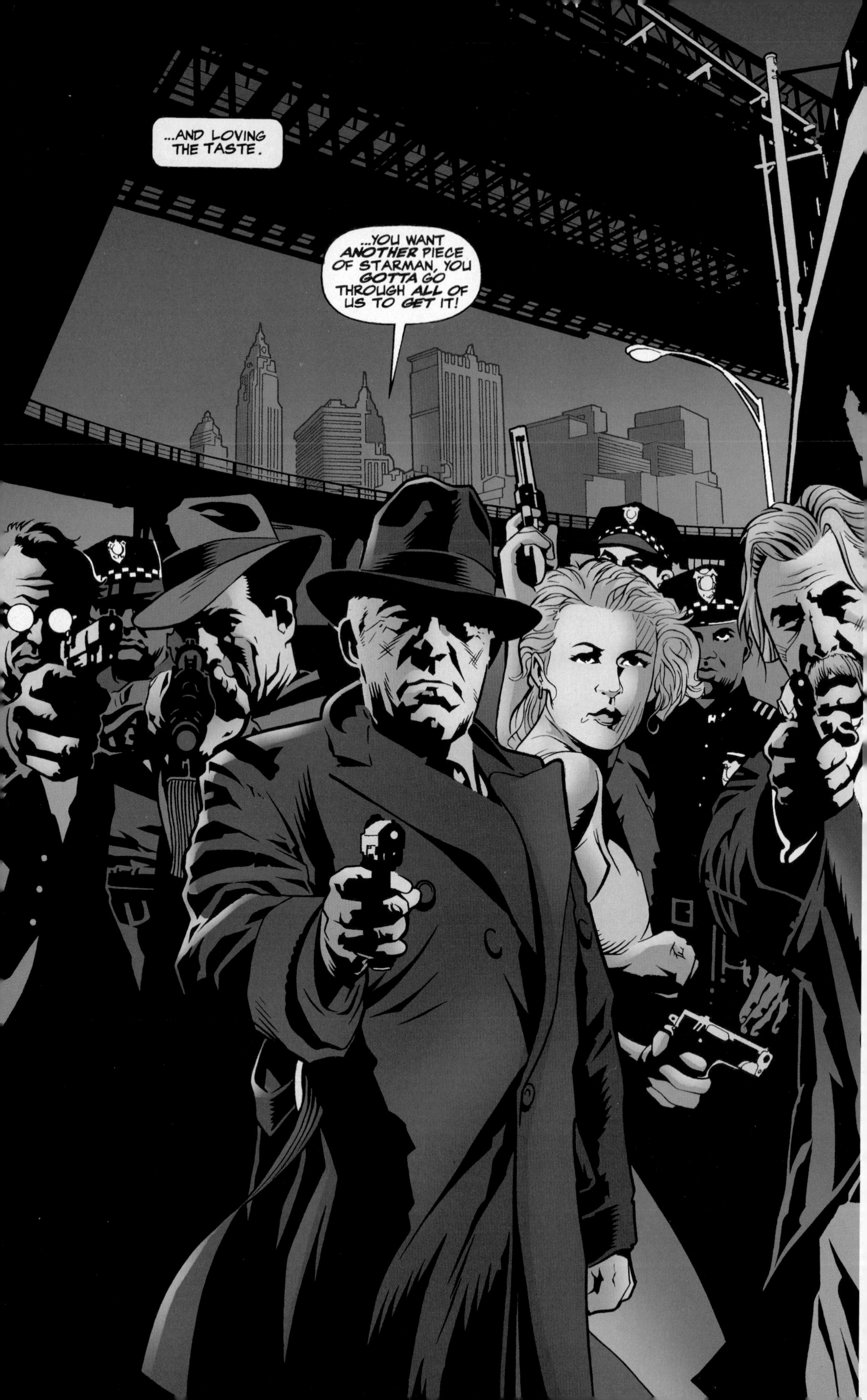
...AND LOVING THE TASTE.
...YOU WANT ANOTHER PIECE OF STARMAN, YOU GOTTA GO THROUGH ALL OF US TO GET IT!

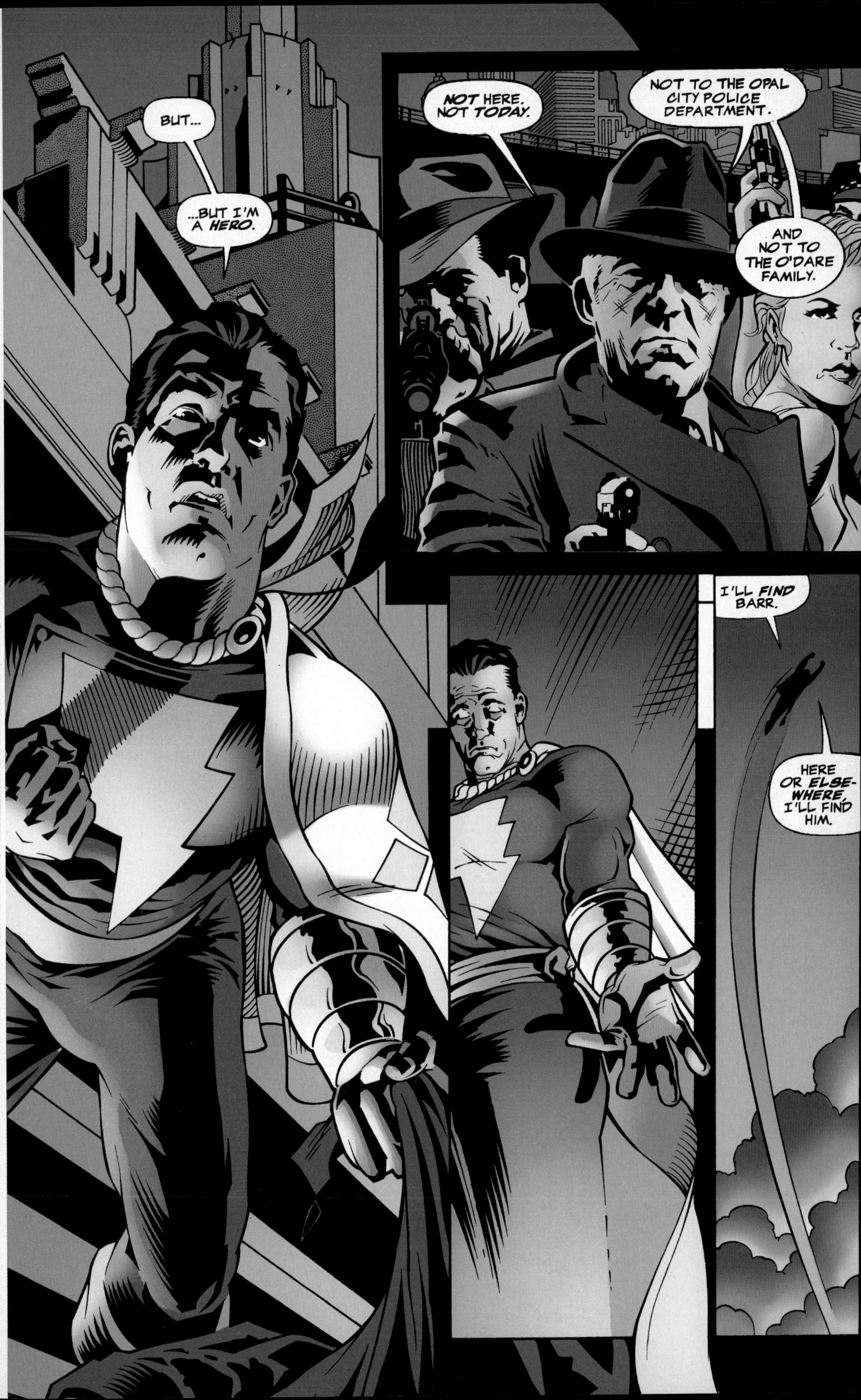
BUT...
...BUT I'M A HERO.
NOT HERE. NOT TODAY.
NOT TO THE OPAL CITY POLICE DEPARTMENT.
AND NOT TO THE O'DARE FAMILY.
I'LL FIND BARR.
HERE OR ELSE-WHERE, I'LL FIND HIM.

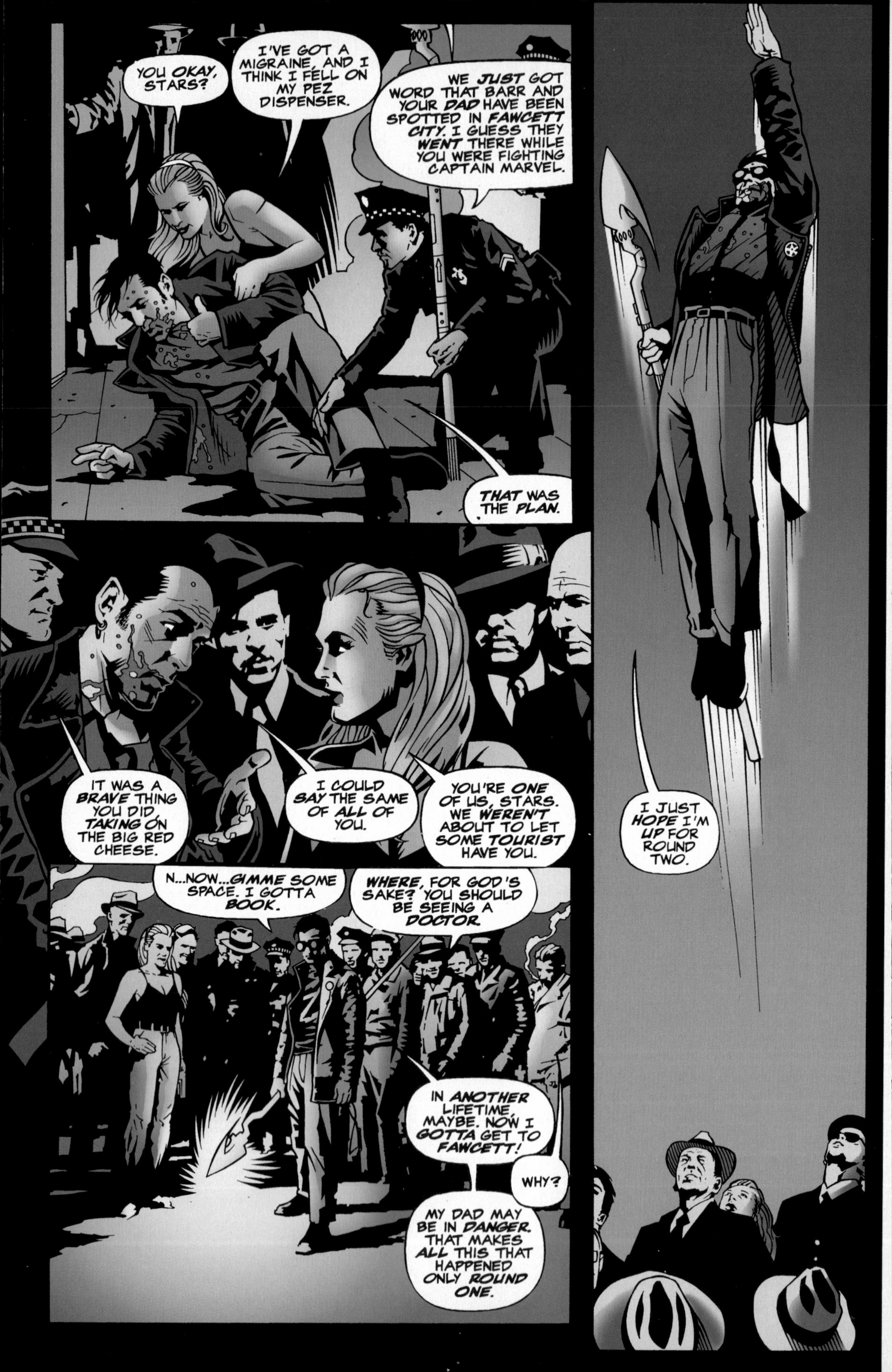

YOU OKAY, STARS?
I'VE GOT A MIGRAINE, AND I THINK I FELL ON MY PEZ DISPENSER.
WE JUST GOT WORD THAT BARR AND YOUR DAD HAVE BEEN SPOTTED IN FAWCETT CITY. I GUESS THEY WENT THERE WHILE YOU WERE FIGHTING CAPTAIN MARVEL.
THAT WAS THE PLAN.
IT WAS A BRAVE THING YOU DID, TAKING ON THE BIG RED CHEESE.
I COULD SAY THE SAME OF ALL OF YOU.
YOU'RE ONE OF US, STARS. WE WEREN'T ABOUT TO LET SOME TOURIST HAVE YOU.
N...NOW...GIMME SOME SPACE. I GOTTA BOOK.
WHERE, FOR GOD'S SAKE? YOU SHOULD BE SEEING A DOCTOR.
IN ANOTHER LIFETIME, MAYBE. NOW I GOTTA GET TO FAWCETT!
WHY?
MY DAD MAY BE IN DANGER. THAT MAKES ALL THIS THAT HAPPENED ONLY ROUND ONE.
I JUST HOPE I'M UP FOR ROUND TWO.

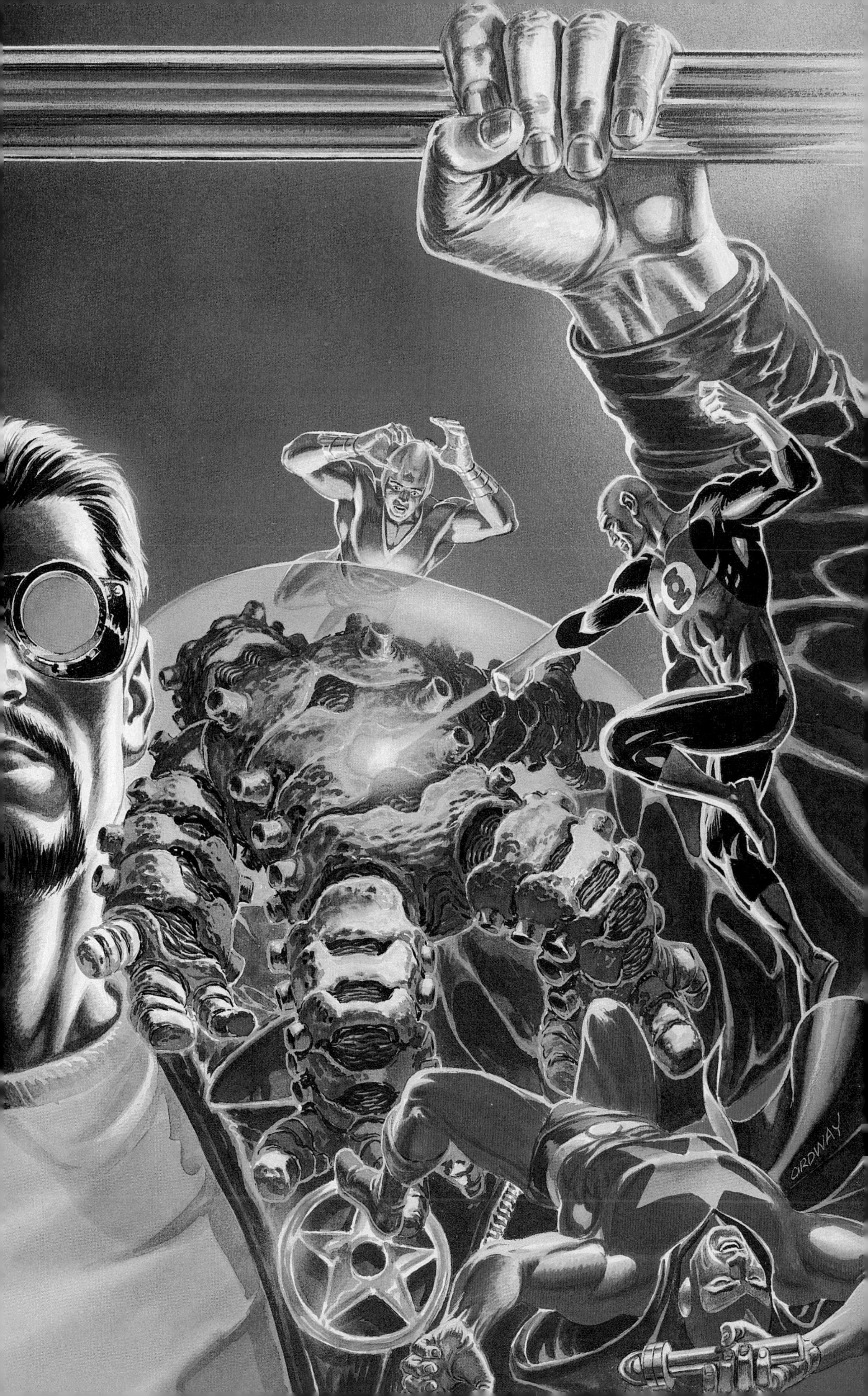
ORDWAY

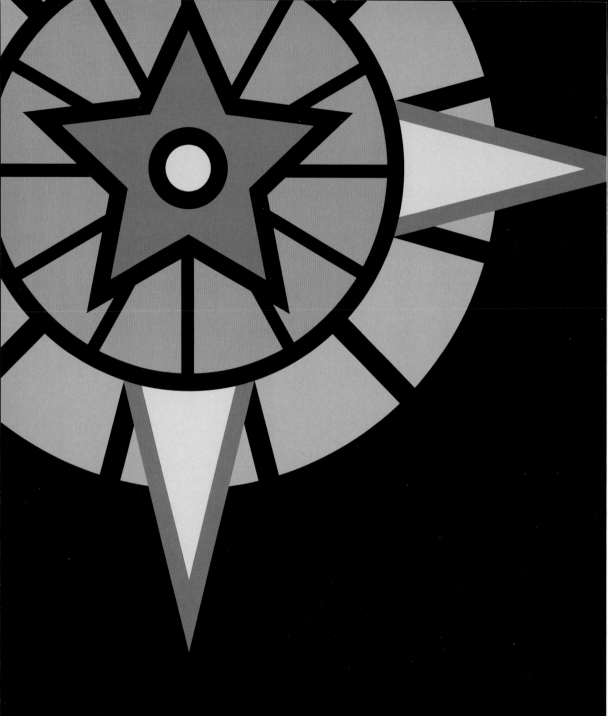

THE POWER OF SHAZAM 36

Cover and script by Jerry Ordway

Pencils by Pete Krause

with inks by Dick Giordano

and colors by Glenn Whitmore

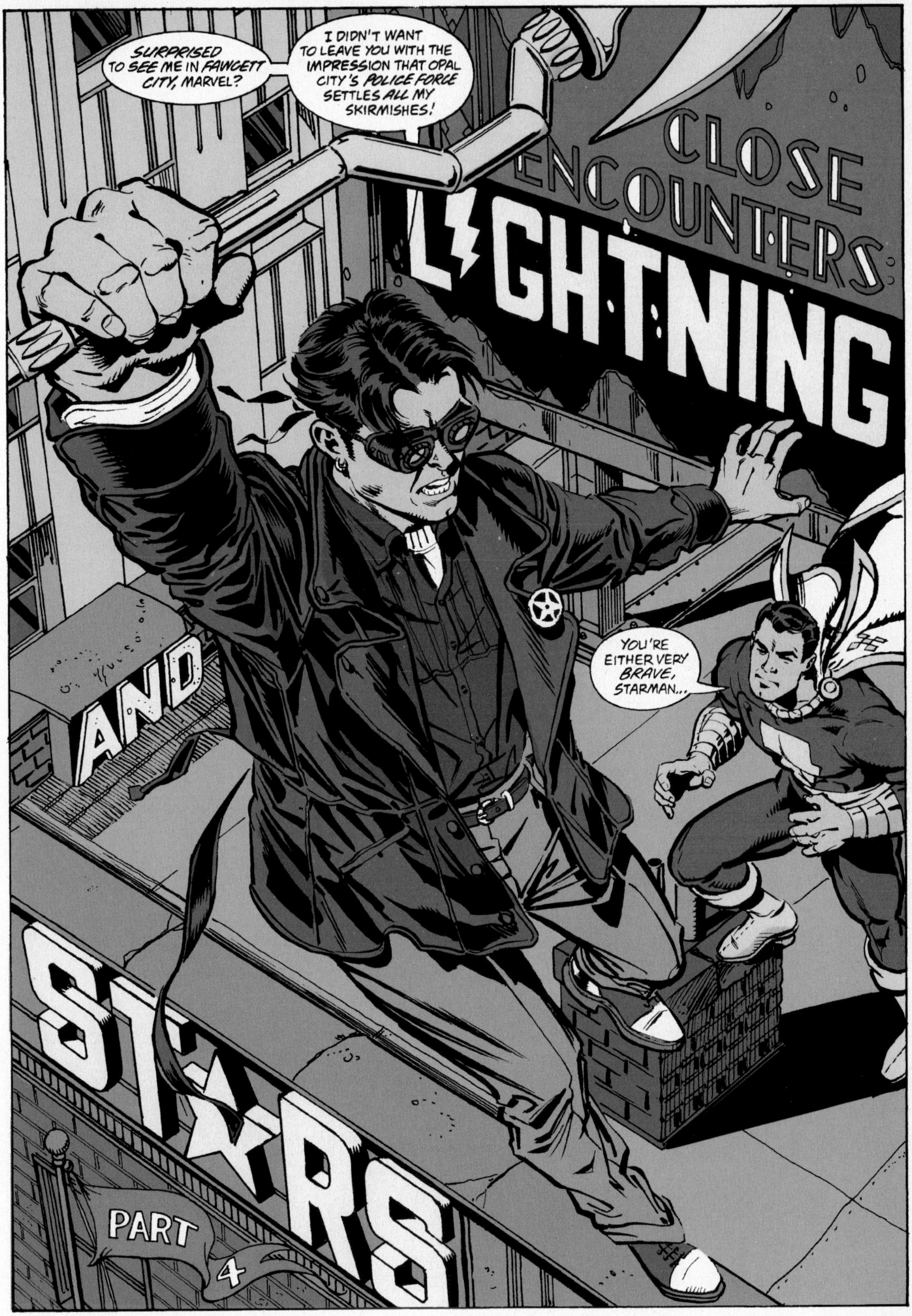
SURPRISED TO SEE ME IN FAWCETT CITY, MARVEL?
I DIDN'T WANT TO LEAVE YOU WITH THE IMPRESSION THAT OPAL CITY'S POLICE FORCE SETTLES ALL MY SKIRMISHES!
CLOSE ENCOUNTERS
LIGHTNING
AND
YOU'RE EITHER VERY BRAVE, STARMAN...
STARS
PART 4

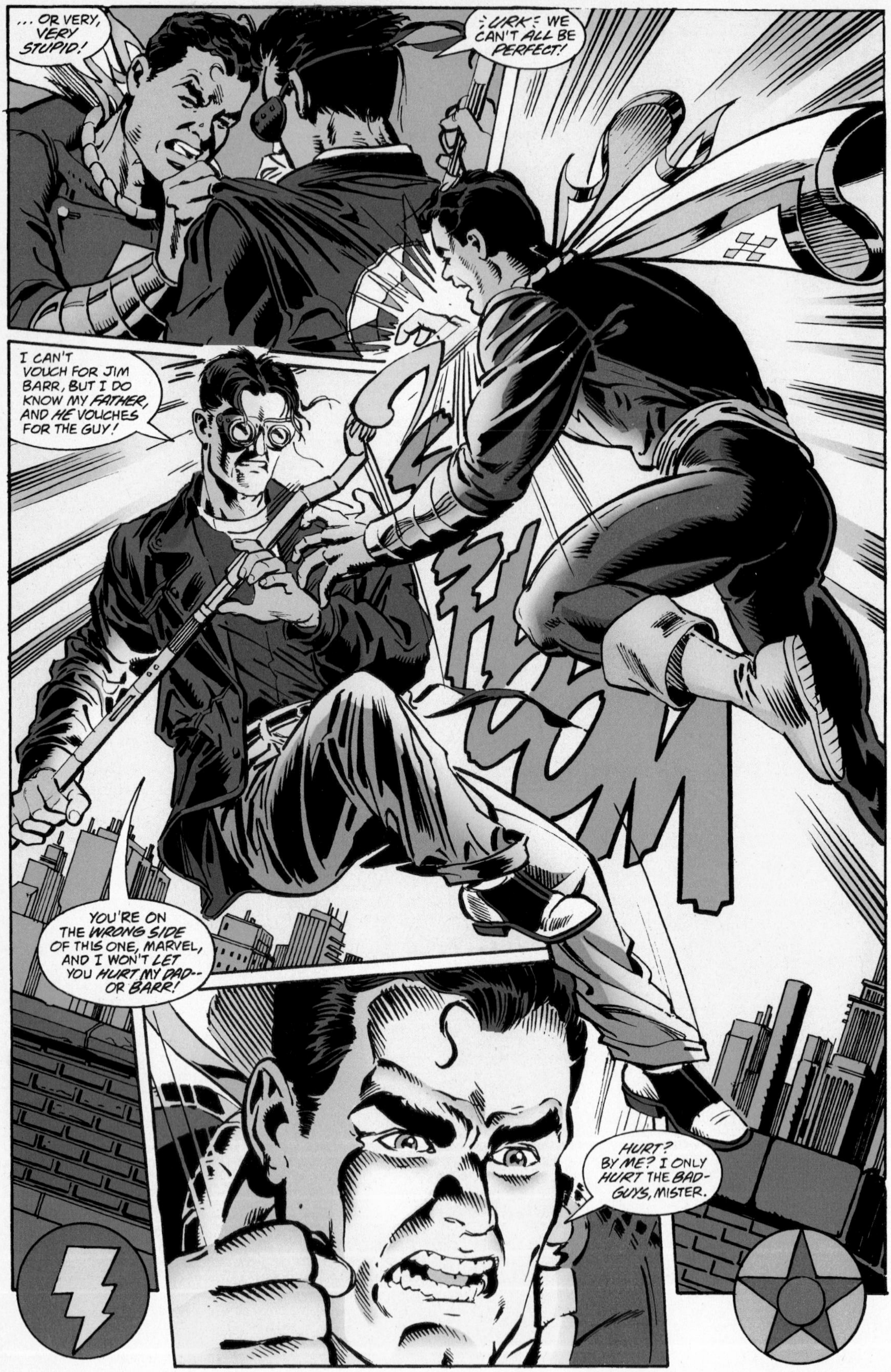

... OR VERY, VERY STUPID!
URK WE CAN'T ALL BE PERFECT!
I CAN'T VOUCH FOR JIM BARR, BUT I DO KNOW MY FATHER, AND HE VOUCHES FOR THE GUY!
YOU'RE ON THE WRONG SIDE OF THIS ONE, MARVEL, AND I WON'T LET YOU HURT MY DAD-- OR BARR!
HURT? BY ME? I ONLY HURT THE BAD-GUYS, MISTER.

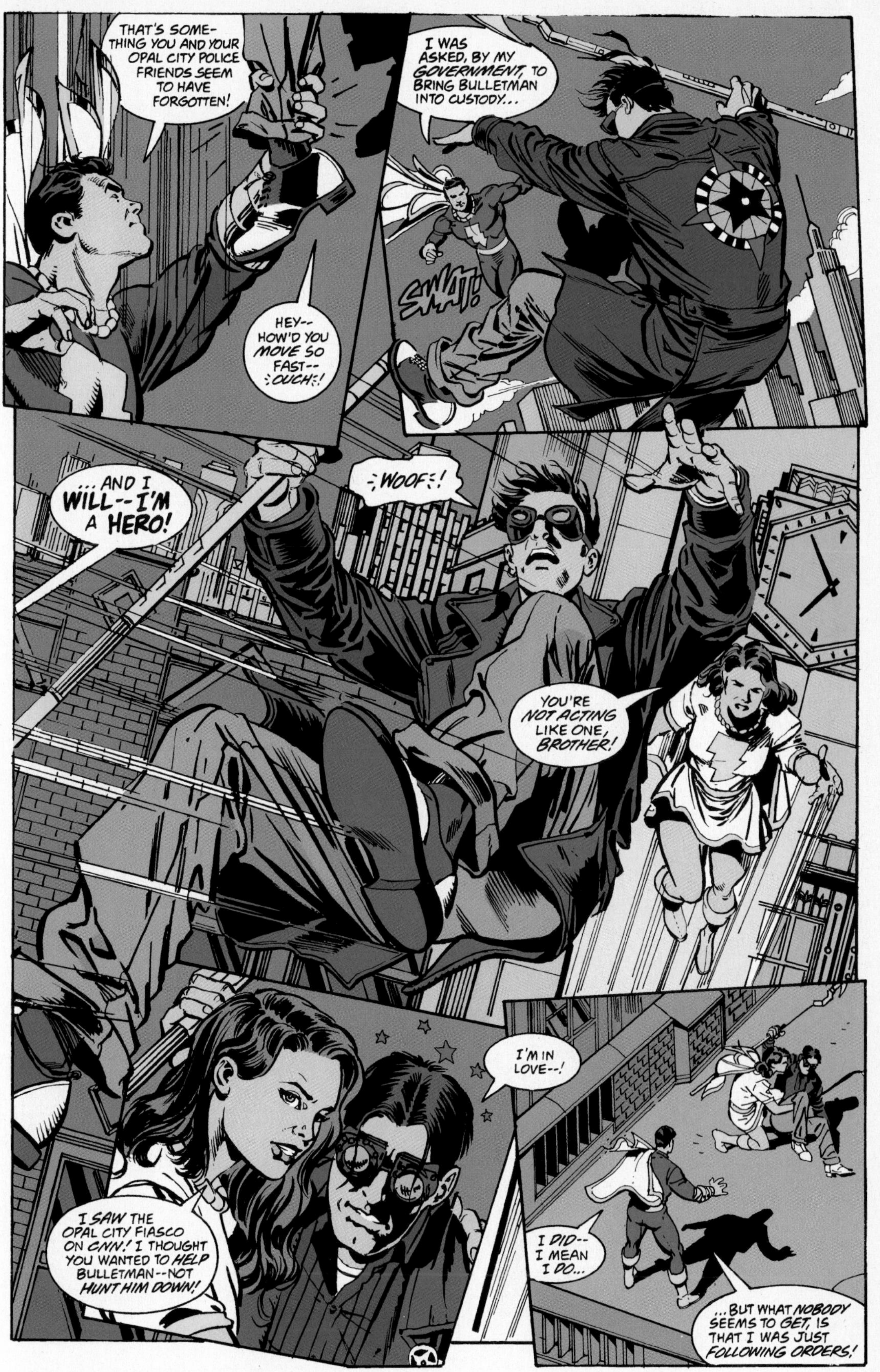

THAT'S SOMETHING YOU AND YOUR OPAL CITY POLICE FRIENDS SEEM TO HAVE FORGOTTEN!
HEY--HOW'D YOU MOVE SO FAST--OUCH!
I WAS ASKED, BY MY GOVERNMENT, TO BRING BULLETMAN INTO CUSTODY...
SWAT!
...AND I WILL--I'M A HERO!
WOOF!
YOU'RE NOT ACTING LIKE ONE, BROTHER!
I'M IN LOVE--!
I SAW THE OPAL CITY FIASCO ON CNN! I THOUGHT YOU WANTED TO HELP BULLETMAN--NOT HUNT HIM DOWN!
I DID--I MEAN I DO...
...BUT WHAT NOBODY SEEMS TO GET, IS THAT I WAS JUST FOLLOWING ORDERS!

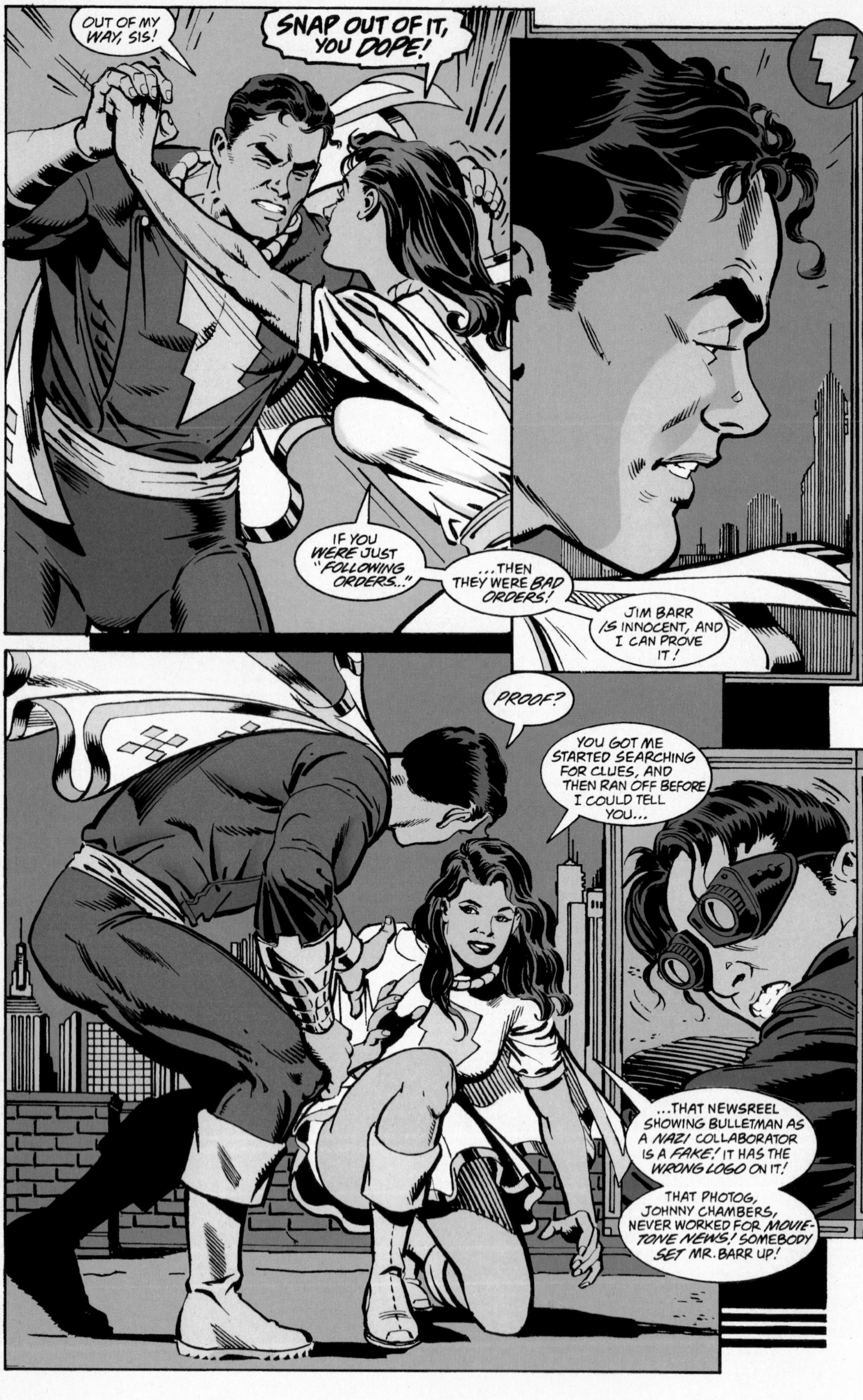
OUT OF MY WAY, SIS!
SNAP OUT OF IT, YOU DOPE!
IF YOU WERE JUST "FOLLOWING ORDERS..."
...THEN THEY WERE BAD ORDERS!
JIM BARR IS INNOCENT, AND I CAN PROVE IT!
PROOF?
YOU GOT ME STARTED SEARCHING FOR CLUES, AND THEN RAN OFF BEFORE I COULD TELL YOU...
...THAT NEWSREEL SHOWING BULLETMAN AS A NAZI COLLABORATOR IS A FAKE! IT HAS THE WRONG LOGO ON IT!
THAT PHOTOG, JOHNNY CHAMBERS, NEVER WORKED FOR MOVIE-TONE NEWS! SOMEBODY SET MR. BARR UP!

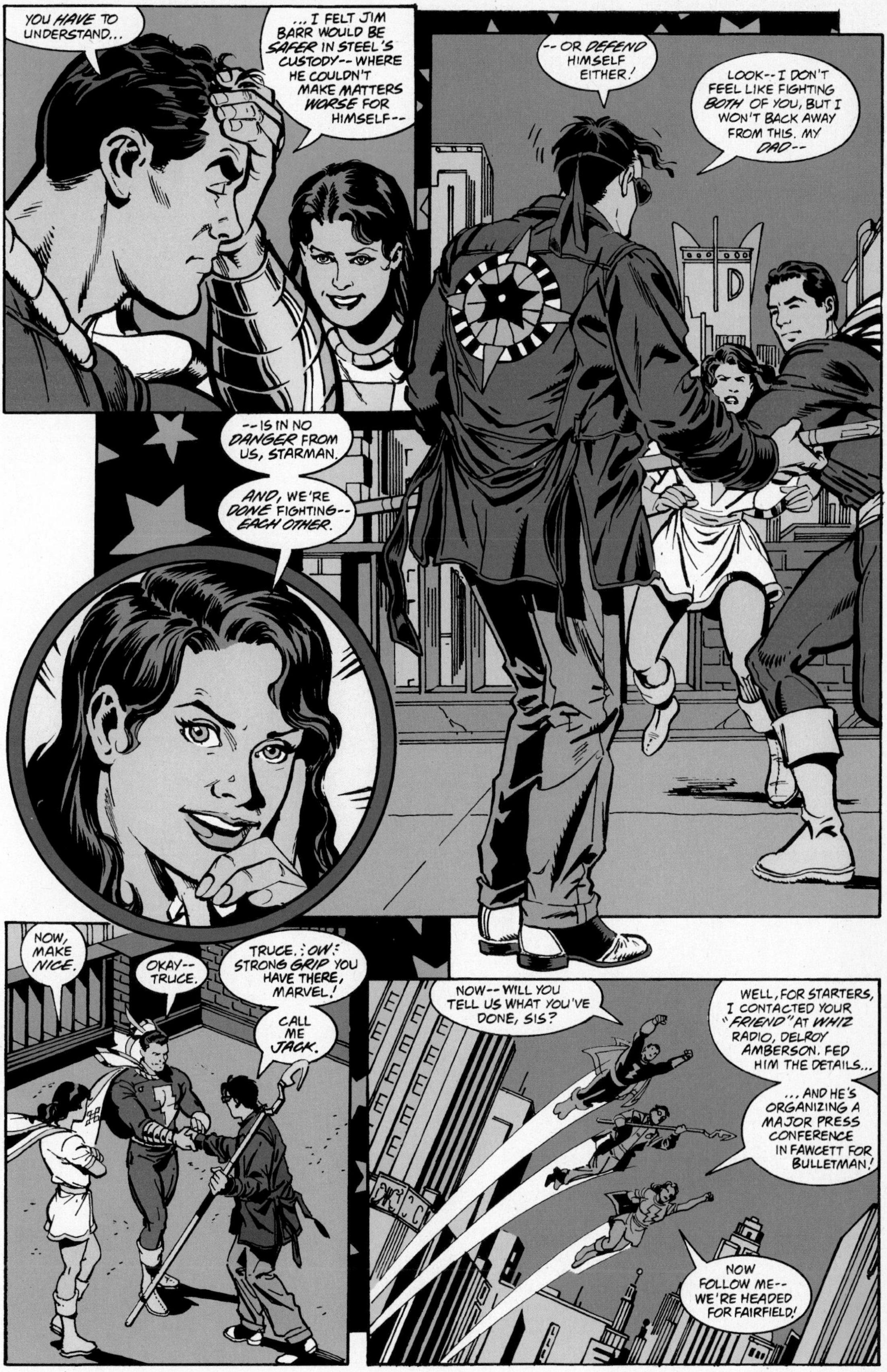
YOU HAVE TO UNDERSTAND...
...I FELT JIM BARR WOULD BE SAFER IN STEEL'S CUSTODY-- WHERE HE COULDN'T MAKE MATTERS WORSE FOR HIMSELF--
--OR DEFEND HIMSELF EITHER!
LOOK--I DON'T FEEL LIKE FIGHTING BOTH OF YOU, BUT I WON'T BACK AWAY FROM THIS. MY DAD--
--IS IN NO DANGER FROM US, STARMAN.
AND, WE'RE DONE FIGHTING-- EACH OTHER.
NOW, MAKE NICE.
OKAY-- TRUCE.
TRUCE. OW STRONG GRIP YOU HAVE THERE, MARVEL!
CALL ME JACK.
NOW--WILL YOU TELL US WHAT YOU'VE DONE, SIS?
WELL, FOR STARTERS, I CONTACTED YOUR "FRIEND" AT WHIZ RADIO, DELROY AMBERSON. FED HIM THE DETAILS...
...AND HE'S ORGANIZING A MAJOR PRESS CONFERENCE IN FAWCETT FOR BULLETMAN!
NOW FOLLOW ME-- WE'RE HEADED FOR FAIRFIELD!

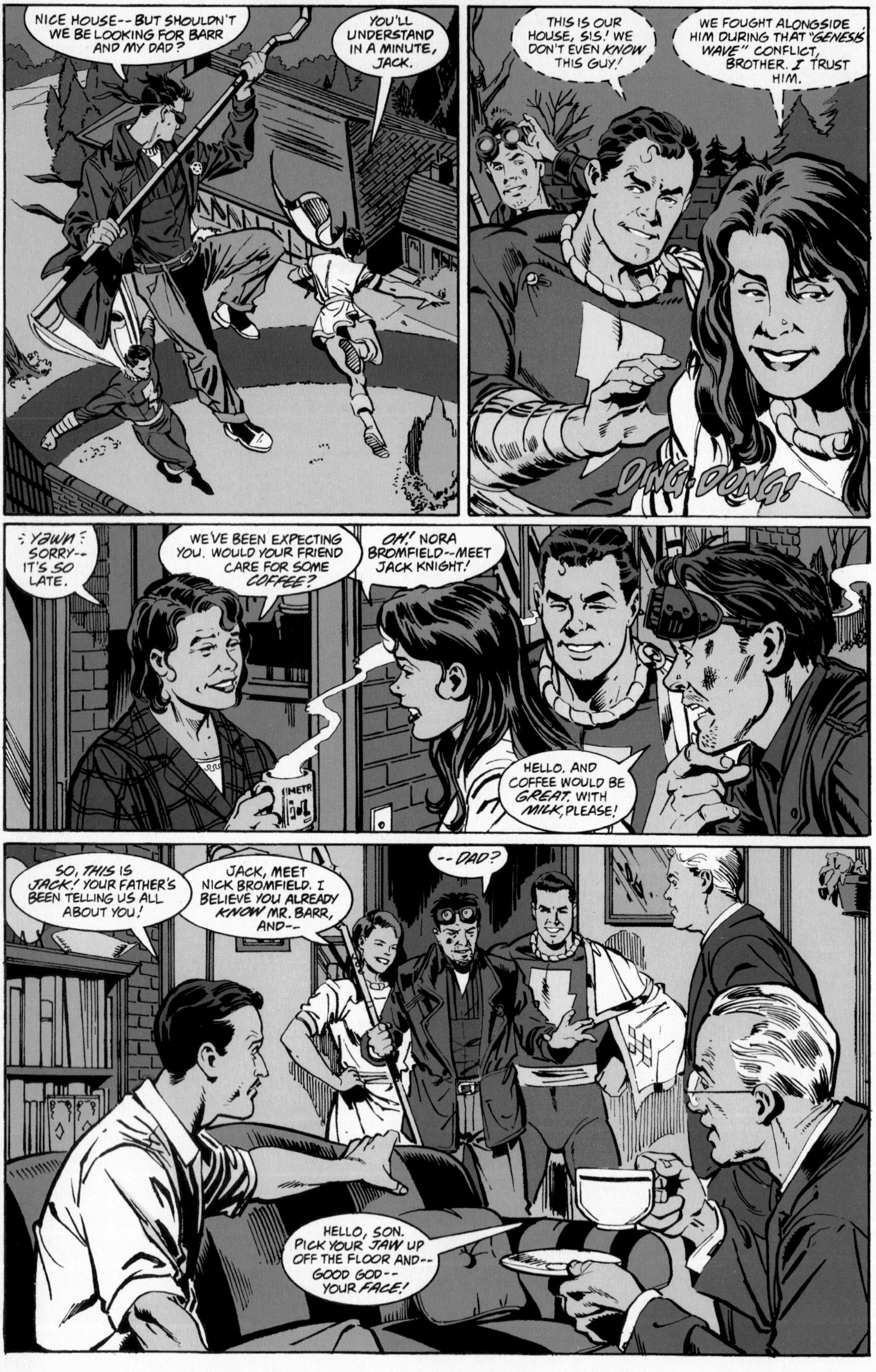

NICE HOUSE--BUT SHOULDN'T WE BE LOOKING FOR BARR AND MY DAD?
YOU'LL UNDERSTAND IN A MINUTE, JACK.
THIS IS OUR HOUSE, SIS! WE DON'T EVEN KNOW THIS GUY!
WE FOUGHT ALONGSIDE HIM DURING THAT "GENESIS WAVE" CONFLICT, BROTHER. I TRUST HIM.
DING-DONG!
YAWN SORRY--IT'S SO LATE.
WE'VE BEEN EXPECTING YOU. WOULD YOUR FRIEND CARE FOR SOME COFFEE?
OH! NORA BROMFIELD--MEET JACK KNIGHT!
HELLO. AND COFFEE WOULD BE GREAT. WITH MILK, PLEASE!
SO, THIS IS JACK! YOUR FATHER'S BEEN TELLING US ALL ABOUT YOU!
JACK, MEET NICK BROMFIELD. I BELIEVE YOU ALREADY KNOW MR. BARR, AND--
--DAD?
HELLO, SON. PICK YOUR JAW UP OFF THE FLOOR AND--GOOD GOD--YOUR FACE!

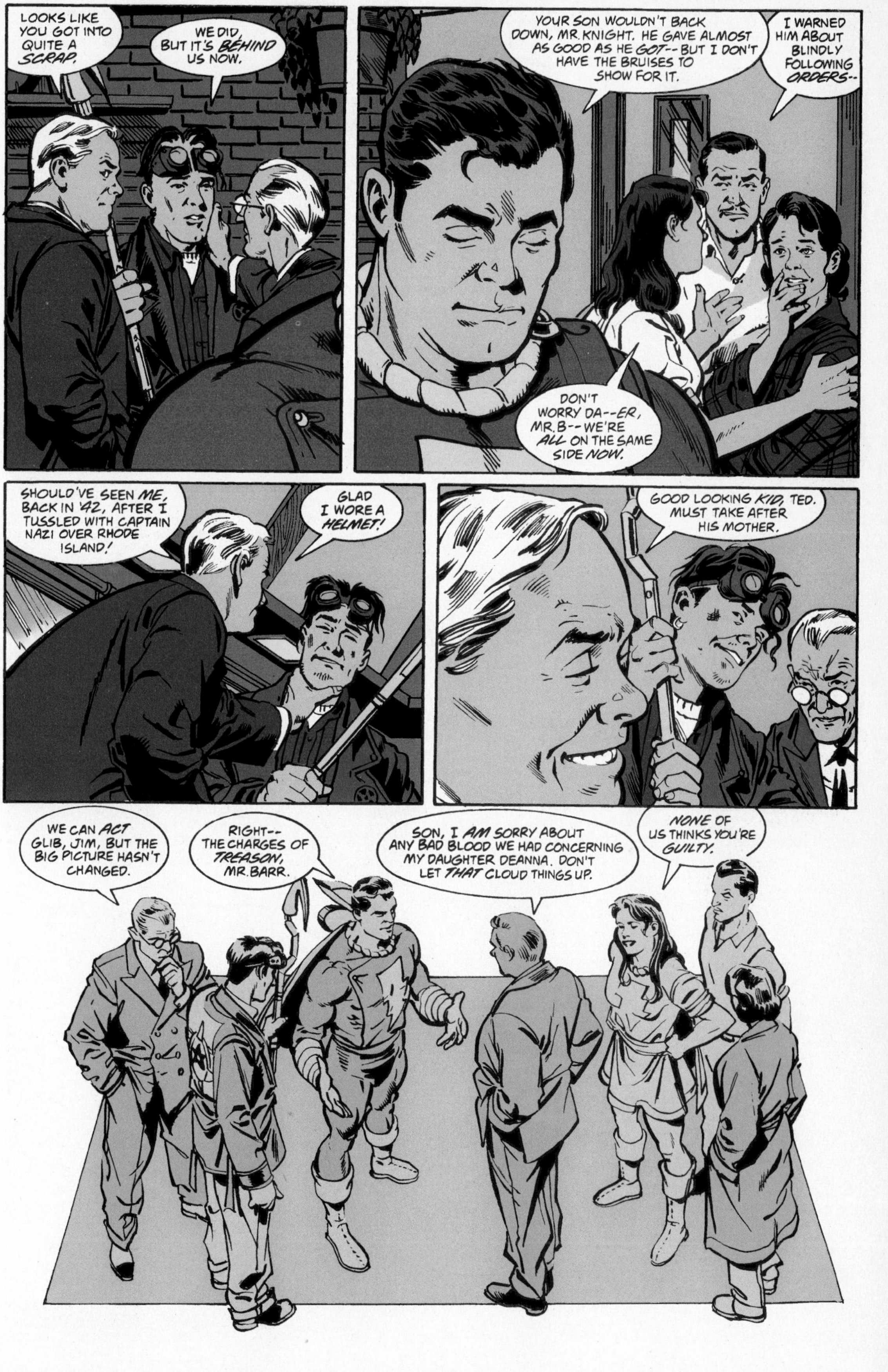
LOOKS LIKE YOU GOT INTO QUITE A SCRAP.
WE DID, BUT IT'S BEHIND US NOW.
YOUR SON WOULDN'T BACK DOWN, MR. KNIGHT. HE GAVE ALMOST AS GOOD AS HE GOT-- BUT I DON'T HAVE THE BRUISES TO SHOW FOR IT.
I WARNED HIM ABOUT BLINDLY FOLLOWING ORDERS--
DON'T WORRY DA--ER, MR. B--WE'RE ALL ON THE SAME SIDE NOW.
SHOULD'VE SEEN ME, BACK IN '42, AFTER I TUSSLED WITH CAPTAIN NAZI OVER RHODE ISLAND!
GLAD I WORE A HELMET!
GOOD LOOKING KID, TED. MUST TAKE AFTER HIS MOTHER.
WE CAN ACT GLIB, JIM, BUT THE BIG PICTURE HASN'T CHANGED.
RIGHT-- THE CHARGES OF TREASON, MR. BARR.
SON, I AM SORRY ABOUT ANY BAD BLOOD WE HAD CONCERNING MY DAUGHTER DEANNA. DON'T LET THAT CLOUD THINGS UP.
NONE OF US THINKS YOU'RE GUILTY.

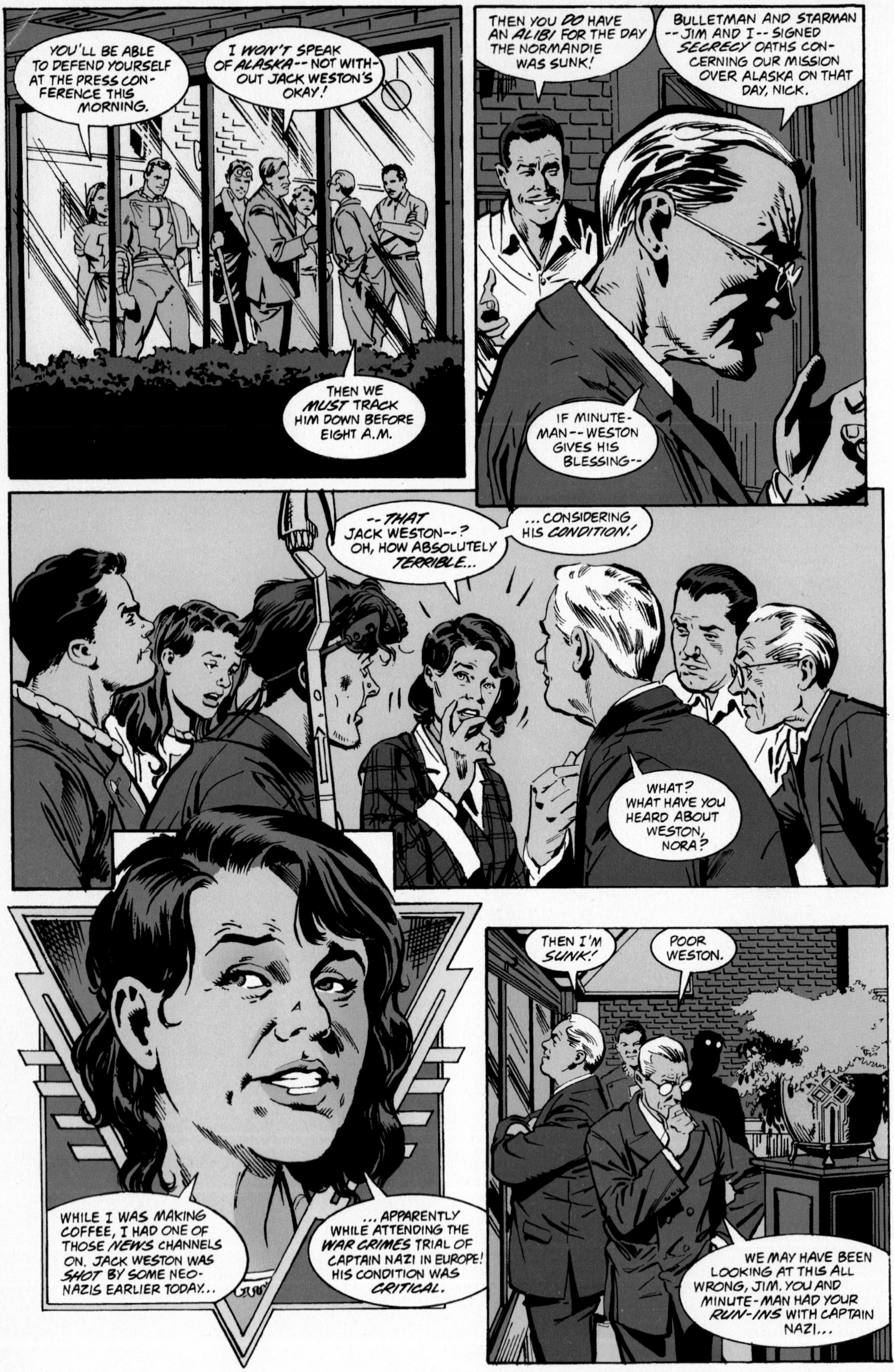
YOU'LL BE ABLE TO DEFEND YOURSELF AT THE PRESS CONFERENCE THIS MORNING.
I WON'T SPEAK OF ALASKA-- NOT WITHOUT JACK WESTON'S OKAY!
THEN WE MUST TRACK HIM DOWN BEFORE EIGHT A.M.
THEN YOU DO HAVE AN ALIBI FOR THE DAY THE NORMANDIE WAS SUNK!
BULLETMAN AND STARMAN --JIM AND I-- SIGNED SECRECY OATHS CONCERNING OUR MISSION OVER ALASKA ON THAT DAY, NICK.
IF MINUTE-MAN--WESTON GIVES HIS BLESSING--
--THAT JACK WESTON--? OH, HOW ABSOLUTELY TERRIBLE...
...CONSIDERING HIS CONDITION!
WHAT? WHAT HAVE YOU HEARD ABOUT WESTON, NORA?
WHILE I WAS MAKING COFFEE, I HAD ONE OF THOSE NEWS CHANNELS ON. JACK WESTON WAS SHOT BY SOME NEO-NAZIS EARLIER TODAY...
...APPARENTLY WHILE ATTENDING THE WAR CRIMES TRIAL OF CAPTAIN NAZI IN EUROPE! HIS CONDITION WAS CRITICAL.
THEN I'M SUNK!
POOR WESTON.
WE MAY HAVE BEEN LOOKING AT THIS ALL WRONG, JIM. YOU AND MINUTE-MAN HAD YOUR RUN-INS WITH CAPTAIN NAZI...

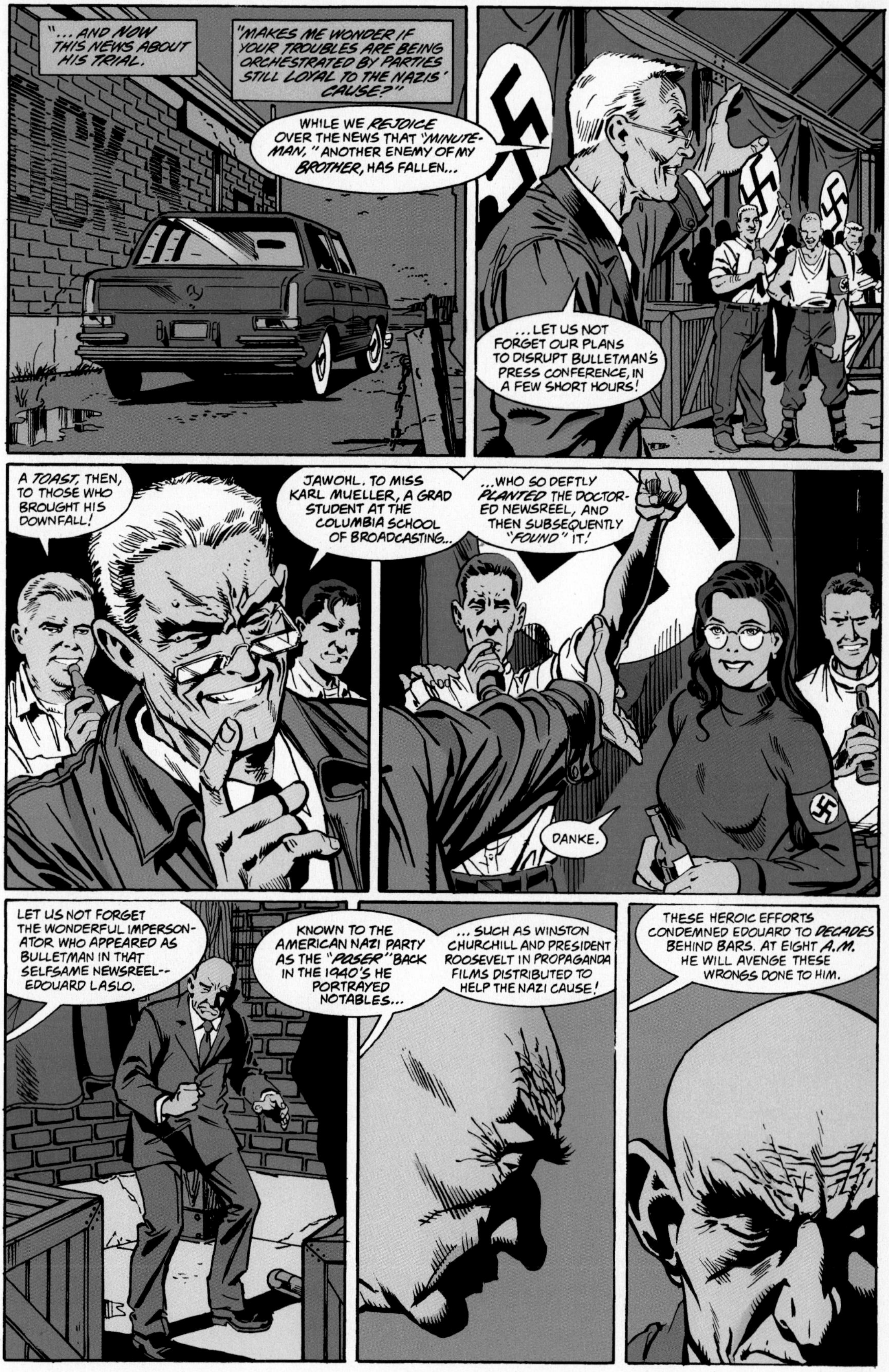
"... AND NOW THIS NEWS ABOUT HIS TRIAL.
"MAKES ME WONDER IF YOUR TROUBLES ARE BEING ORCHESTRATED BY PARTIES STILL LOYAL TO THE NAZIS' CAUSE?"
WHILE WE REJOICE OVER THE NEWS THAT "MINUTE-MAN," ANOTHER ENEMY OF MY BROTHER, HAS FALLEN...
... LET US NOT FORGET OUR PLANS TO DISRUPT BULLETMAN'S PRESS CONFERENCE, IN A FEW SHORT HOURS!
A TOAST, THEN, TO THOSE WHO BROUGHT HIS DOWNFALL!
JAWOHL. TO MISS KARL MUELLER, A GRAD STUDENT AT THE COLUMBIA SCHOOL OF BROADCASTING...
...WHO SO DEFTLY PLANTED THE DOCTOR-ED NEWSREEL, AND THEN SUBSEQUENTLY "FOUND" IT!
DANKE.
LET US NOT FORGET THE WONDERFUL IMPERSON-ATOR WHO APPEARED AS BULLETMAN IN THAT SELFSAME NEWSREEL--EDOUARD LASLO.
KNOWN TO THE AMERICAN NAZI PARTY AS THE "POSER" BACK IN THE 1940'S HE PORTRAYED NOTABLES...
... SUCH AS WINSTON CHURCHILL AND PRESIDENT ROOSEVELT IN PROPAGANDA FILMS DISTRIBUTED TO HELP THE NAZI CAUSE!
THESE HEROIC EFFORTS CONDEMNED EDOUARD TO DECADES BEHIND BARS. AT EIGHT A.M. HE WILL AVENGE THESE WRONGS DONE TO HIM.

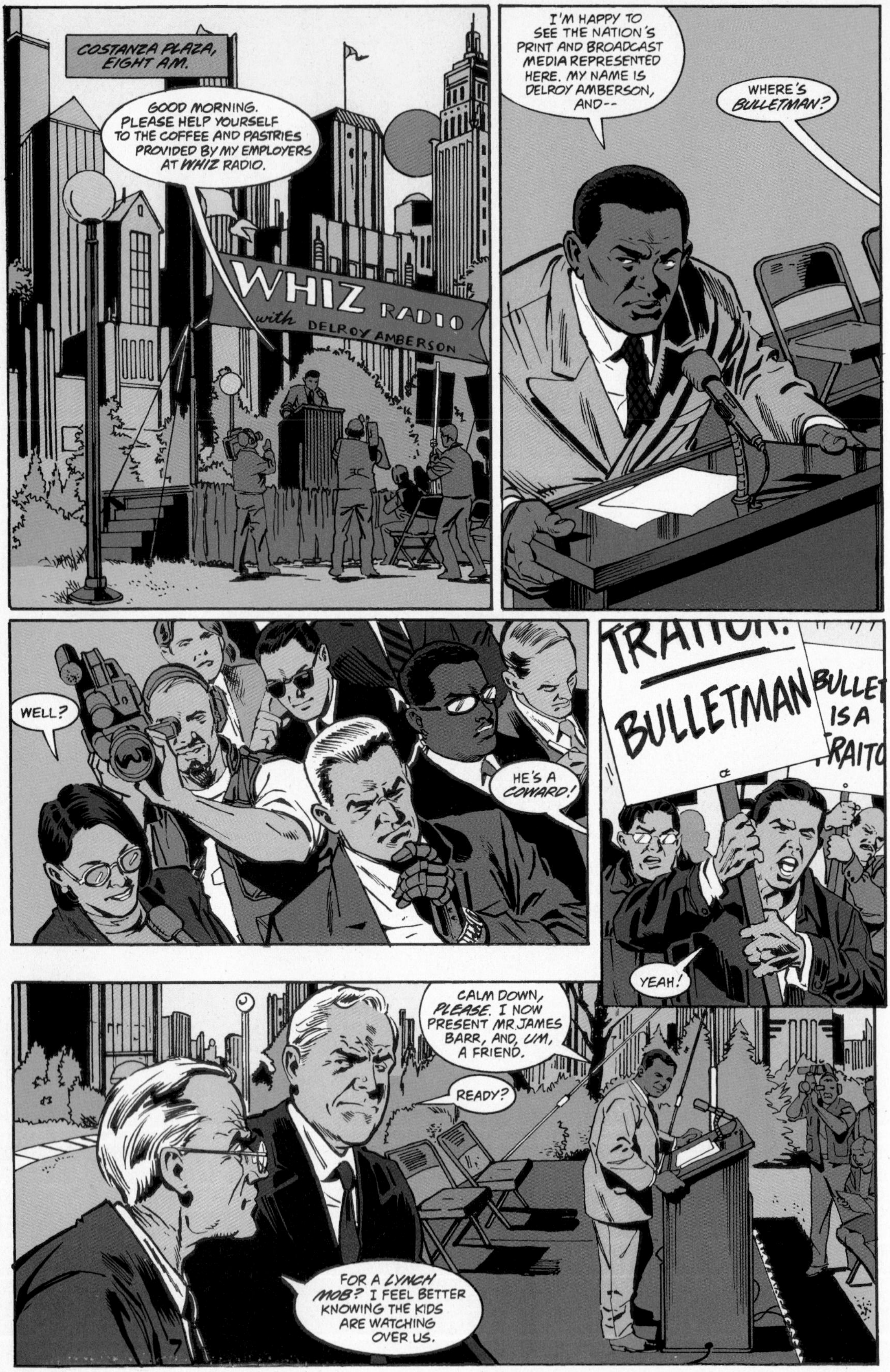
COSTANZA PLAZA, EIGHT AM.
GOOD MORNING. PLEASE HELP YOURSELF TO THE COFFEE AND PASTRIES PROVIDED BY MY EMPLOYERS AT WHIZ RADIO.
WHIZ RADIO with DELROY AMBERSON
I'M HAPPY TO SEE THE NATION'S PRINT AND BROADCAST MEDIA REPRESENTED HERE. MY NAME IS DELROY AMBERSON, AND--
WHERE'S BULLETMAN?
WELL?
HE'S A COWARD!
TRAITOR! BULLETMAN
BULLET IS A TRAITO
YEAH!
CALM DOWN, PLEASE. I NOW PRESENT MR. JAMES BARR, AND, UM, A FRIEND.
READY?
FOR A LYNCH MOB? I FEEL BETTER KNOWING THE KIDS ARE WATCHING OVER US.

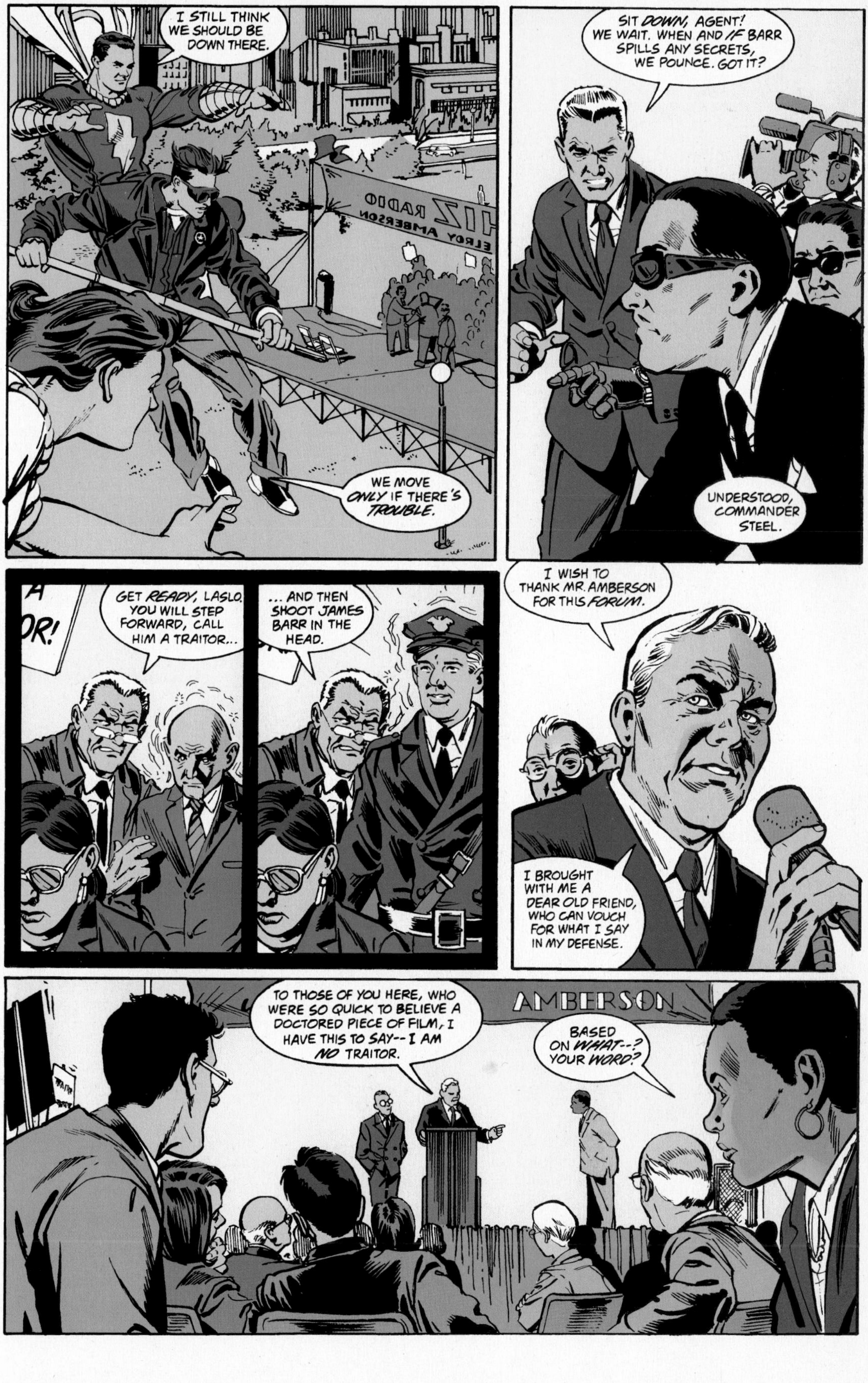

I STILL THINK WE SHOULD BE DOWN THERE.
WE MOVE *ONLY* IF THERE'S *TROUBLE.*
SIT *DOWN,* AGENT! WE WAIT. WHEN AND *IF* BARR SPILLS ANY SECRETS, WE POUNCE. GOT IT?
UNDERSTOOD, COMMANDER STEEL.
GET *READY,* LASLO. YOU WILL STEP FORWARD, CALL HIM A TRAITOR...
... AND THEN SHOOT JAMES BARR IN THE HEAD.
I WISH TO THANK MR. AMBERSON FOR THIS *FORUM.*
I BROUGHT WITH ME A DEAR OLD FRIEND, WHO CAN VOUCH FOR WHAT I SAY IN MY DEFENSE.
AMBERSON
TO THOSE OF YOU HERE, WHO WERE SO QUICK TO BELIEVE A DOCTORED PIECE OF FILM, I HAVE THIS TO *SAY*-- I AM *NO* TRAITOR.
BASED ON *WHAT*--? YOUR *WORD?*

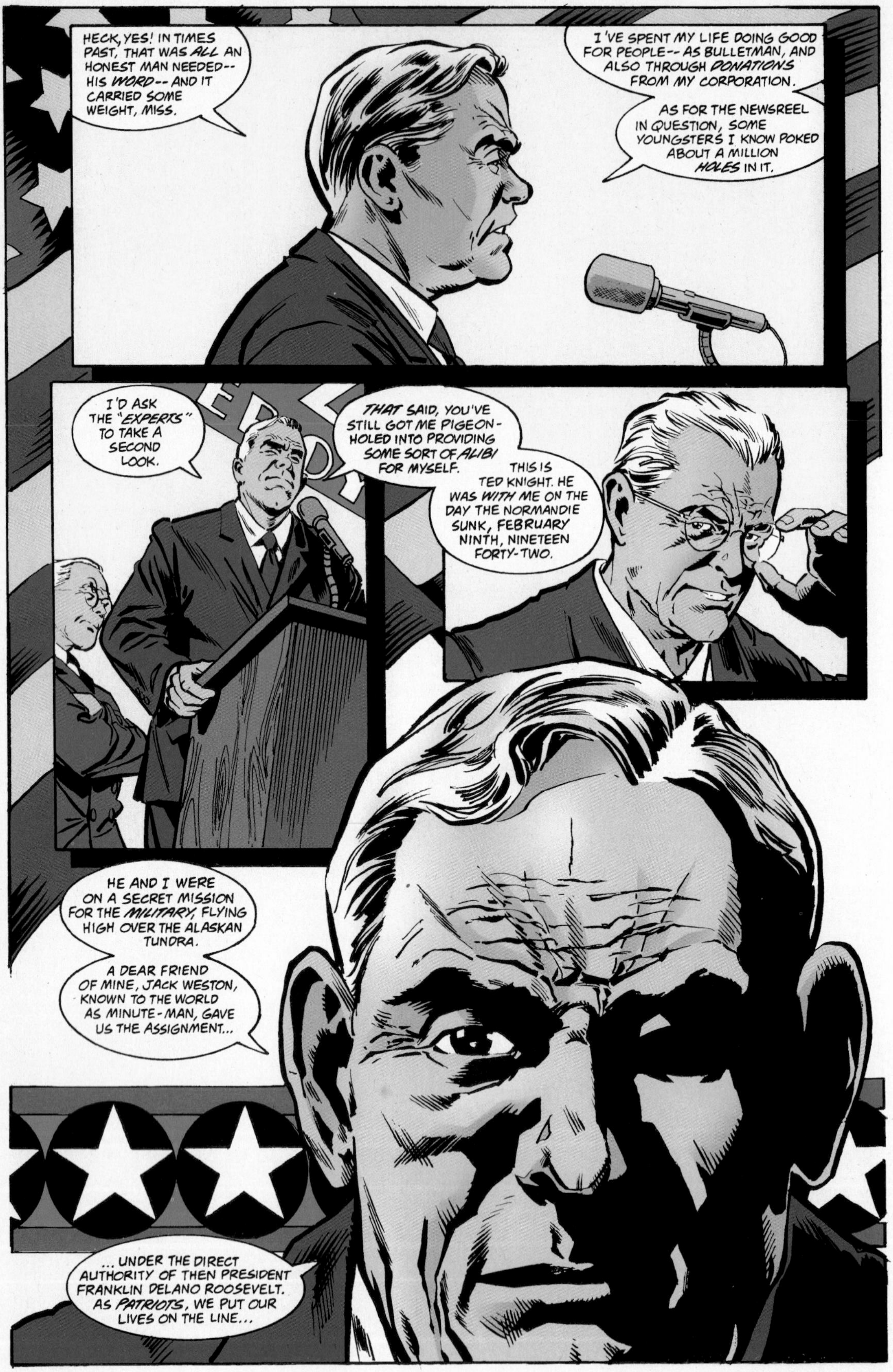
HECK, YES! IN TIMES PAST, THAT WAS ALL AN HONEST MAN NEEDED-- HIS WORD-- AND IT CARRIED SOME WEIGHT, MISS.
I'VE SPENT MY LIFE DOING GOOD FOR PEOPLE-- AS BULLETMAN, AND ALSO THROUGH DONATIONS FROM MY CORPORATION.
AS FOR THE NEWSREEL IN QUESTION, SOME YOUNGSTERS I KNOW POKED ABOUT A MILLION HOLES IN IT.
I'D ASK THE "EXPERTS" TO TAKE A SECOND LOOK.
THAT SAID, YOU'VE STILL GOT ME PIGEON-HOLED INTO PROVIDING SOME SORT OF ALIBI FOR MYSELF.
THIS IS TED KNIGHT. HE WAS WITH ME ON THE DAY THE NORMANDIE SUNK, FEBRUARY NINTH, NINETEEN FORTY-TWO.
HE AND I WERE ON A SECRET MISSION FOR THE MILITARY, FLYING HIGH OVER THE ALASKAN TUNDRA.
A DEAR FRIEND OF MINE, JACK WESTON, KNOWN TO THE WORLD AS MINUTE-MAN, GAVE US THE ASSIGNMENT...
...UNDER THE DIRECT AUTHORITY OF THEN PRESIDENT FRANKLIN DELANO ROOSEVELT. AS PATRIOTS, WE PUT OUR LIVES ON THE LINE...

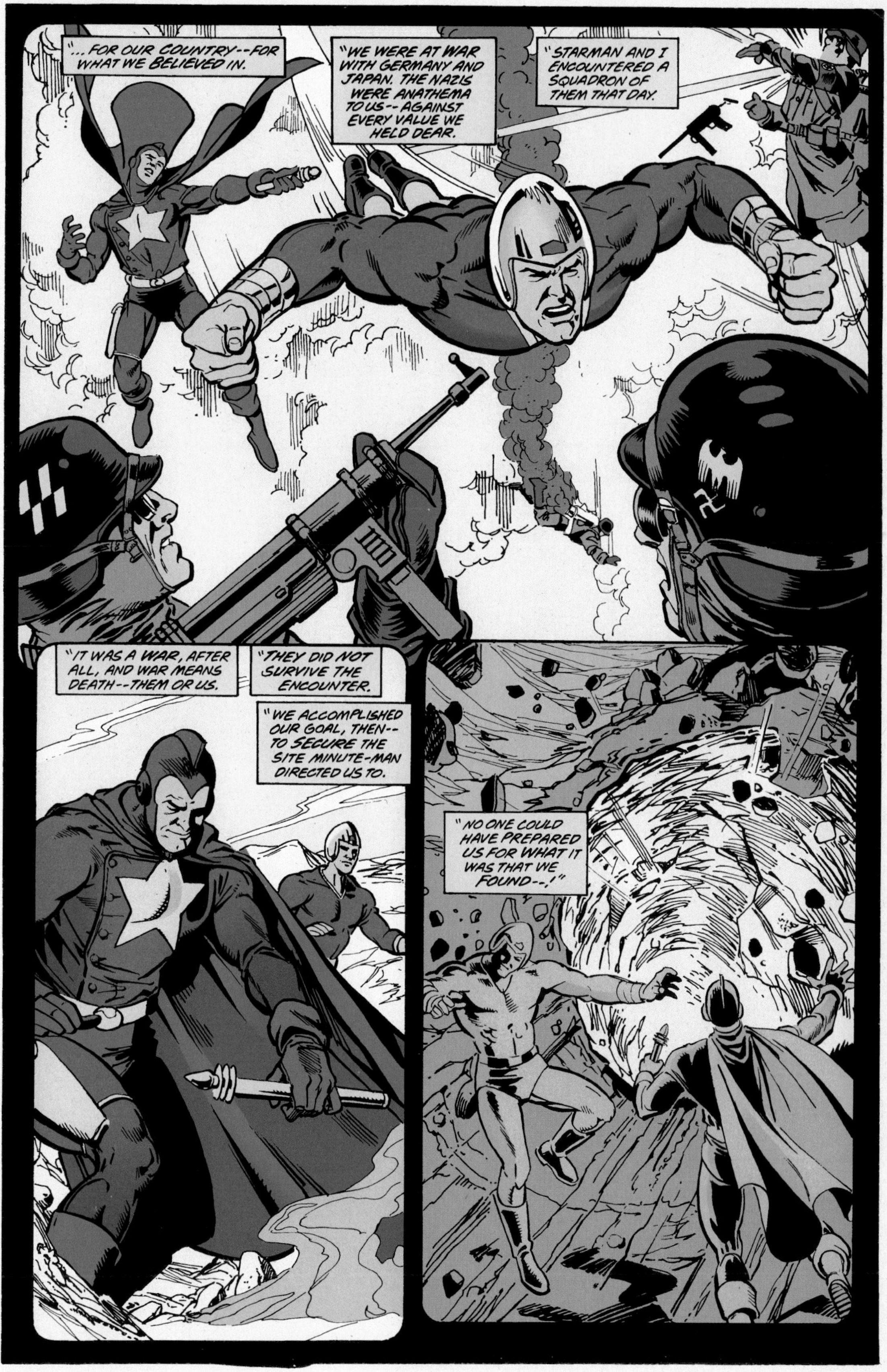
"...FOR OUR COUNTRY--FOR WHAT WE BELIEVED IN.
"WE WERE AT WAR WITH GERMANY AND JAPAN. THE NAZIS WERE ANATHEMA TO US--AGAINST EVERY VALUE WE HELD DEAR.
"STARMAN AND I ENCOUNTERED A SQUADRON OF THEM THAT DAY.
"IT WAS A WAR, AFTER ALL, AND WAR MEANS DEATH--THEM OR US.
"THEY DID NOT SURVIVE THE ENCOUNTER.
"WE ACCOMPLISHED OUR GOAL, THEN--TO SECURE THE SITE MINUTE-MAN DIRECTED US TO.
"NO ONE COULD HAVE PREPARED US FOR WHAT IT WAS THAT WE FOUND--!"

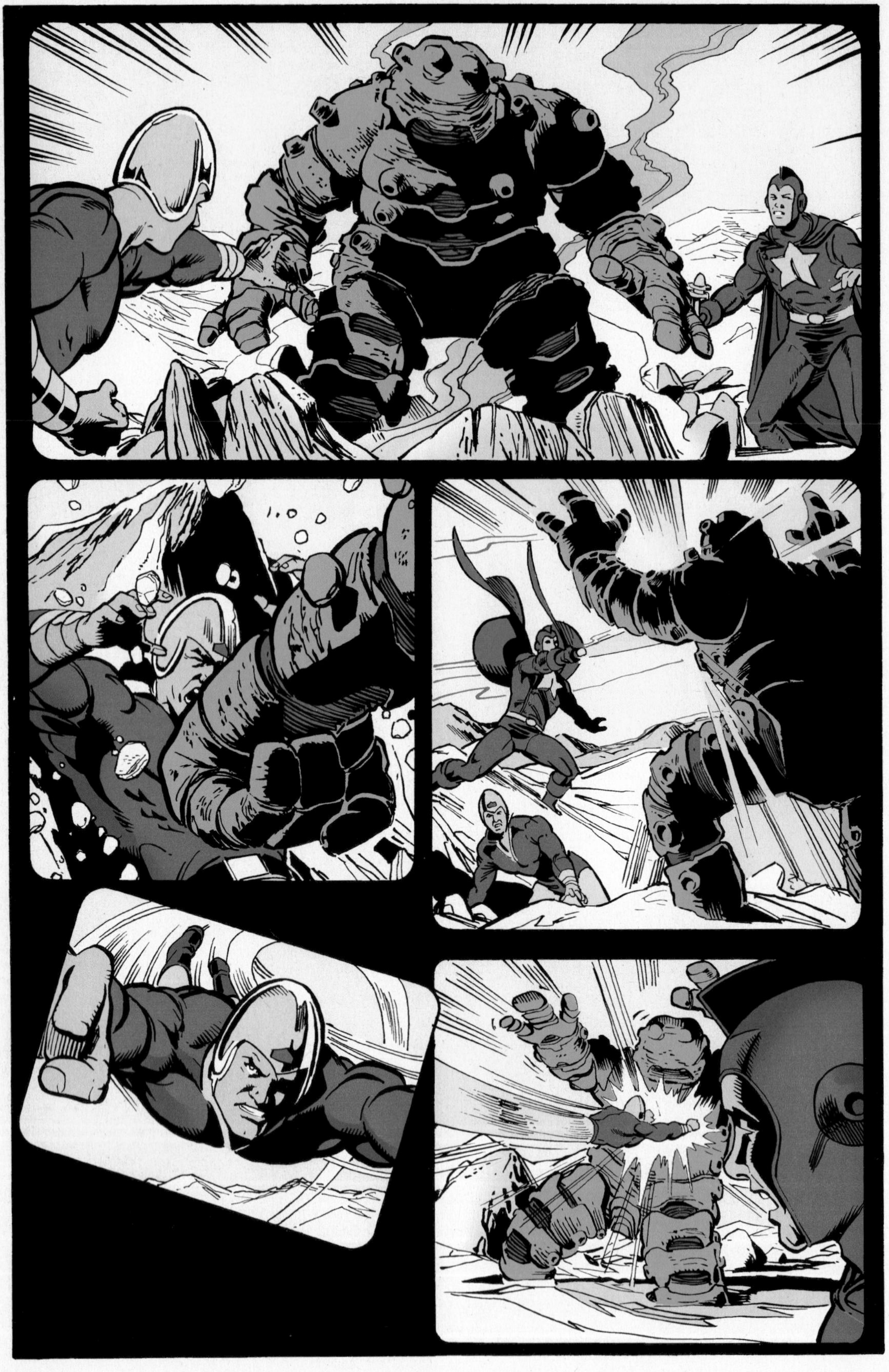

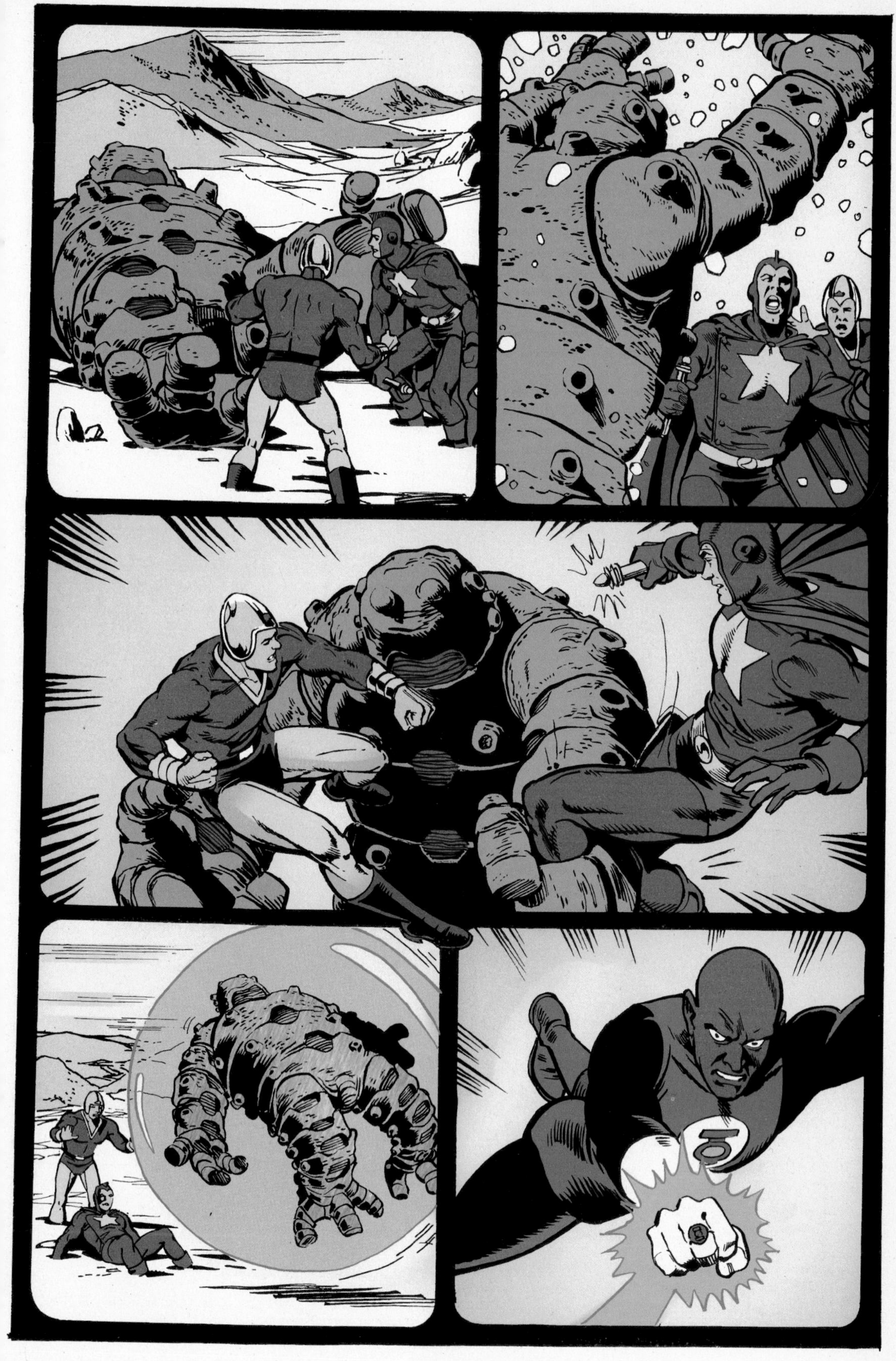

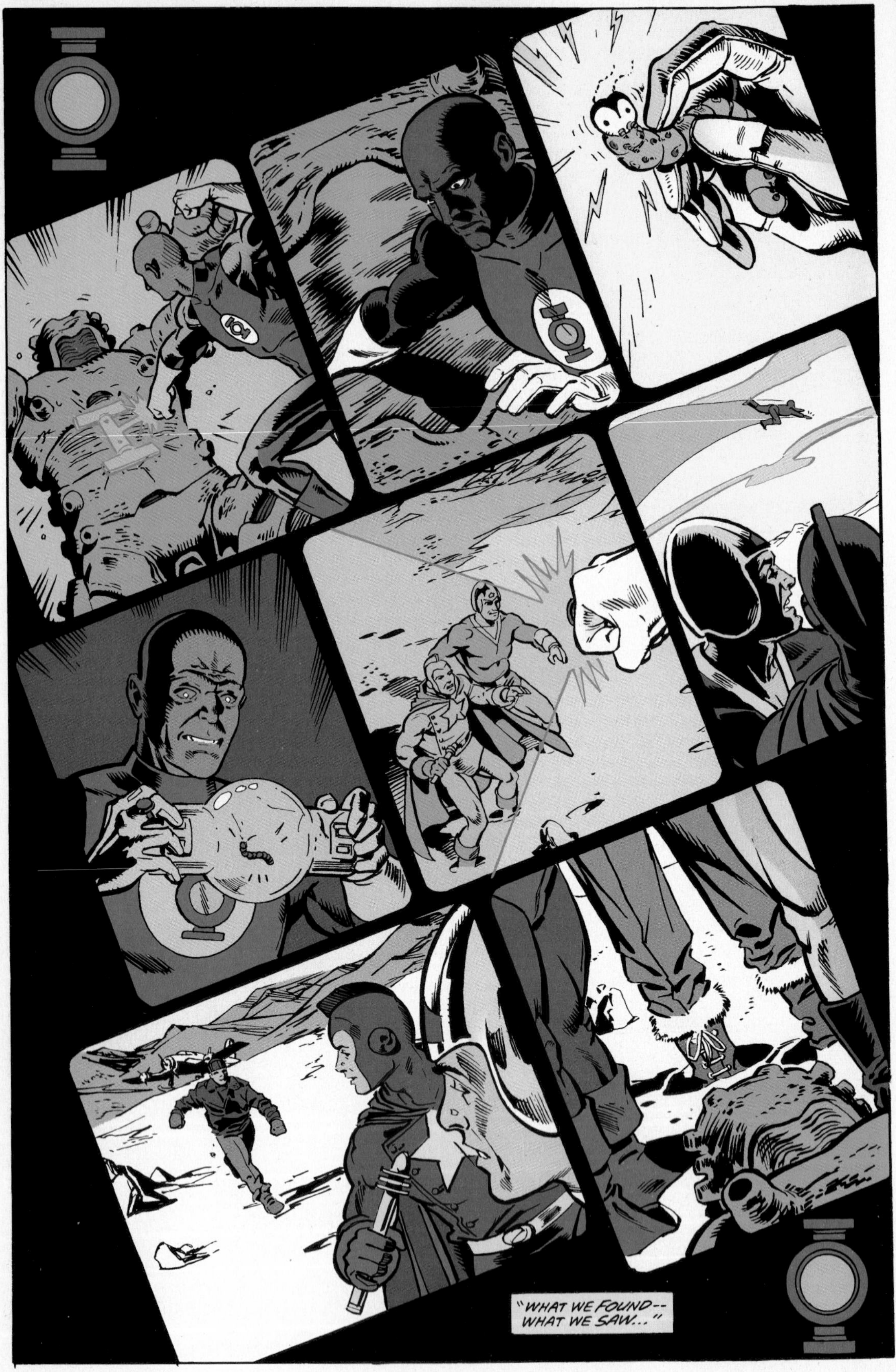
"WHAT WE FOUND--
WHAT WE SAW..."

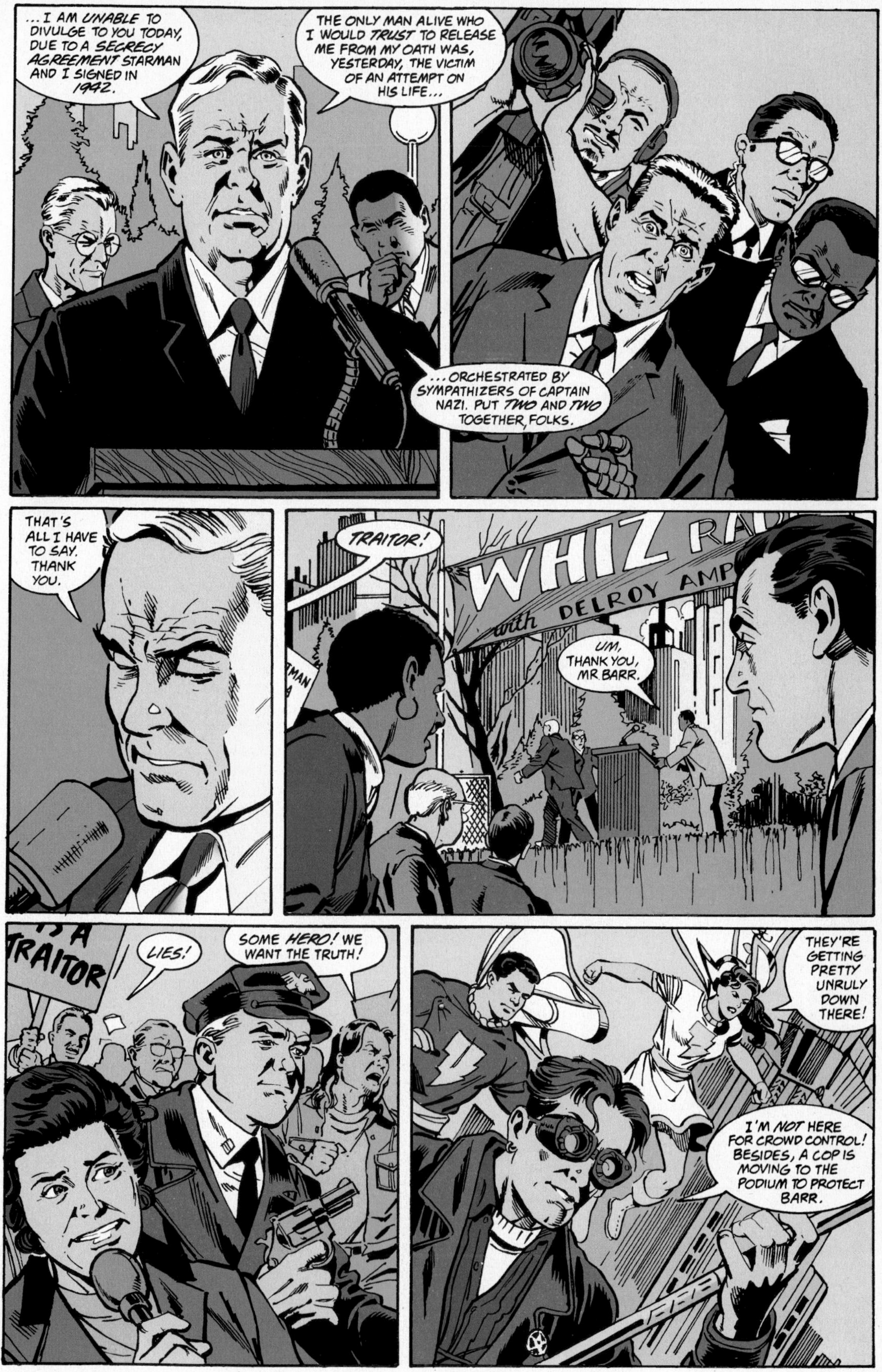
...I AM UNABLE TO DIVULGE TO YOU TODAY, DUE TO A SECRECY AGREEMENT STARMAN AND I SIGNED IN 1942.
THE ONLY MAN ALIVE WHO I WOULD TRUST TO RELEASE ME FROM MY OATH WAS, YESTERDAY, THE VICTIM OF AN ATTEMPT ON HIS LIFE...
...ORCHESTRATED BY SYMPATHIZERS OF CAPTAIN NAZI. PUT TWO AND TWO TOGETHER, FOLKS.
THAT'S ALL I HAVE TO SAY. THANK YOU.
TRAITOR!
WHIZ RA
with DELROY AMP
UM, THANK YOU, MR. BARR.
TRAITOR
LIES!
SOME HERO! WE WANT THE TRUTH!
THEY'RE GETTING PRETTY UNRULY DOWN THERE!
I'M NOT HERE FOR CROWD CONTROL! BESIDES, A COP IS MOVING TO THE PODIUM TO PROTECT BARR.

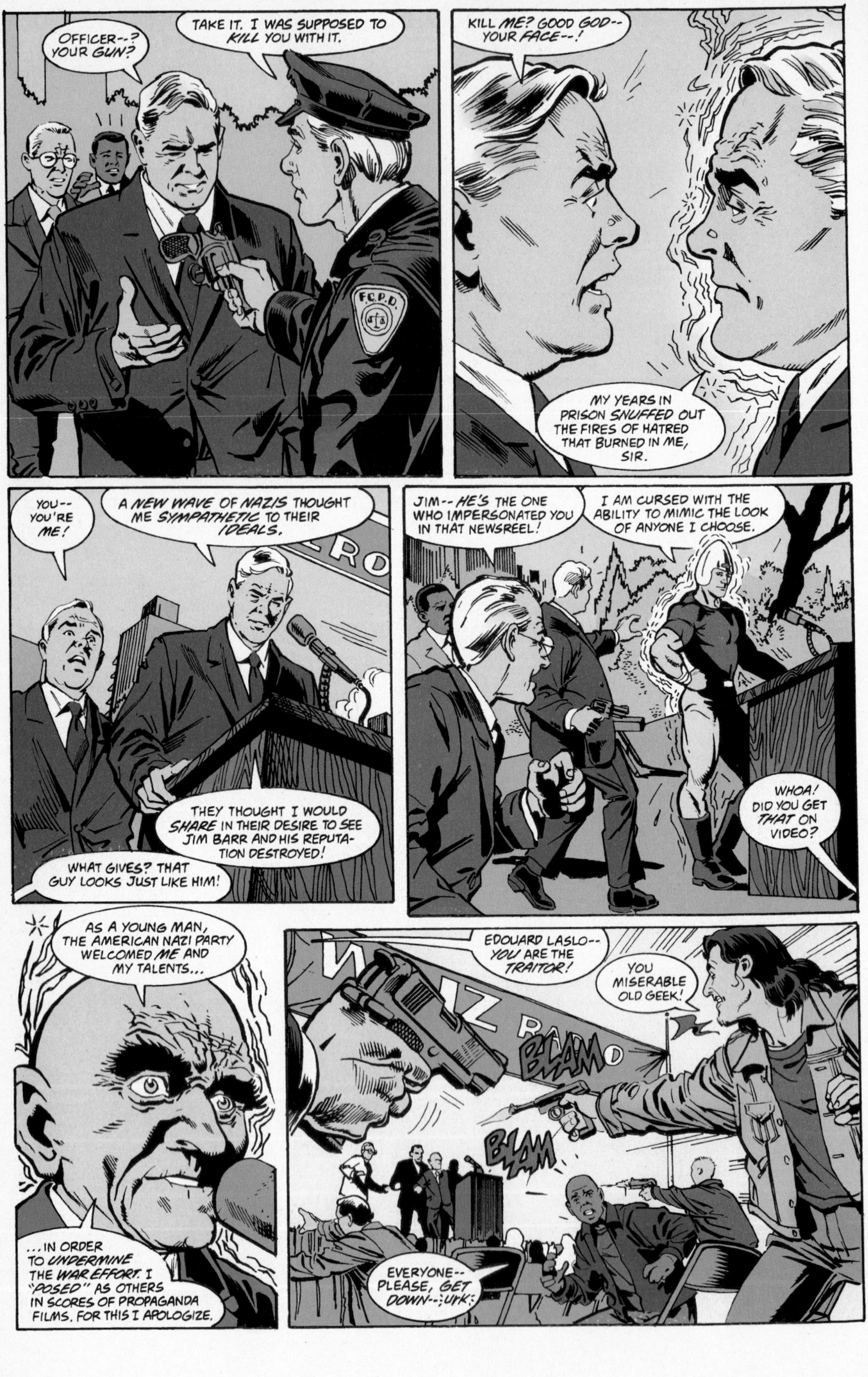
OFFICER--? YOUR GUN?
TAKE IT. I WAS SUPPOSED TO KILL YOU WITH IT.
F.C.P.D.
KILL ME? GOOD GOD-- YOUR FACE--!
MY YEARS IN PRISON SNUFFED OUT THE FIRES OF HATRED THAT BURNED IN ME, SIR.
YOU-- YOU'RE ME!
A NEW WAVE OF NAZIS THOUGHT ME SYMPATHETIC TO THEIR IDEALS.
THEY THOUGHT I WOULD SHARE IN THEIR DESIRE TO SEE JIM BARR AND HIS REPUTATION DESTROYED!
WHAT GIVES? THAT GUY LOOKS JUST LIKE HIM!
JIM-- HE'S THE ONE WHO IMPERSONATED YOU IN THAT NEWSREEL!
I AM CURSED WITH THE ABILITY TO MIMIC THE LOOK OF ANYONE I CHOOSE.
WHOA! DID YOU GET THAT ON VIDEO?
AS A YOUNG MAN, THE AMERICAN NAZI PARTY WELCOMED ME AND MY TALENTS...
...IN ORDER TO UNDERMINE THE WAR EFFORT. I "POSED" AS OTHERS IN SCORES OF PROPAGANDA FILMS. FOR THIS I APOLOGIZE.
EDOUARD LASLO-- YOU ARE THE TRAITOR!
YOU MISERABLE OLD GEEK!
BLAMO
BLAM
EVERYONE-- PLEASE, GET DOWN--; URK!

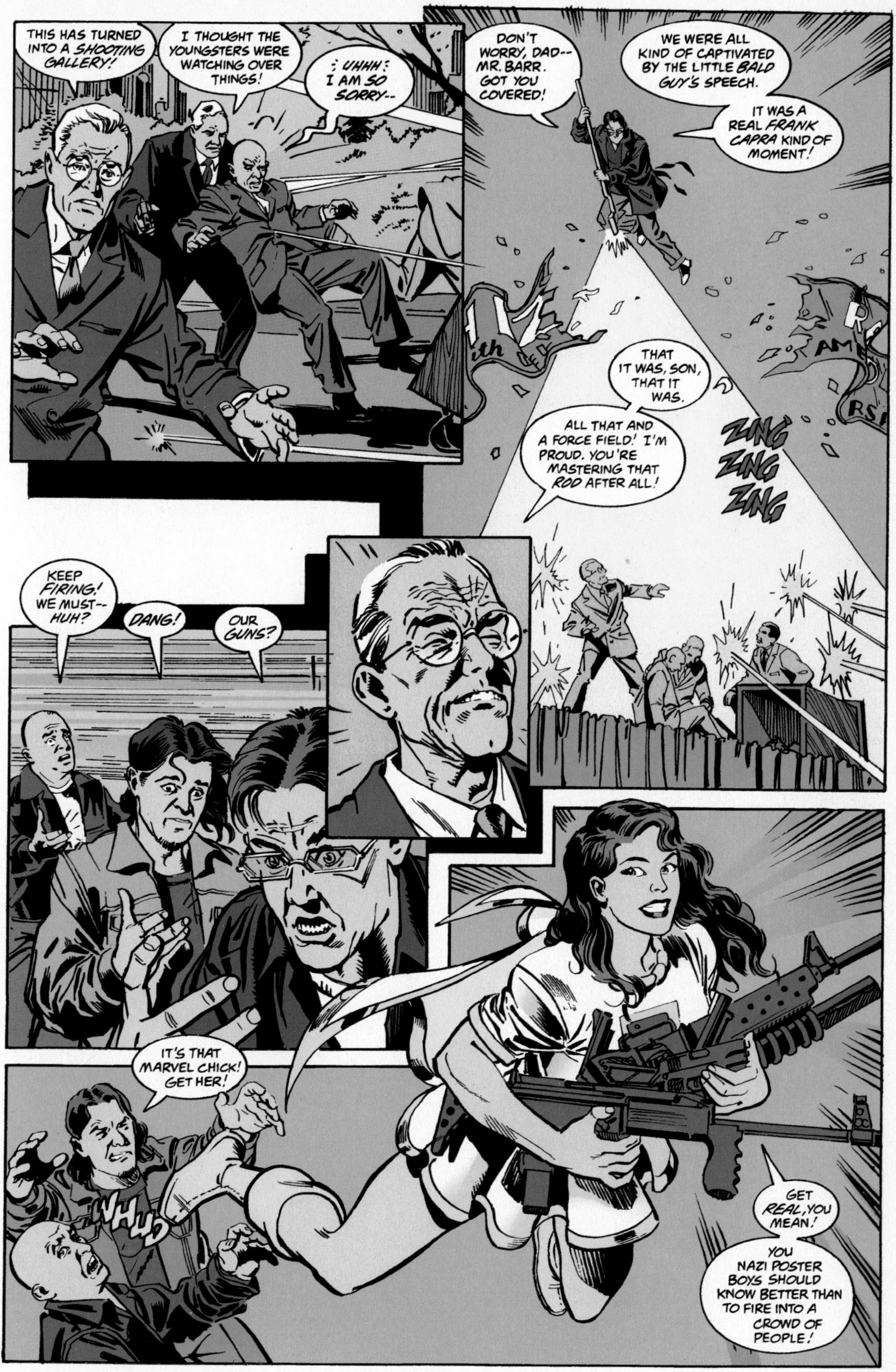
THIS HAS TURNED INTO A SHOOTING GALLERY!
I THOUGHT THE YOUNGSTERS WERE WATCHING OVER THINGS!
UHHH! I AM SO SORRY--
DON'T WORRY, DAD-- MR. BARR. GOT YOU COVERED!
WE WERE ALL KIND OF CAPTIVATED BY THE LITTLE BALD GUY'S SPEECH.
IT WAS A REAL FRANK CAPRA KIND OF MOMENT!
THAT IT WAS, SON, THAT IT WAS.
ALL THAT AND A FORCE FIELD! I'M PROUD. YOU'RE MASTERING THAT ROD AFTER ALL!
ZING ZING ZING
KEEP FIRING! WE MUST-- HUH?
DANG!
OUR GUNS?
IT'S THAT MARVEL CHICK! GET HER!
WHUD
GET REAL, YOU MEAN!
YOU NAZI POSTER BOYS SHOULD KNOW BETTER THAN TO FIRE INTO A CROWD OF PEOPLE!

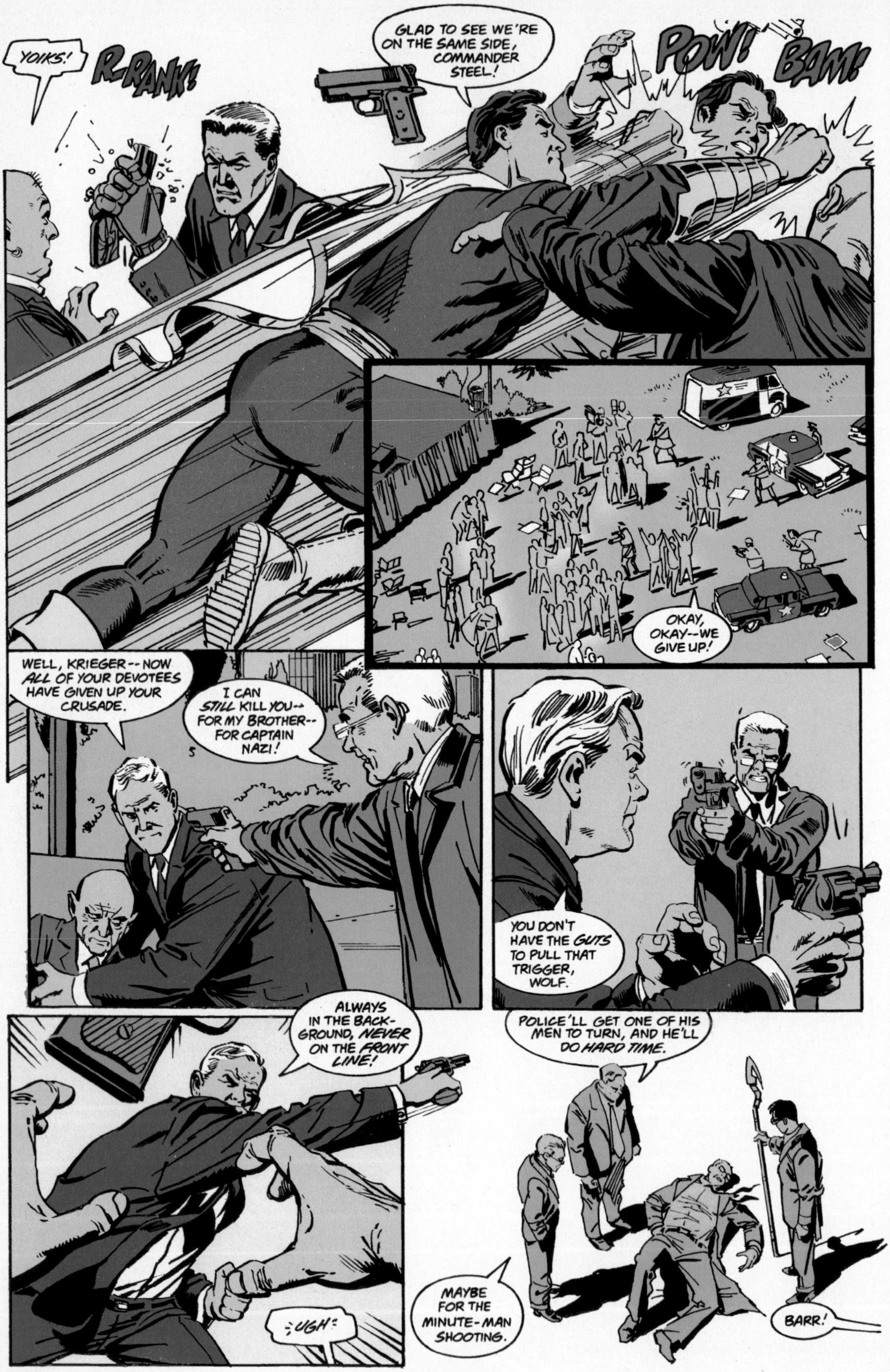
YOIKS!
R-RANK!
GLAD TO SEE WE'RE ON THE SAME SIDE, COMMANDER STEEL!
POW!
BAM!
OKAY, OKAY--WE GIVE UP!
WELL, KRIEGER--NOW ALL OF YOUR DEVOTEES HAVE GIVEN UP YOUR CRUSADE.
I CAN STILL KILL YOU--FOR MY BROTHER--FOR CAPTAIN NAZI!
YOU DON'T HAVE THE GUTS TO PULL THAT TRIGGER, WOLF.
ALWAYS IN THE BACK-GROUND, NEVER ON THE FRONT LINE!
UGH
POLICE'LL GET ONE OF HIS MEN TO TURN, AND HE'LL DO HARD TIME.
MAYBE FOR THE MINUTE-MAN SHOOTING.
BARR!

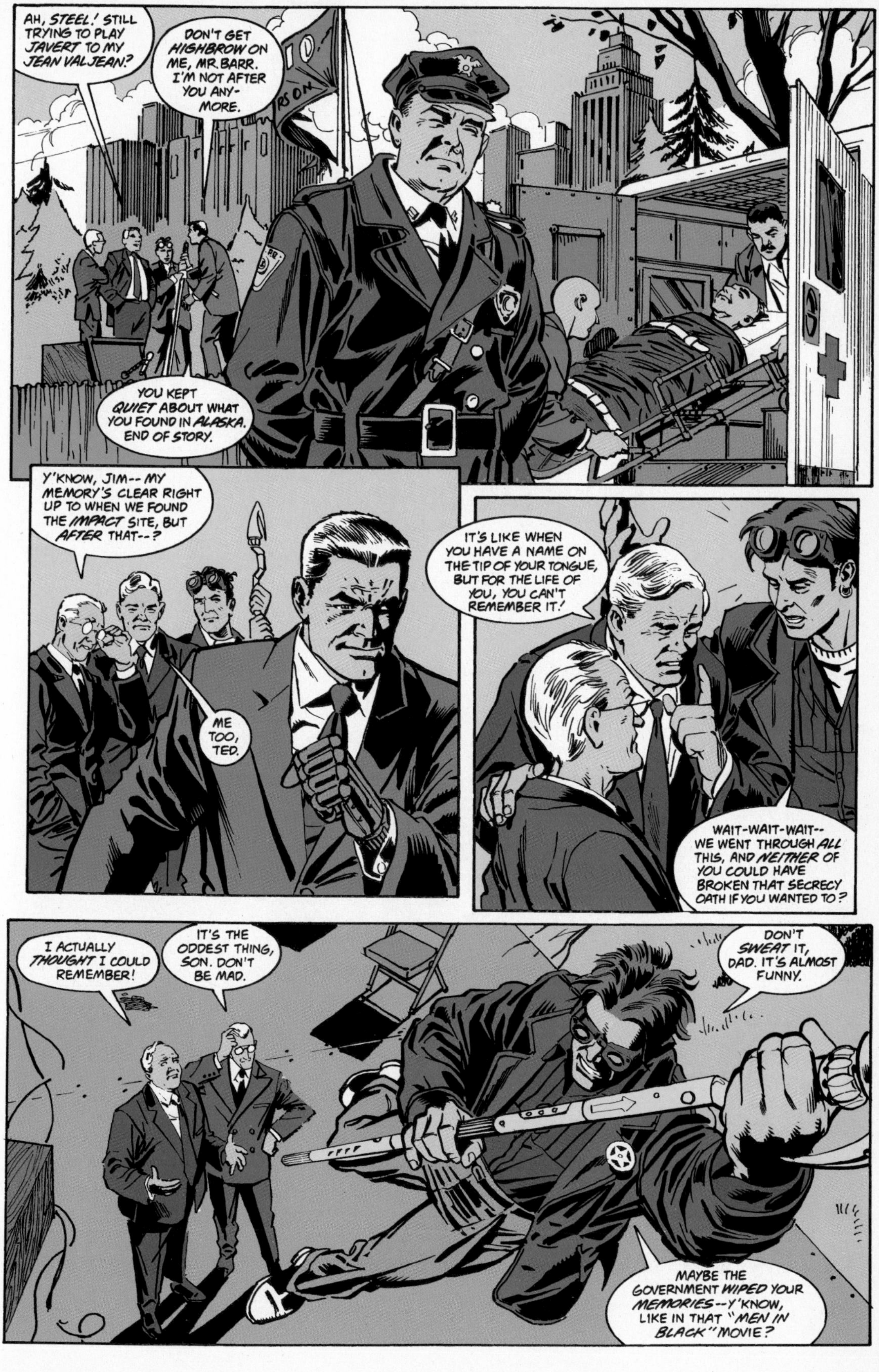
AH, STEEL! STILL TRYING TO PLAY JAVERT TO MY JEAN VALJEAN?
DON'T GET HIGHBROW ON ME, MR. BARR. I'M NOT AFTER YOU ANY-MORE.
YOU KEPT QUIET ABOUT WHAT YOU FOUND IN ALASKA. END OF STORY.
Y'KNOW, JIM-- MY MEMORY'S CLEAR RIGHT UP TO WHEN WE FOUND THE IMPACT SITE, BUT AFTER THAT--?
ME TOO, TED.
IT'S LIKE WHEN YOU HAVE A NAME ON THE TIP OF YOUR TONGUE, BUT FOR THE LIFE OF YOU, YOU CAN'T REMEMBER IT!
WAIT-WAIT-WAIT-- WE WENT THROUGH ALL THIS, AND NEITHER OF YOU COULD HAVE BROKEN THAT SECRECY OATH IF YOU WANTED TO?
I ACTUALLY THOUGHT I COULD REMEMBER!
IT'S THE ODDEST THING, SON. DON'T BE MAD.
DON'T SWEAT IT, DAD. IT'S ALMOST FUNNY.
MAYBE THE GOVERNMENT WIPED YOUR MEMORIES--Y'KNOW, LIKE IN THAT "MEN IN BLACK" MOVIE?

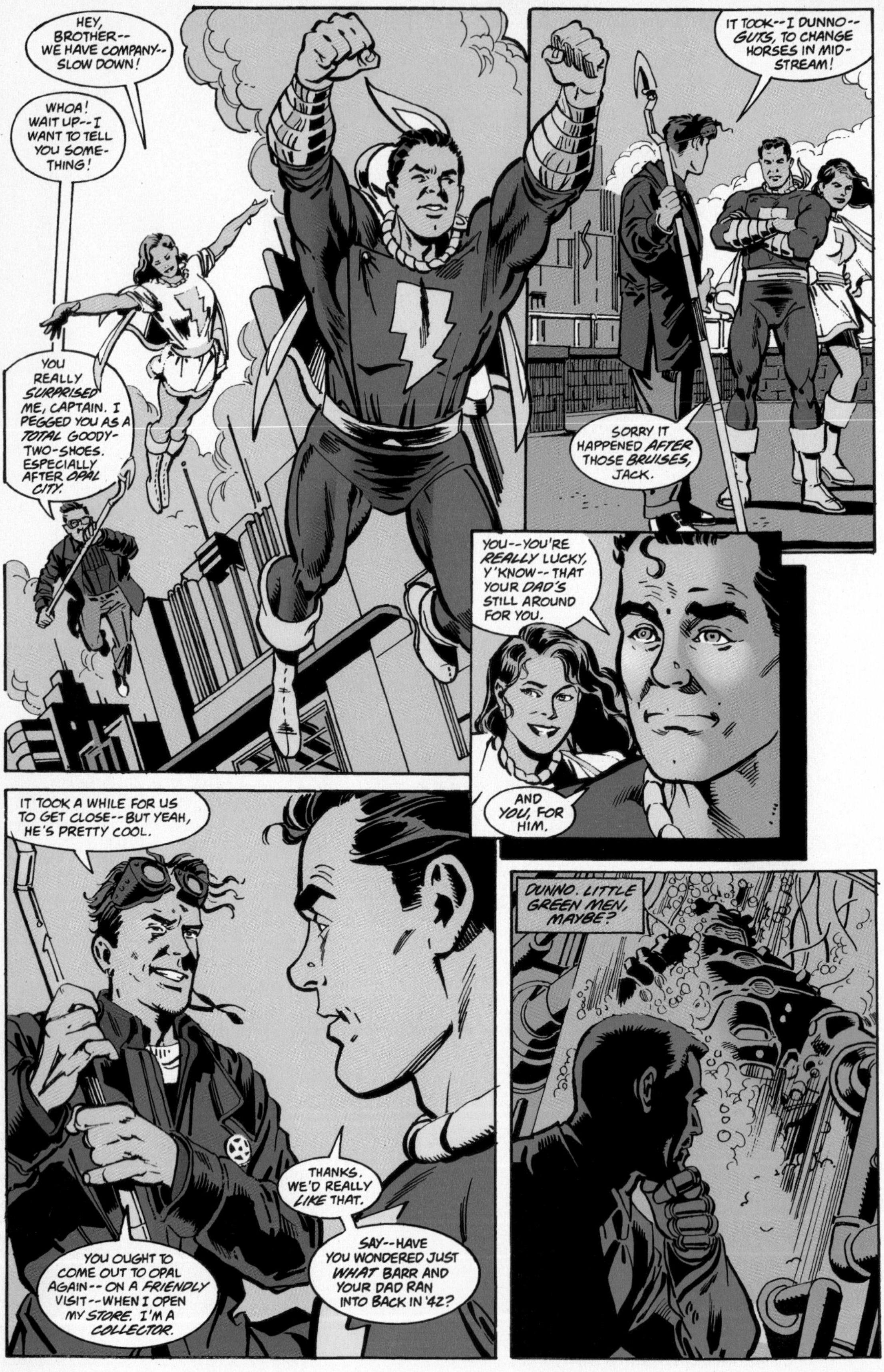
HEY, BROTHER-- WE HAVE COMPANY-- SLOW DOWN!
WHOA! WAIT UP--I WANT TO TELL YOU SOME-THING!
YOU REALLY SURPRISED ME, CAPTAIN. I PEGGED YOU AS A TOTAL GOODY-TWO-SHOES. ESPECIALLY AFTER OPAL CITY.
IT TOOK--I DUNNO--GUTS, TO CHANGE HORSES IN MID-STREAM!
SORRY IT HAPPENED AFTER THOSE BRUISES, JACK.
YOU--YOU'RE REALLY LUCKY, Y'KNOW--THAT YOUR DAD'S STILL AROUND FOR YOU.
AND YOU, FOR HIM.
IT TOOK A WHILE FOR US TO GET CLOSE--BUT YEAH, HE'S PRETTY COOL.
YOU OUGHT TO COME OUT TO OPAL AGAIN--ON A FRIENDLY VISIT--WHEN I OPEN MY STORE. I'M A COLLECTOR.
THANKS. WE'D REALLY LIKE THAT.
SAY--HAVE YOU WONDERED JUST WHAT BARR AND YOUR DAD RAN INTO BACK IN '42?
DUNNO. LITTLE GREEN MEN, MAYBE?

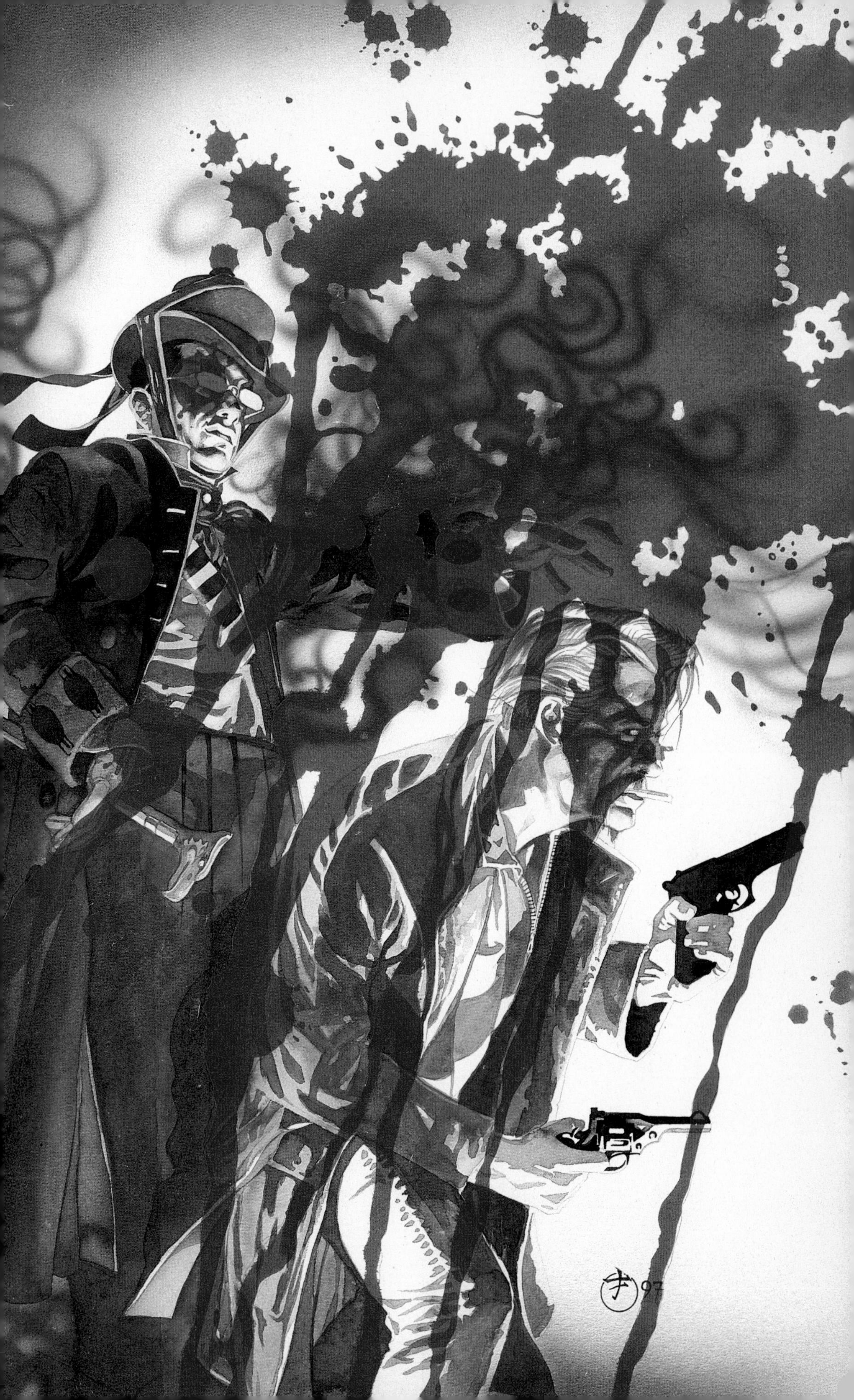

STARMAN 41

Cover by Tony Harris

Written by James Robinson

Art by Gary Erskine

with colors by Gregory Wright

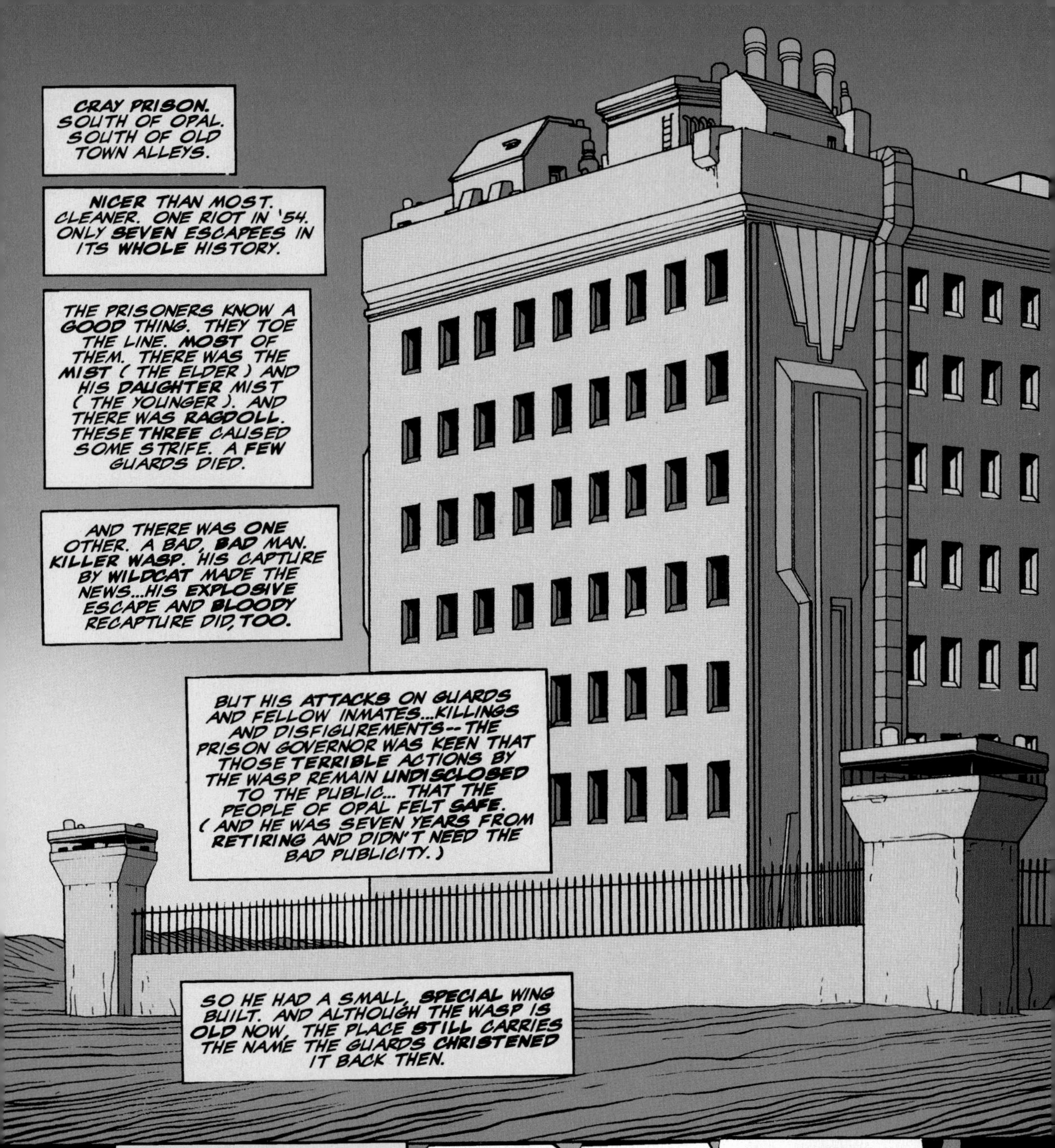
CRAY PRISON. SOUTH OF OPAL. SOUTH OF OLD TOWN ALLEYS.
NICER THAN MOST. CLEANER. ONE RIOT IN '54. ONLY SEVEN ESCAPEES IN ITS WHOLE HISTORY.
THE PRISONERS KNOW A GOOD THING. THEY TOE THE LINE. MOST OF THEM. THERE WAS THE MIST (THE ELDER) AND HIS DAUGHTER MIST (THE YOUNGER). AND THERE WAS RAGDOLL. THESE THREE CAUSED SOME STRIFE. A FEW GUARDS DIED.
AND THERE WAS ONE OTHER. A BAD, BAD MAN. KILLER WASP. HIS CAPTURE BY WILDCAT MADE THE NEWS...HIS EXPLOSIVE ESCAPE AND BLOODY RECAPTURE DID, TOO.
BUT HIS ATTACKS ON GUARDS AND FELLOW INMATES...KILLINGS AND DISFIGUREMENTS-- THE PRISON GOVERNOR WAS KEEN THAT THOSE TERRIBLE ACTIONS BY THE WASP REMAIN UNDISCLOSED TO THE PUBLIC... THAT THE PEOPLE OF OPAL FELT SAFE. (AND HE WAS SEVEN YEARS FROM RETIRING AND DIDN'T NEED THE BAD PUBLICITY.)
SO HE HAD A SMALL, SPECIAL WING BUILT. AND ALTHOUGH THE WASP IS OLD NOW, THE PLACE STILL CARRIES THE NAME THE GUARDS CHRISTENED IT BACK THEN.

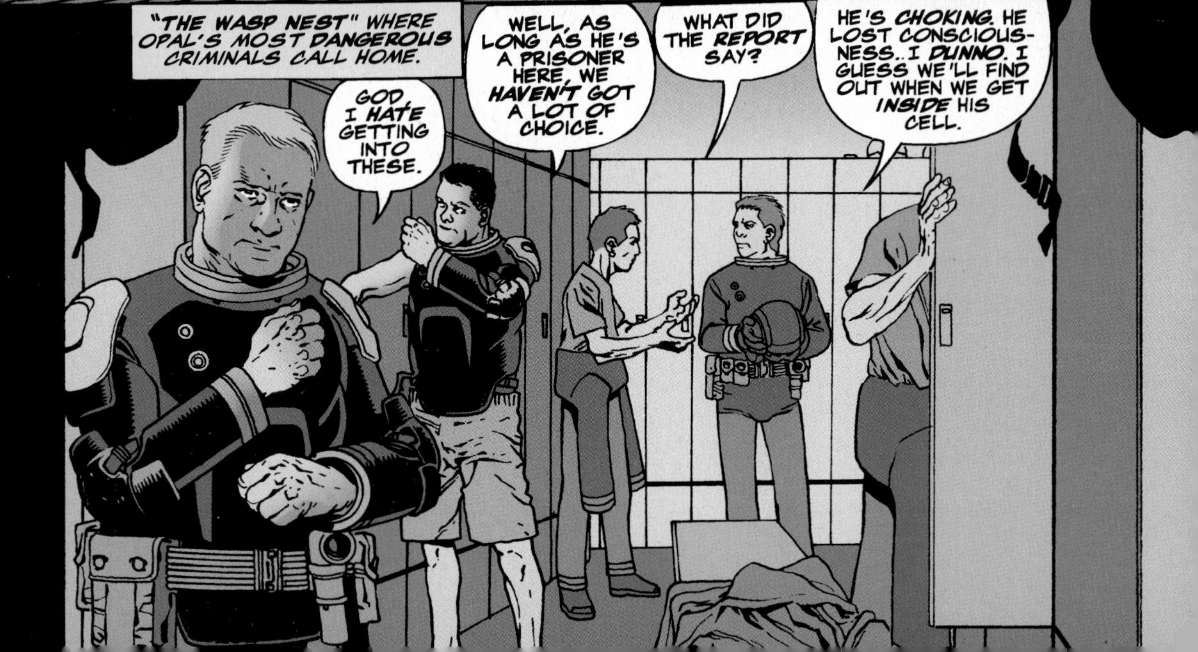
"THE WASP NEST" WHERE OPAL'S MOST DANGEROUS CRIMINALS CALL HOME.
GOD, I HATE GETTING INTO THESE.
WELL, AS LONG AS HE'S A PRISONER HERE, WE HAVEN'T GOT A LOT OF CHOICE.
WHAT DID THE REPORT SAY?
HE'S CHOKING. HE LOST CONSCIOUSNESS..I DUNNO. I GUESS WE'LL FIND OUT WHEN WE GET INSIDE HIS CELL.

I'M THINKING OF CALLING *JUNE* AND ASKING HER OUT.

JUNE? *WHO, JUNE?*

YOUR *SISTER,* DUMMY.

OH, JUNE.

I WAS HOPING YOU *WOULDN'T* MIND.

WHY WOULD I, YOU'RE MY *BUDDY!* 'COURSE IF YOU LAY A FINGER ON HER, I'LL BE SERVING *TIME* HERE FOR KILLING YOU.

NO, I'M *SERIOUS.* I LIKE HER. WE ALWAYS *TALK* AND SHE MAKES ME *LAUGH* WHENEVER I COME OVER WITH THE GUYS FOR POKER.

YEAH, WELL SHE'D *KILL* ME IF I TOLD YOU, BUT HAVE YOU *EVER* WONDERED WHY SHE'S *THERE* ON THOSE NIGHTS?

NO.

POKER NIGHT IS WHEN WIVES AND SISTERS AND MOTHERS *ALL* GO OUT TO MOVIES OR SCRAM SOMEWHERE. NOTHING TURNS THEM OFF MORE THAN SEEING A BUNCH OF GUYS SITTING AROUND A *TABLE* WITH A DECK OF CARDS.

YET MY SISTER *STAYS.*

WHY IS THAT?

'CAUSE SHE *LIKES* YOU, SHERLOCK.

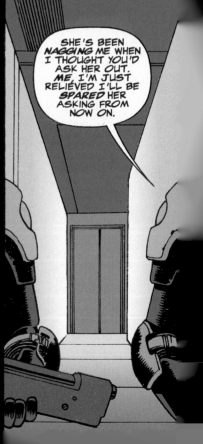

SHE'S BEEN *NAGGING* ME WHEN I THOUGHT YOU'D ASK HER OUT. *ME,* I'M JUST *RELIEVED* I'LL BE *SPARED* HER ASKING FROM NOW ON.

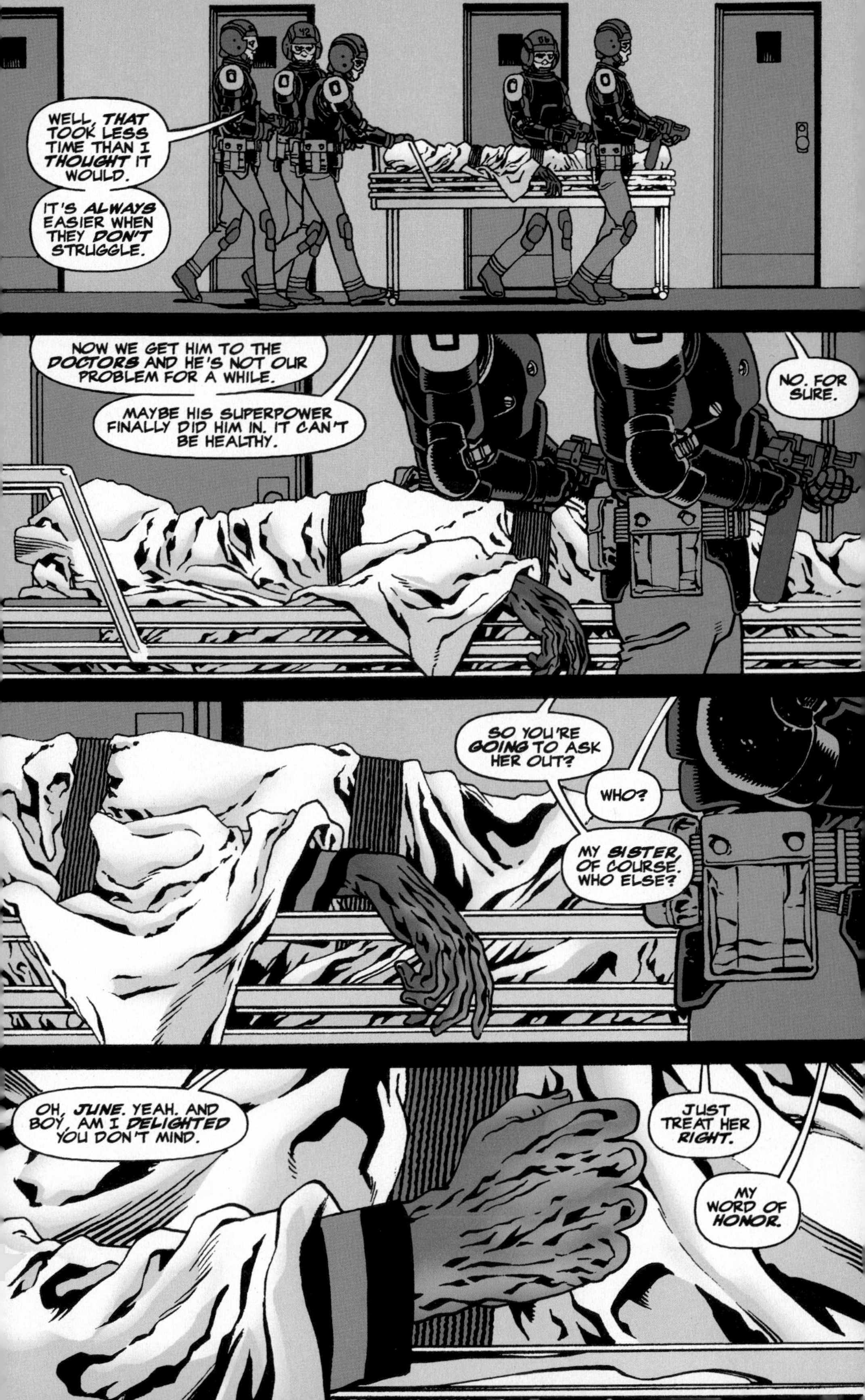
WELL, THAT TOOK LESS TIME THAN I THOUGHT IT WOULD.
IT'S ALWAYS EASIER WHEN THEY DON'T STRUGGLE.
NOW WE GET HIM TO THE DOCTORS AND HE'S NOT OUR PROBLEM FOR A WHILE.
MAYBE HIS SUPERPOWER FINALLY DID HIM IN. IT CAN'T BE HEALTHY.
NO. FOR SURE.
SO YOU'RE GOING TO ASK HER OUT?
WHO?
MY SISTER, OF COURSE. WHO ELSE?
OH, JUNE. YEAH. AND BOY, AM I DELIGHTED YOU DON'T MIND.
JUST TREAT HER RIGHT.
MY WORD OF HONOR.

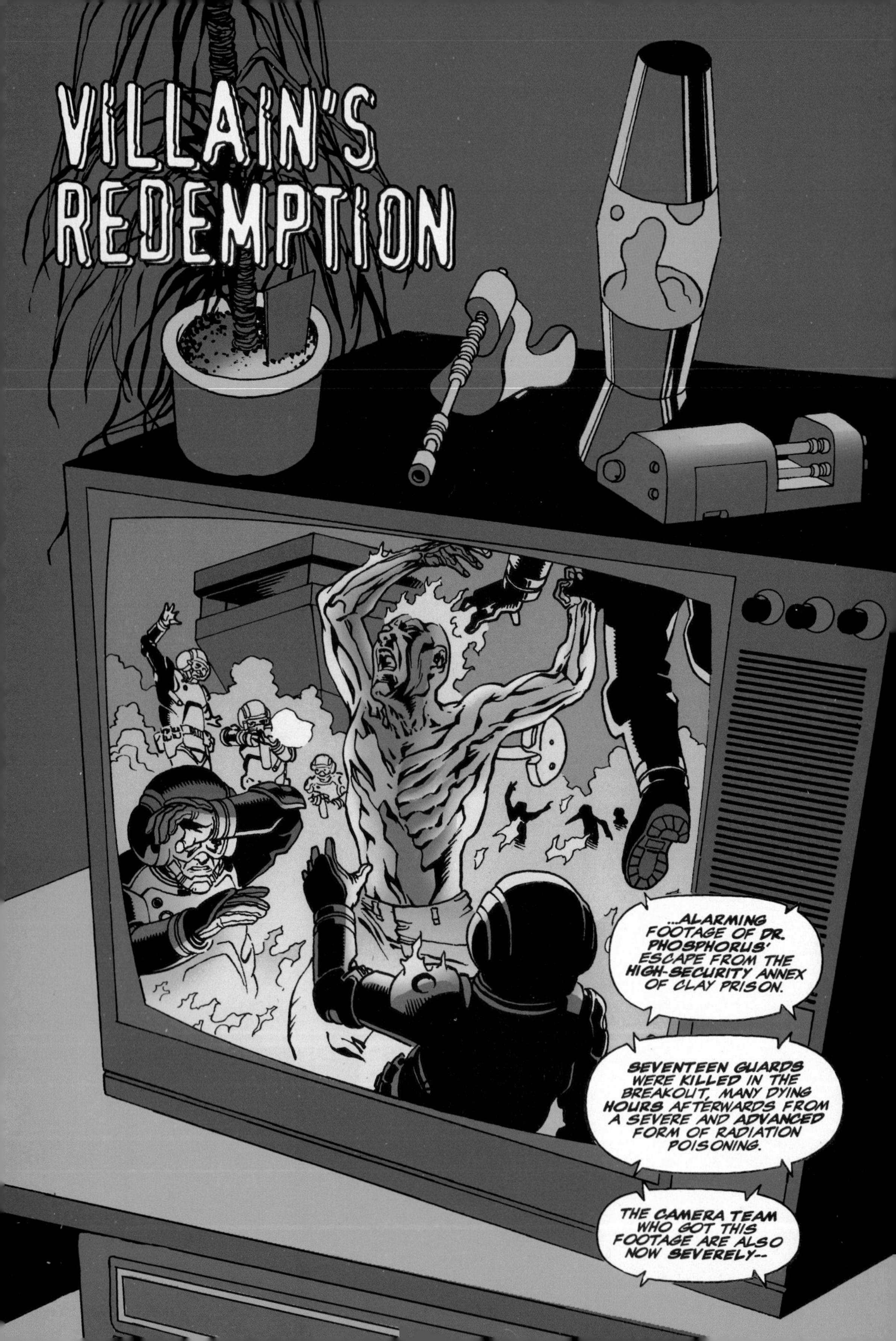
VILLAIN'S REDEMPTION
...ALARMING FOOTAGE OF DR. PHOSPHORUS' ESCAPE FROM THE HIGH-SECURITY ANNEX OF CLAY PRISON.
SEVENTEEN GUARDS WERE KILLED IN THE BREAKOUT, MANY DYING HOURS AFTERWARDS FROM A SEVERE AND ADVANCED FORM OF RADIATION POISONING.
THE CAMERA TEAM WHO GOT THIS FOOTAGE ARE ALSO NOW SEVERELY--

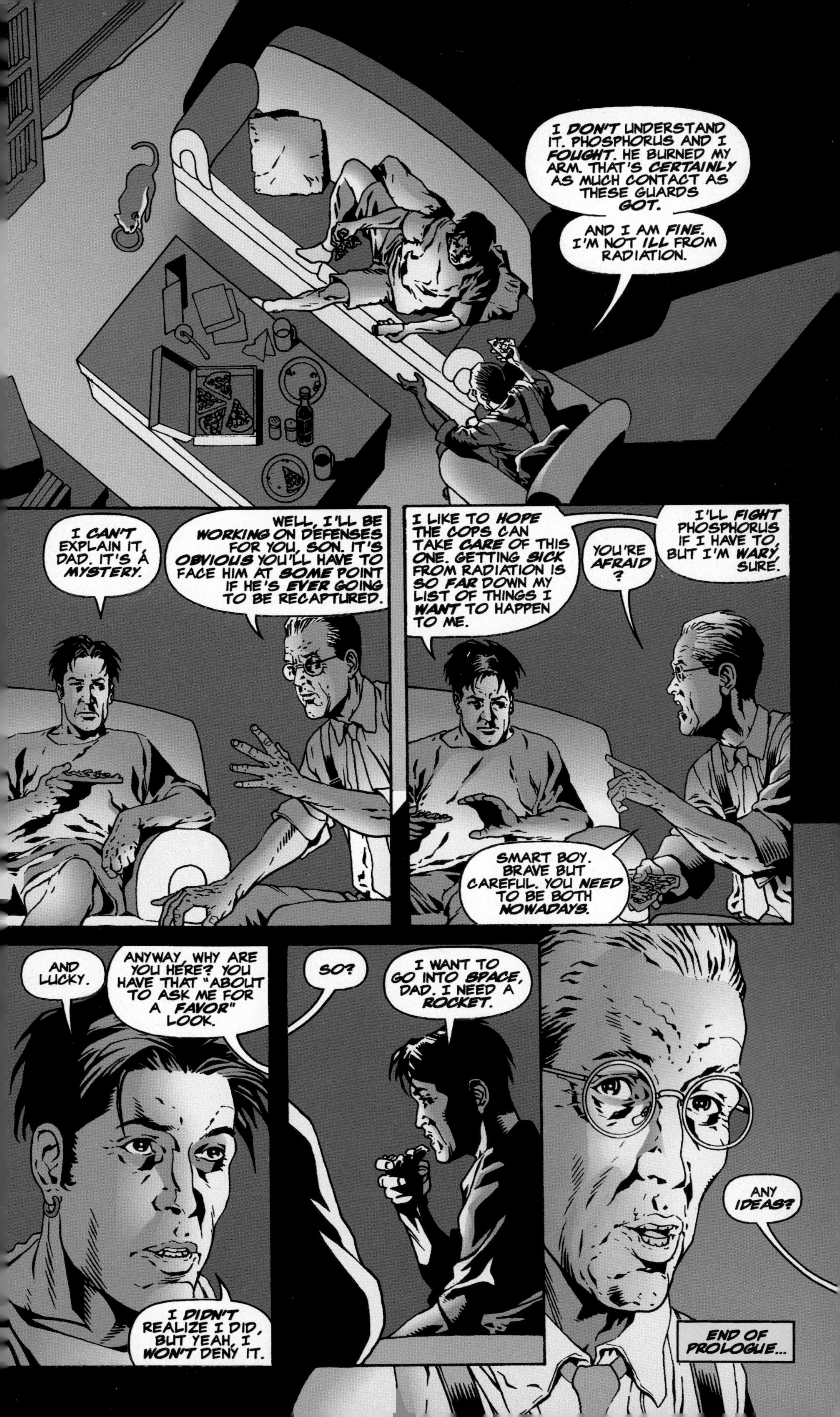
I DON'T UNDERSTAND IT. PHOSPHORUS AND I FOUGHT. HE BURNED MY ARM. THAT'S CERTAINLY AS MUCH CONTACT AS THESE GUARDS GOT.
AND I AM FINE. I'M NOT ILL FROM RADIATION.
I CAN'T EXPLAIN IT, DAD. IT'S A MYSTERY.
WELL, I'LL BE WORKING ON DEFENSES FOR YOU, SON. IT'S OBVIOUS YOU'LL HAVE TO FACE HIM AT SOME POINT IF HE'S EVER GOING TO BE RECAPTURED.
YOU'RE AFRAID?
I'LL FIGHT PHOSPHORUS IF I HAVE TO, BUT I'M WARY, SURE.
I LIKE TO HOPE THE COPS CAN TAKE CARE OF THIS ONE. GETTING SICK FROM RADIATION IS SO FAR DOWN MY LIST OF THINGS I WANT TO HAPPEN TO ME.
SMART BOY. BRAVE BUT CAREFUL. YOU NEED TO BE BOTH NOWADAYS.
AND LUCKY.
ANYWAY, WHY ARE YOU HERE? YOU HAVE THAT "ABOUT TO ASK ME FOR A FAVOR" LOOK.
I DIDN'T REALIZE I DID, BUT YEAH, I WON'T DENY IT.
SO?
I WANT TO GO INTO SPACE, DAD. I NEED A ROCKET.
ANY IDEAS?
END OF PROLOGUE...

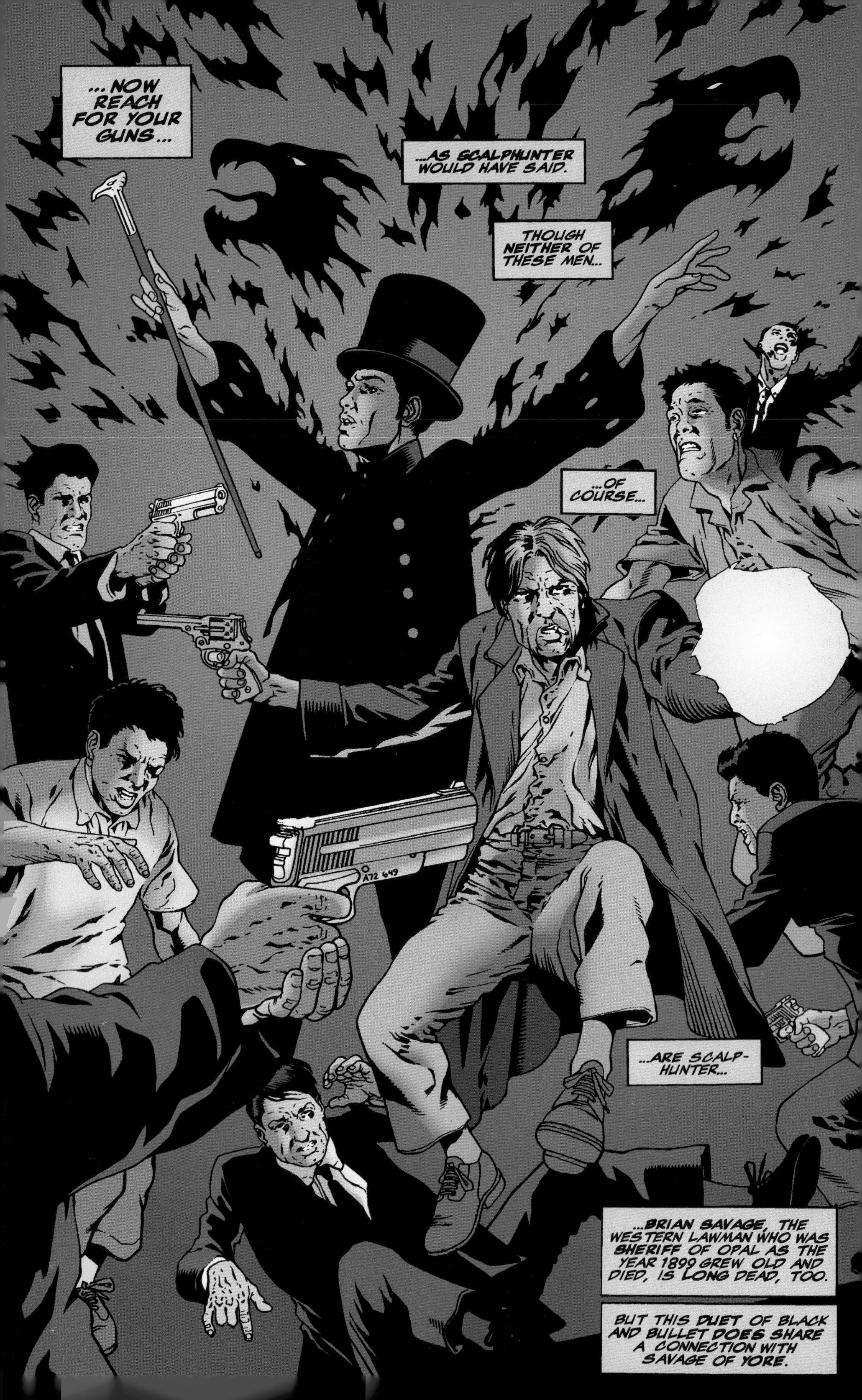
...NOW REACH FOR YOUR GUNS...
...AS SCALPHUNTER WOULD HAVE SAID.
THOUGH NEITHER OF THESE MEN...
...OF COURSE...
...ARE SCALP-HUNTER...
...BRIAN SAVAGE, THE WESTERN LAWMAN WHO WAS SHERIFF OF OPAL AS THE YEAR 1899 GREW OLD AND DIED, IS LONG DEAD, TOO.
BUT THIS DUET OF BLACK AND BULLET DOES SHARE A CONNECTION WITH SAVAGE OF YORE.
A72 649

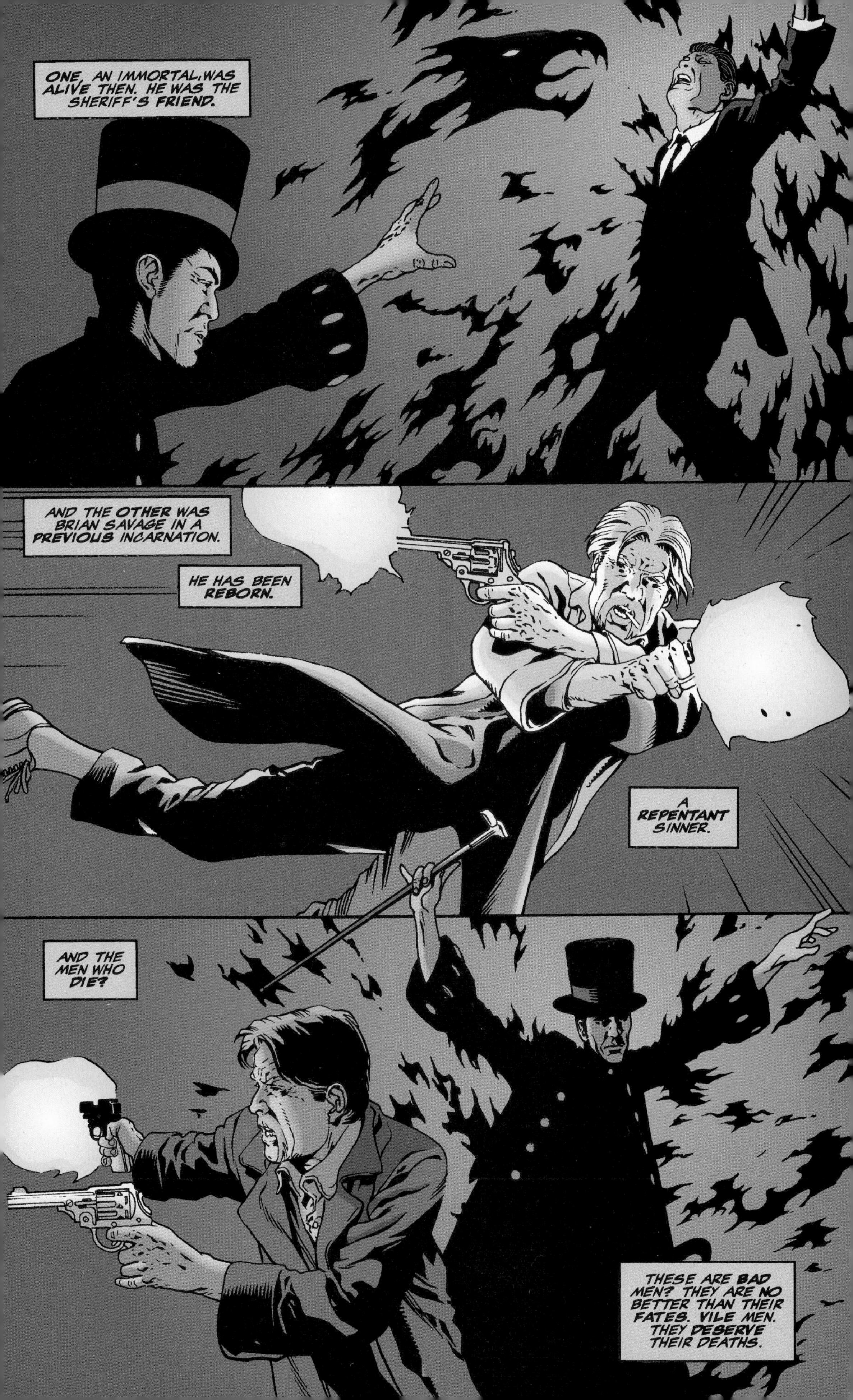
ONE, AN IMMORTAL, WAS ALIVE THEN. HE WAS THE SHERIFF'S FRIEND.
AND THE OTHER WAS BRIAN SAVAGE IN A PREVIOUS INCARNATION.
HE HAS BEEN REBORN.
A REPENTANT SINNER.
AND THE MEN WHO DIE?
THESE ARE BAD MEN? THEY ARE NO BETTER THAN THEIR FATES. VILE MEN. THEY DESERVE THEIR DEATHS.

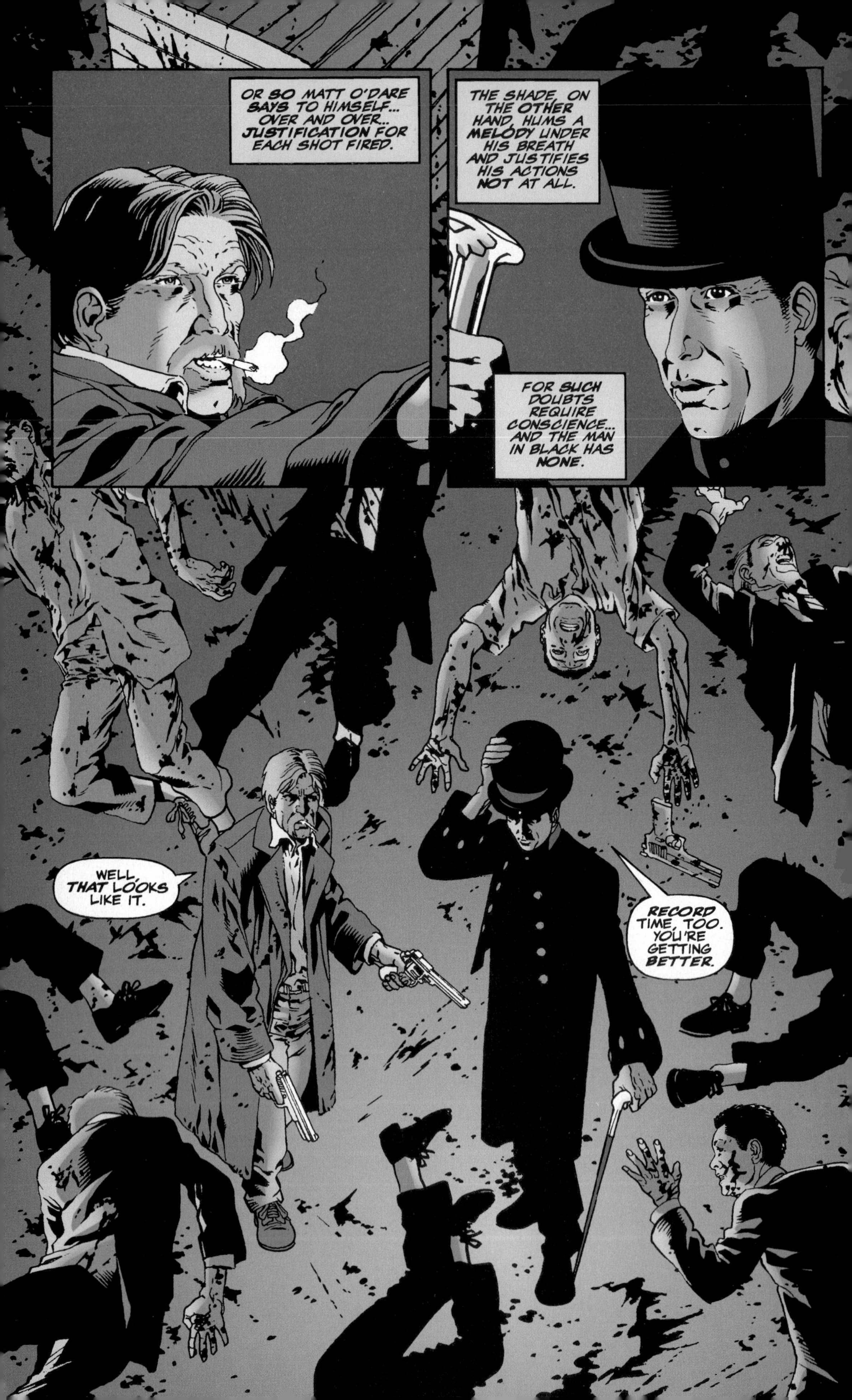
OR SO MATT O'DARE SAYS TO HIMSELF... OVER AND OVER... JUSTIFICATION FOR EACH SHOT FIRED.
THE SHADE, ON THE OTHER HAND, HUMS A MELODY UNDER HIS BREATH AND JUSTIFIES HIS ACTIONS NOT AT ALL.
FOR SUCH DOUBTS REQUIRE CONSCIENCE... AND THE MAN IN BLACK HAS NONE.
WELL, THAT LOOKS LIKE IT.
RECORD TIME, TOO. YOU'RE GETTING BETTER.

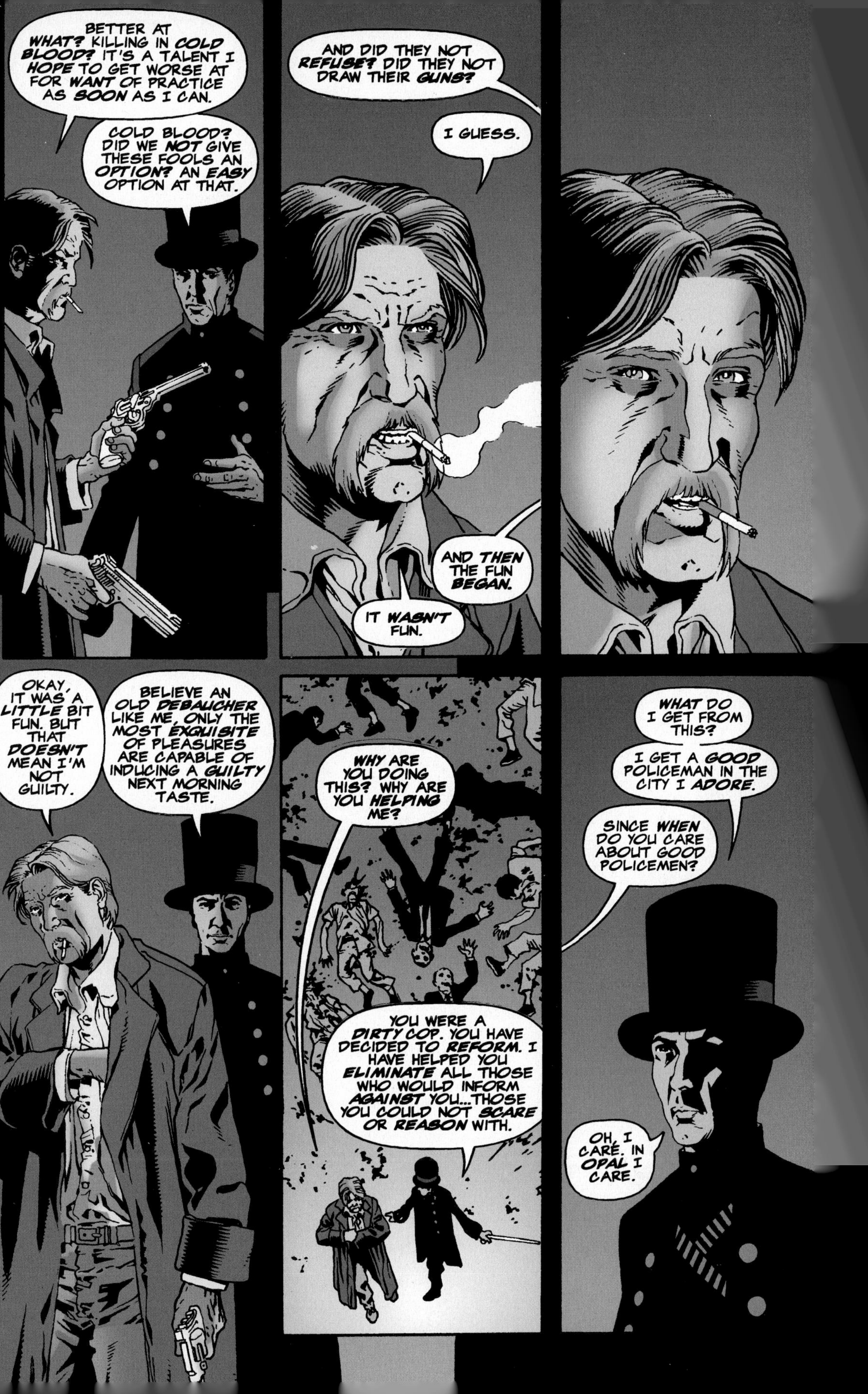

BETTER AT WHAT? KILLING IN COLD BLOOD? IT'S A TALENT I HOPE TO GET WORSE AT FOR WANT OF PRACTICE AS SOON AS I CAN.
COLD BLOOD? DID WE NOT GIVE THESE FOOLS AN OPTION? AN EASY OPTION AT THAT.
AND DID THEY NOT REFUSE? DID THEY NOT DRAW THEIR GUNS?
I GUESS.
AND THEN THE FUN BEGAN.
IT WASN'T FUN.
OKAY, IT WAS A LITTLE BIT FUN. BUT THAT DOESN'T MEAN I'M NOT GUILTY.
BELIEVE AN OLD DEBAUCHER LIKE ME, ONLY THE MOST EXQUISITE OF PLEASURES ARE CAPABLE OF INDUCING A GUILTY NEXT MORNING TASTE.
WHY ARE YOU DOING THIS? WHY ARE YOU HELPING ME?
YOU WERE A DIRTY COP. YOU HAVE DECIDED TO REFORM. I HAVE HELPED YOU ELIMINATE ALL THOSE WHO WOULD INFORM AGAINST YOU...THOSE YOU COULD NOT SCARE OR REASON WITH.
WHAT DO I GET FROM THIS?
I GET A GOOD POLICEMAN IN THE CITY I ADORE.
SINCE WHEN DO YOU CARE ABOUT GOOD POLICEMEN?
OH, I CARE. IN OPAL I CARE.

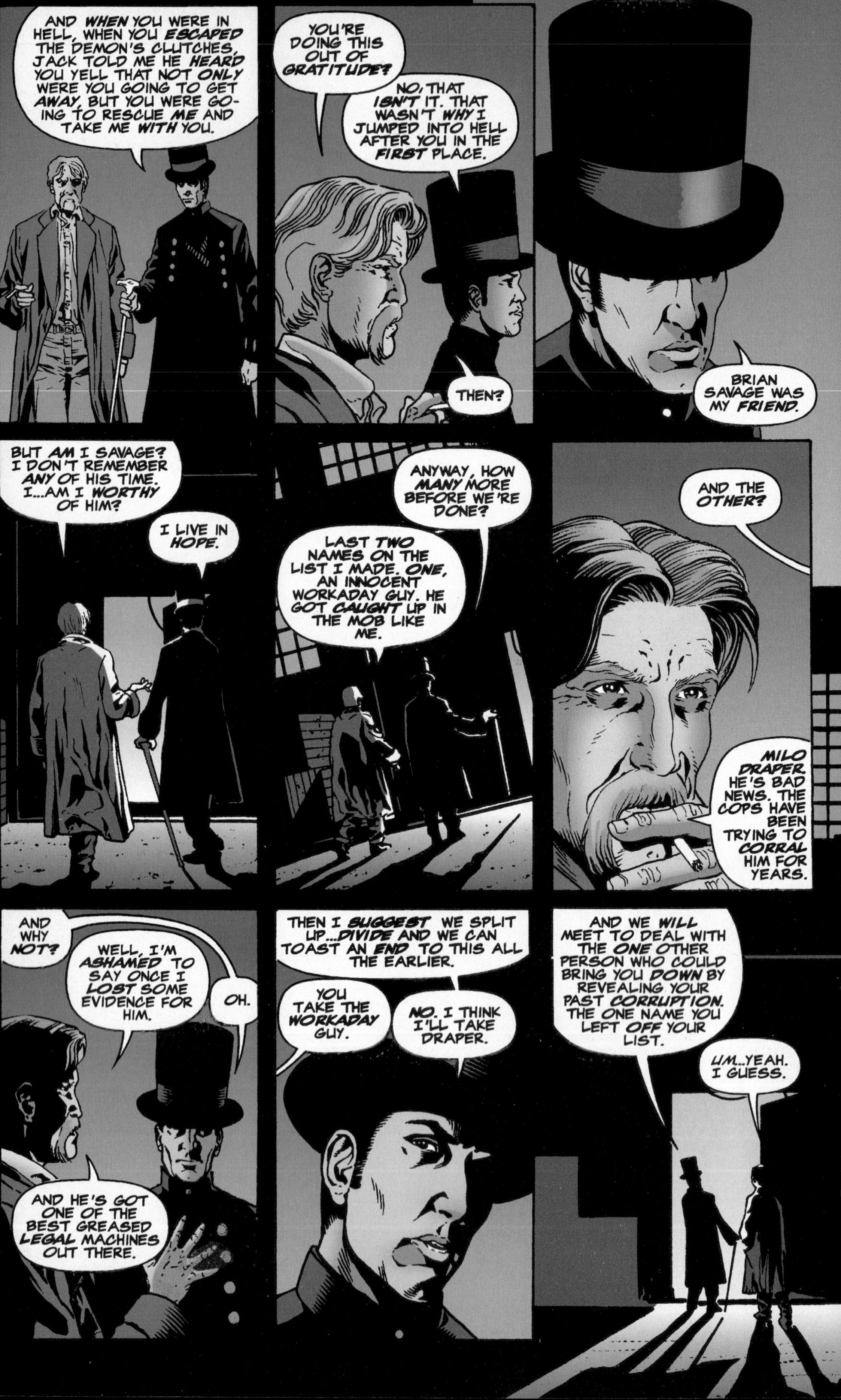
AND WHEN YOU WERE IN HELL, WHEN YOU ESCAPED THE DEMON'S CLUTCHES, JACK TOLD ME HE HEARD YOU YELL THAT NOT ONLY WERE YOU GOING TO GET AWAY, BUT YOU WERE GOING TO RESCUE ME AND TAKE ME WITH YOU.
YOU'RE DOING THIS OUT OF GRATITUDE?
NO, THAT ISN'T IT. THAT WASN'T WHY I JUMPED INTO HELL AFTER YOU IN THE FIRST PLACE.
THEN?
BRIAN SAVAGE WAS MY FRIEND.
BUT AM I SAVAGE? I DON'T REMEMBER ANY OF HIS TIME. I...AM I WORTHY OF HIM?
I LIVE IN HOPE.
ANYWAY, HOW MANY MORE BEFORE WE'RE DONE?
LAST TWO NAMES ON THE LIST I MADE. ONE, AN INNOCENT WORKADAY GUY. HE GOT CAUGHT UP IN THE MOB LIKE ME.
AND THE OTHER?
MILO DRAPER. HE'S BAD NEWS. THE COPS HAVE BEEN TRYING TO CORRAL HIM FOR YEARS.
AND WHY NOT?
WELL, I'M ASHAMED TO SAY ONCE I LOST SOME EVIDENCE FOR HIM.
OH.
AND HE'S GOT ONE OF THE BEST GREASED LEGAL MACHINES OUT THERE.
THEN I SUGGEST WE SPLIT UP...DIVIDE AND WE CAN TOAST AN END TO THIS ALL THE EARLIER.
YOU TAKE THE WORKADAY GUY.
NO. I THINK I'LL TAKE DRAPER.
AND WE WILL MEET TO DEAL WITH THE ONE OTHER PERSON WHO COULD BRING YOU DOWN BY REVEALING YOUR PAST CORRUPTION. THE ONE NAME YOU LEFT OFF YOUR LIST.
UM...YEAH. I GUESS.

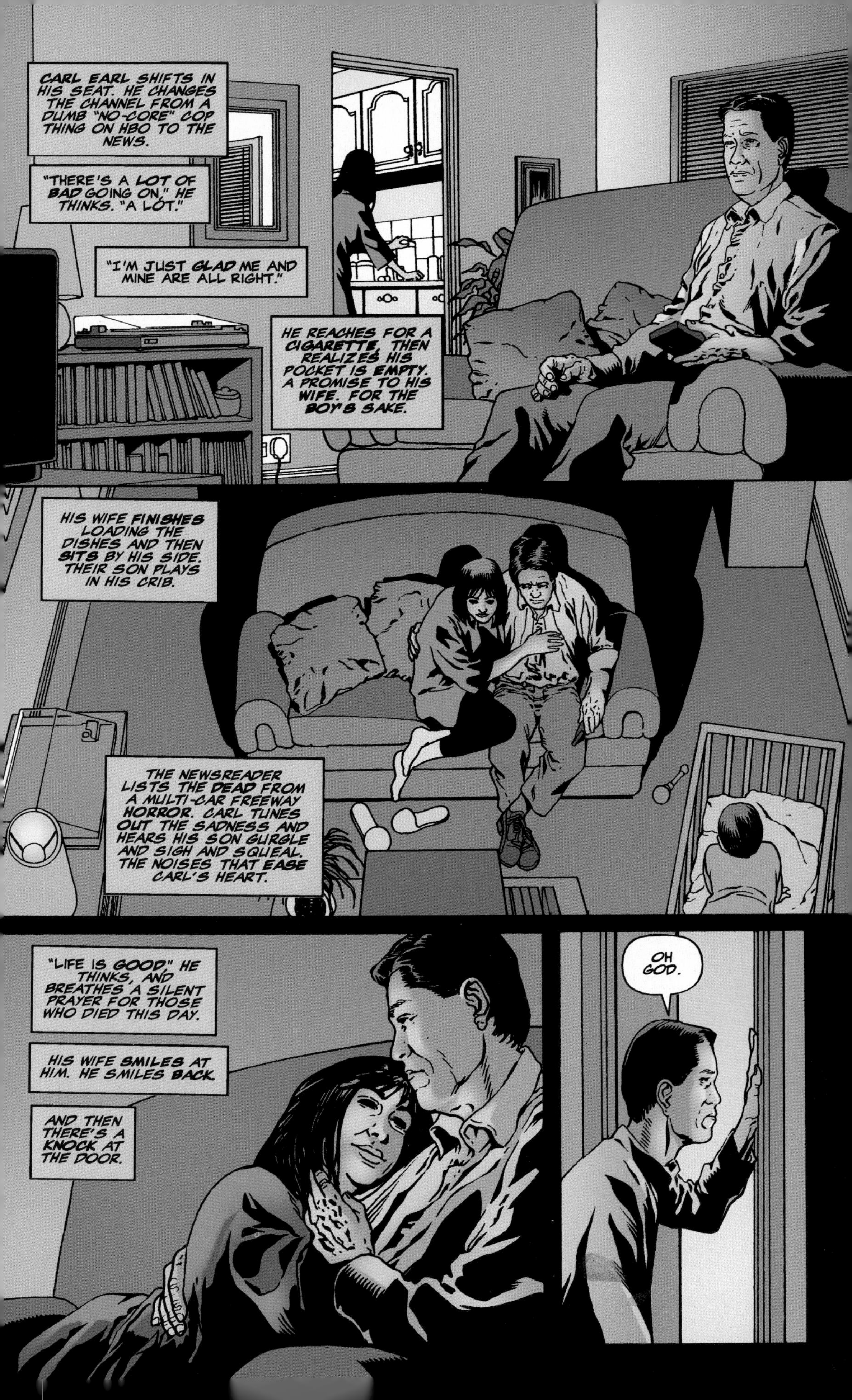
CARL EARL SHIFTS IN HIS SEAT. HE CHANGES THE CHANNEL FROM A DUMB "NO-CORE" COP THING ON HBO TO THE NEWS.
"THERE'S A LOT OF BAD GOING ON," HE THINKS. "A LOT."
"I'M JUST GLAD ME AND MINE ARE ALL RIGHT."
HE REACHES FOR A CIGARETTE, THEN REALIZES HIS POCKET IS EMPTY. A PROMISE TO HIS WIFE. FOR THE BOY'S SAKE.
HIS WIFE FINISHES LOADING THE DISHES AND THEN SITS BY HIS SIDE. THEIR SON PLAYS IN HIS CRIB.
THE NEWSREADER LISTS THE DEAD FROM A MULTI-CAR FREEWAY HORROR. CARL TUNES OUT THE SADNESS AND HEARS HIS SON GURGLE AND SIGH AND SQUEAL. THE NOISES THAT EASE CARL'S HEART.
"LIFE IS GOOD," HE THINKS, AND BREATHES A SILENT PRAYER FOR THOSE WHO DIED THIS DAY.
HIS WIFE SMILES AT HIM. HE SMILES BACK.
AND THEN THERE'S A KNOCK AT THE DOOR.
OH GOD.

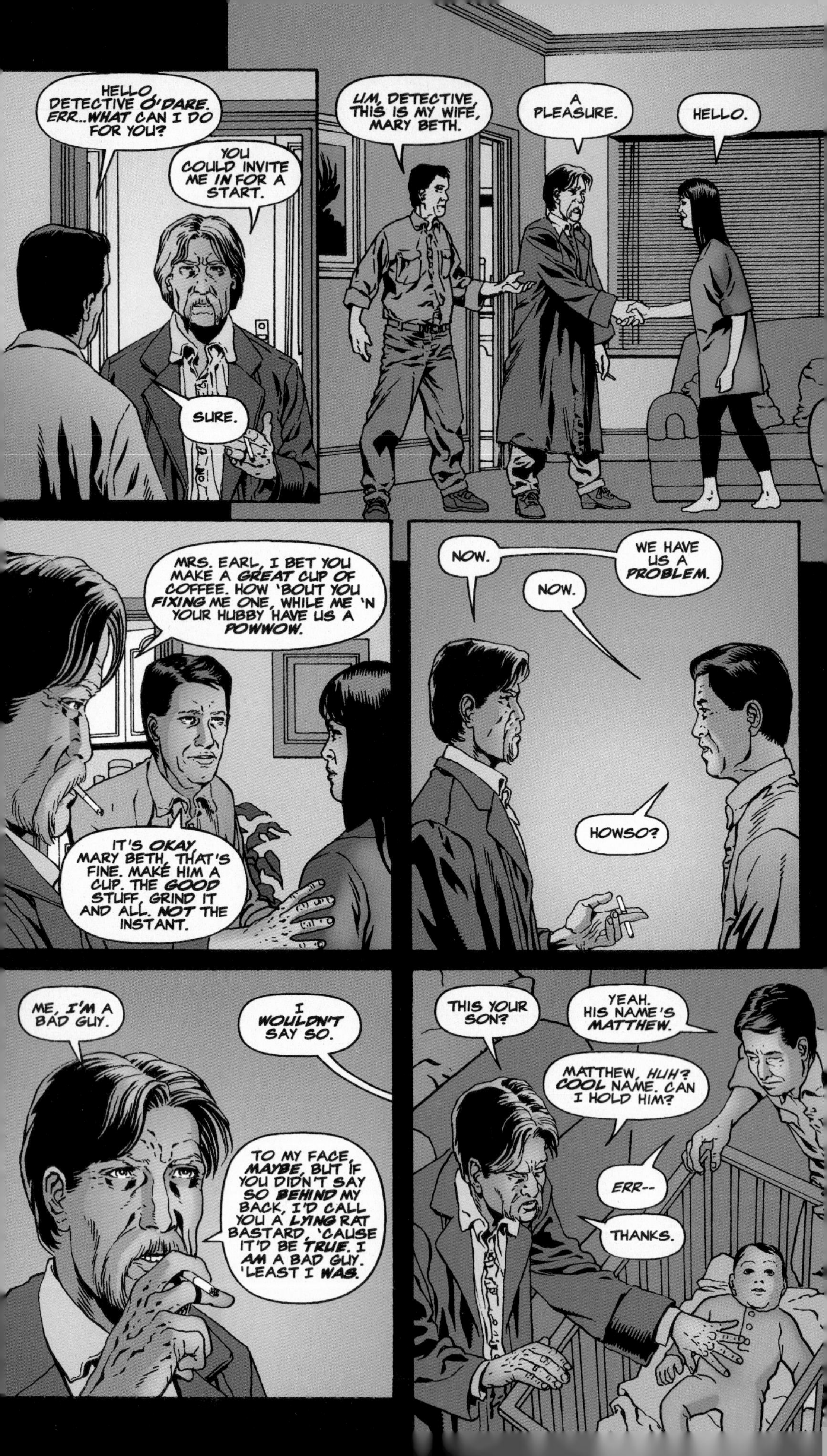
HELLO, DETECTIVE O'DARE. ERR...WHAT CAN I DO FOR YOU?
YOU COULD INVITE ME IN FOR A START.
SURE.
UM, DETECTIVE, THIS IS MY WIFE, MARY BETH.
A PLEASURE.
HELLO.
MRS. EARL, I BET YOU MAKE A GREAT CUP OF COFFEE. HOW 'BOUT YOU FIXING ME ONE, WHILE ME 'N YOUR HUBBY HAVE US A POWWOW.
IT'S OKAY, MARY BETH, THAT'S FINE. MAKE HIM A CUP. THE GOOD STUFF, GRIND IT AND ALL. NOT THE INSTANT.
NOW.
WE HAVE US A PROBLEM.
NOW.
HOWSO?
ME, I'M A BAD GUY.
I WOULDN'T SAY SO.
TO MY FACE, MAYBE, BUT IF YOU DIDN'T SAY SO BEHIND MY BACK, I'D CALL YOU A LYING RAT BASTARD, 'CAUSE IT'D BE TRUE. I AM A BAD GUY. 'LEAST I WAS.
THIS YOUR SON?
YEAH. HIS NAME'S MATTHEW.
MATTHEW, HUH? COOL NAME. CAN I HOLD HIM?
ERR--
THANKS.

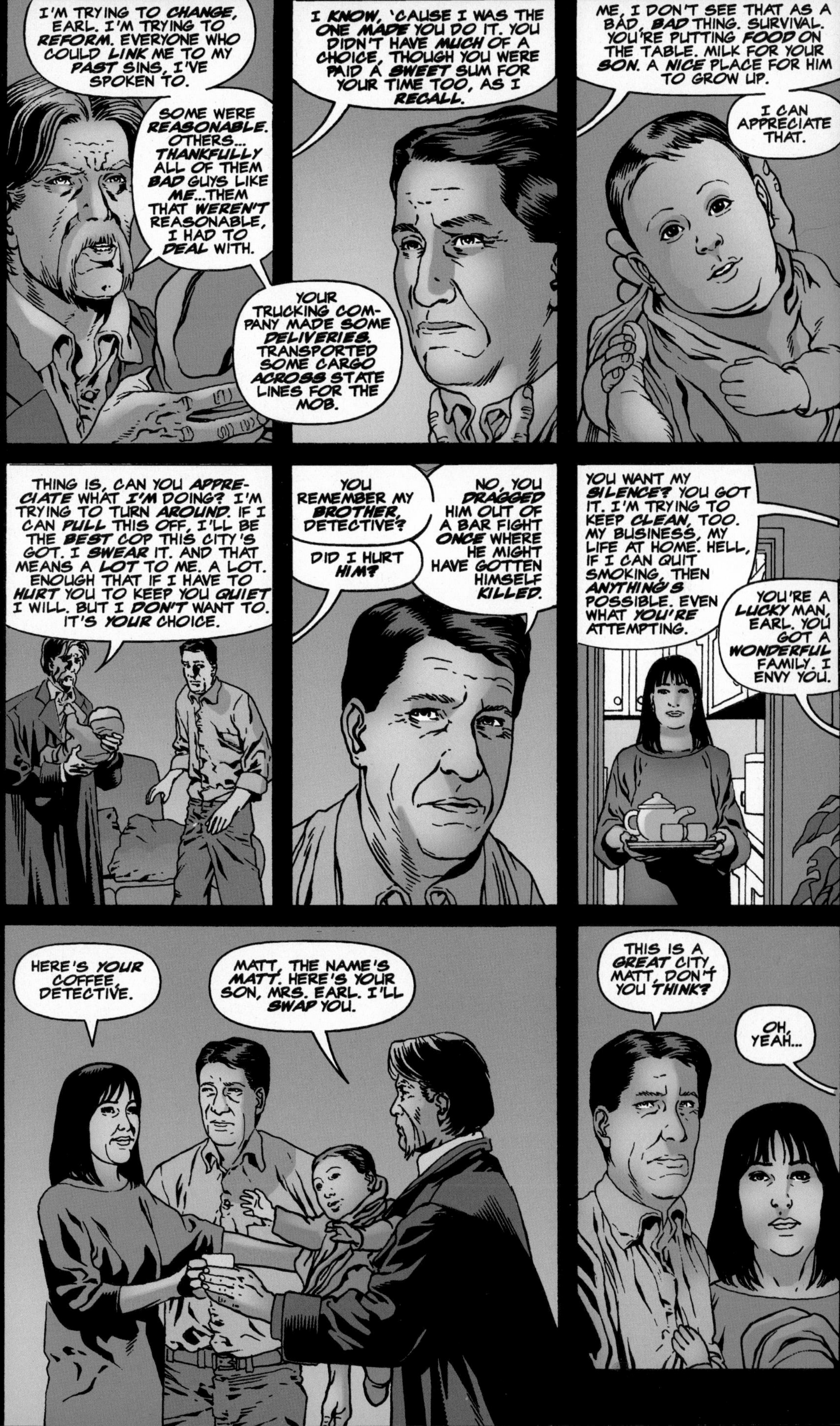
I'M TRYING TO CHANGE, EARL. I'M TRYING TO REFORM. EVERYONE WHO COULD LINK ME TO MY PAST SINS, I'VE SPOKEN TO.
SOME WERE REASONABLE. OTHERS... THANKFULLY ALL OF THEM BAD GUYS LIKE ME...THEM THAT WEREN'T REASONABLE, I HAD TO DEAL WITH.
YOUR TRUCKING COMPANY MADE SOME DELIVERIES. TRANSPORTED SOME CARGO ACROSS STATE LINES FOR THE MOB.
I KNOW, 'CAUSE I WAS THE ONE MADE YOU DO IT. YOU DIDN'T HAVE MUCH OF A CHOICE, THOUGH YOU WERE PAID A SWEET SUM FOR YOUR TIME TOO, AS I RECALL.
ME, I DON'T SEE THAT AS A BAD, BAD THING. SURVIVAL. YOU'RE PUTTING FOOD ON THE TABLE. MILK FOR YOUR SON. A NICE PLACE FOR HIM TO GROW UP.
I CAN APPRECIATE THAT.
THING IS, CAN YOU APPRECIATE WHAT I'M DOING? I'M TRYING TO TURN AROUND. IF I CAN PULL THIS OFF, I'LL BE THE BEST COP THIS CITY'S GOT. I SWEAR IT. AND THAT MEANS A LOT TO ME. A LOT. ENOUGH THAT IF I HAVE TO HURT YOU TO KEEP YOU QUIET I WILL. BUT I DON'T WANT TO. IT'S YOUR CHOICE.
YOU REMEMBER MY BROTHER, DETECTIVE?
DID I HURT HIM?
NO, YOU DRAGGED HIM OUT OF A BAR FIGHT ONCE WHERE HE MIGHT HAVE GOTTEN HIMSELF KILLED.
YOU WANT MY SILENCE? YOU GOT IT. I'M TRYING TO KEEP CLEAN, TOO. MY BUSINESS, MY LIFE AT HOME. HELL, IF I CAN QUIT SMOKING, THEN ANYTHING'S POSSIBLE. EVEN WHAT YOU'RE ATTEMPTING.
YOU'RE A LUCKY MAN, EARL. YOU GOT A WONDERFUL FAMILY. I ENVY YOU.
HERE'S YOUR COFFEE, DETECTIVE.
MATT, THE NAME'S MATT. HERE'S YOUR SON, MRS. EARL. I'LL SWAP YOU.
THIS IS A GREAT CITY, MATT, DON'T YOU THINK?
OH, YEAH...

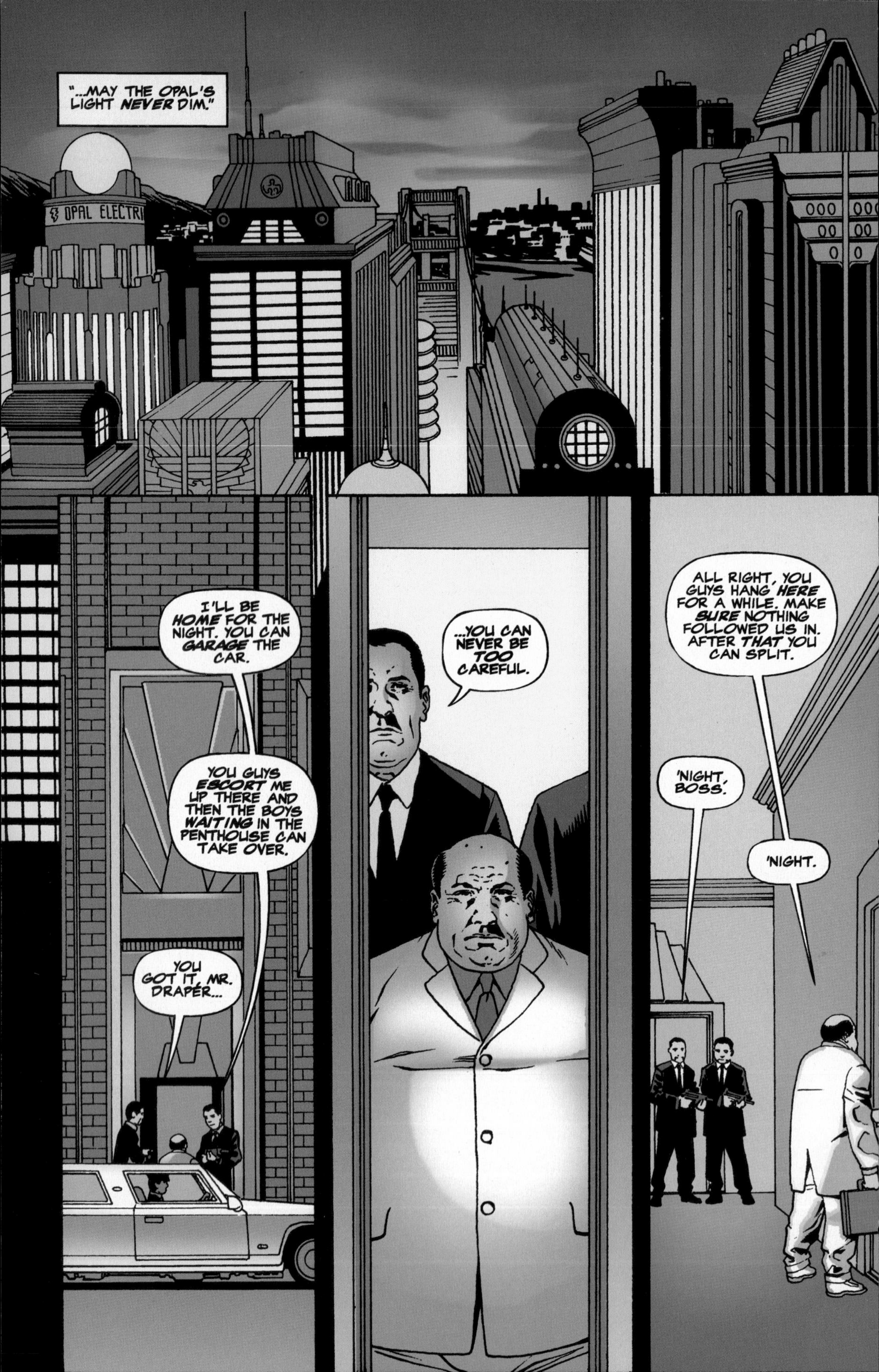
"...MAY THE OPAL'S LIGHT NEVER DIM."
OPAL ELECTRI
I'LL BE HOME FOR THE NIGHT. YOU CAN GARAGE THE CAR.
YOU GUYS ESCORT ME UP THERE AND THEN THE BOYS WAITING IN THE PENTHOUSE CAN TAKE OVER.
YOU GOT IT, MR. DRAPÉR...
...YOU CAN NEVER BE TOO CAREFUL.
ALL RIGHT, YOU GUYS HANG HERE FOR A WHILE. MAKE SURE NOTHING FOLLOWED US IN. AFTER THAT YOU CAN SPLIT.
'NIGHT, BOSS.
'NIGHT.

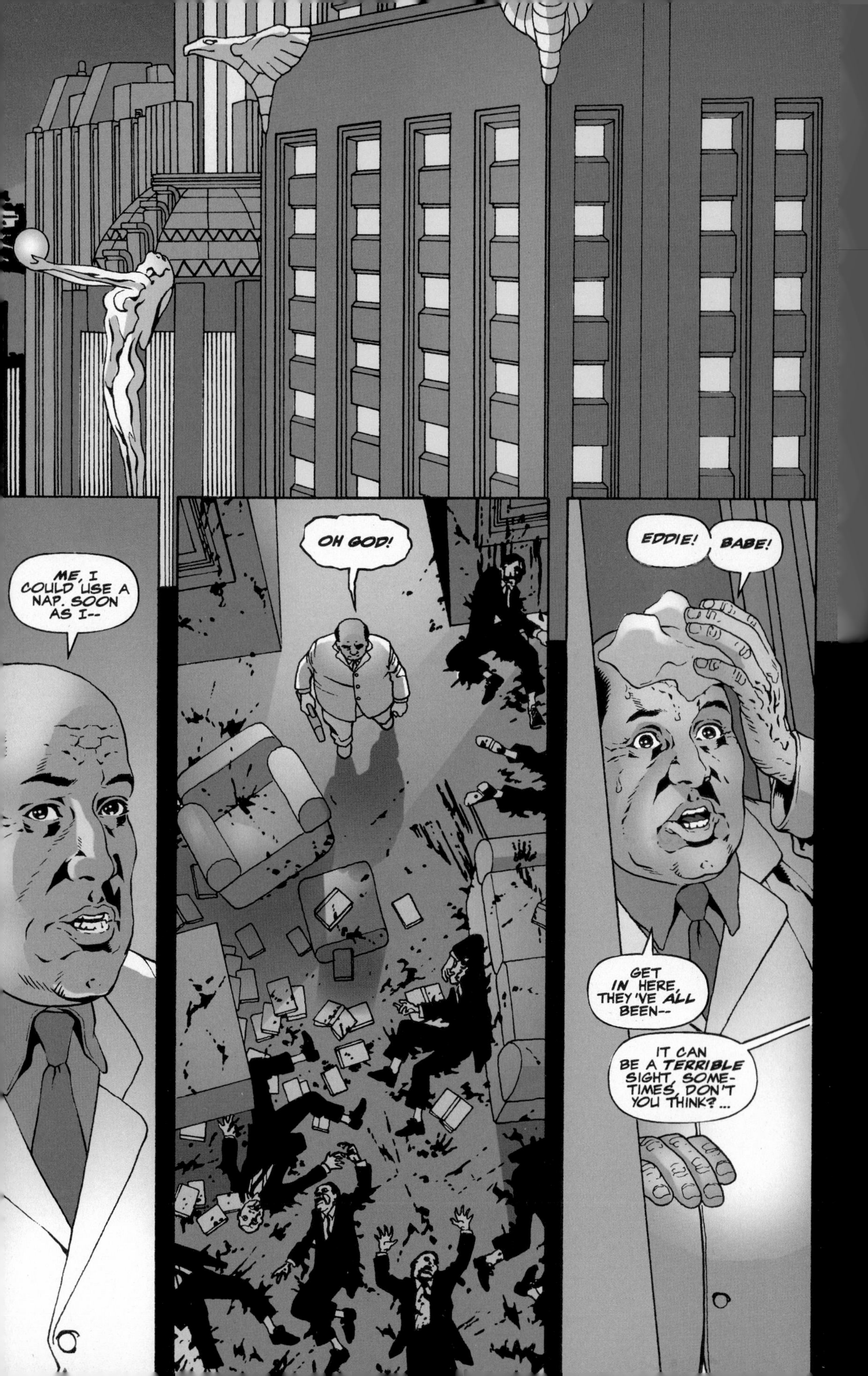
ME, I COULD USE A NAP. SOON AS I--
OH GOD!
EDDIE!
BABE!
GET IN HERE, THEY'VE ALL BEEN--
IT CAN BE A TERRIBLE SIGHT, SOME-TIMES, DON'T YOU THINK?...

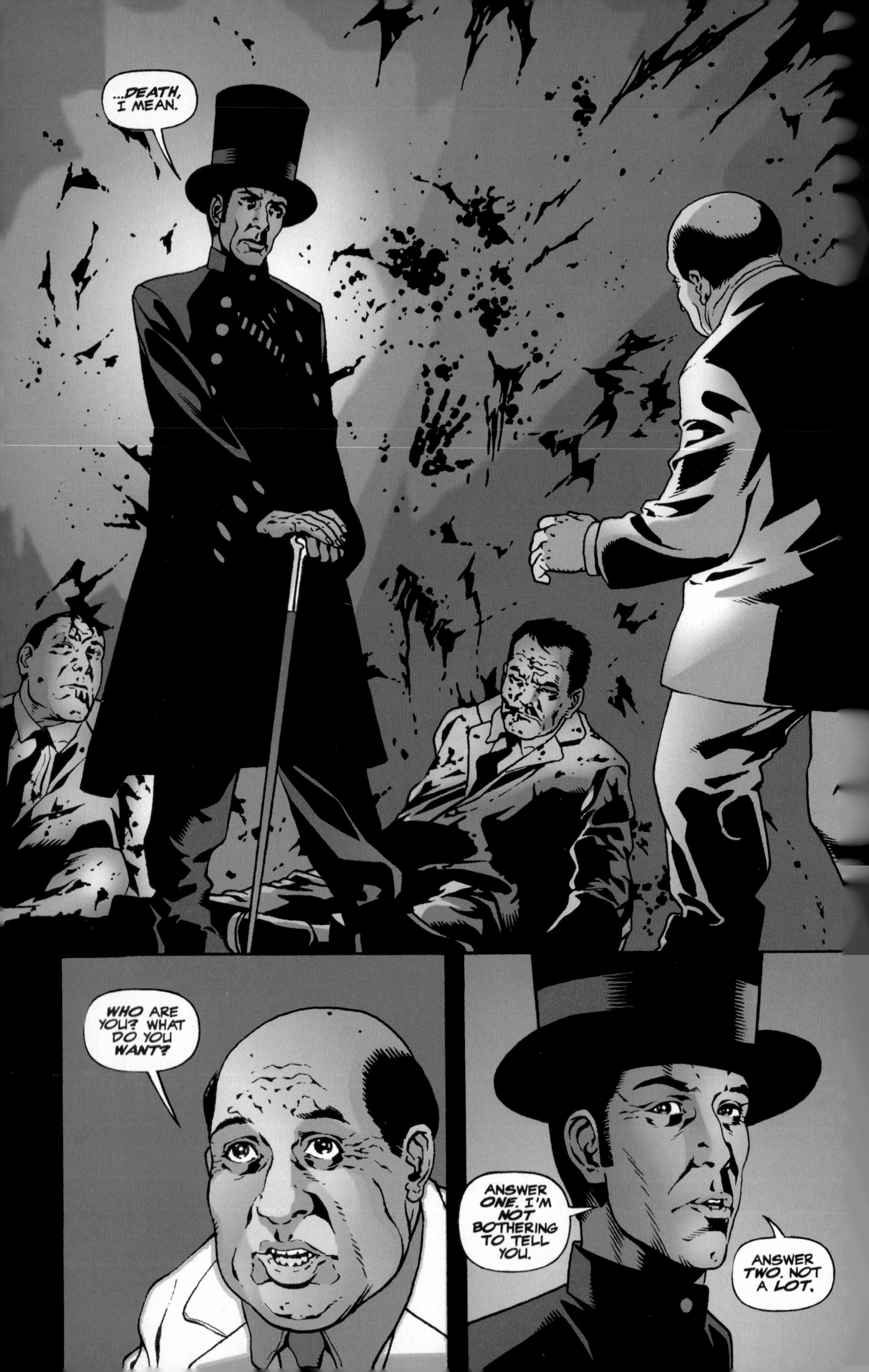
...DEATH, I MEAN.
WHO ARE YOU? WHAT DO YOU WANT?
ANSWER ONE. I'M NOT BOTHERING TO TELL YOU.
ANSWER TWO. NOT A LOT.

WHAT I WANT IS YOUR AGREEMENT ON SOMETHING.
YOU NAME IT. I'M A REASONABLE GUY.
YOU'RE A CROOKED GUY, FROM ALL ACCOUNTS.
HEY, NOTHING WAS EVER PROVEN.
AS FAR AS AMERICAN COURTS GO. I, ON THE OTHER HAND, PREFER THE PRACTICE OF NAPOLEONIC LAW. WHERE THE ACCUSED HAD TO PROVE HIS INNOCENCE, NOT THE LAW PROVE HIS GUILT.
HOW WOULD YOU FARE THEN? WOULD YOU STILL HAVE THE NICE PENTHOUSE VIEW?
ANYWAY, THAT'S ALL INCIDENTAL. WHAT I WANT IS YOUR AGREEMENT THAT MATT O'DARE--
O'DARE WHO THE MOB OWNS? THAT MATT O'DARE?
THAT'S THE THING, O'DARE IS BUYING HIMSELF BACK.
THAT'S WHY SO MANY OF THE GUYS HAVE BEEN KILLED LATELY? ME, I'M SCARED STIFF IT'S SOME RIVAL OUT-OF-TOWN MOB, AND IT'S JUST O'DARE. MAN, HE'S GOT STONES.
WELL, HE DID HAVE SOME HELP.
YOU?
MOI, OUI.
ANYWAY, YOU CAN SEE THAT YOUR PROTECTION MEANS NOTHING. I COULD KILL YOU AT ANY TIME.
I GUESS. YEAH.
THEN FORGET MATT O'DARE WAS EVER CROOKED. FORGET HIS PAST AND YOU CAN ENJOY A BRIGHT AND LENGTHY FUTURE.
ERR..OKAY. O'DARE'S A SAINT. YOU WANT IT, YOU GOT IT.
AHH, WHAT A SHAME.
HUH? WHAT?
I DON'T BELIEVE YOU.

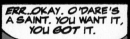

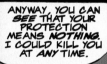

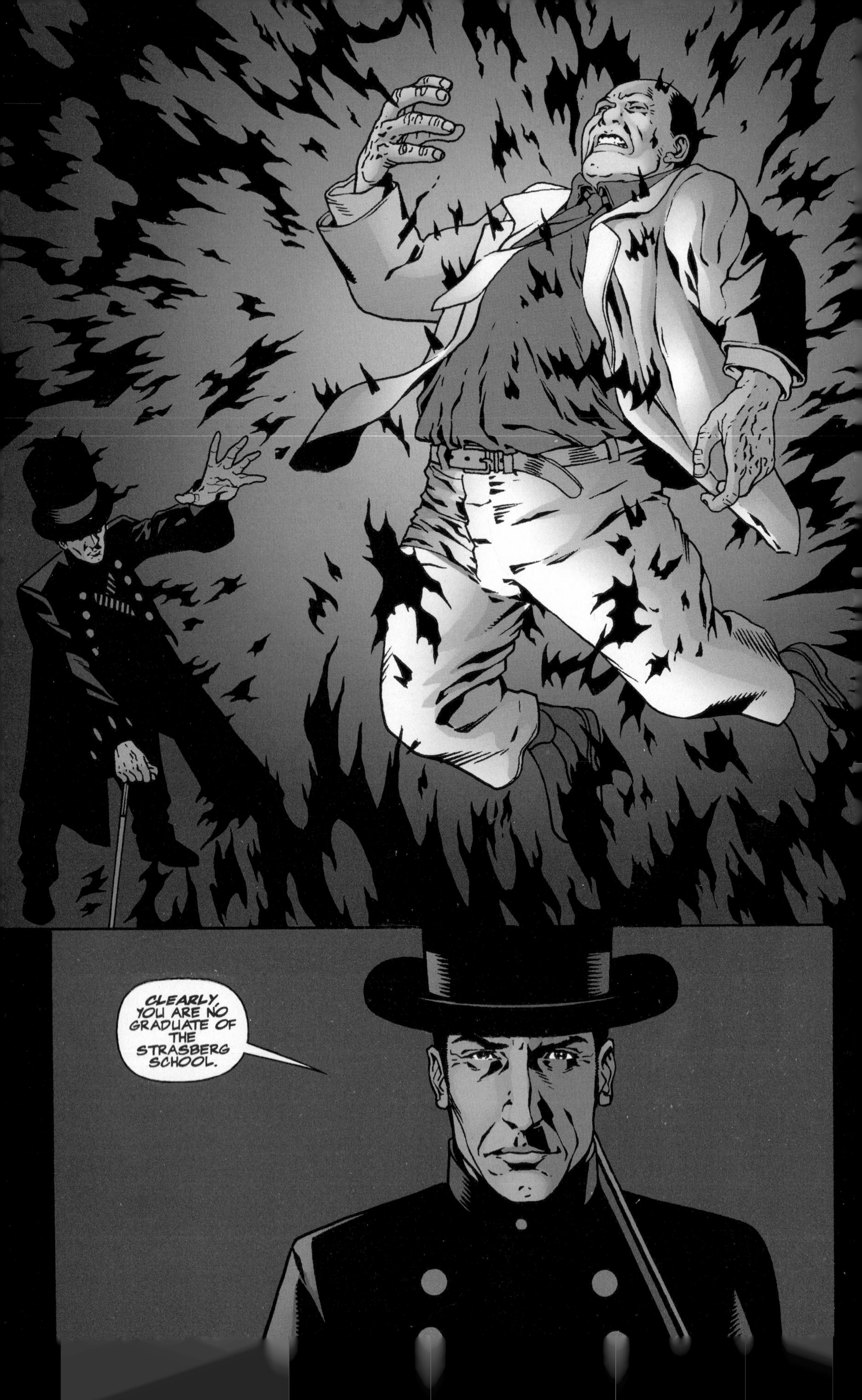
CLEARLY, YOU ARE NO GRADUATE OF THE STRASBERG SCHOOL.

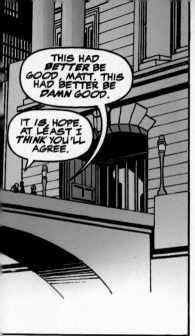

THIS HAD *BETTER* BE GOOD, MATT. THIS HAD BETTER BE *DAMN* GOOD.

IT IS, HOPE. AT LEAST I THINK YOU'LL AGREE.

SHADE AND I HAVE BEEN *BUSY.* EVERYONE WHO *COULD* HAVE REPORTED MY PAST HAS BEEN SEEN AND REASONED WITH.

HOW DID YOU MANAGE *THAT?* YOUR MOB BOSSES WOULD NEVER--

OH. SO ALL THESE KILLINGS WERE YOU TWO?

GUILTY AS CHARGED, MY DEAR.

I'M *NOT* YOUR DEAR, YOU *BLACK-COATED, BLACK-HEARTED* GHOUL.

DON'T TALK TO HIM LIKE THAT, SIS. SHADE'S *OKAY.* HE'S *DIFFERENT.* HE'S...

NO, SHE'S *RIGHT.* I AM EVERYTHING SHE SAYS.

BUT IT *DOESN'T* BOTHER ME, HOPE, SO *WHY* SHOULD IT BOTHER YOU?

ANYWAY, *NO ONE* GOT HURT WHO *DIDN'T* DESERVE IT. ALL THE *LITTLE* GUYS I LEANED ON...THEY WERE MORE THAN HAPPY TO JUST FORGET I EVER ENTERED THEIR LIVES.

AND THE *BIG* BOYS...MOST OF THEM DESERVED ICING.

THAT'S *NOT* FOR YOU TO *DECIDE,* MATT. YOU SAID YOU *WANTED* TO BE A GOOD COP, BUT SPEND YOUR TIME PLAYING *VIGILANTE.*

IT WAS MY *LAST* LOT OF BAD BEFORE THE *GOOD* COULD BEGIN, HOPE. YOU *HAVE* TO UNDERSTAND THAT.

I'LL TRY.

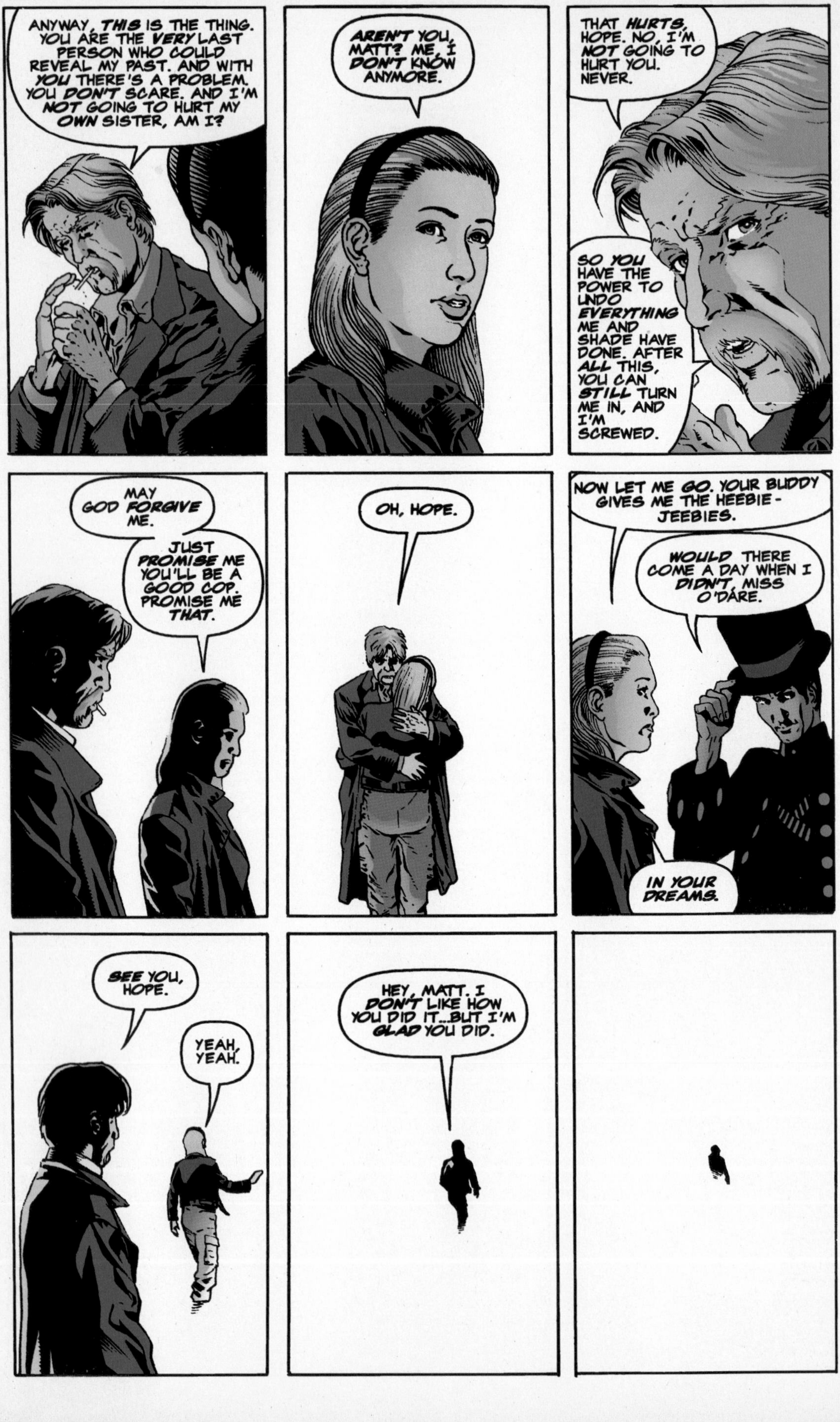
ANYWAY, THIS IS THE THING. YOU ARE THE VERY LAST PERSON WHO COULD REVEAL MY PAST. AND WITH YOU THERE'S A PROBLEM. YOU DON'T SCARE. AND I'M NOT GOING TO HURT MY OWN SISTER, AM I?
AREN'T YOU, MATT? ME, I DON'T KNOW ANYMORE.
THAT HURTS, HOPE. NO, I'M NOT GOING TO HURT YOU. NEVER.
SO YOU HAVE THE POWER TO UNDO EVERYTHING ME AND SHADE HAVE DONE. AFTER ALL THIS, YOU CAN STILL TURN ME IN, AND I'M SCREWED.
MAY GOD FORGIVE ME.
JUST PROMISE ME YOU'LL BE A GOOD COP. PROMISE ME THAT.
OH, HOPE.
NOW LET ME GO. YOUR BUDDY GIVES ME THE HEEBIE-JEEBIES.
WOULD THERE COME A DAY WHEN I DIDN'T, MISS O'DARE.
IN YOUR DREAMS.
SEE YOU, HOPE.
YEAH, YEAH.
HEY, MATT. I DON'T LIKE HOW YOU DID IT...BUT I'M GLAD YOU DID.

YOU *LIKE* MY SISTER?

I HAVE *LEARNED* IT'S NOT WISE FOR ONE SUCH AS *ME* TO LIKE *ANYONE*...NOT IN THE WAY YOU'RE IMPLYING.

SO, YOU AND *ME?* WE'RE *NOT* FRIENDS? YOU DID *ALL* THIS OUT OF *MEMORY* FOR MY PAST INCARNATION?

I *THINK* THAT'S *BEST.*

MY *BEST* FRIEND...

...BRIAN SAVAGE.

...WHEN HE *DIED*... THAT WAS A *TERRIBLE* LOSS.

BUT *ISN'T THAT* LIFE? *LOSING* PEOPLE WE LOVE. ISN'T THAT WHAT *MAKES* US HUMAN BEINGS...*DEALING* WITH THAT?

I AM NOT A HUMAN BEING.

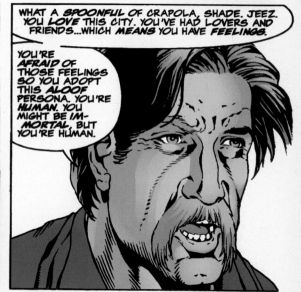

WHAT A *SPOONFUL OF CRAPOLA,* SHADE. JEEZ. YOU *LOVE* THIS CITY. YOU'VE HAD LOVERS AND FRIENDS...WHICH *MEANS* YOU HAVE *FEELINGS.*

YOU'RE *AFRAID* OF THOSE FEELINGS SO YOU ADOPT THIS *ALOOF* PERSONA. YOU'RE *HUMAN.* YOU MIGHT BE IM-*MORTAL,* BUT YOU'RE HUMAN.

ME AND YOU ARE *GONNA* BE FRIENDS, LIKE IT OR *NOT.* I'M *NOT* EVEN GOING TO ARGUE. AND I BET IF YOU *HUNG OUT* WITH ME, 'FORE LONG YOU'D BE ASKING ME FOR HOPE'S *NUMBER.*

IS IT MY *ROSE-TINTED* MEMORIES OF THAT TIME...OR ARE *YOU* BECOMING MORE LIKE BRIAN SAVAGE BY THE *MINUTE?*

WHAT WAS HE LIKE? BRIAN SAVAGE?

DO YOU LIKE *ABSINTHE?* BECAUSE IF I *START* REGALING YOU WITH TALES OF SCALPHUNTER WE MAY BE *UP* ALL NIGHT. I WOULD *PREFER* TO DO IT WITH A LITTLE ABSINTHE ON MY TONGUE.

CAN'T SAY I'VE *EVER* TRIED IT.

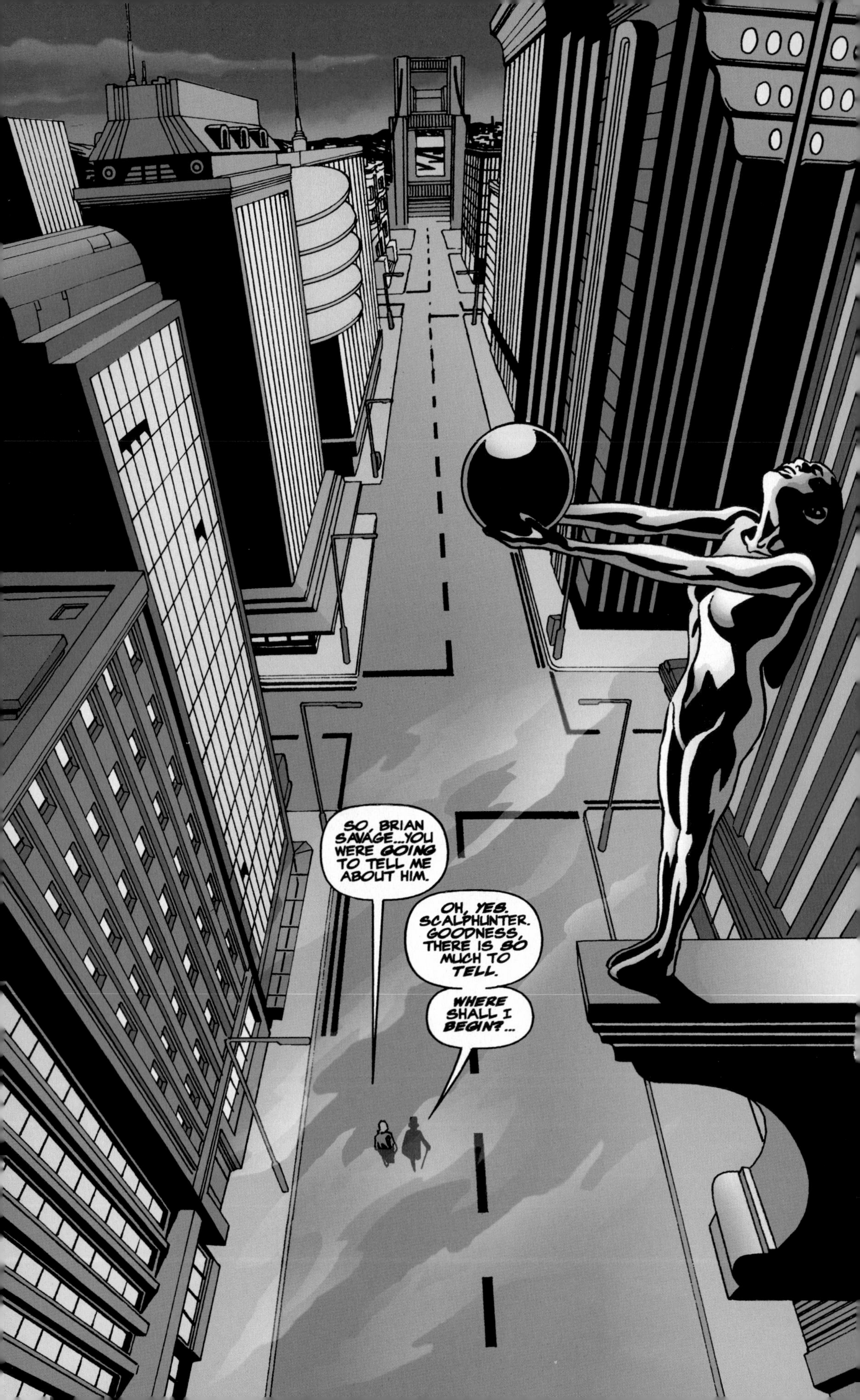
SO, BRIAN SAVAGE...YOU WERE GOING TO TELL ME ABOUT HIM.
OH, YES. SCALPHUNTER. GOODNESS, THERE IS SO MUCH TO TELL.
WHERE SHALL I BEGIN?...

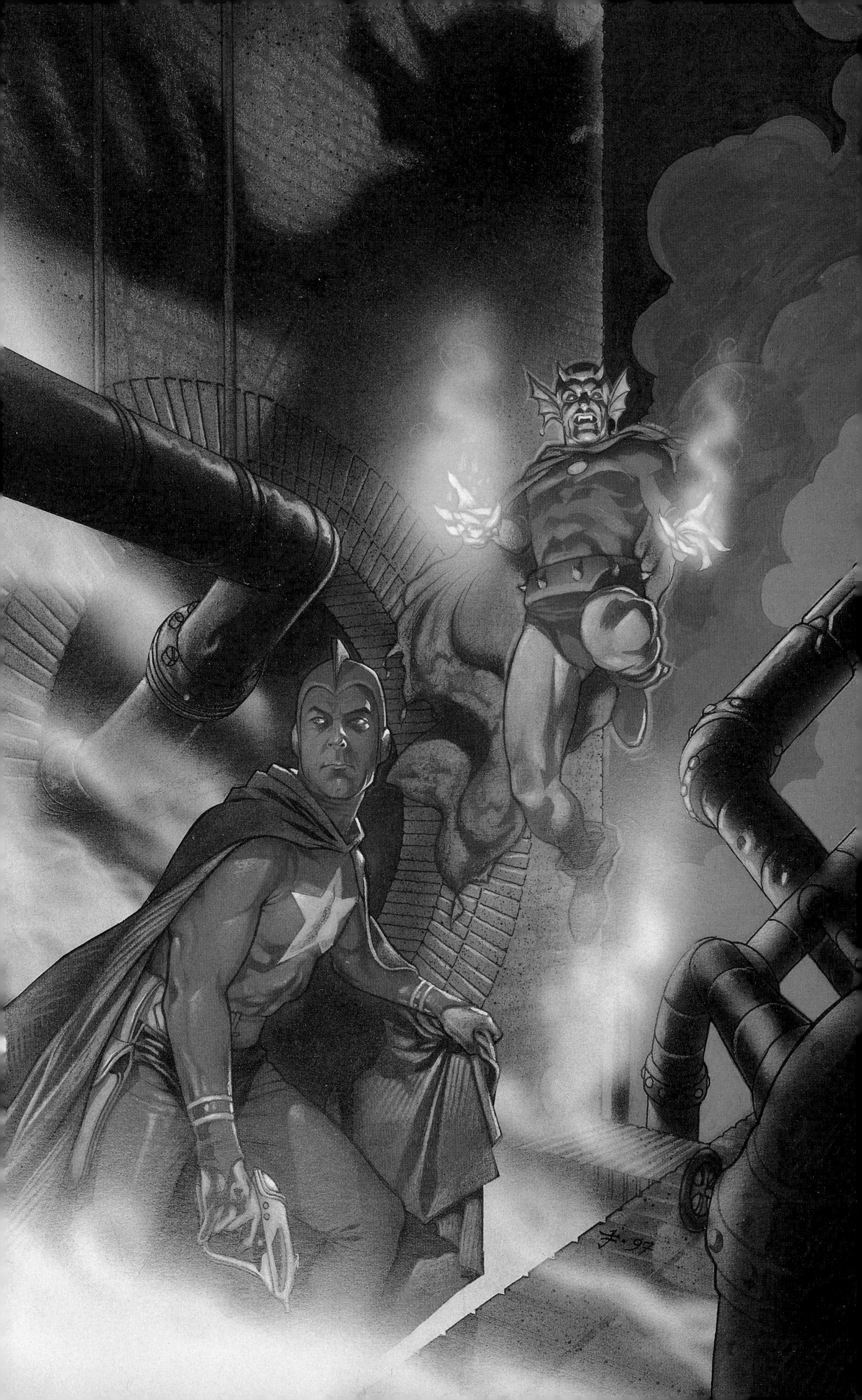

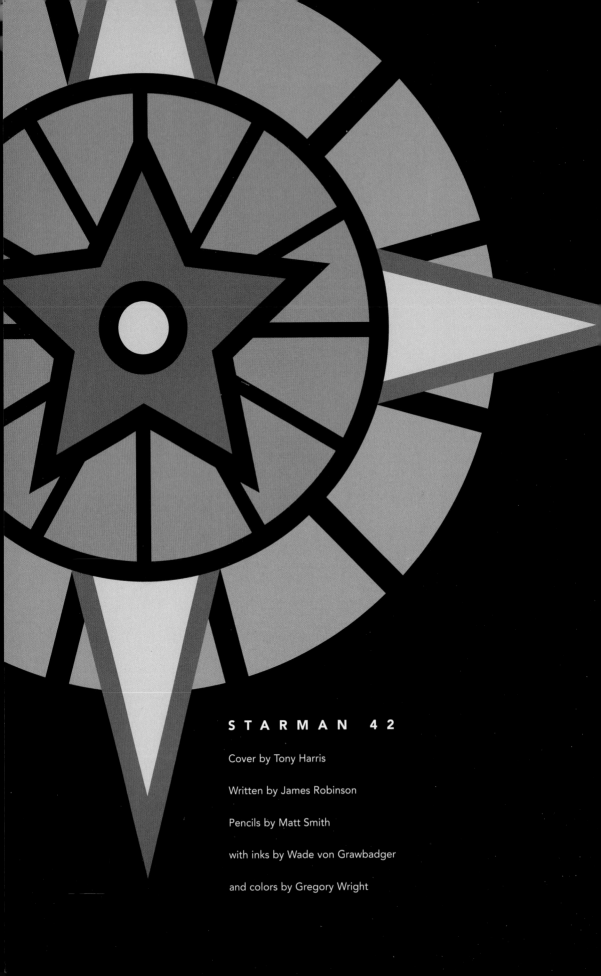

STARMAN 42

Cover by Tony Harris

Written by James Robinson

Pencils by Matt Smith

with inks by Wade von Grawbadger

and colors by Gregory Wright

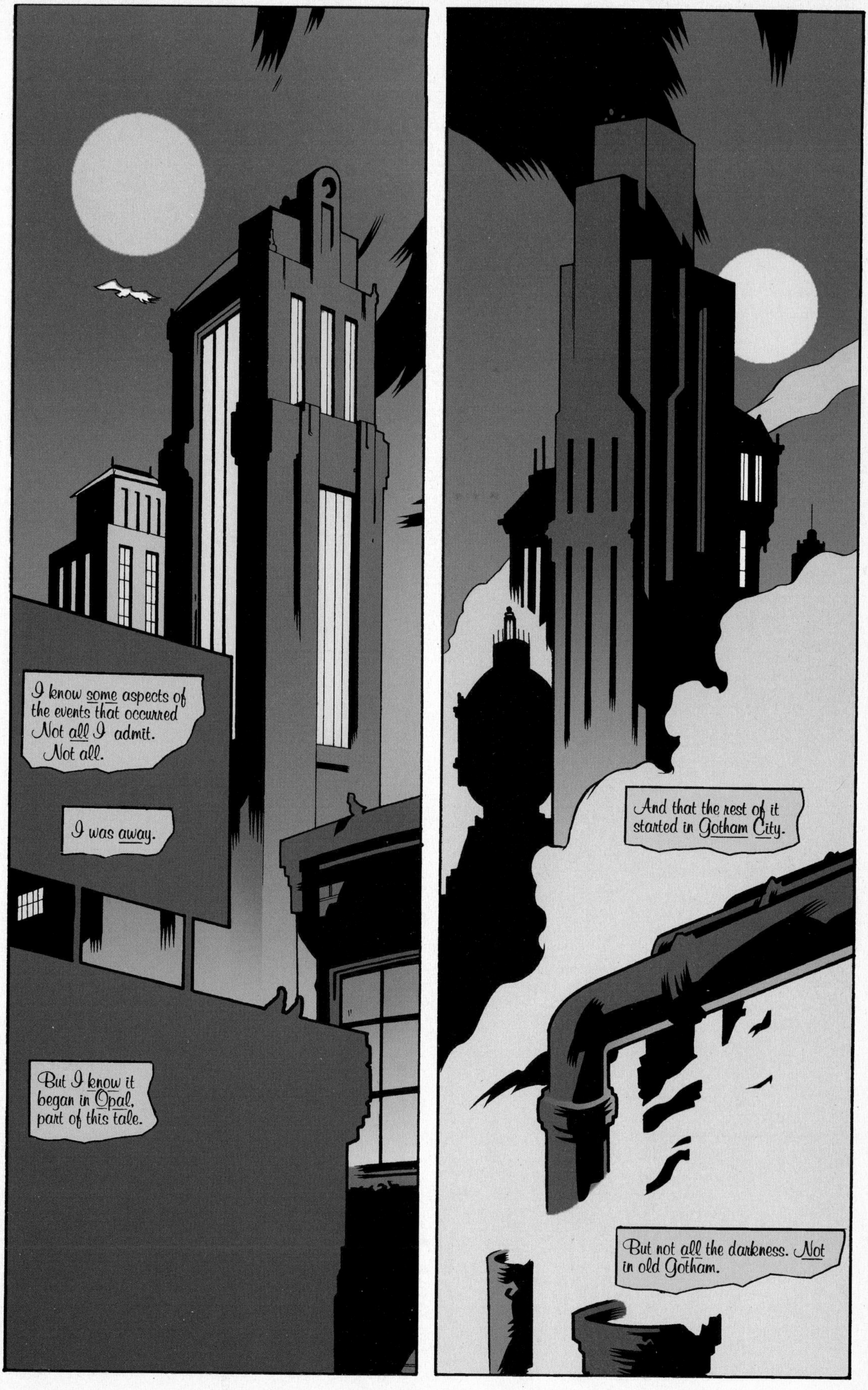
I know some aspects of the events that occurred Not all I admit. Not all.
I was away.
But I know it began in Opal, part of this tale.
And that the rest of it started in Gotham City.
But not all the darkness. Not in old Gotham.

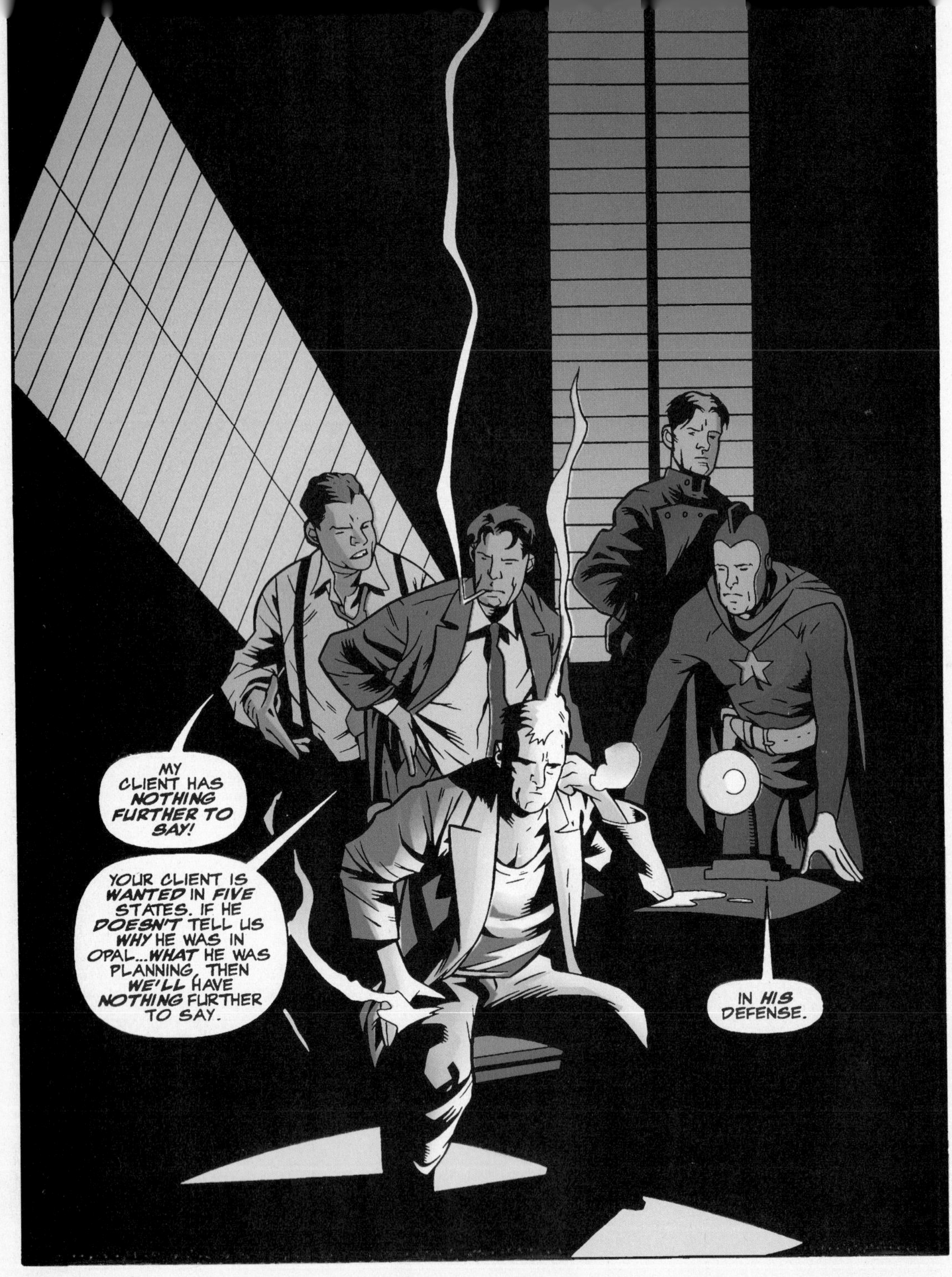
MY CLIENT HAS NOTHING FURTHER TO SAY!
YOUR CLIENT IS WANTED IN FIVE STATES. IF HE DOESN'T TELL US WHY HE WAS IN OPAL...WHAT HE WAS PLANNING, THEN WE'LL HAVE NOTHING FURTHER TO SAY.
IN HIS DEFENSE.

1944: Science and Sorcery

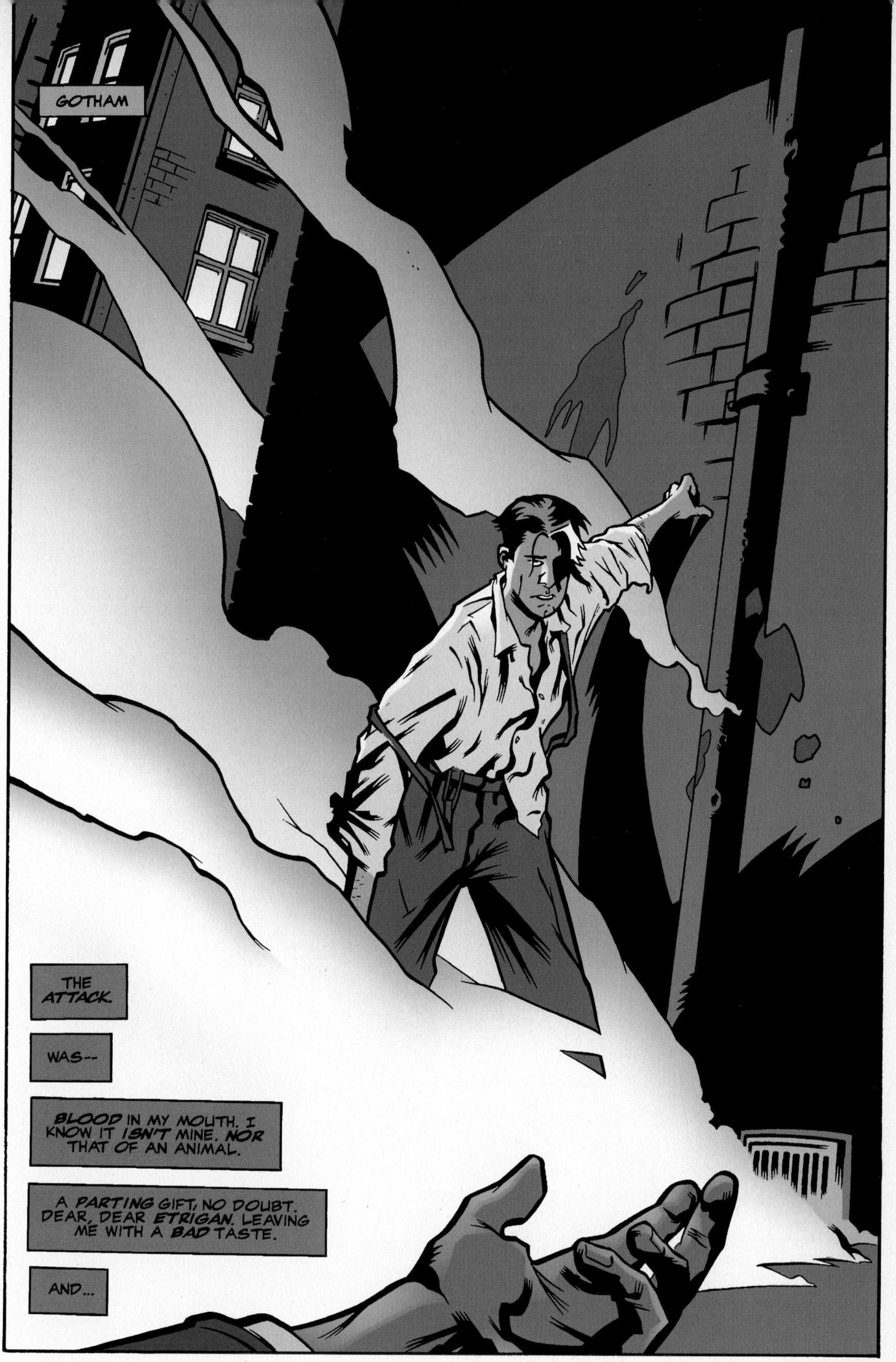
GOTHAM
THE ATTACK.
WAS--
BLOOD IN MY MOUTH. I KNOW IT ISN'T MINE. NOR THAT OF AN ANIMAL.
A PARTING GIFT, NO DOUBT. DEAR, DEAR ETRIGAN. LEAVING ME WITH A BAD TASTE.
AND...

A Tale of Times Past

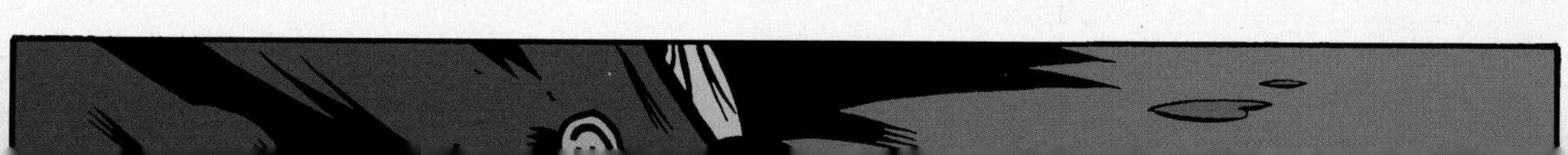

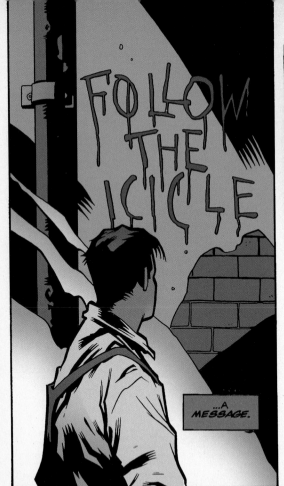

...A MESSAGE.

OPAL

I'M JUST A COURIER.

I WAS PAID TO PICK UP A PACKAGE. DELIVER IT. THEY WANTED MY POWERS AS INSURANCE THAT THE THING WOULD GET HERE.

WHERE'S THE PACKAGE?

I ALREADY HANDED IT OVER TO A GUY IN BURNLEY PARK. IT WAS HEAVY LIKE A BOOK, THOUGH.

WHO HIRED YOU?

THEY SAID NO NAMES. ONLY NAME INTERESTED ME WAS BEN FRANKLIN. FIFTY OF HIM.

SO YOU CAPTURED SOME FIFTH COLUMNISTS, ALAN.

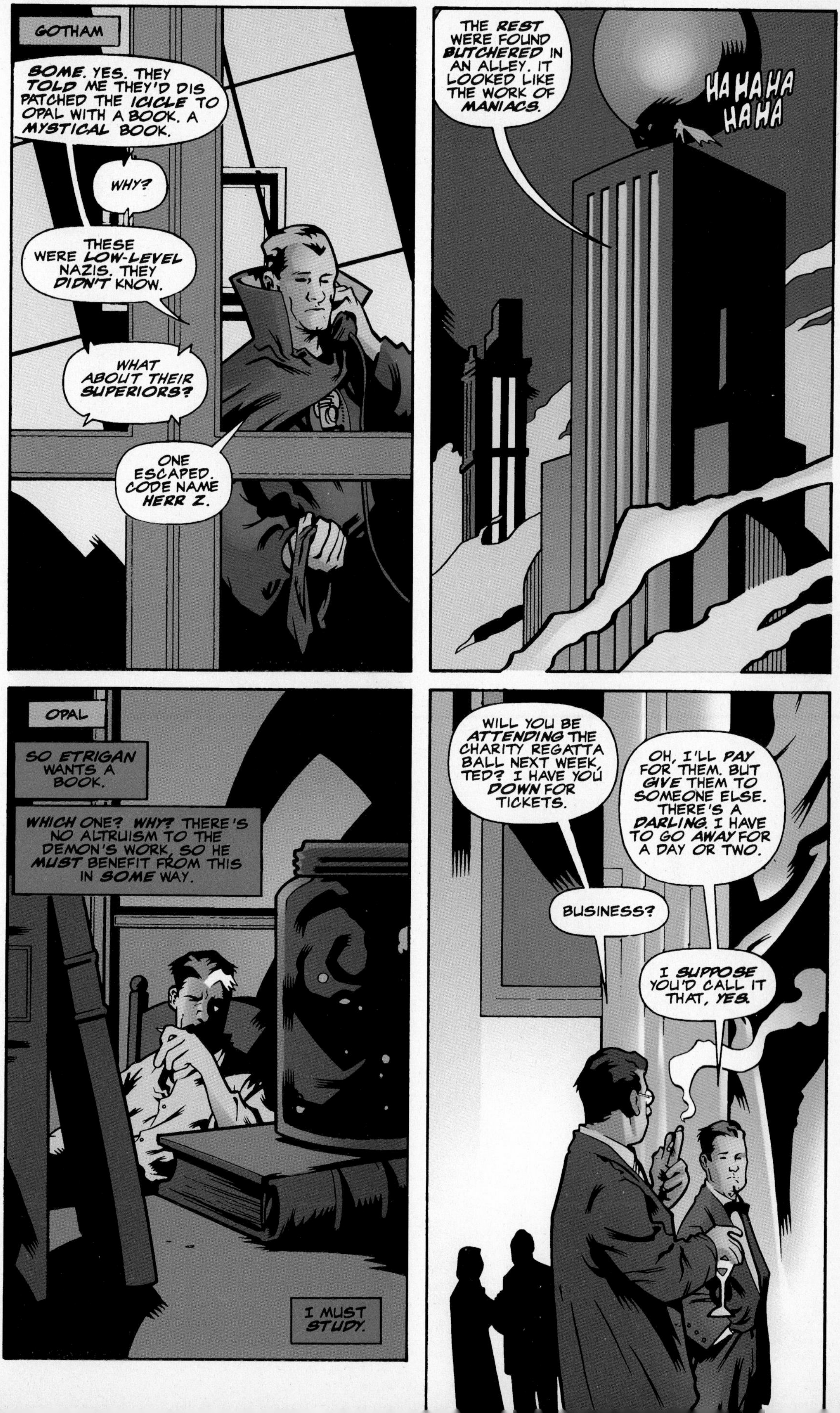
GOTHAM
SOME. YES. THEY TOLD ME THEY'D DIS PATCHED THE ICICLE TO OPAL WITH A BOOK. A MYSTICAL BOOK.
WHY?
THESE WERE LOW-LEVEL NAZIS. THEY DIDN'T KNOW.
WHAT ABOUT THEIR SUPERIORS?
ONE ESCAPED. CODE NAME HERR Z.
THE REST WERE FOUND BUTCHERED IN AN ALLEY. IT LOOKED LIKE THE WORK OF MANIACS.
HA HA HA HA HA
OPAL
SO ETRIGAN WANTS A BOOK.
WHICH ONE? WHY? THERE'S NO ALTRUISM TO THE DEMON'S WORK, SO HE MUST BENEFIT FROM THIS IN SOME WAY.
I MUST STUDY.
WILL YOU BE ATTENDING THE CHARITY REGATTA BALL NEXT WEEK, TED? I HAVE YOU DOWN FOR TICKETS.
OH, I'LL PAY FOR THEM. BUT GIVE THEM TO SOMEONE ELSE. THERE'S A DARLING. I HAVE TO GO AWAY FOR A DAY OR TWO.
BUSINESS?
I SUPPOSE YOU'D CALL IT THAT, YES.

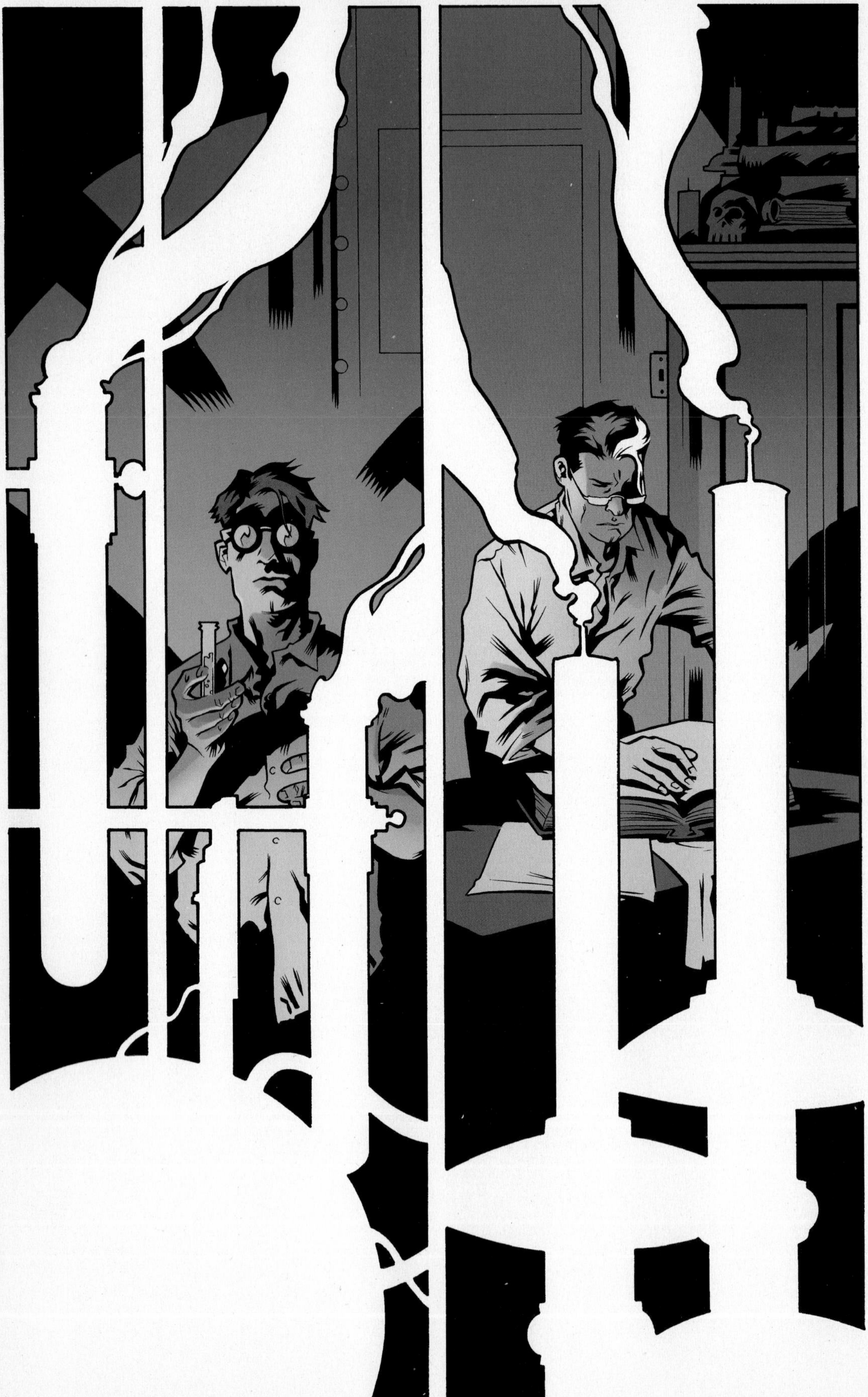

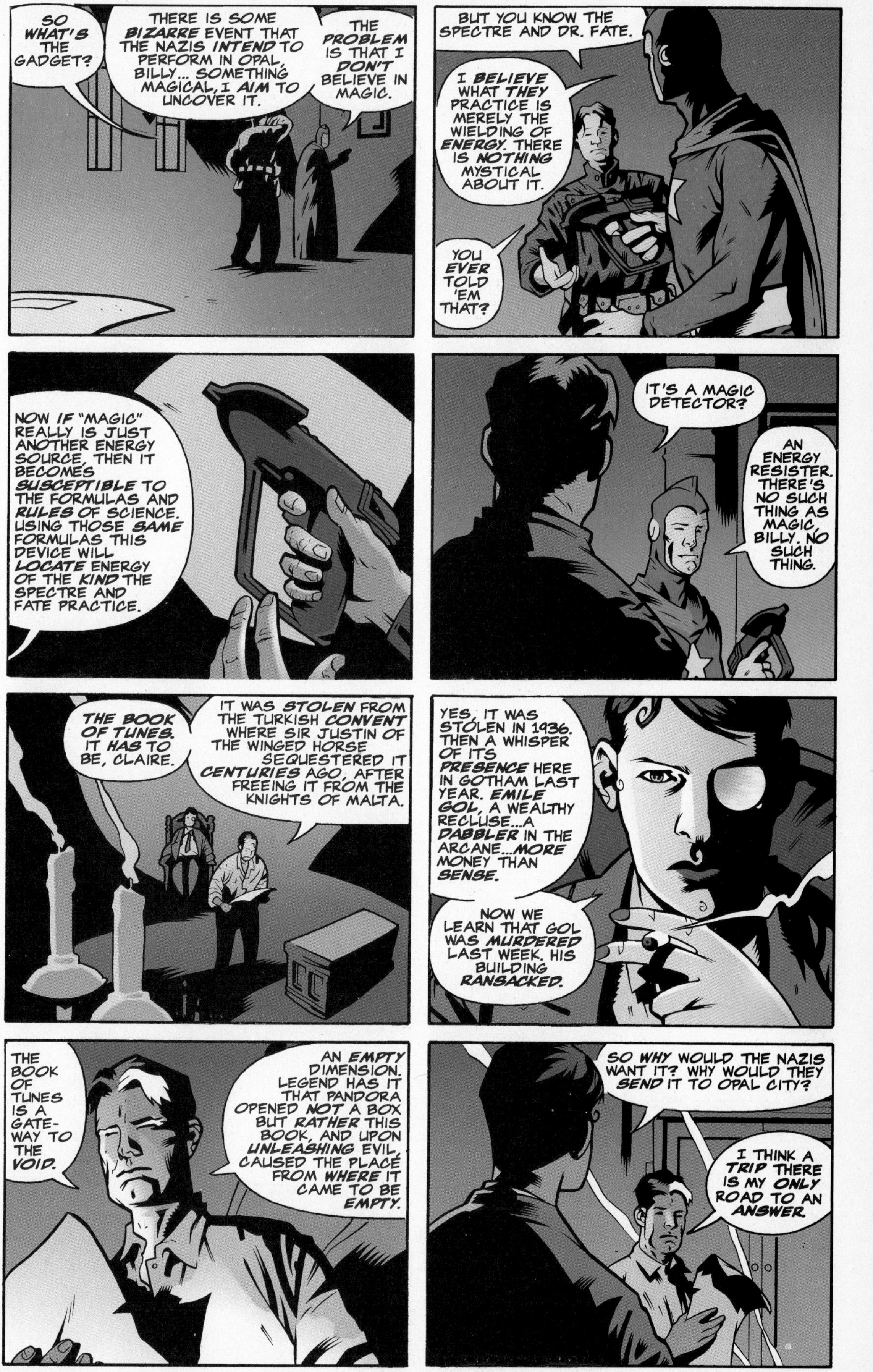
SO WHAT'S THE GADGET?
THERE IS SOME BIZARRE EVENT THAT THE NAZIS INTEND TO PERFORM IN OPAL, BILLY... SOMETHING MAGICAL. I AIM TO UNCOVER IT.
THE PROBLEM IS THAT I DON'T BELIEVE IN MAGIC.
BUT YOU KNOW THE SPECTRE AND DR. FATE.
I BELIEVE WHAT THEY PRACTICE IS MERELY THE WIELDING OF ENERGY. THERE IS NOTHING MYSTICAL ABOUT IT.
YOU EVER TOLD 'EM THAT?
NOW IF "MAGIC" REALLY IS JUST ANOTHER ENERGY SOURCE, THEN IT BECOMES SUSCEPTIBLE TO THE FORMULAS AND RULES OF SCIENCE. USING THOSE SAME FORMULAS THIS DEVICE WILL LOCATE ENERGY OF THE KIND THE SPECTRE AND FATE PRACTICE.
IT'S A MAGIC DETECTOR?
AN ENERGY RESISTER. THERE'S NO SUCH THING AS MAGIC, BILLY. NO SUCH THING.
THE BOOK OF TUNES. IT HAS TO BE, CLAIRE.
IT WAS STOLEN FROM THE TURKISH CONVENT WHERE SIR JUSTIN OF THE WINGED HORSE SEQUESTERED IT CENTURIES AGO, AFTER FREEING IT FROM THE KNIGHTS OF MALTA.
YES, IT WAS STOLEN IN 1936. THEN A WHISPER OF ITS PRESENCE HERE IN GOTHAM LAST YEAR. EMILE GOL, A WEALTHY RECLUSE...A DABBLER IN THE ARCANE...MORE MONEY THAN SENSE.
NOW WE LEARN THAT GOL WAS MURDERED LAST WEEK. HIS BUILDING RANSACKED.
THE BOOK OF TUNES IS A GATE-WAY TO THE VOID.
AN EMPTY DIMENSION. LEGEND HAS IT THAT PANDORA OPENED NOT A BOX BUT RATHER THIS BOOK, AND UPON UNLEASHING EVIL, CAUSED THE PLACE FROM WHERE IT CAME TO BE EMPTY.
SO WHY WOULD THE NAZIS WANT IT? WHY WOULD THEY SEND IT TO OPAL CITY?
I THINK A TRIP THERE IS MY ONLY ROAD TO AN ANSWER.

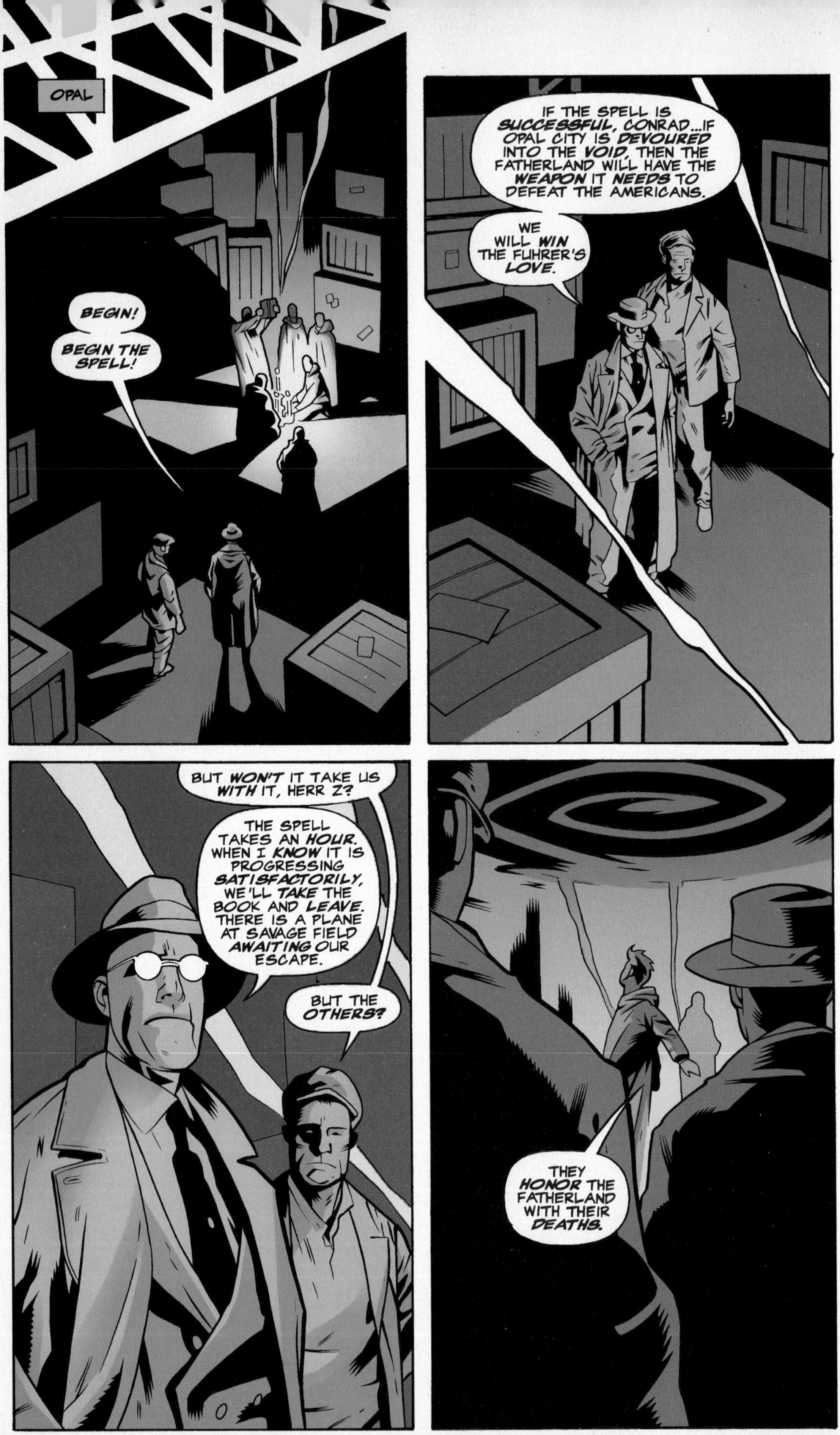
OPAL
BEGIN!
BEGIN THE SPELL!
IF THE SPELL IS SUCCESSFUL, CONRAD...IF OPAL CITY IS DEVOURED INTO THE VOID, THEN THE FATHERLAND WILL HAVE THE WEAPON IT NEEDS TO DEFEAT THE AMERICANS.
WE WILL WIN THE FUHRER'S LOVE.
BUT WON'T IT TAKE US WITH IT, HERR Z?
THE SPELL TAKES AN HOUR. WHEN I KNOW IT IS PROGRESSING SATISFACTORILY, WE'LL TAKE THE BOOK AND LEAVE. THERE IS A PLANE AT SAVAGE FIELD AWAITING OUR ESCAPE.
BUT THE OTHERS?
THEY HONOR THE FATHERLAND WITH THEIR DEATHS.

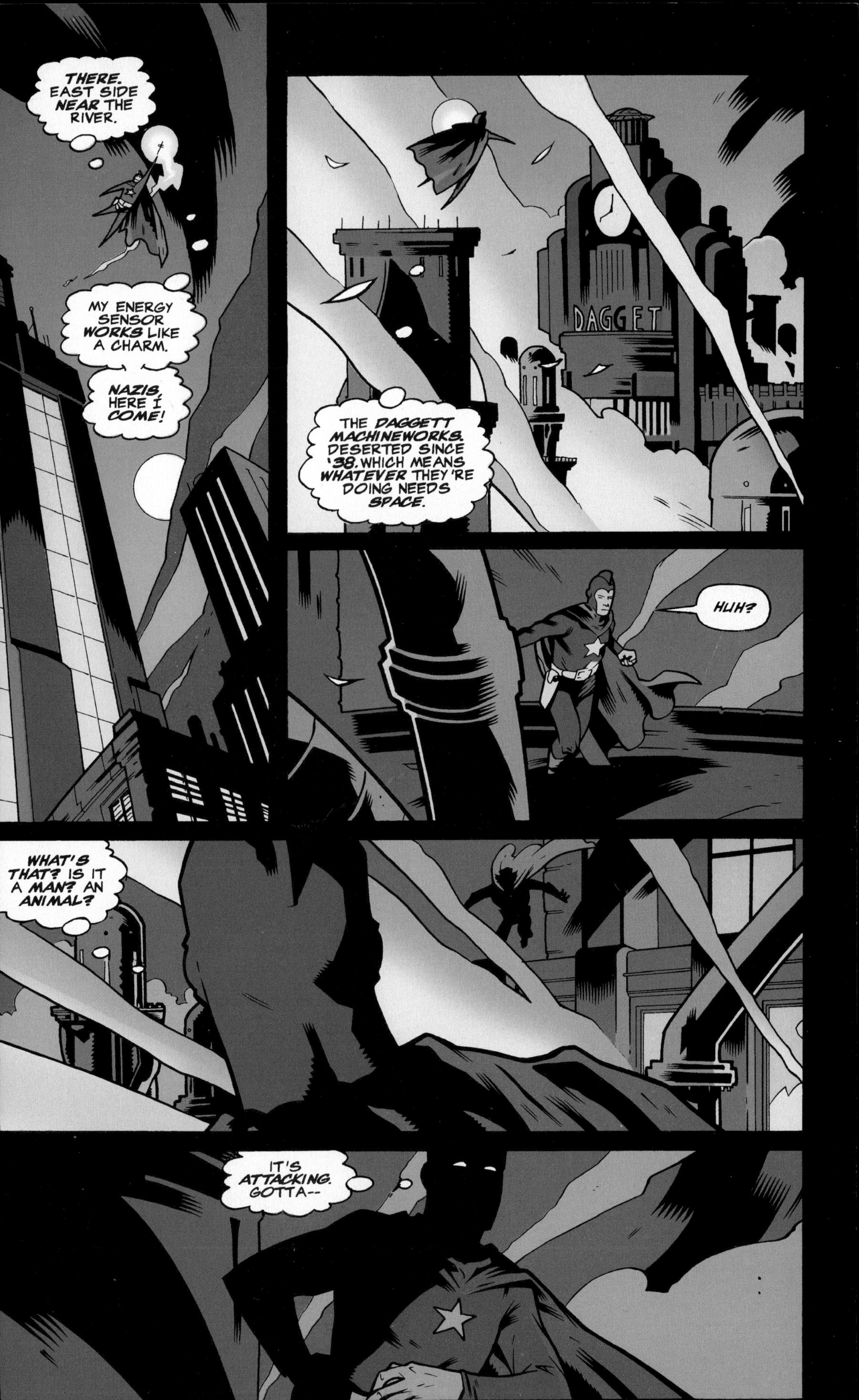
THERE. EAST SIDE NEAR THE RIVER.
MY ENERGY SENSOR WORKS LIKE A CHARM.
NAZIS, HERE I COME!
DAGGET
THE DAGGETT MACHINEWORKS. DESERTED SINCE '38. WHICH MEANS WHATEVER THEY'RE DOING NEEDS SPACE.
HUH?
WHAT'S THAT? IS IT A MAN? AN ANIMAL?
IT'S ATTACKING. GOTTA--

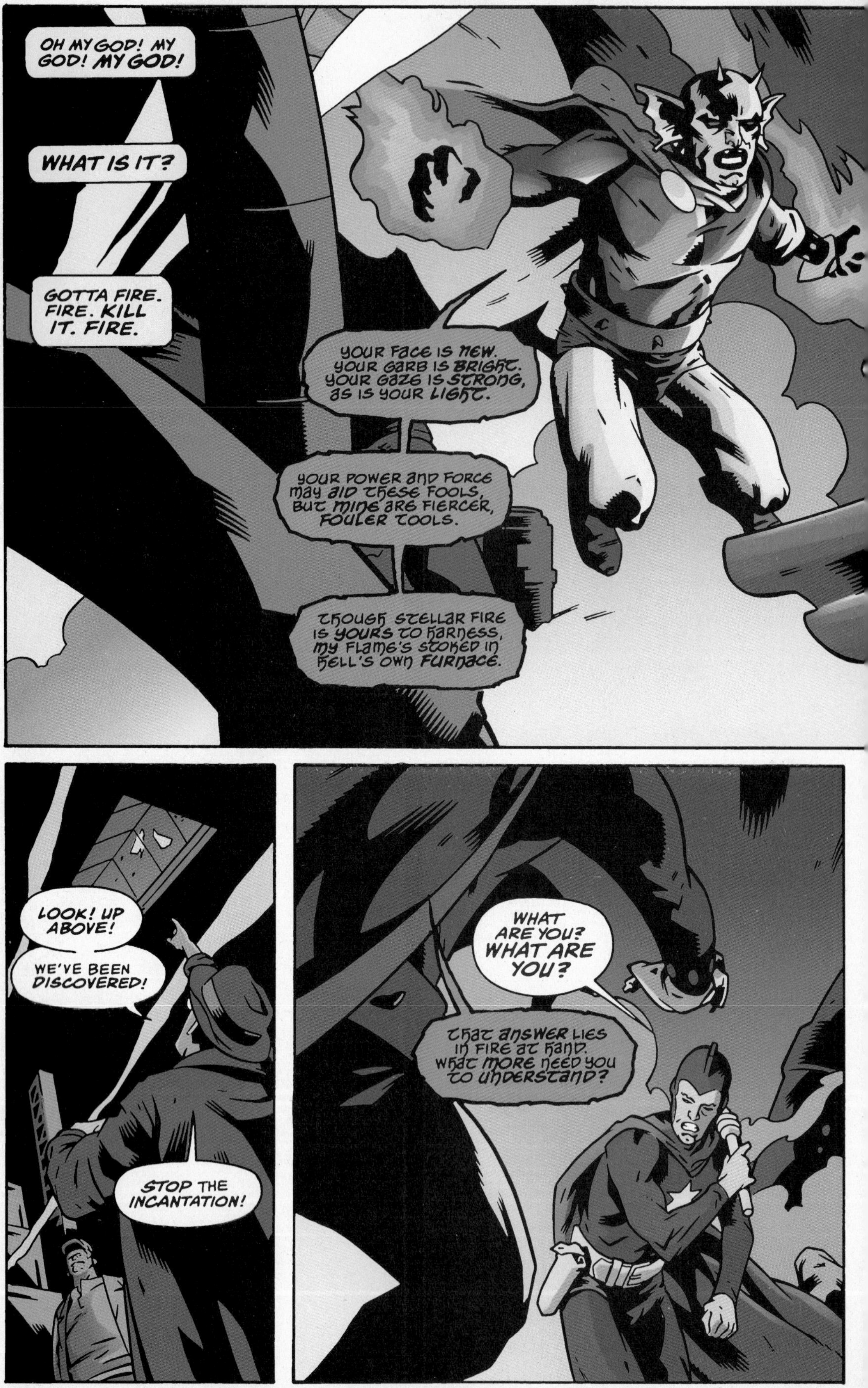
OH MY GOD! MY GOD! MY GOD!
WHAT IS IT?
GOTTA FIRE. FIRE. KILL IT. FIRE.
YOUR FACE IS NEW. YOUR GARB IS BRIGHT. YOUR GAZE IS STRONG, AS IS YOUR LIGHT.
YOUR POWER AND FORCE MAY AID THESE FOOLS, BUT MINE ARE FIERCER, FOULER TOOLS.
THOUGH STELLAR FIRE IS YOURS TO HARNESS, MY FLAME'S STOKED IN HELL'S OWN FURNACE.
LOOK! UP ABOVE!
WE'VE BEEN DISCOVERED!
STOP THE INCANTATION!
WHAT ARE YOU? WHAT ARE YOU?
THAT ANSWER LIES IN FIRE AT HAND. WHAT MORE NEED YOU TO UNDERSTAND?

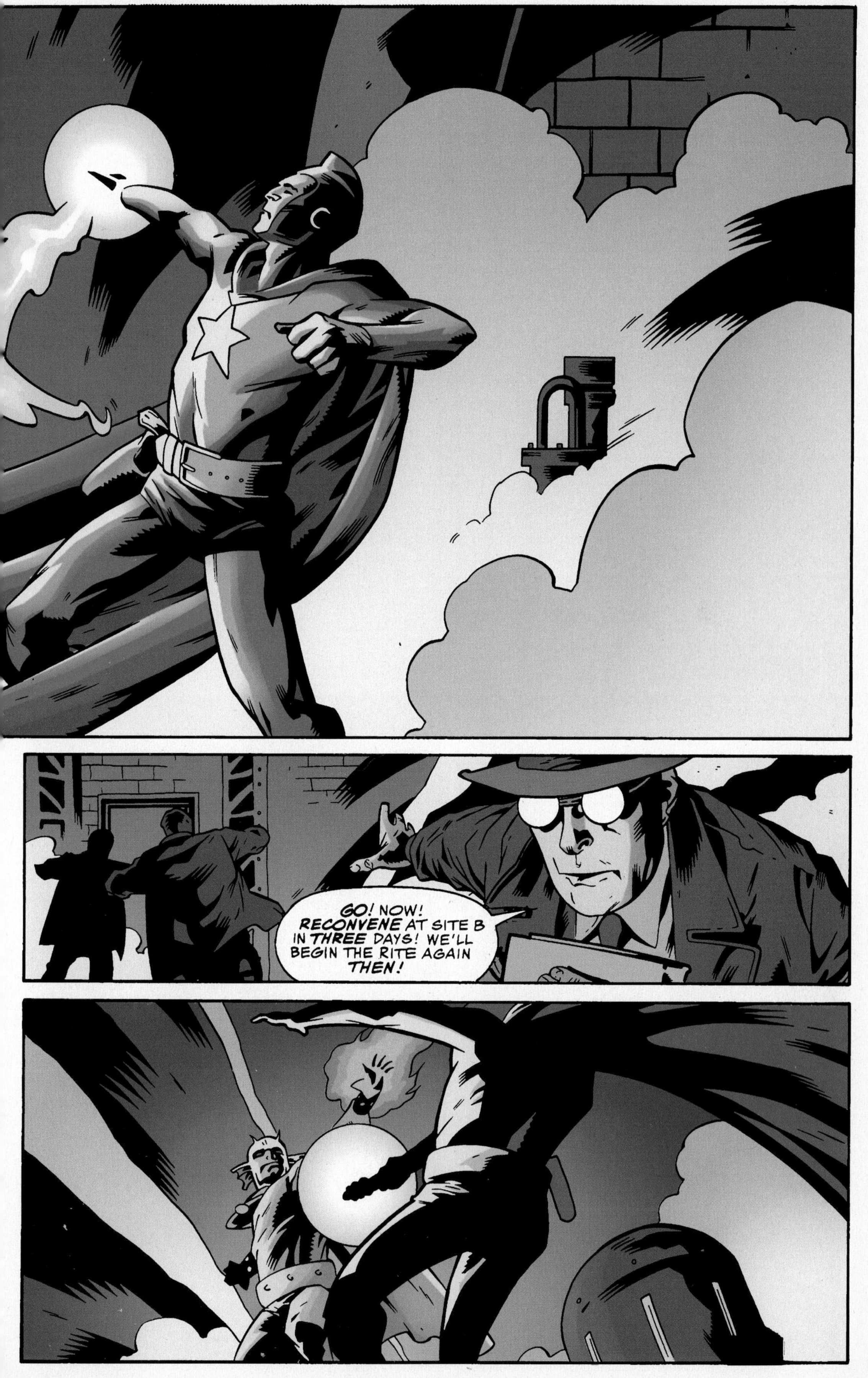
GO! NOW! RECONVENE AT SITE B IN THREE DAYS! WE'LL BEGIN THE RITE AGAIN THEN!

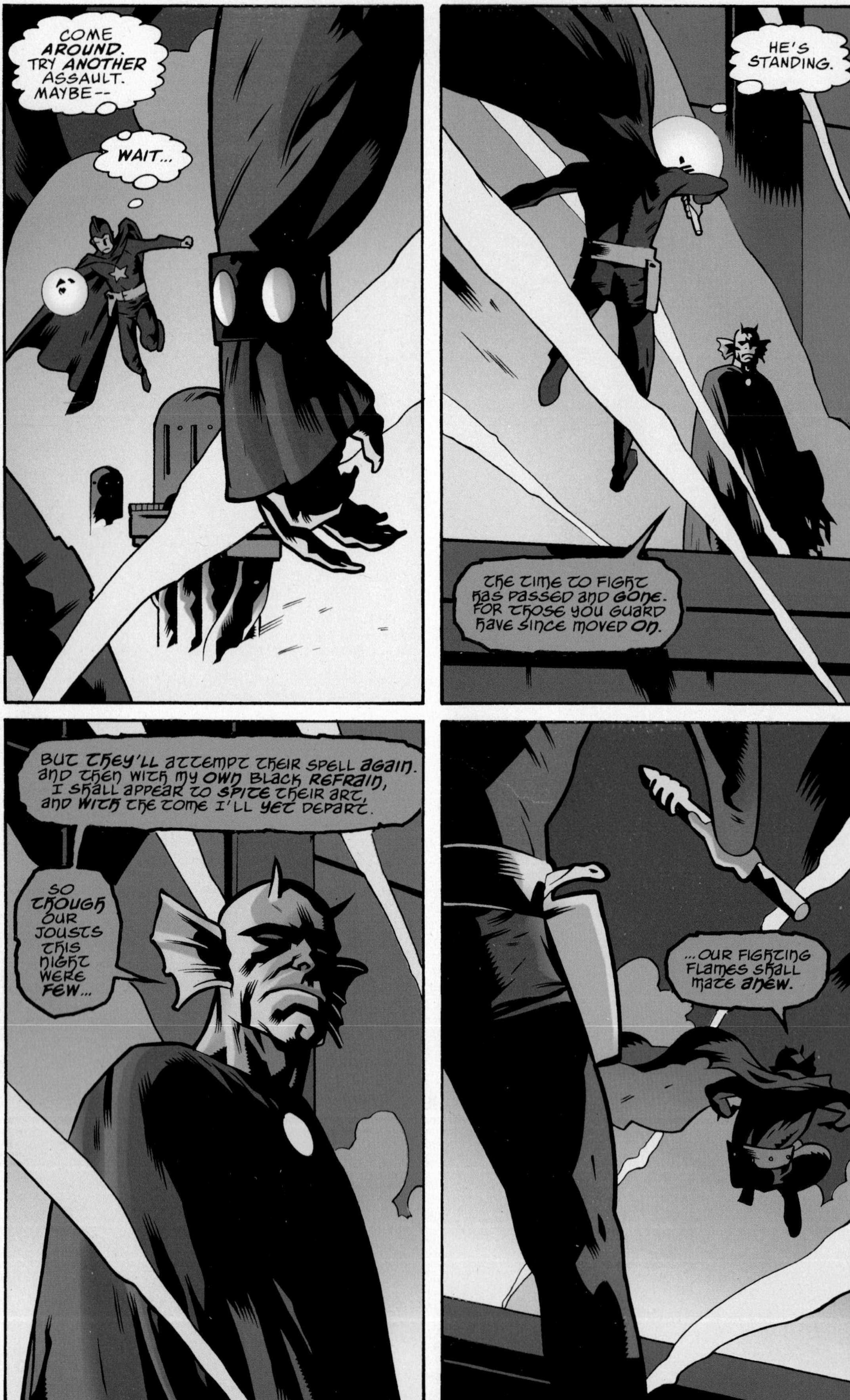
COME AROUND. TRY ANOTHER ASSAULT. MAYBE--
WAIT...
HE'S STANDING.
THE TIME TO FIGHT HAS PASSED AND GONE. FOR THOSE YOU GUARD HAVE SINCE MOVED ON.
BUT THEY'LL ATTEMPT THEIR SPELL AGAIN. AND THEN WITH MY OWN BLACK REFRAIN, I SHALL APPEAR TO SPITE THEIR ART, AND WITH THE TOME I'LL YET DEPART.
SO THOUGH OUR JOUSTS THIS NIGHT WERE FEW...
...OUR FIGHTING FLAMES SHALL MATE ANEW.

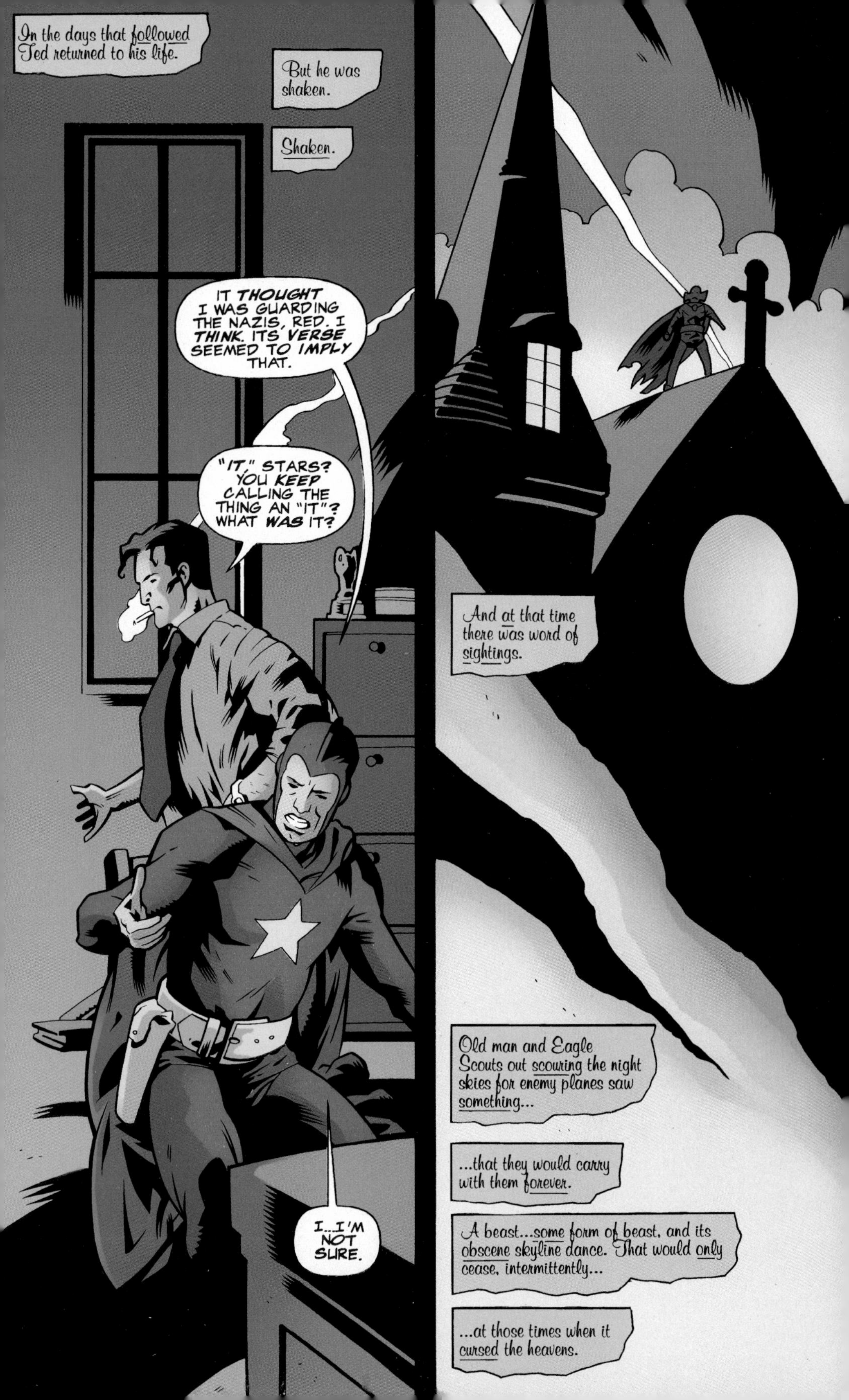

In the days that followed Ted returned to his life.
But he was shaken.
Shaken.
IT THOUGHT I WAS GUARDING THE NAZIS, RED. I THINK. ITS VERSE SEEMED TO IMPLY THAT.
"IT," STARS? YOU KEEP CALLING THE THING AN "IT"? WHAT WAS IT?
I...I'M NOT SURE.
And at that time there was word of sightings.
Old man and Eagle Scouts out scouring the night skies for enemy planes saw something...
...that they would carry with them forever.
A beast...some form of beast, and its obscene skyline dance. That would only cease, intermittently...
...at those times when it cursed the heavens.

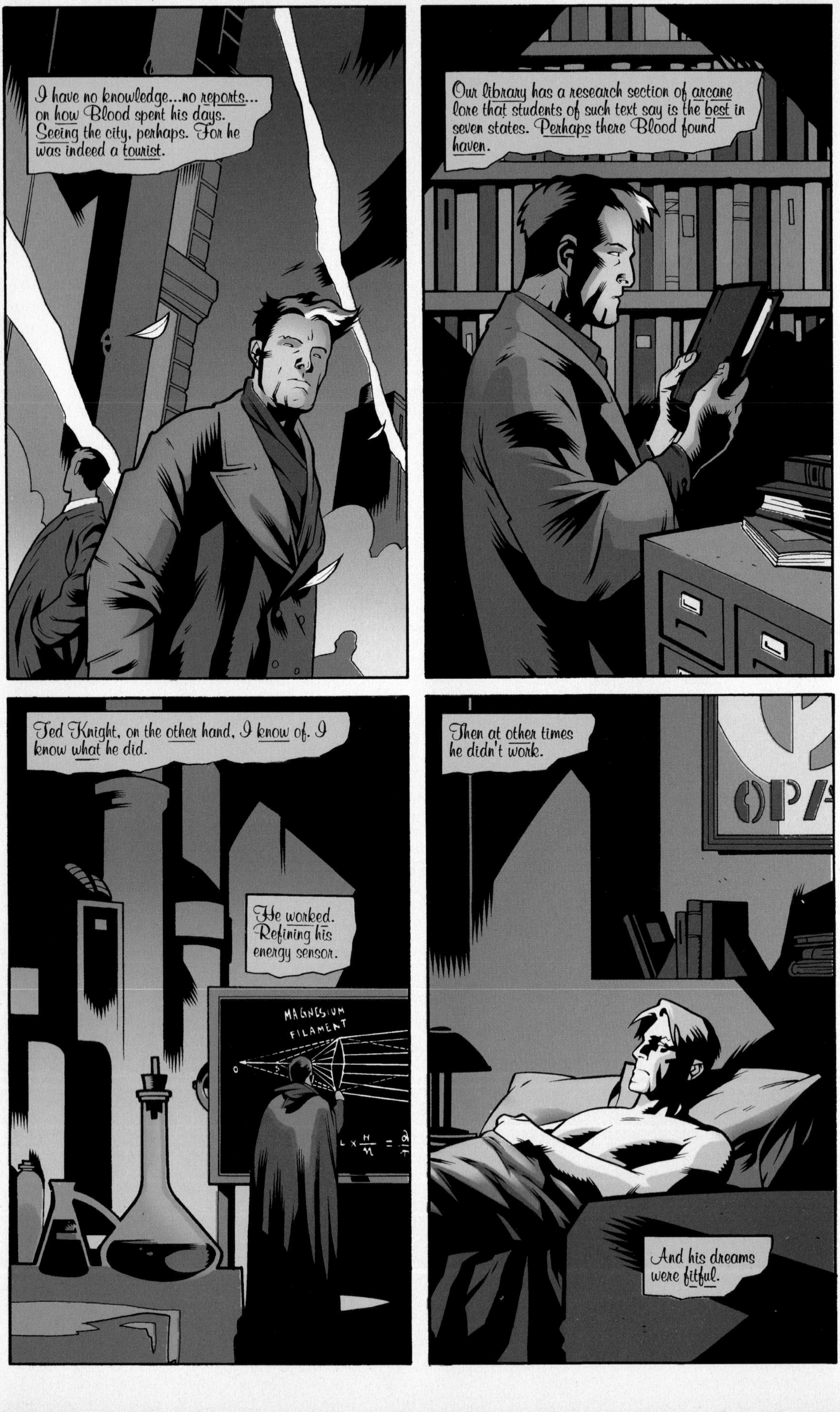
I have no knowledge...no reports... on how Blood spent his days. Seeing the city, perhaps. For he was indeed a tourist.
Our library has a research section of arcane lore that students of such text say is the best in seven states. Perhaps there Blood found haven.
Ted Knight, on the other hand, I know of. I know what he did.
He worked. Refining his energy sensor.
MAGNESIUM FILAMENT
Then at other times he didn't work.
And his dreams were fitful.

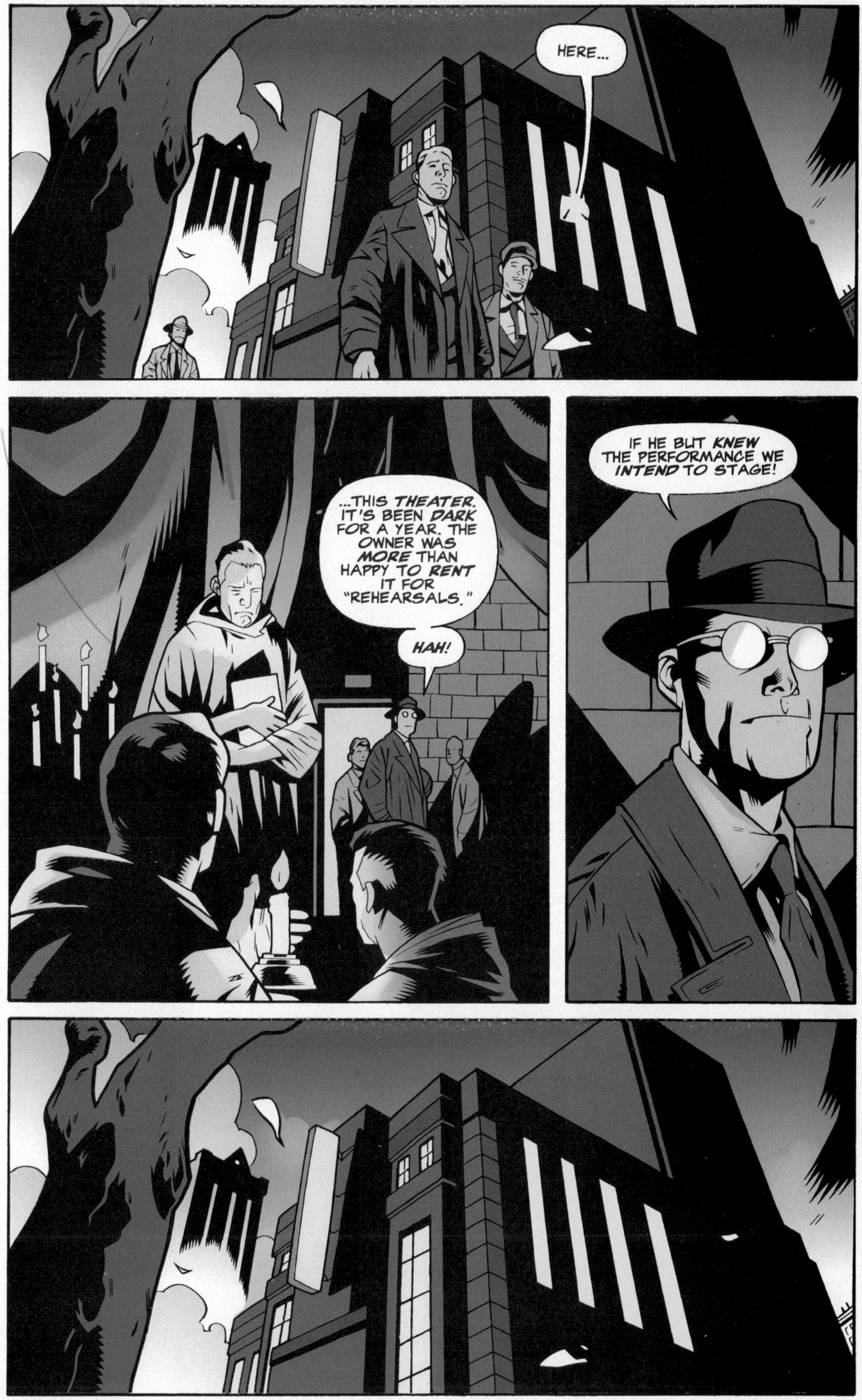
HERE...
...THIS THEATER. IT'S BEEN DARK FOR A YEAR. THE OWNER WAS MORE THAN HAPPY TO RENT IT FOR "REHEARSALS."
HAH!
IF HE BUT KNEW THE PERFORMANCE WE INTEND TO STAGE!

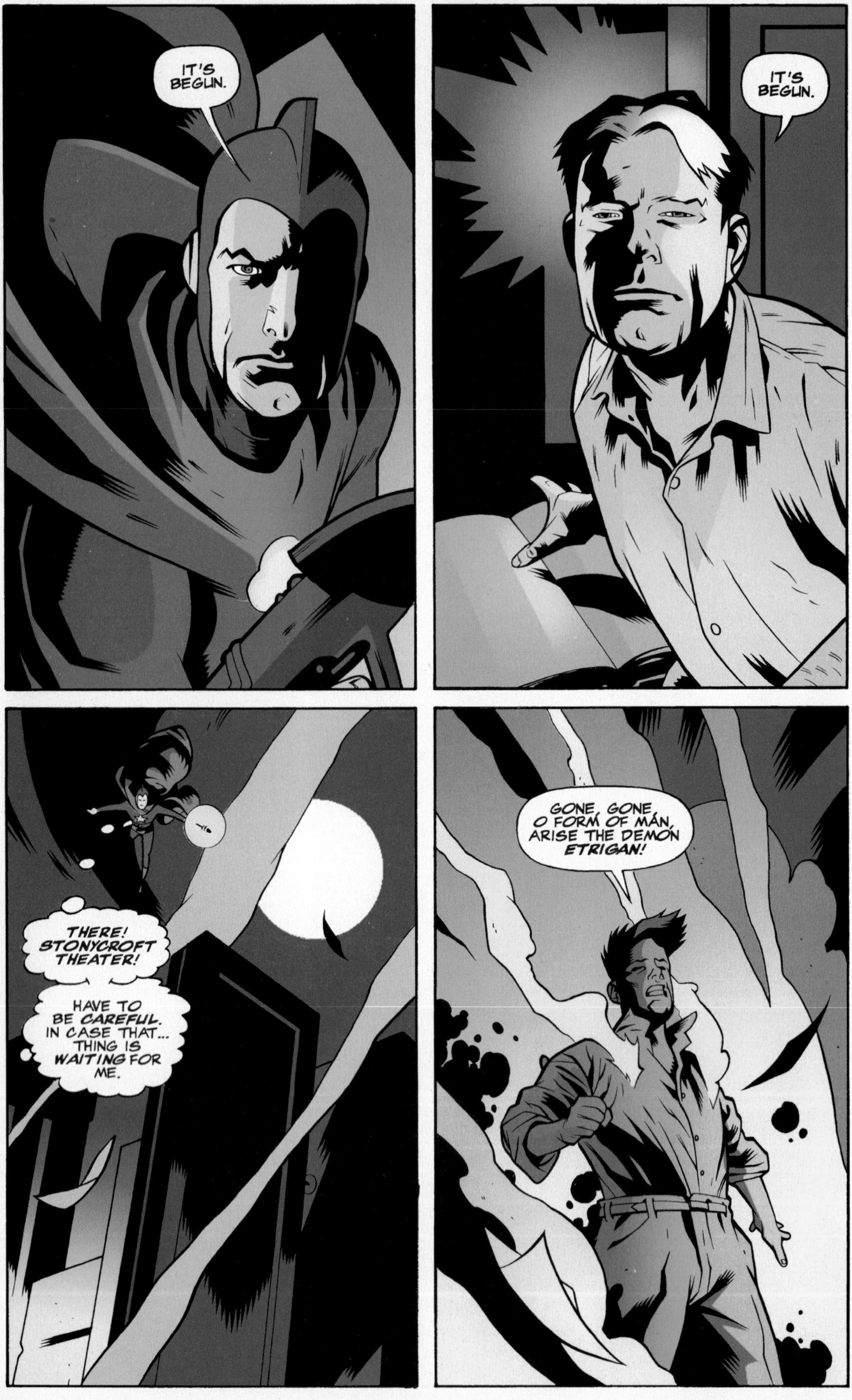
IT'S BEGUN.
IT'S BEGUN.
THERE! STONYCROFT THEATER!
HAVE TO BE CAREFUL. IN CASE THAT... THING IS WAITING FOR ME.
GONE, GONE O FORM OF MÁN, ARISE THE DEMON ETRIGAN!

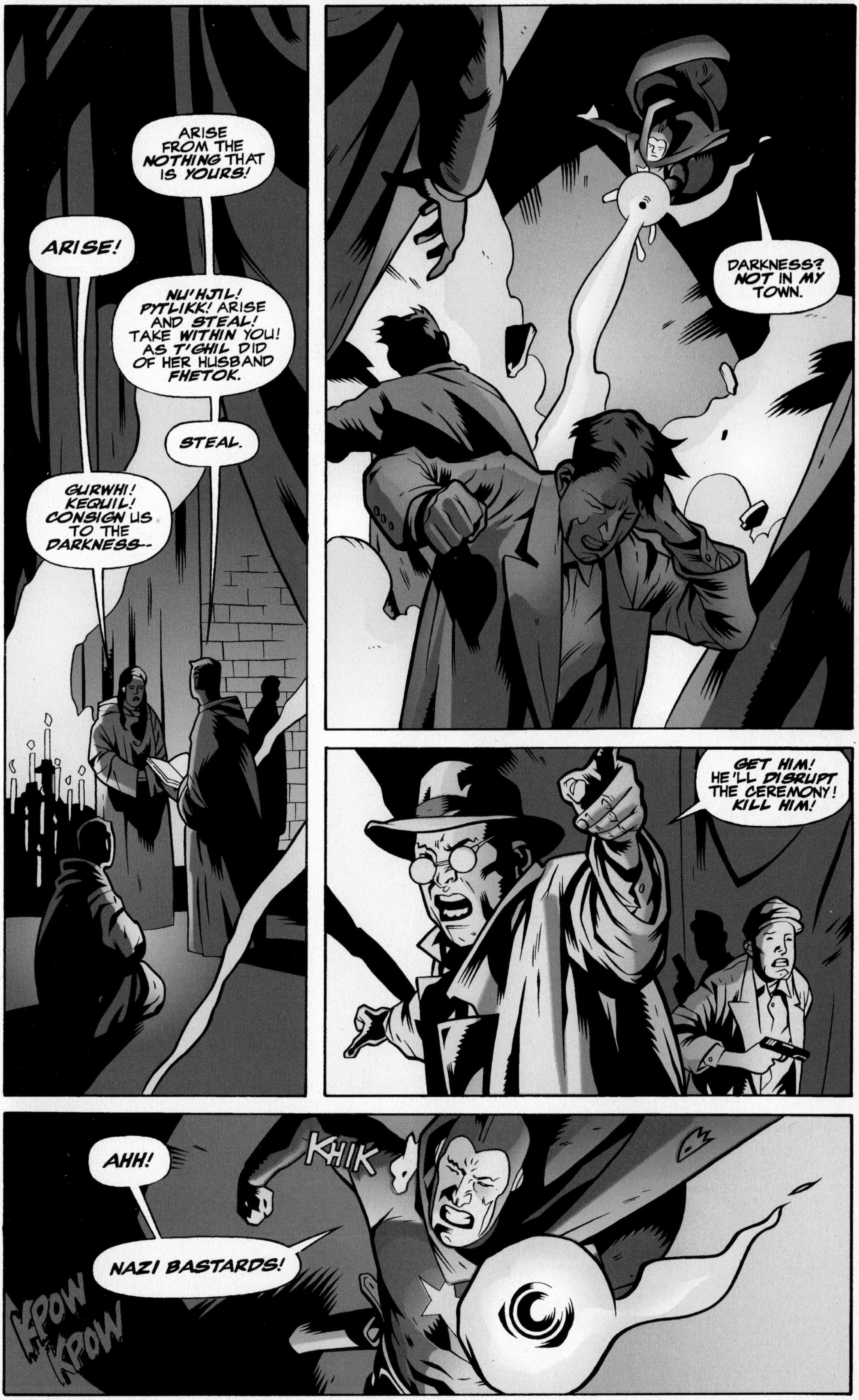
ARISE!
ARISE FROM THE NOTHING THAT IS YOURS!
NU'HJIL! PYTLIKK! ARISE AND STEAL! TAKE WITHIN YOU! AS T'GHIL DID OF HER HUSBAND FHETOK.
STEAL.
GURWHI! KEQUIL! CONSIGN US TO THE DARKNESS--
DARKNESS? NOT IN MY TOWN.
GET HIM! HE'LL DISRUPT THE CEREMONY! KILL HIM!
KHIK
AHH!
NAZI BASTARDS!
KPOW KPOW

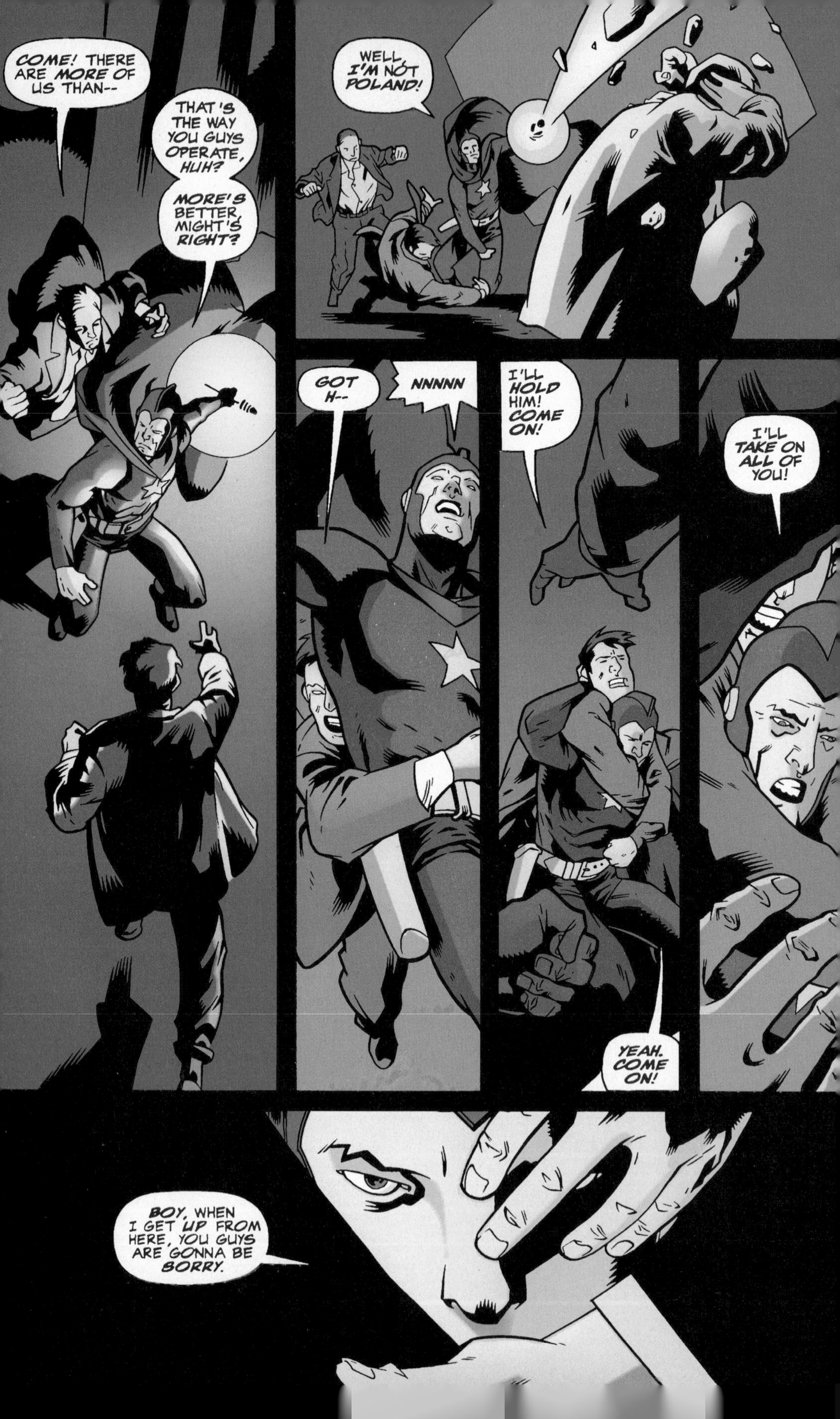
COME! THERE ARE MORE OF US THAN--
THAT'S THE WAY YOU GUYS OPERATE, HUH?
MORE'S BETTER, MIGHT'S RIGHT?
WELL, I'M NOT POLAND!
GOT H--
NNNNN
I'LL HOLD HIM! COME ON!
I'LL TAKE ON ALL OF YOU!
YEAH. COME ON!
BOY, WHEN I GET UP FROM HERE, YOU GUYS ARE GONNA BE SORRY.

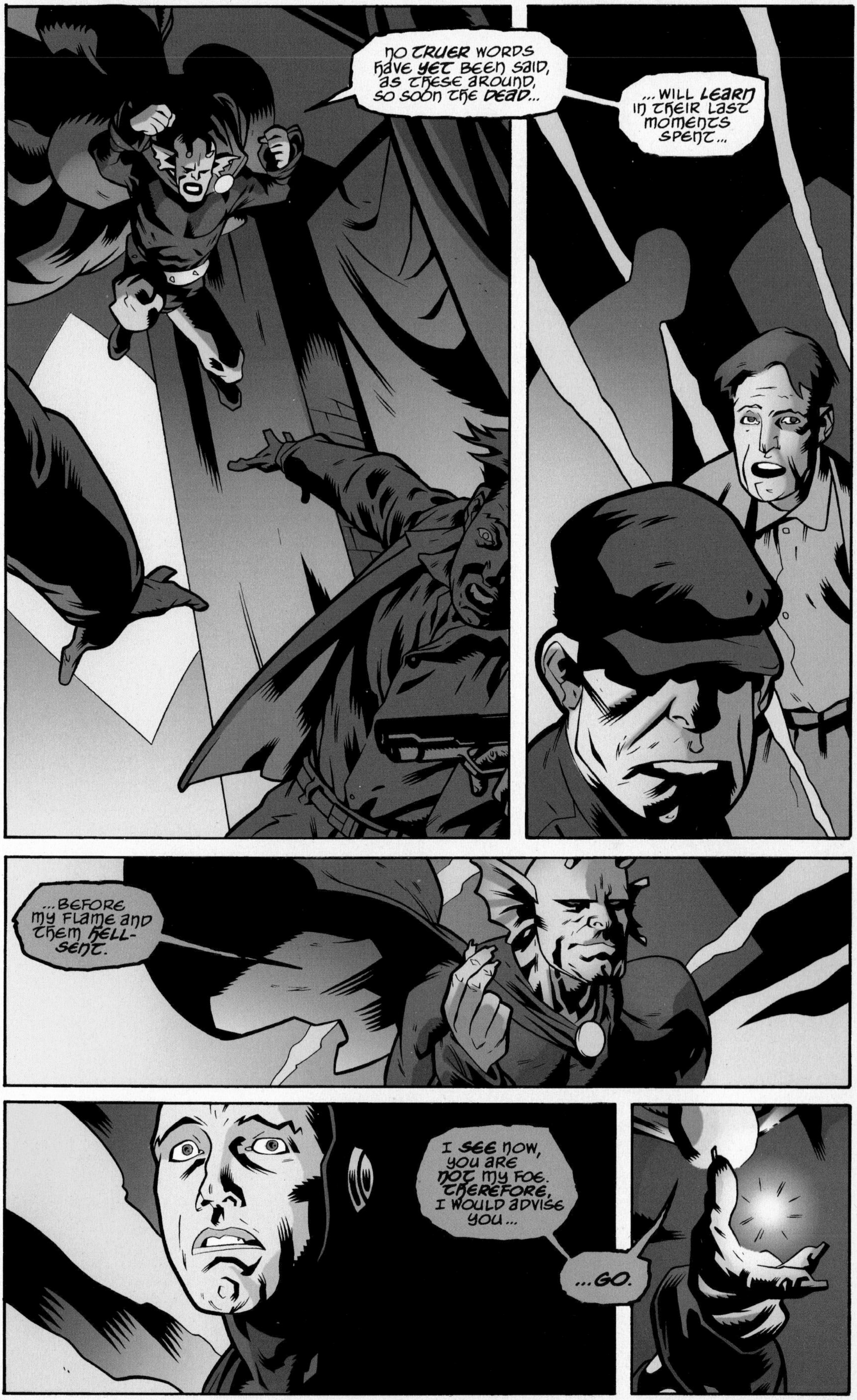

NO TRUER WORDS HAVE YET BEEN SAID, AS THESE AROUND, SO SOON THE DEAD...
...WILL LEARN IN THEIR LAST MOMENTS SPENT...
...BEFORE MY FLAME AND THEM HELL-SENT.
I SEE NOW, YOU ARE NOT MY FOE. THEREFORE, I WOULD ADVISE YOU...
...GO.

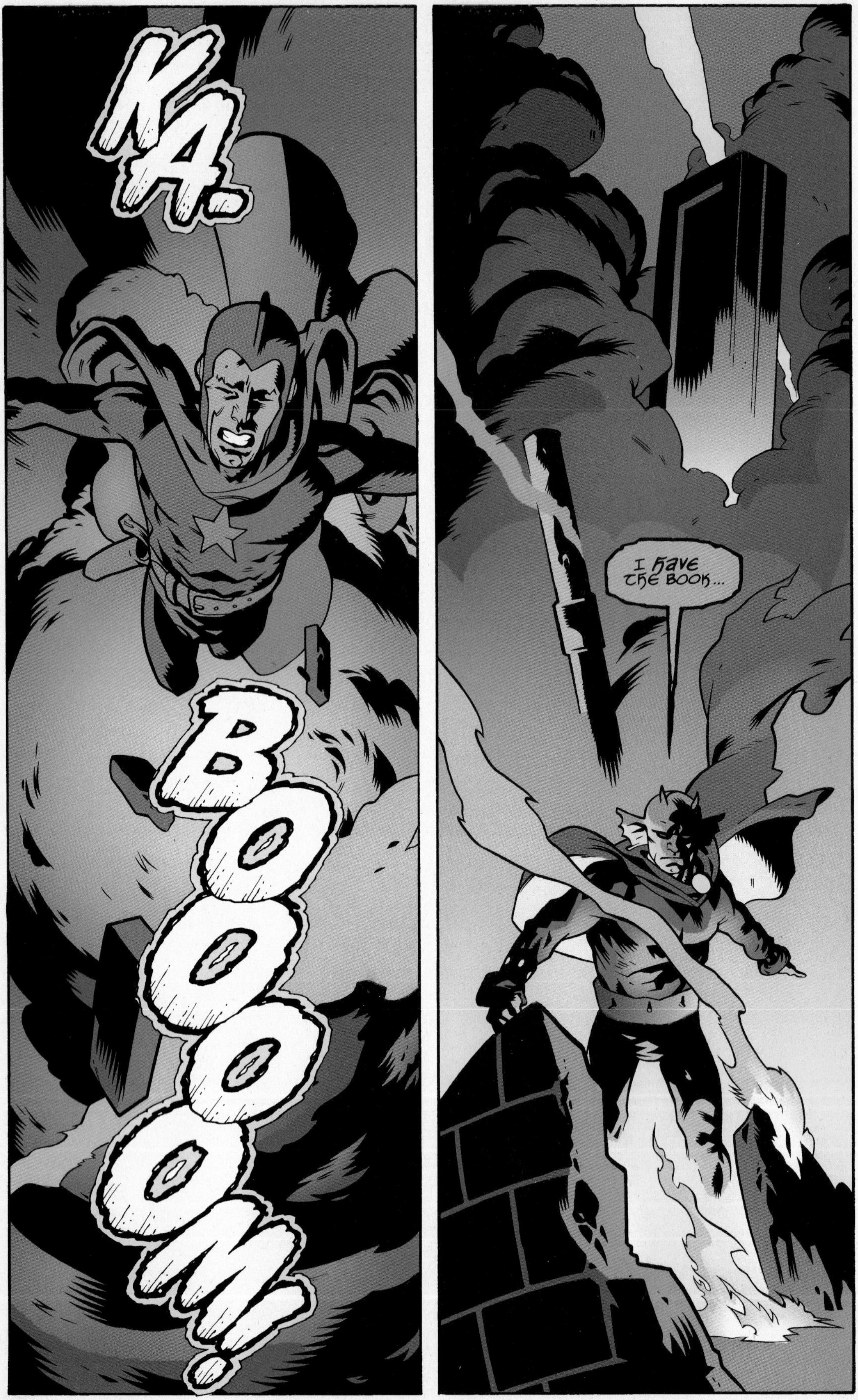
KA-
BOOOOOM!
I HAVE THE BOOK...

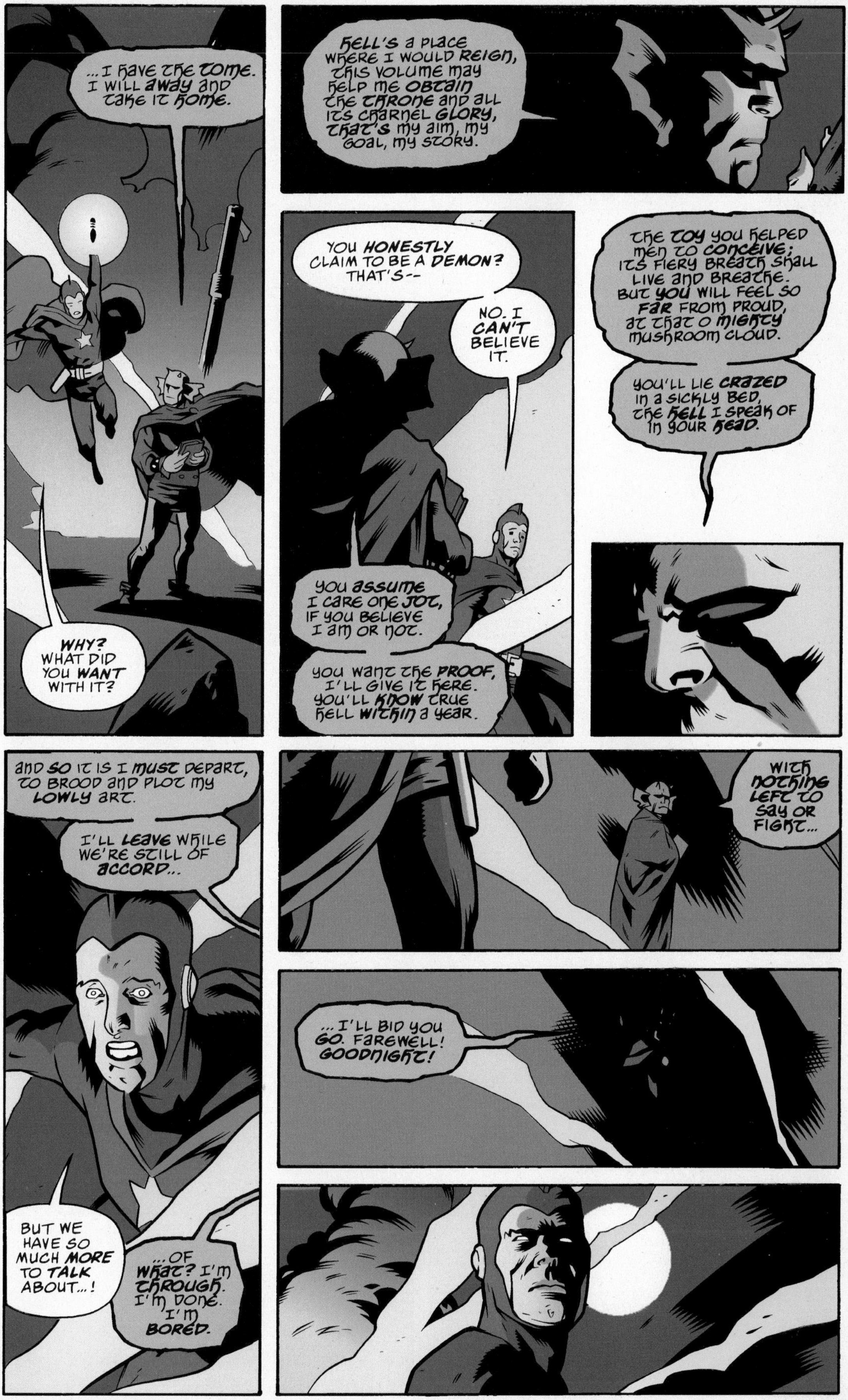
...I HAVE THE TOME. I WILL AWAY AND TAKE IT HOME.
HELL'S A PLACE WHERE I WOULD REIGN, THIS VOLUME MAY HELP ME OBTAIN THE THRONE AND ALL ITS CHARNEL GLORY, THAT'S MY AIM, MY GOAL, MY STORY.
WHY? WHAT DID YOU WANT WITH IT?
YOU HONESTLY CLAIM TO BE A DEMON? THAT'S--
NO. I CAN'T BELIEVE IT.
YOU ASSUME I CARE ONE JOT, IF YOU BELIEVE I AM OR NOT.
YOU WANT THE PROOF, I'LL GIVE IT HERE. YOU'LL KNOW TRUE HELL WITHIN A YEAR.
THE TOY YOU HELPED MEN TO CONCEIVE; ITS FIERY BREATH SHALL LIVE AND BREATHE. BUT YOU WILL FEEL SO FAR FROM PROUD, AT THAT O MIGHTY MUSHROOM CLOUD.
YOU'LL LIE CRAZED IN A SICKLY BED, THE HELL I SPEAK OF IN YOUR HEAD.
AND SO IT IS I MUST DEPART, TO BROOD AND PLOT MY LOWLY ART.
I'LL LEAVE WHILE WE'RE STILL OF ACCORD...
BUT WE HAVE SO MUCH MORE TO TALK ABOUT...!
...OF WHAT? I'M THROUGH. I'M DONE. I'M BORED.
WITH NOTHING LEFT TO SAY OR FIGHT...
...I'LL BID YOU GO. FAREWELL! GOODNIGHT!

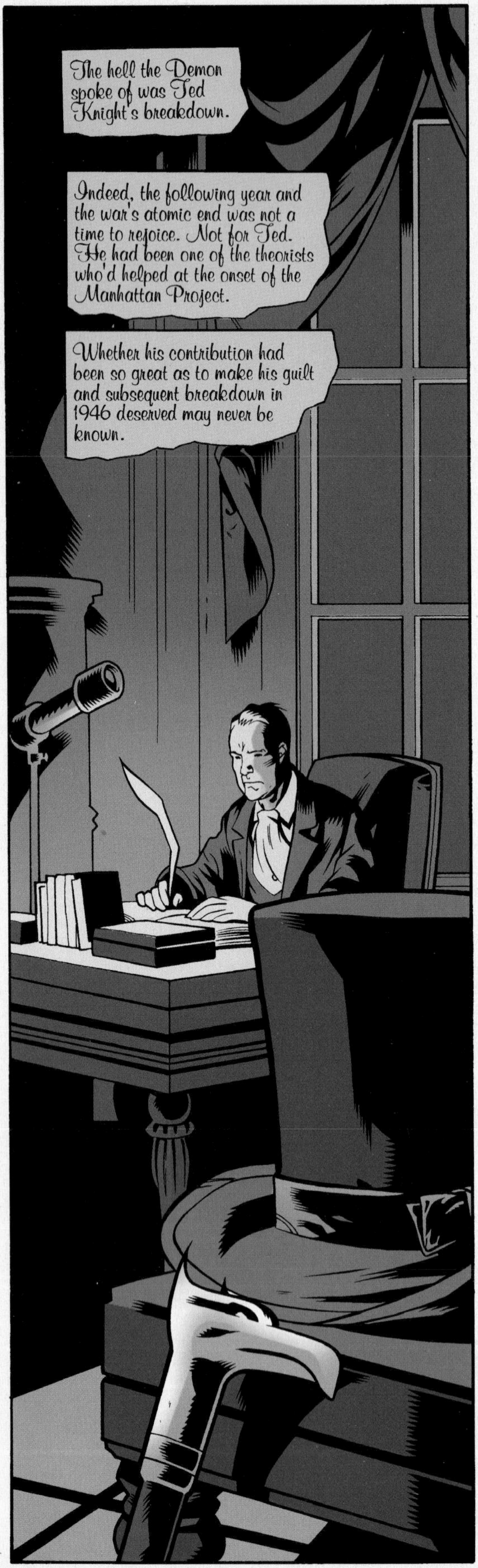
The hell the Demon spoke of was Ted Knight's breakdown.
Indeed, the following year and the war's atomic end was not a time to rejoice. Not for Ted. He had been one of the theorists who'd helped at the onset of the Manhattan Project.
Whether his contribution had been so great as to make his guilt and subsequent breakdown in 1946 deserved may never be known.
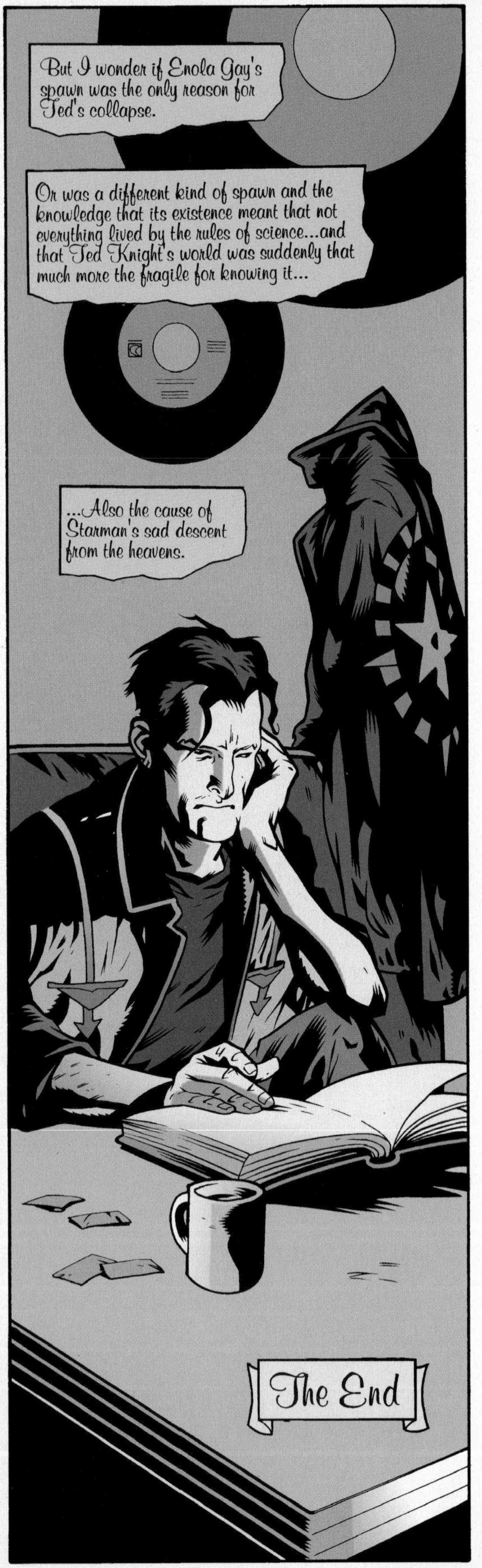
But I wonder if Enola Gay's spawn was the only reason for Ted's collapse.
Or was a different kind of spawn and the knowledge that its existence meant that not everything lived by the rules of science...and that Ted Knight's world was suddenly that much more the fragile for knowing it...
...Also the cause of Starman's sad descent from the heavens.
The End

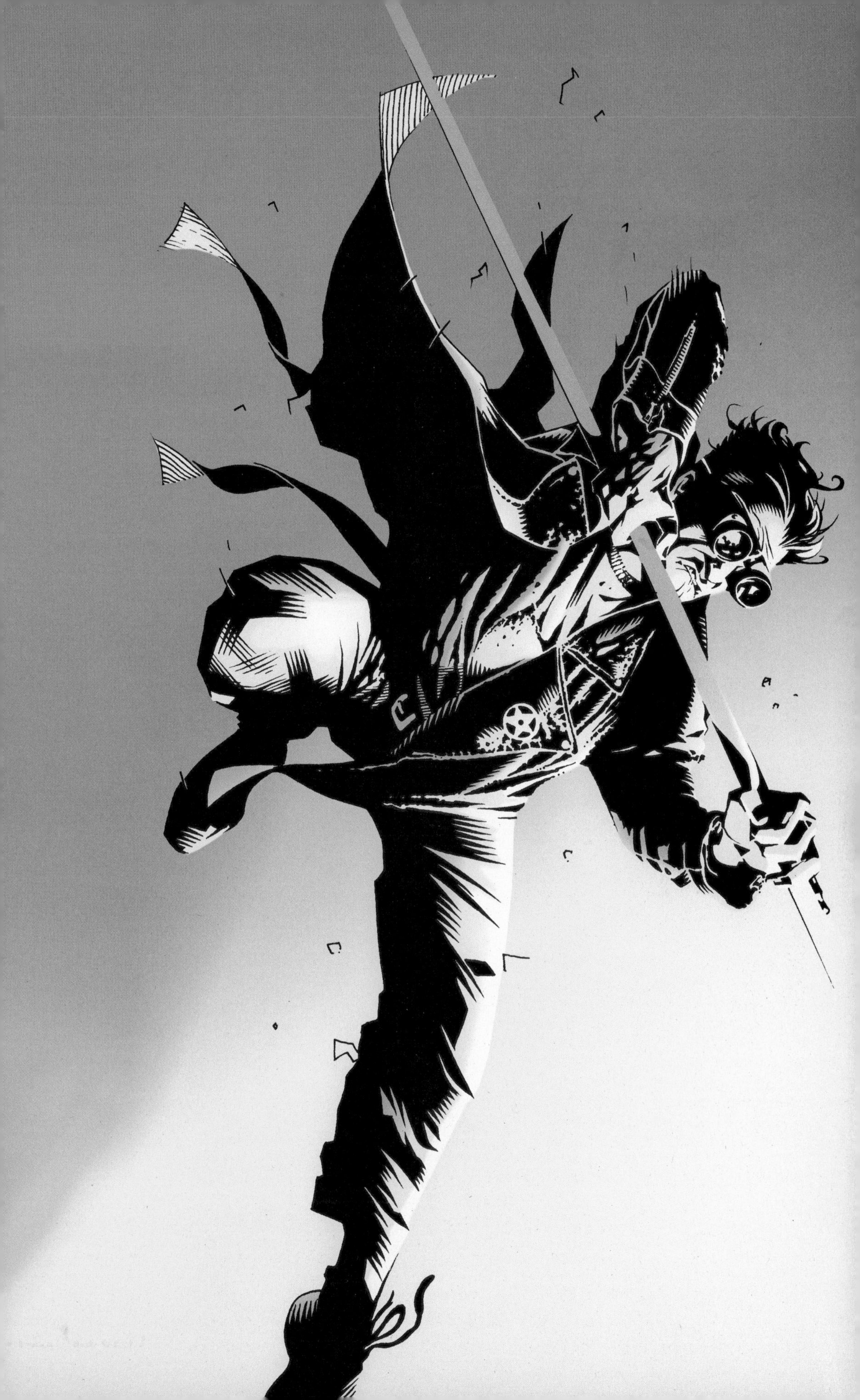

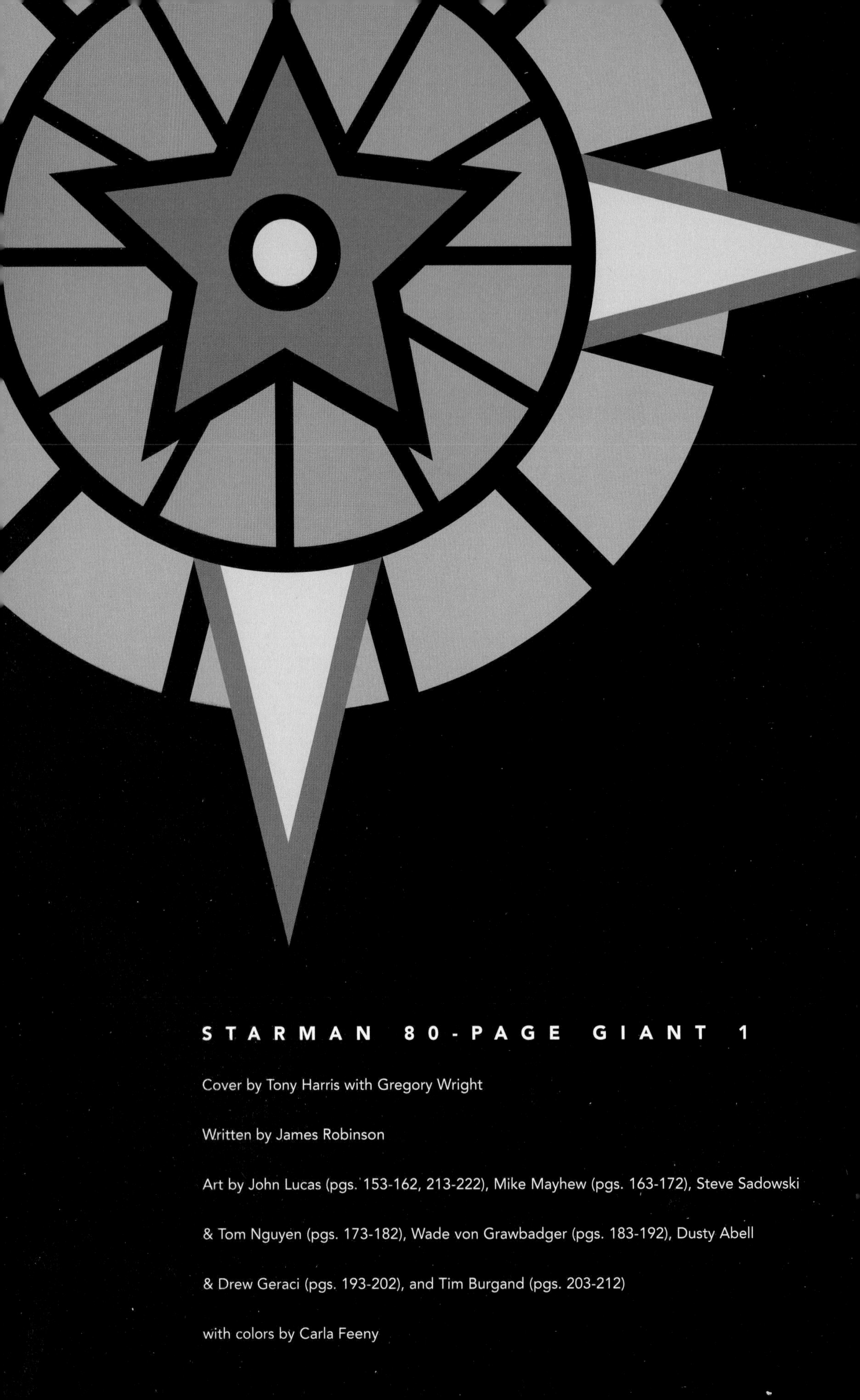

STARMAN 80-PAGE GIANT 1

Cover by Tony Harris with Gregory Wright

Written by James Robinson

Art by John Lucas (pgs. 153-162, 213-222), Mike Mayhew (pgs. 163-172), Steve Sadowski & Tom Nguyen (pgs. 173-182), Wade von Grawbadger (pgs. 183-192), Dusty Abell & Drew Geraci (pgs. 193-202), and Tim Burgand (pgs. 203-212)

with colors by Carla Feeny

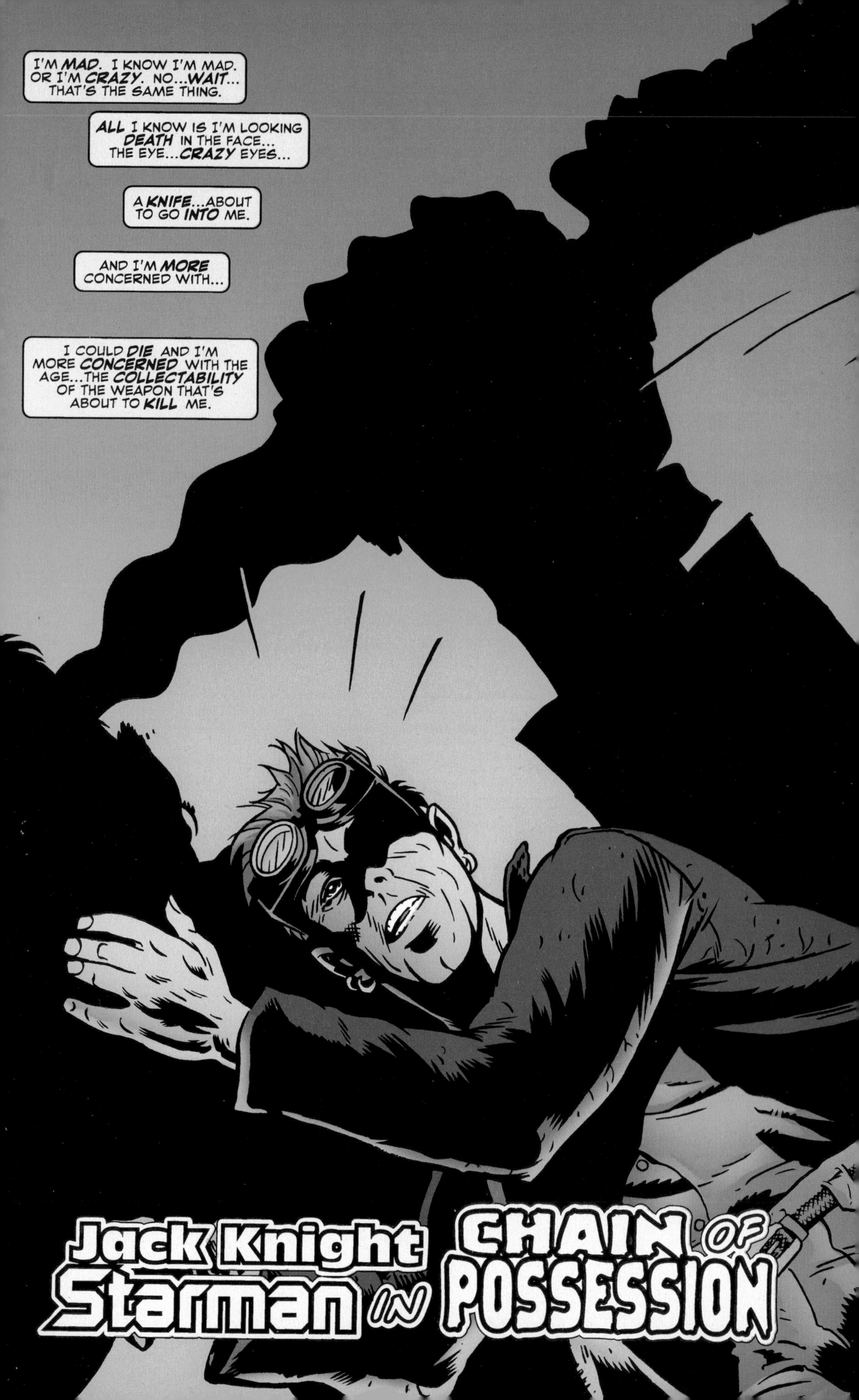

I'M MAD. I KNOW I'M MAD. OR I'M CRAZY. NO...WAIT... THAT'S THE SAME THING.
ALL I KNOW IS I'M LOOKING DEATH IN THE FACE... THE EYE...CRAZY EYES...
A KNIFE...ABOUT TO GO INTO ME.
AND I'M MORE CONCERNED WITH...
I COULD DIE AND I'M MORE CONCERNED WITH THE AGE...THE COLLECTABILITY OF THE WEAPON THAT'S ABOUT TO KILL ME.
Jack Knight Starman IN CHAIN OF POSSESSION

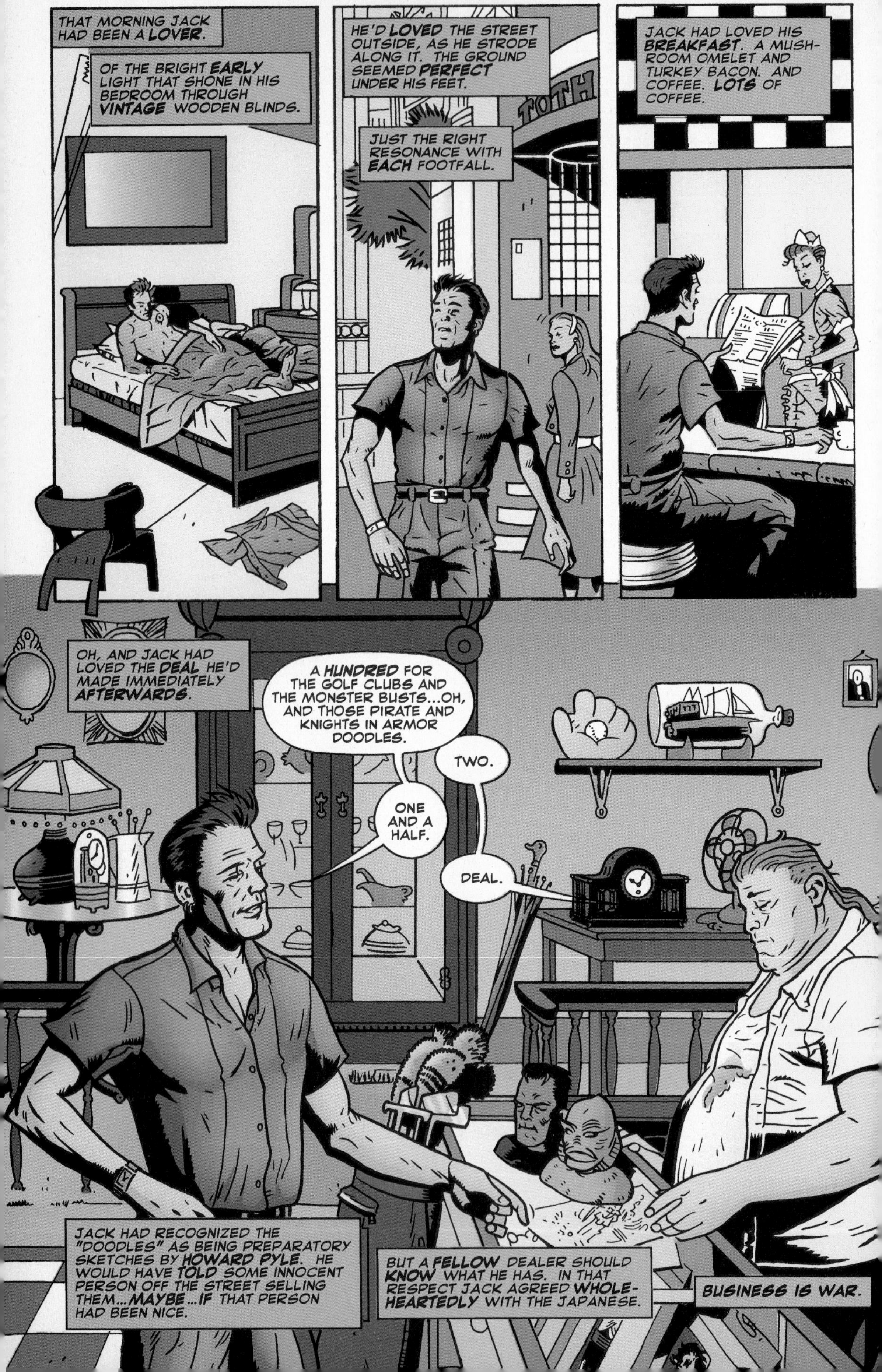
THAT MORNING JACK HAD BEEN A LOVER.
OF THE BRIGHT EARLY LIGHT THAT SHONE IN HIS BEDROOM THROUGH VINTAGE WOODEN BLINDS.
HE'D LOVED THE STREET OUTSIDE, AS HE STRODE ALONG IT. THE GROUND SEEMED PERFECT UNDER HIS FEET.
TOTH
JUST THE RIGHT RESONANCE WITH EACH FOOTFALL.
JACK HAD LOVED HIS BREAKFAST. A MUSH-ROOM OMELET AND TURKEY BACON. AND COFFEE. LOTS OF COFFEE.
OH, AND JACK HAD LOVED THE DEAL HE'D MADE IMMEDIATELY AFTERWARDS.
A HUNDRED FOR THE GOLF CLUBS AND THE MONSTER BUSTS...OH, AND THOSE PIRATE AND KNIGHTS IN ARMOR DOODLES.
TWO.
ONE AND A HALF.
DEAL.
JACK HAD RECOGNIZED THE "DOODLES" AS BEING PREPARATORY SKETCHES BY HOWARD PYLE. HE WOULD HAVE TOLD SOME INNOCENT PERSON OFF THE STREET SELLING THEM...MAYBE...IF THAT PERSON HAD BEEN NICE.
BUT A FELLOW DEALER SHOULD KNOW WHAT HE HAS. IN THAT RESPECT JACK AGREED WHOLE-HEARTEDLY WITH THE JAPANESE.
BUSINESS IS WAR.

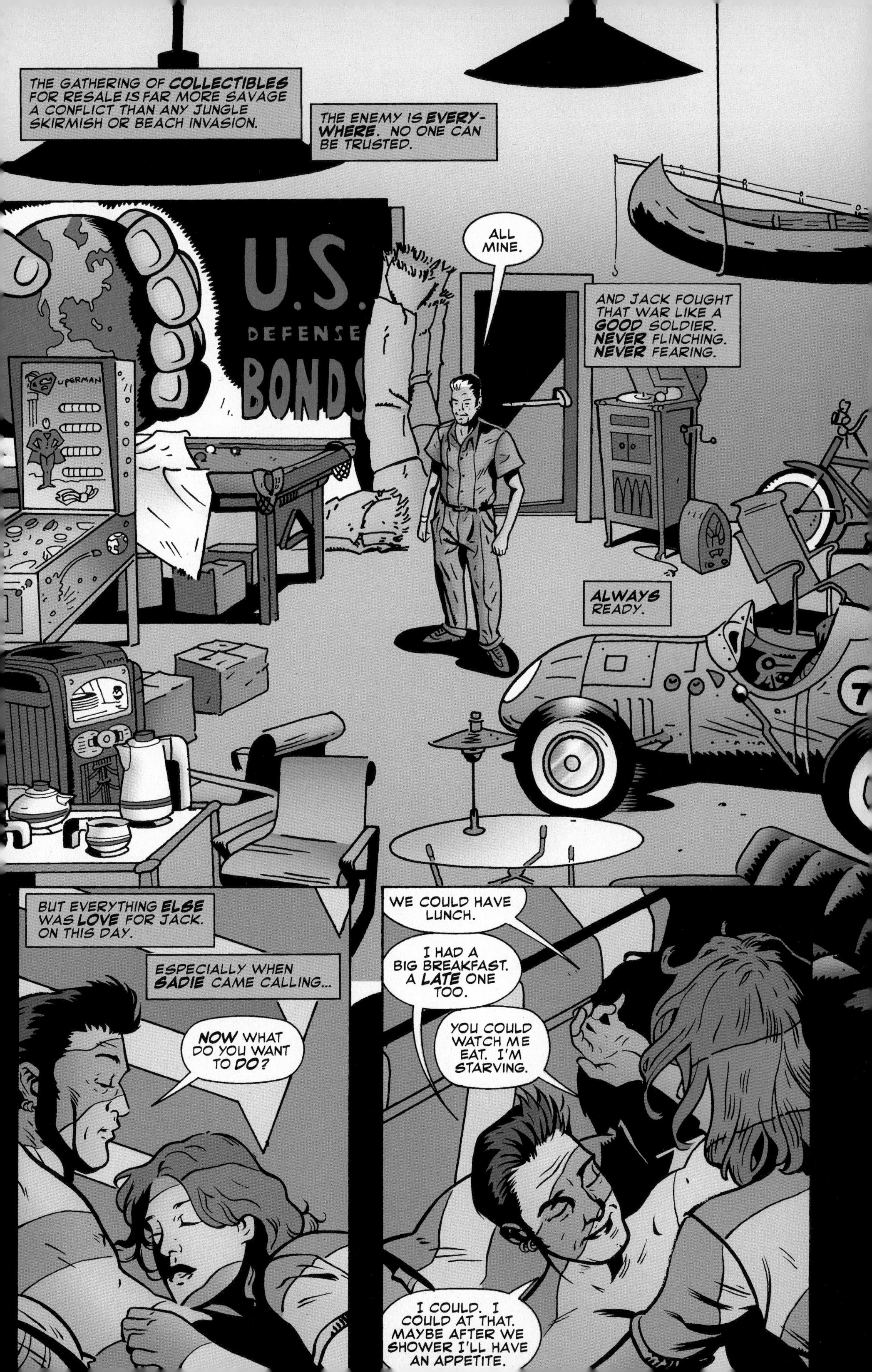
THE GATHERING OF COLLECTIBLES FOR RESALE IS FAR MORE SAVAGE A CONFLICT THAN ANY JUNGLE SKIRMISH OR BEACH INVASION.
THE ENEMY IS EVERY-WHERE. NO ONE CAN BE TRUSTED.
U.S. DEFENSE BONDS
UPERMAN
ALL MINE.
AND JACK FOUGHT THAT WAR LIKE A GOOD SOLDIER. NEVER FLINCHING. NEVER FEARING.
ALWAYS READY.
BUT EVERYTHING ELSE WAS LOVE FOR JACK. ON THIS DAY.
ESPECIALLY WHEN SADIE CAME CALLING...
NOW WHAT DO YOU WANT TO DO?
WE COULD HAVE LUNCH.
I HAD A BIG BREAKFAST. A LATE ONE TOO.
YOU COULD WATCH ME EAT. I'M STARVING.
I COULD. I COULD AT THAT. MAYBE AFTER WE SHOWER I'LL HAVE AN APPETITE.

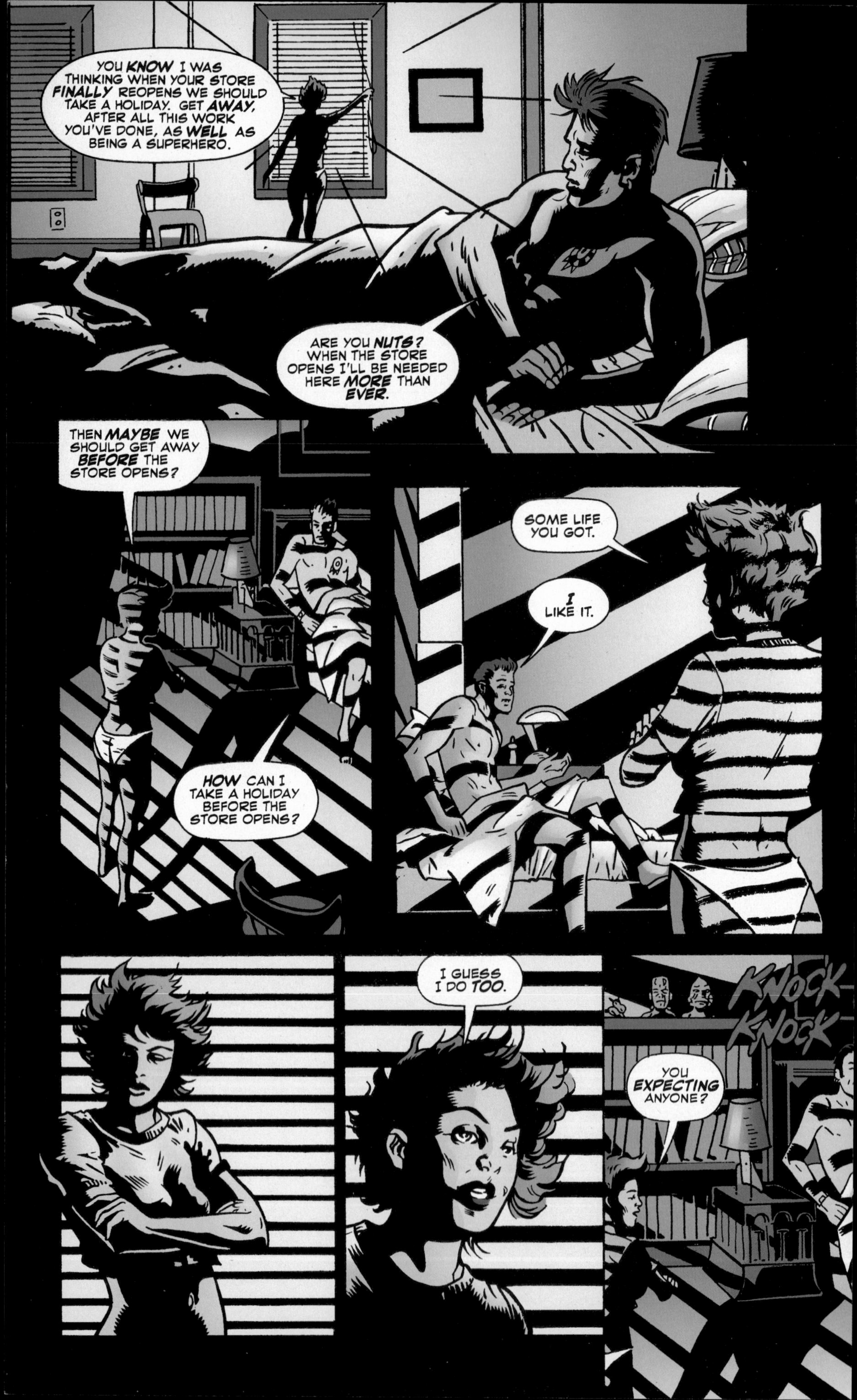
YOU KNOW I WAS THINKING WHEN YOUR STORE FINALLY REOPENS WE SHOULD TAKE A HOLIDAY. GET AWAY, AFTER ALL THIS WORK YOU'VE DONE, AS WELL AS BEING A SUPERHERO.
ARE YOU NUTS? WHEN THE STORE OPENS I'LL BE NEEDED HERE MORE THAN EVER.
THEN MAYBE WE SHOULD GET AWAY BEFORE THE STORE OPENS?
HOW CAN I TAKE A HOLIDAY BEFORE THE STORE OPENS?
SOME LIFE YOU GOT.
I LIKE IT.
I GUESS I DO TOO.
KNOCK KNOCK
YOU EXPECTING ANYONE?

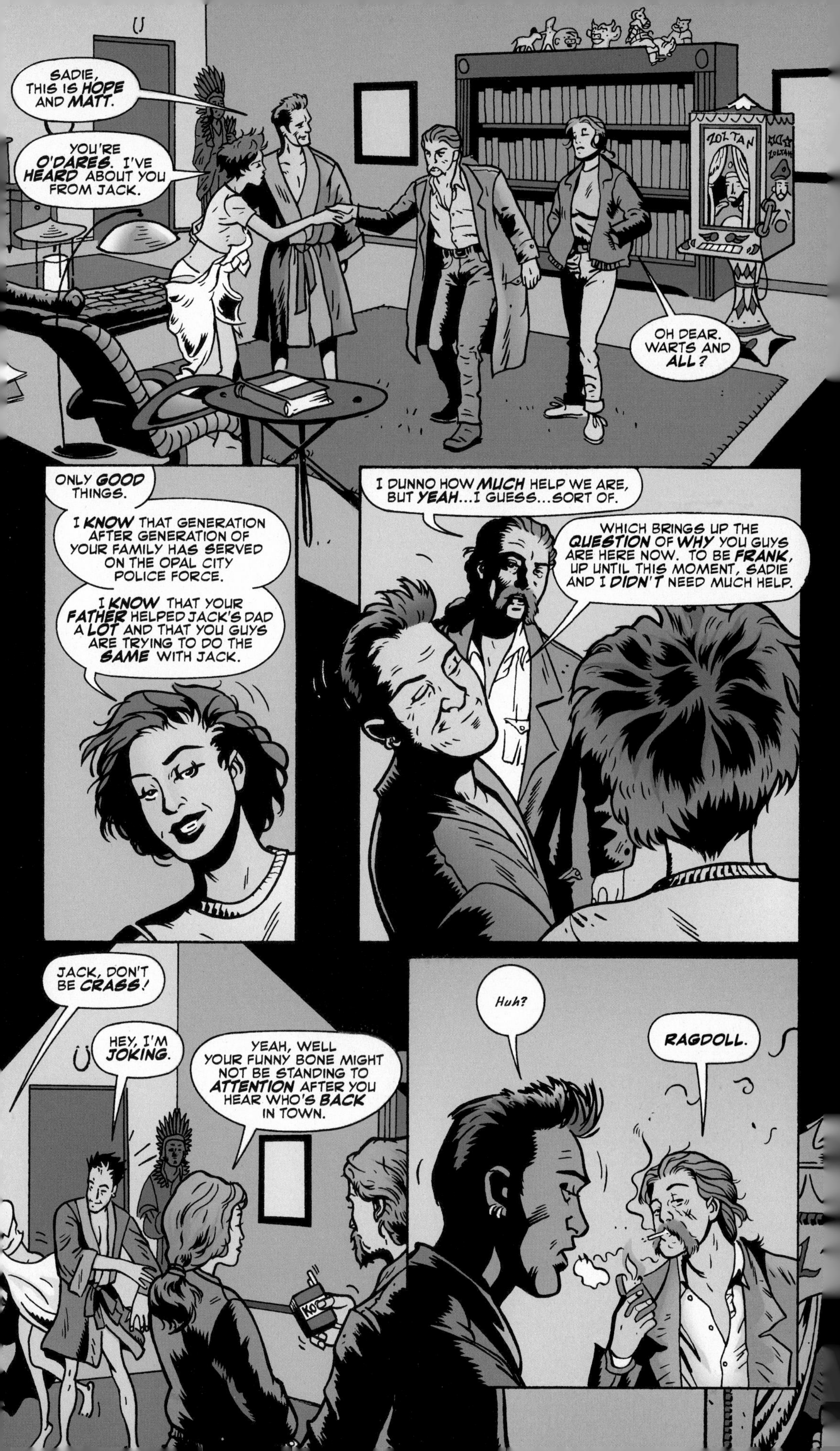
SADIE, THIS IS HOPE AND MATT.
YOU'RE O'DARES. I'VE HEARD ABOUT YOU FROM JACK.
OH DEAR. WARTS AND ALL?
ZOLTAN
ONLY GOOD THINGS.
I KNOW THAT GENERATION AFTER GENERATION OF YOUR FAMILY HAS SERVED ON THE OPAL CITY POLICE FORCE.
I KNOW THAT YOUR FATHER HELPED JACK'S DAD A LOT AND THAT YOU GUYS ARE TRYING TO DO THE SAME WITH JACK.
I DUNNO HOW MUCH HELP WE ARE, BUT YEAH...I GUESS...SORT OF.
WHICH BRINGS UP THE QUESTION OF WHY YOU GUYS ARE HERE NOW. TO BE FRANK, UP UNTIL THIS MOMENT, SADIE AND I DIDN'T NEED MUCH HELP.
JACK, DON'T BE CRASS!
HEY, I'M JOKING.
YEAH, WELL YOUR FUNNY BONE MIGHT NOT BE STANDING TO ATTENTION AFTER YOU HEAR WHO'S BACK IN TOWN.
Huh?
RAGDOLL.

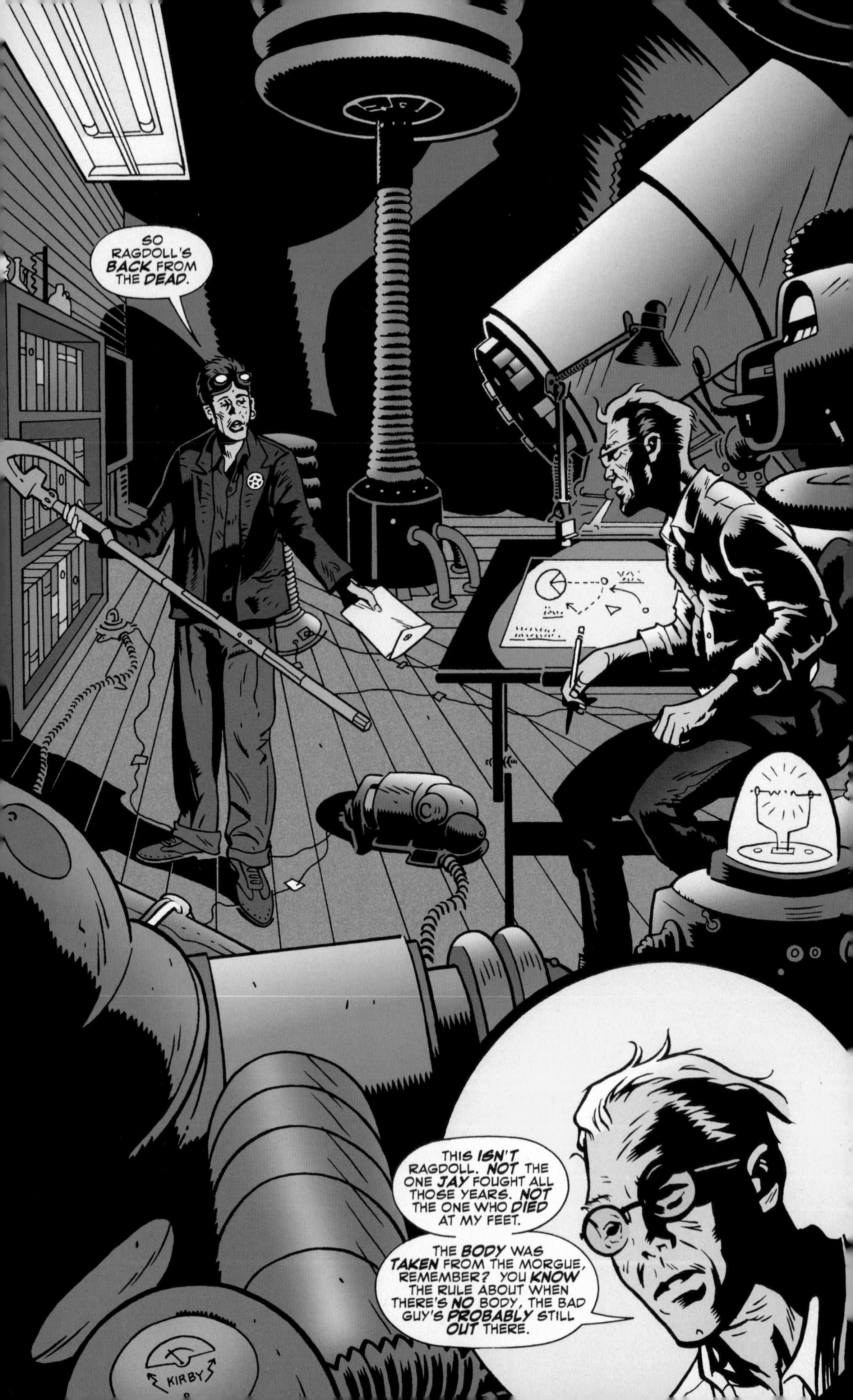
SO RAGDOLL'S BACK FROM THE DEAD.
THIS ISN'T RAGDOLL. NOT THE ONE JAY FOUGHT ALL THOSE YEARS. NOT THE ONE WHO DIED AT MY FEET.
THE BODY WAS TAKEN FROM THE MORGUE, REMEMBER? YOU KNOW THE RULE ABOUT WHEN THERE'S NO BODY, THE BAD GUY'S PROBABLY STILL OUT THERE.
KIRBY

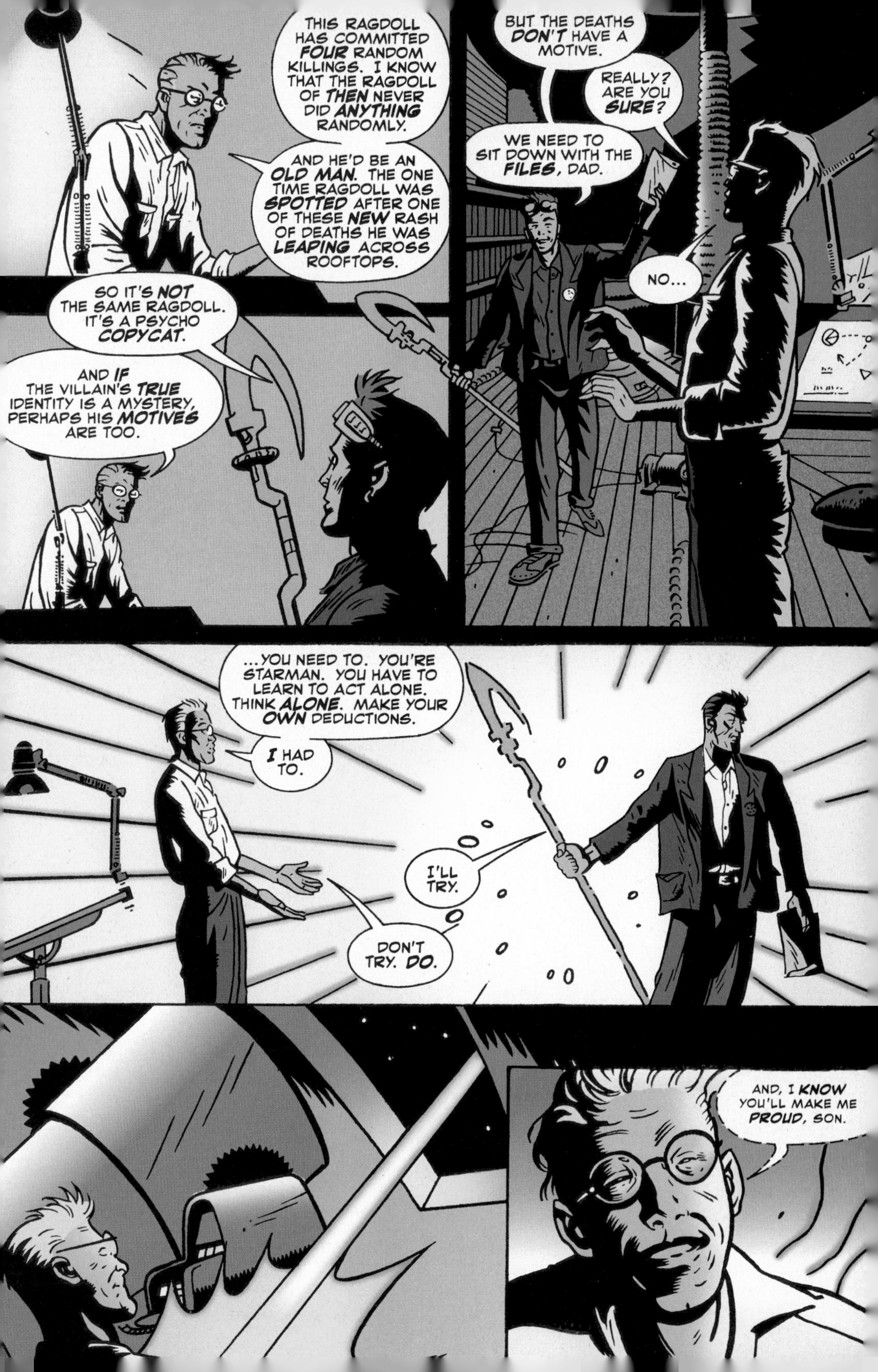
THIS RAGDOLL HAS COMMITTED FOUR RANDOM KILLINGS. I KNOW THAT THE RAGDOLL OF THEN NEVER DID ANYTHING RANDOMLY.
AND HE'D BE AN OLD MAN. THE ONE TIME RAGDOLL WAS SPOTTED AFTER ONE OF THESE NEW RASH OF DEATHS HE WAS LEAPING ACROSS ROOFTOPS.
SO IT'S NOT THE SAME RAGDOLL. IT'S A PSYCHO COPYCAT.
AND IF THE VILLAIN'S TRUE IDENTITY IS A MYSTERY, PERHAPS HIS MOTIVES ARE TOO.
BUT THE DEATHS DON'T HAVE A MOTIVE.
REALLY? ARE YOU SURE?
WE NEED TO SIT DOWN WITH THE FILES, DAD.
NO...
...YOU NEED TO. YOU'RE STARMAN. YOU HAVE TO LEARN TO ACT ALONE. THINK ALONE. MAKE YOUR OWN DEDUCTIONS.
I HAD TO.
I'LL TRY.
DON'T TRY. DO.
AND, I KNOW YOU'LL MAKE ME PROUD, SON.

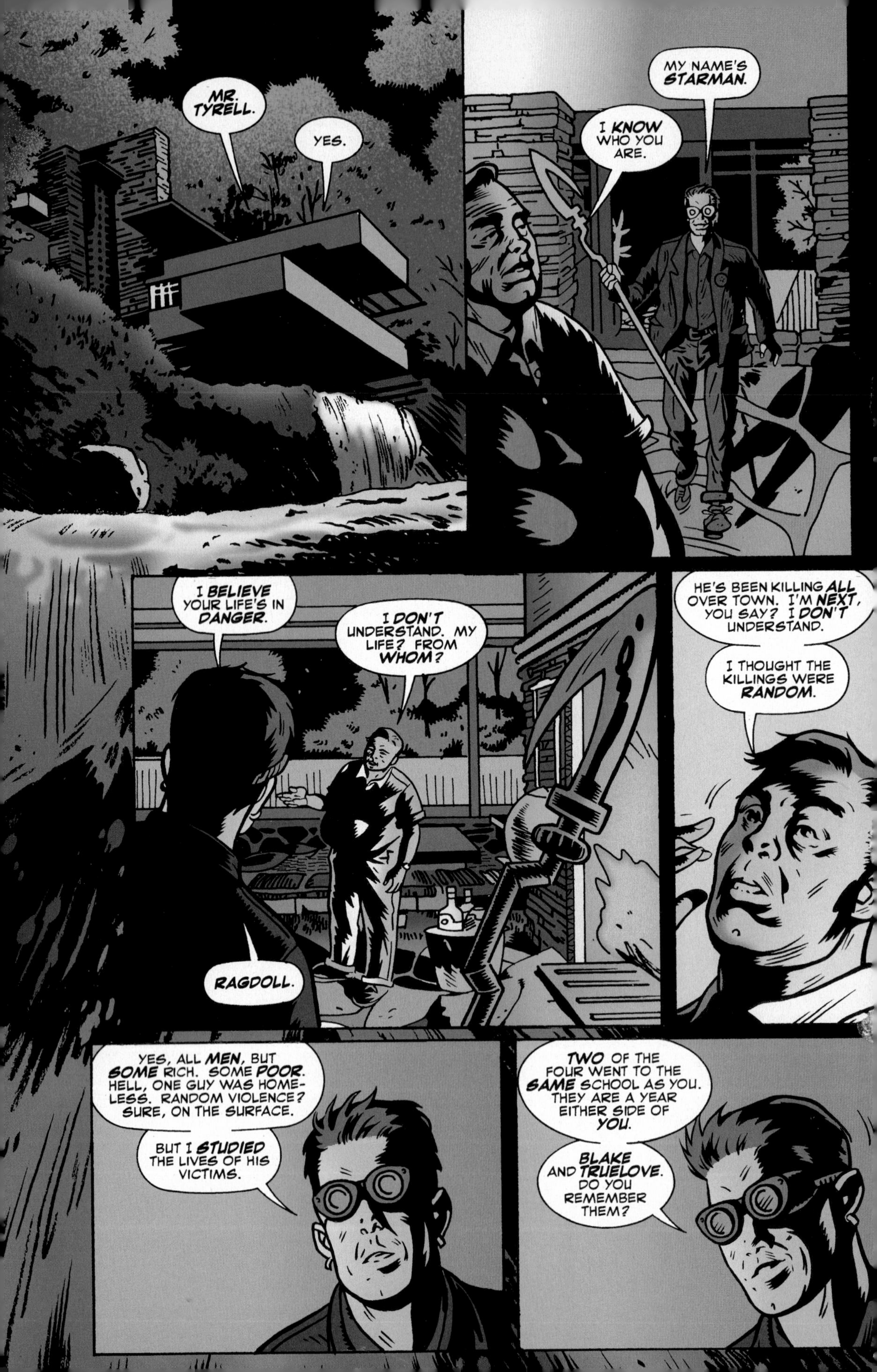
MR. TYRELL.
YES.
MY NAME'S STARMAN.
I KNOW WHO YOU ARE.
I BELIEVE YOUR LIFE'S IN DANGER.
I DON'T UNDERSTAND. MY LIFE? FROM WHOM?
RAGDOLL.
HE'S BEEN KILLING ALL OVER TOWN. I'M NEXT, YOU SAY? I DON'T UNDERSTAND.
I THOUGHT THE KILLINGS WERE RANDOM.
YES, ALL MEN, BUT SOME RICH. SOME POOR. HELL, ONE GUY WAS HOMELESS. RANDOM VIOLENCE? SURE, ON THE SURFACE.
BUT I STUDIED THE LIVES OF HIS VICTIMS.
TWO OF THE FOUR WENT TO THE SAME SCHOOL AS YOU. THEY ARE A YEAR EITHER SIDE OF YOU.
BLAKE AND TRUELOVE. DO YOU REMEMBER THEM?

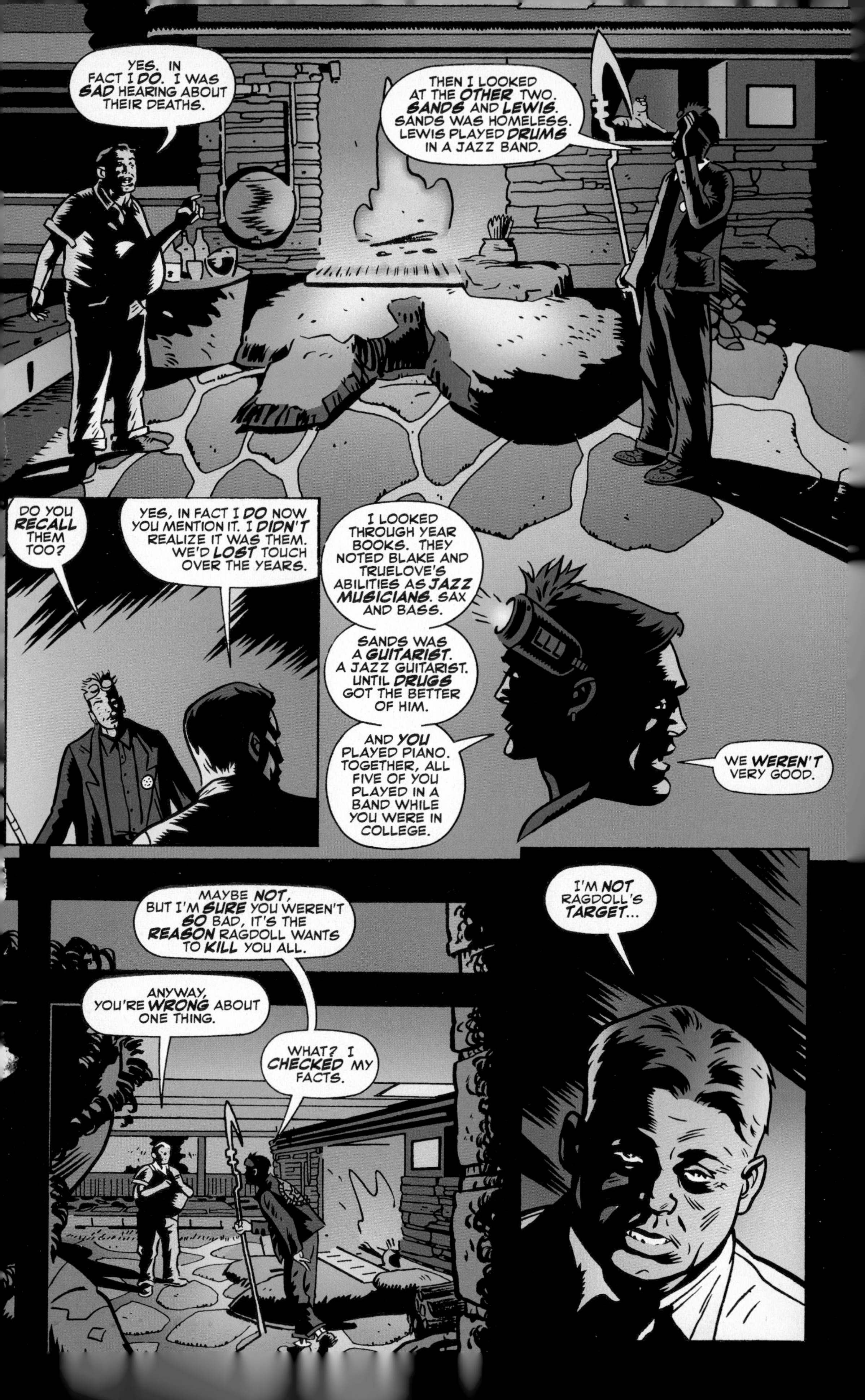
YES. IN FACT I DO. I WAS SAD HEARING ABOUT THEIR DEATHS.
THEN I LOOKED AT THE OTHER TWO. SANDS AND LEWIS. SANDS WAS HOMELESS. LEWIS PLAYED DRUMS IN A JAZZ BAND.
DO YOU RECALL THEM TOO?
YES, IN FACT I DO NOW YOU MENTION IT. I DIDN'T REALIZE IT WAS THEM. WE'D LOST TOUCH OVER THE YEARS.
I LOOKED THROUGH YEAR BOOKS. THEY NOTED BLAKE AND TRUELOVE'S ABILITIES AS JAZZ MUSICIANS. SAX AND BASS.
SANDS WAS A GUITARIST. A JAZZ GUITARIST. UNTIL DRUGS GOT THE BETTER OF HIM.
AND YOU PLAYED PIANO. TOGETHER, ALL FIVE OF YOU PLAYED IN A BAND WHILE YOU WERE IN COLLEGE.
WE WEREN'T VERY GOOD.
MAYBE NOT, BUT I'M SURE YOU WEREN'T SO BAD, IT'S THE REASON RAGDOLL WANTS TO KILL YOU ALL.
ANYWAY, YOU'RE WRONG ABOUT ONE THING.
WHAT? I CHECKED MY FACTS.
I'M NOT RAGDOLL'S TARGET...

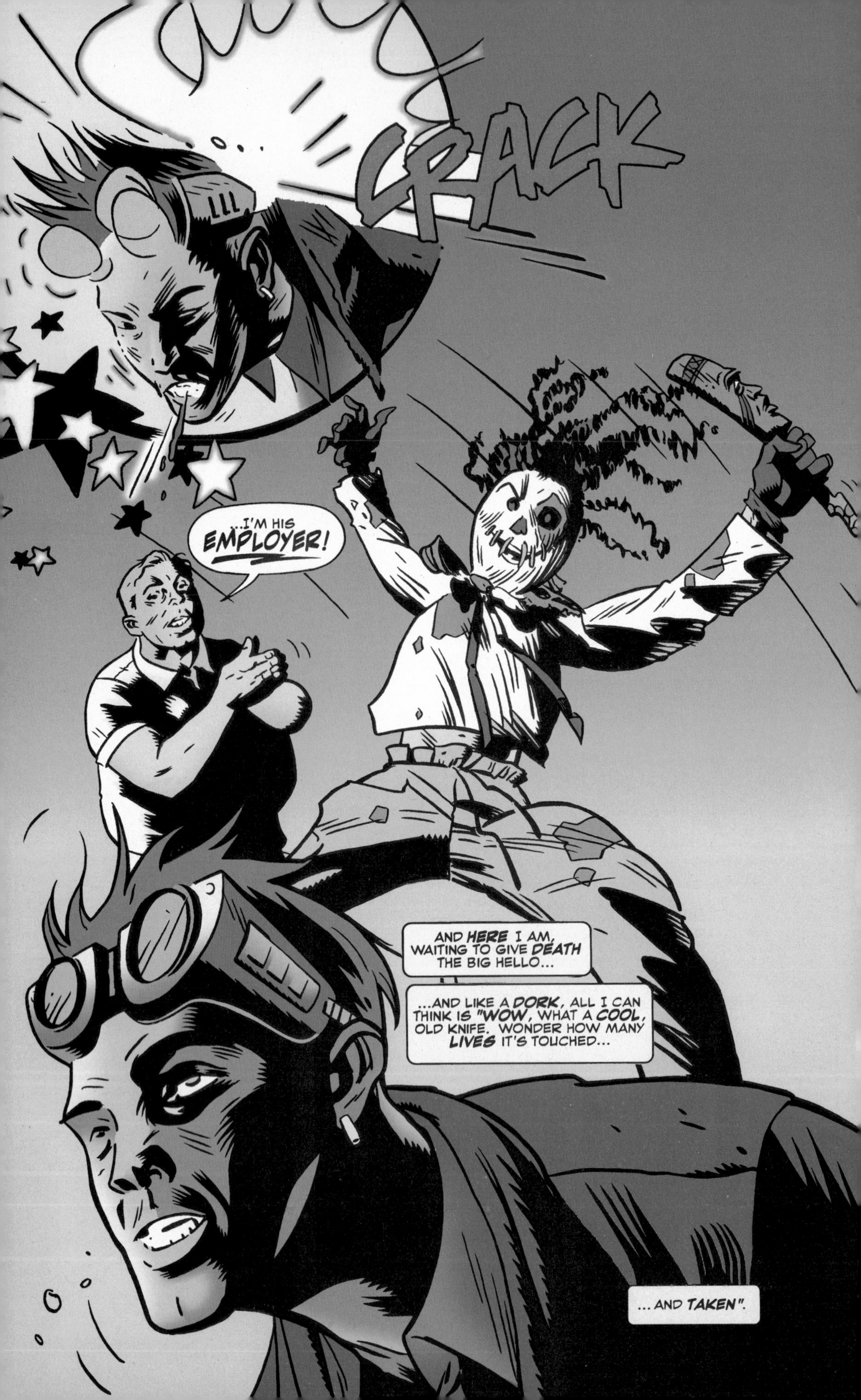
CRACK
...I'M HIS EMPLOYER!
AND HERE I AM, WAITING TO GIVE DEATH THE BIG HELLO...
...AND LIKE A DORK, ALL I CAN THINK IS "WOW, WHAT A COOL, OLD KNIFE. WONDER HOW MANY LIVES IT'S TOUCHED...
... AND TAKEN".

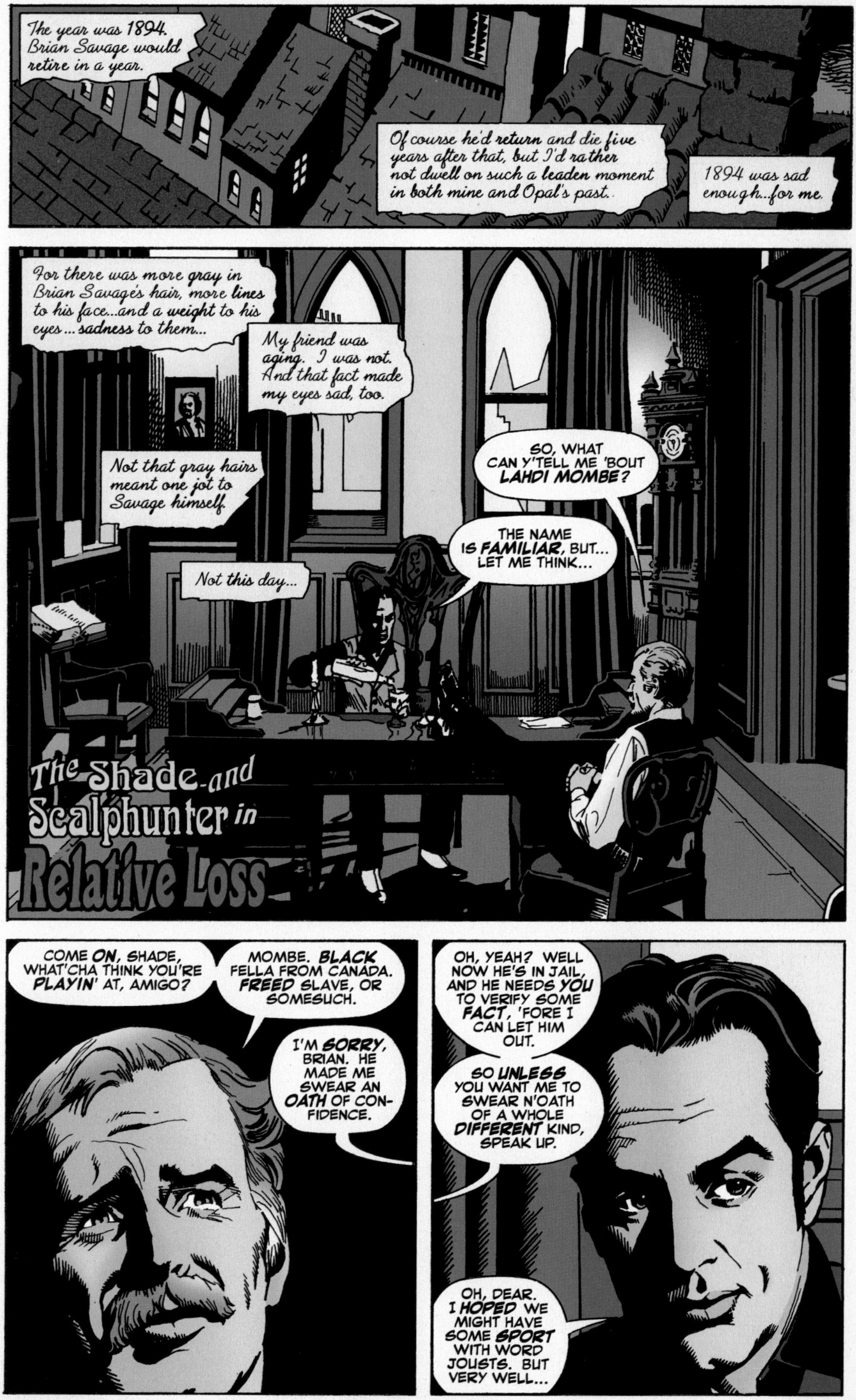
The year was 1894. Brian Savage would retire in a year.
Of course he'd return and die five years after that, but I'd rather not dwell on such a leaden moment in both mine and Opal's past.
1894 was sad enough...for me.
For there was more gray in Brian Savage's hair, more lines to his face...and a weight to his eyes... sadness to them...
My friend was aging. I was not. And that fact made my eyes sad, too.
Not that gray hairs meant one jot to Savage himself.
Not this day...
SO, WHAT CAN Y'TELL ME 'BOUT LAHDI MOMBE?
THE NAME IS FAMILIAR, BUT... LET ME THINK...
The Shade and Scalphunter in
Relative Loss
COME ON, SHADE, WHAT'CHA THINK YOU'RE PLAYIN' AT, AMIGO?
MOMBE. BLACK FELLA FROM CANADA. FREED SLAVE, OR SOMESUCH.
I'M SORRY, BRIAN. HE MADE ME SWEAR AN OATH OF CONFIDENCE.
OH, YEAH? WELL NOW HE'S IN JAIL, AND HE NEEDS YOU TO VERIFY SOME FACT, 'FORE I CAN LET HIM OUT.
SO UNLESS YOU WANT ME TO SWEAR N'OATH OF A WHOLE DIFFERENT KIND, SPEAK UP.
OH, DEAR. I HOPED WE MIGHT HAVE SOME SPORT WITH WORD JOUSTS. BUT VERY WELL...

...Lahdi Mombe contacted me several days ago...

MY **GRANDFATHER** AND HIS BROTHER WERE BROUGHT **HERE** FROM AFRICA.

AS SLAVES?

HOW ELSE?

BUT THEIR OWNER...MASTER... **HIM**, HE HAD ENEMIES. A GROUP WHO WANTED HIS LAND. THEY SENT PISTOLEROS FROM SOUTH OF THE BORDER TO GUN HIM OFF IT.

THE MAN **HELD** HIS LAND, BUT HE WAS **WOUNDED**. THE ATTACKING PARTY WENT FOR THE MAN'S **WIFE** AND **CHILDREN**.

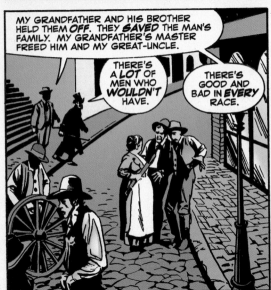

MY GRANDFATHER AND HIS BROTHER HELD THEM **OFF**. THEY **SAVED** THE MAN'S FAMILY. MY GRANDFATHER'S MASTER FREED HIM AND MY GREAT-UNCLE.

THERE'S A **LOT** OF MEN WHO **WOULDN'T** HAVE.

THERE'S GOOD AND BAD IN **EVERY** RACE.

ANYWAY, MY GRANDFATHER WENT **NORTH** WHERE THE COLOR OF A MAN'S SKIN MATTERED LESS...A **LITTLE** LESS. MY GREAT-UNCLE'S FAMILY MOVED NORTH **TOO**, BUT **NOT** AS FAR. **OPAL CITY**.

WHERE THEY WORKED IN **MENIAL** JOBS. SERVANTS. MY UNCLE WAS A **BLACKSMITH**. MY COUSIN WILL WAS A **VALET**. AT LEAST **THAT'S** WHAT HE TOLD ME IN A LETTER HE WROTE.

I **STILL** DON'T KNOW WHERE **I** COME IN.

HE'S THE **LAST** OF HIS FAMILY. HE'S VANISHED AND THERE'S **NO ONE** I CAN ASK WHO MIGHT **KNOW**.

I KNOW HE'D **JUST** GOTTEN **NEW** EMPLOYMENT. HE WROTE THAT, BUT DIDN'T SAY **WHERE** EXACTLY.

I KNOW YOU TAKE ON **JOBS**. THAT YOU GET **RESULTS** IN WAYS PEOPLE ARE SCARED TO TALK ABOUT.

I'M **PAID** FOR SUCH DEEDS. MY PRICE IS **NOT** CHEAP.

MY GRANDFATHER **KEPT** MOVING NORTH. CANADA TOOK HIM **IN**. HE MADE A **FORTUNE** IN FURS. FURS AND GOLD. I'M **WEALTHY** ENOUGH I CAN PAY **WHATEVER** PRICE YOU ASK.

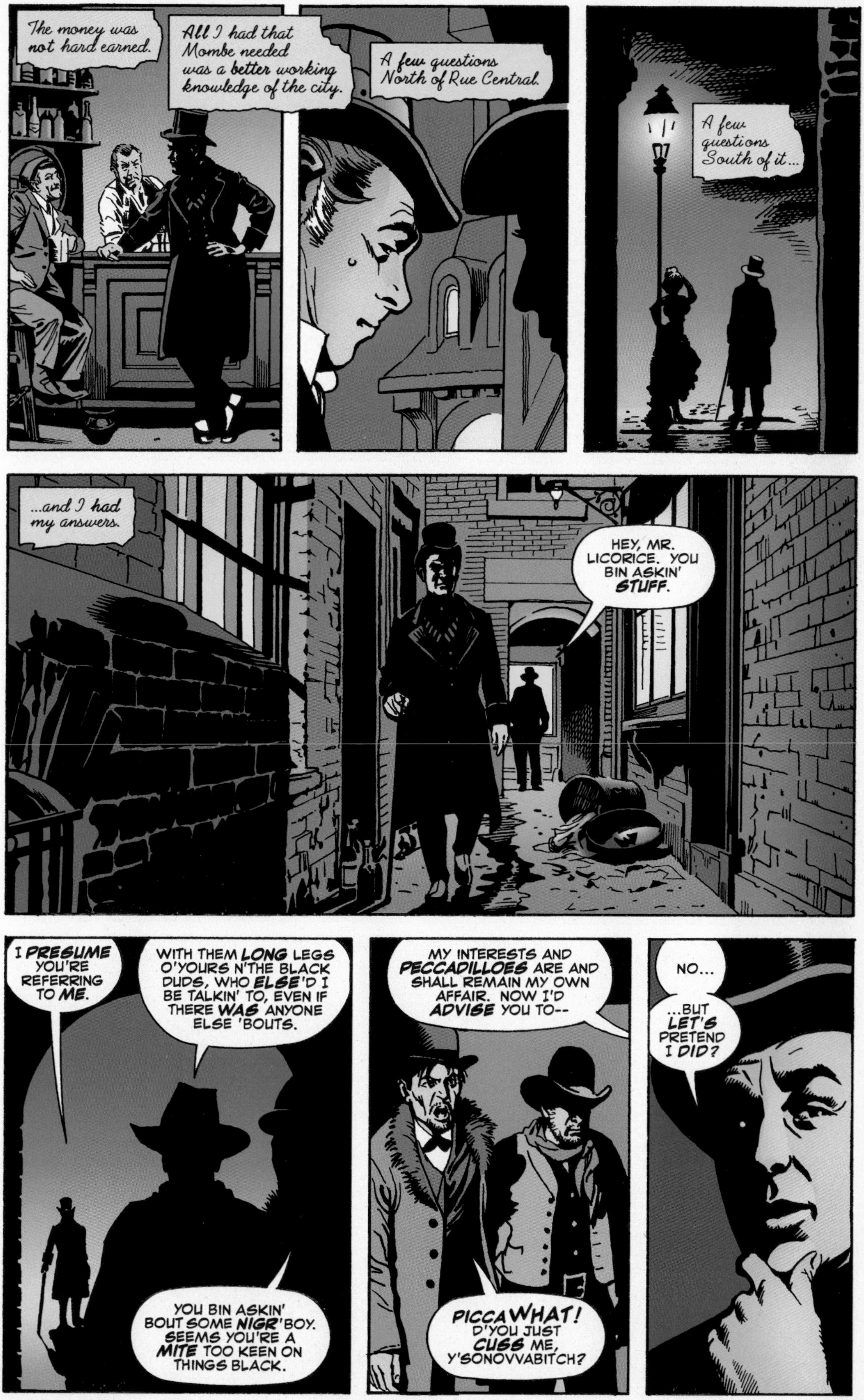
The money was not hard earned.
All I had that Mombe needed was a better working knowledge of the city.
A few questions North of Rue Central.
A few questions South of it...
...and I had my answers.
HEY, MR. LICORICE. YOU BIN ASKIN' STUFF.
I PRESUME YOU'RE REFERRING TO ME.
WITH THEM LONG LEGS O'YOURS N'THE BLACK DUDS, WHO ELSE'D I BE TALKIN' TO, EVEN IF THERE WAS ANYONE ELSE 'BOUTS.
YOU BIN ASKIN' BOUT SOME NIGR'BOY. SEEMS YOU'RE A MITE TOO KEEN ON THINGS BLACK.
MY INTERESTS AND PECCADILLOES ARE AND SHALL REMAIN MY OWN AFFAIR. NOW I'D ADVISE YOU TO--
PICCAWHAT! D'YOU JUST CUSS ME, Y'SONOVVABITCH?
NO...
...BUT LET'S PRETEND I DID?

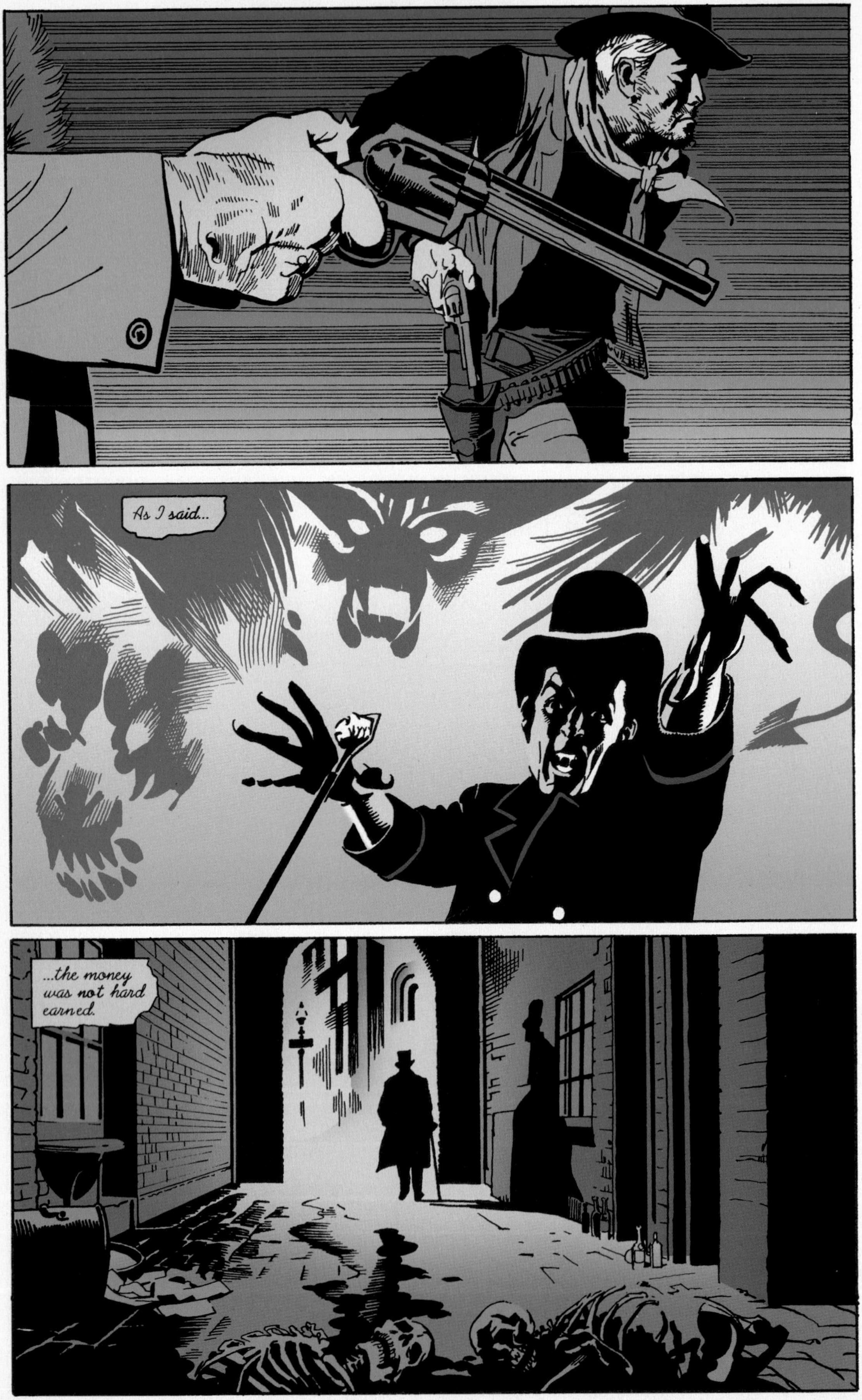
As I said...
...the money was not hard earned.

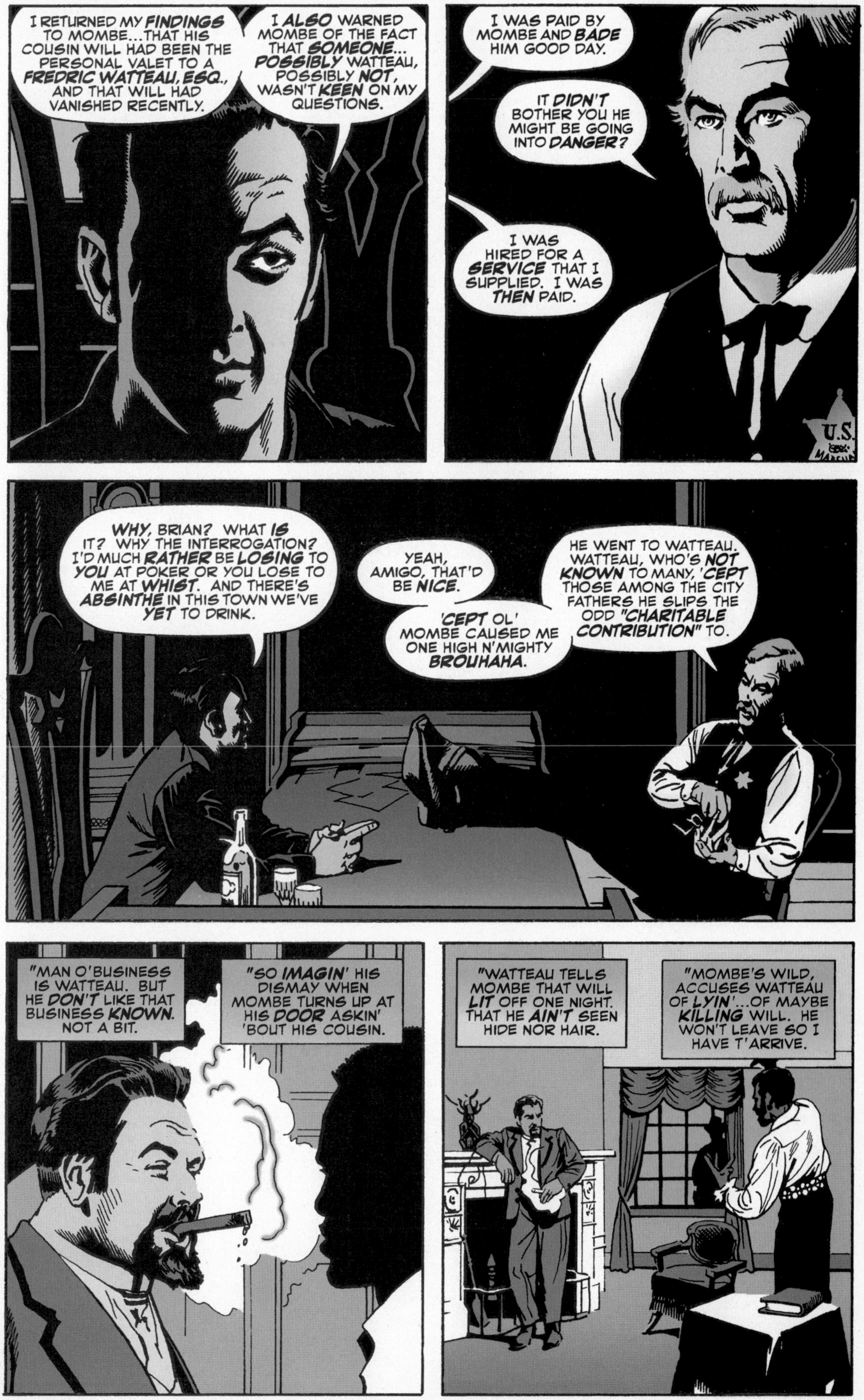

I RETURNED MY FINDINGS TO MOMBE...THAT HIS COUSIN WILL HAD BEEN THE PERSONAL VALET TO A FREDRIC WATTEAU, ESQ., AND THAT WILL HAD VANISHED RECENTLY.
I ALSO WARNED MOMBE OF THE FACT THAT SOMEONE... POSSIBLY WATTEAU, POSSIBLY NOT, WASN'T KEEN ON MY QUESTIONS.
I WAS PAID BY MOMBE AND BADE HIM GOOD DAY.
IT DIDN'T BOTHER YOU HE MIGHT BE GOING INTO DANGER?
I WAS HIRED FOR A SERVICE THAT I SUPPLIED. I WAS THEN PAID.
U.S. MARSHAL
WHY, BRIAN? WHAT IS IT? WHY THE INTERROGATION? I'D MUCH RATHER BE LOSING TO YOU AT POKER OR YOU LOSE TO ME AT WHIST. AND THERE'S ABSINTHE IN THIS TOWN WE'VE YET TO DRINK.
YEAH, AMIGO, THAT'D BE NICE.
'CEPT OL' MOMBE CAUSED ME ONE HIGH N'MIGHTY BROUHAHA.
HE WENT TO WATTEAU. WATTEAU, WHO'S NOT KNOWN TO MANY, 'CEPT THOSE AMONG THE CITY FATHERS HE SLIPS THE ODD "CHARITABLE CONTRIBUTION" TO.
"MAN O'BUSINESS IS WATTEAU. BUT HE DON'T LIKE THAT BUSINESS KNOWN. NOT A BIT.
"SO IMAGIN' HIS DISMAY WHEN MOMBE TURNS UP AT HIS DOOR ASKIN' 'BOUT HIS COUSIN.
"WATTEAU TELLS MOMBE THAT WILL LIT OFF ONE NIGHT. THAT HE AIN'T SEEN HIDE NOR HAIR.
"MOMBE'S WILD, ACCUSES WATTEAU OF LYIN'...OF MAYBE KILLING WILL. HE WON'T LEAVE SO I HAVE T'ARRIVE.

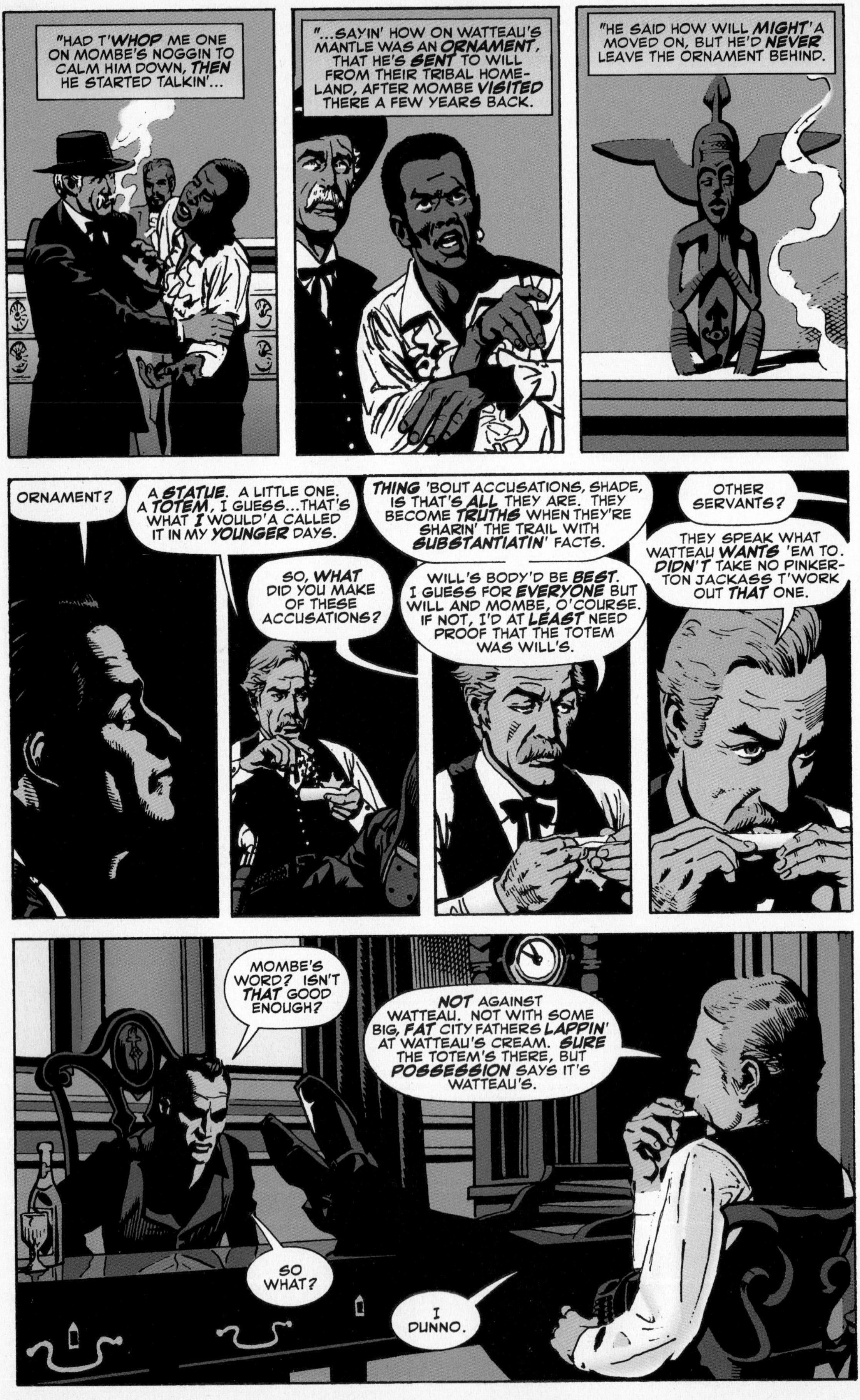

"HAD T'WHOP ME ONE ON MOMBE'S NOGGIN TO CALM HIM DOWN, THEN HE STARTED TALKIN'...
"...SAYIN' HOW ON WATTEAU'S MANTLE WAS AN ORNAMENT, THAT HE'S SENT TO WILL FROM THEIR TRIBAL HOMELAND, AFTER MOMBE VISITED THERE A FEW YEARS BACK.
"HE SAID HOW WILL MIGHT'A MOVED ON, BUT HE'D NEVER LEAVE THE ORNAMENT BEHIND.
ORNAMENT?
A STATUE. A LITTLE ONE. A TOTEM, I GUESS...THAT'S WHAT I WOULD'A CALLED IT IN MY YOUNGER DAYS.
SO, WHAT DID YOU MAKE OF THESE ACCUSATIONS?
THING 'BOUT ACCUSATIONS, SHADE, IS THAT'S ALL THEY ARE. THEY BECOME TRUTHS WHEN THEY'RE SHARIN' THE TRAIL WITH SUBSTANTIATIN' FACTS.
WILL'S BODY'D BE BEST. I GUESS FOR EVERYONE BUT WILL AND MOMBE, O'COURSE. IF NOT, I'D AT LEAST NEED PROOF THAT THE TOTEM WAS WILL'S.
OTHER SERVANTS?
THEY SPEAK WHAT WATTEAU WANTS 'EM TO. DIDN'T TAKE NO PINKERTON JACKASS T'WORK OUT THAT ONE.
MOMBE'S WORD? ISN'T THAT GOOD ENOUGH?
NOT AGAINST WATTEAU. NOT WITH SOME BIG, FAT CITY FATHERS LAPPIN' AT WATTEAU'S CREAM. SURE THE TOTEM'S THERE, BUT POSSESSION SAYS IT'S WATTEAU'S.
SO WHAT?
I DUNNO.

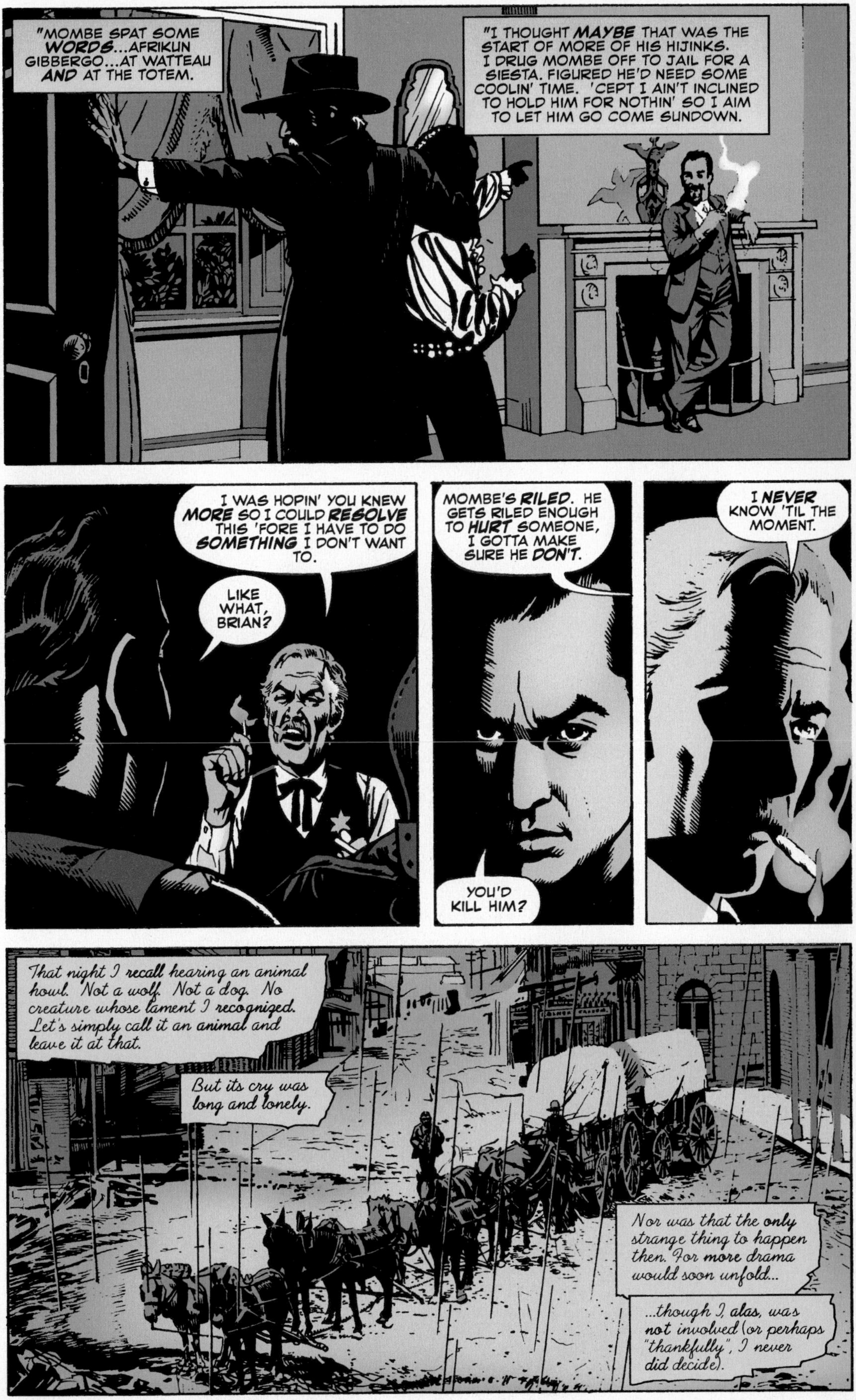
"MOMBE SPAT SOME WORDS...AFRIKUN GIBBERGO...AT WATTEAU AND AT THE TOTEM.
"I THOUGHT MAYBE THAT WAS THE START OF MORE OF HIS HIJINKS. I DRUG MOMBE OFF TO JAIL FOR A SIESTA. FIGURED HE'D NEED SOME COOLIN' TIME. 'CEPT I AIN'T INCLINED TO HOLD HIM FOR NOTHIN' SO I AIM TO LET HIM GO COME SUNDOWN.
I WAS HOPIN' YOU KNEW MORE SO I COULD RESOLVE THIS 'FORE I HAVE TO DO SOMETHING I DON'T WANT TO.
LIKE WHAT, BRIAN?
MOMBE'S RILED. HE GETS RILED ENOUGH TO HURT SOMEONE, I GOTTA MAKE SURE HE DON'T.
YOU'D KILL HIM?
I NEVER KNOW 'TIL THE MOMENT.
That night I recall hearing an animal howl. Not a wolf. Not a dog. No creature whose lament I recognized. Let's simply call it an animal and leave it at that.
But its cry was long and lonely.
Nor was that the only strange thing to happen then. For more drama would soon unfold...
...though I, alas, was not involved (or perhaps "thankfully", I never did decide).

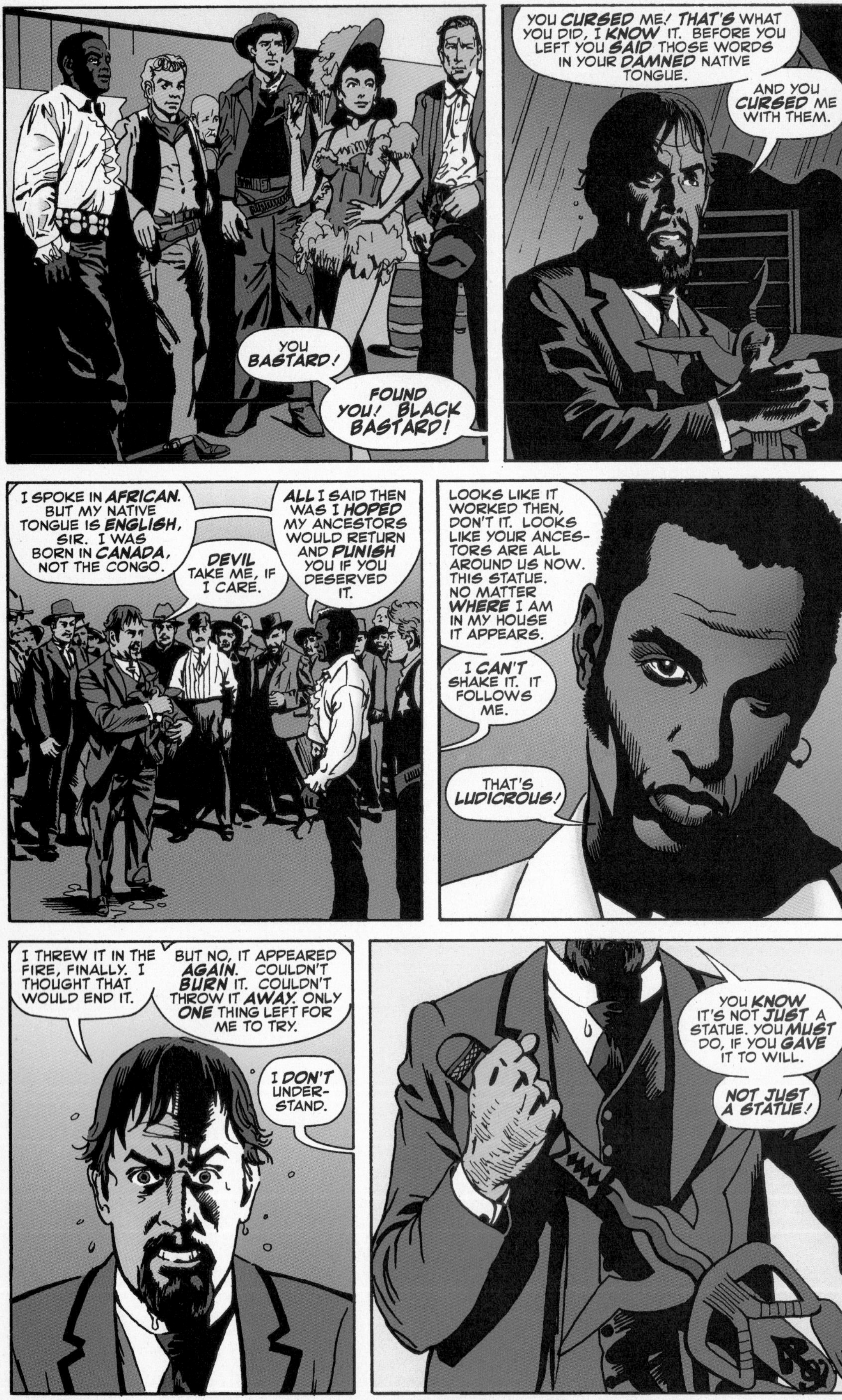
YOU BASTARD!
FOUND YOU! BLACK BASTARD!
YOU CURSED ME! THAT'S WHAT YOU DID, I KNOW IT. BEFORE YOU LEFT YOU SAID THOSE WORDS IN YOUR DAMNED NATIVE TONGUE.
AND YOU CURSED ME WITH THEM.
I SPOKE IN AFRICAN. BUT MY NATIVE TONGUE IS ENGLISH, SIR. I WAS BORN IN CANADA, NOT THE CONGO.
DEVIL TAKE ME, IF I CARE.
ALL I SAID THEN WAS I HOPED MY ANCESTORS WOULD RETURN AND PUNISH YOU IF YOU DESERVED IT.
LOOKS LIKE IT WORKED THEN, DON'T IT. LOOKS LIKE YOUR ANCESTORS ARE ALL AROUND US NOW. THIS STATUE. NO MATTER WHERE I AM IN MY HOUSE IT APPEARS.
I CAN'T SHAKE IT. IT FOLLOWS ME.
THAT'S LUDICROUS!
I THREW IT IN THE FIRE, FINALLY. I THOUGHT THAT WOULD END IT.
BUT NO, IT APPEARED AGAIN. COULDN'T BURN IT. COULDN'T THROW IT AWAY. ONLY ONE THING LEFT FOR ME TO TRY.
I DON'T UNDERSTAND.
YOU KNOW IT'S NOT JUST A STATUE. YOU MUST DO, IF YOU GAVE IT TO WILL.
NOT JUST A STATUE!

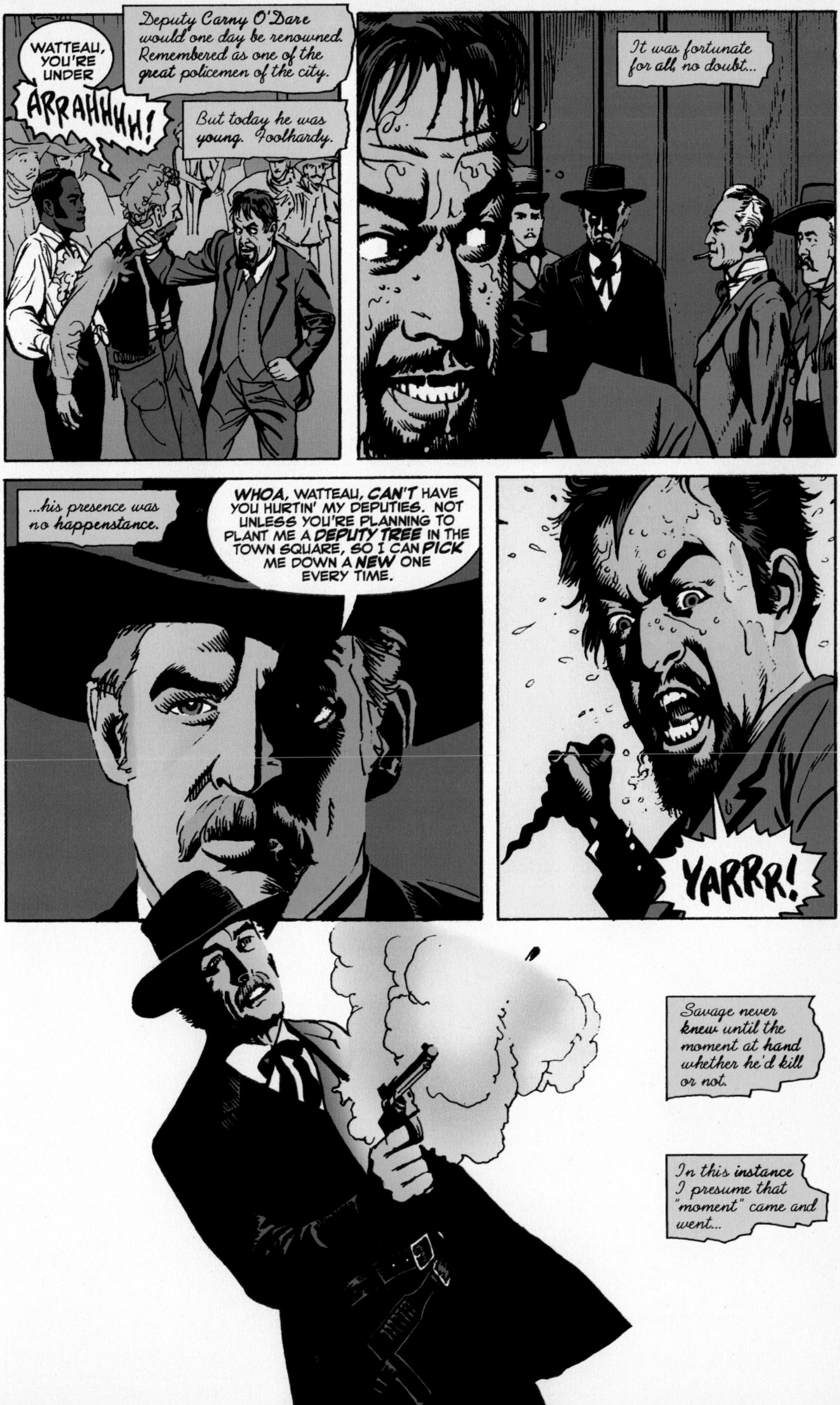

WATTEAU, YOU'RE UNDER
Deputy Carny O'Dare would one day be renowned. Remembered as one of the great policemen of the city.
ARRAHHHH!
But today he was young. Foolhardy.
It was fortunate for all, no doubt...
...his presence was no happenstance.
WHOA, WATTEAU, CAN'T HAVE YOU HURTIN' MY DEPUTIES. NOT UNLESS YOU'RE PLANNING TO PLANT ME A DEPUTY TREE IN THE TOWN SQUARE, SO I CAN PICK ME DOWN A NEW ONE EVERY TIME.
YARRR!
Savage never knew until the moment at hand whether he'd kill or not.
In this instance I presume that "moment" came and went...

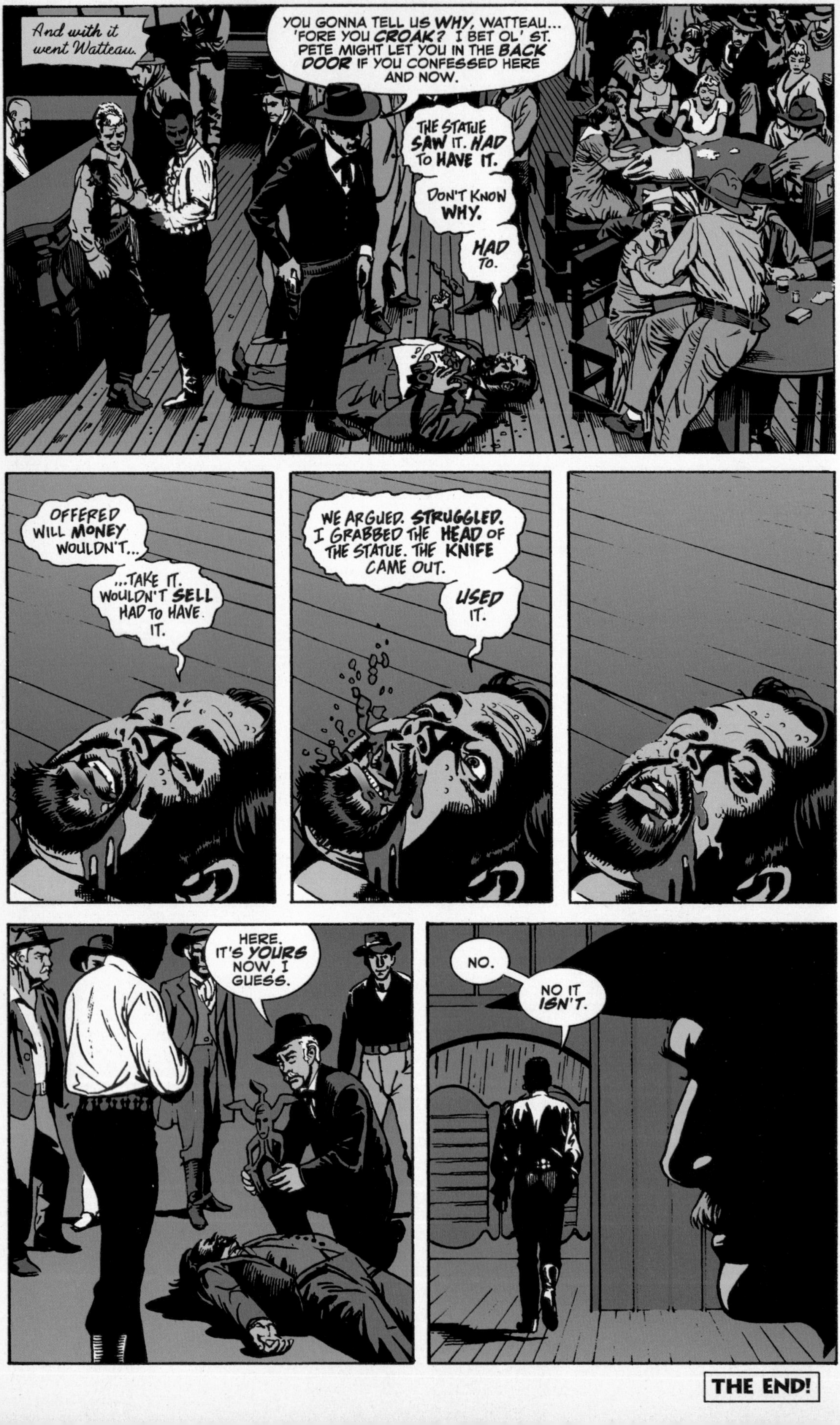
And with it went Watteau.
YOU GONNA TELL US WHY, WATTEAU... 'FORE YOU CROAK? I BET OL' ST. PETE MIGHT LET YOU IN THE BACK DOOR IF YOU CONFESSED HERE AND NOW.
THE STATUE SAW IT. HAD TO HAVE IT.
DON'T KNOW WHY.
HAD TO.
OFFERED WILL MONEY WOULDN'T...
...TAKE IT. WOULDN'T SELL HAD TO HAVE IT.
WE ARGUED. STRUGGLED. I GRABBED THE HEAD OF THE STATUE. THE KNIFE CAME OUT.
USED IT.
HERE. IT'S YOURS NOW, I GUESS.
NO.
NO IT ISN'T.
THE END!

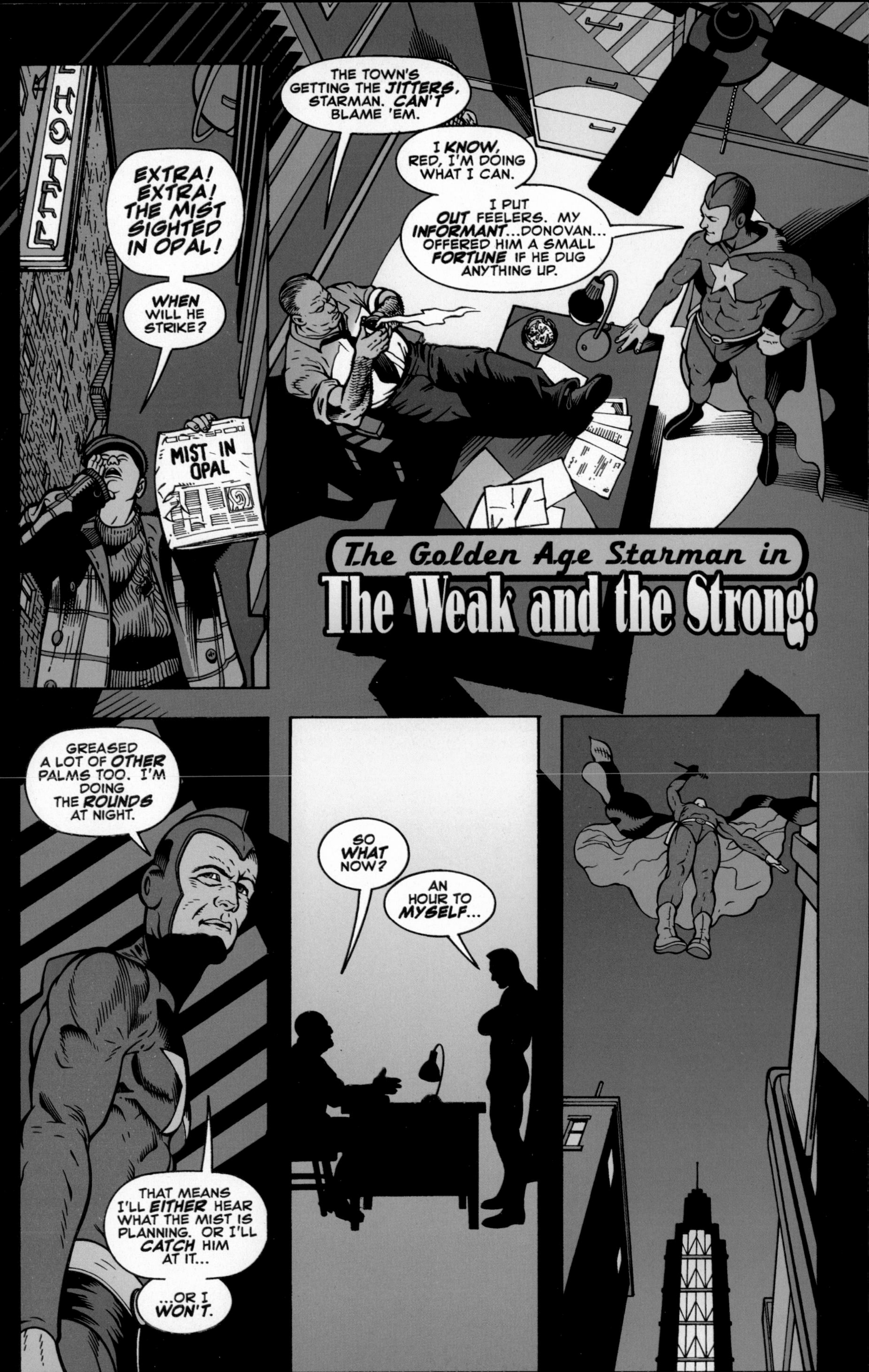
HOTEL
EXTRA! EXTRA! THE MIST SIGHTED IN OPAL!
WHEN WILL HE STRIKE?
MIST IN OPAL
THE TOWN'S GETTING THE JITTERS, STARMAN. CAN'T BLAME 'EM.
I KNOW, RED, I'M DOING WHAT I CAN.
I PUT OUT FEELERS. MY INFORMANT...DONOVAN... OFFERED HIM A SMALL FORTUNE IF HE DUG ANYTHING UP.
The Golden Age Starman in
The Weak and the Strong!
GREASED A LOT OF OTHER PALMS TOO. I'M DOING THE ROUNDS AT NIGHT.
THAT MEANS I'LL EITHER HEAR WHAT THE MIST IS PLANNING, OR I'LL CATCH HIM AT IT...
...OR I WON'T.
SO WHAT NOW?
AN HOUR TO MYSELF...

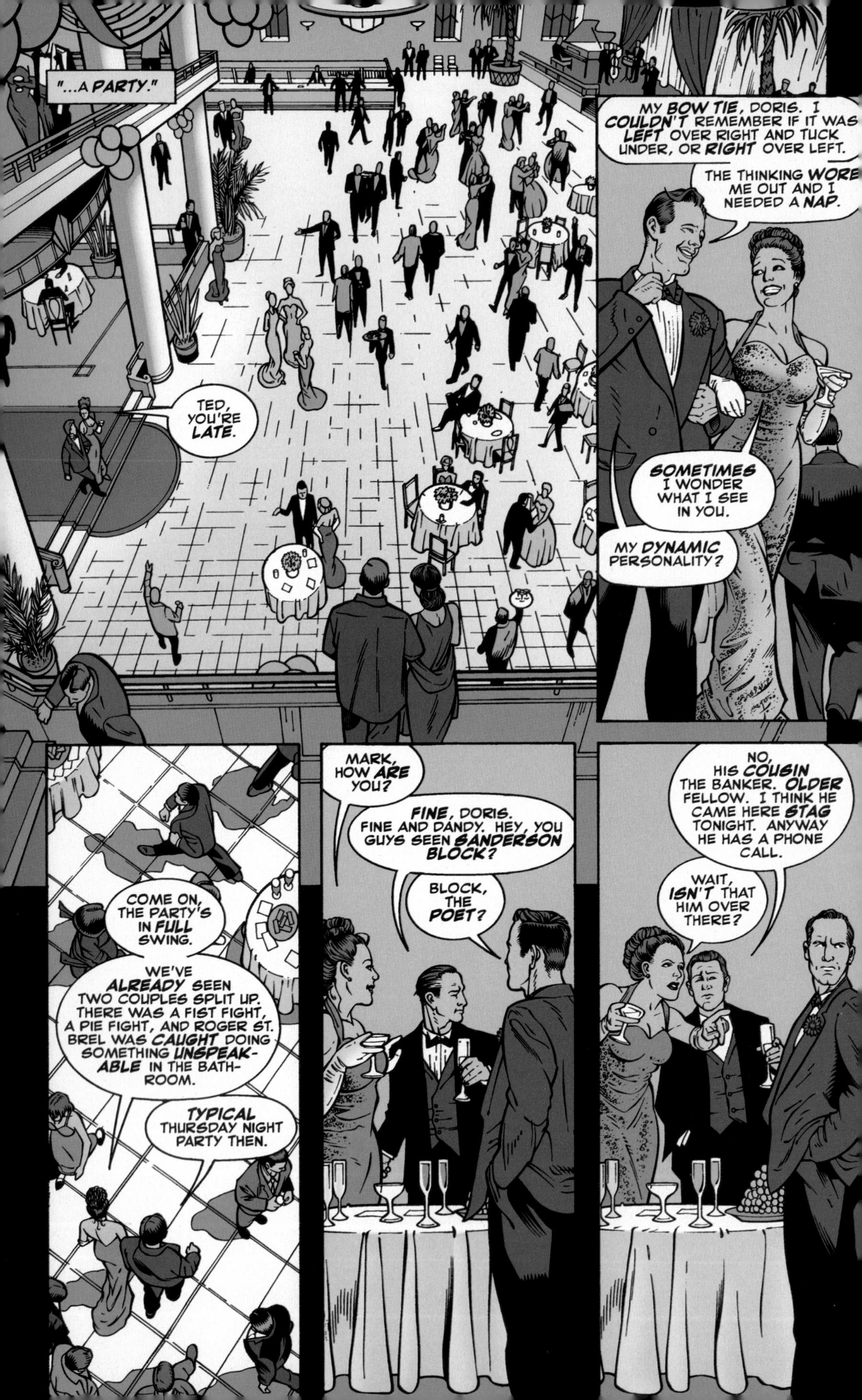

"...A PARTY."
TED, YOU'RE LATE.
MY BOW TIE, DORIS. I COULDN'T REMEMBER IF IT WAS LEFT OVER RIGHT AND TUCK UNDER, OR RIGHT OVER LEFT.
THE THINKING WORE ME OUT AND I NEEDED A NAP.
SOMETIMES I WONDER WHAT I SEE IN YOU.
MY DYNAMIC PERSONALITY?
COME ON, THE PARTY'S IN FULL SWING.
WE'VE ALREADY SEEN TWO COUPLES SPLIT UP. THERE WAS A FIST FIGHT, A PIE FIGHT, AND ROGER ST. BREL WAS CAUGHT DOING SOMETHING UNSPEAK-ABLE IN THE BATH-ROOM.
TYPICAL THURSDAY NIGHT PARTY THEN.
MARK, HOW ARE YOU?
FINE, DORIS. FINE AND DANDY. HEY, YOU GUYS SEEN SANDERSON BLOCK?
BLOCK, THE POET?
NO, HIS COUSIN THE BANKER. OLDER FELLOW. I THINK HE CAME HERE STAG TONIGHT. ANYWAY HE HAS A PHONE CALL.
WAIT, ISN'T THAT HIM OVER THERE?

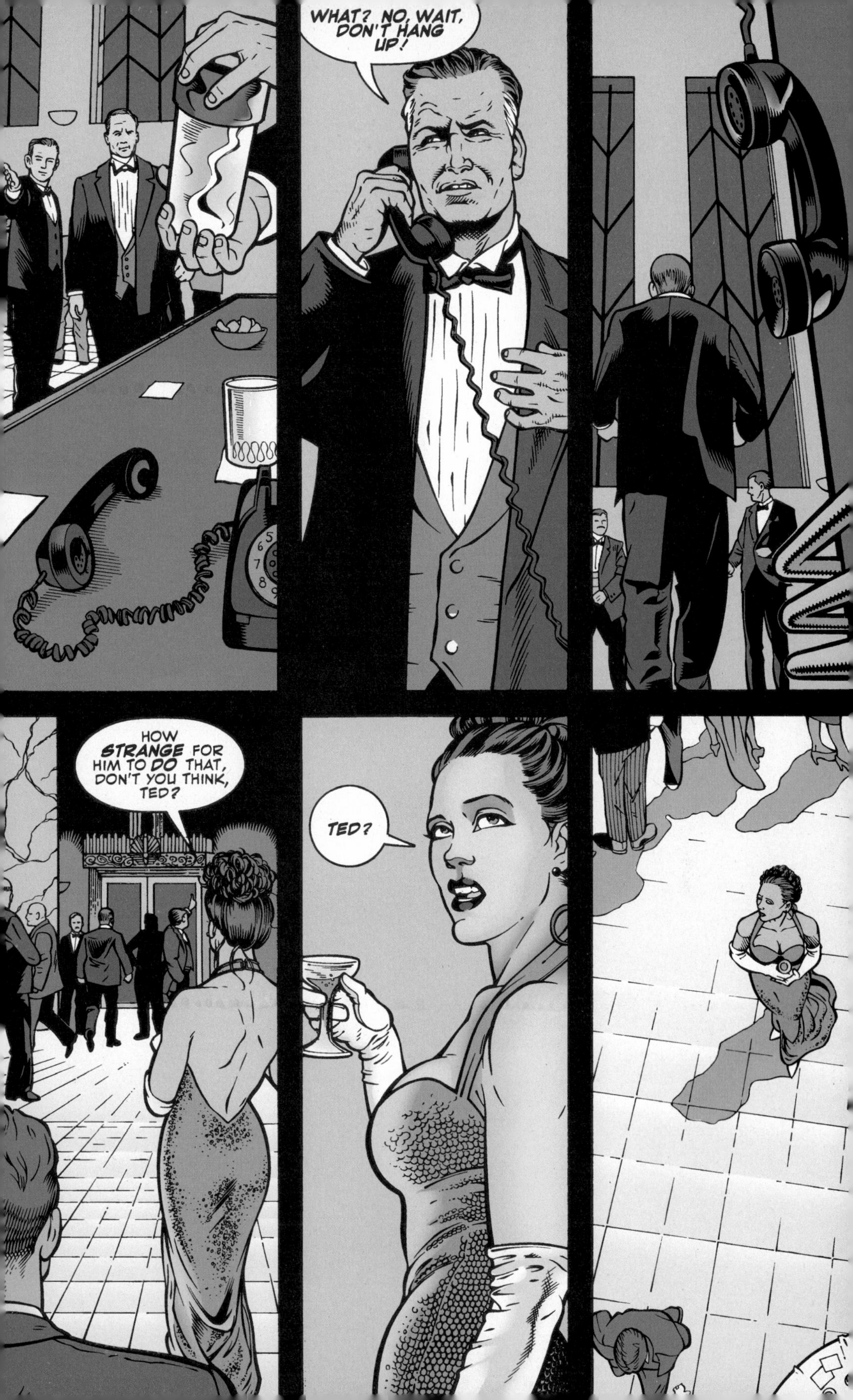
WHAT? NO, WAIT, DON'T HANG UP!
HOW STRANGE FOR HIM TO DO THAT, DON'T YOU THINK, TED?
TED?

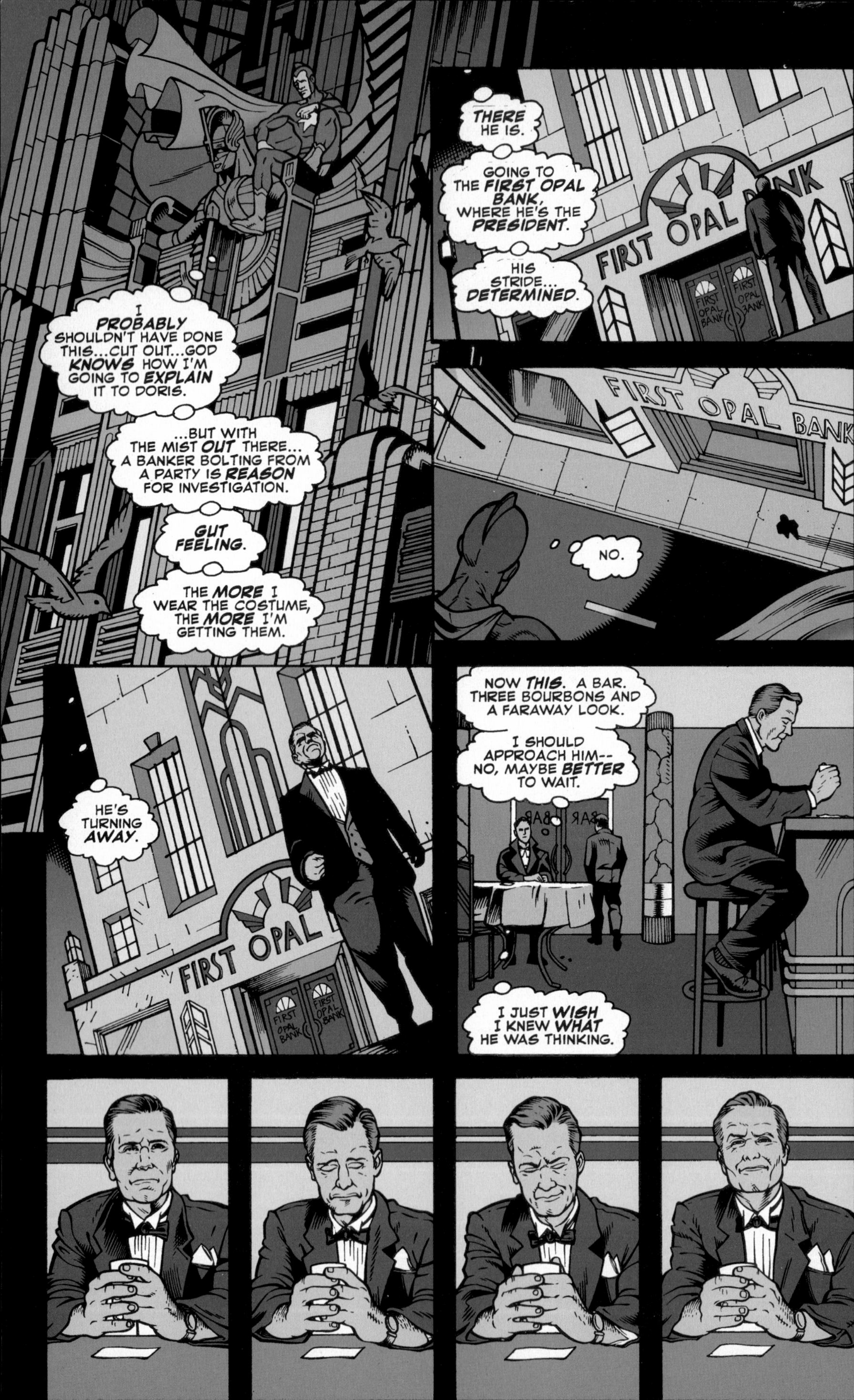
I PROBABLY SHOULDN'T HAVE DONE THIS...CUT OUT...GOD KNOWS HOW I'M GOING TO EXPLAIN IT TO DORIS.
...BUT WITH THE MIST OUT THERE... A BANKER BOLTING FROM A PARTY IS REASON FOR INVESTIGATION.
GUT FEELING.
THE MORE I WEAR THE COSTUME, THE MORE I'M GETTING THEM.
THERE HE IS.
GOING TO THE FIRST OPAL BANK, WHERE HE'S THE PRESIDENT.
HIS STRIDE... DETERMINED.
FIRST OPAL BANK
NO.
HE'S TURNING AWAY.
FIRST OPAL
NOW THIS. A BAR. THREE BOURBONS AND A FARAWAY LOOK.
I SHOULD APPROACH HIM-- NO, MAYBE BETTER TO WAIT.
I JUST WISH I KNEW WHAT HE WAS THINKING.

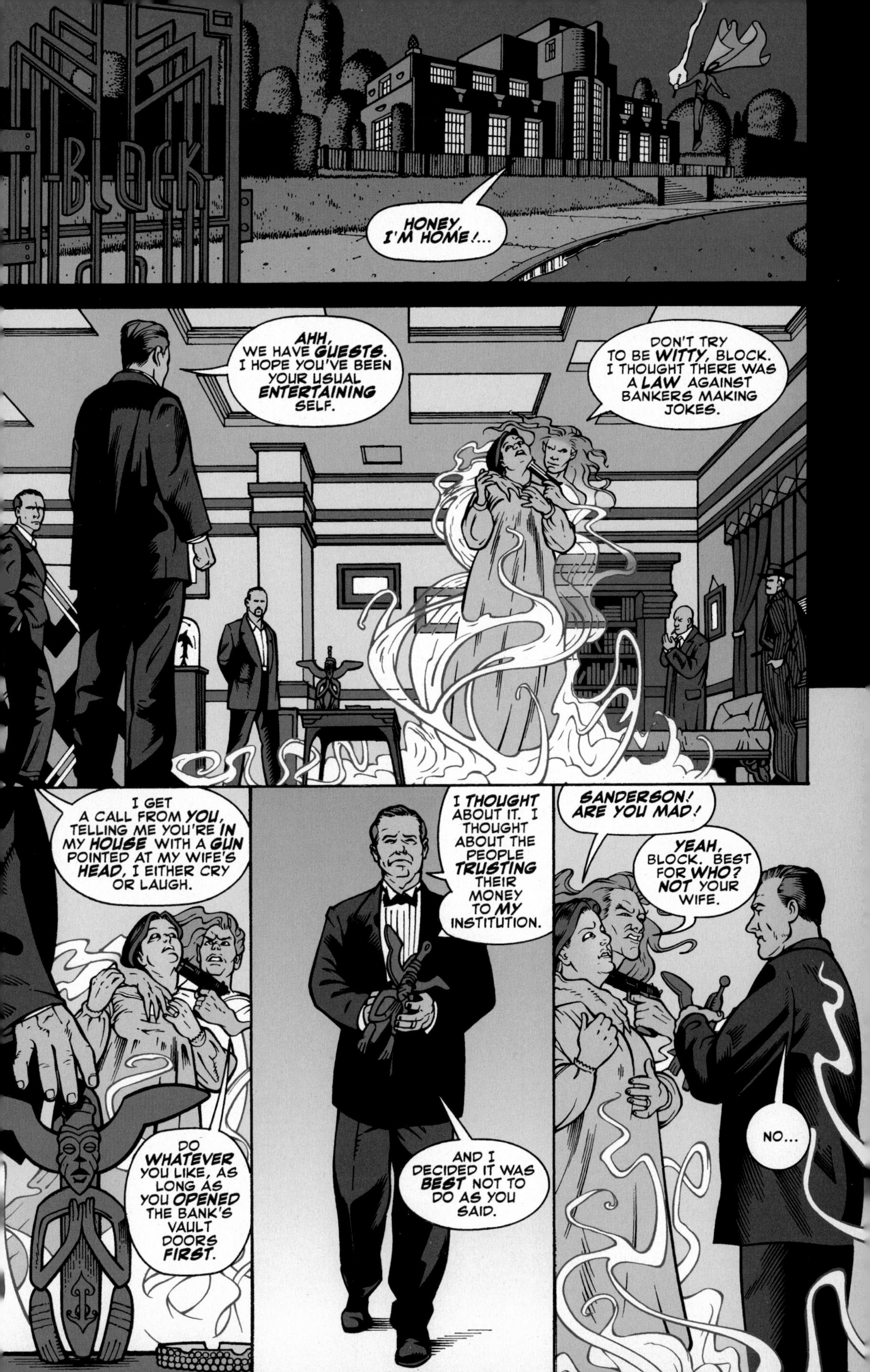
BLOCK
HONEY, I'M HOME!...
AHH, WE HAVE GUESTS. I HOPE YOU'VE BEEN YOUR USUAL ENTERTAINING SELF.
DON'T TRY TO BE WITTY, BLOCK. I THOUGHT THERE WAS A LAW AGAINST BANKERS MAKING JOKES.
I GET A CALL FROM YOU, TELLING ME YOU'RE IN MY HOUSE WITH A GUN POINTED AT MY WIFE'S HEAD, I EITHER CRY OR LAUGH.
DO WHATEVER YOU LIKE, AS LONG AS YOU OPENED THE BANK'S VAULT DOORS FIRST.
I THOUGHT ABOUT IT. I THOUGHT ABOUT THE PEOPLE TRUSTING THEIR MONEY TO MY INSTITUTION.
AND I DECIDED IT WAS BEST NOT TO DO AS YOU SAID.
SANDERSON! ARE YOU MAD!
YEAH, BLOCK. BEST FOR WHO? NOT YOUR WIFE.
NO...

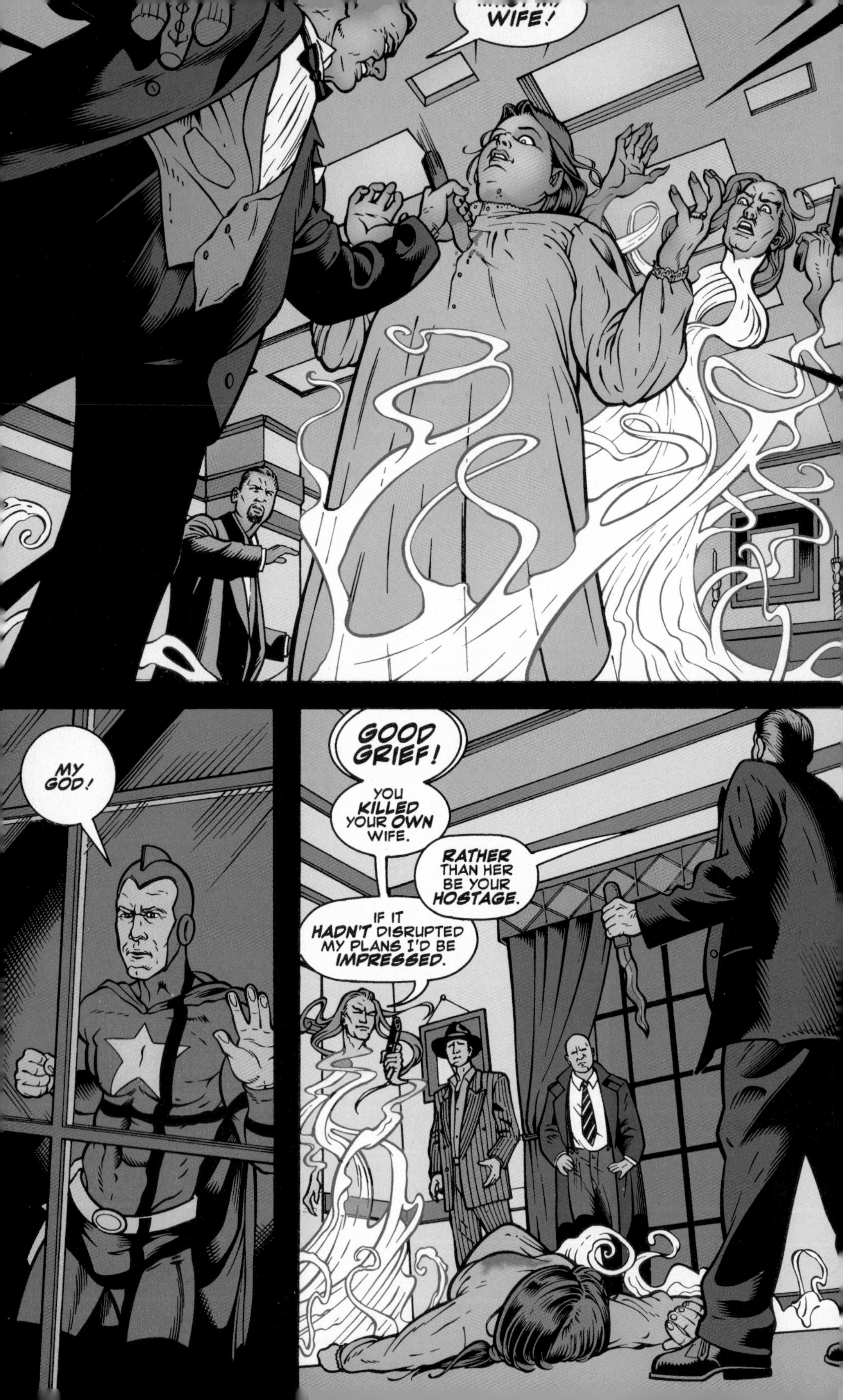
WIFE!
MY GOD!
GOOD GRIEF!
YOU KILLED YOUR OWN WIFE.
RATHER THAN HER BE YOUR HOSTAGE.
IF IT HADN'T DISRUPTED MY PLANS I'D BE IMPRESSED.

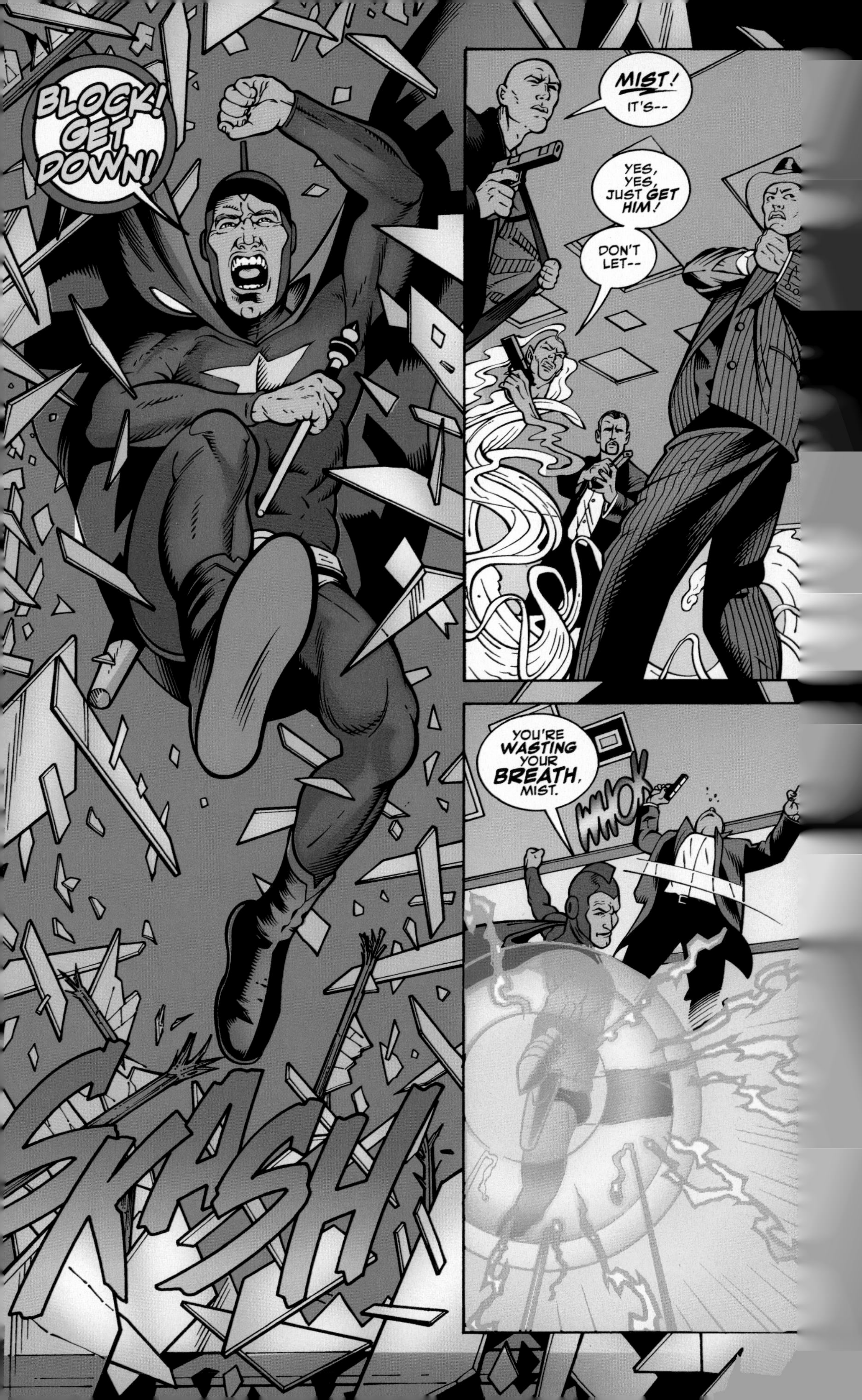
BLOCK! GET DOWN!
KSSH
MIST! IT'S--
YES, YES, JUST GET HIM!
DON'T LET--
YOU'RE WASTING YOUR BREATH, MIST.
WHOK

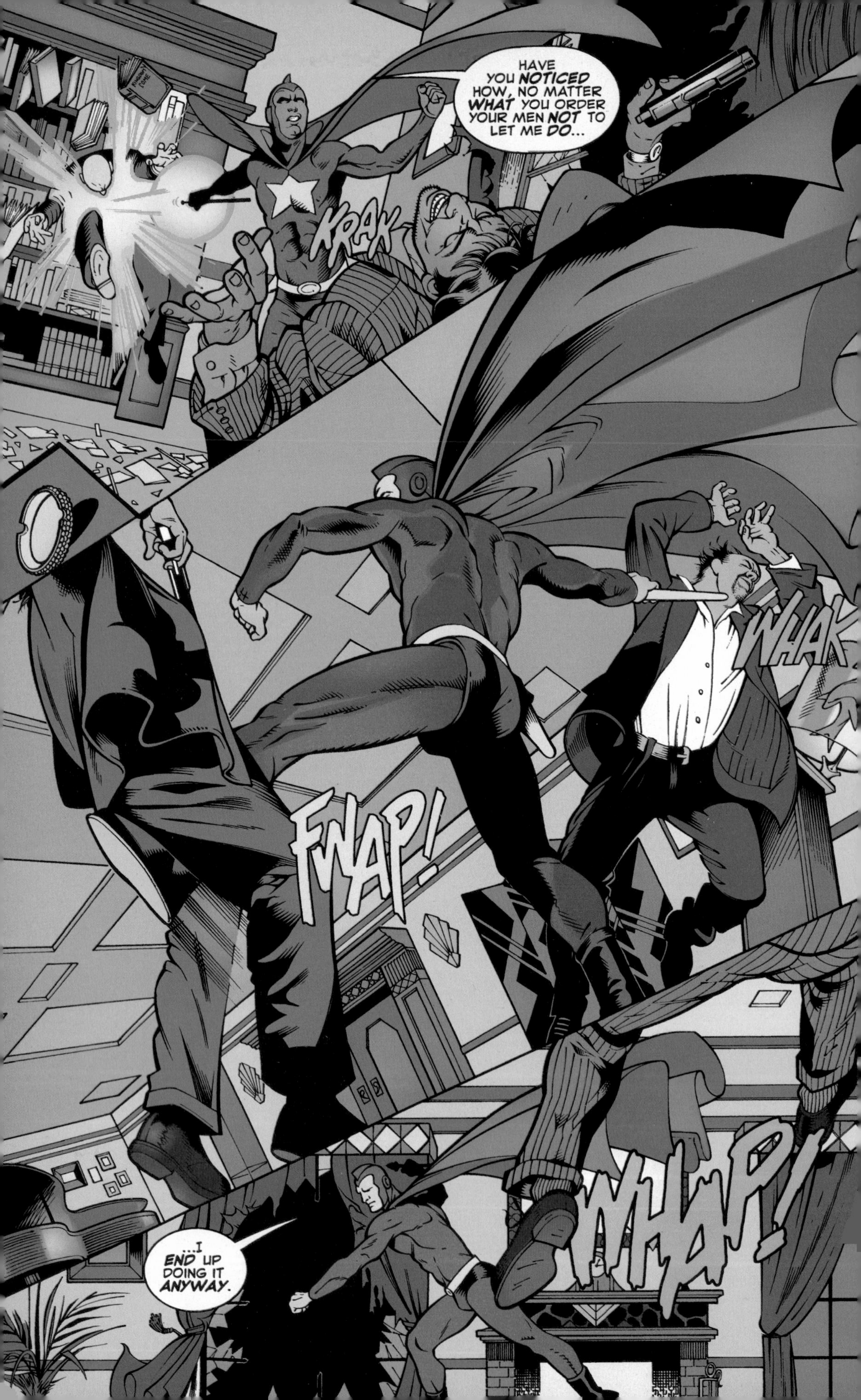
HAVE YOU NOTICED HOW, NO MATTER WHAT YOU ORDER YOUR MEN NOT TO LET ME DO...
KRAK
WHAK
FWAP!
WHAP!
...I END UP DOING IT ANYWAY.

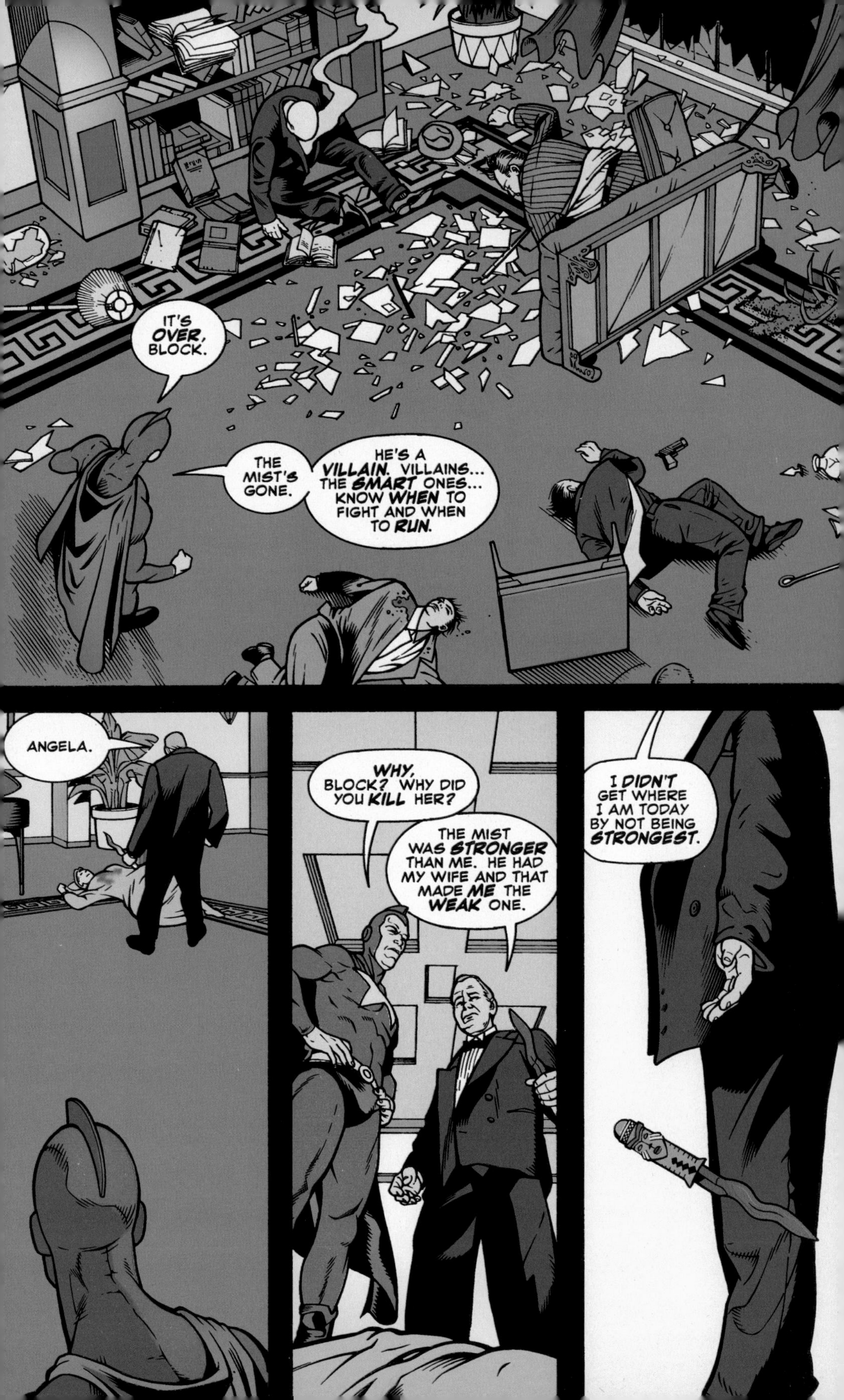
IT'S OVER, BLOCK.
THE MIST'S GONE.
HE'S A VILLAIN. VILLAINS... THE SMART ONES... KNOW WHEN TO FIGHT AND WHEN TO RUN.
ANGELA.
WHY, BLOCK? WHY DID YOU KILL HER?
THE MIST WAS STRONGER THAN ME. HE HAD MY WIFE AND THAT MADE ME THE WEAK ONE.
I DIDN'T GET WHERE I AM TODAY BY NOT BEING STRONGEST.

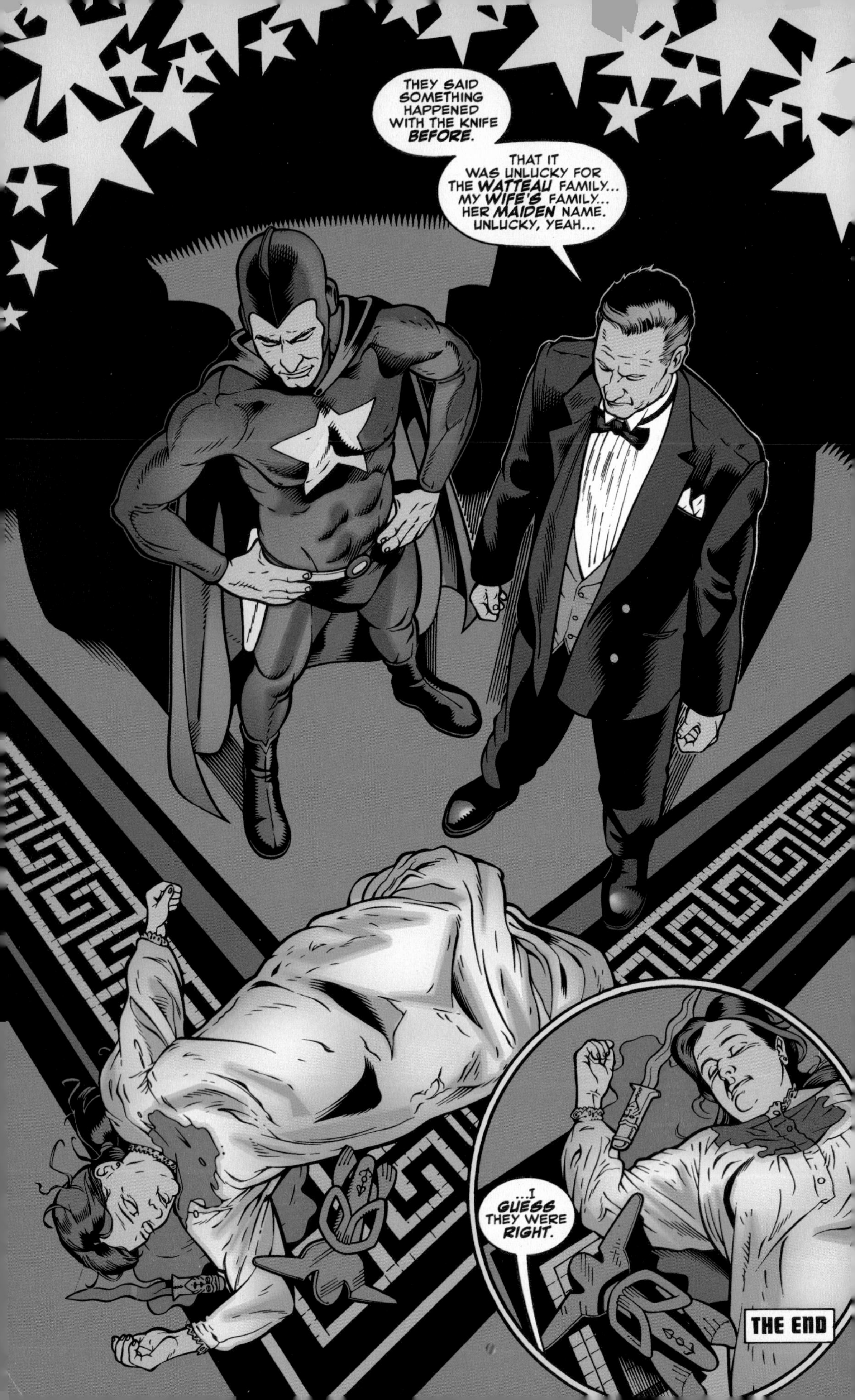
THEY SAID SOMETHING HAPPENED WITH THE KNIFE *BEFORE*.
THAT IT WAS UNLUCKY FOR THE *WATTEAU* FAMILY... MY *WIFE'S* FAMILY... HER *MAIDEN* NAME. UNLUCKY, YEAH...
...I *GUESS* THEY WERE *RIGHT*.
THE END

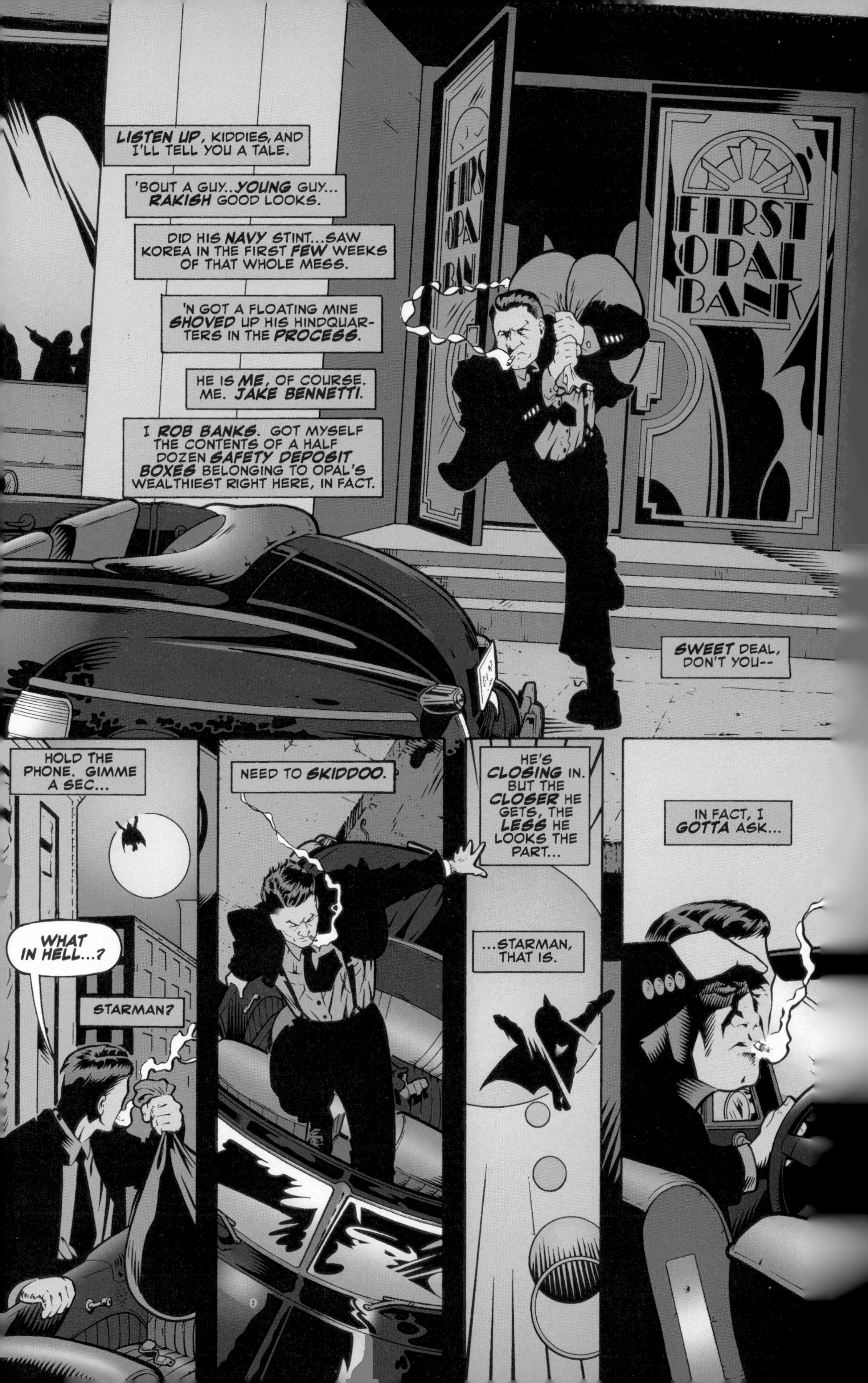
LISTEN UP, KIDDIES, AND I'LL TELL YOU A TALE.
'BOUT A GUY...YOUNG GUY... RAKISH GOOD LOOKS.
DID HIS NAVY STINT...SAW KOREA IN THE FIRST FEW WEEKS OF THAT WHOLE MESS.
'N GOT A FLOATING MINE SHOVED UP HIS HINDQUARTERS IN THE PROCESS.
HE IS ME, OF COURSE. ME. JAKE BENNETTI.
I ROB BANKS. GOT MYSELF THE CONTENTS OF A HALF DOZEN SAFETY DEPOSIT BOXES BELONGING TO OPAL'S WEALTHIEST RIGHT HERE, IN FACT.
FIRST OPAL BANK
SWEET DEAL, DON'T YOU--
HOLD THE PHONE. GIMME A SEC...
WHAT IN HELL...?
STARMAN?
NEED TO SKIDDOO.
HE'S CLOSING IN. BUT THE CLOSER HE GETS, THE LESS HE LOOKS THE PART...
...STARMAN, THAT IS.
IN FACT, I GOTTA ASK...

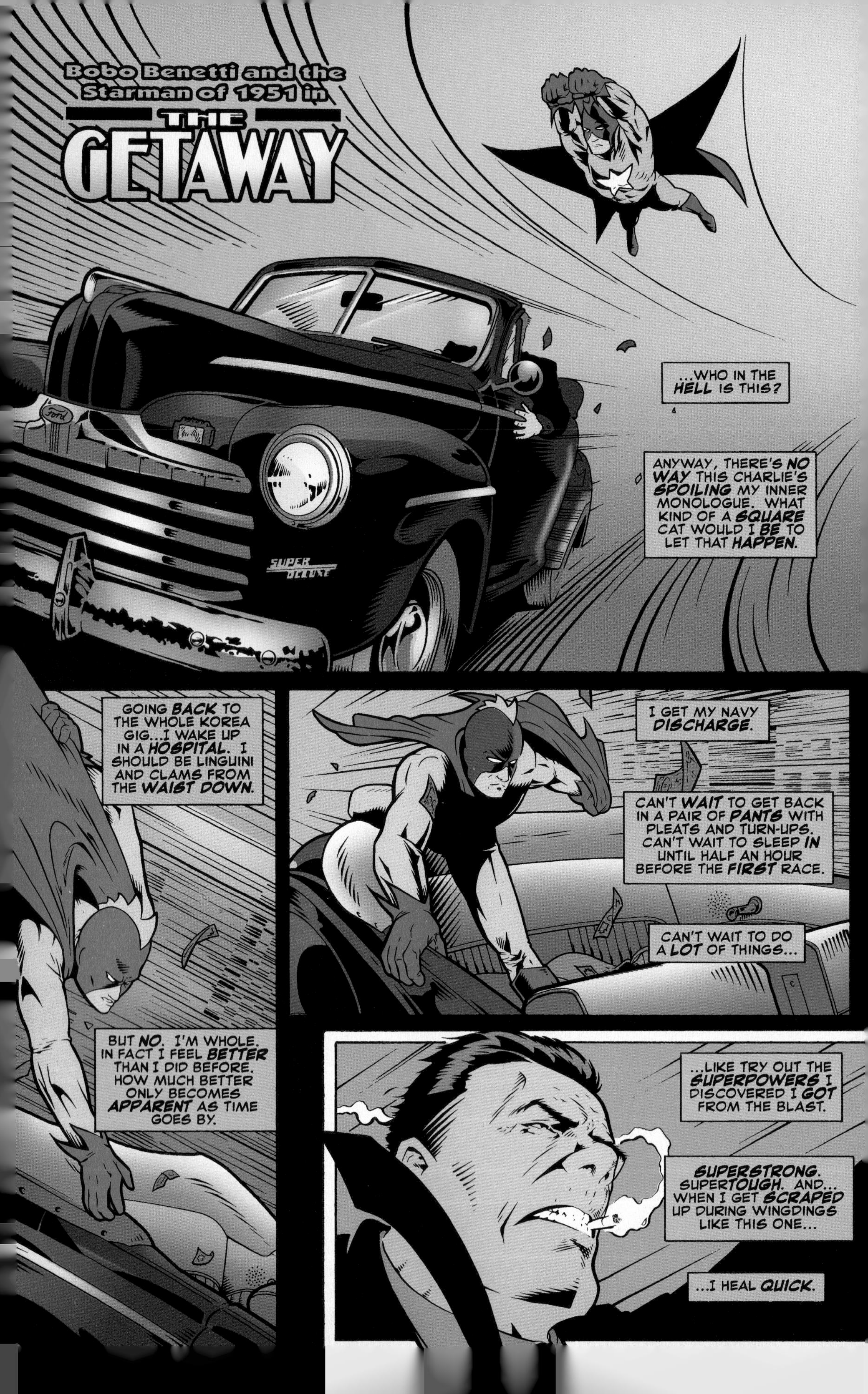

Bobo Benetti and the Starman of 1951 in
THE GETAWAY
...WHO IN THE HELL IS THIS?
ANYWAY, THERE'S NO WAY THIS CHARLIE'S SPOILING MY INNER MONOLOGUE. WHAT KIND OF A SQUARE CAT WOULD I BE TO LET THAT HAPPEN.
GOING BACK TO THE WHOLE KOREA GIG...I WAKE UP IN A HOSPITAL. I SHOULD BE LINGUINI AND CLAMS FROM THE WAIST DOWN.
BUT NO. I'M WHOLE. IN FACT I FEEL BETTER THAN I DID BEFORE. HOW MUCH BETTER ONLY BECOMES APPARENT AS TIME GOES BY.
I GET MY NAVY DISCHARGE.
CAN'T WAIT TO GET BACK IN A PAIR OF PANTS WITH PLEATS AND TURN-UPS. CAN'T WAIT TO SLEEP IN UNTIL HALF AN HOUR BEFORE THE FIRST RACE.
CAN'T WAIT TO DO A LOT OF THINGS...
...LIKE TRY OUT THE SUPERPOWERS I DISCOVERED I GOT FROM THE BLAST.
SUPERSTRONG. SUPERTOUGH. AND... WHEN I GET SCRAPED UP DURING WINGDINGS LIKE THIS ONE...
...I HEAL QUICK.

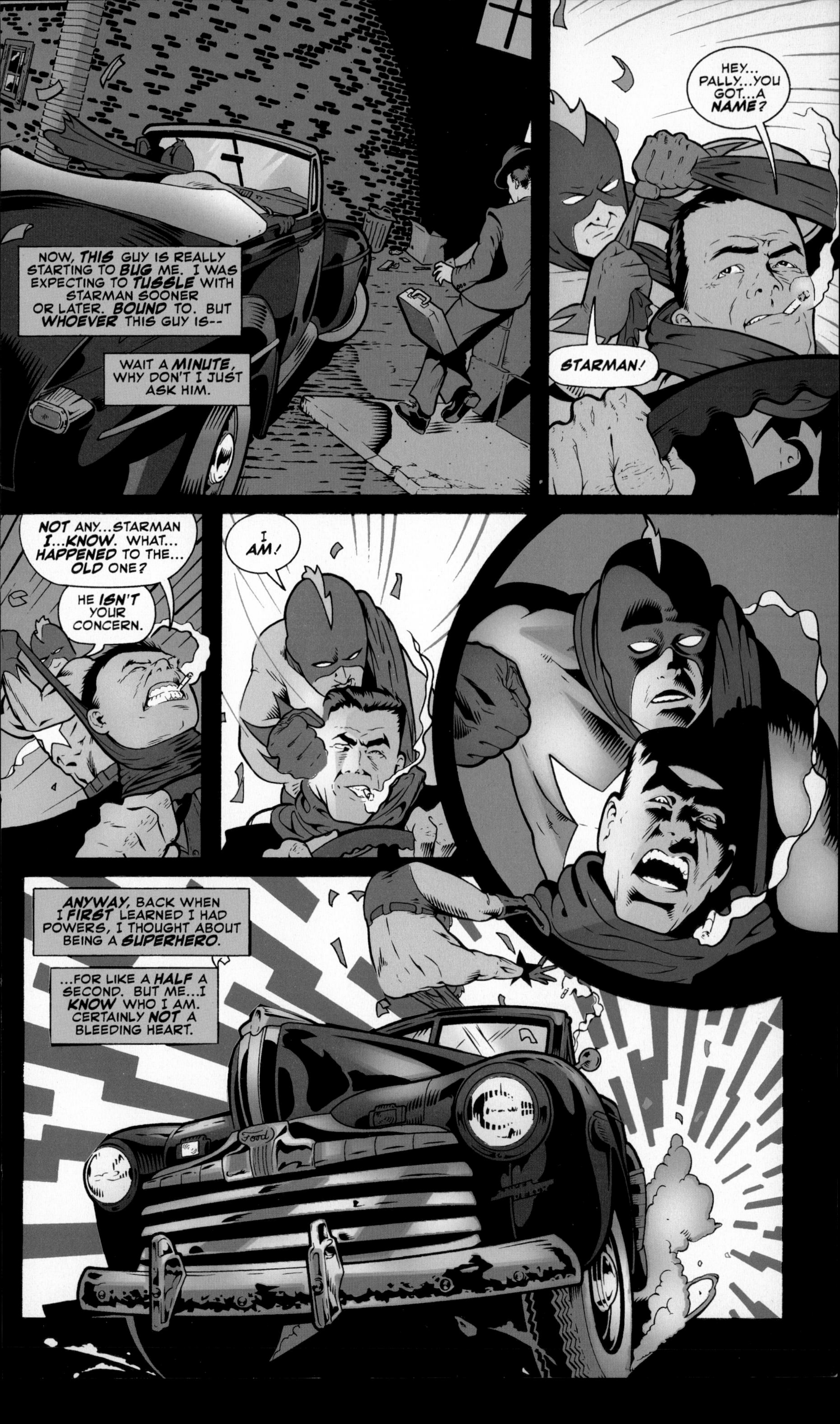
NOW, THIS GUY IS REALLY STARTING TO BUG ME. I WAS EXPECTING TO TUSSLE WITH STARMAN SOONER OR LATER. BOUND TO. BUT WHOEVER THIS GUY IS--
WAIT A MINUTE, WHY DON'T I JUST ASK HIM.
HEY... PALLY...YOU GOT...A NAME?
STARMAN!
NOT ANY...STARMAN I...KNOW. WHAT... HAPPENED TO THE... OLD ONE?
HE ISN'T YOUR CONCERN.
I AM!
ANYWAY, BACK WHEN I FIRST LEARNED I HAD POWERS, I THOUGHT ABOUT BEING A SUPERHERO.
...FOR LIKE A HALF A SECOND. BUT ME...I KNOW WHO I AM. CERTAINLY NOT A BLEEDING HEART.

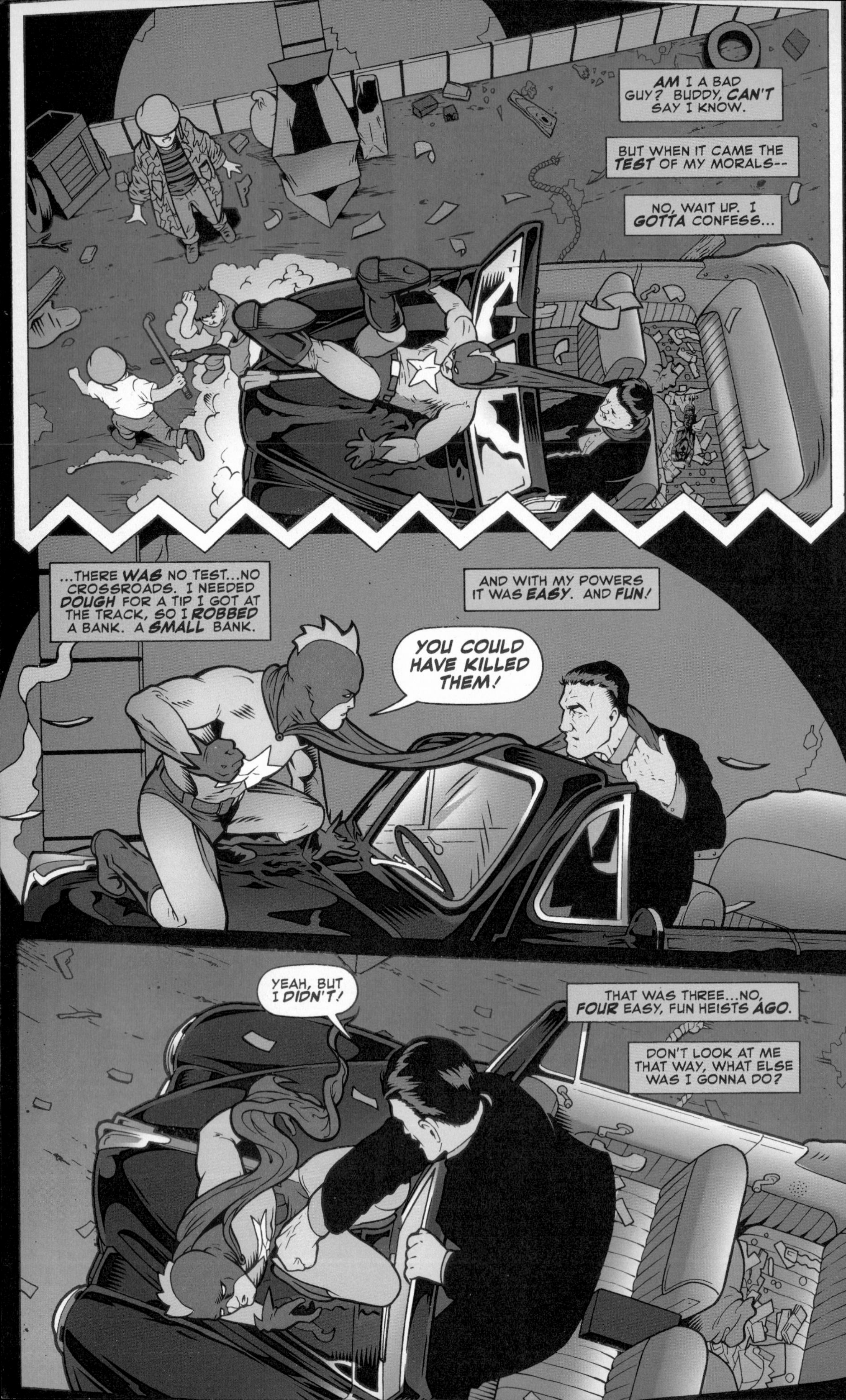
AM I A BAD GUY? BUDDY, CAN'T SAY I KNOW.
BUT WHEN IT CAME THE TEST OF MY MORALS--
NO, WAIT UP. I GOTTA CONFESS...
...THERE WAS NO TEST...NO CROSSROADS. I NEEDED DOUGH FOR A TIP I GOT AT THE TRACK, SO I ROBBED A BANK. A SMALL BANK.
AND WITH MY POWERS IT WAS EASY. AND FUN!
YOU COULD HAVE KILLED THEM!
YEAH, BUT I DIDN'T!
THAT WAS THREE...NO, FOUR EASY, FUN HEISTS AGO.
DON'T LOOK AT ME THAT WAY, WHAT ELSE WAS I GONNA DO?

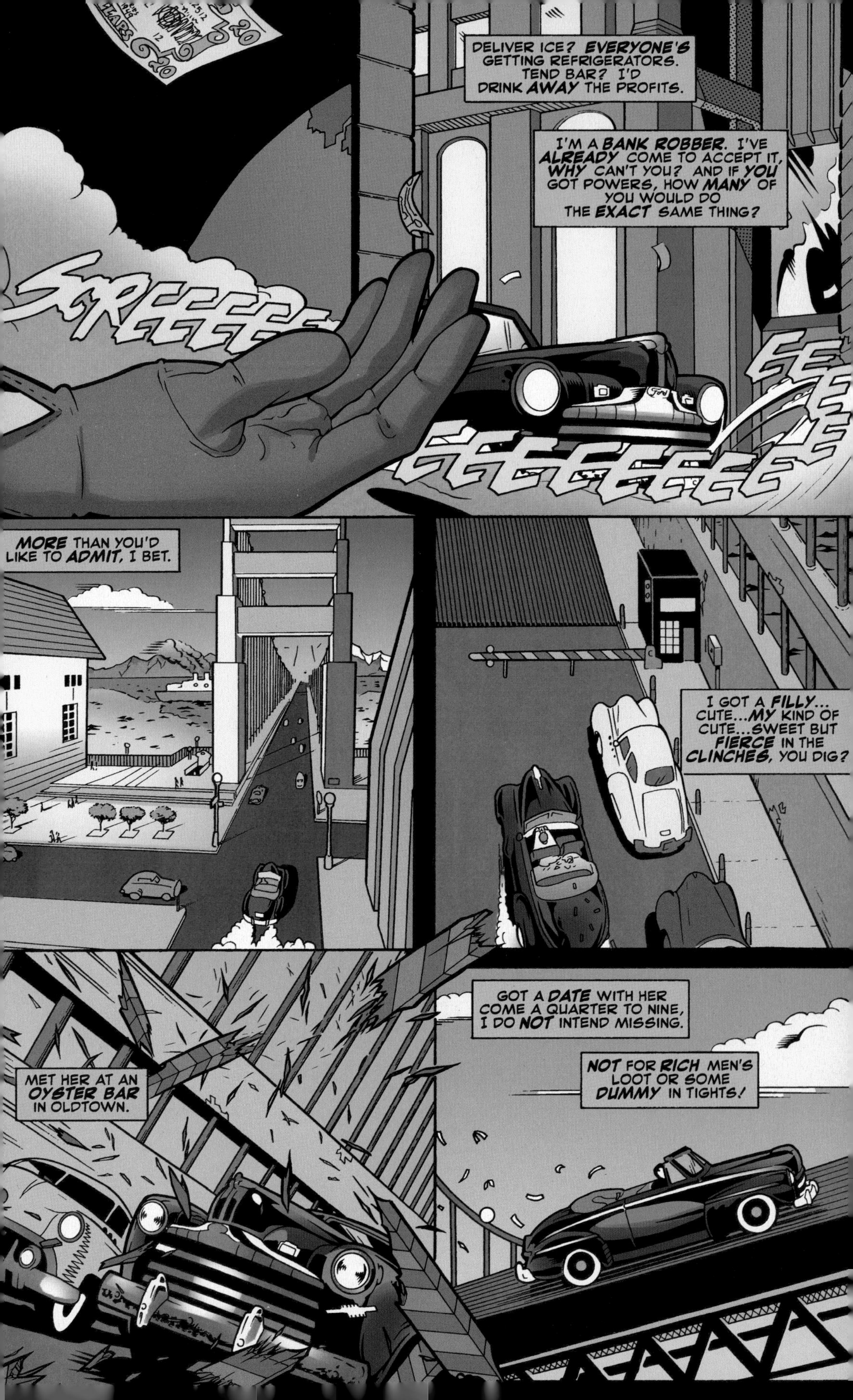

DELIVER ICE? EVERYONE'S GETTING REFRIGERATORS. TEND BAR? I'D DRINK AWAY THE PROFITS.
I'M A BANK ROBBER. I'VE ALREADY COME TO ACCEPT IT, WHY CAN'T YOU? AND IF YOU GOT POWERS, HOW MANY OF YOU WOULD DO THE EXACT SAME THING?
SCREEEEEEEEEEEEEEEEEEEEE
MORE THAN YOU'D LIKE TO ADMIT, I BET.
I GOT A FILLY... CUTE...MY KIND OF CUTE...SWEET BUT FIERCE IN THE CLINCHES, YOU DIG?
MET HER AT AN OYSTER BAR IN OLDTOWN.
GOT A DATE WITH HER COME A QUARTER TO NINE, I DO NOT INTEND MISSING.
NOT FOR RICH MEN'S LOOT OR SOME DUMMY IN TIGHTS!

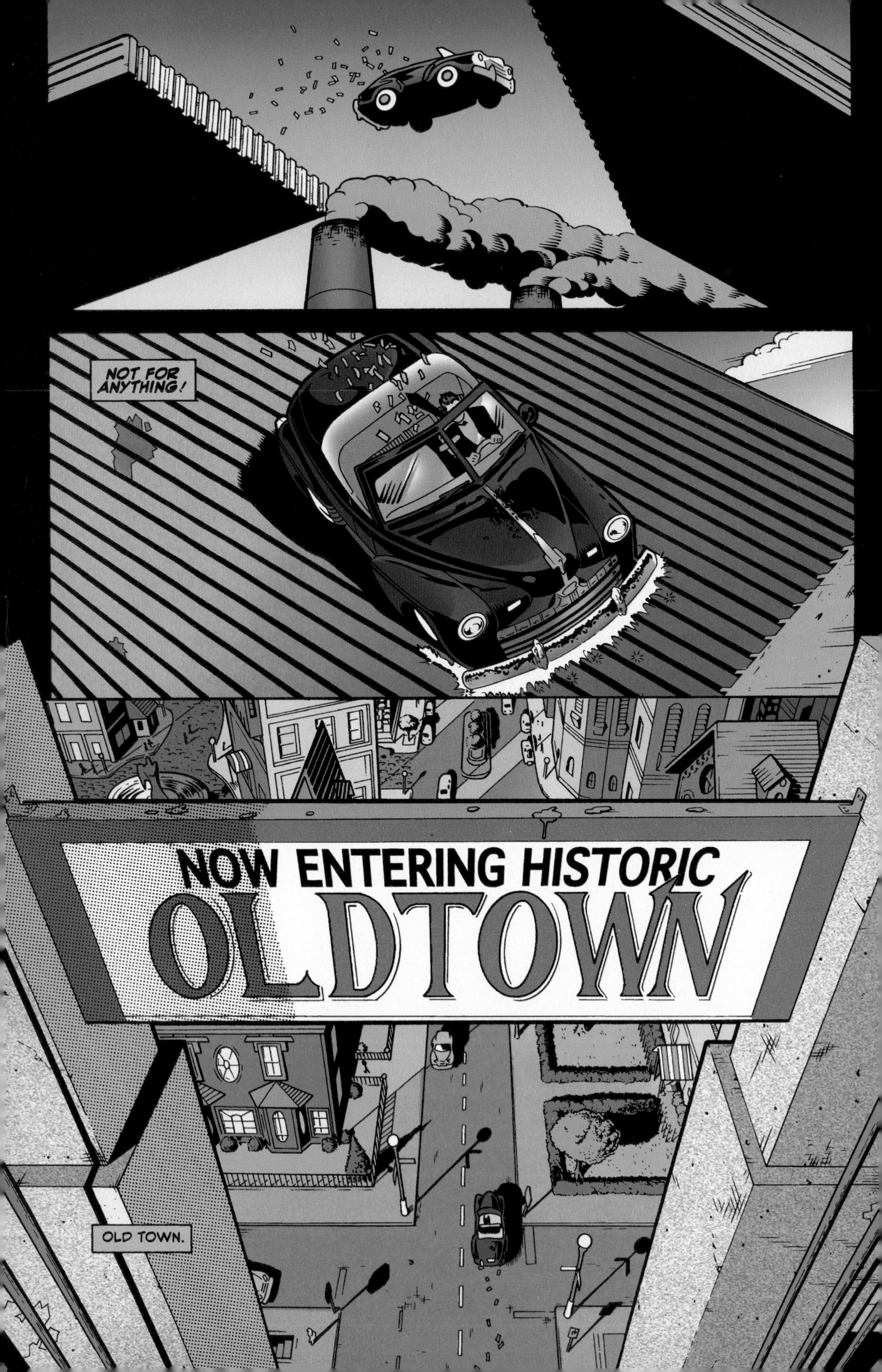

NOT FOR ANYTHING!
NOW ENTERING HISTORIC
OLDTOWN
OLD TOWN.

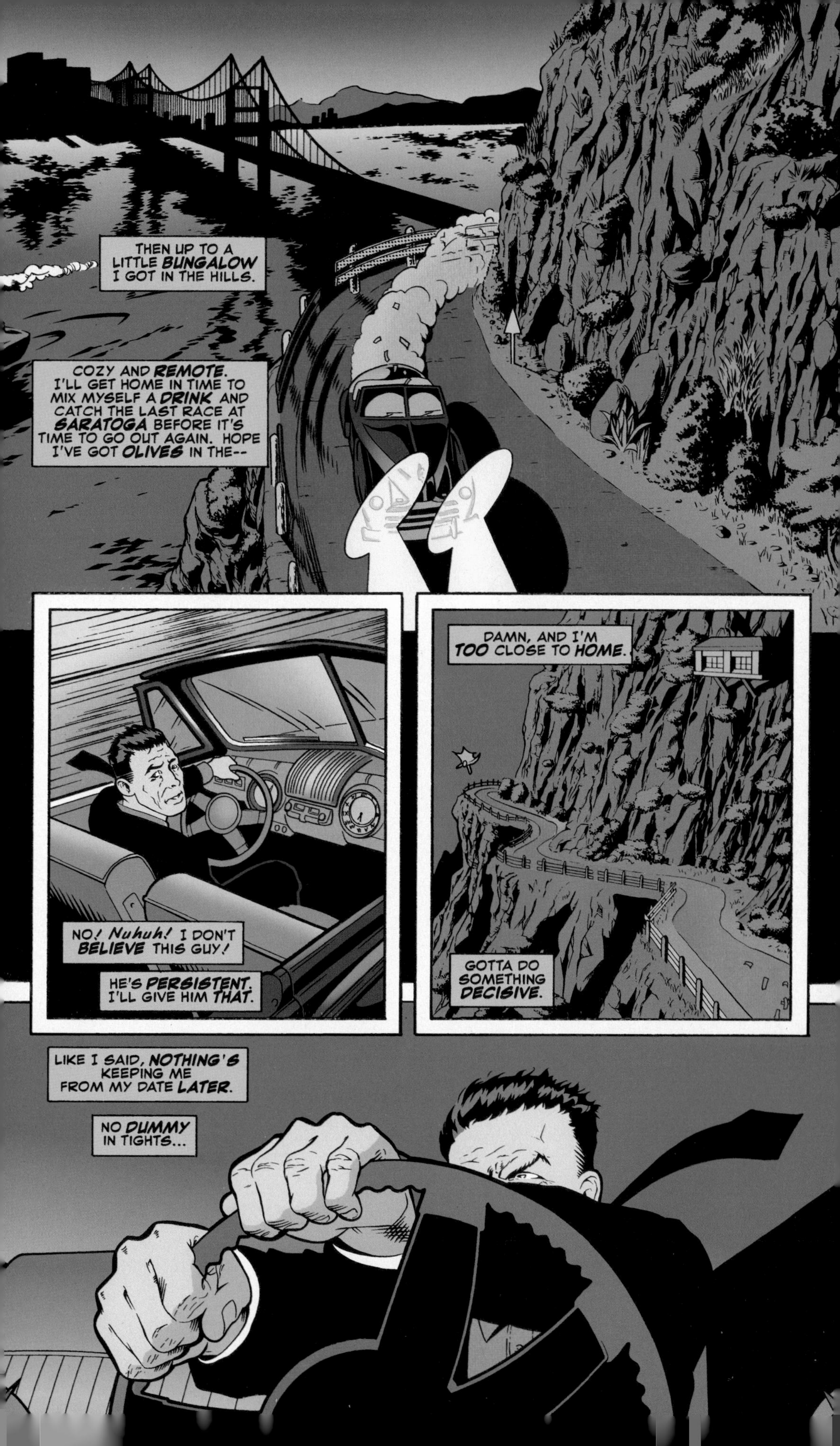
THEN UP TO A LITTLE BUNGALOW I GOT IN THE HILLS.
COZY AND REMOTE. I'LL GET HOME IN TIME TO MIX MYSELF A DRINK AND CATCH THE LAST RACE AT SARATOGA BEFORE IT'S TIME TO GO OUT AGAIN. HOPE I'VE GOT OLIVES IN THE--
NO! Nuhuh! I DON'T BELIEVE THIS GUY!
HE'S PERSISTENT. I'LL GIVE HIM THAT.
DAMN, AND I'M TOO CLOSE TO HOME.
GOTTA DO SOMETHING DECISIVE.
LIKE I SAID, NOTHING'S KEEPING ME FROM MY DATE LATER.
NO DUMMY IN TIGHTS...

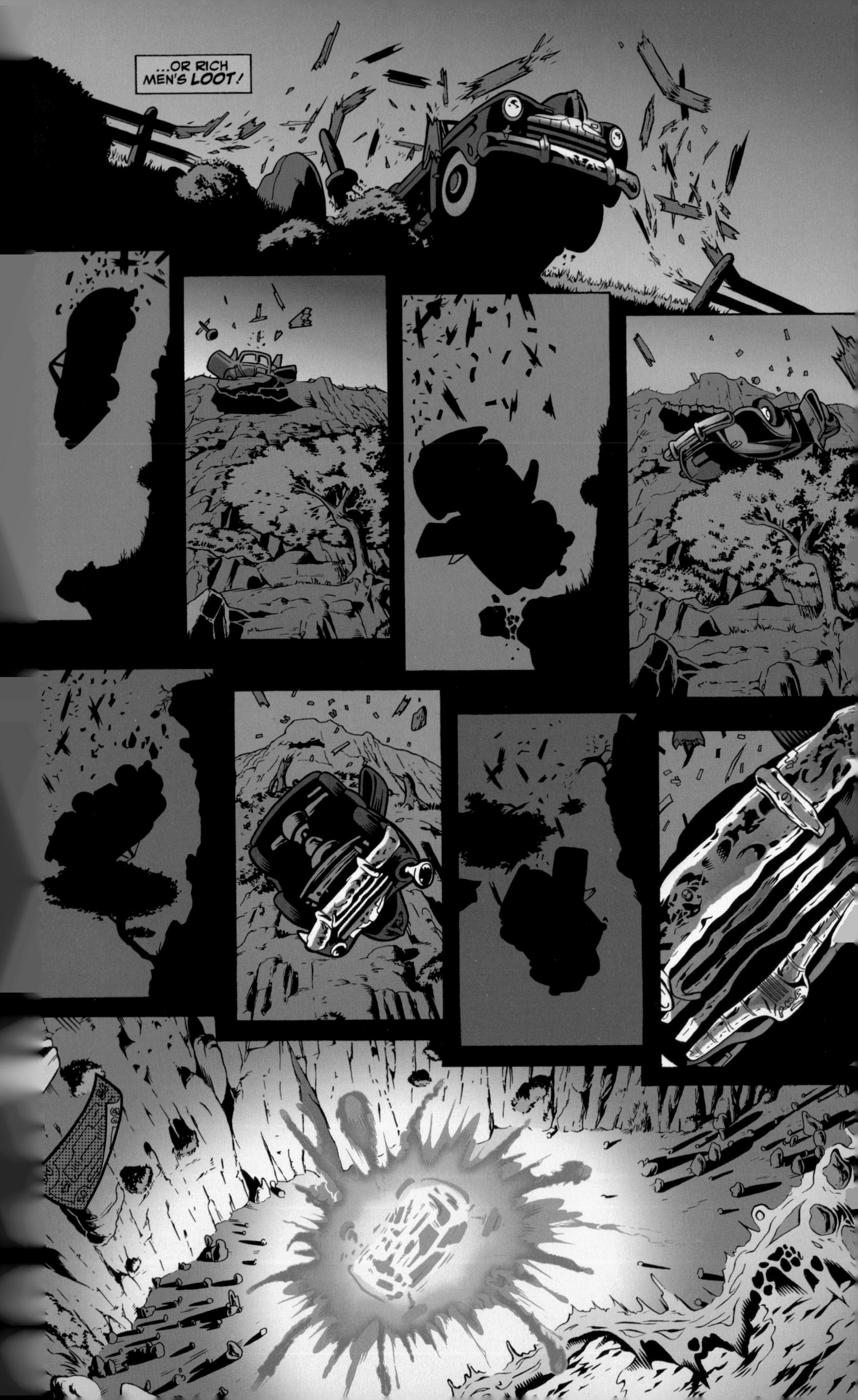
...OR RICH MEN'S LOOT!

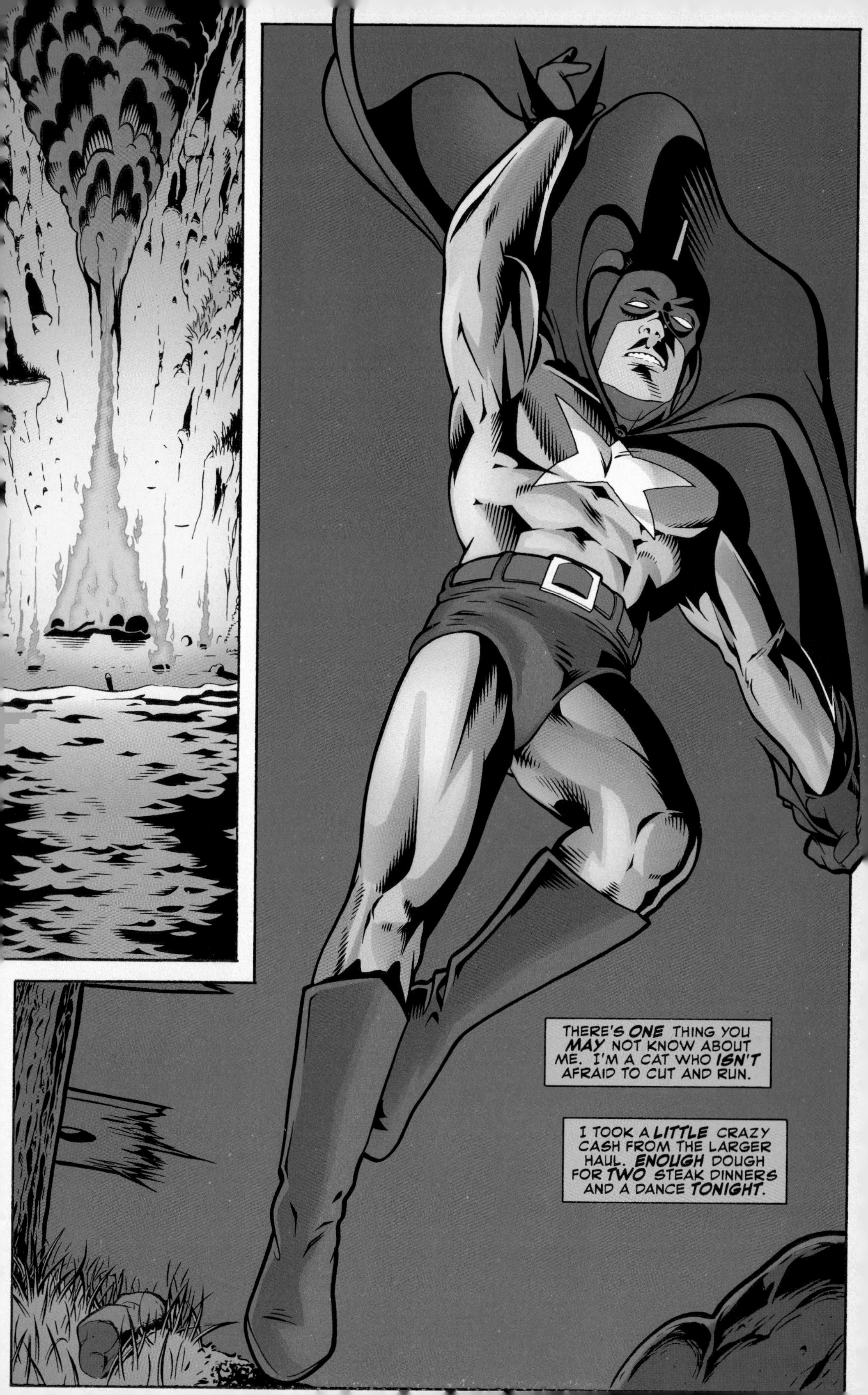
THERE'S ONE THING YOU MAY NOT KNOW ABOUT ME. I'M A CAT WHO ISN'T AFRAID TO CUT AND RUN.
I TOOK A LITTLE CRAZY CASH FROM THE LARGER HAUL. ENOUGH DOUGH FOR TWO STEAK DINNERS AND A DANCE TONIGHT.

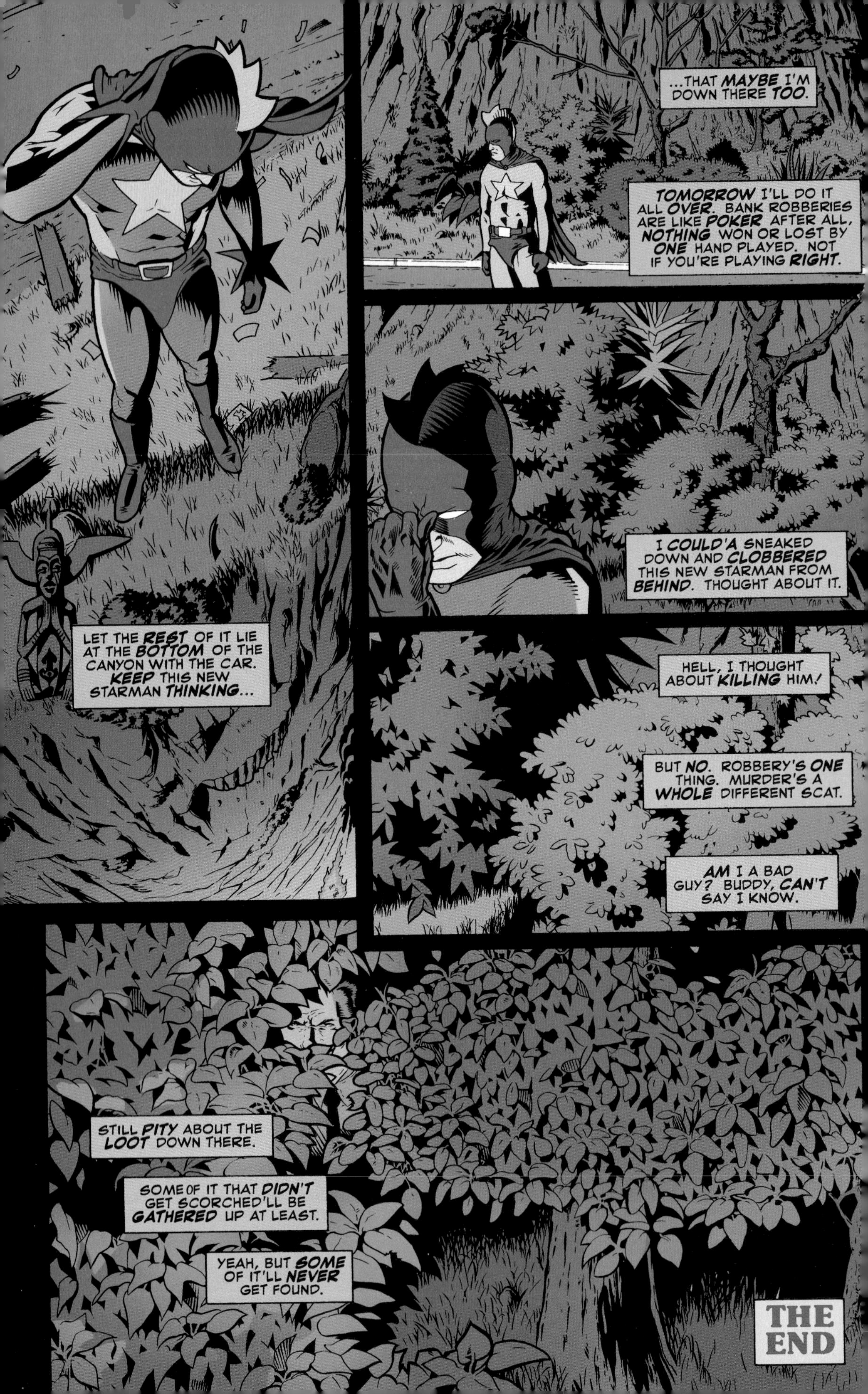

...THAT MAYBE I'M DOWN THERE TOO.
TOMORROW I'LL DO IT ALL OVER. BANK ROBBERIES ARE LIKE POKER AFTER ALL, NOTHING WON OR LOST BY ONE HAND PLAYED. NOT IF YOU'RE PLAYING RIGHT.
LET THE REST OF IT LIE AT THE BOTTOM OF THE CANYON WITH THE CAR. KEEP THIS NEW STARMAN THINKING...
I COULD'A SNEAKED DOWN AND CLOBBERED THIS NEW STARMAN FROM BEHIND. THOUGHT ABOUT IT.
HELL, I THOUGHT ABOUT KILLING HIM!
BUT NO. ROBBERY'S ONE THING. MURDER'S A WHOLE DIFFERENT SCAT.
AM I A BAD GUY? BUDDY, CAN'T SAY I KNOW.
STILL PITY ABOUT THE LOOT DOWN THERE.
SOME OF IT THAT DIDN'T GET SCORCHED'LL BE GATHERED UP AT LEAST.
YEAH, BUT SOME OF IT'LL NEVER GET FOUND.
THE END

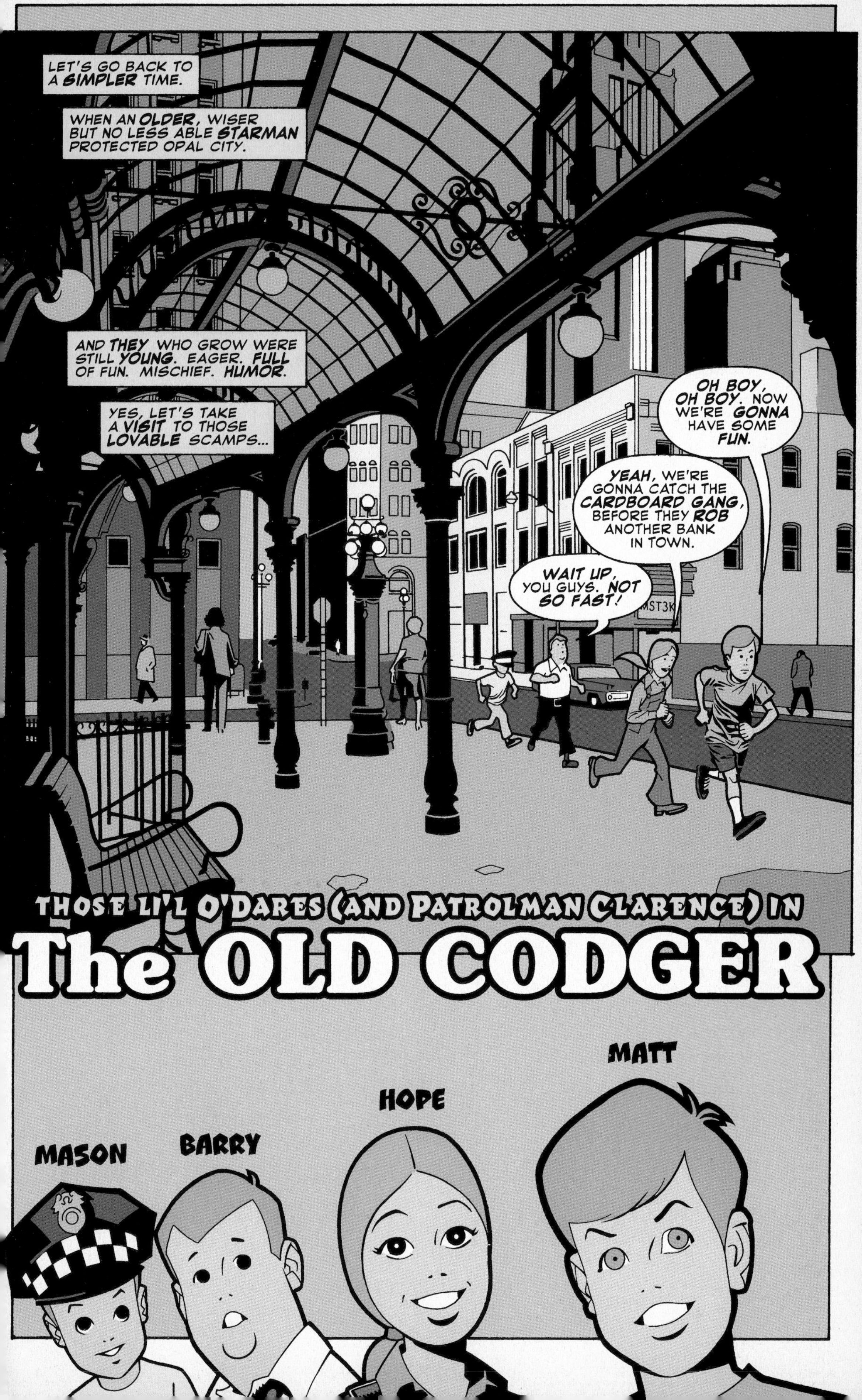

LET'S GO BACK TO A SIMPLER TIME.
WHEN AN OLDER, WISER BUT NO LESS ABLE STARMAN PROTECTED OPAL CITY.
AND THEY WHO GROW WERE STILL YOUNG. EAGER. FULL OF FUN. MISCHIEF. HUMOR.
YES, LET'S TAKE A VISIT TO THOSE LOVABLE SCAMPS...
OH BOY, OH BOY. NOW WE'RE GONNA HAVE SOME FUN.
YEAH, WE'RE GONNA CATCH THE CARDBOARD GANG, BEFORE THEY ROB ANOTHER BANK IN TOWN.
WAIT UP, YOU GUYS. NOT SO FAST!
MST3K
THOSE LI'L O'DARES (AND PATROLMAN CLARENCE) IN
The OLD CODGER
MASON
BARRY
HOPE
MATT

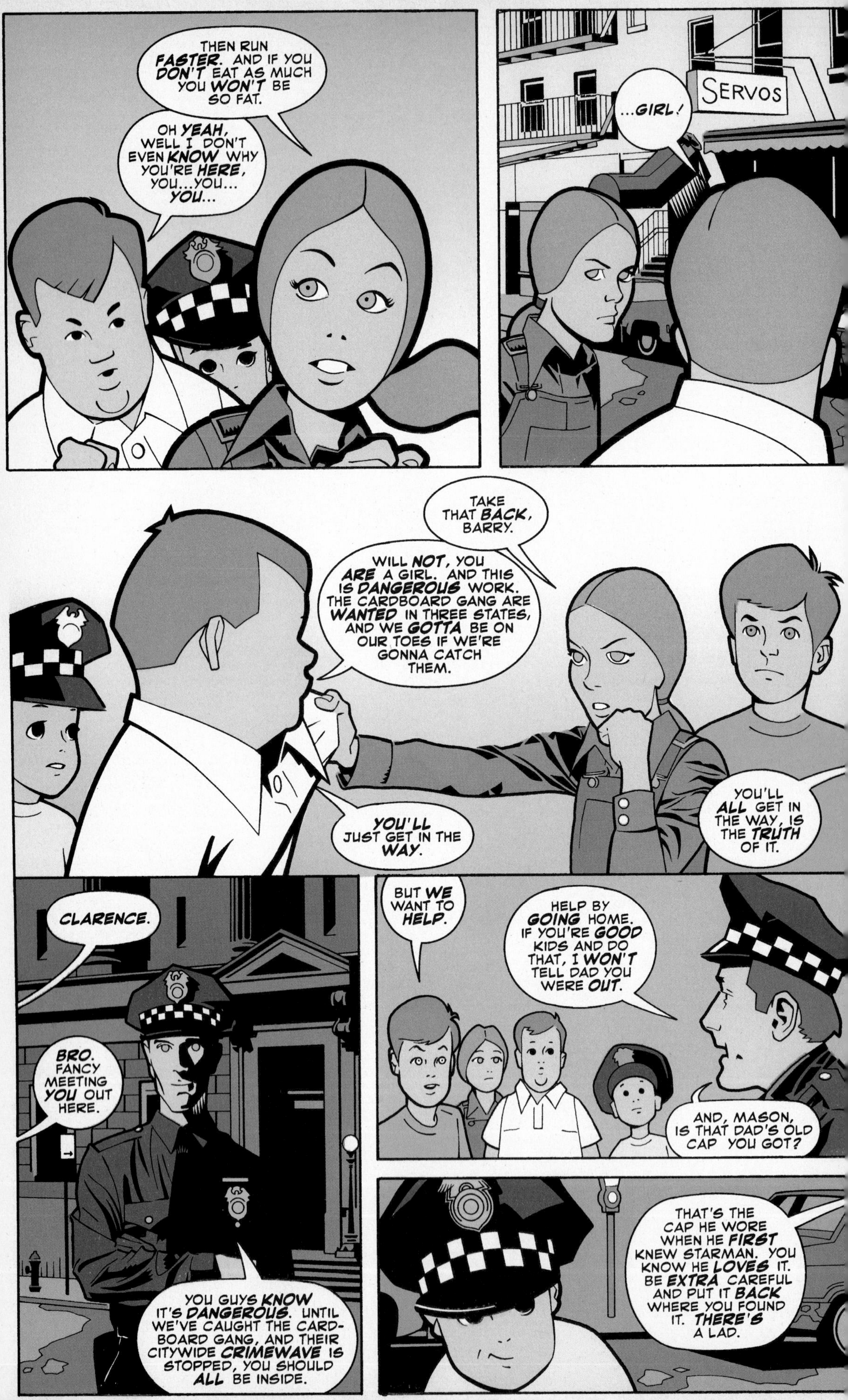
THEN RUN FASTER. AND IF YOU DON'T EAT AS MUCH YOU WON'T BE SO FAT.
OH YEAH, WELL I DON'T EVEN KNOW WHY YOU'RE HERE, YOU...YOU... YOU...
SERVOS
...GIRL!
TAKE THAT BACK, BARRY.
WILL NOT, YOU ARE A GIRL. AND THIS IS DANGEROUS WORK. THE CARDBOARD GANG ARE WANTED IN THREE STATES, AND WE GOTTA BE ON OUR TOES IF WE'RE GONNA CATCH THEM.
YOU'LL JUST GET IN THE WAY.
YOU'LL ALL GET IN THE WAY, IS THE TRUTH OF IT.
CLARENCE.
BRO. FANCY MEETING YOU OUT HERE.
YOU GUYS KNOW IT'S DANGEROUS. UNTIL WE'VE CAUGHT THE CARD-BOARD GANG, AND THEIR CITYWIDE CRIMEWAVE IS STOPPED, YOU SHOULD ALL BE INSIDE.
BUT WE WANT TO HELP.
HELP BY GOING HOME. IF YOU'RE GOOD KIDS AND DO THAT, I WON'T TELL DAD YOU WERE OUT.
AND, MASON, IS THAT DAD'S OLD CAP YOU GOT?
THAT'S THE CAP HE WORE WHEN HE FIRST KNEW STARMAN. YOU KNOW HE LOVES IT. BE EXTRA CAREFUL AND PUT IT BACK WHERE YOU FOUND IT. THERE'S A LAD.

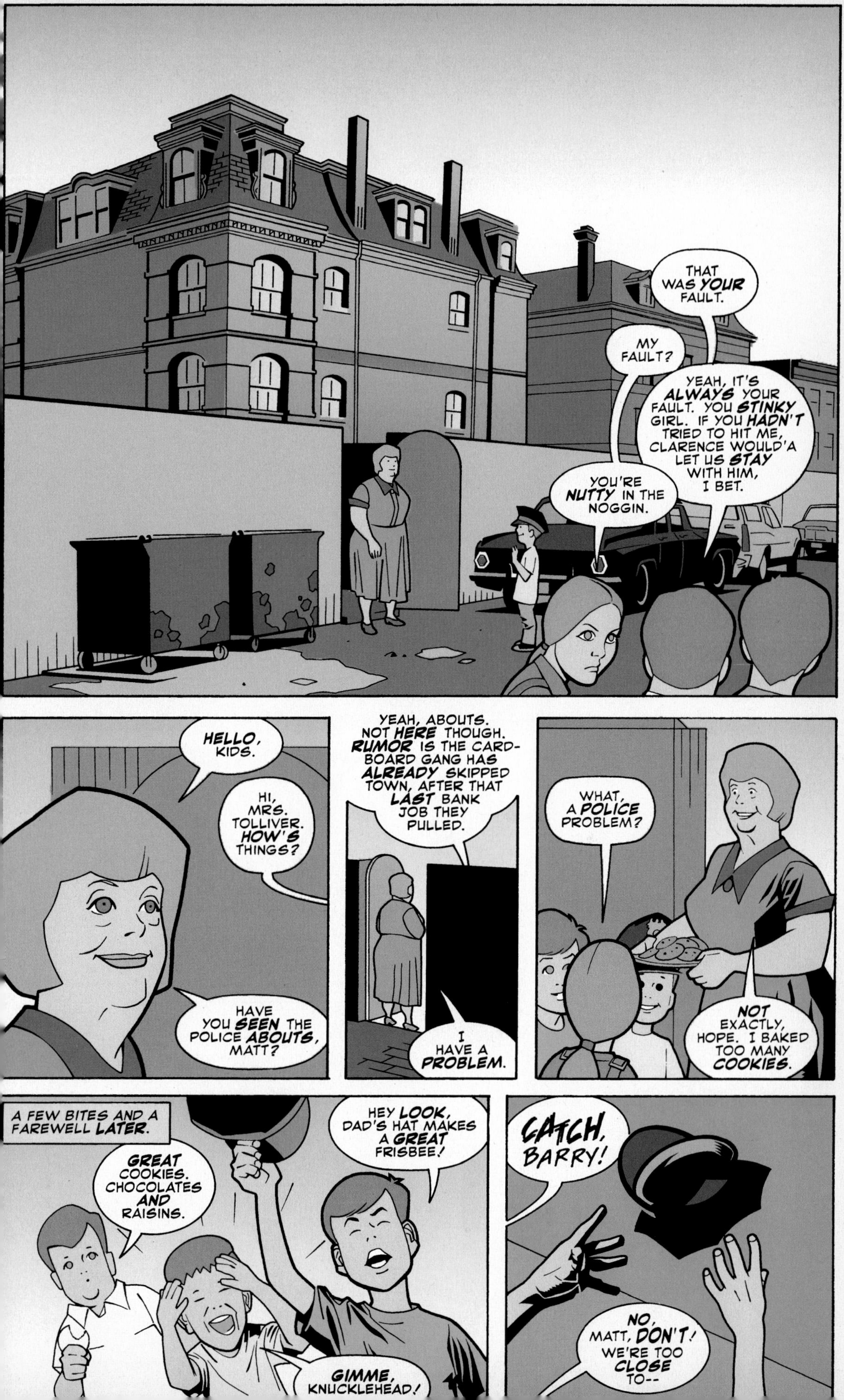
THAT WAS YOUR FAULT.
MY FAULT?
YEAH, IT'S ALWAYS YOUR FAULT. YOU STINKY GIRL. IF YOU HADN'T TRIED TO HIT ME, CLARENCE WOULD'A LET US STAY WITH HIM, I BET.
YOU'RE NUTTY IN THE NOGGIN.
HELLO, KIDS.
HI, MRS. TOLLIVER. HOW'S THINGS?
HAVE YOU SEEN THE POLICE ABOUTS, MATT?
YEAH, ABOUTS. NOT HERE THOUGH. RUMOR IS THE CARD-BOARD GANG HAS ALREADY SKIPPED TOWN, AFTER THAT LAST BANK JOB THEY PULLED.
I HAVE A PROBLEM.
WHAT, A POLICE PROBLEM?
NOT EXACTLY, HOPE. I BAKED TOO MANY COOKIES.
A FEW BITES AND A FAREWELL LATER.
GREAT COOKIES. CHOCOLATES AND RAISINS.
HEY LOOK, DAD'S HAT MAKES A GREAT FRISBEE!
GIMME, KNUCKLEHEAD!
CATCH, BARRY!
NO, MATT, DON'T! WE'RE TOO CLOSE TO--

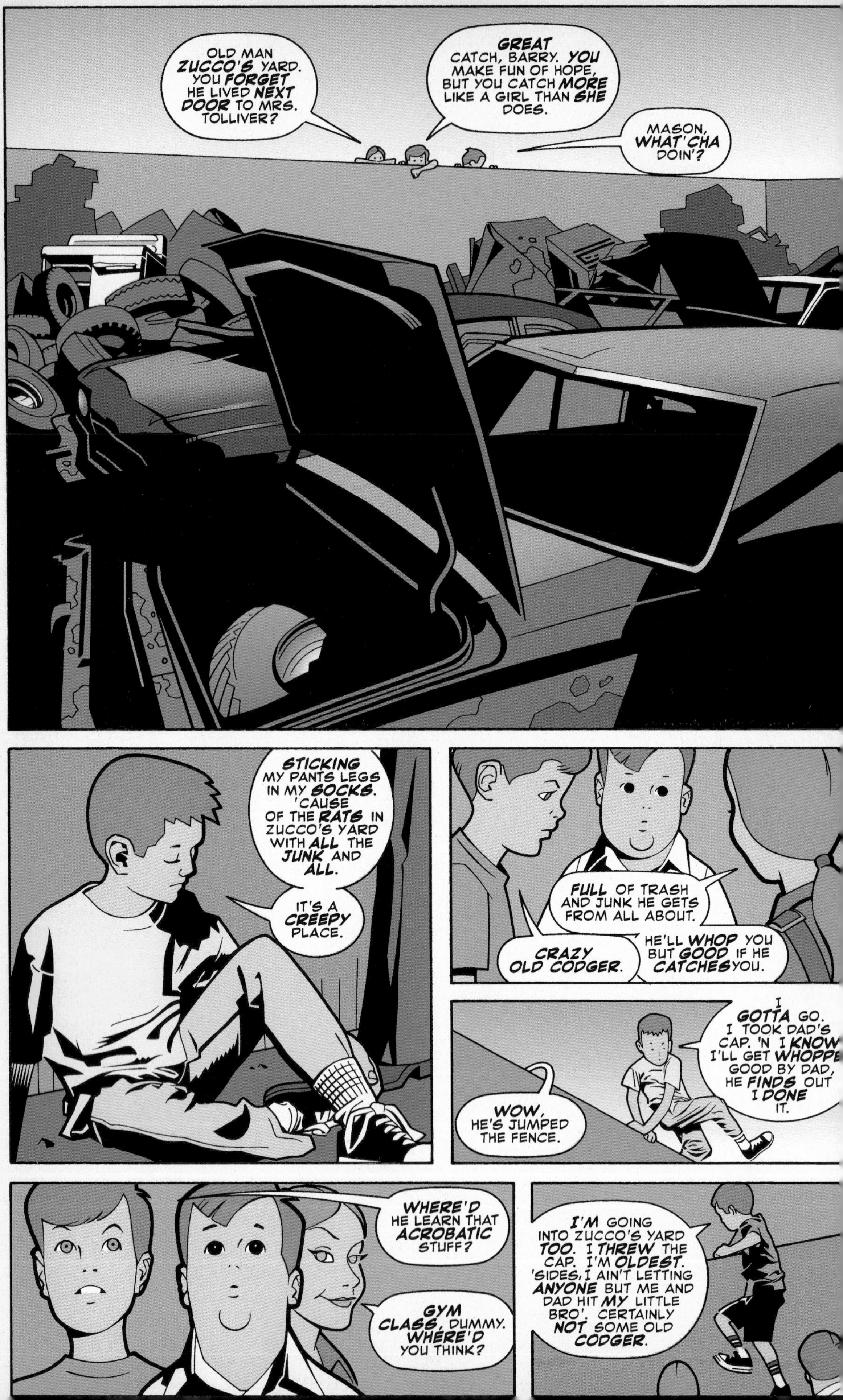
OLD MAN ZUCCO'S YARD. YOU FORGET HE LIVED NEXT DOOR TO MRS. TOLLIVER?
GREAT CATCH, BARRY. YOU MAKE FUN OF HOPE, BUT YOU CATCH MORE LIKE A GIRL THAN SHE DOES.
MASON, WHAT'CHA DOIN'?
STICKING MY PANTS LEGS IN MY SOCKS. 'CAUSE OF THE RATS IN ZUCCO'S YARD WITH ALL THE JUNK AND ALL.
IT'S A CREEPY PLACE.
FULL OF TRASH AND JUNK HE GETS FROM ALL ABOUT.
CRAZY OLD CODGER.
HE'LL WHOP YOU BUT GOOD IF HE CATCHES YOU.
WOW, HE'S JUMPED THE FENCE.
I GOTTA GO. I TOOK DAD'S CAP. 'N I KNOW I'LL GET WHOPPE GOOD BY DAD, HE FINDS OUT I DONE IT.
WHERE'D HE LEARN THAT ACROBATIC STUFF?
GYM CLASS, DUMMY. WHERE'D YOU THINK?
I'M GOING INTO ZUCCO'S YARD TOO. I THREW THE CAP. I'M OLDEST. 'SIDES, I AIN'T LETTING ANYONE BUT ME AND DAD HIT MY LITTLE BRO'. CERTAINLY NOT SOME OLD CODGER.

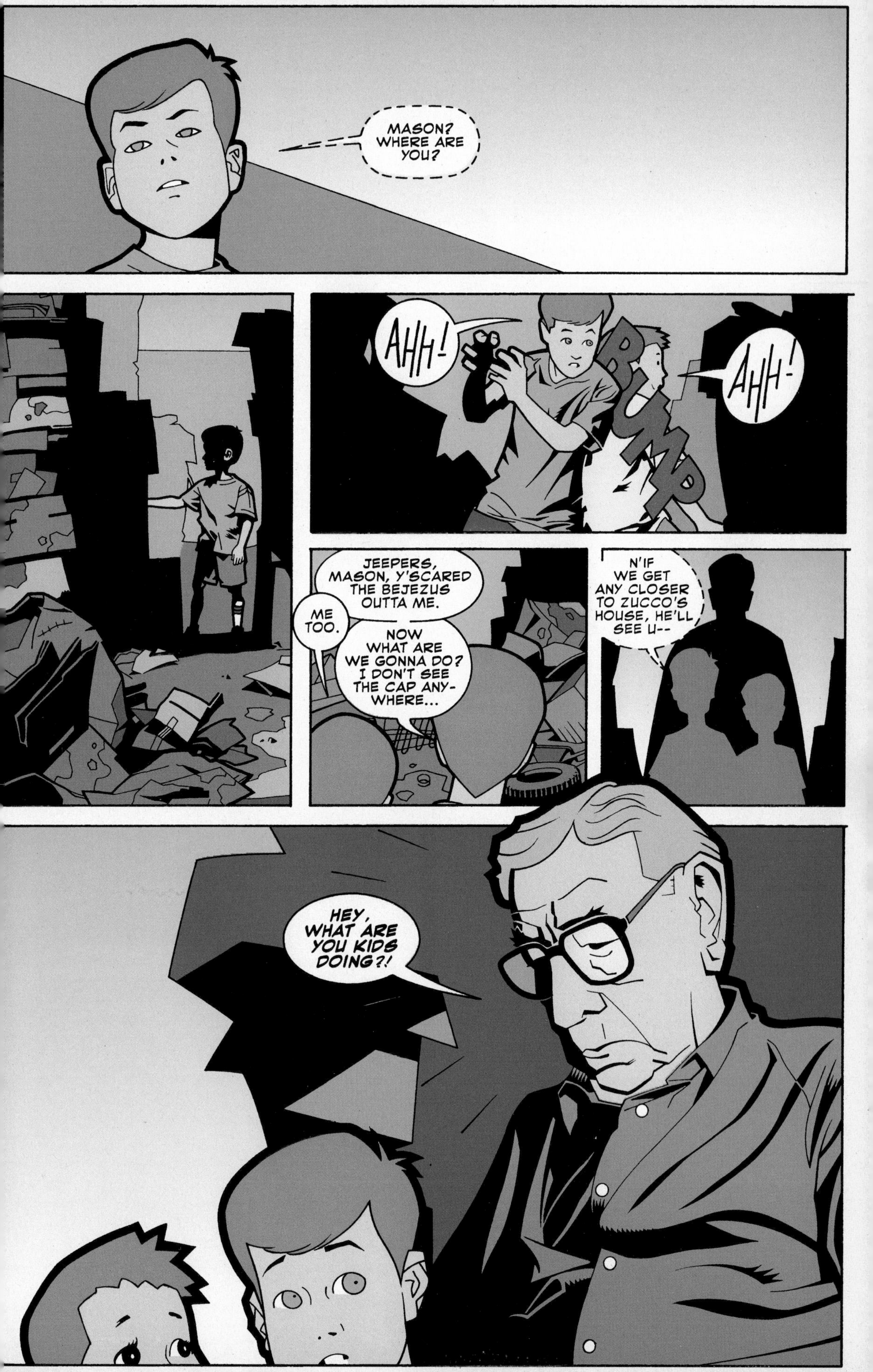
MASON? WHERE ARE YOU?
AHH!
BUMP
AHH!
JEEPERS, MASON, Y'SCARED THE BEJEZUS OUTTA ME.
ME TOO.
NOW WHAT ARE WE GONNA DO? I DON'T SEE THE CAP ANYWHERE...
N'IF WE GET ANY CLOSER TO ZUCCO'S HOUSE, HE'LL SEE U--
HEY, WHAT ARE YOU KIDS DOING?!

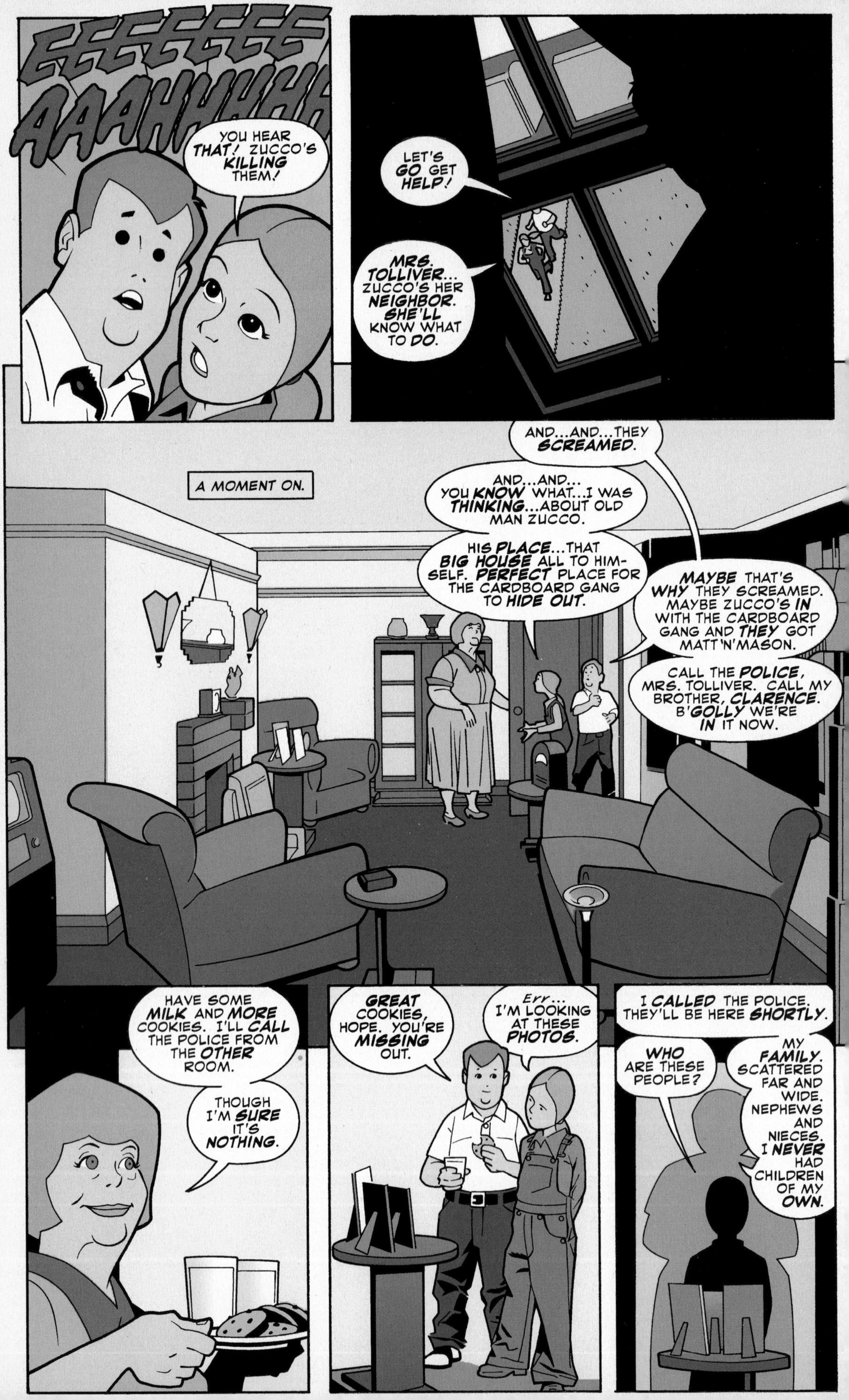
EEEEEEEE AAAHHHHH
YOU HEAR THAT! ZUCCO'S KILLING THEM!
LET'S GO GET HELP!
MRS. TOLLIVER... ZUCCO'S HER NEIGHBOR. SHE'LL KNOW WHAT TO DO.
A MOMENT ON.
AND...AND...THEY SCREAMED.
AND...AND... YOU KNOW WHAT...I WAS THINKING...ABOUT OLD MAN ZUCCO.
HIS PLACE...THAT BIG HOUSE ALL TO HIM-SELF. PERFECT PLACE FOR THE CARDBOARD GANG TO HIDE OUT.
MAYBE THAT'S WHY THEY SCREAMED. MAYBE ZUCCO'S IN WITH THE CARDBOARD GANG AND THEY GOT MATT'N'MASON.
CALL THE POLICE, MRS. TOLLIVER. CALL MY BROTHER, CLARENCE. B'GOLLY WE'RE IN IT NOW.
HAVE SOME MILK AND MORE COOKIES. I'LL CALL THE POLICE FROM THE OTHER ROOM.
THOUGH I'M SURE IT'S NOTHING.
GREAT COOKIES, HOPE. YOU'RE MISSING OUT.
Err... I'M LOOKING AT THESE PHOTOS.
I CALLED THE POLICE. THEY'LL BE HERE SHORTLY.
WHO ARE THESE PEOPLE?
MY FAMILY. SCATTERED FAR AND WIDE. NEPHEWS AND NIECES. I NEVER HAD CHILDREN OF MY OWN.

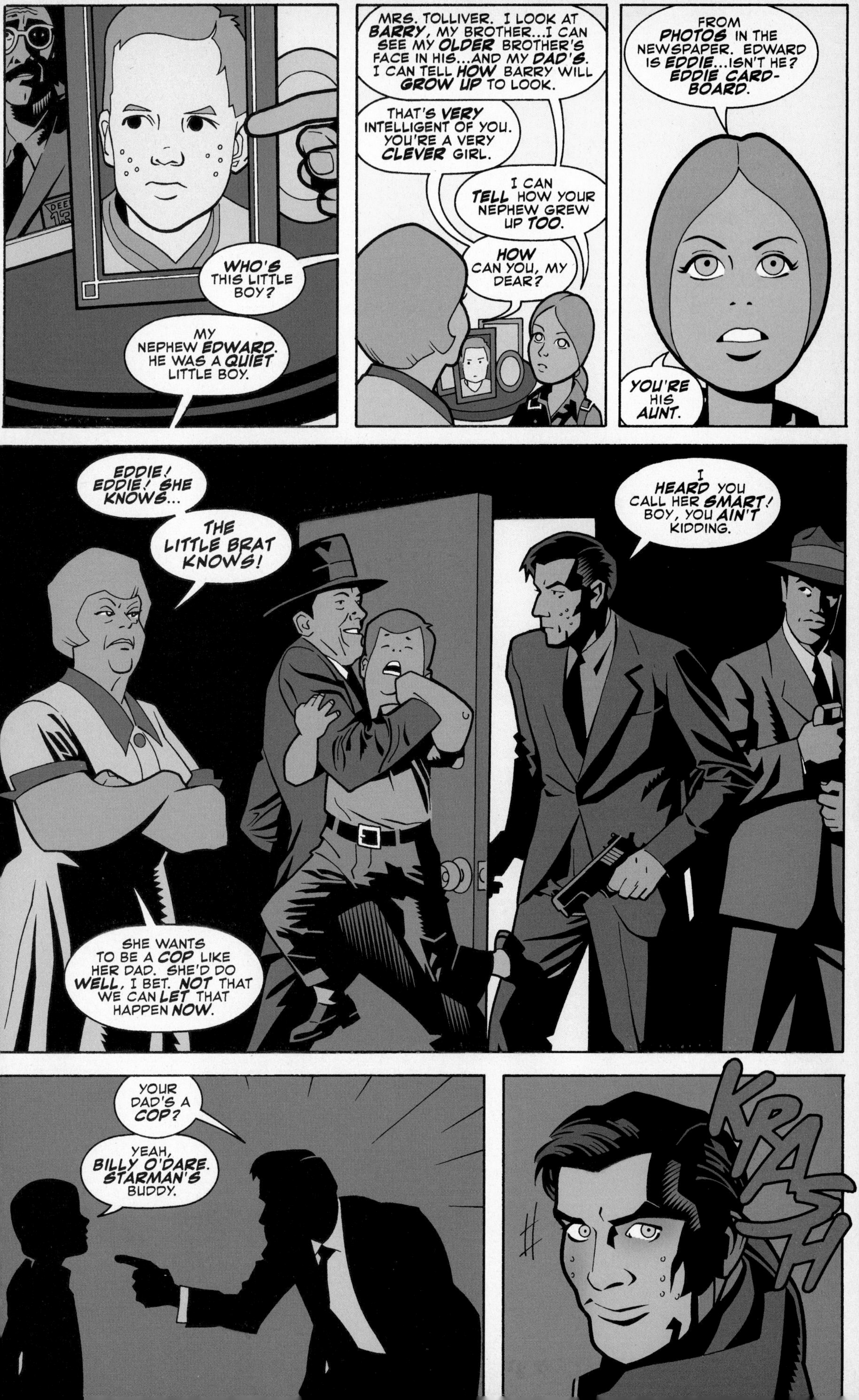
WHO'S THIS LITTLE BOY?
MY NEPHEW EDWARD. HE WAS A QUIET LITTLE BOY.
MRS. TOLLIVER. I LOOK AT BARRY, MY BROTHER...I CAN SEE MY OLDER BROTHER'S FACE IN HIS...AND MY DAD'S. I CAN TELL HOW BARRY WILL GROW UP TO LOOK.
THAT'S VERY INTELLIGENT OF YOU. YOU'RE A VERY CLEVER GIRL.
I CAN TELL HOW YOUR NEPHEW GREW UP TOO.
HOW CAN YOU, MY DEAR?
FROM PHOTOS IN THE NEWSPAPER. EDWARD IS EDDIE...ISN'T HE? EDDIE CARD-BOARD.
YOU'RE HIS AUNT.
EDDIE! EDDIE! SHE KNOWS...
THE LITTLE BRAT KNOWS!
I HEARD YOU CALL HER SMART! BOY, YOU AIN'T KIDDING.
SHE WANTS TO BE A COP LIKE HER DAD. SHE'D DO WELL, I BET. NOT THAT WE CAN LET THAT HAPPEN NOW.
YOUR DAD'S A COP?
YEAH, BILLY O'DARE. STARMAN'S BUDDY.
KRASH

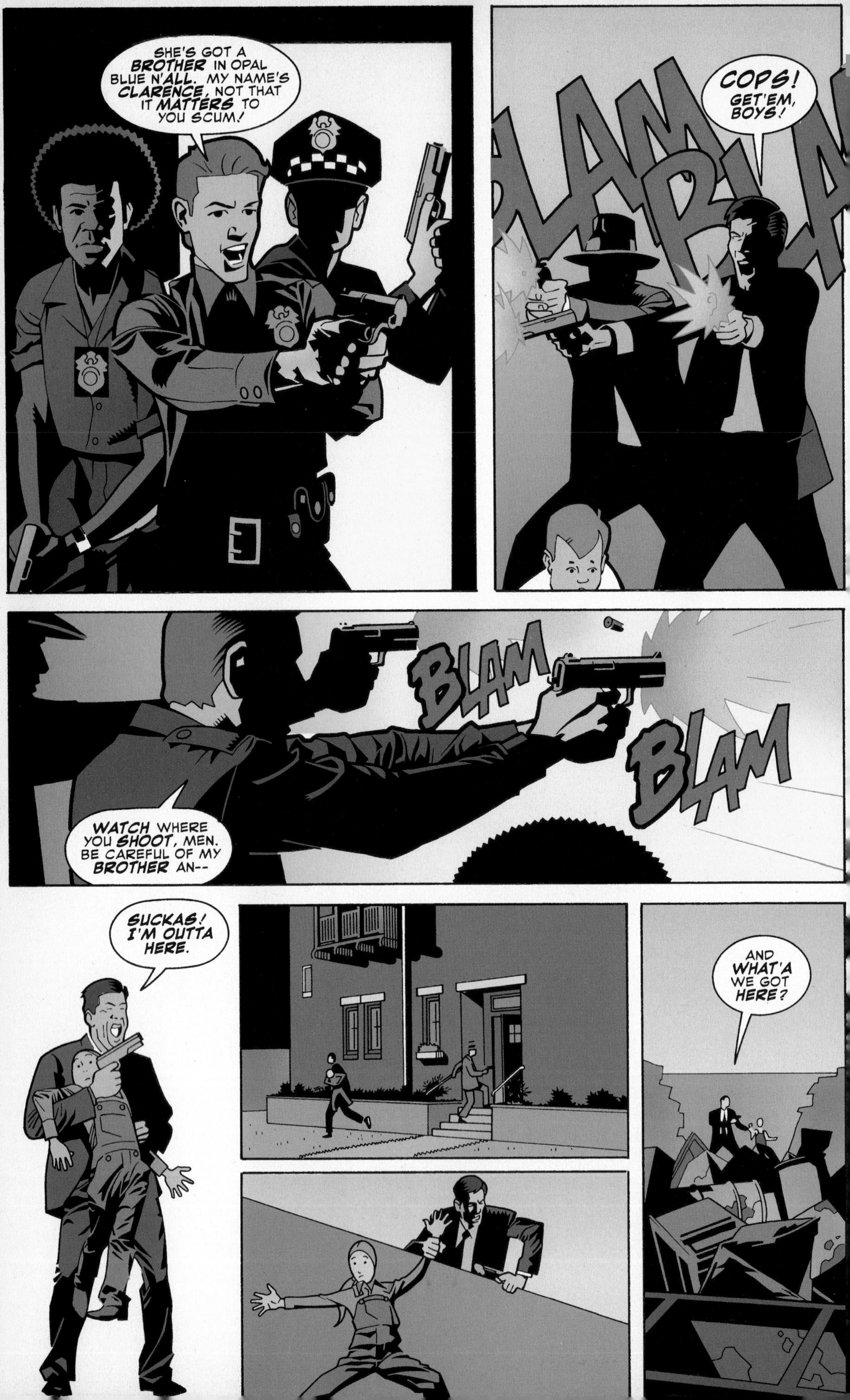
SHE'S GOT A BROTHER IN OPAL BLUE N'ALL. MY NAME'S CLARENCE, NOT THAT IT MATTERS TO YOU SCUM!
BLAM
BLAM
COPS! GET'EM, BOYS!
BLAM
BLAM
WATCH WHERE YOU SHOOT, MEN. BE CAREFUL OF MY BROTHER AN--
SUCKAS! I'M OUTTA HERE.
AND WHAT'A WE GOT HERE?

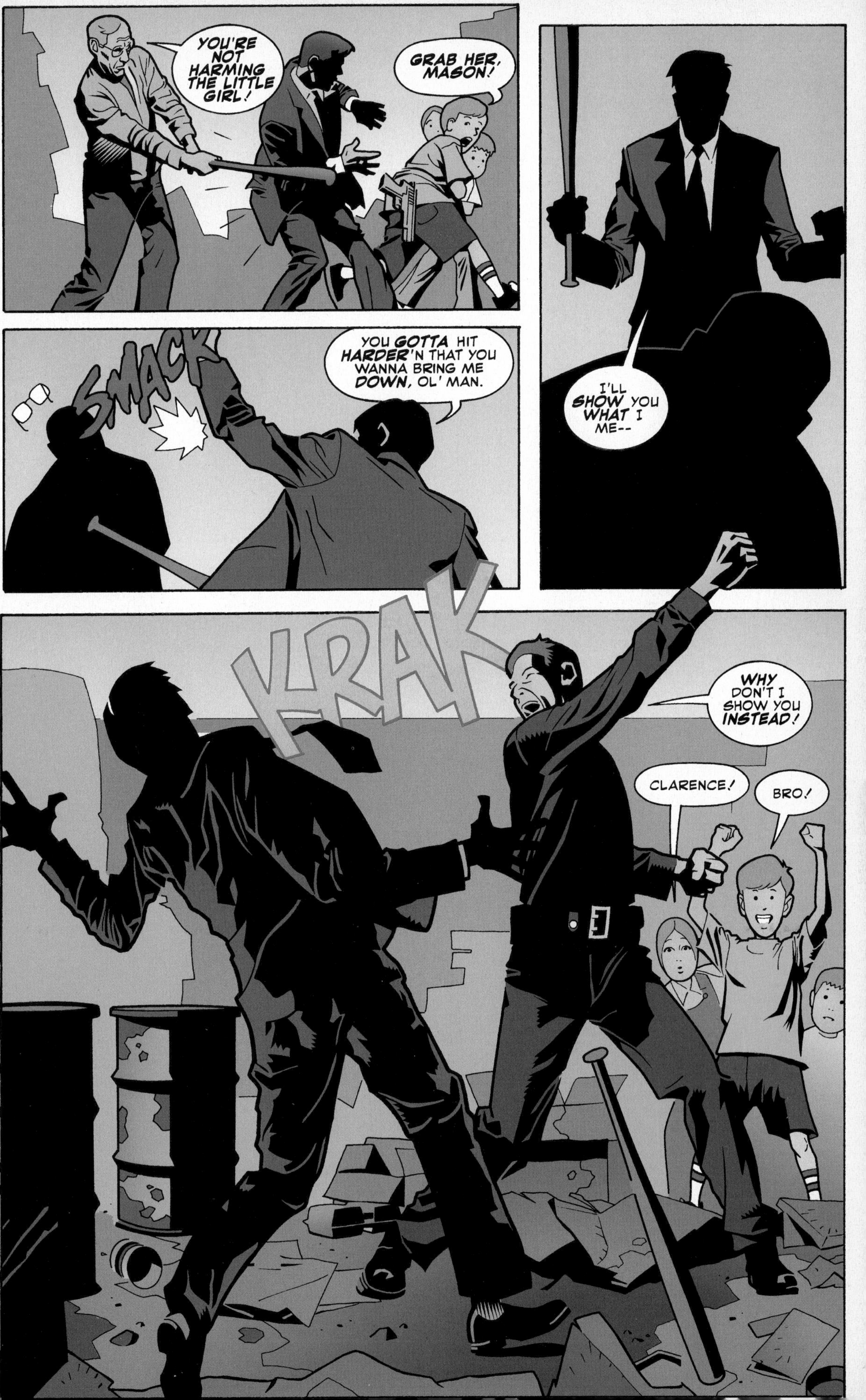
YOU'RE NOT HARMING THE LITTLE GIRL!
GRAB HER, MASON!
SMACK
YOU GOTTA HIT HARDER'N THAT YOU WANNA BRING ME DOWN, OL' MAN.
I'LL SHOW YOU WHAT I ME--
KRAK
WHY DON'T I SHOW YOU INSTEAD!
CLARENCE!
BRO!

LATER.

AND MR. ZUCCO WAS SHOWING US *ALL* THE *NEAT* STUFF IN HIS HOUSE, WHEN WE HEARD THE *GUNS.*

BUT YOU SCREAMED.

HE *SURPRISED* US, SURE, BUT IT WAS AN *ACCIDENT.*

I'M *OLD* AND NO ONE VISITS ME, SO I *GUESS* I'VE GROWN A LITTLE *ODD* IN MY WAYS...

...BUT I'D *NEVER* HARM A *CHILD.*

YOU'RE A *HERO,* MR. ZUCCO. *THAT'S* WHAT YOU *ARE.*

GOOD THING WE KNEW ABOUT MRS. TOLLIVER'S FAMILY *LINK* TO EDDIE AND WE HAD THE HOUSE *STAKED OUT.* OTHERWISE WE MIGHT *NOT* HAVE THESE *SMILES* ON OUR FACES.

CAN I HAVE MY DAD'S *CAP* BACK?

SURE. I TOOK IT *INSIDE* SO I COULD *CLEAN* IT UP BEFORE I *HANDED* IT IN AT THE POLICE STATION. I *WASN'T* GOING TO KEEP IT.

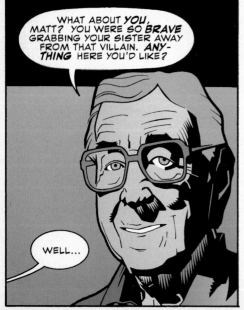

WHAT ABOUT *YOU,* MATT? YOU WERE SO *BRAVE* GRABBING YOUR SISTER AWAY FROM THAT VILLAIN. *ANYTHING* HERE YOU'D LIKE?

WELL...

...THAT *AFRICAN* STATUE THING IS KINDA *NEAT.*

THAT *OLD* THING? I FOUND IT OUT IN THE *HILLS* ONE DAY. YOU WANT IT...

...IT'S *YOURS.*

THE END

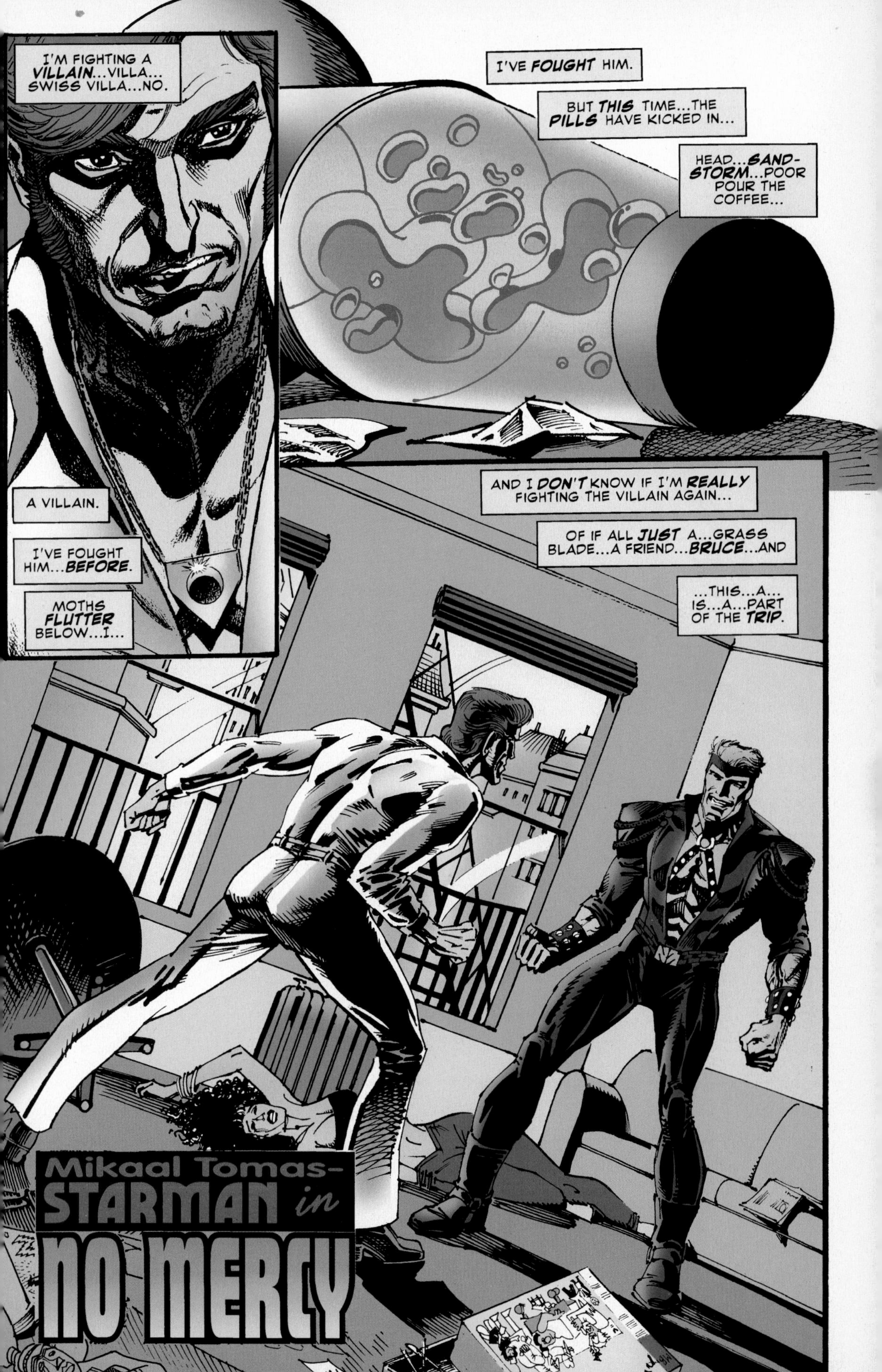

I'M FIGHTING A VILLAIN...VILLA... SWISS VILLA...NO.
I'VE FOUGHT HIM.
BUT THIS TIME...THE PILLS HAVE KICKED IN...
HEAD...SAND-STORM...POOR POUR THE COFFEE...
A VILLAIN.
I'VE FOUGHT HIM...BEFORE.
MOTHS FLUTTER BELOW...I...
AND I DON'T KNOW IF I'M REALLY FIGHTING THE VILLAIN AGAIN...
OF IF ALL JUST A...GRASS BLADE...A FRIEND...BRUCE...AND
...THIS...A... IS...A...PART OF THE TRIP.
Mikaal Tomas-
STARMAN in
NO MERCY

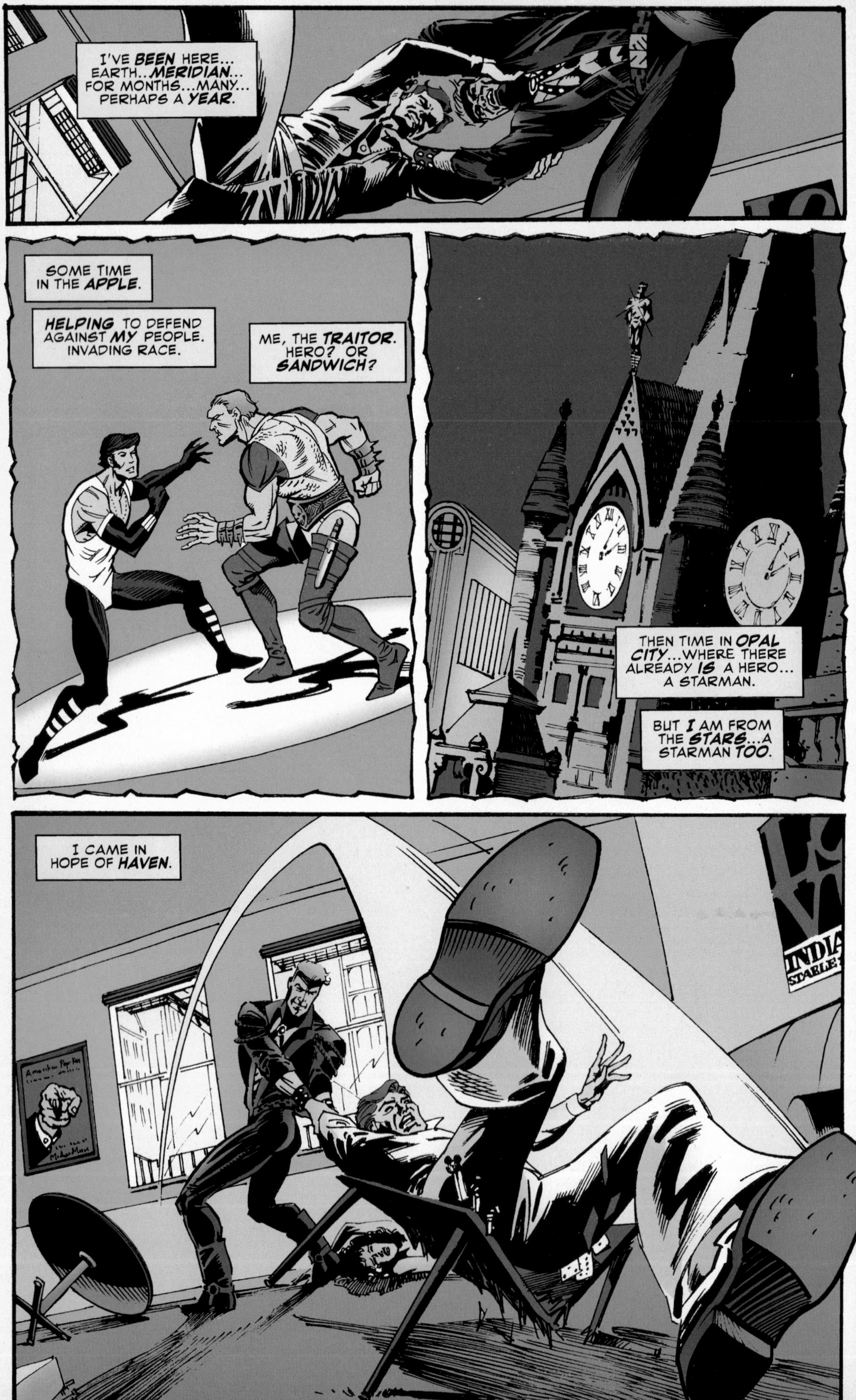
I'VE BEEN HERE... EARTH...MERIDIAN... FOR MONTHS...MANY... PERHAPS A YEAR.
SOME TIME IN THE APPLE.
HELPING TO DEFEND AGAINST MY PEOPLE. INVADING RACE.
ME, THE TRAITOR. HERO? OR SANDWICH?
THEN TIME IN OPAL CITY...WHERE THERE ALREADY IS A HERO... A STARMAN.
BUT I AM FROM THE STARS...A STARMAN TOO.
I CAME IN HOPE OF HAVEN.

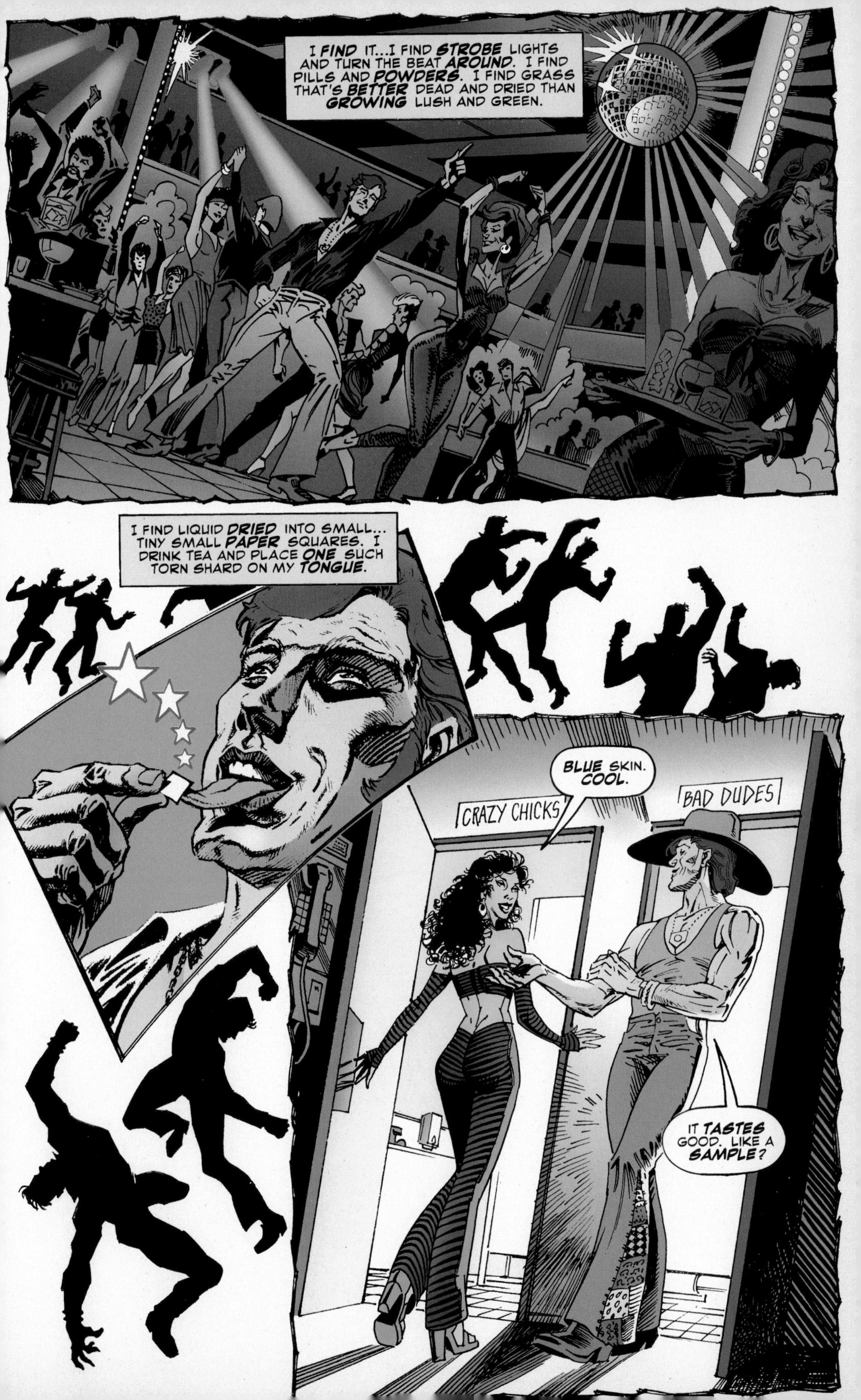

I FIND IT...I FIND STROBE LIGHTS AND TURN THE BEAT AROUND. I FIND PILLS AND POWDERS. I FIND GRASS THAT'S BETTER DEAD AND DRIED THAN GROWING LUSH AND GREEN.
I FIND LIQUID DRIED INTO SMALL... TINY SMALL PAPER SQUARES. I DRINK TEA AND PLACE ONE SUCH TORN SHARD ON MY TONGUE.
BLUE SKIN. COOL.
CRAZY CHICKS
BAD DUDES
IT TASTES GOOD. LIKE A SAMPLE?

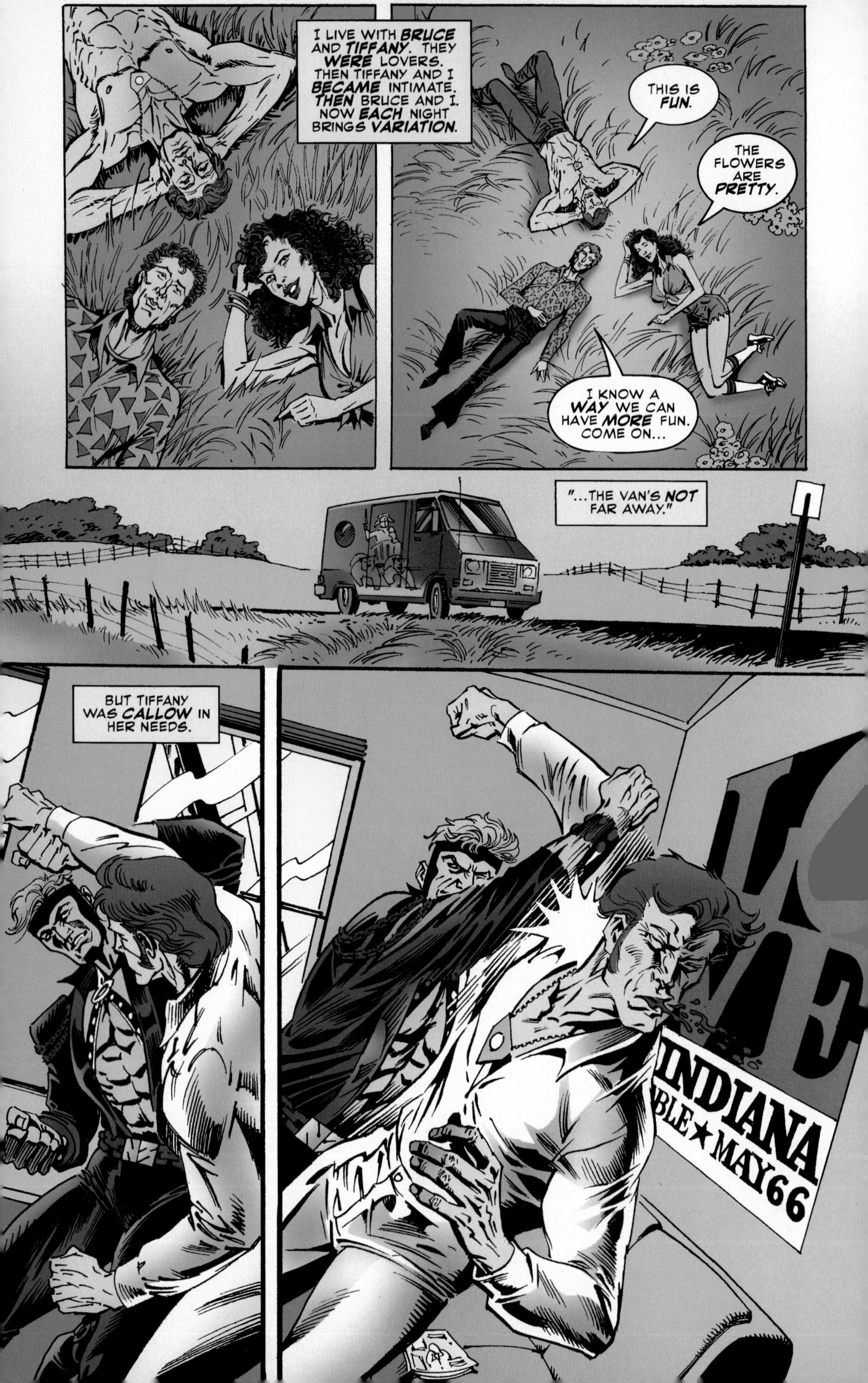
I LIVE WITH BRUCE AND TIFFANY. THEY WERE LOVERS. THEN TIFFANY AND I BECAME INTIMATE. THEN BRUCE AND I. NOW EACH NIGHT BRINGS VARIATION.
THIS IS FUN.
THE FLOWERS ARE PRETTY.
I KNOW A WAY WE CAN HAVE MORE FUN. COME ON...
"...THE VAN'S NOT FAR AWAY."
BUT TIFFANY WAS CALLOW IN HER NEEDS.
INDIANA
BLE★MAY 66

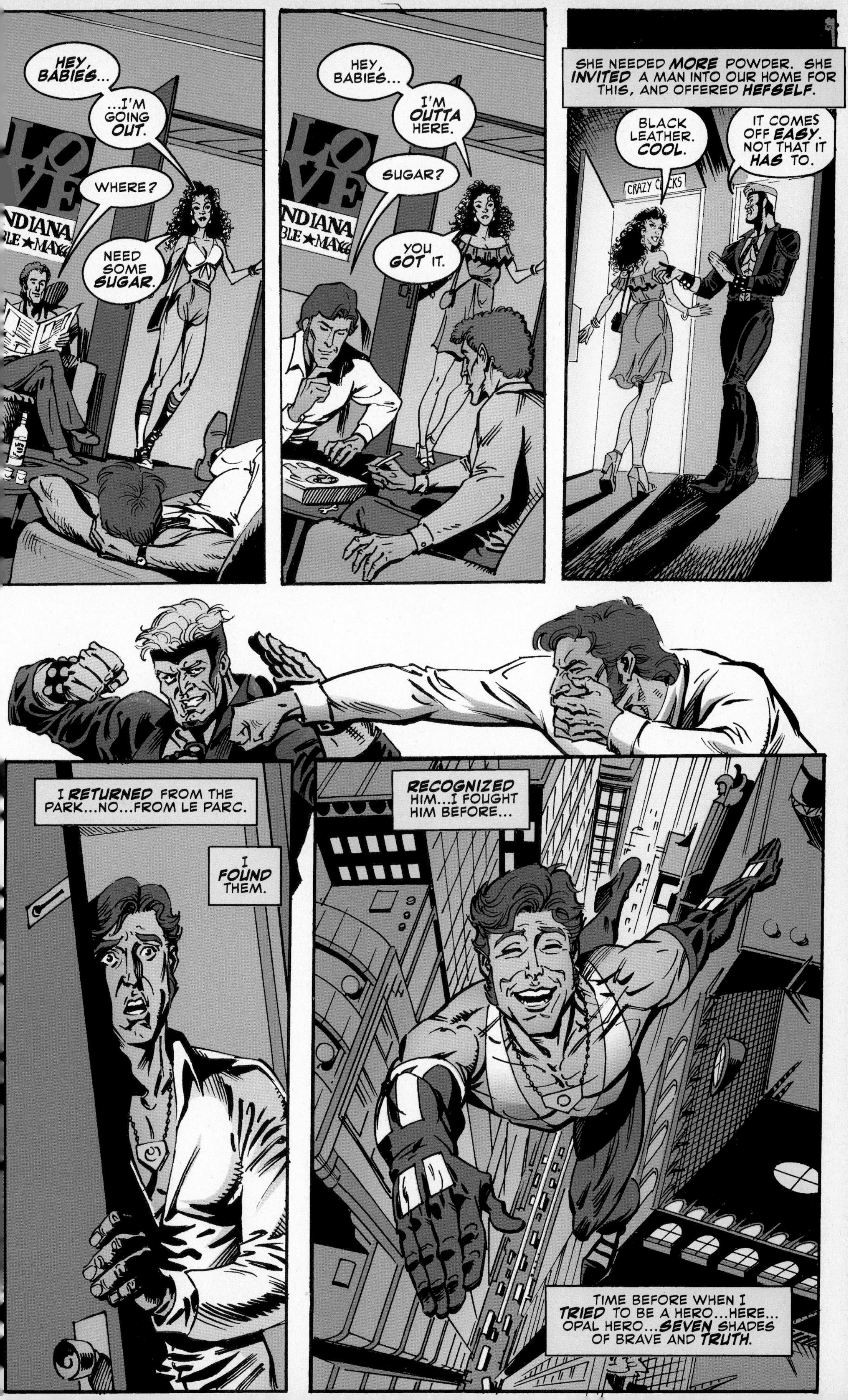
HEY, BABIES...
...I'M GOING OUT.
WHERE?
NEED SOME SUGAR.
HEY, BABIES...
I'M OUTTA HERE.
SUGAR?
YOU GOT IT.
SHE NEEDED MORE POWDER. SHE INVITED A MAN INTO OUR HOME FOR THIS, AND OFFERED HEFSELF.
BLACK LEATHER. COOL.
IT COMES OFF EASY. NOT THAT IT HAS TO.
I RETURNED FROM THE PARK...NO...FROM LE PARC.
I FOUND THEM.
RECOGNIZED HIM...I FOUGHT HIM BEFORE...
TIME BEFORE WHEN I TRIED TO BE A HERO...HERE... OPAL HERO...SEVEN SHADES OF BRAVE AND TRUTH.

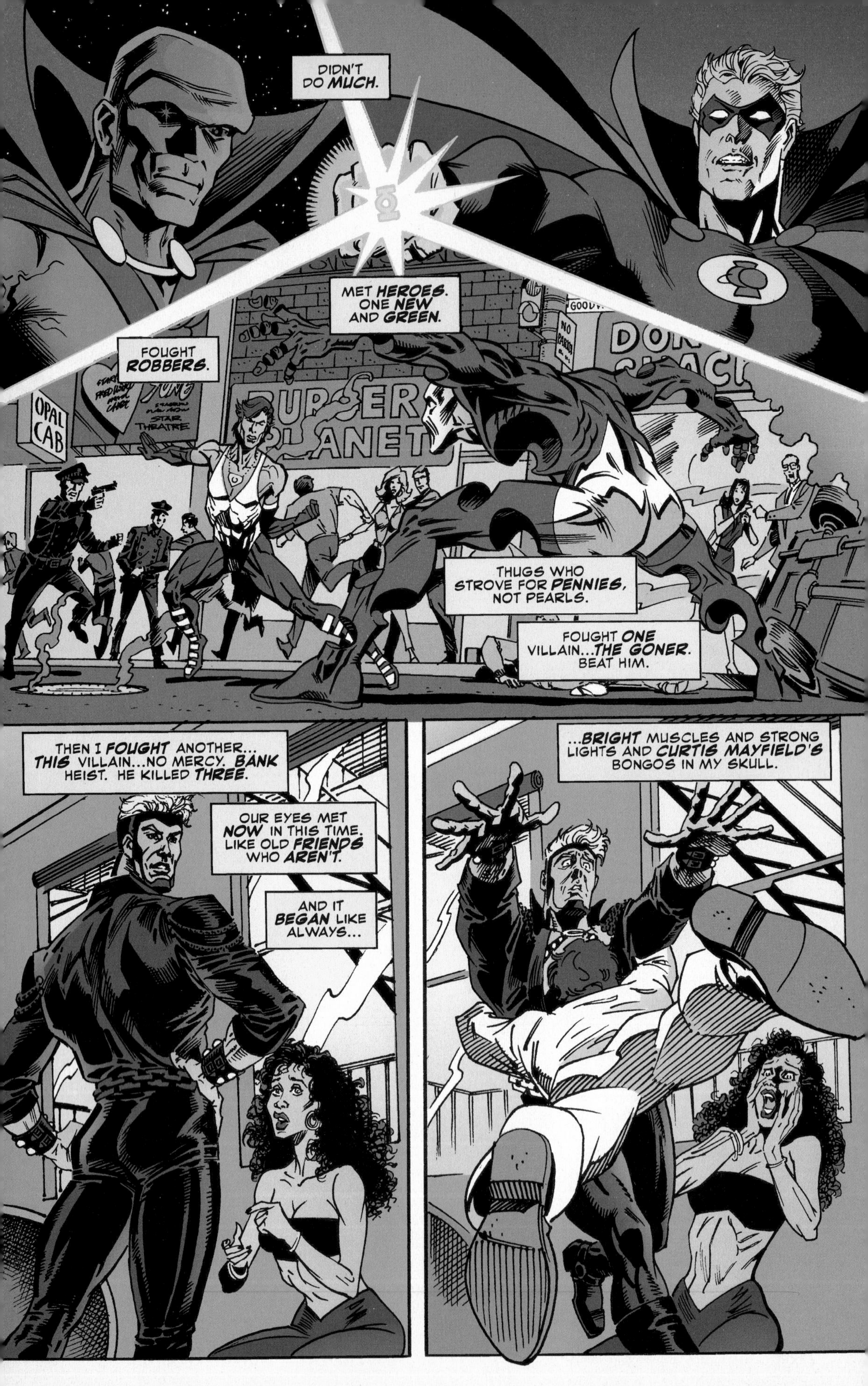
DIDN'T DO MUCH.
MET HEROES. ONE NEW AND GREEN.
FOUGHT ROBBERS.
OPAL CAB
STAR THEATRE
THUGS WHO STROVE FOR PENNIES, NOT PEARLS.
FOUGHT ONE VILLAIN...THE GONER. BEAT HIM.
THEN I FOUGHT ANOTHER... THIS VILLAIN...NO MERCY. BANK HEIST. HE KILLED THREE.
OUR EYES MET NOW IN THIS TIME. LIKE OLD FRIENDS WHO AREN'T.
AND IT BEGAN LIKE ALWAYS...
...BRIGHT MUSCLES AND STRONG LIGHTS AND CURTIS MAYFIELD'S BONGOS IN MY SKULL.

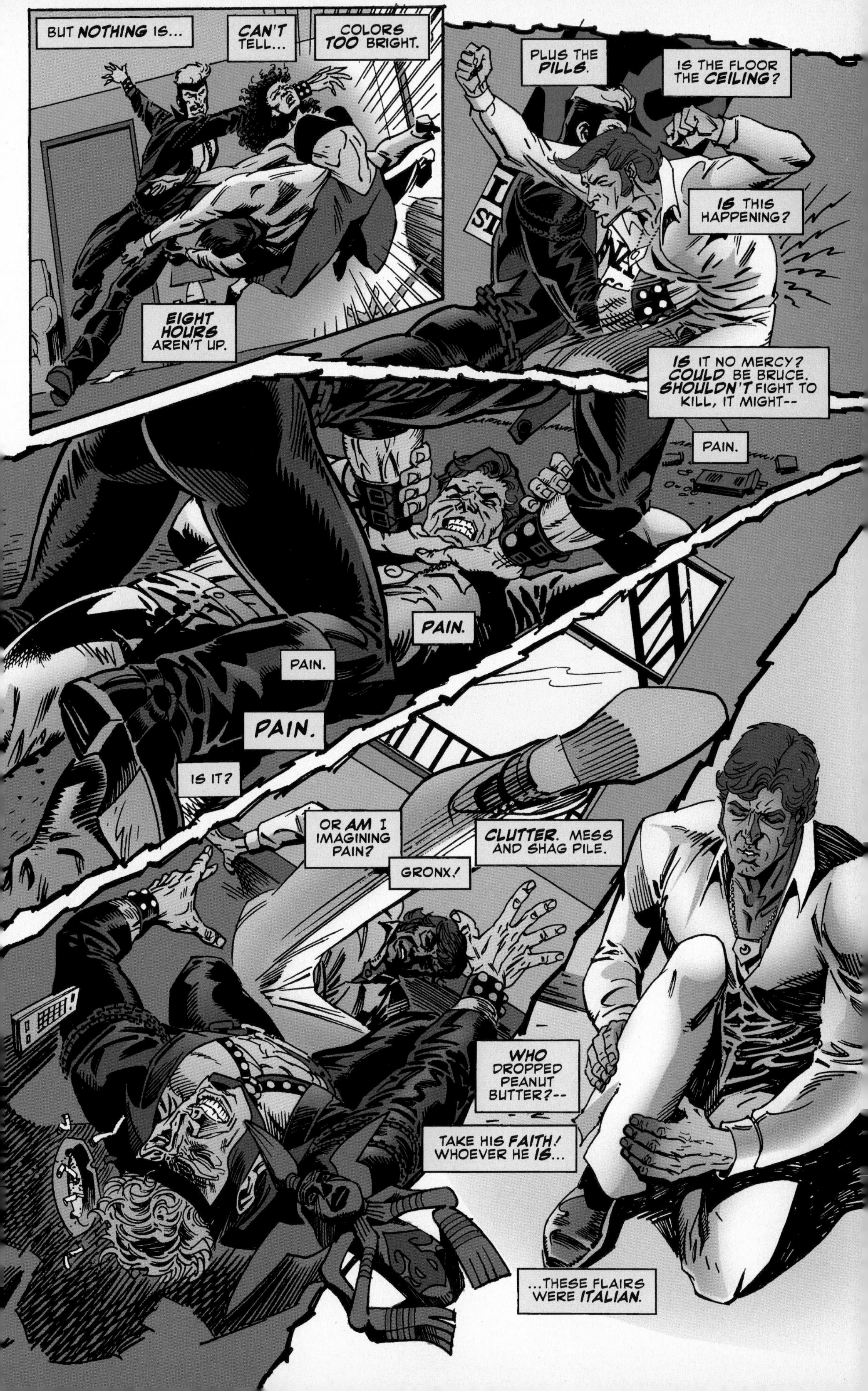
BUT NOTHING IS...
CAN'T TELL...
COLORS TOO BRIGHT.
EIGHT HOURS AREN'T UP.
PLUS THE PILLS.
IS THE FLOOR THE CEILING?
IS THIS HAPPENING?
IS IT NO MERCY? COULD BE BRUCE. SHOULDN'T FIGHT TO KILL, IT MIGHT--
PAIN.
PAIN.
PAIN.
PAIN.
IS IT?
OR AM I IMAGINING PAIN?
CLUTTER. MESS AND SHAG PILE.
GRONX!
WHO DROPPED PEANUT BUTTER?--
TAKE HIS FAITH! WHOEVER HE IS...
...THESE FLAIRS WERE ITALIAN.

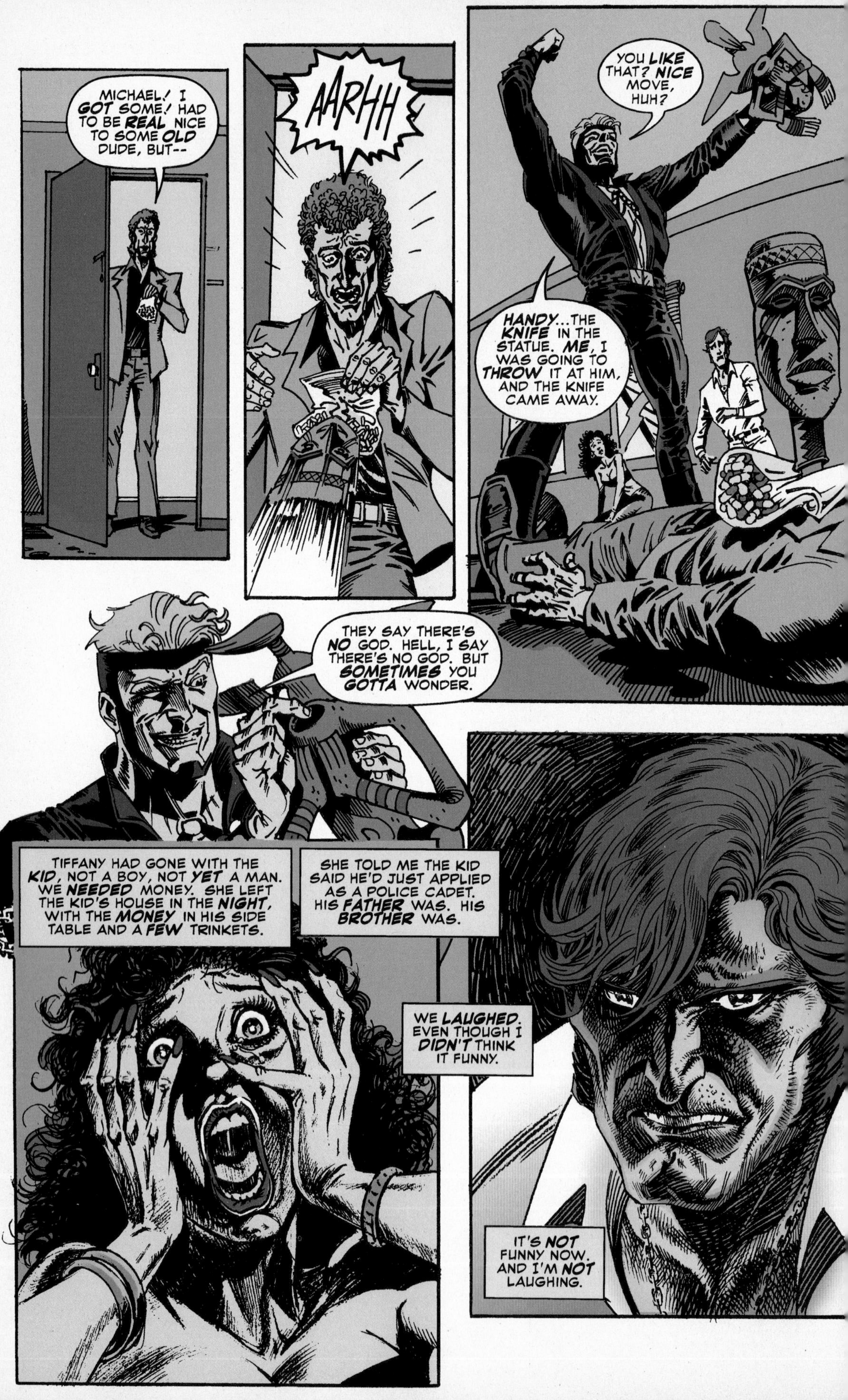
MICHAEL! I GOT SOME! HAD TO BE REAL NICE TO SOME OLD DUDE, BUT--
AARHH
YOU LIKE THAT? NICE MOVE, HUH?
HANDY...THE KNIFE IN THE STATUE. ME, I WAS GOING TO THROW IT AT HIM, AND THE KNIFE CAME AWAY.
THEY SAY THERE'S NO GOD. HELL, I SAY THERE'S NO GOD. BUT SOMETIMES YOU GOTTA WONDER.
TIFFANY HAD GONE WITH THE KID, NOT A BOY, NOT YET A MAN. WE NEEDED MONEY. SHE LEFT THE KID'S HOUSE IN THE NIGHT, WITH THE MONEY IN HIS SIDE TABLE AND A FEW TRINKETS.
SHE TOLD ME THE KID SAID HE'D JUST APPLIED AS A POLICE CADET. HIS FATHER WAS. HIS BROTHER WAS.
WE LAUGHED. EVEN THOUGH I DIDN'T THINK IT FUNNY.
IT'S NOT FUNNY NOW. AND I'M NOT LAUGHING.

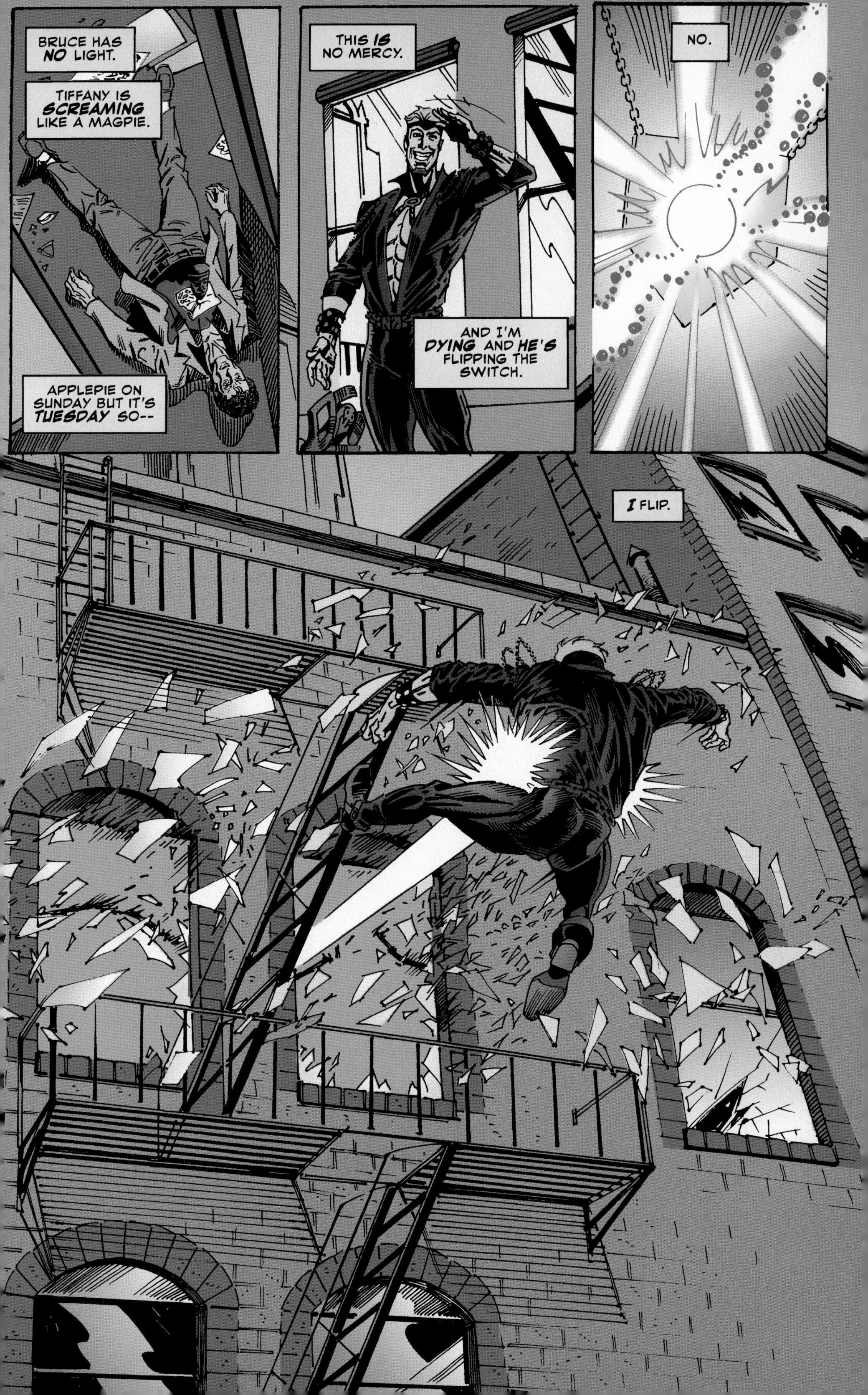
BRUCE HAS NO LIGHT.
TIFFANY IS SCREAMING LIKE A MAGPIE.
APPLEPIE ON SUNDAY BUT IT'S TUESDAY SO--
THIS IS NO MERCY.
AND I'M DYING AND HE'S FLIPPING THE SWITCH.
NO.
I FLIP.

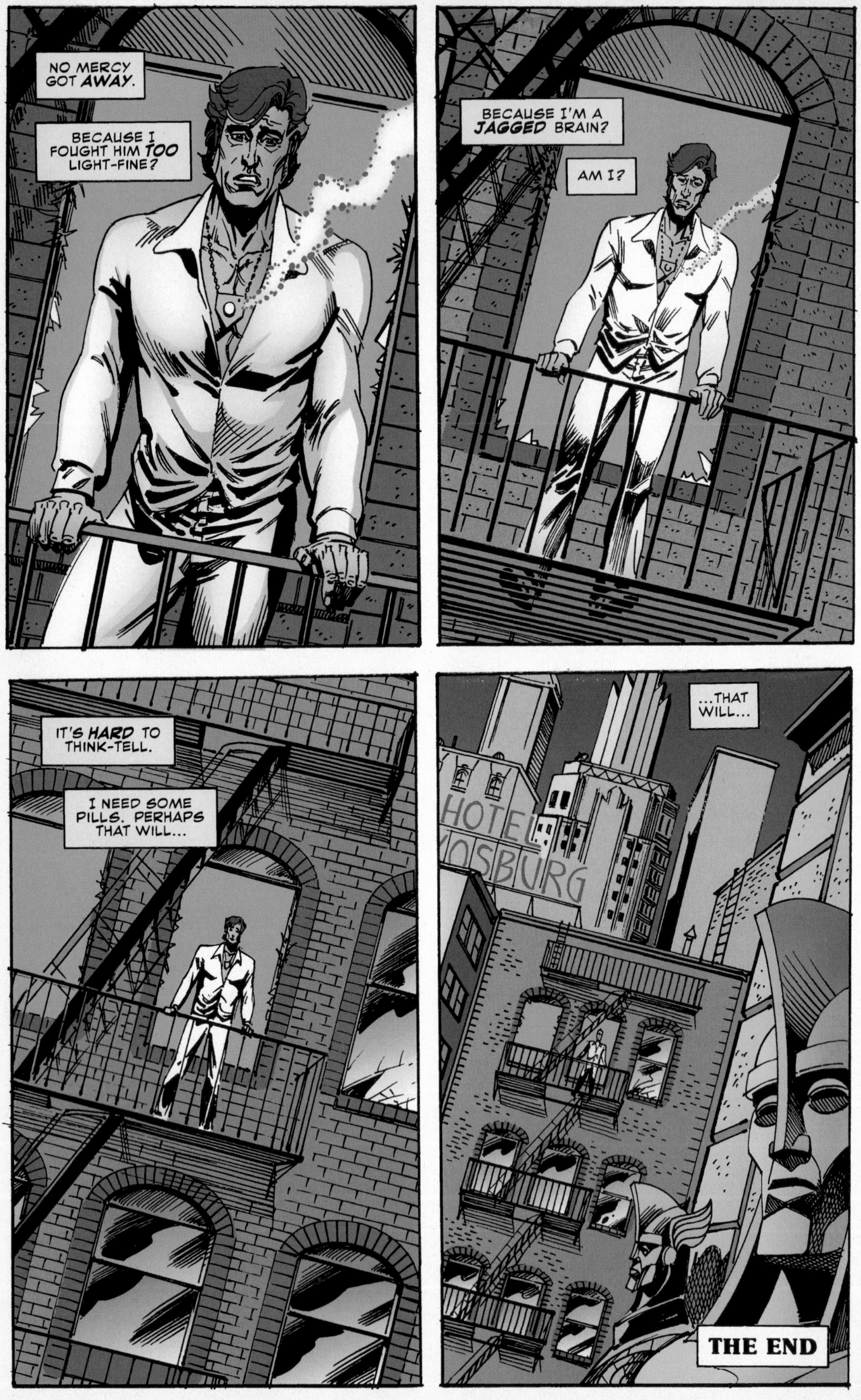
NO MERCY GOT AWAY.
BECAUSE I FOUGHT HIM TOO LIGHT-FINE?
BECAUSE I'M A JAGGED BRAIN?
AM I?
IT'S HARD TO THINK-TELL.
I NEED SOME PILLS. PERHAPS THAT WILL...
HOTEL VOSBURG
...THAT WILL...
THE END

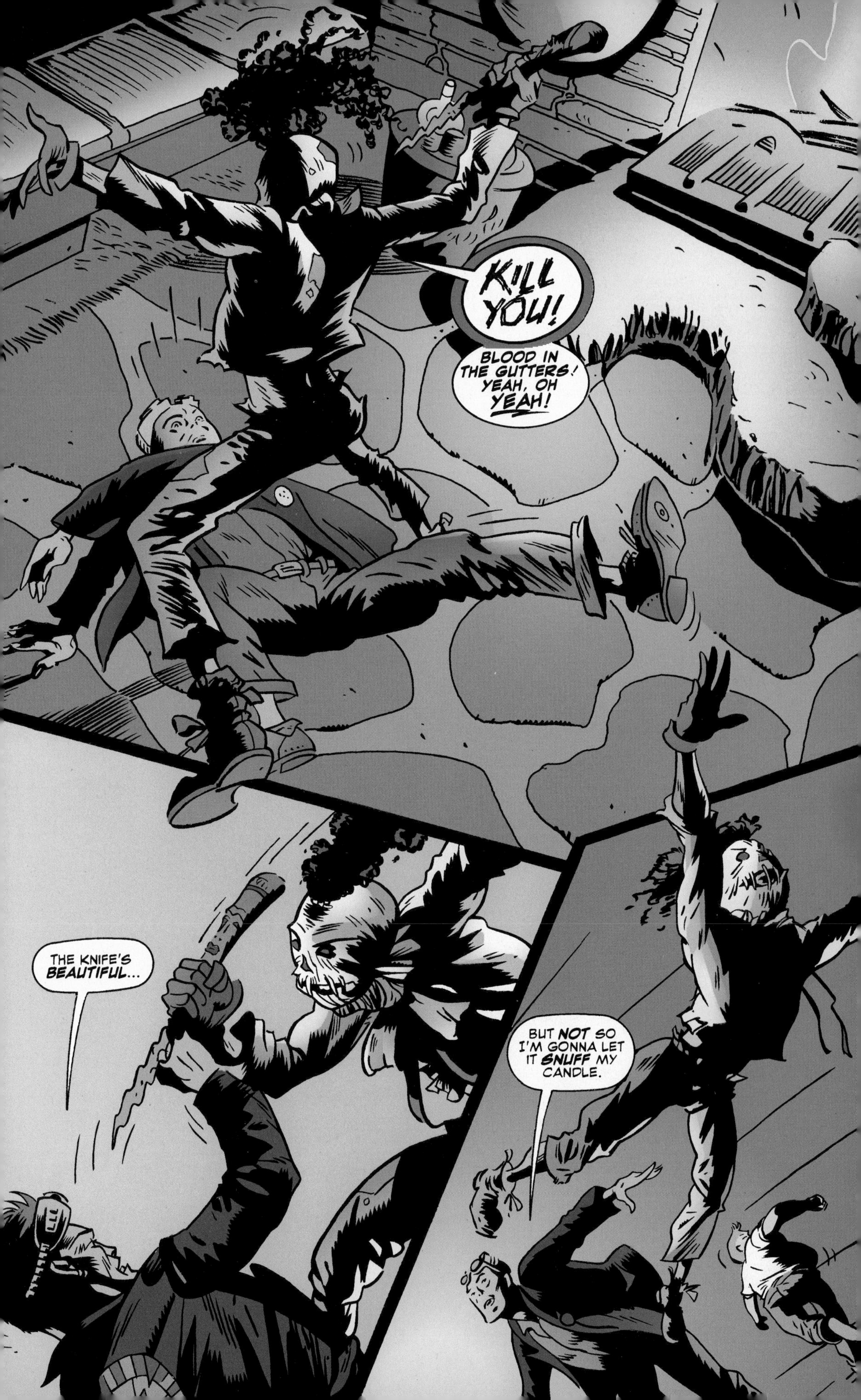
KILL YOU!
BLOOD IN THE GUTTERS! YEAH, OH YEAH!
THE KNIFE'S BEAUTIFUL...
BUT NOT SO I'M GONNA LET IT SNUFF MY CANDLE.

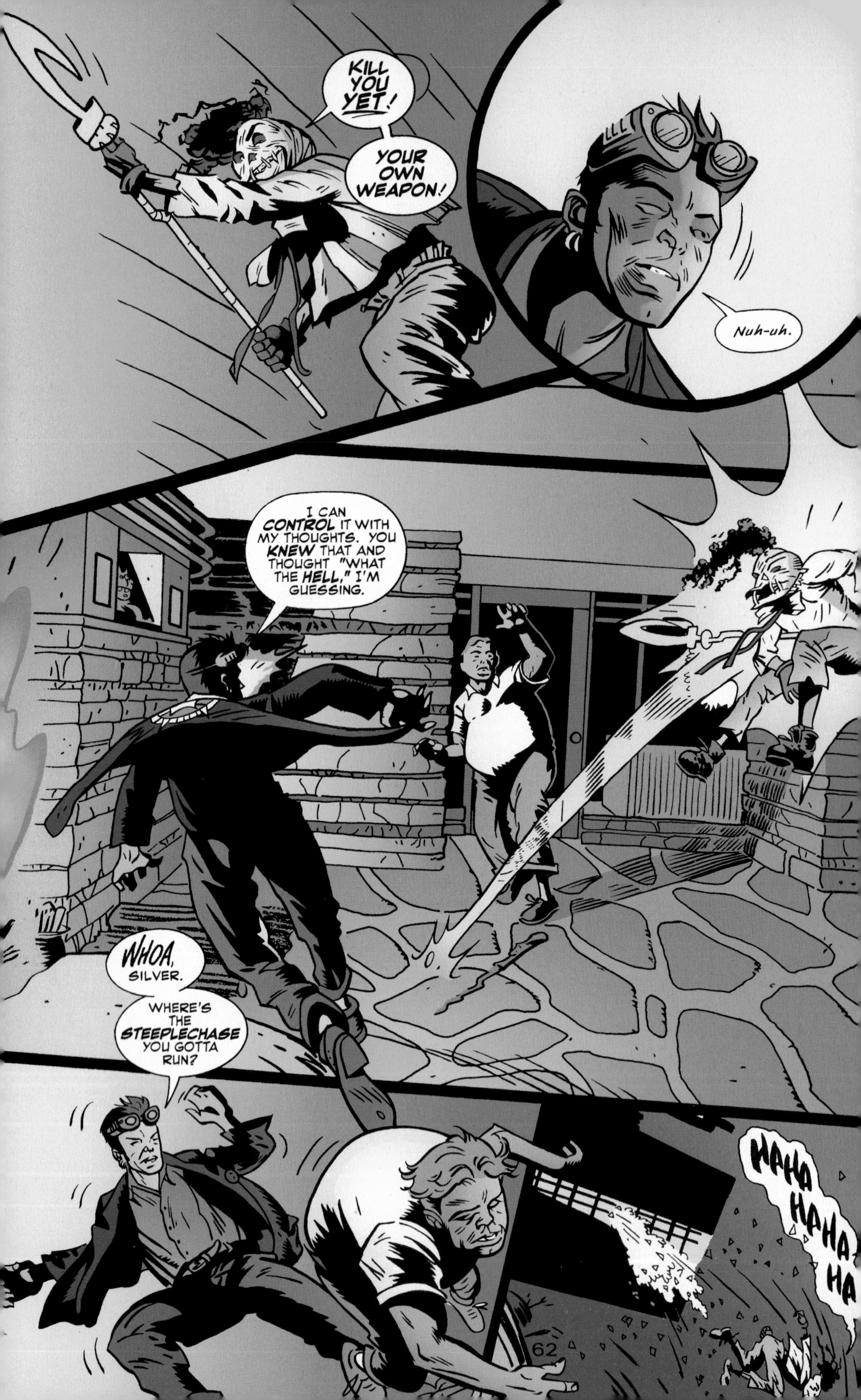
KILL YOU YET!
YOUR OWN WEAPON!
Nuh-uh.
I CAN CONTROL IT WITH MY THOUGHTS. YOU KNEW THAT AND THOUGHT "WHAT THE HELL," I'M GUESSING.
WHOA, SILVER.
WHERE'S THE STEEPLECHASE YOU GOTTA RUN?
HAHA HAHA HA HA

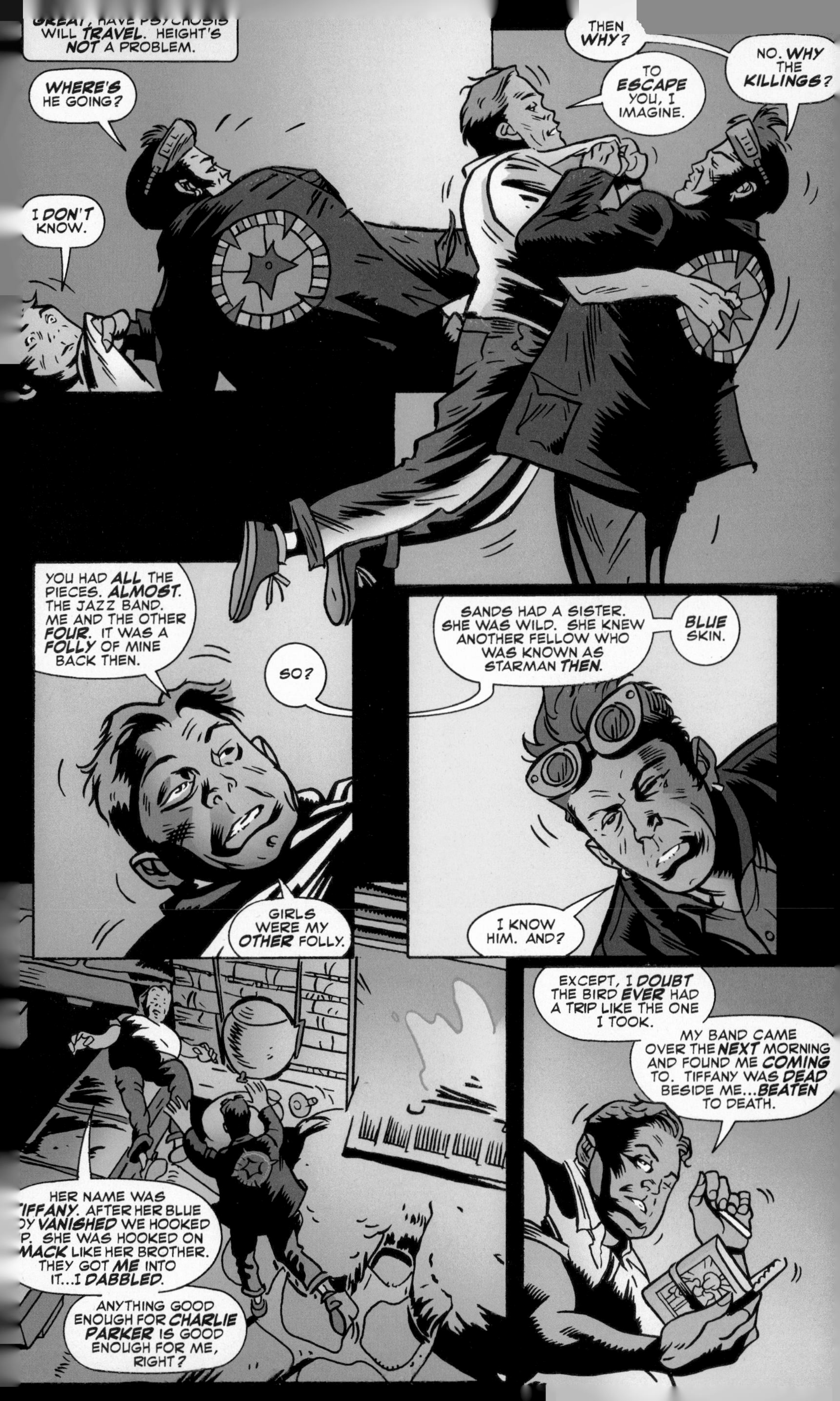

GREAT, HAVE PSYCHOSIS WILL TRAVEL. HEIGHT'S NOT A PROBLEM.
WHERE'S HE GOING?
I DON'T KNOW.
THEN WHY?
TO ESCAPE YOU, I IMAGINE.
NO. WHY THE KILLINGS?
YOU HAD ALL THE PIECES. ALMOST. THE JAZZ BAND. ME AND THE OTHER FOUR. IT WAS A FOLLY OF MINE BACK THEN.
SO?
GIRLS WERE MY OTHER FOLLY.
SANDS HAD A SISTER. SHE WAS WILD. SHE KNEW ANOTHER FELLOW WHO WAS KNOWN AS STARMAN THEN.
BLUE SKIN.
I KNOW HIM. AND?
HER NAME WAS IFFANY. AFTER HER BLUE OY VANISHED WE HOOKED P. SHE WAS HOOKED ON MACK LIKE HER BROTHER. THEY GOT ME INTO IT...I DABBLED.
ANYTHING GOOD ENOUGH FOR CHARLIE PARKER IS GOOD ENOUGH FOR ME, RIGHT?
EXCEPT, I DOUBT THE BIRD EVER HAD A TRIP LIKE THE ONE I TOOK.
MY BAND CAME OVER THE NEXT MORNING AND FOUND ME COMING TO. TIFFANY WAS DEAD BESIDE ME...BEATEN TO DEATH.

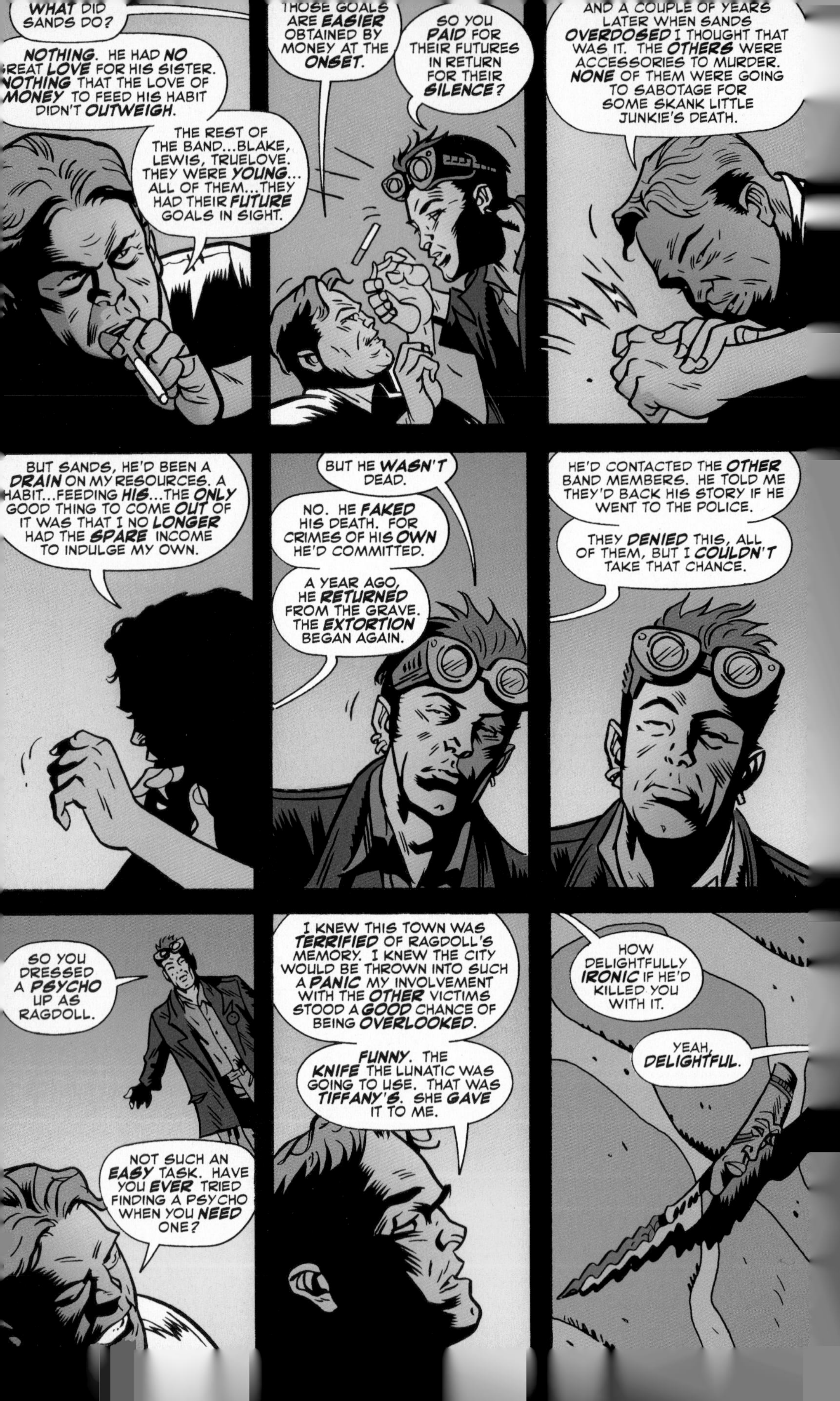
WHAT DID SANDS DO?
NOTHING. HE HAD NO GREAT LOVE FOR HIS SISTER. NOTHING THAT THE LOVE OF MONEY TO FEED HIS HABIT DIDN'T OUTWEIGH.
THE REST OF THE BAND...BLAKE, LEWIS, TRUELOVE. THEY WERE YOUNG... ALL OF THEM...THEY HAD THEIR FUTURE GOALS IN SIGHT.
THOSE GOALS ARE EASIER OBTAINED BY MONEY AT THE ONSET.
SO YOU PAID FOR THEIR FUTURES IN RETURN FOR THEIR SILENCE?
AND A COUPLE OF YEARS LATER WHEN SANDS OVERDOSED I THOUGHT THAT WAS IT. THE OTHERS WERE ACCESSORIES TO MURDER. NONE OF THEM WERE GOING TO SABOTAGE FOR SOME SKANK LITTLE JUNKIE'S DEATH.
BUT SANDS, HE'D BEEN A DRAIN ON MY RESOURCES. A HABIT...FEEDING HIS...THE ONLY GOOD THING TO COME OUT OF IT WAS THAT I NO LONGER HAD THE SPARE INCOME TO INDULGE MY OWN.
BUT HE WASN'T DEAD.
NO. HE FAKED HIS DEATH. FOR CRIMES OF HIS OWN HE'D COMMITTED.
A YEAR AGO, HE RETURNED FROM THE GRAVE. THE EXTORTION BEGAN AGAIN.
HE'D CONTACTED THE OTHER BAND MEMBERS. HE TOLD ME THEY'D BACK HIS STORY IF HE WENT TO THE POLICE.
THEY DENIED THIS, ALL OF THEM, BUT I COULDN'T TAKE THAT CHANCE.
SO YOU DRESSED A PSYCHO UP AS RAGDOLL.
NOT SUCH AN EASY TASK. HAVE YOU EVER TRIED FINDING A PSYCHO WHEN YOU NEED ONE?
I KNEW THIS TOWN WAS TERRIFIED OF RAGDOLL'S MEMORY. I KNEW THE CITY WOULD BE THROWN INTO SUCH A PANIC MY INVOLVEMENT WITH THE OTHER VICTIMS STOOD A GOOD CHANCE OF BEING OVERLOOKED.
FUNNY. THE KNIFE THE LUNATIC WAS GOING TO USE. THAT WAS TIFFANY'S. SHE GAVE IT TO ME.
HOW DELIGHTFULLY IRONIC IF HE'D KILLED YOU WITH IT.
YEAH, DELIGHTFUL.

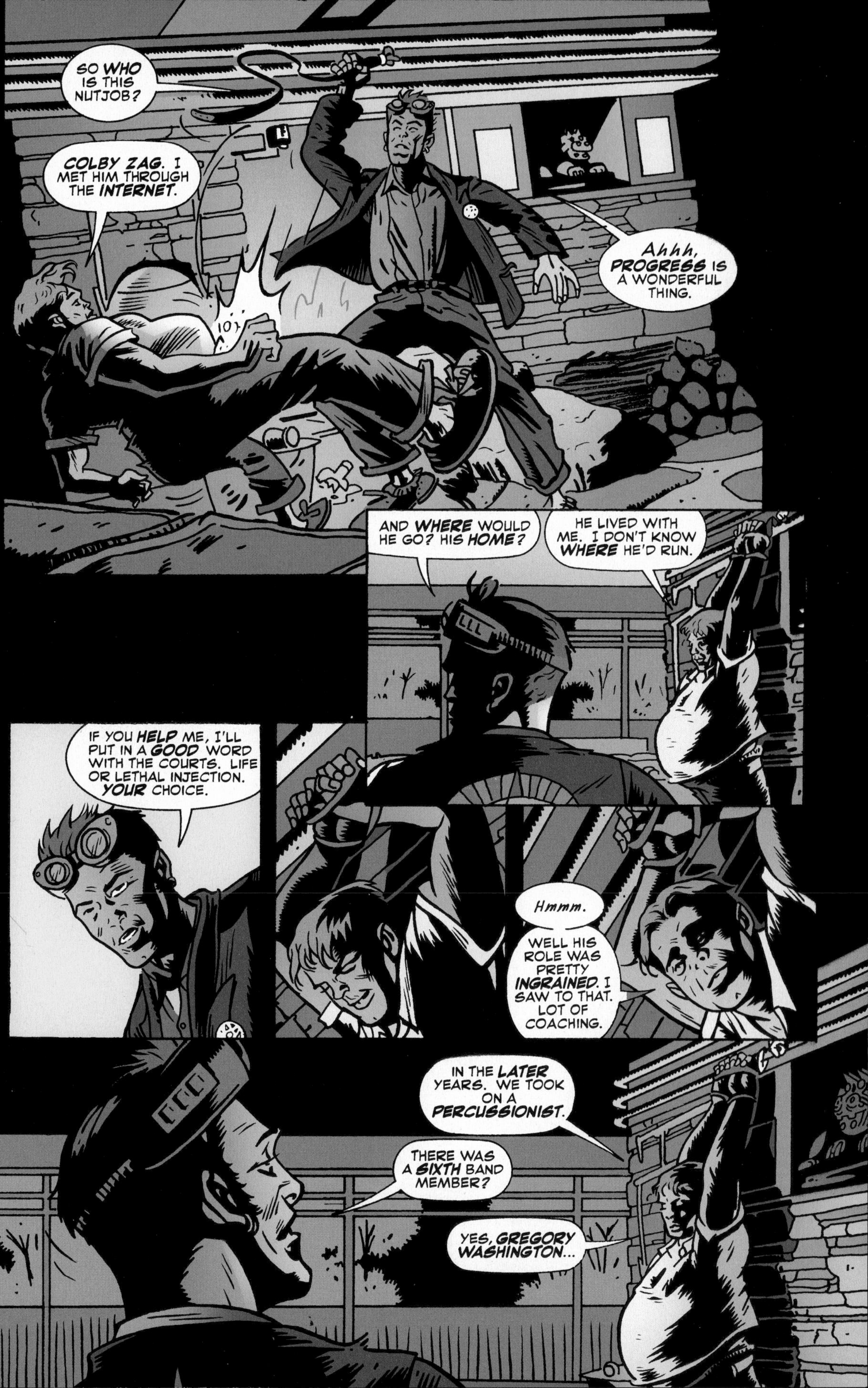
SO WHO IS THIS NUTJOB?
COLBY ZAG. I MET HIM THROUGH THE INTERNET.
Ahhh, PROGRESS IS A WONDERFUL THING.
AND WHERE WOULD HE GO? HIS HOME?
HE LIVED WITH ME. I DON'T KNOW WHERE HE'D RUN.
IF YOU HELP ME, I'LL PUT IN A GOOD WORD WITH THE COURTS. LIFE OR LETHAL INJECTION. YOUR CHOICE.
Hmmm.
WELL HIS ROLE WAS PRETTY INGRAINED. I SAW TO THAT. LOT OF COACHING.
IN THE LATER YEARS. WE TOOK ON A PERCUSSIONIST.
THERE WAS A SIXTH BAND MEMBER?
YES, GREGORY WASHINGTON...

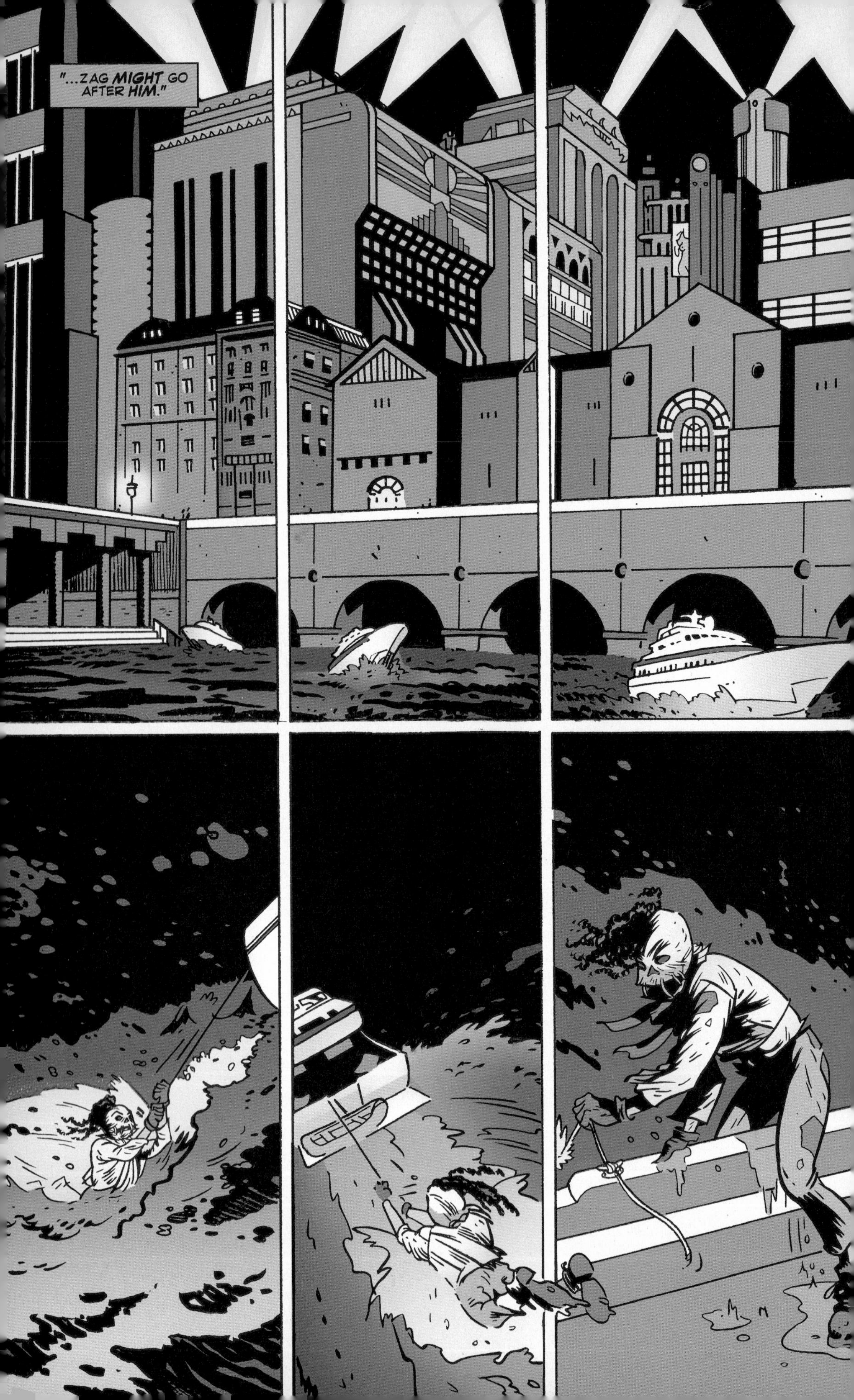
"...ZAG MIGHT GO AFTER HIM."

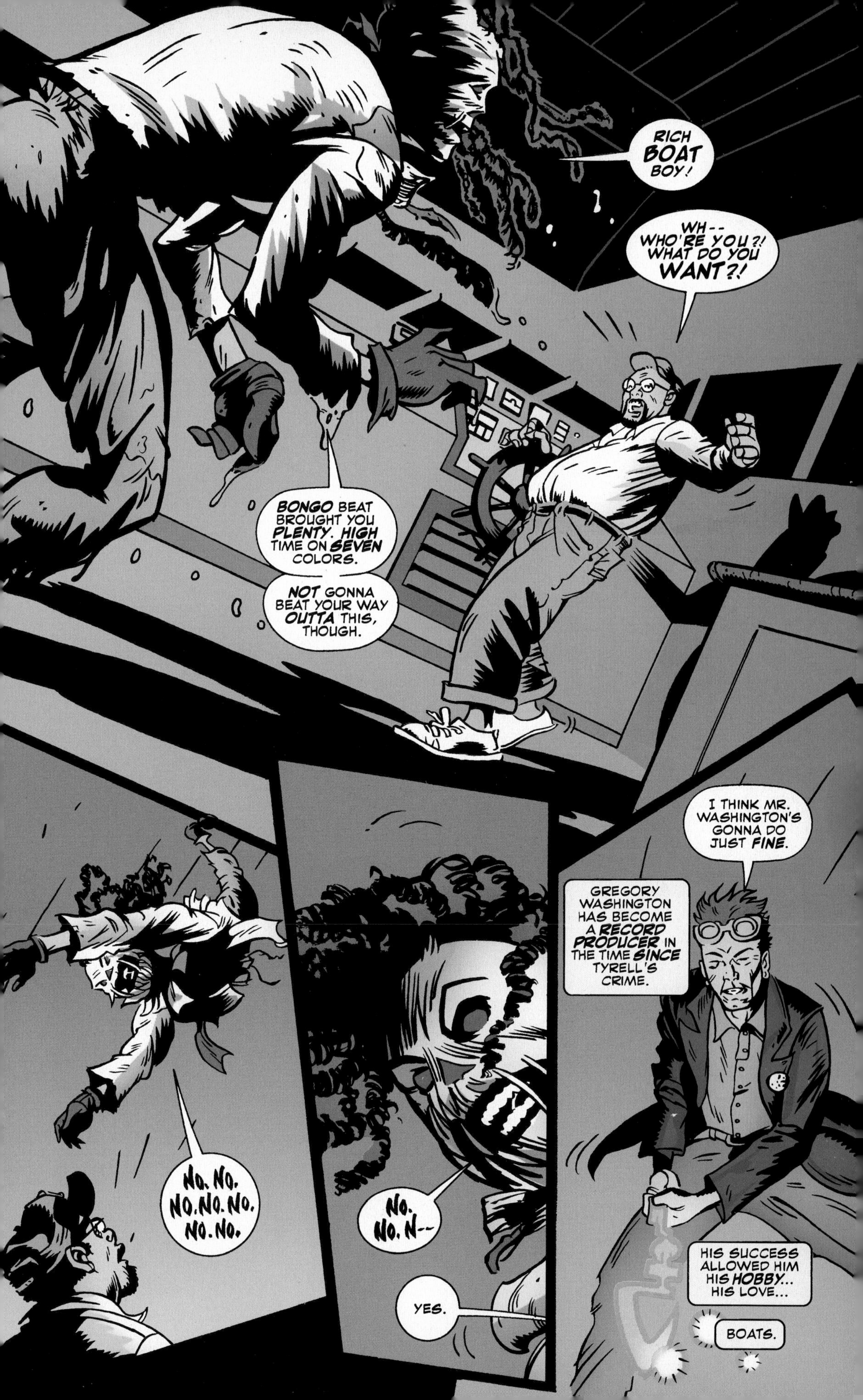
RICH BOAT BOY!
WH-- WHO'RE YOU?! WHAT DO YOU WANT?!
BONGO BEAT BROUGHT YOU PLENTY. HIGH TIME ON SEVEN COLORS.
NOT GONNA BEAT YOUR WAY OUTTA THIS, THOUGH.
NO. NO. NO. NO. NO. NO. NO.
NO. NO. N--
YES.
I THINK MR. WASHINGTON'S GONNA DO JUST FINE.
GREGORY WASHINGTON HAS BECOME A RECORD PRODUCER IN THE TIME SINCE TYRELL'S CRIME.
HIS SUCCESS ALLOWED HIM HIS HOBBY... HIS LOVE...
BOATS.

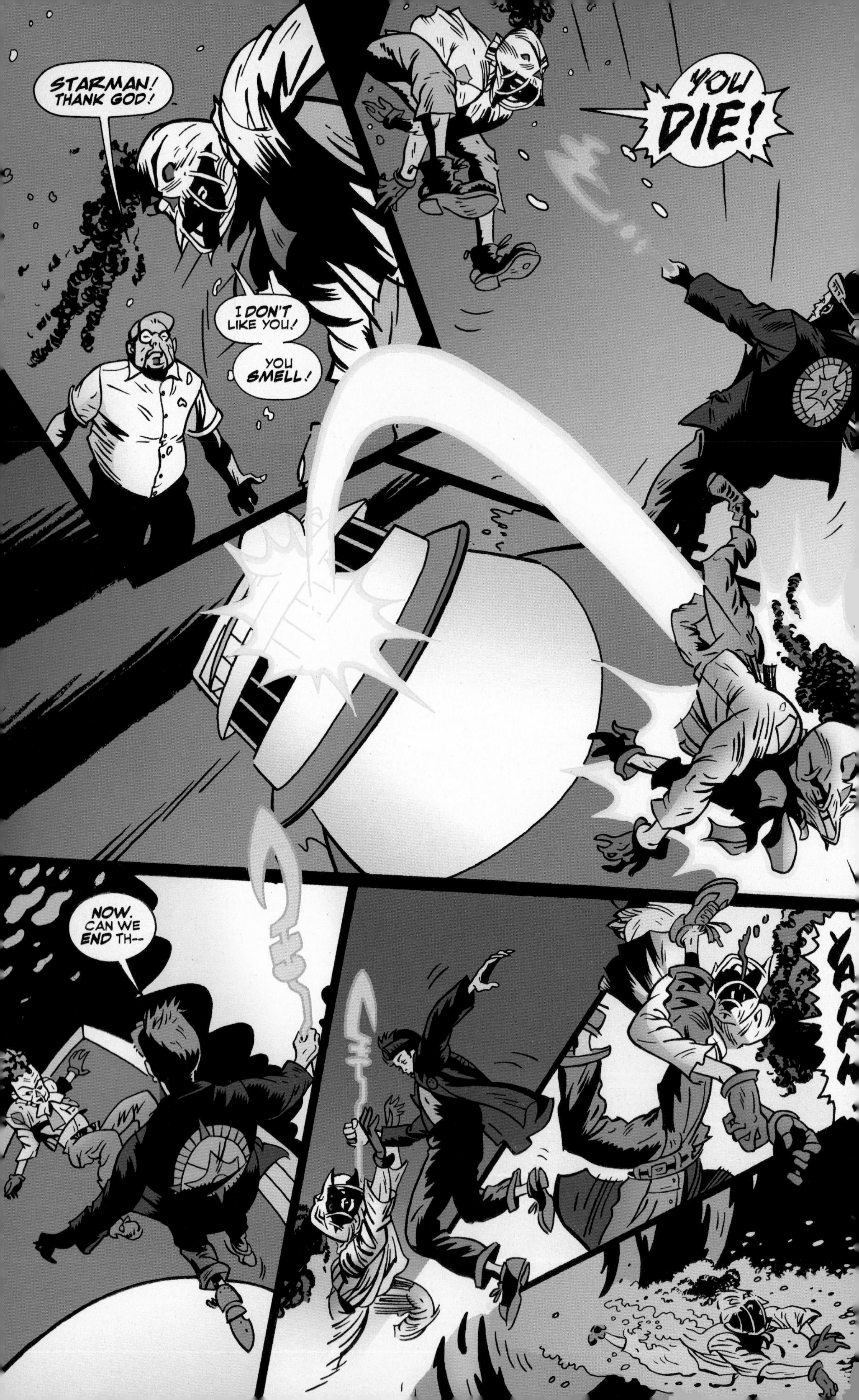
STARMAN! THANK GOD!
YOU DIE!
I DON'T LIKE YOU!
YOU SMELL!
NOW. CAN WE END TH--
YARR

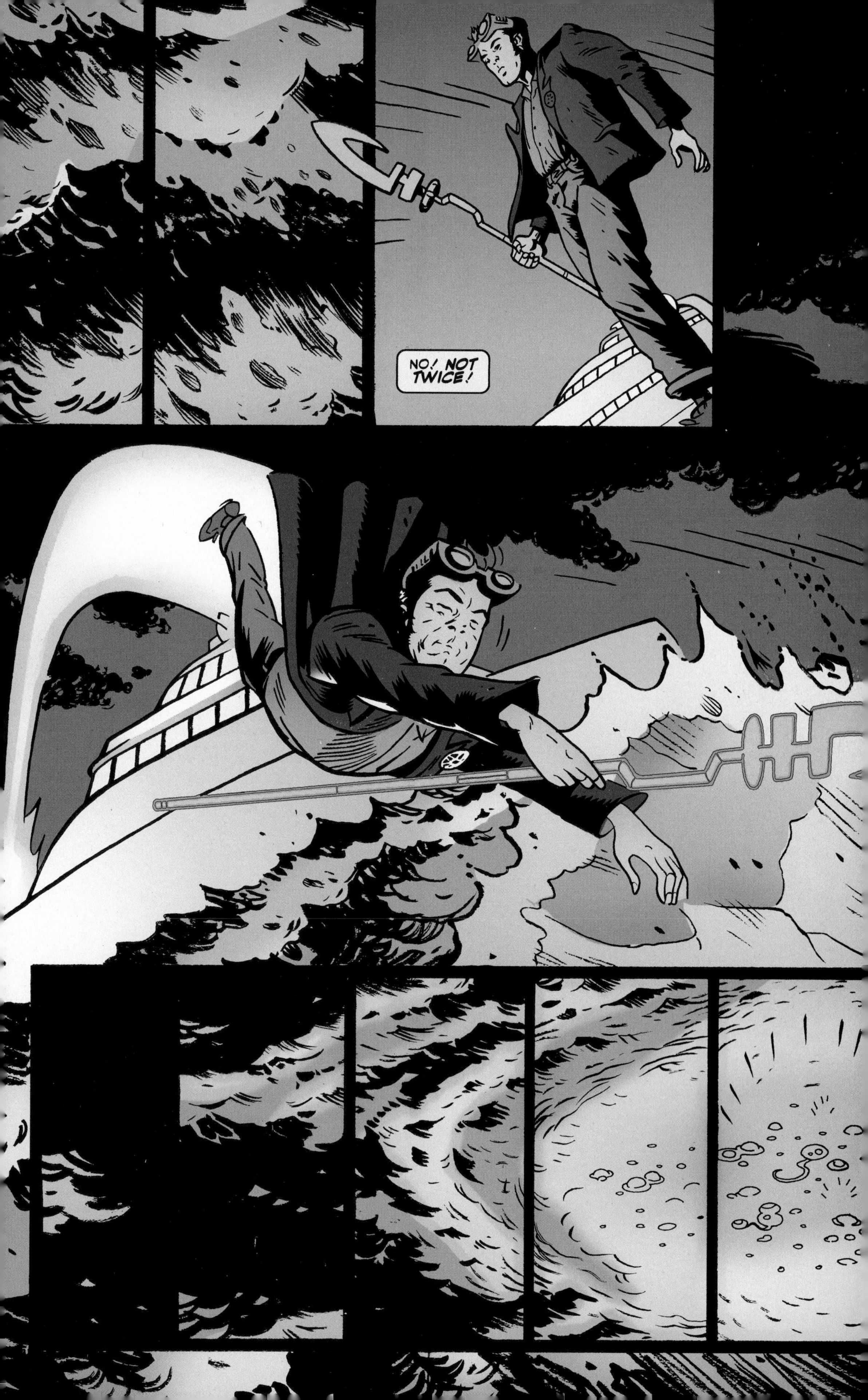
NO! NOT TWICE!

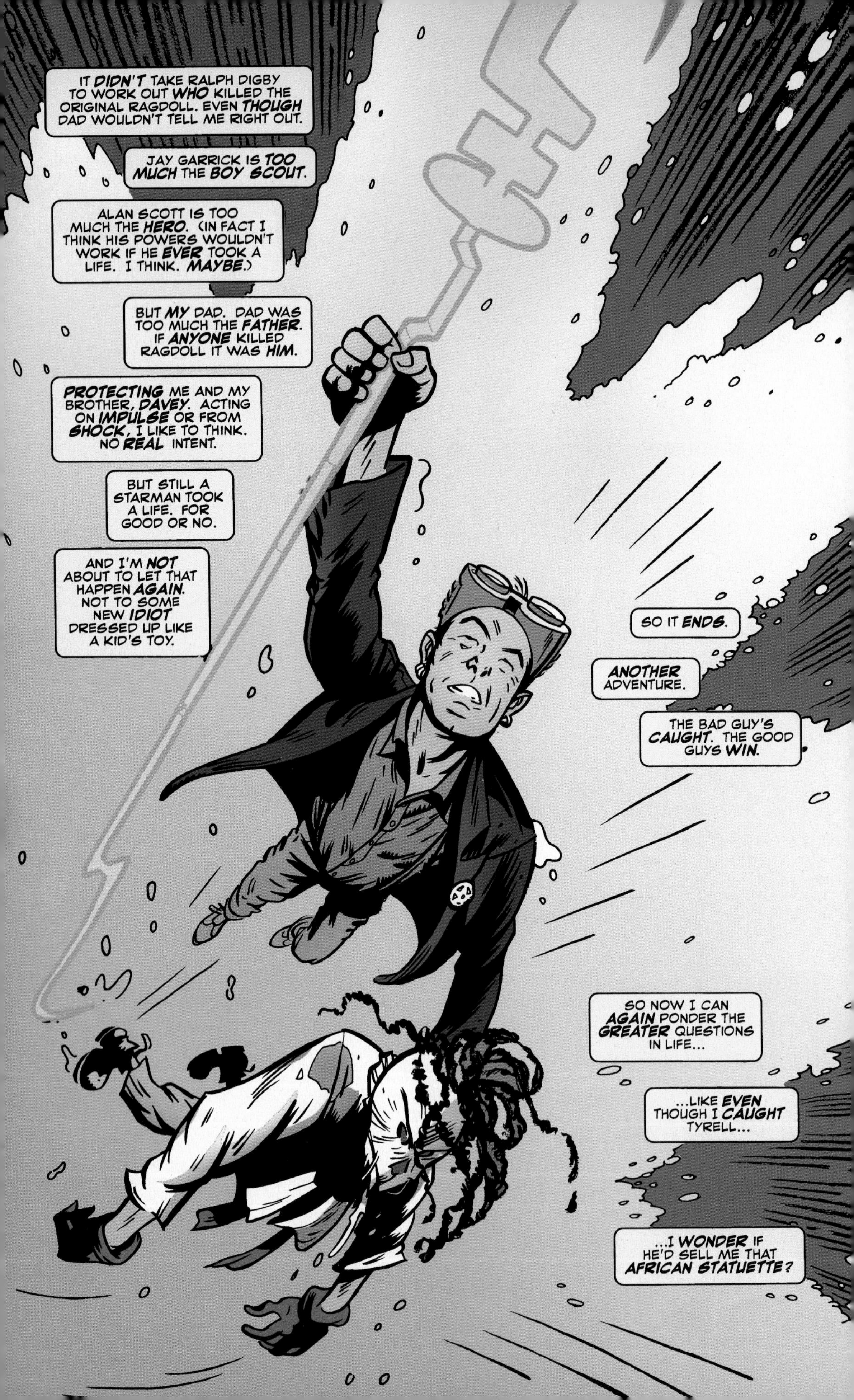
IT DIDN'T TAKE RALPH DIGBY TO WORK OUT WHO KILLED THE ORIGINAL RAGDOLL. EVEN THOUGH DAD WOULDN'T TELL ME RIGHT OUT.
JAY GARRICK IS TOO MUCH THE BOY SCOUT.
ALAN SCOTT IS TOO MUCH THE HERO. (IN FACT I THINK HIS POWERS WOULDN'T WORK IF HE EVER TOOK A LIFE. I THINK. MAYBE.)
BUT MY DAD. DAD WAS TOO MUCH THE FATHER. IF ANYONE KILLED RAGDOLL IT WAS HIM.
PROTECTING ME AND MY BROTHER, DAVEY. ACTING ON IMPULSE OR FROM SHOCK, I LIKE TO THINK. NO REAL INTENT.
BUT STILL A STARMAN TOOK A LIFE. FOR GOOD OR NO.
AND I'M NOT ABOUT TO LET THAT HAPPEN AGAIN. NOT TO SOME NEW IDIOT DRESSED UP LIKE A KID'S TOY.
SO IT ENDS.
ANOTHER ADVENTURE.
THE BAD GUY'S CAUGHT. THE GOOD GUYS WIN.
SO NOW I CAN AGAIN PONDER THE GREATER QUESTIONS IN LIFE...
...LIKE EVEN THOUGH I CAUGHT TYRELL...
...I WONDER IF HE'D SELL ME THAT AFRICAN STATUETTE?

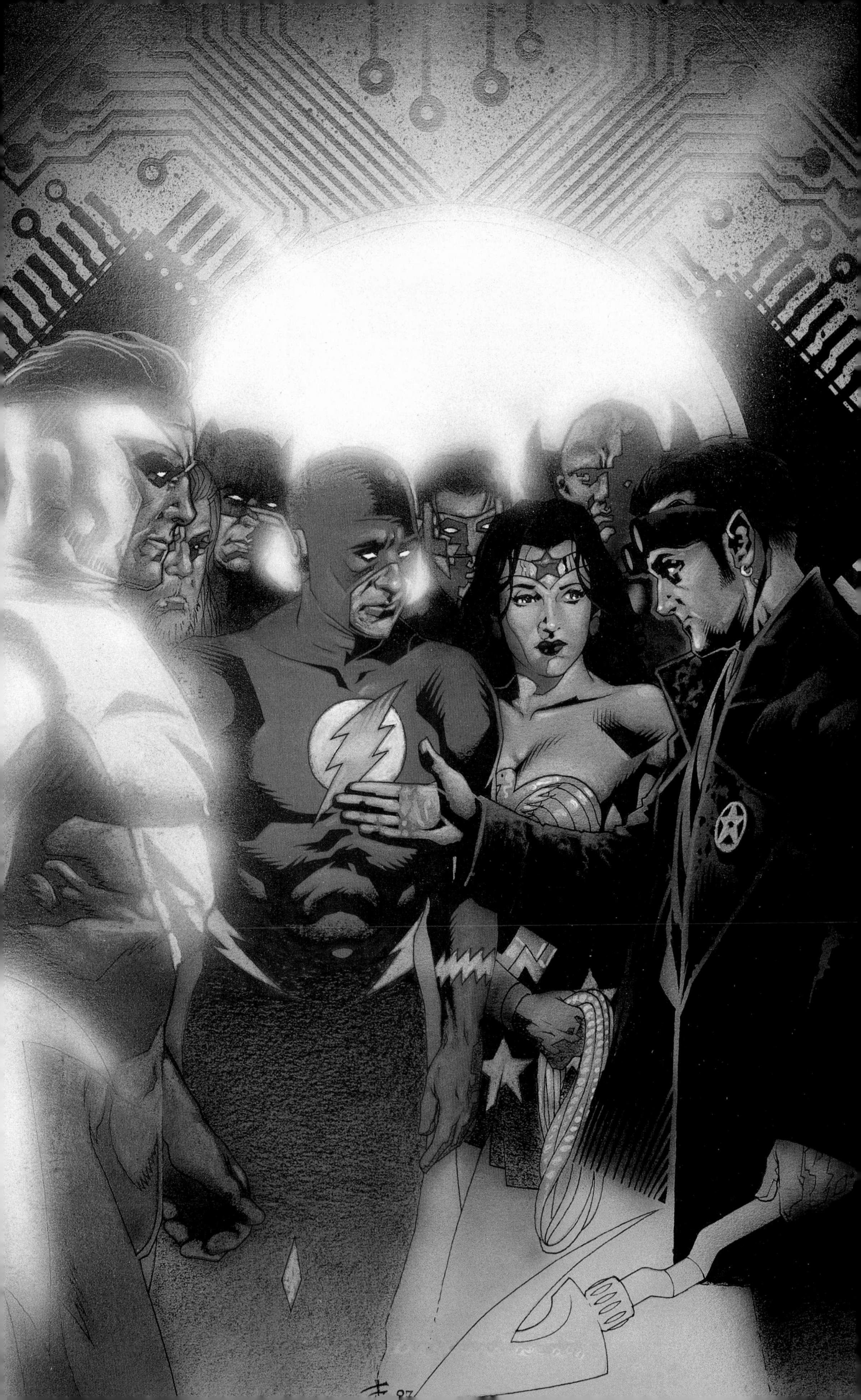

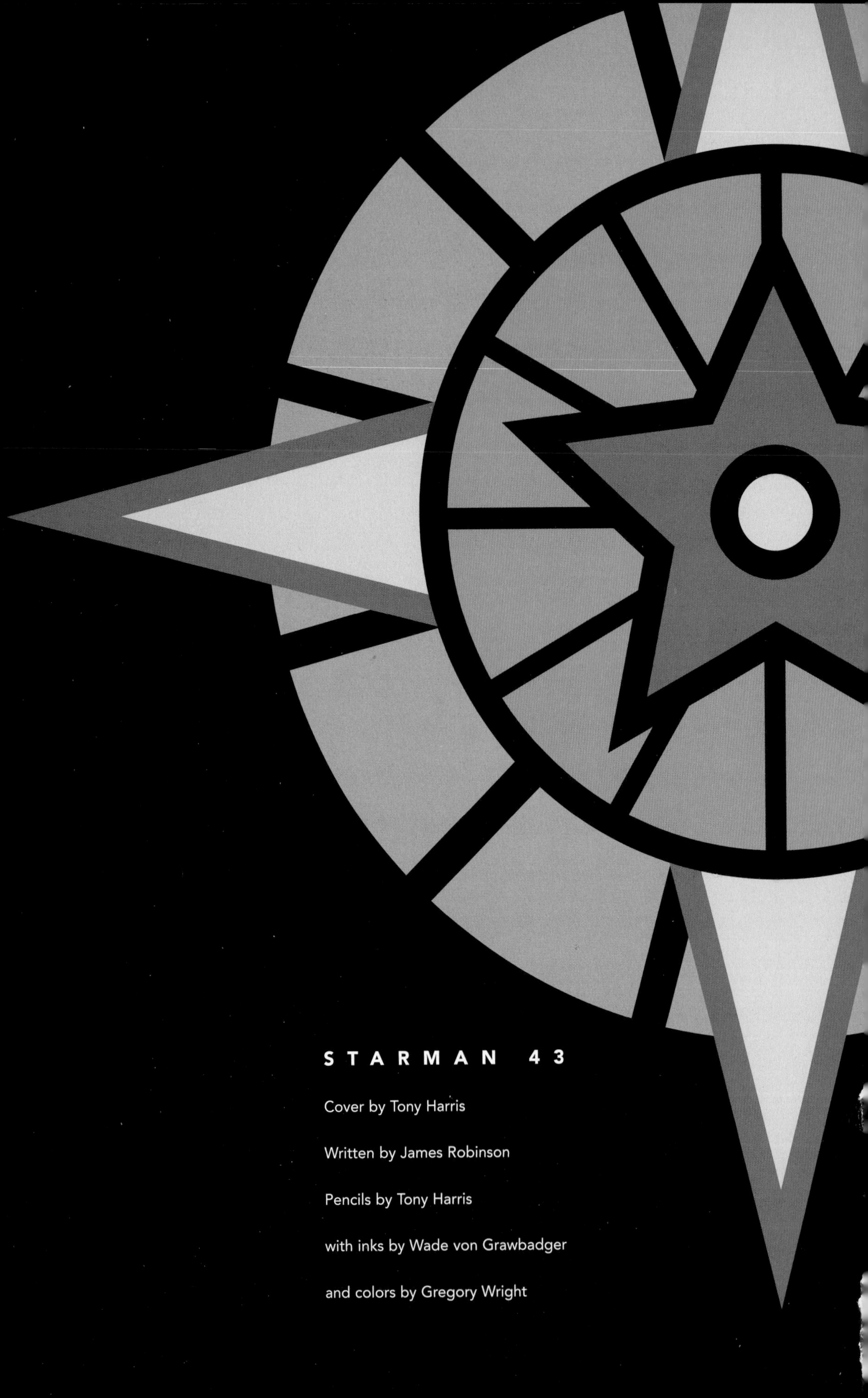

S T A R M A N   4 3

Cover by Tony Harris

Written by James Robinson

Pencils by Tony Harris

with inks by Wade von Grawbadger

and colors by Gregory Wright

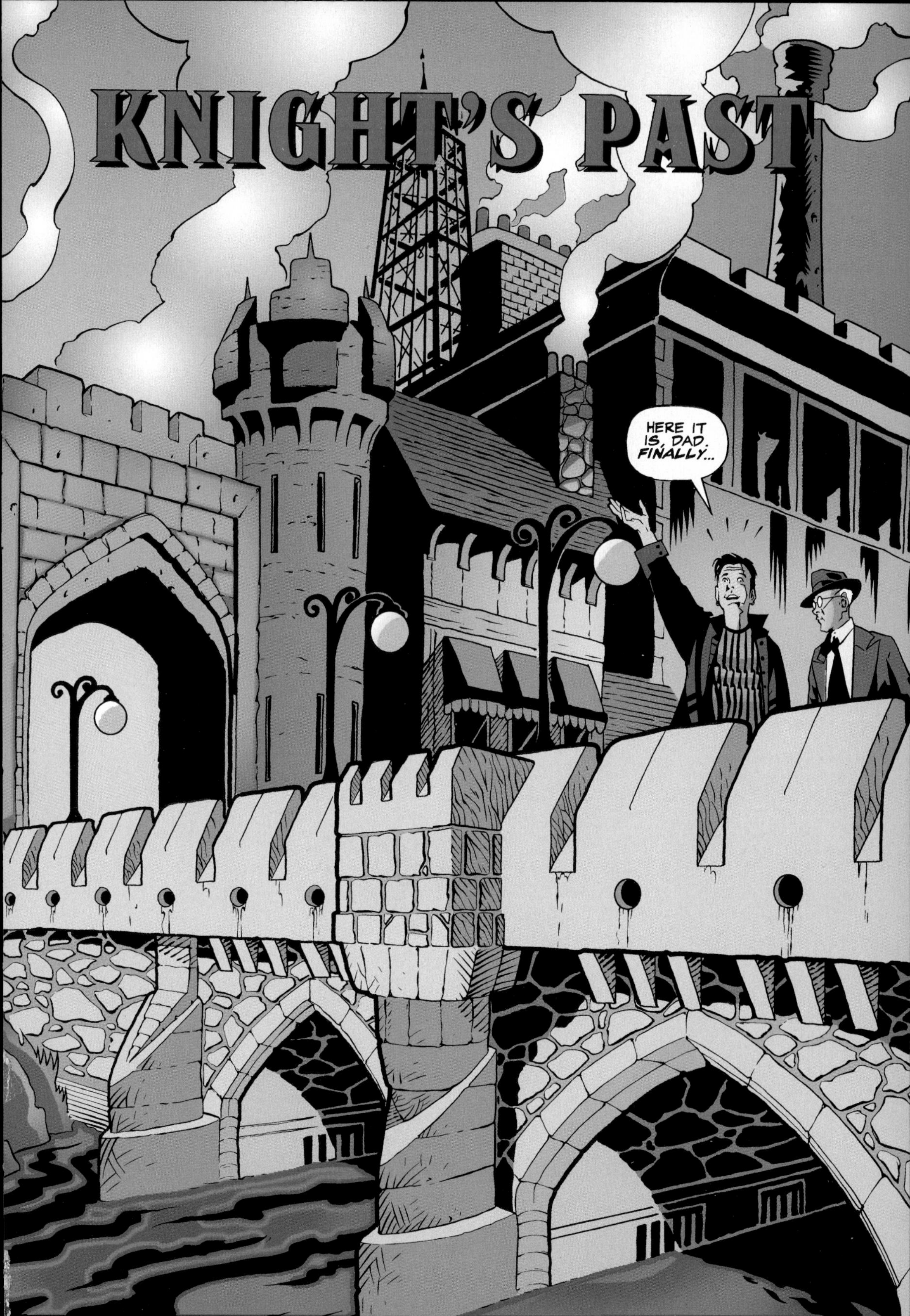
KNIGHT'S PAST
HERE IT IS, DAD. FINALLY...

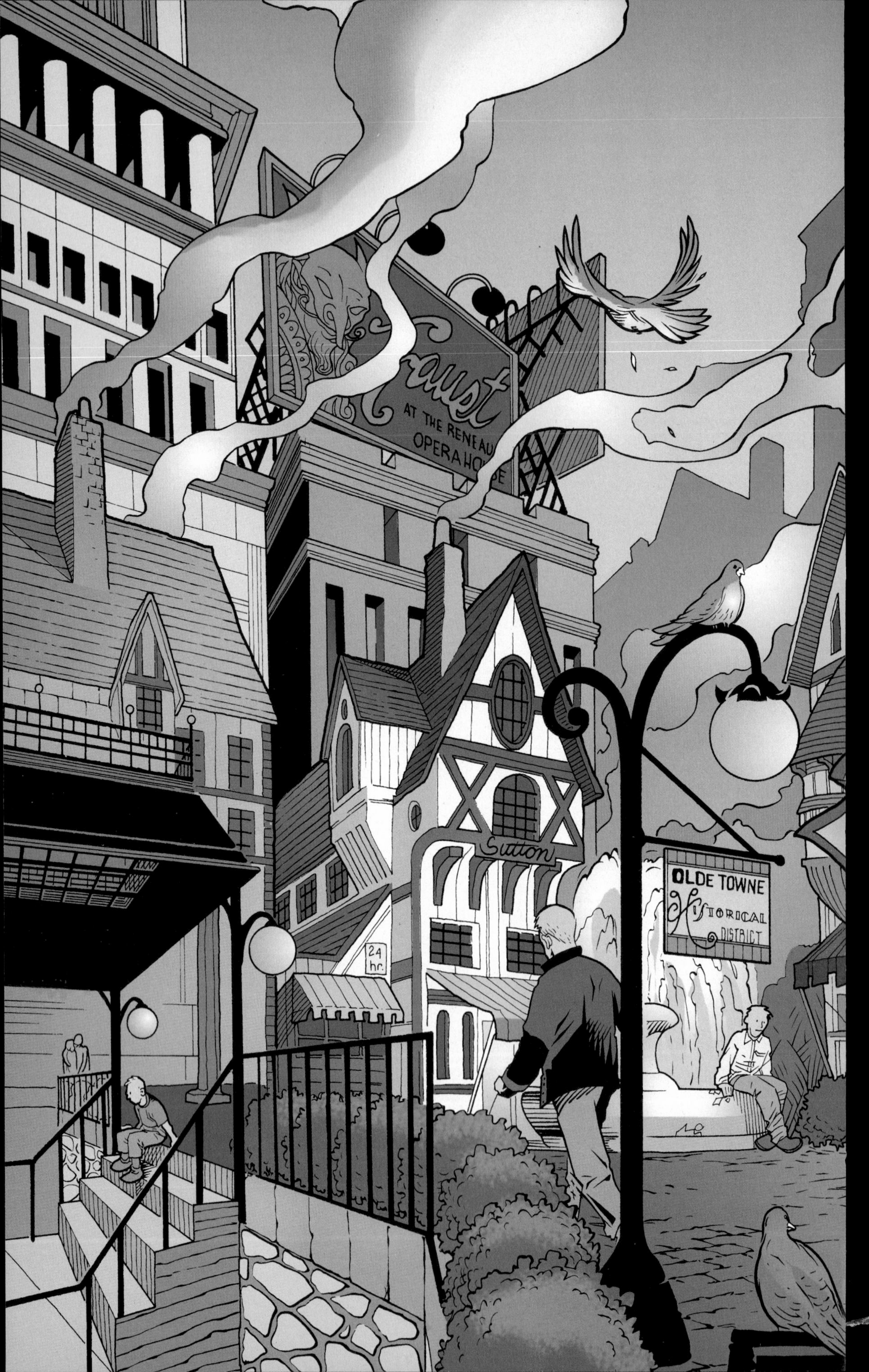
Faust
AT THE RENEAU
OPERA HOUSE
Sutton
24 hr.
OLDE TOWNE
Historical
DISTRICT

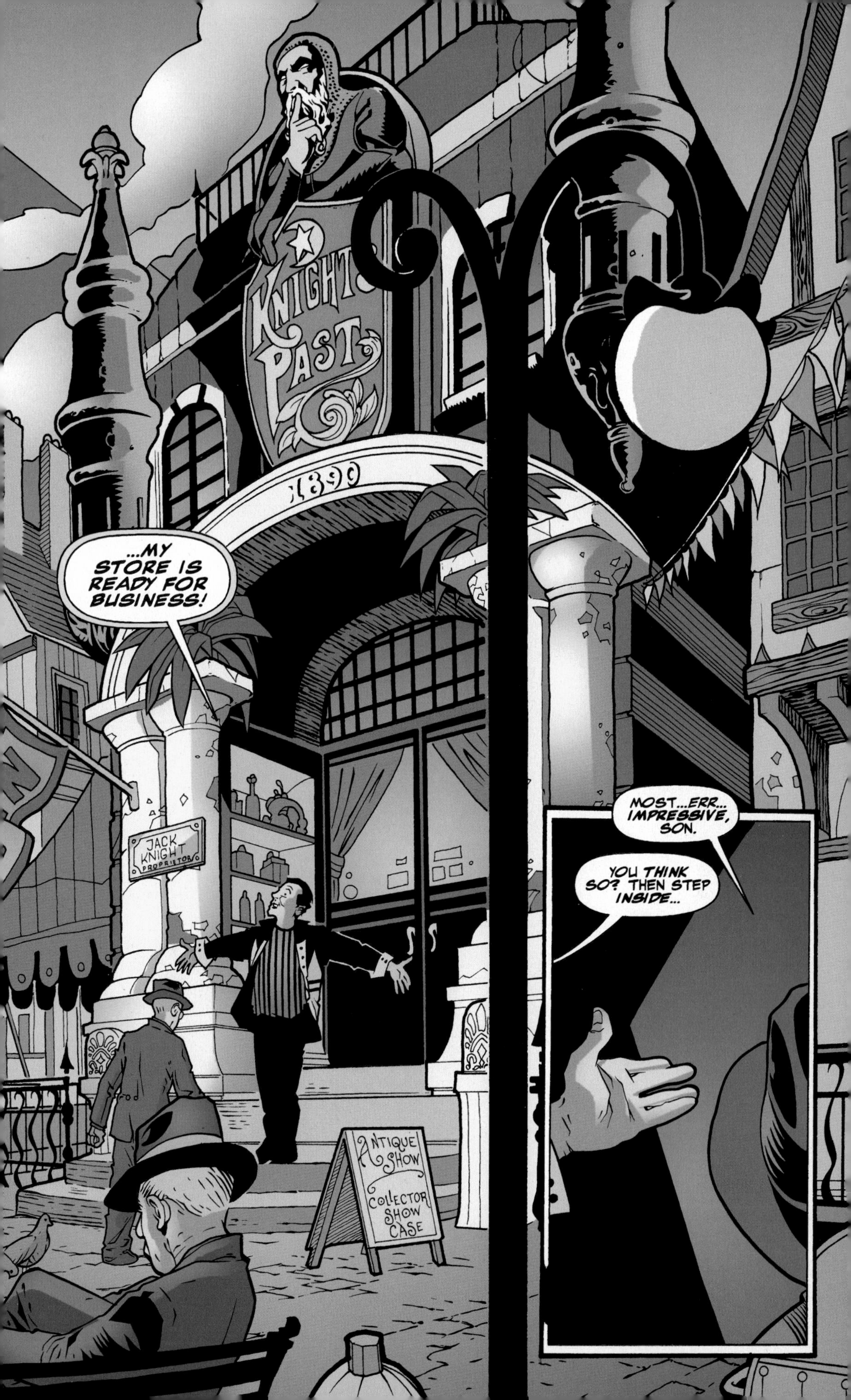
KNIGHTS PAST
1890
...MY STORE IS READY FOR BUSINESS!
JACK KNIGHT PROPRIETOR
MOST...ERR... IMPRESSIVE, SON.
YOU THINK SO? THEN STEP INSIDE...
ANTIQUE SHOW
COLLECTOR SHOW CASE

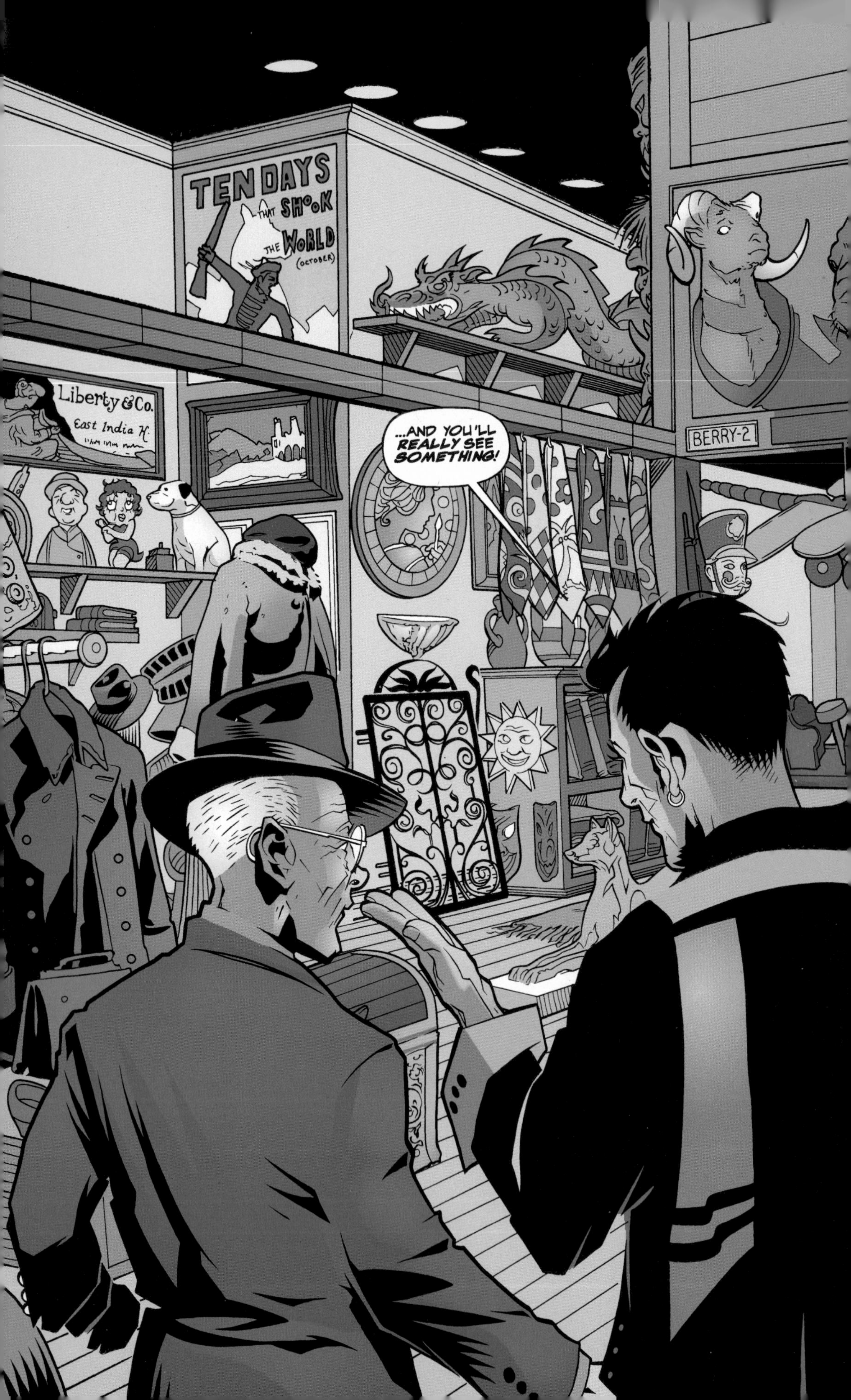

TEN DAYS THAT SHOOK THE WORLD
(OCTOBER)
Liberty & Co.
East India H.
...AND YOU'LL REALLY SEE SOMETHING!
BERRY-2

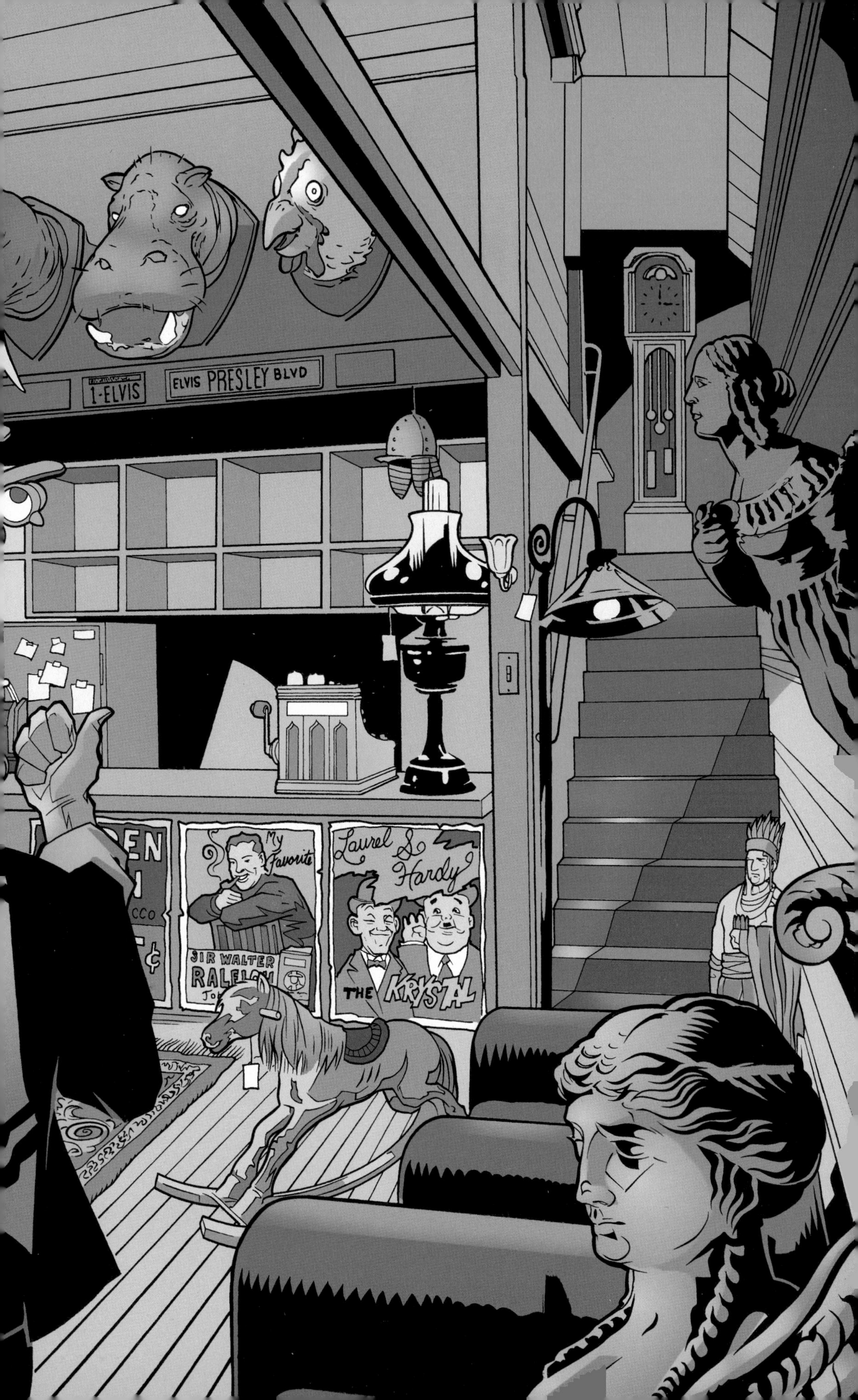

1-ELVIS
ELVIS PRESLEY BLVD
My Favorite
SIR WALTER RALEIGH
Laurel & Hardy
THE KRYSTAL

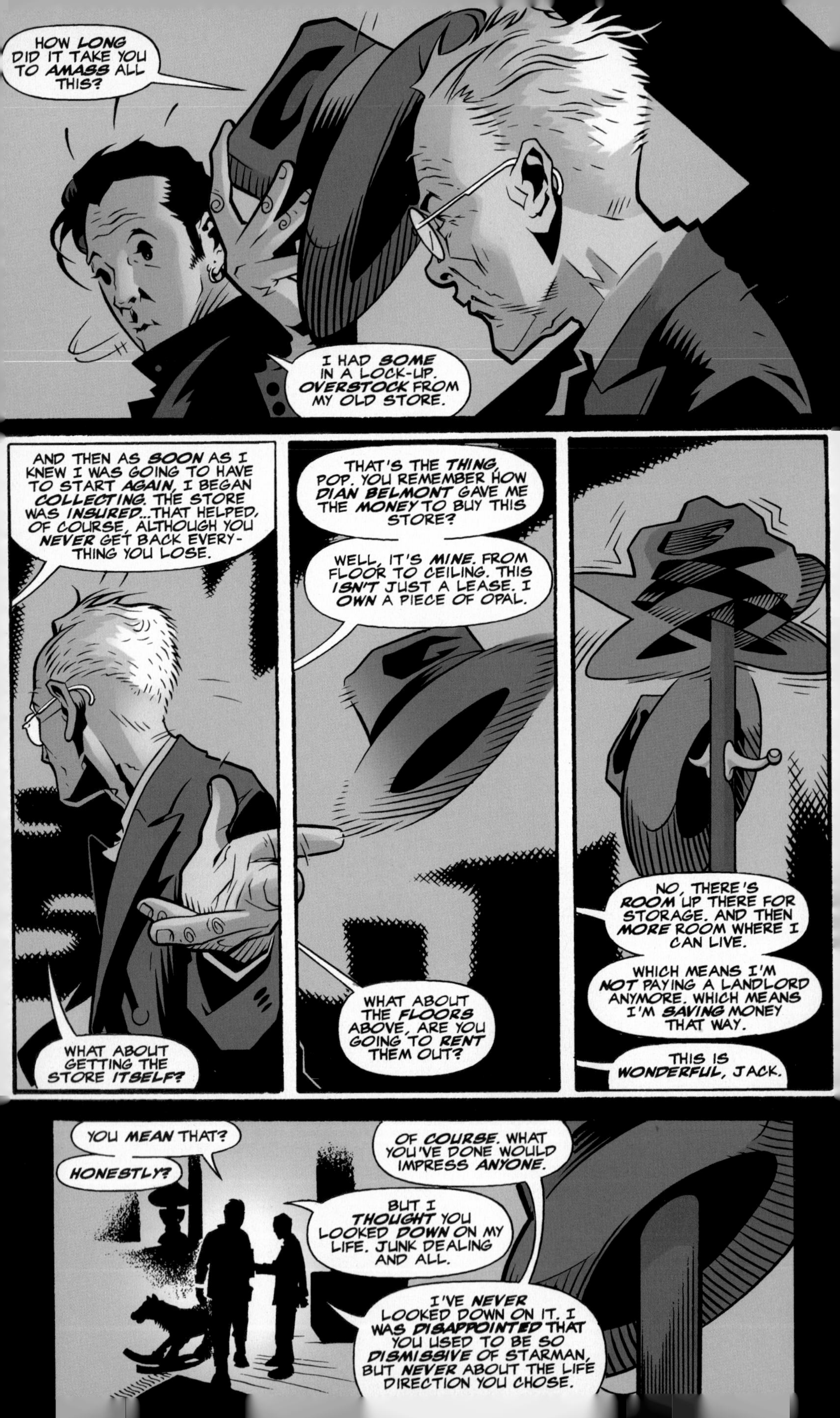
HOW LONG DID IT TAKE YOU TO AMASS ALL THIS?
I HAD SOME IN A LOCK-UP. OVERSTOCK FROM MY OLD STORE.
AND THEN AS SOON AS I KNEW I WAS GOING TO HAVE TO START AGAIN, I BEGAN COLLECTING. THE STORE WAS INSURED...THAT HELPED, OF COURSE, ALTHOUGH YOU NEVER GET BACK EVERY-THING YOU LOSE.
WHAT ABOUT GETTING THE STORE ITSELF?
THAT'S THE THING, POP. YOU REMEMBER HOW DIAN BELMONT GAVE ME THE MONEY TO BUY THIS STORE?
WELL, IT'S MINE. FROM FLOOR TO CEILING. THIS ISN'T JUST A LEASE. I OWN A PIECE OF OPAL.
WHAT ABOUT THE FLOORS ABOVE, ARE YOU GOING TO RENT THEM OUT?
NO, THERE'S ROOM UP THERE FOR STORAGE. AND THEN MORE ROOM WHERE I CAN LIVE.
WHICH MEANS I'M NOT PAYING A LANDLORD ANYMORE. WHICH MEANS I'M SAVING MONEY THAT WAY.
THIS IS WONDERFUL, JACK.
YOU MEAN THAT?
HONESTLY?
OF COURSE. WHAT YOU'VE DONE WOULD IMPRESS ANYONE.
BUT I THOUGHT YOU LOOKED DOWN ON MY LIFE. JUNK DEALING AND ALL.
I'VE NEVER LOOKED DOWN ON IT. I WAS DISAPPOINTED THAT YOU USED TO BE SO DISMISSIVE OF STARMAN, BUT NEVER ABOUT THE LIFE DIRECTION YOU CHOSE.

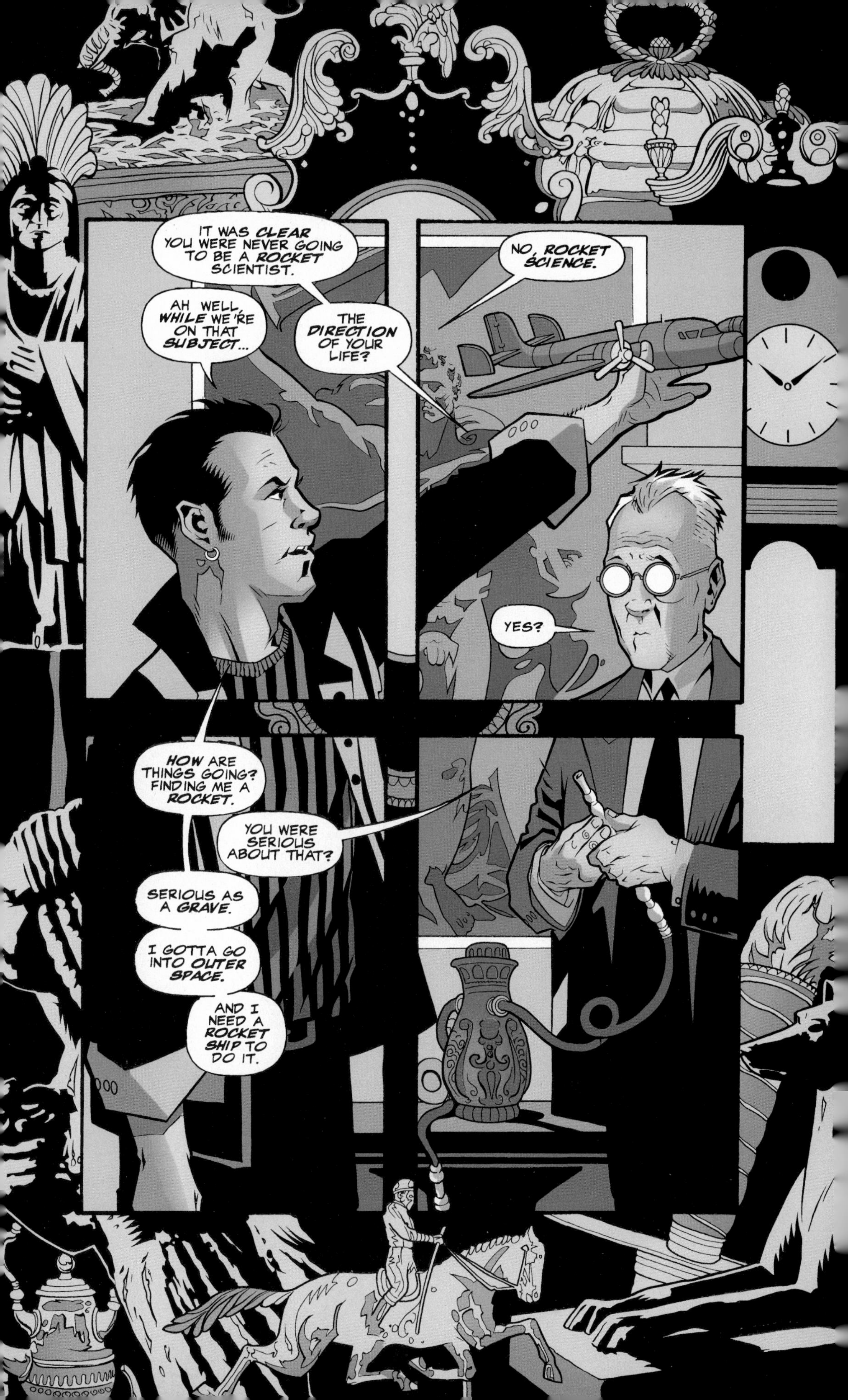
IT WAS CLEAR YOU WERE NEVER GOING TO BE A ROCKET SCIENTIST.
NO, ROCKET SCIENCE.
AH WELL, WHILE WE'RE ON THAT SUBJECT...
THE DIRECTION OF YOUR LIFE?
YES?
HOW ARE THINGS GOING? FINDING ME A ROCKET.
YOU WERE SERIOUS ABOUT THAT?
SERIOUS AS A GRAVE.
I GOTTA GO INTO OUTER SPACE.
AND I NEED A ROCKET SHIP TO DO IT.

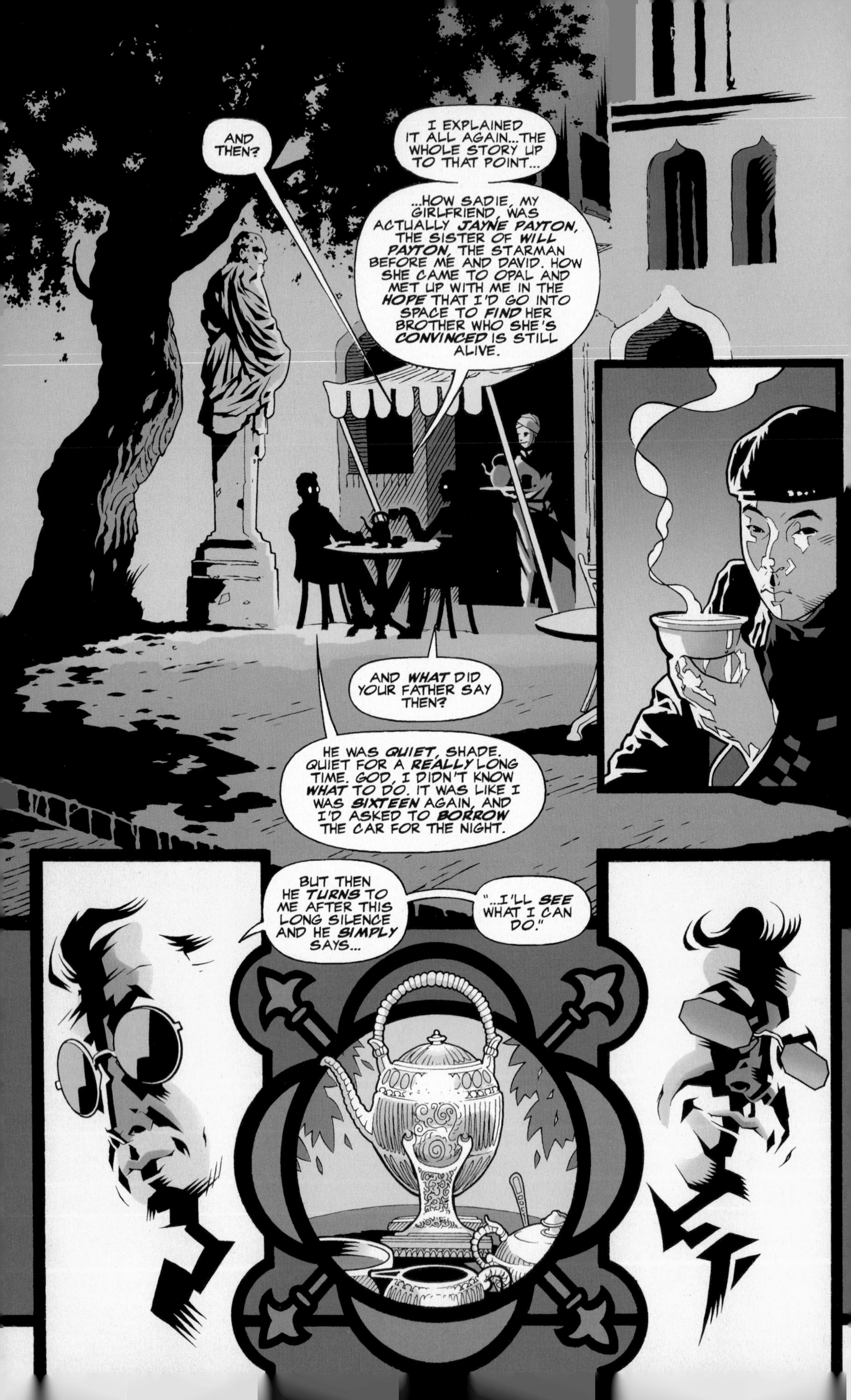
AND THEN?
I EXPLAINED IT ALL AGAIN... THE WHOLE STORY UP TO THAT POINT...
...HOW SADIE, MY GIRLFRIEND, WAS ACTUALLY JAYNE PAYTON, THE SISTER OF WILL PAYTON, THE STARMAN BEFORE ME AND DAVID. HOW SHE CAME TO OPAL AND MET UP WITH ME IN THE HOPE THAT I'D GO INTO SPACE TO FIND HER BROTHER WHO SHE'S CONVINCED IS STILL ALIVE.
AND WHAT DID YOUR FATHER SAY THEN?
HE WAS QUIET, SHADE. QUIET FOR A REALLY LONG TIME. GOD, I DIDN'T KNOW WHAT TO DO. IT WAS LIKE I WAS SIXTEEN AGAIN, AND I'D ASKED TO BORROW THE CAR FOR THE NIGHT.
BUT THEN HE TURNS TO ME AFTER THIS LONG SILENCE AND HE SIMPLY SAYS...
"...I'LL SEE WHAT I CAN DO."

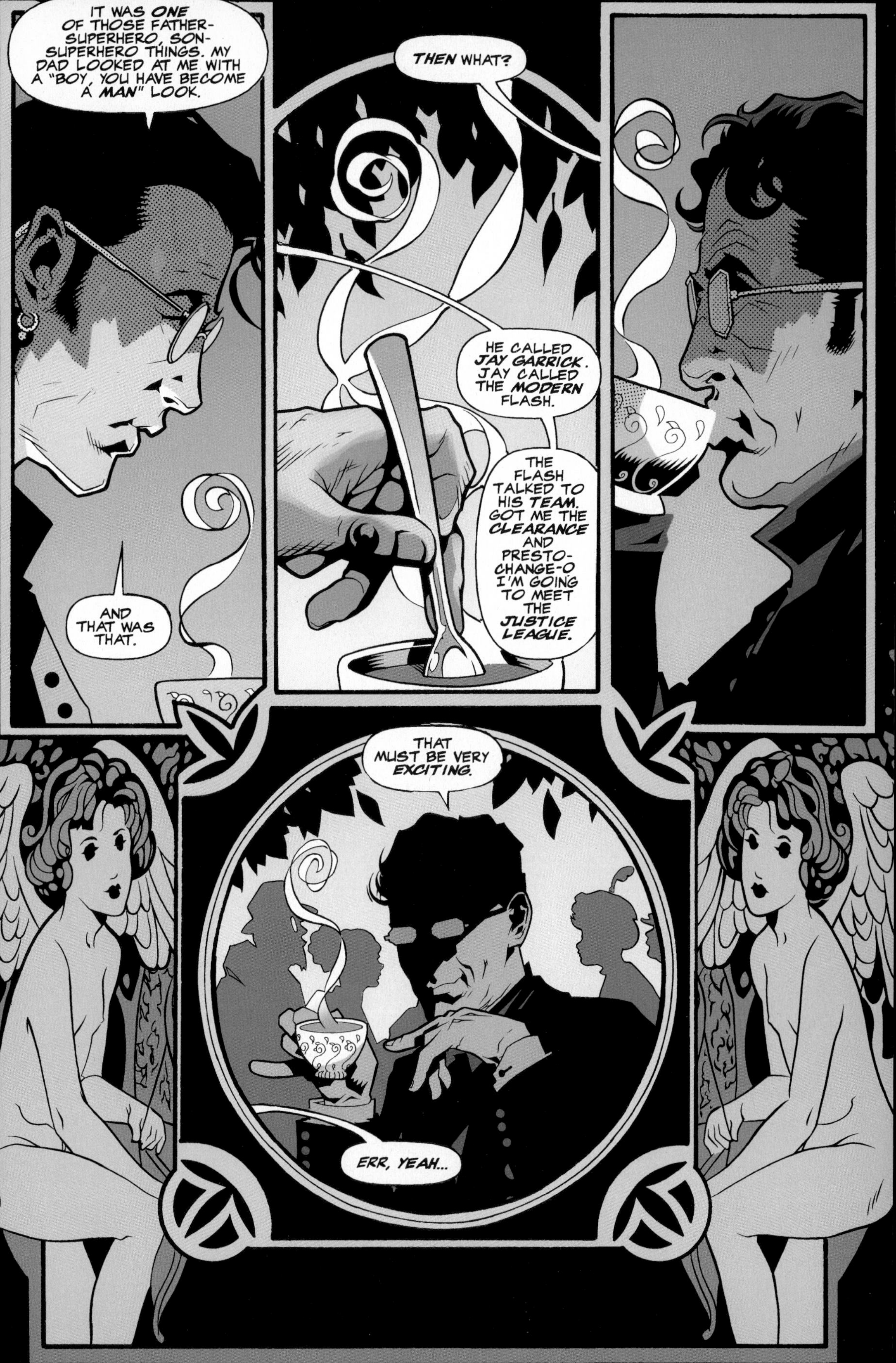

IT WAS ONE OF THOSE FATHER-SUPERHERO, SON-SUPERHERO THINGS. MY DAD LOOKED AT ME WITH A "BOY, YOU HAVE BECOME A MAN" LOOK.
AND THAT WAS THAT.
THEN WHAT?
HE CALLED JAY GARRICK. JAY CALLED THE MODERN FLASH.
THE FLASH TALKED TO HIS TEAM. GOT ME THE CLEARANCE AND PRESTO-CHANGE-O I'M GOING TO MEET THE JUSTICE LEAGUE.
THAT MUST BE VERY EXCITING.
ERR, YEAH...

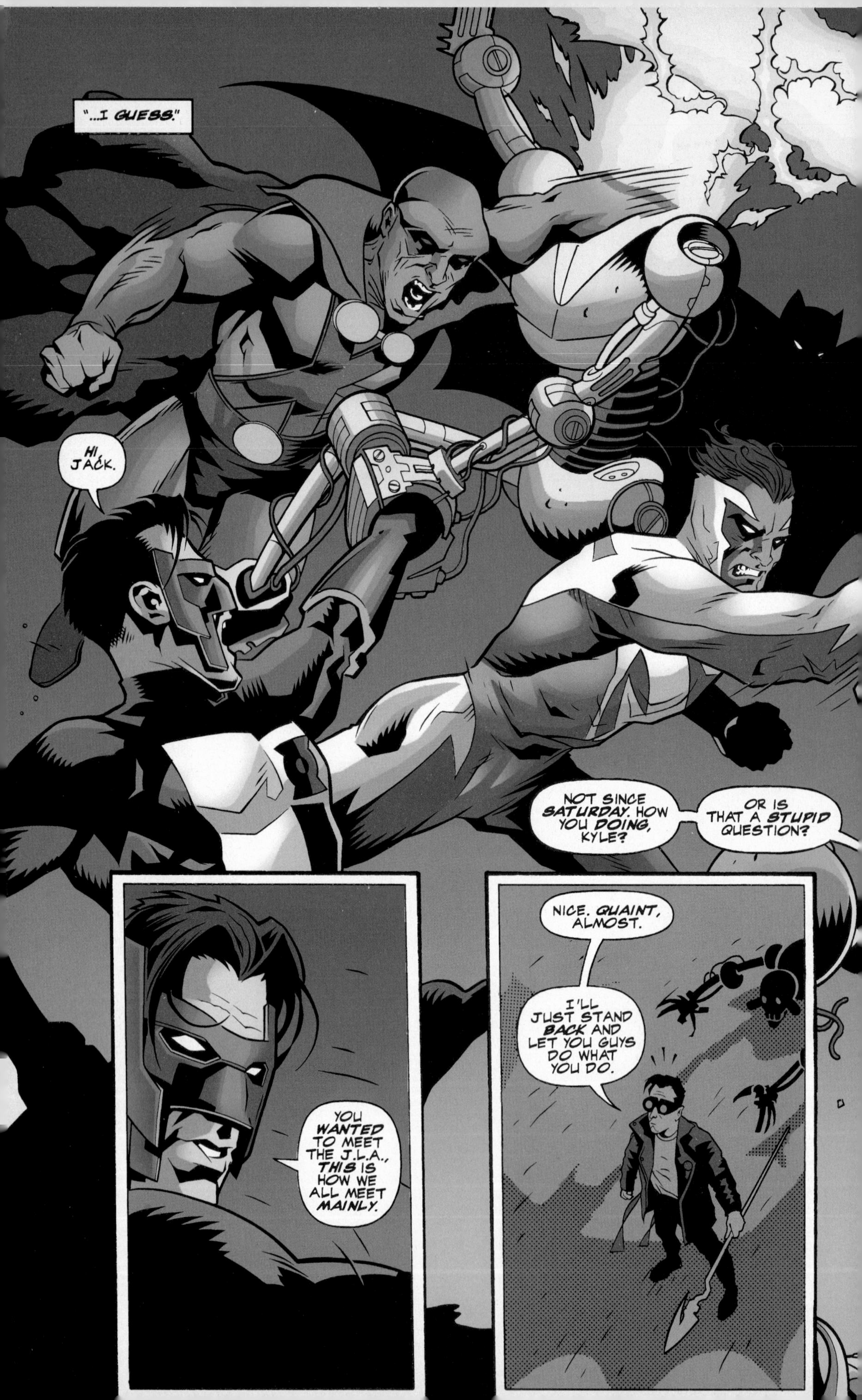
"...I GUESS."
HI JACK.
NOT SINCE SATURDAY. HOW YOU DOING, KYLE?
OR IS THAT A STUPID QUESTION?
YOU WANTED TO MEET THE J.L.A., THIS IS HOW WE ALL MEET MAINLY.
NICE. QUAINT, ALMOST.
I'LL JUST STAND BACK AND LET YOU GUYS DO WHAT YOU DO.

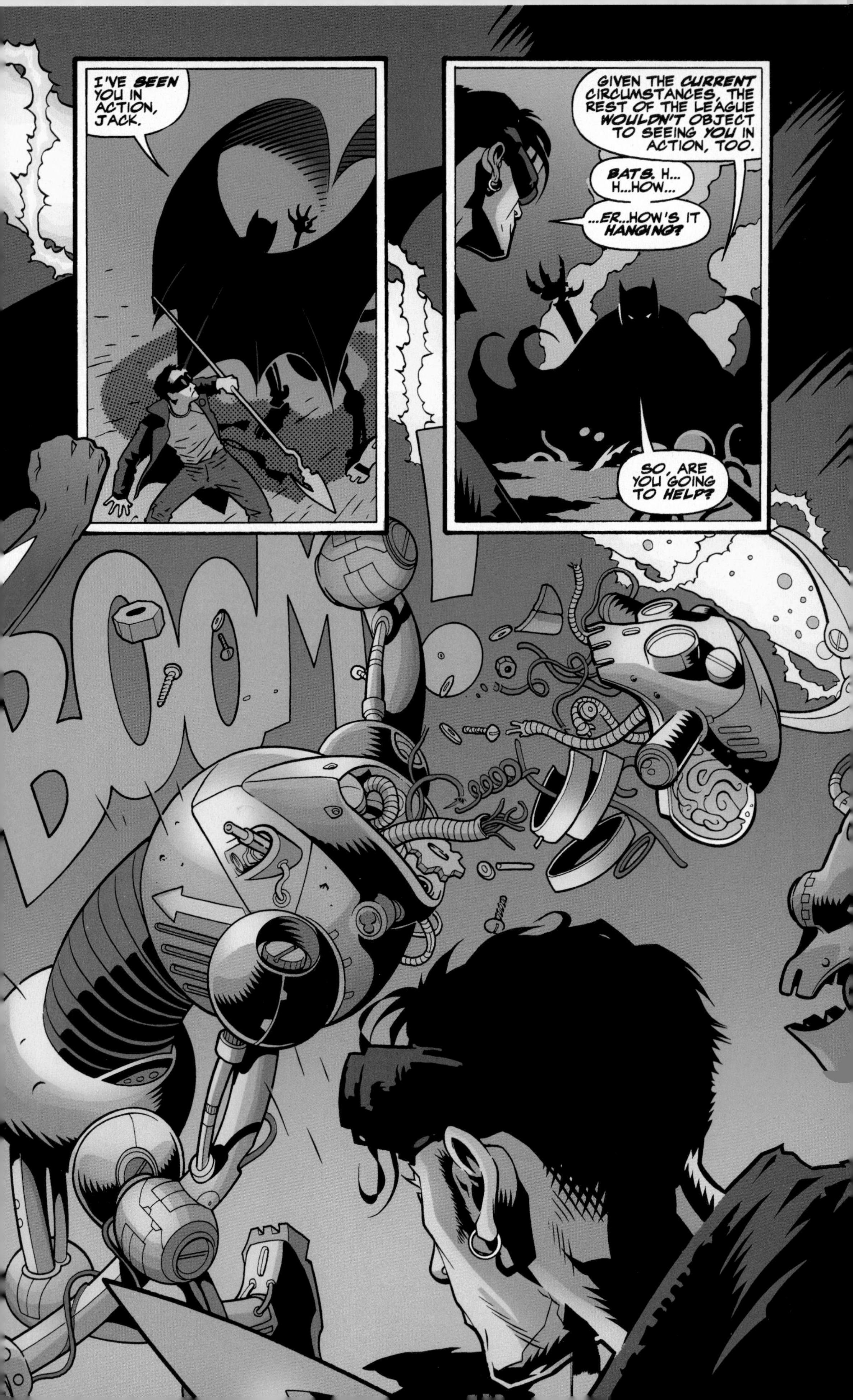
I'VE SEEN YOU IN ACTION, JACK.
GIVEN THE CURRENT CIRCUMSTANCES, THE REST OF THE LEAGUE WOULDN'T OBJECT TO SEEING YOU IN ACTION, TOO.
BATS. H... H...HOW...
...ER...HOW'S IT HANGING?
SO, ARE YOU GOING TO HELP?
BOOM!

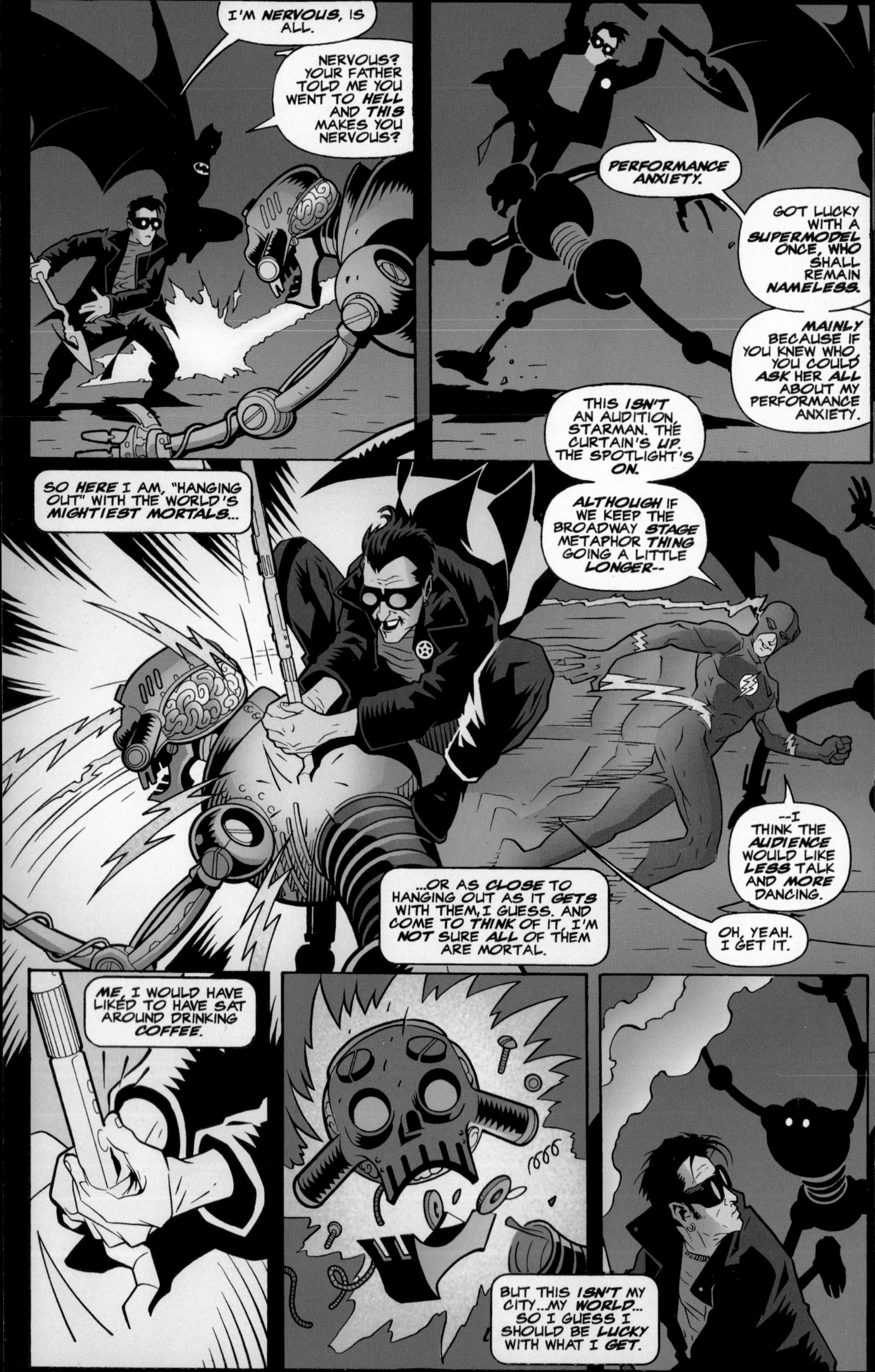

I'M NERVOUS, IS ALL.
NERVOUS? YOUR FATHER TOLD ME YOU WENT TO HELL AND THIS MAKES YOU NERVOUS?
PERFORMANCE ANXIETY.
GOT LUCKY WITH A SUPERMODEL ONCE, WHO SHALL REMAIN NAMELESS.
MAINLY BECAUSE IF YOU KNEW WHO, YOU COULD ASK HER ALL ABOUT MY PERFORMANCE ANXIETY.
THIS ISN'T AN AUDITION, STARMAN. THE CURTAIN'S UP. THE SPOTLIGHT'S ON.
SO HERE I AM, "HANGING OUT" WITH THE WORLD'S MIGHTIEST MORTALS...
ALTHOUGH IF WE KEEP THE BROADWAY STAGE METAPHOR THING GOING A LITTLE LONGER--
--I THINK THE AUDIENCE WOULD LIKE LESS TALK AND MORE DANCING.
...OR AS CLOSE TO HANGING OUT AS IT GETS WITH THEM, I GUESS. AND COME TO THINK OF IT, I'M NOT SURE ALL OF THEM ARE MORTAL.
OH, YEAH. I GET IT.
ME, I WOULD HAVE LIKED TO HAVE SAT AROUND DRINKING COFFEE.
BUT THIS ISN'T MY CITY...MY WORLD... SO I GUESS I SHOULD BE LUCKY WITH WHAT I GET.

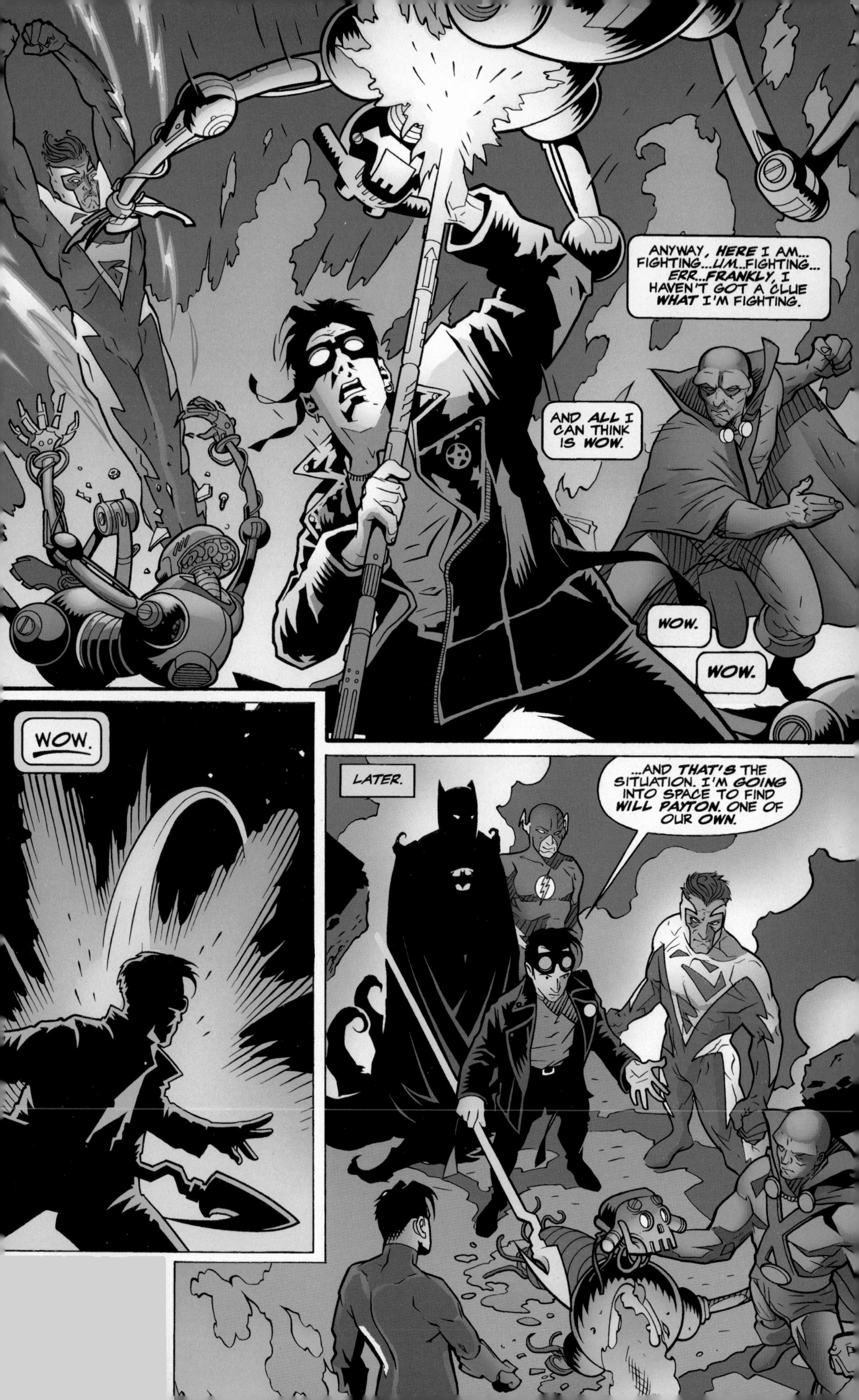
ANYWAY, HERE I AM... FIGHTING...UM...FIGHTING... ERR...FRANKLY, I HAVEN'T GOT A CLUE WHAT I'M FIGHTING.
AND ALL I CAN THINK IS WOW.
WOW.
WOW.
WOW.
LATER.
...AND THAT'S THE SITUATION. I'M GOING INTO SPACE TO FIND WILL PAYTON. ONE OF OUR OWN.

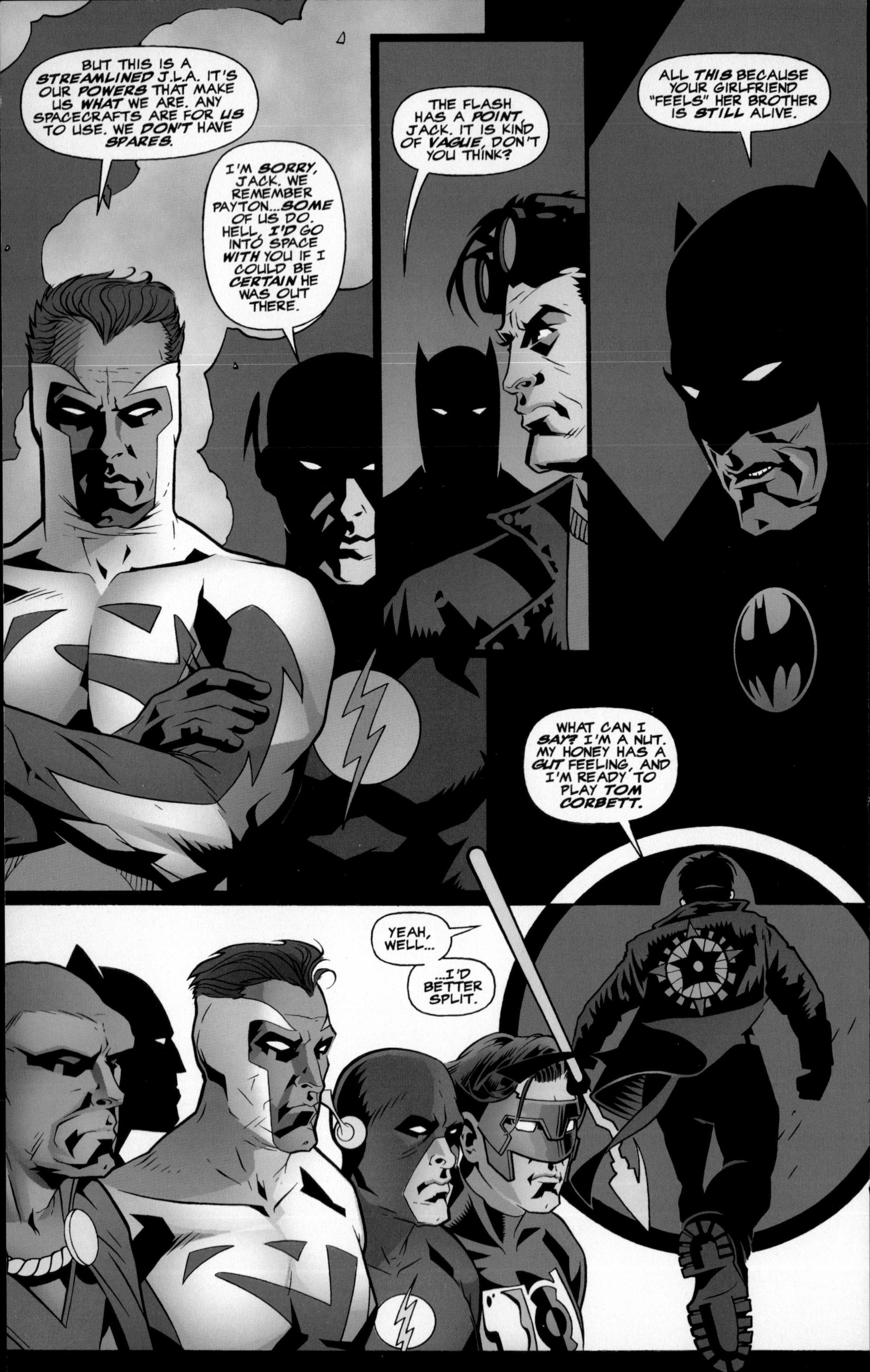
BUT THIS IS A STREAMLINED J.L.A. IT'S OUR POWERS THAT MAKE US WHAT WE ARE. ANY SPACECRAFTS ARE FOR US TO USE. WE DON'T HAVE SPARES.
I'M SORRY, JACK. WE REMEMBER PAYTON...SOME OF US DO. HELL, I'D GO INTO SPACE WITH YOU IF I COULD BE CERTAIN HE WAS OUT THERE.
THE FLASH HAS A POINT, JACK. IT IS KIND OF VAGUE, DON'T YOU THINK?
ALL THIS BECAUSE YOUR GIRLFRIEND "FEELS" HER BROTHER IS STILL ALIVE.
WHAT CAN I SAY? I'M A NUT. MY HONEY HAS A GUT FEELING, AND I'M READY TO PLAY TOM CORBETT.
YEAH, WELL...
...I'D BETTER SPLIT.

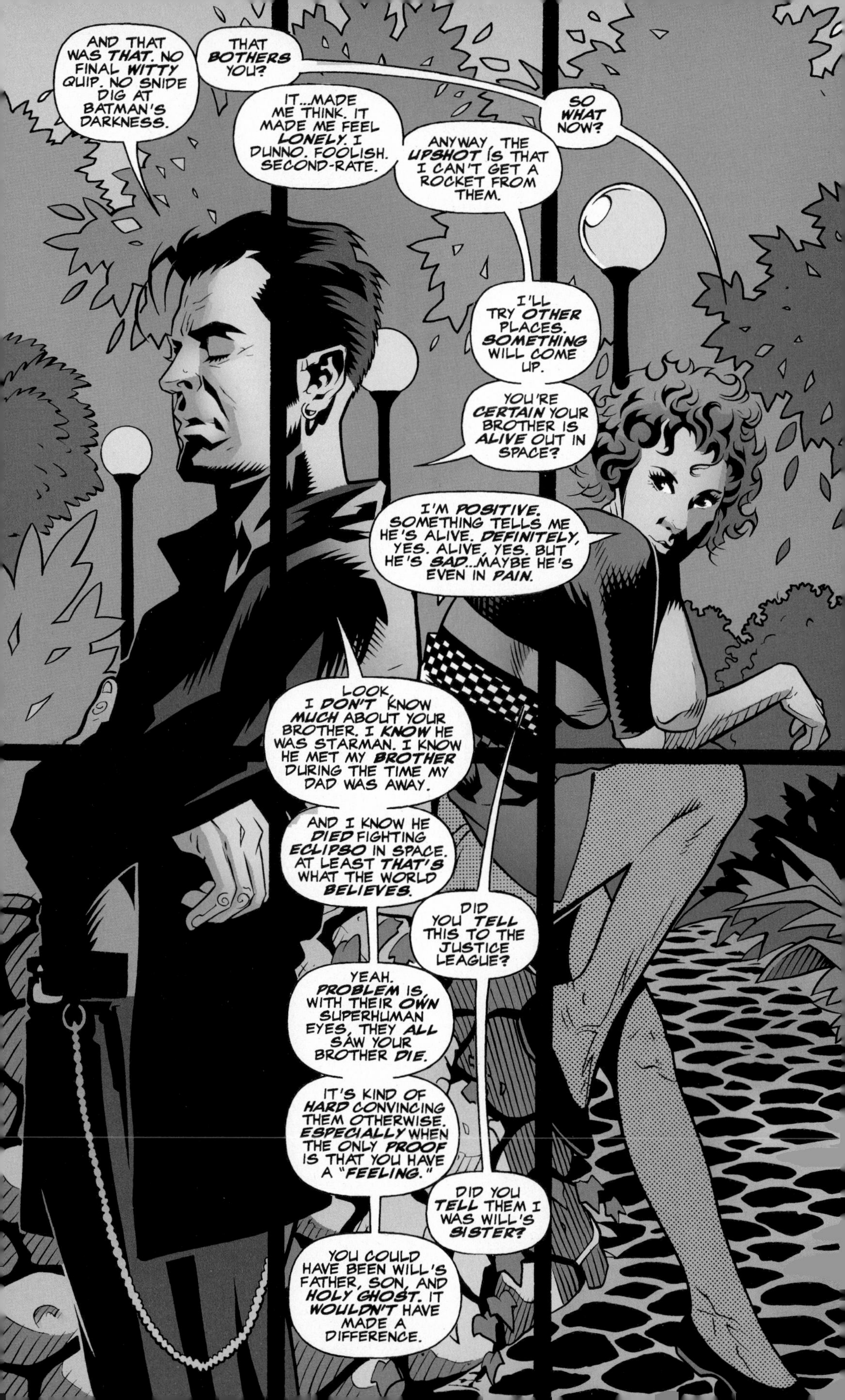

AND THAT WAS THAT. NO FINAL WITTY QUIP. NO SNIDE DIG AT BATMAN'S DARKNESS.
THAT BOTHERS YOU?
IT...MADE ME THINK. IT MADE ME FEEL LONELY. I DUNNO. FOOLISH. SECOND-RATE.
SO WHAT NOW?
ANYWAY, THE UPSHOT IS THAT I CAN'T GET A ROCKET FROM THEM.
I'LL TRY OTHER PLACES. SOMETHING WILL COME UP.
YOU'RE CERTAIN YOUR BROTHER IS ALIVE OUT IN SPACE?
I'M POSITIVE. SOMETHING TELLS ME HE'S ALIVE. DEFINITELY, YES. ALIVE, YES. BUT HE'S SAD...MAYBE HE'S EVEN IN PAIN.
LOOK, I DON'T KNOW MUCH ABOUT YOUR BROTHER. I KNOW HE WAS STARMAN. I KNOW HE MET MY BROTHER DURING THE TIME MY DAD WAS AWAY.
AND I KNOW HE DIED FIGHTING ECLIPSO IN SPACE. AT LEAST THAT'S WHAT THE WORLD BELIEVES.
DID YOU TELL THIS TO THE JUSTICE LEAGUE?
YEAH. PROBLEM IS, WITH THEIR OWN SUPERHUMAN EYES, THEY ALL SAW YOUR BROTHER DIE.
IT'S KIND OF HARD CONVINCING THEM OTHERWISE. ESPECIALLY WHEN THE ONLY PROOF IS THAT YOU HAVE A "FEELING."
DID YOU TELL THEM I WAS WILL'S SISTER?
YOU COULD HAVE BEEN WILL'S FATHER, SON, AND HOLY GHOST. IT WOULDN'T HAVE MADE A DIFFERENCE.

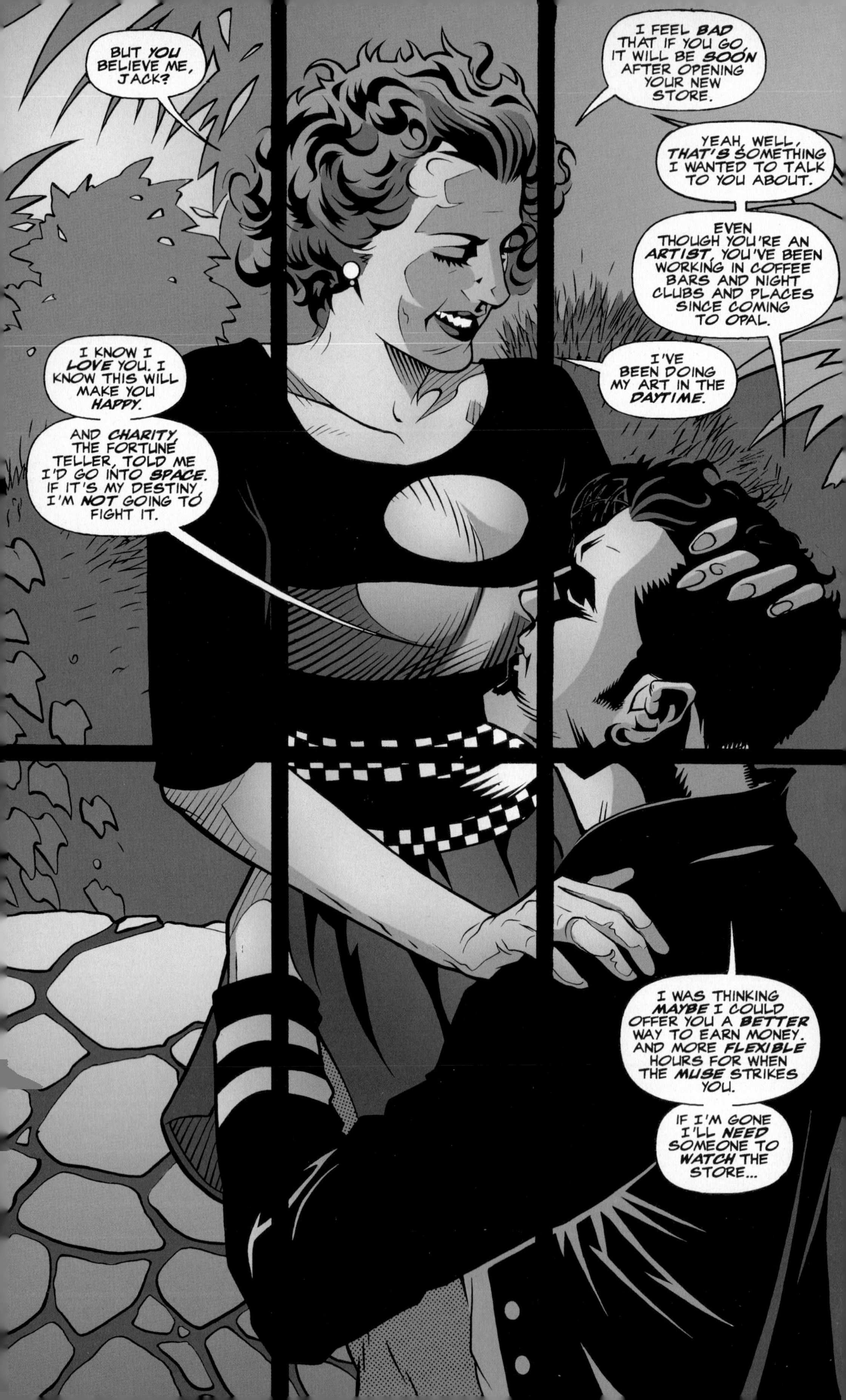

BUT YOU BELIEVE ME, JACK?
I FEEL BAD THAT IF YOU GO, IT WILL BE SOON AFTER OPENING YOUR NEW STORE.
YEAH, WELL, THAT'S SOMETHING I WANTED TO TALK TO YOU ABOUT.
EVEN THOUGH YOU'RE AN ARTIST, YOU'VE BEEN WORKING IN COFFEE BARS AND NIGHT CLUBS AND PLACES SINCE COMING TO OPAL.
I KNOW I LOVE YOU. I KNOW THIS WILL MAKE YOU HAPPY.
AND CHARITY, THE FORTUNE TELLER, TOLD ME I'D GO INTO SPACE. IF IT'S MY DESTINY, I'M NOT GOING TO FIGHT IT.
I'VE BEEN DOING MY ART IN THE DAYTIME.
I WAS THINKING MAYBE I COULD OFFER YOU A BETTER WAY TO EARN MONEY. AND MORE FLEXIBLE HOURS FOR WHEN THE MUSE STRIKES YOU.
IF I'M GONE I'LL NEED SOMEONE TO WATCH THE STORE...

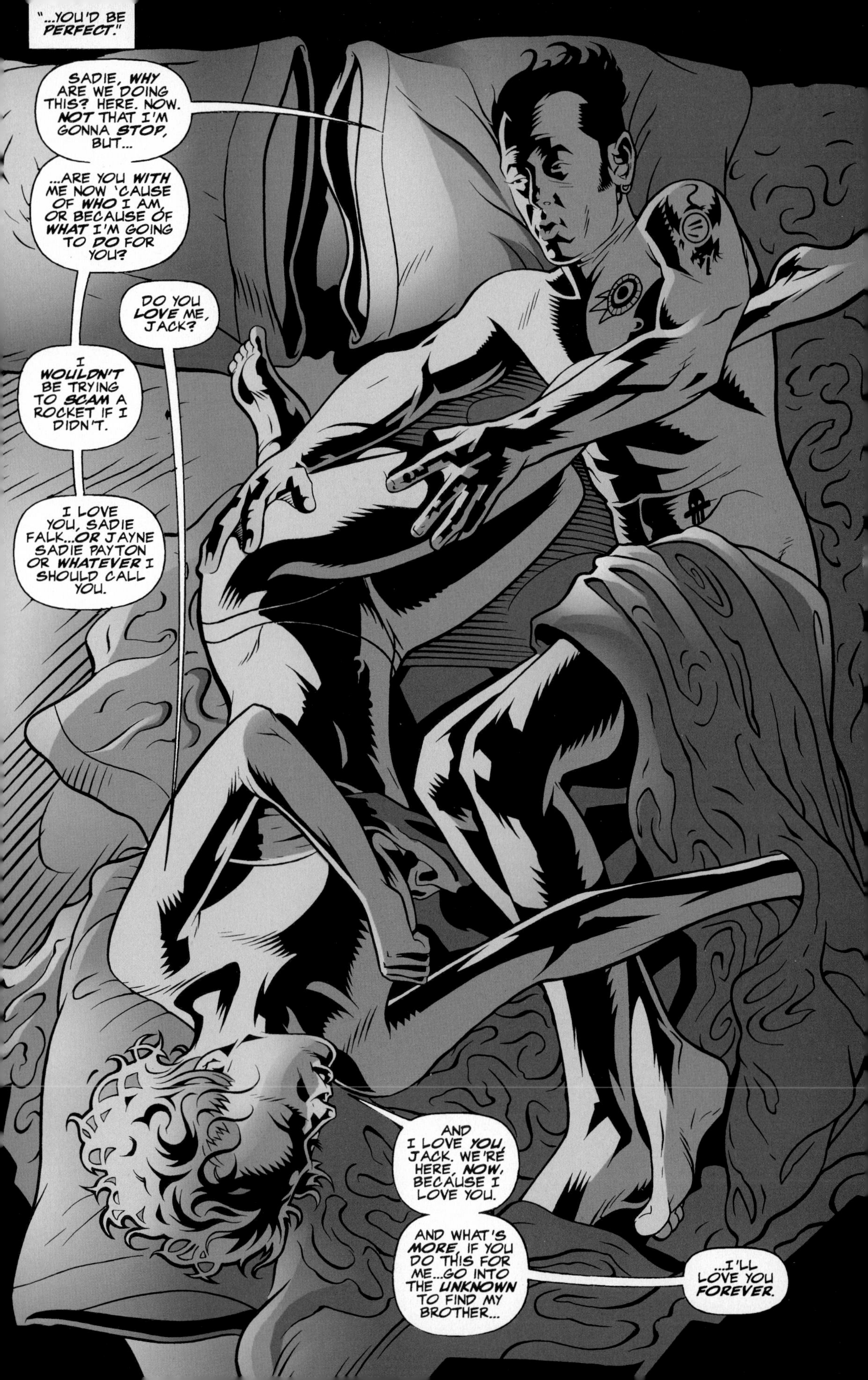

"...YOU'D BE *PERFECT*."
SADIE, *WHY* ARE WE DOING THIS? HERE. NOW. *NOT* THAT I'M GONNA *STOP*, BUT...
...ARE YOU *WITH* ME NOW 'CAUSE OF *WHO* I AM, OR BECAUSE OF *WHAT* I'M GOING TO *DO* FOR YOU?
DO YOU *LOVE* ME, JACK?
I *WOULDN'T* BE TRYING TO *SCAM* A ROCKET IF I DIDN'T.
I LOVE YOU, SADIE FALK...*OR* JAYNE SADIE PAYTON *OR WHATEVER* I SHOULD CALL YOU.
AND I LOVE *YOU*, JACK. WE'RE HERE, *NOW*, BECAUSE I LOVE YOU.
AND WHAT'S *MORE*, IF YOU DO THIS FOR ME...GO INTO THE *UNKNOWN* TO FIND MY BROTHER...
...I'LL LOVE YOU *FOREVER*.

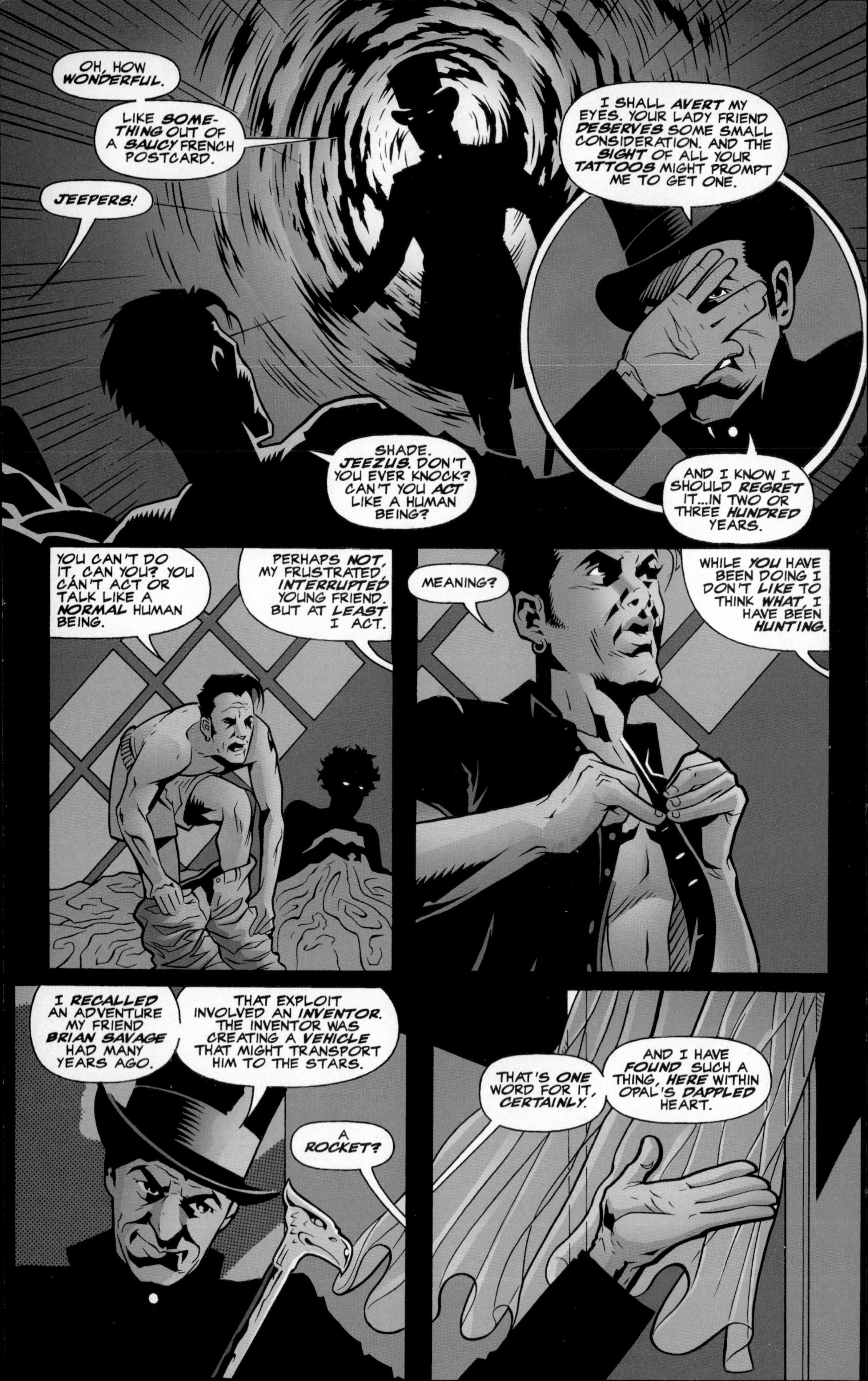
OH, HOW WONDERFUL.
LIKE SOMETHING OUT OF A SAUCY FRENCH POSTCARD.
JEEPERS!
I SHALL AVERT MY EYES. YOUR LADY FRIEND DESERVES SOME SMALL CONSIDERATION. AND THE SIGHT OF ALL YOUR TATTOOS MIGHT PROMPT ME TO GET ONE.
SHADE. JEEZUS. DON'T YOU EVER KNOCK? CAN'T YOU ACT LIKE A HUMAN BEING?
AND I KNOW I SHOULD REGRET IT...IN TWO OR THREE HUNDRED YEARS.
YOU CAN'T DO IT, CAN YOU? YOU CAN'T ACT OR TALK LIKE A NORMAL HUMAN BEING.
PERHAPS NOT, MY FRUSTRATED, INTERRUPTED YOUNG FRIEND. BUT AT LEAST I ACT.
MEANING?
WHILE YOU HAVE BEEN DOING I DON'T LIKE TO THINK WHAT, I HAVE BEEN HUNTING.
I RECALLED AN ADVENTURE MY FRIEND BRIAN SAVAGE HAD MANY YEARS AGO.
THAT EXPLOIT INVOLVED AN INVENTOR. THE INVENTOR WAS CREATING A VEHICLE THAT MIGHT TRANSPORT HIM TO THE STARS.
A ROCKET?
THAT'S ONE WORD FOR IT, CERTAINLY.
AND I HAVE FOUND SUCH A THING, HERE WITHIN OPAL'S DAPPLED HEART.

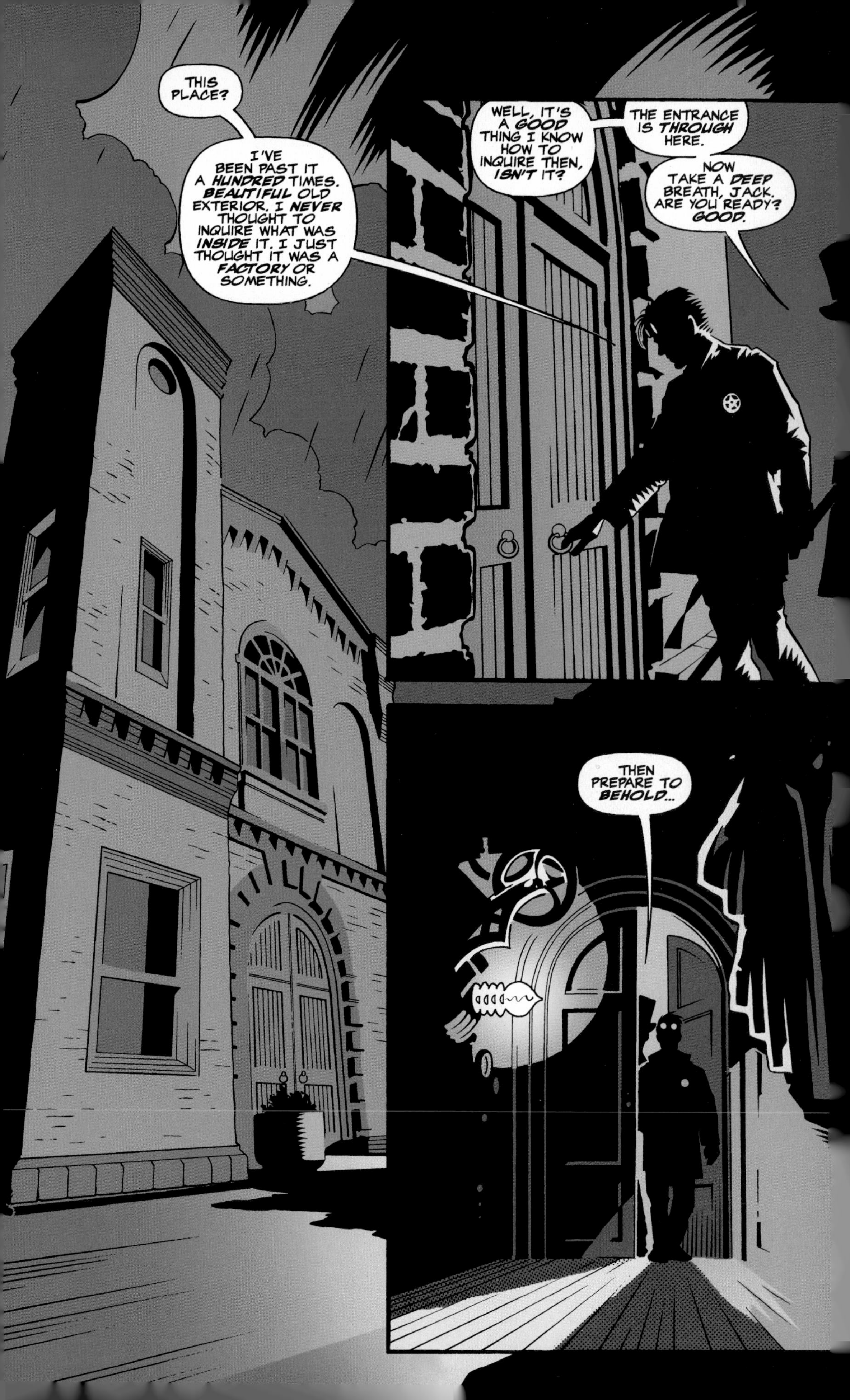
THIS PLACE?
I'VE BEEN PAST IT A HUNDRED TIMES. BEAUTIFUL OLD EXTERIOR. I NEVER THOUGHT TO INQUIRE WHAT WAS INSIDE IT. I JUST THOUGHT IT WAS A FACTORY OR SOMETHING.
WELL, IT'S A GOOD THING I KNOW HOW TO INQUIRE THEN, ISN'T IT?
THE ENTRANCE IS THROUGH HERE.
NOW TAKE A DEEP BREATH, JACK. ARE YOU READY? GOOD.
THEN PREPARE TO BEHOLD...

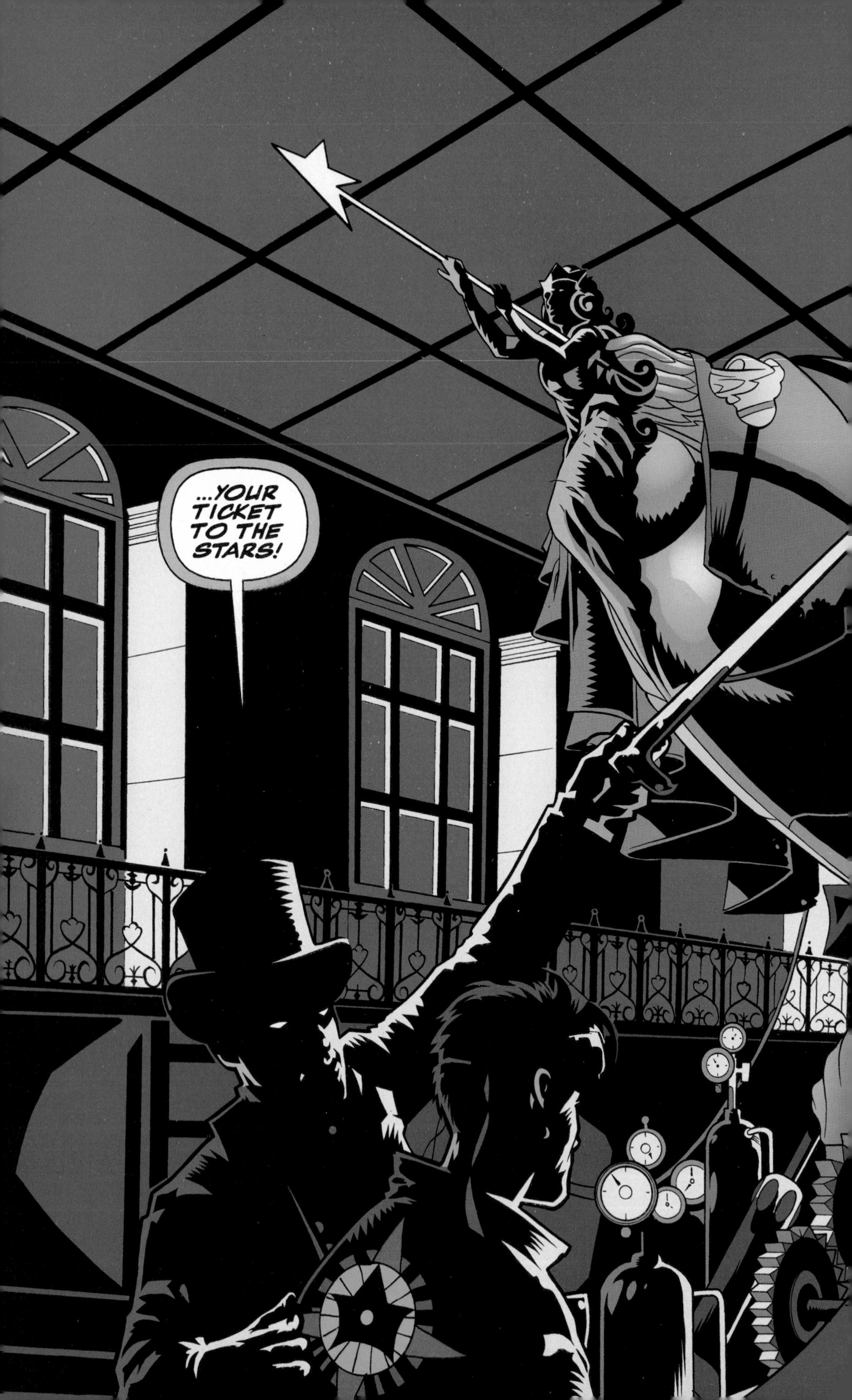
...YOUR TICKET TO THE STARS!

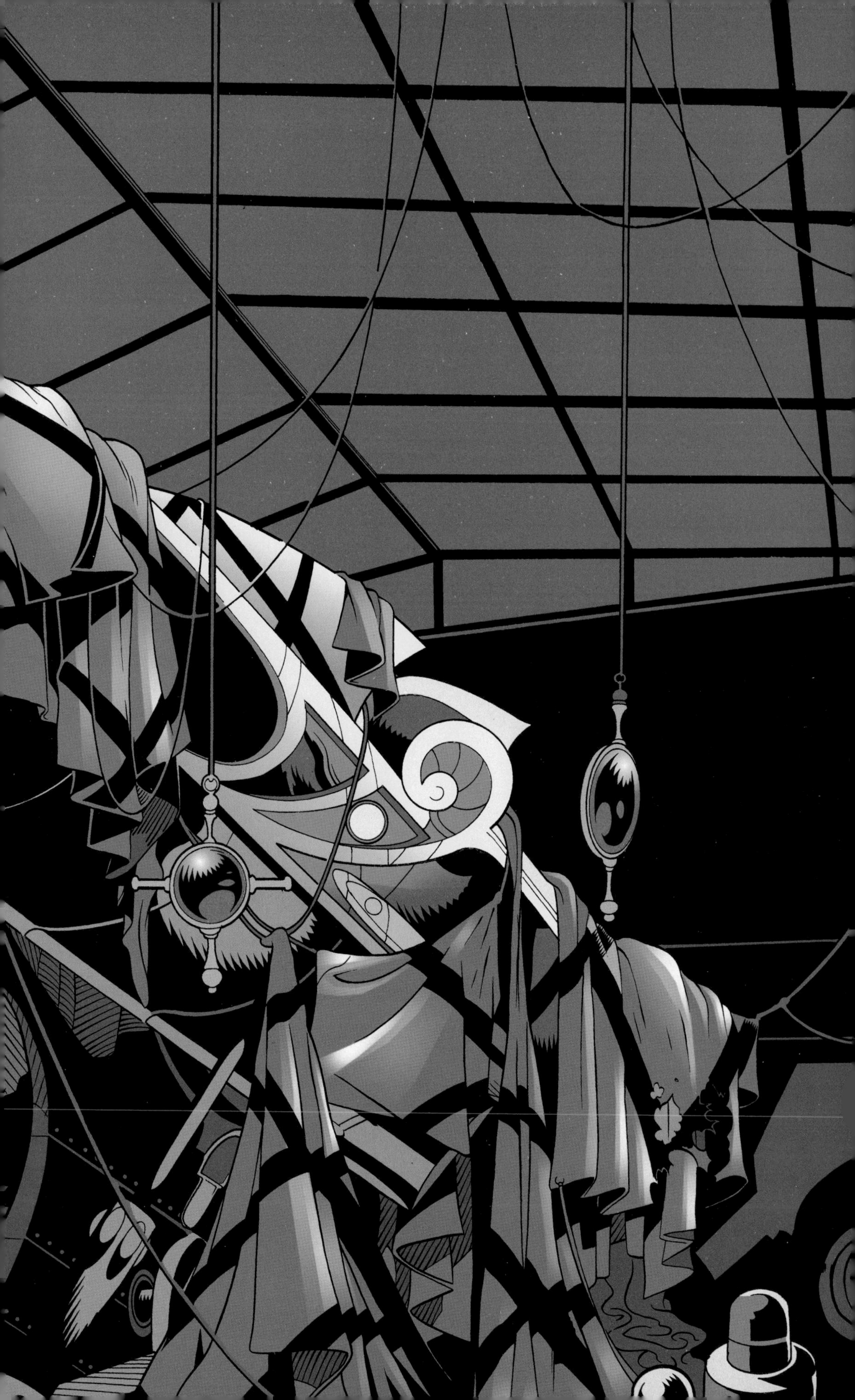

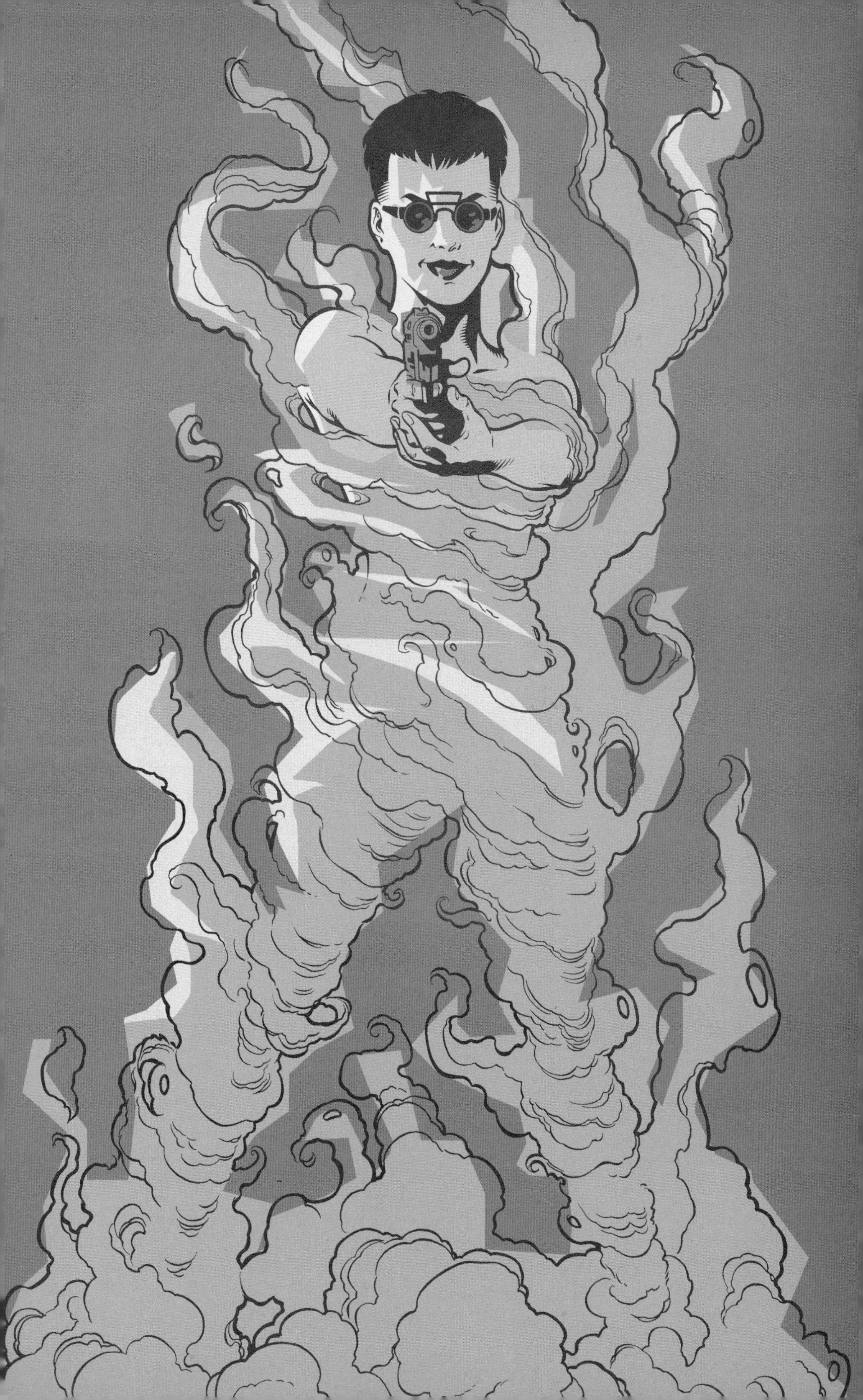

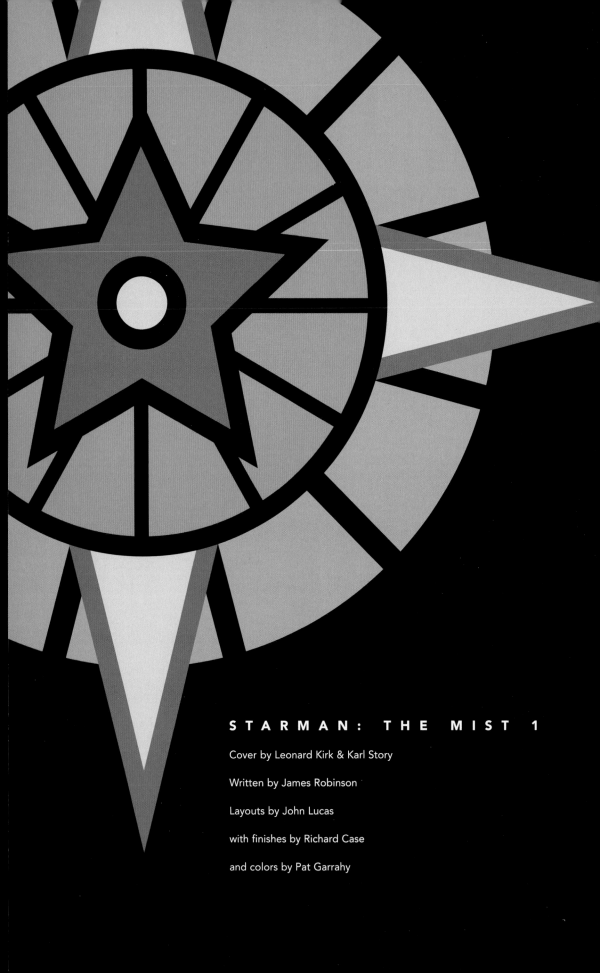

STARMAN: THE MIST 1

Cover by Leonard Kirk & Karl Story

Written by James Robinson

Layouts by John Lucas

with finishes by Richard Case

and colors by Pat Garrahy

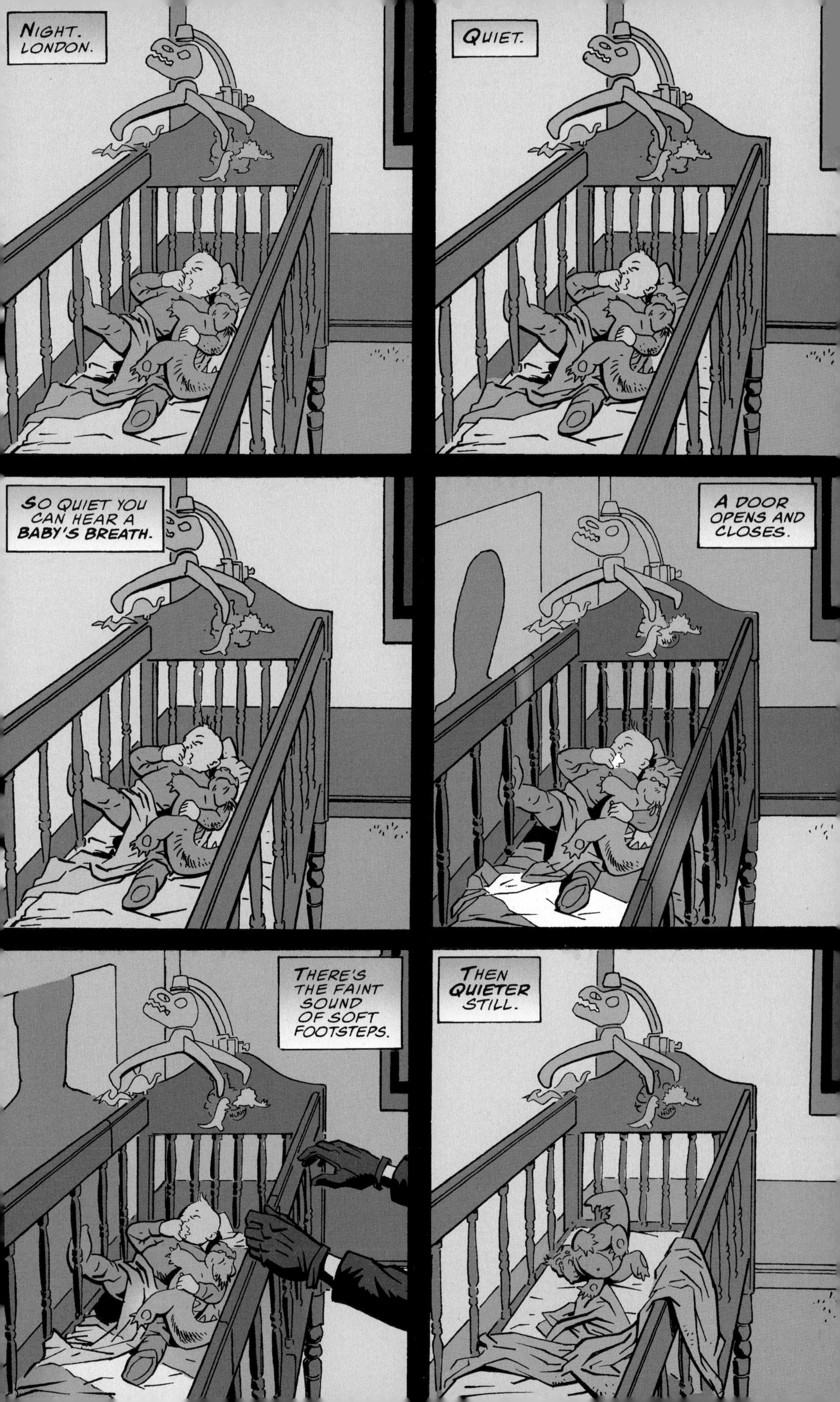
NIGHT. LONDON.
QUIET.
SO QUIET YOU CAN HEAR A BABY'S BREATH.
A DOOR OPENS AND CLOSES.
HUM
THERE'S THE FAINT SOUND OF SOFT FOOTSTEPS.
HUM
THEN QUIETER STILL.
HUM

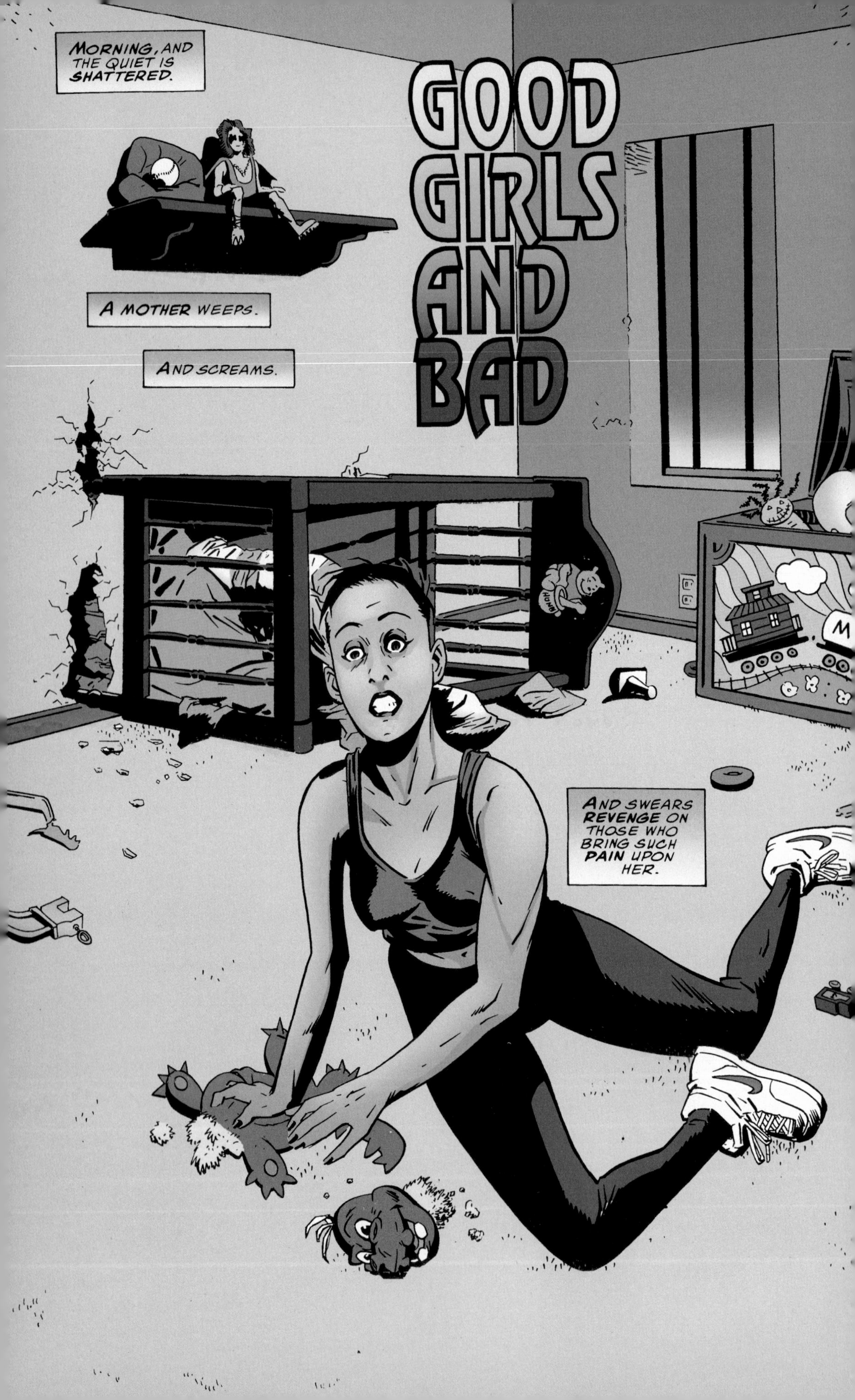
MORNING, AND THE QUIET IS SHATTERED.
GOOD GIRLS AND BAD
A MOTHER WEEPS.
AND SCREAMS.
AND SWEARS REVENGE ON THOSE WHO BRING SUCH PAIN UPON HER.

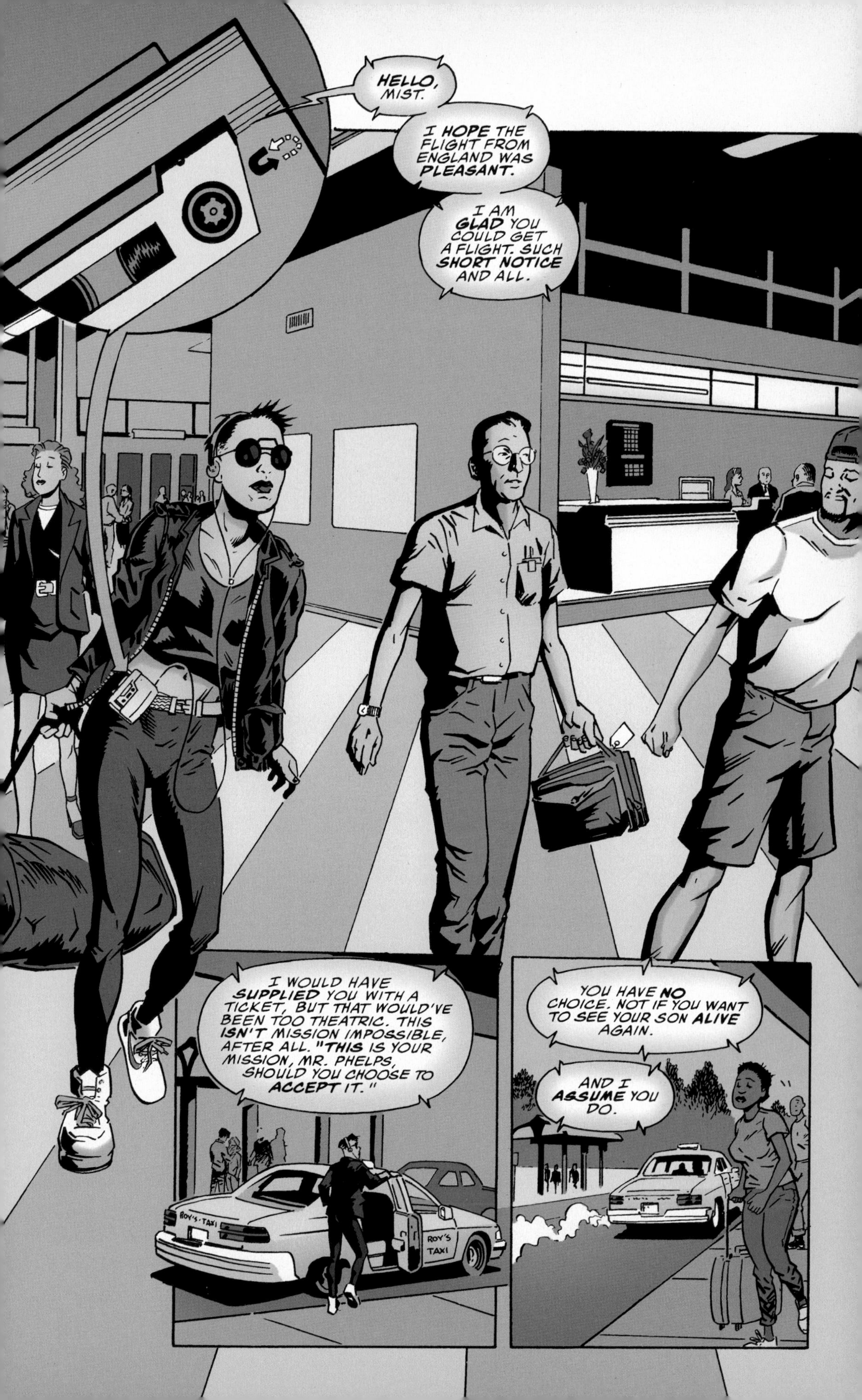
HELLO, MIST.
I HOPE THE FLIGHT FROM ENGLAND WAS PLEASANT.
I AM GLAD YOU COULD GET A FLIGHT. SUCH SHORT NOTICE AND ALL.
I WOULD HAVE SUPPLIED YOU WITH A TICKET, BUT THAT WOULD'VE BEEN TOO THEATRIC. THIS ISN'T MISSION IMPOSSIBLE, AFTER ALL. "THIS IS YOUR MISSION, MR. PHELPS, SHOULD YOU CHOOSE TO ACCEPT IT."
ROY'S TAXI
ROY'S TAXI
YOU HAVE NO CHOICE. NOT IF YOU WANT TO SEE YOUR SON ALIVE AGAIN.
AND I ASSUME YOU DO.

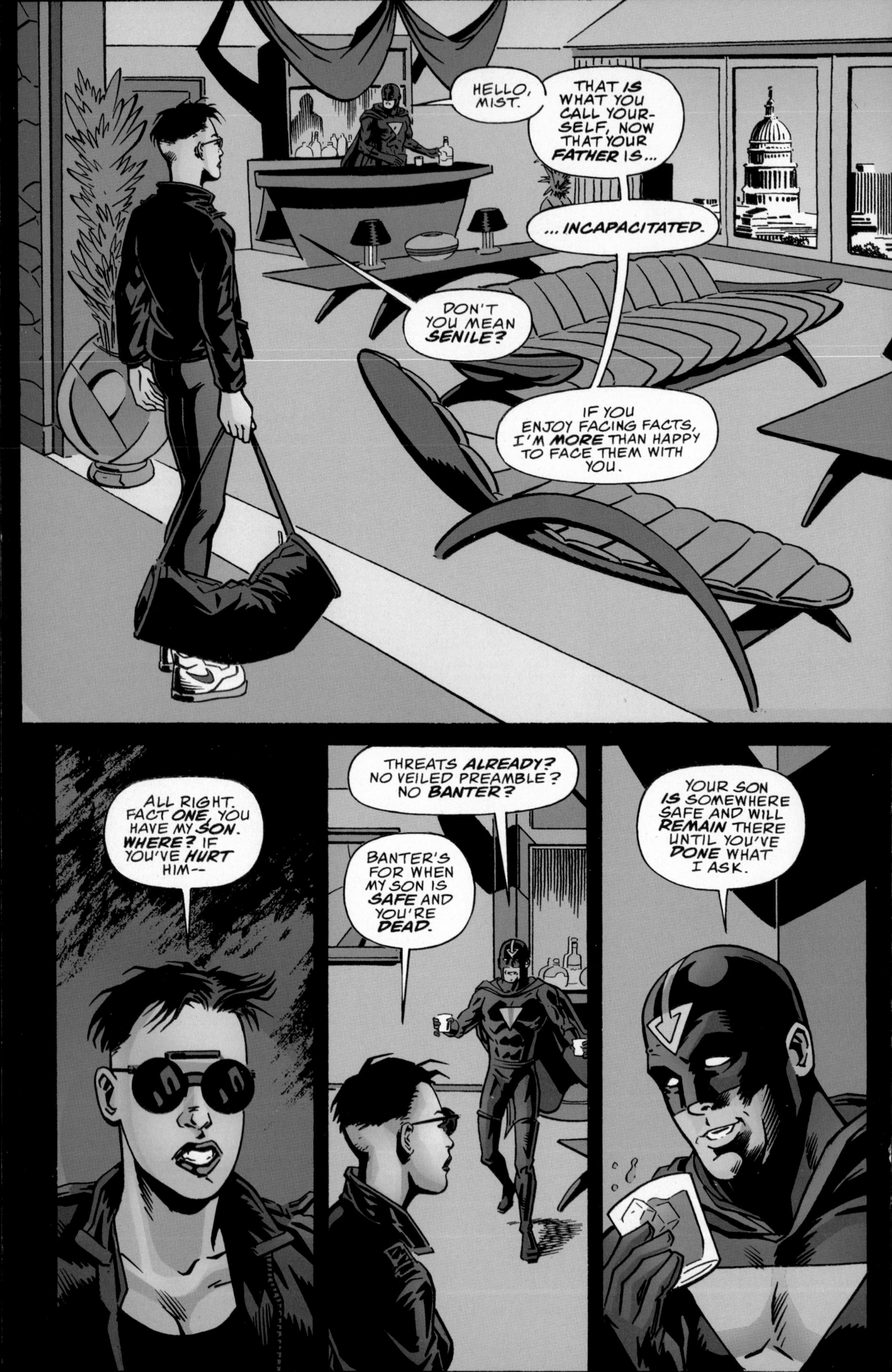
HELLO, MIST.
THAT IS WHAT YOU CALL YOURSELF, NOW THAT YOUR FATHER IS...
...INCAPACITATED.
DON'T YOU MEAN SENILE?
IF YOU ENJOY FACING FACTS, I'M MORE THAN HAPPY TO FACE THEM WITH YOU.
ALL RIGHT. FACT ONE, YOU HAVE MY SON. WHERE? IF YOU'VE HURT HIM--
THREATS ALREADY? NO VEILED PREAMBLE? NO BANTER?
BANTER'S FOR WHEN MY SON IS SAFE AND YOU'RE DEAD.
YOUR SON IS SOMEWHERE SAFE AND WILL REMAIN THERE UNTIL YOU'VE DONE WHAT I ASK.

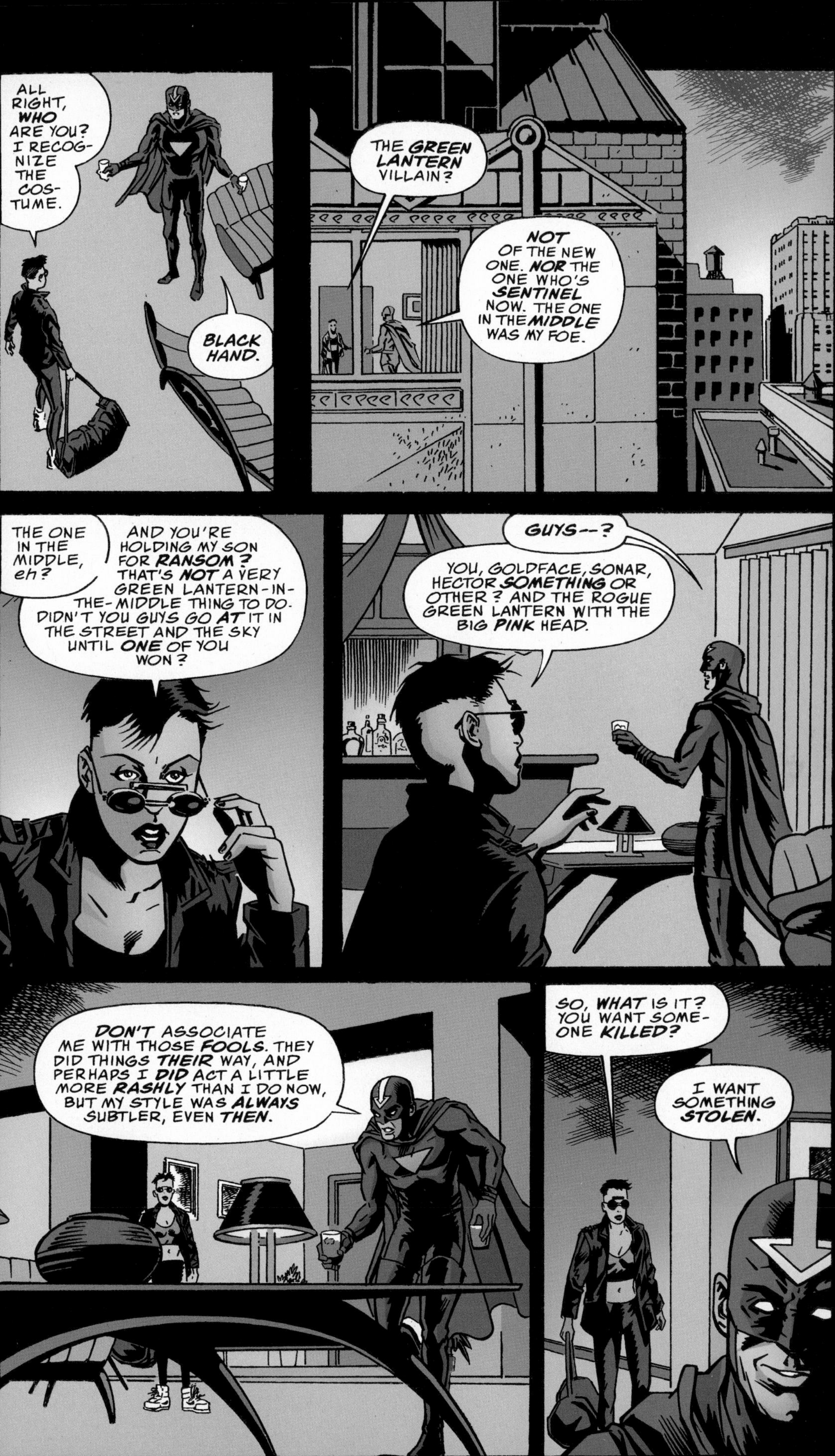
ALL RIGHT, WHO ARE YOU? I RECOGNIZE THE COSTUME.
BLACK HAND.
THE GREEN LANTERN VILLAIN?
NOT OF THE NEW ONE. NOR THE ONE WHO'S SENTINEL NOW. THE ONE IN THE MIDDLE WAS MY FOE.
THE ONE IN THE MIDDLE, eh?
AND YOU'RE HOLDING MY SON FOR RANSOM? THAT'S NOT A VERY GREEN LANTERN-IN-THE-MIDDLE THING TO DO. DIDN'T YOU GUYS GO AT IT IN THE STREET AND THE SKY UNTIL ONE OF YOU WON?
GUYS--?
YOU, GOLDFACE, SONAR, HECTOR SOMETHING OR OTHER? AND THE ROGUE GREEN LANTERN WITH THE BIG PINK HEAD.
DON'T ASSOCIATE ME WITH THOSE FOOLS. THEY DID THINGS THEIR WAY, AND PERHAPS I DID ACT A LITTLE MORE RASHLY THAN I DO NOW, BUT MY STYLE WAS ALWAYS SUBTLER, EVEN THEN.
SO, WHAT IS IT? YOU WANT SOMEONE KILLED?
I WANT SOMETHING STOLEN.

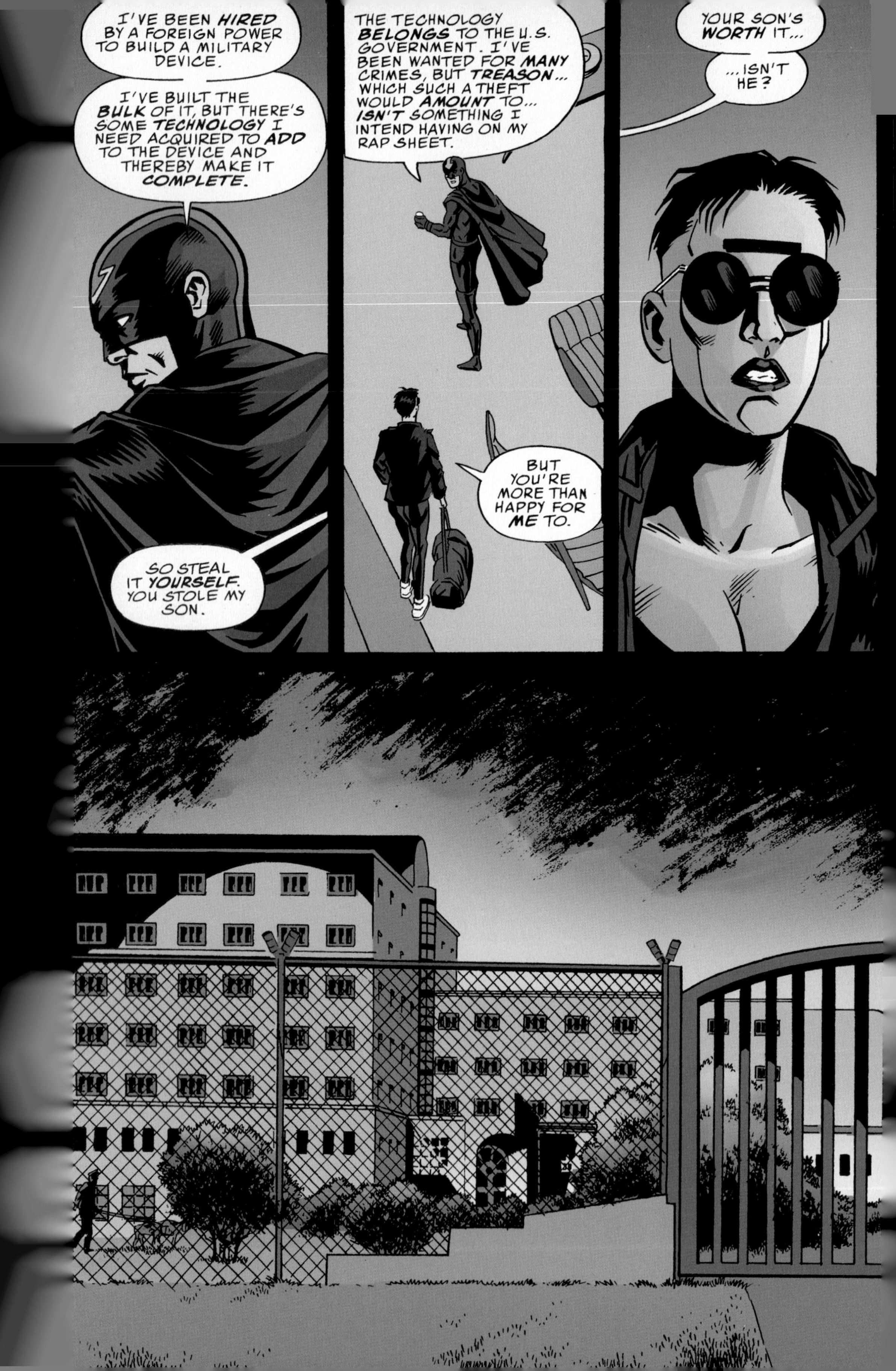
I'VE BEEN HIRED BY A FOREIGN POWER TO BUILD A MILITARY DEVICE.
I'VE BUILT THE BULK OF IT, BUT THERE'S SOME TECHNOLOGY I NEED ACQUIRED TO ADD TO THE DEVICE AND THEREBY MAKE IT COMPLETE.
SO STEAL IT YOURSELF. YOU STOLE MY SON.
THE TECHNOLOGY BELONGS TO THE U.S. GOVERNMENT. I'VE BEEN WANTED FOR MANY CRIMES, BUT TREASON... WHICH SUCH A THEFT WOULD AMOUNT TO... ISN'T SOMETHING I INTEND HAVING ON MY RAP SHEET.
BUT YOU'RE MORE THAN HAPPY FOR ME TO.
YOUR SON'S WORTH IT...
...ISN'T HE?

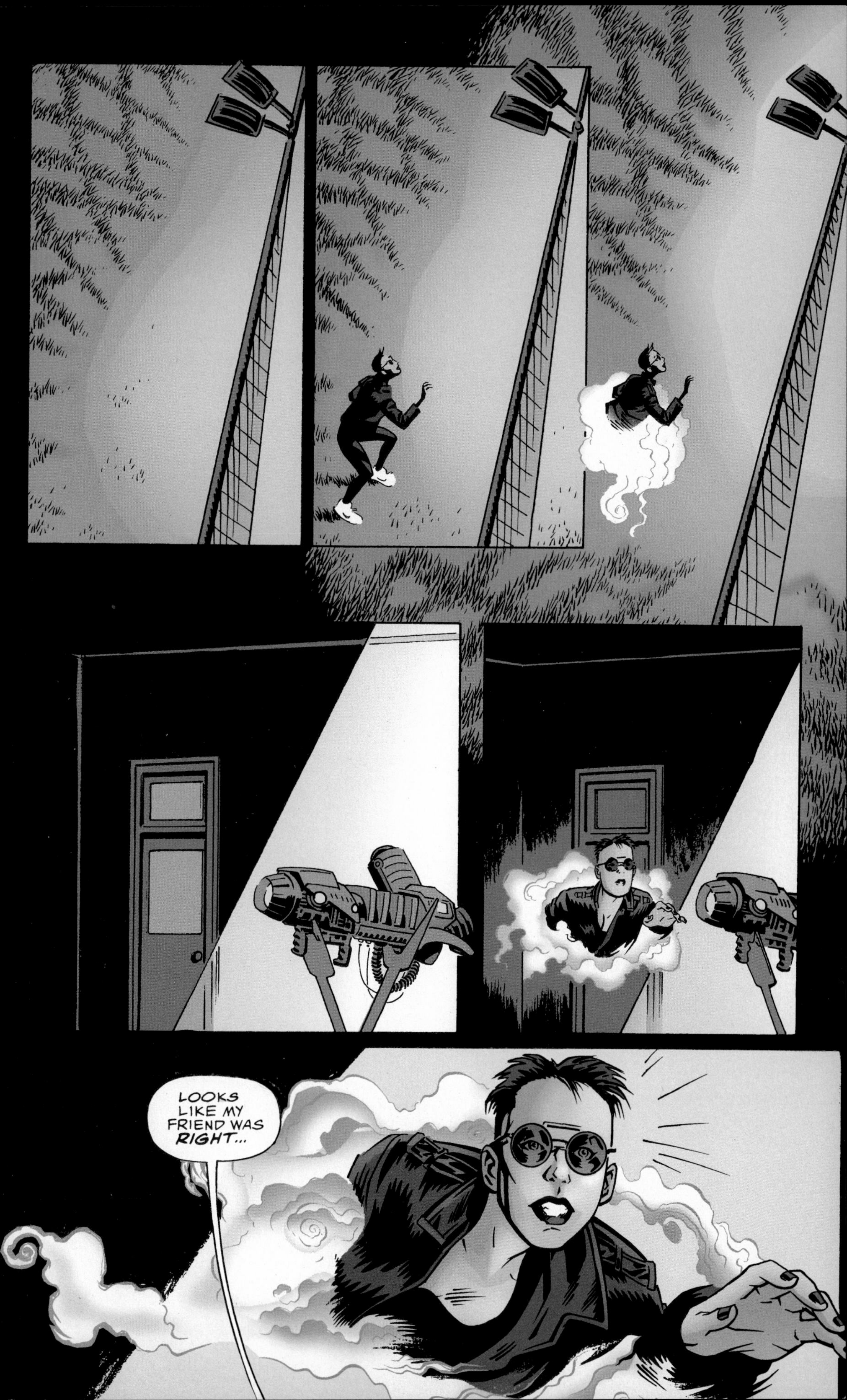
LOOKS LIKE MY FRIEND WAS RIGHT...

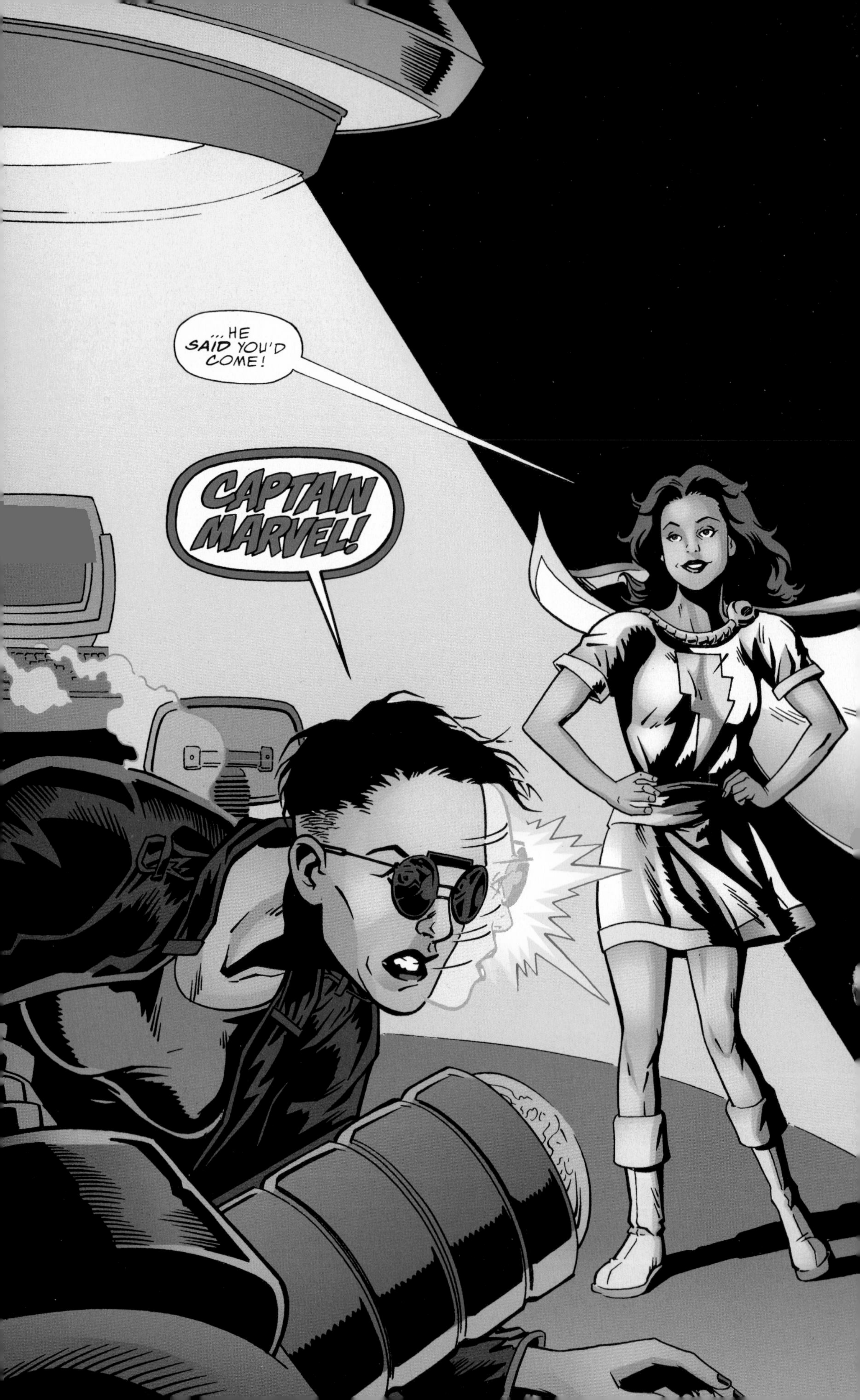

CAPTAIN MARVEL!
...HE SAID YOU'D COME!

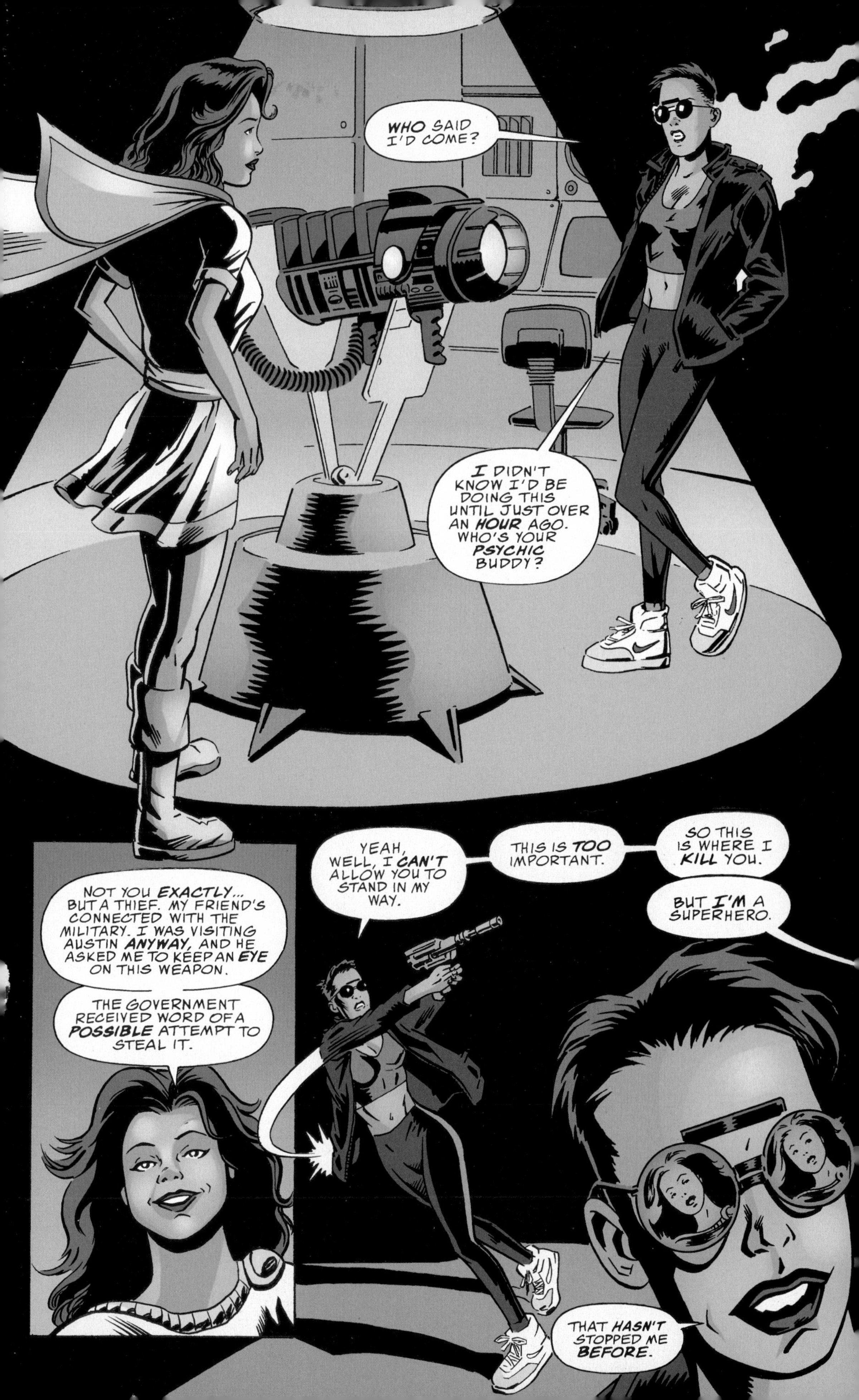

WHO SAID I'D COME?
I DIDN'T KNOW I'D BE DOING THIS UNTIL JUST OVER AN HOUR AGO. WHO'S YOUR PSYCHIC BUDDY?
NOT YOU EXACTLY... BUT A THIEF. MY FRIEND'S CONNECTED WITH THE MILITARY. I WAS VISITING AUSTIN ANYWAY, AND HE ASKED ME TO KEEP AN EYE ON THIS WEAPON.
THE GOVERNMENT RECEIVED WORD OF A POSSIBLE ATTEMPT TO STEAL IT.
YEAH, WELL, I CAN'T ALLOW YOU TO STAND IN MY WAY.
THIS IS TOO IMPORTANT.
SO THIS IS WHERE I KILL YOU.
BUT I'M A SUPERHERO.
THAT HASN'T STOPPED ME BEFORE.

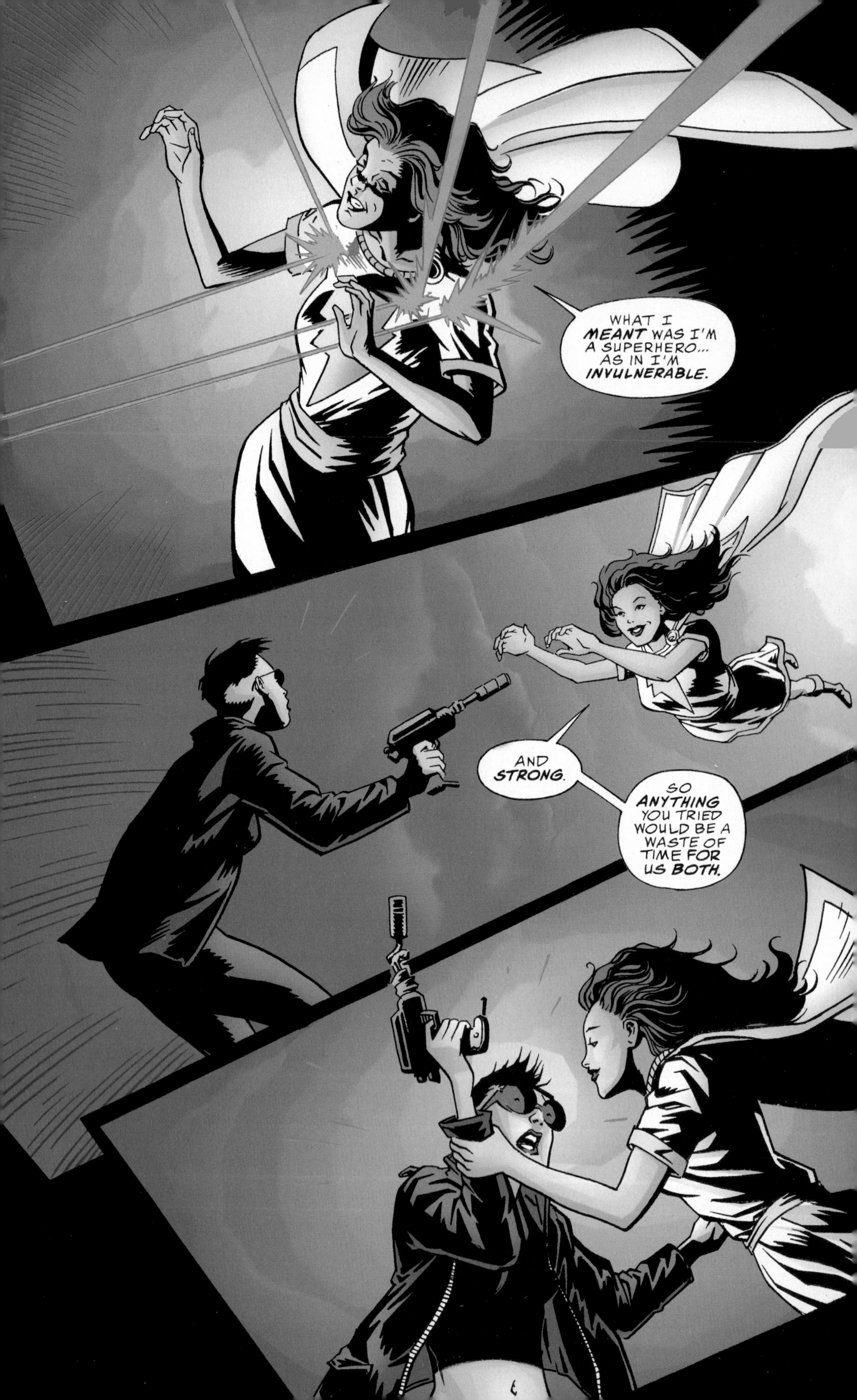
WHAT I MEANT WAS I'M A SUPERHERO... AS IN I'M INVULNERABLE.
AND STRONG.
SO ANYTHING YOU TRIED WOULD BE A WASTE OF TIME FOR US BOTH.

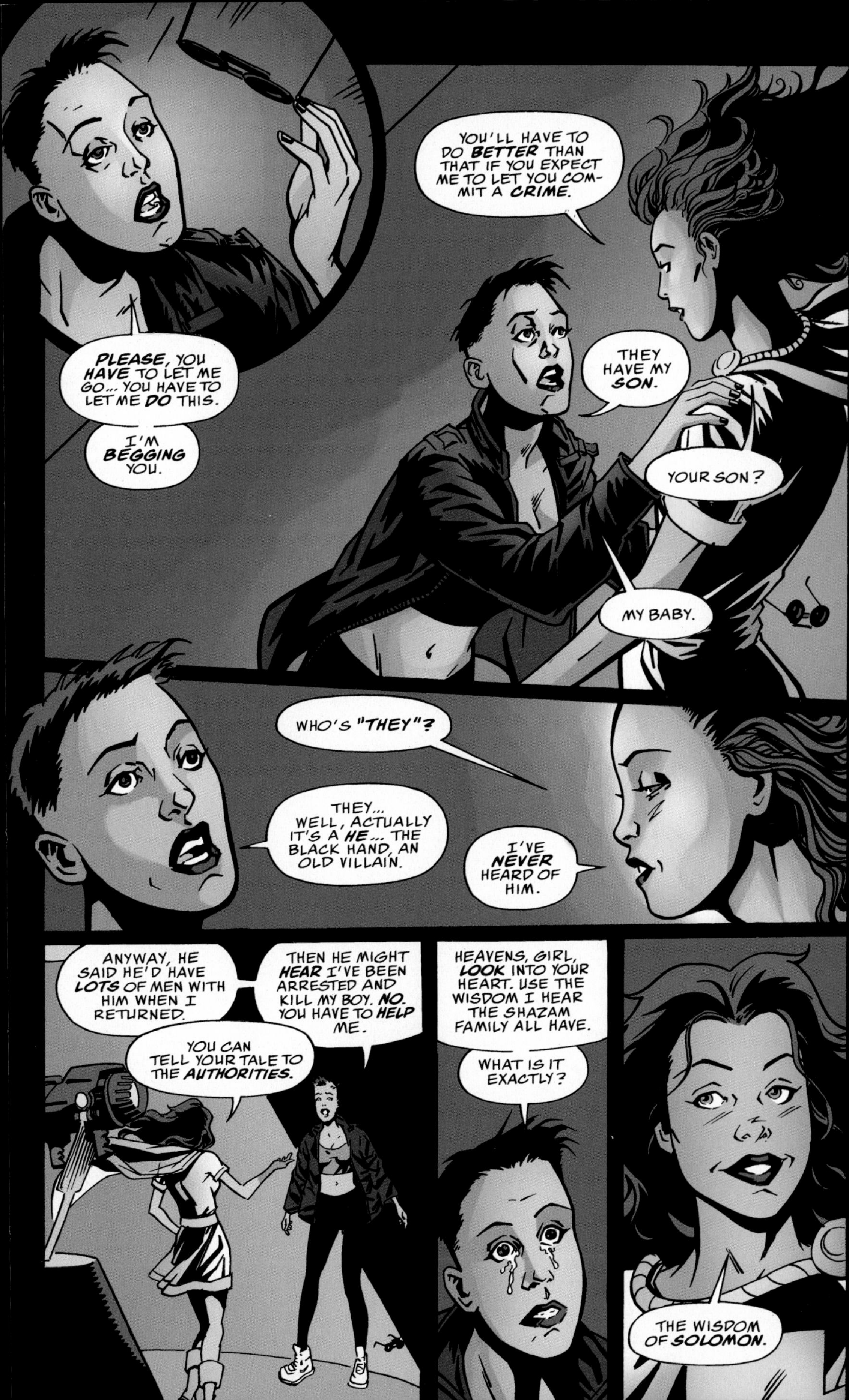

PLEASE, YOU HAVE TO LET ME GO... YOU HAVE TO LET ME DO THIS.
I'M BEGGING YOU.
YOU'LL HAVE TO DO BETTER THAN THAT IF YOU EXPECT ME TO LET YOU COMMIT A CRIME.
THEY HAVE MY SON.
YOUR SON?
MY BABY.
WHO'S "THEY"?
THEY... WELL, ACTUALLY IT'S A HE... THE BLACK HAND, AN OLD VILLAIN.
I'VE NEVER HEARD OF HIM.
ANYWAY, HE SAID HE'D HAVE LOTS OF MEN WITH HIM WHEN I RETURNED.
THEN HE MIGHT HEAR I'VE BEEN ARRESTED AND KILL MY BOY. NO. YOU HAVE TO HELP ME.
YOU CAN TELL YOUR TALE TO THE AUTHORITIES.
HEAVENS, GIRL, LOOK INTO YOUR HEART. USE THE WISDOM I HEAR THE SHAZAM FAMILY ALL HAVE.
WHAT IS IT EXACTLY?
THE WISDOM OF SOLOMON.

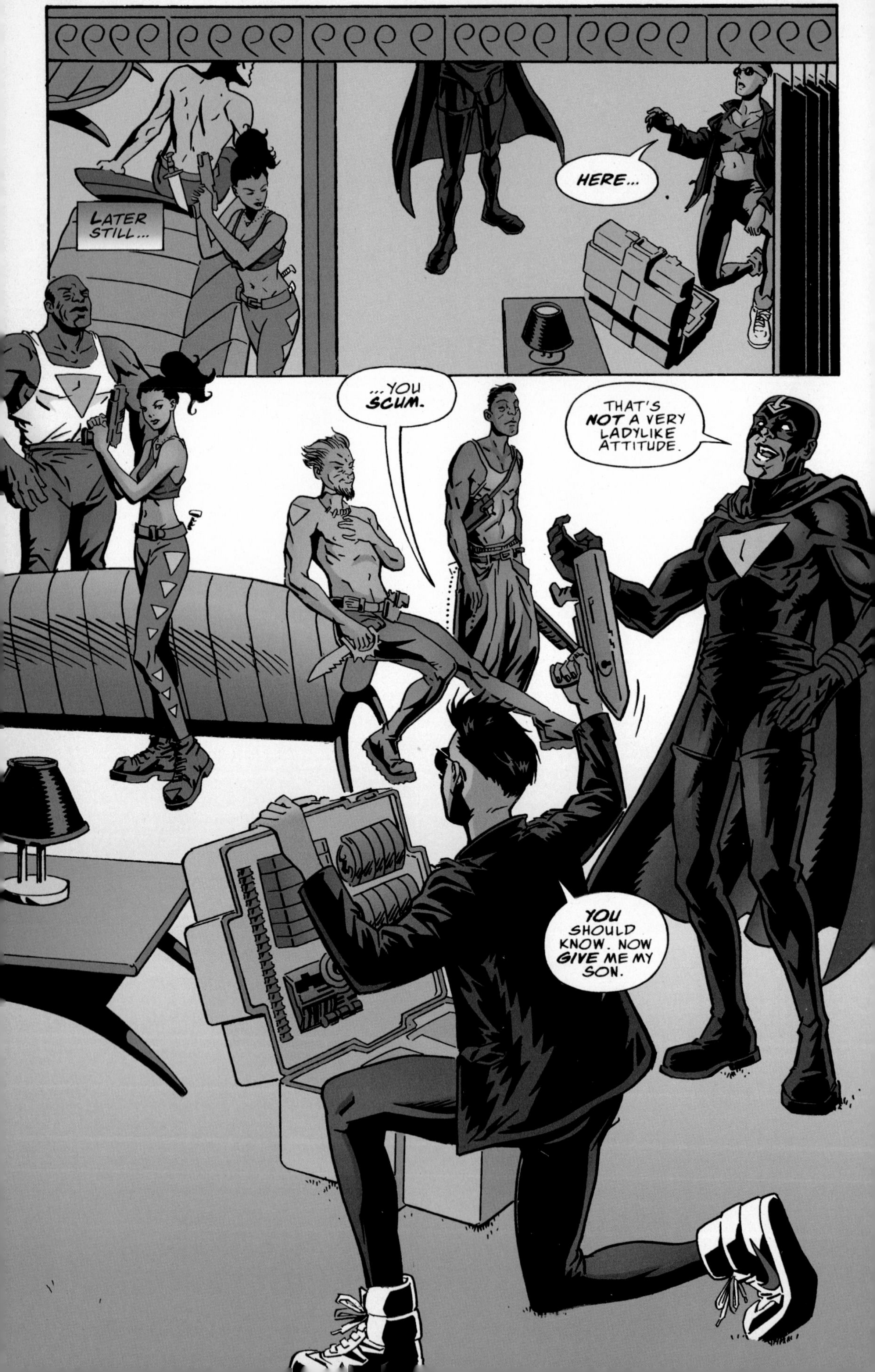
LATER STILL...
HERE...
...YOU SCUM.
THAT'S NOT A VERY LADYLIKE ATTITUDE.
YOU SHOULD KNOW. NOW GIVE ME MY SON.

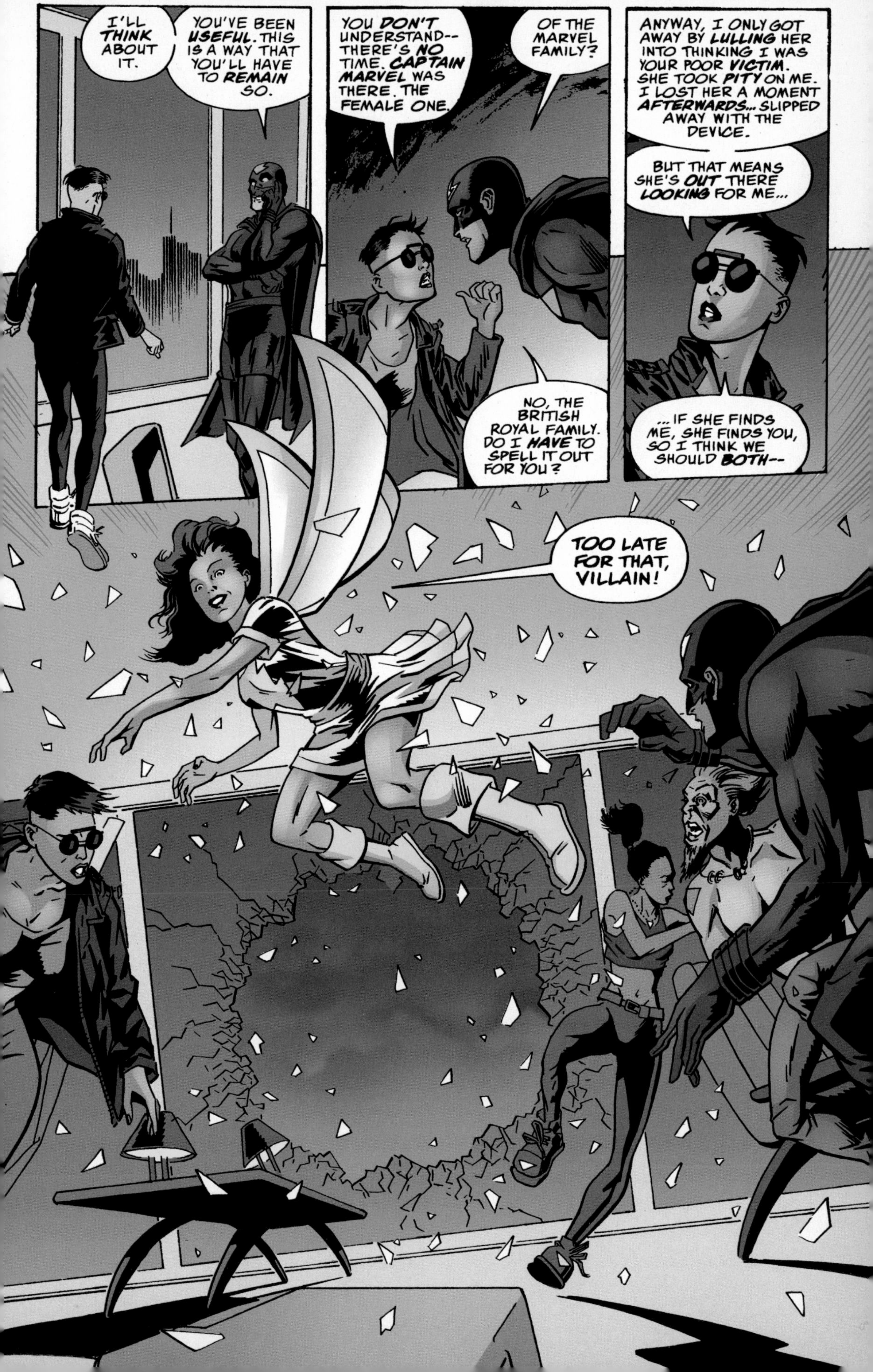
I'LL THINK ABOUT IT.
YOU'VE BEEN USEFUL. THIS IS A WAY THAT YOU'LL HAVE TO REMAIN SO.
YOU DON'T UNDERSTAND-- THERE'S NO TIME. CAPTAIN MARVEL WAS THERE. THE FEMALE ONE.
OF THE MARVEL FAMILY?
NO, THE BRITISH ROYAL FAMILY. DO I HAVE TO SPELL IT OUT FOR YOU?
ANYWAY, I ONLY GOT AWAY BY LULLING HER INTO THINKING I WAS YOUR POOR VICTIM. SHE TOOK PITY ON ME. I LOST HER A MOMENT AFTERWARDS... SLIPPED AWAY WITH THE DEVICE.
BUT THAT MEANS SHE'S OUT THERE LOOKING FOR ME...
...IF SHE FINDS ME, SHE FINDS YOU, SO I THINK WE SHOULD BOTH--
TOO LATE FOR THAT, VILLAIN!

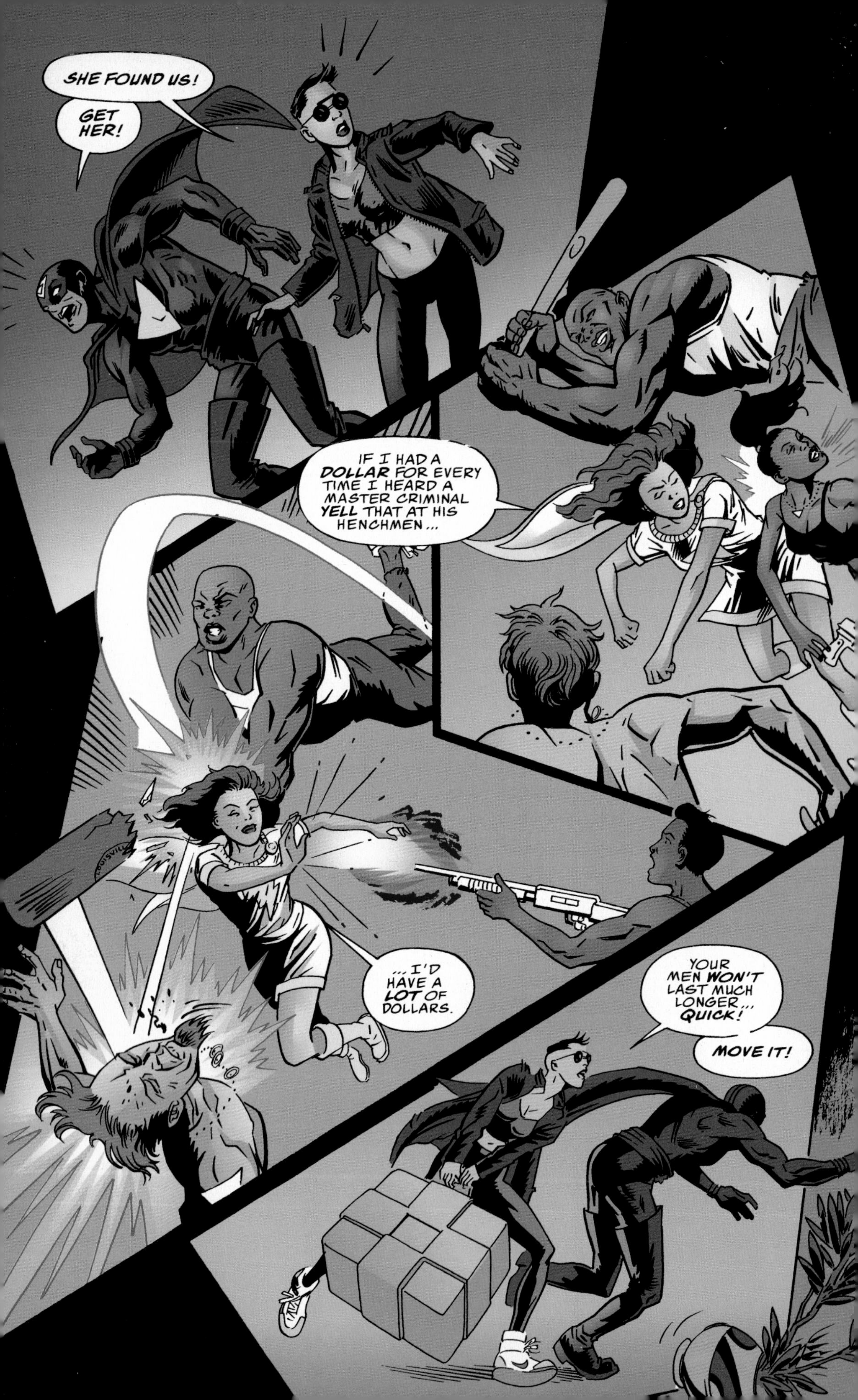
SHE FOUND US!
GET HER!
IF I HAD A DOLLAR FOR EVERY TIME I HEARD A MASTER CRIMINAL YELL THAT AT HIS HENCHMEN...
...I'D HAVE A LOT OF DOLLARS.
YOUR MEN WON'T LAST MUCH LONGER... QUICK!
MOVE IT!

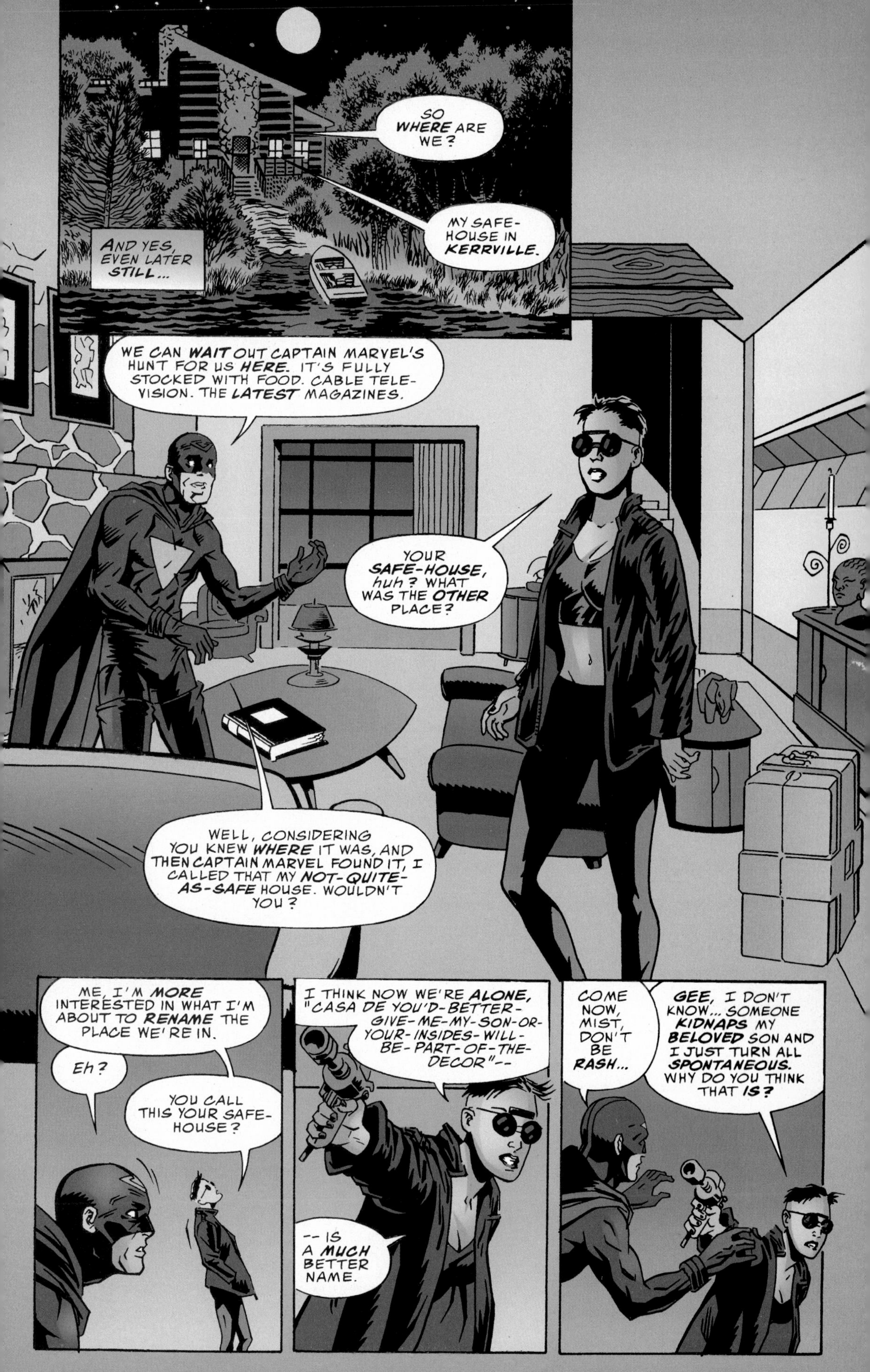

AND YES, EVEN LATER STILL...
SO WHERE ARE WE?
MY SAFE-HOUSE IN KERRVILLE.
WE CAN WAIT OUT CAPTAIN MARVEL'S HUNT FOR US HERE. IT'S FULLY STOCKED WITH FOOD. CABLE TELEVISION. THE LATEST MAGAZINES.
YOUR SAFE-HOUSE, huh? WHAT WAS THE OTHER PLACE?
WELL, CONSIDERING YOU KNEW WHERE IT WAS, AND THEN CAPTAIN MARVEL FOUND IT, I CALLED THAT MY NOT-QUITE-AS-SAFE HOUSE. WOULDN'T YOU?
ME, I'M MORE INTERESTED IN WHAT I'M ABOUT TO RENAME THE PLACE WE'RE IN.
Eh?
YOU CALL THIS YOUR SAFE-HOUSE?
I THINK NOW WE'RE ALONE, "CASA DE YOU'D-BETTER-GIVE-ME-MY-SON-OR-YOUR-INSIDES-WILL-BE-PART-OF-THE-DECOR"--
-- IS A MUCH BETTER NAME.
COME NOW, MIST, DON'T BE RASH...
GEE, I DON'T KNOW... SOMEONE KIDNAPS MY BELOVED SON AND I JUST TURN ALL SPONTANEOUS. WHY DO YOU THINK THAT IS?

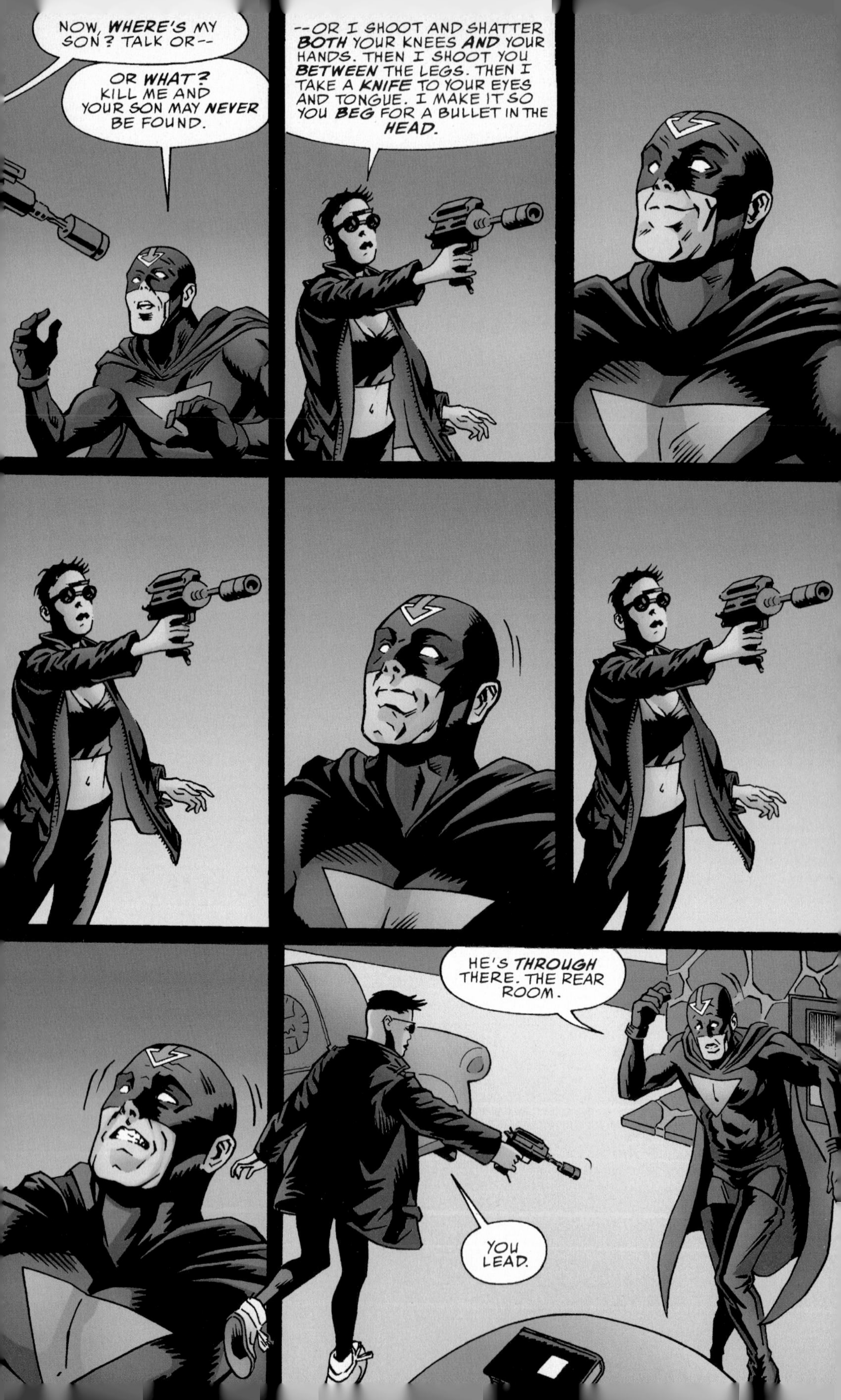
NOW, WHERE'S MY SON? TALK OR--
OR WHAT? KILL ME AND YOUR SON MAY NEVER BE FOUND.
--OR I SHOOT AND SHATTER BOTH YOUR KNEES AND YOUR HANDS. THEN I SHOOT YOU BETWEEN THE LEGS. THEN I TAKE A KNIFE TO YOUR EYES AND TONGUE. I MAKE IT SO YOU BEG FOR A BULLET IN THE HEAD.
HE'S THROUGH THERE. THE REAR ROOM.
YOU LEAD.

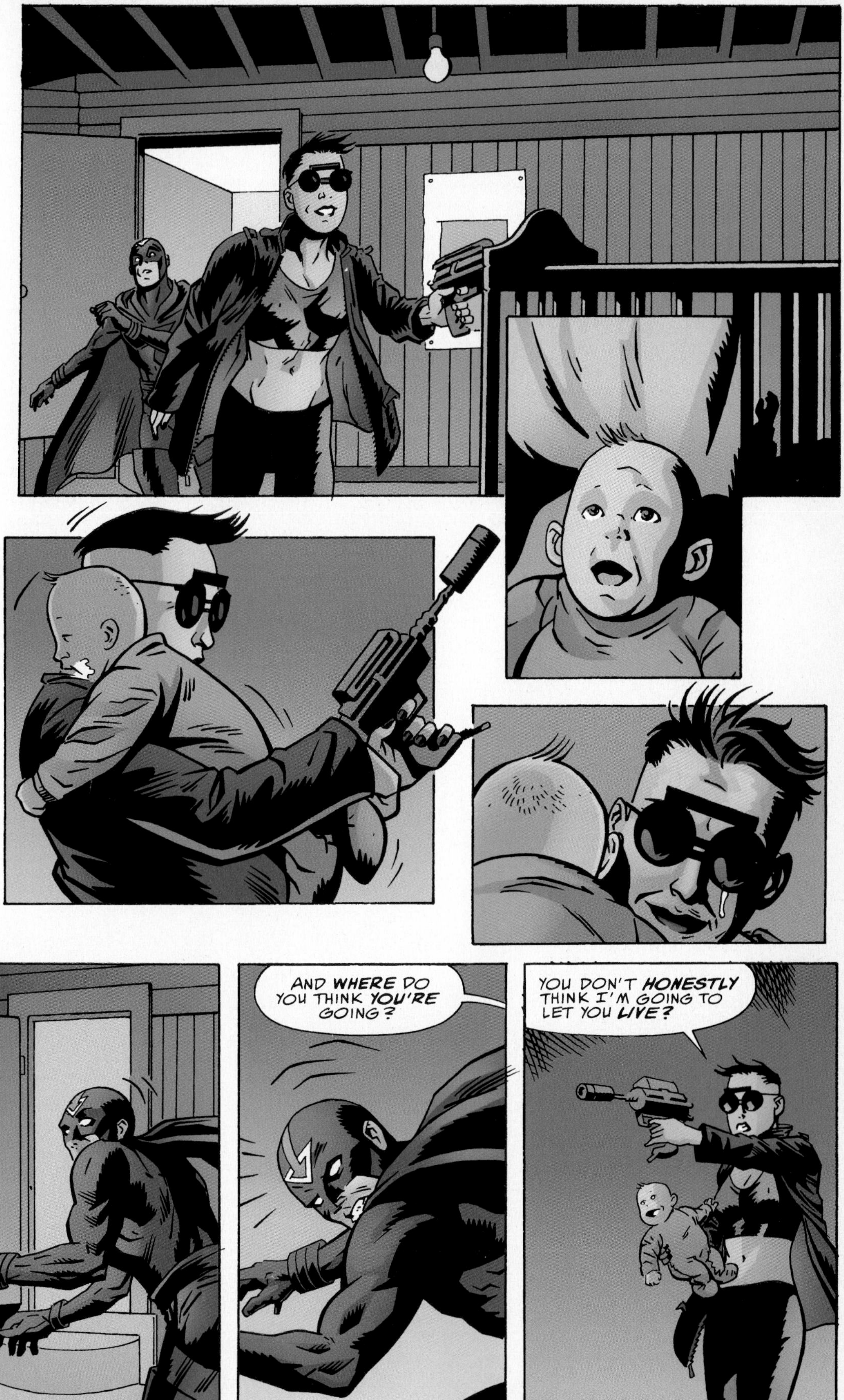
AND WHERE DO YOU THINK YOU'RE GOING?
YOU DON'T HONESTLY THINK I'M GOING TO LET YOU LIVE?

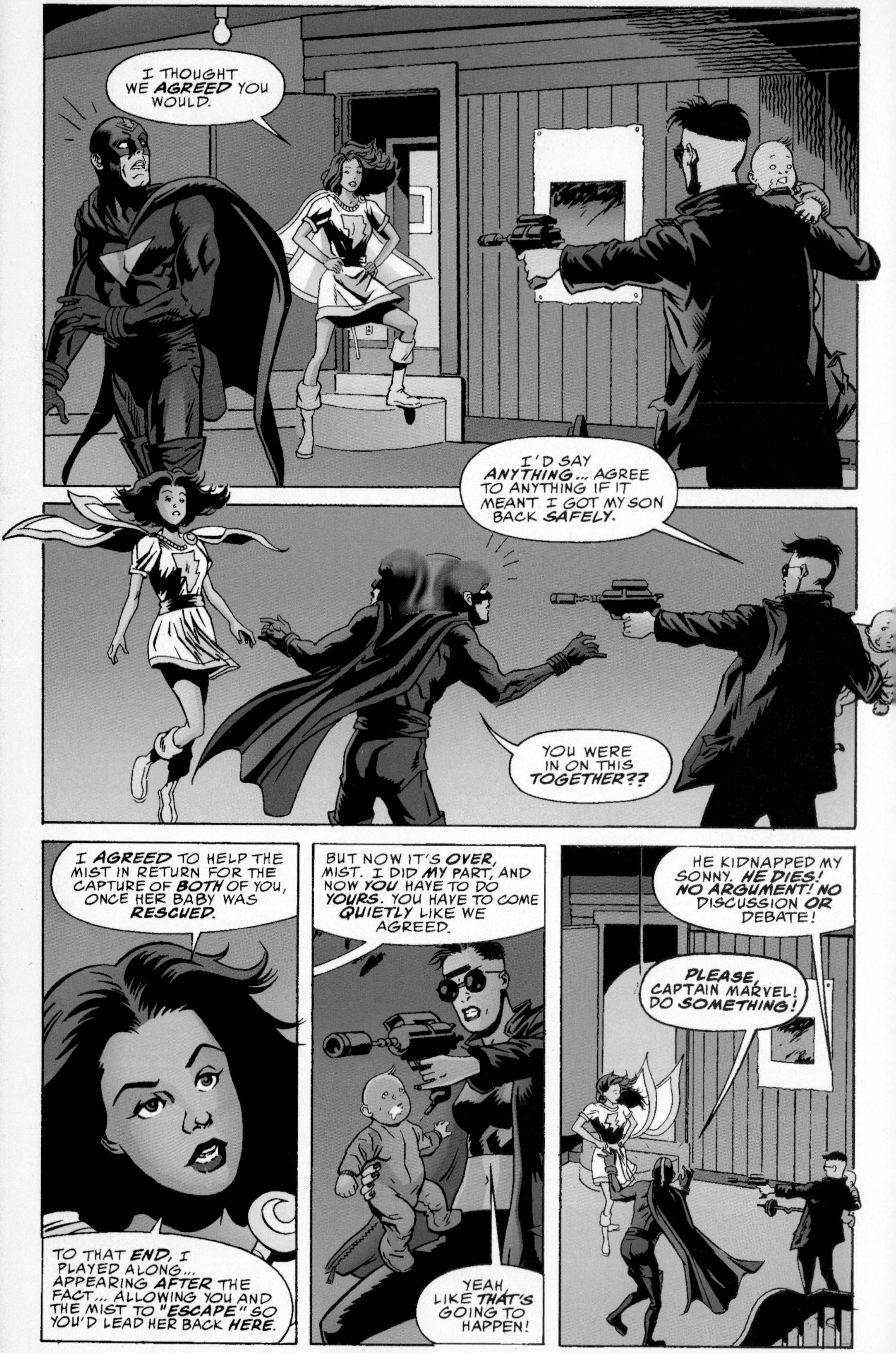
I THOUGHT WE AGREED YOU WOULD.
I'D SAY ANYTHING... AGREE TO ANYTHING IF IT MEANT I GOT MY SON BACK SAFELY.
YOU WERE IN ON THIS TOGETHER??
I AGREED TO HELP THE MIST IN RETURN FOR THE CAPTURE OF BOTH OF YOU, ONCE HER BABY WAS RESCUED.
TO THAT END, I PLAYED ALONG... APPEARING AFTER THE FACT... ALLOWING YOU AND THE MIST TO "ESCAPE" SO YOU'D LEAD HER BACK HERE.
BUT NOW IT'S OVER, MIST. I DID MY PART, AND NOW YOU HAVE TO DO YOURS. YOU HAVE TO COME QUIETLY LIKE WE AGREED.
YEAH LIKE THAT'S GOING TO HAPPEN!
HE KIDNAPPED MY SONNY. HE DIES! NO ARGUMENT! NO DISCUSSION OR DEBATE!
PLEASE, CAPTAIN MARVEL! DO SOMETHING!

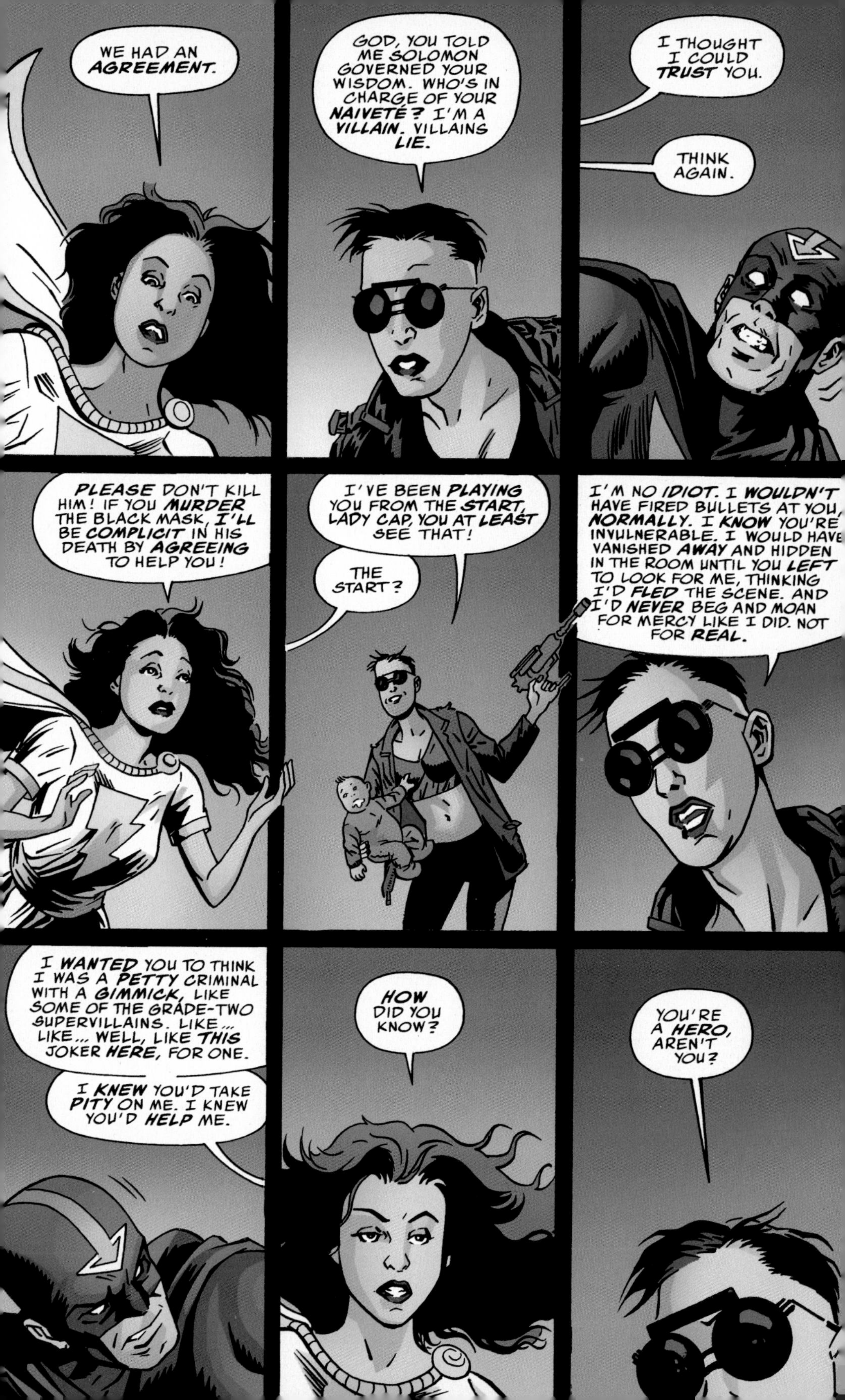
WE HAD AN AGREEMENT.
GOD, YOU TOLD ME SOLOMON GOVERNED YOUR WISDOM. WHO'S IN CHARGE OF YOUR NAIVETÉ? I'M A VILLAIN. VILLAINS LIE.
I THOUGHT I COULD TRUST YOU.
THINK AGAIN.
PLEASE DON'T KILL HIM! IF YOU MURDER THE BLACK MASK, I'LL BE COMPLICIT IN HIS DEATH BY AGREEING TO HELP YOU!
I'VE BEEN PLAYING YOU FROM THE START, LADY CAP, YOU AT LEAST SEE THAT!
THE START?
I'M NO IDIOT. I WOULDN'T HAVE FIRED BULLETS AT YOU, NORMALLY. I KNOW YOU'RE INVULNERABLE. I WOULD HAVE VANISHED AWAY AND HIDDEN IN THE ROOM UNTIL YOU LEFT TO LOOK FOR ME, THINKING I'D FLED THE SCENE. AND I'D NEVER BEG AND MOAN FOR MERCY LIKE I DID. NOT FOR REAL.
I WANTED YOU TO THINK I WAS A PETTY CRIMINAL WITH A GIMMICK, LIKE SOME OF THE GRADE-TWO SUPERVILLAINS. LIKE... LIKE... WELL, LIKE THIS JOKER HERE, FOR ONE.
I KNEW YOU'D TAKE PITY ON ME. I KNEW YOU'D HELP ME.
HOW DID YOU KNOW?
YOU'RE A HERO, AREN'T YOU?

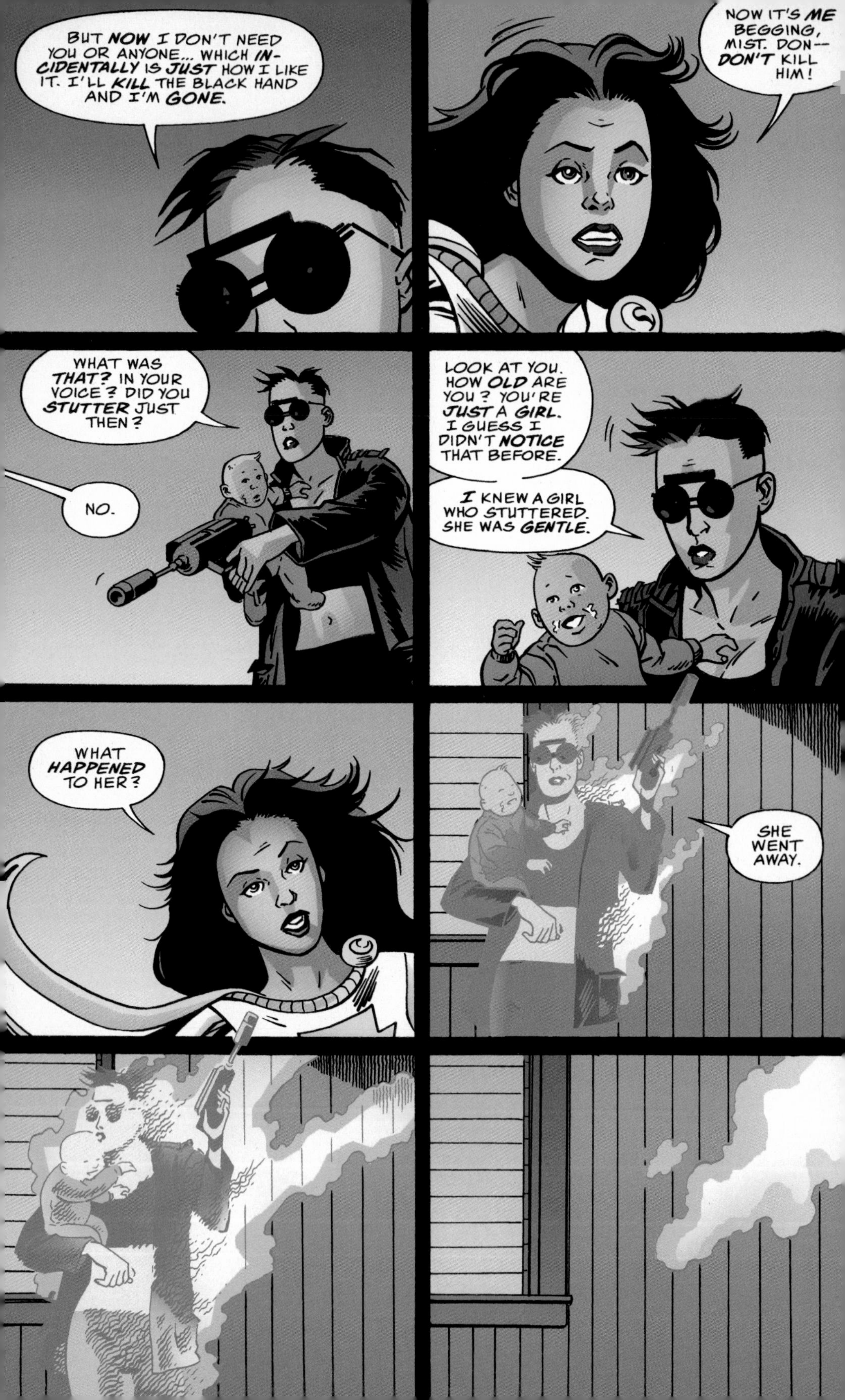
BUT NOW I DON'T NEED YOU OR ANYONE... WHICH INCIDENTALLY IS JUST HOW I LIKE IT. I'LL KILL THE BLACK HAND AND I'M GONE.
NOW IT'S ME BEGGING, MIST. DON-- DON'T KILL HIM!
WHAT WAS THAT? IN YOUR VOICE? DID YOU STUTTER JUST THEN?
NO.
LOOK AT YOU. HOW OLD ARE YOU? YOU'RE JUST A GIRL. I GUESS I DIDN'T NOTICE THAT BEFORE.
I KNEW A GIRL WHO STUTTERED. SHE WAS GENTLE.
WHAT HAPPENED TO HER?
SHE WENT AWAY.

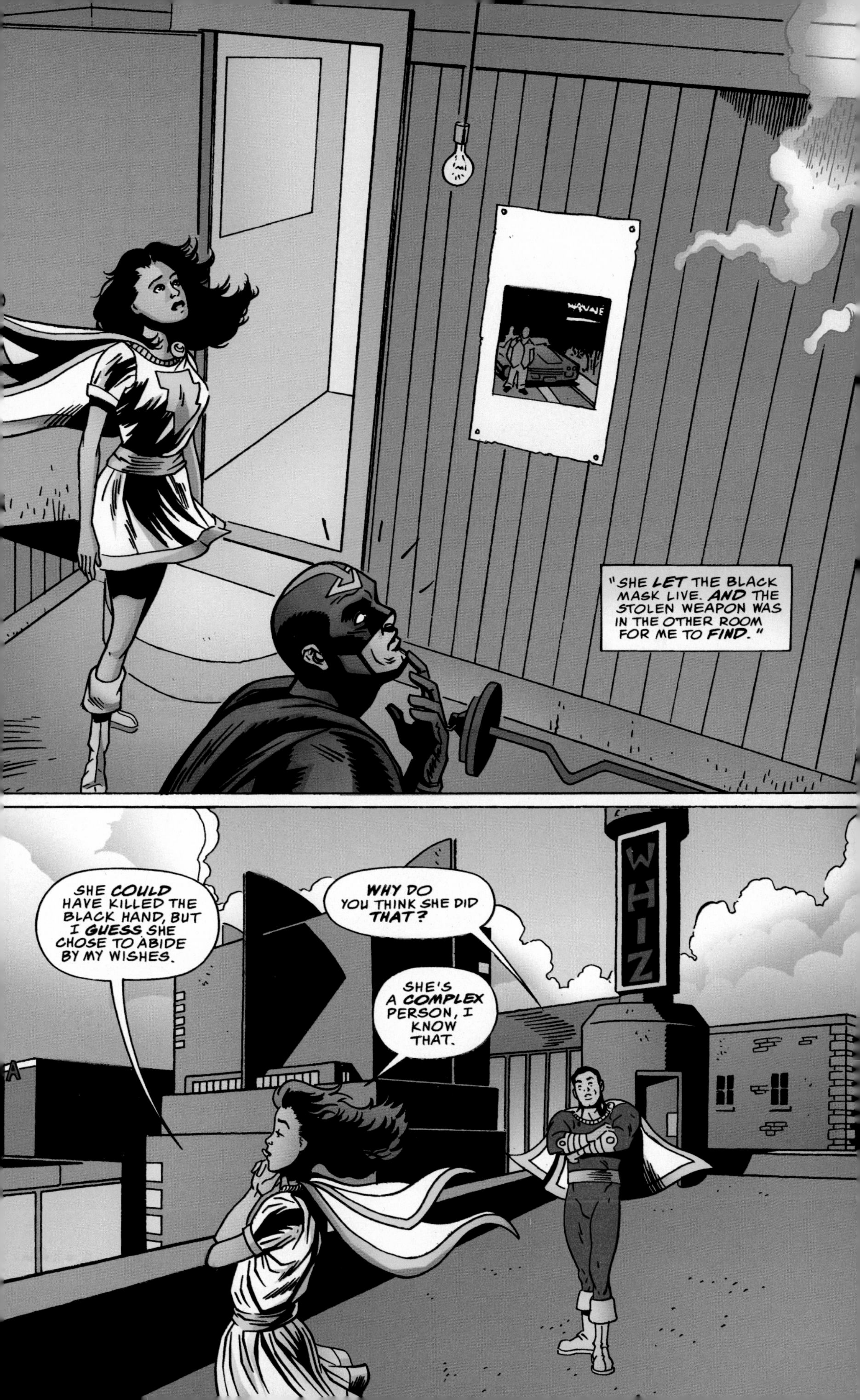
"SHE LET THE BLACK MASK LIVE. AND THE STOLEN WEAPON WAS IN THE OTHER ROOM FOR ME TO FIND."
SHE COULD HAVE KILLED THE BLACK HAND, BUT I GUESS SHE CHOSE TO ABIDE BY MY WISHES.
WHY DO YOU THINK SHE DID THAT?
SHE'S A COMPLEX PERSON, I KNOW THAT.
WHIZ

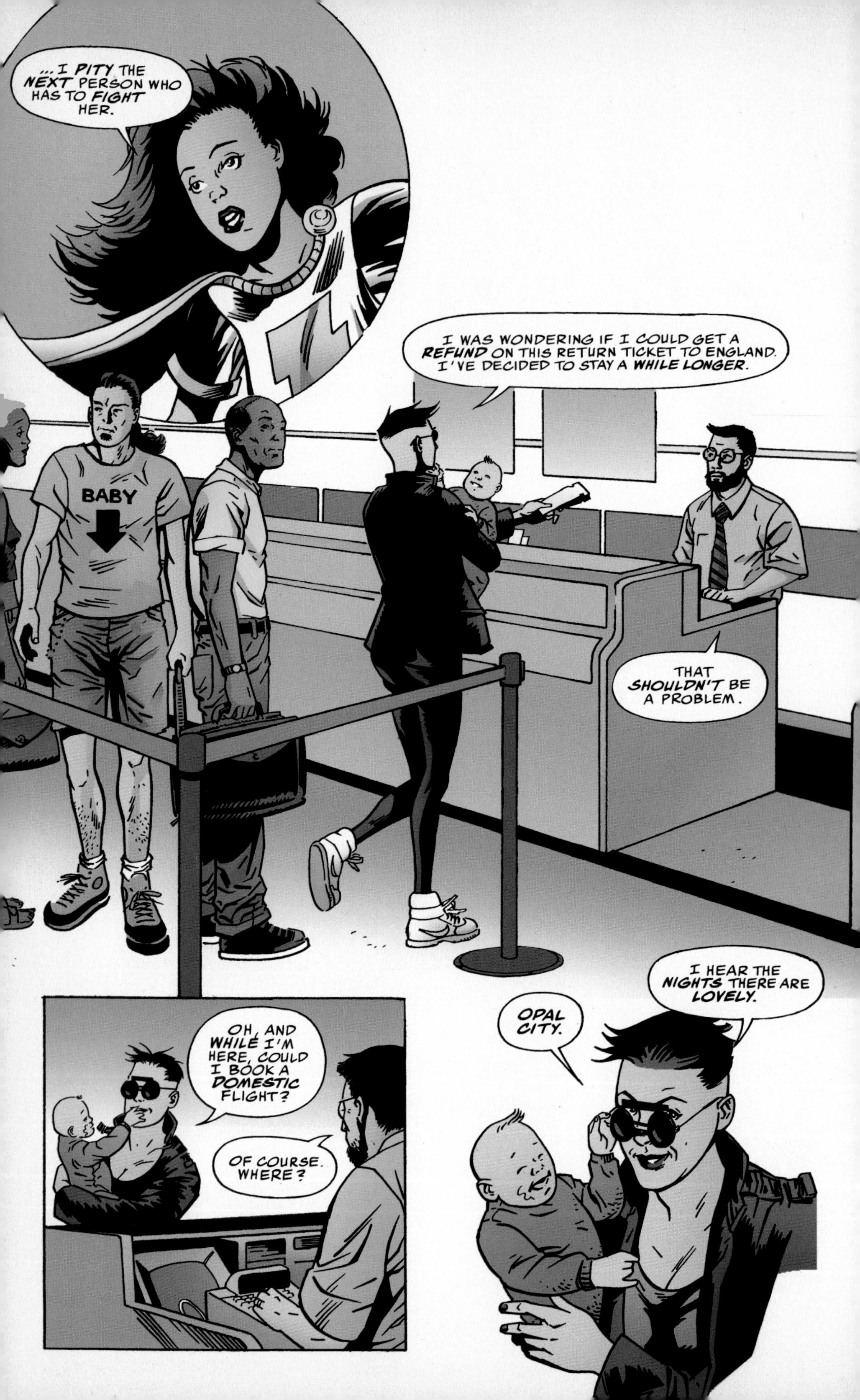
...I PITY THE NEXT PERSON WHO HAS TO FIGHT HER.
I WAS WONDERING IF I COULD GET A REFUND ON THIS RETURN TICKET TO ENGLAND. I'VE DECIDED TO STAY A WHILE LONGER.
BABY
THAT SHOULDN'T BE A PROBLEM.
OH, AND WHILE I'M HERE, COULD I BOOK A DOMESTIC FLIGHT?
OF COURSE. WHERE?
OPAL CITY.
I HEAR THE NIGHTS THERE ARE LOVELY.

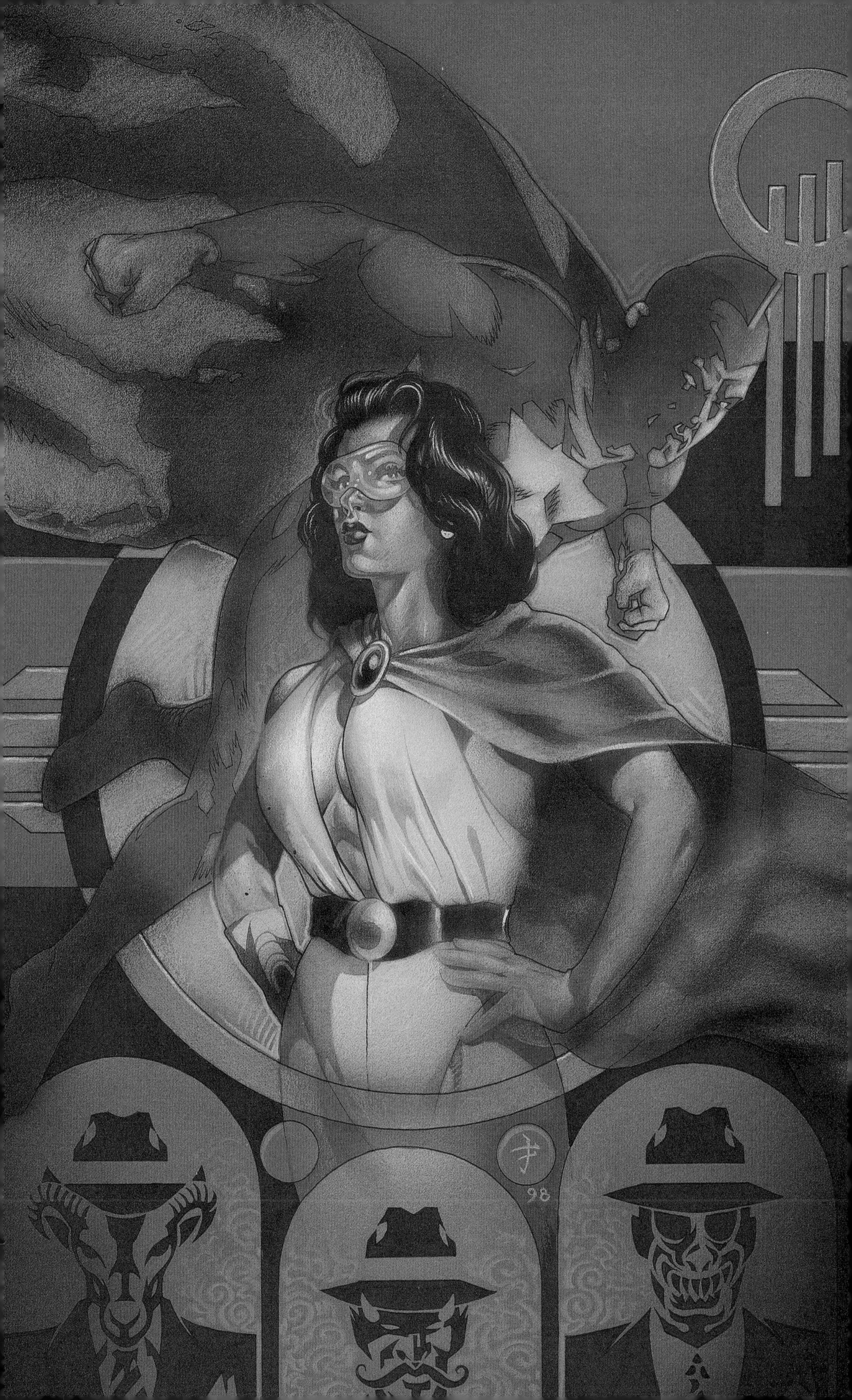

STARMAN 44

Cover by Tony Harris

Written by James Robinson

Pencils by Mike Mayhew

with inks by Wade von Grawbadger

and colors by Gregory Wright

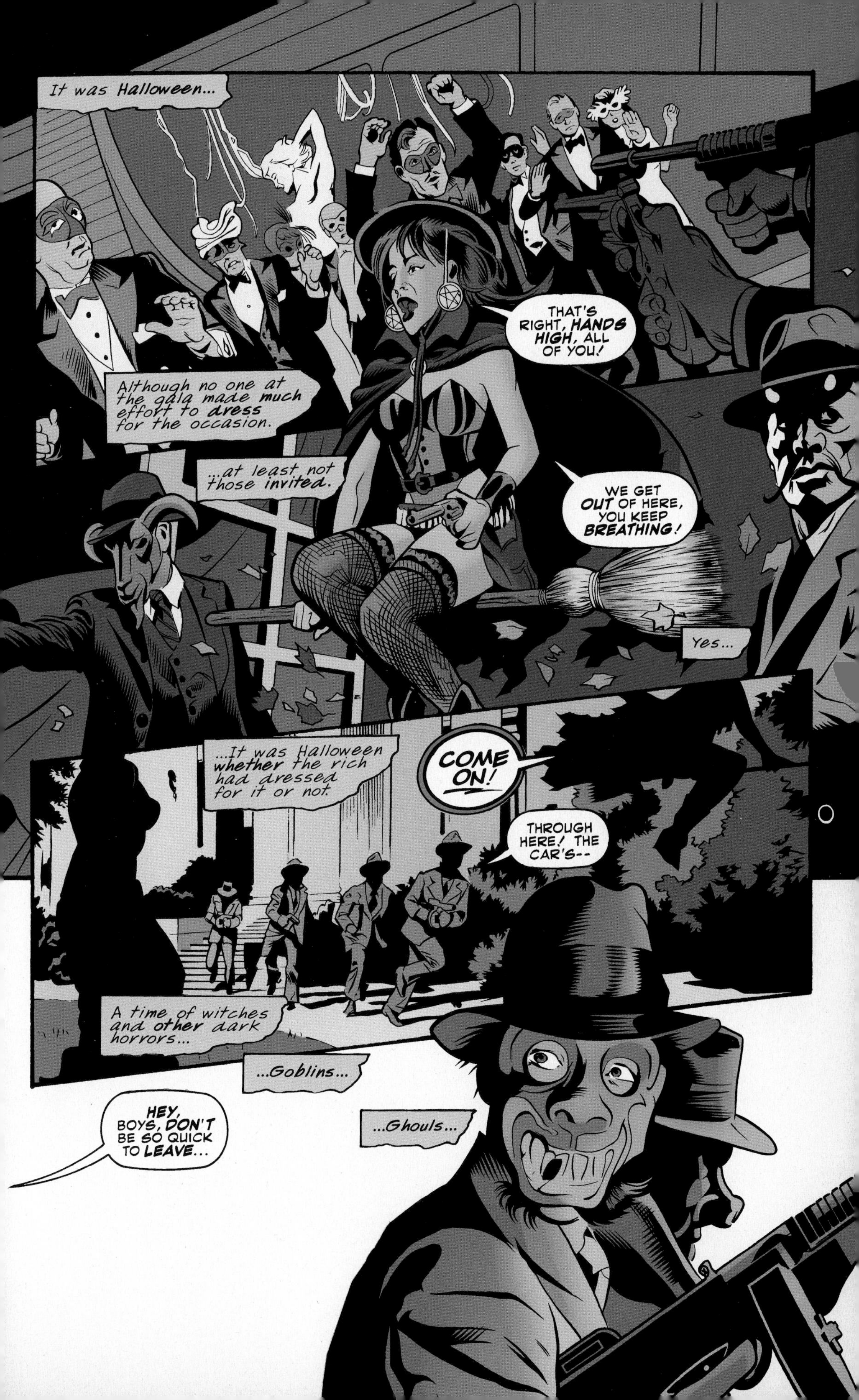

It was Halloween...
THAT'S RIGHT, HANDS HIGH, ALL OF YOU!
Although no one at the gala made much effort to dress for the occasion.
...at least not those invited.
WE GET OUT OF HERE, YOU KEEP BREATHING!
Yes...
...It was Halloween whether the rich had dressed for it or not.
COME ON!
THROUGH HERE! THE CAR'S--
A time of witches and other dark horrors...
...Goblins...
...Ghouls...
HEY, BOYS, DON'T BE SO QUICK TO LEAVE...

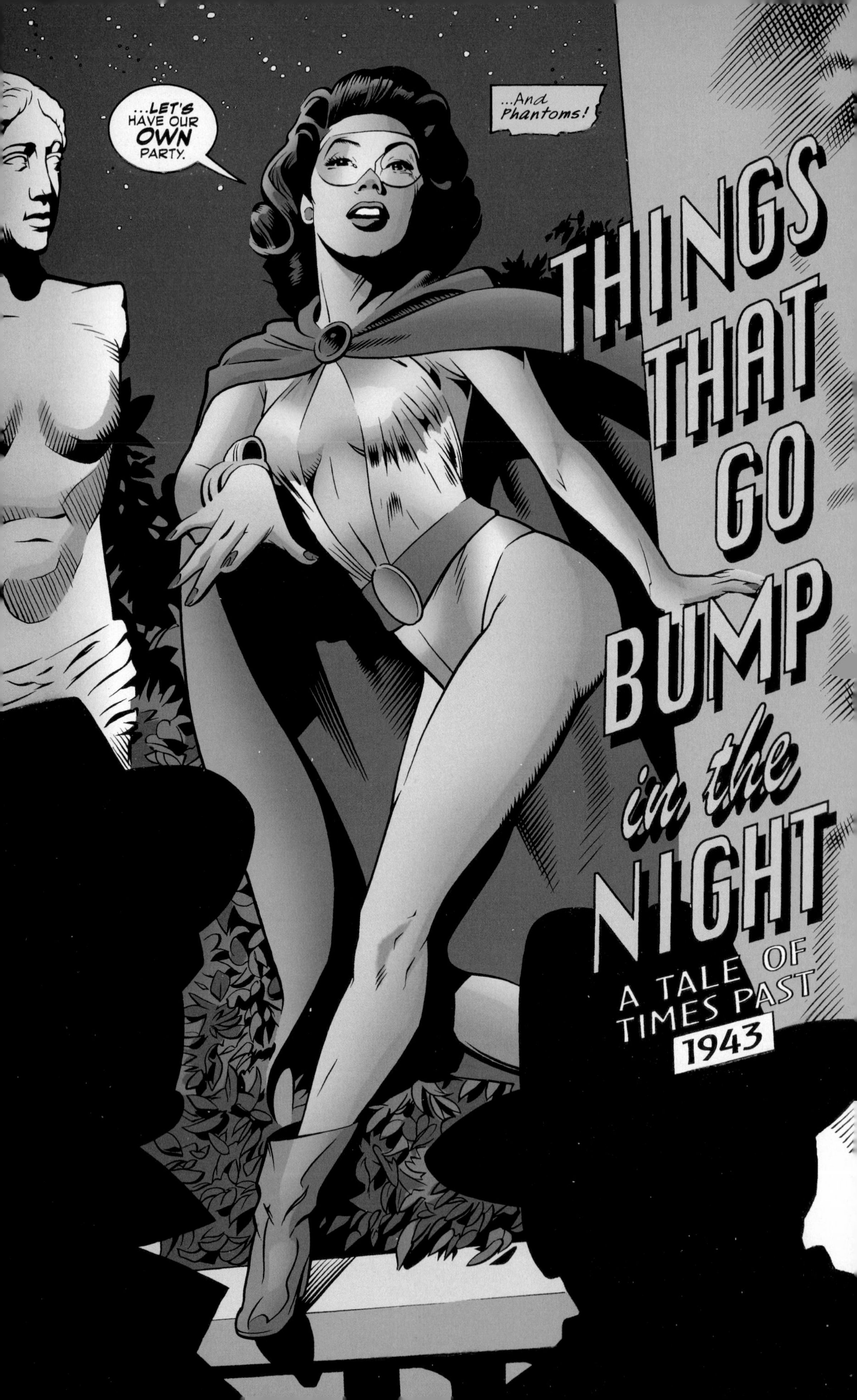
...LET'S HAVE OUR OWN PARTY.
...And Phantoms!
THINGS THAT GO BUMP in the NIGHT
A TALE OF TIMES PAST
1943

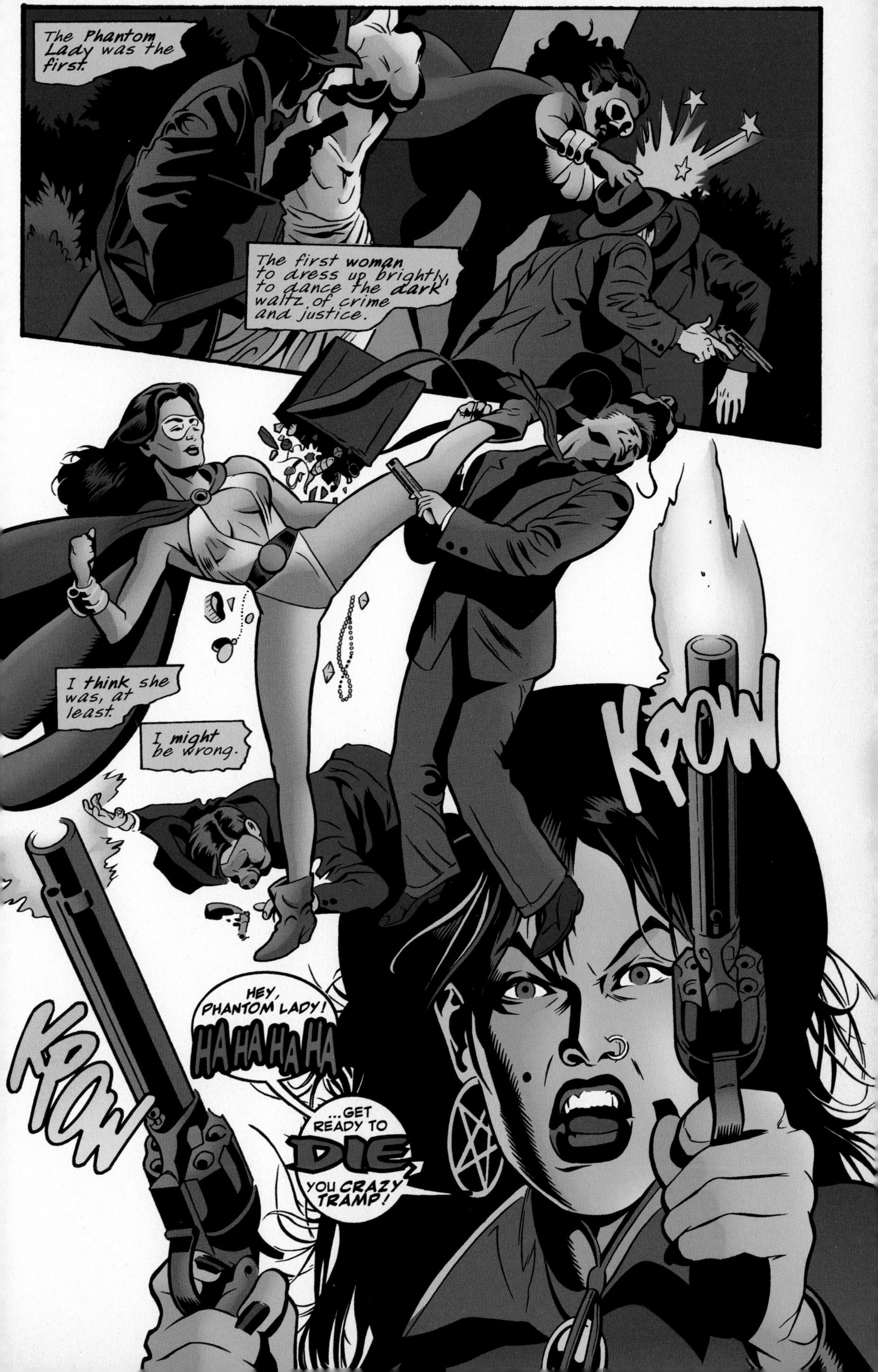

The Phantom Lady was the first.
The first woman to dress up brightly, to dance the dark waltz of crime and justice.
I think she was, at least.
I might be wrong.
KPOW
HEY, PHANTOM LADY!
HA HA HA HA
...GET READY TO
DIE
YOU CRAZY TRAMP!
KPOW

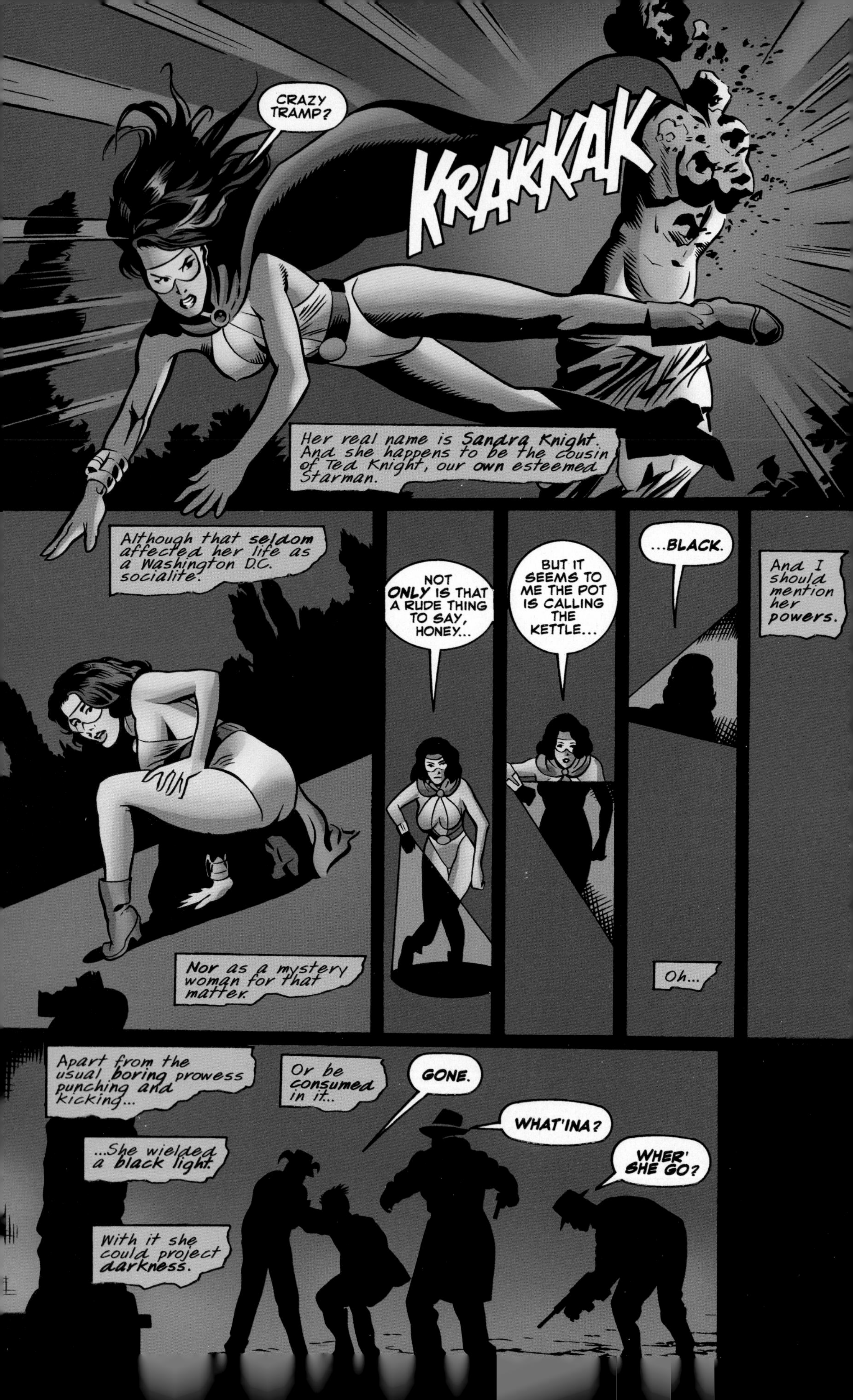
CRAZY TRAMP?
KRAKKAK
Her real name is Sandra Knight. And she happens to be the cousin of Ted Knight, our own esteemed Starman.
Although that seldom affected her life as a Washington D.C. socialite.
Nor as a mystery woman for that matter.
NOT ONLY IS THAT A RUDE THING TO SAY, HONEY...
BUT IT SEEMS TO ME THE POT IS CALLING THE KETTLE...
...BLACK.
Oh...
And I should mention her powers.
Apart from the usual boring prowess punching and kicking...
...She wielded a black light.
With it she could project darkness.
Or be consumed in it...
GONE.
WHAT'INA?
WHER' SHE GO?

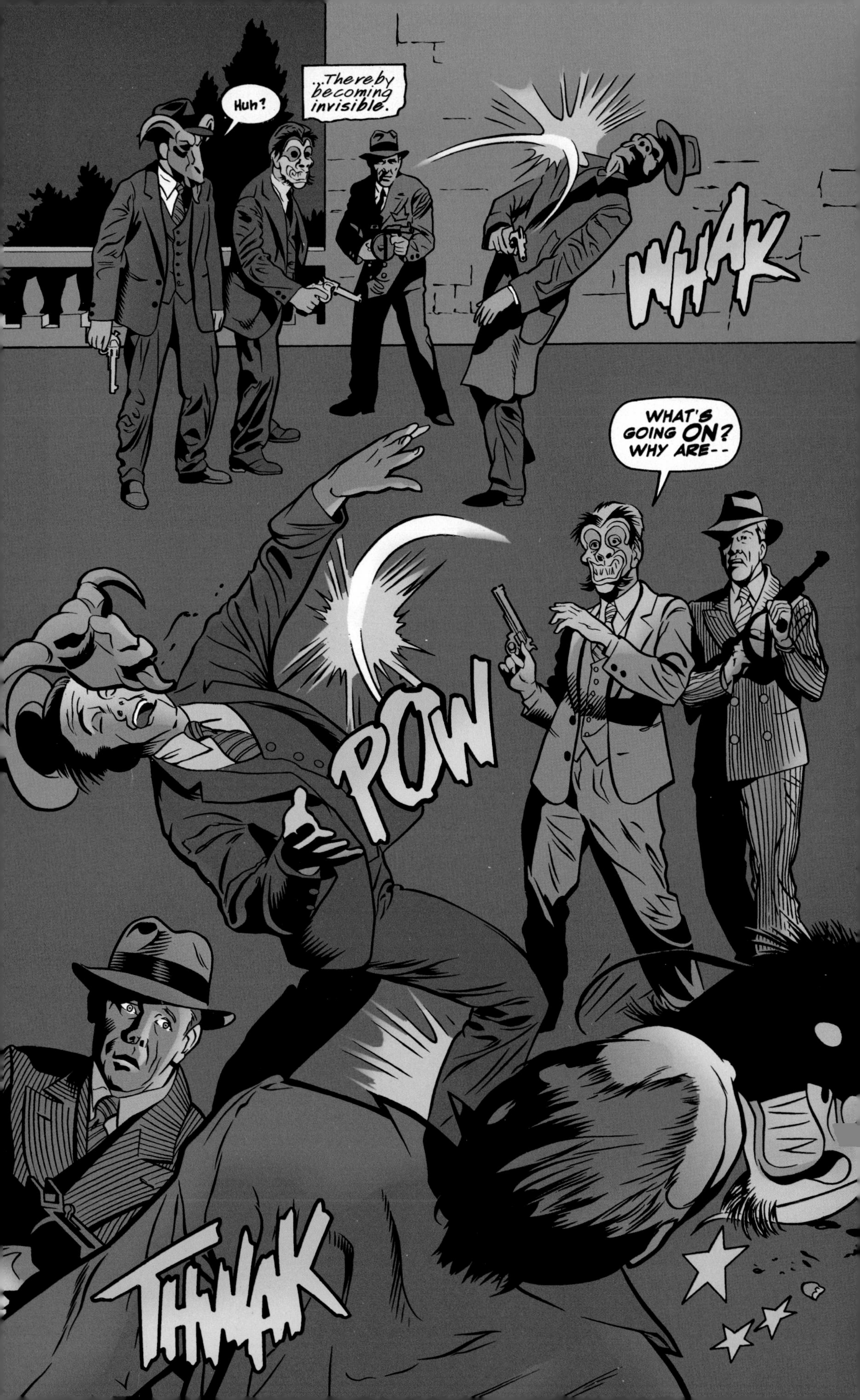
Huh?
...Thereby becoming invisible.
WHAK
WHAT'S GOING ON? WHY ARE--
POW
THWAK

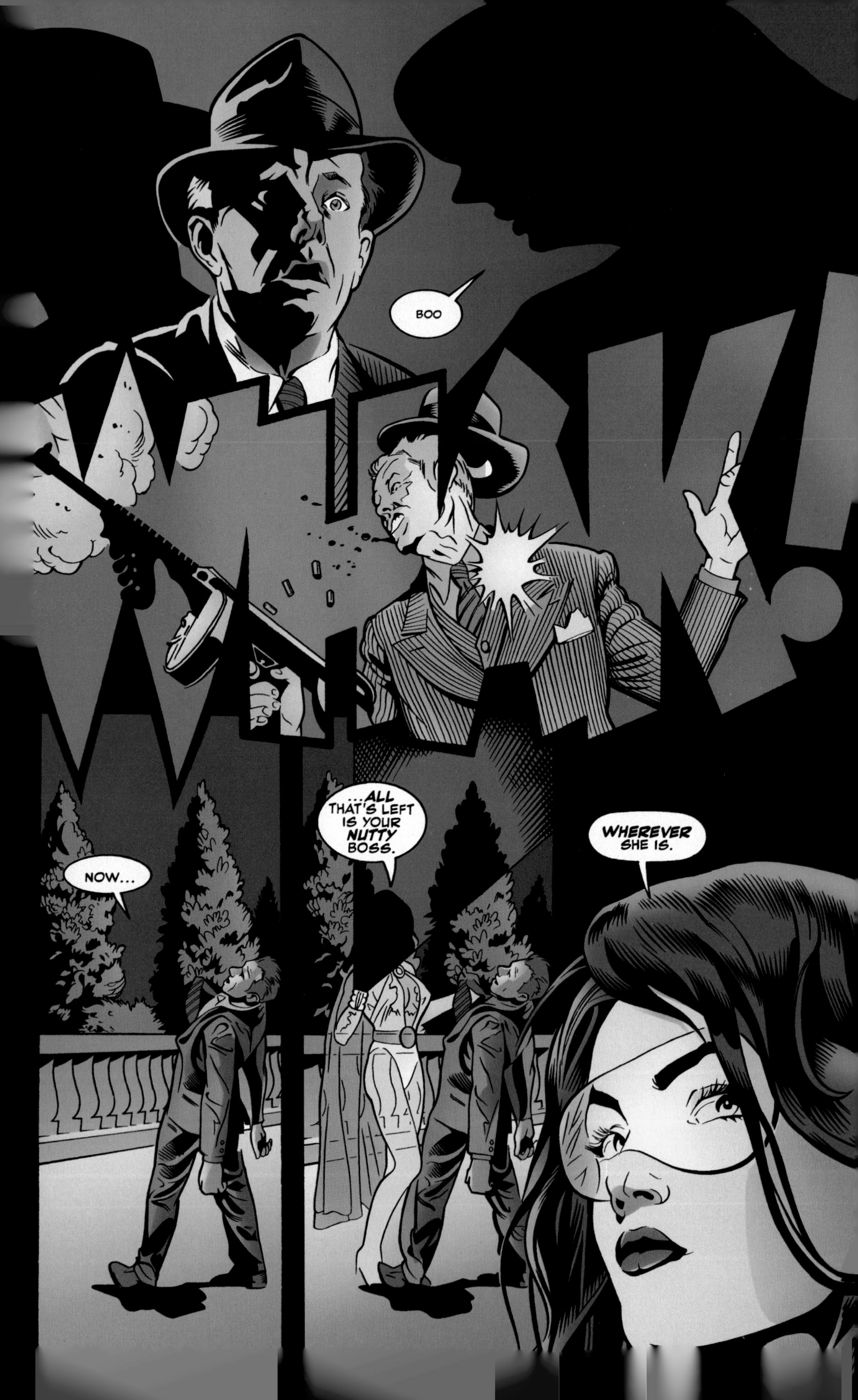
BOO
NOW...
...ALL THAT'S LEFT IS YOUR NUTTY BOSS.
WHEREVER SHE IS.

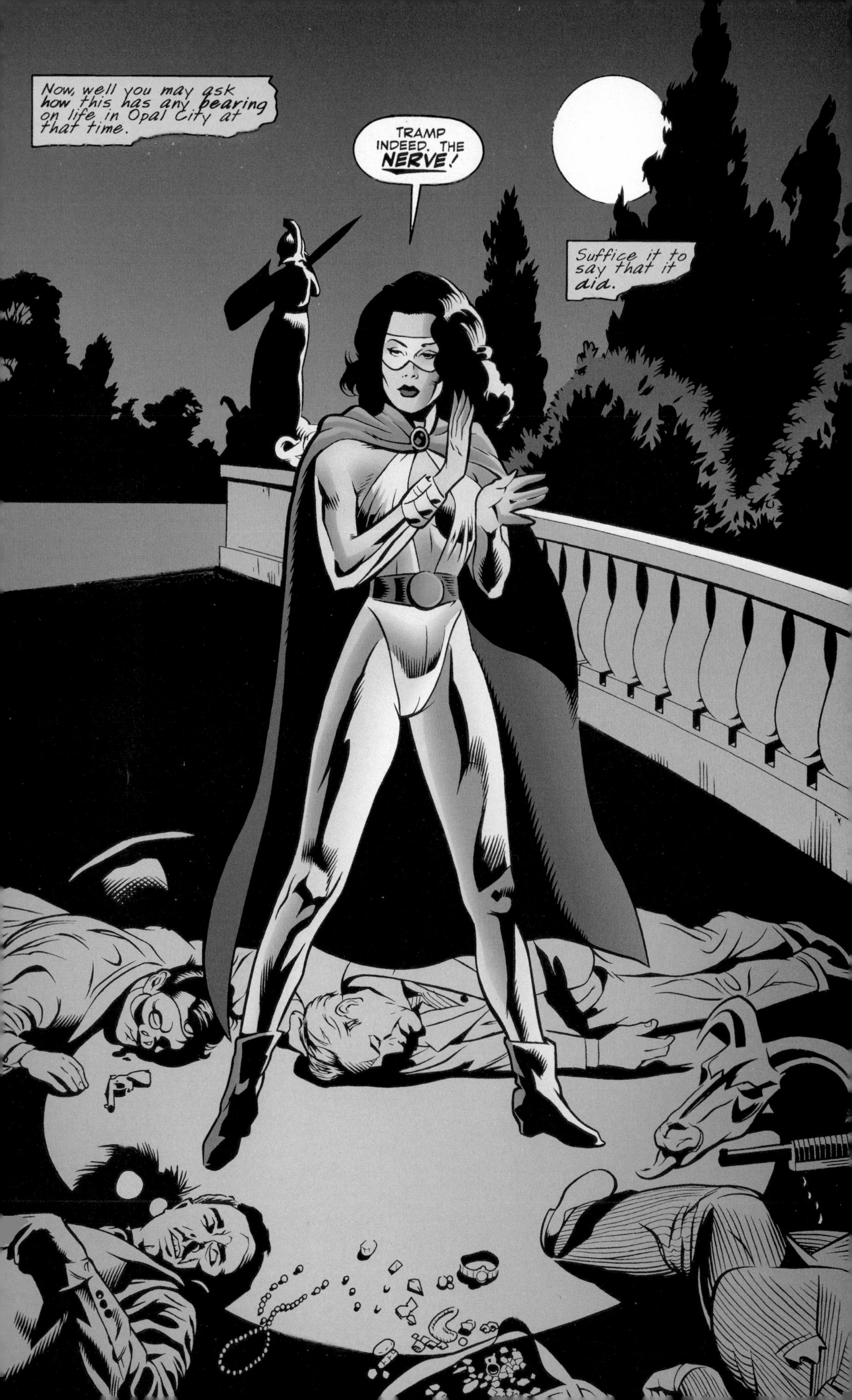
Now, well you may ask how this has any bearing on life in Opal City at that time.
TRAMP INDEED. THE NERVE!
Suffice it to say that it did.

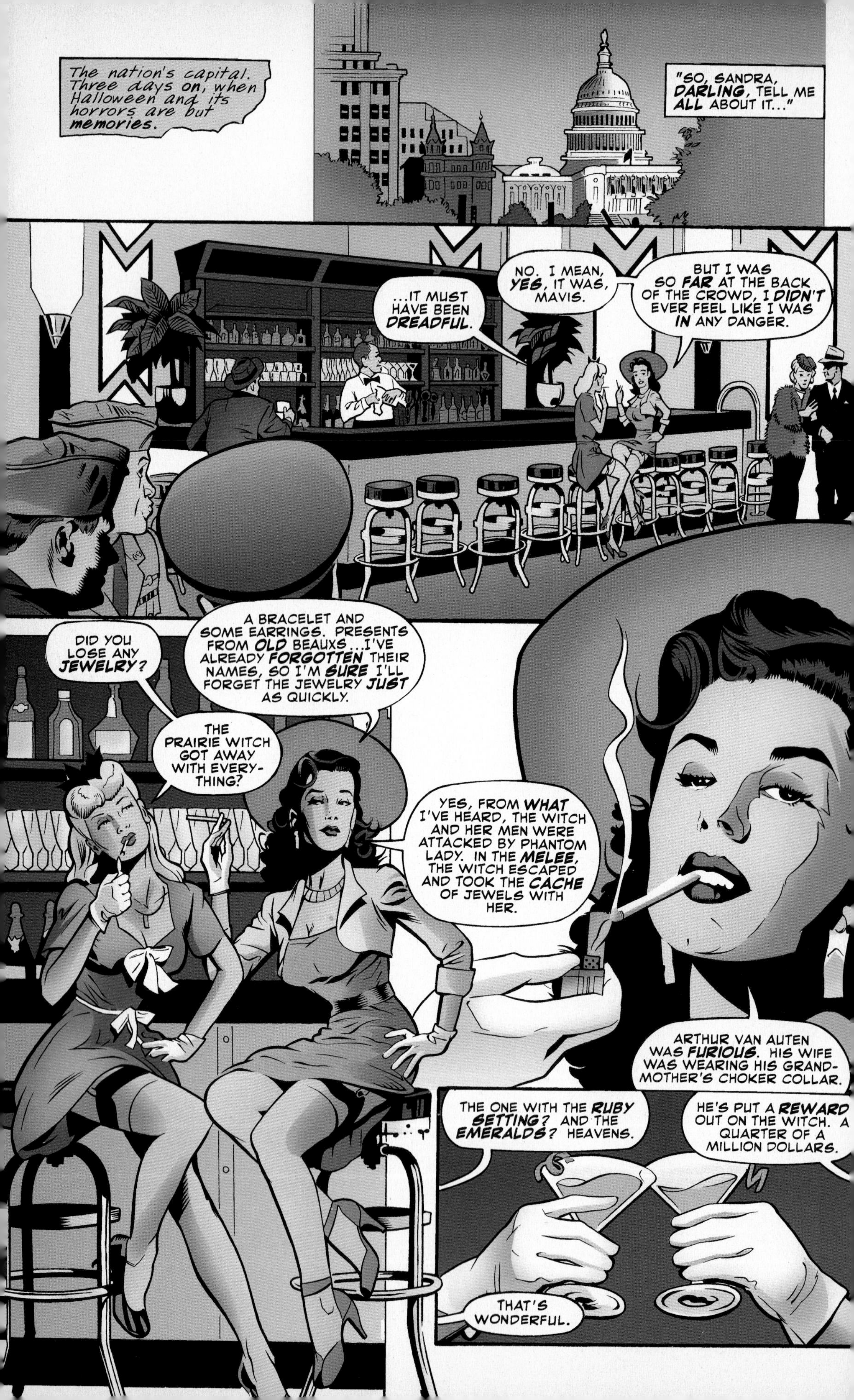

The nation's capital. Three days on, when Halloween and its horrors are but memories.
"SO, SANDRA, DARLING, TELL ME ALL ABOUT IT..."
...IT MUST HAVE BEEN DREADFUL.
NO. I MEAN, YES, IT WAS, MAVIS.
BUT I WAS SO FAR AT THE BACK OF THE CROWD, I DIDN'T EVER FEEL LIKE I WAS IN ANY DANGER.
DID YOU LOSE ANY JEWELRY?
A BRACELET AND SOME EARRINGS. PRESENTS FROM OLD BEAUXS...I'VE ALREADY FORGOTTEN THEIR NAMES, SO I'M SURE I'LL FORGET THE JEWELRY JUST AS QUICKLY.
THE PRAIRIE WITCH GOT AWAY WITH EVERY-THING?
YES, FROM WHAT I'VE HEARD, THE WITCH AND HER MEN WERE ATTACKED BY PHANTOM LADY. IN THE MELEE, THE WITCH ESCAPED AND TOOK THE CACHE OF JEWELS WITH HER.
ARTHUR VAN AUTEN WAS FURIOUS. HIS WIFE WAS WEARING HIS GRAND-MOTHER'S CHOKER COLLAR.
THE ONE WITH THE RUBY SETTING? AND THE EMERALDS? HEAVENS.
HE'S PUT A REWARD OUT ON THE WITCH. A QUARTER OF A MILLION DOLLARS.
THAT'S WONDERFUL.

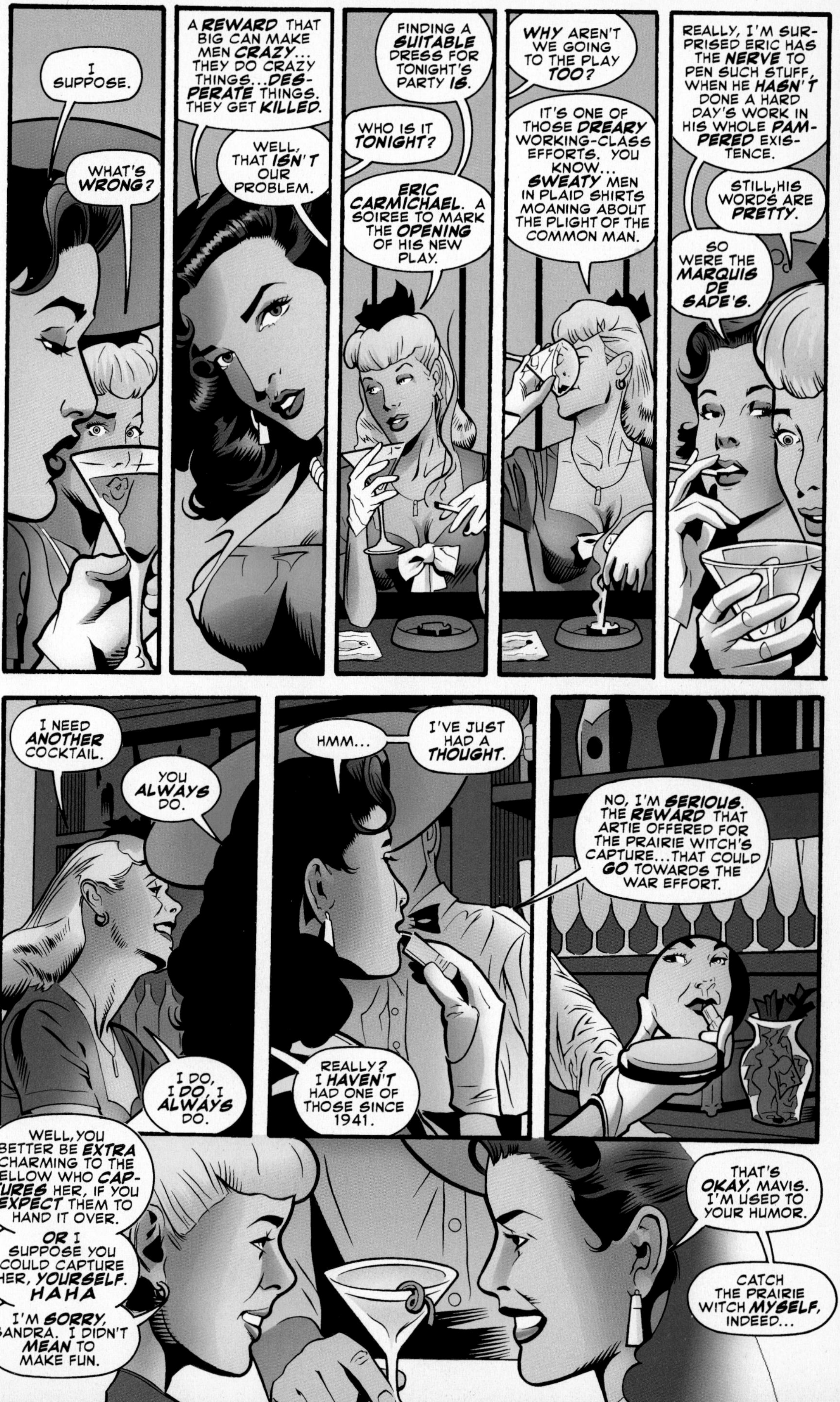

I SUPPOSE.
WHAT'S WRONG?
A REWARD THAT BIG CAN MAKE MEN CRAZY... THEY DO CRAZY THINGS...DESPERATE THINGS. THEY GET KILLED.
WELL, THAT ISN'T OUR PROBLEM.
FINDING A SUITABLE DRESS FOR TONIGHT'S PARTY IS.
WHO IS IT TONIGHT?
ERIC CARMICHAEL. A SOIREE TO MARK THE OPENING OF HIS NEW PLAY.
WHY AREN'T WE GOING TO THE PLAY TOO?
IT'S ONE OF THOSE DREARY WORKING-CLASS EFFORTS. YOU KNOW... SWEATY MEN IN PLAID SHIRTS MOANING ABOUT THE PLIGHT OF THE COMMON MAN.
REALLY, I'M SURPRISED ERIC HAS THE NERVE TO PEN SUCH STUFF, WHEN HE HASN'T DONE A HARD DAY'S WORK IN HIS WHOLE PAMPERED EXISTENCE.
STILL, HIS WORDS ARE PRETTY.
SO WERE THE MARQUIS DE SADE'S.
I NEED ANOTHER COCKTAIL.
YOU ALWAYS DO.
I DO, I DO, I ALWAYS DO.
HMM...
I'VE JUST HAD A THOUGHT.
REALLY? I HAVEN'T HAD ONE OF THOSE SINCE 1941.
NO, I'M SERIOUS. THE REWARD THAT ARTIE OFFERED FOR THE PRAIRIE WITCH'S CAPTURE...THAT COULD GO TOWARDS THE WAR EFFORT.
WELL, YOU BETTER BE EXTRA CHARMING TO THE FELLOW WHO CAPTURES HER, IF YOU EXPECT THEM TO HAND IT OVER.
OR I SUPPOSE YOU COULD CAPTURE HER, YOURSELF. HAHA
I'M SORRY, SANDRA. I DIDN'T MEAN TO MAKE FUN.
THAT'S OKAY, MAVIS. I'M USED TO YOUR HUMOR.
CATCH THE PRAIRIE WITCH MYSELF, INDEED...

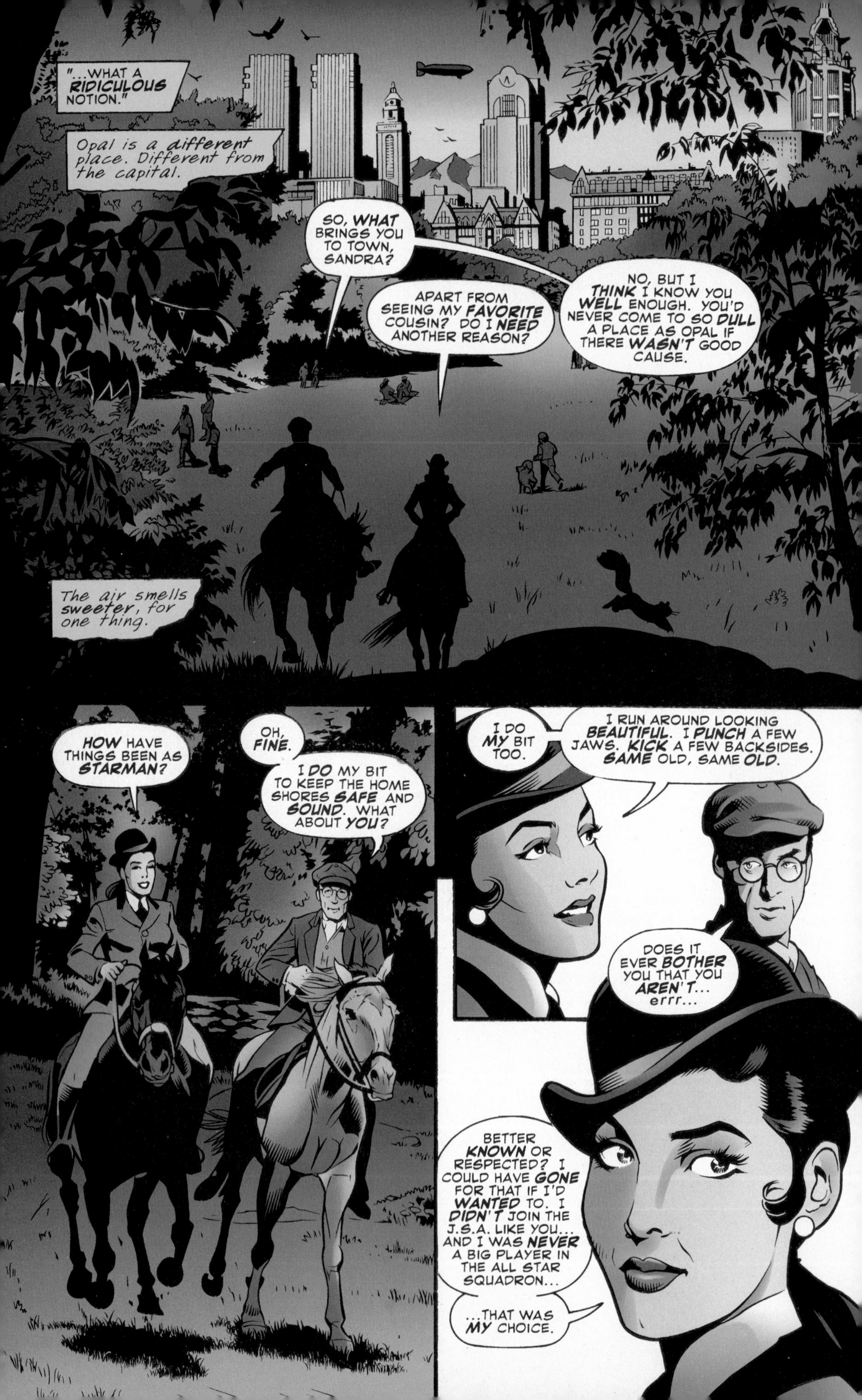
"...WHAT A RIDICULOUS NOTION."
Opal is a different place. Different from the capital.
SO, WHAT BRINGS YOU TO TOWN, SANDRA?
APART FROM SEEING MY FAVORITE COUSIN? DO I NEED ANOTHER REASON?
NO, BUT I THINK I KNOW YOU WELL ENOUGH. YOU'D NEVER COME TO SO DULL A PLACE AS OPAL IF THERE WASN'T GOOD CAUSE.
The air smells sweeter, for one thing.
HOW HAVE THINGS BEEN AS STARMAN?
OH, FINE.
I DO MY BIT TO KEEP THE HOME SHORES SAFE AND SOUND. WHAT ABOUT YOU?
I DO MY BIT TOO.
I RUN AROUND LOOKING BEAUTIFUL. I PUNCH A FEW JAWS. KICK A FEW BACKSIDES. SAME OLD, SAME OLD.
DOES IT EVER BOTHER YOU THAT YOU AREN'T... errr...
BETTER KNOWN OR RESPECTED? I COULD HAVE GONE FOR THAT IF I'D WANTED TO. I DIDN'T JOIN THE J.S.A. LIKE YOU... AND I WAS NEVER A BIG PLAYER IN THE ALL STAR SQUADRON...
...THAT WAS MY CHOICE.

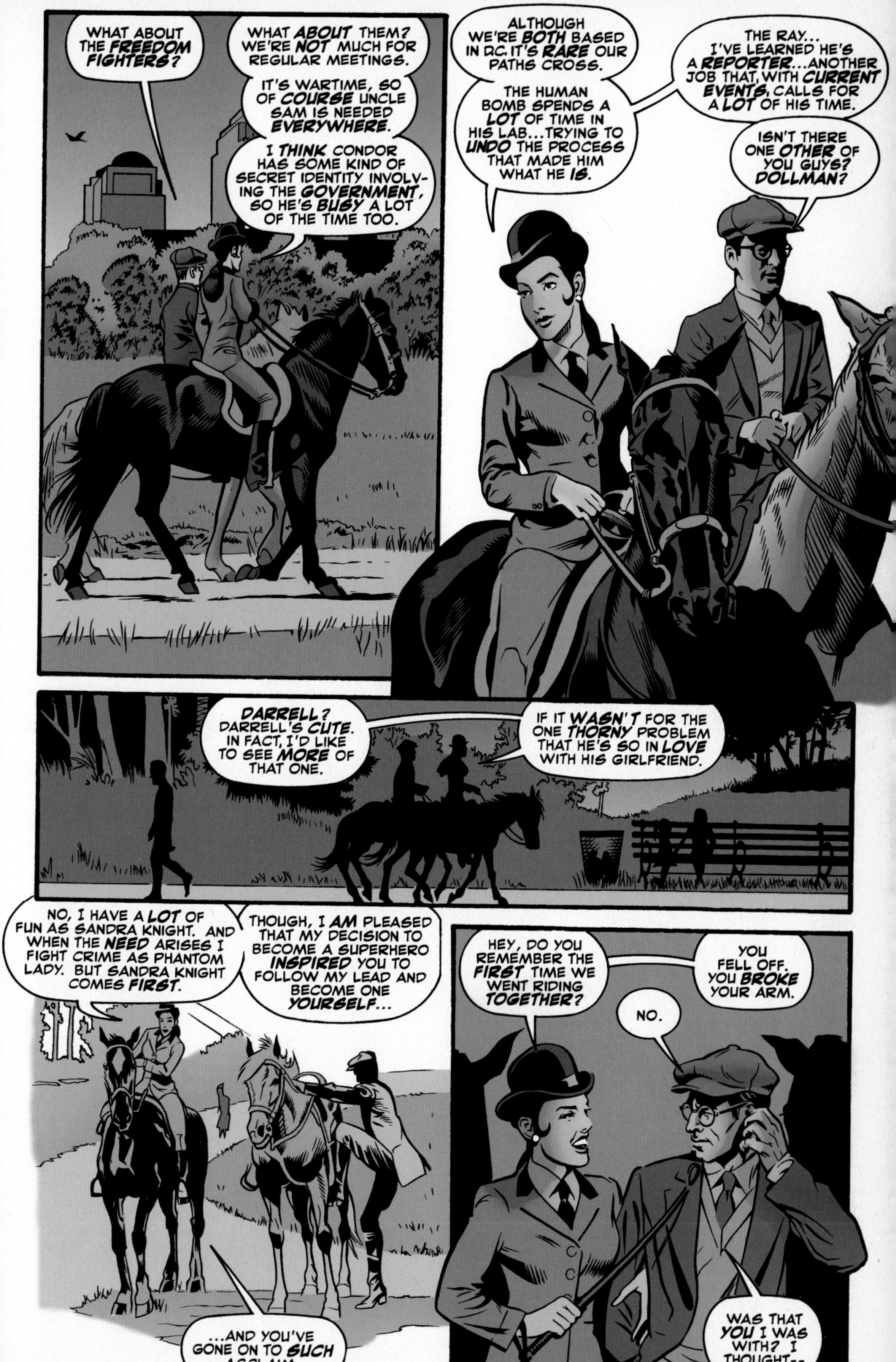
WHAT ABOUT THE FREEDOM FIGHTERS?
WHAT ABOUT THEM? WE'RE NOT MUCH FOR REGULAR MEETINGS.
IT'S WARTIME, SO OF COURSE UNCLE SAM IS NEEDED EVERYWHERE.
I THINK CONDOR HAS SOME KIND OF SECRET IDENTITY INVOLVING THE GOVERNMENT, SO HE'S BUSY A LOT OF THE TIME TOO.
ALTHOUGH WE'RE BOTH BASED IN D.C. IT'S RARE OUR PATHS CROSS.
THE HUMAN BOMB SPENDS A LOT OF TIME IN HIS LAB...TRYING TO UNDO THE PROCESS THAT MADE HIM WHAT HE IS.
THE RAY... I'VE LEARNED HE'S A REPORTER...ANOTHER JOB THAT, WITH CURRENT EVENTS, CALLS FOR A LOT OF HIS TIME.
ISN'T THERE ONE OTHER OF YOU GUYS? DOLLMAN?
DARRELL? DARRELL'S CUTE. IN FACT, I'D LIKE TO SEE MORE OF THAT ONE.
IF IT WASN'T FOR THE ONE THORNY PROBLEM THAT HE'S SO IN LOVE WITH HIS GIRLFRIEND.
NO, I HAVE A LOT OF FUN AS SANDRA KNIGHT. AND WHEN THE NEED ARISES I FIGHT CRIME AS PHANTOM LADY. BUT SANDRA KNIGHT COMES FIRST.
THOUGH, I AM PLEASED THAT MY DECISION TO BECOME A SUPERHERO INSPIRED YOU TO FOLLOW MY LEAD AND BECOME ONE YOURSELF...
...AND YOU'VE GONE ON TO SUCH ACCLAIM.
HEY, DO YOU REMEMBER THE FIRST TIME WE WENT RIDING TOGETHER?
NO.
YOU FELL OFF. YOU BROKE YOUR ARM.
WAS THAT YOU I WAS WITH? I THOUGHT--

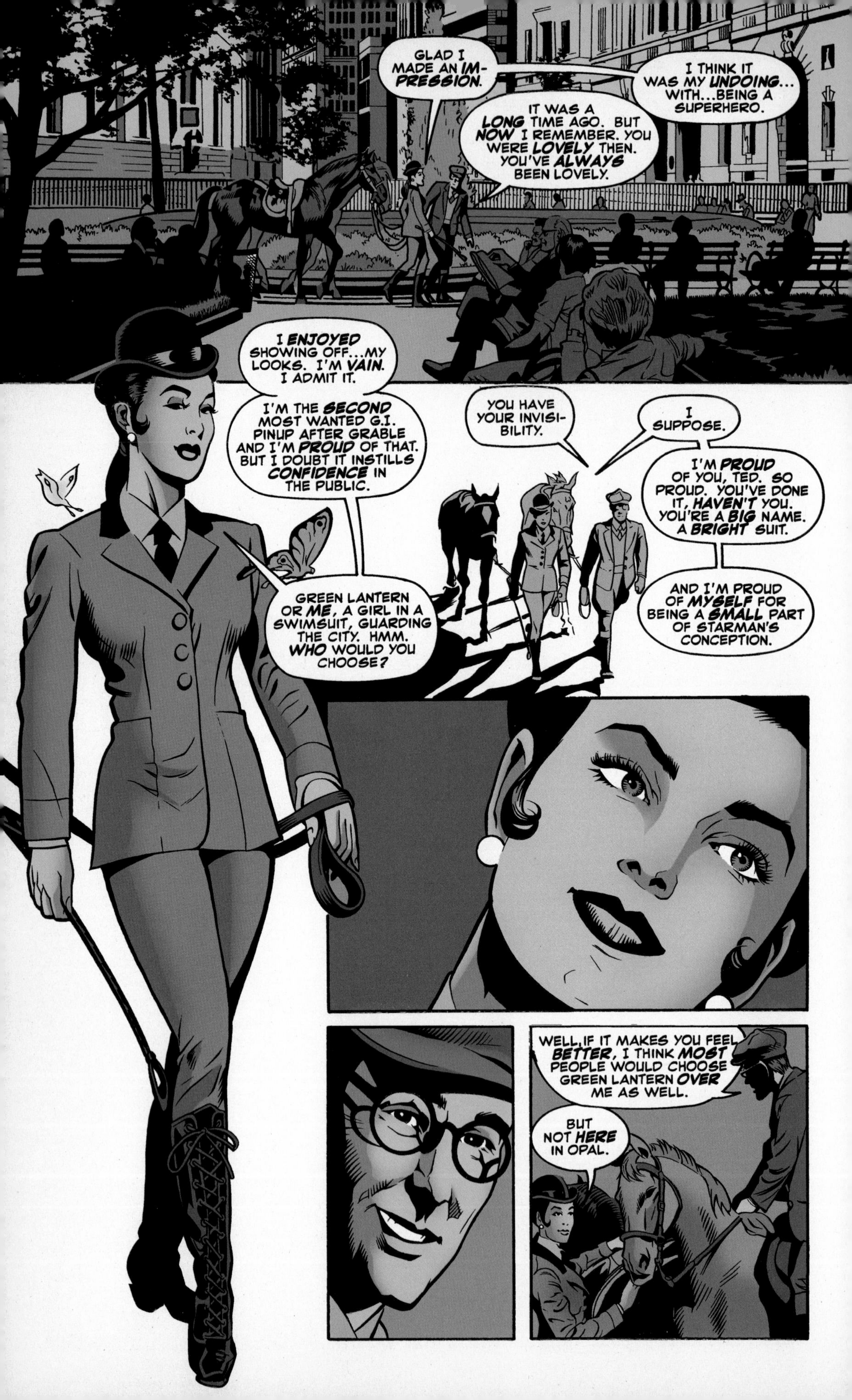
GLAD I MADE AN IM-PRESSION.
I THINK IT WAS MY UNDOING... WITH...BEING A SUPERHERO.
IT WAS A LONG TIME AGO. BUT NOW I REMEMBER. YOU WERE LOVELY THEN. YOU'VE ALWAYS BEEN LOVELY.
I ENJOYED SHOWING OFF...MY LOOKS. I'M VAIN. I ADMIT IT.
I'M THE SECOND MOST WANTED G.I. PINUP AFTER GRABLE AND I'M PROUD OF THAT. BUT I DOUBT IT INSTILLS CONFIDENCE IN THE PUBLIC.
GREEN LANTERN OR ME, A GIRL IN A SWIMSUIT, GUARDING THE CITY. HMM. WHO WOULD YOU CHOOSE?
YOU HAVE YOUR INVISI-BILITY.
I SUPPOSE.
I'M PROUD OF YOU, TED. SO PROUD. YOU'VE DONE IT, HAVEN'T YOU. YOU'RE A BIG NAME. A BRIGHT SUIT.
AND I'M PROUD OF MYSELF FOR BEING A SMALL PART OF STARMAN'S CONCEPTION.
WELL, IF IT MAKES YOU FEEL BETTER, I THINK MOST PEOPLE WOULD CHOOSE GREEN LANTERN OVER ME AS WELL.
BUT NOT HERE IN OPAL.

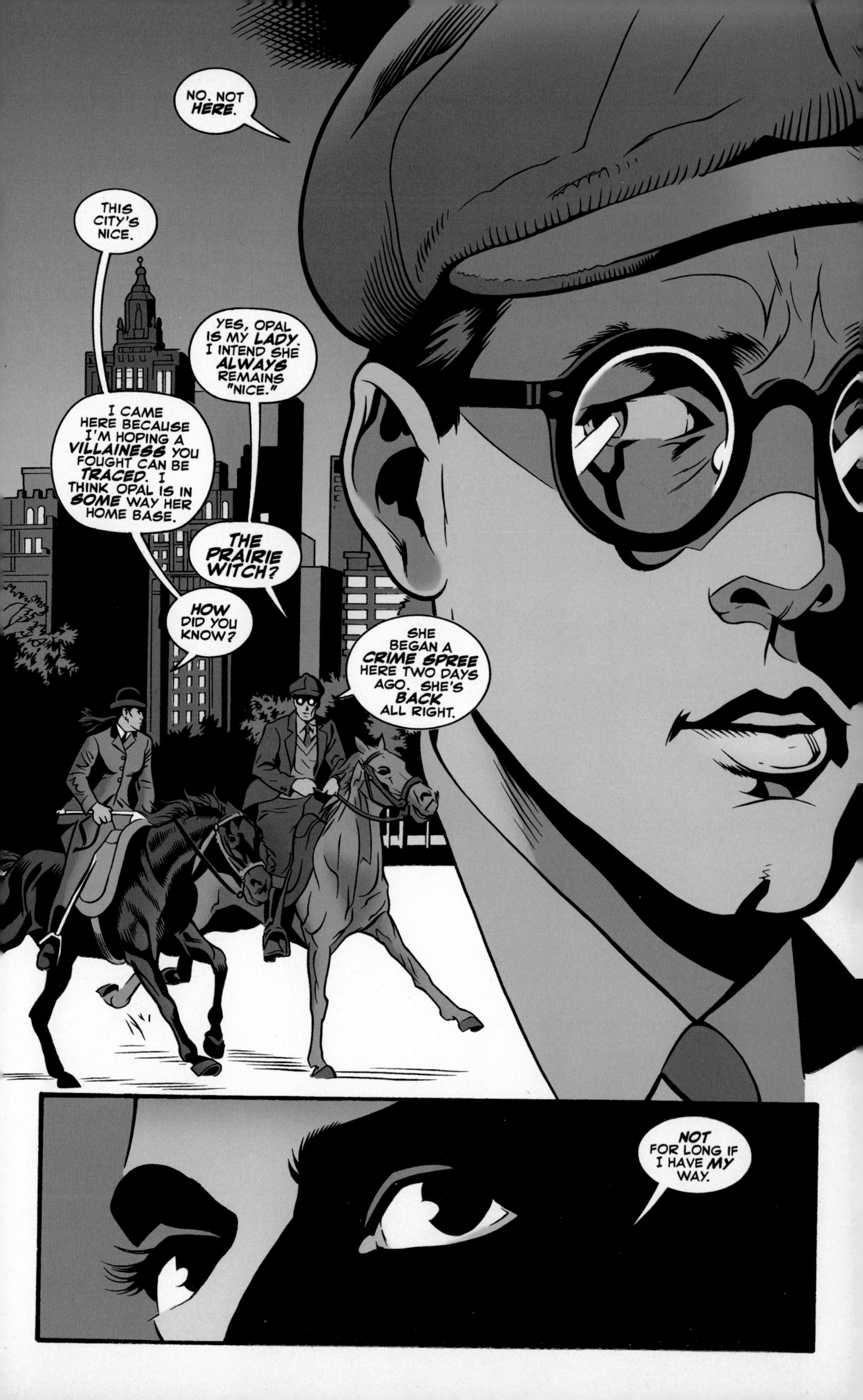
NO. NOT HERE.
THIS CITY'S NICE.
YES, OPAL IS MY LADY. I INTEND SHE ALWAYS REMAINS "NICE."
I CAME HERE BECAUSE I'M HOPING A VILLAINESS YOU FOUGHT CAN BE TRACED. I THINK OPAL IS IN SOME WAY HER HOME BASE.
THE PRAIRIE WITCH?
HOW DID YOU KNOW?
SHE BEGAN A CRIME SPREE HERE TWO DAYS AGO. SHE'S BACK ALL RIGHT.
NOT FOR LONG IF I HAVE MY WAY.

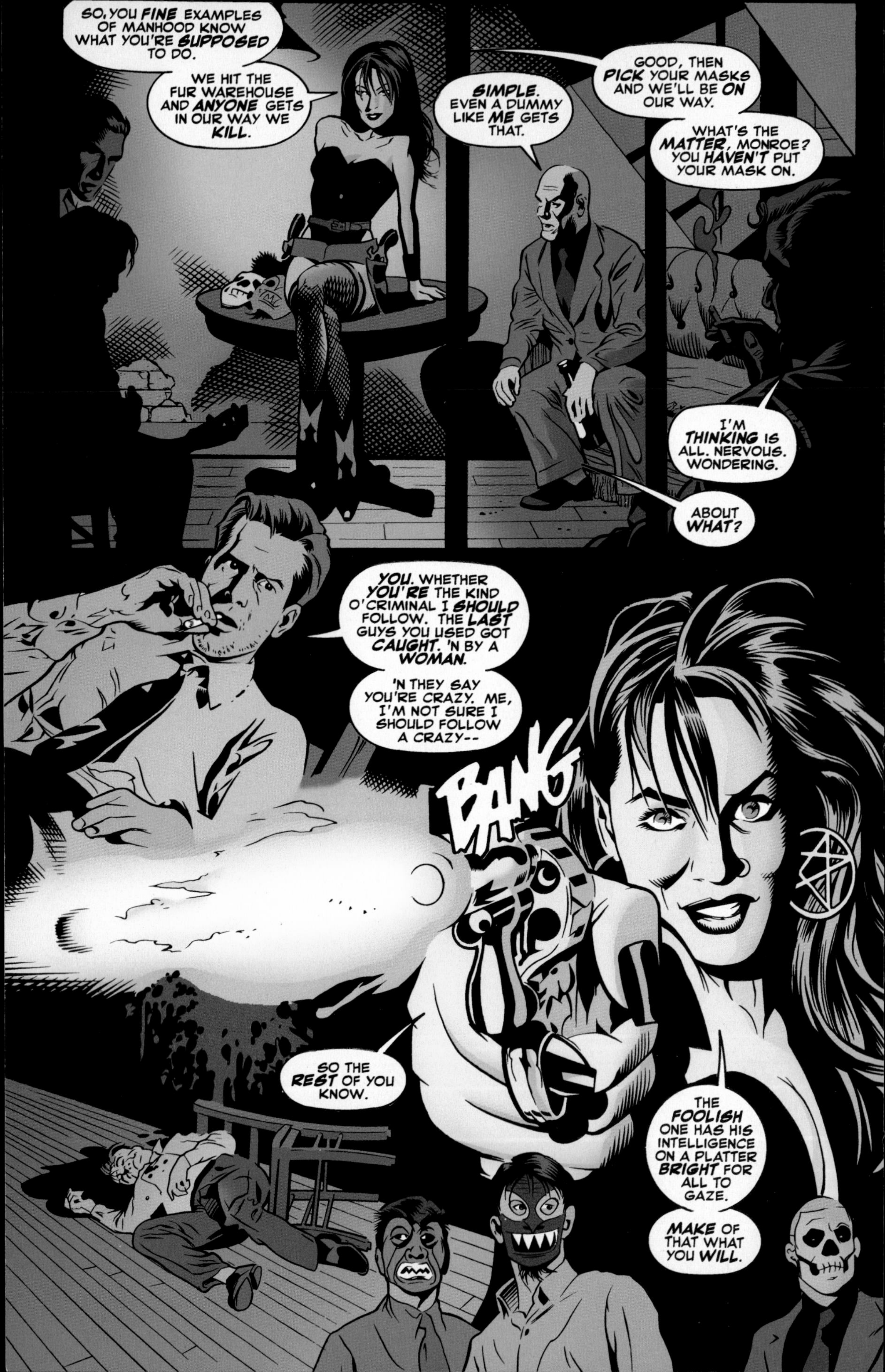
SO, YOU FINE EXAMPLES OF MANHOOD KNOW WHAT YOU'RE SUPPOSED TO DO.
WE HIT THE FUR WAREHOUSE AND ANYONE GETS IN OUR WAY WE KILL.
SIMPLE. EVEN A DUMMY LIKE ME GETS THAT.
GOOD, THEN PICK YOUR MASKS AND WE'LL BE ON OUR WAY.
WHAT'S THE MATTER, MONROE? YOU HAVEN'T PUT YOUR MASK ON.
I'M THINKING IS ALL. NERVOUS. WONDERING.
ABOUT WHAT?
YOU. WHETHER YOU'RE THE KIND O'CRIMINAL I SHOULD FOLLOW. THE LAST GUYS YOU USED GOT CAUGHT. 'N BY A WOMAN.
'N THEY SAY YOU'RE CRAZY. ME, I'M NOT SURE I SHOULD FOLLOW A CRAZY--
BANG
SO THE REST OF YOU KNOW.
THE FOOLISH ONE HAS HIS INTELLIGENCE ON A PLATTER BRIGHT FOR ALL TO GAZE.
MAKE OF THAT WHAT YOU WILL.

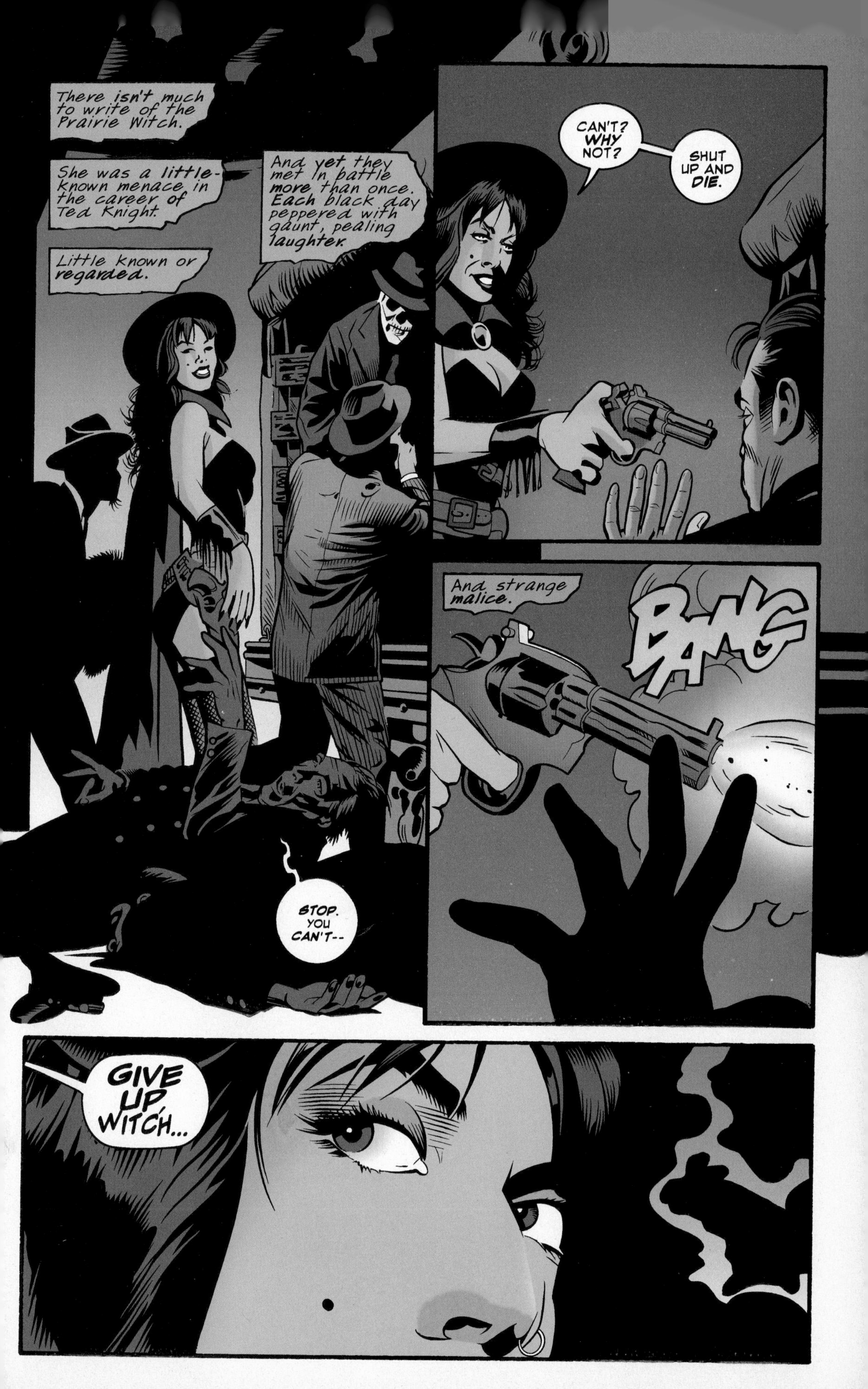
There isn't much to write of the Prairie Witch.
She was a little-known menace in the career of Ted Knight.
Little known or regarded.
And yet they met in battle more than once. Each black day peppered with gaunt, pealing laughter.
STOP. YOU CAN'T--
CAN'T? WHY NOT?
SHUT UP AND DIE.
And strange malice.
BANG
GIVE UP, WITCH...

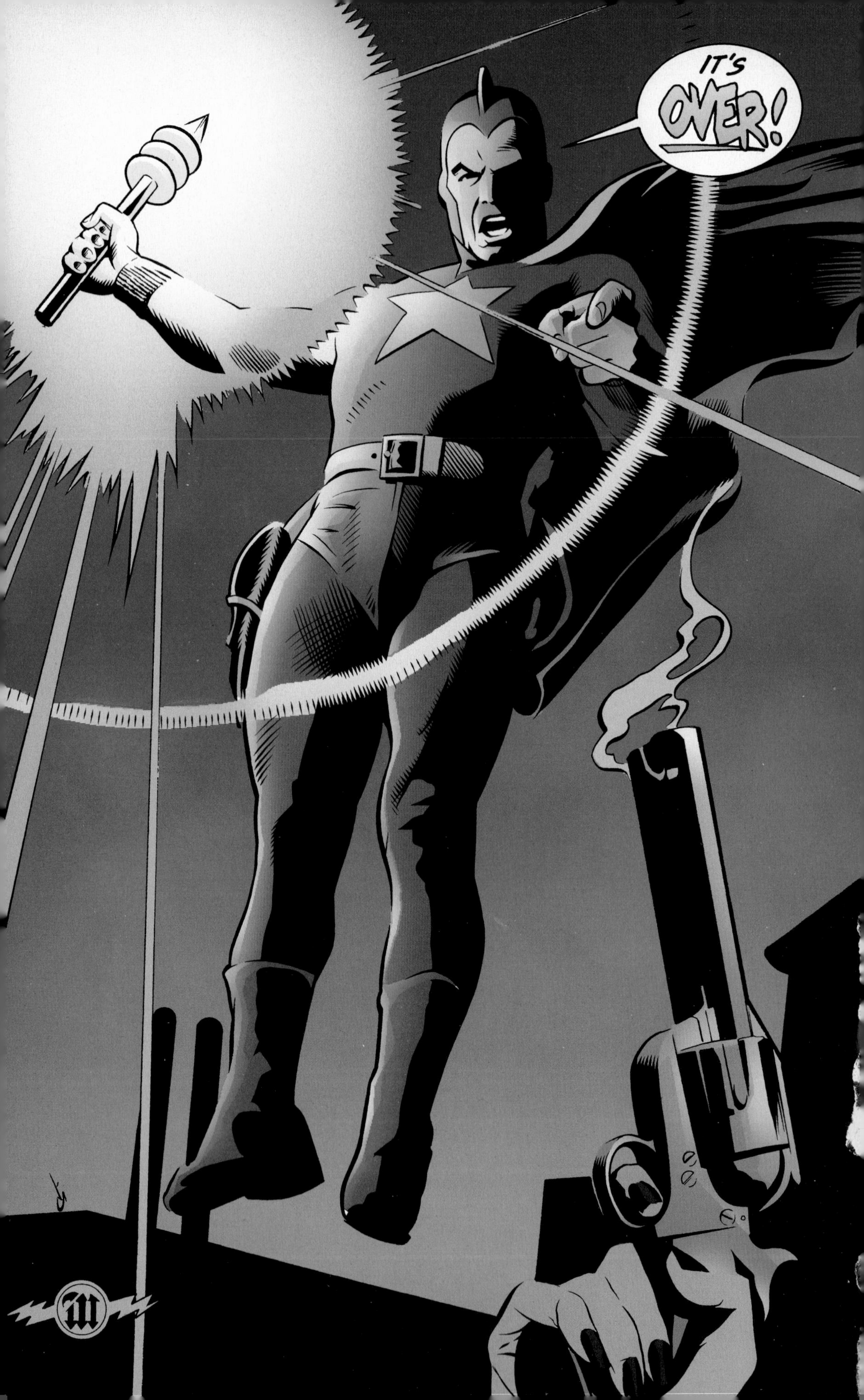
IT'S OVER!

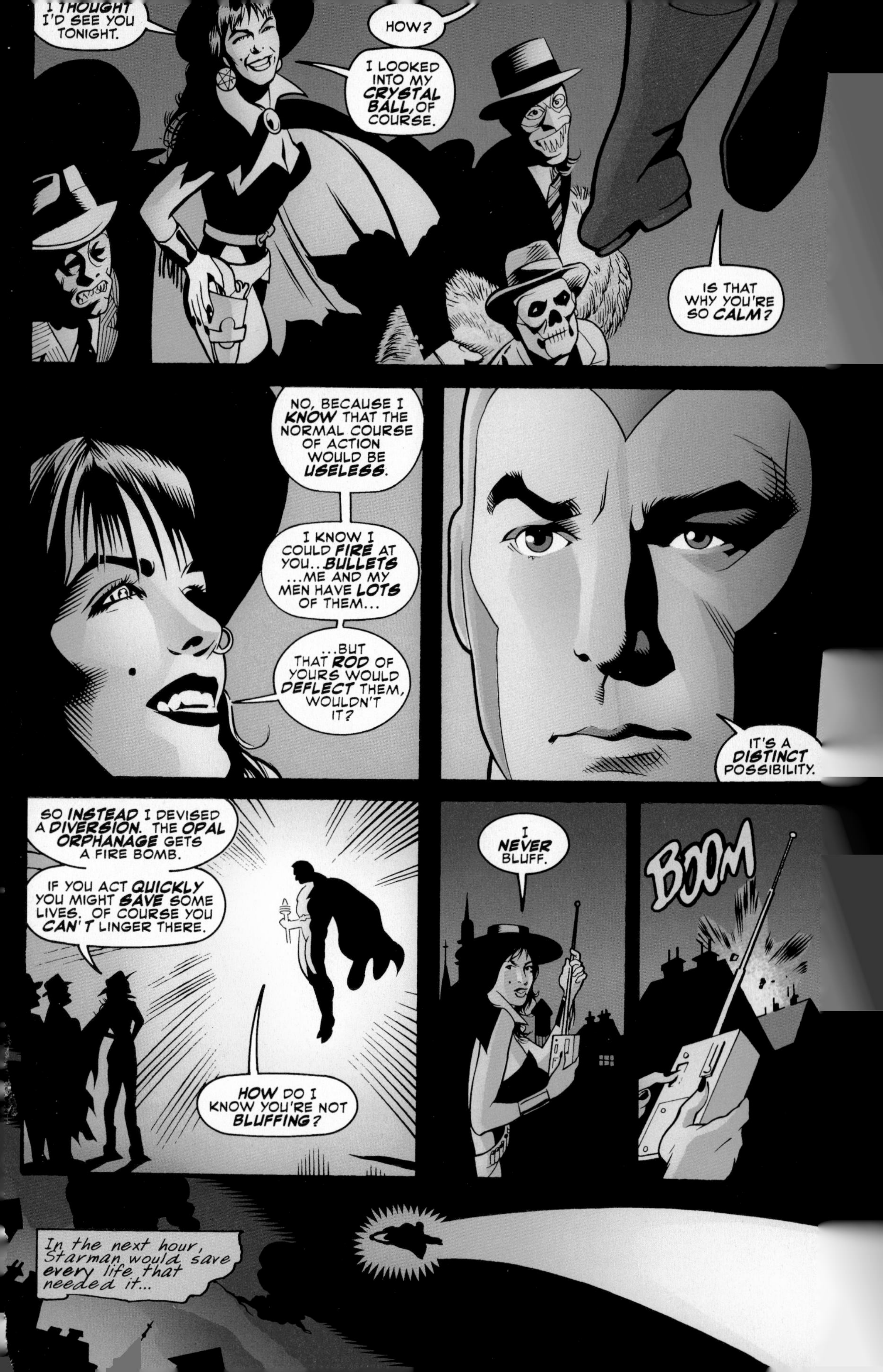
I THOUGHT I'D SEE YOU TONIGHT.
HOW?
I LOOKED INTO MY CRYSTAL BALL, OF COURSE.
IS THAT WHY YOU'RE SO CALM?
NO, BECAUSE I KNOW THAT THE NORMAL COURSE OF ACTION WOULD BE USELESS.
I KNOW I COULD FIRE AT YOU...BULLETS ...ME AND MY MEN HAVE LOTS OF THEM...
...BUT THAT ROD OF YOURS WOULD DEFLECT THEM, WOULDN'T IT?
IT'S A DISTINCT POSSIBILITY.
SO INSTEAD I DEVISED A DIVERSION. THE OPAL ORPHANAGE GETS A FIRE BOMB.
IF YOU ACT QUICKLY YOU MIGHT SAVE SOME LIVES. OF COURSE YOU CAN'T LINGER THERE.
HOW DO I KNOW YOU'RE NOT BLUFFING?
I NEVER BLUFF.
BOOM
In the next hour, Starman would save every life that needed it...

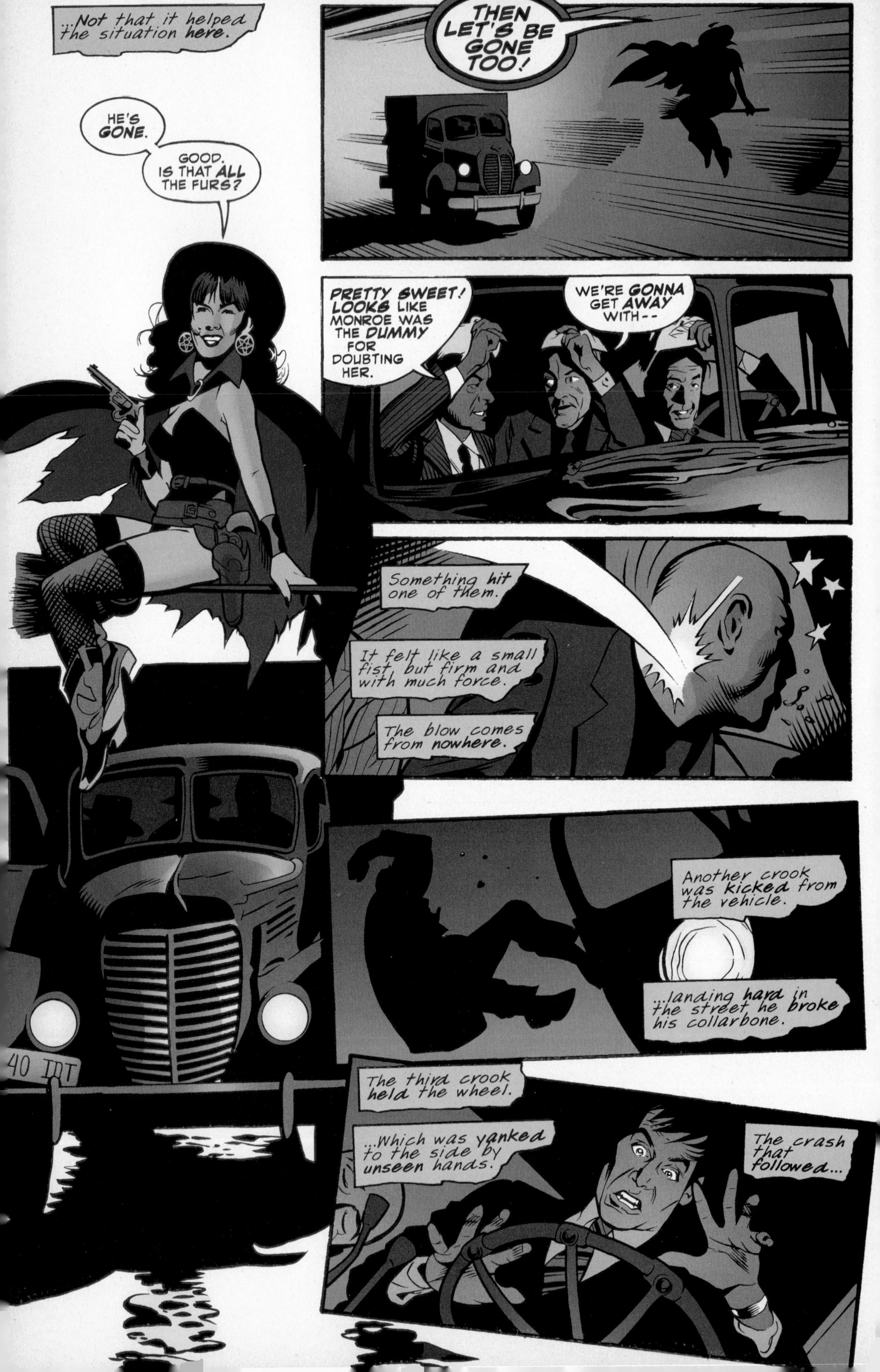
...Not that it helped the situation here.
HE'S GONE.
GOOD. IS THAT ALL THE FURS?
THEN LET'S BE GONE TOO!
PRETTY SWEET! LOOKS LIKE MONROE WAS THE DUMMY FOR DOUBTING HER.
WE'RE GONNA GET AWAY WITH--
Something hit one of them.
It felt like a small fist, but firm and with much force.
The blow comes from nowhere.
Another crook was kicked from the vehicle.
...landing hard in the street he broke his collarbone.
The third crook held the wheel.
...Which was yanked to the side by unseen hands.
The crash that followed...

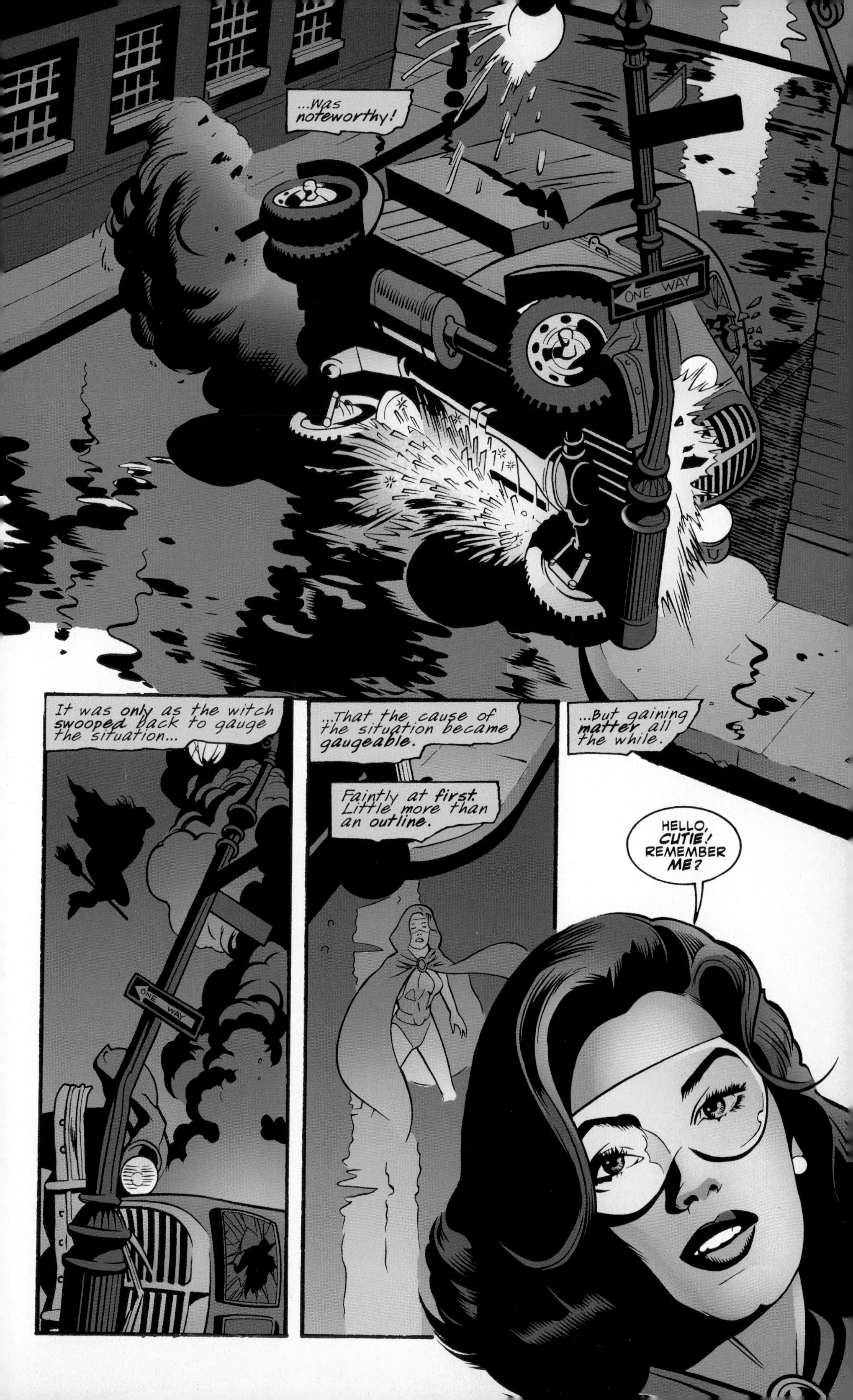
...Was noteworthy!
ONE WAY
It was only as the witch swooped back to gauge the situation...
ONE WAY
...That the cause of the situation became gaugeable.
Faintly at first. Little more than an outline.
...But gaining matter all the while.
HELLO, CUTIE! REMEMBER ME?

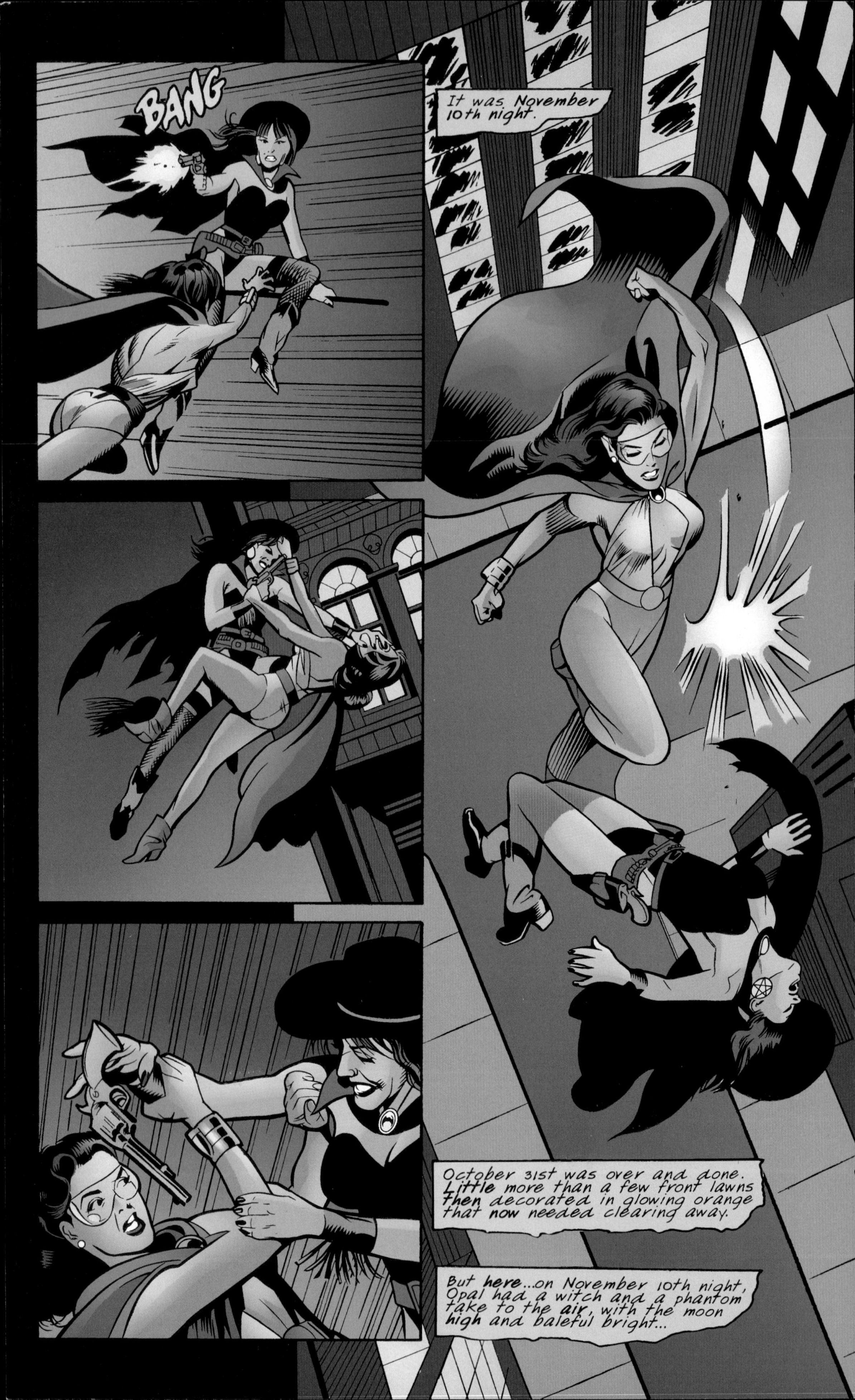
BANG
It was November 10th night.
October 31st was over and done. Little more than a few front lawns then decorated in glowing orange that now needed clearing away.
But here...on November 10th night, Opal had a witch and a phantom take to the air, with the moon high and baleful bright...

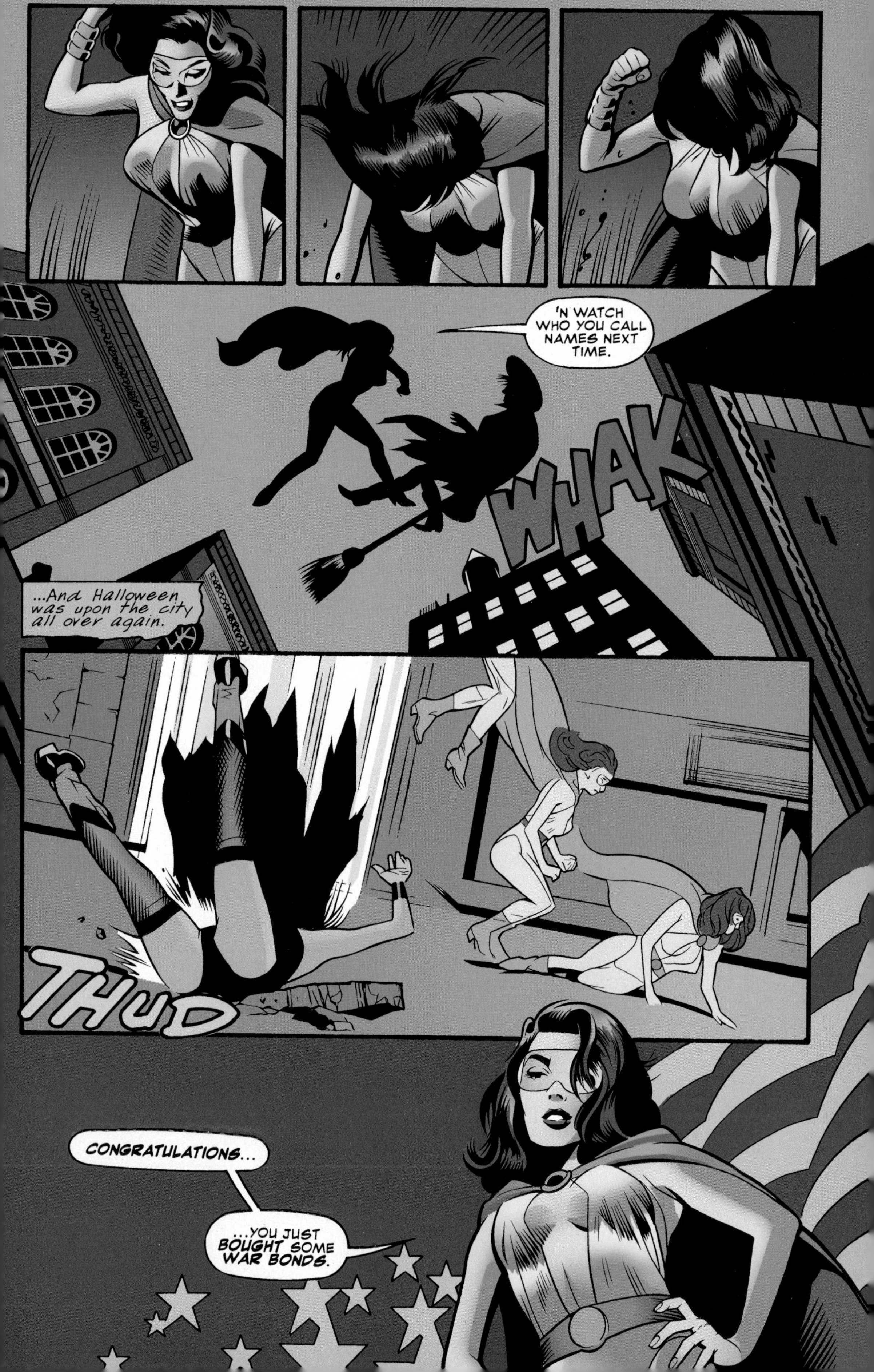
'N WATCH WHO YOU CALL NAMES NEXT TIME.
WHAK
...And Halloween was upon the city all over again.
THUD
CONGRATULATIONS...
...YOU JUST BOUGHT SOME WAR BONDS.

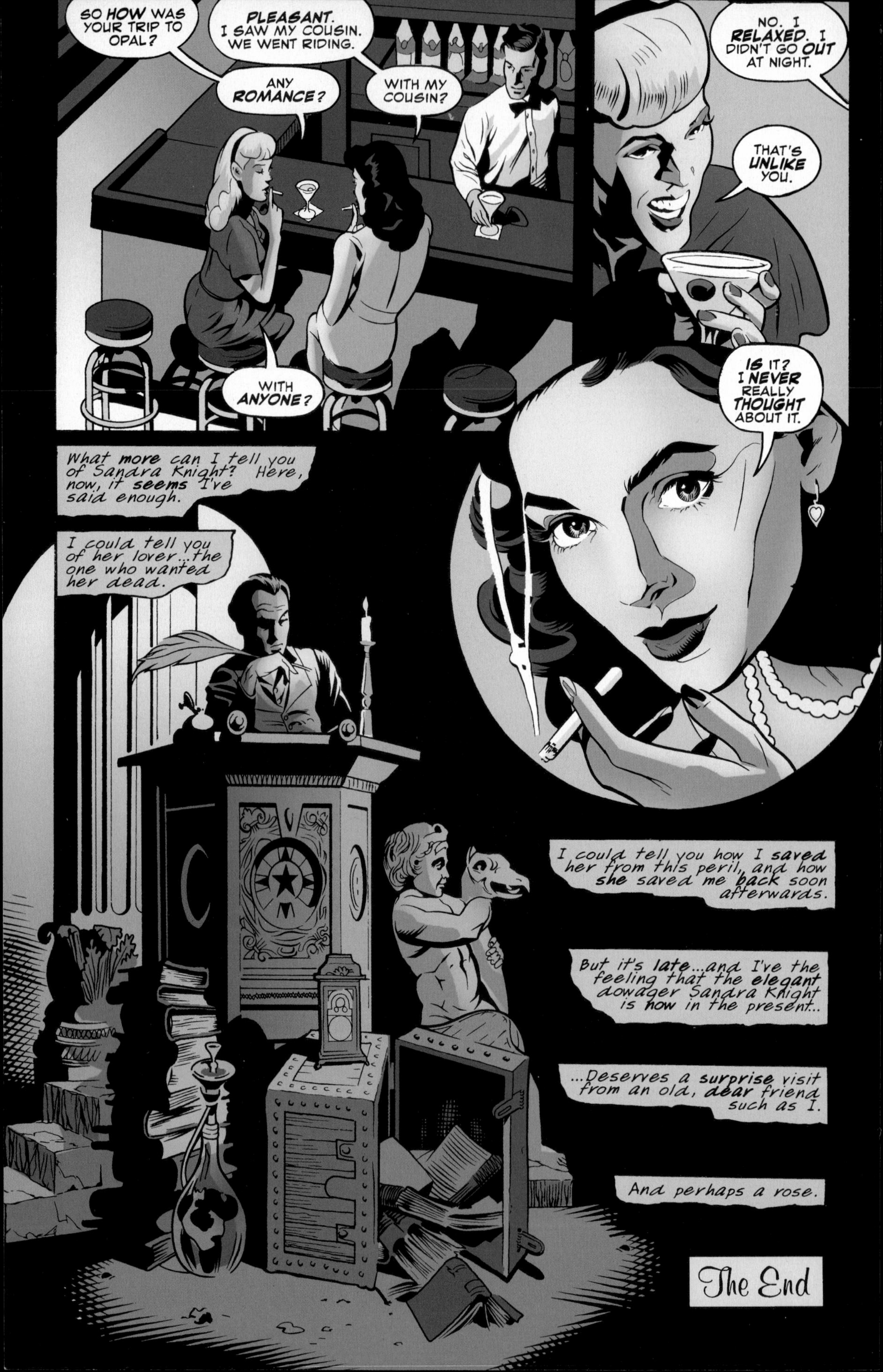

SO HOW WAS YOUR TRIP TO OPAL?
PLEASANT. I SAW MY COUSIN. WE WENT RIDING.
ANY ROMANCE?
WITH MY COUSIN?
WITH ANYONE?
NO. I RELAXED. I DIDN'T GO OUT AT NIGHT.
THAT'S UNLIKE YOU.
IS IT? I NEVER REALLY THOUGHT ABOUT IT.
What more can I tell you of Sandra Knight? Here, now, it seems I've said enough.
I could tell you of her lover...the one who wanted her dead.
I could tell you how I saved her from this peril, and how she saved me back soon afterwards.
But it's late...and I've the feeling that the elegant dowager Sandra Knight is now in the present...
...Deserves a surprise visit from an old, dear friend such as I.
And perhaps a rose.
The End

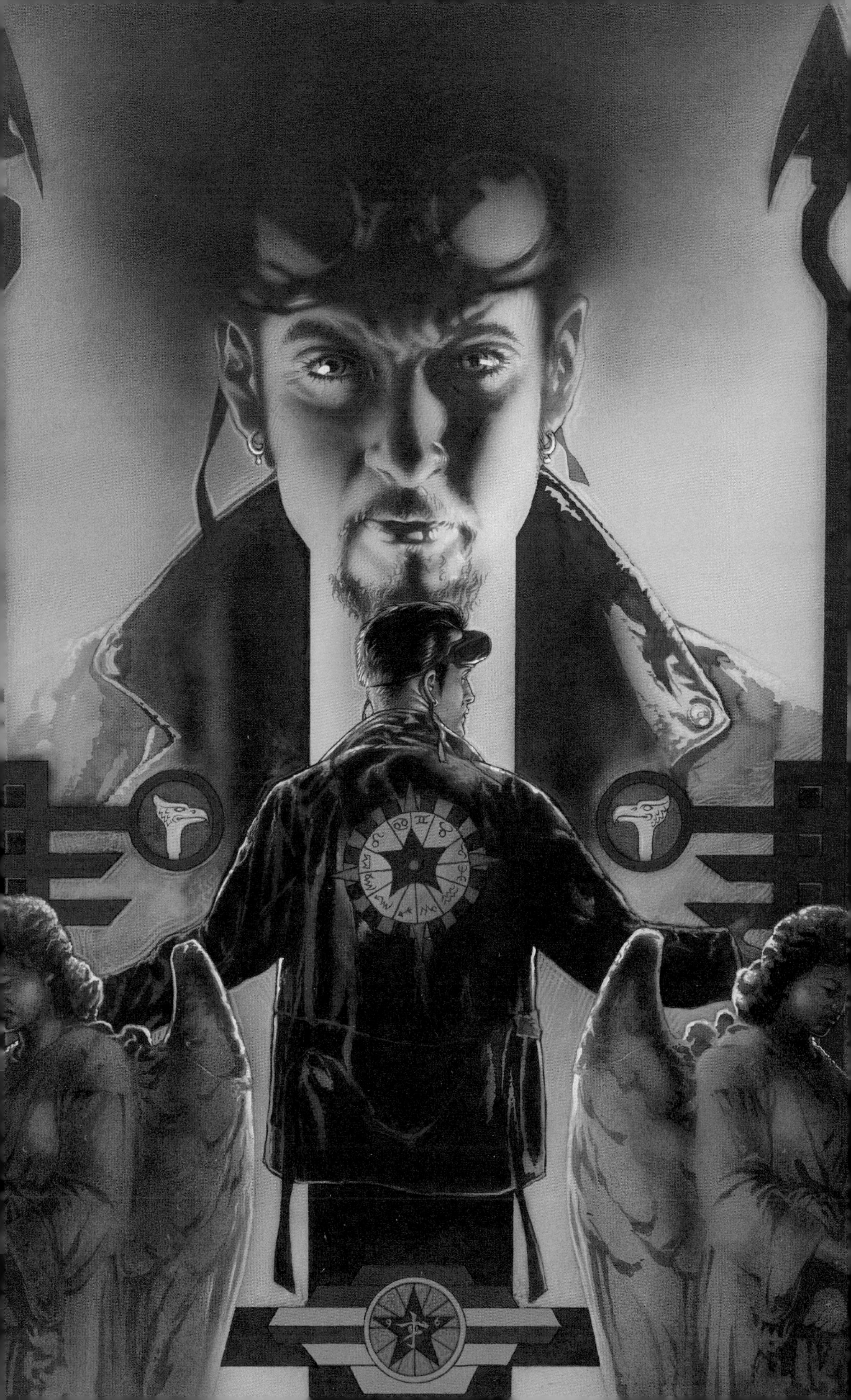

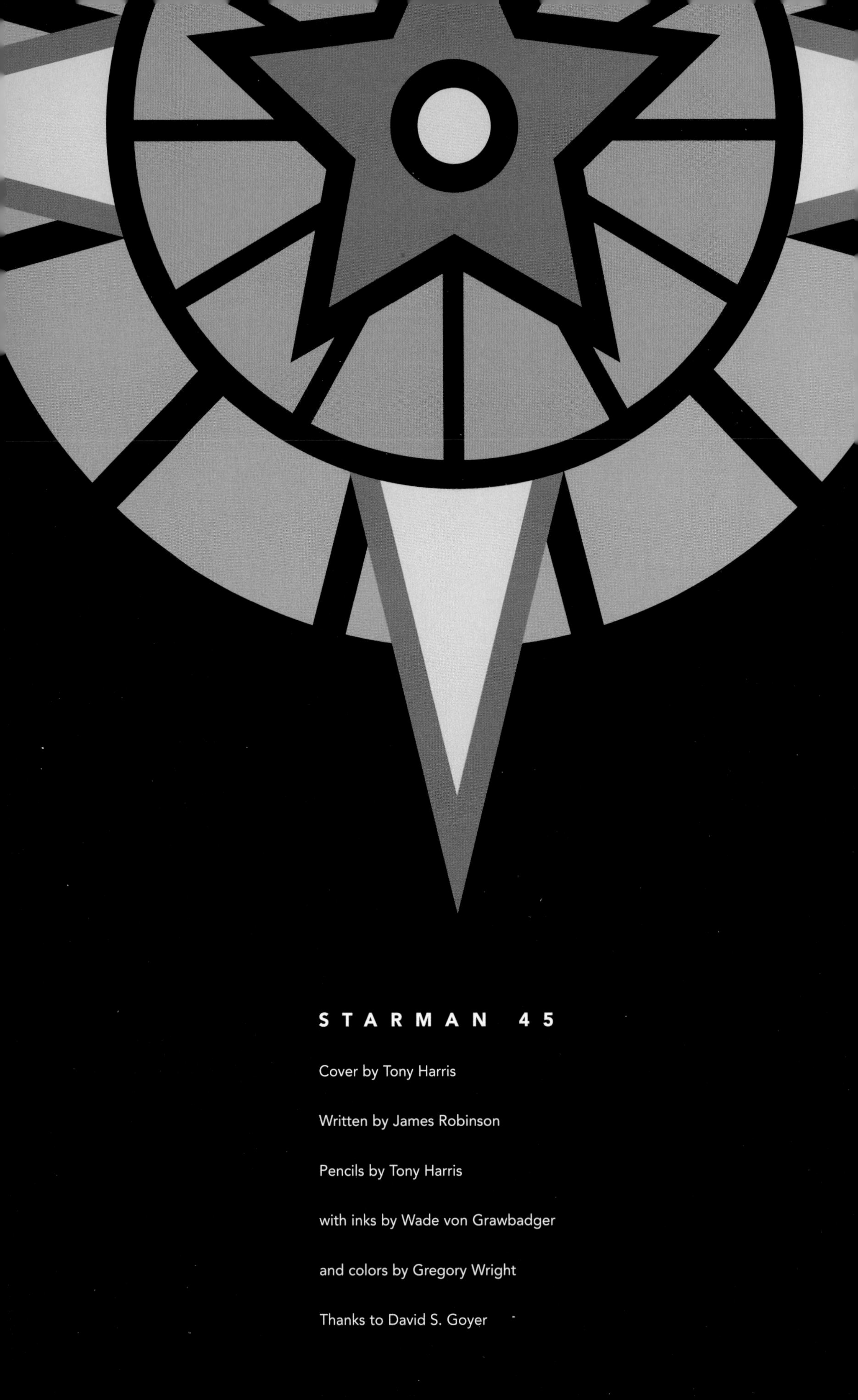

S T A R M A N   4 5

Cover by Tony Harris

Written by James Robinson

Pencils by Tony Harris

with inks by Wade von Grawbadger

and colors by Gregory Wright

Thanks to David S. Goyer

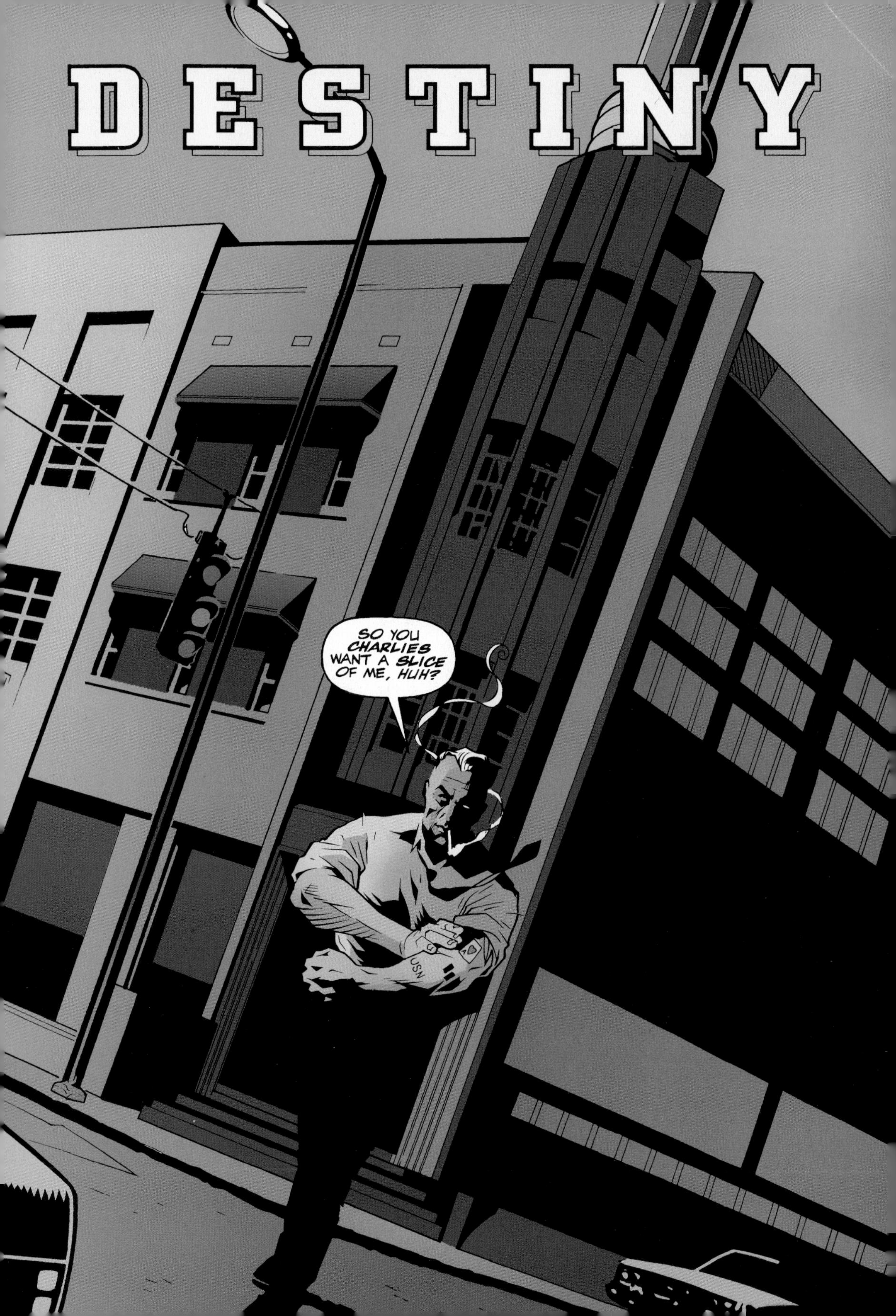
DESTINY
SO YOU CHARLIES WANT A SLICE OF ME, HUH?
USN

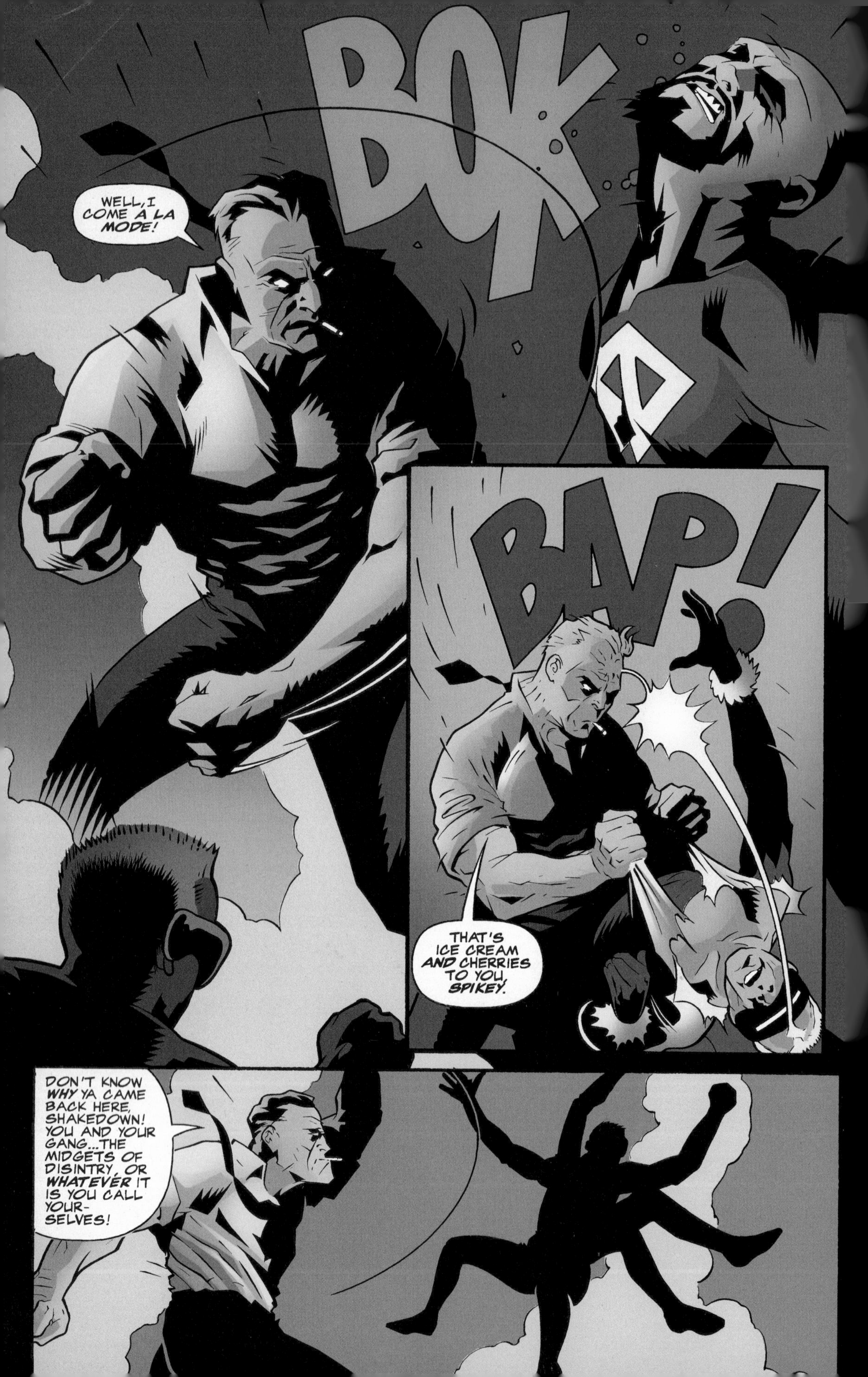
BOK
WELL, I COME A LA MODE!
BAP!
THAT'S ICE CREAM AND CHERRIES TO YOU, SPIKEY.
DON'T KNOW WHY YA CAME BACK HERE, SHAKEDOWN! YOU AND YOUR GANG...THE MIDGETS OF DISINTRY, OR WHATEVER IT IS YOU CALL YOUR-SELVES!

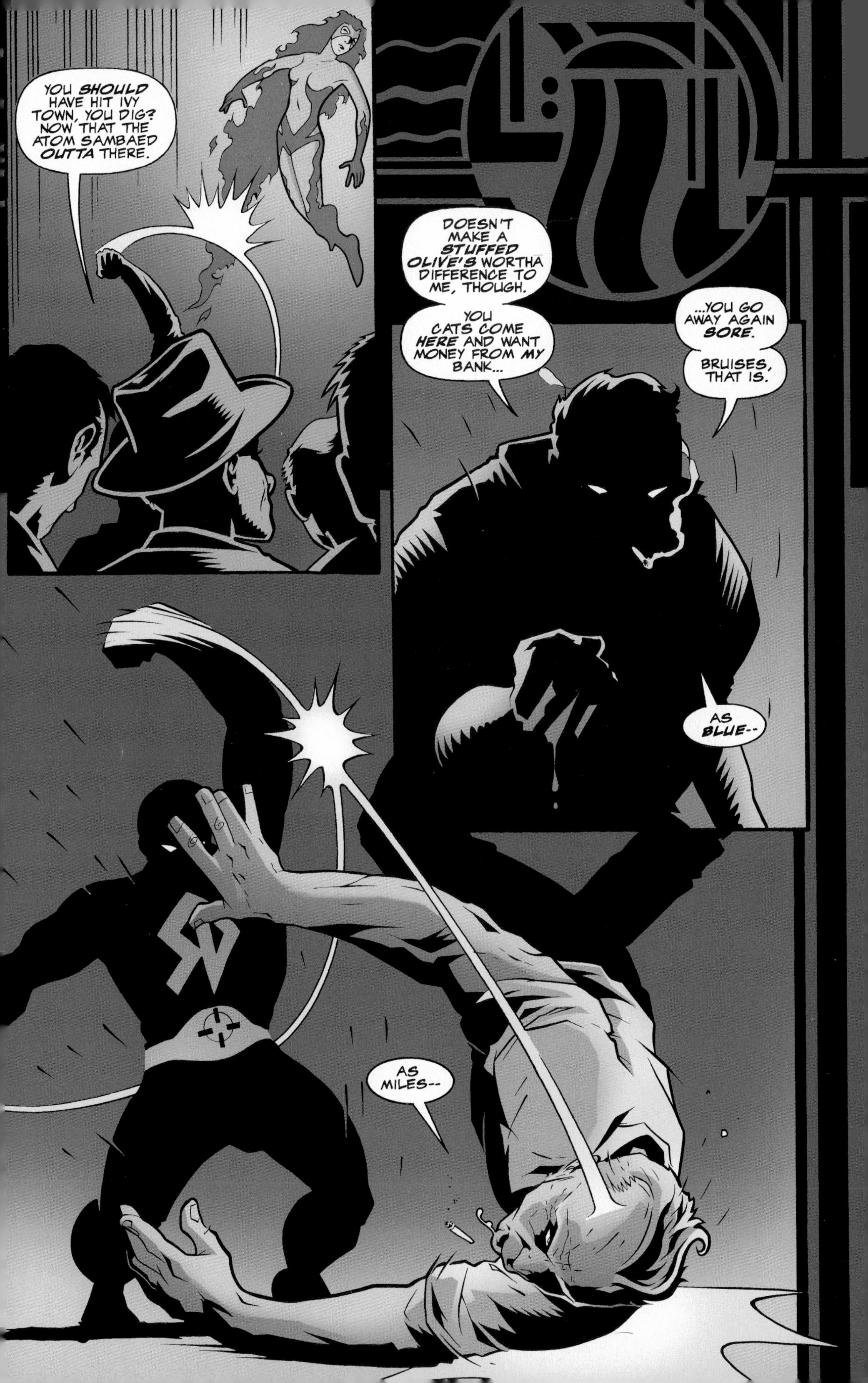
YOU SHOULD HAVE HIT IVY TOWN, YOU DIG? NOW THAT THE ATOM SAMBAED OUTTA THERE.
DOESN'T MAKE A STUFFED OLIVE'S WORTHA DIFFERENCE TO ME, THOUGH.
YOU CATS COME HERE AND WANT MONEY FROM MY BANK...
...YOU GO AWAY AGAIN SORE.
BRUISES, THAT IS.
AS BLUE--
AS MILES--

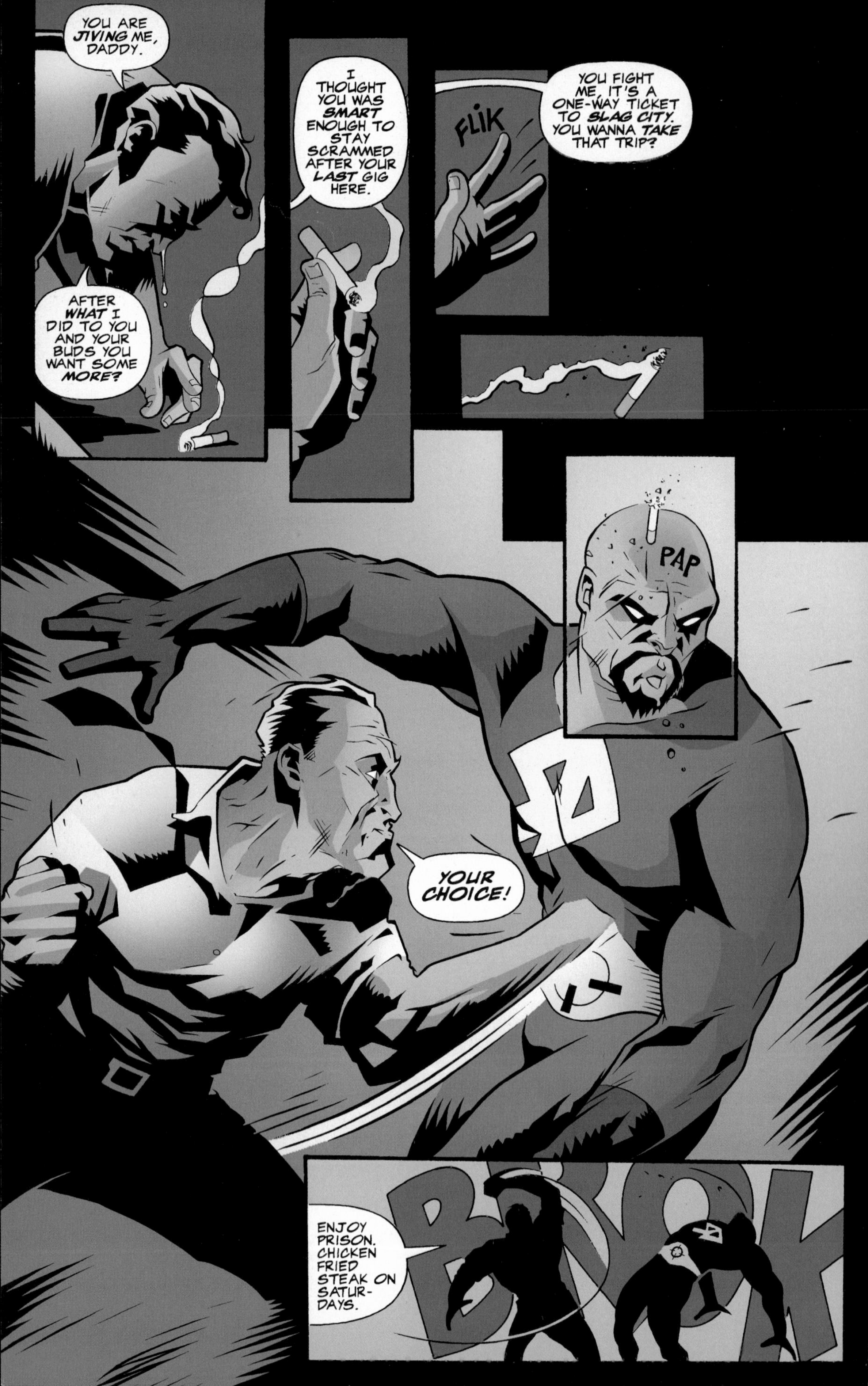
YOU ARE JIVING ME, DADDY.
AFTER WHAT I DID TO YOU AND YOUR BUDS YOU WANT SOME MORE?
I THOUGHT YOU WAS SMART ENOUGH TO STAY SCRAMMED AFTER YOUR LAST GIG HERE.
FLIK
YOU FIGHT ME, IT'S A ONE-WAY TICKET TO SLAG CITY. YOU WANNA TAKE THAT TRIP?
PAP
YOUR CHOICE!
ENJOY PRISON. CHICKEN FRIED STEAK ON SATUR-DAYS.

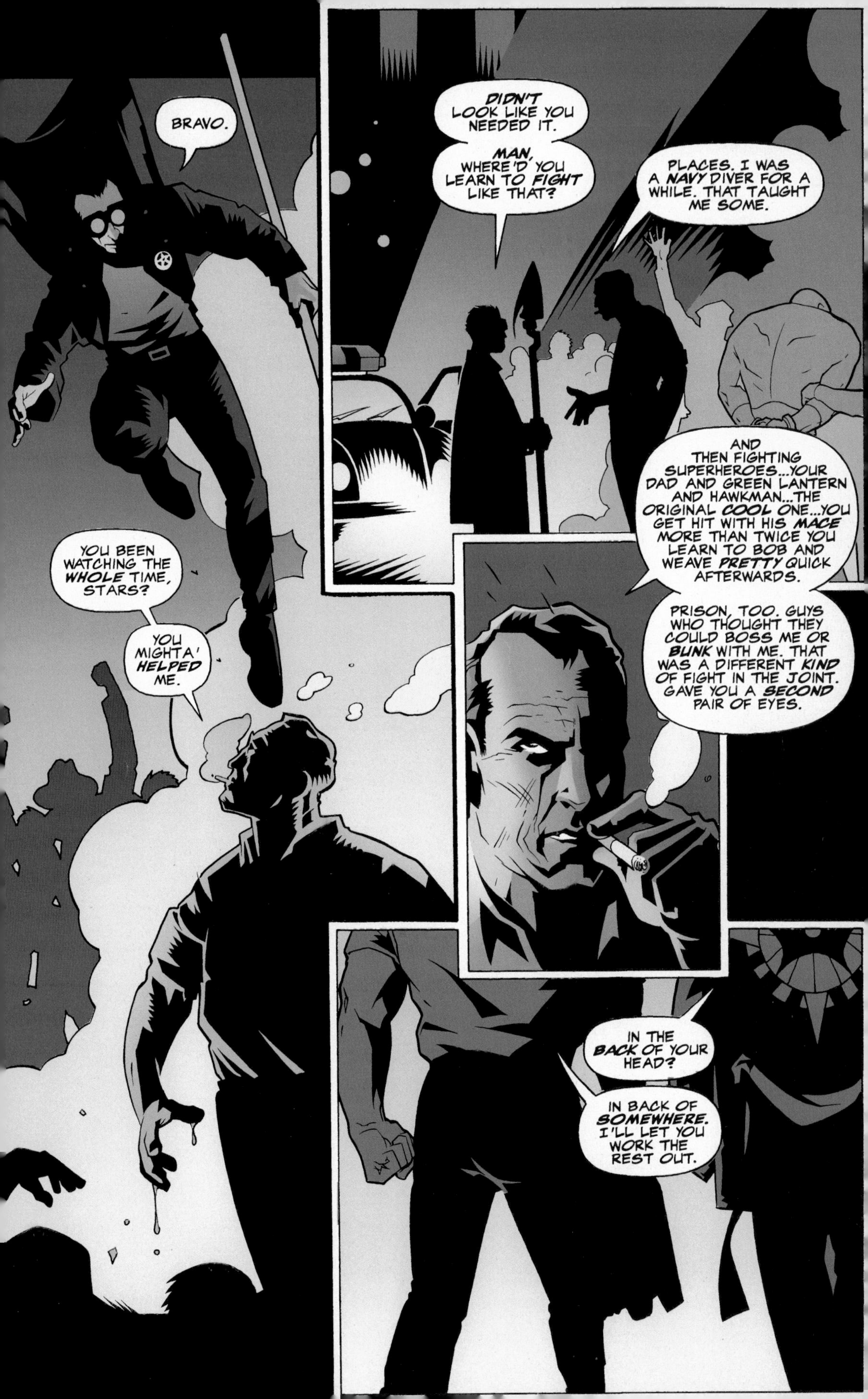

BRAVO.
YOU BEEN WATCHING THE WHOLE TIME, STARS?
YOU MIGHTA' HELPED ME.
DIDN'T LOOK LIKE YOU NEEDED IT.
MAN, WHERE'D YOU LEARN TO FIGHT LIKE THAT?
PLACES. I WAS A NAVY DIVER FOR A WHILE. THAT TAUGHT ME SOME.
AND THEN FIGHTING SUPERHEROES...YOUR DAD AND GREEN LANTERN AND HAWKMAN...THE ORIGINAL COOL ONE...YOU GET HIT WITH HIS MACE MORE THAN TWICE YOU LEARN TO BOB AND WEAVE PRETTY QUICK AFTERWARDS.
PRISON, TOO. GUYS WHO THOUGHT THEY COULD BOSS ME OR BUNK WITH ME. THAT WAS A DIFFERENT KIND OF FIGHT IN THE JOINT. GAVE YOU A SECOND PAIR OF EYES.
IN THE BACK OF YOUR HEAD?
IN BACK OF SOMEWHERE. I'LL LET YOU WORK THE REST OUT.

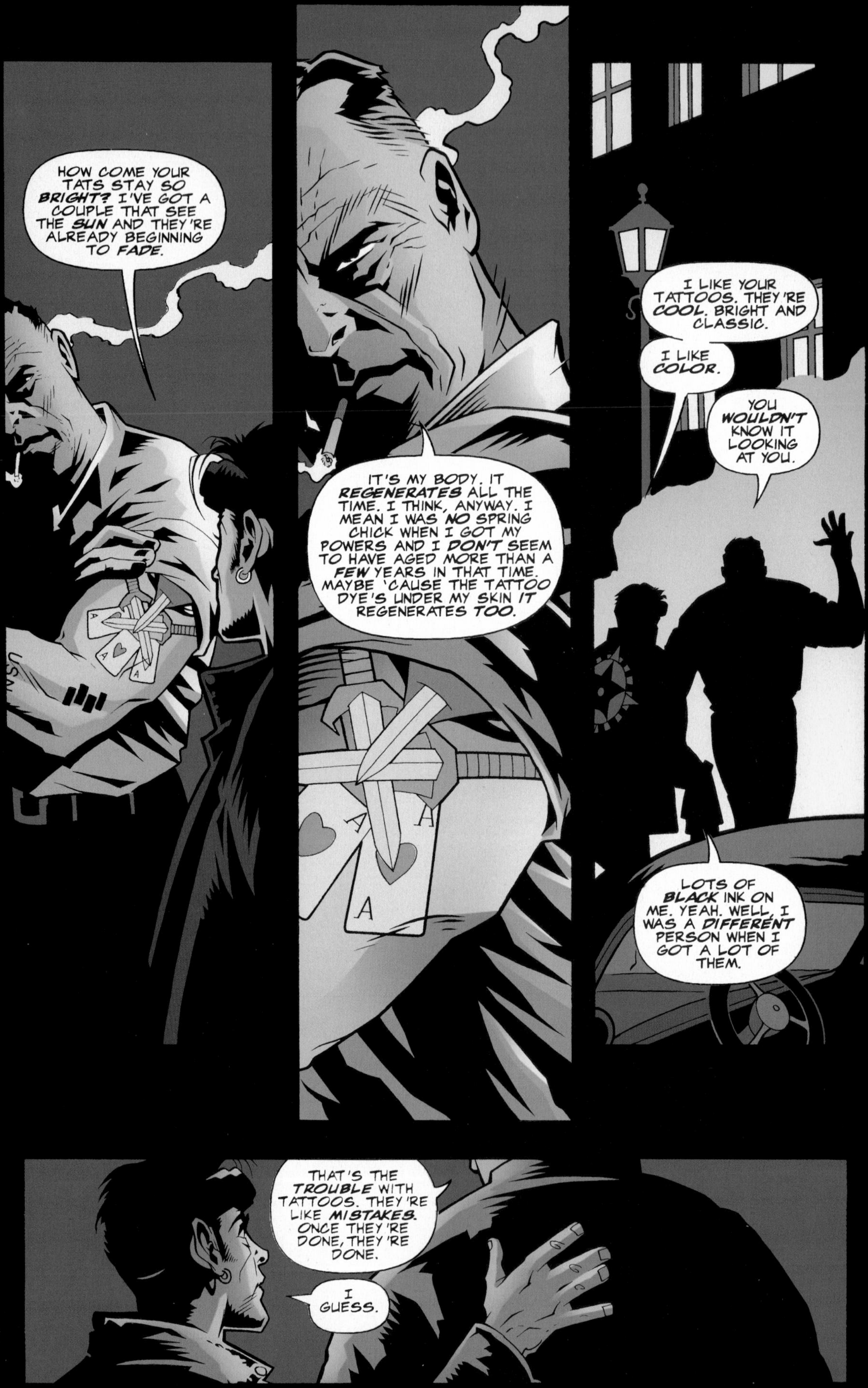

HOW COME YOUR TATS STAY SO BRIGHT? I'VE GOT A COUPLE THAT SEE THE SUN AND THEY'RE ALREADY BEGINNING TO FADE.
IT'S MY BODY. IT REGENERATES ALL THE TIME. I THINK, ANYWAY. I MEAN I WAS NO SPRING CHICK WHEN I GOT MY POWERS AND I DON'T SEEM TO HAVE AGED MORE THAN A FEW YEARS IN THAT TIME. MAYBE 'CAUSE THE TATTOO DYE'S UNDER MY SKIN IT REGENERATES TOO.
I LIKE YOUR TATTOOS. THEY'RE COOL. BRIGHT AND CLASSIC.
I LIKE COLOR.
YOU WOULDN'T KNOW IT LOOKING AT YOU.
LOTS OF BLACK INK ON ME. YEAH. WELL, I WAS A DIFFERENT PERSON WHEN I GOT A LOT OF THEM.
THAT'S THE TROUBLE WITH TATTOOS. THEY'RE LIKE MISTAKES. ONCE THEY'RE DONE, THEY'RE DONE.
I GUESS.

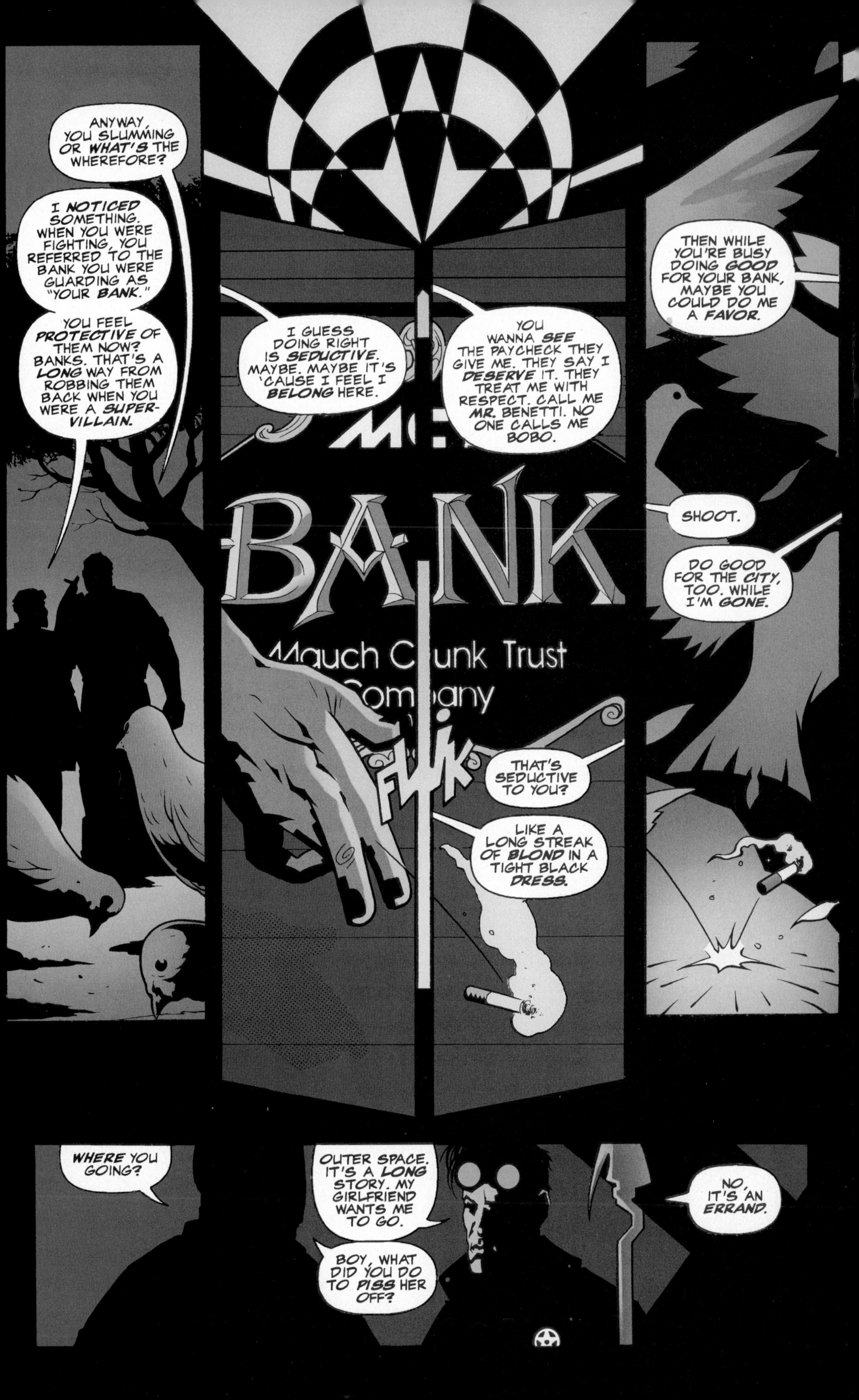

ANYWAY, YOU SLUMMING OR WHAT'S THE WHEREFORE?
I NOTICED SOMETHING. WHEN YOU WERE FIGHTING, YOU REFERRED TO THE BANK YOU WERE GUARDING AS "YOUR BANK."
YOU FEEL PROTECTIVE OF THEM NOW? BANKS. THAT'S A LONG WAY FROM ROBBING THEM BACK WHEN YOU WERE A SUPER-VILLAIN.
I GUESS DOING RIGHT IS SEDUCTIVE. MAYBE. MAYBE IT'S 'CAUSE I FEEL I BELONG HERE.
YOU WANNA SEE THE PAYCHECK THEY GIVE ME. THEY SAY I DESERVE IT. THEY TREAT ME WITH RESPECT. CALL ME MR. BENETTI. NO ONE CALLS ME BOBO.
THEN WHILE YOU'RE BUSY DOING GOOD FOR YOUR BANK, MAYBE YOU COULD DO ME A FAVOR.
BANK
Mauch Chunk Trust Company
SHOOT.
DO GOOD FOR THE CITY, TOO. WHILE I'M GONE.
FLIK
THAT'S SEDUCTIVE TO YOU?
LIKE A LONG STREAK OF BLOND IN A TIGHT BLACK DRESS.
WHERE YOU GOING?
OUTER SPACE. IT'S A LONG STORY. MY GIRLFRIEND WANTS ME TO GO.
BOY, WHAT DID YOU DO TO PISS HER OFF?
NO, IT'S AN ERRAND.

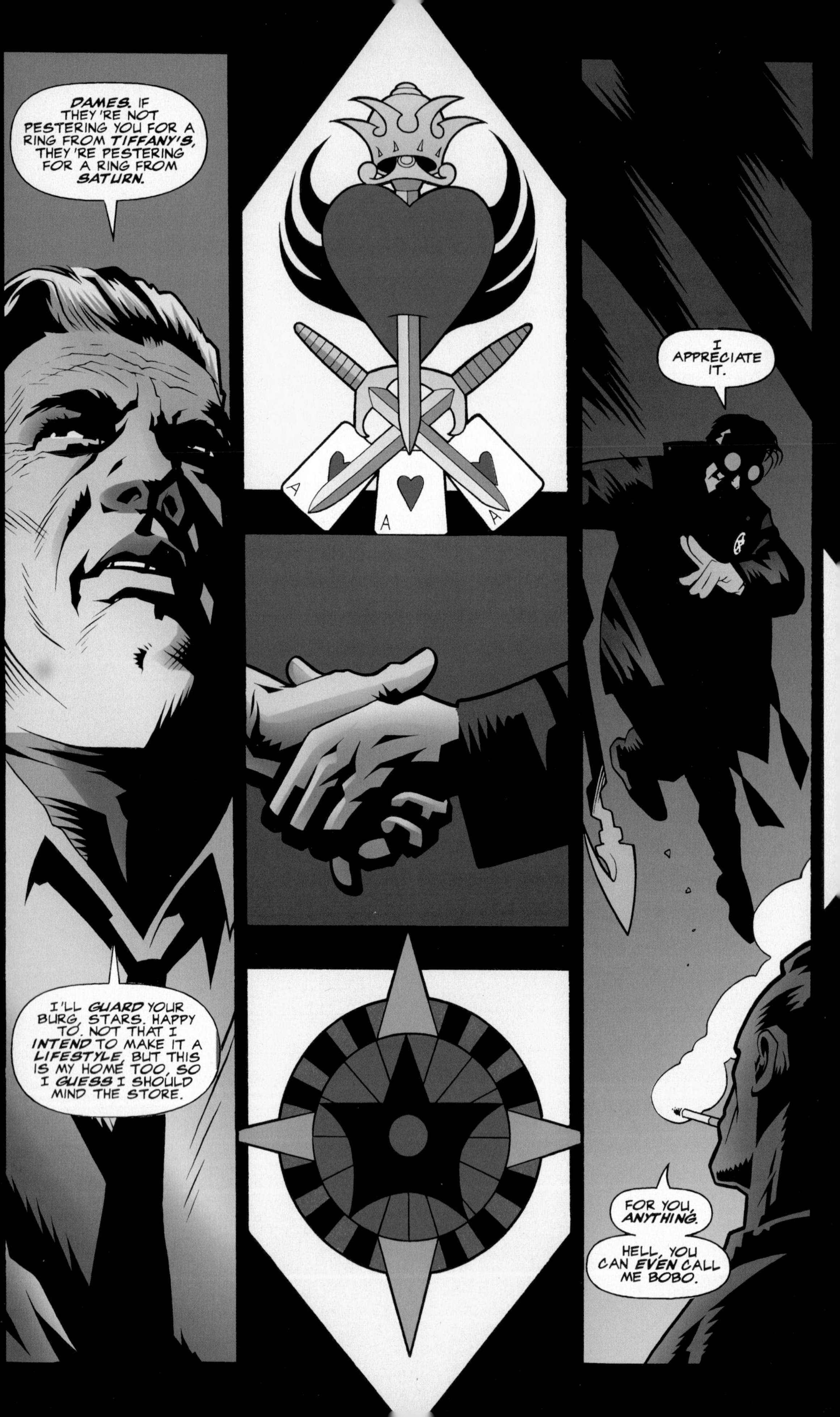
DAMES. IF THEY'RE NOT PESTERING YOU FOR A RING FROM TIFFANY'S, THEY'RE PESTERING FOR A RING FROM SATURN.
I'LL GUARD YOUR BURG, STARS. HAPPY TO. NOT THAT I INTEND TO MAKE IT A LIFESTYLE, BUT THIS IS MY HOME TOO, SO I GUESS I SHOULD MIND THE STORE.
I APPRECIATE IT.
FOR YOU, ANYTHING.
HELL, YOU CAN EVEN CALL ME BOBO.

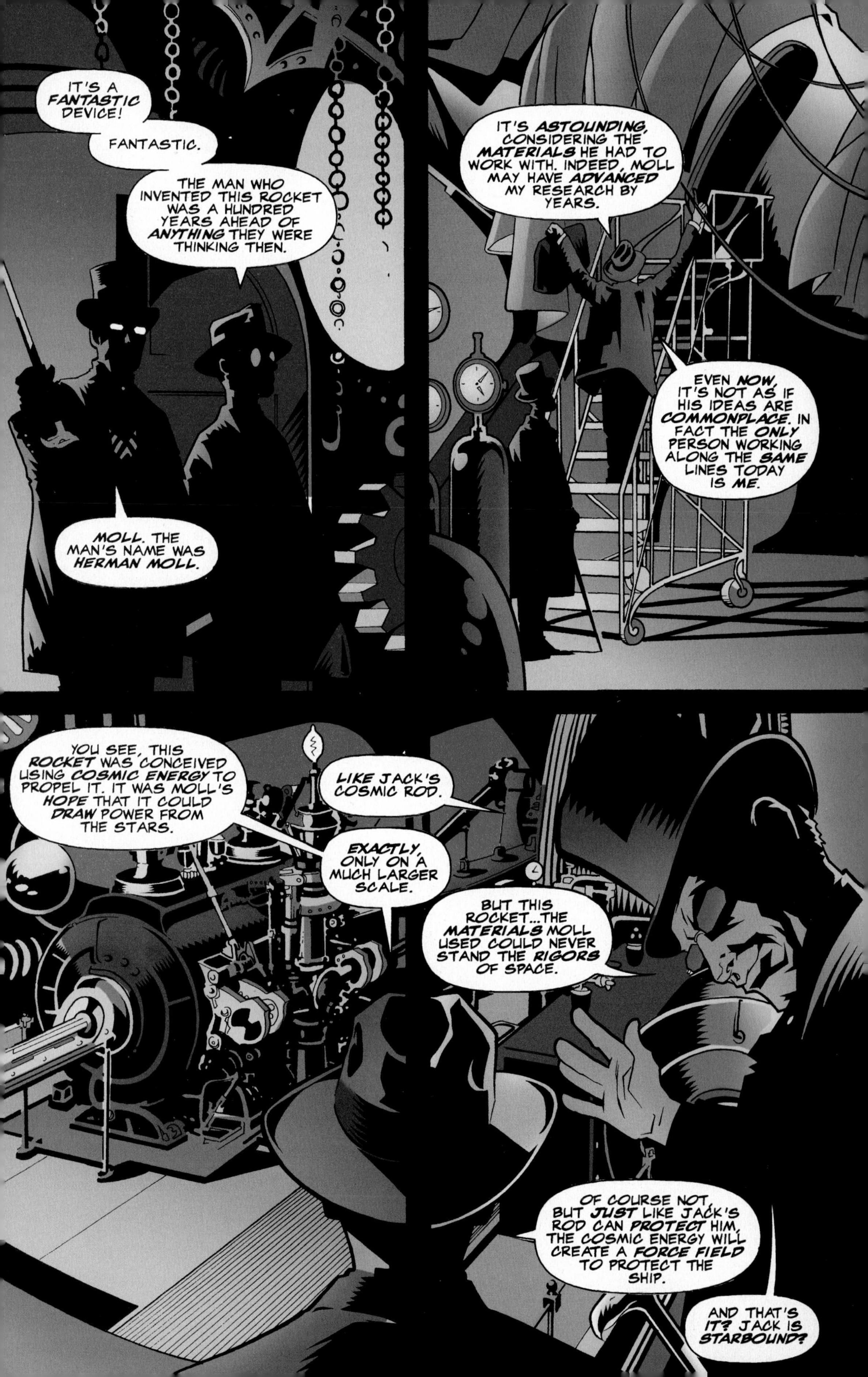

IT'S A FANTASTIC DEVICE!
FANTASTIC.
THE MAN WHO INVENTED THIS ROCKET WAS A HUNDRED YEARS AHEAD OF ANYTHING THEY WERE THINKING THEN.
MOLL. THE MAN'S NAME WAS HERMAN MOLL.
IT'S ASTOUNDING, CONSIDERING THE MATERIALS HE HAD TO WORK WITH. INDEED, MOLL MAY HAVE ADVANCED MY RESEARCH BY YEARS.
EVEN NOW, IT'S NOT AS IF HIS IDEAS ARE COMMONPLACE. IN FACT THE ONLY PERSON WORKING ALONG THE SAME LINES TODAY IS ME.
YOU SEE, THIS ROCKET WAS CONCEIVED USING COSMIC ENERGY TO PROPEL IT. IT WAS MOLL'S HOPE THAT IT COULD DRAW POWER FROM THE STARS.
LIKE JACK'S COSMIC ROD.
EXACTLY, ONLY ON A MUCH LARGER SCALE.
BUT THIS ROCKET...THE MATERIALS MOLL USED COULD NEVER STAND THE RIGORS OF SPACE.
OF COURSE NOT, BUT JUST LIKE JACK'S ROD CAN PROTECT HIM, THE COSMIC ENERGY WILL CREATE A FORCE FIELD TO PROTECT THE SHIP.
AND THAT'S IT? JACK IS STARBOUND?

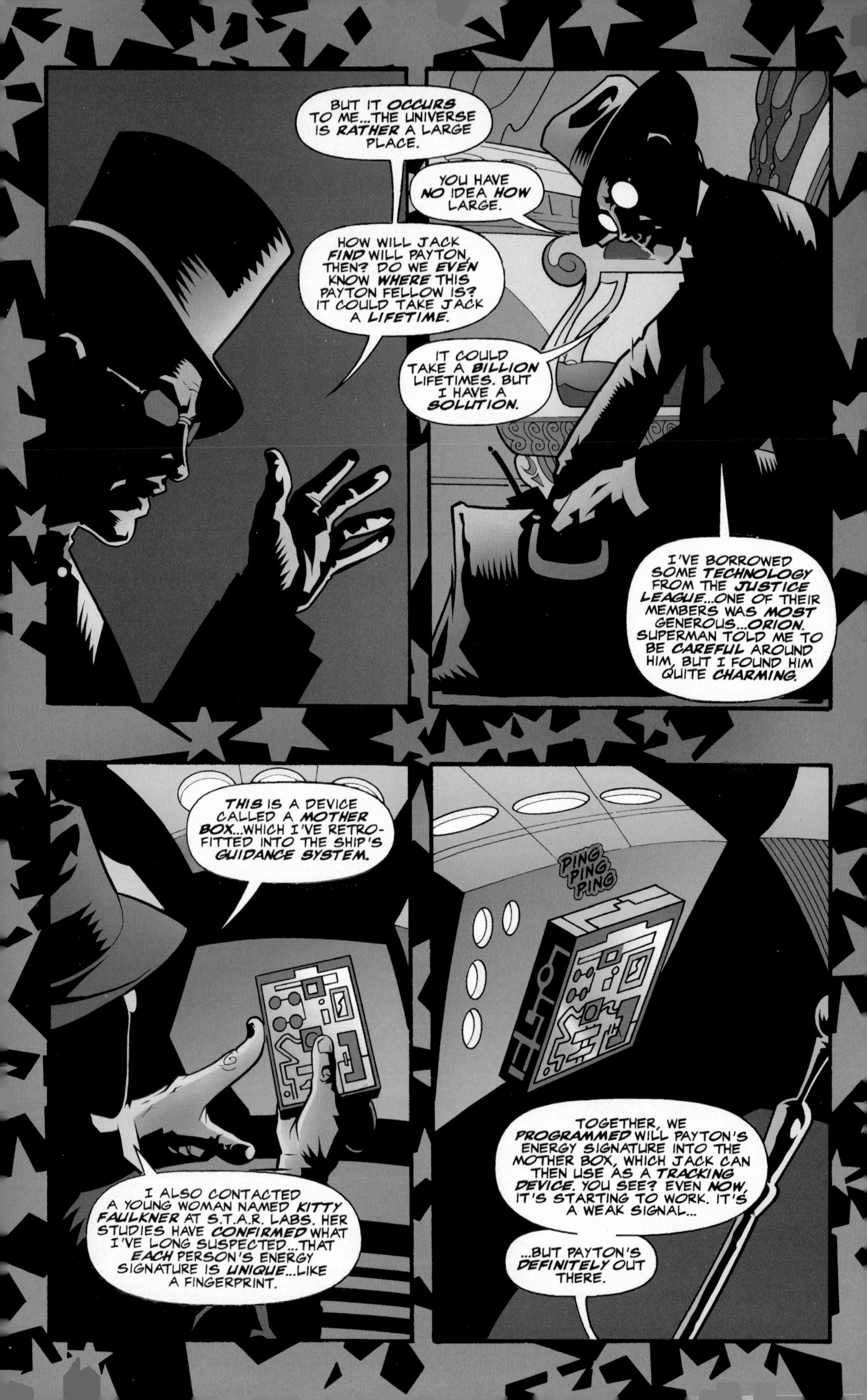
BUT IT OCCURS TO ME...THE UNIVERSE IS RATHER A LARGE PLACE.
YOU HAVE NO IDEA HOW LARGE.
HOW WILL JACK FIND WILL PAYTON, THEN? DO WE EVEN KNOW WHERE THIS PAYTON FELLOW IS? IT COULD TAKE JACK A LIFETIME.
IT COULD TAKE A BILLION LIFETIMES. BUT I HAVE A SOLUTION.
I'VE BORROWED SOME TECHNOLOGY FROM THE JUSTICE LEAGUE...ONE OF THEIR MEMBERS WAS MOST GENEROUS...ORION. SUPERMAN TOLD ME TO BE CAREFUL AROUND HIM, BUT I FOUND HIM QUITE CHARMING.
THIS IS A DEVICE CALLED A MOTHER BOX...WHICH I'VE RETRO-FITTED INTO THE SHIP'S GUIDANCE SYSTEM.
I ALSO CONTACTED A YOUNG WOMAN NAMED KITTY FAULKNER AT S.T.A.R. LABS. HER STUDIES HAVE CONFIRMED WHAT I'VE LONG SUSPECTED...THAT EACH PERSON'S ENERGY SIGNATURE IS UNIQUE...LIKE A FINGERPRINT.
PING PING PING
TOGETHER, WE PROGRAMMED WILL PAYTON'S ENERGY SIGNATURE INTO THE MOTHER BOX, WHICH JACK CAN THEN USE AS A TRACKING DEVICE. YOU SEE? EVEN NOW, IT'S STARTING TO WORK. IT'S A WEAK SIGNAL...
...BUT PAYTON'S DEFINITELY OUT THERE.

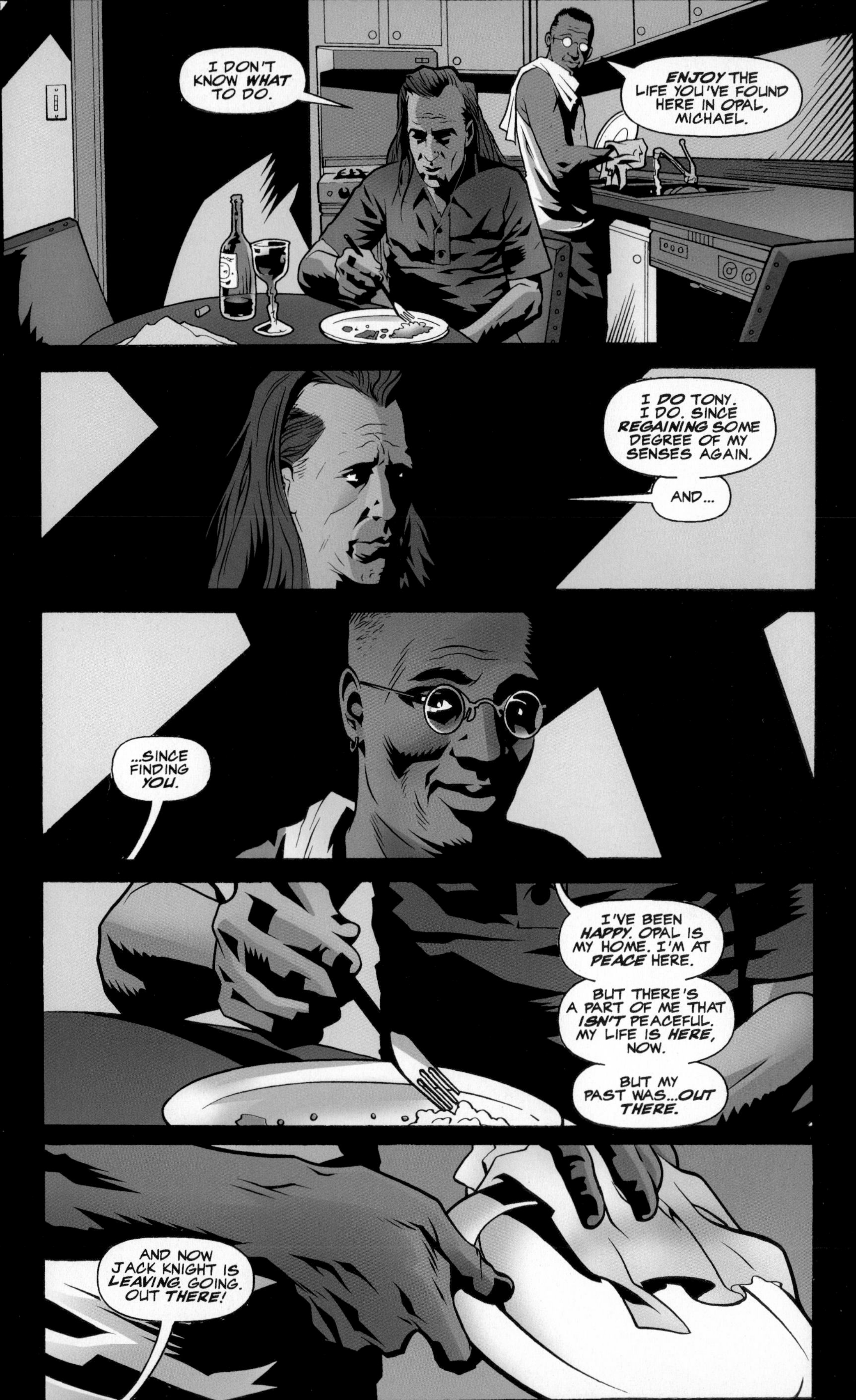
I DON'T KNOW WHAT TO DO.
ENJOY THE LIFE YOU'VE FOUND HERE IN OPAL, MICHAEL.
I DO TONY. I DO. SINCE REGAINING SOME DEGREE OF MY SENSES AGAIN.
AND...
...SINCE FINDING YOU.
I'VE BEEN HAPPY. OPAL IS MY HOME. I'M AT PEACE HERE.
BUT THERE'S A PART OF ME THAT ISN'T PEACEFUL. MY LIFE IS HERE, NOW.
BUT MY PAST WAS...OUT THERE.
AND NOW JACK KNIGHT IS LEAVING. GOING. OUT THERE!

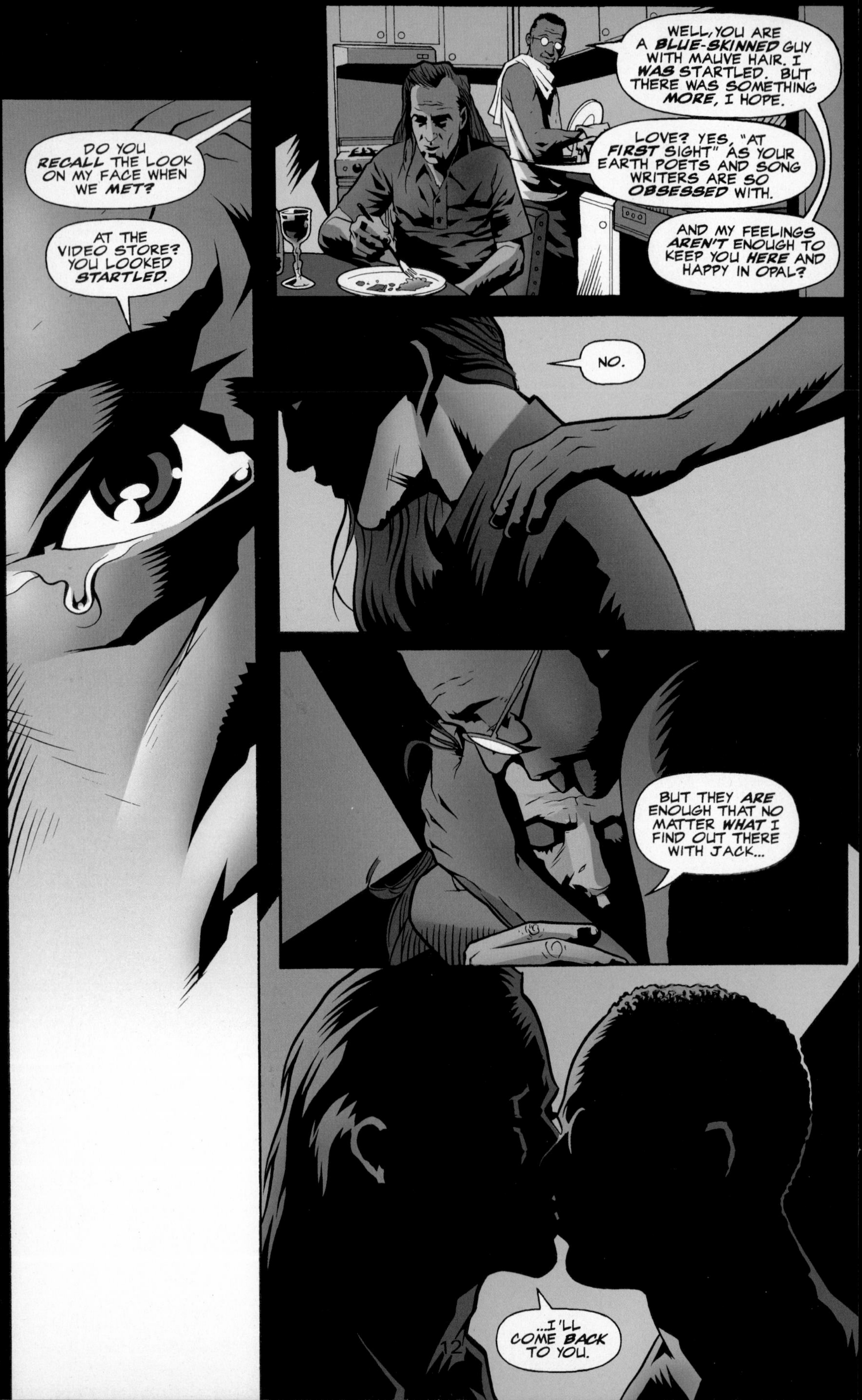

DO YOU RECALL THE LOOK ON MY FACE WHEN WE MET?
AT THE VIDEO STORE? YOU LOOKED STARTLED.
WELL, YOU ARE A BLUE-SKINNED GUY WITH MAUVE HAIR. I WAS STARTLED. BUT THERE WAS SOMETHING MORE, I HOPE.
LOVE? YES, "AT FIRST SIGHT" AS YOUR EARTH POETS AND SONG WRITERS ARE SO OBSESSED WITH.
AND MY FEELINGS AREN'T ENOUGH TO KEEP YOU HERE AND HAPPY IN OPAL?
NO.
BUT THEY ARE ENOUGH THAT NO MATTER WHAT I FIND OUT THERE WITH JACK...
...I'LL COME BACK TO YOU.

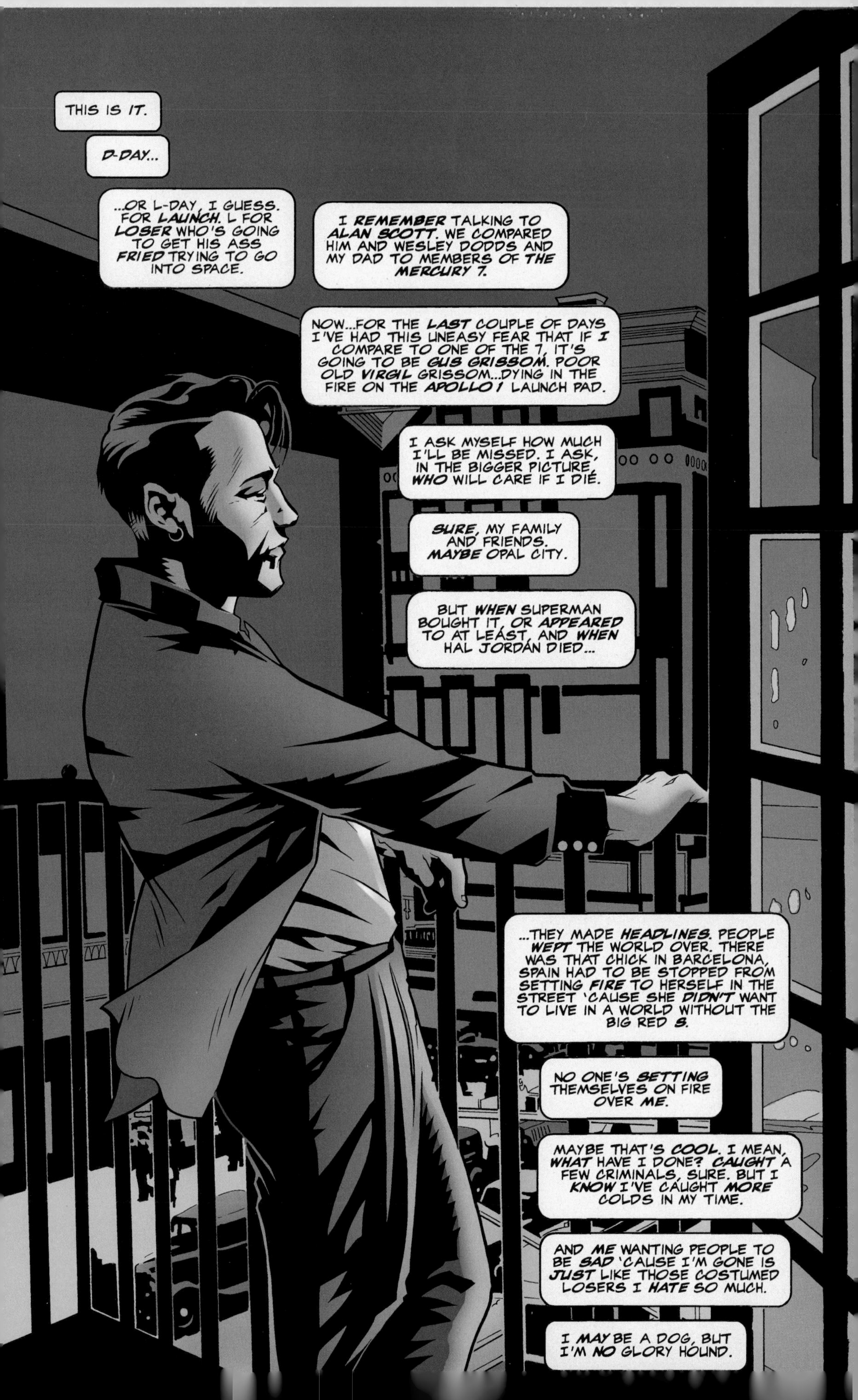
THIS IS IT.
D-DAY...
...OR L-DAY, I GUESS. FOR LAUNCH. L FOR LOSER WHO'S GOING TO GET HIS ASS FRIED TRYING TO GO INTO SPACE.
I REMEMBER TALKING TO ALAN SCOTT. WE COMPARED HIM AND WESLEY DODDS AND MY DAD TO MEMBERS OF THE MERCURY 7.
NOW...FOR THE LAST COUPLE OF DAYS I'VE HAD THIS UNEASY FEAR THAT IF I COMPARE TO ONE OF THE 7, IT'S GOING TO BE GUS GRISSOM. POOR OLD VIRGIL GRISSOM...DYING IN THE FIRE ON THE APOLLO 1 LAUNCH PAD.
I ASK MYSELF HOW MUCH I'LL BE MISSED. I ASK, IN THE BIGGER PICTURE, WHO WILL CARE IF I DIE.
SURE, MY FAMILY AND FRIENDS. MAYBE OPAL CITY.
BUT WHEN SUPERMAN BOUGHT IT, OR APPEARED TO AT LEAST, AND WHEN HAL JORDAN DIED...
...THEY MADE HEADLINES. PEOPLE WEPT THE WORLD OVER. THERE WAS THAT CHICK IN BARCELONA, SPAIN HAD TO BE STOPPED FROM SETTING FIRE TO HERSELF IN THE STREET 'CAUSE SHE DIDN'T WANT TO LIVE IN A WORLD WITHOUT THE BIG RED S.
NO ONE'S SETTING THEMSELVES ON FIRE OVER ME.
MAYBE THAT'S COOL. I MEAN, WHAT HAVE I DONE? CAUGHT A FEW CRIMINALS, SURE. BUT I KNOW I'VE CAUGHT MORE COLDS IN MY TIME.
AND ME WANTING PEOPLE TO BE SAD 'CAUSE I'M GONE IS JUST LIKE THOSE COSTUMED LOSERS I HATE SO MUCH.
I MAY BE A DOG, BUT I'M NO GLORY HOUND.

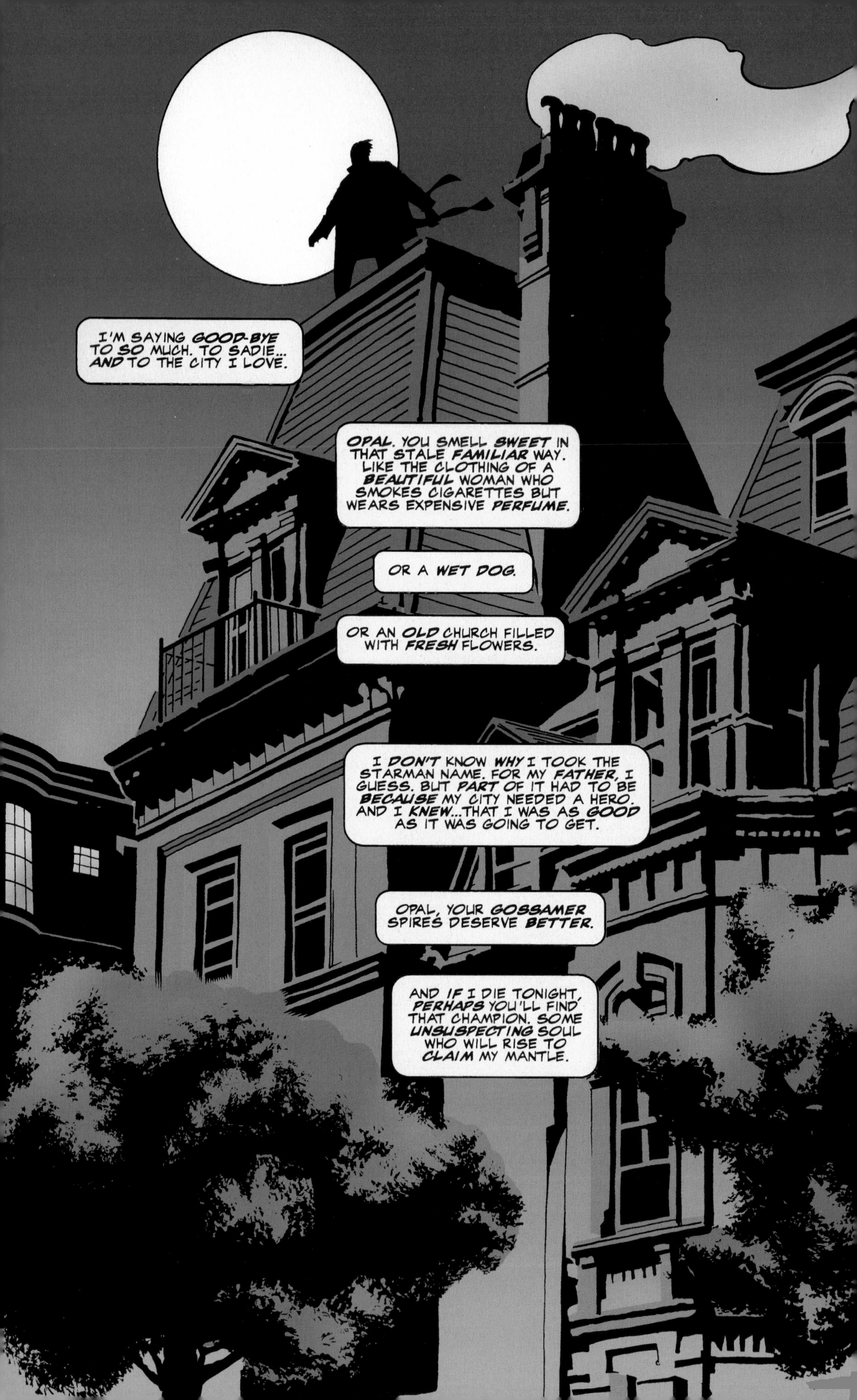
I'M SAYING GOOD-BYE TO SO MUCH. TO SADIE... AND TO THE CITY I LOVE.
OPAL. YOU SMELL SWEET IN THAT STALE FAMILIAR WAY. LIKE THE CLOTHING OF A BEAUTIFUL WOMAN WHO SMOKES CIGARETTES BUT WEARS EXPENSIVE PERFUME.
OR A WET DOG.
OR AN OLD CHURCH FILLED WITH FRESH FLOWERS.
I DON'T KNOW WHY I TOOK THE STARMAN NAME. FOR MY FATHER, I GUESS. BUT PART OF IT HAD TO BE BECAUSE MY CITY NEEDED A HERO. AND I KNEW...THAT I WAS AS GOOD AS IT WAS GOING TO GET.
OPAL, YOUR GOSSAMER SPIRES DESERVE BETTER.
AND IF I DIE TONIGHT, PERHAPS YOU'LL FIND THAT CHAMPION. SOME UNSUSPECTING SOUL WHO WILL RISE TO CLAIM MY MANTLE.

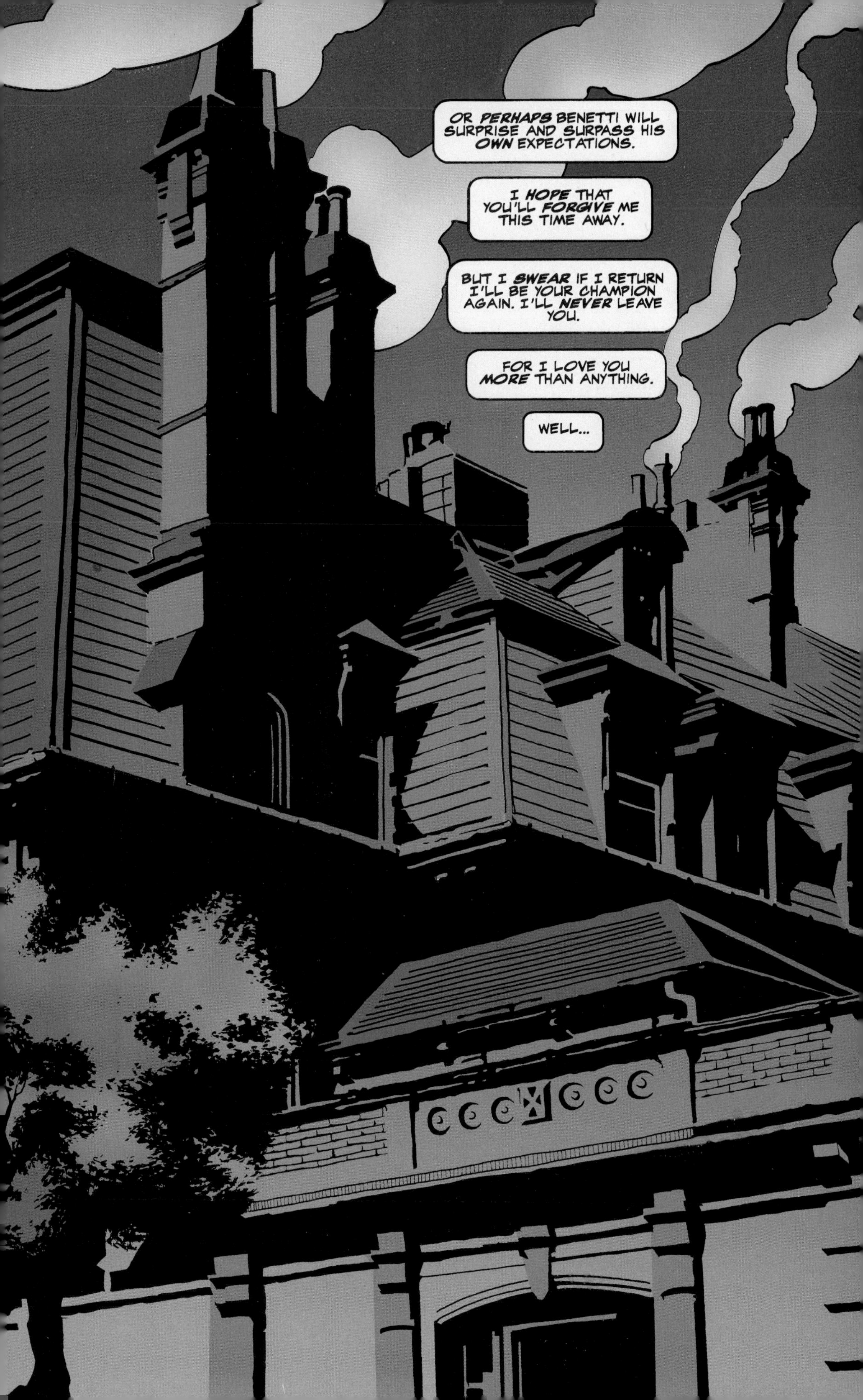
OR PERHAPS BENETTI WILL SURPRISE AND SURPASS HIS OWN EXPECTATIONS.
I HOPE THAT YOU'LL FORGIVE ME THIS TIME AWAY.
BUT I SWEAR IF I RETURN I'LL BE YOUR CHAMPION AGAIN. I'LL NEVER LEAVE YOU.
FOR I LOVE YOU MORE THAN ANYTHING.
WELL...

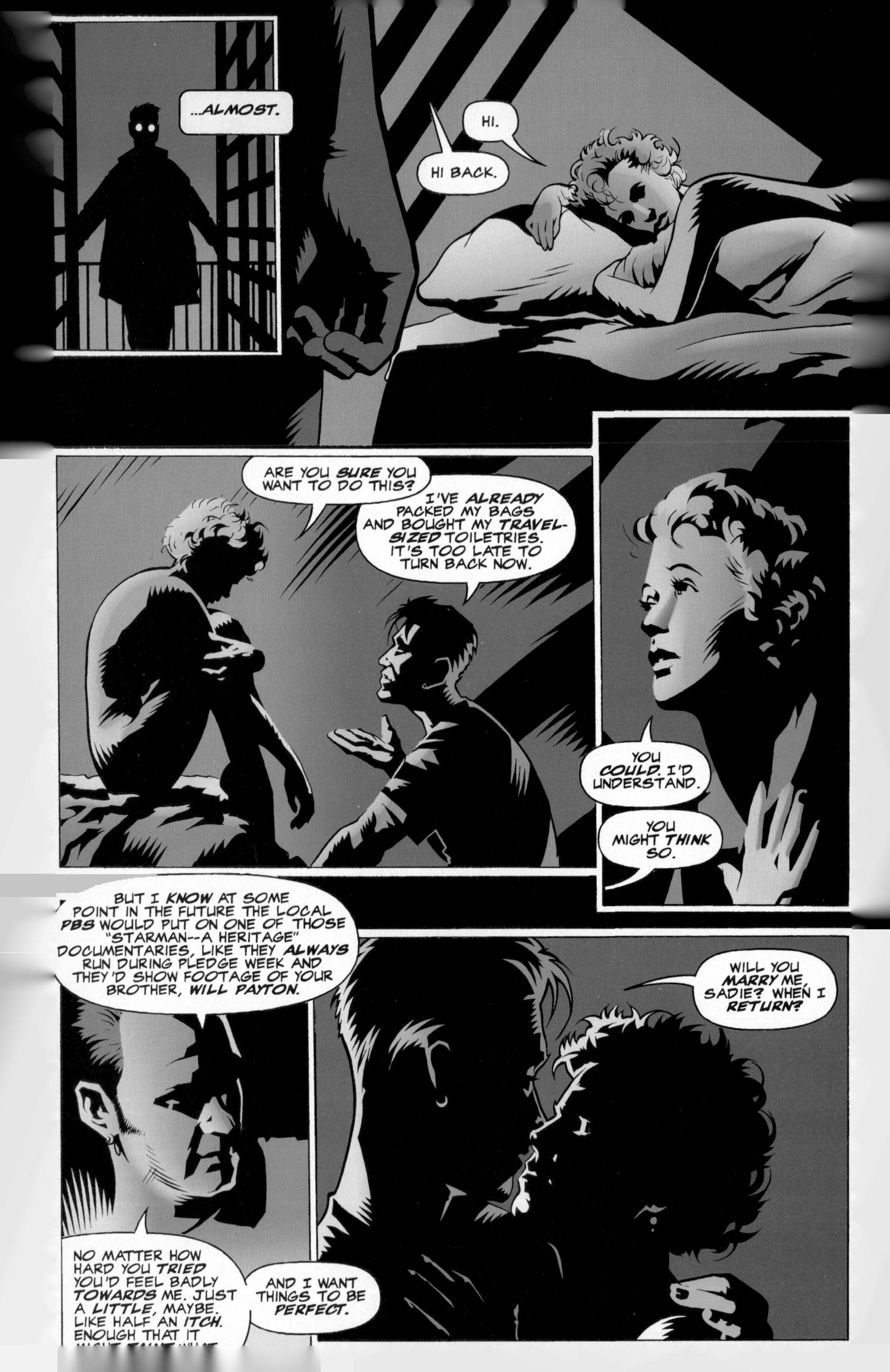
...ALMOST.
HI.
HI BACK.
ARE YOU SURE YOU WANT TO DO THIS?
I'VE ALREADY PACKED MY BAGS AND BOUGHT MY TRAVEL-SIZED TOILETRIES. IT'S TOO LATE TO TURN BACK NOW.
YOU COULD. I'D UNDERSTAND.
YOU MIGHT THINK SO.
BUT I KNOW AT SOME POINT IN THE FUTURE THE LOCAL PBS WOULD PUT ON ONE OF THOSE "STARMAN--A HERITAGE" DOCUMENTARIES, LIKE THEY ALWAYS RUN DURING PLEDGE WEEK AND THEY'D SHOW FOOTAGE OF YOUR BROTHER, WILL PAYTON.
NO MATTER HOW HARD YOU TRIED YOU'D FEEL BADLY TOWARDS ME. JUST A LITTLE, MAYBE. LIKE HALF AN ITCH. ENOUGH THAT IT
AND I WANT THINGS TO BE PERFECT.
WILL YOU MARRY ME, SADIE? WHEN I RETURN?

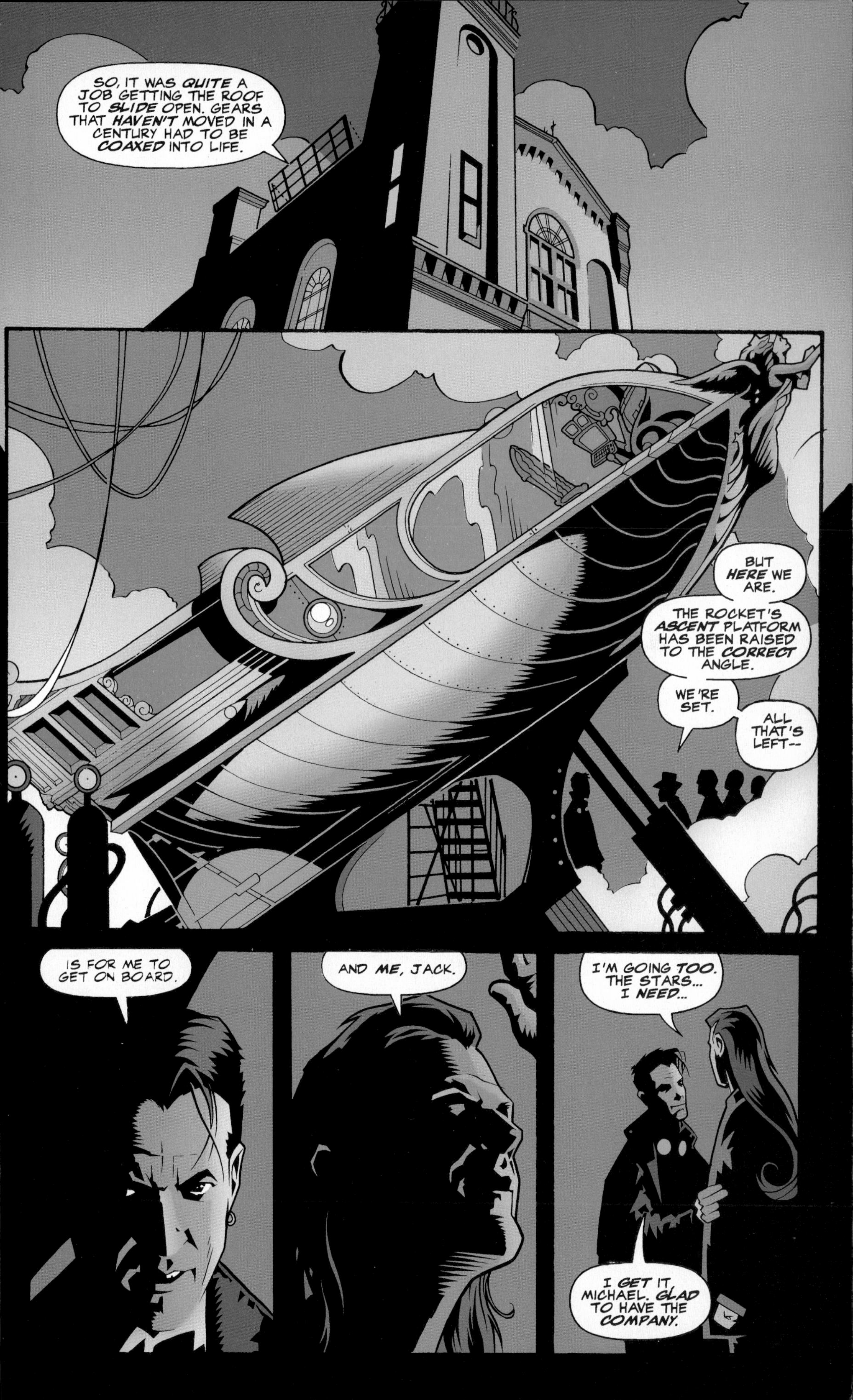
SO, IT WAS QUITE A JOB GETTING THE ROOF TO SLIDE OPEN. GEARS THAT HAVEN'T MOVED IN A CENTURY HAD TO BE COAXED INTO LIFE.
BUT HERE WE ARE.
THE ROCKET'S ASCENT PLATFORM HAS BEEN RAISED TO THE CORRECT ANGLE.
WE'RE SET.
ALL THAT'S LEFT--
IS FOR ME TO GET ON BOARD.
AND ME, JACK.
I'M GOING TOO. THE STARS... I NEED...
I GET IT, MICHAEL. GLAD TO HAVE THE COMPANY.

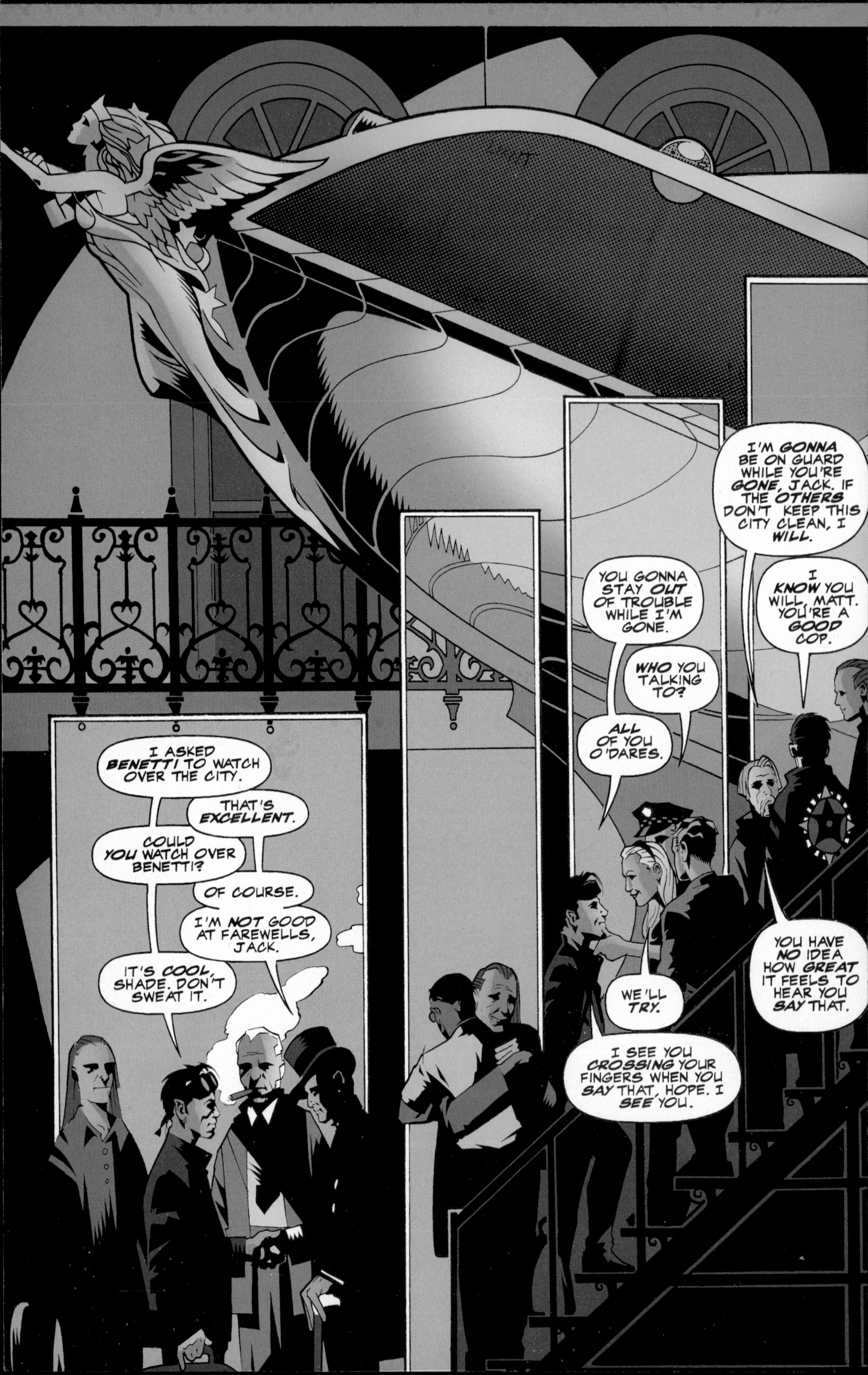
I ASKED BENETTI TO WATCH OVER THE CITY.
THAT'S EXCELLENT.
COULD YOU WATCH OVER BENETTI?
OF COURSE.
I'M NOT GOOD AT FAREWELLS, JACK.
IT'S COOL, SHADE. DON'T SWEAT IT.
YOU GONNA STAY OUT OF TROUBLE WHILE I'M GONE.
WHO YOU TALKING TO?
ALL OF YOU O'DARES.
WE'LL TRY.
I SEE YOU CROSSING YOUR FINGERS WHEN YOU SAY THAT, HOPE. I SEE YOU.
I'M GONNA BE ON GUARD WHILE YOU'RE GONE, JACK. IF THE OTHERS DON'T KEEP THIS CITY CLEAN, I WILL.
I KNOW YOU WILL, MATT. YOU'RE A GOOD COP.
YOU HAVE NO IDEA HOW GREAT IT FEELS TO HEAR YOU SAY THAT.

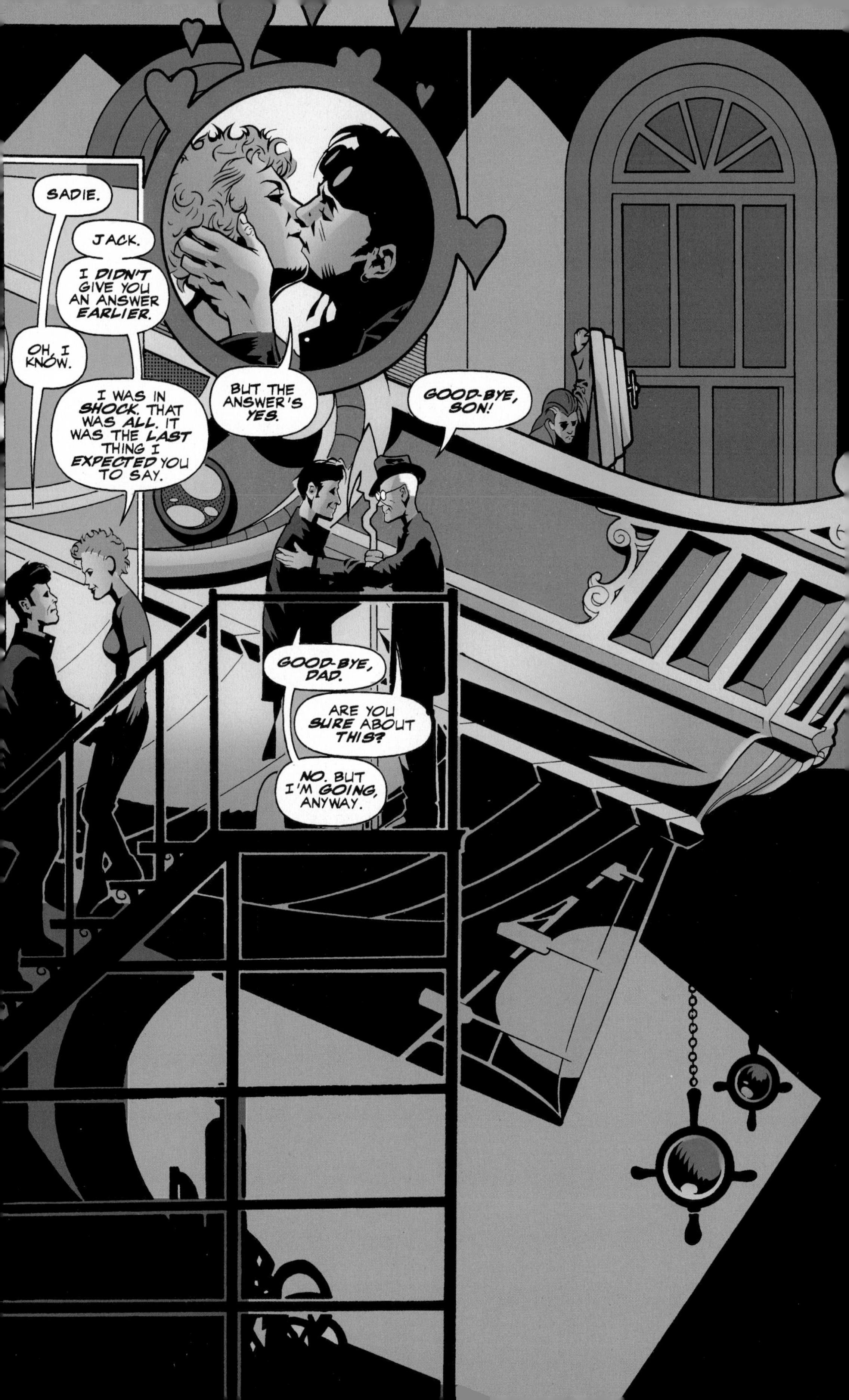
SADIE.
JACK.
I DIDN'T GIVE YOU AN ANSWER EARLIER.
OH, I KNOW.
I WAS IN SHOCK. THAT WAS ALL. IT WAS THE LAST THING I EXPECTED YOU TO SAY.
BUT THE ANSWER'S YES.
GOOD-BYE, SON!
GOOD-BYE, DAD.
ARE YOU SURE ABOUT THIS?
NO. BUT I'M GOING, ANYWAY.

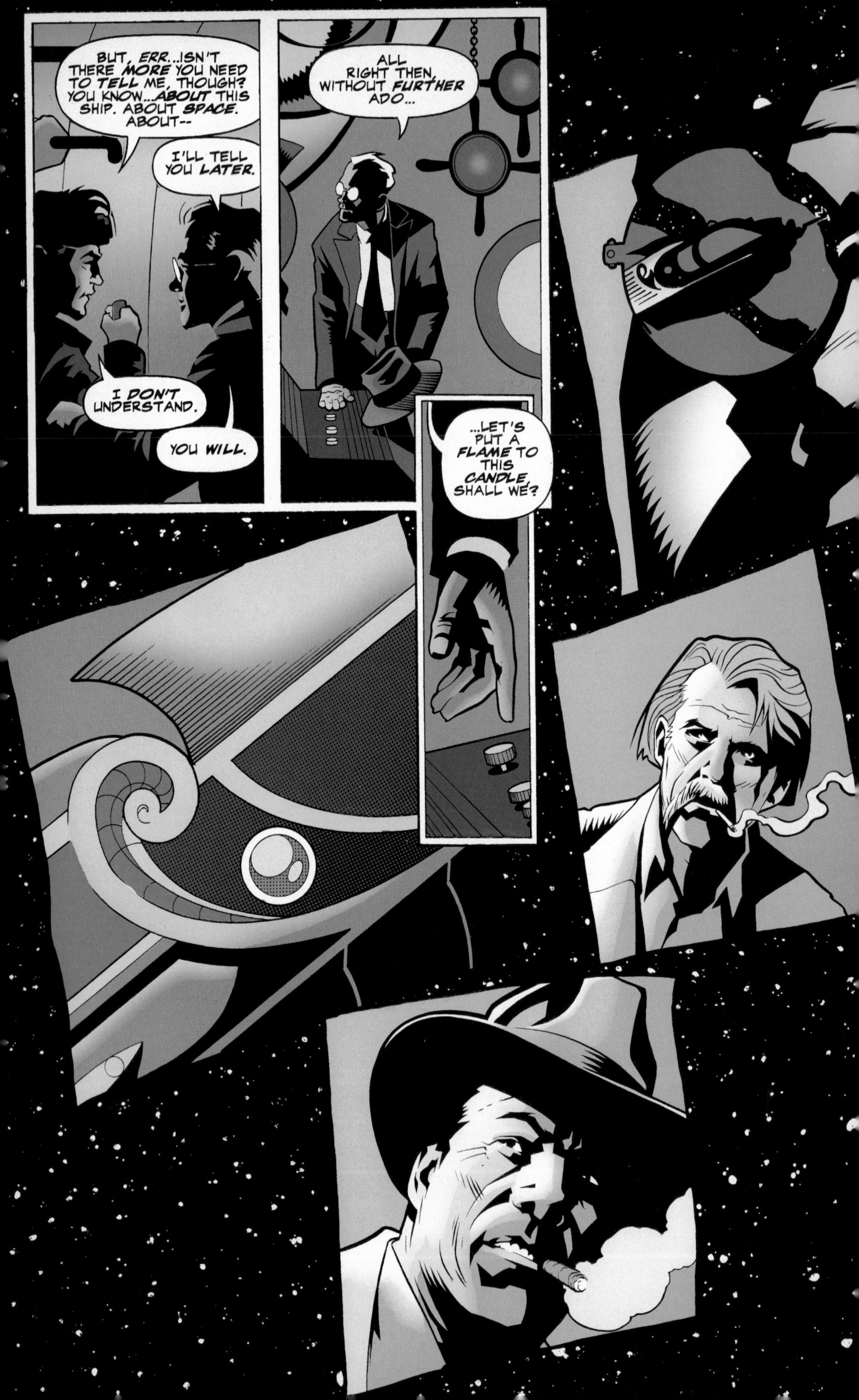
BUT, ERR...ISN'T THERE MORE YOU NEED TO TELL ME, THOUGH? YOU KNOW...ABOUT THIS SHIP. ABOUT SPACE. ABOUT--
I'LL TELL YOU LATER.
I DON'T UNDERSTAND.
YOU WILL.
ALL RIGHT THEN, WITHOUT FURTHER ADO...
...LET'S PUT A FLAME TO THIS CANDLE, SHALL WE?

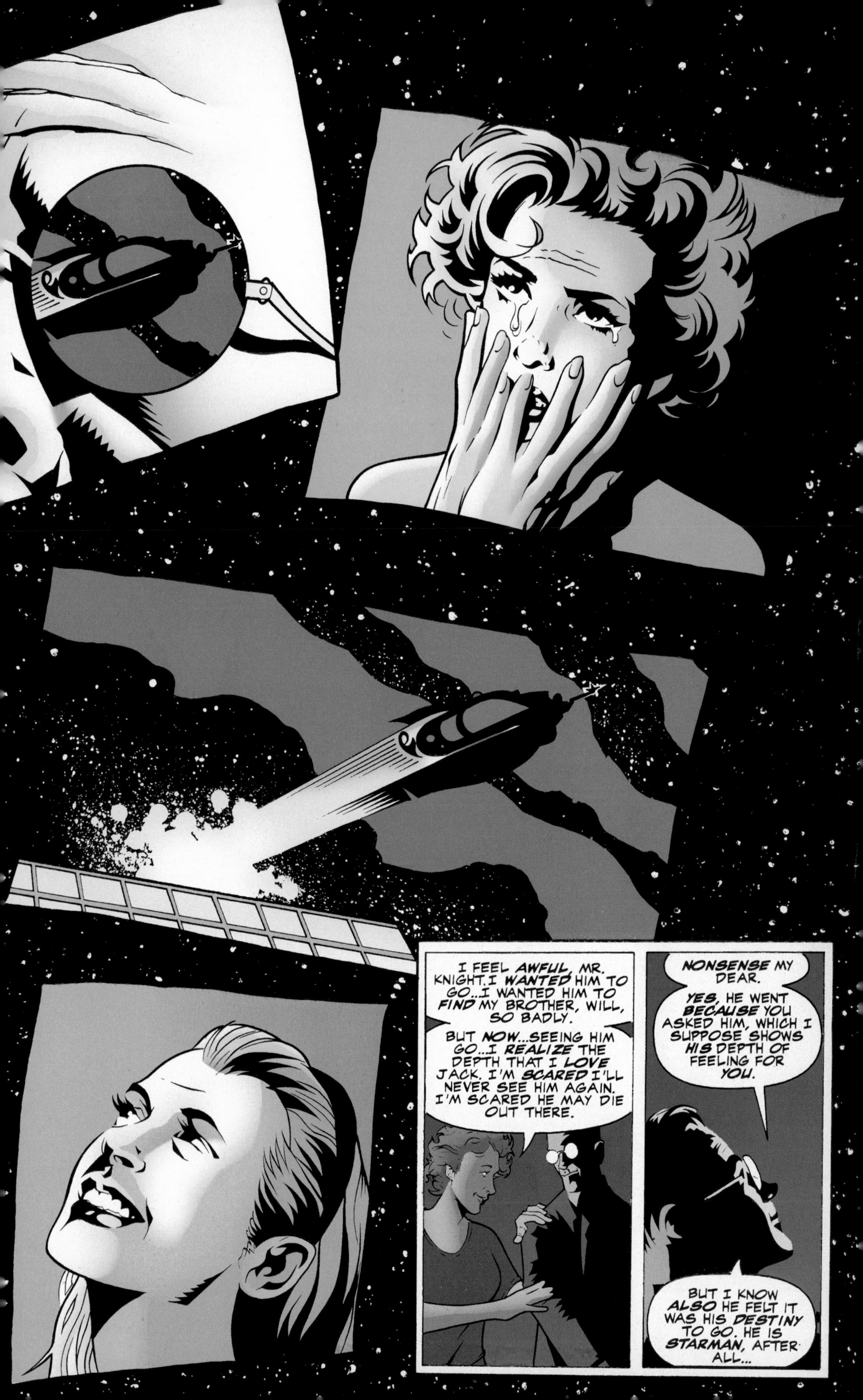
I FEEL AWFUL, MR. KNIGHT. I WANTED HIM TO GO...I WANTED HIM TO FIND MY BROTHER, WILL, SO BADLY.
BUT NOW...SEEING HIM GO...I REALIZE THE DEPTH THAT I LOVE JACK. I'M SCARED I'LL NEVER SEE HIM AGAIN. I'M SCARED HE MAY DIE OUT THERE.
NONSENSE MY DEAR.
YES, HE WENT BECAUSE YOU ASKED HIM, WHICH I SUPPOSE SHOWS HIS DEPTH OF FEELING FOR YOU.
BUT I KNOW ALSO HE FELT IT WAS HIS DESTINY TO GO. HE IS STARMAN, AFTER ALL...

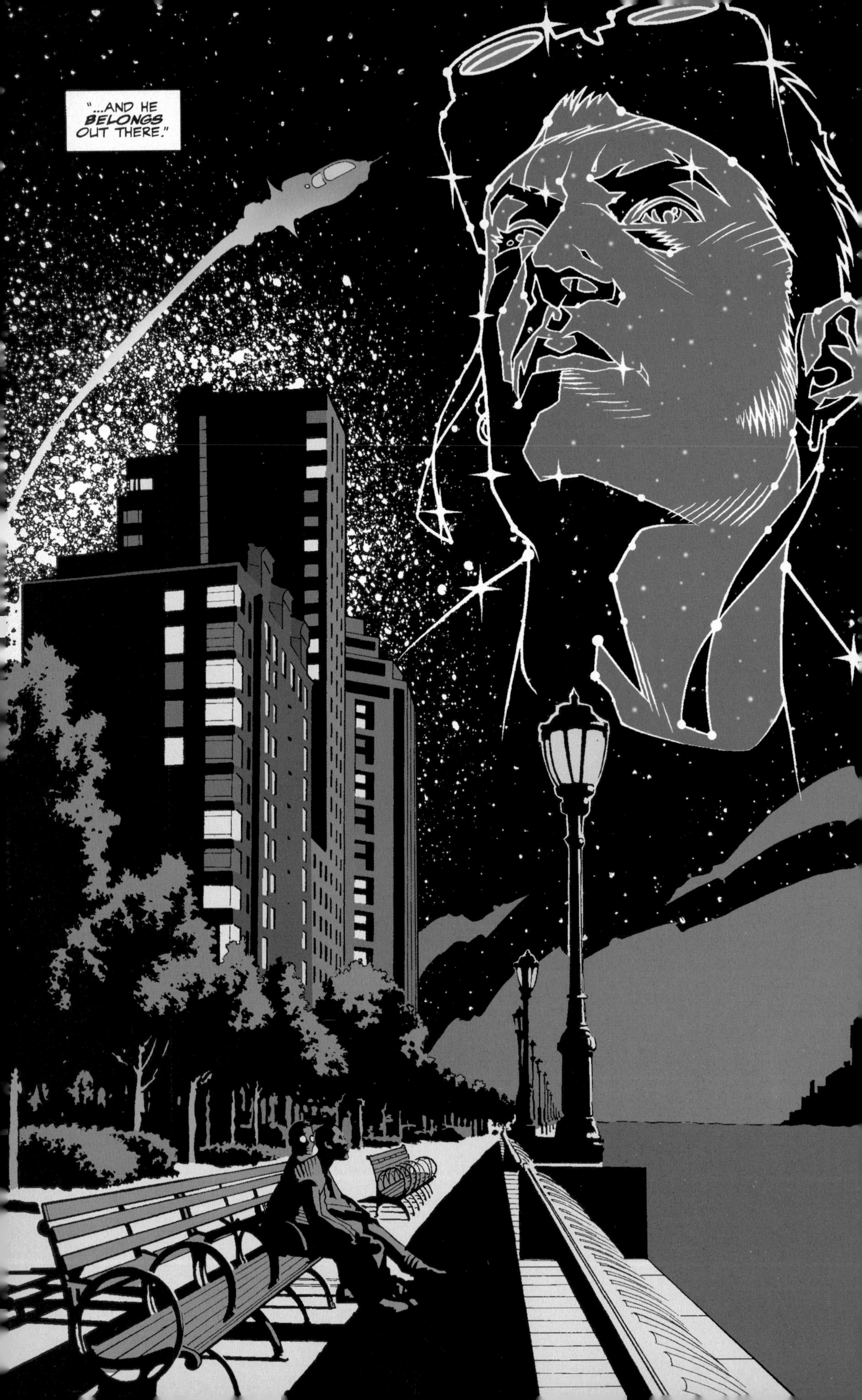
"...AND HE BELONGS OUT THERE."

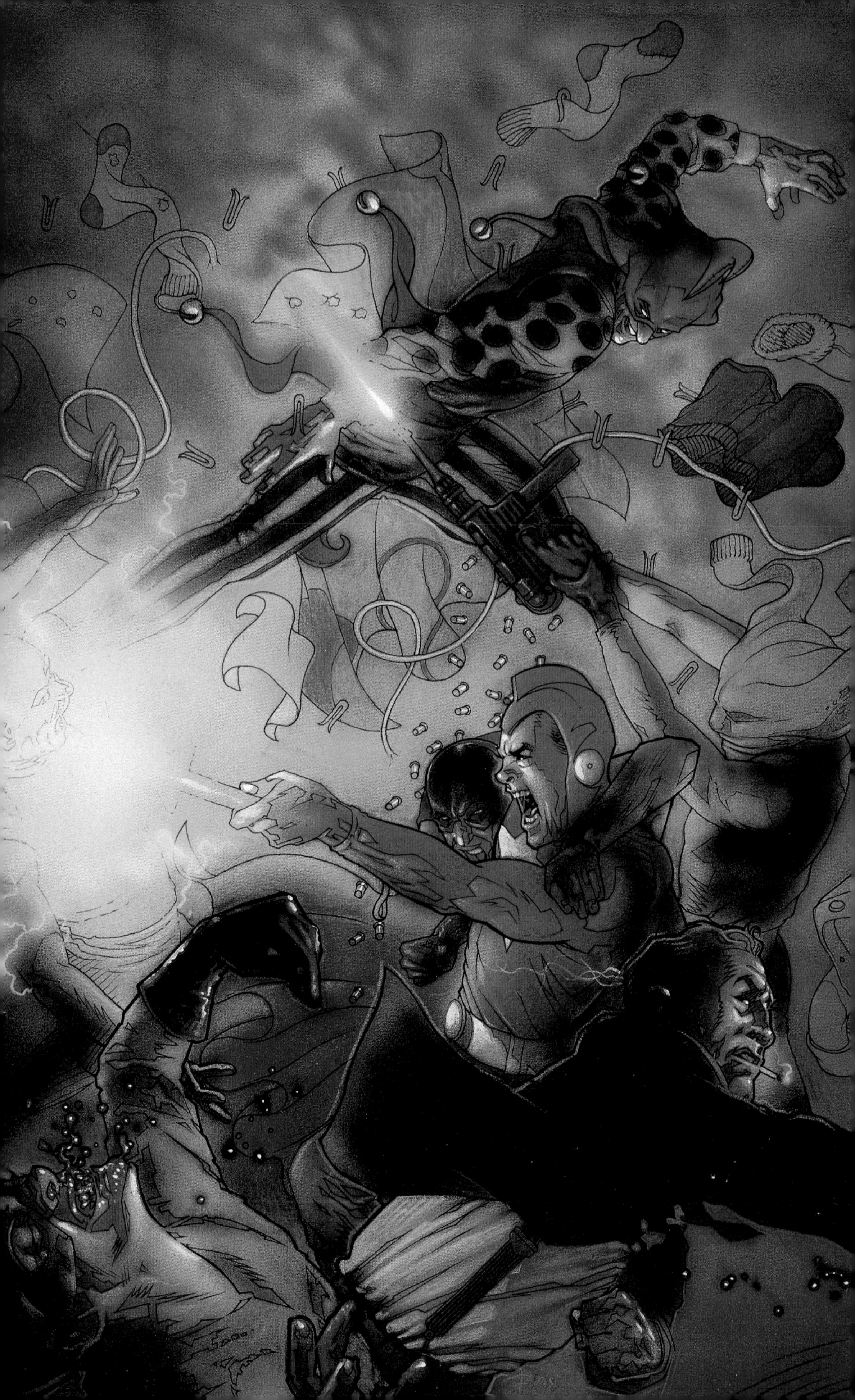

STARMAN 46

Cover by Tony Harris

Written by James Robinson

Art and colors by Gene Ha

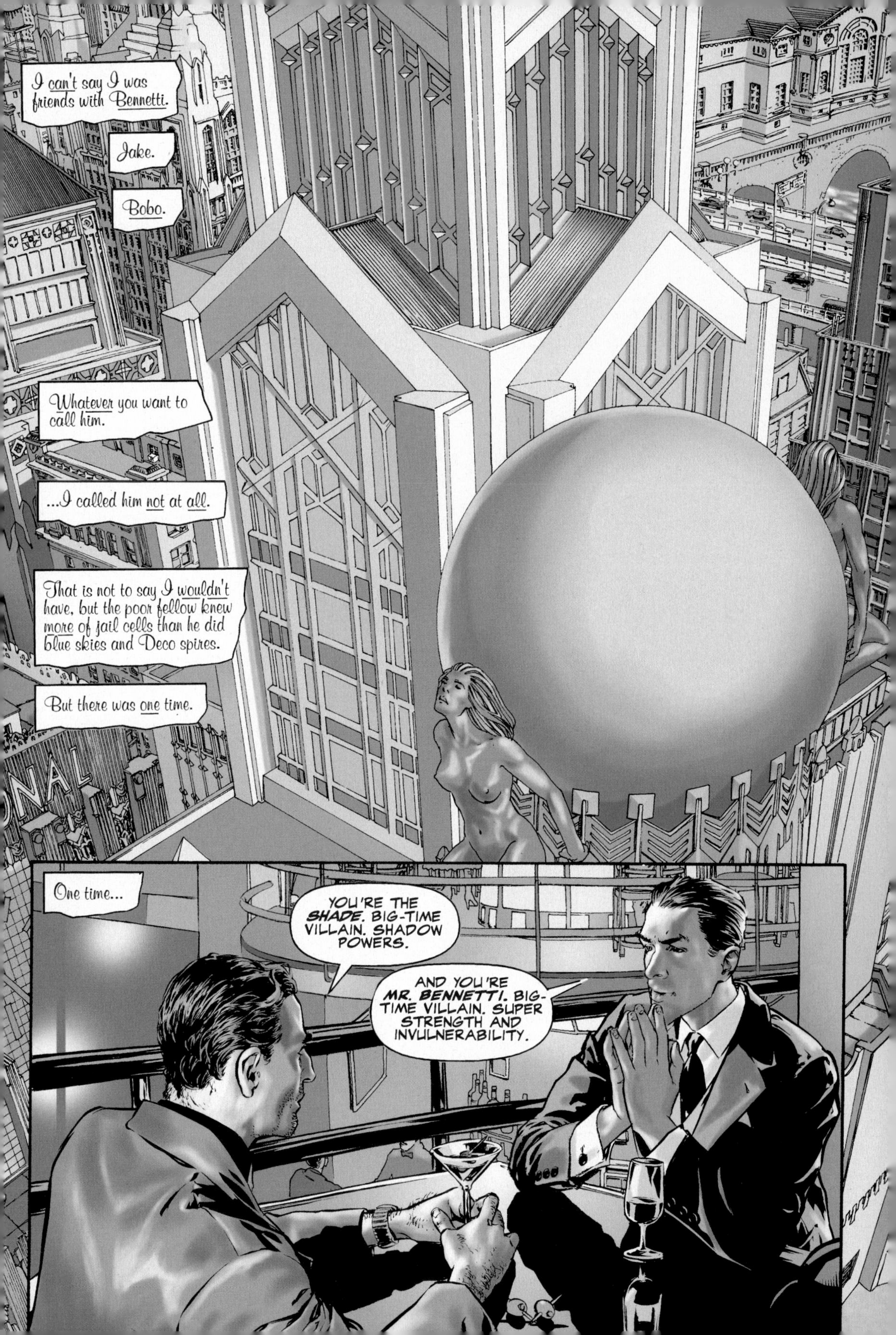
I can't say I was friends with Bennetti.
Jake.
Bobo.
Whatever you want to call him.
...I called him not at all.
That is not to say I wouldn't have, but the poor fellow knew more of jail cells than he did blue skies and Deco spires.
But there was one time.
One time...
YOU'RE THE SHADE. BIG-TIME VILLAIN. SHADOW POWERS.
AND YOU'RE MR. BENNETTI. BIG-TIME VILLAIN. SUPER STRENGTH AND INVULNERABILITY.

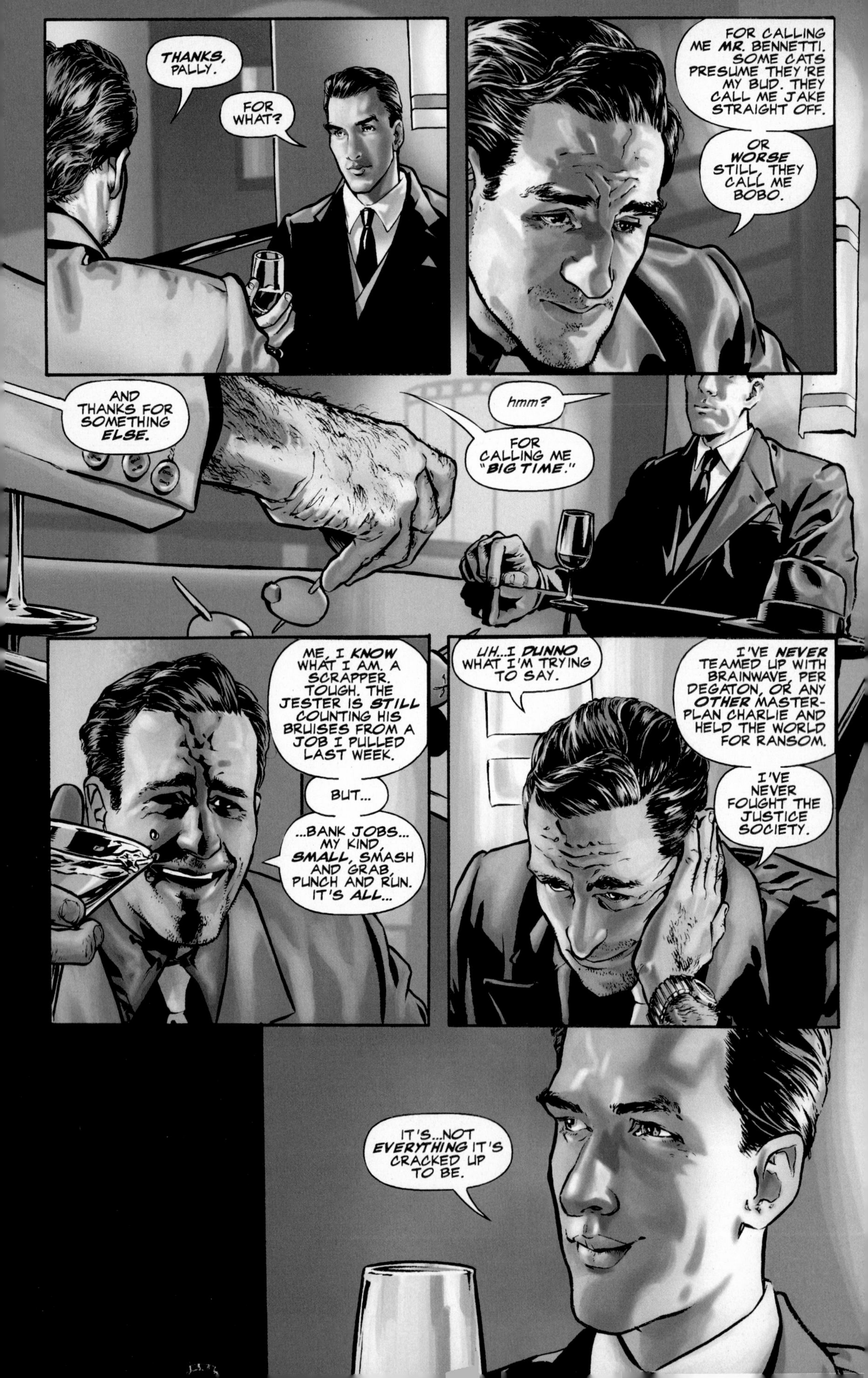
THANKS, PALLY.
FOR WHAT?
FOR CALLING ME MR. BENNETTI. SOME CATS PRESUME THEY'RE MY BUD. THEY CALL ME JAKE STRAIGHT OFF.
OR WORSE STILL, THEY CALL ME BOBO.
AND THANKS FOR SOMETHING ELSE.
hmm?
FOR CALLING ME "BIG TIME."
ME, I KNOW WHAT I AM. A SCRAPPER. TOUGH. THE JESTER IS STILL COUNTING HIS BRUISES FROM A JOB I PULLED LAST WEEK.
BUT...
...BANK JOBS... MY KIND, SMALL, SMASH AND GRAB, PUNCH AND RUN. IT'S ALL...
UH...I DUNNO WHAT I'M TRYING TO SAY.
I'VE NEVER TEAMED UP WITH BRAINWAVE, PER DEGATON, OR ANY OTHER MASTER-PLAN CHARLIE AND HELD THE WORLD FOR RANSOM.
I'VE NEVER FOUGHT THE JUSTICE SOCIETY.
IT'S...NOT EVERYTHING IT'S CRACKED UP TO BE.

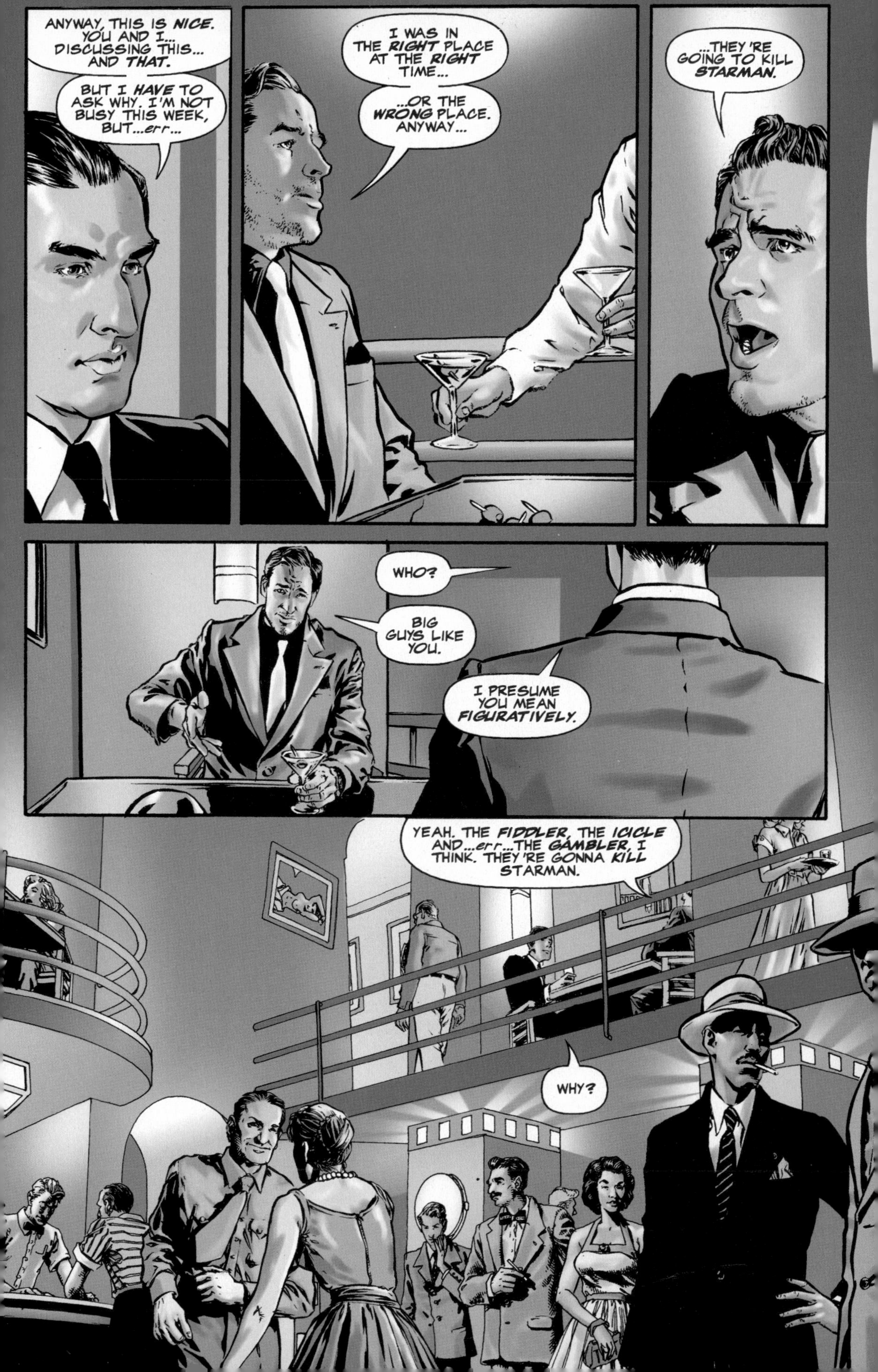
ANYWAY, THIS IS NICE. YOU AND I... DISCUSSING THIS... AND THAT.
BUT I HAVE TO ASK WHY. I'M NOT BUSY THIS WEEK, BUT...err...
I WAS IN THE RIGHT PLACE AT THE RIGHT TIME...
...OR THE WRONG PLACE. ANYWAY...
...THEY'RE GOING TO KILL STARMAN.
WHO?
BIG GUYS LIKE YOU.
I PRESUME YOU MEAN FIGURATIVELY.
YEAH. THE FIDDLER, THE ICICLE AND...err...THE GAMBLER, I THINK. THEY'RE GONNA KILL STARMAN.
WHY?

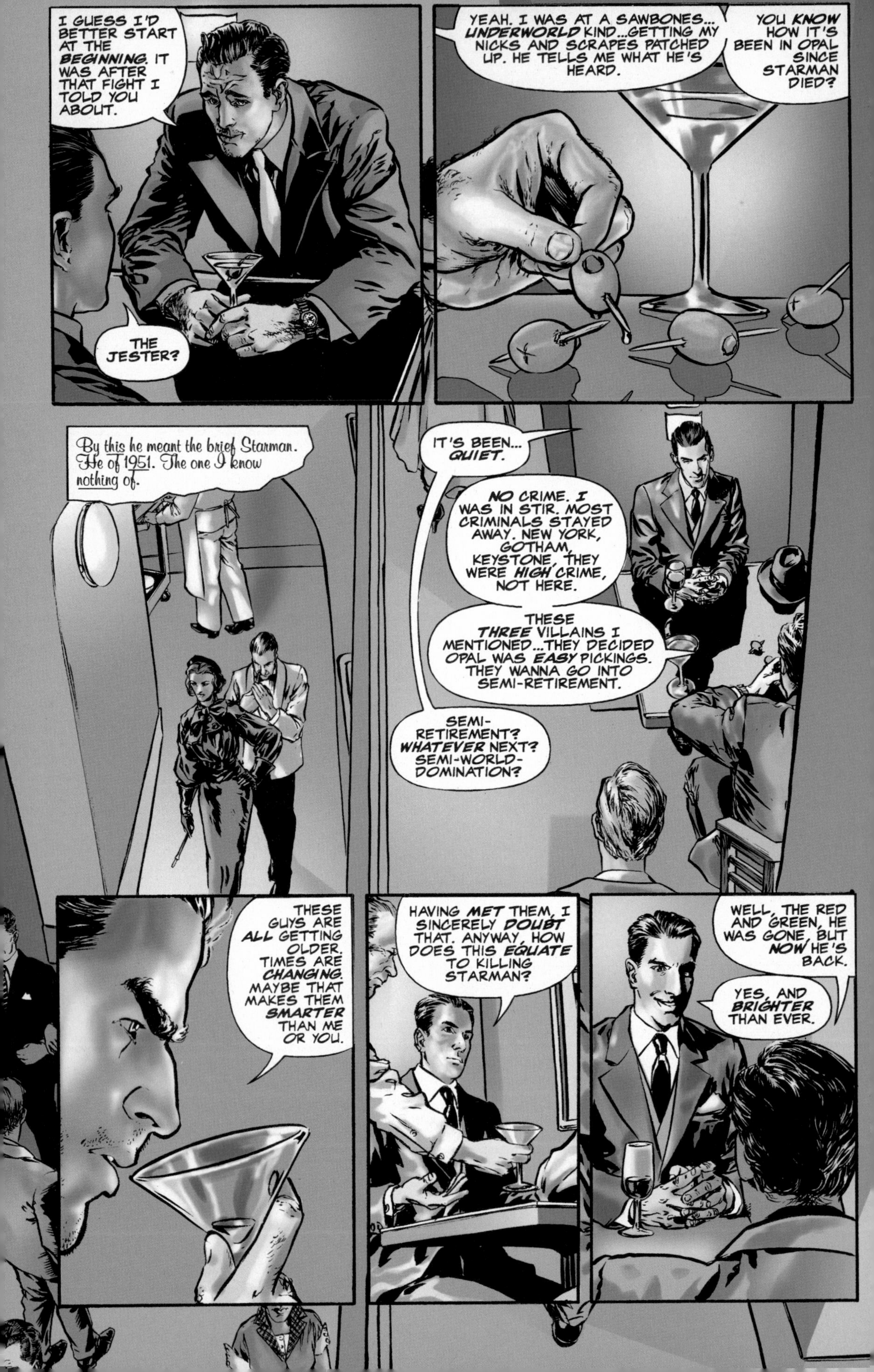

I GUESS I'D BETTER START AT THE BEGINNING. IT WAS AFTER THAT FIGHT I TOLD YOU ABOUT.
THE JESTER?
YEAH. I WAS AT A SAWBONES... UNDERWORLD KIND...GETTING MY NICKS AND SCRAPES PATCHED UP. HE TELLS ME WHAT HE'S HEARD.
YOU KNOW HOW IT'S BEEN IN OPAL SINCE STARMAN DIED?
By this he meant the brief Starman. He of 1951. The one I know nothing of.
IT'S BEEN... QUIET.
NO CRIME. I WAS IN STIR. MOST CRIMINALS STAYED AWAY. NEW YORK, GOTHAM, KEYSTONE, THEY WERE HIGH CRIME, NOT HERE.
THESE THREE VILLAINS I MENTIONED...THEY DECIDED OPAL WAS EASY PICKINGS. THEY WANNA GO INTO SEMI-RETIREMENT.
SEMI-RETIREMENT? WHATEVER NEXT? SEMI-WORLD-DOMINATION?
THESE GUYS ARE ALL GETTING OLDER. TIMES ARE CHANGING. MAYBE THAT MAKES THEM SMARTER THAN ME OR YOU.
HAVING MET THEM, I SINCERELY DOUBT THAT. ANYWAY, HOW DOES THIS EQUATE TO KILLING STARMAN?
WELL, THE RED AND GREEN, HE WAS GONE, BUT NOW HE'S BACK.
YES, AND BRIGHTER THAN EVER.

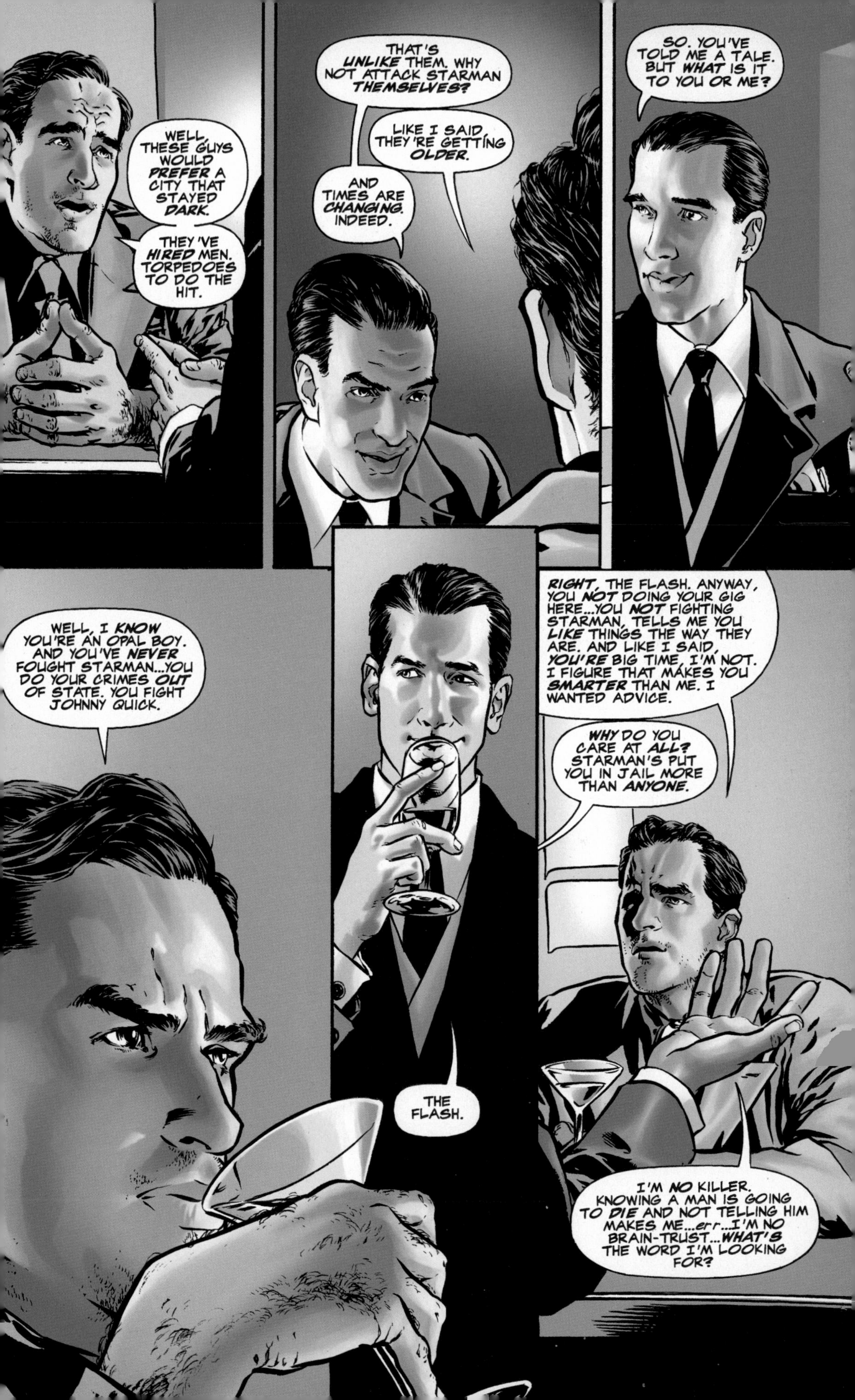
WELL, THESE GUYS WOULD PREFER A CITY THAT STAYED DARK.
THEY'VE HIRED MEN. TORPEDOES TO DO THE HIT.
THAT'S UNLIKE THEM. WHY NOT ATTACK STARMAN THEMSELVES?
LIKE I SAID, THEY'RE GETTING OLDER.
AND TIMES ARE CHANGING. INDEED.
SO. YOU'VE TOLD ME A TALE. BUT WHAT IS IT TO YOU OR ME?
WELL, I KNOW YOU'RE AN OPAL BOY. AND YOU'VE NEVER FOUGHT STARMAN...YOU DO YOUR CRIMES OUT OF STATE. YOU FIGHT JOHNNY QUICK.
THE FLASH.
RIGHT, THE FLASH. ANYWAY, YOU NOT DOING YOUR GIG HERE...YOU NOT FIGHTING STARMAN, TELLS ME YOU LIKE THINGS THE WAY THEY ARE. AND LIKE I SAID, YOU'RE BIG TIME, I'M NOT. I FIGURE THAT MAKES YOU SMARTER THAN ME. I WANTED ADVICE.
WHY DO YOU CARE AT ALL? STARMAN'S PUT YOU IN JAIL MORE THAN ANYONE.
I'M NO KILLER. KNOWING A MAN IS GOING TO DIE AND NOT TELLING HIM MAKES ME...err...I'M NO BRAIN-TRUST...WHAT'S THE WORD I'M LOOKING FOR?

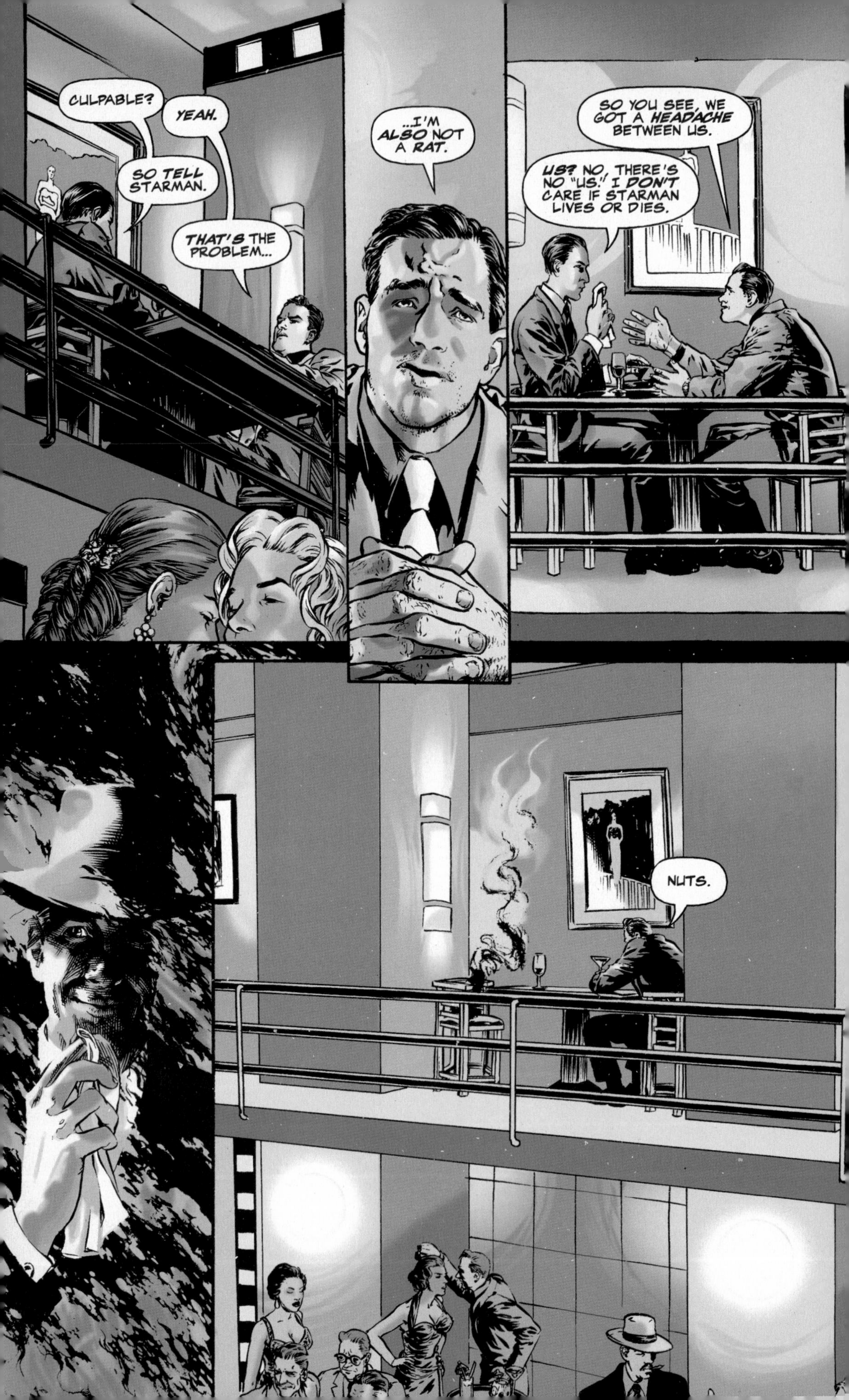
CULPABLE?
YEAH.
SO TELL STARMAN.
THAT'S THE PROBLEM...
...I'M ALSO NOT A RAT.
SO YOU SEE, WE GOT A HEADACHE BETWEEN US.
US? NO, THERE'S NO "US." I DON'T CARE IF STARMAN LIVES OR DIES.
NUTS.

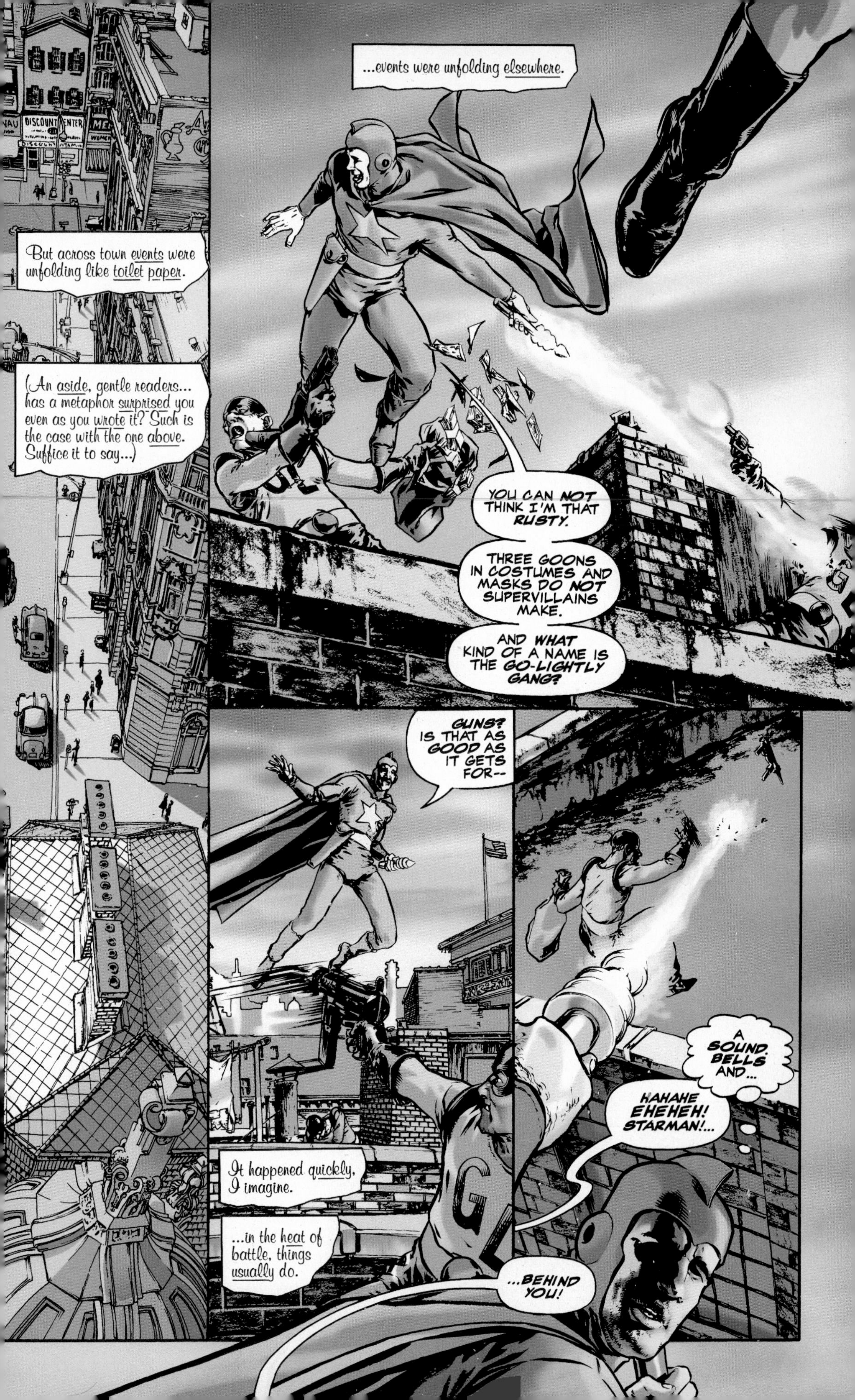

...events were unfolding elsewhere.
But across town events were unfolding like toilet paper.
(An aside, gentle readers... has a metaphor surprised you even as you wrote it? Such is the case with the one above. Suffice it to say...)
YOU CAN NOT THINK I'M THAT RUSTY.
THREE GOONS IN COSTUMES AND MASKS DO NOT SUPERVILLAINS MAKE.
AND WHAT KIND OF A NAME IS THE GO-LIGHTLY GANG?
GUNS? IS THAT AS GOOD AS IT GETS FOR--
It happened quickly, I imagine.
...in the heat of battle, things usually do.
A SOUND. BELLS AND...
HAHAHE EHEHEH! STARMAN!...
...BEHIND YOU!

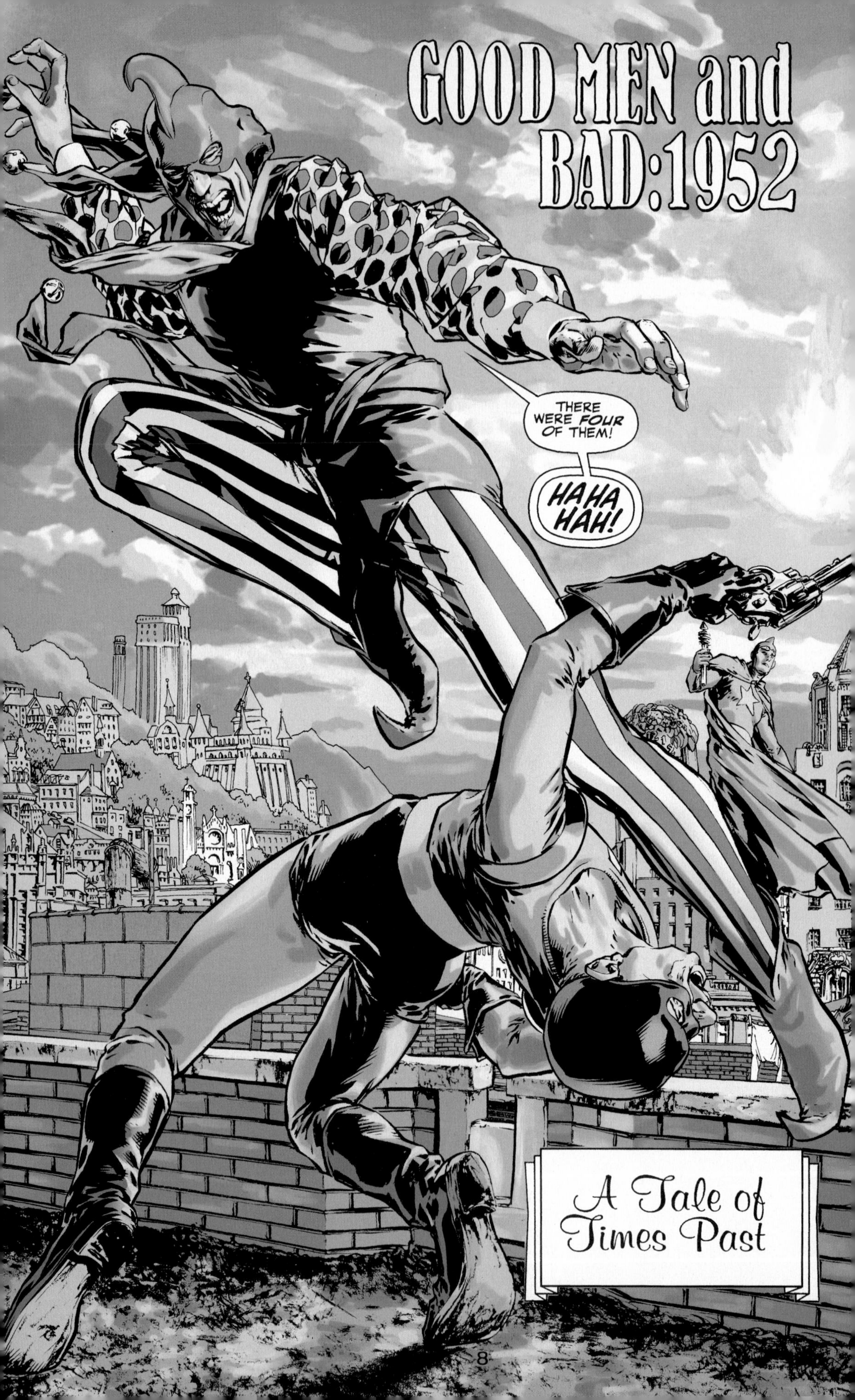
GOOD MEN and BAD:1952
THERE WERE FOUR OF THEM!
HAHA HAH!
A Tale of Times Past

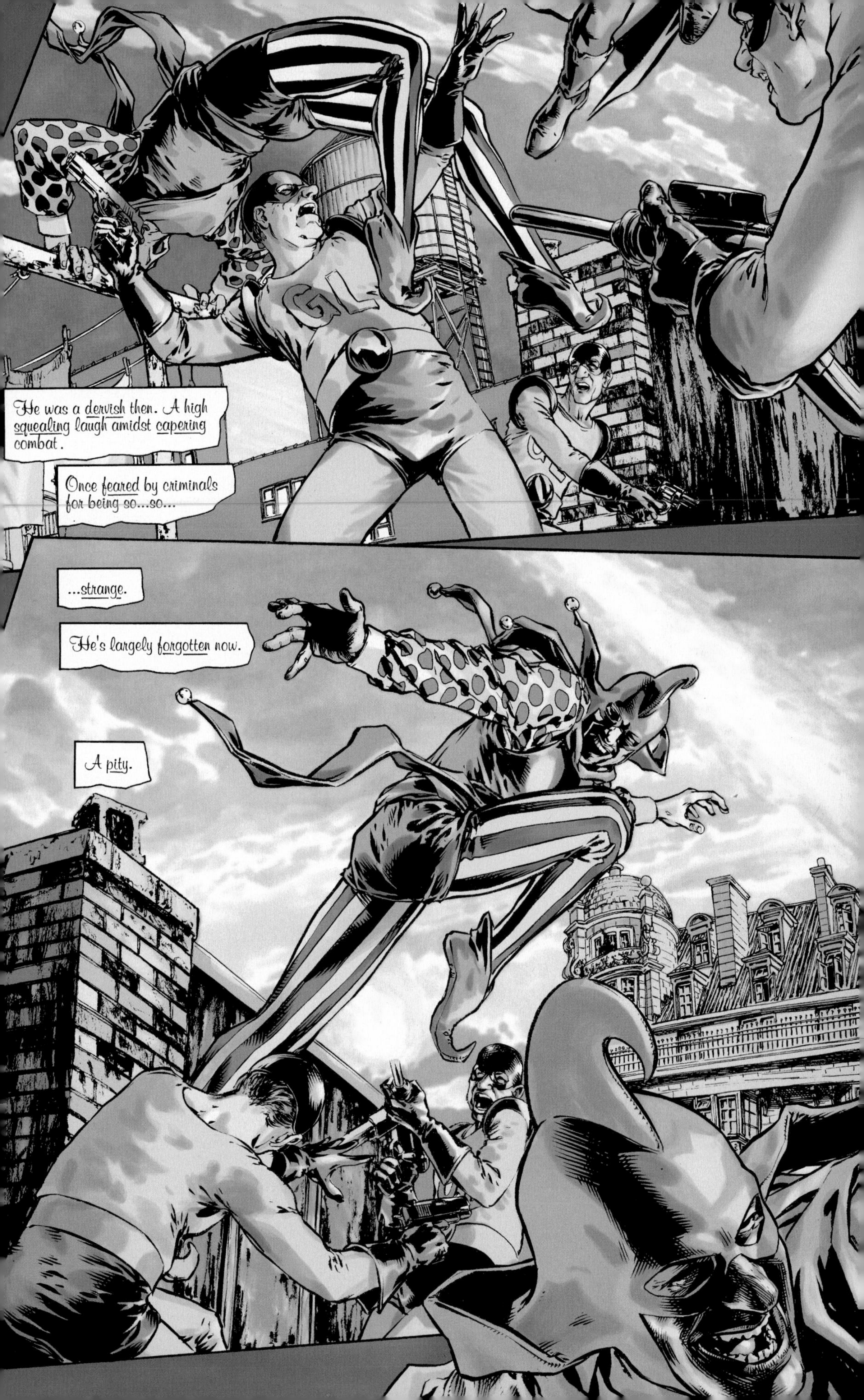
He was a dervish then. A high squealing laugh amidst capering combat.
Once feared by criminals for being so...so...
...strange.
He's largely forgotten now.
A pity.

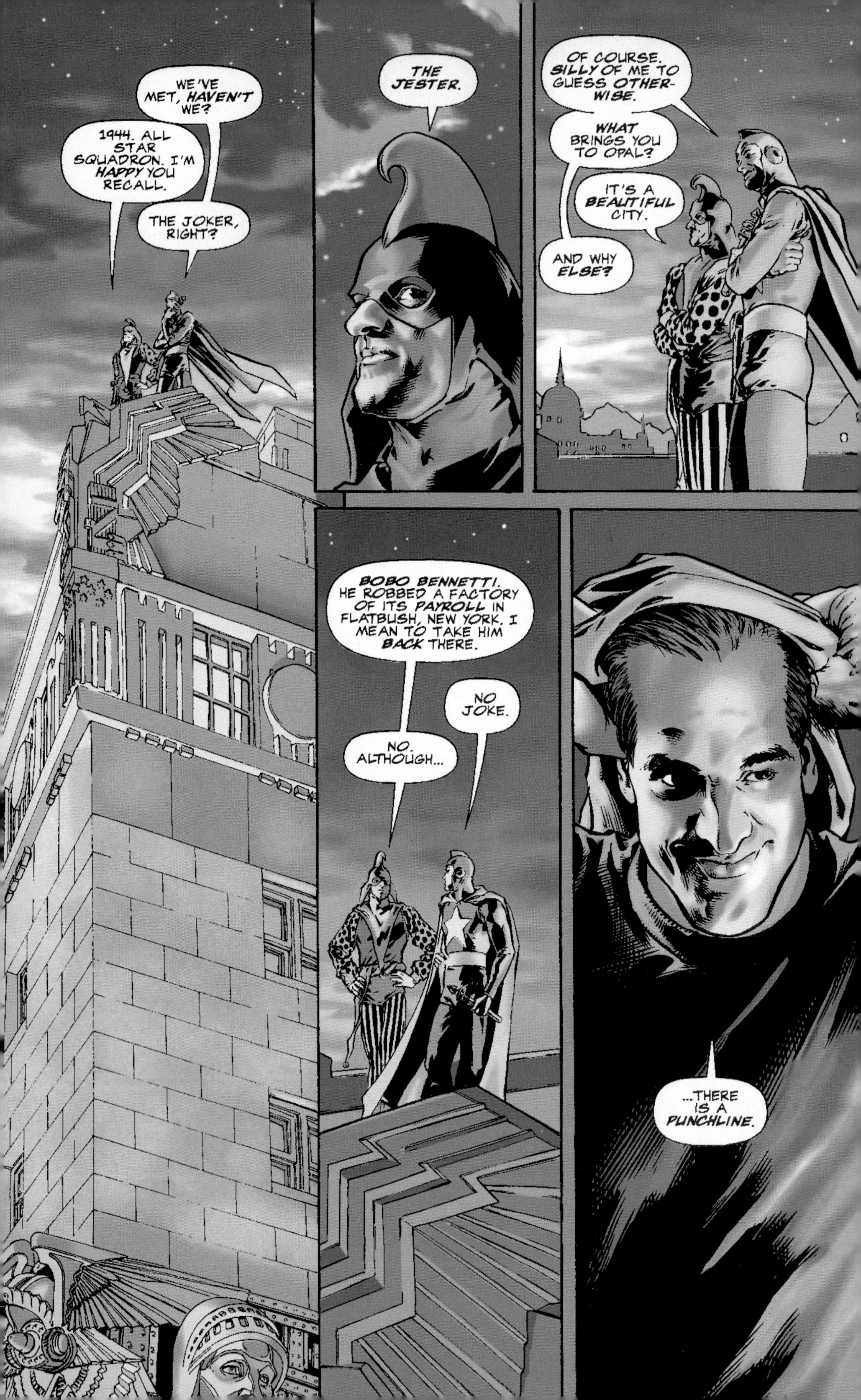
WE'VE MET, HAVEN'T WE?
1944. ALL STAR SQUADRON. I'M HAPPY YOU RECALL.
THE JOKER, RIGHT?
THE JESTER.
OF COURSE. SILLY OF ME TO GUESS OTHERWISE.
WHAT BRINGS YOU TO OPAL?
IT'S A BEAUTIFUL CITY.
AND WHY ELSE?
BOBO BENNETTI. HE ROBBED A FACTORY OF ITS PAYROLL IN FLATBUSH, NEW YORK. I MEAN TO TAKE HIM BACK THERE.
NO JOKE.
NO. ALTHOUGH...
...THERE IS A PUNCHLINE.

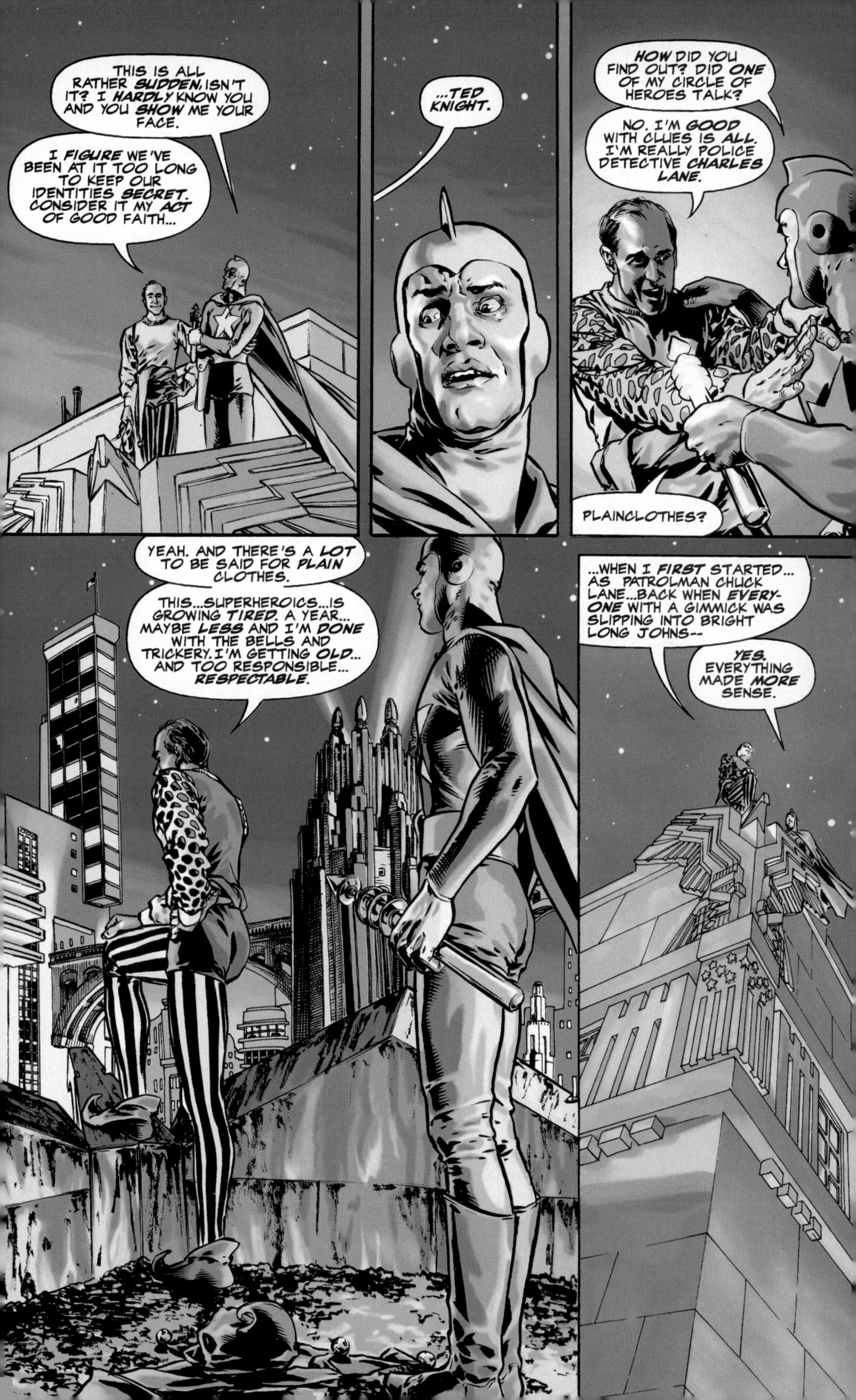

THIS IS ALL RATHER SUDDEN, ISN'T IT? I HARDLY KNOW YOU AND YOU SHOW ME YOUR FACE.
I FIGURE WE'VE BEEN AT IT TOO LONG TO KEEP OUR IDENTITIES SECRET. CONSIDER IT MY ACT OF GOOD FAITH...
...TED KNIGHT.
HOW DID YOU FIND OUT? DID ONE OF MY CIRCLE OF HEROES TALK?
NO. I'M GOOD WITH CLUES IS ALL. I'M REALLY POLICE DETECTIVE CHARLES LANE.
PLAINCLOTHES?
YEAH. AND THERE'S A LOT TO BE SAID FOR PLAIN CLOTHES.
THIS...SUPERHEROICS...IS GROWING TIRED. A YEAR... MAYBE LESS AND I'M DONE WITH THE BELLS AND TRICKERY. I'M GETTING OLD... AND TOO RESPONSIBLE... RESPECTABLE.
...WHEN I FIRST STARTED... AS PATROLMAN CHUCK LANE...BACK WHEN EVERY-ONE WITH A GIMMICK WAS SLIPPING INTO BRIGHT LONG JOHNS--
YES. EVERYTHING MADE MORE SENSE.

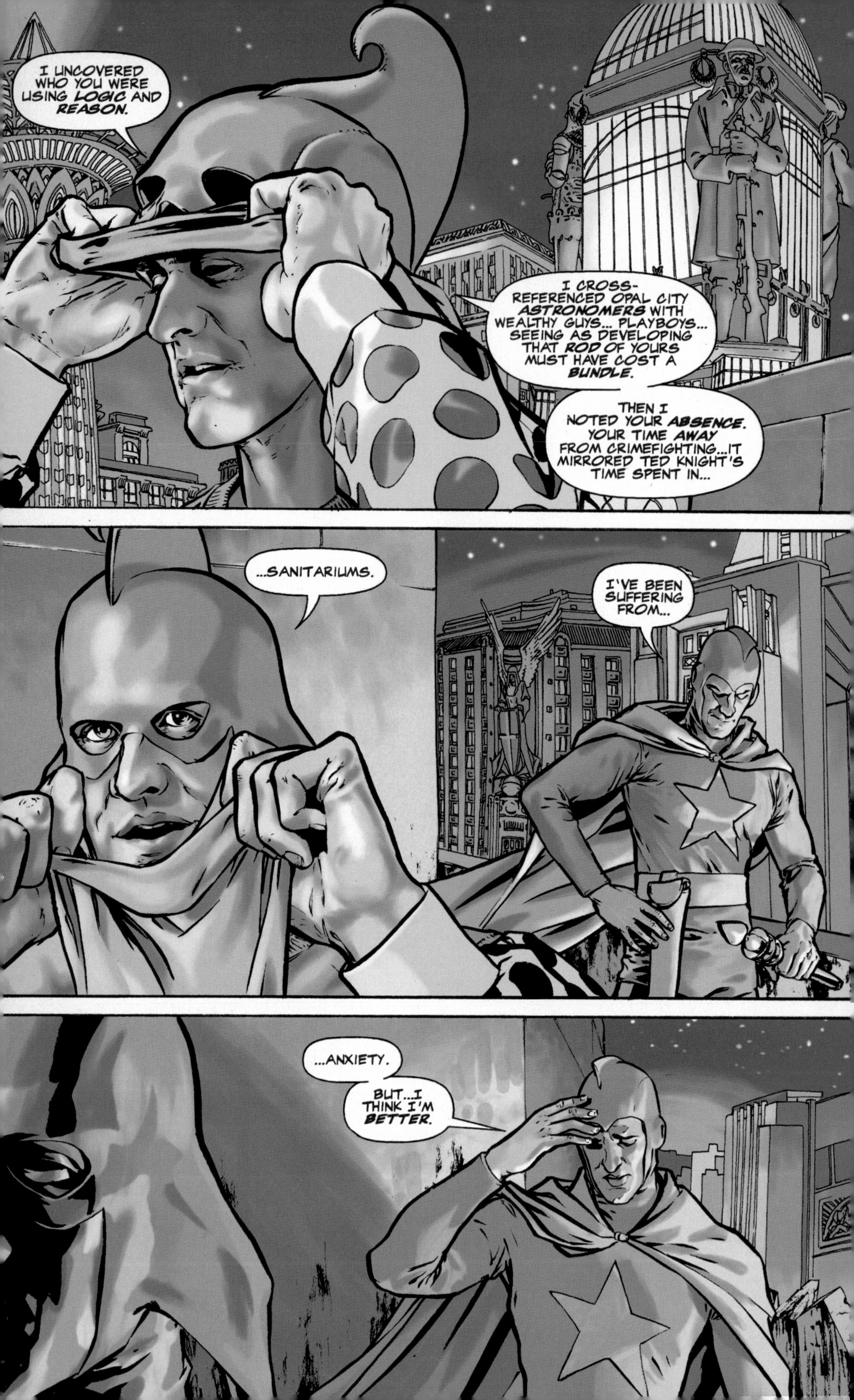
I UNCOVERED WHO YOU WERE USING LOGIC AND REASON.
I CROSS-REFERENCED OPAL CITY ASTRONOMERS WITH WEALTHY GUYS... PLAYBOYS... SEEING AS DEVELOPING THAT ROD OF YOURS MUST HAVE COST A BUNDLE.
THEN I NOTED YOUR ABSENCE. YOUR TIME AWAY FROM CRIMEFIGHTING...IT MIRRORED TED KNIGHT'S TIME SPENT IN...
...SANITARIUMS.
I'VE BEEN SUFFERING FROM...
...ANXIETY.
BUT...I THINK I'M BETTER.

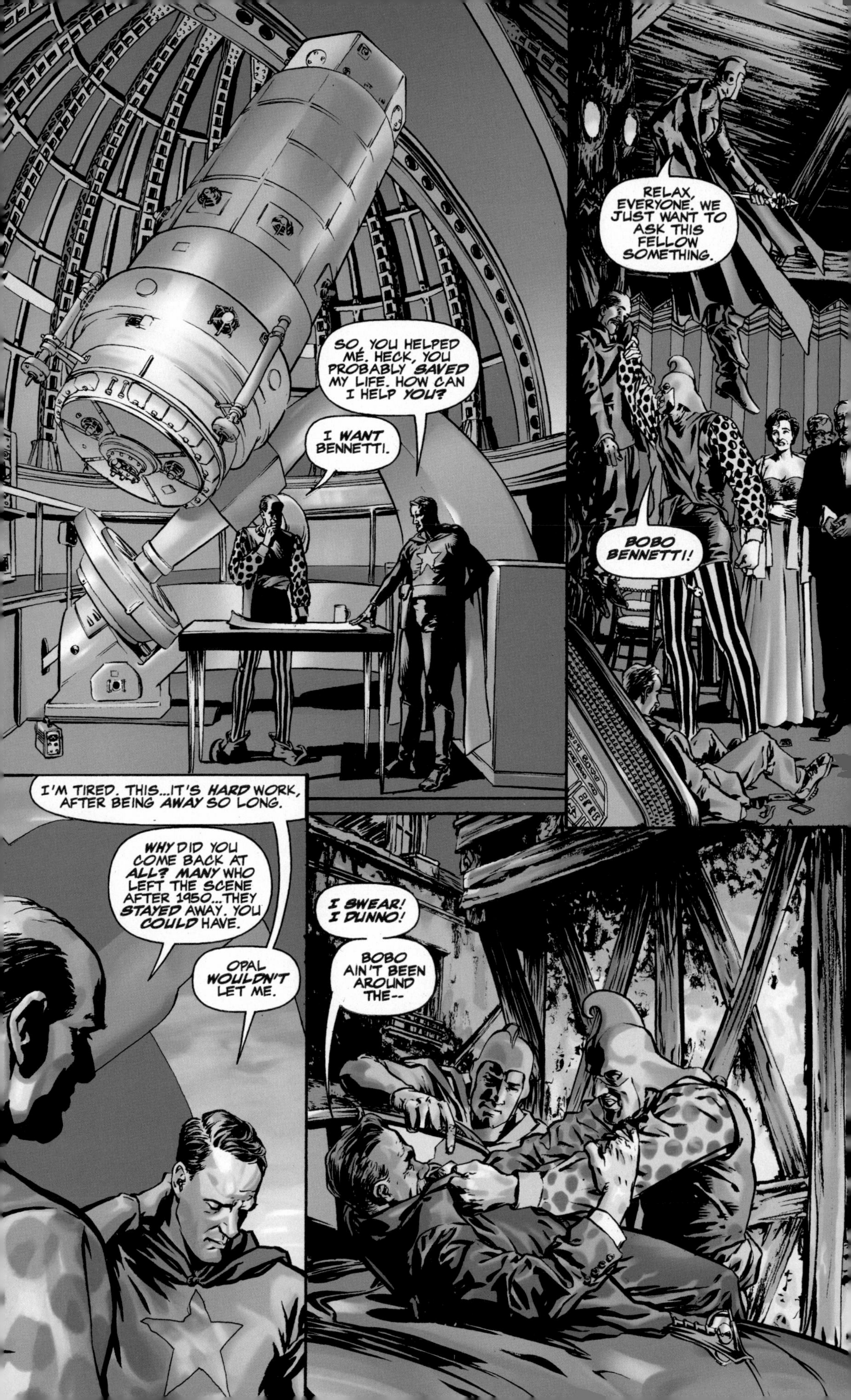
SO, YOU HELPED ME. HECK, YOU PROBABLY SAVED MY LIFE. HOW CAN I HELP YOU?
I WANT BENNETTI.
RELAX, EVERYONE. WE JUST WANT TO ASK THIS FELLOW SOMETHING.
BOBO BENNETTI!
I'M TIRED. THIS...IT'S HARD WORK, AFTER BEING AWAY SO LONG.
WHY DID YOU COME BACK AT ALL? MANY WHO LEFT THE SCENE AFTER 1950...THEY STAYED AWAY. YOU COULD HAVE.
OPAL WOULDN'T LET ME.
I SWEAR! I DUNNO!
BOBO AIN'T BEEN AROUND THE--

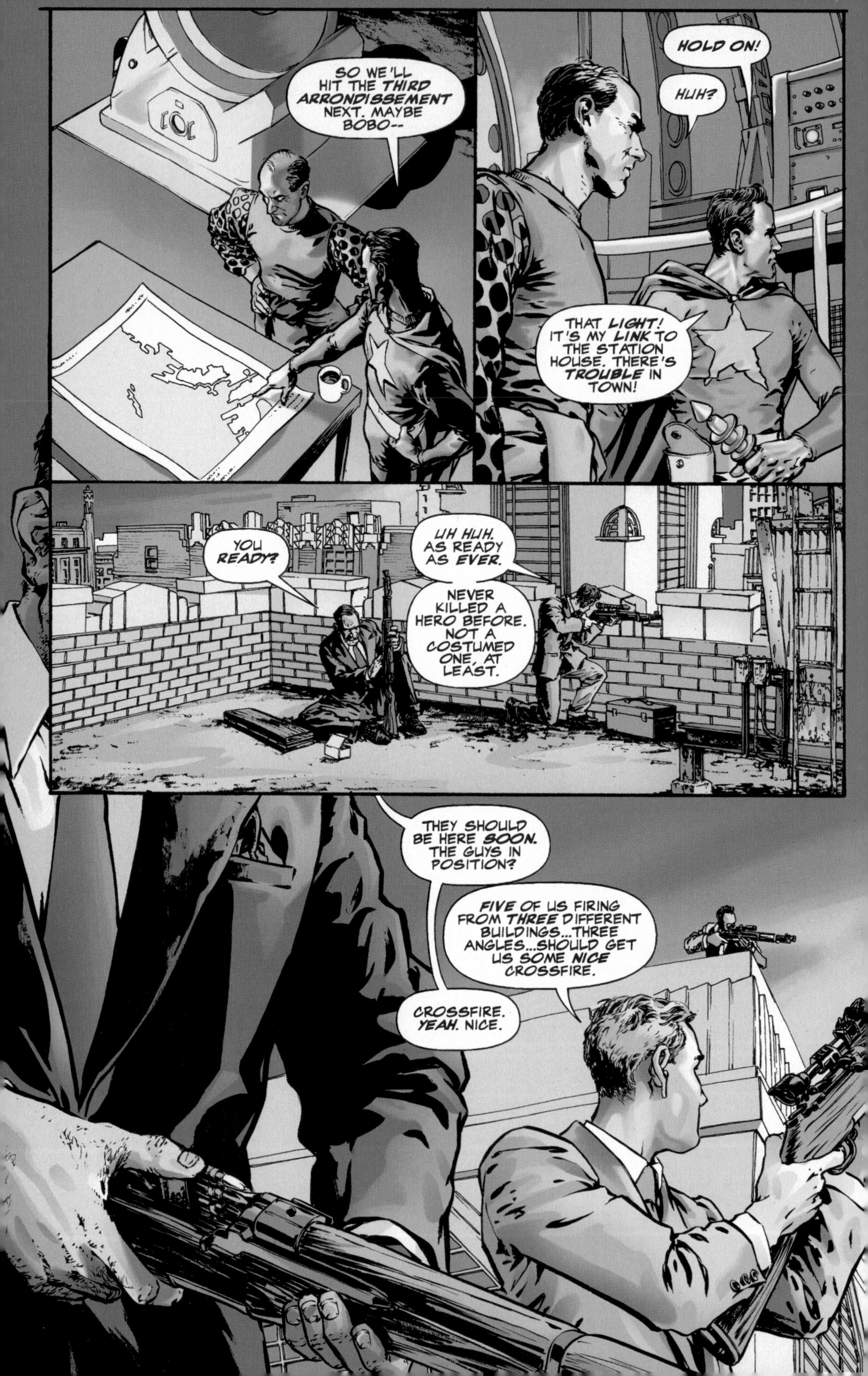

SO WE'LL HIT THE THIRD ARRONDISSEMENT NEXT. MAYBE BOBO--
HOLD ON!
HUH?
THAT LIGHT! IT'S MY LINK TO THE STATION HOUSE. THERE'S TROUBLE IN TOWN!
YOU READY?
UH HUH. AS READY AS EVER.
NEVER KILLED A HERO BEFORE. NOT A COSTUMED ONE, AT LEAST.
THEY SHOULD BE HERE SOON. THE GUYS IN POSITION?
FIVE OF US FIRING FROM THREE DIFFERENT BUILDINGS...THREE ANGLES...SHOULD GET US SOME NICE CROSSFIRE.
CROSSFIRE. YEAH. NICE.

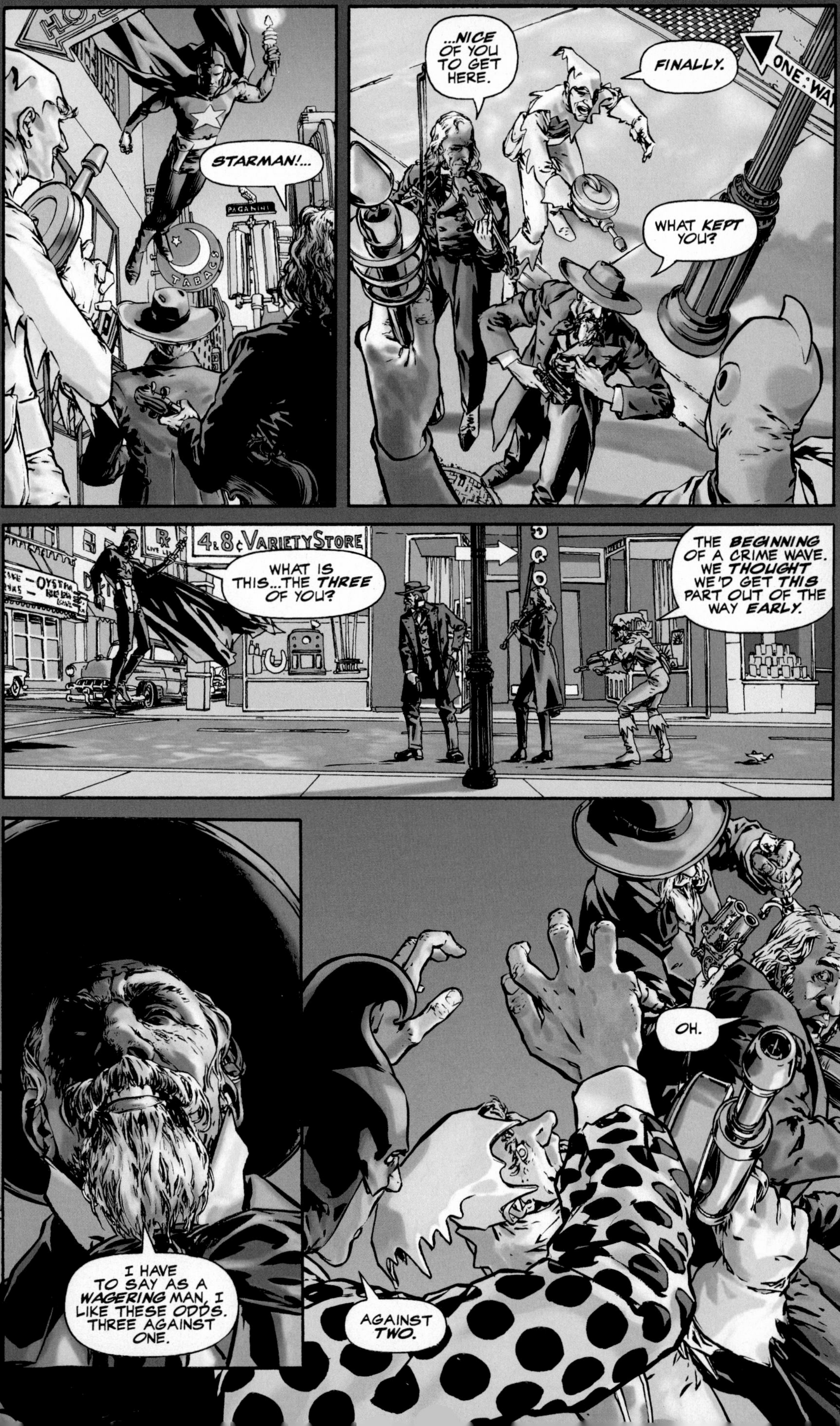
STARMAN!...
PAGANINI
TABACS
...NICE OF YOU TO GET HERE.
FINALLY.
ONE WAY
WHAT KEPT YOU?
4&8¢ VARIETY STORE
WHAT IS THIS...THE THREE OF YOU?
THE BEGINNING OF A CRIME WAVE. WE THOUGHT WE'D GET THIS PART OUT OF THE WAY EARLY.
OH.
I HAVE TO SAY AS A WAGERING MAN, I LIKE THESE ODDS. THREE AGAINST ONE.
AGAINST TWO.

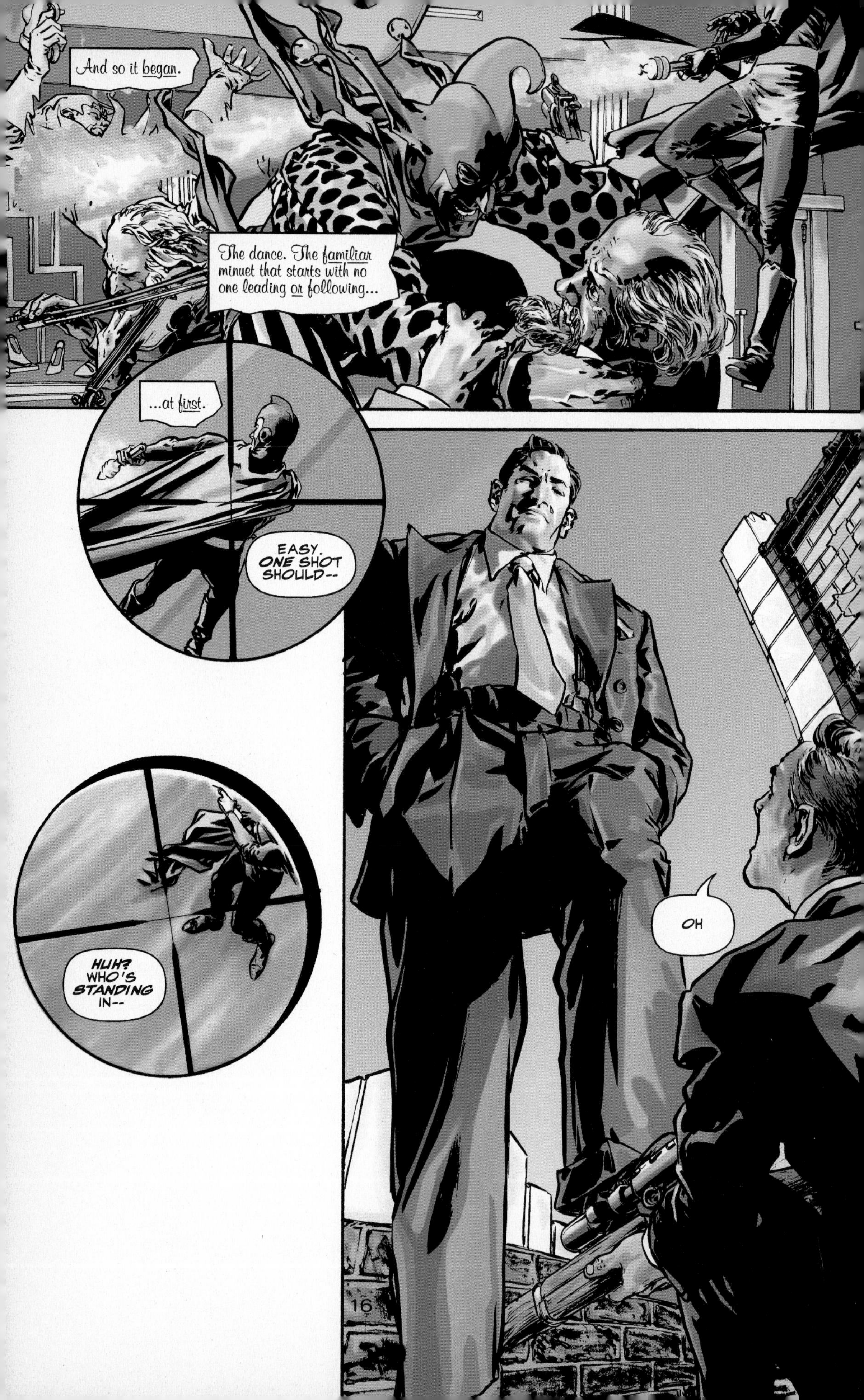

And so it began.
The dance. The familiar minuet that starts with no one leading or following...
...at first.
EASY. ONE SHOT SHOULD--
HUH? WHO'S STANDING IN--
OH

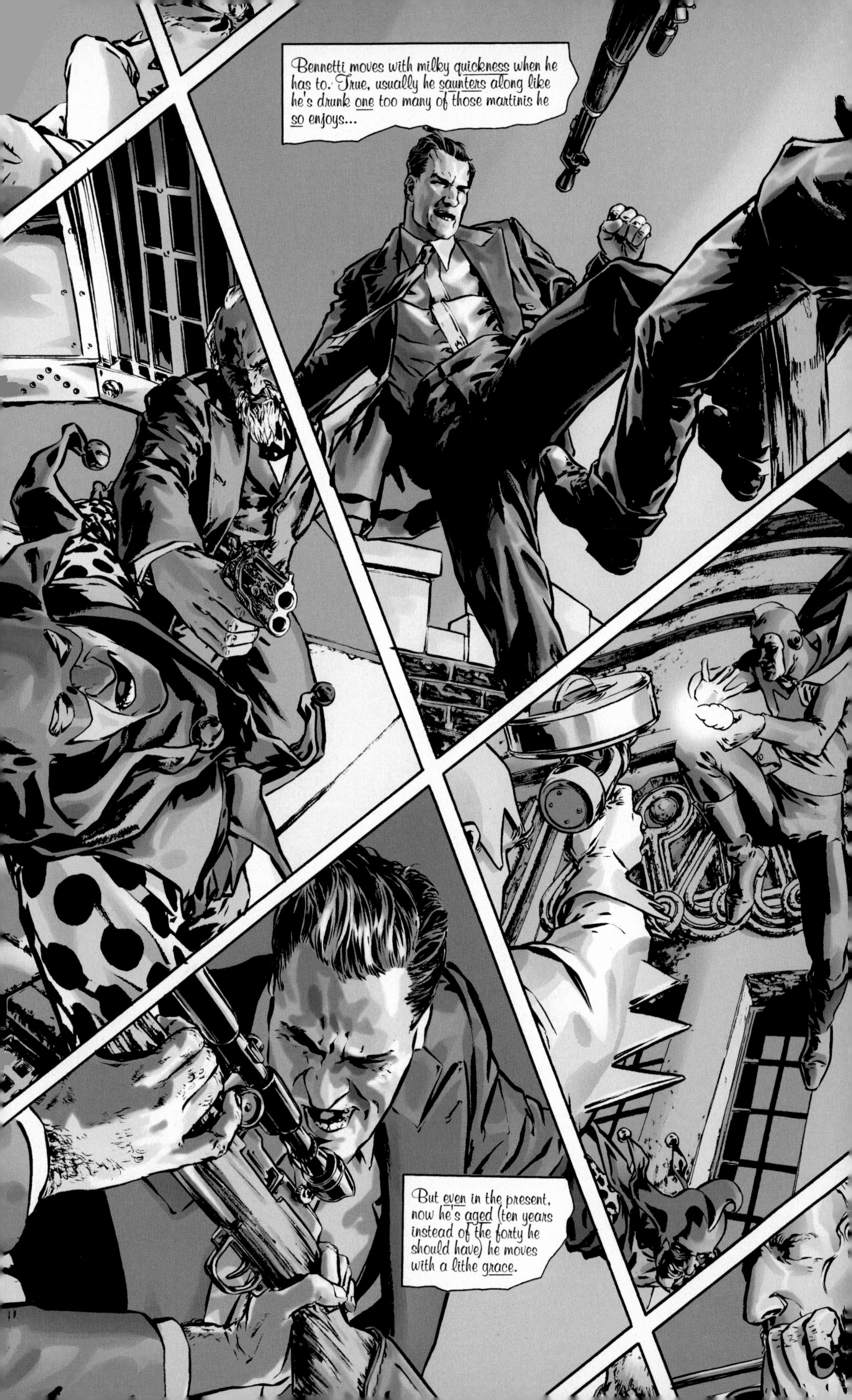
Bennetti moves with milky quickness when he has to. True, usually he saunters along like he's drunk one too many of those martinis he so enjoys...
But even in the present, now he's aged (ten years instead of the forty he should have) he moves with a lithe grace.

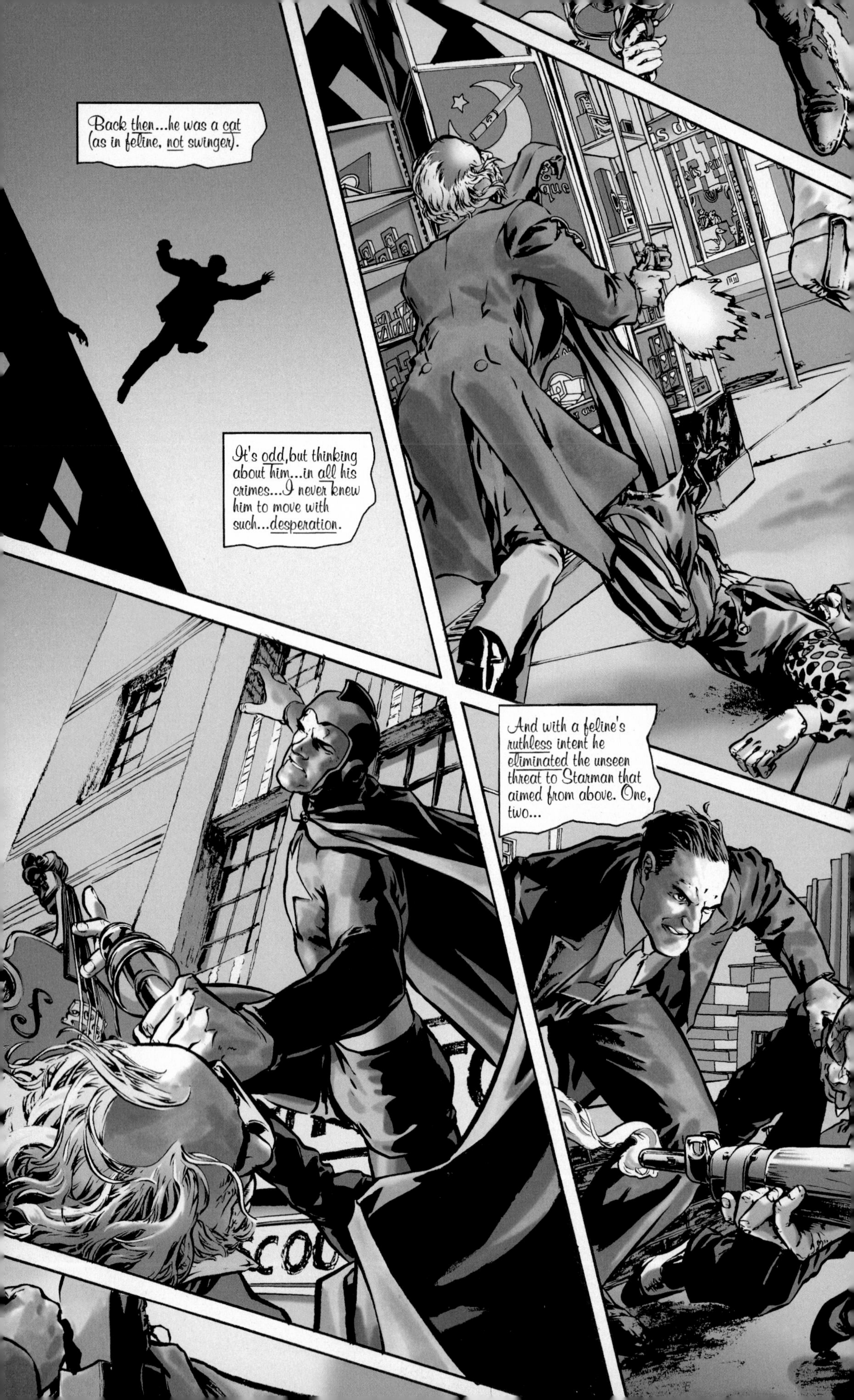
Back then...he was a cat (as in feline, not swinger).
It's odd, but thinking about him...in all his crimes...I never knew him to move with such...desperation.
And with a feline's ruthless intent he eliminated the unseen threat to Starman that aimed from above. One, two...

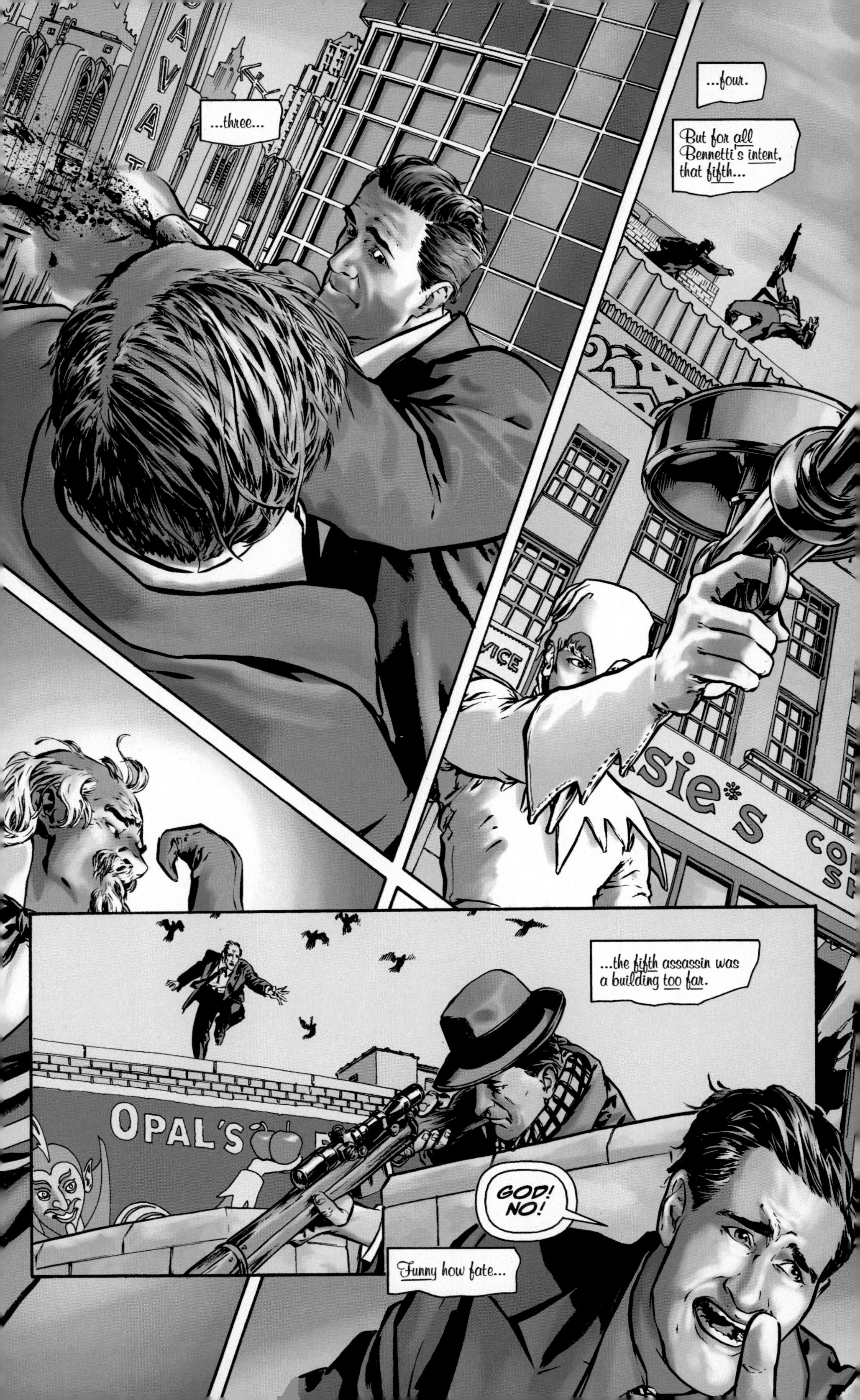
...three...
...four.
But for all Bennetti's intent, that fifth...
sie's
...the fifth assassin was a building too far.
OPAL'S
GOD! NO!
Funny how fate...

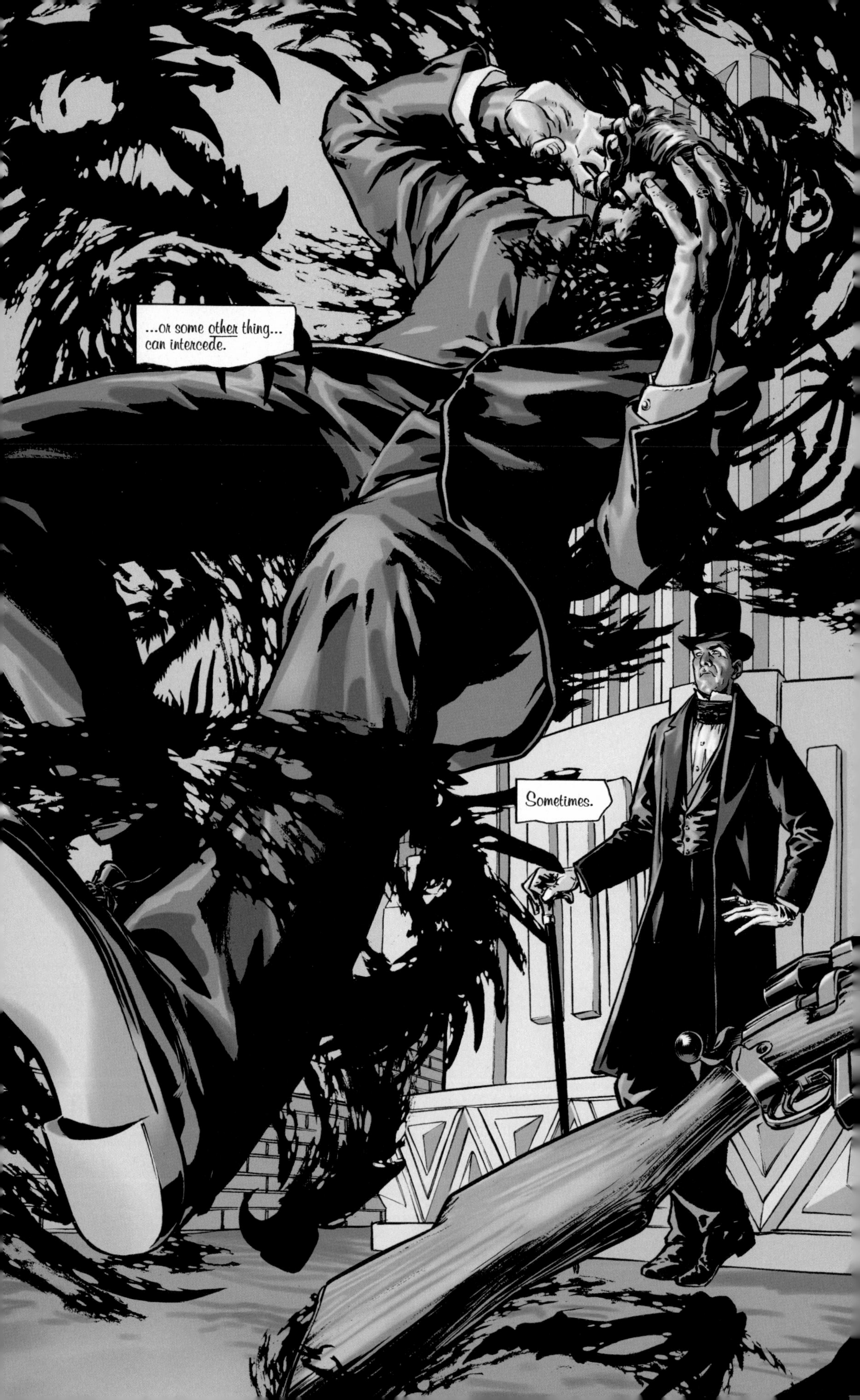
...or some other thing... can intercede.
Sometimes.

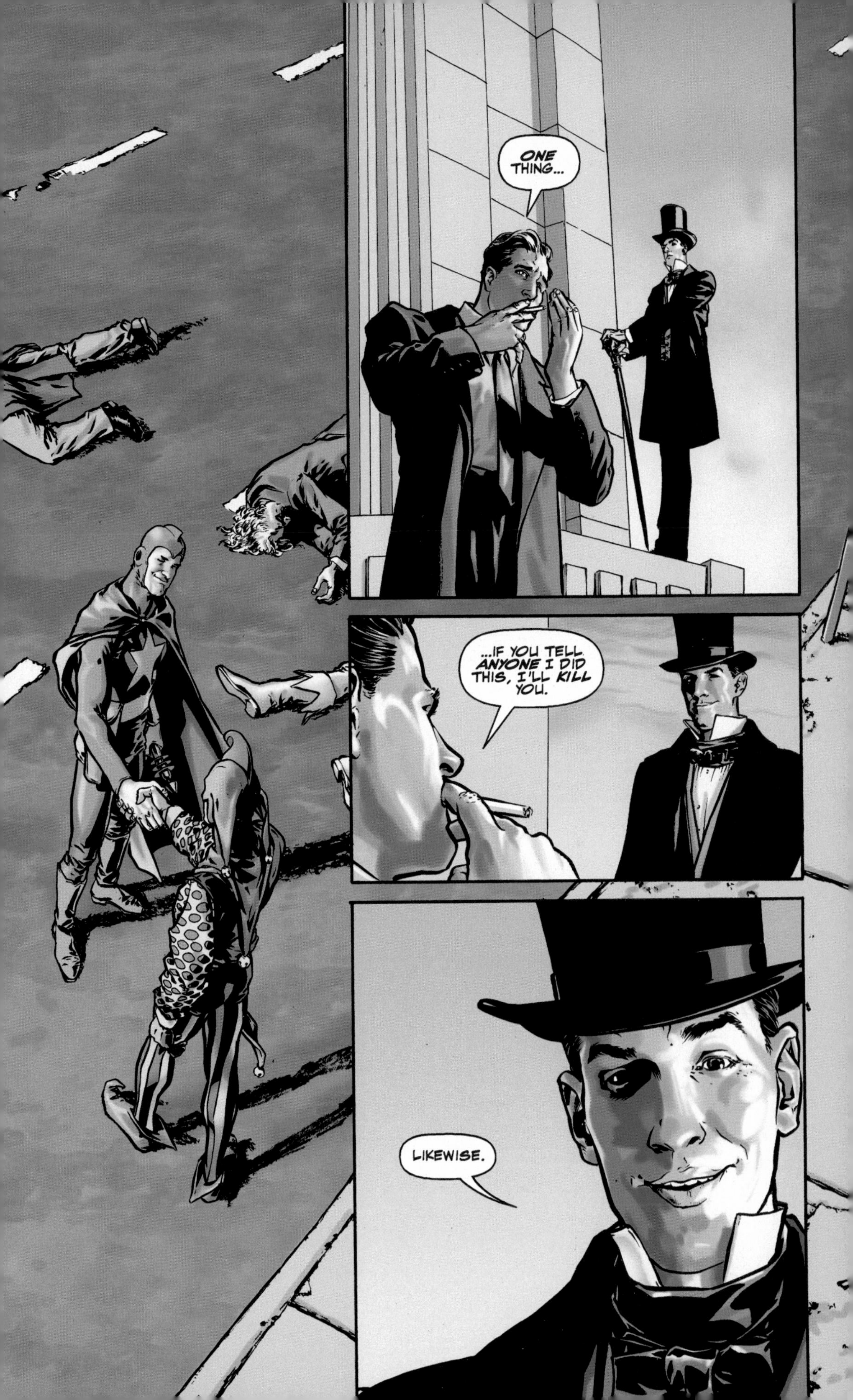
ONE THING...
...IF YOU TELL ANYONE I DID THIS, I'LL KILL YOU.
LIKEWISE.

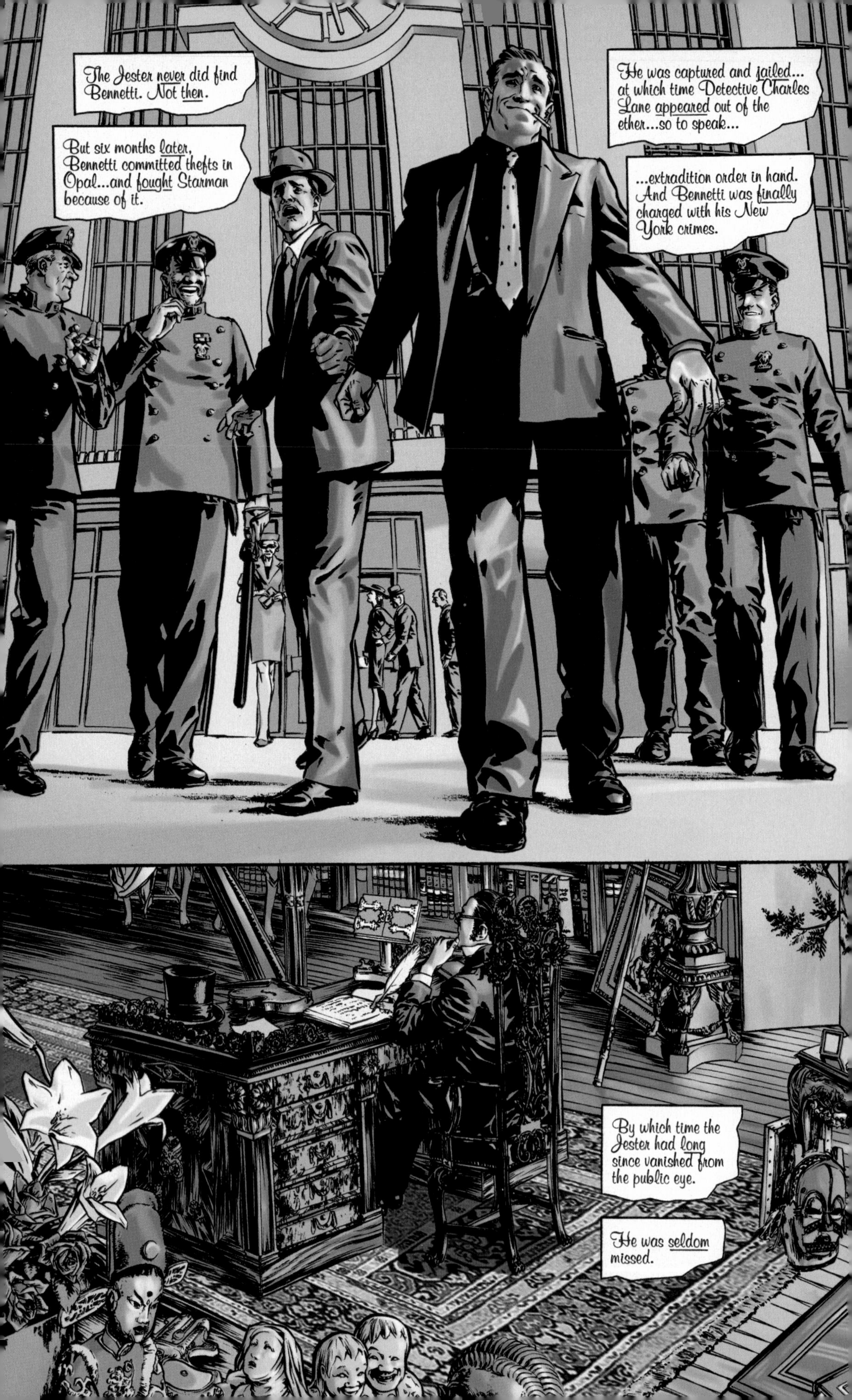
The Jester never did find Bennetti. Not then.
But six months later, Bennetti committed thefts in Opal...and fought Starman because of it.
He was captured and jailed... at which time Detective Charles Lane appeared out of the ether...so to speak...
...extradition order in hand. And Bennetti was finally charged with his New York crimes.
By which time the Jester had long since vanished from the public eye.
He was seldom missed.

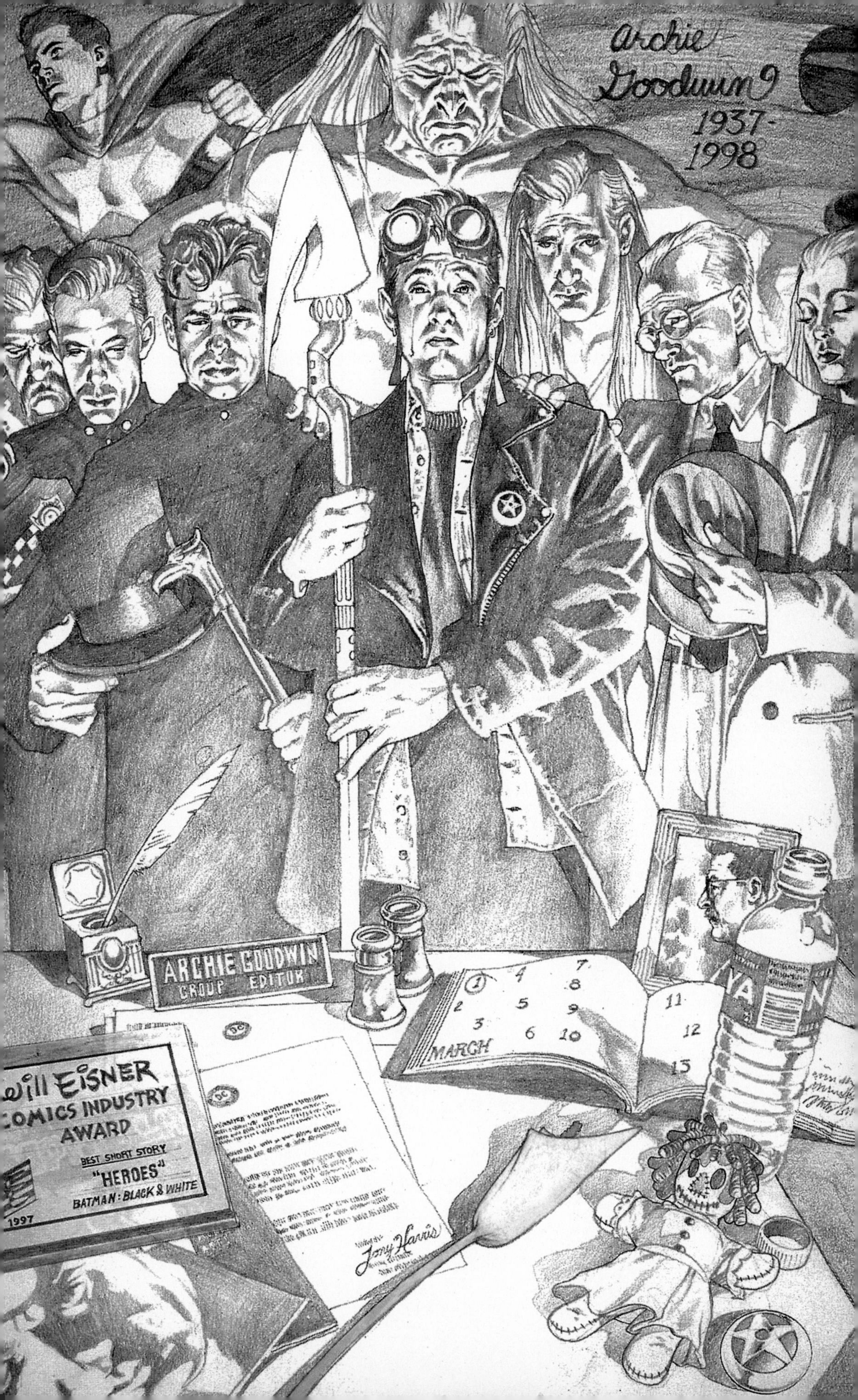
Archie Goodwin 1937-1998
ARCHIE GOODWIN GROUP EDITOR
MARCH
1 2 3 4 5 6 7 8 9 10 11 12 13
WILL EISNER COMICS INDUSTRY AWARD
BEST SHORT STORY
"HEROES"
BATMAN: BLACK & WHITE
1997
Tony Harris

From the Shade's Journal...

Eddy Gomez had a natural talent for the kind of dancing he performed for me that night. *I suppose the closest thing to it would be an "Apache Dance" that you might see in a Parisian revue — you know, where the man wears a beret and a striped vest, the woman is dressed like a mademoiselle of the night, and with grace and agility the pair beat each other up for the amusement of patrons.*

Of course, the "Apache Dance" is artifice. No one is really hurt.

In my "Apache Dance," in the washroom of Musso & Frank's on Hollywood Boulevard, things were a little more improvised. Eddy, I suppose, was playing the female role, though he was dressed in a rather spectacular lavender zoot suit instead of a split skirt and fishnet stockings. However, in the dance it's the female who appears to take the beating and Eddy was certainly taking one as he jerked and jived and pirouetted with each punch and kick he received. The "male" of the dance was all that and more, although if you'd asked him to sport a beret and striped shirt while he made his assault, he might as well have hit you as hard as he was pummeling poor Eddy. Sam Mild had a cigarette in his mouth the whole time. The nonchalance of this only added to the scene's surrealism.

Sam blew smoke from the side of his mouth. "Why won't you talk?" he asked for the twentieth time.

"I'm not a squealer," Eddy spat back, along with one of his incisors.

"Since when? Are you not the Eddy Gomez who sold his own mother to the cops for a hundred and fifty bucks?"

I smiled. Mild's joke wasn't that funny, but I thought it the polite thing to do. Then Gomez replied with a cough of blood...

"It was two hundred. And the old bitch had it coming."

...And then I realized Mild wasn't joking at all.

"Hey! What's going on in there?!" It was one of the waiters. He pounded at the locked door. His voice was shrill. "If you guys don't stop whatever it is you're doing, we'll call the cops. We got laws, you know."

"Shut up," Mild yelled in reply, giving Eddy another punch as he did so.

"We got laws!" The waiter was not to be put off. "And we got famous people who want to use the facilities. We got Sidney Greenstreet out here, and he wants in."

"Tell the fat bastard not to eat so much..."

Another punch, this one to the side of Gomez's head.

"...And he might hold out for the little boy's room longer."

A snort could be heard, which I'm guessing was Greenstreet himself, and then a thud as the waiter threw himself against the door. I presume the man was slight, as he made little effect on the door, hinge, lock, or the stream of punches that Eddy Gomez enjoyed.

"That's it, to hell with bad publicity," the waiter screamed out in his high-pitched tone, "I'm calling the cops."

"Damn." Mild kicked Eddy between the legs. "They don't mind the bad publicity but I'm paid to make sure none of it washes up outside Mr. Hughes' cabana." He dragged Gomez toward the door. "Come on, Eddy. Let's take a drive. I love the canyons at night. How about you?"

★ ★ ★ ★ ★ ★

We had arrived at Musso & Frank's a quarter of an hour before that. The place was full. It was a popular eatery after all, with its cozy wood-lined booths and its familiar menu of tried and true meals. Sometimes a star would drop by for a sandwich or some soup, so it was also a place where tourists visited in the hope of sighting their big-screen favorite. As we entered, I immediately saw Greenstreet in a corner booth devouring a chicken. Apart from that, it had been the usual mixture of Hollywood Boulevard flotsam.

Mild had walked through the place, pushing aside a waiter who had tried to seat him. We were looking for Eddy Gomez, and Mild fully intended that this would be the final port of call in our evening's hunt for the little fellow.

Our search had begun in a pool hall down near the Santa Monica pier. A large fellow named Gunny had told Mild and myself that a friend of a friend of a friend of his had heard "some news about Hughes" but he wasn't sure what.

From there we drove to Fairfax and a small motel where Gunny's friend of a friend of a friend was enjoying the favors of a middle-aged lady with a quite spectacular amount of hair growth on her upper lip. In fact, had the lady in question not scurried from bed to bathroom sans apparel when Mild kicked the door in on them, I might have questioned her sex more so and assumed her a man with a taste for wigs and rouge. The friend of a friend of a friend was nervous. He didn't want to get anyone in trouble. But when Mild put the fellow's genitals in the drawer of the bedside table and threatened to slam it shut on them, the friend of a friend of a friend all of a sudden didn't care how hard a rain was going to fall on the next fellow as long as his favorite little chap and he stayed together to play together.

And so we again drove through the night. It had begun to rain by now, but the car had good wipers and Mild's handling of slippery L.A. roads was assured. I sat, a passenger content.

The friend of a friend was a drummer in a fairly acceptable dance band. They were play-ing in a little basement club over on Los Feliz. It was a mixed crowd there. Latinos in their zoot suits. Some servicemen. Some shady white men with sallow complexions and shifty eyes.

The drummer's name was Jerry.

"Hey, man," he said in his coolest half-whisper, "you a friend of Gunny's? Gunny owes me $40."

Mild backhanded him across the cheek. "I don't care if he owes you his life. I want to know who was talking about Howard Hughes."

"I forgot."

Mild sighed. "You know, if I smashed your hands you might heal to play the drums some more. But if I held them down while my buddy drove over them with our car, buddy, you ain't never gonna be hitting the high hat again. So why don't you think a little harder and maybe your memory will come back."

I looked at Jerry's eyes. They spun like plates on the vaudeville stage.

"This man is a drug user," I said.

Mild looked more closely into his face. "Yeah, for sure. Should have noticed." He shook Jerry. "You hopped up? Wouldn't be the first jazzer I met with the habit. Still, it makes getting information out of him easy."

Mild reached into his jacket. For his gun, I thought. Or perhaps a cosh. Instead he produced four crisp twenty-dollar bills.

"Gunny owes you forty? Here's that and that again. You want it? Buys a lot of junk, that much dough. Just give me a name and you can bliss yourself silly, friend."

Jerry stared at the cash. He seemed transfixed. It was as if he were trying to put all these scattered fragments of information together in his head — money...for information....tell him information...I get money...with money I buy dope...with money...for information...

After what seemed like an eternity, Jerry opened his mouth.

"You cats know Eddy Gomez?"

★ ★ ★ ★ ★ ★

And so we arrived at Musso & Frank's. We found Eddy making the acquaintance of an egg salad sandwich. Mild stood Eddy up and marched him to the men's room. The questions turn into a beating. Then the waiter's high-pitched threats and his news of Greenstreet's full bladder. Out the back door, as the police arrives in the front. Into the car we had parked...and away.

Our car was parked high up on a deserted stretch of Mulholland. Mild looked out at the lights of the San Fernando Valley.

"You like the canyons?" he asked Eddy.

"I guess. I like to bring girls up here."

"So do I. Isn't that why God created them?"

"Girls?"

"No, canyons."

Sitting in the back, listening to this repartee, I suppressed a smile.

"I don't get you, Eddy," Mild said.

"I'm a simple guy. What's not to get?"

"I beat the hell out of you. Why didn't you tell me what you heard about Hughes? If you'd ask me for money, I'd have given it to you. You could have come out of this ahead."

"I got my reasons."

"You got reasons? You got reasons? I admire your guts, kid. Even if you are a sap."

"So what'cho gonna do to me now?"

"I'm going to kill you."

"Just like that."

"Just like that. I'm going to put a bullet in you and roll you off the road and down the canyonside into the brush. By the time the cops find you, you'll probably have been torn up some by the coyotes. Messy death. Gomez...that's a Mex name, right? You from South of the border?"

"I was born in San Francisco. My father worked in the vineyards."

"You're Catholic with a name like that, though. Gotta be. No open casket burial for you if the dogs chew you up."

Eddy sat in the passenger seat for a short while. He stared at the twinkling lights below him. Tears began to roll down his cheeks.

"I love this town. I'd hate to leave it."

Mild rolled his eyes. "Then why not stay? Tell me what you know, Eddy. Believe me. I will kill you and not think twice, but I don't enjoy the taking of lives and I would rather drive you back to some nice corner of town and drop you off. Hell, spill what you know and I'll even kick in a thousand bucks. Call it my apology for the beating you took earlier."

"I'm scared."

"Of what? I'm going to kill you in about a minute if you don't talk. What could you be more scared of than that?"

"My soul."

"Come again?"

"What I heard is that Mr. Hughes is being attacked by characters from a children's book, right?"

"Maybe," Mild replied blowing a perfect ring of smoke.

"Maybe nothing. Am I right?"

"Yeah."

"Word is that the guy behind the attacks is a magician. Word is he knows black magic and stuff. Word is he has an army of soulless helpers who do his bidding."

"Oh, yeah?" Mild sounded skeptical.

"He was a film director," Eddy continued, oblivious to Mild's tone. "Until recently. He used to be a big name, too. Horror movies. Stuff with Lon Chaney. Big name. Then his career went downhill. He quit in '38 or '39, about."

Mild shook Eddy's collar. "I don't want his life story, just his name."

Eddy swallowed and sighed. "The guy's name is Tod Browning," he said, and shivered a little as he did so.

"So what do you know about Tod Browning?"

"Less than you, I'm sure."

This was how Sam Mild broke the silence we had enjoyed since dropping off young Eddy Gomez at the corner of Beverly and Fairfax. Mild had been true to his word and had stuffed money in the lad's pocket as he heaved him out of his car.

Eddy had turned to Mild as he stood on the sidewalk dusting himself off. "Thanks for not killing me, you bastard," he said. "But next time try not to hit me so hard, huh?"

"You better hope there isn't a next time, kid. I was feeling good tonight. Tomorrow might find me in a different mood."

"Please don't repeat what I told you about Tod Browning," Eddy said nervously.

"Oh, I'll repeat it," Mild replied. "I've got to tell my superiors. You know that." Eddy looked at Mild with fearful uneasiness. "But they don't have to know who told me," Mild continued. "So relax."

"I'm scared, man."

"Of this Browning cat?"

"Oh, yeah. Man. He's gonna be the death of you if you dig too deeply in whatever he's got going."

"Yeah, well, we all gotta die." He turned to me. "Ain't that right, Shade?"

I smiled and said nothing.

"Watch yourself, kid," Mild said as our car pulled away.

And so we drove. Along Beverly to La Brea and left up Fountain, passing through Fairfax, and then left again on La Cienega back down to Beverly. I realized Mild had driven us in and enormous square and was about to break the silence by remarking upon it, when Mild spoke first just ahead of me.

"So, what do you know about Tod Browning?"

"Less than you, I'm sure," I replied.

"He's a film director," he said. "We know that. I think...didn't he direct a horror film? Maybe. The Wolfman? Or....I dunno."

"No. And neither do I. I find all horror films tiresome and foolish and refrain from seeing them."

"Me, I got no time for films," Mild offered. "I see too much of the dirt that goes into making them. The actors and their boys on the side. The actresses whose stag films I have to locate the negatives for. Or they have the prostitution records I have to bribe free of the law to destroy. Or they've had abortions. Or there's an ex-husband kicking around who needs paying off or killing. And that's just the weak goddamn actors. Bunch of stupid kids with more money than smarts. The big guys...Mayer and Warner and Cohn and Selznick...all of them have dirty secrets too, that me or someone like me has had to sweep under the rug for them."

"The only name I recognize out of those you mention is Mayer," I said. "I hate the man."

"What did he do to you?"

"Nothing. In fact, I've never even met him."

"Then what gives?"

"Through chance and happenstance I met an actor named John Gilbert. We became friends." I coughed slightly as Mild lit one of his cheap cigarettes. "Anyway," I continued, "Gilbert ran afoul of his then boss Louis B. Mayer. Mayer responded to this by driving Gilbert out of the industry. Messing with the man's voice test when the actors were all making the transition from silents to talkies. He drove poor John to an early grave."

"Yeah, I heard that too," Mild muttered. "But don't let it rile you. Stuff like that happens all the time."

"I'm afraid I've already been riled. And one day, Mayer will pay."

Mild placed a hand on my arm. "Look, the one thing I have learned about this town is it's a great leveler. Everybody who is up will one day be down. That's this place. Mayer, as powerful as he is now, will get his one day. Trust me on that."

I sighed a sigh of dissatisfaction and pondered how my revenge on Mayer might one day take shape, when Mild interrupted my thoughts.

"Anyway, I don't see Louis B. Mayer in the car with us, helping us with info on Tod Browning, so I don't want to think about him now. And neither should you, Shade. We've got us a culprit behind this crazy mess, but because we're both ignorant of things movie-like in this land of cinema, we're both of us stymied." He took a drag of his cigarette. "You thirsty?"

"I could take a drink if one was offered to me."

"I know a little after-hours place. Let's go there."

The place in question was actually quite near. A little room with a bar, above a camera store on Cherokee just south of Hollywood Boulevard. Mild parked the car in an alleyway close by and we entered through a side door, taking the creaking wooden staircase upwards to it slowly and with the solemn reverence of two who were entering a temple.

The drinking club itself had been a living quarters at some point, but the owner had seen profit in the lonely who drink when even the moon is telling them they should be home abed. Indeed, one or two men were still there talking about the world to their whiskey sours. The bar itself was cracked marble, old and warred upon, having countless skirmishes with glass and tankard to its credit. Although it was now early the following morning, Larry, the establishment's owner, a fat, happy man with a large disfiguring mole on his cheek, still stood behind the bar awaiting orders.

"What will it be, gentlemen?"

"Vodka gimlet for me. Shade?"

"Sherry," I answered.

"Not in this joint," both Mild and Larry said in unison.

"No?" I asked. "Then what about wine?"

"Got a red somewhere," Larry replied.

"I'm sure in this land of sun-warmed vineyards your red has a humble charm. A glass of that."

Mild and I took our drinks to a side table close to a young man and an older woman. Mild and I sat there in silence for a moment or two, as we sipped our drinks (the red was acceptable), and in that quiet time, I overheard the young man near us making a final negotiation with the woman before the pair of them stepped out for some kind of illicit coupling.

Then Mild called over to Larry. "Hey, Lar! You ever heard of Tod Browning?"

"Yeah. Director. He don't work much now, but didn't he direct Dracula with Lugosi?"

Mild and I looked at each other with relief. In an instant we both knew that Larry was right, and that irritation when a nagging question refuses to be answered had been eased.

"What else do you know about him?"

"You got the sum and total, brother."

"So what do we do now?" I asked.

"We grab some sleep," Mild said. "We got a name. That's a good going for one night. I'll report it to Mr. Hughes and he can use his power to locate Browning. We'll drag him somewhere deserted and I'll introduce Browning to my leather cosh and a couple of yards of rubber hose. He'll talk before long, tell us what's going on and why. We'll have the complete picture. Then we'll drive him out to the desert. Pop him in the head. And you can go back to Opal City the richer for having known me and Mr. Hughes, having actually done very little yourself in terms of solving this mystery."

My face was expressionless.

"Though I must admit to finding your company surprisingly agreeable, on this, a very disagreeable night of hurting folks," Mild said with a smile.

I smiled too.

"You don't enjoy the hurting part of the work?" I asked.

"Never hire someone for that kind of work who enjoys it. They'll go nuts on you when you need them straight. No, the hurting is just part of the job. Nothing more than that." Mild downed his drink. "Come on," he said. "I'm tired. I bet you are too."

I nodded and drained my wine. We left with a wave to Larry, who looked to be beginning to close up shop himself.

It was still night as we left Larry's bar and walked to the alley. The alley was dark. Very dark. Darker than the night and street around it suggested that it should be.

"Come on," Mild said. "The car's—"

Then he stopped. He, like I, could hear a noise. Soft at first, but growing louder. A purring. Purring. Purring. And then there was a smile. A large, toothy, feline smile, shining forth from the black of the alley like a beacon.

Mild whistled through his teeth. "You see that?"

"How could I not?"

Mild took his pistol out and fired two shots into the alley. Both passed through the smiling mouth, but the shattering of glass told us that Mild had managed to hit his car's windscreen further within the blackness. He turned to me. "Your shadow gonna be any use?"

"I doubt it. Not if your bullets aren't." I sent shards of shadows at the smile anyway. No use.

The smile then proceeded to advance from the blackness towards us, getting larger all the while. Presently from the gloom an enormous cat's head became visible. If the size of this was anything to go by, then the beast's body would be immense.

"I think we should split," Mild said.

"I concur," I replied, and we both began sprinting for Hollywood Boulevard.

It was four in the morning or thereabouts, and no one was in sight. Looking over my shoulder I could see the Cheshire Cat (for that was what it was) appear from the alley and begin its chase after us. Its body more resembled a panther's, being lithe and muscular, and indeed it was bigger than any normal animal, being ten feet high at the shoulder.

One bound covered many yards and we were but a few seconds from being pounced upon, when salvation came in the shape of a lonely yellow cab. It's "for hire" sign was down, but that didn't stop Mild, who stood in front of the oncoming car aiming his gun at the driver in order to make him stop. The driver did and we threw ourselves inside the car, as the Cheshire Cat bounded onto the spot upon which we had been standing but seconds before. The driver looked on with dismay.

"What's the matter with you?" Mild screamed. "Drive this heap!"

The driver did. Accelerating as the Cheshire Cat gave chase. Faster and faster the hack sped down the deserted 4:00 A.M. of Hollywood Boulevard. All the while the Cheshire Cat maintained its pursuit. Indeed, it seemed to be getting faster as it bounded after us.

"It's gaining!" Mild screamed. "You call yourself a driver?"

The driver glared over his shoulder at Mild and put all his weight on the gas. The car sped up and away finally, leaving the Cheshire Cat behind. With a final spiteful grin at us, from far in the distance, the Cat vanished as the first lights of dawn arose behind it, far to the East.

"What was that all about?" the driver asked. "What was that thing?"

"A special effect gone crazy," Mild replied. "Movie hijinks, you know?"

"No. I don't know. It looked pretty damn real to me."

"You wanna make some dough? I mean big dough?"

"I guess."

Mild pulled a card and wrote an address down on the back of it. "Here. Come to this address tomorrow. Tell them I sent you. You'll be well paid. You know what for?"

"No."

"You forget all about this. If you don't, I gotta kill you. Understand?"

The driver looked nervous. "Like the gospels, buddy. Me, I'm already developing amnesia."

"Smart," Mild said. "Now take us to our hotel and we'll call it a night? You got it?"

Mild settled back and glanced my way. I could see the anger in his eyes, burning like the dawn we drove away from.

"Man," he said. "When I get my hands on the Browning guy, I am gonna give him such a beating."

The morning after the night of our escape from the large Cheshire Cat (yes, how delightfully benign the whole affair sounds by the light of day)...the morning after that I slept late. I am a being with little need for sleep, but I do find it such an exquisite pleasure. And I knew Mild was out there "packing a wallop" as he so succinctly put it, trying to uncover the whereabouts and activities of Tod Browning.

I never dream. But after waking with the light that shone as glints through the gaps in my curtains, I tried to go back to sleep and in that semi-slumber state imagined meeting Tod Browning. I didn't know what he looked like, so I imagined him resembling Raymond Massey (for no reason at all). I imagined us fighting (well, in truth it would be my shadow demons who'd be doing the fighting while I stood around making delightfully pithy remarks).

...So, in the haze of dreaming not, Browning brought his monsters to fight mine. Shadow Demons fought March Hare and Mock Turtle while the Queen of Hearts screamed "off with his head"...referring to mine. And then when all else failed, Browning called upon his ultimate agent of fear and death, Dracula. Here I imagined Bela Lugosi, but with a long and elegantly groomed mustache. It looked strangely at odd with the smooth, slick hair he'd given his cinematic interpretation of the character.

And that was how it was as I dozed and slept and dozed and slept, until sometime in the very late morning when a timid knock at my door aroused me.

"Come in," I said, sitting up in bed and stretching.

The door was opened by a maid, a small scared girl. She had the look of a beaten dog whose spirit had long ago been broken.

"I was sent to ask you if you'd like some breakfast?"

"Breakfast. That sounds just the thing." I smile. "Tell me my dear, what in this land of sun and oranges passes for breakfast?"

"Gee, I dunno."

"You were sent here to ask me if I wanted breakfast, yet you have no idea what breakfasts are on the menu?"

"No," she countered. "It was the way you asked. It confused me. I thought you were asking me how food here was different from other parts of America."

"I'm sorry, I didn't mean to do that."

"Breakfast can be anything you want, sir. You're a guest of Mr. Hughes, so the kitchen will cook you anything."

"Well, in that case I would like deviled kidneys and scrambled eggs. Toast. And tea with milk. Oh, and perhaps a glass of the fine, sweet juice of oranges that this land is known for."

"You mean orange juice?"

"I mean exactly that."

She moved to leave, then dropped, turning with a questioning expression on her face marked by a slight creasing of her forehead.

"Err...what are deviled kidneys?"

"I take it offal isn't part of the Californian breakfast cuisine," I said. "Yes, you can take the man out of his country, but you can never quite take the desire for that country's food out of the man." I thought for a moment before answering.

"Tell the cook to take, say...two kidneys. Pig's kidneys. Or one large cow's kidney and cut it into bite-size pieces. Fry them with a little pepper and some hot sauce. That's a close approximation of what I have in mind."

The maid looked stunned. "I...I've never heard of it."

"I'm English," I replied. "What can I say? If you really want to be delighted, let me tell you of a singular dish the Northerners in my country created. They call it black pudding."

"Oh, I rather you didn't, sir."

"As you wish. What's your name?"

"Mary."

"You look tired, Mary."

"I was late for work. I've missed my coffee. I have to admit I'm flagging."

"Well, go get my food and we'll discuss your fatigue when you return with it. How does that sound?"

Mary left warily. It was clear few guests before me had ever stopped to ask her name or state of being. I entered the bathroom and brushed my teeth. I then donned a silk kimono I'd acquired during an exploit in Japan, and awaited my food. But then as the moments passed, a thought came to me, and I reached for the telephone.

"Hello. Is this room service?" I asked. "I'd like to add something to my breakfast order. No, not a substitution. An addition to it, that's right. I'd like a big pot of coffee. And cream and sugar. And what goes well with coffee? Strudel? Just the thing. That, too. Oh, and I don't like to eat unattended, so the maid who you sent up earlier, Mary. I'd like her to stay with me while I eat. Yes, that's right, I am a guest of Mr. Hughes."

A while later, Mary returned.

"I ordered you coffee, Mary. We can't have a sleepy maid in the hotel, can we?"

She appeared nervous. "But I should be getting back."

"No. I asked for your company. Sit and take a break."

We sat. She seemed pensive at first, but as the coffee and strudel began to vanish, so did her concerns.

"Where do you live, Mary?"

"Los Feliz."

"So you know the Los Angeles area?"

"As good as anyone."

"Then let's take the time to talk about it. After all, we have the time. I've asked for your company for the whole time I'm eating. And I am a very slow eater."

"All tight," Mary said, shaking off the drab and tired moment by moment. She smiled and suddenly the room was all the brighter for it. "What do you want to know?"

Mary, the maid, stood before me. She was naked. And not unappealing, for I can only presume it was the hard work she did which had made her body firm and shapely. A fine sight. So quickly gone.

In her place was Marguerite Ludlow. She too was naked, and as comely a sight as I have ever beheld. My breath stumbled from my lungs. My eyes became hubcaps. Marguerite. My Marguerite. She was back.

"How are you, my love?"

She said this with the familiar warm, slow curve of her mouth I knew.

"I'm fine, Marguerite. I'm surprised, but I'm fine."

"Surprised?"

"Well, you are dead, after all. I did kill you…after all."

"Did you? I don't recall."

"Wait a minute," I said. "This is a dream. This has to be a dream." Indeed, Marguerite is dead. "If you stand before me now, you are a wraith, or you are a figment."

"Dreams are their own reality," she replied. "If I am here before you, I am here…in this existence I am alive. Close your eyes and take a breath."

"A breath?"

"Smell me."

"Oh."

I did as I was bid and smelled Marguerite's perfume, lavender and rose, made by the local chemist in a town just outside of Paris where we visited often. That sweet aroma bonded with the warm natural smell of her own skin, and combined it smelled of springtime. Even in the coldest weather, around Marguerite it smelled like spring.

"I miss you," she said.

"And I you," I replied, the first frail tear forming in the corner of my eye.

"I'm sorry I tried to kill you," she said.

"And I'm sorry I succeeded," I said back.

She smiled. "What was, was. What will be, will. You shouldn't hate yourself. Do you remember the opera?"

"Which one?"

"The marriage of Figaro. You were disappointed at the end. You had so looked forward to hearing the 'Figaro chorus,' as you called it." (At which point Marguerite began to sing..."Figaro. Figaro, Figaro, Figaro"...then looked at me with a grin.) "You didn't realize that the music you wanted to hear was from the Barber of Seville."

"Yes," I said awkwardly. "Well. Two operas with characters called Figaro. Who would have guessed."

"The walk back from the opera house was wonderful. The cool night. All those stars. We found a courtyard. It was asleep...everyone in the houses around. I made you forget your disappointment in that courtyard."

I closed my eyes again. The pain of remembering those happier times before I discovered Marguerite was really one of the Ludlow clan bent upon my death...it was almost too much to bear. I who had lived so long. I who had endured so much. Yet, all I had to do was see my lost love again and I was close to destruction, my heart close to breaking. I was beyond forlorn. I took another breath of her sweet, springtime perfume...

...And almost retched upon the ground. Gone was spring in all its lavender freshness. I smelled brimstone and human waste and rotting flesh. I recall India, one summer of sickness when I had visited the Ganges. The banks of it were lined with the corpses of untouchables the Indian caste system forbids others to move. The dead stayed where they had fallen to bake and rot in the afternoon rays. The stench I smelled now was akin to the rancid odor on that day in India once. Only worse.

I opened my eyes and saw the Devil.

"Hello again," he said.

He was as naked as Marguerite had been. The sight was not as pleasing.

"When was it last," he asked. "Iceland?"

"Where's Marguerite?"

"Dead, I imagine," he said in an offhand Devil's fashion. "Yes, quite dead."

"You're telling me she was never here?"

"It's your dreams. You tell me."

"No, I suppose not. I suppose she remains as dead as when I left her. Why are you here?"

"You're my son. Of sorts. I fear for you."

"I am no one's son," I sneered back.

"Nevertheless I fear for you. I fear for you this day."

"Why?"

"People come to crossroads. Life is a series of them."

"Like the day you decided to defy your father?"

"Hmm," the Devil said, pausing to think for a moment. "I suppose that was one of those times." He looked off for a moment. "I've never been able to decide if that was one of my better choices...or one of my worst."

"It's my dream. You tell me."

"Touché. I fear for you, Shade," he said, rapidly changing the subject as if the topic of his fall from grace made him uncomfortable. "I fear this adventure you're on. A word...of advice. Beware the demon."

"The demon? Which demon?"

"That is for you to discover. My warning is the beginning and end. You must give the menace a name other than that."

"Is there nothing else you can tell me?" I asked, twitching a little as I said this, like a little boy caught doing something bad.

"Yes, I have to say..." A pause. "...We're here," the Devil said.

"We're here?"

"Yes," he said. "Look around you..."

I looked and in doing so opened my eyes. I had indeed been asleep the whole time. Now, upon waking, I saw sand and palm trees.

Mary was in the driver's seat of a small, gray Ford roadster (which actually was black, but had so many layers of dirt as to disguise this fact). She turned to me, sitting next to her as her passenger as I was.

"Look around," she said with a smile.

"Where are we?"

"Why, don't you remember?" she asked. "I had the afternoon off. I told you I was going to the beach. You asked if you could come with me. And here we are."

"Oh," I said. "Oh yes. Now I recall."

I smiled back at her and got out of the car, breathing fresh sea air that quickly cleared the lingering smell of brimstone.

"It's a beautiful afternoon," Mary said.

"Yes. Yes, it is," I replied, looking out.

The Pacific was before me. Blue and calm. I closed my eyes, said a final farewell to Marguerite who lingered still on my mind, and then stepped towards the water.

TO BE CONTINUED...

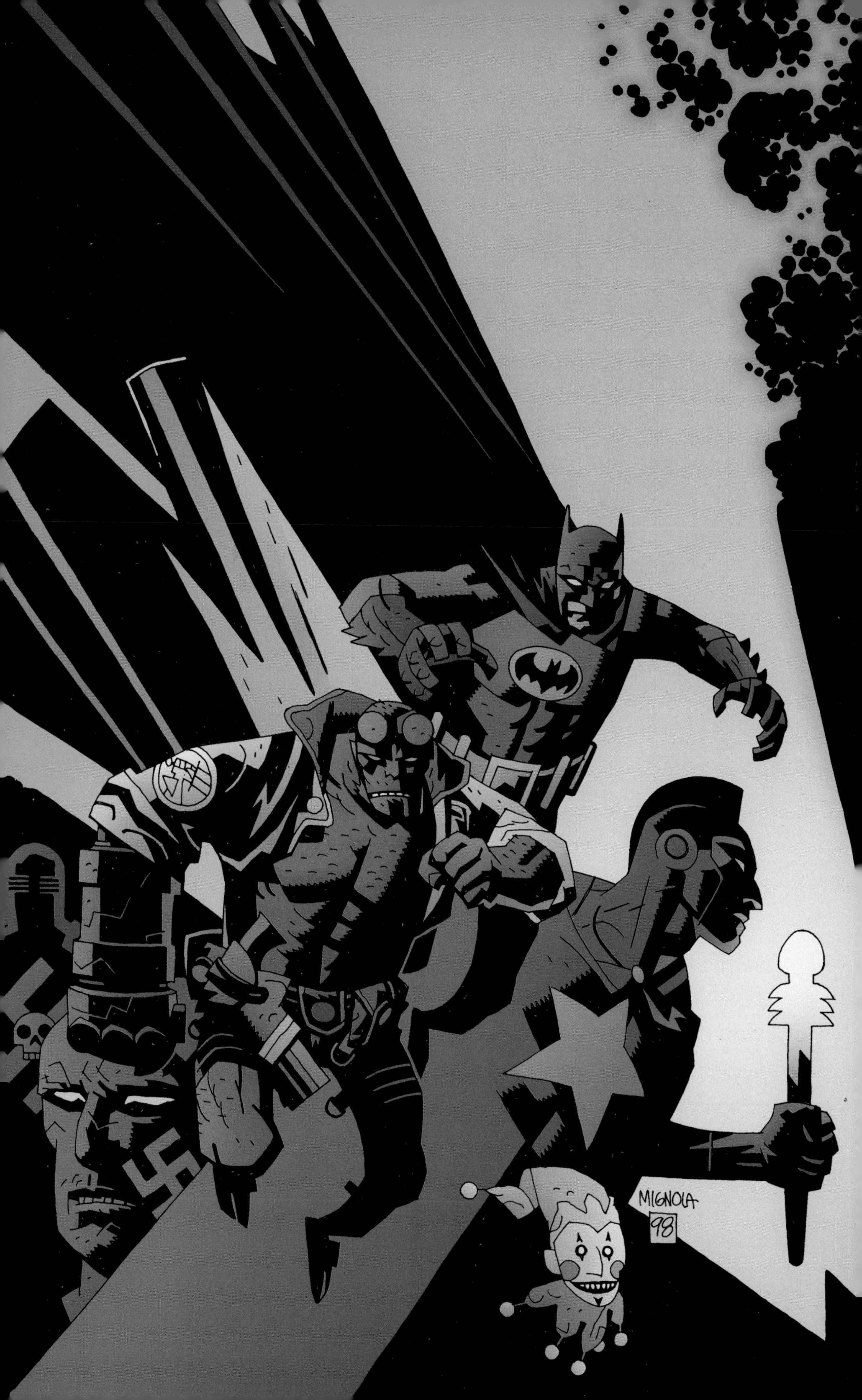
MIGNOLA
98

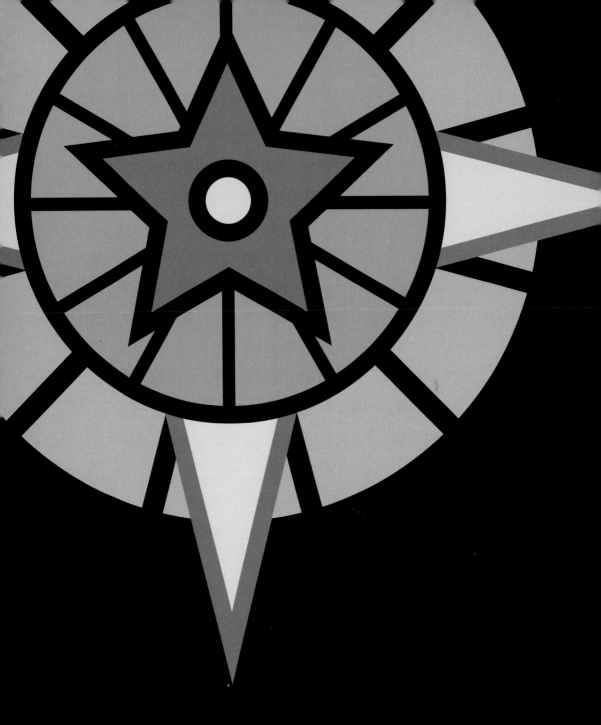

BATMAN/HELLBOY/STARMAN 1

Cover by Mike Mignola

Written by James Robinson

Art by Mike Mignola

with colors by Matt Hollingsworth

Special thanks to Archie Goodwin

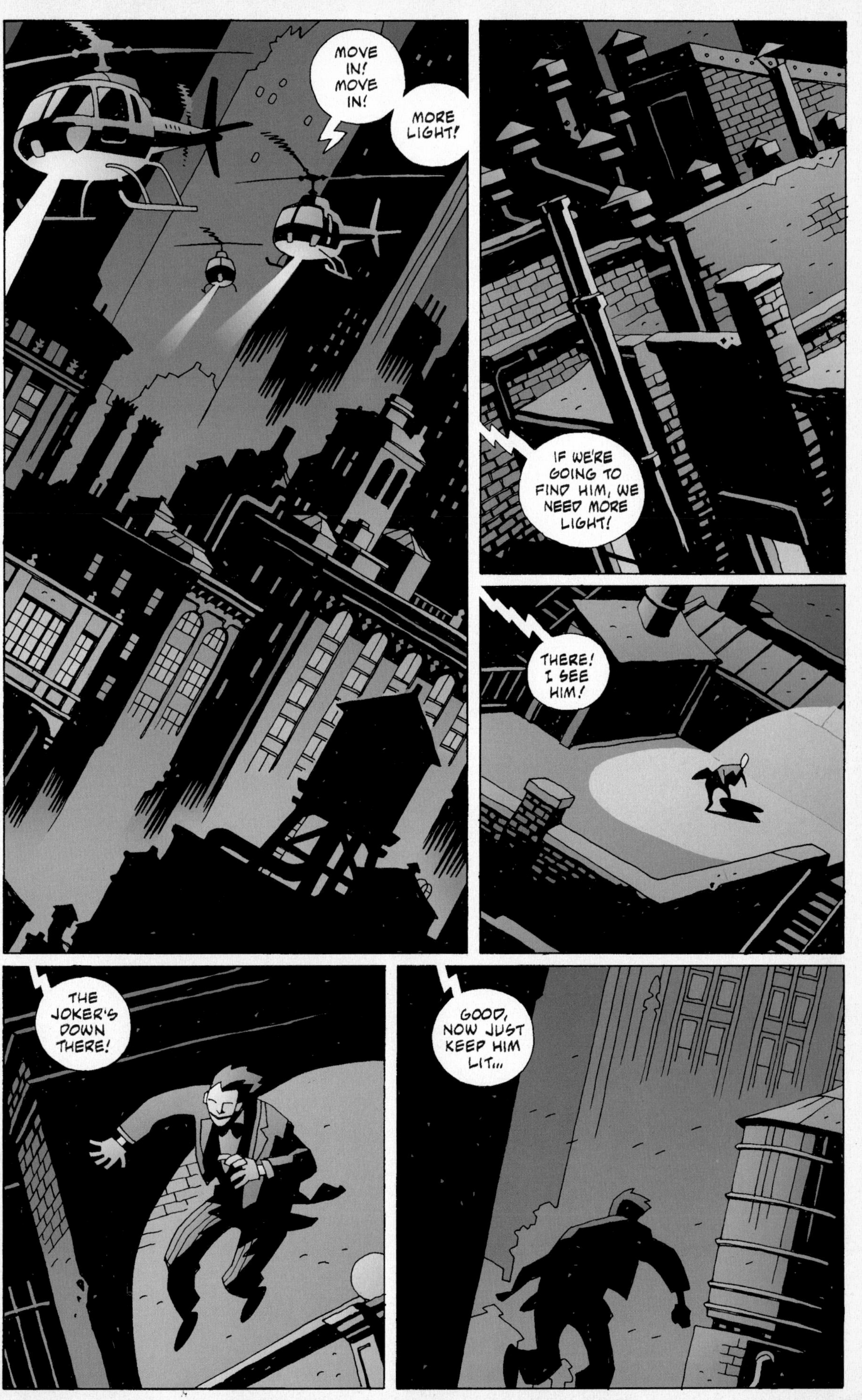
MOVE IN! MOVE IN!
MORE LIGHT!
IF WE'RE GOING TO FIND HIM, WE NEED MORE LIGHT!
THERE! I SEE HIM!
THE JOKER'S DOWN THERE!
GOOD, NOW JUST KEEP HIM LIT...

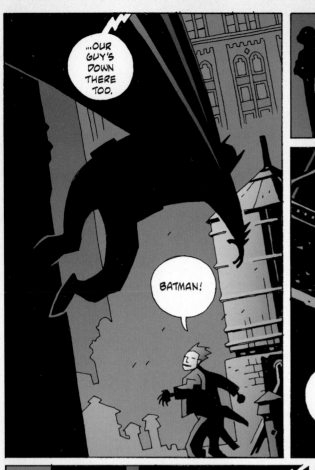

...OUR GUY'S DOWN THERE TOO.

BATMAN!

THEY'RE MOVING TOO FAST. HARD TO SEE WITH ALL THE SPIRES.

KEEP ON THEM! DO YOUR BEST.

YOU CAN'T GET AWAY, MANIAC!

THE DEVIL YOU SAY.

BATMAN'S GAINING!

GIVE UP, JOKER!

SURRENDER? YOU MUST THINK I'M CRAZY!

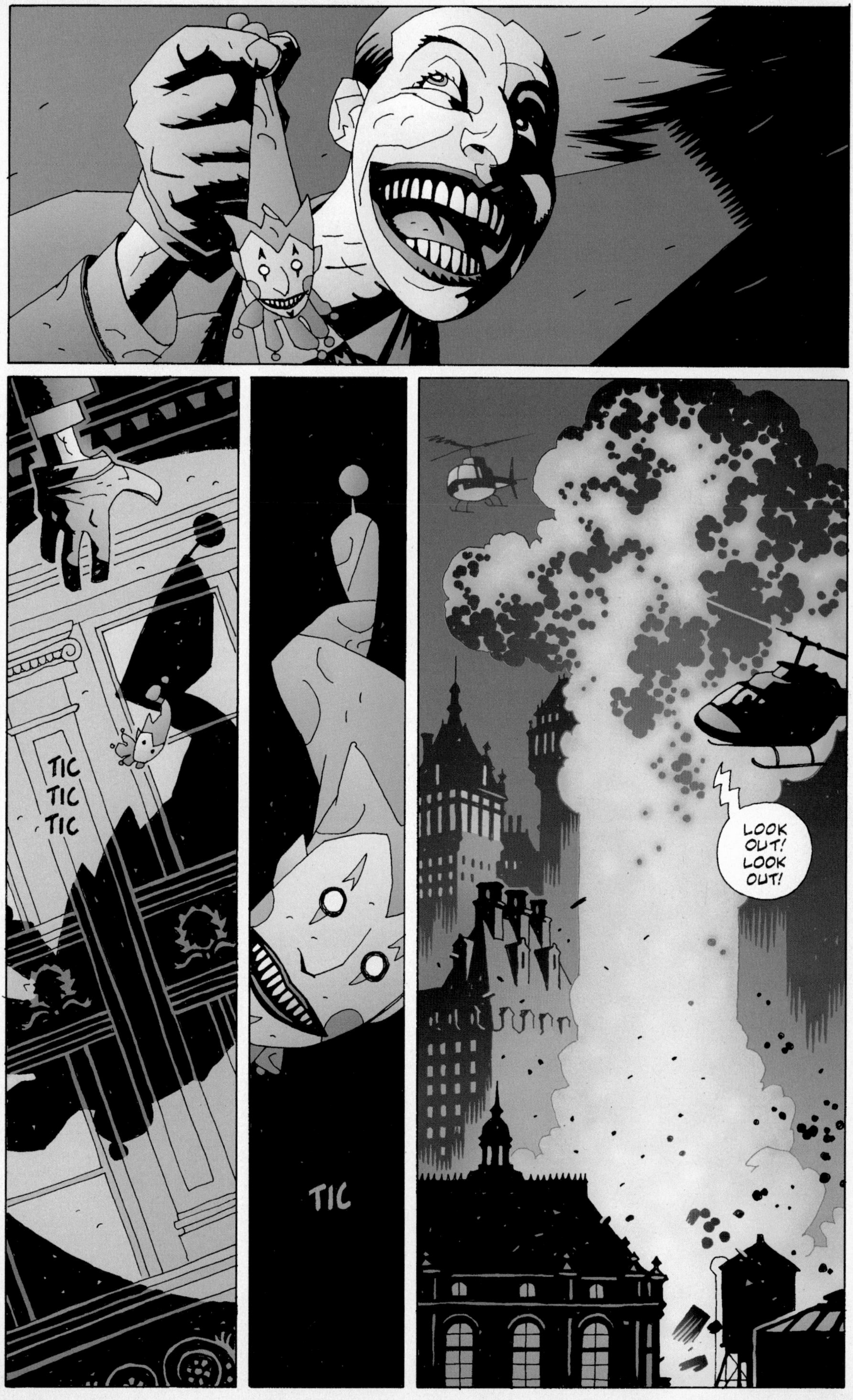
TIC
TIC
TIC
TIC
LOOK OUT! LOOK OUT!

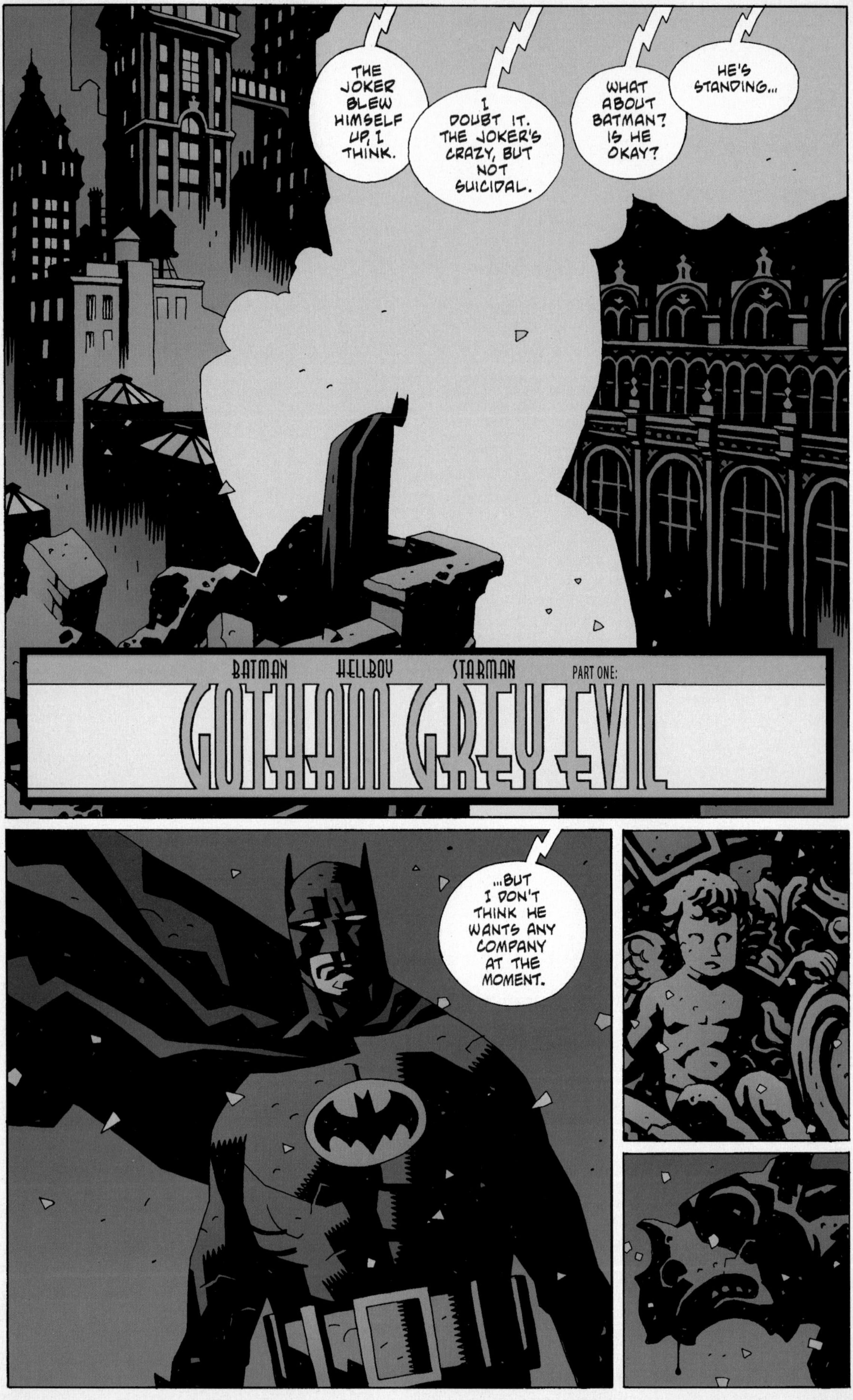
THE JOKER BLEW HIMSELF UP, I THINK.
I DOUBT IT. THE JOKER'S CRAZY, BUT NOT SUICIDAL.
WHAT ABOUT BATMAN? IS HE OKAY?
HE'S STANDING...
BATMAN HELLBOY STARMAN PART ONE:
GOTHAM GREY EVIL
...BUT I DON'T THINK HE WANTS ANY COMPANY AT THE MOMENT.

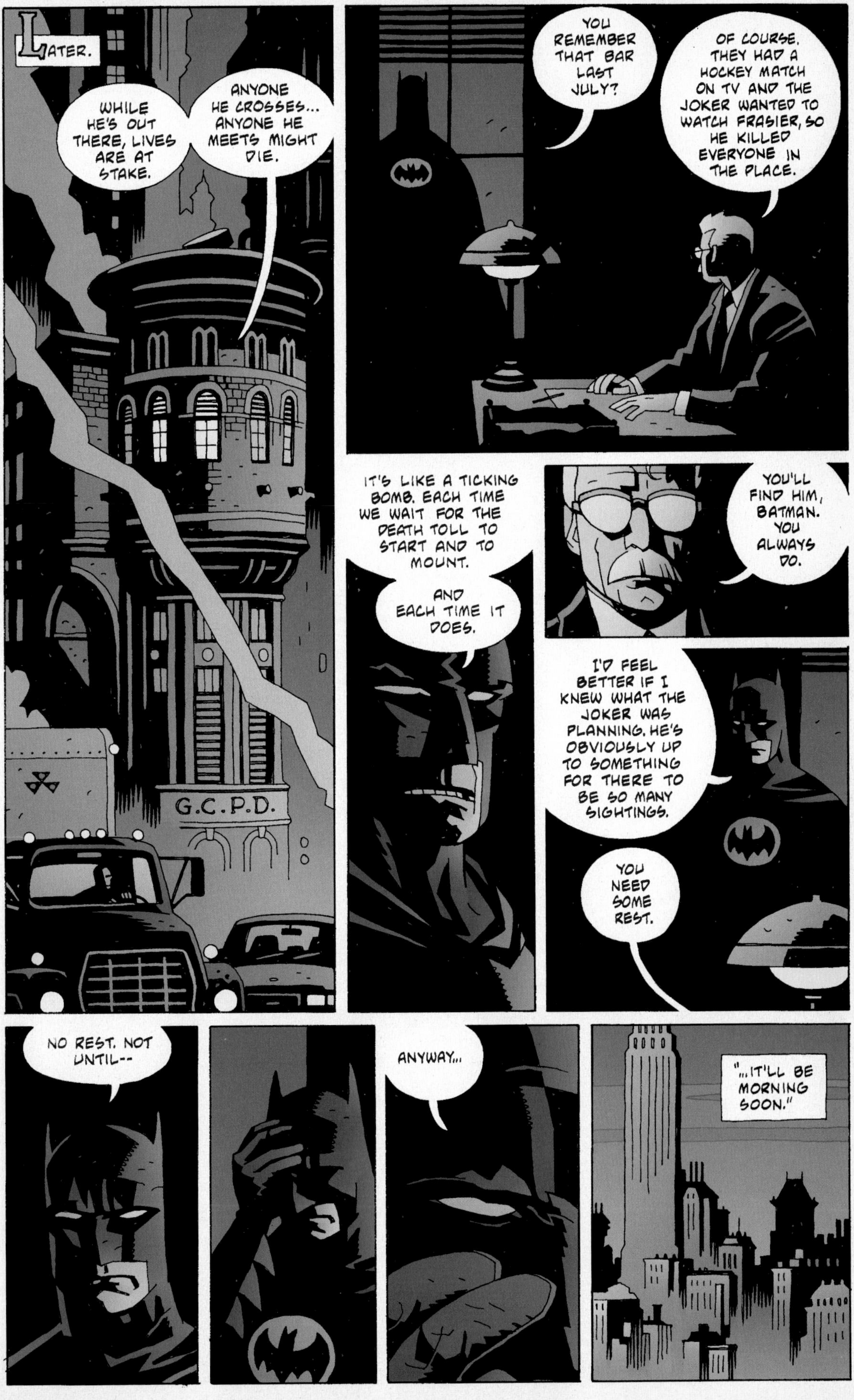
LATER.
WHILE HE'S OUT THERE, LIVES ARE AT STAKE.
ANYONE HE CROSSES... ANYONE HE MEETS MIGHT DIE.
G.C.P.D.
YOU REMEMBER THAT BAR LAST JULY?
OF COURSE. THEY HAD A HOCKEY MATCH ON TV AND THE JOKER WANTED TO WATCH FRASIER, SO HE KILLED EVERYONE IN THE PLACE.
IT'S LIKE A TICKING BOMB. EACH TIME WE WAIT FOR THE DEATH TOLL TO START AND TO MOUNT.
AND EACH TIME IT DOES.
YOU'LL FIND HIM, BATMAN. YOU ALWAYS DO.
I'D FEEL BETTER IF I KNEW WHAT THE JOKER WAS PLANNING. HE'S OBVIOUSLY UP TO SOMETHING FOR THERE TO BE SO MANY SIGHTINGS.
YOU NEED SOME REST.
NO REST. NOT UNTIL--
ANYWAY...
"...IT'LL BE MORNING SOON."

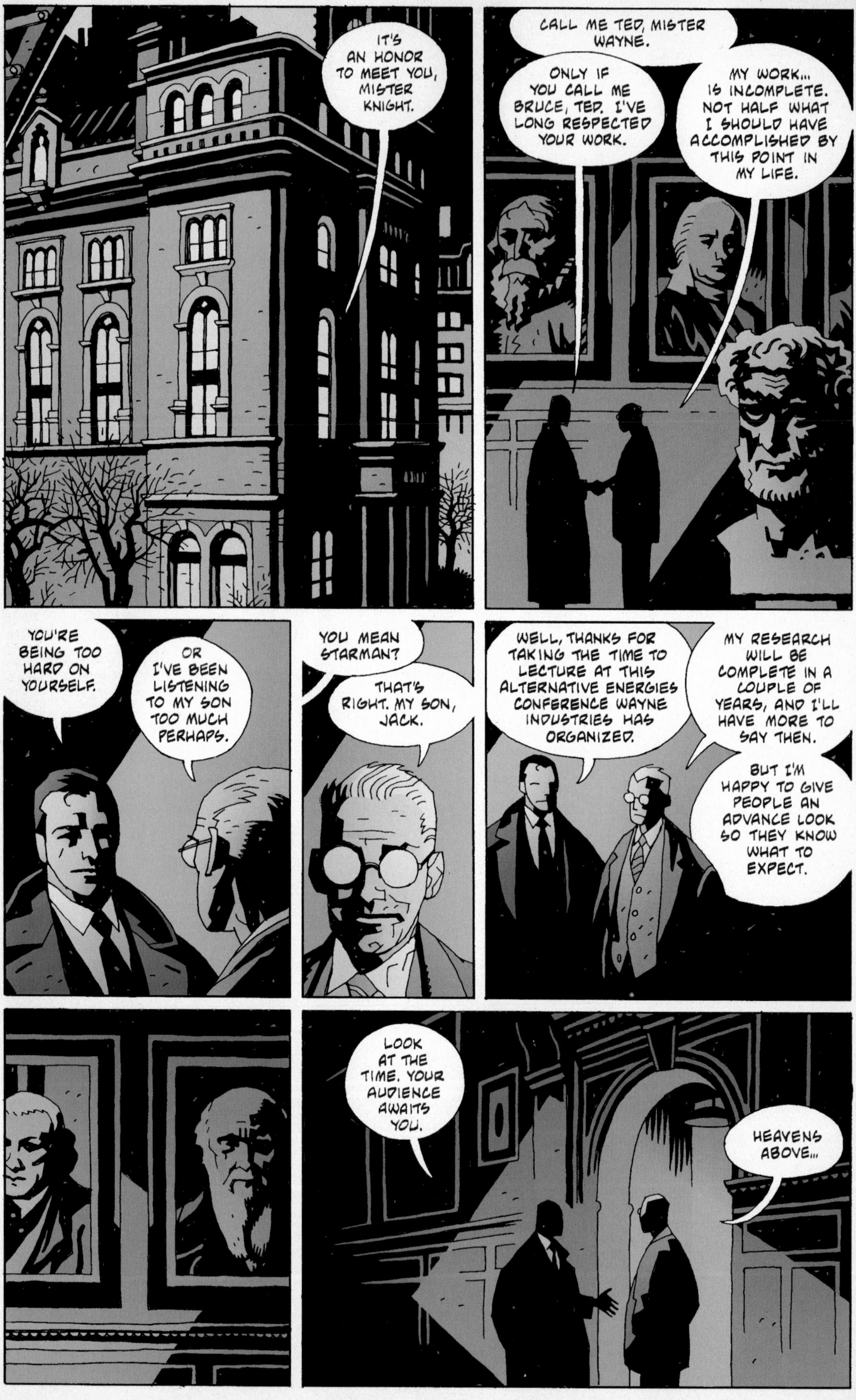
IT'S AN HONOR TO MEET YOU, MISTER KNIGHT.
CALL ME TED, MISTER WAYNE.
ONLY IF YOU CALL ME BRUCE, TED. I'VE LONG RESPECTED YOUR WORK.
MY WORK... IS INCOMPLETE. NOT HALF WHAT I SHOULD HAVE ACCOMPLISHED BY THIS POINT IN MY LIFE.
YOU'RE BEING TOO HARD ON YOURSELF.
OR I'VE BEEN LISTENING TO MY SON TOO MUCH PERHAPS.
YOU MEAN STARMAN?
THAT'S RIGHT. MY SON, JACK.
WELL, THANKS FOR TAKING THE TIME TO LECTURE AT THIS ALTERNATIVE ENERGIES CONFERENCE WAYNE INDUSTRIES HAS ORGANIZED.
MY RESEARCH WILL BE COMPLETE IN A COUPLE OF YEARS, AND I'LL HAVE MORE TO SAY THEN.
BUT I'M HAPPY TO GIVE PEOPLE AN ADVANCE LOOK SO THEY KNOW WHAT TO EXPECT.
LOOK AT THE TIME. YOUR AUDIENCE AWAITS YOU.
HEAVENS ABOVE...

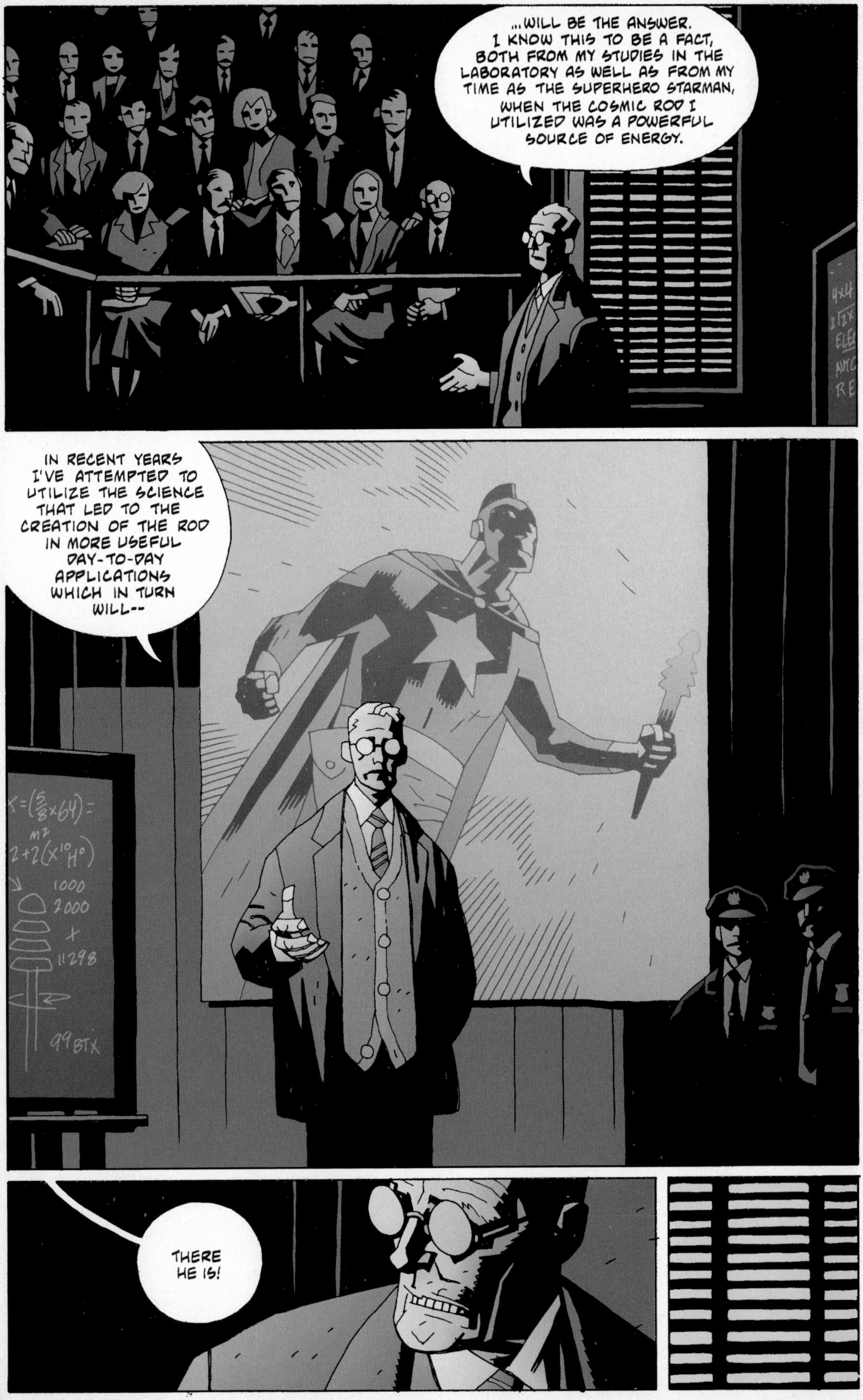
...WILL BE THE ANSWER. I KNOW THIS TO BE A FACT, BOTH FROM MY STUDIES IN THE LABORATORY AS WELL AS FROM MY TIME AS THE SUPERHERO STARMAN, WHEN THE COSMIC ROD I UTILIZED WAS A POWERFUL SOURCE OF ENERGY.
IN RECENT YEARS I'VE ATTEMPTED TO UTILIZE THE SCIENCE THAT LED TO THE CREATION OF THE ROD IN MORE USEFUL DAY-TO-DAY APPLICATIONS WHICH IN TURN WILL--
THERE HE IS!

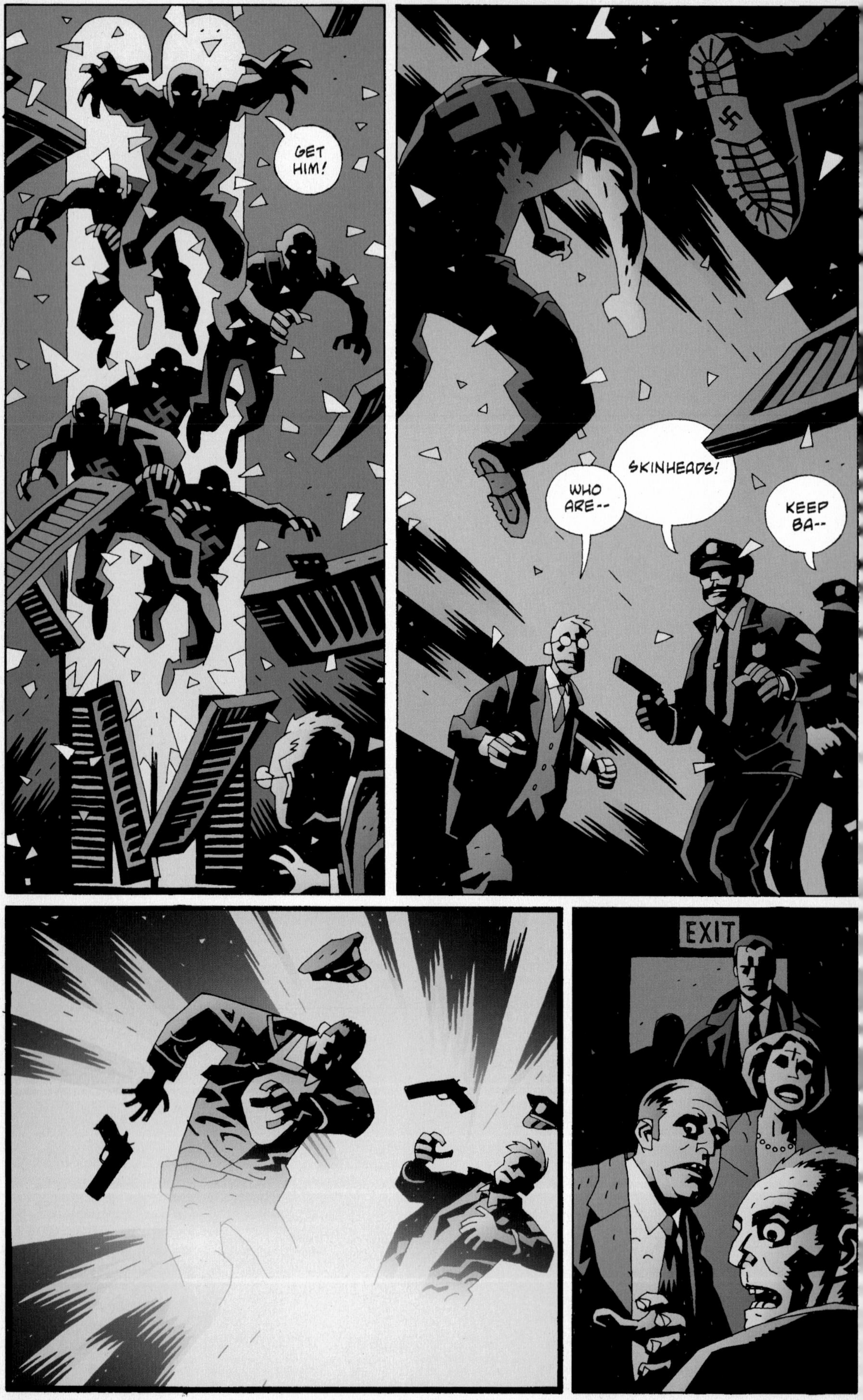
GET HIM!
WHO ARE--
SKINHEADS!
KEEP BA--
EXIT

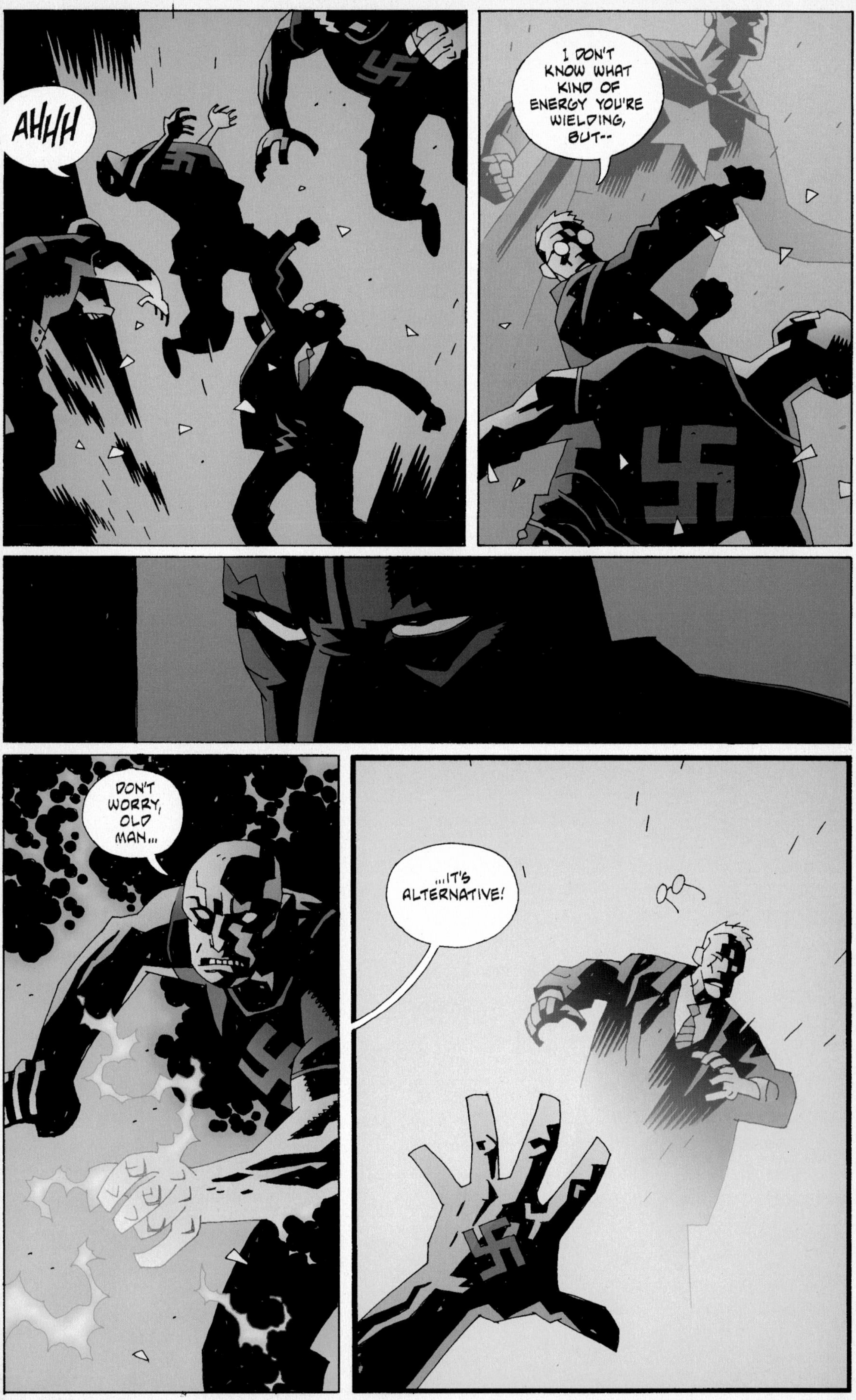
AHHH
I DON'T KNOW WHAT KIND OF ENERGY YOU'RE WIELDING, BUT--
DON'T WORRY, OLD MAN...
...IT'S ALTERNATIVE!

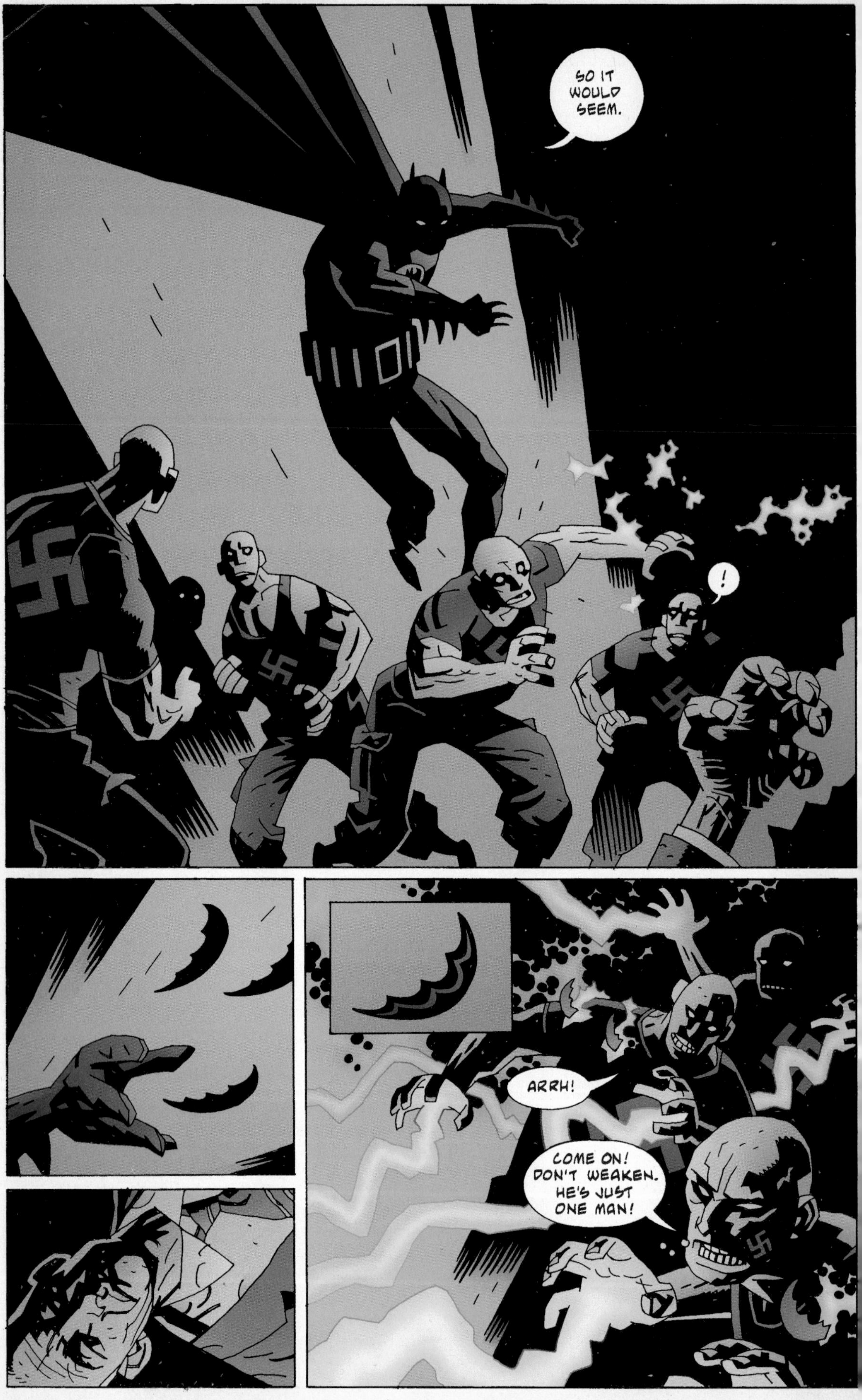
SO IT WOULD SEEM.
!
ARRH!
COME ON! DON'T WEAKEN. HE'S JUST ONE MAN!

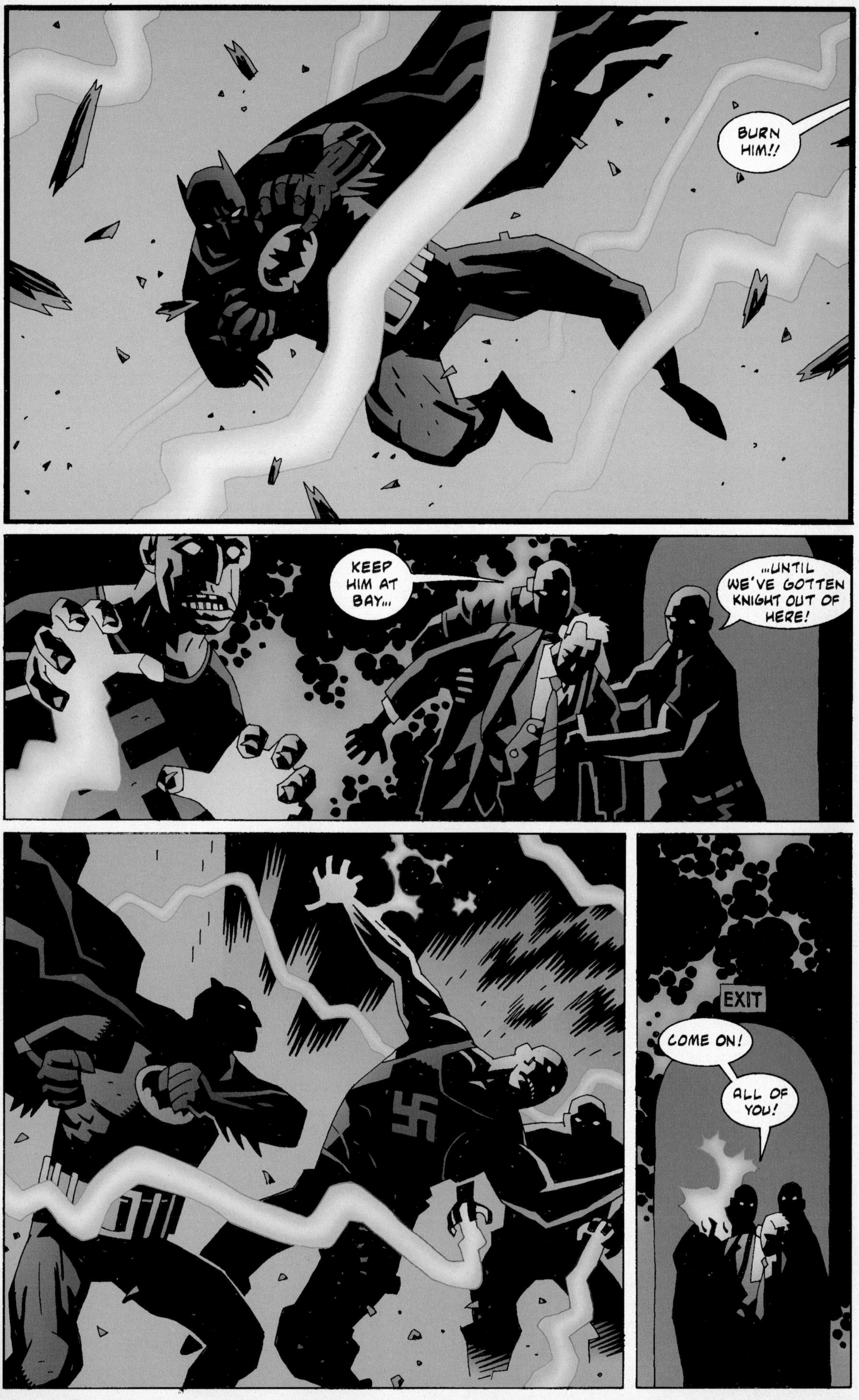
BURN HIM!!
KEEP HIM AT BAY...
...UNTIL WE'VE GOTTEN KNIGHT OUT OF HERE!
EXIT
COME ON!
ALL OF YOU!

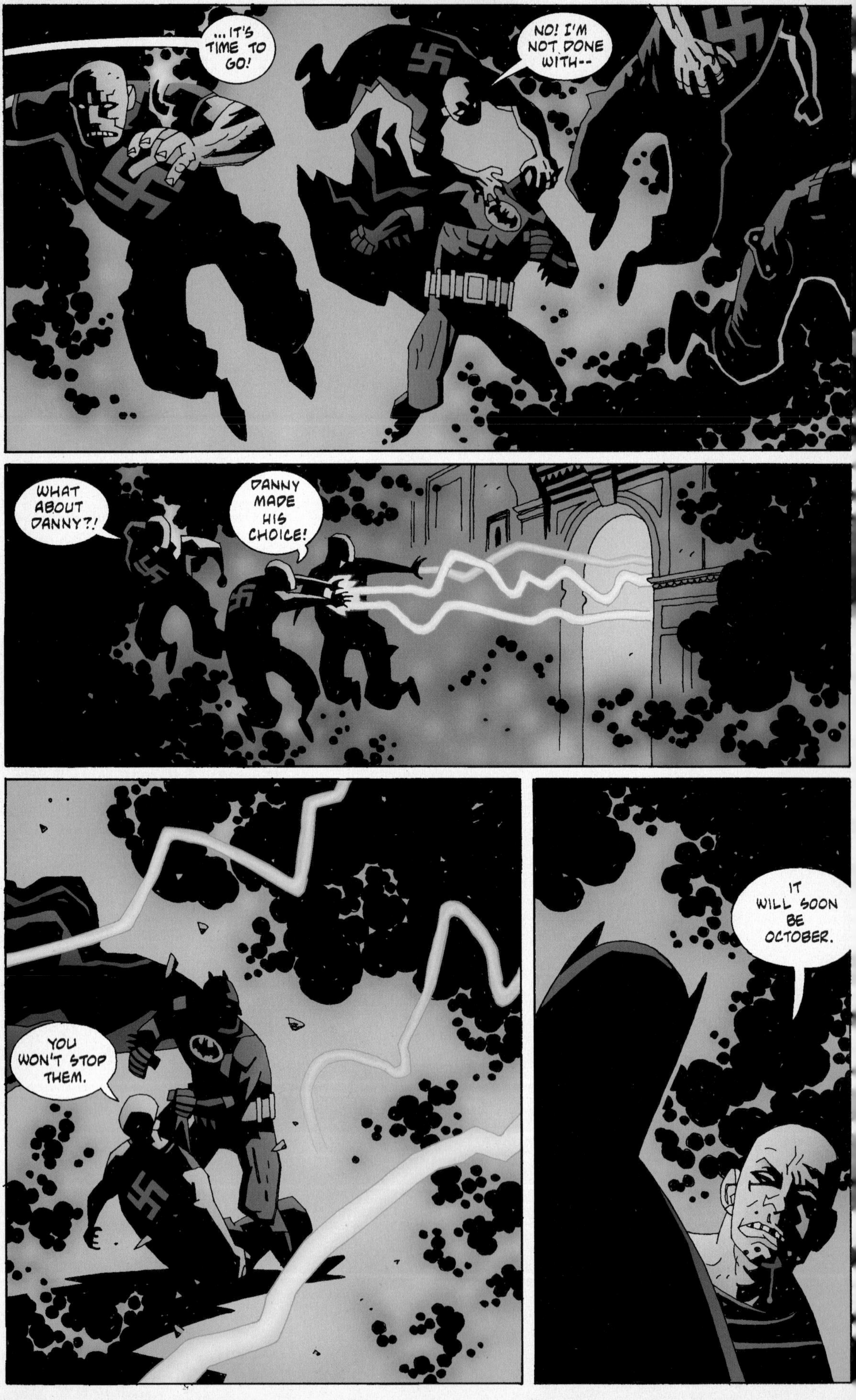
...IT'S TIME TO GO!
NO! I'M NOT DONE WITH--
WHAT ABOUT DANNY?!
DANNY MADE HIS CHOICE!
YOU WON'T STOP THEM.
IT WILL SOON BE OCTOBER.

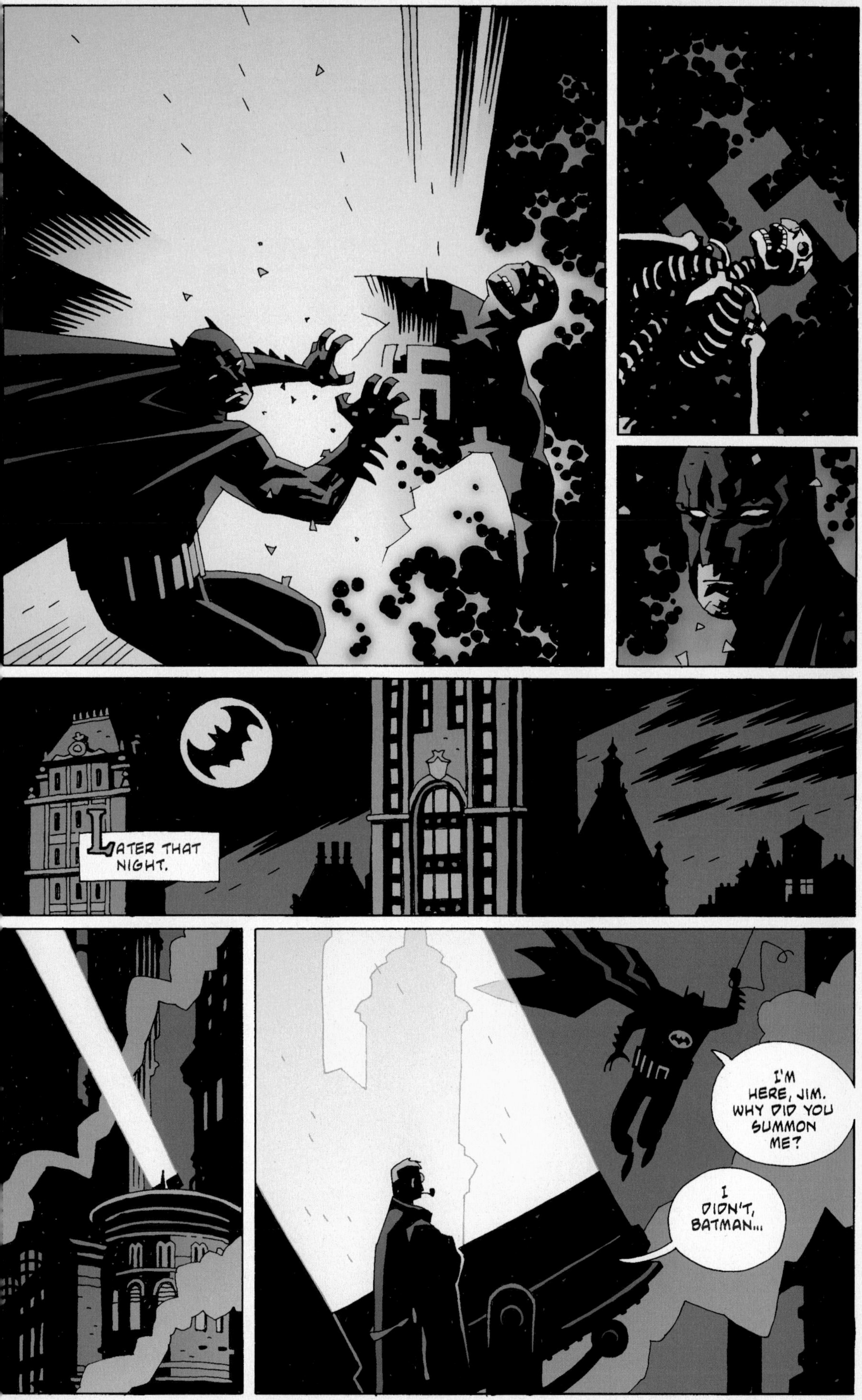
LATER THAT NIGHT.
I'M HERE, JIM. WHY DID YOU SUMMON ME?
I DIDN'T, BATMAN...

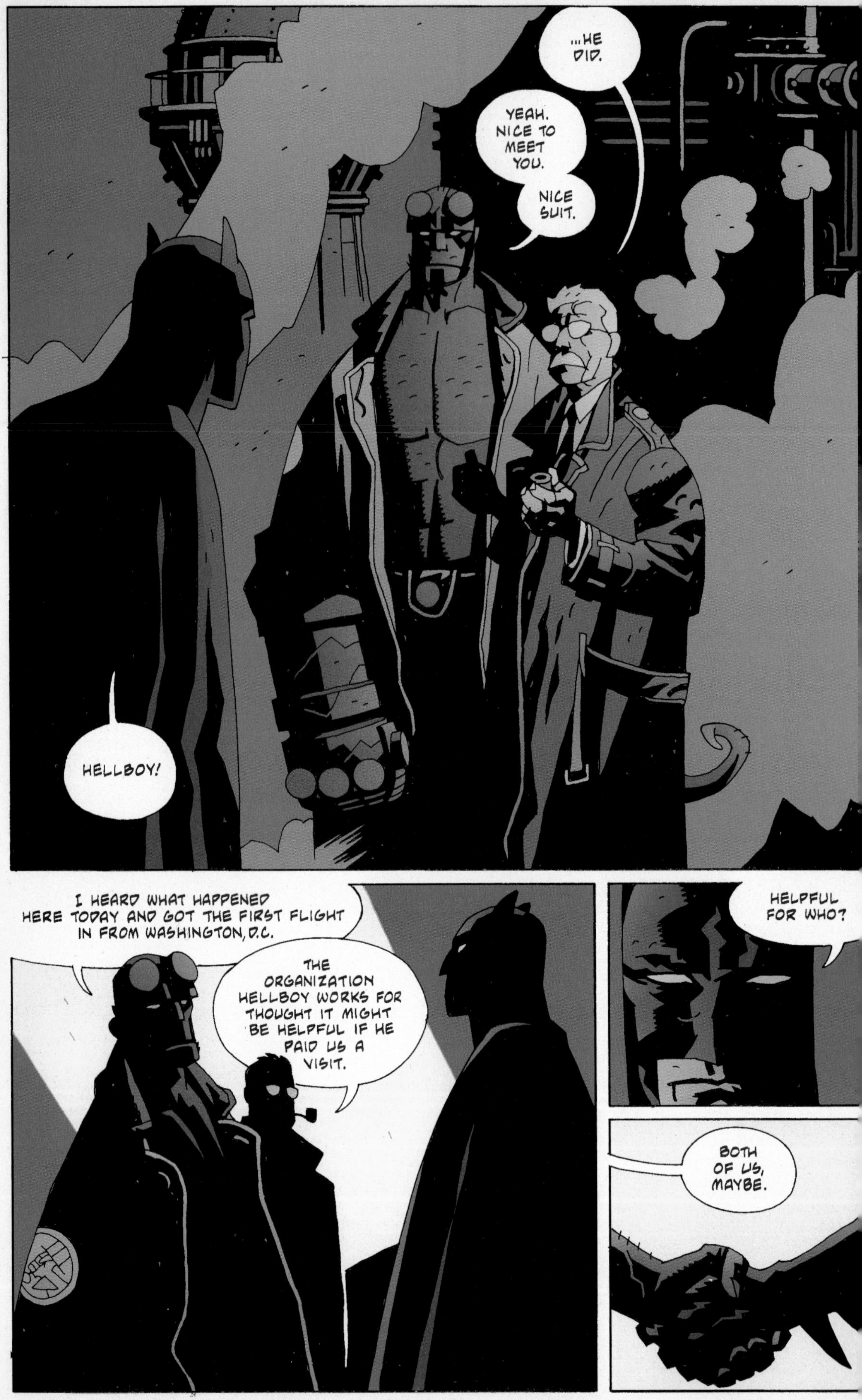
...HE DID.
YEAH. NICE TO MEET YOU.
NICE SUIT.
HELLBOY!
I HEARD WHAT HAPPENED HERE TODAY AND GOT THE FIRST FLIGHT IN FROM WASHINGTON, D.C.
THE ORGANIZATION HELLBOY WORKS FOR THOUGHT IT MIGHT BE HELPFUL IF HE PAID US A VISIT.
HELPFUL FOR WHO?
BOTH OF US, MAYBE.

THERE ARE ASPECTS OF THIS CASE THAT FIT WITH REPORTS THE B.P.R.D.* HAS BEEN LOOKING INTO.

*BUREAU OF PARANORMAL RESEARCH AND DEFENSE.

ASPECTS?

THE NEO-NAZI WHO BLEW HIMSELF UP... BEFORE HE DIED HE SAID "IT WILL SOON BE OCTOBER."

EVEN THOUGH IT'S MARCH. YES, THAT WAS STRANGE.

A GROUP OF NAZIS... THE REAL OLD-FASHIONED KIND... BASED SOMEWHERE IN SOUTH AMERICA...

...THEY GO BY THE NAME KNIGHTS OF OCTOBER.

WORD'S REACHED US THEY'RE PLANNING SOMETHING USING MAGIC BEST LEFT ALONE.

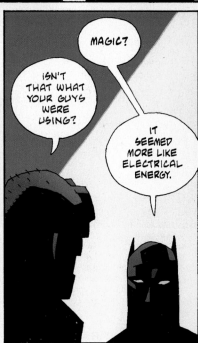

MAGIC?

ISN'T THAT WHAT YOUR GUYS WERE USING?

IT SEEMED MORE LIKE ELECTRICAL ENERGY.

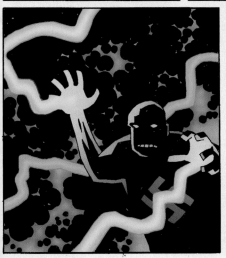

SURE.

IT'S HARD TO TELL THE DIFFERENCE AT FIRST, BUT THIS IS SORT OF MY THING SO YOU'RE GONNA HAVE TO TRUST ME.

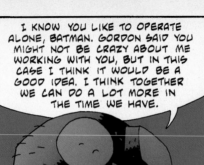
I'LL TAKE EVERYTHING YOU'VE SAID UNDER ADVISEMENT, HELLBOY, AS I CONTINUE MY INVESTIGATION.

I KNOW YOU LIKE TO OPERATE ALONE, BATMAN. GORDON SAID YOU MIGHT NOT BE CRAZY ABOUT ME WORKING WITH YOU, BUT IN THIS CASE I THINK IT WOULD BE A GOOD IDEA. I THINK TOGETHER WE CAN DO A LOT MORE IN THE TIME WE HAVE.

AND HOW MUCH TIME IS THAT?

CLICK

I DON'T KNOW. BUT MAYBE WE SHOULD BE ASKING HOW MUCH TIME DOES TED KNIGHT HAVE.

WITH ALL DUE RESPECT, YOU MAY THINK YOU'RE EXPERIENCED WITH MAGIC, BATMAN. BUT REALLY, COMPARED TO ME...

HE CAN HELP YOU, BATMAN.

...YOU HAVE NO IDEA.

WHY DO YOU THINK THEY WANTED TED KNIGHT? A SCIENTIST.

I'M NOT SURE. BUT SPELLS AND RITES USE FORMULAS AND PHYSICS AS MUCH AS THEY USE CHARMS AND POTIONS. SCIENCE...THE ALIGNMENT OF PLANETS...THAT'S ALL STUFF MISTER KNIGHT MIGHT BE NEEDED TO HELP THEM WITH.

WELL, I SUPPOSE WE'LL KNOW WHEN KNIGHT'S LOCATED.

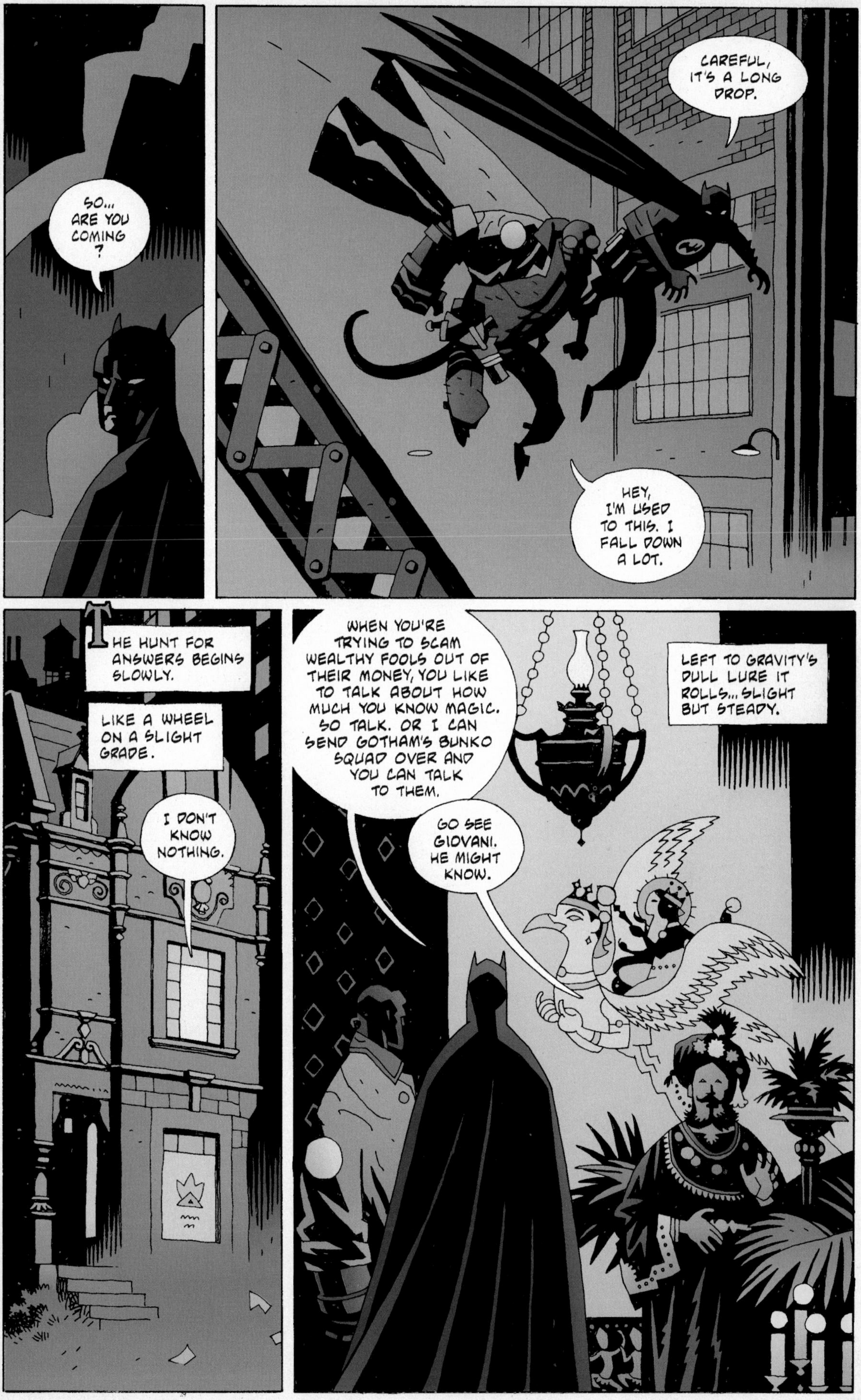
SO... ARE YOU COMING ?
CAREFUL, IT'S A LONG DROP.
HEY, I'M USED TO THIS. I FALL DOWN A LOT.
THE HUNT FOR ANSWERS BEGINS SLOWLY.
LIKE A WHEEL ON A SLIGHT GRADE.
I DON'T KNOW NOTHING.
WHEN YOU'RE TRYING TO SCAM WEALTHY FOOLS OUT OF THEIR MONEY, YOU LIKE TO TALK ABOUT HOW MUCH YOU KNOW MAGIC. SO TALK. OR I CAN SEND GOTHAM'S BUNKO SQUAD OVER AND YOU CAN TALK TO THEM.
GO SEE GIOVANI. HE MIGHT KNOW.
LEFT TO GRAVITY'S DULL LURE IT ROLLS... SLIGHT BUT STEADY.

JERRY GIOVANI'S A TWO-BIT NOTHING. HE *DOESN'T* KNOW MAGIC, HE STEALS CARS FOR GETAWAYS.

STILL, I HEARD HIM TALKING...

AND BEFORE LONG IT GAINS *MOMENTUM.*

YEAH, SURE, I KNOW SOMETHING, MAYBE.

YOU AREN'T HARD TO GET ANSWERS FROM, GIOVANI.

ME, I'M CIVIL MINDED. PLUS THE FACT THAT YOU AND BIG RED OVER THERE ARE SCARING ME TO THE POINT I CAN BARELY HOLD MY BLADDER.

GO SEE MORTY SLADE. HE'S GOT THE SCOOP.

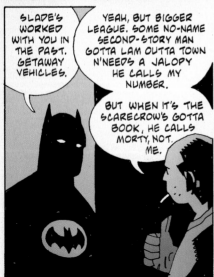

SLADE'S WORKED WITH YOU IN THE PAST. GETAWAY VEHICLES.

YEAH, BUT BIGGER LEAGUE. SOME NO-NAME SECOND-STORY MAN GOTTA LAM OUTTA TOWN N'NEEDS A JALOPY HE CALLS MY NUMBER.

BUT WHEN IT'S THE SCARECROW'S GOTTA BOOK, HE CALLS MORTY, NOT ME.

AND WHO WAS IT HAD TO "BOOK"?

THAT I DON'T KNOW. I'M SMART ENOUGH NOT TO ASK TOO MANY QUESTIONS, IN CASE SITUATIONS LIKE THIS ONE EVER ARISE WHEN I GOTTA YACK.

MORTY JUST TOLD ME HE WAS HIRED FOR A GIG... SOMETHING ABOUT AN AIRFIELD...

"...SOMETHING ABOUT A PLANE."

MORTY.

IT WASN'T ME.

IT WASN'T YOU WHAT?

I DON'T KNOW ANYTHING.

ABOUT WHAT?

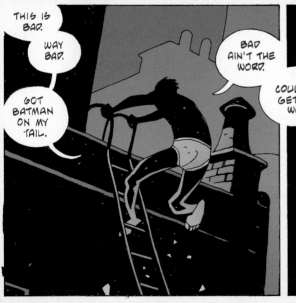

THIS IS BAD.

WAY BAD.

GOT BATMAN ON MY TAIL.

BAD AIN'T THE WORD.

COULDN'T GET ANY WOR--

BOO.

!

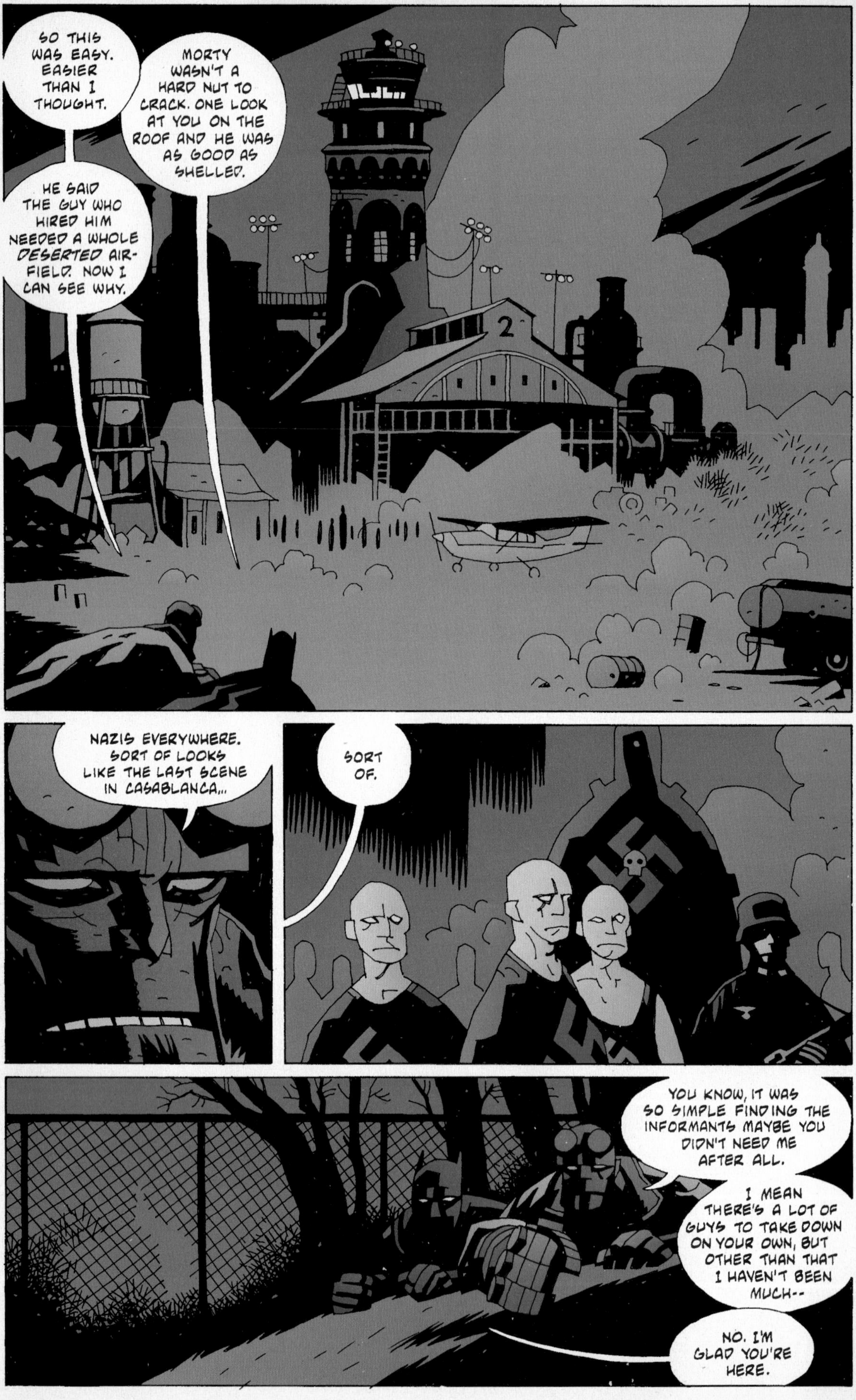
SO THIS WAS EASY. EASIER THAN I THOUGHT.
MORTY WASN'T A HARD NUT TO CRACK. ONE LOOK AT YOU ON THE ROOF AND HE WAS AS GOOD AS SHELLED.
HE SAID THE GUY WHO HIRED HIM NEEDED A WHOLE *DESERTED* AIR-FIELD. NOW I CAN SEE WHY.
2
NAZIS EVERYWHERE. SORT OF LOOKS LIKE THE LAST SCENE IN CASABLANCA...
SORT OF.
YOU KNOW, IT WAS SO SIMPLE FINDING THE INFORMANTS MAYBE YOU DIDN'T NEED ME AFTER ALL.
I MEAN THERE'S A LOT OF GUYS TO TAKE DOWN ON YOUR OWN, BUT OTHER THAN THAT I HAVEN'T BEEN MUCH--
NO. I'M GLAD YOU'RE HERE.

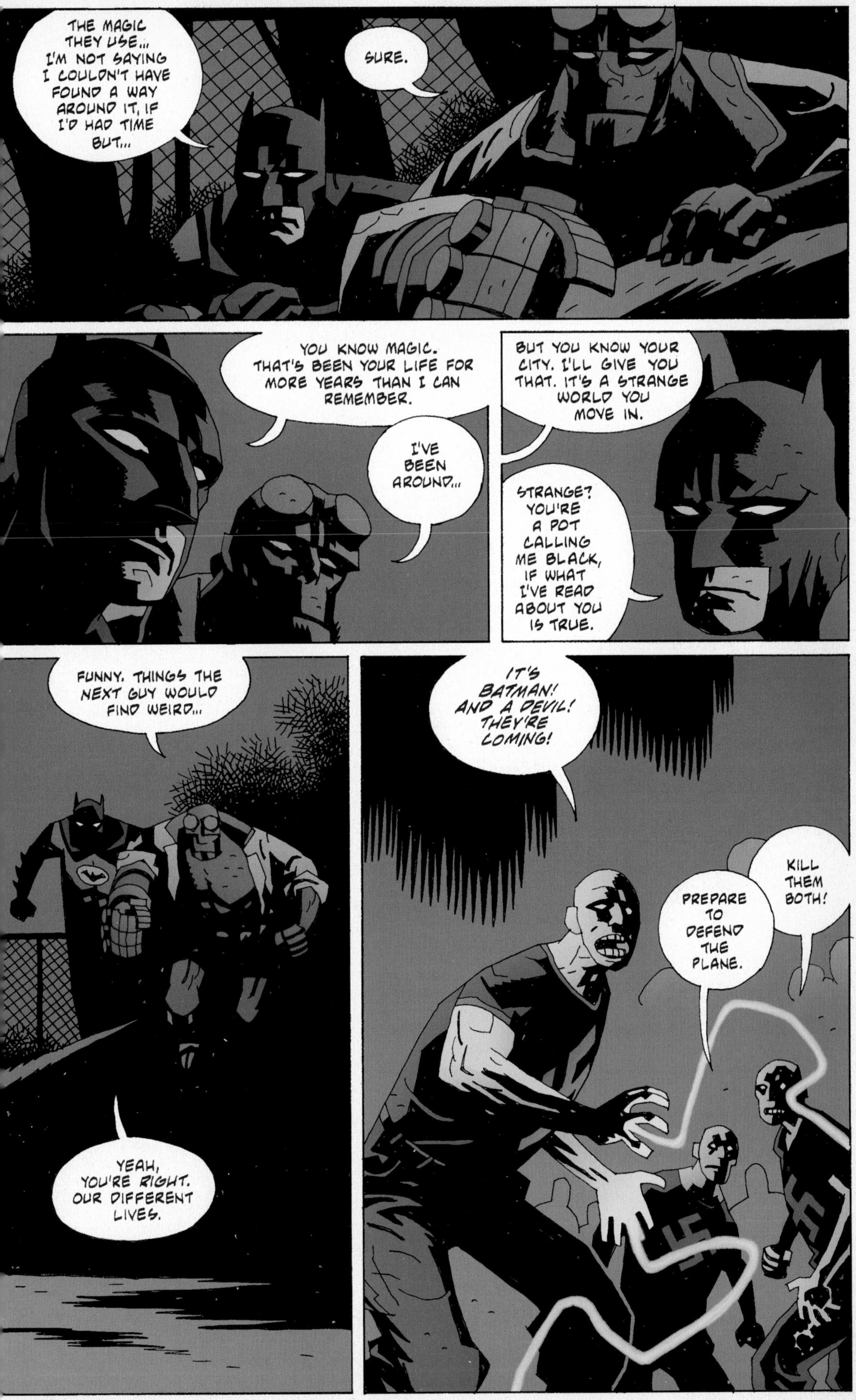
THE MAGIC THEY USE... I'M NOT SAYING I COULDN'T HAVE FOUND A WAY AROUND IT, IF I'D HAD TIME BUT...
SURE.
YOU KNOW MAGIC. THAT'S BEEN YOUR LIFE FOR MORE YEARS THAN I CAN REMEMBER.
I'VE BEEN AROUND...
BUT YOU KNOW YOUR CITY. I'LL GIVE YOU THAT. IT'S A STRANGE WORLD YOU MOVE IN.
STRANGE? YOU'RE A POT CALLING ME BLACK, IF WHAT I'VE READ ABOUT YOU IS TRUE.
FUNNY. THINGS THE NEXT GUY WOULD FIND WEIRD...
YEAH, YOU'RE RIGHT. OUR DIFFERENT LIVES.
IT'S BATMAN! AND A DEVIL! THEY'RE COMING!
PREPARE TO DEFEND THE PLANE.
KILL THEM BOTH!

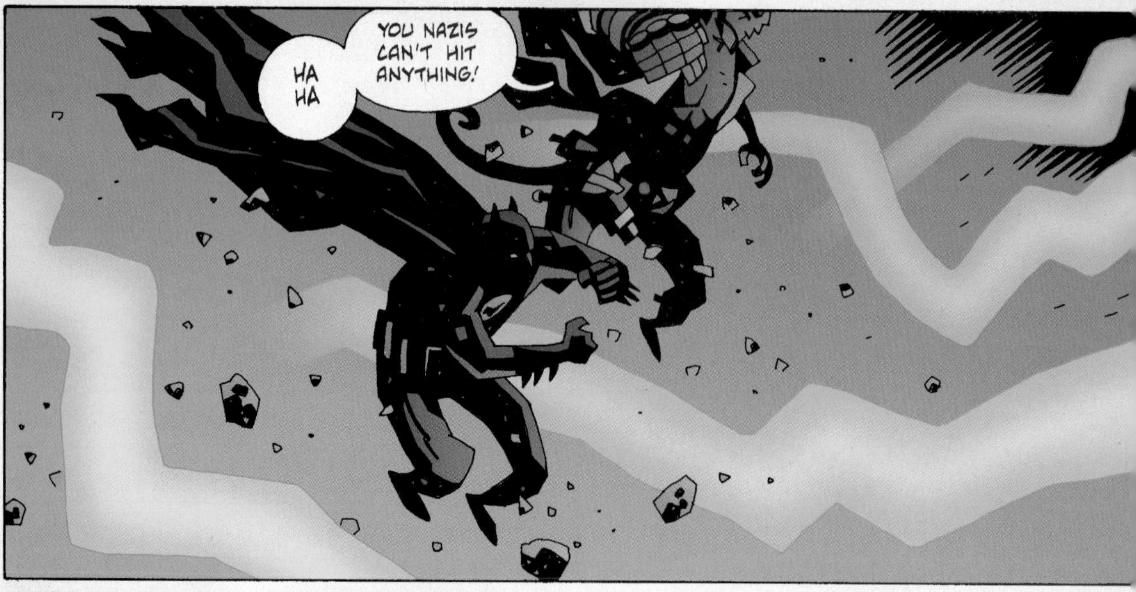
HA HA
YOU NAZIS CAN'T HIT ANYTHING!

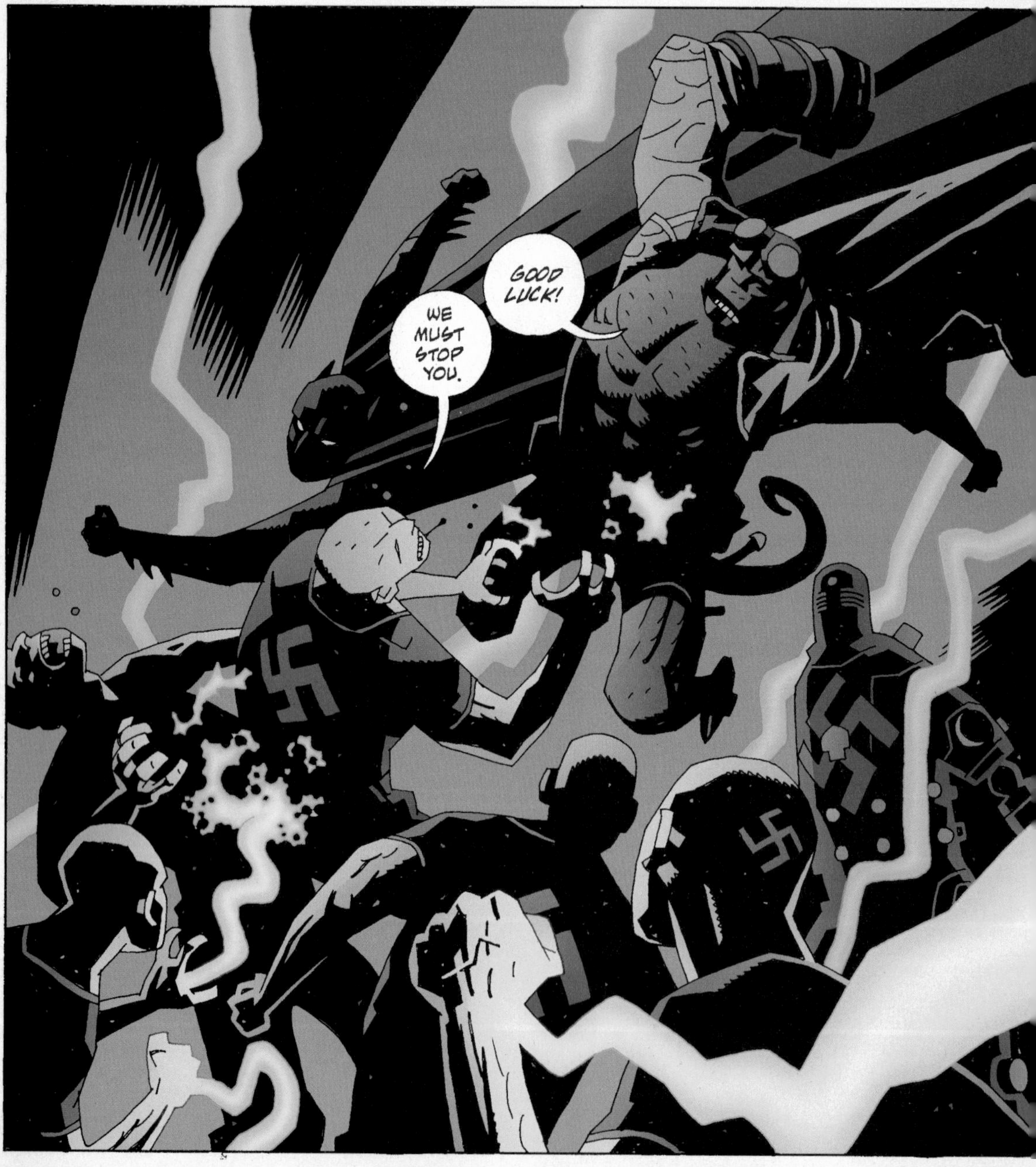
GOOD LUCK!
WE MUST STOP YOU.

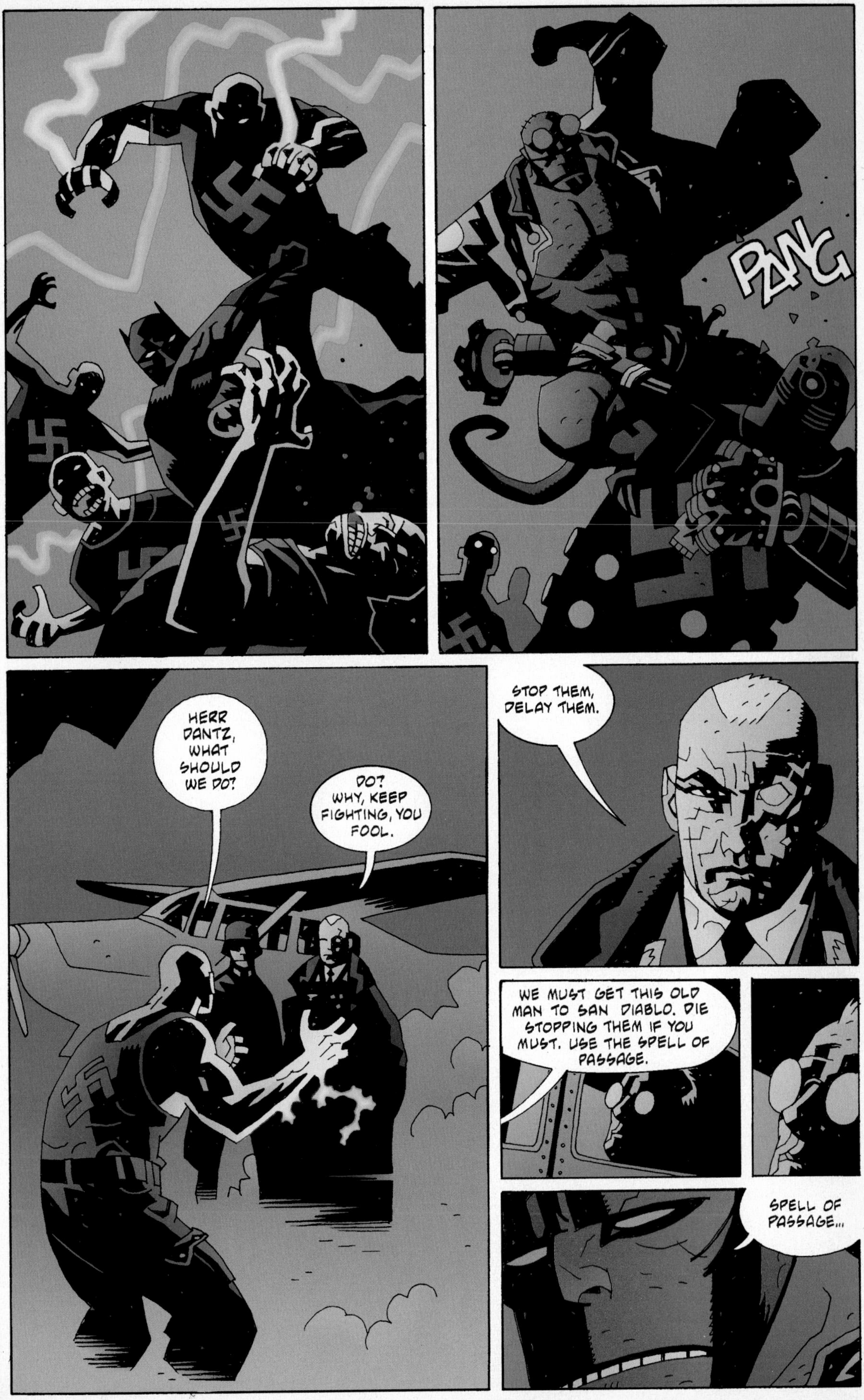
PANG
HERR DANTZ, WHAT SHOULD WE DO?
DO? WHY, KEEP FIGHTING, YOU FOOL.
STOP THEM, DELAY THEM.
WE MUST GET THIS OLD MAN TO SAN DIABLO. DIE STOPPING THEM IF YOU MUST. USE THE SPELL OF PASSAGE.
SPELL OF PASSAGE...

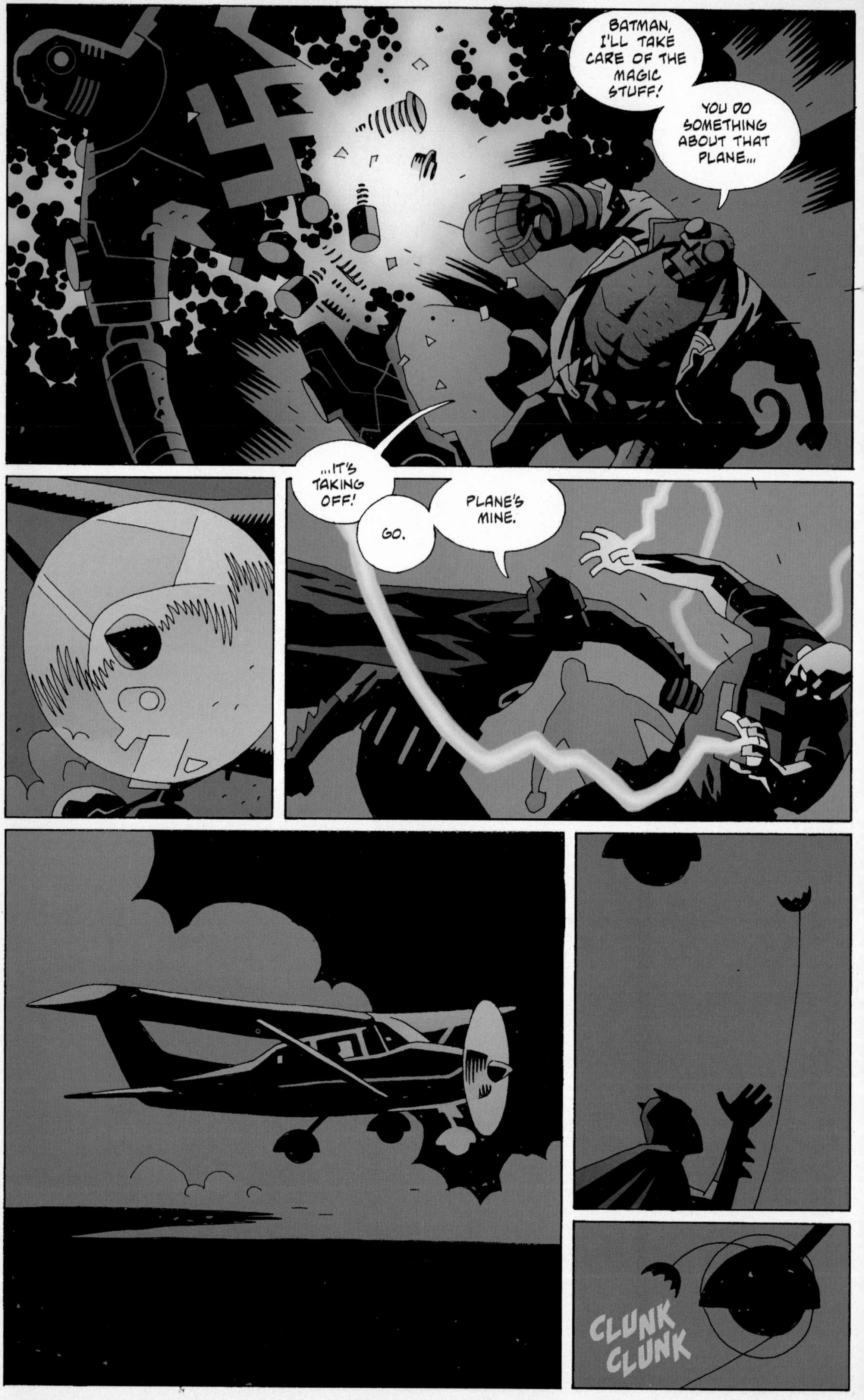
BATMAN, I'LL TAKE CARE OF THE MAGIC STUFF!
YOU DO SOMETHING ABOUT THAT PLANE...
...IT'S TAKING OFF!
GO.
PLANE'S MINE.
CLUNK CLUNK

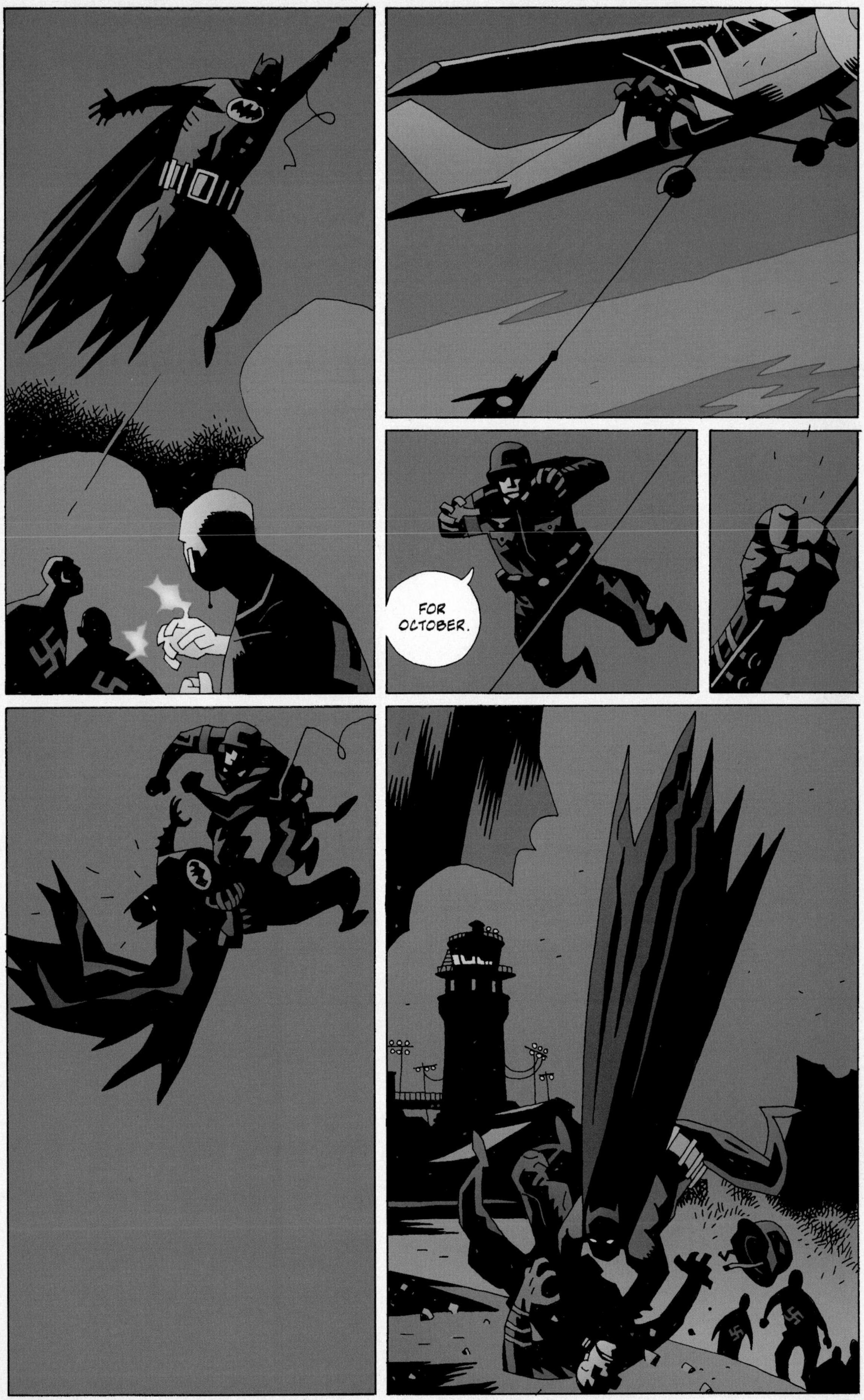
FOR OCTOBER.

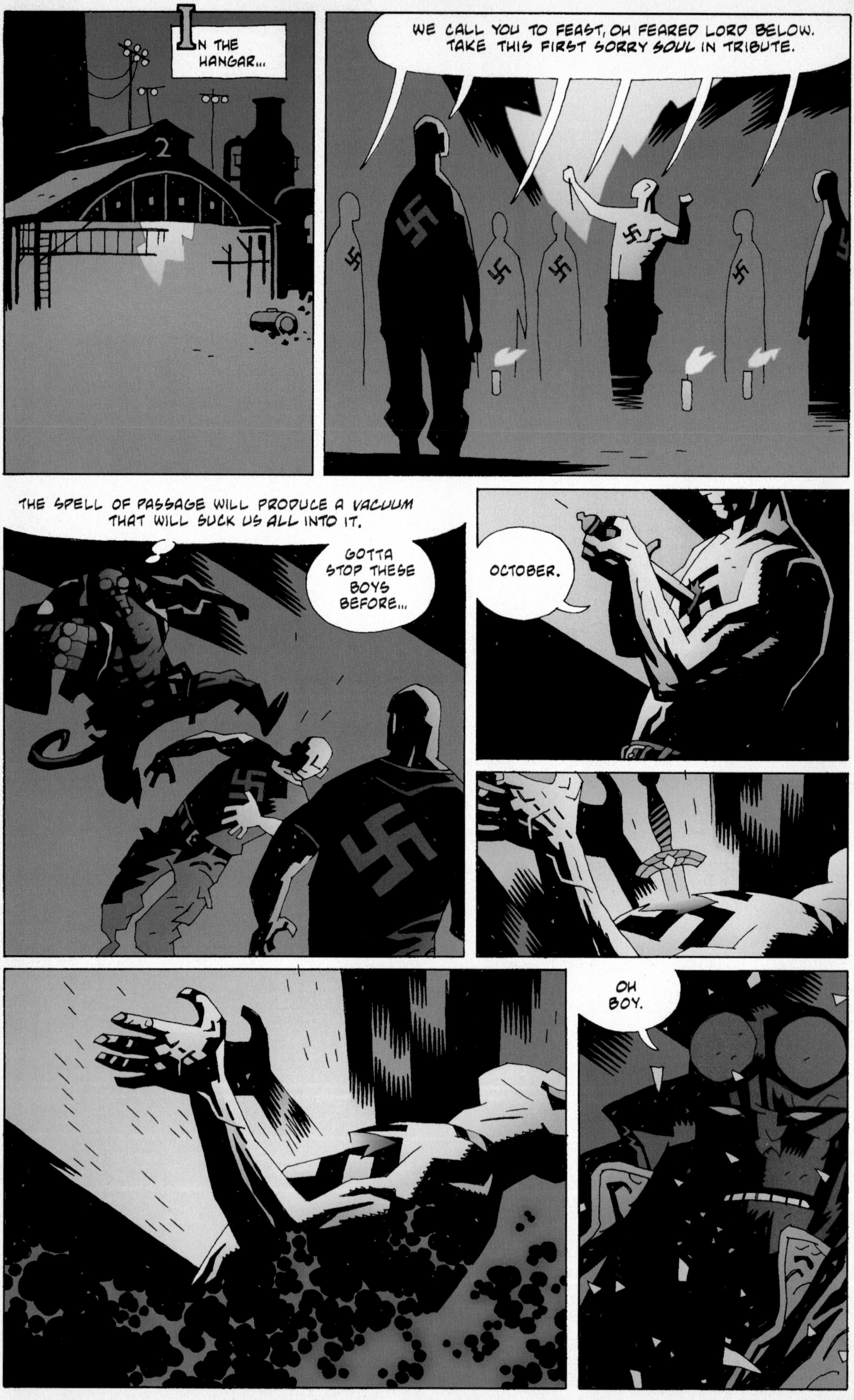
IN THE HANGAR...
WE CALL YOU TO FEAST, OH FEARED LORD BELOW. TAKE THIS FIRST SORRY SOUL IN TRIBUTE.
THE SPELL OF PASSAGE WILL PRODUCE A VACUUM THAT WILL SUCK US ALL INTO IT.
GOTTA STOP THESE BOYS BEFORE...
OCTOBER.
OH BOY.

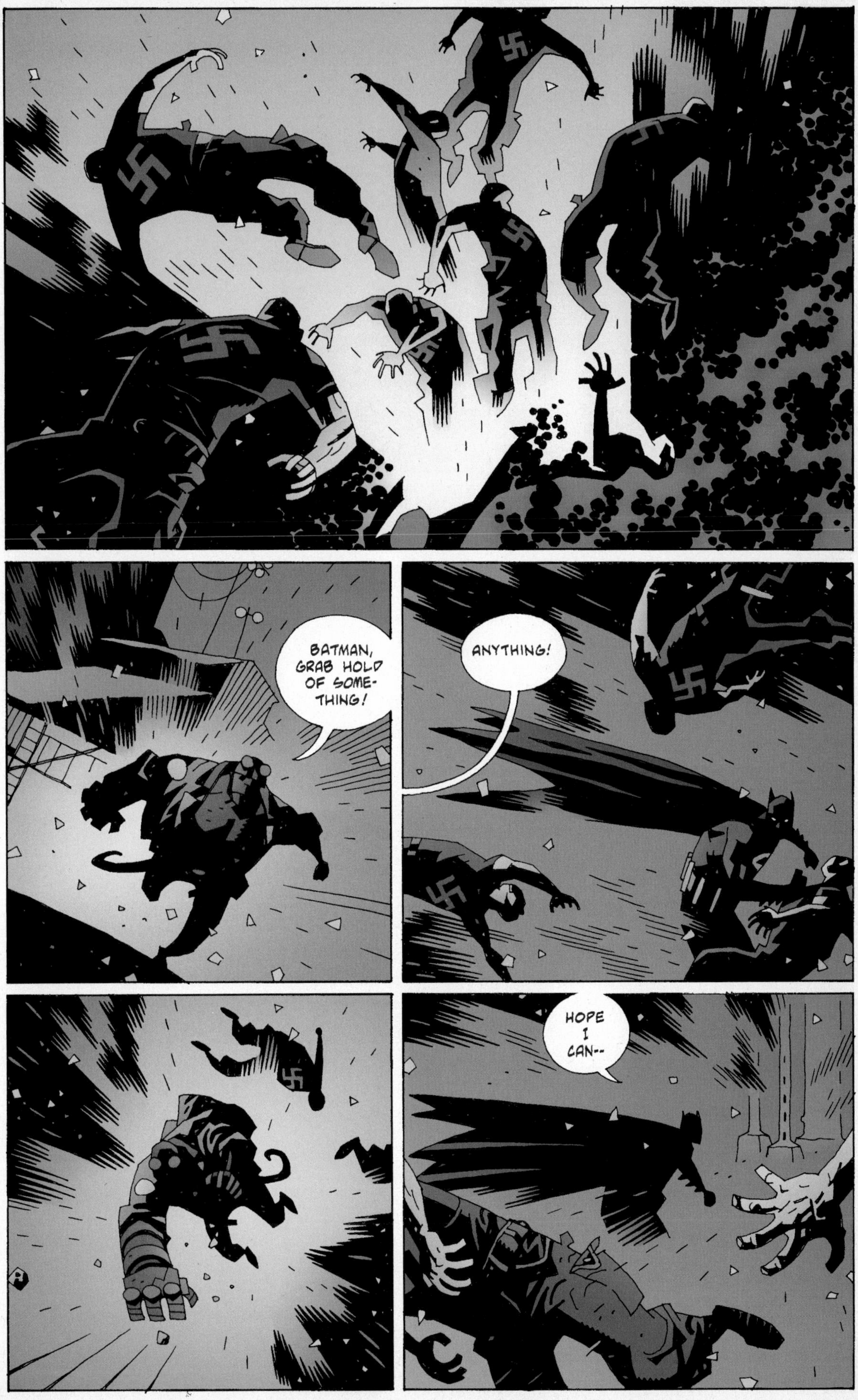
BATMAN, GRAB HOLD OF SOME-THING!
ANYTHING!
HOPE I CAN--

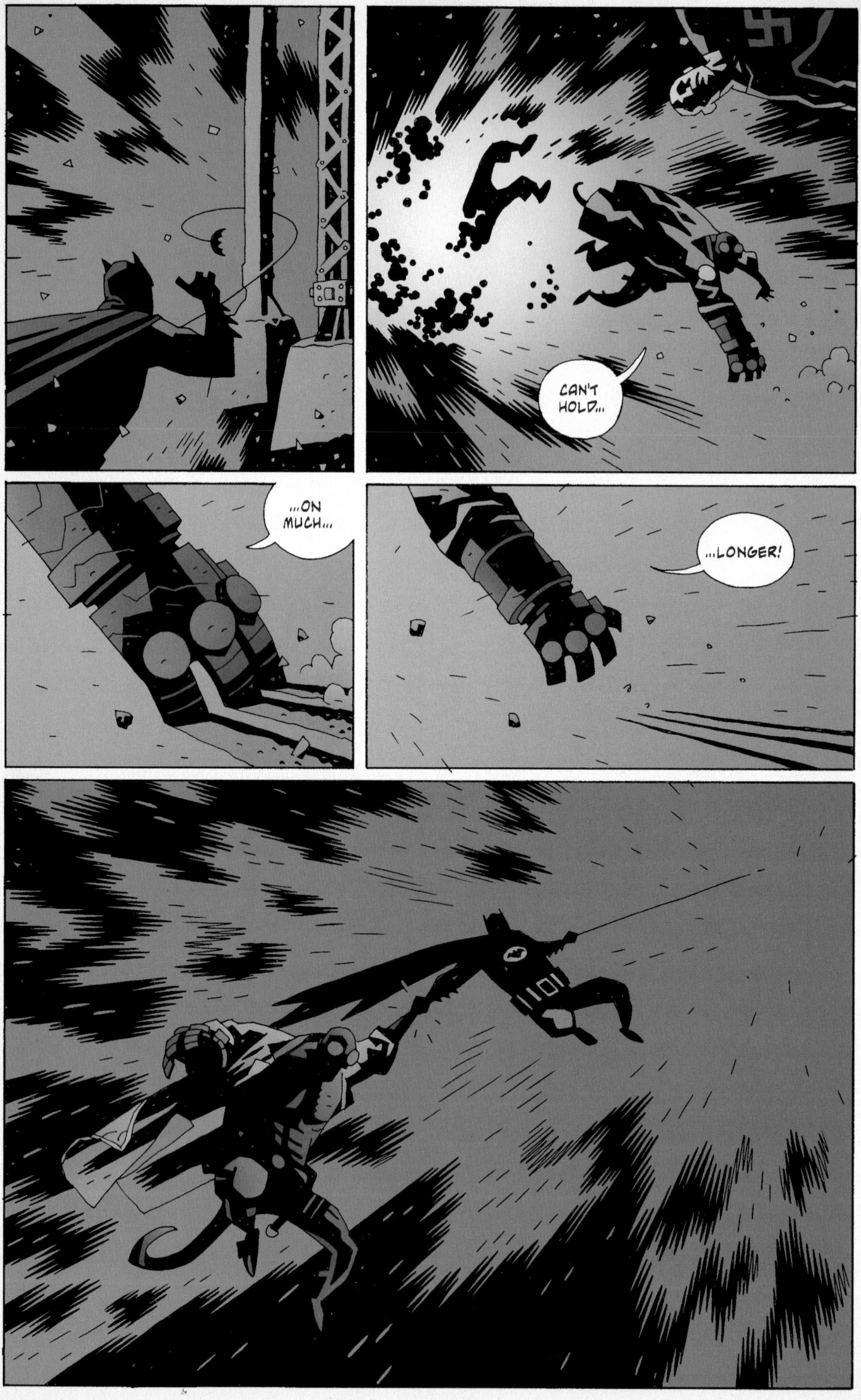
CAN'T HOLD...
...ON MUCH...
...LONGER!

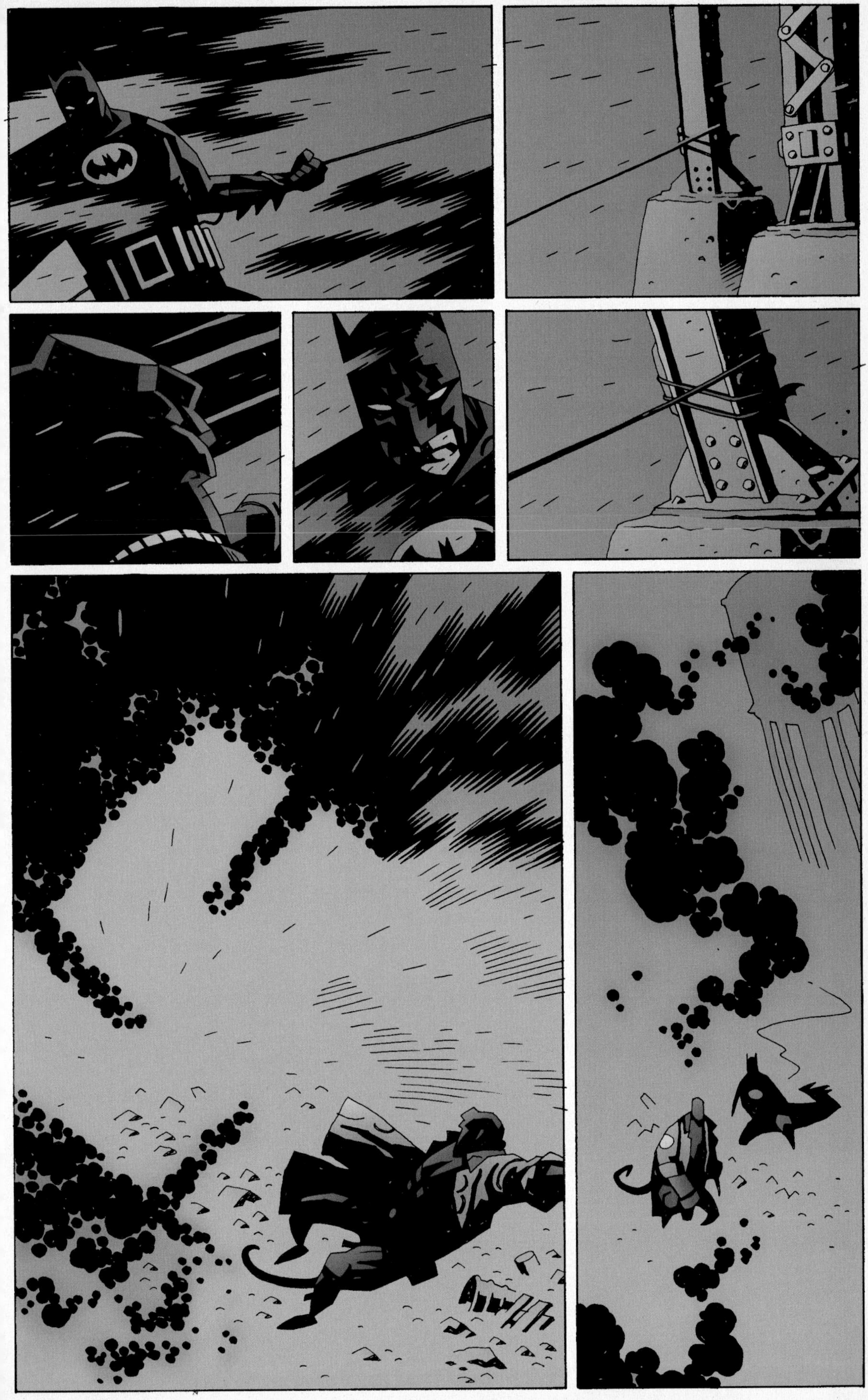

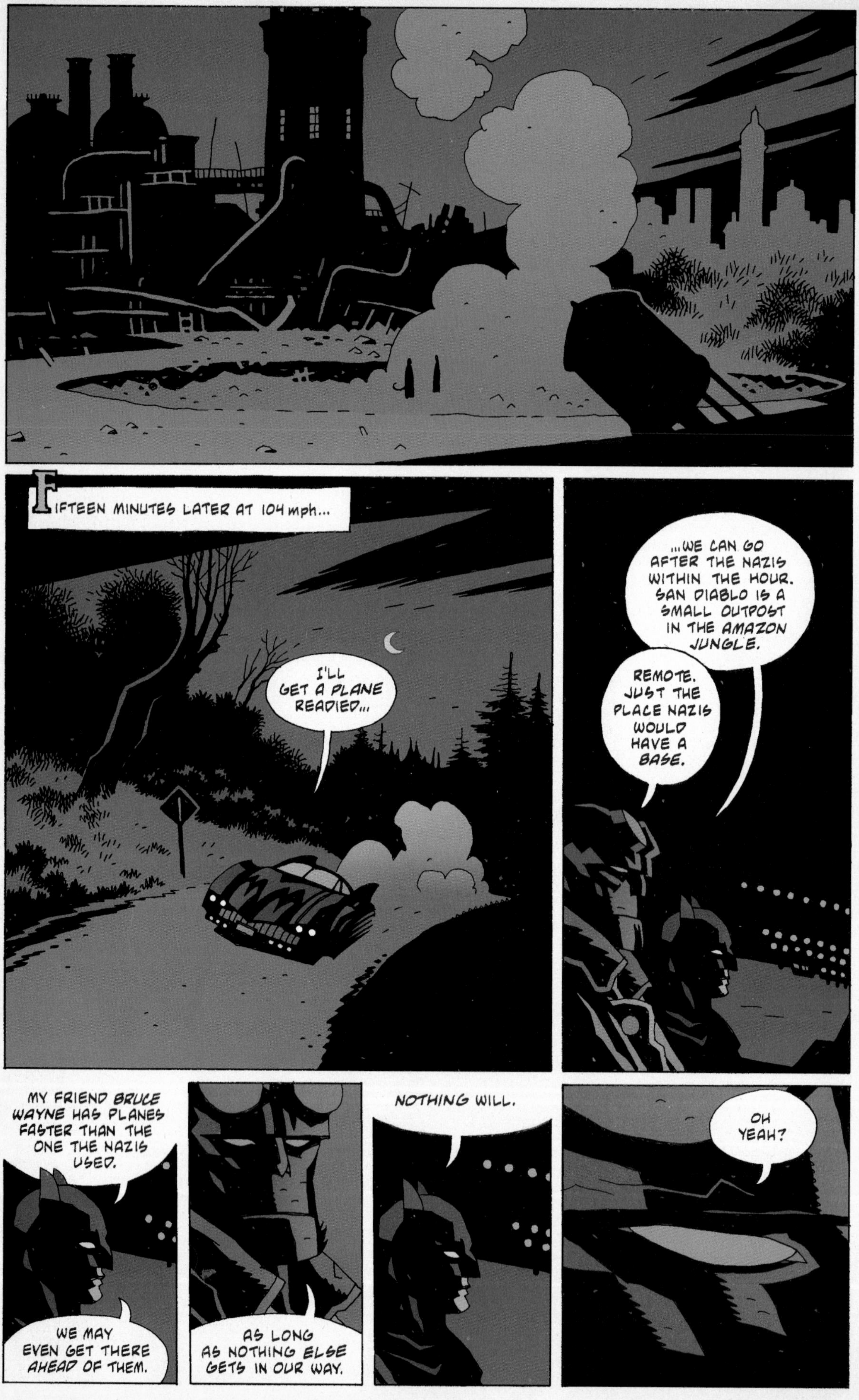
FIFTEEN MINUTES LATER AT 104 mph...
I'LL GET A PLANE READIED...
...WE CAN GO AFTER THE NAZIS WITHIN THE HOUR. SAN DIABLO IS A SMALL OUTPOST IN THE AMAZON JUNGLE.
REMOTE. JUST THE PLACE NAZIS WOULD HAVE A BASE.
MY FRIEND BRUCE WAYNE HAS PLANES FASTER THAN THE ONE THE NAZIS USED.
WE MAY EVEN GET THERE AHEAD OF THEM.
AS LONG AS NOTHING ELSE GETS IN OUR WAY.
NOTHING WILL.
OH YEAH?

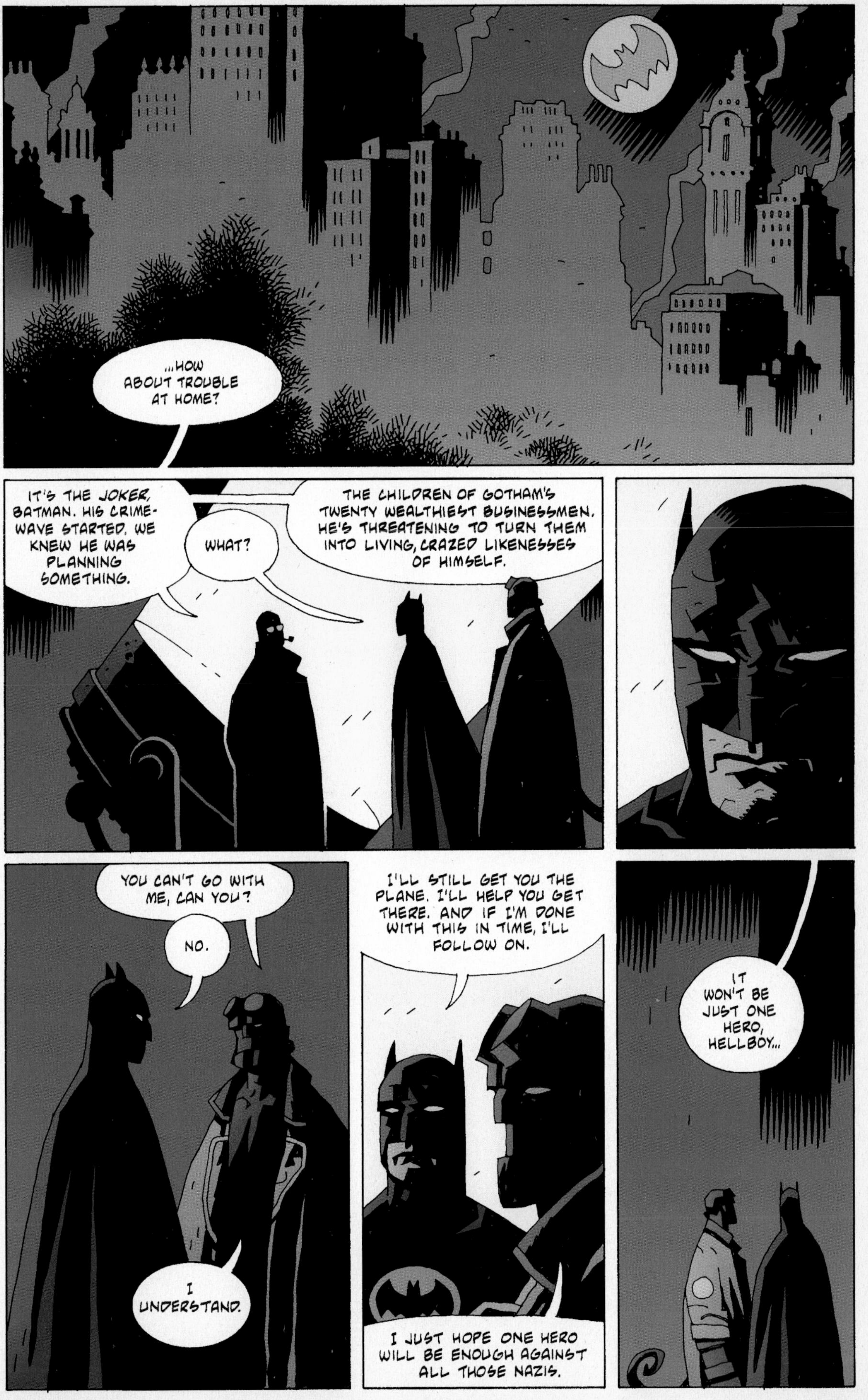
...HOW ABOUT TROUBLE AT HOME?
IT'S THE JOKER, BATMAN. HIS CRIME-WAVE STARTED. WE KNEW HE WAS PLANNING SOMETHING.
WHAT?
THE CHILDREN OF GOTHAM'S TWENTY WEALTHIEST BUSINESSMEN. HE'S THREATENING TO TURN THEM INTO LIVING, CRAZED LIKENESSES OF HIMSELF.
YOU CAN'T GO WITH ME, CAN YOU?
NO.
I UNDERSTAND.
I'LL STILL GET YOU THE PLANE. I'LL HELP YOU GET THERE. AND IF I'M DONE WITH THIS IN TIME, I'LL FOLLOW ON.
I JUST HOPE ONE HERO WILL BE ENOUGH AGAINST ALL THOSE NAZIS.
IT WON'T BE JUST ONE HERO, HELLBOY...

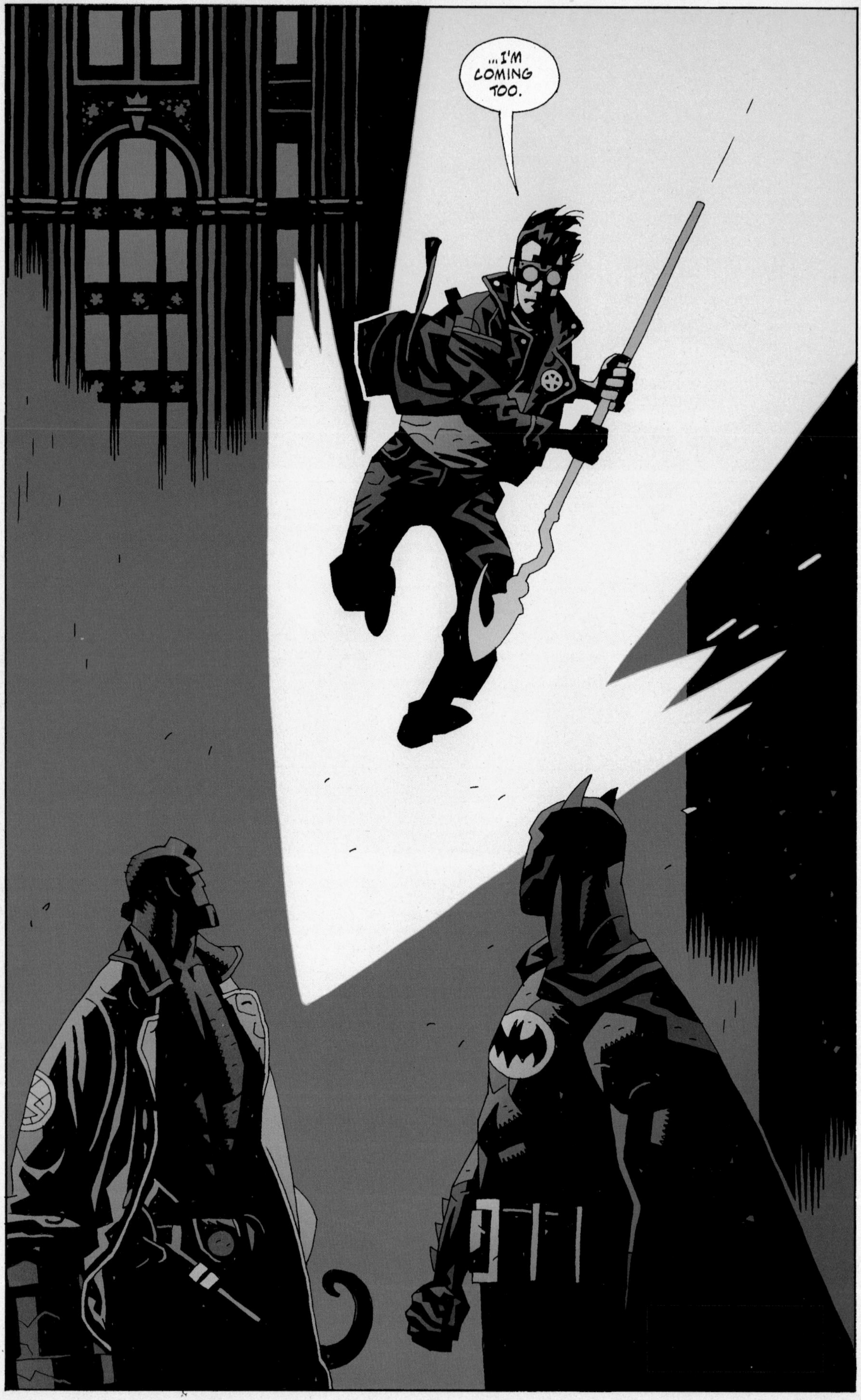
...I'M COMING TOO.

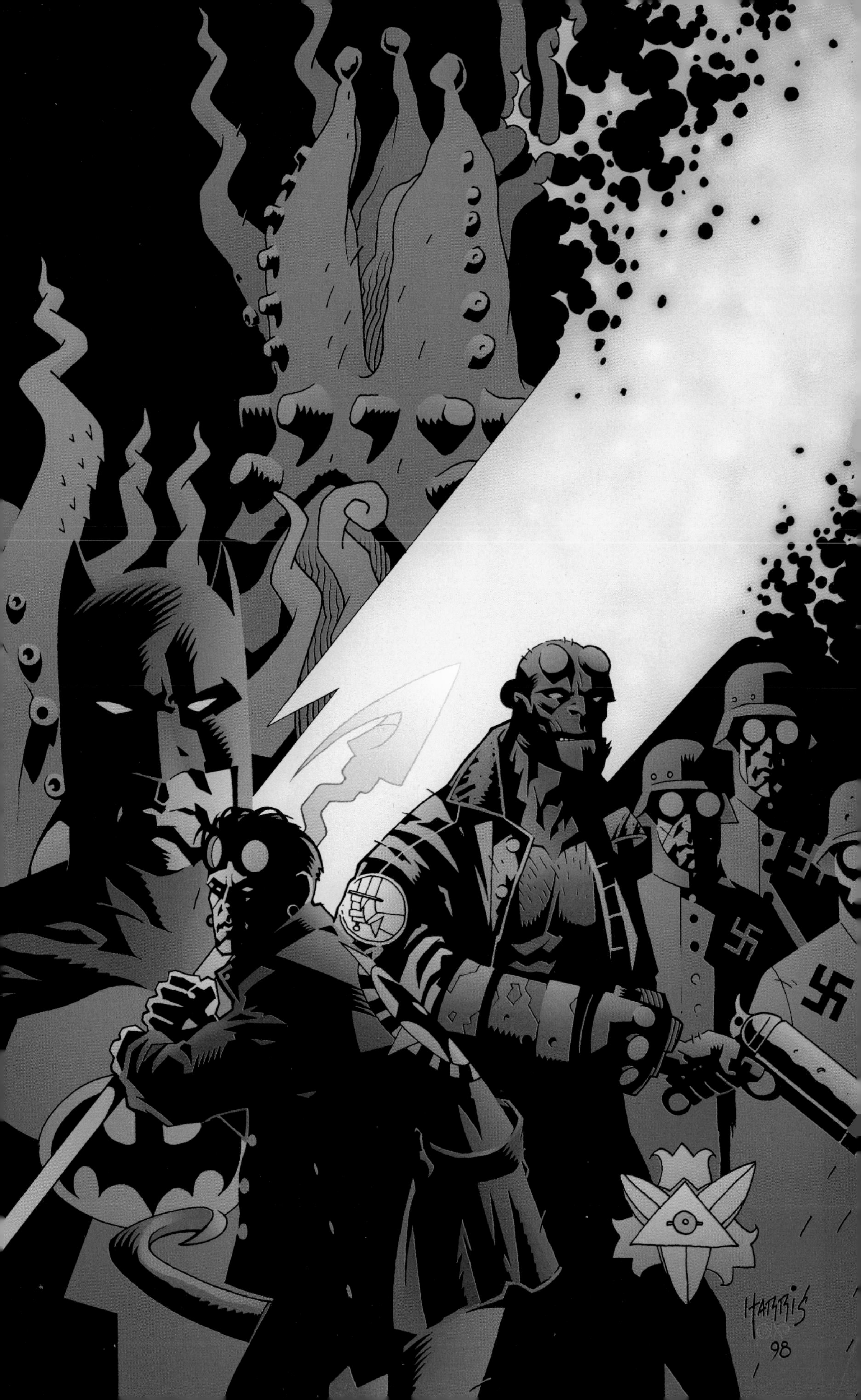
HARRIS
98

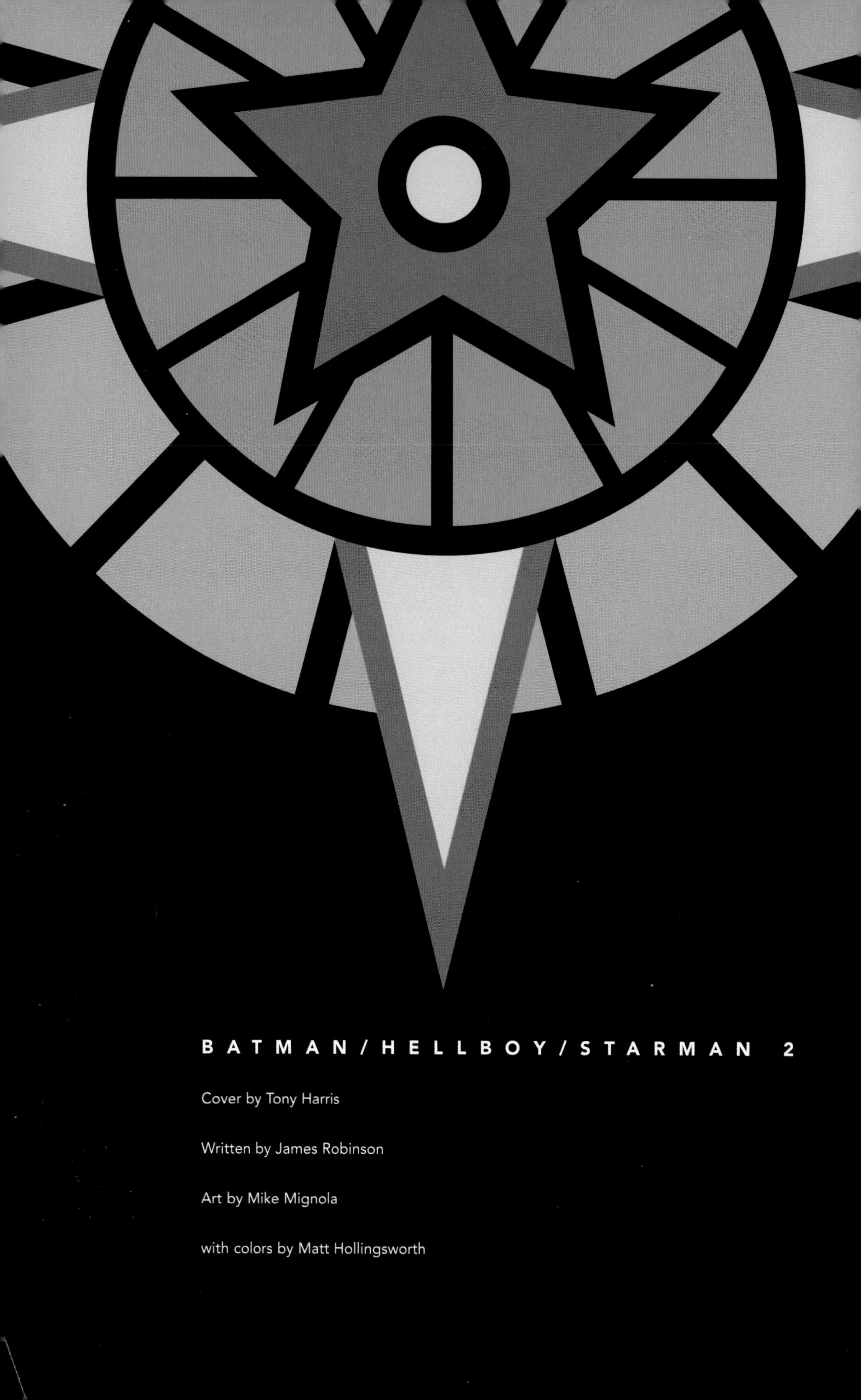

BATMAN/HELLBOY/STARMAN 2

Cover by Tony Harris

Written by James Robinson

Art by Mike Mignola

with colors by Matt Hollingsworth

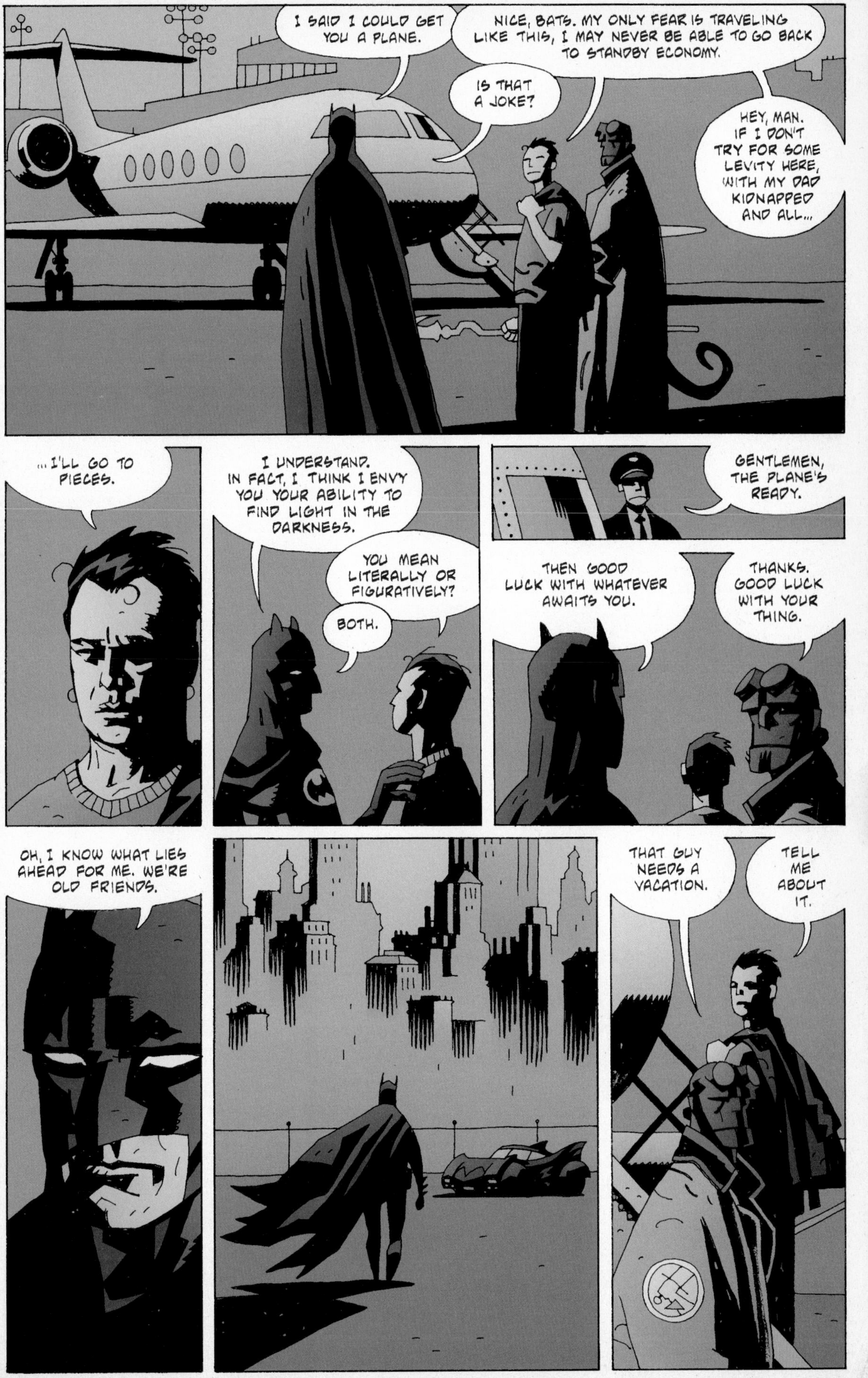
I SAID I COULD GET YOU A PLANE.
NICE, BATS. MY ONLY FEAR IS TRAVELING LIKE THIS, I MAY NEVER BE ABLE TO GO BACK TO STANDBY ECONOMY.
IS THAT A JOKE?
HEY, MAN. IF I DON'T TRY FOR SOME LEVITY HERE, WITH MY DAD KIDNAPPED AND ALL...
...I'LL GO TO PIECES.
I UNDERSTAND. IN FACT, I THINK I ENVY YOU YOUR ABILITY TO FIND LIGHT IN THE DARKNESS.
YOU MEAN LITERALLY OR FIGURATIVELY?
BOTH.
GENTLEMEN, THE PLANE'S READY.
THEN GOOD LUCK WITH WHATEVER AWAITS YOU.
THANKS. GOOD LUCK WITH YOUR THING.
OH, I KNOW WHAT LIES AHEAD FOR ME. WE'RE OLD FRIENDS.
THAT GUY NEEDS A VACATION.
TELL ME ABOUT IT.

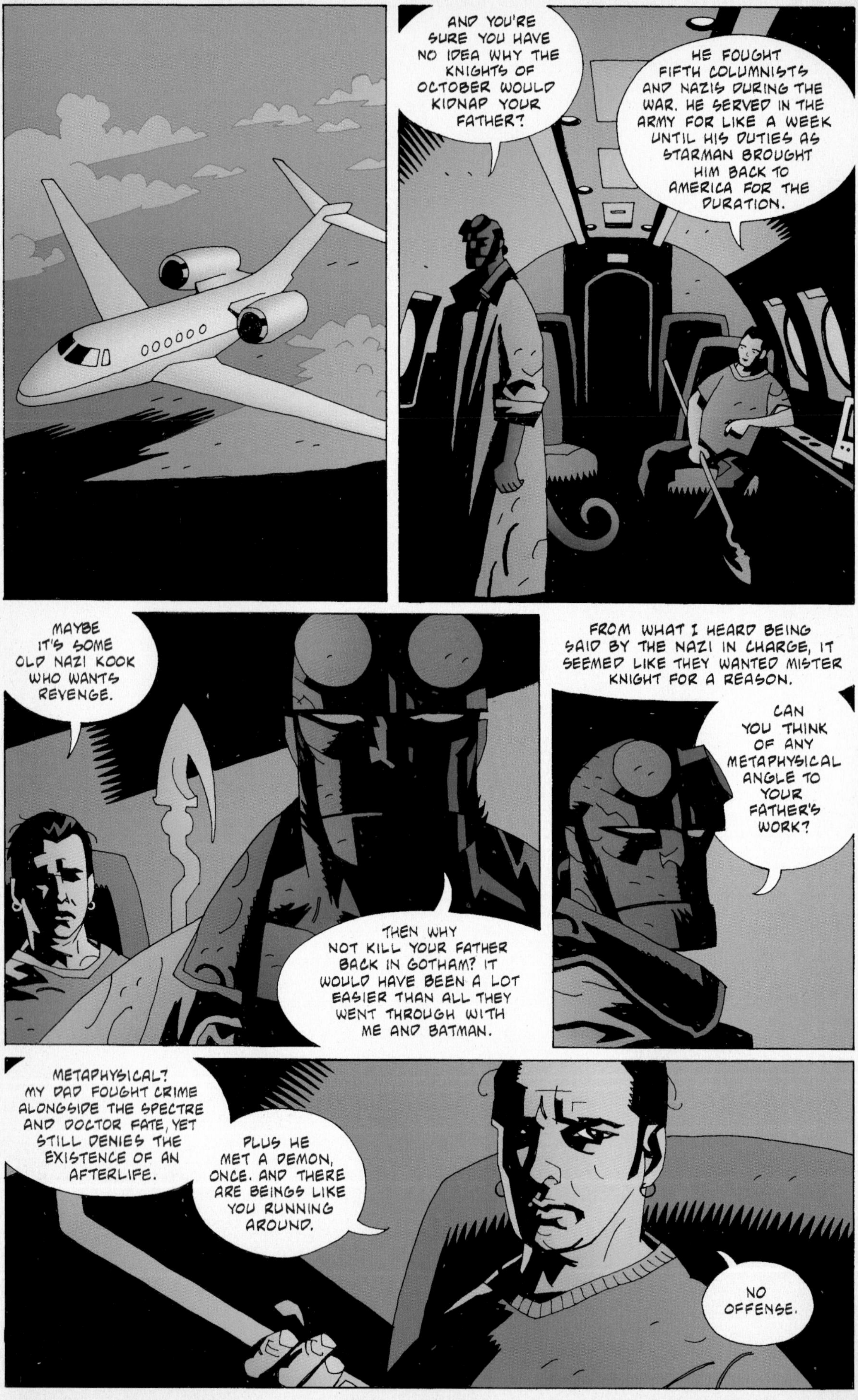
AND YOU'RE SURE YOU HAVE NO IDEA WHY THE KNIGHTS OF OCTOBER WOULD KIDNAP YOUR FATHER?
HE FOUGHT FIFTH COLUMNISTS AND NAZIS DURING THE WAR. HE SERVED IN THE ARMY FOR LIKE A WEEK UNTIL HIS DUTIES AS STARMAN BROUGHT HIM BACK TO AMERICA FOR THE DURATION.
MAYBE IT'S SOME OLD NAZI KOOK WHO WANTS REVENGE.
THEN WHY NOT KILL YOUR FATHER BACK IN GOTHAM? IT WOULD HAVE BEEN A LOT EASIER THAN ALL THEY WENT THROUGH WITH ME AND BATMAN.
FROM WHAT I HEARD BEING SAID BY THE NAZI IN CHARGE, IT SEEMED LIKE THEY WANTED MISTER KNIGHT FOR A REASON.
CAN YOU THINK OF ANY METAPHYSICAL ANGLE TO YOUR FATHER'S WORK?
METAPHYSICAL? MY DAD FOUGHT CRIME ALONGSIDE THE SPECTRE AND DOCTOR FATE, YET STILL DENIES THE EXISTENCE OF AN AFTERLIFE.
PLUS HE MET A DEMON, ONCE. AND THERE ARE BEINGS LIKE YOU RUNNING AROUND.
NO OFFENSE.

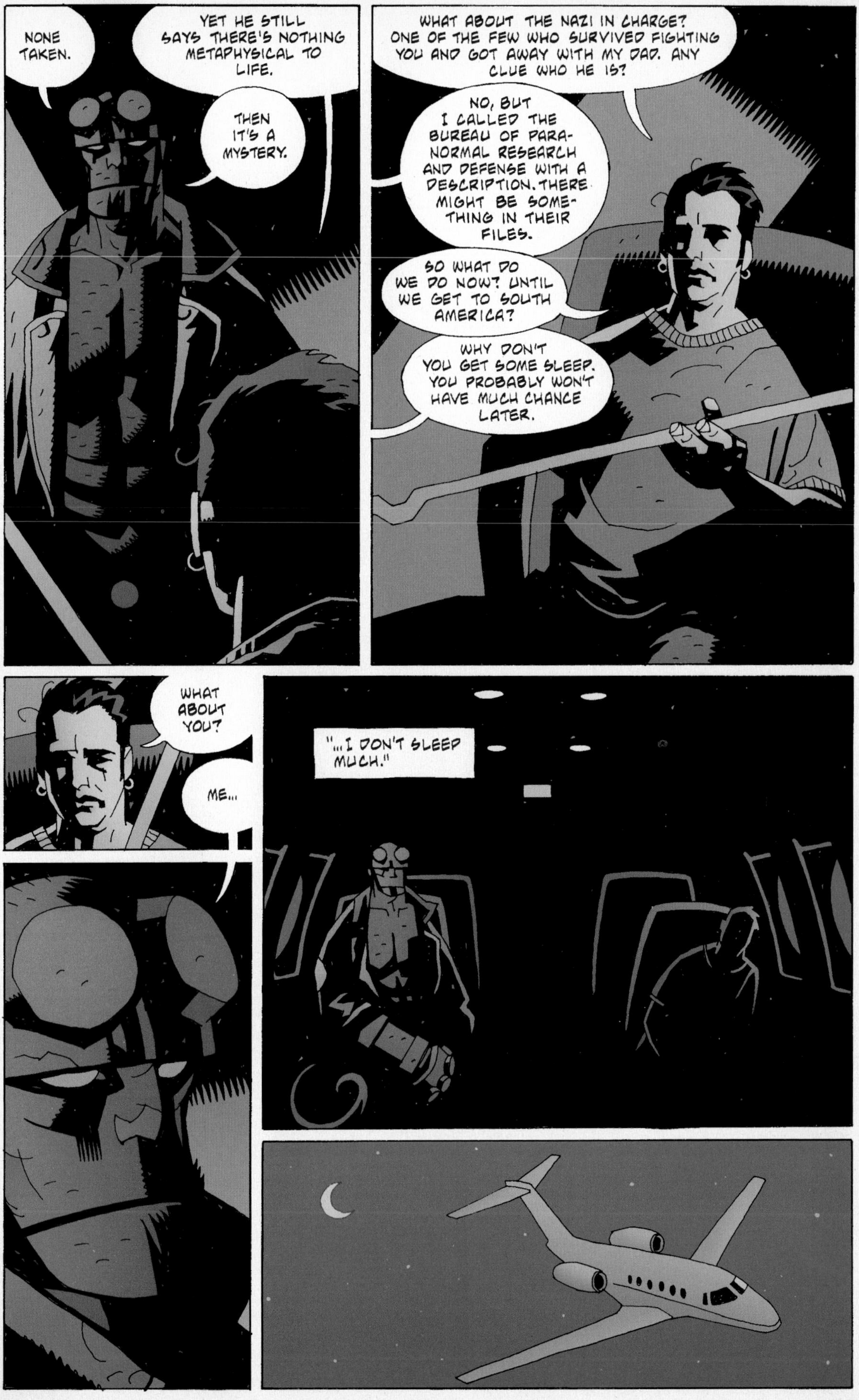
NONE TAKEN.
YET HE STILL SAYS THERE'S NOTHING METAPHYSICAL TO LIFE.
THEN IT'S A MYSTERY.
WHAT ABOUT THE NAZI IN CHARGE? ONE OF THE FEW WHO SURVIVED FIGHTING YOU AND GOT AWAY WITH MY DAD. ANY CLUE WHO HE IS?
NO, BUT I CALLED THE BUREAU OF PARA-NORMAL RESEARCH AND DEFENSE WITH A DESCRIPTION. THERE MIGHT BE SOME-THING IN THEIR FILES.
SO WHAT DO WE DO NOW? UNTIL WE GET TO SOUTH AMERICA?
WHY DON'T YOU GET SOME SLEEP. YOU PROBABLY WON'T HAVE MUCH CHANCE LATER.
WHAT ABOUT YOU?
ME...
"...I DON'T SLEEP MUCH."

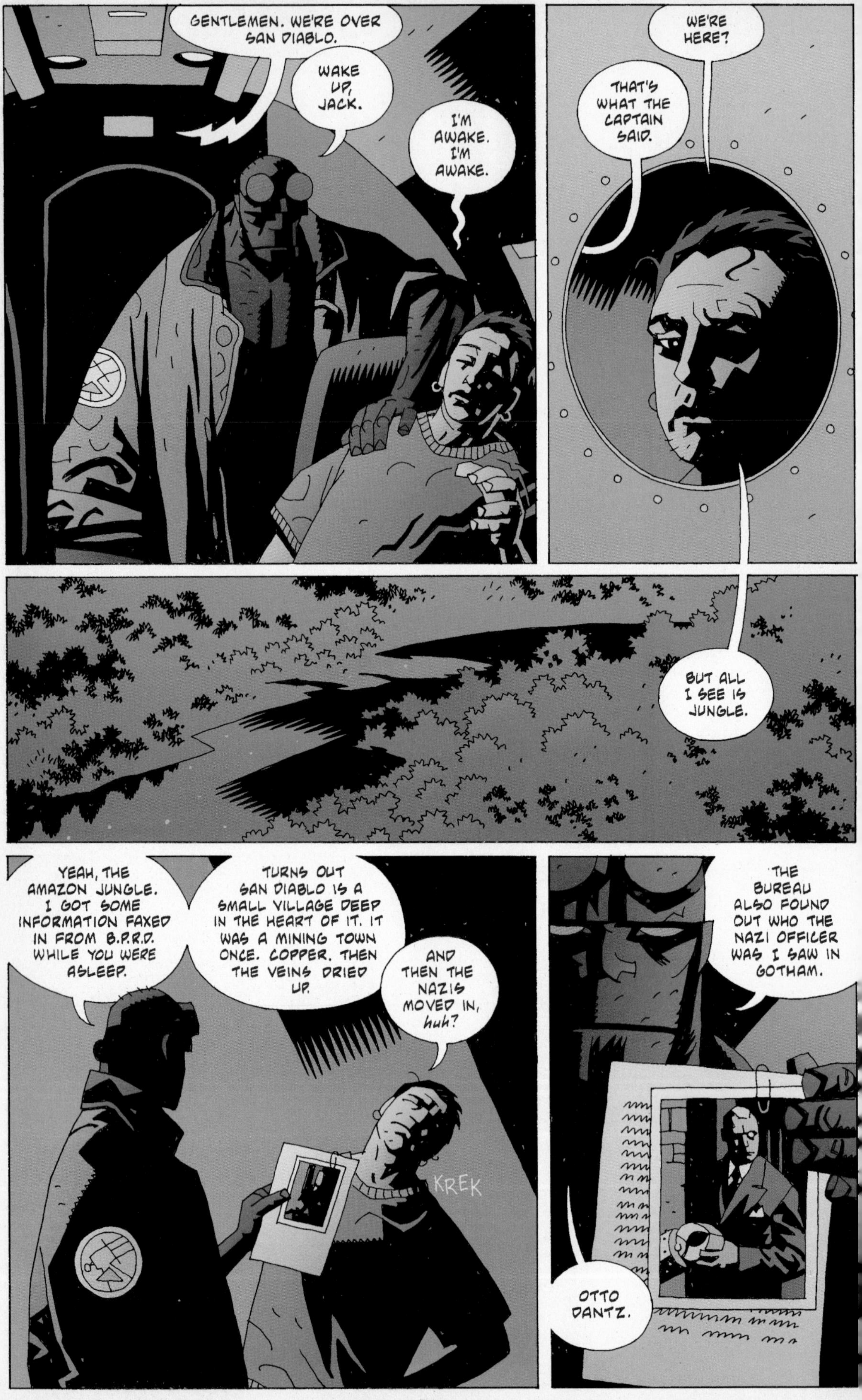

GENTLEMEN. WE'RE OVER SAN DIABLO.
WAKE UP, JACK.
I'M AWAKE. I'M AWAKE.
WE'RE HERE?
THAT'S WHAT THE CAPTAIN SAID.
BUT ALL I SEE IS JUNGLE.
YEAH, THE AMAZON JUNGLE. I GOT SOME INFORMATION FAXED IN FROM B.P.R.D. WHILE YOU WERE ASLEEP.
TURNS OUT SAN DIABLO IS A SMALL VILLAGE DEEP IN THE HEART OF IT. IT WAS A MINING TOWN ONCE. COPPER. THEN THE VEINS DRIED UP.
AND THEN THE NAZIS MOVED IN, *huh?*
KREK
THE BUREAU ALSO FOUND OUT WHO THE NAZI OFFICER WAS I SAW IN GOTHAM.
OTTO DANTZ.

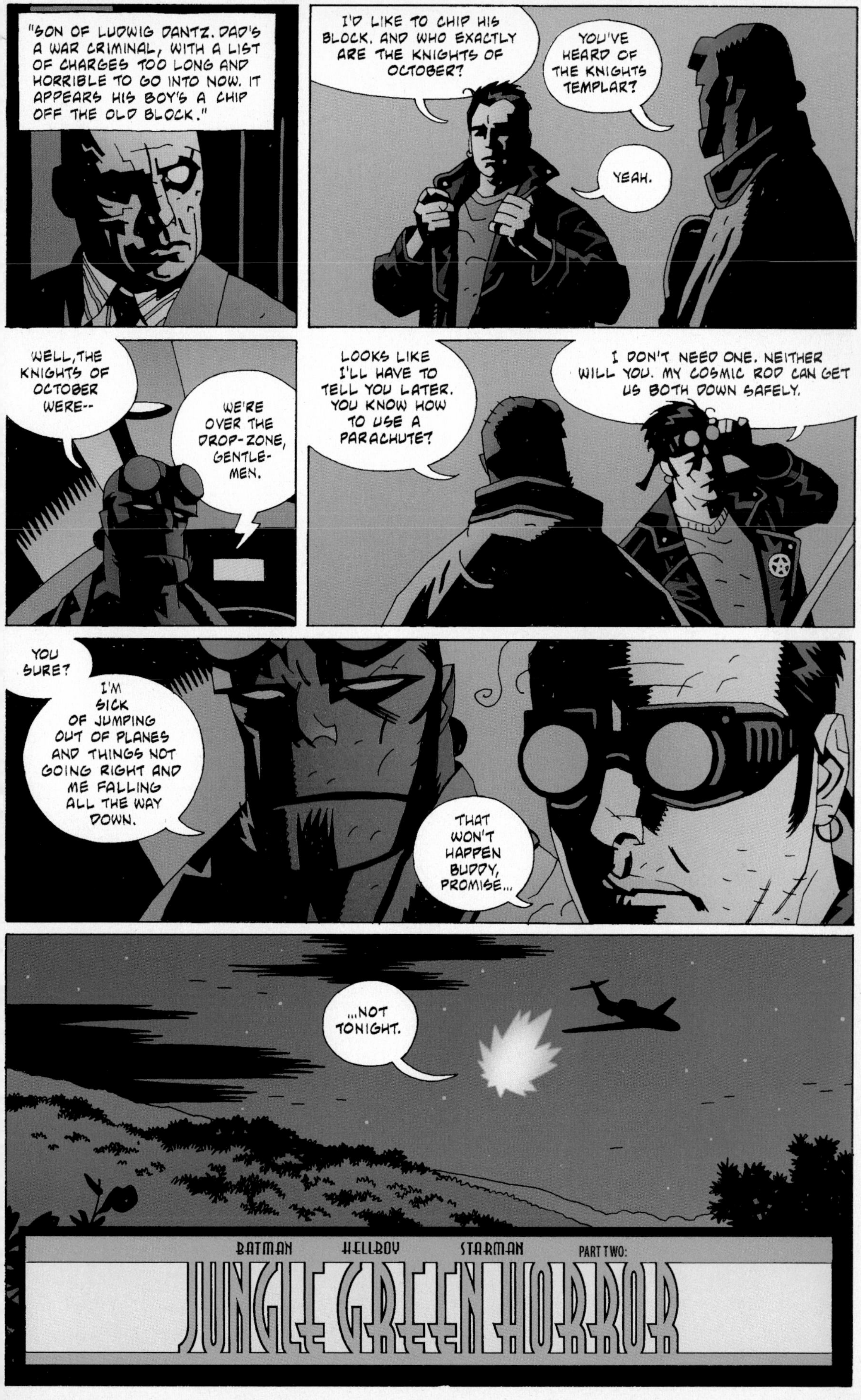
"SON OF LUDWIG DANTZ. DAD'S A WAR CRIMINAL, WITH A LIST OF CHARGES TOO LONG AND HORRIBLE TO GO INTO NOW. IT APPEARS HIS BOY'S A CHIP OFF THE OLD BLOCK."
I'D LIKE TO CHIP HIS BLOCK. AND WHO EXACTLY ARE THE KNIGHTS OF OCTOBER?
YOU'VE HEARD OF THE KNIGHTS TEMPLAR?
YEAH.
WELL, THE KNIGHTS OF OCTOBER WERE--
WE'RE OVER THE DROP-ZONE, GENTLE-MEN.
LOOKS LIKE I'LL HAVE TO TELL YOU LATER. YOU KNOW HOW TO USE A PARACHUTE?
I DON'T NEED ONE. NEITHER WILL YOU. MY COSMIC ROD CAN GET US BOTH DOWN SAFELY.
YOU SURE?
I'M SICK OF JUMPING OUT OF PLANES AND THINGS NOT GOING RIGHT AND ME FALLING ALL THE WAY DOWN.
THAT WON'T HAPPEN BUDDY, PROMISE...
...NOT TONIGHT.
BATMAN
HELLBOY
STARMAN
PART TWO:
JUNGLE GREEN HORROR

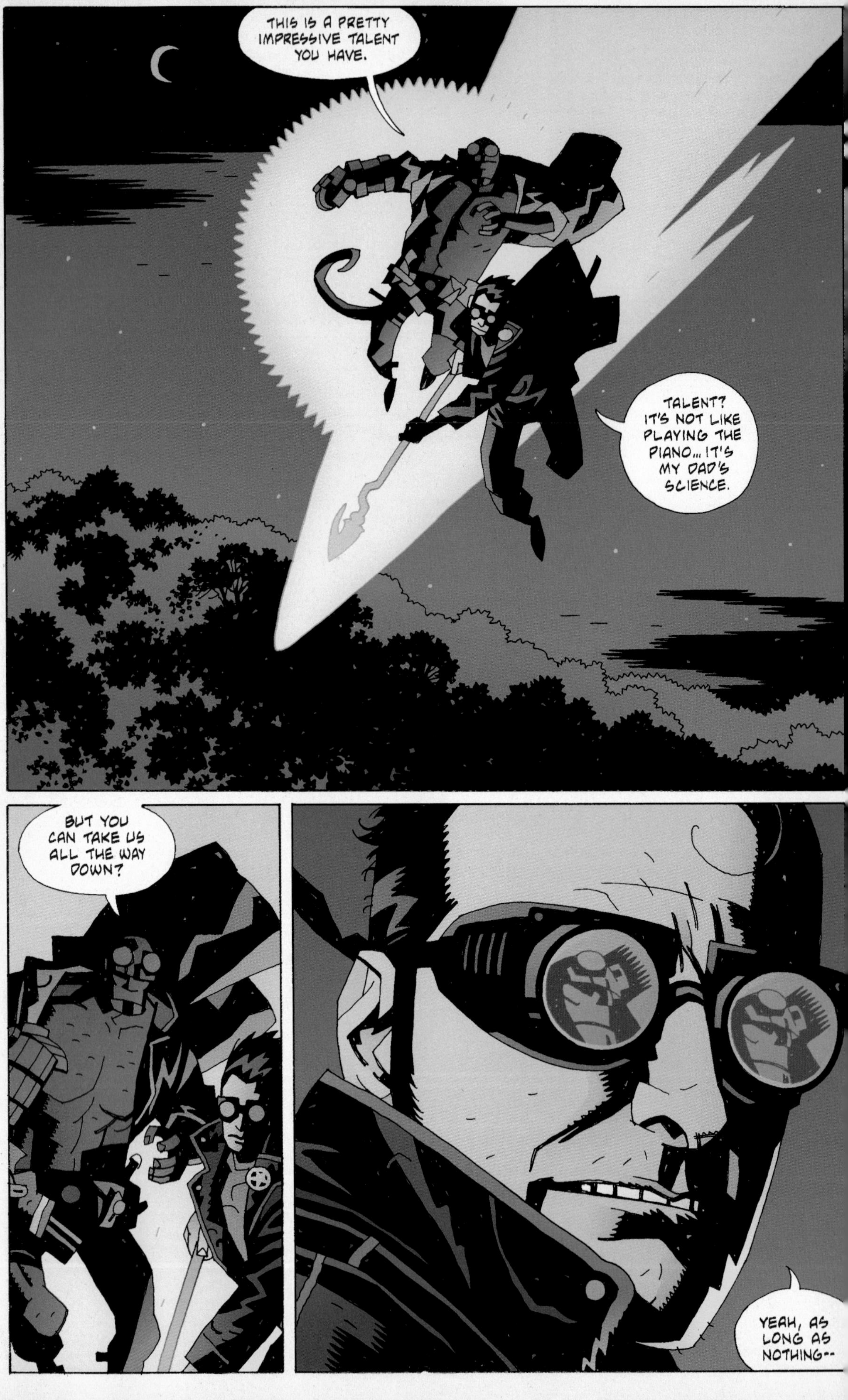
THIS IS A PRETTY IMPRESSIVE TALENT YOU HAVE.
TALENT? IT'S NOT LIKE PLAYING THE PIANO... IT'S MY DAD'S SCIENCE.
BUT YOU CAN TAKE US ALL THE WAY DOWN?
YEAH, AS LONG AS NOTHING--

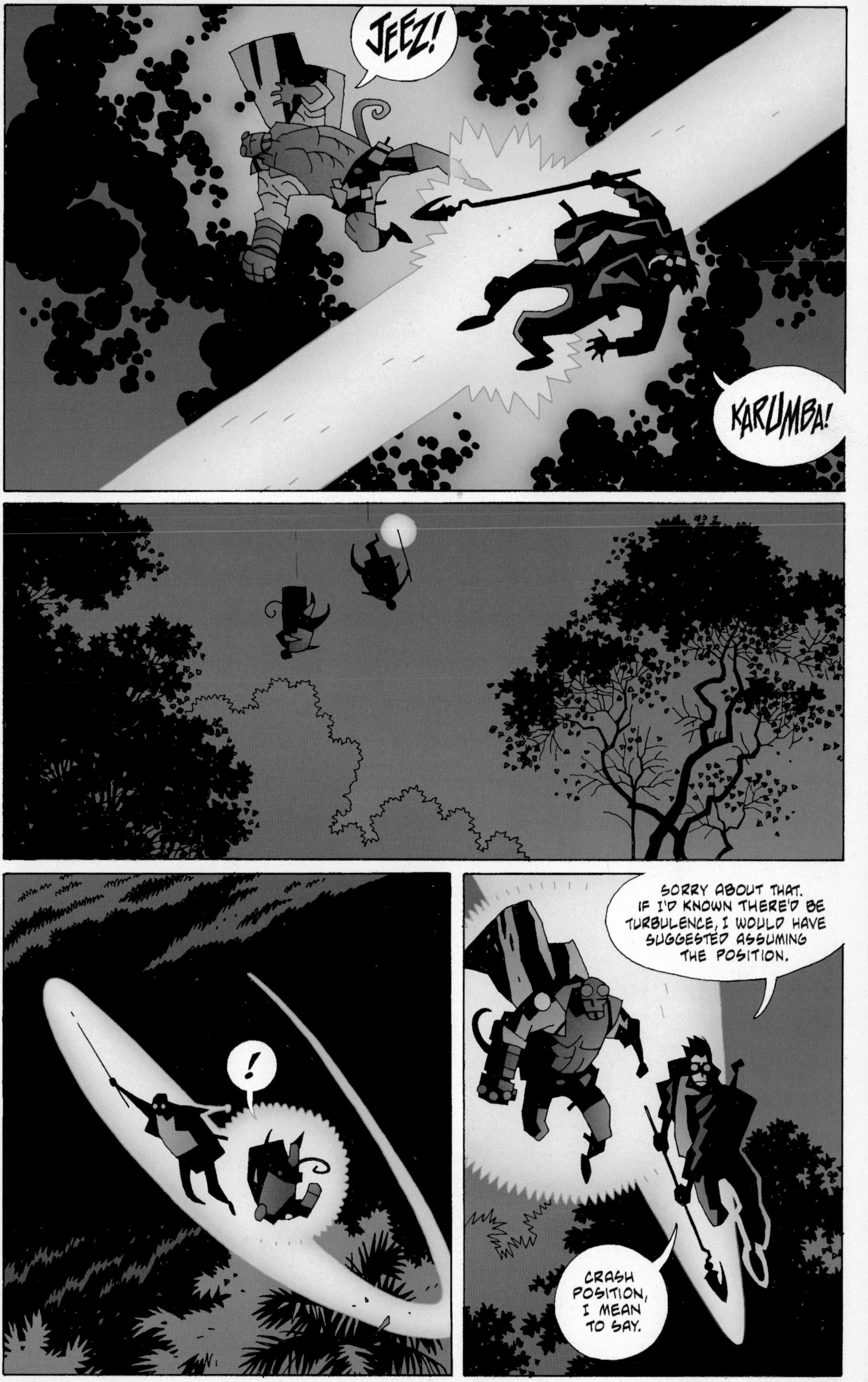
JEEZ!
KARUMBA!
!
SORRY ABOUT THAT. IF I'D KNOWN THERE'D BE TURBULENCE, I WOULD HAVE SUGGESTED ASSUMING THE POSITION.
CRASH POSITION, I MEAN TO SAY.

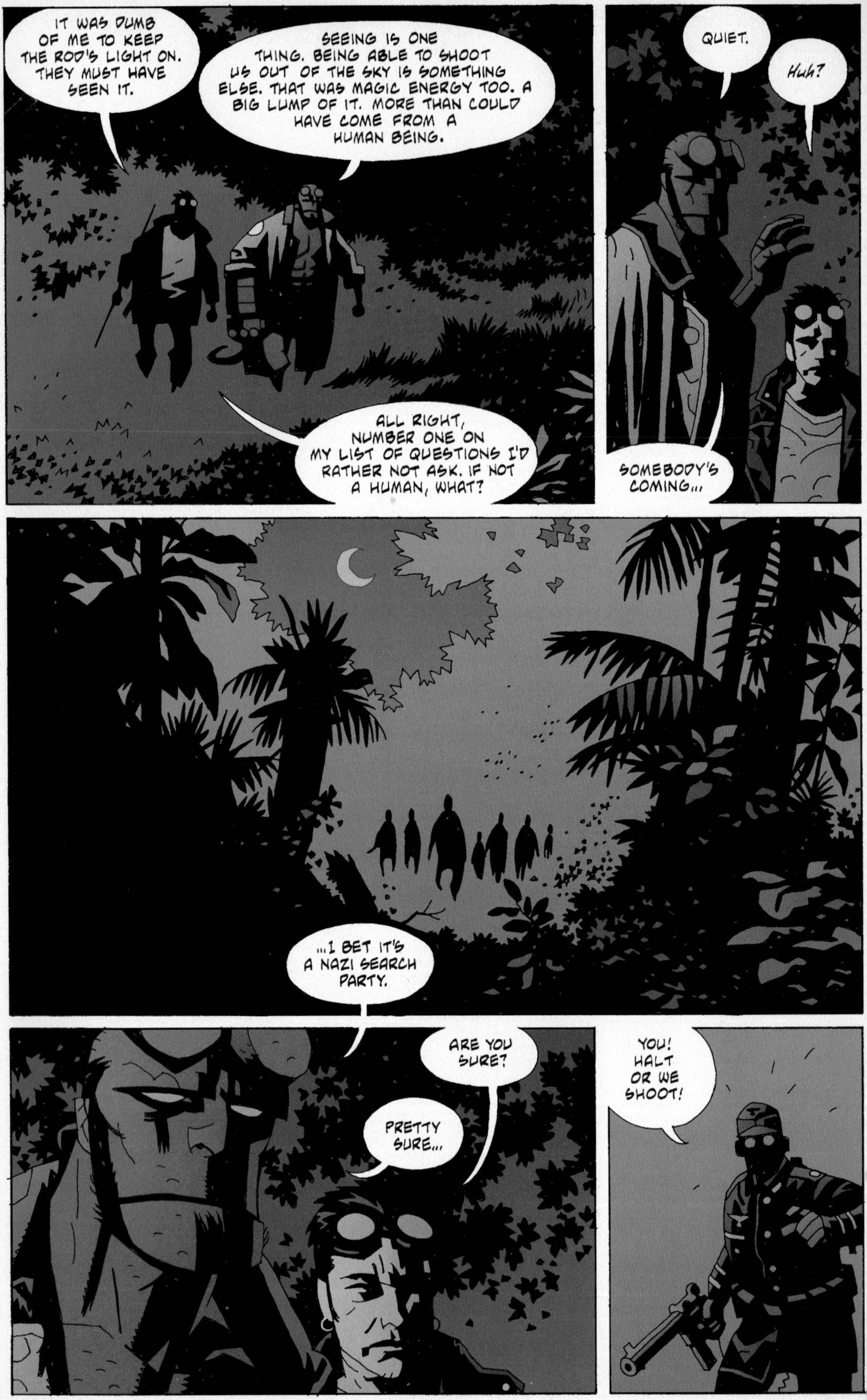
IT WAS DUMB OF ME TO KEEP THE ROD'S LIGHT ON. THEY MUST HAVE SEEN IT.
SEEING IS ONE THING. BEING ABLE TO SHOOT US OUT OF THE SKY IS SOMETHING ELSE. THAT WAS MAGIC ENERGY TOO. A BIG LUMP OF IT. MORE THAN COULD HAVE COME FROM A HUMAN BEING.
ALL RIGHT, NUMBER ONE ON MY LIST OF QUESTIONS I'D RATHER NOT ASK. IF NOT A HUMAN, WHAT?
QUIET.
Huh?
SOMEBODY'S COMING...
...I BET IT'S A NAZI SEARCH PARTY.
ARE YOU SURE?
PRETTY SURE...
YOU! HALT OR WE SHOOT!

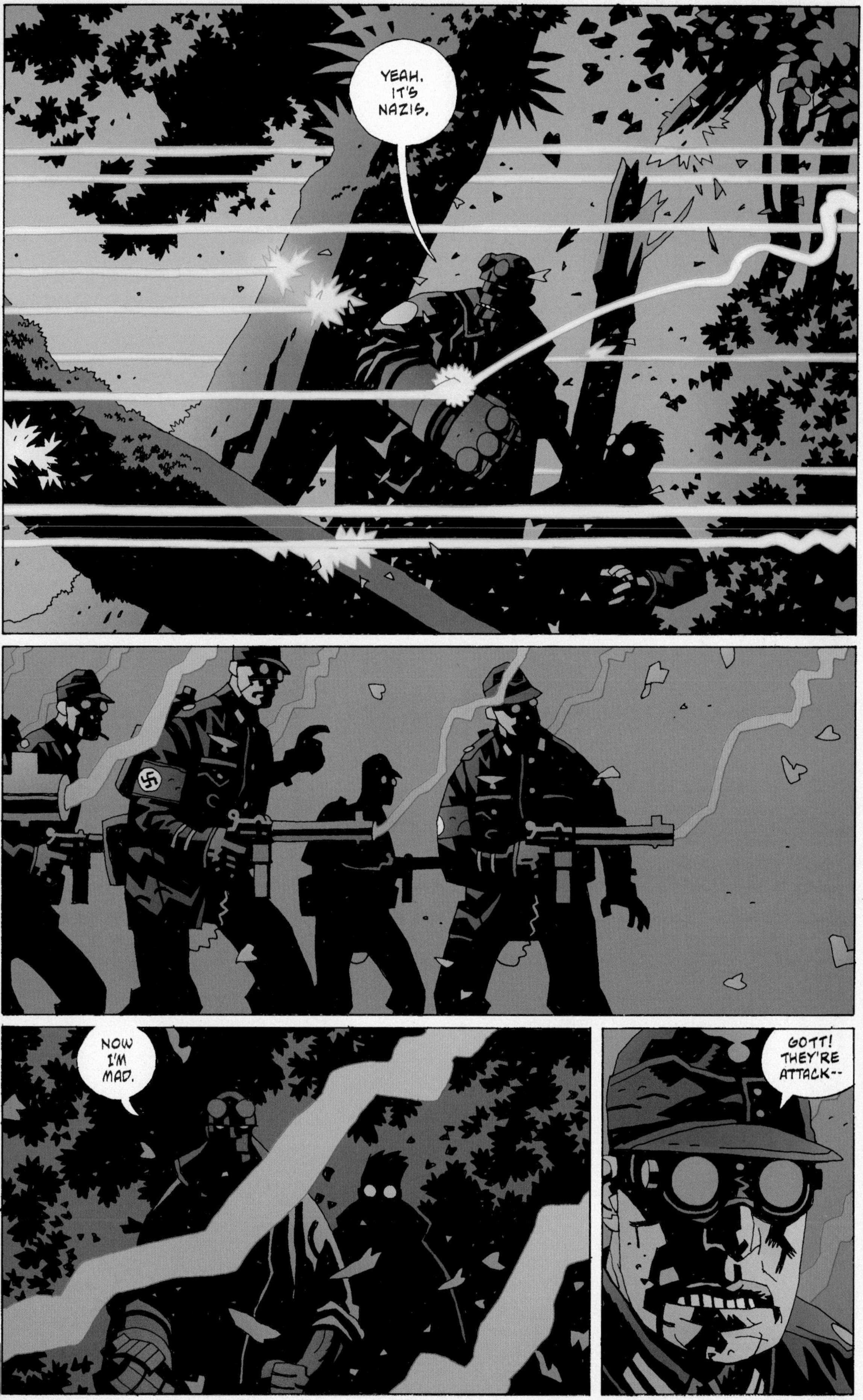
YEAH. IT'S NAZIS.
NOW I'M MAD.
GOTT! THEY'RE ATTACK--

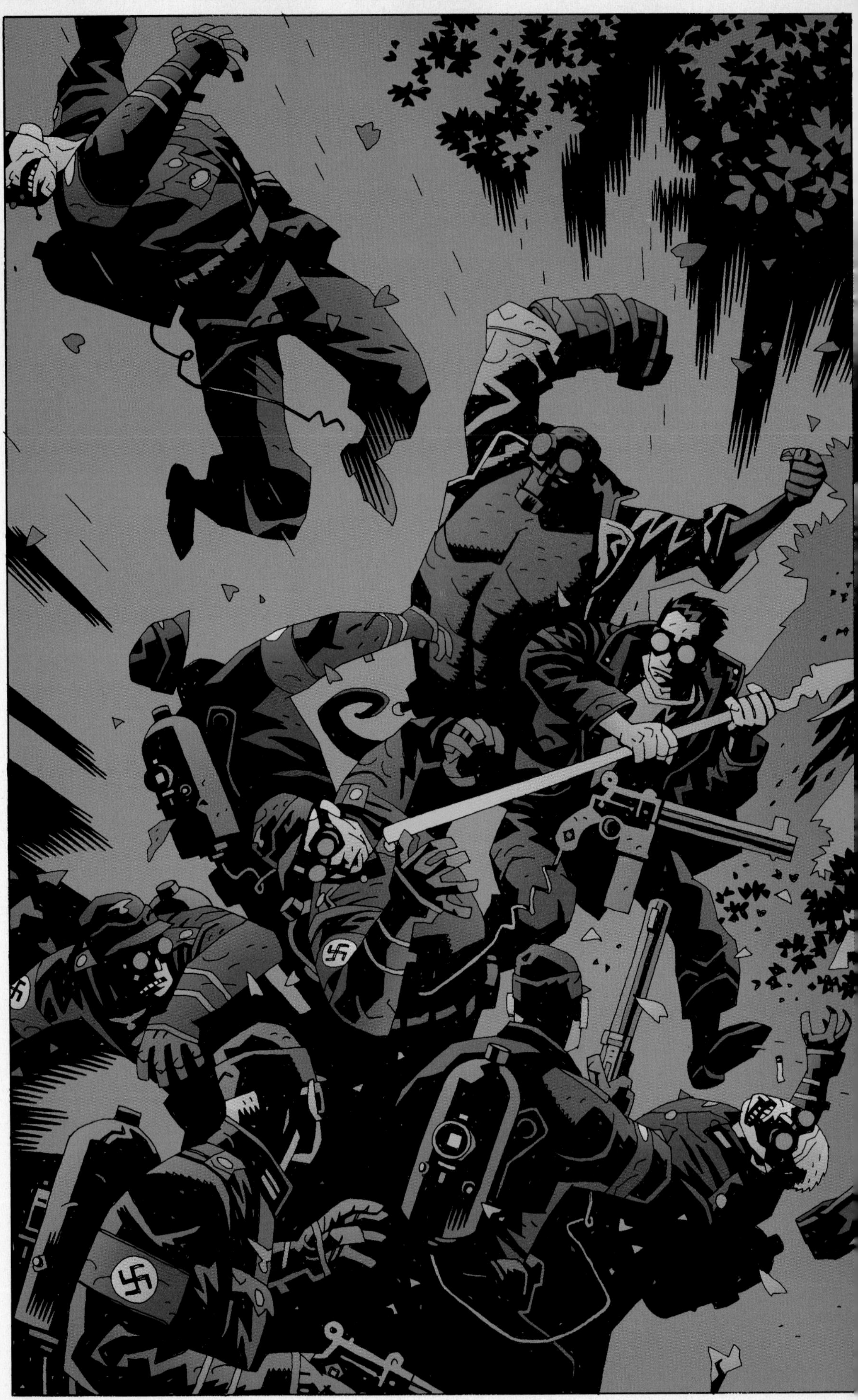

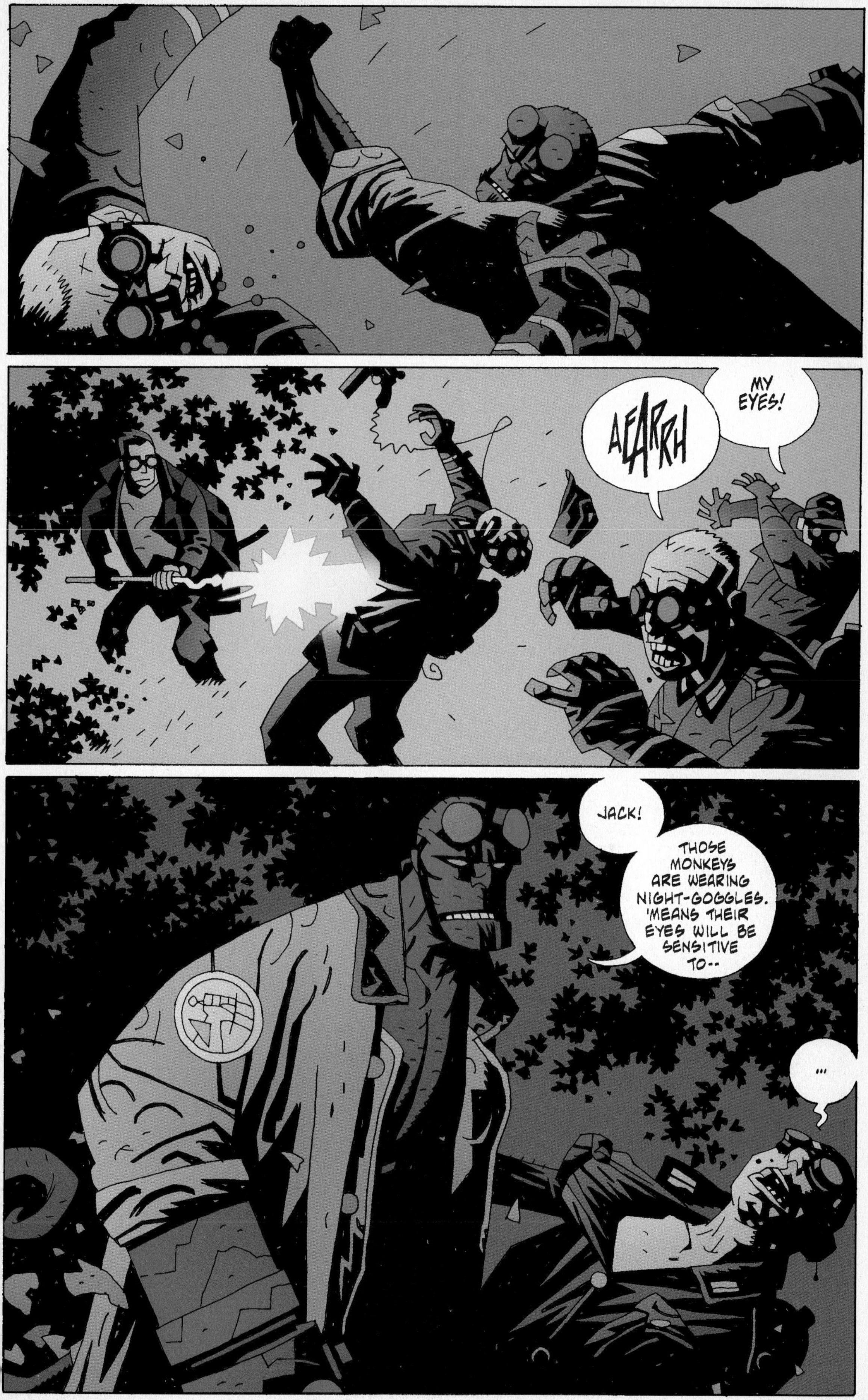
AEARRH
MY EYES!
JACK!
THOSE MONKEYS ARE WEARING NIGHT-GOGGLES. 'MEANS THEIR EYES WILL BE SENSITIVE TO--
...

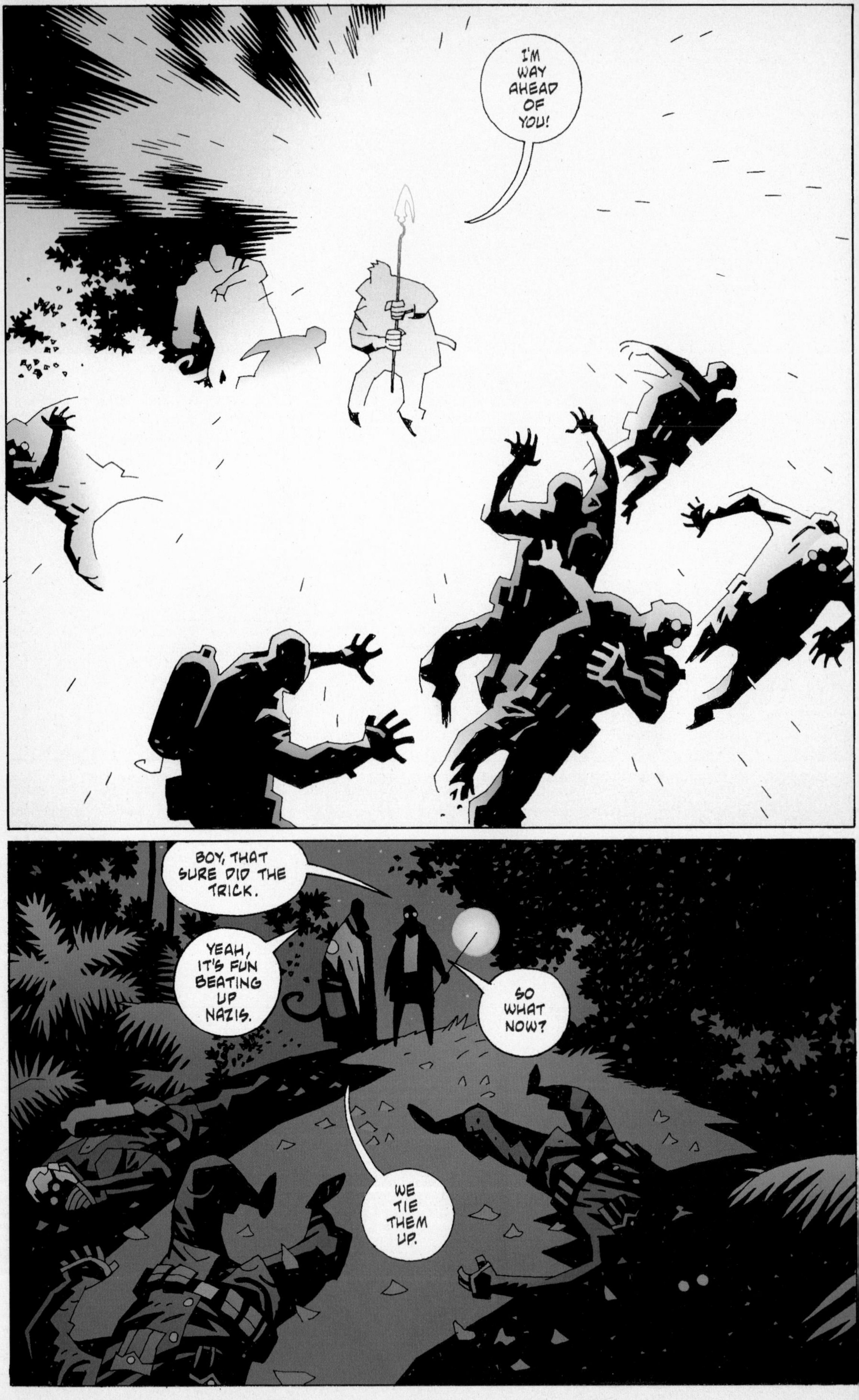
I'M WAY AHEAD OF YOU!
BOY, THAT SURE DID THE TRICK.
YEAH, IT'S FUN BEATING UP NAZIS.
SO WHAT NOW?
WE TIE THEM UP.

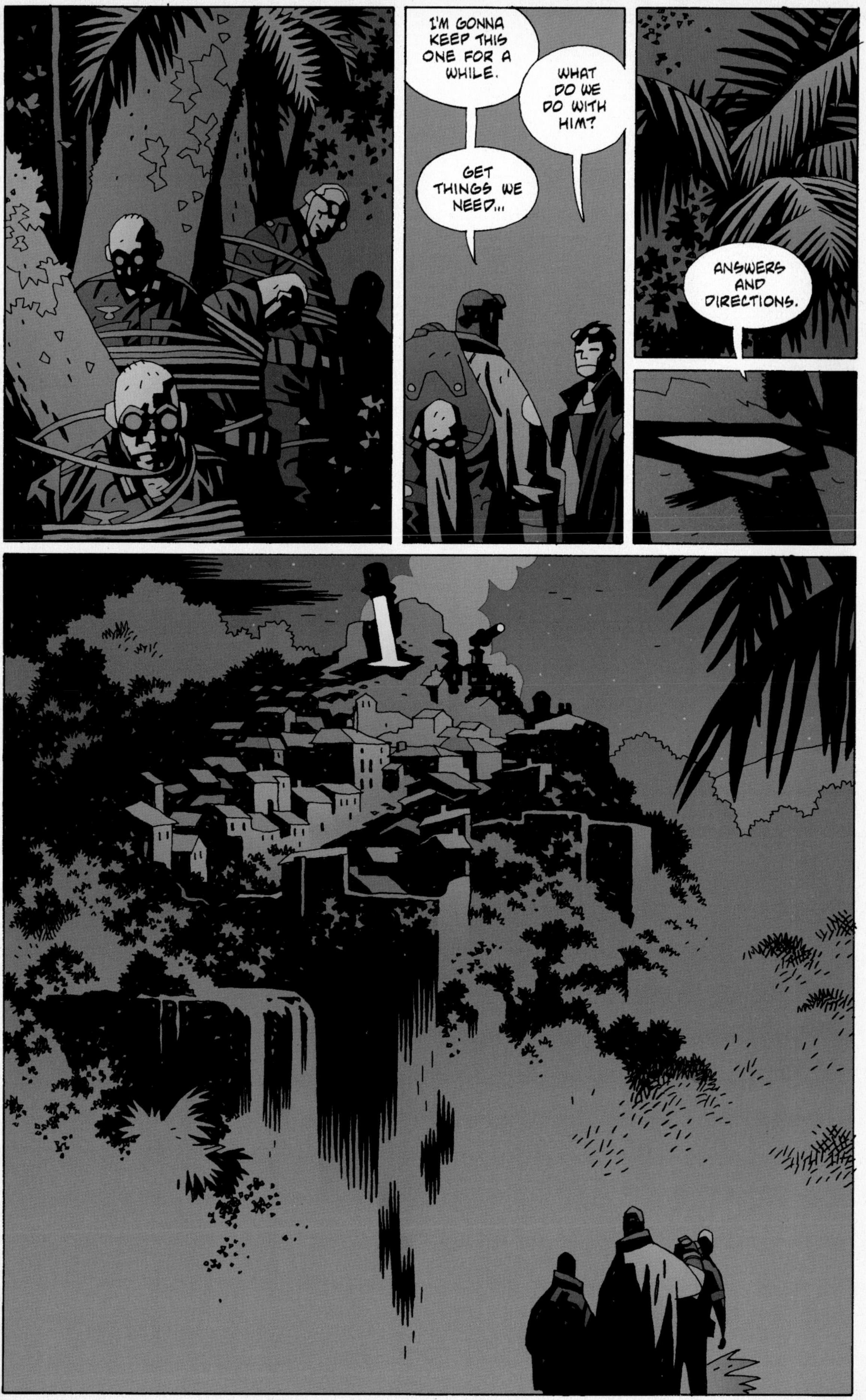
I'M GONNA KEEP THIS ONE FOR A WHILE.
WHAT DO WE DO WITH HIM?
GET THINGS WE NEED...
ANSWERS AND DIRECTIONS.

NICE. HOMEY.

REMINDS ME OF A PLACE I STAYED ONE NIGHT ON THE ROAD BACK WHEN I PLAYED BASS IN A GARAGE BAND.

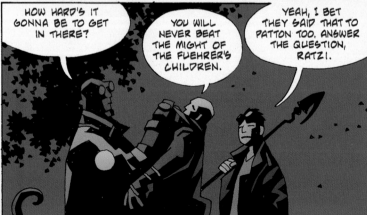

HOW HARD'S IT GONNA BE TO GET IN THERE?

YOU WILL NEVER BEAT THE MIGHT OF THE FUEHRER'S CHILDREN.

YEAH, I BET THEY SAID THAT TO PATTON TOO. ANSWER THE QUESTION, RATZI.

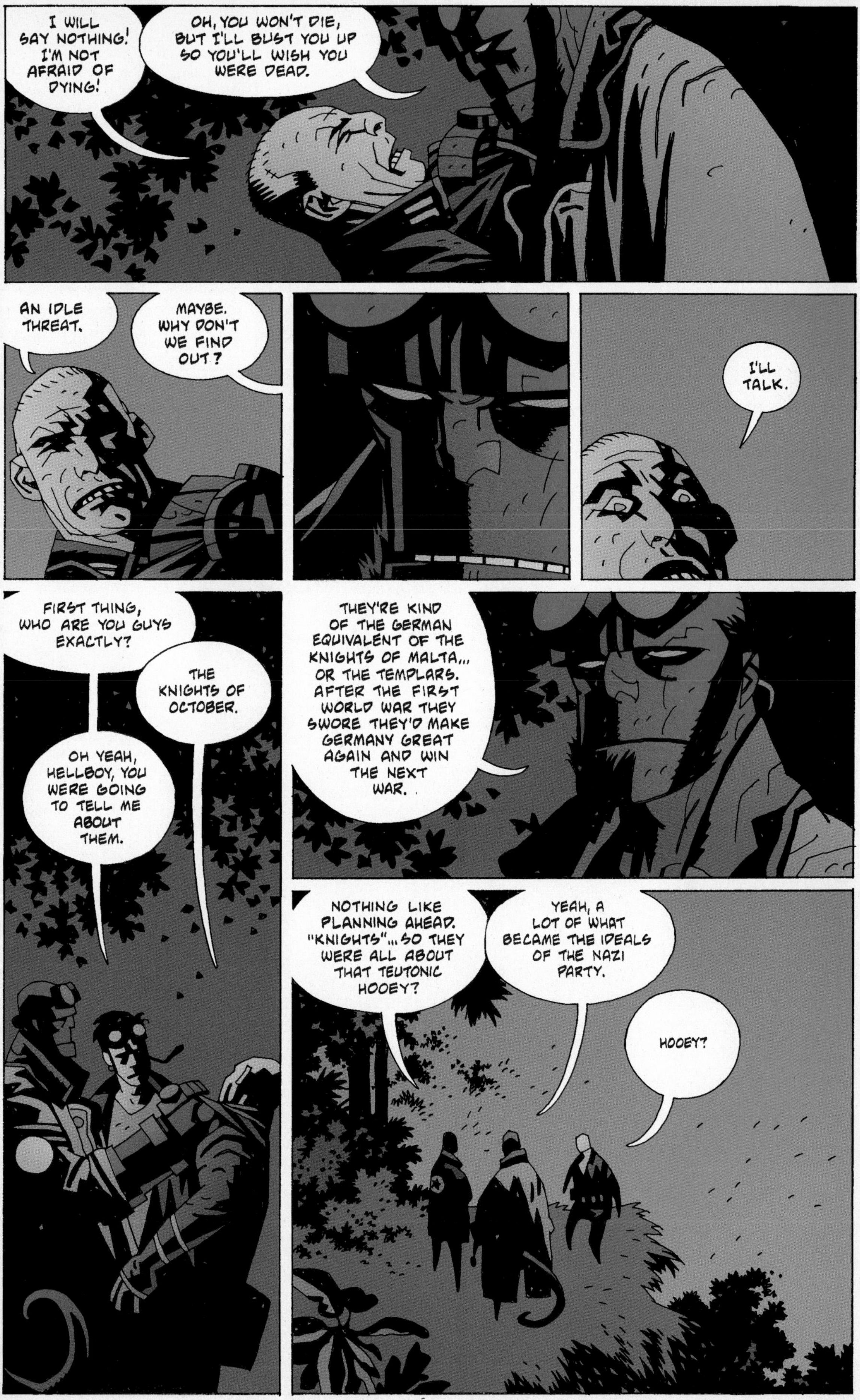
I WILL SAY NOTHING! I'M NOT AFRAID OF DYING!
OH, YOU WON'T DIE, BUT I'LL BUST YOU UP SO YOU'LL WISH YOU WERE DEAD.
AN IDLE THREAT.
MAYBE. WHY DON'T WE FIND OUT?
I'LL TALK.
FIRST THING, WHO ARE YOU GUYS EXACTLY?
THE KNIGHTS OF OCTOBER.
OH YEAH, HELLBOY, YOU WERE GOING TO TELL ME ABOUT THEM.
THEY'RE KIND OF THE GERMAN EQUIVALENT OF THE KNIGHTS OF MALTA... OR THE TEMPLARS. AFTER THE FIRST WORLD WAR THEY SWORE THEY'D MAKE GERMANY GREAT AGAIN AND WIN THE NEXT WAR.
NOTHING LIKE PLANNING AHEAD. "KNIGHTS"... SO THEY WERE ALL ABOUT THAT TEUTONIC HOOEY?
YEAH, A LOT OF WHAT BECAME THE IDEALS OF THE NAZI PARTY.
HOOEY?

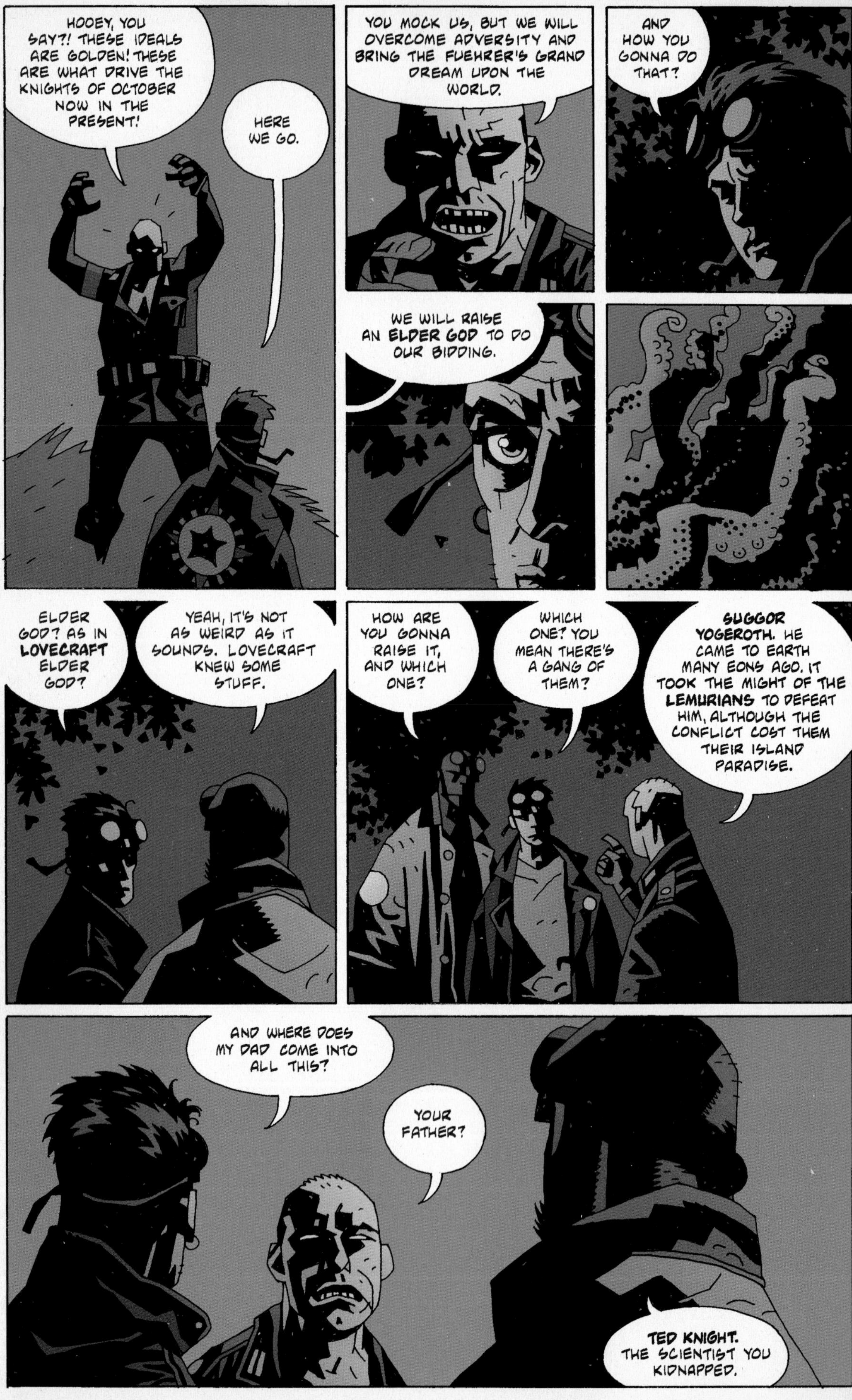
HOOEY, YOU SAY?! THESE IDEALS ARE GOLDEN! THESE ARE WHAT DRIVE THE KNIGHTS OF OCTOBER NOW IN THE PRESENT!
HERE WE GO.
YOU MOCK US, BUT WE WILL OVERCOME ADVERSITY AND BRING THE FUEHRER'S GRAND DREAM UPON THE WORLD.
AND HOW YOU GONNA DO THAT?
WE WILL RAISE AN ELDER GOD TO DO OUR BIDDING.
ELDER GOD? AS IN LOVECRAFT ELDER GOD?
YEAH, IT'S NOT AS WEIRD AS IT SOUNDS. LOVECRAFT KNEW SOME STUFF.
HOW ARE YOU GONNA RAISE IT, AND WHICH ONE?
WHICH ONE? YOU MEAN THERE'S A GANG OF THEM?
SUGGOR YOGEROTH. HE CAME TO EARTH MANY EONS AGO. IT TOOK THE MIGHT OF THE LEMURIANS TO DEFEAT HIM, ALTHOUGH THE CONFLICT COST THEM THEIR ISLAND PARADISE.
AND WHERE DOES MY DAD COME INTO ALL THIS?
YOUR FATHER?
TED KNIGHT. THE SCIENTIST YOU KIDNAPPED.

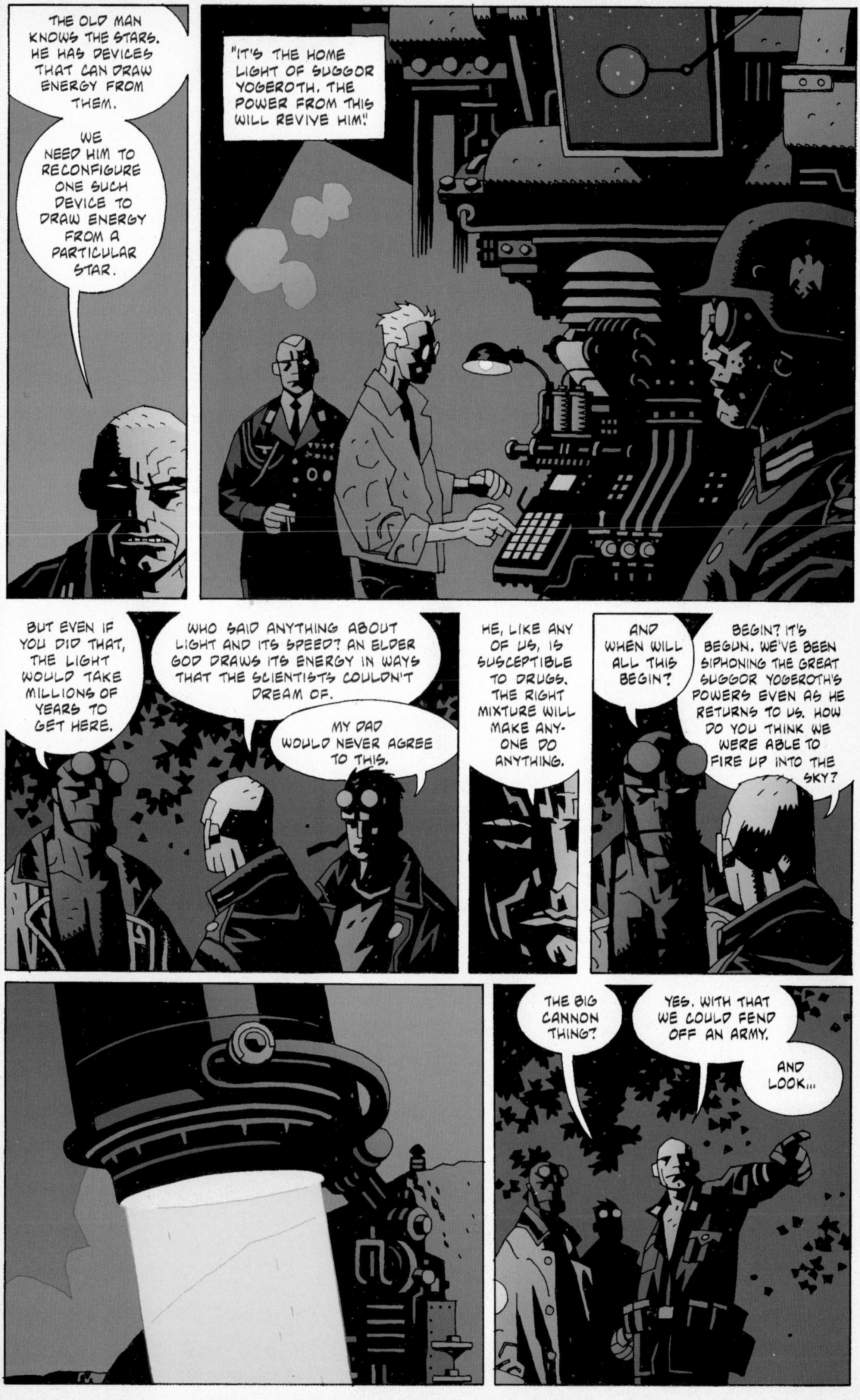
THE OLD MAN KNOWS THE STARS. HE HAS DEVICES THAT CAN DRAW ENERGY FROM THEM.
WE NEED HIM TO RECONFIGURE ONE SUCH DEVICE TO DRAW ENERGY FROM A PARTICULAR STAR.
"IT'S THE HOME LIGHT OF SUGGOR YOGEROTH. THE POWER FROM THIS WILL REVIVE HIM."
BUT EVEN IF YOU DID THAT, THE LIGHT WOULD TAKE MILLIONS OF YEARS TO GET HERE.
WHO SAID ANYTHING ABOUT LIGHT AND ITS SPEED? AN ELDER GOD DRAWS ITS ENERGY IN WAYS THAT THE SCIENTISTS COULDN'T DREAM OF.
MY DAD WOULD NEVER AGREE TO THIS.
HE, LIKE ANY OF US, IS SUSCEPTIBLE TO DRUGS. THE RIGHT MIXTURE WILL MAKE ANY-ONE DO ANYTHING.
AND WHEN WILL ALL THIS BEGIN?
BEGIN? IT'S BEGUN. WE'VE BEEN SIPHONING THE GREAT SUGGOR YOGEROTH'S POWERS EVEN AS HE RETURNS TO US. HOW DO YOU THINK WE WERE ABLE TO FIRE UP INTO THE SKY?
THE BIG CANNON THING?
YES. WITH THAT WE COULD FEND OFF AN ARMY.
AND LOOK...

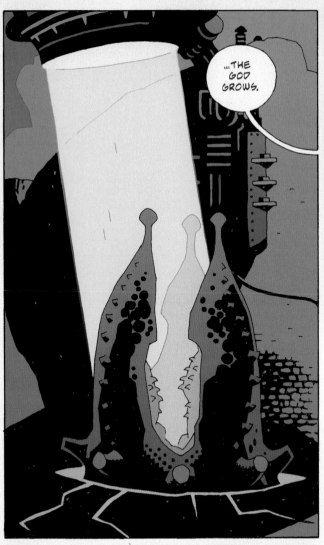

"...THE GOD GROWS.

WHOA, HE'S A BIG BOY.

AND MANY-SIDED.

NOW THAT WAS FROM LOVECRAFT. DON'T BE TRYING TO IMPRESS ME WITH WATERED-DOWN H.P.

YEAH, YOU'RE GIVING ME A HEADACHE.

KLONK

NOW WHAT?

WE ATTACK AND GET YOUR FATHER OUT. THEN WE STOP THAT THING FROM GETTING ANY BIGGER.

ATTACK? YOU GOT A PLAN?

NOPE.

JUST ASKING.

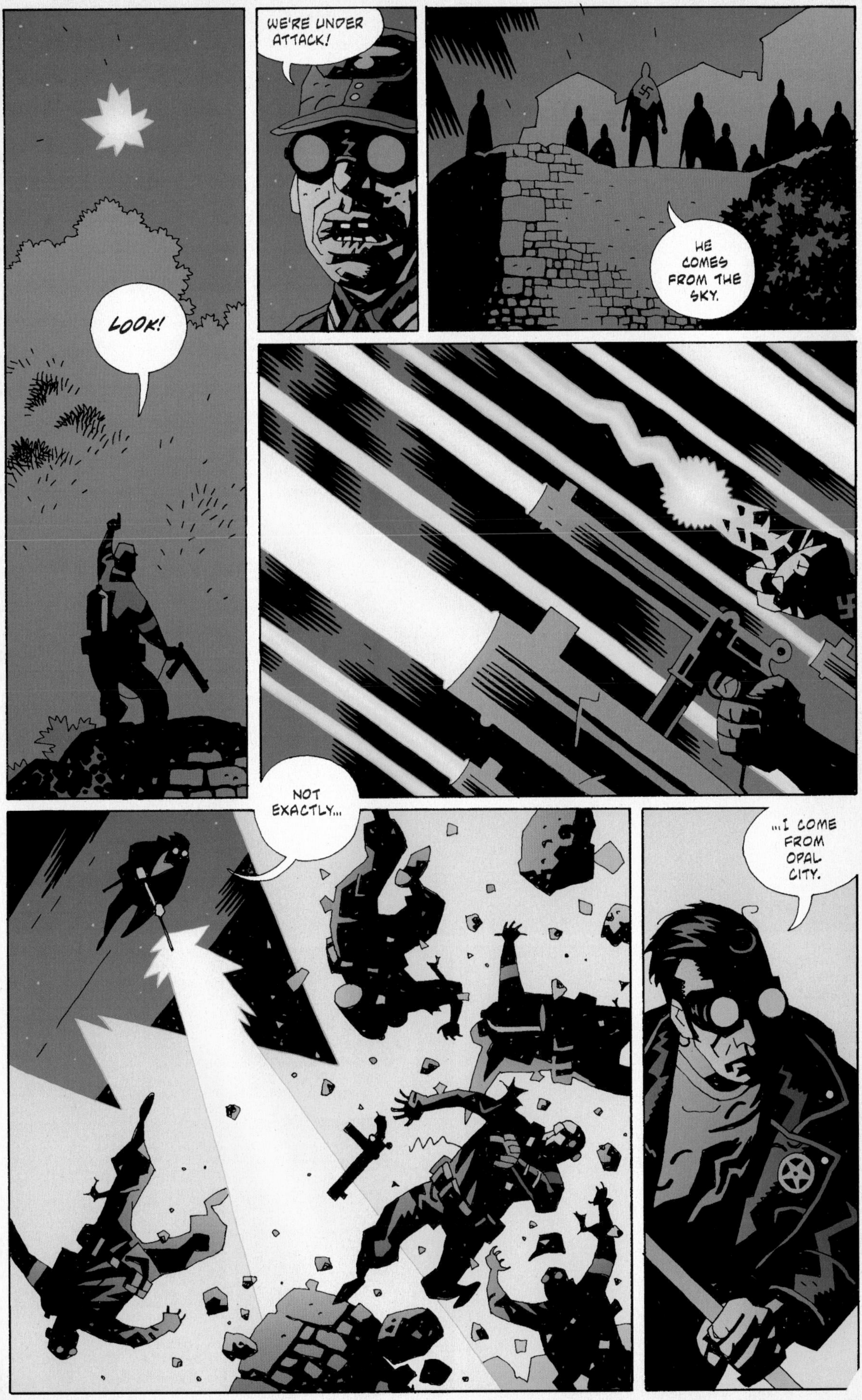
LOOK!
WE'RE UNDER ATTACK!
HE COMES FROM THE SKY.
NOT EXACTLY...
...I COME FROM OPAL CITY.

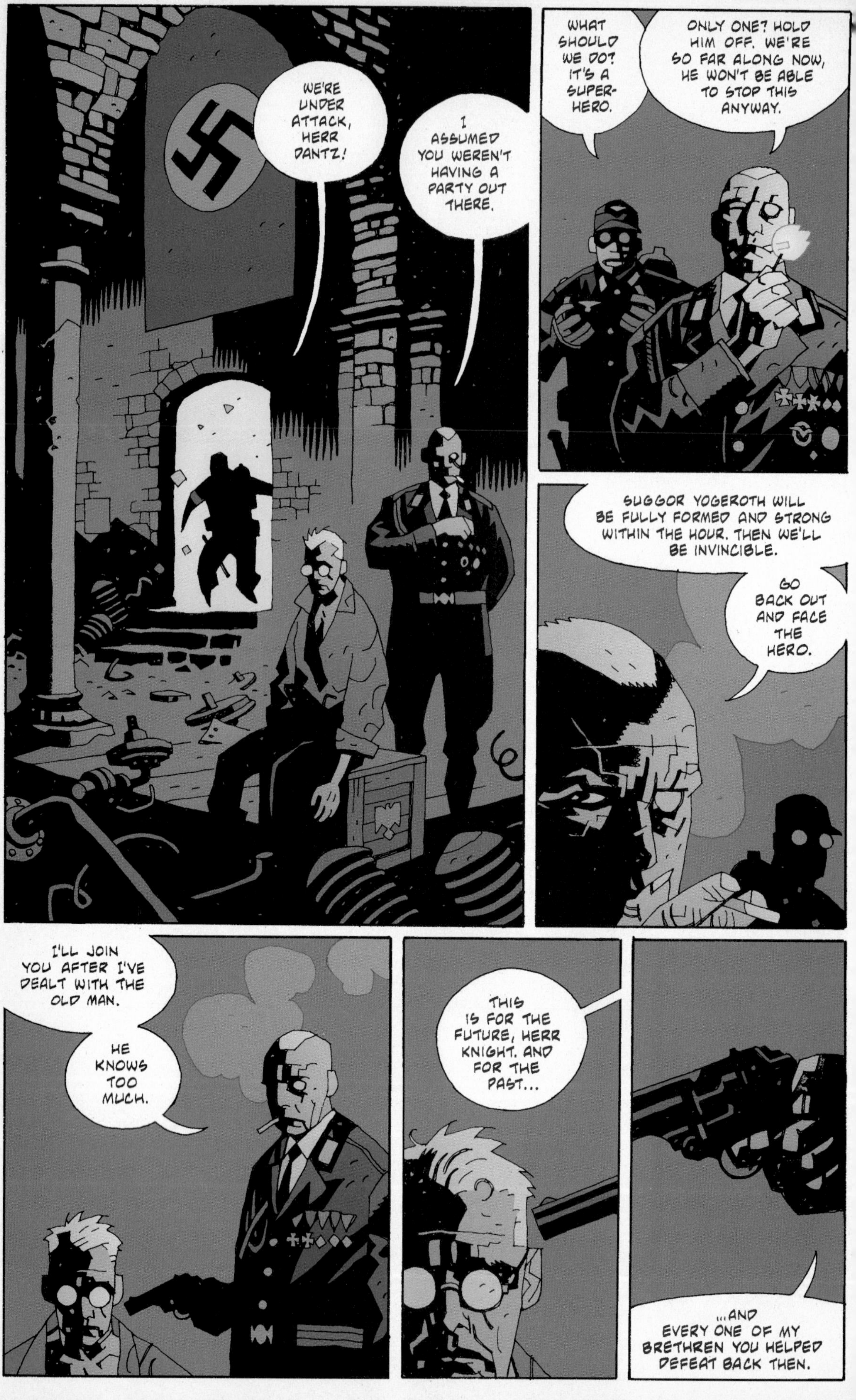
WE'RE UNDER ATTACK, HERR DANTZ!
I ASSUMED YOU WEREN'T HAVING A PARTY OUT THERE.
WHAT SHOULD WE DO? IT'S A SUPER-HERO.
ONLY ONE? HOLD HIM OFF. WE'RE SO FAR ALONG NOW, HE WON'T BE ABLE TO STOP THIS ANYWAY.
SUGGOR YOGEROTH WILL BE FULLY FORMED AND STRONG WITHIN THE HOUR. THEN WE'LL BE INVINCIBLE.
GO BACK OUT AND FACE THE HERO.
I'LL JOIN YOU AFTER I'VE DEALT WITH THE OLD MAN.
HE KNOWS TOO MUCH.
THIS IS FOR THE FUTURE, HERR KNIGHT. AND FOR THE PAST...
...AND EVERY ONE OF MY BRETHREN YOU HELPED DEFEAT BACK THEN.

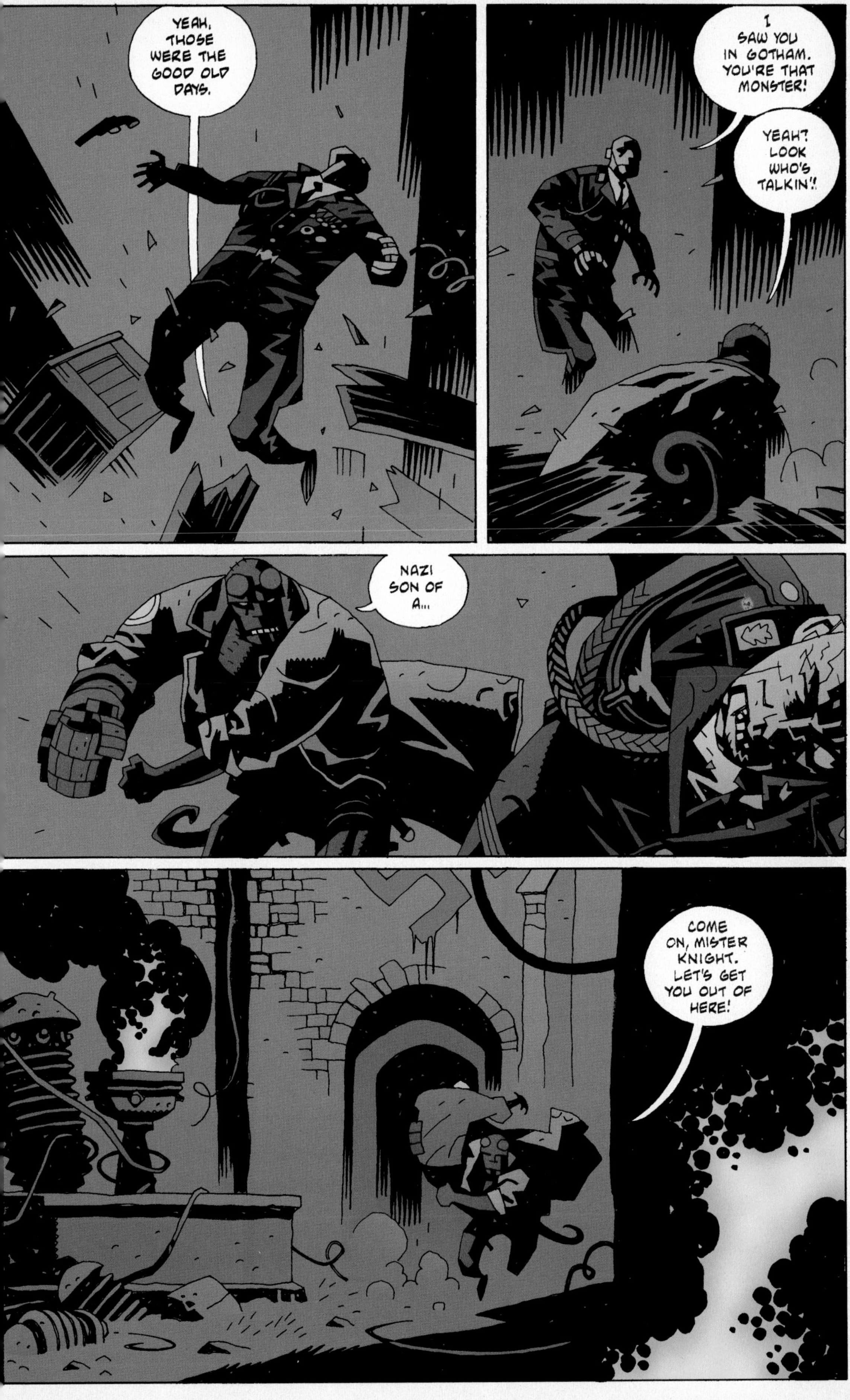
YEAH, THOSE WERE THE GOOD OLD DAYS.
I SAW YOU IN GOTHAM. YOU'RE THAT MONSTER!
YEAH? LOOK WHO'S TALKIN'!
NAZI SON OF A...
COME ON, MISTER KNIGHT. LET'S GET YOU OUT OF HERE!

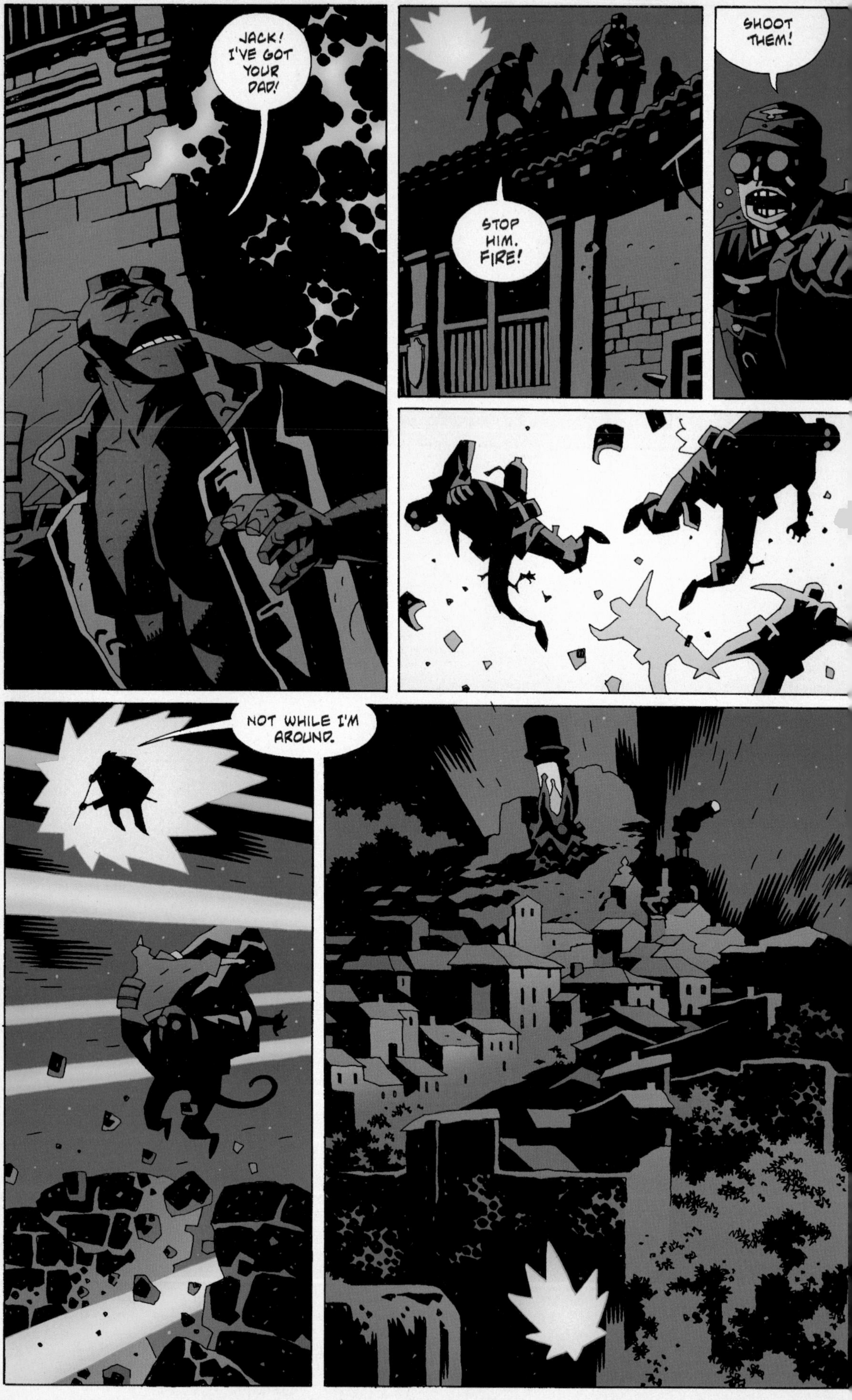
JACK! I'VE GOT YOUR DAD!
STOP HIM. FIRE!
SHOOT THEM!
NOT WHILE I'M AROUND.

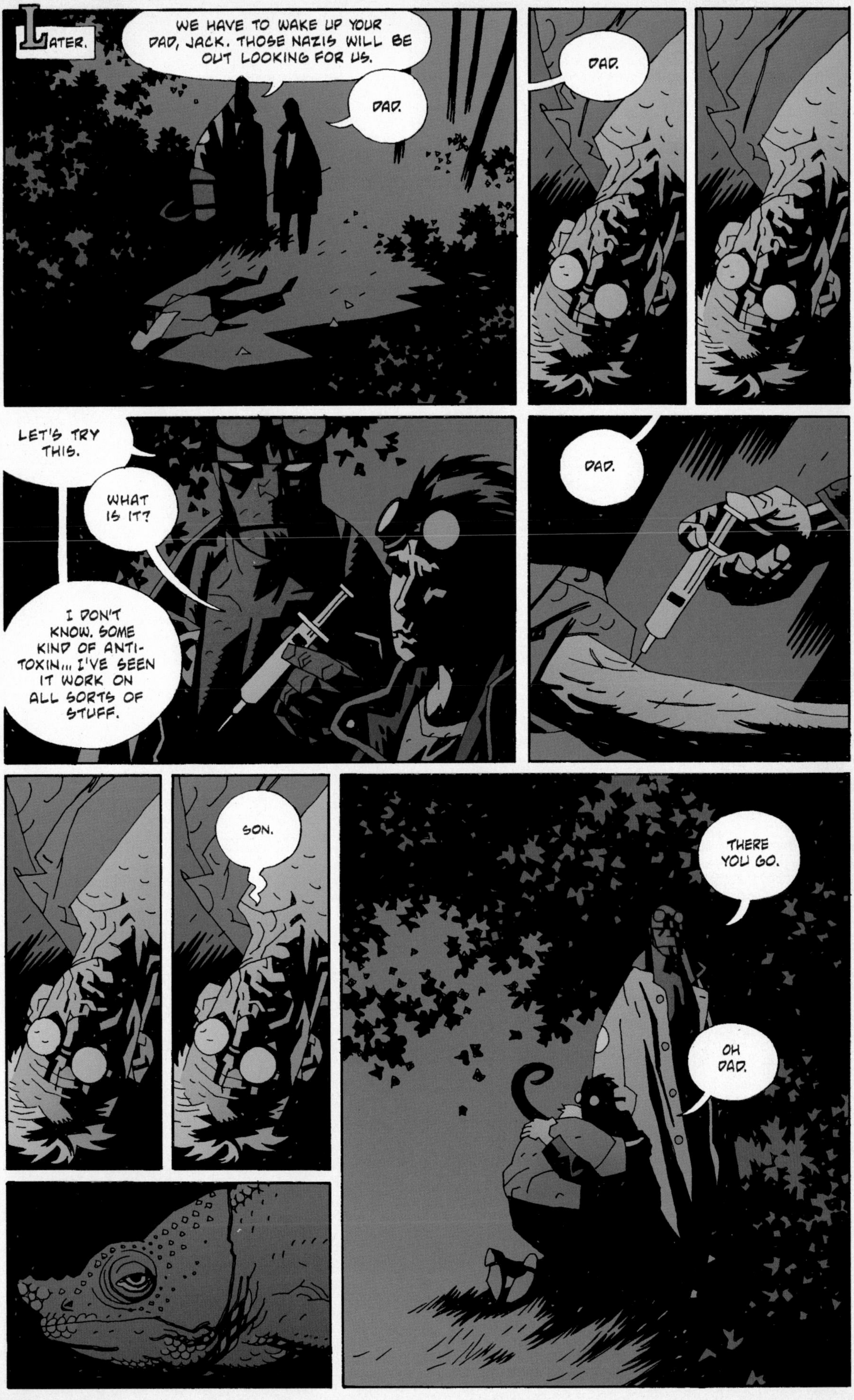
LATER.
WE HAVE TO WAKE UP YOUR DAD, JACK. THOSE NAZIS WILL BE OUT LOOKING FOR US.
DAD.
DAD.
LET'S TRY THIS.
WHAT IS IT?
I DON'T KNOW. SOME KIND OF ANTI-TOXIN... I'VE SEEN IT WORK ON ALL SORTS OF STUFF.
DAD.
SON.
THERE YOU GO.
OH DAD.

MISTER KNIGHT, DO YOU KNOW WHAT'S HAPPENED SINCE YOUR ABDUCTION?

IT WAS LIKE I WAS IN A SMALL PART OF MY HEAD, SCREAMING TO GET OUT, WHILE MY BODY ACTED INDEPENDENT OF ME.

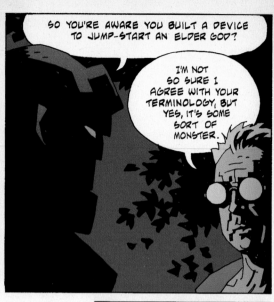

SO YOU'RE AWARE YOU BUILT A DEVICE TO JUMP-START AN ELDER GOD?

I'M NOT SO SURE I AGREE WITH YOUR TERMINOLOGY, BUT YES, IT'S SOME SORT OF MONSTER.

IS THERE ANY INSIGHT INTO THE DEVICE? ANY WAY WE CAN WEAKEN IT?

LIKE I SAID, MY BODY WAS INDEPENDENT OF MY MIND. I COULDN'T STOP MYSELF FROM DOING WHAT I DID.

BUT...

...I ALSO COULDN'T SPEAK. I WAS AWARE THAT THE NAZIS WERE USING THE WRONG GAUGE OF WIRING FOR THE DEVICES BUT DIDN'T TELL THEM.

I'M SORRY, MISTER KNIGHT. SCIENCE ISN'T ONE OF MY STRONG POINTS.

IF JACK ATTACKS THE DEVICE, ENOUGH COSMIC BLASTS... ENERGY FROM OTHER STARS COULD OVER-LOAD THE DEVICE'S POWER CORE.

I DON'T KNOW IF THAT WILL DEFEAT THE MONSTER, BUT SAN DIABLO WOULD CERTAINLY NEED A NEW LICK OF PAINT.

THAT'S A BIG BOY UP THERE... HE'LL GO AFTER YOU.

I'M NOT AFRAID.

THEN YOU'RE NOT AS SMART AS YOU LOOK.

I'VE GOT AN OLD PRAYER... THAT MIGHT SEND THE THING BACK WHERE IT CAME FROM.

YOU'RE SAYING WE ATTACK THE GOD FIRST BEFORE WE ATTACK THE DEVICE POWERING IT?

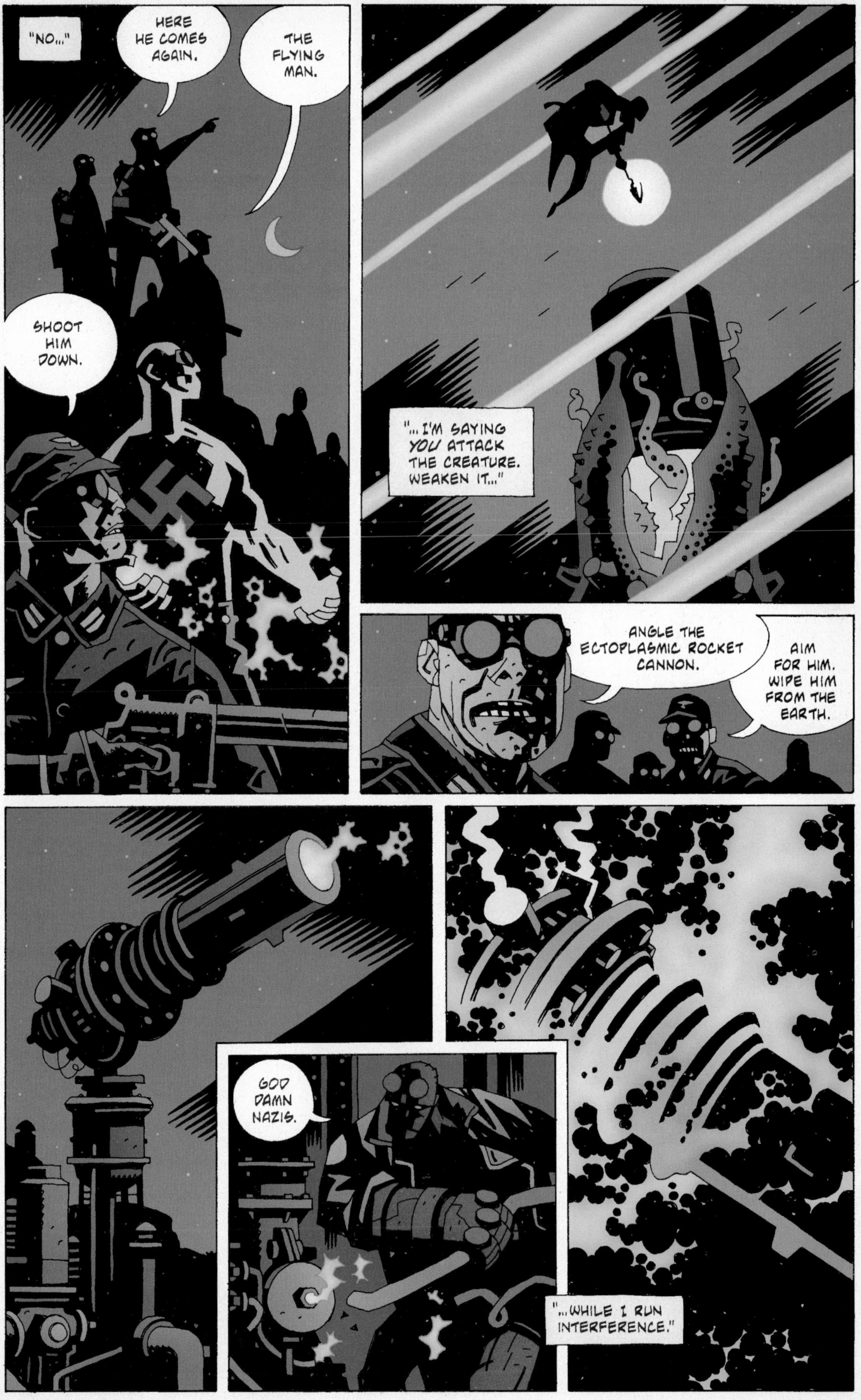
"NO..."
HERE HE COMES AGAIN.
THE FLYING MAN.
SHOOT HIM DOWN.
"...I'M SAYING YOU ATTACK THE CREATURE. WEAKEN IT..."
ANGLE THE ECTOPLASMIC ROCKET CANNON.
AIM FOR HIM. WIPE HIM FROM THE EARTH.
GOD DAMN NAZIS.
"...WHILE I RUN INTERFERENCE."

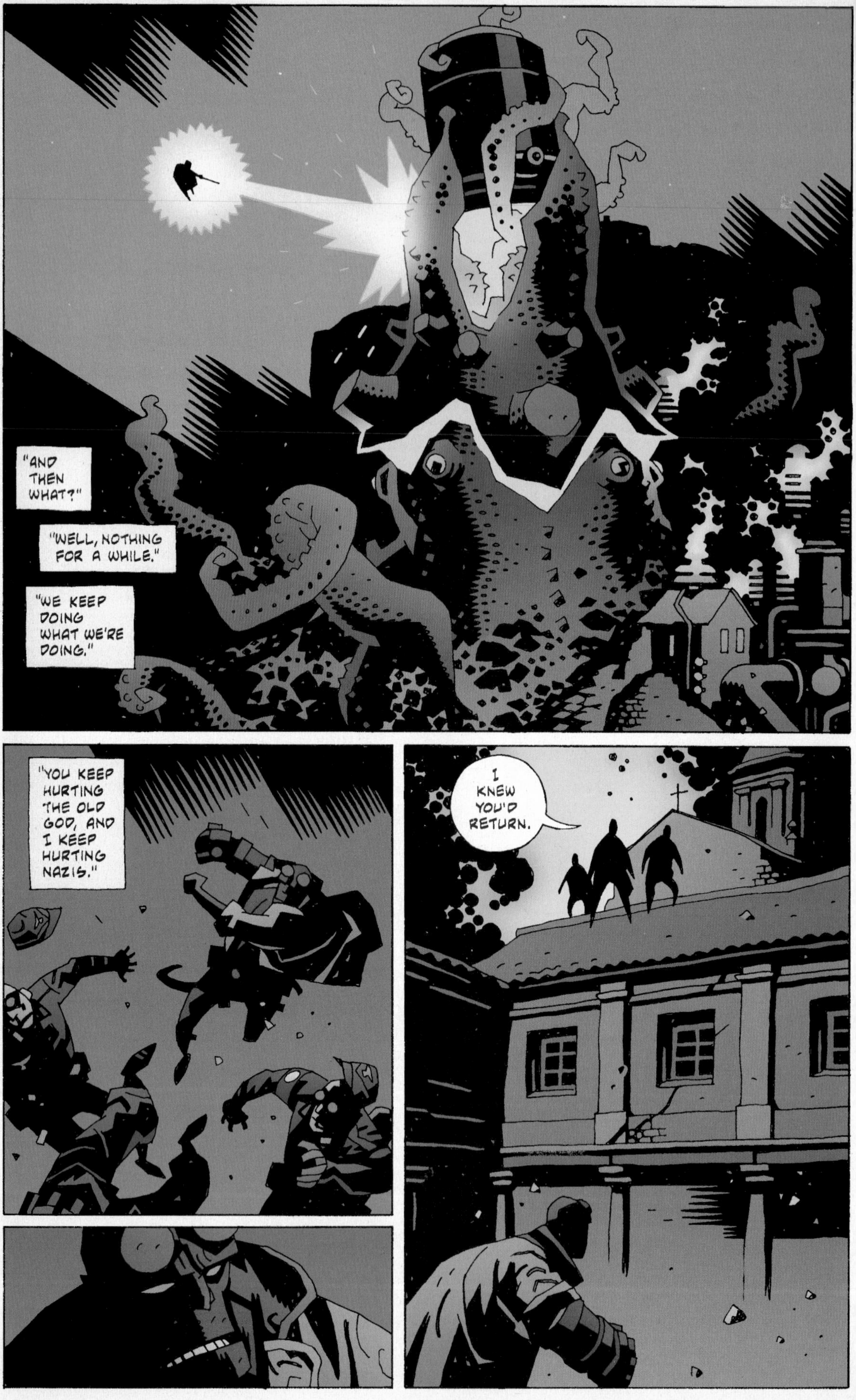
"AND THEN WHAT?"
"WELL, NOTHING FOR A WHILE."
"WE KEEP DOING WHAT WE'RE DOING."
"YOU KEEP HURTING THE OLD GOD, AND I KEEP HURTING NAZIS."
I KNEW YOU'D RETURN.

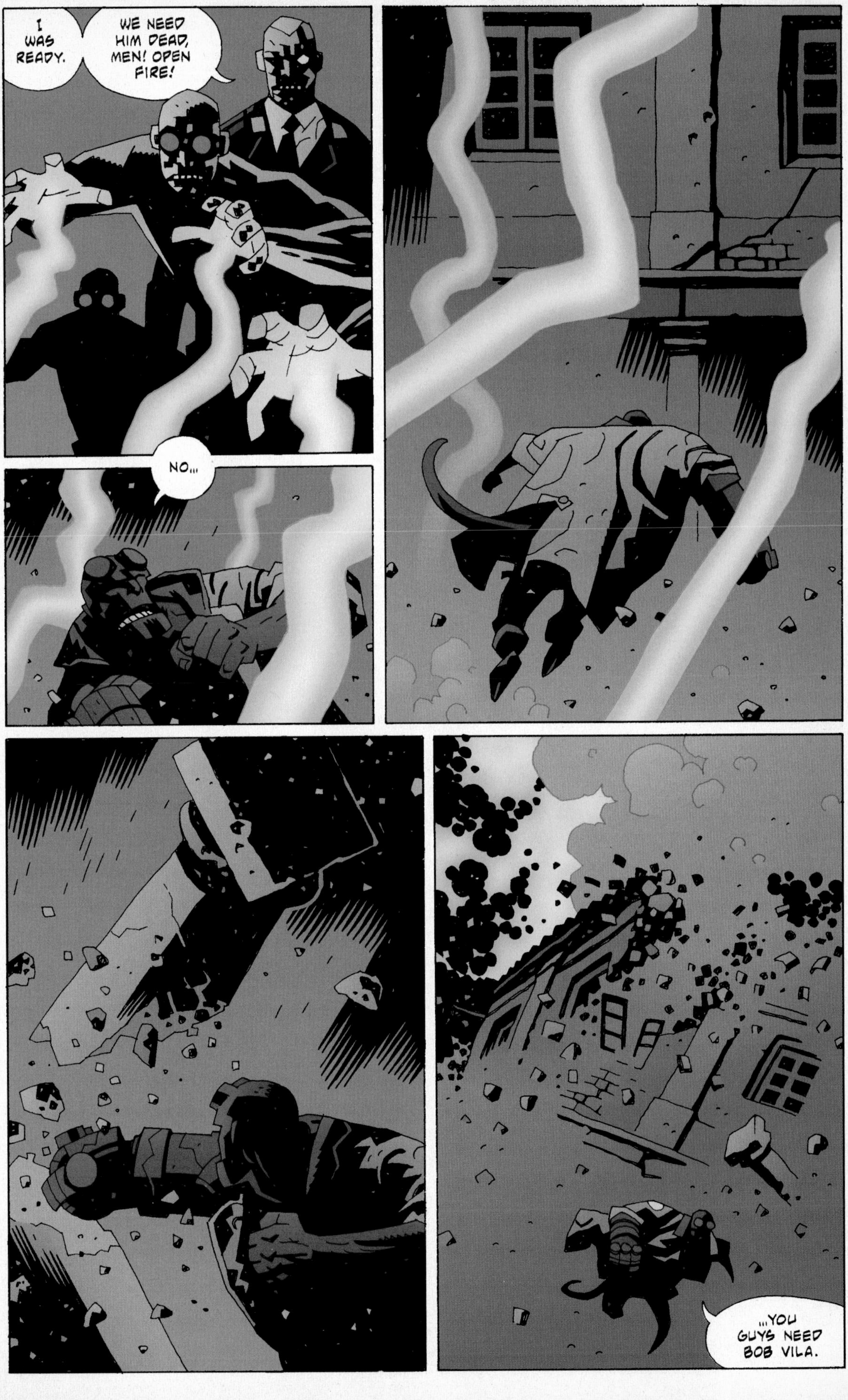

I WAS READY.
WE NEED HIM DEAD, MEN! OPEN FIRE!
NO...
...YOU GUYS NEED BOB VILA.

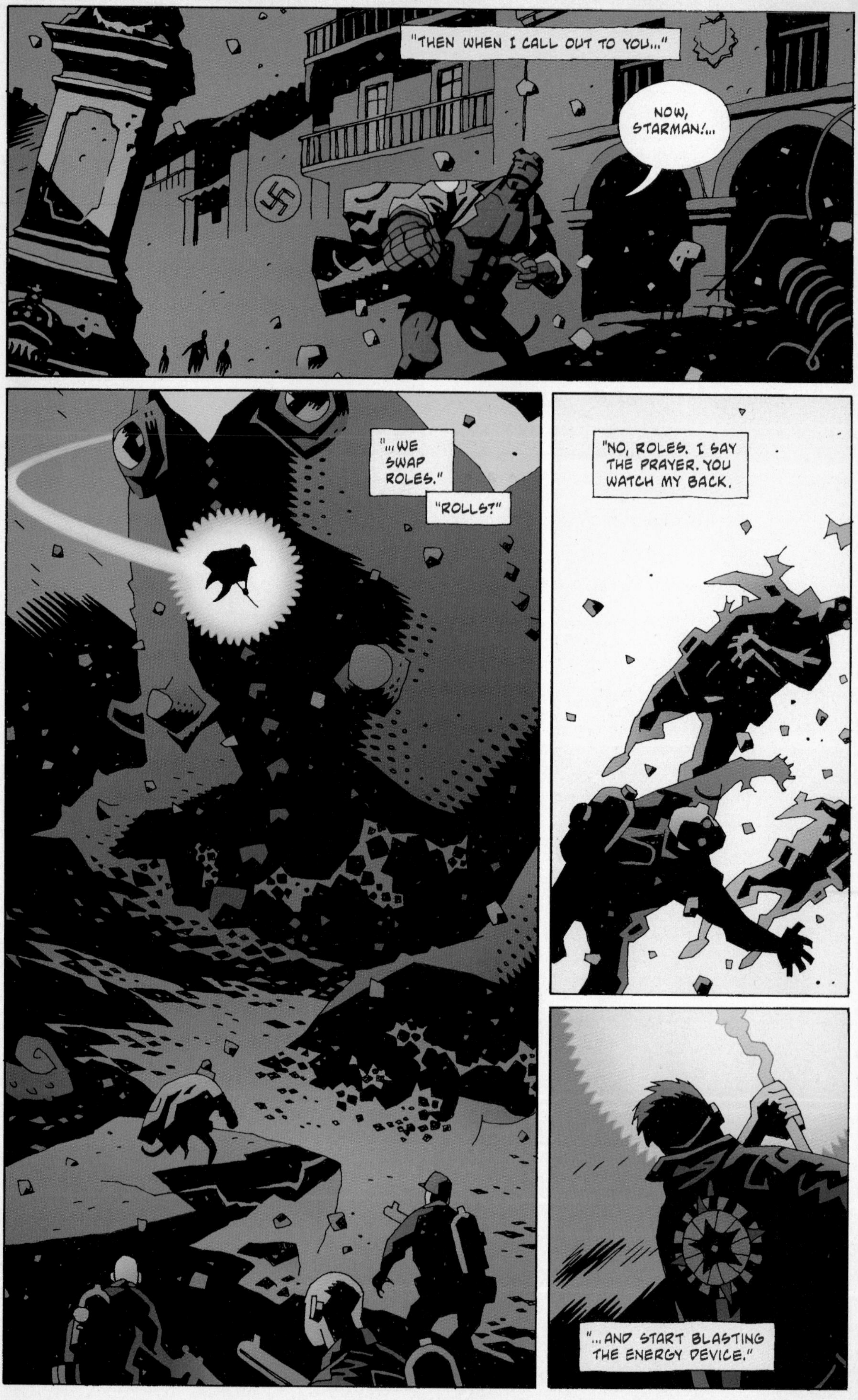
"THEN WHEN I CALL OUT TO YOU..."
NOW, STARMAN!...
"...WE SWAP ROLES."
"ROLLS?"
"NO, ROLES. I SAY THE PRAYER. YOU WATCH MY BACK.
"...AND START BLASTING THE ENERGY DEVICE."

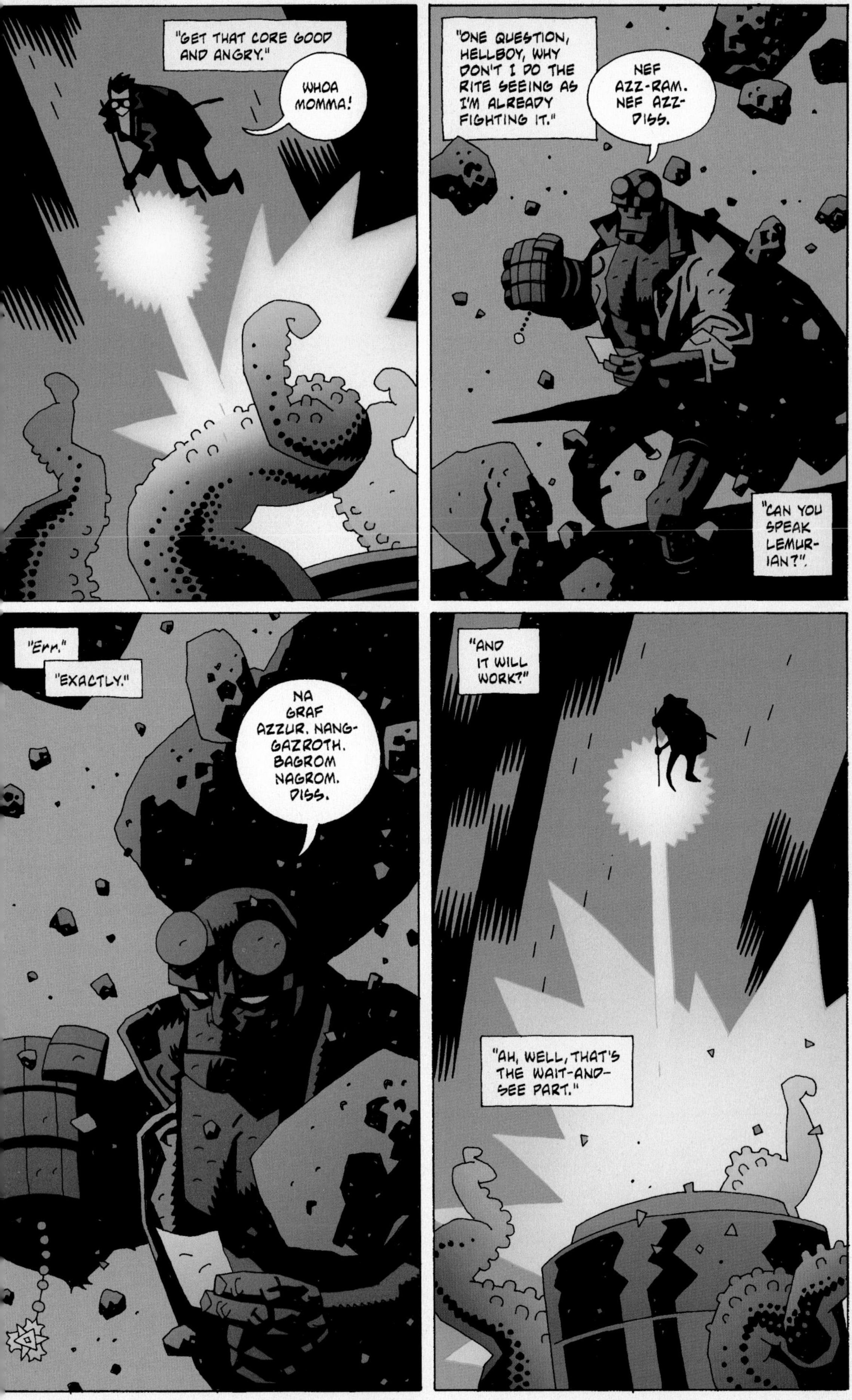
"GET THAT CORE GOOD AND ANGRY."
WHOA MOMMA!
"ONE QUESTION, HELLBOY, WHY DON'T I DO THE RITE SEEING AS I'M ALREADY FIGHTING IT."
NEF AZZ-RAM. NEF AZZ-DISS.
"CAN YOU SPEAK LEMURIAN?".
"Err."
"EXACTLY."
NA GRAF AZZUR. NANG-GAZROTH. BAGROM NAGROM. DISS.
"AND IT WILL WORK?"
"AH, WELL, THAT'S THE WAIT-AND-SEE PART."

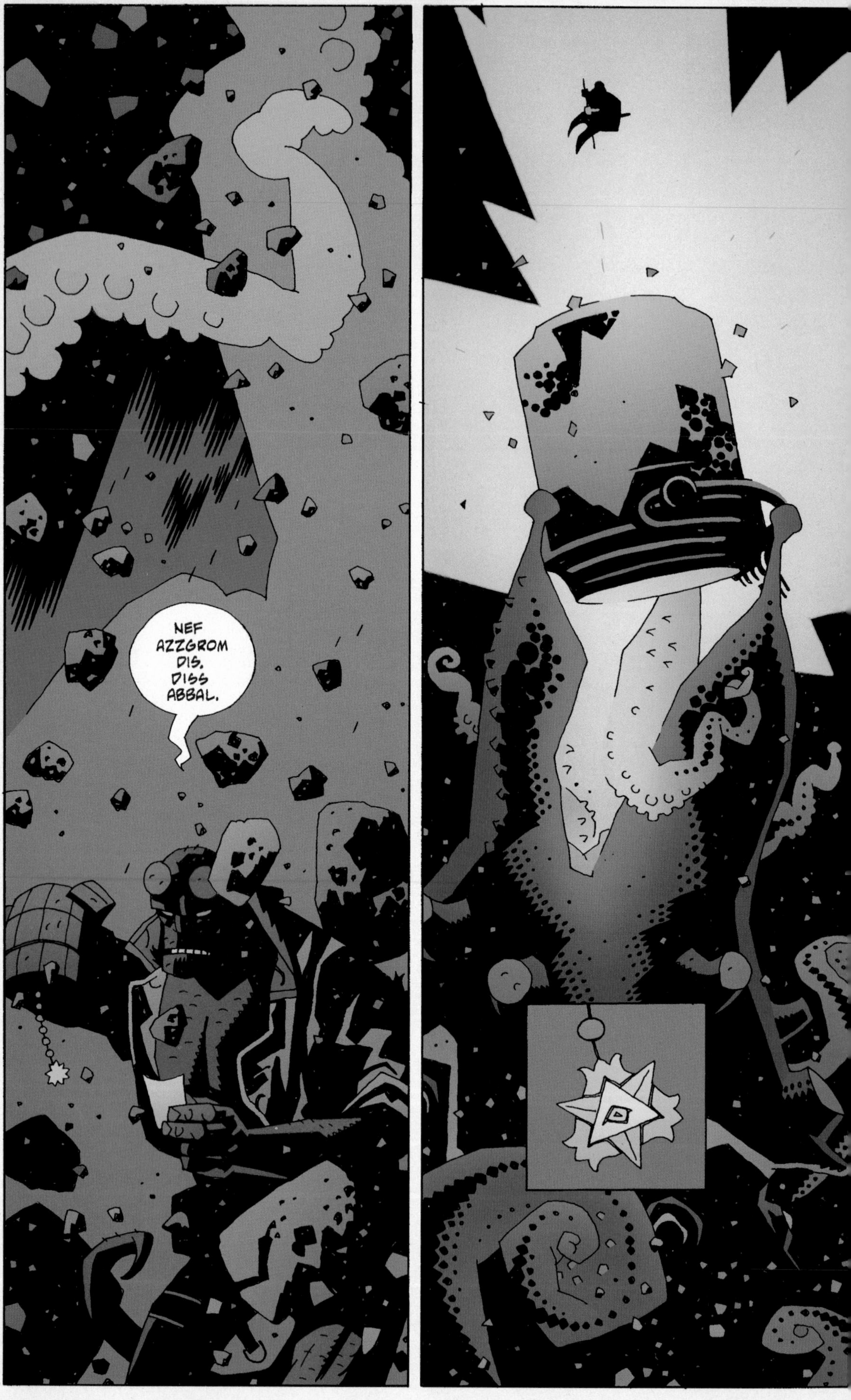
NEF AZZGROM DIS. DISS ABBAL.

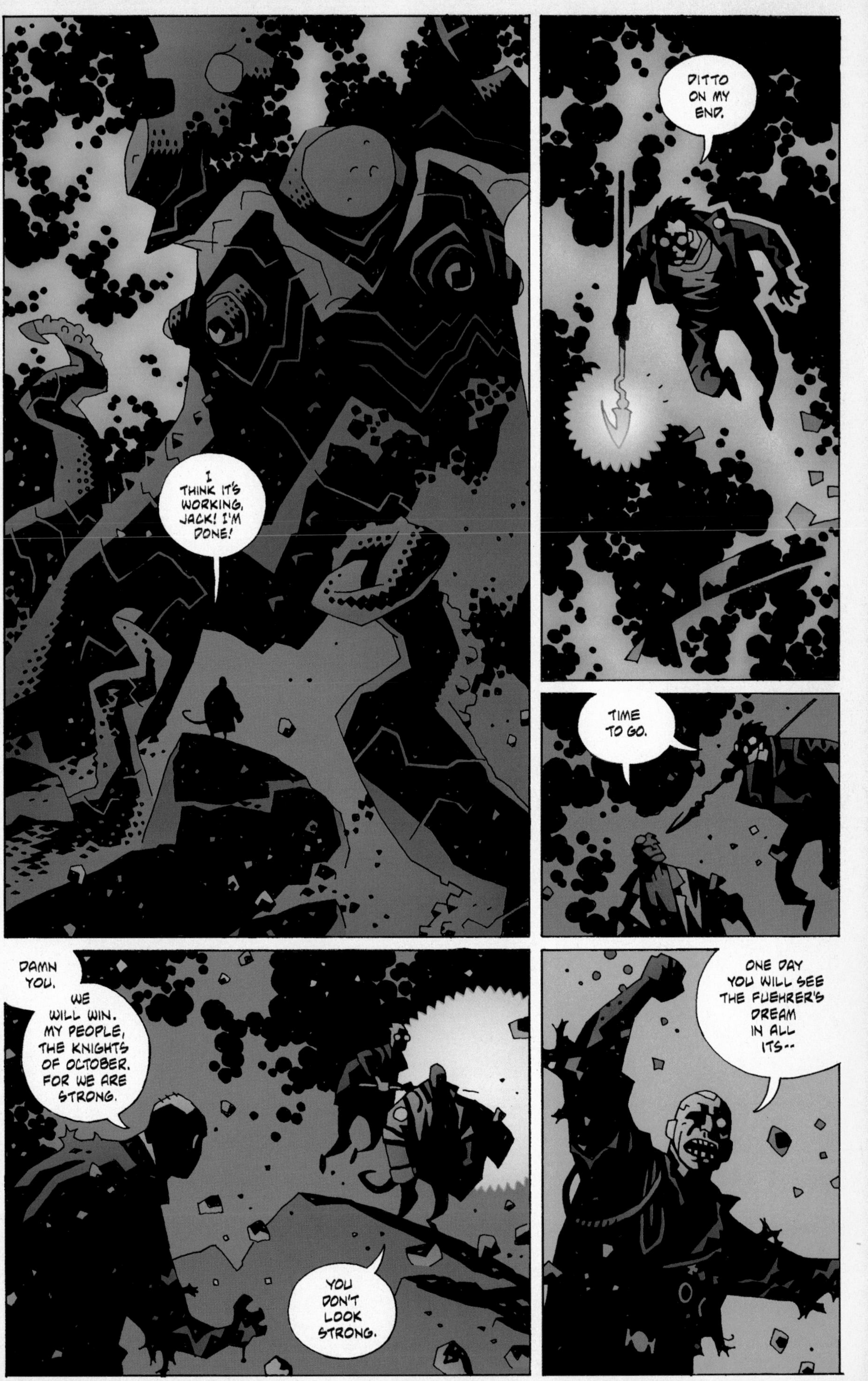
I THINK IT'S WORKING, JACK! I'M DONE!
DITTO ON MY END.
TIME TO GO.
DAMN YOU.
WE WILL WIN. MY PEOPLE, THE KNIGHTS OF OCTOBER. FOR WE ARE STRONG.
YOU DON'T LOOK STRONG.
ONE DAY YOU WILL SEE THE FUEHRER'S DREAM IN ALL ITS--

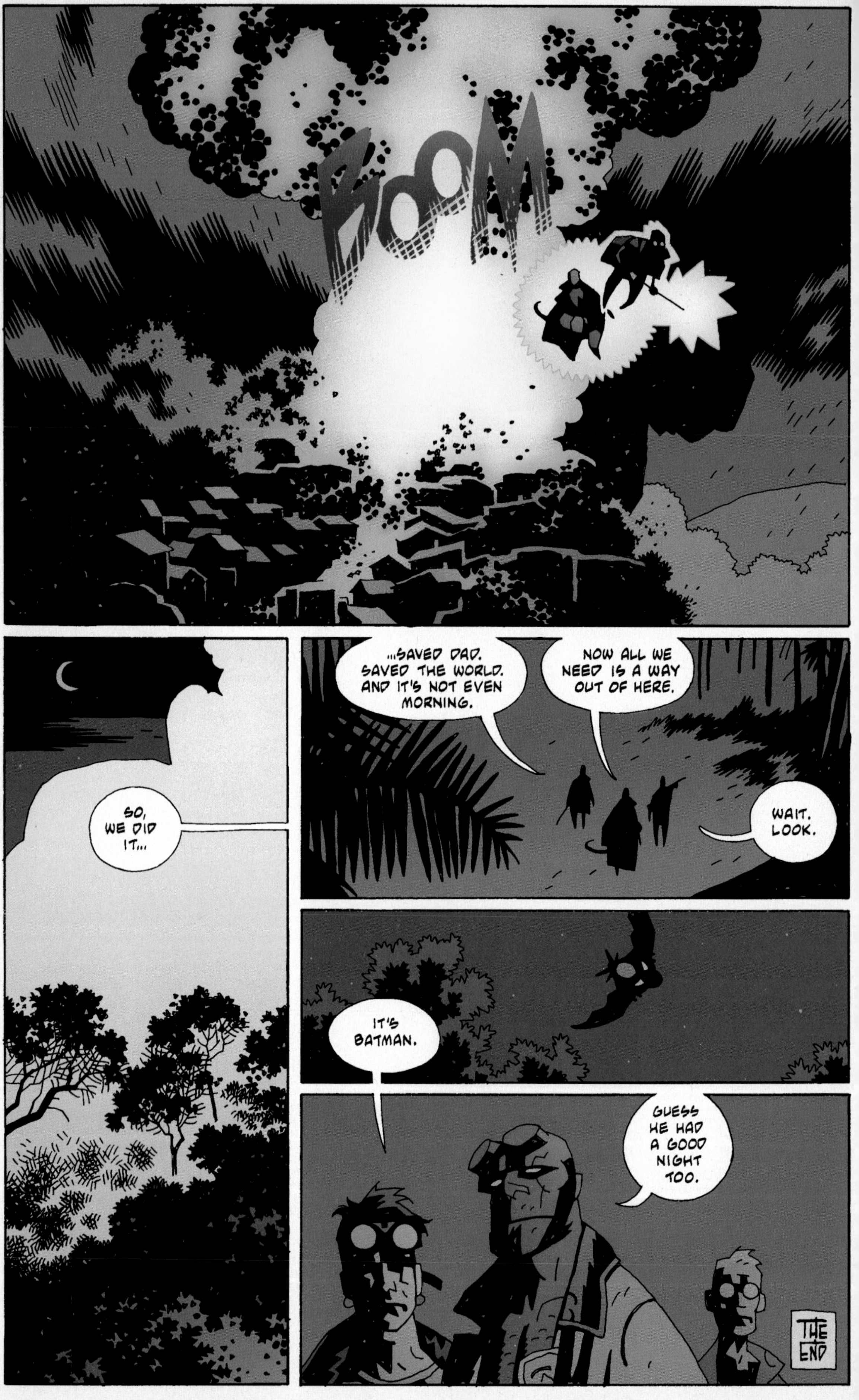
BOOM
SO, WE DID IT...
...SAVED DAD. SAVED THE WORLD. AND IT'S NOT EVEN MORNING.
NOW ALL WE NEED IS A WAY OUT OF HERE.
WAIT. LOOK.
IT'S BATMAN.
GUESS HE HAD A GOOD NIGHT TOO.
THE END

TIMES PAST An (ongoing) afterword

Memory. Like most of us, I value and fear it in equal measure.

I'll explain why in a minute, but let me first say that in the "rules" that I set myself in terms of these afterwords, I decided that there would be no holding back. I would be completely honest. No cool patina belying the fears and insecurities that all we creators carry with us...no, have dragging behind us like Marley's chains. I'm as messed up as anyone and as I get older, I feel, unlike a cloud lifting, the haze of doubt and wistful regret lays more heavily upon me. But honesty. For these afterwords that's the key.

My mother was crazy. I grew up poor and with a crazy mother and the fact I'm not a basket case myself is a miracle. I thank the sequence of events that got me into art classes and art schools and film schools and onwards in the direction of a creative life that I'm not instead sitting on a park bench somewhere in England, talking to myself, having imaginary conversations with my dead mum and everyone who ever wronged me, swatting at imaginary flies while wearing the heady laden aroma of urine and pain.

Thank God for origami and Henri Cartier-Bresson, that's all I have to say.

But the fact is that as my now dead mother drifted into her dotage, she lost her faculties. She began to forget. I have no idea if this loss of memory was due to dementia or Alzheimer's. If it was the latter, and if I share that hereditary gene, then I myself may one day no longer recall names and events. Or indeed who all the Magnificent Seven were. Yes, I value memory greatly while I have it.

And so as I begin to write about this volume of STARMAN, I realize that memory, while ironclad in terms of singular events, may still be a liquid thing in terms of the exact order that one thing or another occurred.

This volume features tales I am proud that you now read, in that they're somewhat unheralded and unknown and as such stand resolute in that they don't deserve the ignoble fate they were meted prior to this. (Boy, what a pretentious sentence. James, you are such a wanker.) Basically, what you're going to read in this volume is a lot of stuff that prior to now for one reason or another hadn't been reprinted.

In my memory Archie is still editing all of it. I could have sworn that I had conversations with him about specific aspects of certain stories. I could have sworn. But memory is elusive and playful. It tricks us. I know Archie was a part of BATMAN/

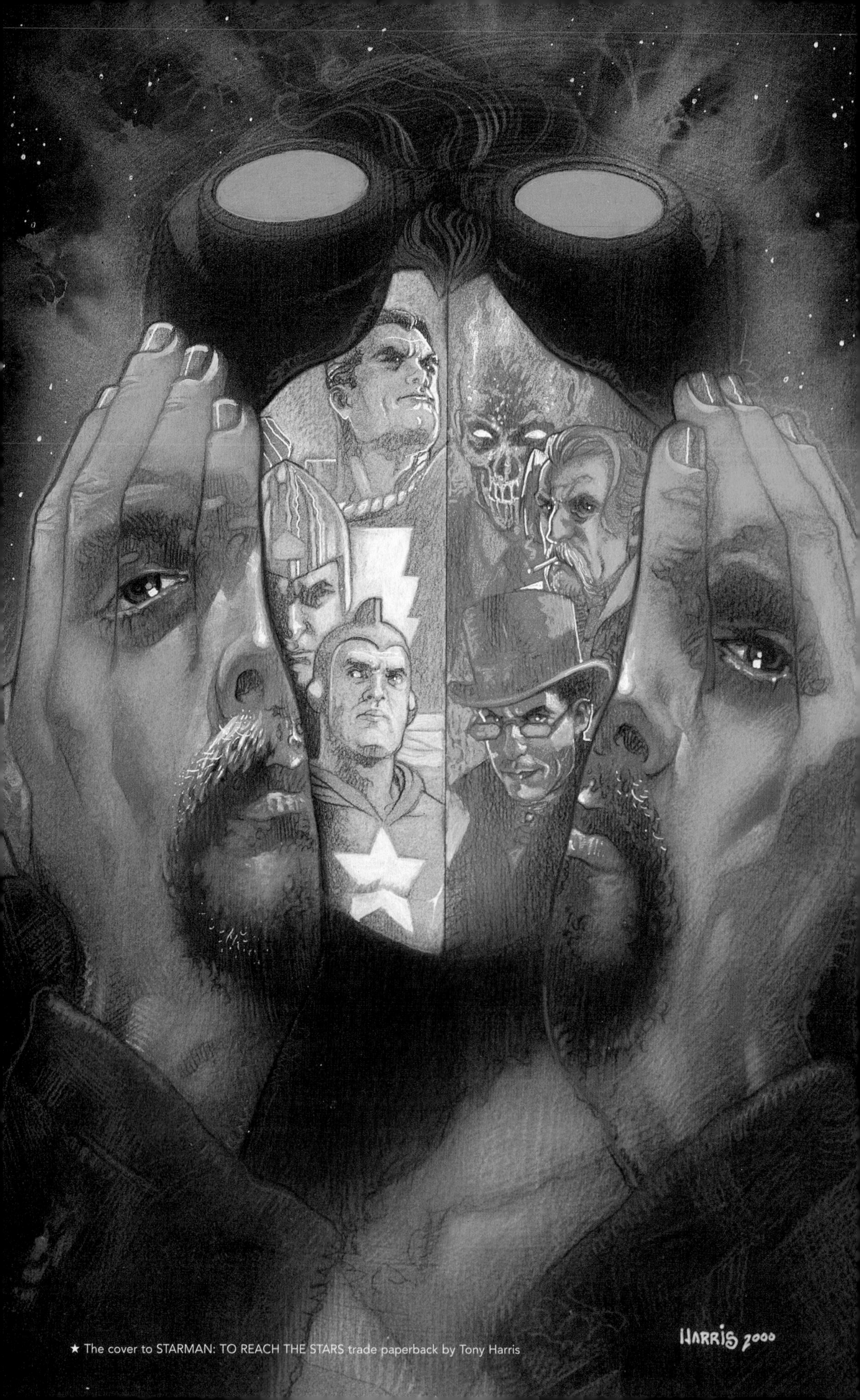
HARRIS 2000

★ The cover to STARMAN: TO REACH THE STARS trade paperback by Tony Harris

HELLBOY/STARMAN, but apart from that…was it Assistant Editor Chuck Kim still filling in for Archie? Was it the new editor, Pete Tomasi? I consult the credits of the actual comics and see who did what, and yet it isn't how I remember it. I recall looking at pages and discussing script with Peter and/or Archie when it was the other who worked on that particular issue. But perhaps that's to be expected with someone who has written as many comics as me. And genetic time bomb or not, my memory has never been that good.

I think of how things were at that time. Still living in Burbank, still married, living in the house where I was awoken one morning by a phone call from Chuck to tell me that Archie was dead. This was a house where I'd sit outside in the garden, alone save for a beloved dog who'd run around and chase crows while I read through my writing for the day. That was more than a decade ago. The house is gone. So is the wife. The beloved dog is dead. Now I live in San Francisco with a new fiancée and new beloved dog. It's a different life with less of the drinking and debauched/abject behavior that filled the intervening years between the divorce of then and the marriage of soon. A calmer and more peaceful life. Not the life I thought I'd have then, though. I imagined more success for myself, although thinking back I'm not sure what form I expected that success to take. Money? I guess, although as the slalom run that my writing career has been will show, I've never been one for taking a gig just for cash…not often, anyway. It's more often been that the job felt right for me (more on this topic when I get to talking about BATMAN/HELLBOY/STARMAN in a bit.) I guess the "success" I wanted so badly then was for people to like what I did. I guess that's indeed success in its purest form for those of us driven to create. And to

this day, I've never really known if my work was liked or not. No, I'm not being coy. Yeah, I know that STARMAN has a following, and God bless one and all of you, but I have no idea how I'll be perceived as a writer by the time I pop my clogs. Not just STARMAN, but all of it. It's something I ponder a lot — moreso as I age, looking back at all the creative missteps I've made since first sitting down to write for a living.

Further to that, of late I've been thinking about death. *My* death. No, I haven't had bad news from the doctor, and fully intend to outlive all of you. But still. I was thinking the other day about the departed and sorely missed Mike Wieringo. I only worked with him once, and only met him once in Charlotte at a Heroes Con, but I knew instantly he was a nice man and someone I liked. When Mike passed, there was a legitimate outpouring of grief that the guy was gone. Yes, he died far too young and far too suddenly. That would account for some of the sadness, of course. But beyond that…people loved him. Not just the man's work, but the man himself. (By the way, his sketch image of Mon-El that I dug up on the internet – Google it, it's easy to find – is I think my personal favorite image of a character I have so taken to my heart. It's the image I look at whenever I want to focus on Mon-El before I write him. For what that's worth.) Anyway, I wonder, as do we all if we care to admit it, what level of grief I will trigger when I die. I am not so well liked. I am not a popular guy. I know that. In fact, stories I hear secondhand about me oftentimes paint me as a nasty piece of work. Am I? I hope not. Honestly, I try to be a good guy. I try to be a nice guy. Somehow, more often than I'd like, that gets lost in translation.

Boy this is a fun afterword, isn't it? All we need is

some Leonard Cohen playing in the background, and maybe some dead roses on a dusty vase off to the side of the room.

I guess I'm this way — writing this melancholy and admittedly somewhat aimless piece — because it makes me sad to recall life then. I'm putting off thinking about it too clearly. My memories of this period of STARMAN are coupled with a feeling of my life changing, my focus and direction meandering as my marriage began to fall by the wayside. My dog had died. I felt lost and distracted. Prone to depression. Ideas came hard for me then. In fact, when Tony left, and with Archie dead, this was a time when I actually thought of ending my involvement with STARMAN... sending Jack Knight off into space for another writer to pick up and continue. This will sound like a lie. Even as I write it, I know it reads like I'm making this up. But the only reason I didn't leave the book was because I felt I owed the loyal group of readers who'd stuck with it and allowed sales to maintain so STARMAN didn't fall by the wayside like so many other titles. I felt they should read Jack's saga through to the end, as I'd originally imagined it. Thinking about it now, I guess that was kind of arrogant. But as I've said before, echoing the words of others, creativity is not just the desire to create but the need for that work to be seen and enjoyed by others.

So what else do I remember of that period? Lingering sadness. Sleeplessness. Always feeling tired. Oh, and being really skinny.

Don't worry, the next afterword in Volume Five, when Jack and I begin our journey through space (with the assistance of David Goyer, who was something of a life-saver), will be a much jollier romp. But

I think it's best I end it here, with an apology to everyone for this ramble down a dark path of memory...especially those among you now eyeing the bottle of sleeping pills in the bathroom with intent. Don't do it. Life is wonderful. It's not just a line in a musical...the sun will come out tomorrow. This I have found to be true, as I sit here now working and living...happily.

I know, let's jump to the issue-by-issue breakdown part. We should be safe with that.

Issues #39 and 40. These were a bit of an experiment. STARMAN, while periodically tipping the hat to the DCU as a whole, still remained off in its own little corner of it. These issues, tying in with THE POWER OF SHAZAM!, was seeing how it felt to allow Jack more into the overall DC world as a whole. I was very much a fan of Jerry Ordway's work on SHAZAM!, loving the timeless feel it had, unique in its own way like I felt STARMAN was in its own way, too. I have always been a sucker for the Fawcett hero Bulletman too, for no reason except that I liked him, so getting to write him in an untold wartime adventure with Ted was fun for me. Was the crossover experiment a success? I don't know, honestly. Part of me thinks it works. Part of me feels that the worlds of Starman and Shazam! were too unique to themselves and that it's an odd marriage. You be the judge.

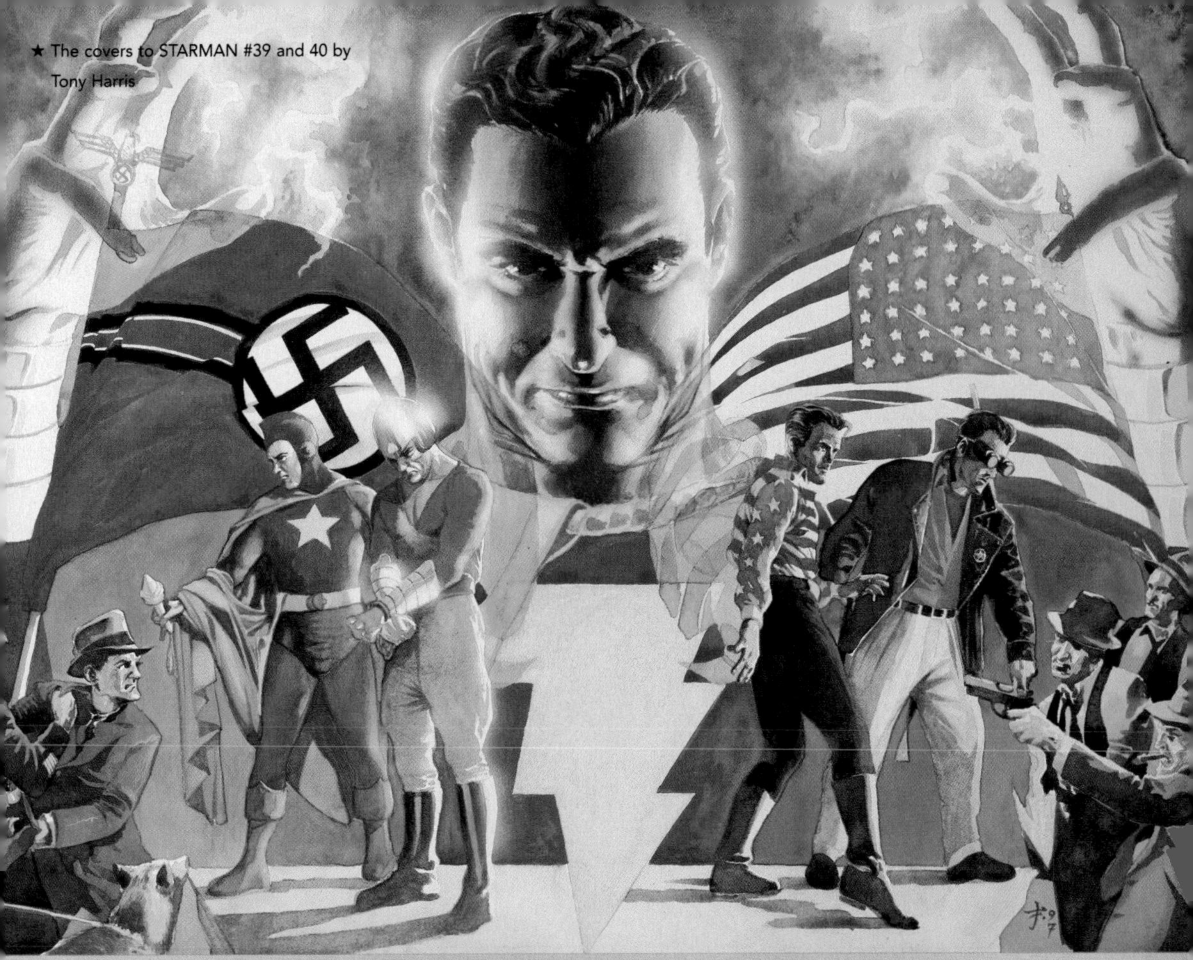

★ The covers to STARMAN #39 and 40 by Tony Harris

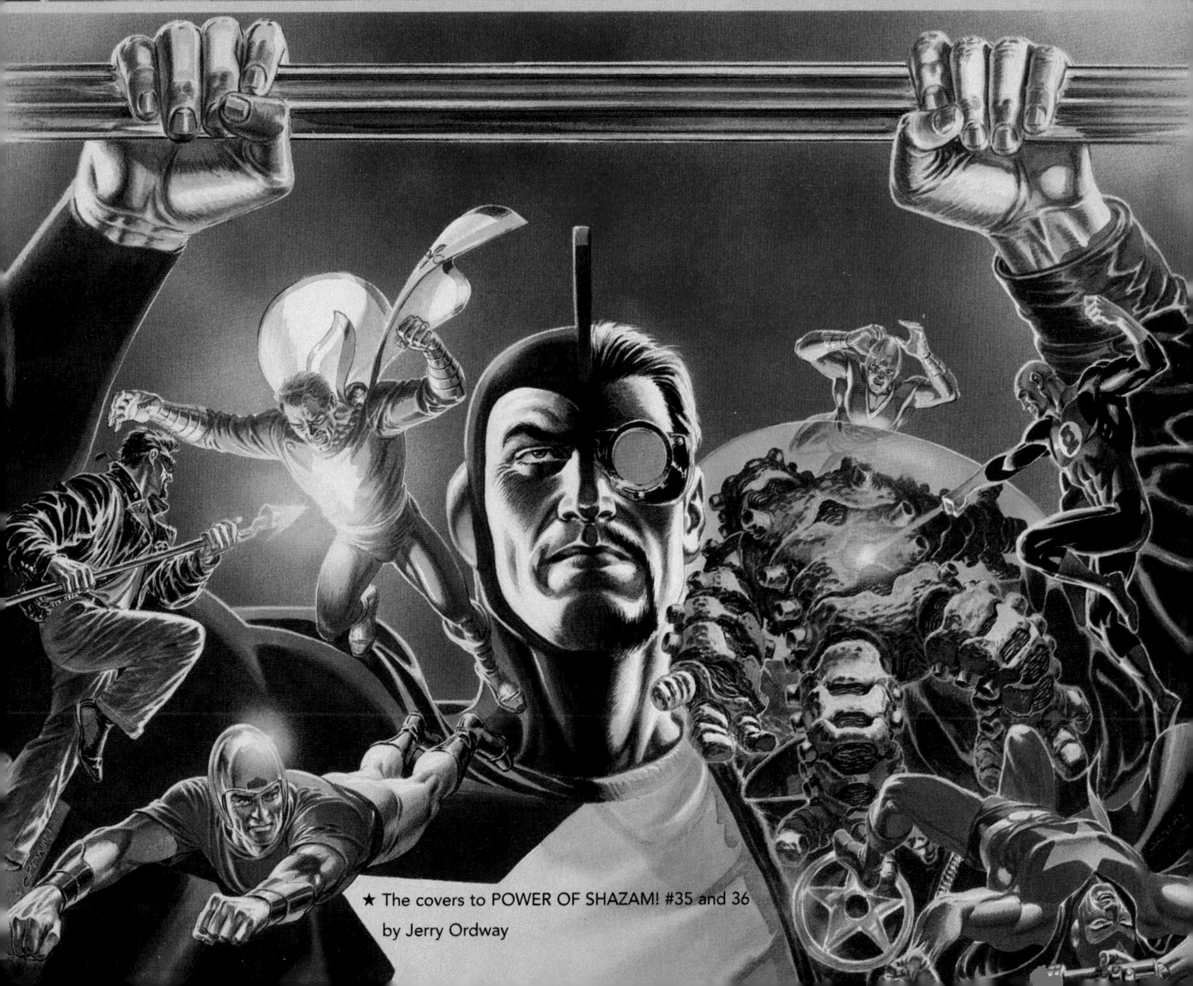

★ The covers to POWER OF SHAZAM! #35 and 36 by Jerry Ordway

Issue #41. This issue featured The Shade and Matt O'Dare and their growing friendship, mirroring the friendship that the Shade had had with Scalphunter many years prior. A quieter tale. I got to work with Gary Erskine again many years after we did a fun and violent John Woo-inspired two issues of *Firearm*. What an amazing artist.

Issue #42. This is the first of the non-reprinted STARMAN material. It was my idea that we do the original "Times Past" trade paperback collections as two separate volumes and in the rush to get STARMAN TPBs finished up and out of the way, the second batch of these stories were overlooked and then I believe deemed not important enough to collect in light of all of Jack's present day adventures being collected. It always disappointed me in that smaller pieces of the larger narrative that were revealed in these tales, especially how Jack and Mikaal get the spacecraft that gets them into space — which, as you read the series back then just in trade form, kind of appears out of nowhere courtesy of the Shade, with no explanation as to how in the Hell he got it.

Anyway, here's the first of those puzzle pieces. It's my second collaboration with Matt Smith, and it's interesting to see how more refined his art is here compared to the earlier "Times Past" tale he did back in Issue #11. The tale features the Demon, and I got to write him speaking in rhyme. Originally Jack Kirby hadn't had this. It was Len Wein who introduced the notion and Alan Moore who took this new aspect to Etigran to even loftier heights in the pages of THE SAGA OF THE SWAMP THING. Since then some writers have refrained from doing it, which I think is a shame. Yes, it's a bit of work to come up

with, but it's fun — and you definitely get a sense of achievement when you're done. I'm quite proud of this tale, both for Etigran's verse and the story itself which I wrote to show by example how much Ted Knight didn't believe in an afterlife (something important for later in his own arc). I think Matt did a superb job here and looking at it so much later, I really enjoyed revisiting it.

Issue #43. This was an issue that I needed to write to fill in some important narrative bits before Jack goes into space. We see his new shop opened finally. It also allowed me space to show more of Jack and Sadie's relationship as well as our boy meeting with the Justice League. This was at a time when Superman in the League was "Superman Blue" — an energy being. It was another time Jack fitted in with the DCU as a whole and I think it works fairly well. And of course this issue is where Jack gets his aforementioned rocket — where it came from to be explained in a "Times Past" adventure in an omnibus to come.

Issue #44. Another "Times Past." Another never-before reprinted tale. One of my two collaborations with Mike Mayhew that you'll see in this volume. I had met Mike years prior at San Diego and very much liked the pencilled art that I'd seen for a Praxis backup feature he was doing in JLA QUARTERLY. It took a while until we got to work together, and by then, his great art had refined and improved even more for this, what is basically a Golden Age Phantom Lady solo story. I'd written it to show the family link between Ted and Sandra Knight, something Roy Thomas had come up with way back when in ALL-STAR SQUADRON. I think it's a fun romp. I recall having fun writing the dialogue of Sandra and her drinking buddy. And I wanted to show the Prairie Witch again, for no other reason than I dreamed her up and I think she's cool.

This also marks the first issue of STARMAN edited by Peter Tomasi. And so things change and the torch is passed. (More of Peter and his amazing contribution to the book, next afterword.)

Issue #45. This is it. Tony's last issue. Jack's farewell to Opal and the people in it. It also features Mikaal's farewell to his boyfriend Tony, which I believe may be the first gay male kiss in a mainstream comic. Kind of proud of that, gotta say. I also have to say how much fun it is to write Bobo's dialogue. Also of note is Tony's one-page drawn farewell to Archie Goodwin featuring the whole Starman cast, which is truly a work of love and thing of beauty.

Issue #46. Another "Times Past" previously uncollected and one that I'm especially proud of. In it I got to use the Jester, an old Quality hero, in his first major and to my knowledge only appearance since the Golden Age. And, patting myself on the back, I think I did a pretty good job of giving the guy character and personality in the brief amount of time I had. This is another collaboration with Gene Ha, my second after THE SHADE #1. I love his color choices, making the book feel old and of a past time. But more importantly, I love his art, period. Yeah, I really am very proud of this one.

80-PAGE GIANT #1. Also never-before collected. This was a weird one. I decided to have one item, an African totem, be an element in each tale I told, linking characters throughout time in the STARMAN series and affording me the chance to write in different time periods with the whole thing bookended by Jack in the present and his conflict with Ragdoll.

It was fun to do. And challenging in that while linked by the totem passing from owner to owner through time, I nevertheless wanted each tale to stand alone. Highlights for me include –

Well, all the artists. I was very lucky with the talent I got to work with on this book, all so varied, but I feel each artist suited the tale he told.
– John Lucas in the present. A young artist with a lot of energy. A lot of fun to write for.

– My second collaboration with Mike Mayhew on the Scalphunter tale.

– Steve Sadowski doing the Golden Age Starman (a guy I'd go on to work with bringing back the JSA with David Goyer.)

– Wade Von Grawbadger got the next story, a Bobo tale where I chose to also include the Starman of 1951 – trickier than it seemed in that I had to feature him, yet not reveal anything about him.

– Dusty Abel and I doing Those L'il O'Dares and Patrolman Clarence. I like this tale in that I modeled it on old Jack Kirby style kid gang stories where they get into a fix/solve a crime and then have their butts saved by the adult character in the story at the end. I like how it feels like there have been other tales of the young O'Dares when this is the only one.

– Tim Burgard and I have a long history, one of my longest in comics. We did a "Secret Origin of Dinosaur Island" story many years prior. SECRET ORIGINS was cancelled before the story could be published, and Tim's art was subsequently lost by DC when they moved from their old address to the one they're in now, so the work was never to be seen. So this was Tim and I getting to work together so many years later.

Looking at this tale, like Mikaal's "Times Past" in STARMAN #28...I'm amazed by how much we got away with. Drugs and bisexuality in a mainstream book. And flared pants.

THE MIST #1. This was part of a series of comics that DC did with the banner title of "Girl Frenzy." It was a chance for me to flesh out The Mist a little more, prior to the events of "Grand Guignol" that I knew would come one day. I note now that I also got to write The Black Hand, who was a pretty forgotten villain then and thanks to Geoff Johns is forgotten no longer.

And finally, **BATMAN/HELLBOY/STARMAN #1 and 2.** Actually I don't have much to say about this. No, maybe I do. Firstly, this is where me not always taking the most lucrative gig comes into play. As some of you may know, I was the first guy offered KINGDOM COME. After kicking the idea around for a bit, I passed on — because with so much of the story beats fleshed out by Alex Ross at the onset, I didn't feel I could offer enough to the project. It shows

★ The back cover to BATMAN/HELLBOY/STARMAN #1 by Mike Mignola with Matt Hollingsworth

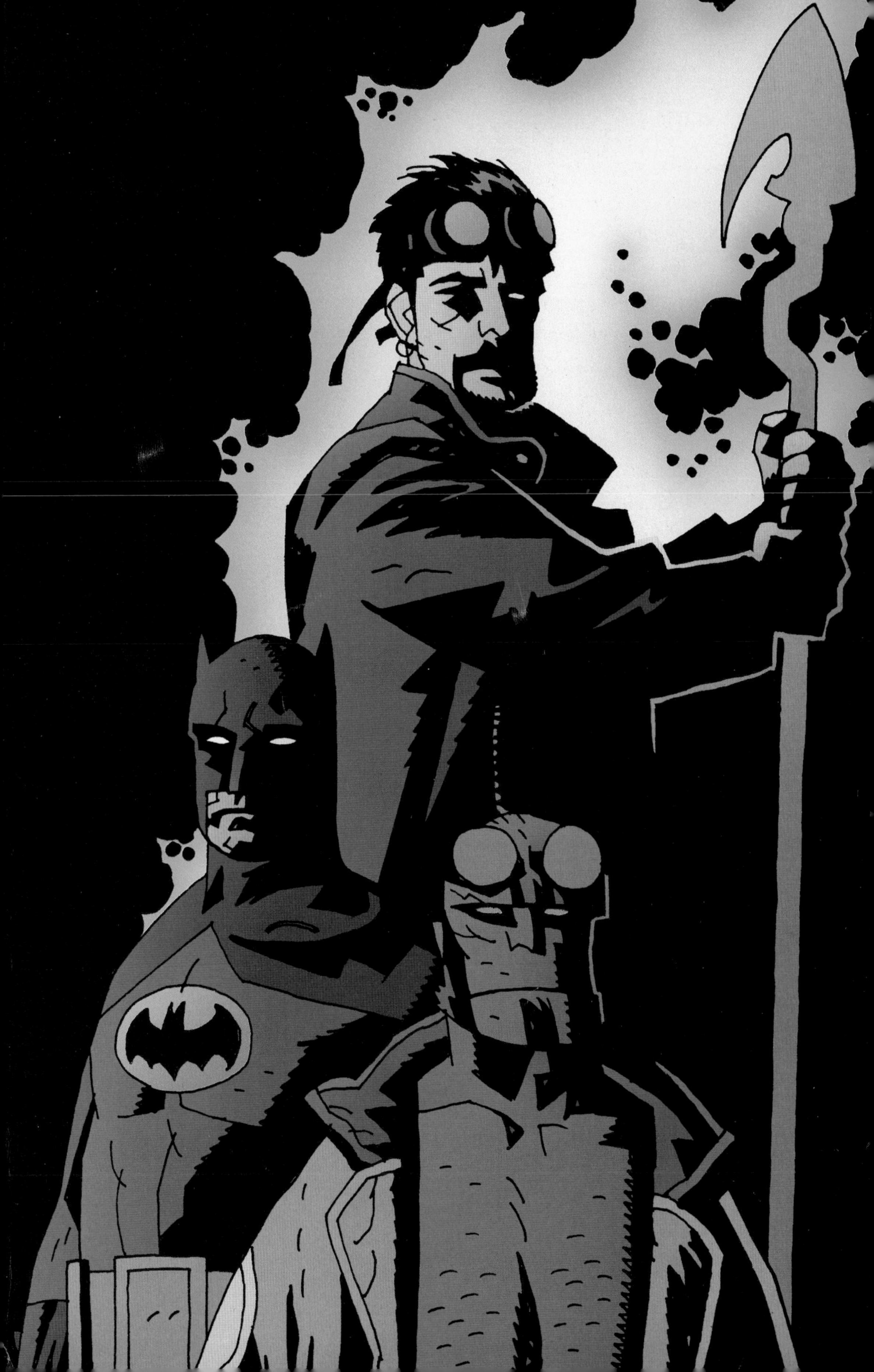

Mark Waid's skill that ultimately he was able to very much make the book his own, so the job went to the right guy in the end. But, oh the money I would have made if I'd taken it.

Instead, another project came my way. The chance to work with Mignola. It wasn't an either/or scenario, but I think I turned it into that in my head to justify my turning down the chance to work with Alex Ross. Instead I got to work with Mike Mignola on his fabulous creation and got to add in Batman and Jack Knight along with it. I was thrilled by how hands-off Mike was too, letting me do my thing, but I in turn took great pains to make it feel like a Hellboy tale. I

think it's a great yarn and of the many crossovers Hellboy was having with other characters at that time it's the one I believe Mike is most happy with.

So there we go. Going. Gone.

Again apologies for the dour afterword. Next time it'll be laughter and cherry pies. Promise.

James Robinson
San Francisco, November 2009

★ Tony Harris often uses himself as a model for his own art, filling in for characters like Jack Knight and others.